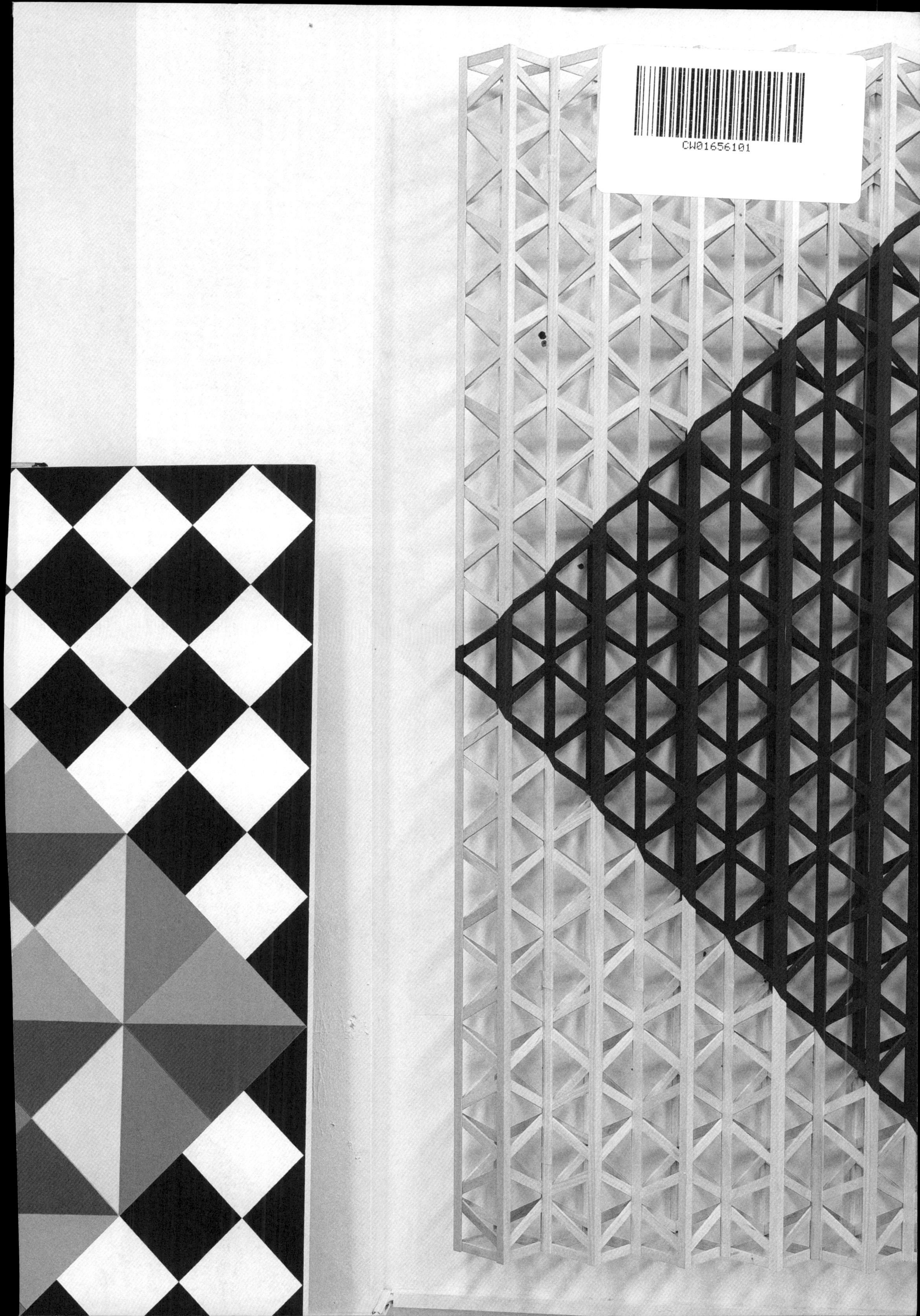

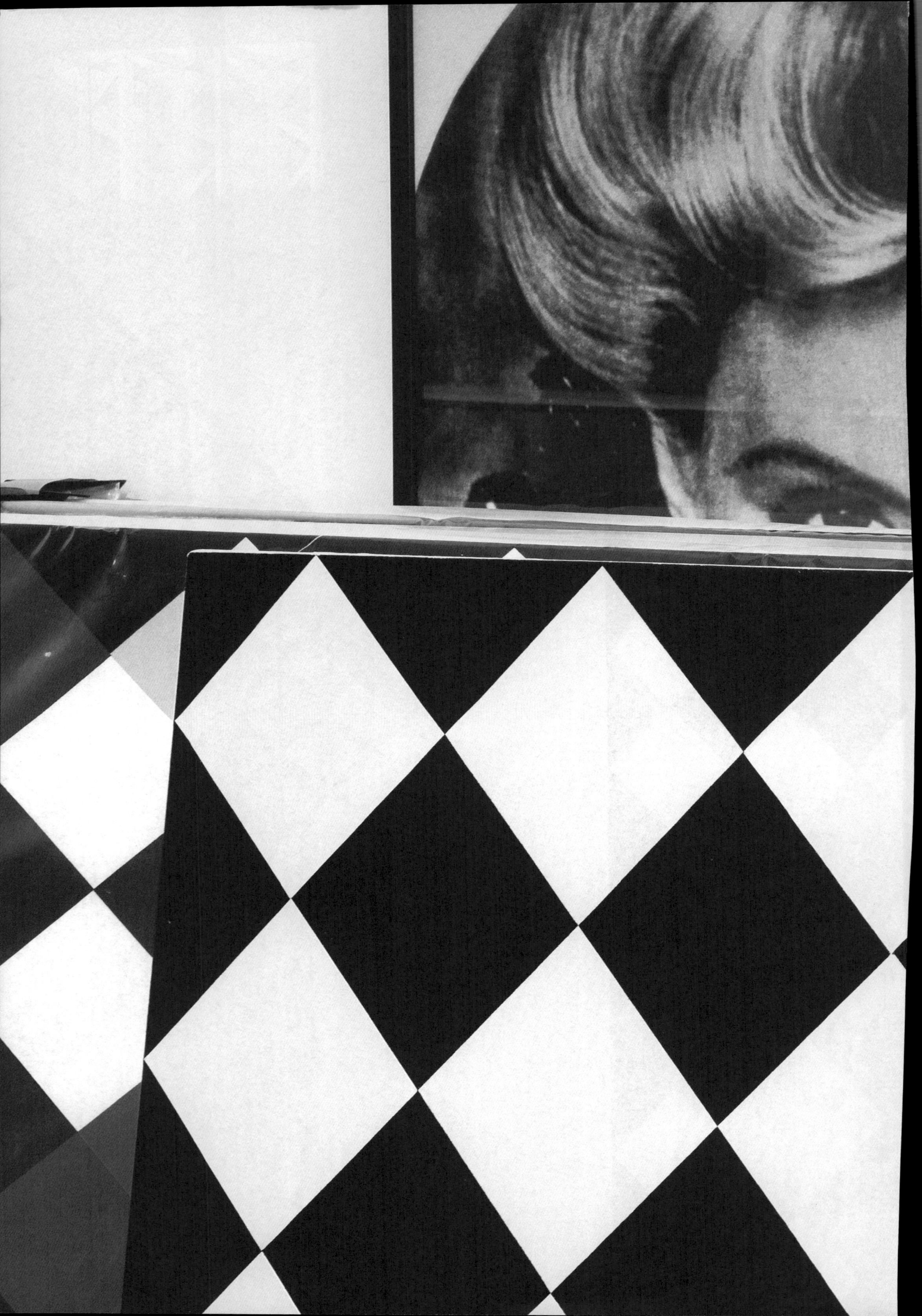

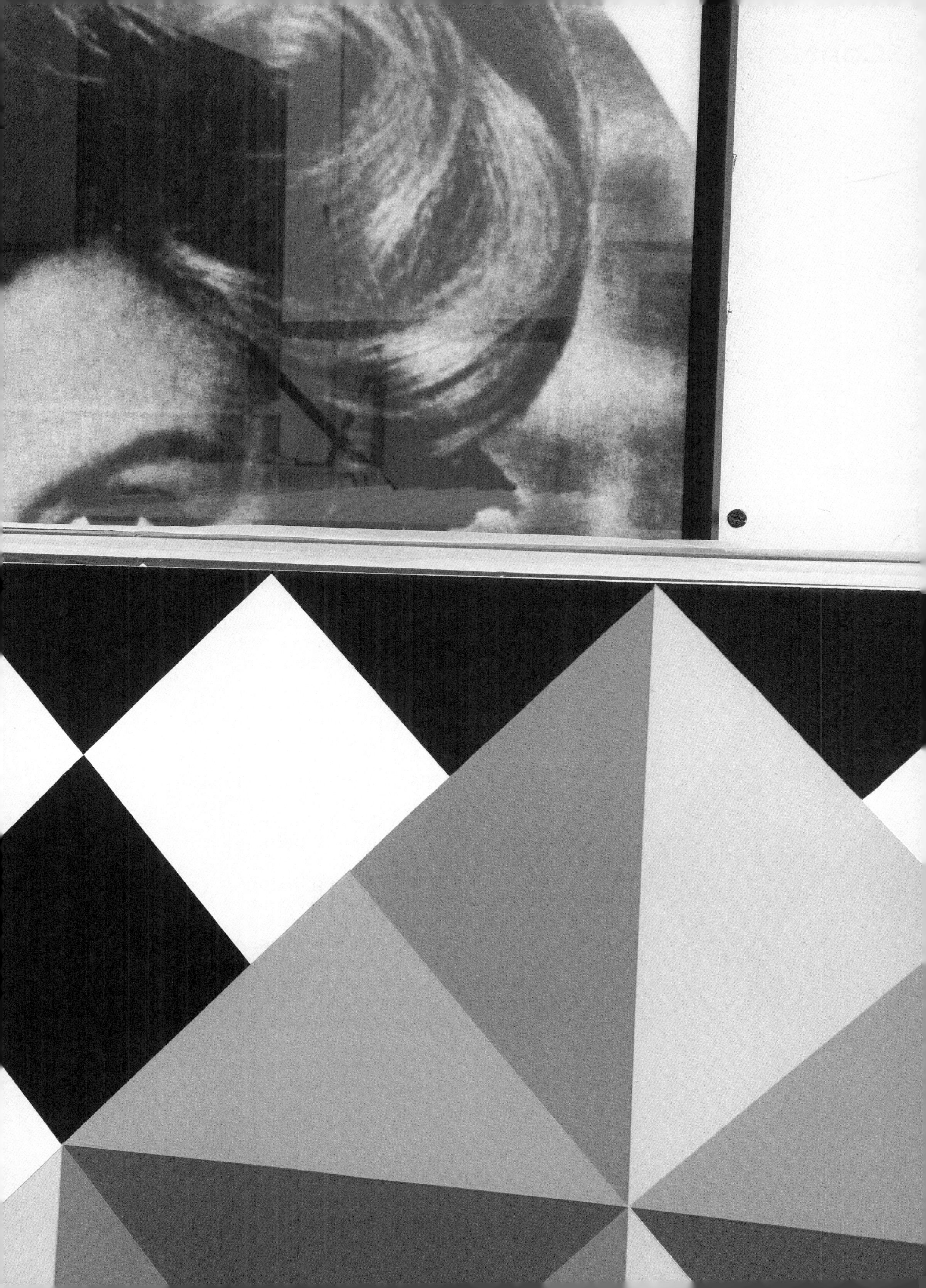

Contents

Preface

Charles Esche

It is an honour to open this publication that accompanies Rasheed Araeen's retrospective.[1] One might rightly think that this exhibition and book are long overdue. The Van Abbemuseum, from where I write, has been as culpable as others in marginalizing the work of women artists and/or artists of non-European origin. Those from the greatest part of the world were regularly deemed to be not (yet) modern enough, and disallowed from taking their place in the canon of mainstream avant-garde practices. One might be tempted to think that our current attempts at opening up to a wider geographic and disciplinary basis is more timely. There is a widespread idea that such artists and practices were simply invisible to twentieth-century art institutions. Araeen's work gives the lie to that assumption. As an artist, writer, publisher, and curator, he has been making work for over sixty years. He has been a resident of the British imperial capital for most of that time and has consistently claimed the right to be seen and heard alongside his London-based colleagues, often as loudly as he could. The fact that this is one of the first times that it is possible to judge his work over the course of his whole working period within a British or European museum retrospective is a signal to both the longevity of the art world's refusal to listen to voices beyond its own familiar social matrix, and Araeen's ultimate success in getting his point across to the current generation of artists and curators.

One of the many persistent investigations Araeen has been working on during these last sixty years is the partiality and blindness of Eurocentric modernism, that practice of art that emerges in the nineteenth century to become the dominant form of visual expression in the century or so that followed. This modernism that we inherit today is one still in need of reshaping. Its claims to universality, emancipation, mutuality, and equality have long been hollow when only certain variants of the human race are allowed to enter fully into its discourse. While various forms of inclusion and expansion have taken place under rubrics such as postmodernism, alter-modernism, or trans-modernism, the core of the effectively white, male story is only now, and only just, beginning to shift significantly. Probably, this is a partial sign that modernism (and modernity, its larger and more powerful ally) is leaving us. Yet its influence over our imagination and capacity for thought is still so great today that it requires urgent undoing and repurposing just in the time of its departure. As Araeen himself has written in his proposal for the project *The Whole Story: Art in Post-War Britain*, discussed at length by curator Kate Fowle: 'Art reflects the society in which it is produced; it conforms to its nature by reflecting it but it also questions and challenges what may be an obstruction to its development as a humane and enlightened society.' He goes on: 'Unfortunately, we do not find this reflection or recognition within the prevailing dominant historical narratives, because they are still part of a history which is constructed on the basis that modernism is exclusive to the West and its indigenous people.' I am confident that the research for *The Whole Story*, should it be realized, will have a long and influential impact on how the modern past comes to be understood in the future.

The Van Abbemuseum is an institution born of the expropriation of wealth in South East Asia, just as many institutions are founded on the appropriated wealth and geopolitics of colonial histories. Yet, as with others, its activities focused exclusively on the modernism of Europe and its majority white colonies. We therefore have much to learn and be grateful for in Araeen's efforts. They allow us to look back at the collections and histories held within our modern institutions with a less blinkered gaze, to observe partiality while understanding where it originated – not to try to correct what happened but to take account of it in the ways we tell the stories of our coming into being and our reasons to continue to exist.

It is equally crucial that Araeen is presented as a contemporary artist in this exhibition – one who continues to challenge and develop his ideas restlessly. It is important to understanding his trajectory as an artist that has gained a completely new following in recent years among his younger peers. His time has come, one might say, as can most obviously be seen in his participation in the 2017 documenta, which presented two substantial projects marking the breadth of his practice: *Shamiyaana–Food for Thought: Thought for Change*, a free restaurant serving lunch to anyone in the centre of Athens for the duration of the exhibition and *The Reading Room Kassel*, comprising thirty-six of his painted wooden Structures on which lay the remarkable archive of words and ideas contained in the history of *Third Text*, the room lined with his fizzing new 'Opus' paintings.

This monograph, though produced to accompany Araeen's retrospective, is conceived as an attempt to add to what an exhibition can offer – particularly one that insists on a chronologically structured display of objects and images. In keeping with the spirit of this retrospective, we have structured the book around a chronological inventory of works made by Araeen from 1953 until the present day. While a central motivation for this is to provide a record of Araeen's production and, we hope, an important resource, it serves as a conceptual grid through which to assess the practice. Thumbing through the 500-odd works reveals the moments in which new ideas are generated and formal propositions offered, while underscoring the formal and conceptual consistency that spans these sixty years of work. This is visible, for example, in the manner in which the transformative motif of fire first emerges in *Burning Bicycle Tyres* (1959) as a way out of representation's limitations, then reappears in *Burning Ties* (1976), and later again in the candle flames of the 'cruciform' work *Bismullah* (1988). It is evidenced in the number nine, first deployed in the aptly titled *Nine* (1968–1975), consisting of a 3 x 3 Structure that would reappear in installations such as *Once Upon a Time* (1994), *Aflatoon (So You Think You Are Plato)* (1994), and *Tigerjee* (1992–1997), but also as the structuring principle of the nine-panel 'cruciform' works.

The format of the publication also allows for an assessment of elements of Araeen's practice that are less sympathetically referenced through the exhibition but that nevertheless are central to understanding the range of his ideas and strategies. This is perhaps most clear in the pieces by Kate Fowle as well as theorists Gene Ray and John Roberts, each of which examine Araeen's founding and editorship of the journal *Third Text* (1987–2011), his exhibition and art historical projects *The Other Story: Afro-Asian Artists in Post-War Britain* (1989–1990), and *The Whole Story* (2001 – ongoing), and his recent manifesto *Art Beyond Art, Ecoaesthetics: A Manifesto for the 21st Century* (2010), respectively. Whilst these vital components of Araeen's practice are brought into the exhibition through drawings, archival material, documents, and *The Reading Room* installation, the format of the book allows for a more detailed, critical assessment of the manner in which they have fed into Araeen's work – or what he describes in his conversation with curator and editor of this monograph Nick Aikens as a 'conceptual extension of what I was producing as art objects'.

I would like to thank all the writers in this book and especially to recognize the work of my colleague Nick Aikens, who has worked so closely with the artist and curated such a perceptive and stimulating exhibition. We are happy that this important body of work has been met with enthusiasm by some of our colleagues in the art world. Their support, both spiritual and financial, has made it possible for the exhibition to happen and given it different contexts varying from the offshore United Kingdom to locations in Western, central, and Eastern Europe.

In the UK, Araeen's home, the work will speak to a renewed imperial context in which British exceptionalism is peppered with xenophobic and supremacist exclusions that lie at its heart. In Western and central Europe, the challenge of the work is more directly to the artistic exclusions of Eurocentric modernism, one that is also rooted in the legacy of colonialism. Finally, in Russia, the histories of the revolutionary avant-garde will resonate with the work in different ways, while also attesting to the particular forms of ethnic and political marginalization that continue there. I would therefore like to thank you, our colleagues at MAMCO, BALTIC, and Garage, who have been such a supportive group with which to work. Primarily our thanks go to Araeen himself of course, for his inspiring generosity and wonderful dedication in allowing us to realize this show – thank you for your work and your commitment over the past decades; you are a model for engaged artists and thinkers everywhere today.

1 This publication accompanies Rasheed Araeen's retrospective at the Van Abbemuseum, Eindhoven; MAMCO, Musée d'art moderne et contemporain, Geneva; BALTIC Centre for Contemporary Art, Gateshead; and Garage Museum of Contemporary Art, Moscow. See colophon for full exhibition information, 411.

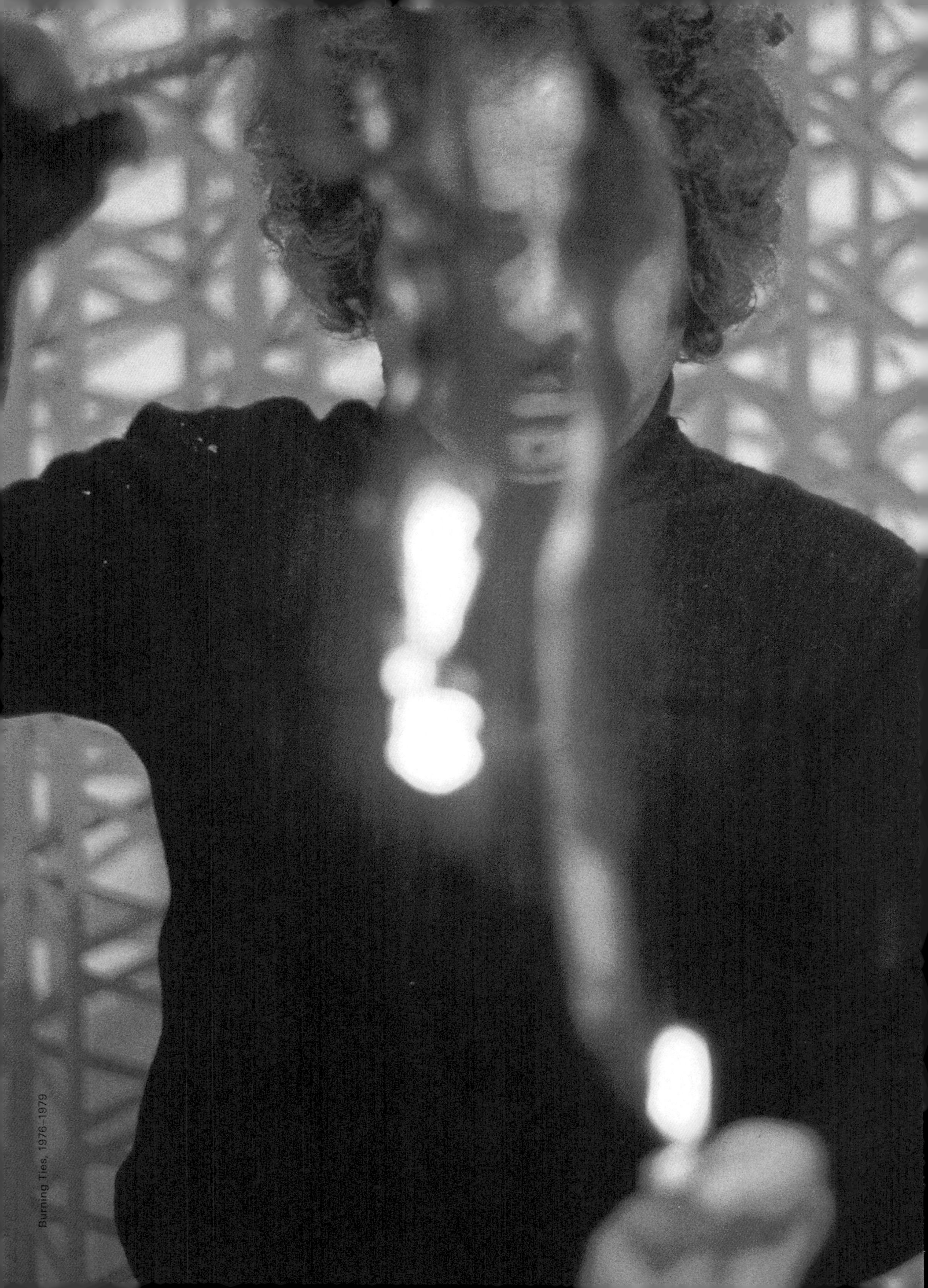

Burning Ties, 1976–1979

Introduction: Burning Ties

Nick Aikens

> Art cannot be developed by a set of rules but only through an evolving life process that generates new ideas at every stage of its transformation.[1]

In his performance *Burning Ties* (London, 1979), Rasheed Araeen is dressed in black. With his gloved right hand he holds a stick above his head, from which hang five differently patterned red neckties. He lights one with his free hand, and the four remaining ties quickly catch fire. A wall of flames then obscures Araeen's face and upper body. As they die down and the ties turn to ash, the artist comes into view, positioned in front of the red diagonal struts of his lattice reliefs on the wall behind him. The photo documentation of the performance comprises a series of eight powerful images; they are slightly out of focus: the reds of the ties, flames, and lattice bleed into one another with Araeen's silhouette emerging through them to fill the frame. The sequence reveals an artist in total command of the formal and symbolic arsenal at his disposal. Indeed, the performance takes place at a critical juncture within the 'journey' of Araeen's ideas as his practice moves from a sculptural language of abstraction to one both personal and overtly politicized. Art historian Courtney J. Martin lays this out in her essay in this volume charting the evolution of Araeen's work in the 1970s from a studio-centric practice to a performance, writing, and an outwardly political practice. *Burning Ties* shows the manner in which he began to position himself – his struggles, his image, his body – at the nexus of his critical investigations.

The operation taking place in *Burning Ties*, like many throughout the extraordinary trajectory of Araeen's practice, is calculated and precise. I read it firstly as standing for the destruction of an archetypal bourgeois symbol, of English propriety, of corporate boardroom formality. It is destruction in the name of creativity, enacted by an artist who has chosen to confront a system from which he has been excluded and to borrow the title of his 1984 book, who insists on making himself visible. I also read the setting alight of ties as a confrontation with a set of institutions that had – and to a large extent still do – operated within the spheres of influence of white privilege. This included a British art establishment that seemed to have told Araeen, following his arrival from Pakistan in 1964, that his contribution to modernism and Minimalism was not valid as each were the domain of white European and American men. By setting fire to that genealogy and standing before his unmistakably Minimalist, modernist works, Araeen confronts and undoes such assumptions. 'The issue of genealogy', as critic Jean Fisher notes 'lies at the centre of the art establishment's antagonism to Araeen's counter-history and illuminates the radicality of his position'.[2]

Araeen chose to carry out this performance in front of one of his abstract lattice pieces. These works, painted wooden reliefs and freestanding columns that used intersecting diagonals, were integral to his investigations into the non-hierarchical and egalitarian properties of geometry and symmetry in the 1960s. As with all of his Structures (a term Araeen also uses more broadly to describe the Minimalist work of which his lattices are part) – including his open cubes of different sizes and colours – the lattice works have been central features and conceptual devices within his work ever since. Yet, when he took steps away from abstraction towards an interrogation of systems of representation he opted to use one of these works as a backdrop. Araeen's *Burning Ties* is not meant as a break from the formal language of his past work. Rather, it insists on infusing that language, repositioning it within a new visual vocabulary and political agenda. As the epigraph to this introduction alludes, the lattice is incorporated into a new stage of transformation. This is also true of the act of burning itself. Araeen's encounter with a burnt bicycle tyre on the side of a street in Karachi in 1959 while he was, by his own admission, an artist-hobbyist painting portraits and landscapes, was a formative moment. It opened up an understanding of art that did not need to be confined by representation – that could be first and foremost conceptually and formally generative. That Araeen revisits the act of burning to re-engage with the question of representation as an artist in the context of a structurally racist Britain, is a testament to the manner in which his ideas and aesthetic strategies evolve and revolve, unsettling our reading of what came before and creating new avenues through which to understand his work.

Universality and Geometric Thinking

> My ultimate aim is to create symmetry within human relationships. Not just between humans but humans and other forms of life. That is the political aspect of my work. You can use geometry and symmetry in art to realize equality in the world.[3]

At the core of Araeen's artistic project are enduring themes that resurface over sixty years of work. Arguably the most striking of these is that of universality, which appears in the title of the opening text by writer Michael Newman and throughout the volume's pages. As Newman rightly points out the universal might seem a strange frame within which to assess Araeen's work given that one of the central projects of postcolonial theory – or more fittingly for Araeen, anti-colonial positions – has been to take on and dismantle the Western notion of Enlightenment universalism that was both blind to cultural difference and to the position of power from which it was conceived. Yet Araeen's understanding of the universal, or what Newman terms 'critical universalism' points to a way past the hegemonic reading of the term imposed on us by Enlightenment thinkers. Indeed, in light of art theorist Zoë Sutherland's observation that Araeen's chosen strategy is to work *within and against* institutional structures or systems of knowledge, it seems entirely fitting that his work allows us to decouple the concept of the universal from the violent confines of Western modern-colonial thinking towards a genuine proposition for equality and mutuality. Araeen's engagement with universality, therefore, is a mark of his ongoing resistance to the loss of terms and ideas to a central, hegemonic position, insisting that we re-engage them from different grounds – or, as Edward Said argued when considering the role of the contemporary intellectual it shows 'a perpetual willingness not to let half-truths or received ideas steer one along'.[4] As Newman's essay points out, Araeen's method for repositioning universality is through his use of geometry and abstraction: 'The space of abstraction, understood as axiomatic and based in equality, facilitates the critique of the entwinement of power and representation, and relation of representation to exclusion.' What is compelling about Newman's appraisal is that it reads the artist's geometric forms – that we would most readily, though mistakenly, place within a modernist, Western aesthetic paradigm – as a conceptual device through which Araeen has wrested the concept of universality away from modern Europe. First through the Structures themselves and the use of geometry as an organizing principle that eschews hierarchy. And second, in the Structures including the lattices becoming backdrops in Araeen's politicized performances – most noticeably seeing the artist gagged and blindfolded in *'Paki Bastard' (Portrait of the Artist as a Black Person)* (1977) – as an equalizing counter to the image of the artist as ethnic 'other', which he so fervently takes on.

Writer Kaelen Wilson-Goldie describes Araeen's 'late' work, his most recent paintings in the 'Homecoming' (2010–2014) and 'Opus' (2014 – present) series', as 'purely joyful, dryly mathematical, archly conceptual, and decidedly mischievous all at once'. Following Newman's analysis, she reads these paintings as reframing abstraction and geometry – widely considered by Europe and America as *their* twentieth-century avant-garde invention – as pushed by Islamic thinkers and mathematicians in the eighth, ninth, and tenth centuries for being an embodiment of equality and universality on a societal level that funnels through into the arts. These paintings, which Wilson-Goldie persuasively loops back to Araeen's time in Karachi and his Minimalist Structures, appear as the latest iteration of the artist's persistent challenges put to the suppositions of Eurocentric modernism, and the ideas and formal languages in art that it professed to invent. By doing so Wilson-Goldie argues Araeen's Structures reframe modernism, both geographically and temporally, transferring it from the twentieth-century artistic centres of Paris, Amsterdam, and New York to Umayyad Damascus or Abbasid Baghdad over 1,000 years ago. They are part of Araeen's evolving relationship with Islam – not as a system of beliefs to which he adheres, but as a body of knowledge and aesthetic language that, as he tells Wilson-Goldie, opens up our understanding of 'the history of humanity' where 'geometric thinking allows us to perceive the world in terms of equality for all'.

Interestingly, mathematics professor Marcus du Sautoy positions Araeen's use of geometry and symmetry away from the sphere of modern art altogether. He recognizes in Araeen a desire, like that of the mathematician 'to extract the patterns and universal structures underlying the particularities of the physical world'. Significantly Du Sautoy sees in Araeen's geometric forms a pull towards 'shapes that are universal and *not bound by cultural reference*' (italics added). Araeen's insistence on not being 'bound by cultural reference' connects what at first seem different facets of his practice – allowing us to see his use of geometry in line with his outspoken resolve that artists are acknowledged for the work they produce, not through the framing of racial or ethnic identity that has, since the 1980s, become endemic in both the globalized contemporary art world and the discourse of postcolonialism.

As Sutherland lays out in her close reading of the 'cruciform' works of the 1980s and 1990s, reclaiming universality and by inference equality away from a Western paradigm extends beyond Araeen's use of geometry and symmetry, even if this remains its most potent and accessible articulation. His use of green monochrome in the four corners of the nine-panel works, she points out, evokes a set of references, 'the core colour of Arab and Islamic universalisms – religious and secular – and nationalisms' that offer 'parallel[s] between these connotations of a universalism rooted in a world religion and those of the colour white in Western
tradition'. By framing images that span sacrificial killings (*Green Painting I*, 1985), 262
gender and class struggles (*Tableau Noir*, 1987) or the equating of Western 266
imperial aggression with its manifestation in the images and myths of modern
art (*Golden Calf*, 1987) with the green monochrome, the 'cruciform' works cut 269
through the binary positioning of East and West and their cultural manifestations, asking us to consider them as entangled and co-constituting. As with Araeen's recent paintings, abstraction is thus lifted away from the domain of autonomous art production as understood through mainstream art history and replayed back to the West, revealed as complicit in what Frantz Fanon called the violence of praxis that is central to the condition of both colonizer and colonized.[5]

Collectivity and Mutuality

> The real aim of the work is to show that it is possible to confront and challenge the established view of things [...] This challenge is not carried out by an individual, but is realized through a process that recognizes the collective creativity of people, so as not only to re-define and construct

radically a new premise of art but also the role of the artists as well as of the public in its conception and execution.[6]

Tied closely to Araeen's conjuring of a reclaimed form of universality is that of equality, evidenced in his repeated push for collective action. The Conceptual beginnings of this approach lie in his Minimalist experiments in works such as *Chakras* (1969–1970) and *Zero to Infinity* (first proposed to the Institute of Contemporary Arts as *Biostructural Play* in 1968) – the subject of a close reading by art historian Dominic Rahtz. The first step in breaking systems of hierarchy is to set up the conditions through which outcomes remain undetermined; grappling with this process in the late 1960s Araeen experimented with ways to break open the limitations of a static work of art. By releasing discs into the water next to his studio in London's Docklands in 1970 or inviting the public to rearrange his cubic Structures in *Zero to Infinity*, the artist becomes an initiator but not the author of an artistic process. This approach pushes against the logic of artist-as-genius, central to the paradigm of Western modernism and, through a modest act, aims to harness the potential of the multiple over the singular. Rahtz rightly contextualizes these works within the contemporaneous tendency in Conceptual art practices to 'explore the social and political potential of participation and play'. For Araeen, the infinite possibilities afforded by the audience's continued rearranging of the cubic Structures, extends what Du Sautoy calls 'the politics of symmetry', pointing to a proposition that breaks the binary between symmetry and asymmetry.[7] Araeen tells us that he sees symmetry when considered the flattening and equalizing of all subjects as having its most latent manifestation in communism, and the asymmetry of capitalism is its supposedly dynamic binary. *Zero to Infinity* enacts a dialectic between the two – the symmetry of the 10 x 10 cubes will be broken, but it remains latent in the work. What's more, it is the creativity of individuals that enacts this dialectic. While works such as *Zero to Infinity* and *Chakras* eschew any direct political references, in their structure and formation they point to Araeen's long-held belief in the political potential of creative action. 136, 305

Six years after the first iteration of *Chakras*, Araeen returned to these principles in the closing section of his seminal text 'Preliminary Notes for a BLACK MANIFESTO', referenced by multiple authors in the book, but addressed specifically by Martin as part of her analysis of the overt politicization of Araeen's work in the 1970s. In the closing section of the text Araeen puts forward the idea of a jointly conceived Third World Praxis. Araeen's 'proposed work' would be constructed with and through collective action, by people submitting material and texts, and critically engaging with its content. This engagement, Araeen stated should be premised on the 'DENUNCIATION OF AND CONFRONTATION WITH IMPERIALIST CULTURE and THE SYSTEM that perpetuates international domination'.[8] Like the releasing of *Chakras* into the water in London's Docklands, though now infused with a newfound political charge, this closing section of the 'BLACK MANIFESTO' 'provides a [conceptual] starting point in a direction towards a new-dynamism' that is neither defined nor wholly understood. It is driven by an impulse to unleash a creative force that is not restricted 'by a set of rules' but determined by the collective will, intellect, and artistic drive of those involved. Like many of his propositions, Araeen's ideas would only be fully realized some years later. In the case of the gauntlet laid down by the call for a Third World Praxis, Araeen's initiation and stewardship of *Third Text* stands as its most coherent and potent manifestation. 230

Thirty-five years after 'BLACK MANIFESTO', Araeen wrote his latest manifesto *Art Beyond Art, Ecoaesthetics: A Manifesto for the 21st Century*. The propositional, collective impulse behind *Chakras* and 'BLACK MANIFESTO' resurface here. As critical theorist Gene Ray notes, the manifesto combines 'various metaphors, stories, project proposals, and a running dialogue with art history' in seeking 'nothing less than the kinds of elusive inspirations, which, sometimes in history, move and encourage people to alter the restricting patterns of everyday life'. In the essay 'Food for Thought: Thought for Change' Araeen introduces a vision for how collective creativity might serve as a model to counter the systemic, life-threatening damage inflicted on the Earth by capitalist consumption. As with the conceptual proposition of *Chakras*, the collaborative creation required for *Zero to Infinity*, or the counter-hegemonic offer of Third World Praxis, Araeen asks us to imagine the open-ended potential of creativity to forge new, localized, decentralized infrastructures. It is an ambitious, utopian vision, placing artistic thinking at the centre of a call to radically rethink the dynamic between public, land, and production. Such a vision may seem out of reach, but so too have many of Araeen's proposals that have ultimately come to fruition. The possibility in 1987, for example, of a journal premised on the promise of offering a 'shift away from the centre of the dominant culture to its periphery in order to consider the centre critically' sustaining itself in a homogenized, closed, and xenophobic Britain would itself have seemed like utopian thinking.[9] The collective efforts of those involved in that endeavour ensured it delivered on its founding aims.

Whose Modernism?

> I'm not doing it for myself, for black artists, or for the Third World. My main focus is modernism.[10]

Connecting the many different facets of Araeen's practice is a relentless quest to rethink the formal, ideological, and political assumptions of Eurocentric modernism – one of the central threads running through my conversation with the artist. An outspoken articulation of this can again be traced back to 'BLACK MANIFESTO'. It opens by chastising the impact of colonialism and imperialism on contemporary art in the third world: 'THE ESTABLISHMENT OF EUROPEAN CIVILIZATION AS THE MAINSTREAM IS ONE OF THE MOST CATASTROPHIC DEVELOPMENTS THAT HAVE TAKEN PLACE IN HUMAN HISTORY, DESTROYING OR SUPPRESSING OTHER CULTURES AND CIVILIZATIONS.'[11] This statement inflects our reading of the whole range of work within Araeen's practice – it is at the core of his burning persistence to counter the effect of enforced Eurocentrism on other cultures and the subsequent possibilities for genuine equality. It drives Araeen's practice – his art production, writing, editing, and curatorial projects from the 1970s onwards – fuelling the images he produced and the political discourse he became engaged in, first through the Black Panther movement in London (1972–1973), Artists for Democracy (1975–1976), and the co-founding of *Black Phoenix: Journal of Contemporary Art & Culture in the Third World* (1978) and founding of *Third Text* (1987). It is what is set fire to in *Burning Ties*. It is what he directly challenges in a series such as *Ethnic Drawings* (1986) that combine self-portraits of the artist, overlaid with Urdu script indecipherable to the vast majority of Western viewers along with excerpts of the children's nursery rhyme 'Baa Baa Black Sheep'. Here, Araeen's mischievous, precise rattling of the laziness and centrality of the Western subject – both through the image of the artist that is presented and the language that the Western viewer for the most part cannot read – is Araeen telling us, as he has done so often, that the mainstream cannot be allowed to remain as it is, comfortable in its ignorance.

It was what ultimately drove Araeen to found *Third Text* in 1987, the project for which he is perhaps, to some at least, most widely known. The journal is the subject of theorist John Roberts' cogent essay in this book 'Third Text: Modernism, Negritude, and the Critique of Ethnicity'. Roberts maps the context out of which the journal arose and that Araeen as an artist and political subject was confronting – namely Margaret Thatcher's Britain that since the conservative politician Enoch Powell had inflamed race relations with his infamous 'Rivers of Blood' speech denouncing the effects of immigration on Britain, had been venomously articulating its desire to both distinguish and divide those living on its shores. This imperial logic contended, as Araeen describes in 'BLACK MANIFESTO' that those from elsewhere should be subject to the power of the ruling class, and that their histories, knowledge, and culture should serve as the example to be followed. Over the twenty-five years of Araeen's editorship the journal's insistence on confronting that logic provided a forum for unparalleled debate and intellectual exchange. While for Araeen the roots of this debate were in Britain the far-reaching scope of *Third Text*'s activities by 2012 had, once again reconfigured the centre-periphery dynamic.

And it is within the context of shifting dynamics and evolving ideas that I am honoured to introduce this publication, produced to accompany Araeen's first comprehensive retrospective. The format of both the retrospective and monograph – their capacity to lay out the trajectory of forms, ideas, and concerns that have driven an artistic practice – feels not only necessary but timely for Araeen. Timely, in that it is remarkable that this will be the first time the different stages of his oeuvre are presented in a public institution. Such surprise is tempered when reading curator and writer Kate Fowle's detailed analysis of the manner in which Araeen has struggled to have his ideas heard within the art establishment of his adopted country. Fowle frames this struggle with the example of Araeen's groundbreaking exhibition *The Other Story* (1989) and the subsequent unrealized proposal '*The Whole Story: Art in Postwar Britain*, projects that are symptomatic of the artist's pursuit in overturning what he sees as 'the prevailing history of modernism [being] the history of only white artists'. Timely, also for the fact that Araeen's ongoing negotiation of what he calls 'aesthetic sensibility and political awareness' invites us in 2017 and at a moment of unnerving, global political disquiet, to consider enduring themes of equality and mutuality, regardless of race, culture, or creed. His insistence on the power of the imagination and creativity, as a political project that can combat and overcome systemic hierarchies, as well as the veracious greed of capitalist production, is a mantra with which we need to repeatedly re-engage.

The format of the retrospective – conventionally conceived as a chronological survey of an artist's work and in the case of Araeen's exhibition articulated through five stages – was a strategic choice. Throughout his career, as Sutherland astutely points out, Araeen has been consistent in insisting on operating both 'within and against the institutionalized spaces of the art world'. This approach was integral in his decision to deploy the format of the self-portrait in the 1980s, that archetypal symbol that embodies Western Enlightenment universalism – one (white) man, standing for all – to explore the systems and projections of representation operative in a racially divided and divisive Britain. It drove the projects of *The Other Story* and *The Whole Story*, initiated at the same time, to address what Fowle rightly terms 'the seat of power', by insisting that the contribution of 'African' and 'Asian' artists to British modernism was acknowledged, and paid for, by the very institutions that had hitherto kept them out. It therefore feels necessary that the retrospective, that revered institutional apparatus with which to ratify an artist, should be the format *within* which to understand how Araeen has consistently operated *against* institutionalized forms of knowledge and the problematics they embody.

Returning to the epigraph, then, it is informative to view the different elements of Araeen's work – the stages of his object and image making, his writing, editing, and his dogged insistence on speaking truth to power – as a journey that has 'generate[d] new ideas at every stage of its transformation'. It is for Araeen, as he wrote in 1975, a 'life process', informed by but critically never subjugated to the cultural, political, and personal context from which he speaks. As Said reminds us such committed intellectual and artistic work is 'a complicated struggle', but 'an everlasting effort, constitutively unfinished and necessarily imperfect'.[12] Araeen's is a process that presses us, time and again, to comprehend the potential of creativity and the imagination as forces for equality in the world – to insist that the continual transformation of ideas is the means through which we can foster more complex relationships to history, ourselves, and each other. That, I would suggest, is what drove Araeen to set fire to five ties in 1975 – to undo one set of genealogies in order to make space for another.

1 Rasheed Araeen, 'Preliminary Notes for a BLACK MANIFESTO', *Black Phoenix*, no. 1 (winter 1978):12.
2 Jean Fisher, 'Introduction', in *The Triumph of Icarus: Life and Art of Rasheed Araeen*, ed. Jean Fisher (Karachi: Millennium Media, 2014), 6.
3 See Marcus du Sautoy, 'The Politics of Symmetry', in this volume.
4 Edward Said, *Representations of the Intellectual* (New York: Vintage Books, 1996), 23.
5 Frantz Fanon, *The Wretched of the Earth* (New York: Grove Press, 2004 [1961]), 44.
6 Rasheed Araeen, *Art Beyond Art, Ecoaesthetics: A Manifesto for the 21st Century* (London: Third Text Publications, 2010), 48.
7 Ibid., 47.
8 Araeen, 'BLACK MANIFESTO', 4.
9 'Why Third Text?', *Third Text* 1, no 1 (fall 1987):5.
10 See Kate Fowle, 'Missing History', in this volume.
11 Araeen, 'BLACK MANIFESTO', 12.
12 Said, *Representations*, 23.

Selected Works 1953–2017

R
as
heed
Araeen

Araeen
heed
as
R

The following is an inventory of works made by Rasheed Araeen from 1953–2017. It is not exhaustive, but based on available information at the time of publishing.

A Memory of My Childhood in Punjab, 1953
watercolour on paper, 25 x 36 cm

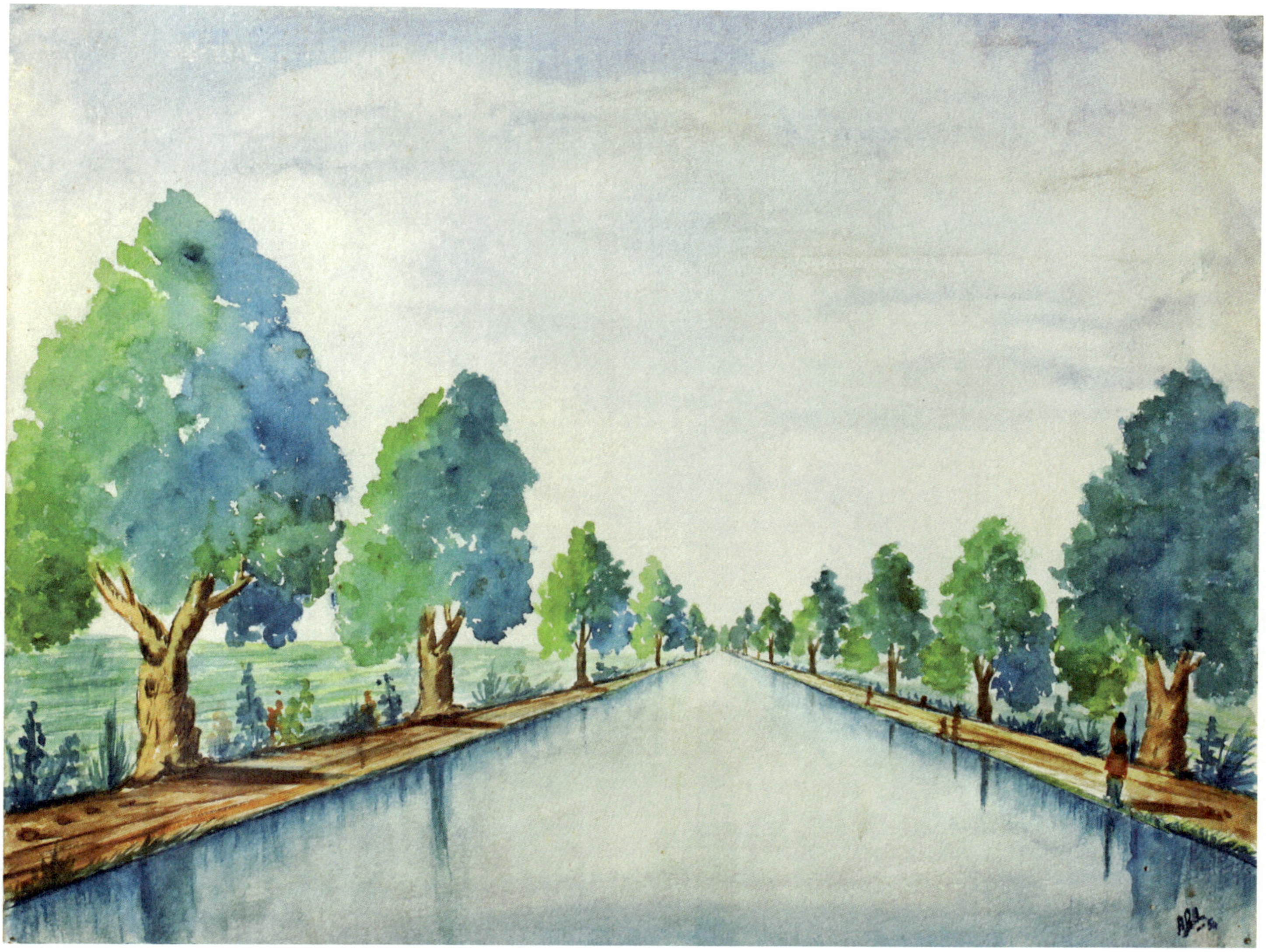

Views of Karachi, 1953–1956
series of 11 watercolours on paper
various dimensions (selection)

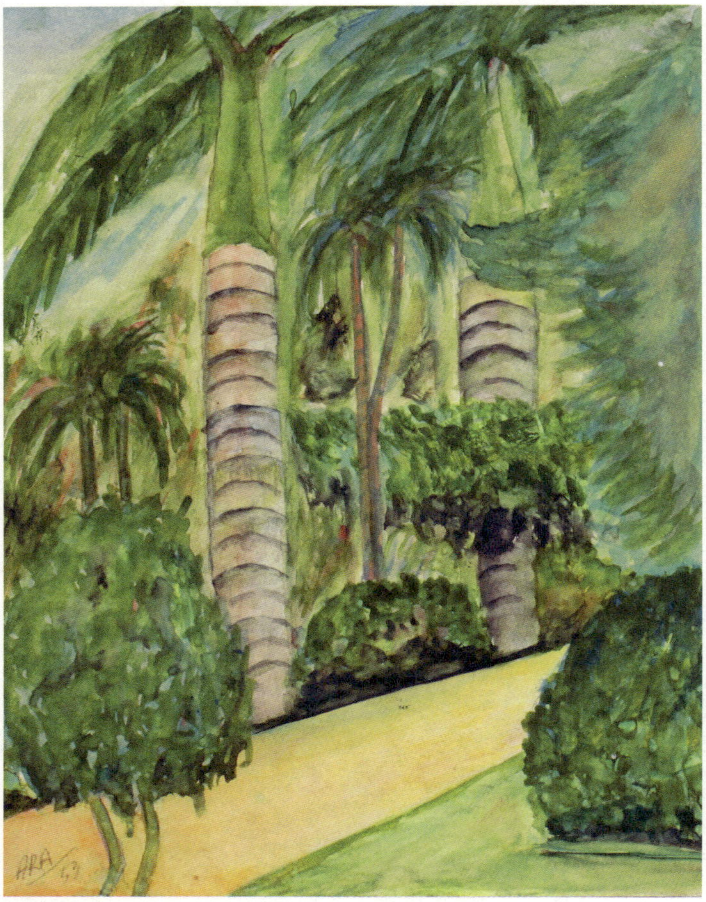

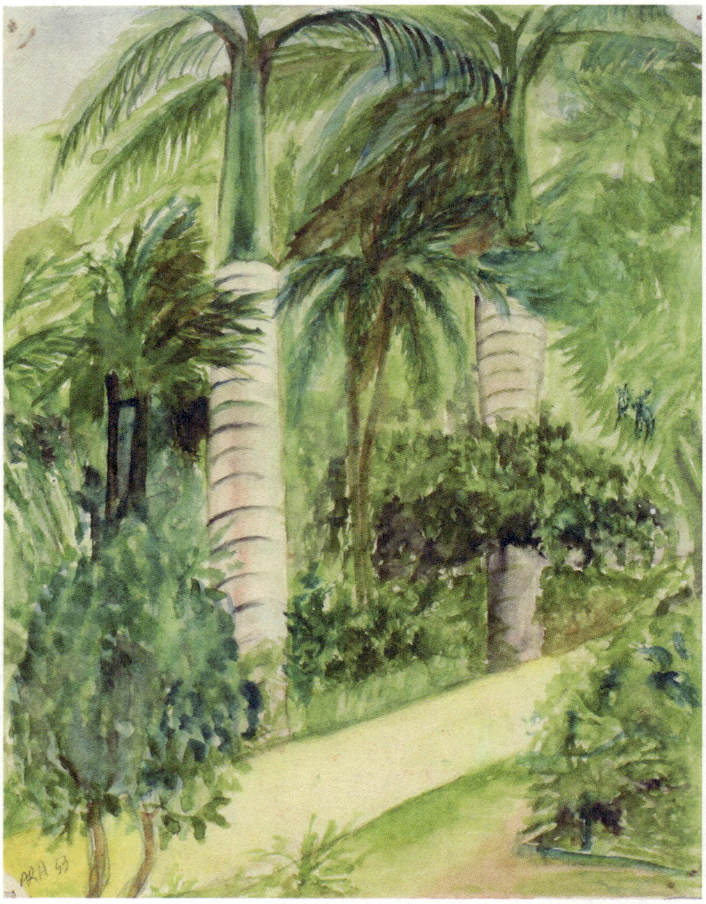

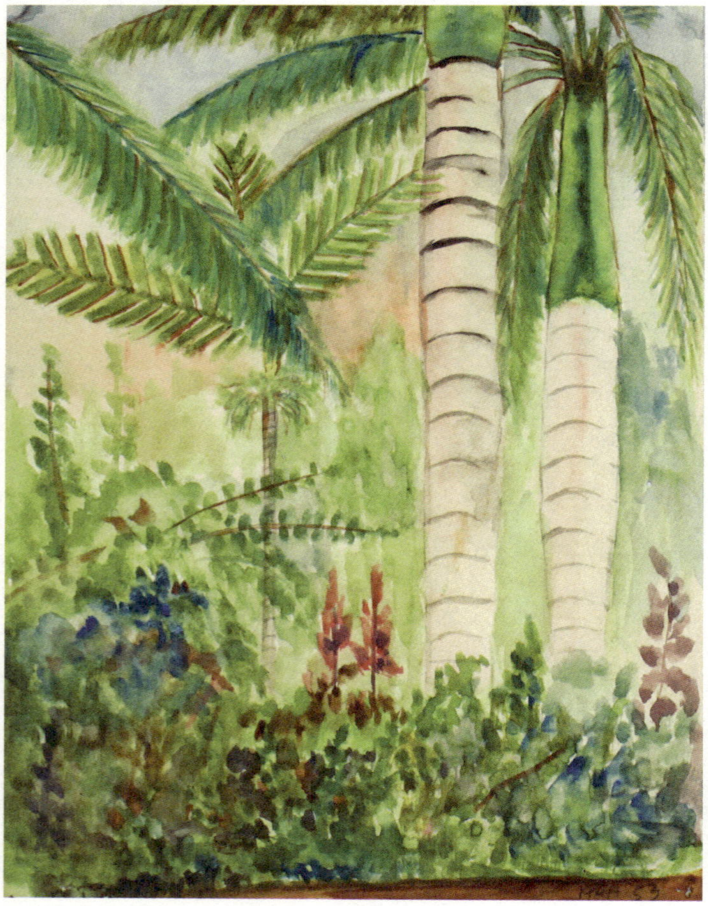

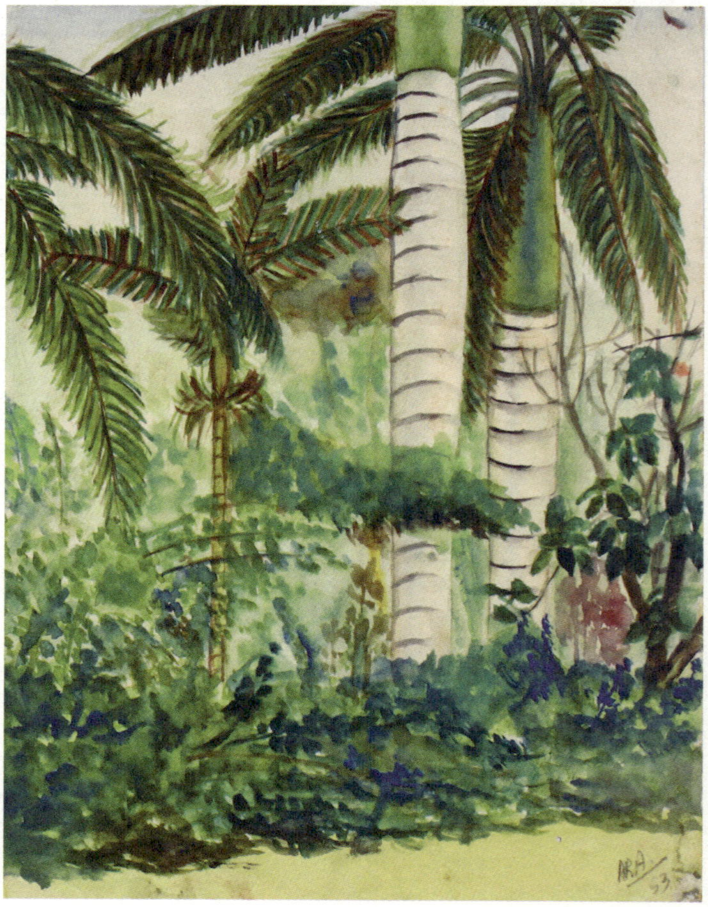

People of Karachi I, 1955–1959
series of 24 works on paper
56 x 41 cm each (selection)

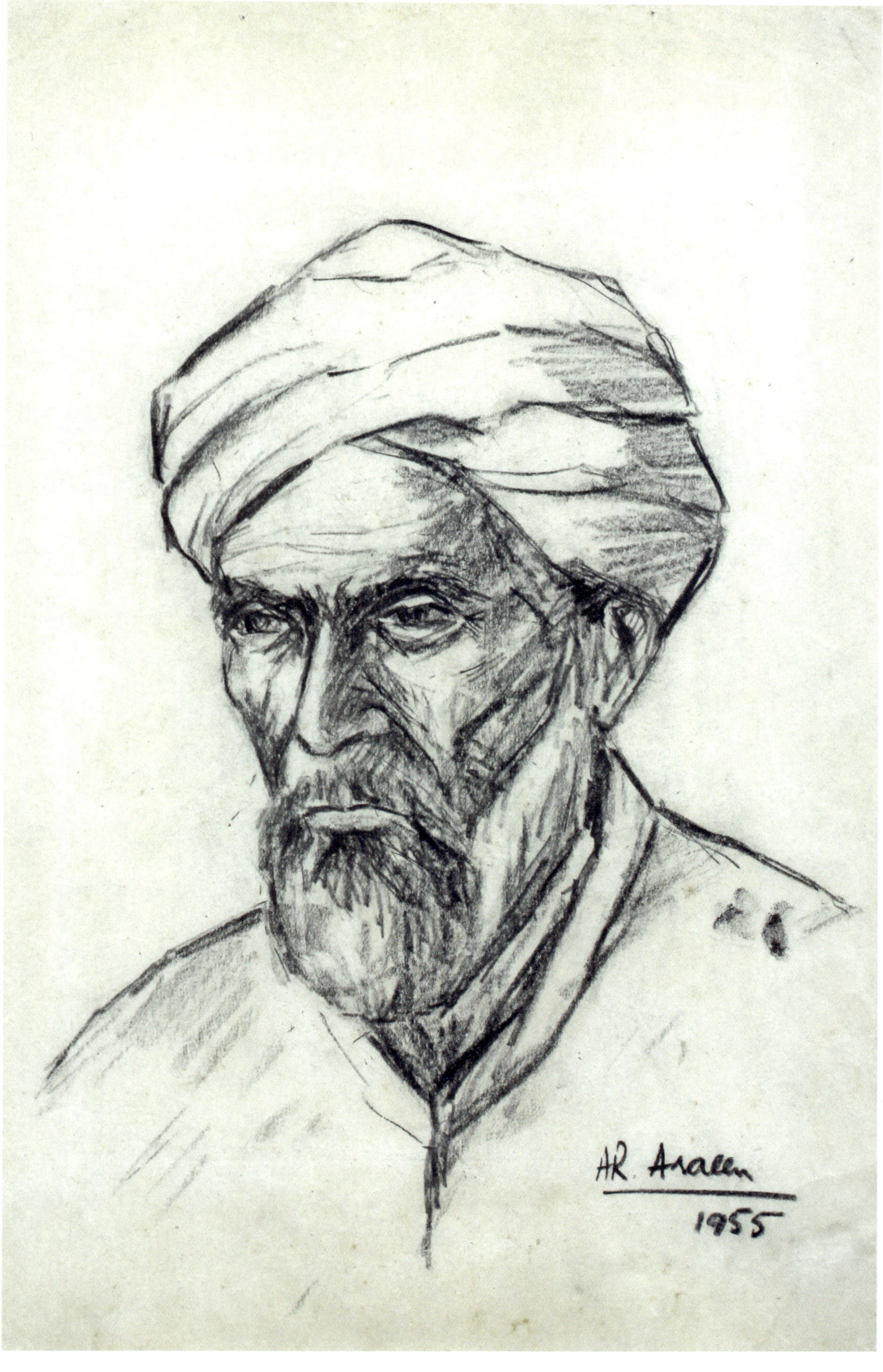

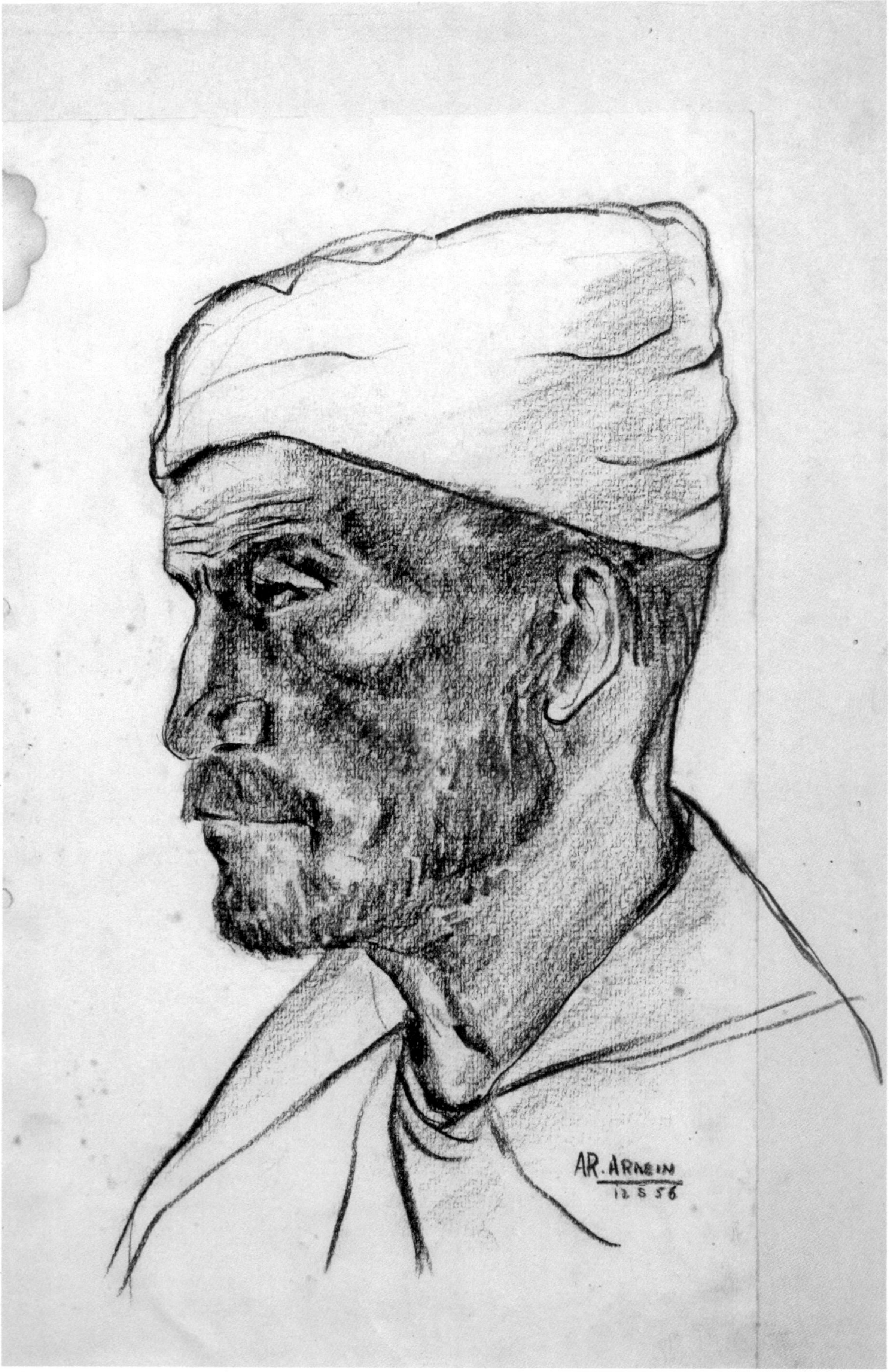
AR. ARAGIN
12 8 56

People of Karachi II, 1957–1959
series of 6 works on paper
56 x 41 cm each (selection)

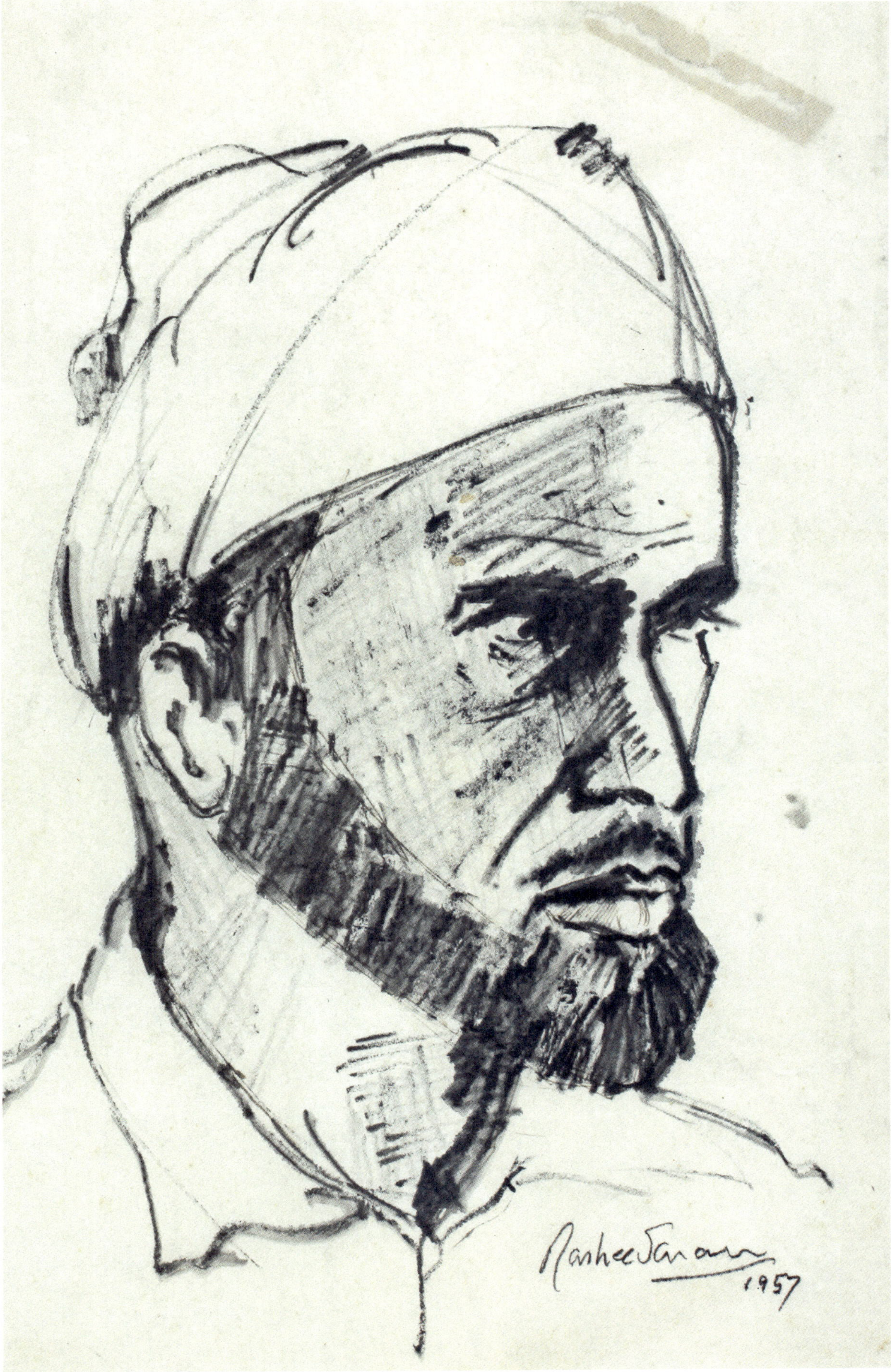

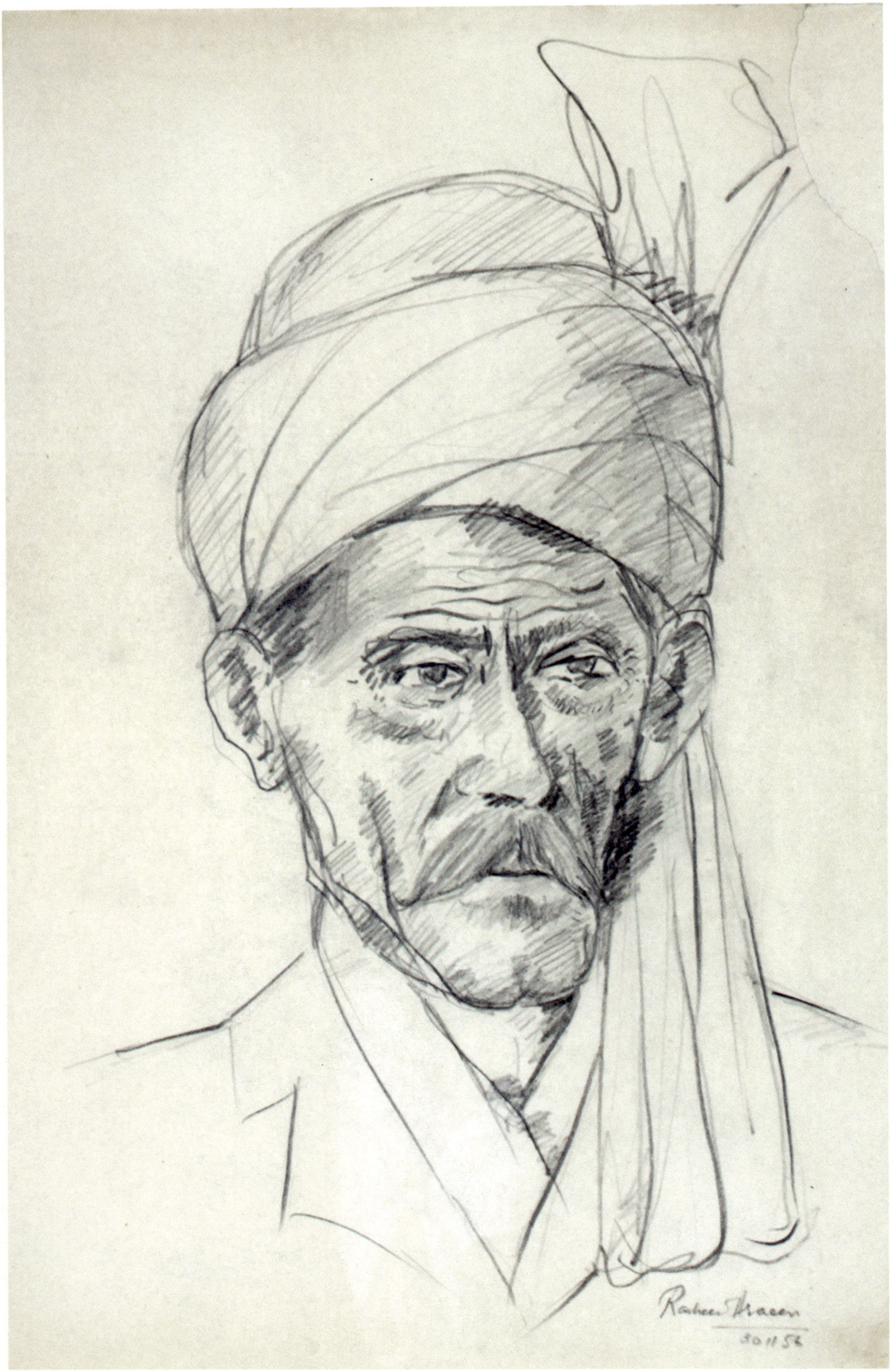

People of Karachi III, 1957–1959
series of 4 works on paper
56 x 41 cm each (selection)

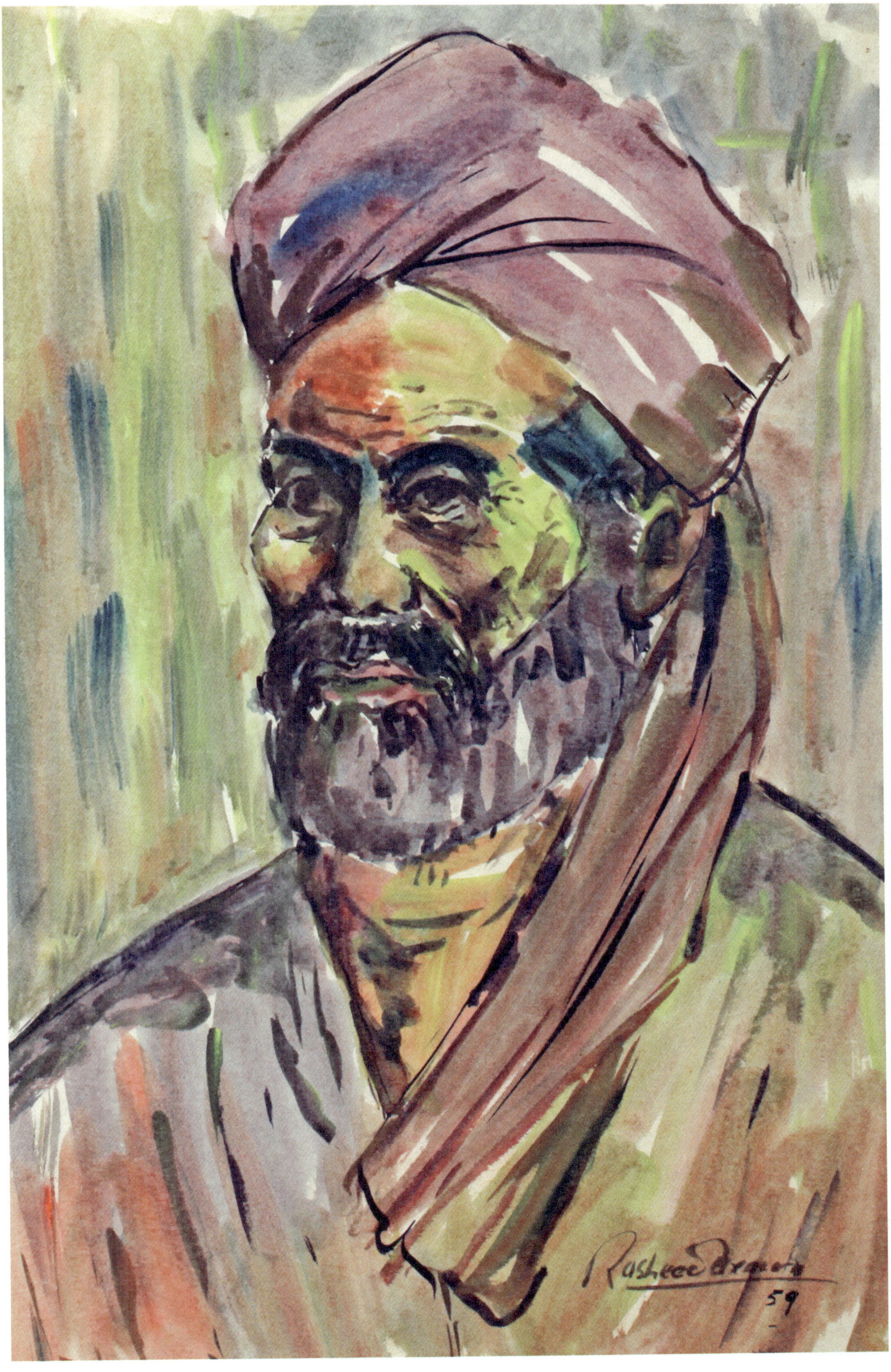

Waves at Sandspit, 1956
watercolour on paper, 27 x 38 cm

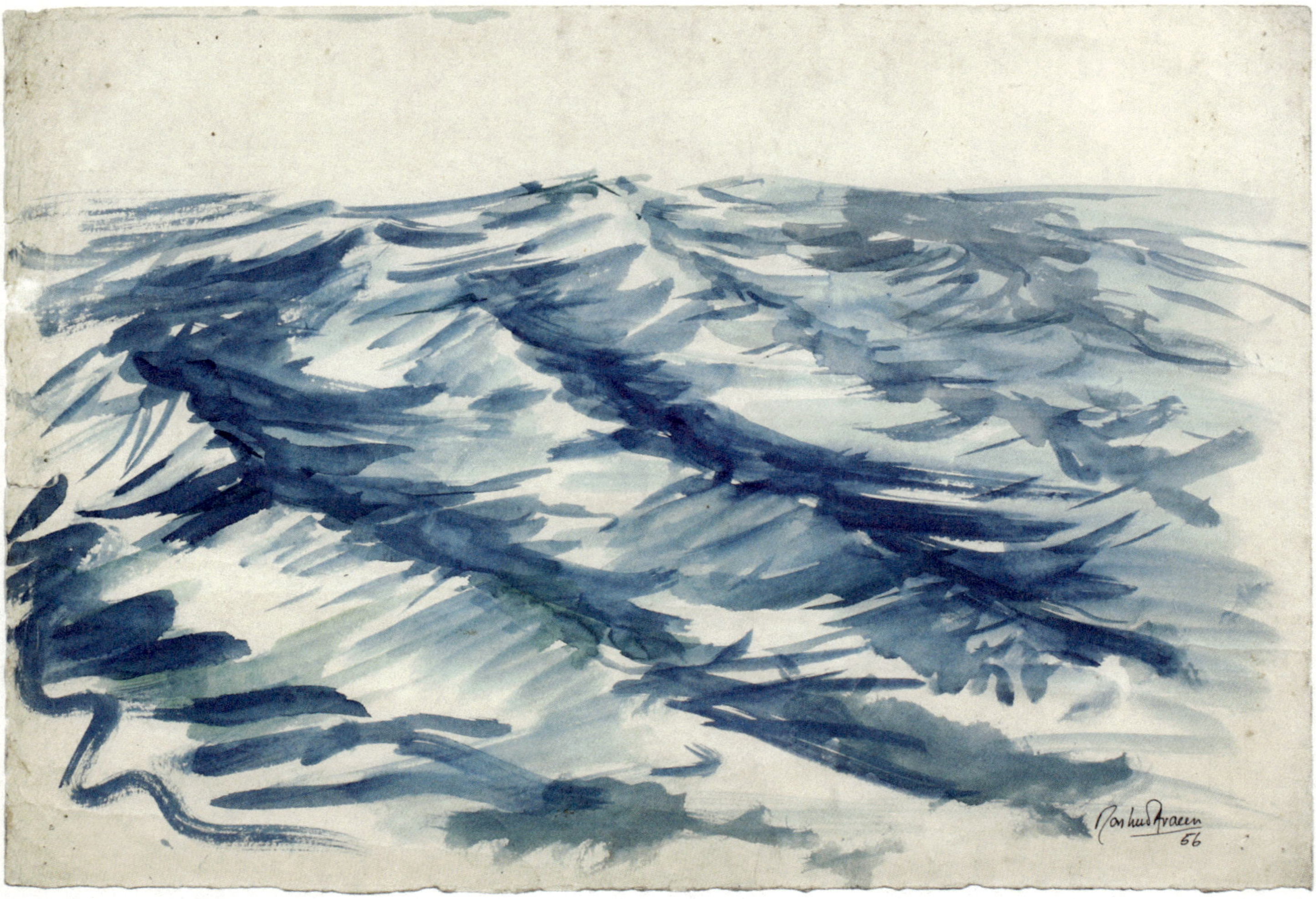

Window Design for a House, 1957
photograph, dimensions unknown

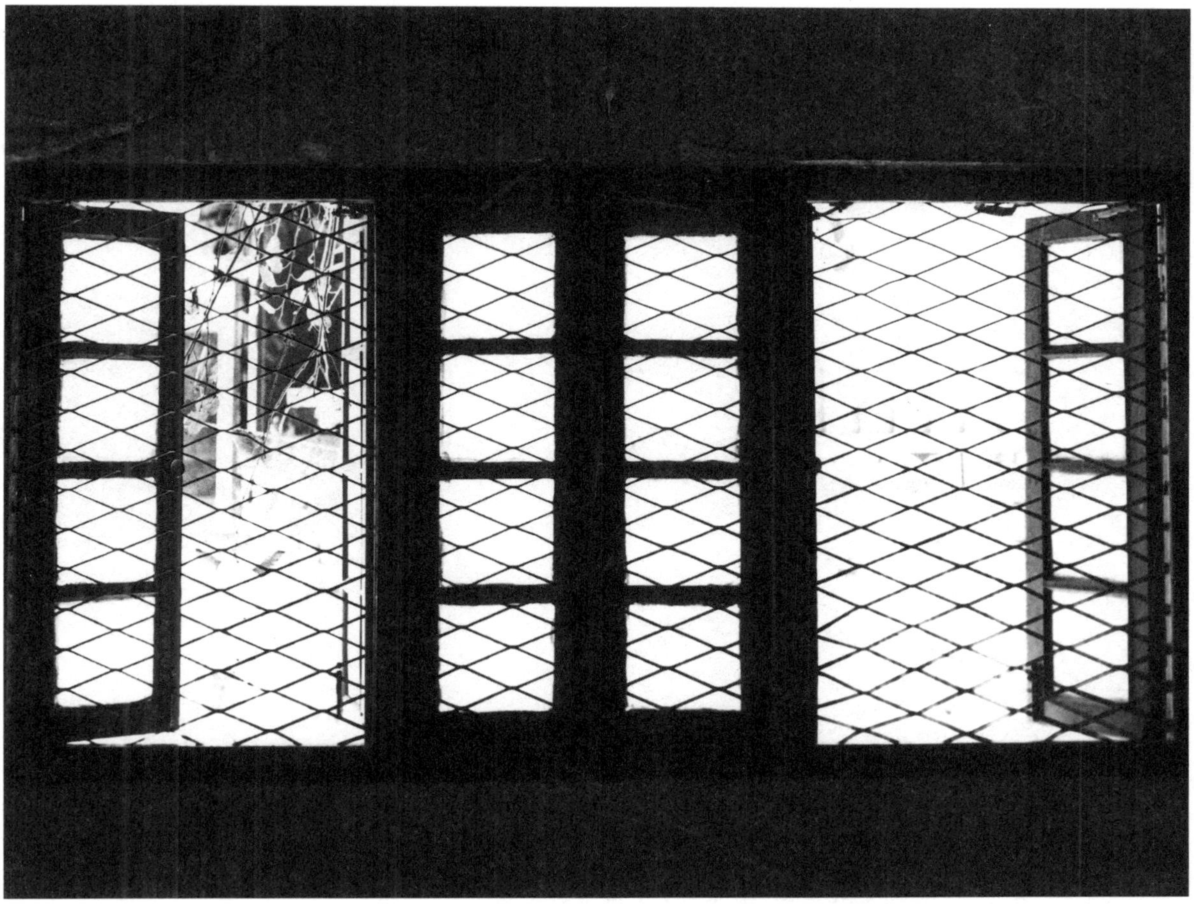

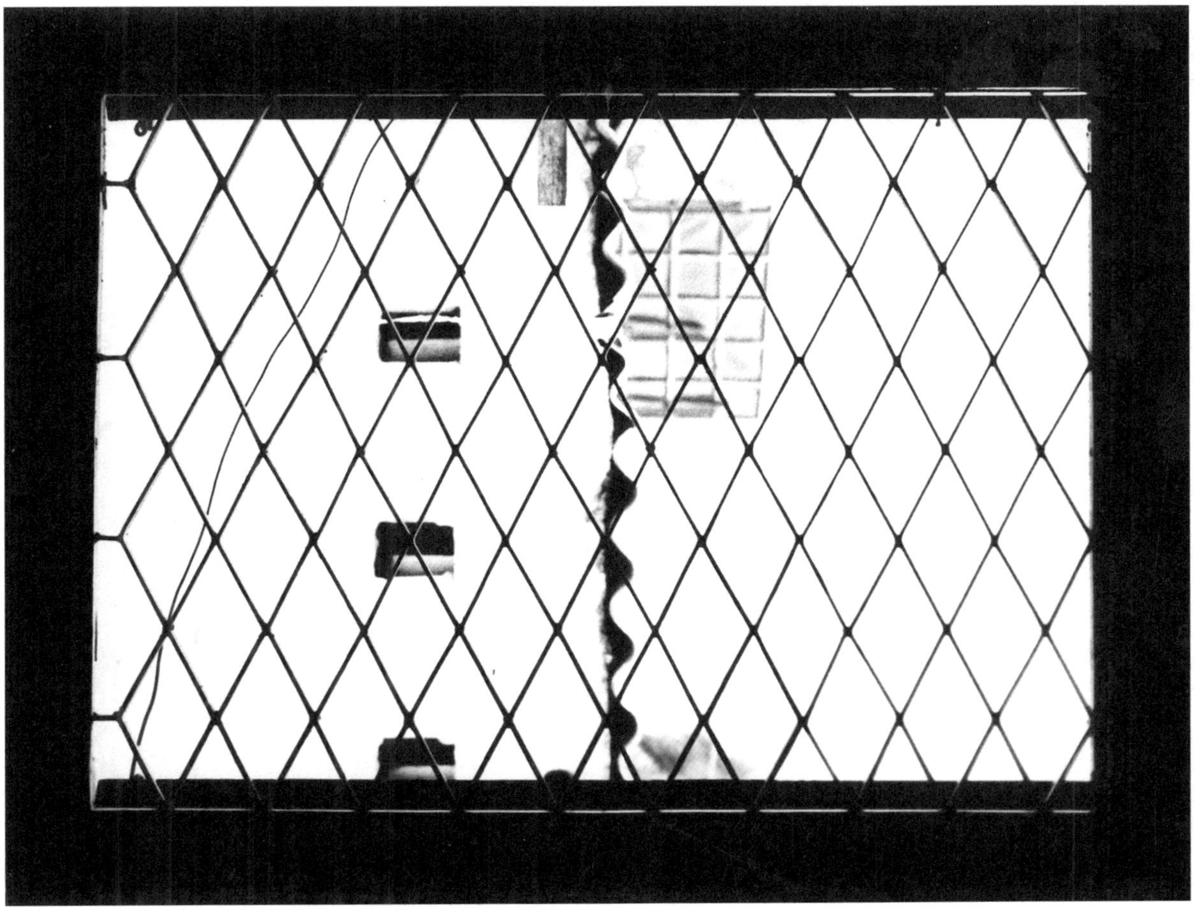

Untitled Green I, 1958
watercolour and ink on paper, 34 x 25 cm
Nightmare, 1958
watercolour and ink on paper, 34 x 25 cm

Untitled Green II, 1958
watercolour and ink on paper, 34 x 25 cm

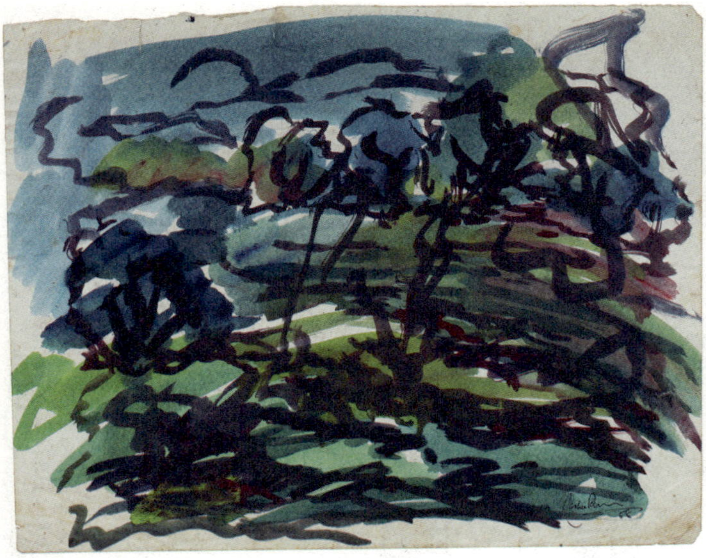

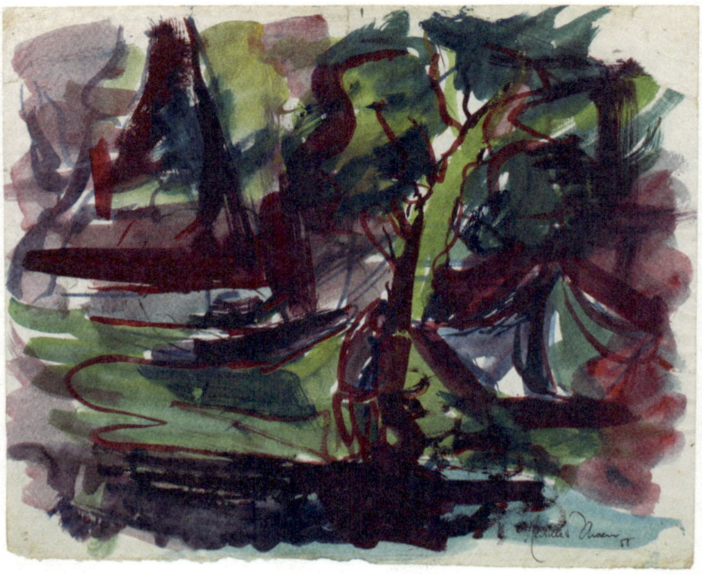

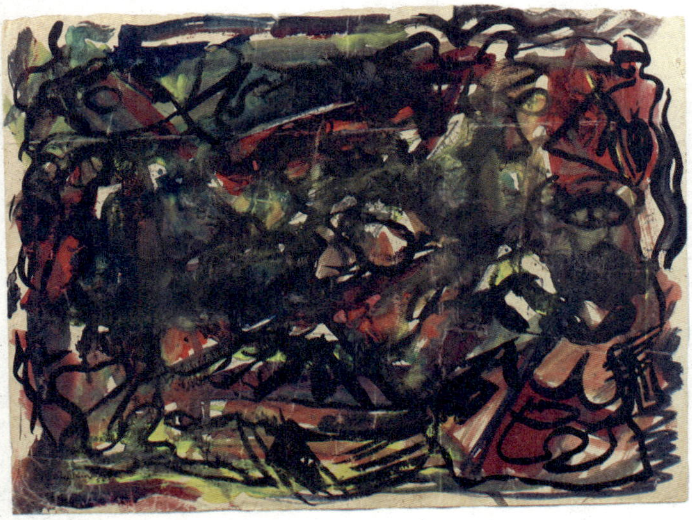

Boats at Keamari, 1958
series of 6 watercolours on paper, 23 x 33 cm each

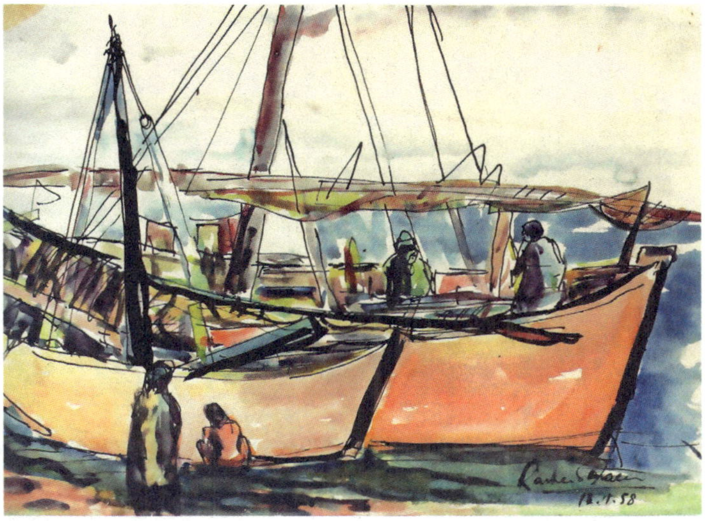

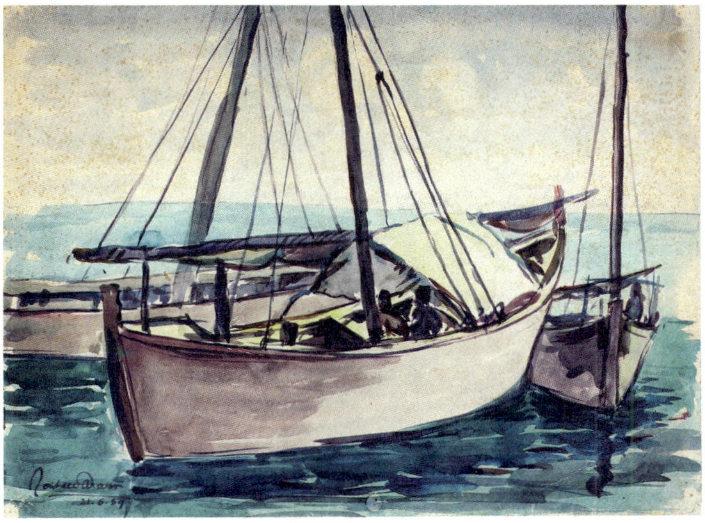

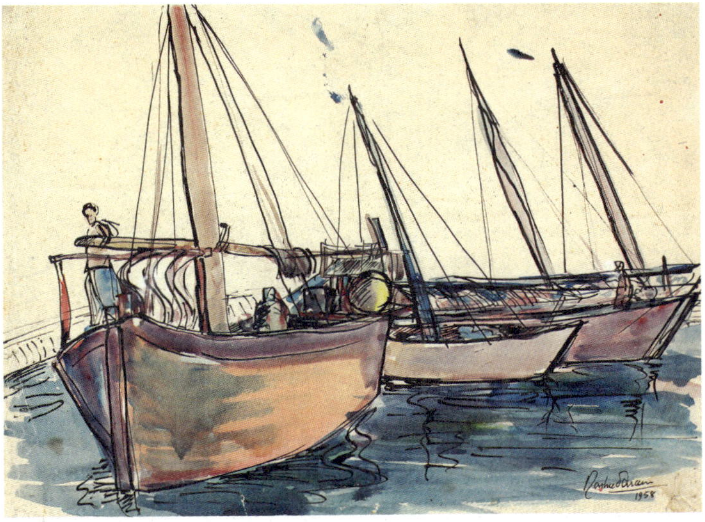

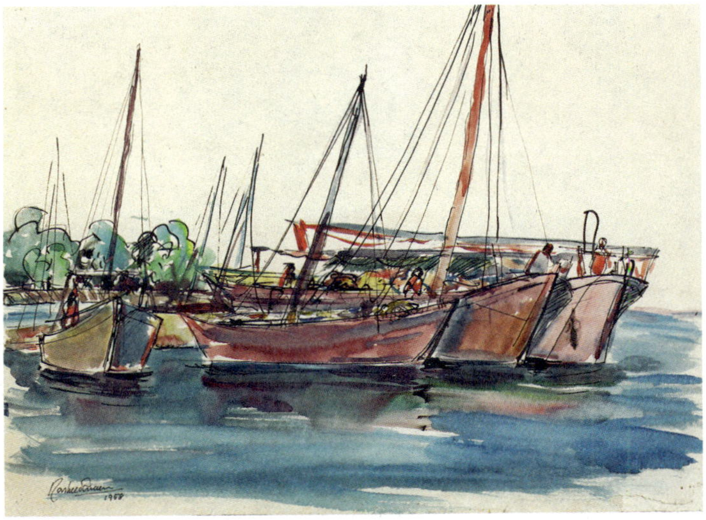

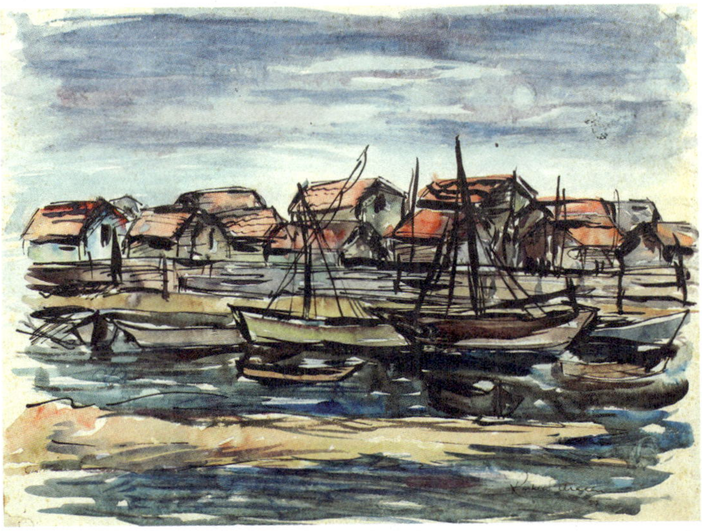

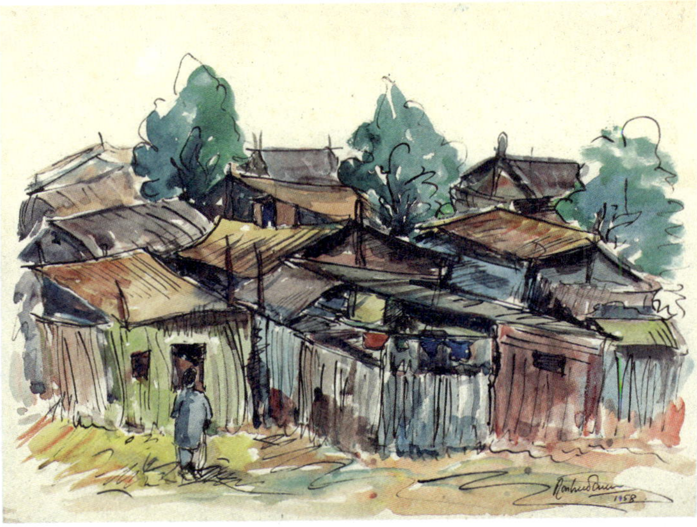

Boats: Towards Abstraction, 1958–1962
series of 9 works on paper, various dimensions
M+ Collection, Hong Kong

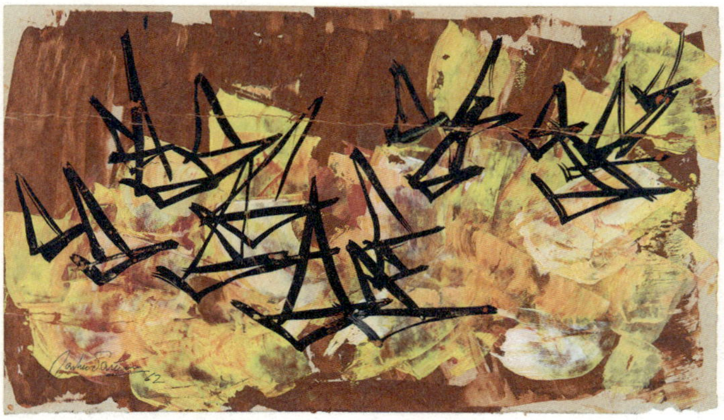

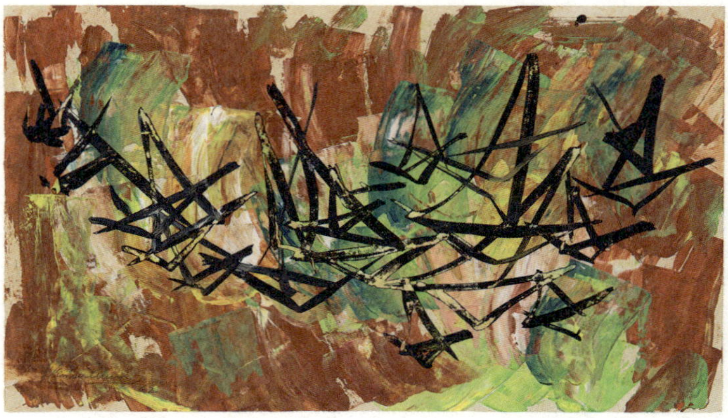

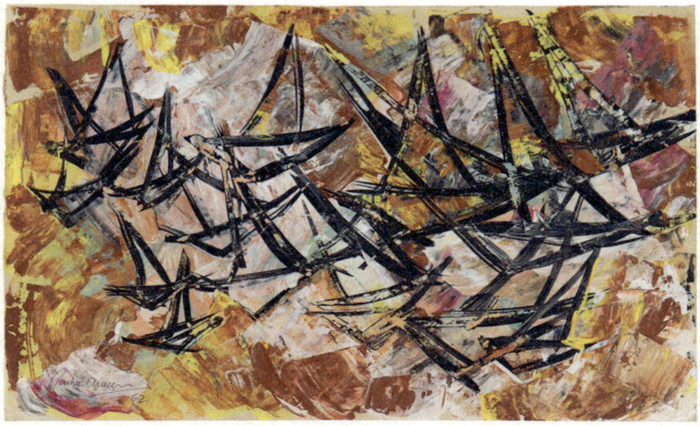

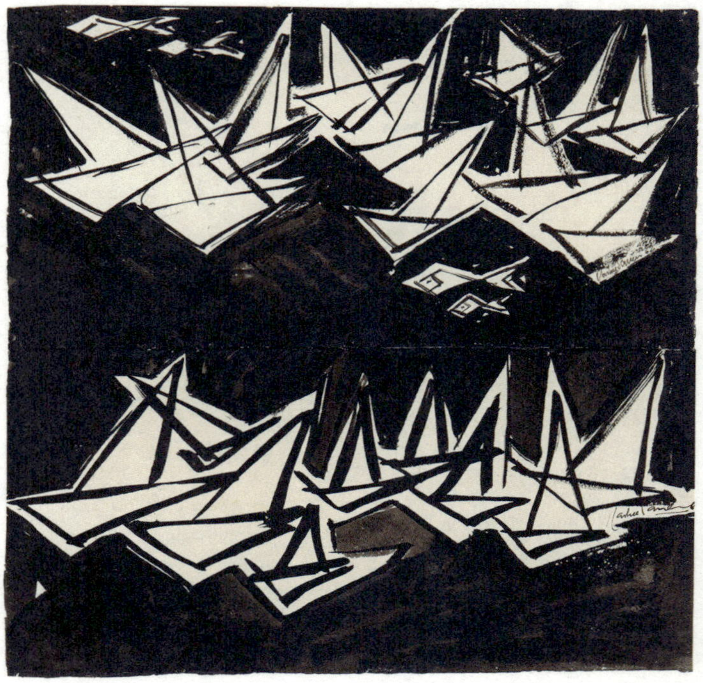

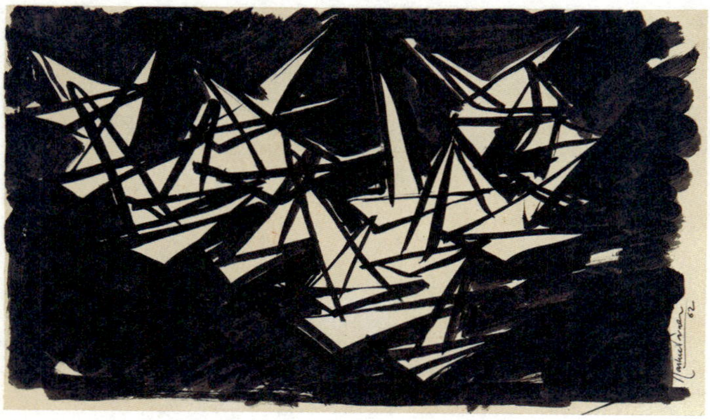

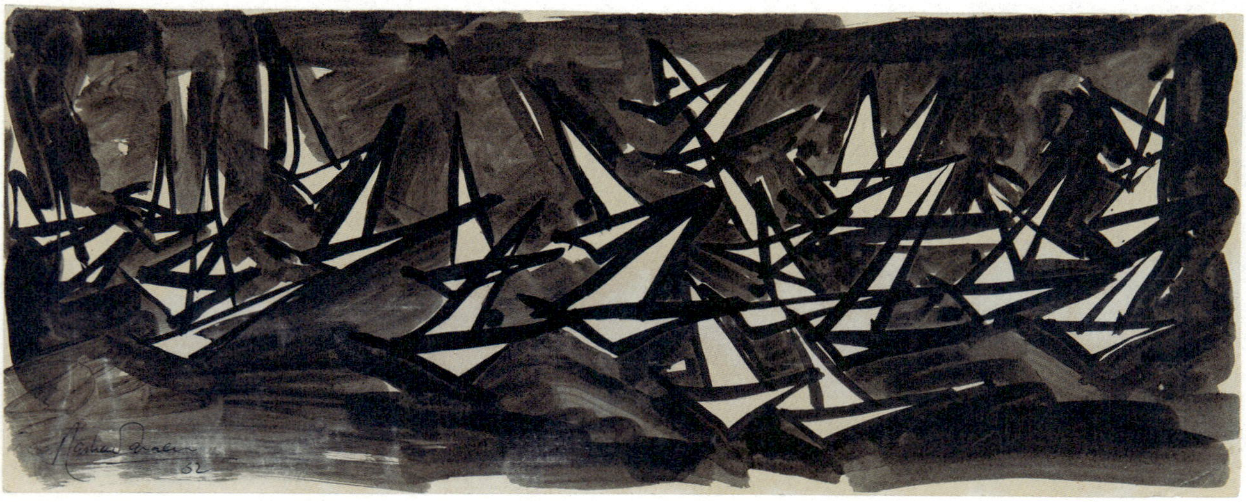

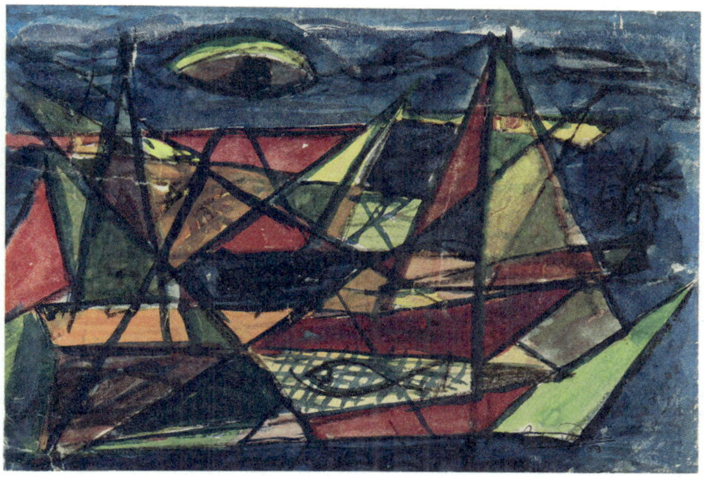

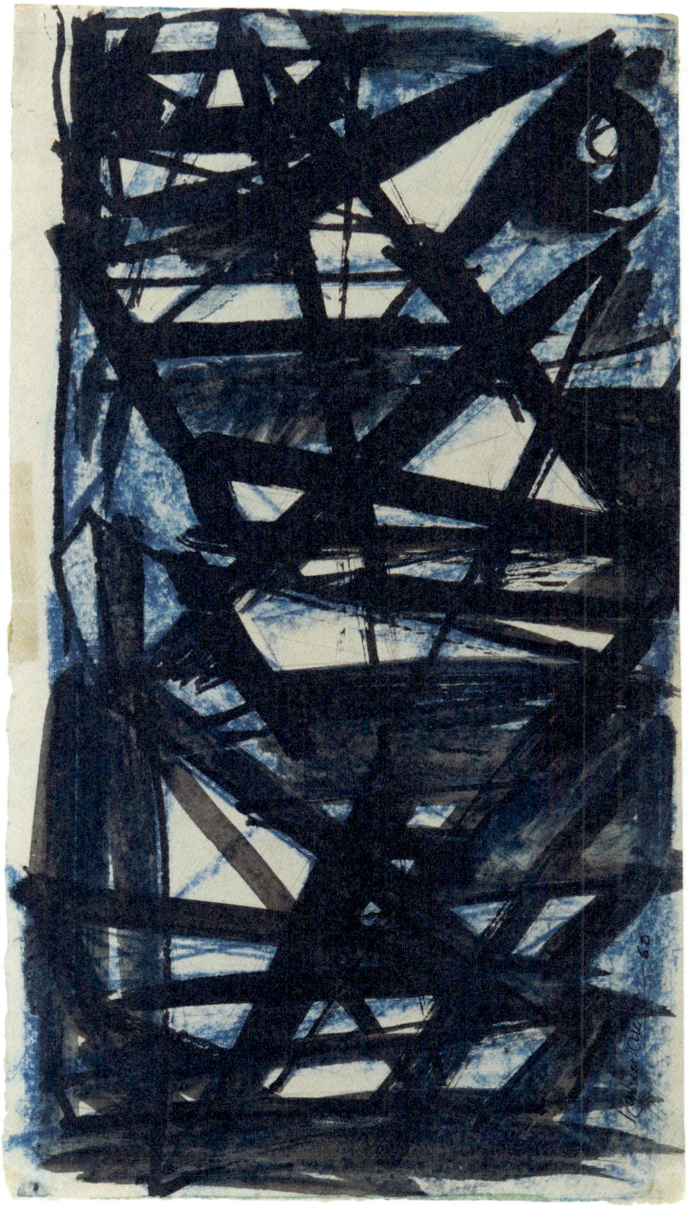

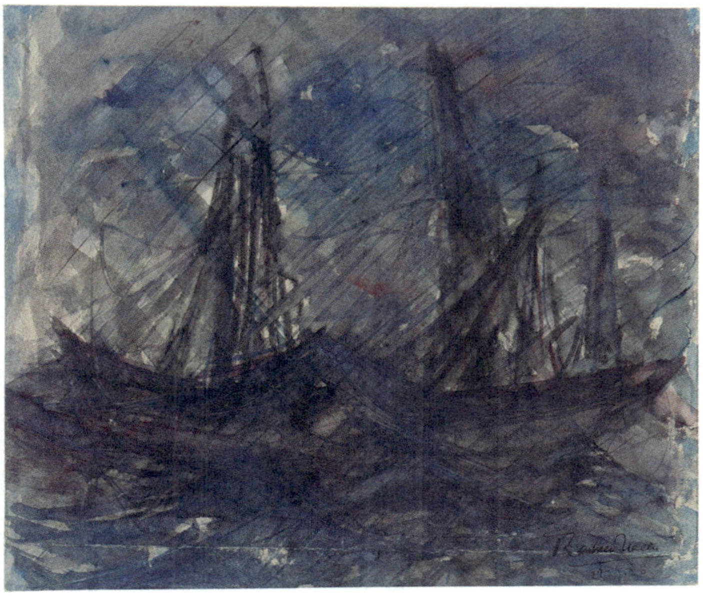

My First Sculpture, 1959
steel wire, dimensions variable

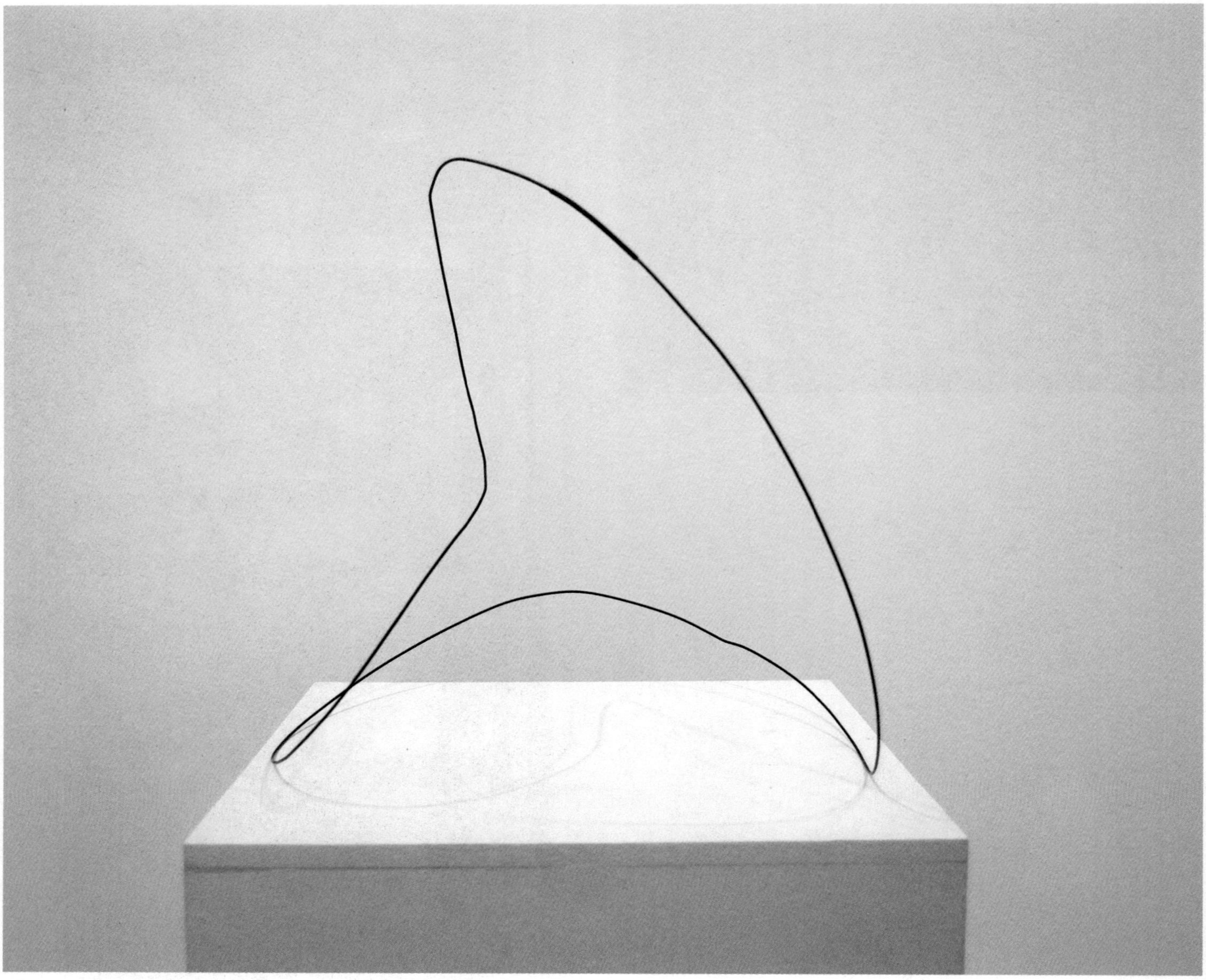

Ham Raqs, 1959
oil on canvas, 64 x 41 cm

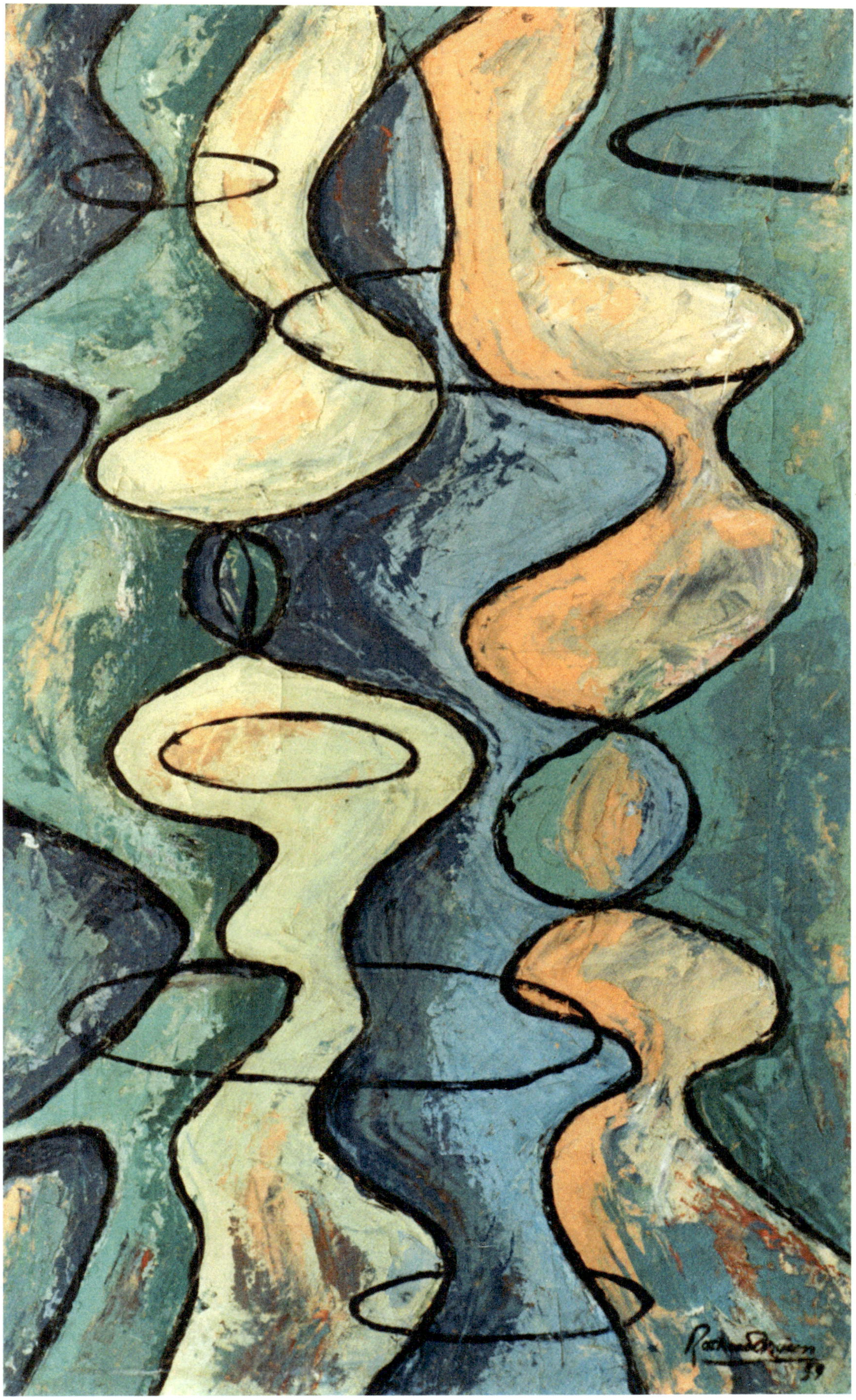

Untitled Yellow, 1959
gouache on paper, 35 x 25 cm

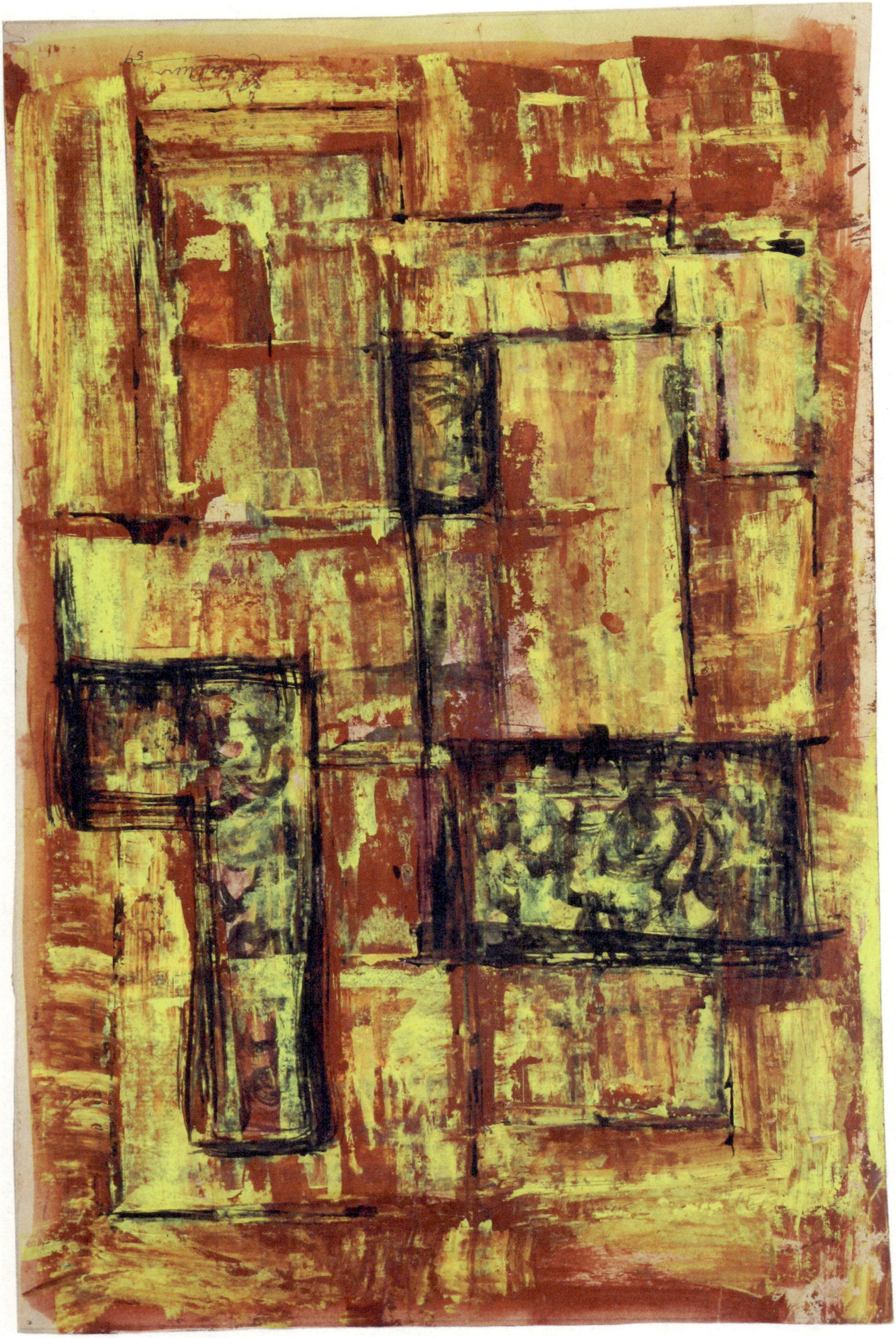

Dancing Bodies (Hula-Hoop Series), 1959–1962
series of 10 works on paper
various dimensions (selection)
Sharjah Art Foundation Collection

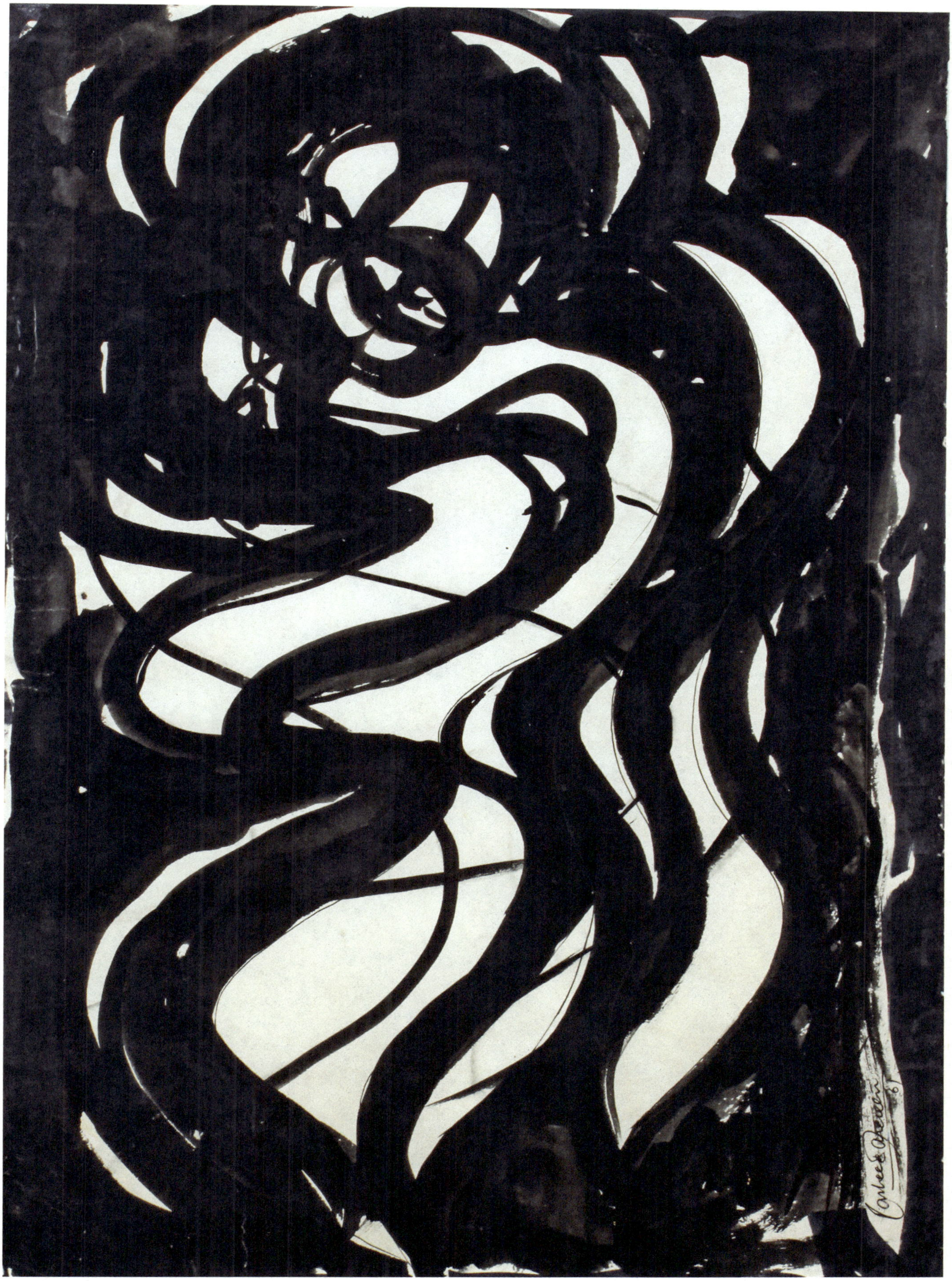

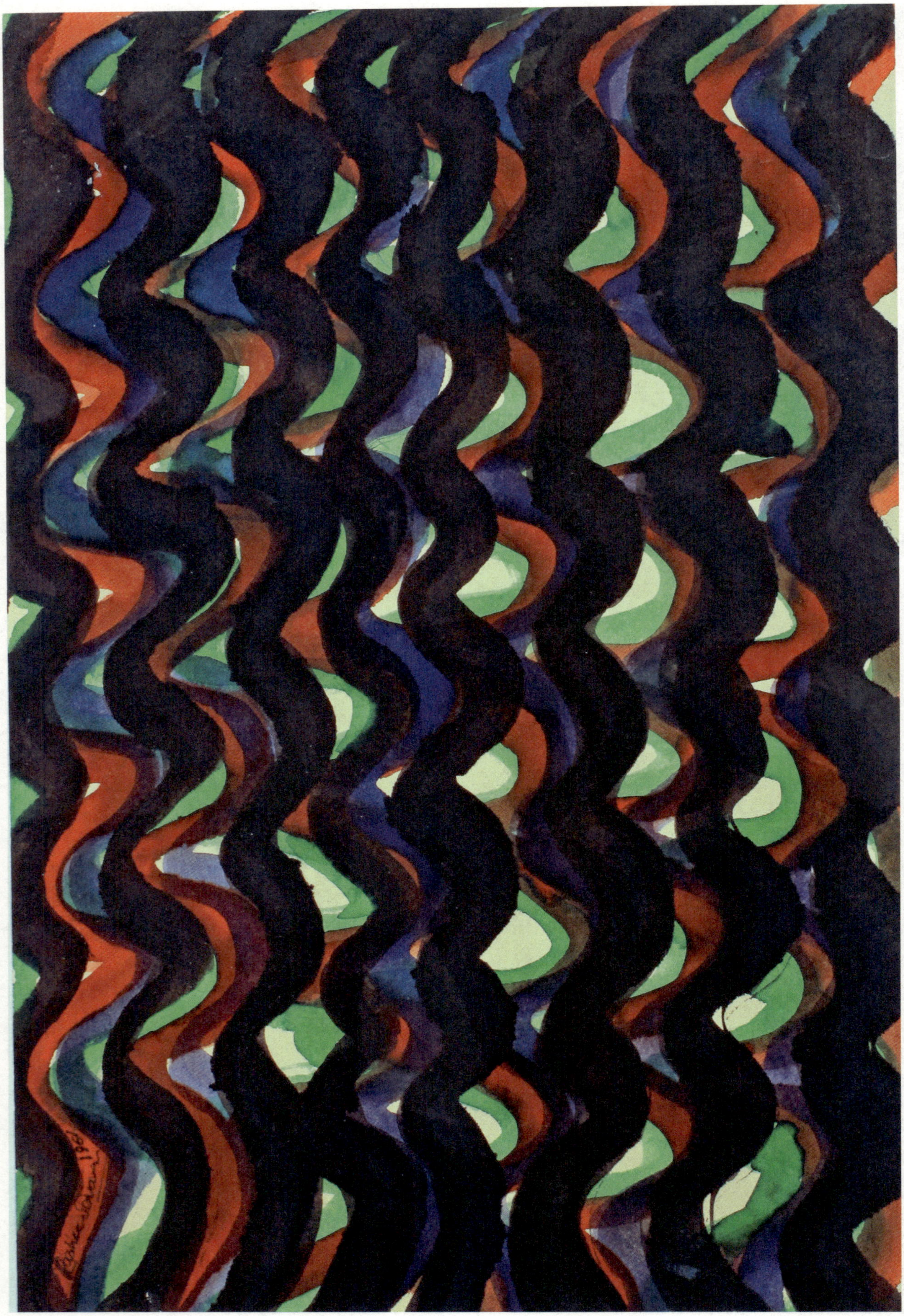

Untitled, 1961
ink on paper, 28 x 20 cm

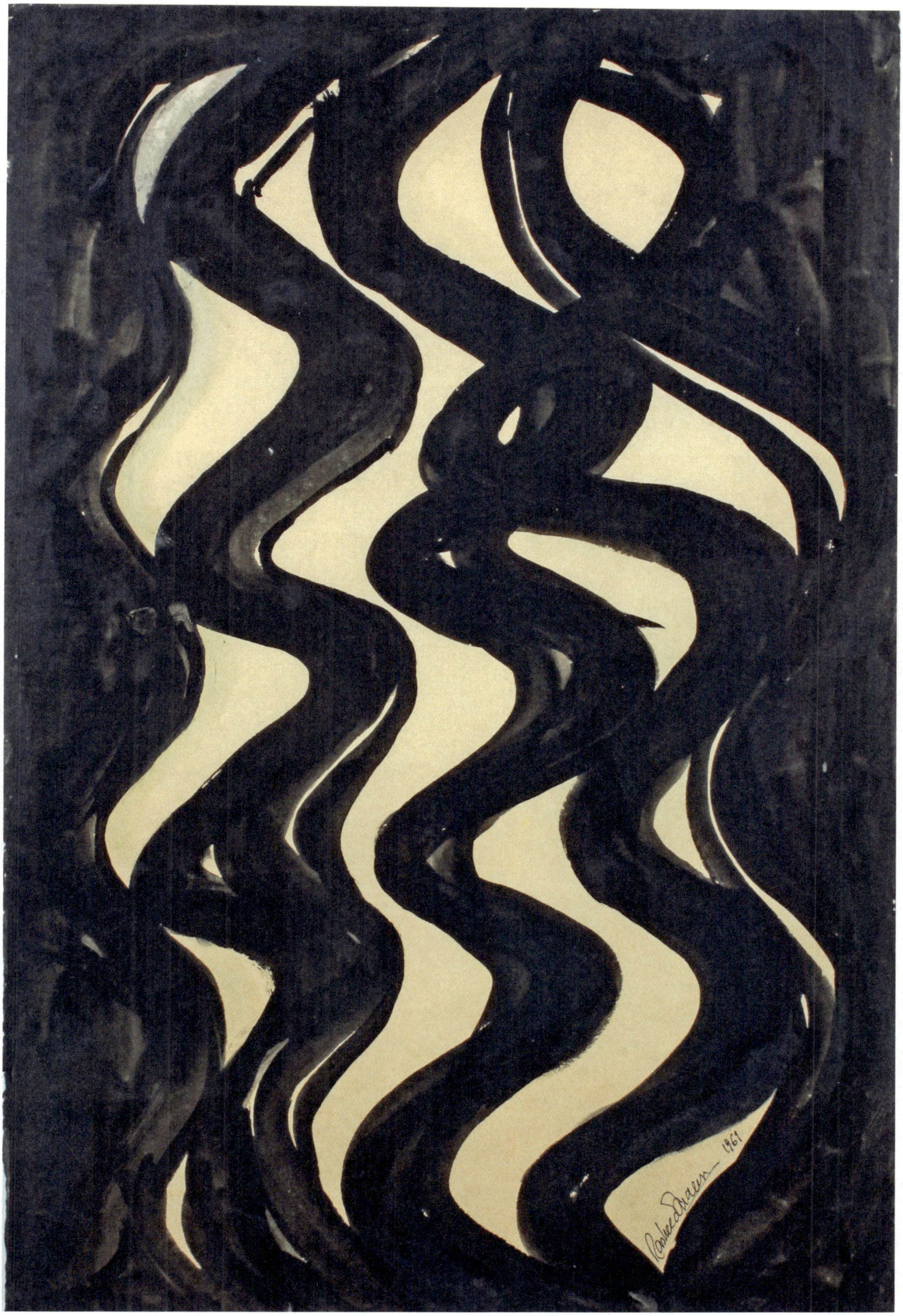

Burning Bicycle Tyres, 1959 / 1975
series of 9 photographs, dimensions variable

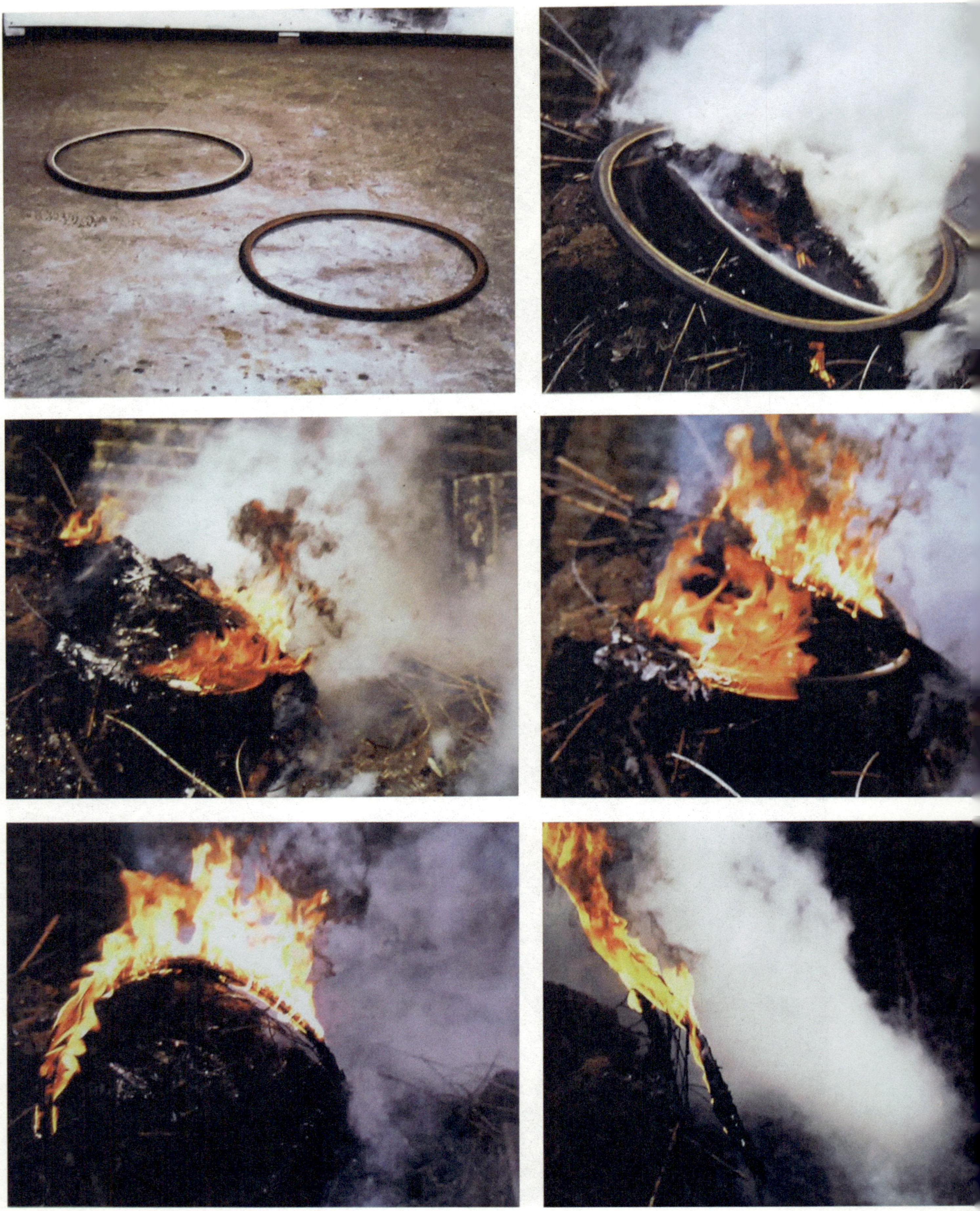

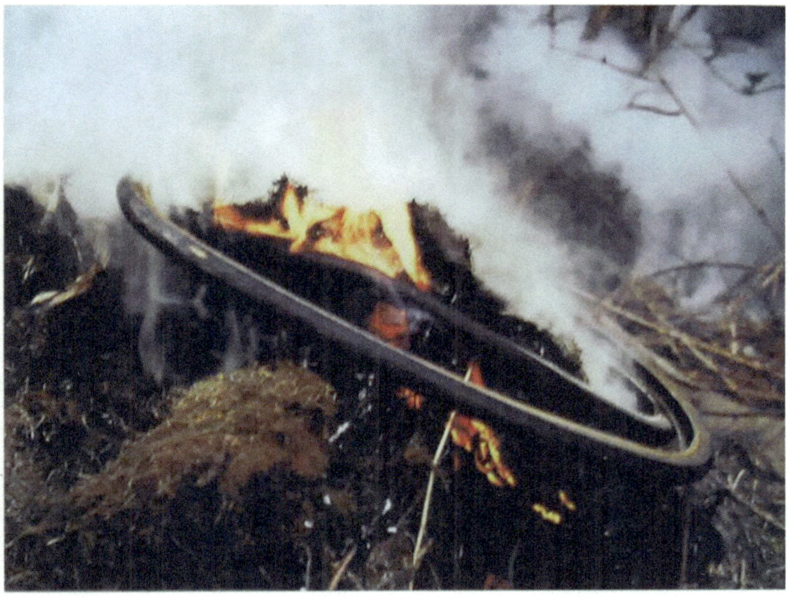

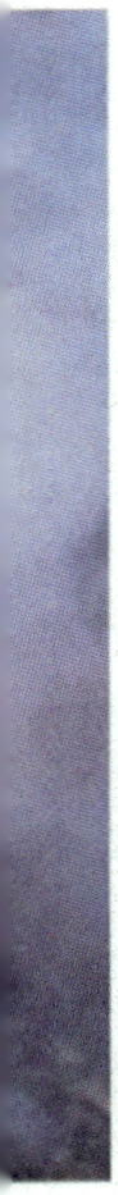

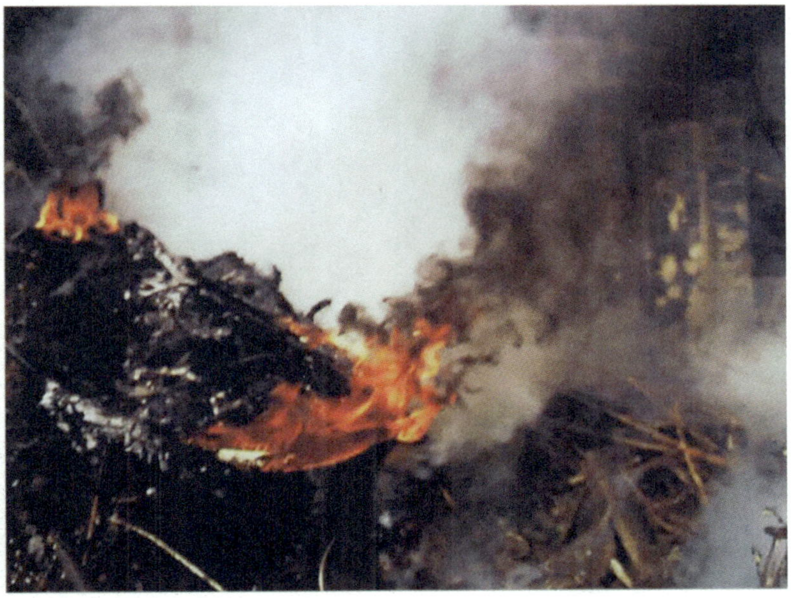

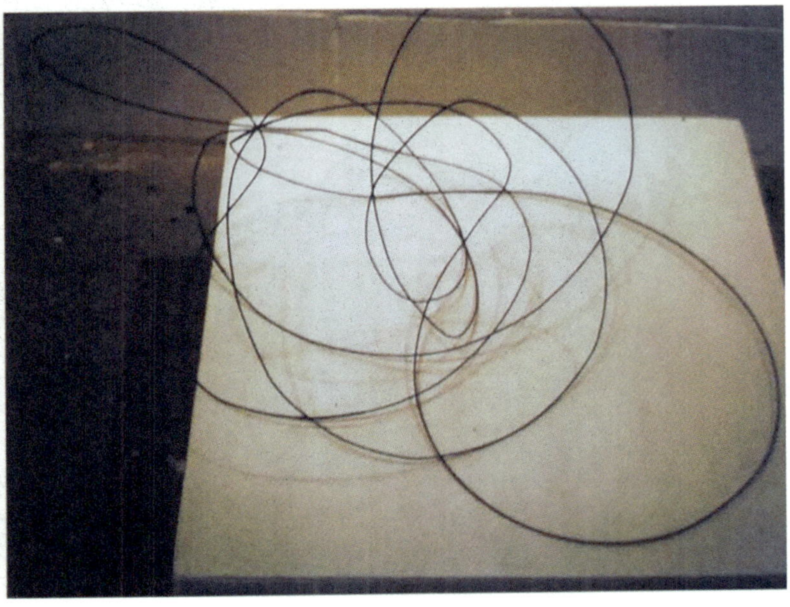

Burning Bicycle Tyres, 1959 / 1975
photograph, dimensions unknown

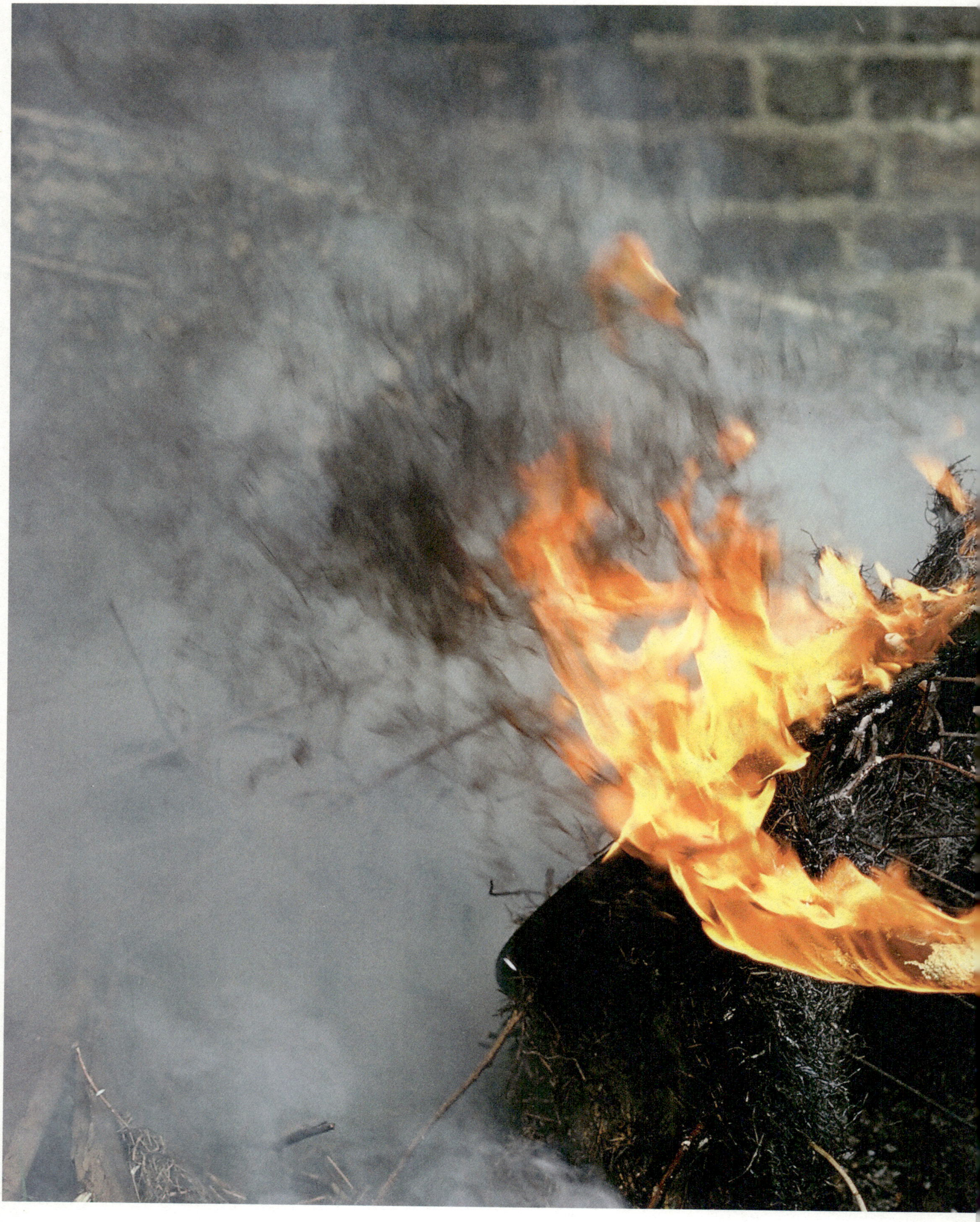

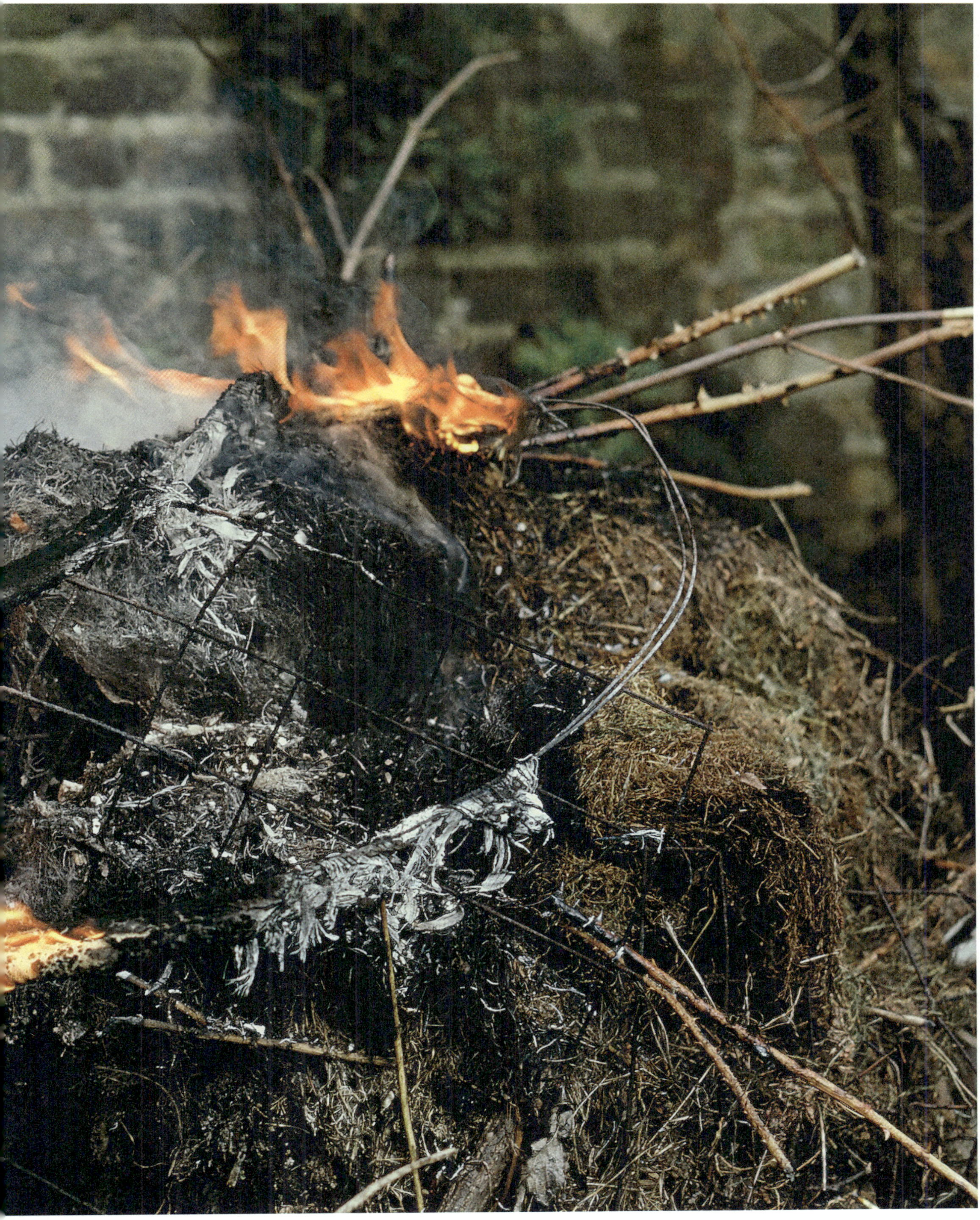

Red and Yellow, 1961
oil on board, 92 x 61 cm

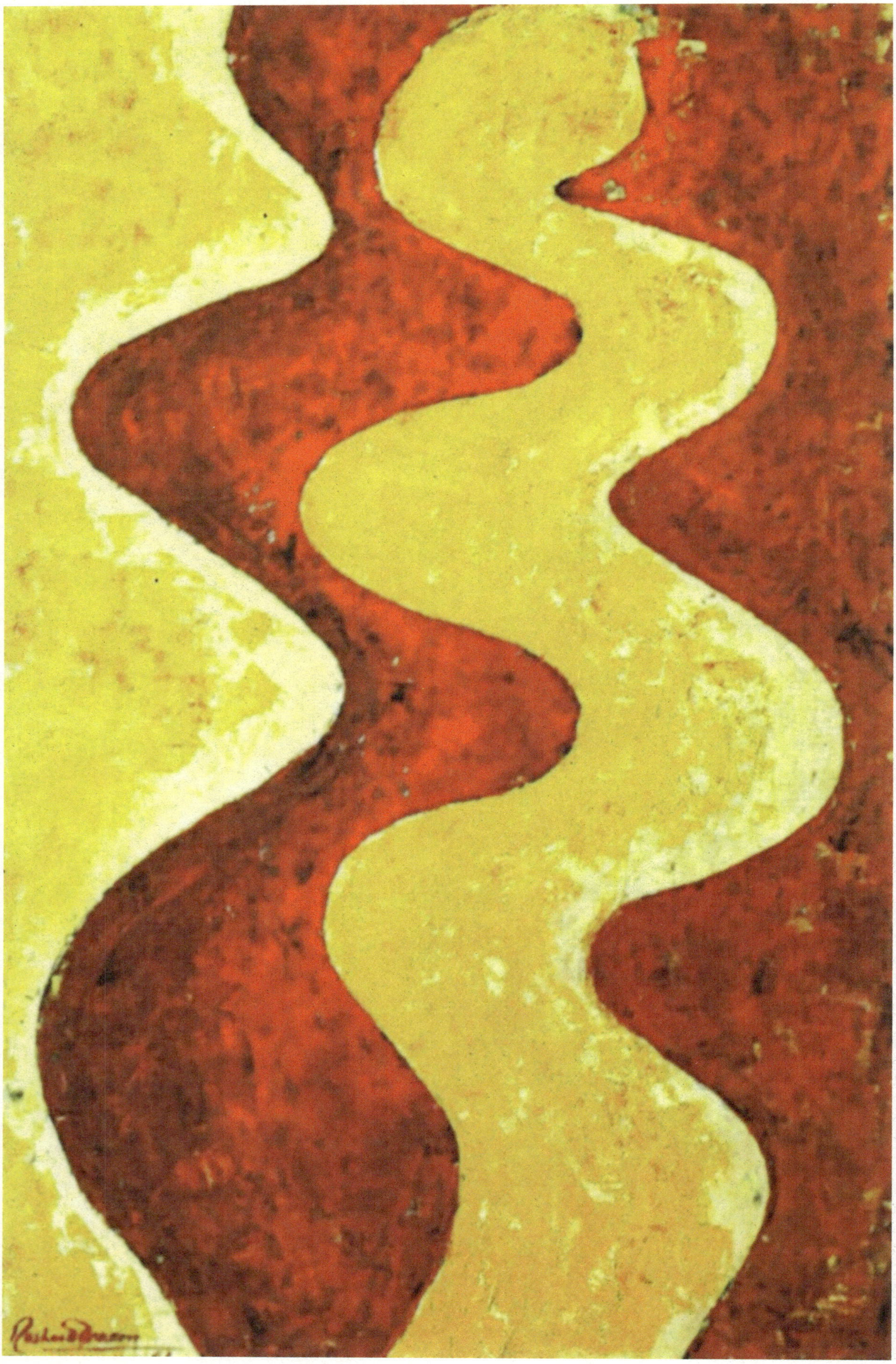

Aag, 1961
oil on board, 91 x 61 cm

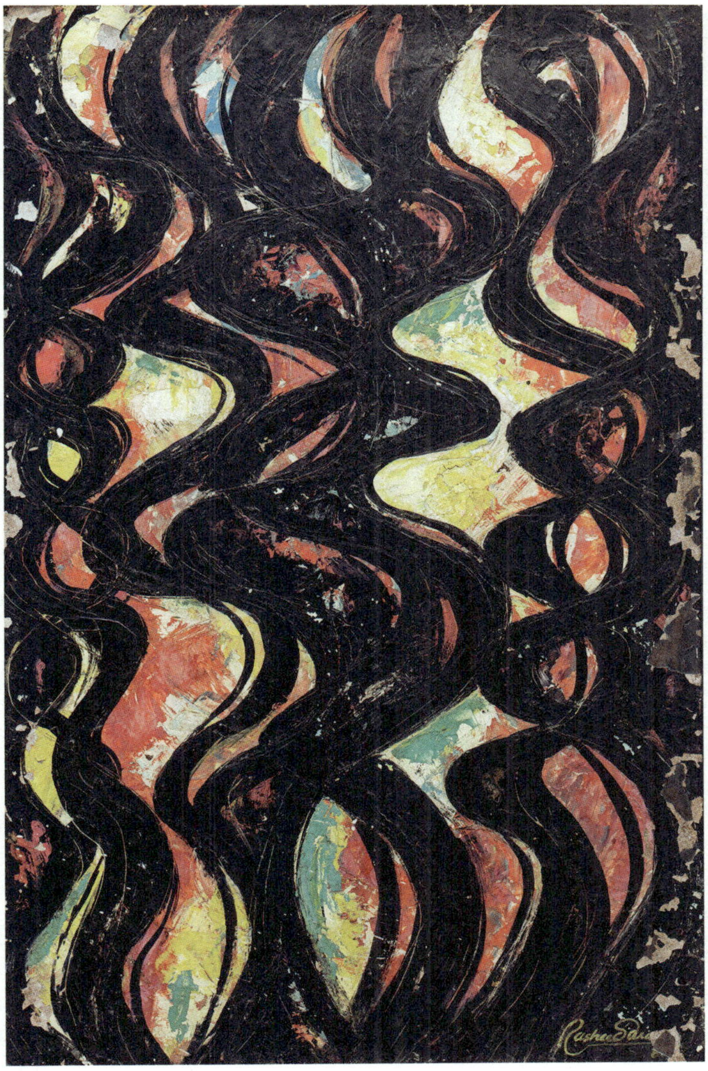

Aag ka Naach, 1961
oil on board, 91 x 61 cm

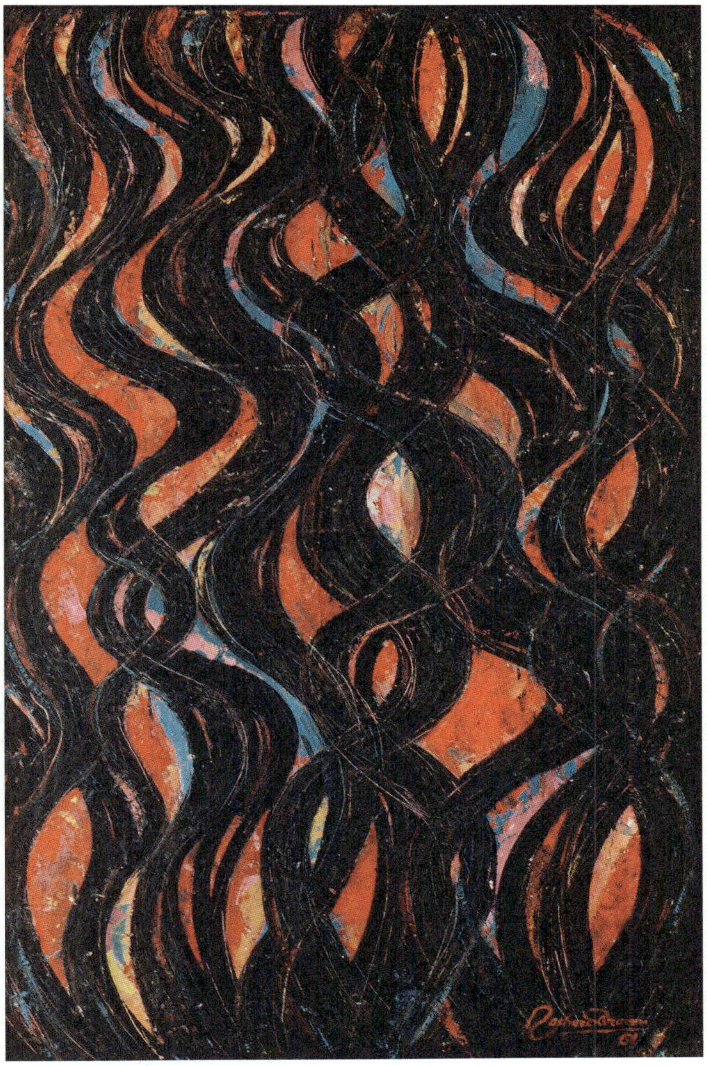

Window Design, 1961
painted steel, dimensions unknown

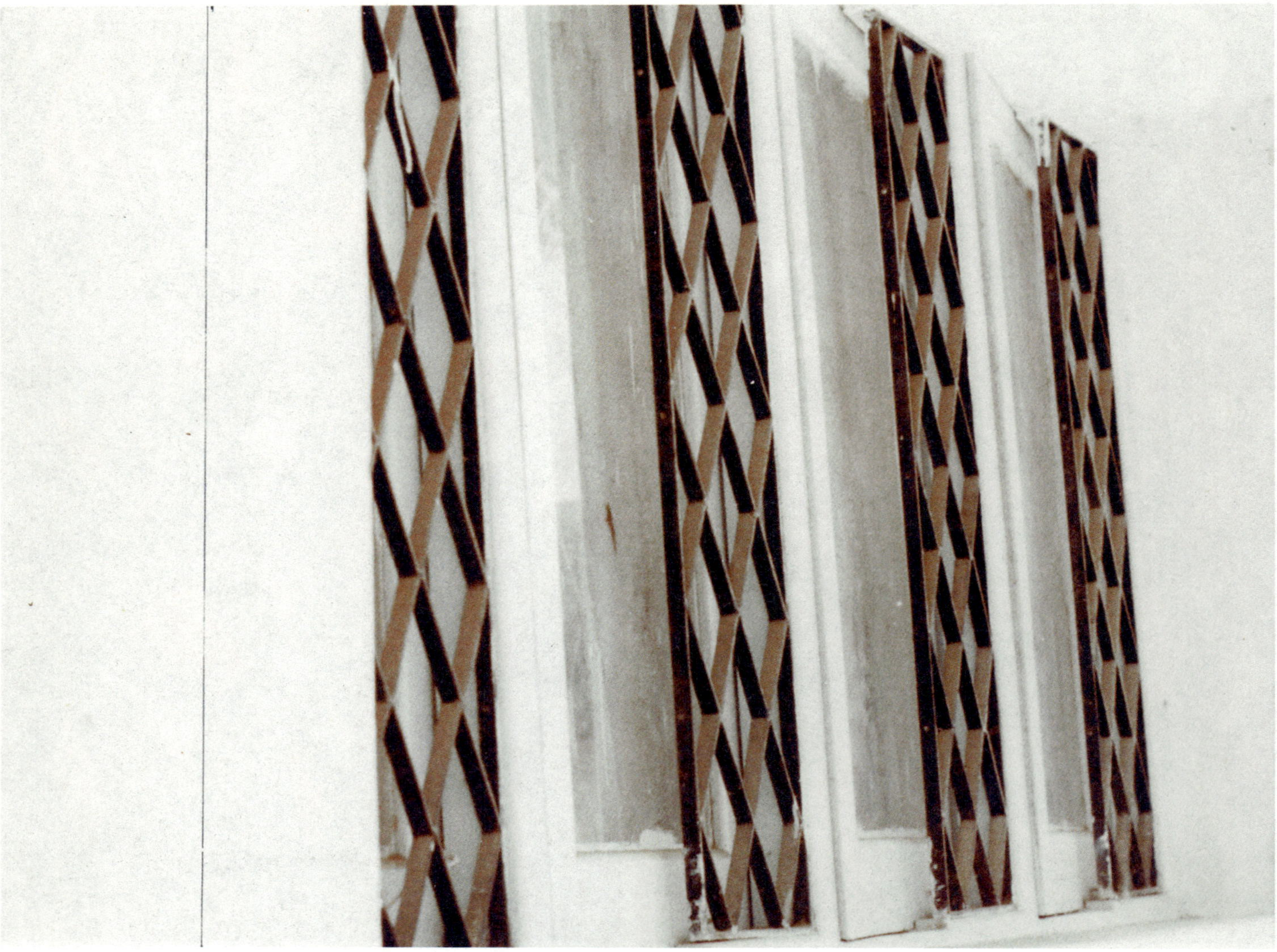

Demand of Life (A Scribble), 1961
watercolour and biro on paper, 38 x 28 cm

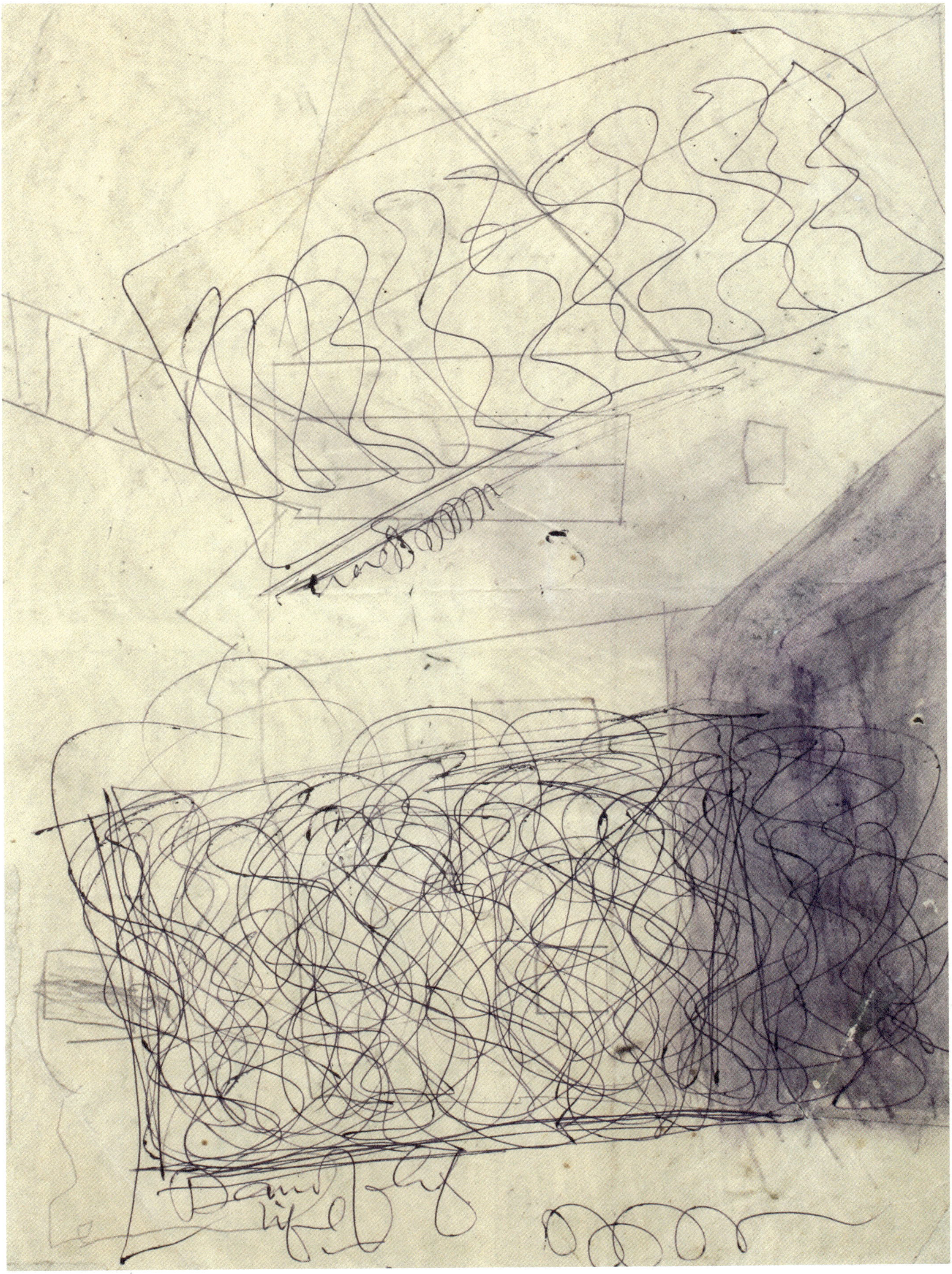

Untitled A, 1961
series of 6 drawings, ink on paper, 28 x 20 cm each

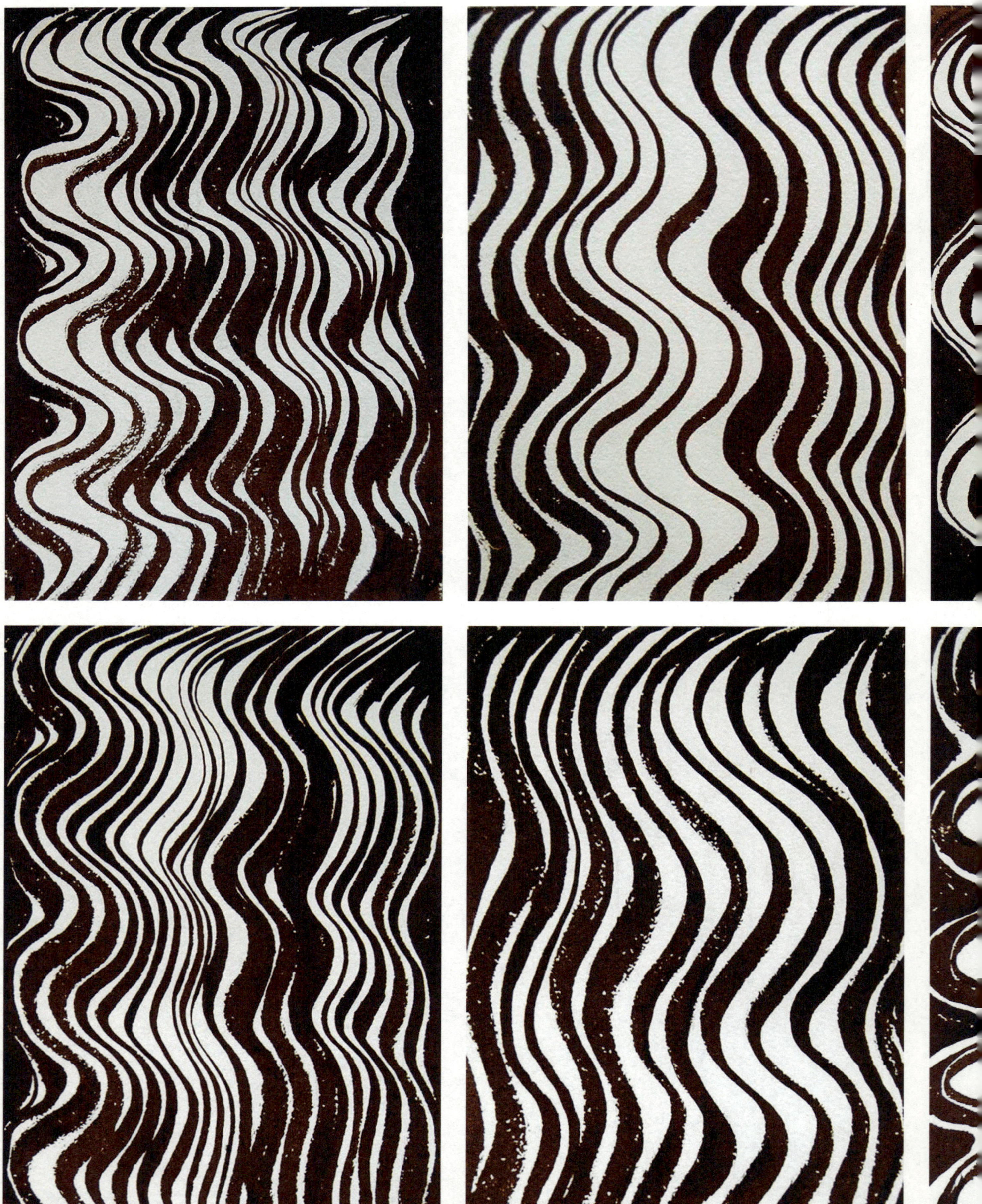

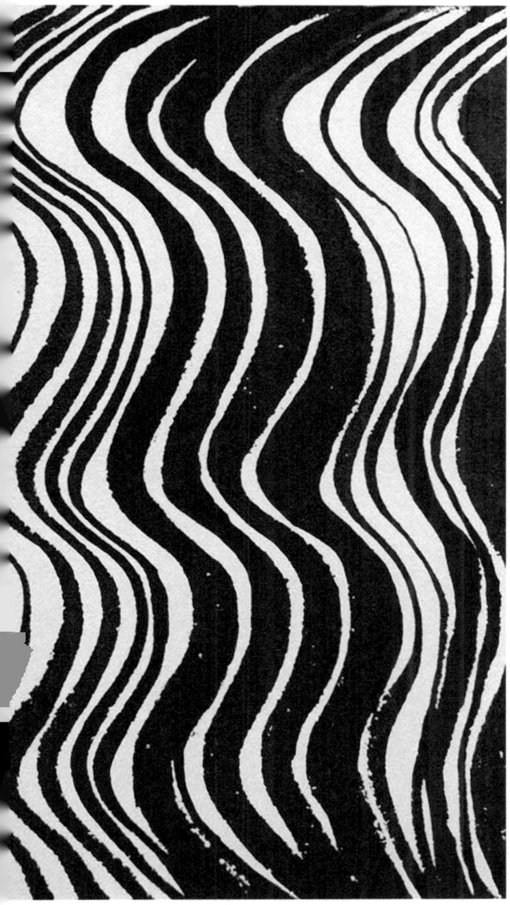

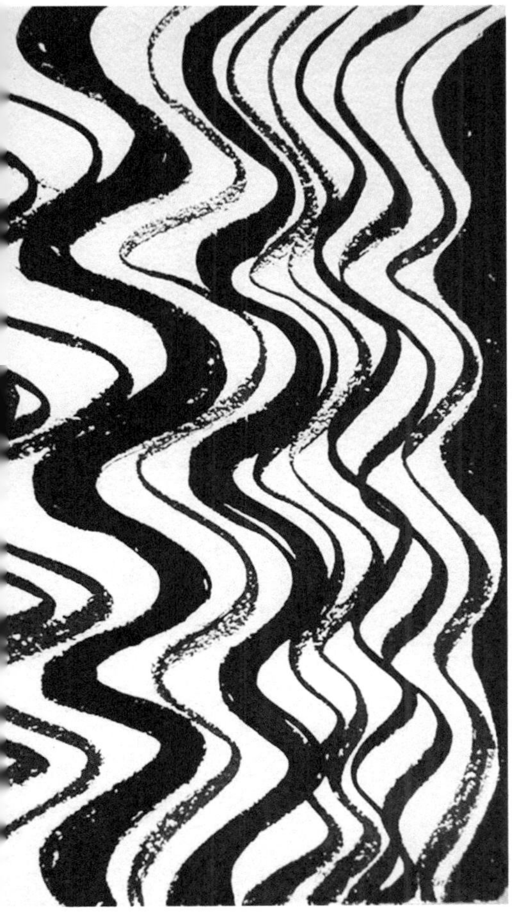

Untitled (B Series), 1962
series of 6 drawings, felt-tip marker on paper, 28 x 41 cm

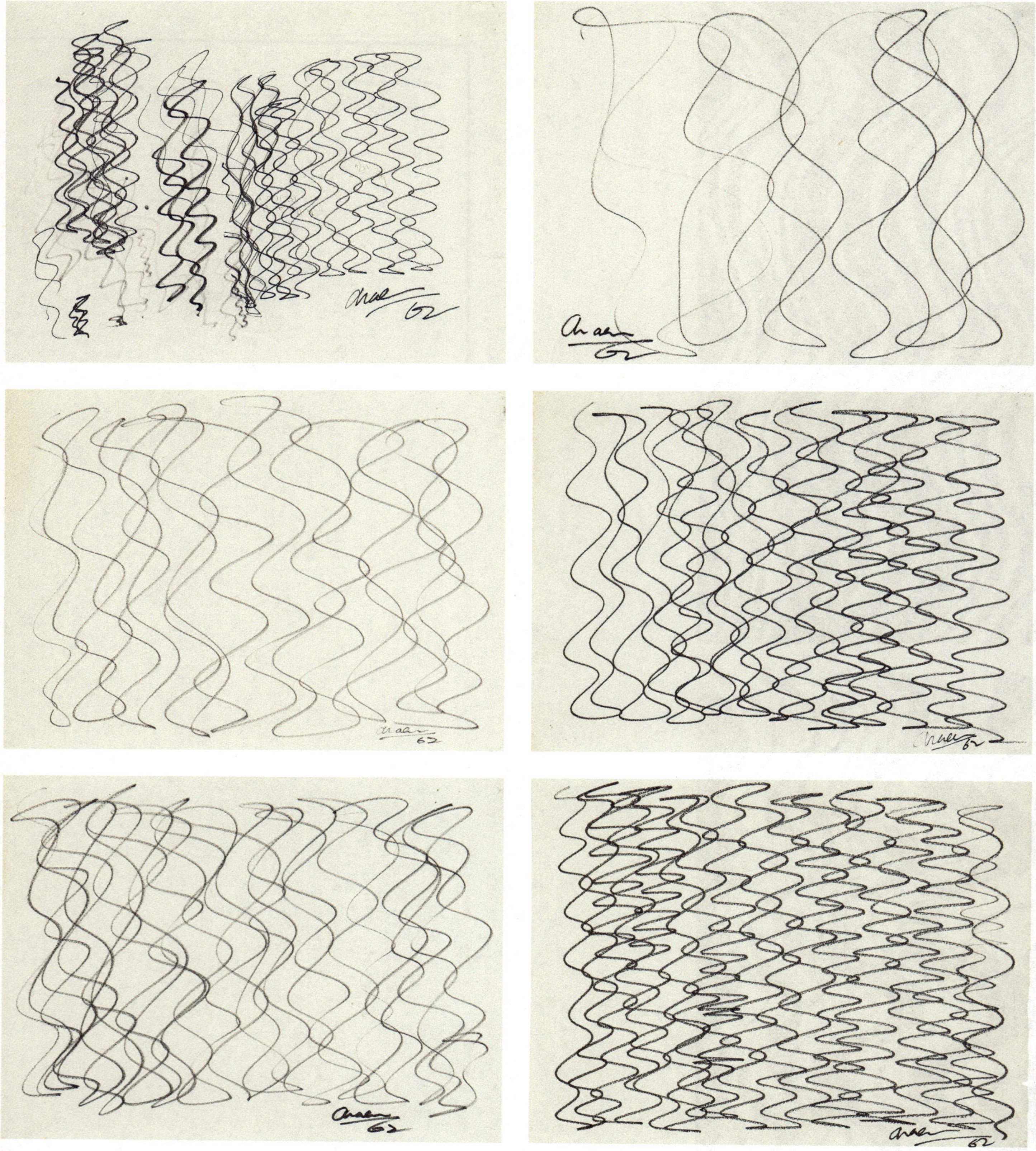

Untitled B10, 1962, felt-tip marker on paper, 28 x 38 cm
Untitled B9, 1962, felt-tip marker on paper, 28 x 38 cm

Untitled B7, 1962, felt-tip marker on paper, 28 x 38 cm
Untitled B8, 1962, felt-tip marker on paper, 28 x 38 cm

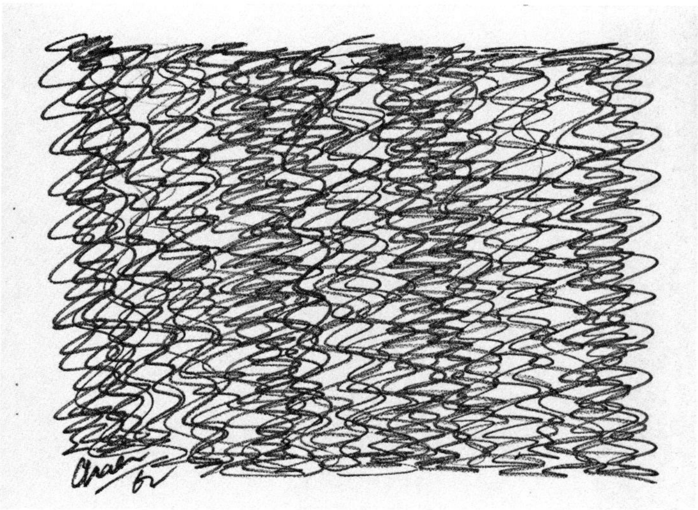

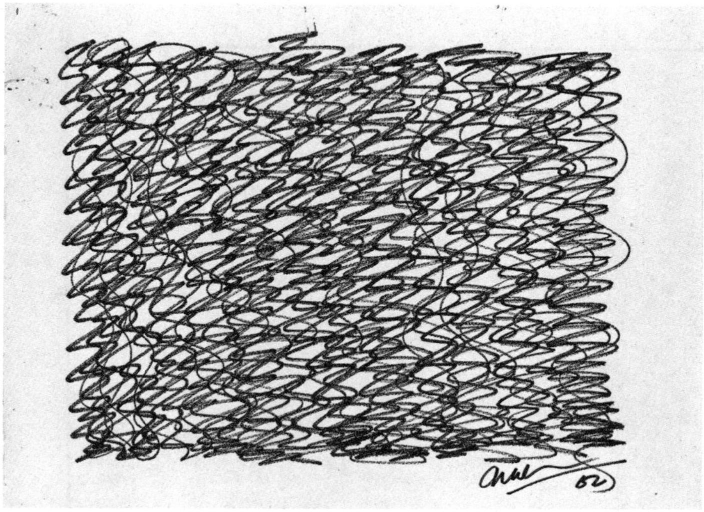

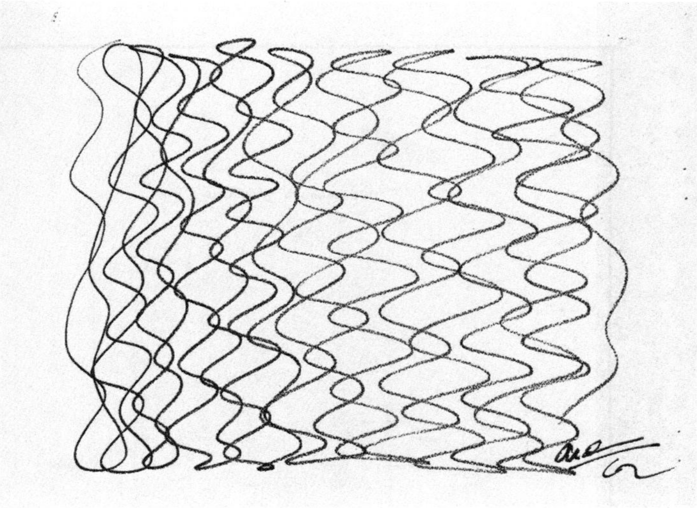

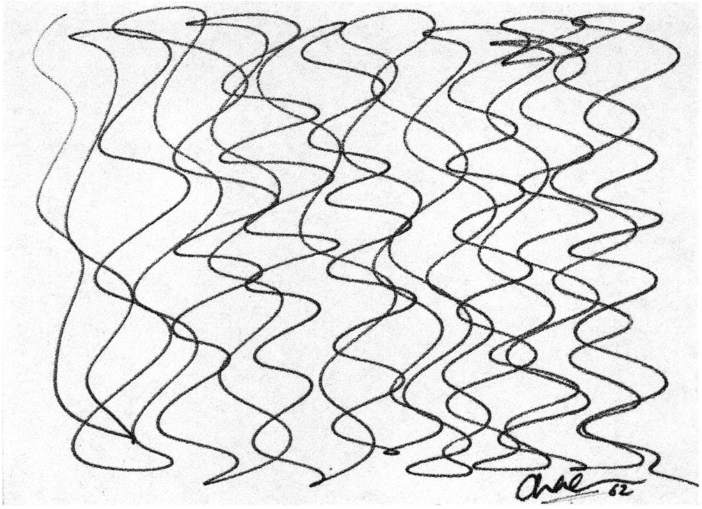

Cats and Lips, 1962
oil on board, 76 x 33 cm

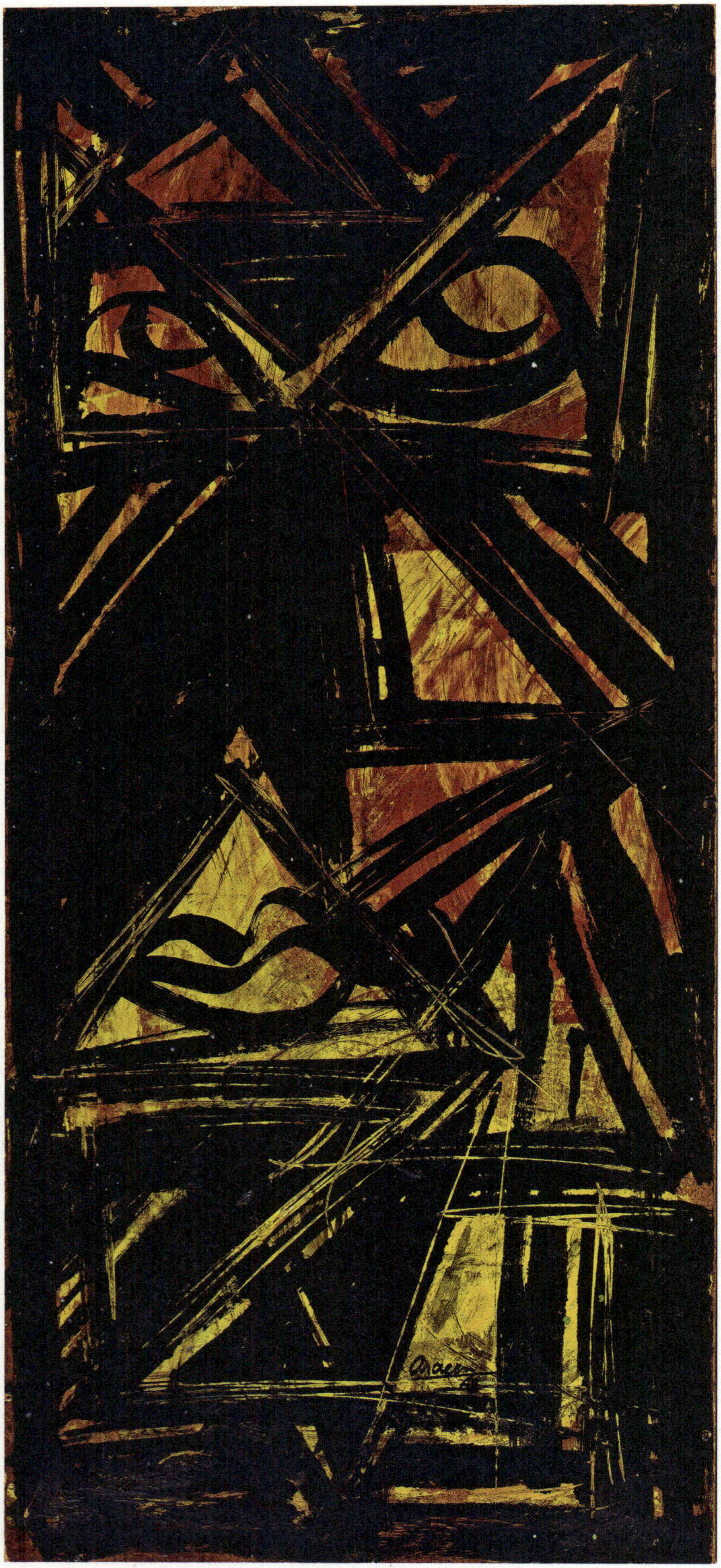

Self-Portrait, 1963
oil on board, dimensions unknown

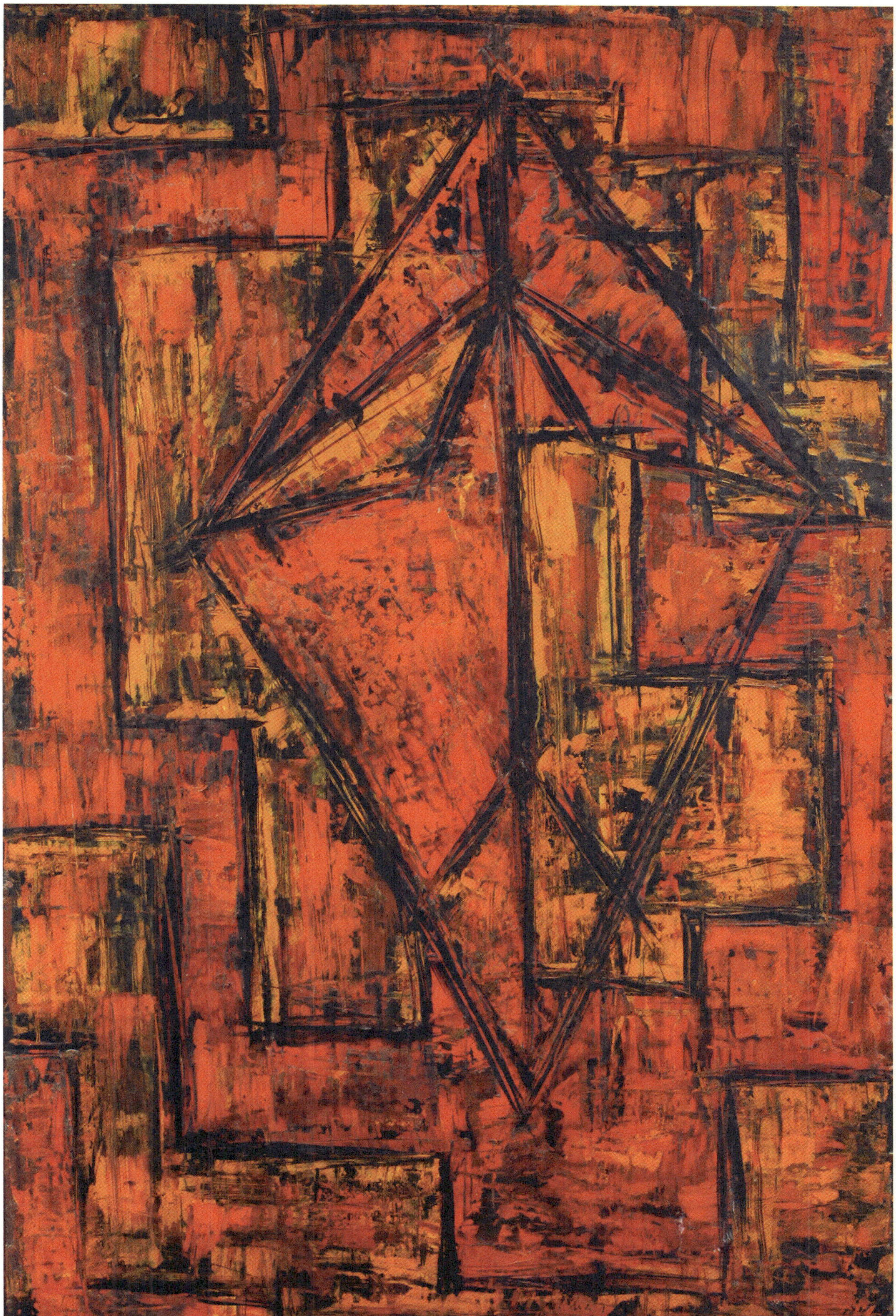

Windcatchers in Pink, 1963
watercolour, pastel and ink on paper, 20 x 30 cm

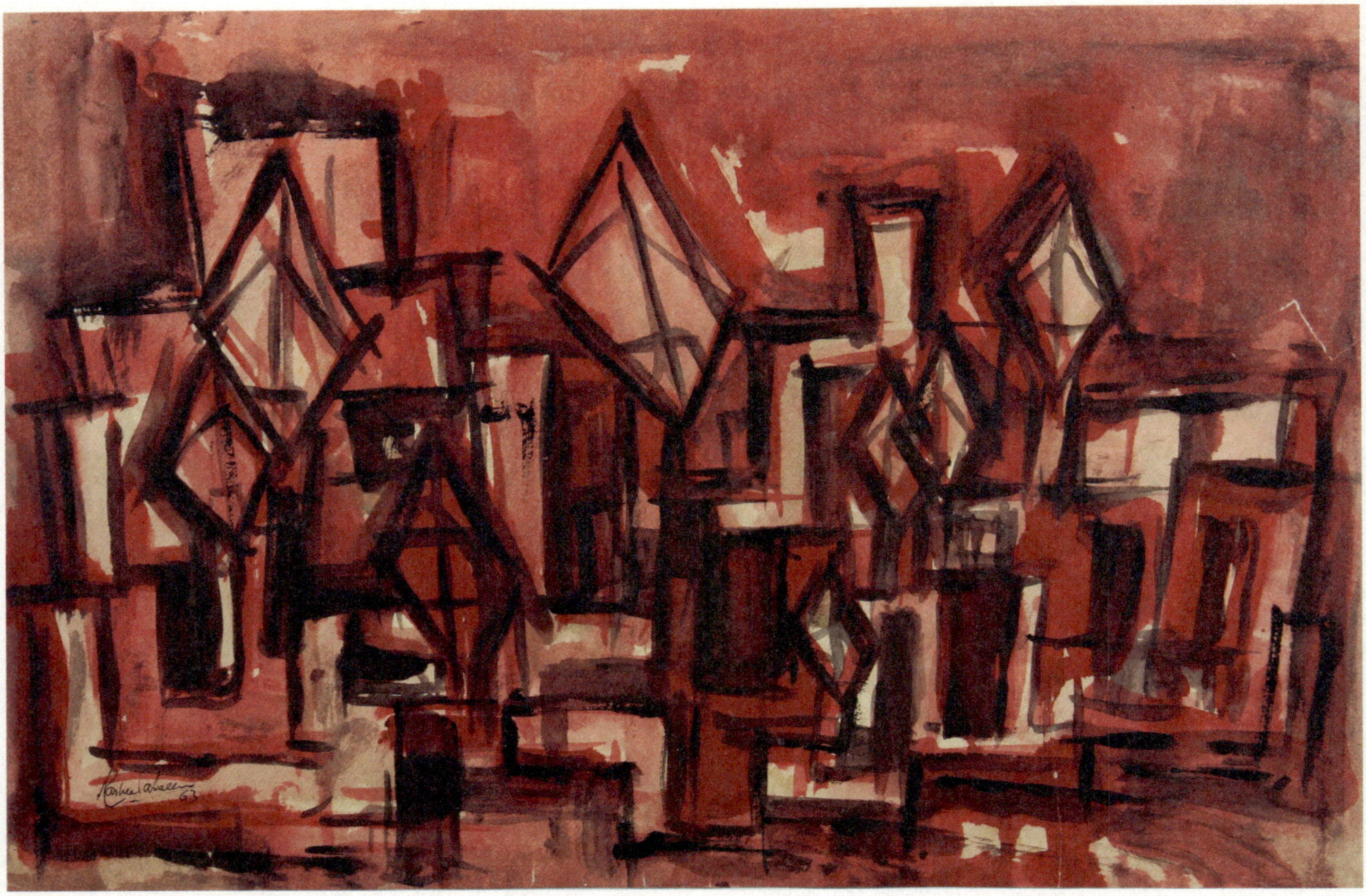

Hyderabad Abstraction, 1963
watercolour and ink on paper, 56 x 46 cm

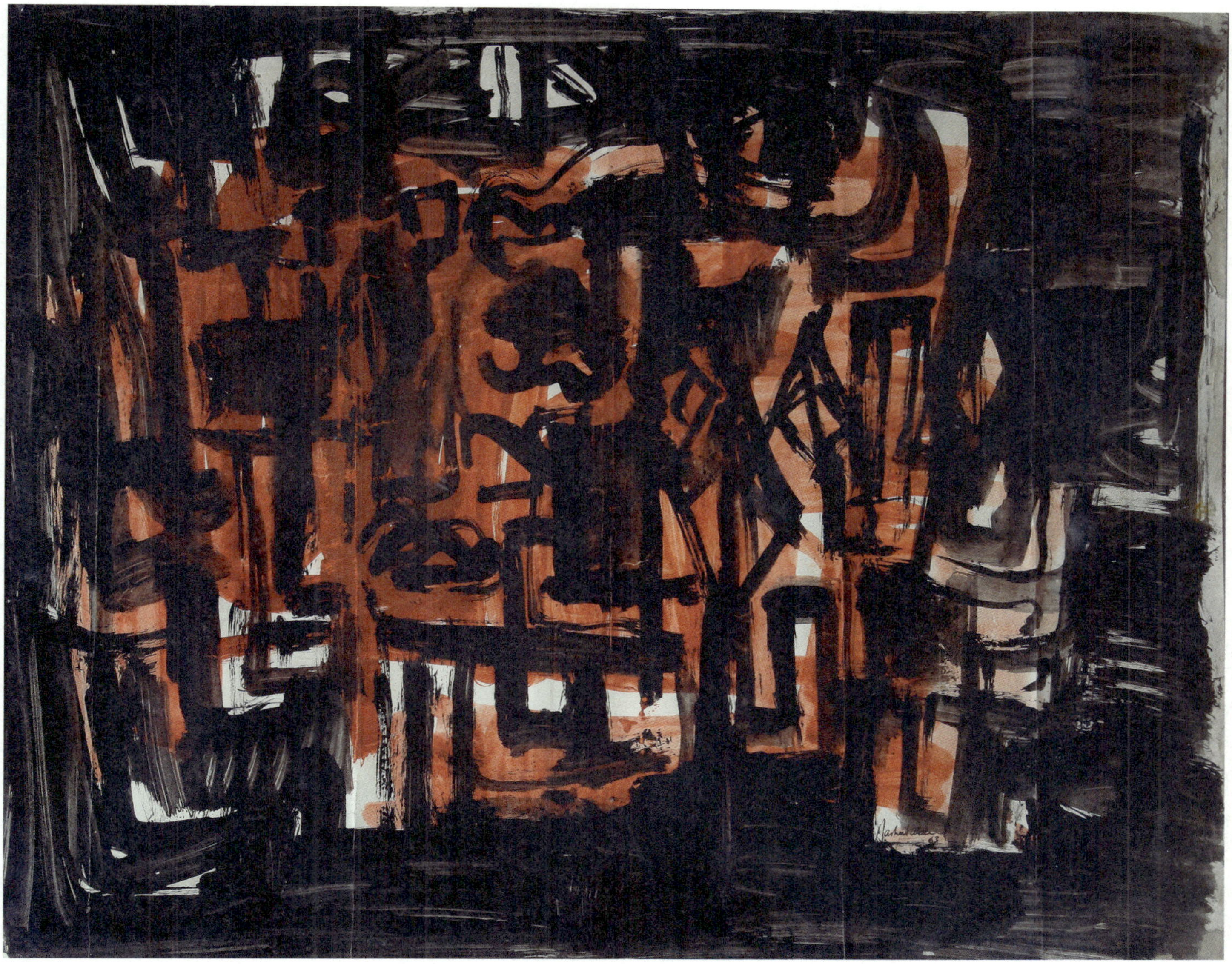

Peace, 1963
oil on board, dimensions unknown

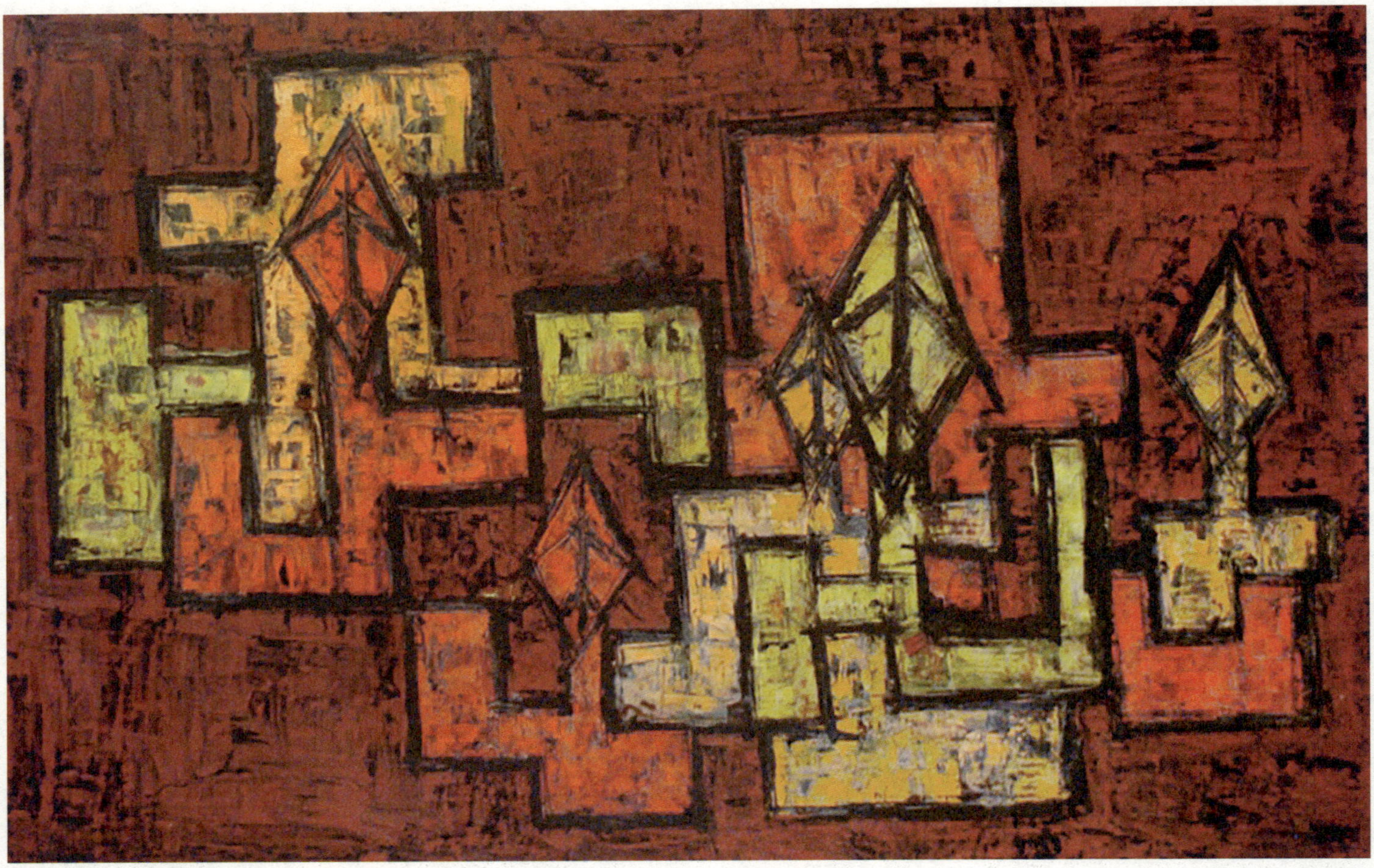

Hyderabad, 1962
watercolour, pastel, and ink on paper
40 x 50 cm

Houses, 1963
watercolour, pastel, and ink on paper
40 x 50 cm

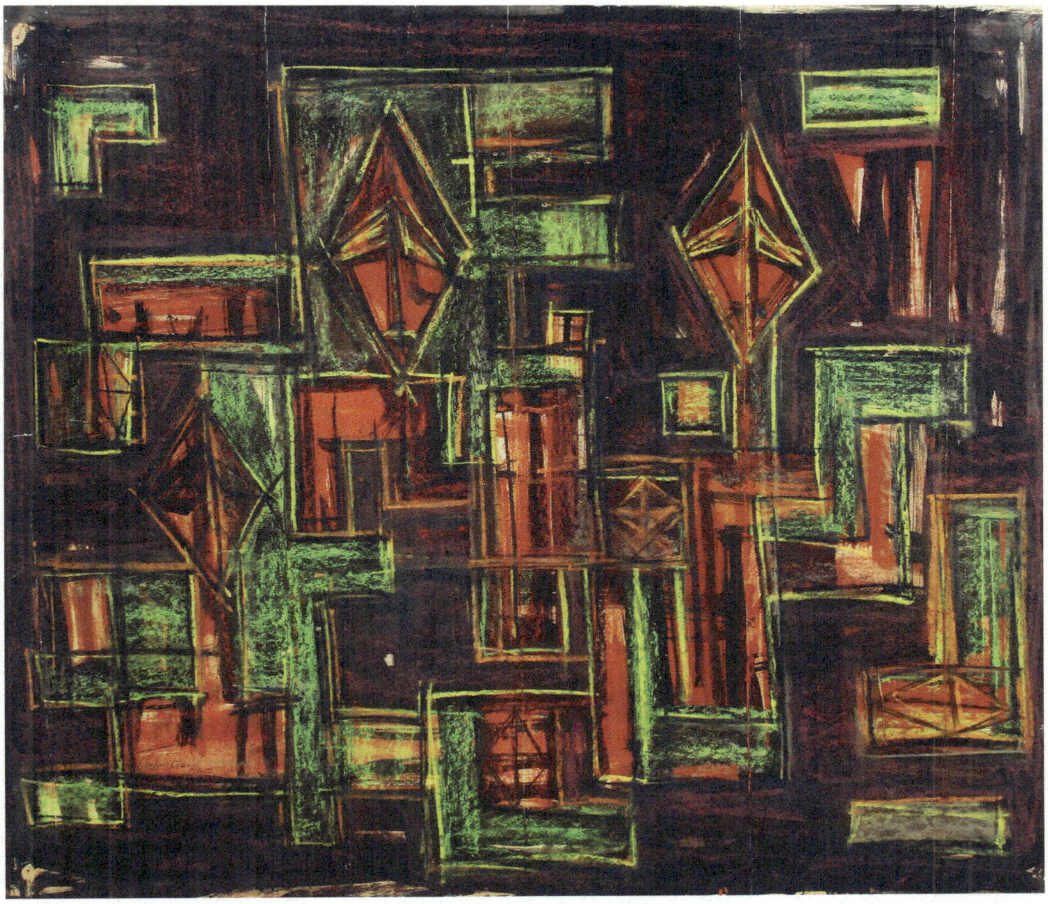

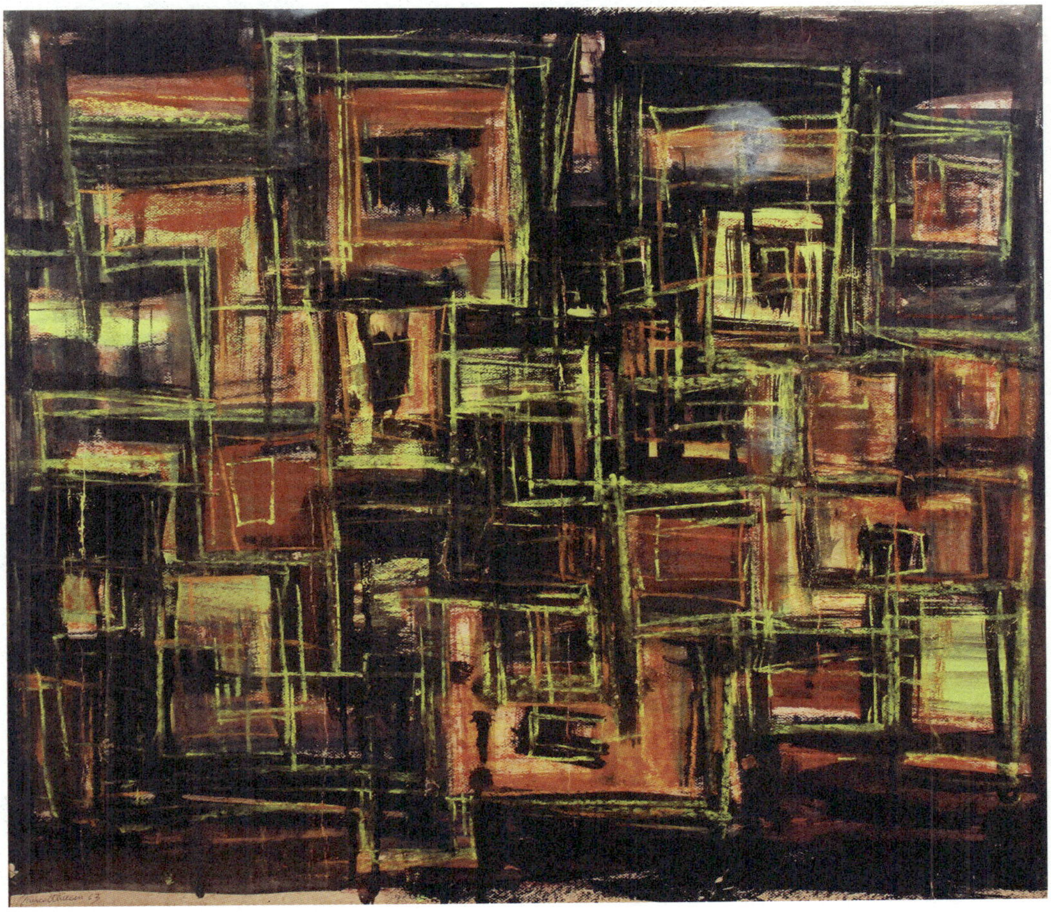

Untitled (Hyderabad 1), 1962
watercolour, pastel, and ink on paper, 37 x 56 cm
Untitled (Hyderabad 3), 1963
watercolour, pastel, and ink on paper, 37 x 56 cm

Untitled (Hyderabad 2), 1963
watercolour, pastel, and ink on paper, 37 x 56 cm

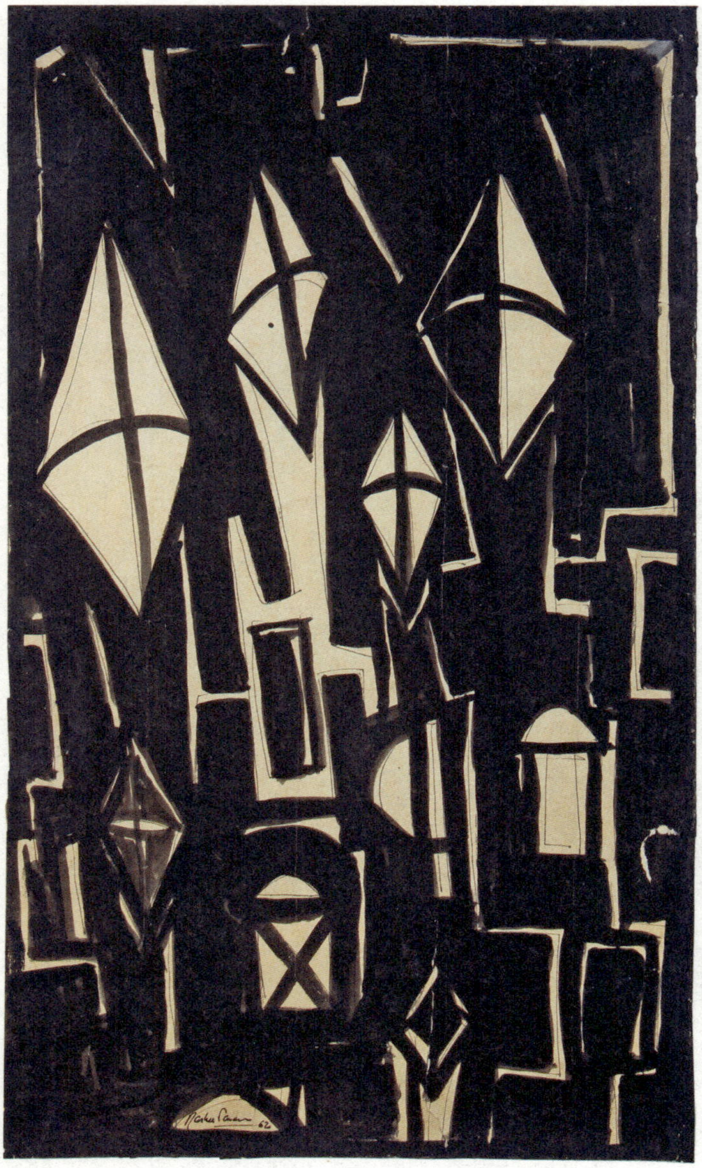

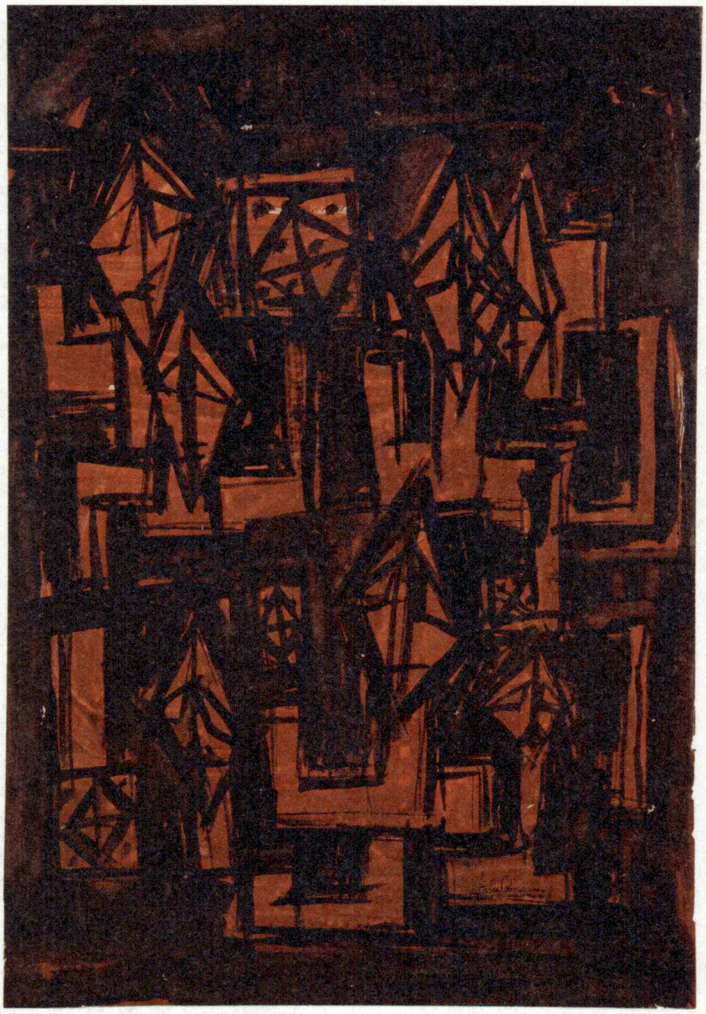

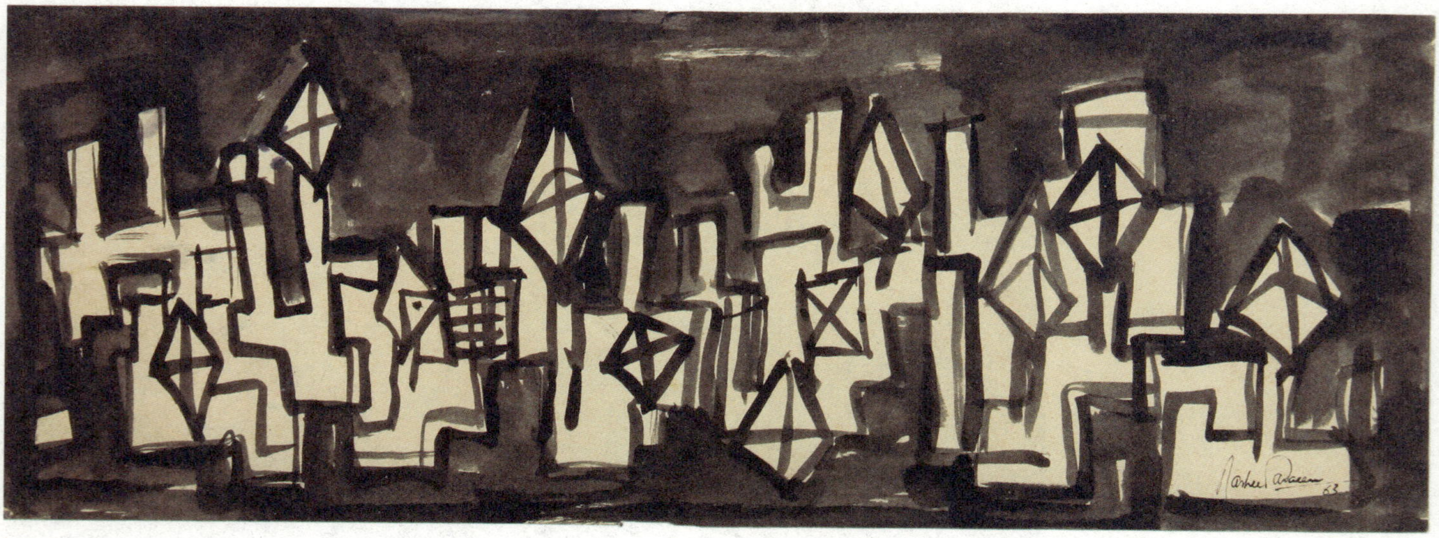

Untitled (Hyderabad 4), 1963
watercolour, pastel, and ink on paper, 37 x 56 cm

Untitled (Hyderabad 5), 1963
watercolour, pastel, and ink on paper, 37 x 56 cm

Untitled (Hyderabad 6), 1963
watercolour and ink on paper, 10 x 25 cm

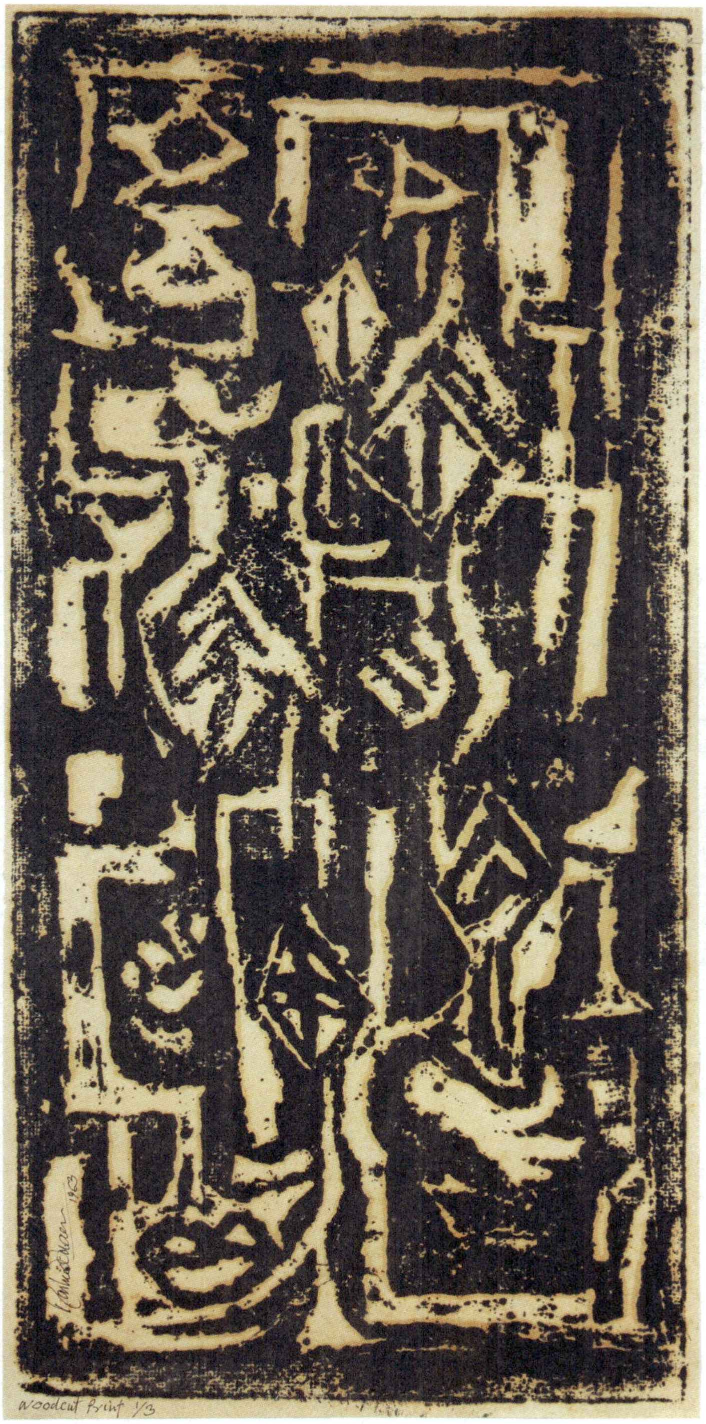

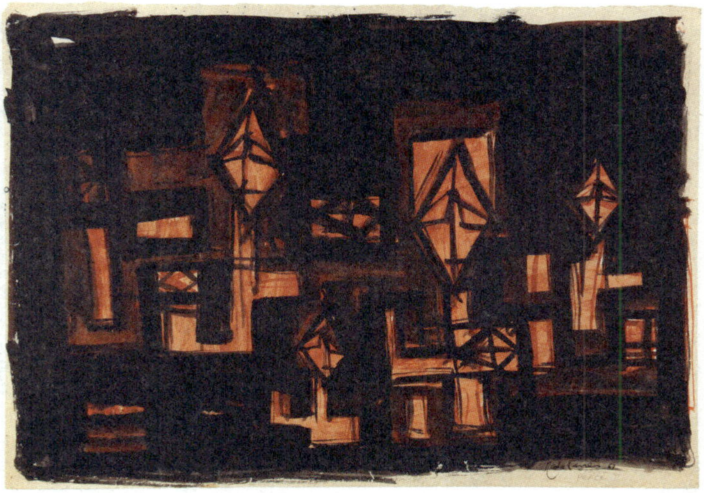

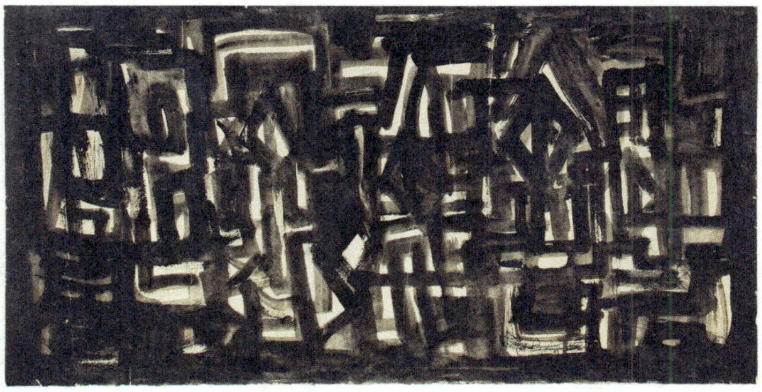

City of Hyderabad, 1963
watercolour and ink on paper, 56 x 75 cm

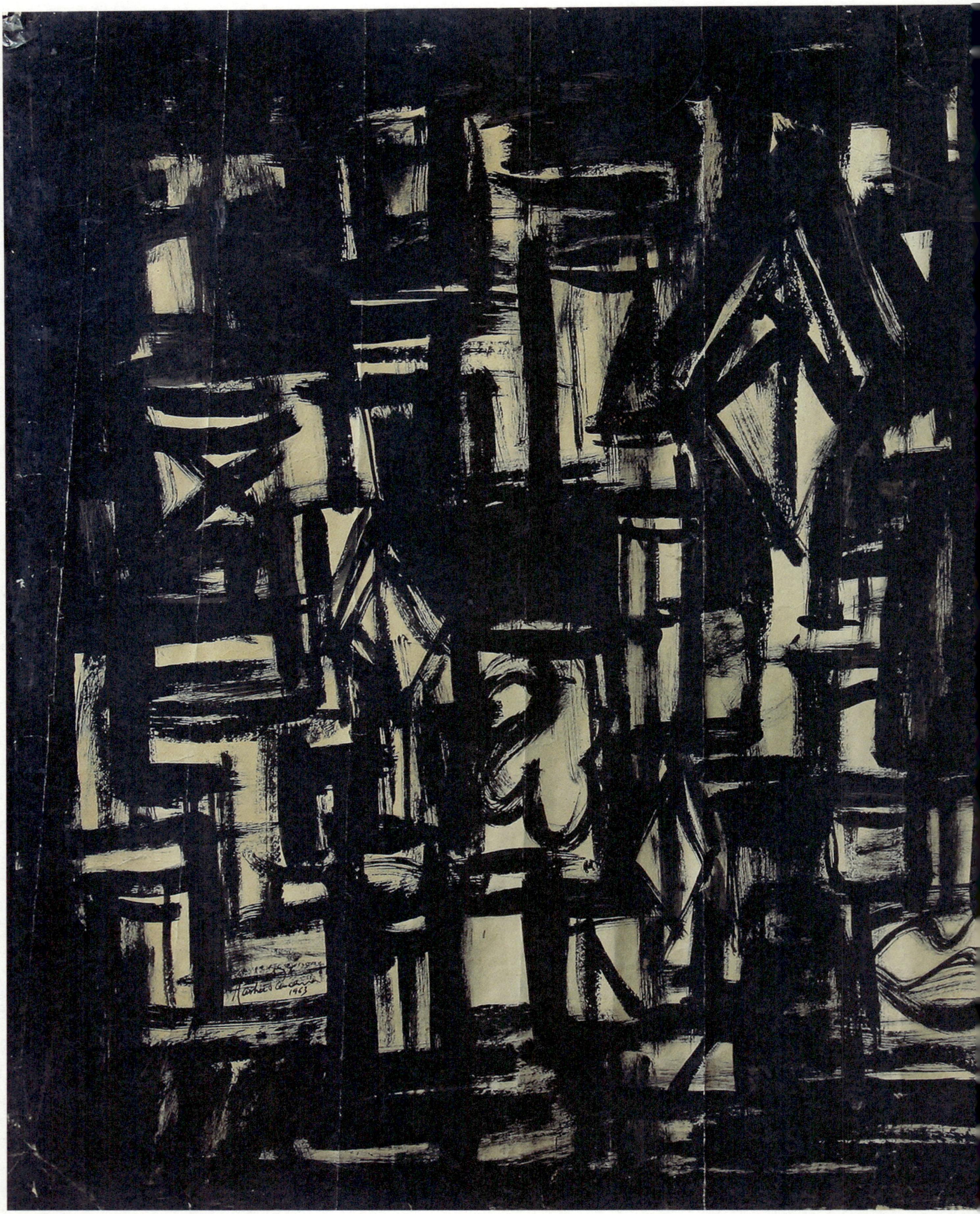

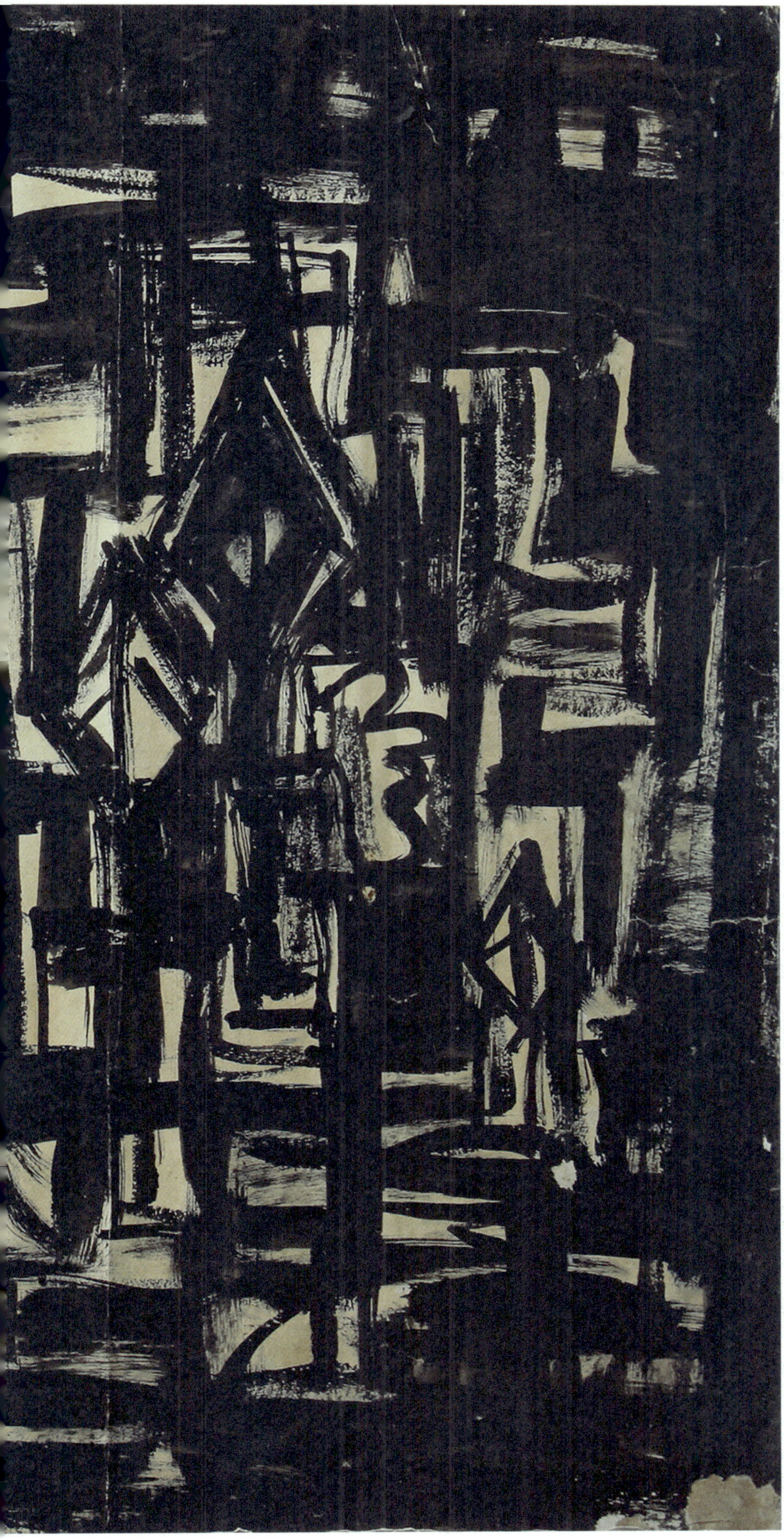

Before Departure (Black Painting No. IV), 1963
oil on canvas, 91 x 99 cm
Sharjah Art Foundation Collection

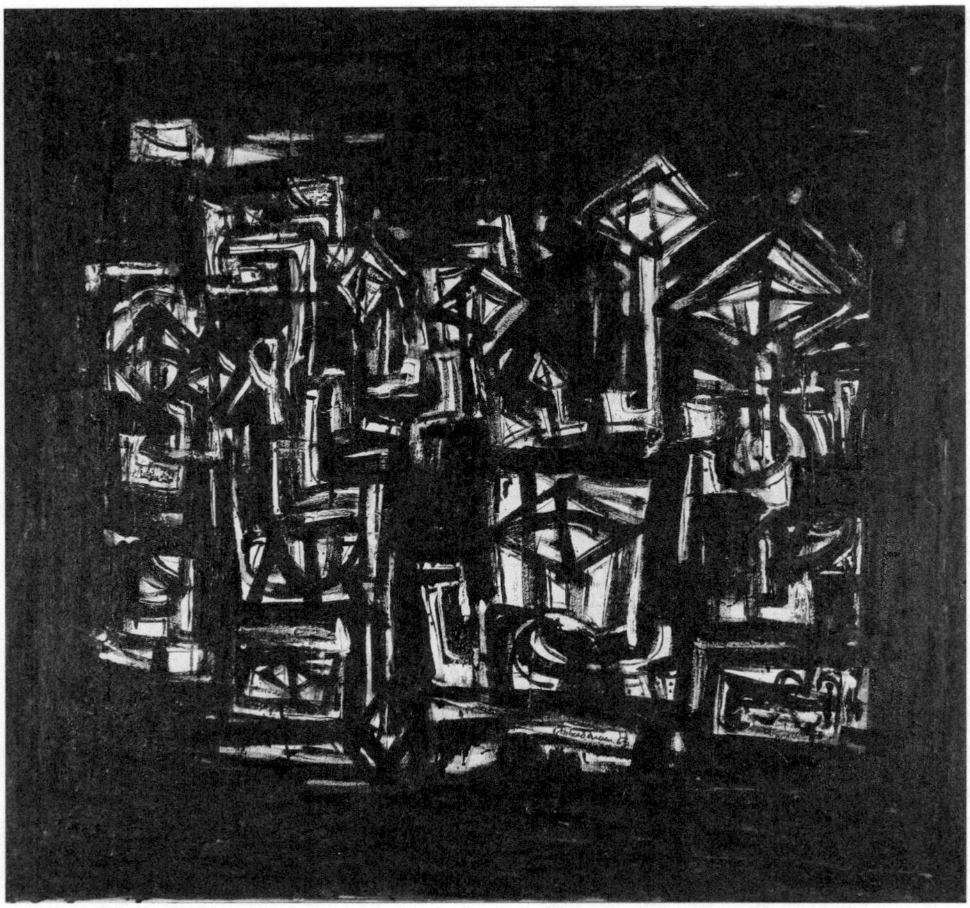

Before Departure (Black Painting No. V), 1963
oil on canvas, 92 x 122 cm
Sharjah Art Foundation Collection

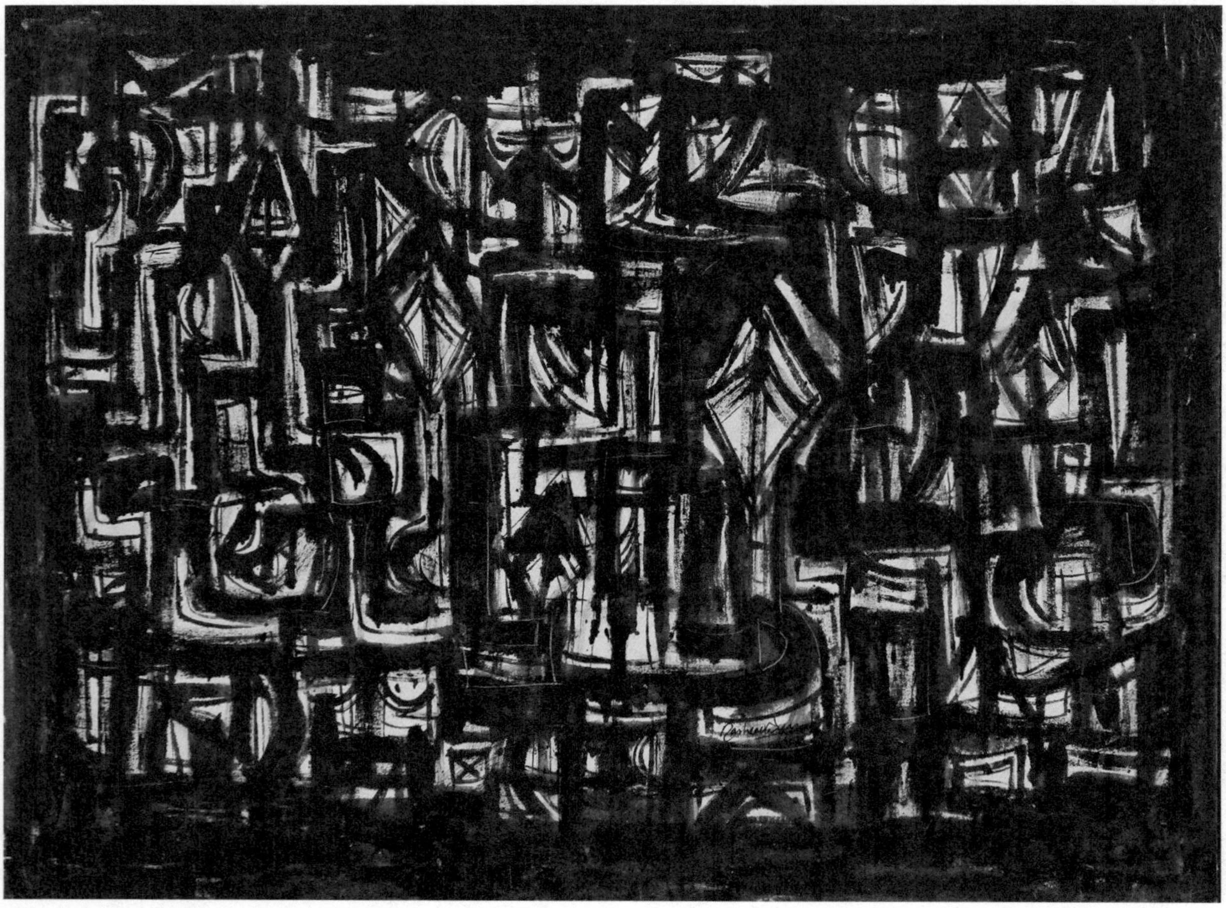

Before Departure (Black Painting No. VI), 1963
oil on canvas, 91 x 73 cm
Sharjah Art Foundation Collection

Before Departure (Painting 71), 1964
oil on canvas, 91 x 91 cm
Sharjah Art Foundation Collection

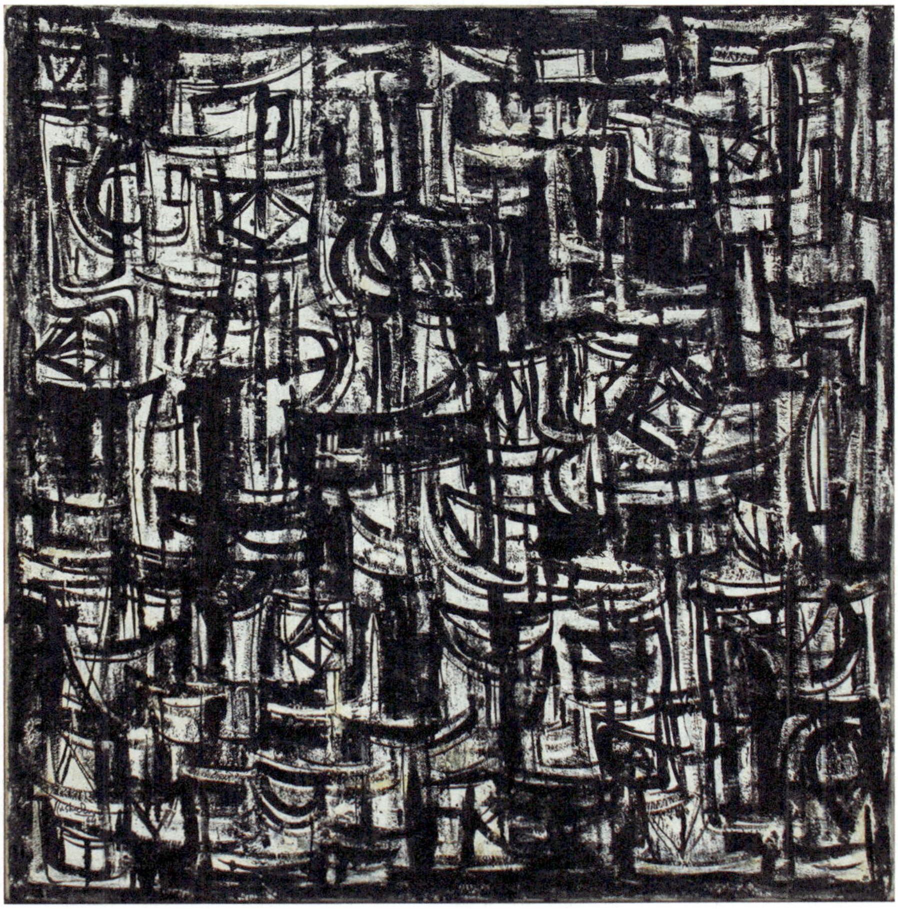

Before Departure (Black Painting No. VIII), 1964
oil on canvas, 92 x 139 cm
Sharjah Art Foundation Collection

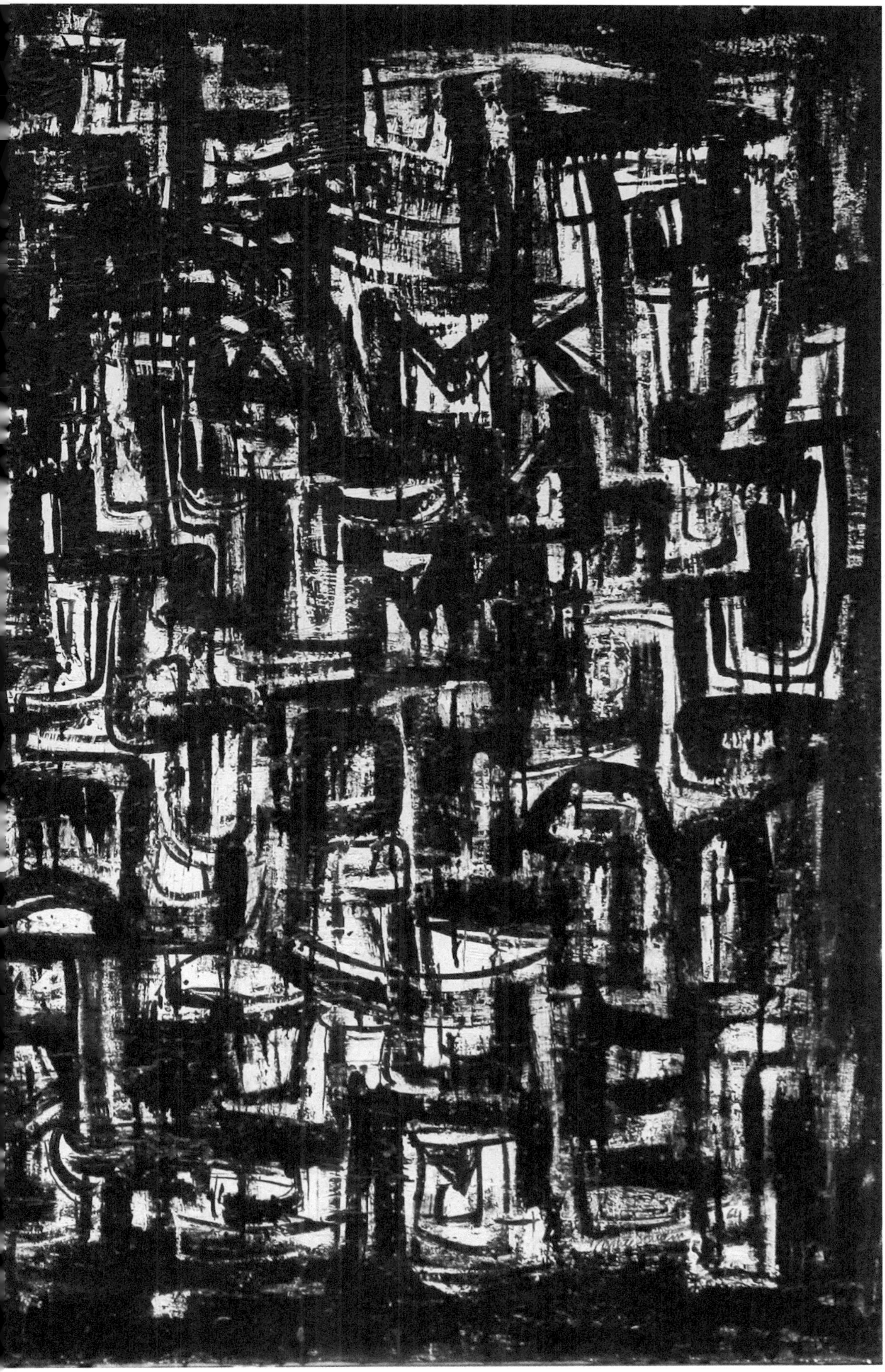

Self-Portrait, 1964
felt-tip marker on paper, dimensions unknown
Collection Sheikha Hoor Al Qasimi

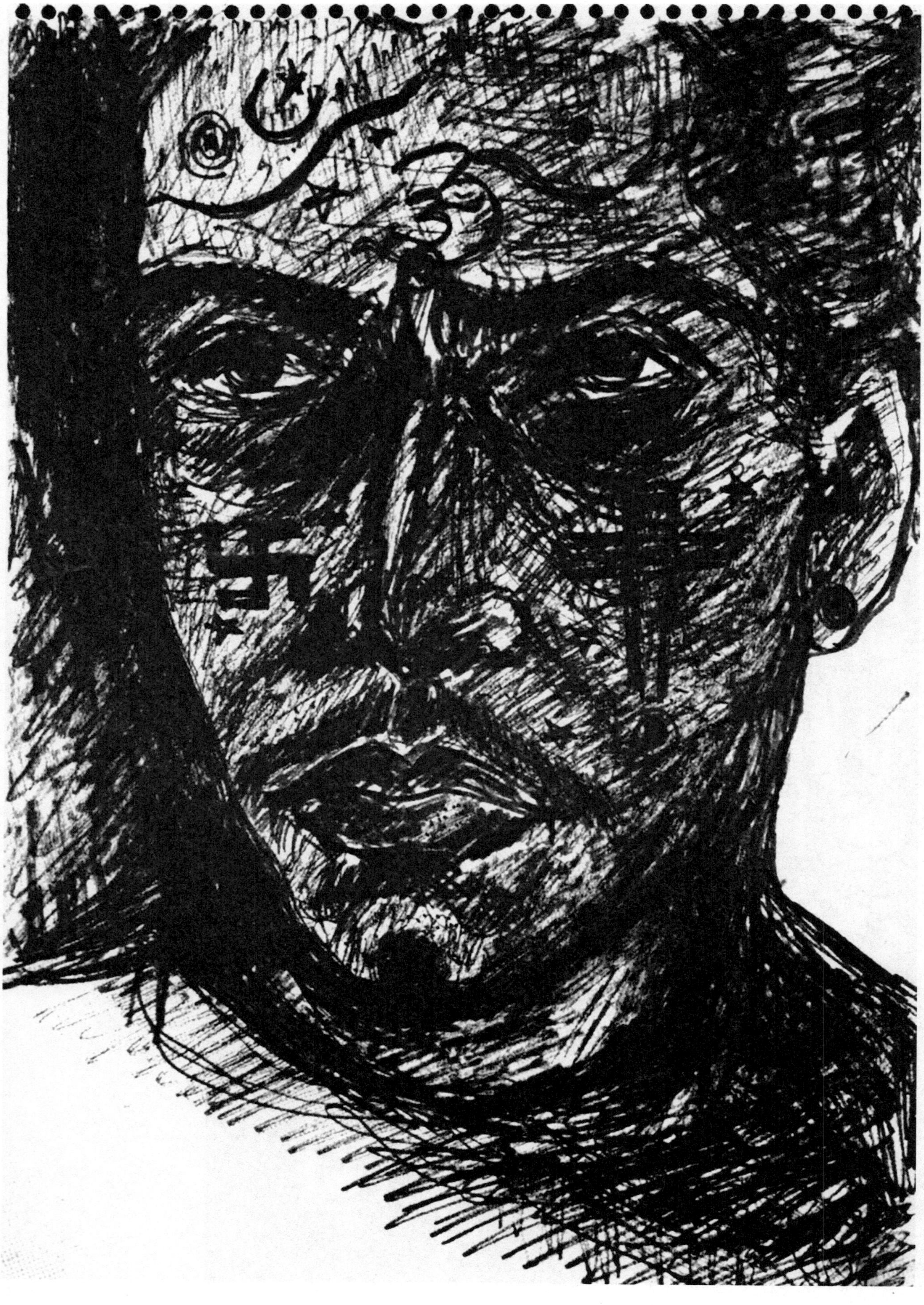

Equality, Resistance, Hospitality: Abstraction and Universality in the Work of Rasheed Araeen

Michael Newman

Rasheed Araeen's work as an artist can be understood according to different perspectives and histories, and undergoes quite drastic shifts in approach. Yet there is an underlying consistency, which to my mind has a rather surprising source given his struggle for the visibility of black artists and the powerful critique of colonialism conducted through the journal he founded *Third Text*, namely a commitment to a concept of universality. This is most plausible in relation to his abstract Structures, but is also implicit in the basis for the critique within the works and activities concerning representation of racial identity. Seen sequentially – with the proviso that such a view is very partial – I will address four stages in Araeen's work. In Karachi, Pakistan, during the mid- to late 1950s, following the study of engineering, joining the Artists Club, and practising drawing in the Sketch Club at the United States Information Service,[1] his work moves from drawing in conventional Western portrait and landscape genres to abstraction and Arte Povera. In London, which he reached via Paris after leaving Karachi in 1964, through the 1960s into the 1970s, he mainly makes abstract sculpture using I-beams and lattice structures evocative of engineering and architecture, and a work releasing red-coloured floating disks into St. Katharine's Docks in London. From the late '70s into the '80s, he engages with the ways in which he is positioned and marginalized as a black artist of South Asian origin, using photography, video, and performance. From 1978, in the context of black power and civil rights struggles, he writes polemical texts and publishes the *Black Phoenix: Journal of Contemporary Art & Culture in the Third World*, and in 1987 he founds *Third Text*, which becomes the most influential journal on issues of postcolonialism and critical art outside the Western mainstream in relation to globalization; the activity of writing and publishing should be considered an integral part of Araeen's activity as an artist. In the latest phase Araeen develops the combination of abstraction and participation, which was already there in his work of the '60s, both as autonomous works, and into art involving social activity and transformation.[2]

Of course, these four stages are not strictly speaking sequential: they overlap, and cross back and forth. The assumptions concerning what an artist is and does changes – or perhaps one should say broadens – as it does for other artists throughout the '60s and '70s. From making art objects to what has come to be called 'practice' in an expanded field, extended more recently to social art orientated towards use by different publics, Araeen was primed for this change in the concept of art partly by his training as an engineer. This background aligns him with the pre-history of this transformation in Constructivism. The expansion of his practice was also a critical response to the marginalization he experienced after the initial success of his I-beam sculptures and lattice structures in the second half of the 1960s.[3] It was then that the art establishment started to position the work of black and Asian artists in terms of ethnic identities. The situation was made more complex by the shift on the political left from solidarity with liberation struggles and movements of the left in the 'Third World' to identity politics in the context of globalization. Thus, the assertion of marginalized and oppressed identities as a political project and ground for critique met the establishment's assigning of a role to black artists on the basis of which they were provided with funding and visibility, while remaining marginal with respect to the dominant modes of art making.

The problem, then, was how to lay a claim to difference without being marginalized and being excluded once again by the power relations that sustained a largely white, male, Western 'mainstream'. One possible strategy that gained a great deal of support and chimed with post-'68 developments in philosophy – was to attribute a fundamental status to difference. This was not Araeen's solution, which is rather rooted in the Afro-Caribbean and Asian anti-racist alliances from the 1960s into the early 1980s in the UK.[4] He did indeed make work that presented his 'difference' or 'otherness' as a black artist of South Asian origin, but at the same time these works reflected back the way he was positioned as such by social and art-world institutions. The implication was that to simply assert his difference or otherness would reinforce those power relations. Returning to the West's colonial origins – and there is no West without the history of colonization and indeed of slavery – it is a truism to say that the West imposed its hegemony by 'universalizing' its values; be it through religion or teleological philosophies and pseudo-science, and ultimately through violent repression and ethnic cleansing by settler colonialism. As a result, the deconstruction of universality has been a crucial aspect of postcolonial critique in philosophy and the arts, to which Araeen has made an important contribution through his writing, editing, and publishing as well as his artworks.

In this context, it may come as a surprise to confront the claim that a notion of universality has been central to Araeen's work, and indeed underlies the abstract sculptures, lattice Structures, and paintings on the one hand, and the photo, video, and performance works concerned with identity and marginalization on the other: we could say that it is this universality, rather than identity, that gives his diverse work its consistency. In order to argue this, it is essential to distinguish what we could call the 'critical universality' on which Araeen draws, from the ideological universality that is rightly the object of postcolonial critique. It is the relation to critical universality and its implication of equality that gives Araeen's work its urgency and exemplary importance today. The limitations of political approaches based on identity in confronting both white supremacist racism and renascent nationalism, and the crushing injustice of growing economic inequality, is becoming alarmingly apparent.

Coming to art from engineering (and without formal training as an artist) has fed Araeen's insights. It is no coincidence that he called his early lattice-work objects and reliefs Structures rather than sculptures. Structural principles are universal and immutable: unless a building or structure is made in a certain way, calculated according to geometry and a science of forces, it will fall down. This universality has nothing to do with context, identity, or representation. If Araeen's Structures are non-hierarchical and egalitarian, this too is not only a matter of representation or allegory: it is based on the fact that structural principles or laws are universally applicable. Everyone and everything is subject to gravity.

What the work proposes is a relation between difference and universality. The public of the work is differentiated, with those differences involving power relations, something that Araeen forces to explicitness in his late '70s and early '80s photographic and performance works: for example, in the central panel of
Look Mamma…Macho! (1986), which includes, behind the text of Mrs. Thatcher's 256
infamous 'Swamped' speech of 1978 concerning the fear of immigrants from other cultures, an image from the performance *'Paki Bastard' (Portrait of the Artist as a Black Person)* (1977), of Araeen blinded by dark glasses, gagged, holding 234
a broom or mop handle to suggest labour as a cleaner, while over his body is projected the image of a lattice Structure. Araeen's resistance by assuming the

way in which otherness is projected onto him by the dominant white Western colonialist culture is 'felt' with respect to the universality of the lattice that in effect is his projection onto himself. The universality implied by the lattice is distinct from the ideological 'universality' of modernism, both in its teleological/purist Constructivist and Greenbergian high modernist moments.

It would be a mistake to equate the critical universality behind Araeen's work with the identity of identity-and-difference or the sameness of same-and-other. The universality of geometry and mathematics (the basis of engineering) is unrelated to difference and otherness – it is not the identity of difference or the sameness of otherness. Of course, art is not engineering – even if Araeen and others dream of assimilating art into real-life projects. It always involves an element of representation and allegory. The same is true of politics. So, the question is not that of the universality of art (the false question of 'Civilization', and the modernism advocated by the American critic Clement Greenberg based on the supposed disinterestedness of judgement), but rather of art's potential relation to universality, and to the abuses of particular, partial representations of universality in the name of hierarchy and domination.

There are two key moments in the development of Araeen's approach to
making art after the portraits, landscapes, and abstract paintings of the 1950s in
Karachi. The first was his discovery in November 1959 of a twisted metal spiral
from a bicycle tyre that had been burned as a form of sculpture (Araeen keeps
it in his studio to this day) that lead to the work *My First Sculpture* (1959). The 32
finding of this spiral resulted in an action shortly afterwards to produce more
(reconstructed in London in 1975).[5] This form, a loose spiral achieved through a
process of burning as purification, could be seen as standing for dynamism and
transformation. In terms of method, we might see a parallel with Arte Povera
in the incorporation of poor materials into art using an anti-form approach.
The *Chakras* (water disks) event first staged in 1970 at St. Katherine's Docks 136
in London, where Araeen had a studio, might be seen as a continuation of this
project, using water rather than fire: sixteen discs painted in fluorescent red
were cast into the water by volunteers, and floated out of the dock into the
River Thames.

The second moment is the development of the I-beam sculptures in 1965
during his early period in London, and the lattice forms from 1966, both
influenced by Araeen's engineering experience. The first of the I-beam sculptures,
Sculpture No. 1 (1965), involved four steel beams painted in a neutral colour 98
simply laid side by side with an equal gap between them to make a 72-inch
square. The first lattice work *First Structure* (1966–1967), was a 55-inch square 101
quadrilateral with a bracing diagonal on each side, dividing them further into
quadrilateral triangles. *Second Structure* (1966–1967) took the form of a squat 103
tower 72 inches high with three diagonals on each side, initiating the sense of a
spiralling movement that was increased in the narrower multiple Structures such
as *BoO* (1969). All these works were lucid, transparent, and without interiors,
involving repetition and clearly accessible, non-mysterious modes of construction.
This marks his particular engagement with Constructivism, Anthony Caro, and
the New Generation sculpture, as well as a parallel practice that differentiates
Araeen's work from American Minimalism.[6] The combination of repetition with
flow and change can be seen in abstract oil paintings such as *Ham Raqs* (dance 33
partners) (1959) and *Aag Ka Naach* (dance of fire) (1961) (the relation between 43
modes is in no sense teleological: the turn to sculpture or performance and
Conceptual art does not imply a break with painting that continues to be an
aspect of his practice). Amid these two moments we can discern the critical
potential of the encounter between anti-form and participation in a situation
with a universalist abstraction.

During the '70s and '80s a large-scale model of Vladimir Tatlin's *Tower* occupied a terrace of the Marylebone Road building of the Polytechnic of Central London (PCL) (now University of Westminster).[7] Tatlin's *Tower or Monument to the Third International*, a project developed for Petrograd in 1919–1920 but never built, relates to Araeen's work in three ways: it combines the two forms of his breakthrough, the spiral from the bicycle tyres with the struts and the lattice of the beams, which in the *Tower* were to be of steel; and there is a strong emphasis on the diagonal, both structurally and in the dynamism of its iconography, and the conception of the work of art not so much as a sculptural object but as a feat of architecture and engineering: it was intended as a challenge to the Eiffel Tower. There are also two important ways in which the *Tower* differs from Araeen's lattice Structures. First, Tatlin's *Tower* has the outline of a cone, which suggests a hierarchical structure like a pyramid – after all conceived as a monument. Second, it was supposed to function as an information and propaganda projector for a mass public, teleologically orientated towards the development of an ideal society in the future in which it would have been instrumental as a functioning structure.

Araeen's approach repudiates monumentality and hierarchy, even if it is occasionally made on a large scale. While the eschewal of monumentality is consistent with the sculpture of Caro and the New Generation sculptors, who Araeen admired, and anticipates or parallels the approach of Minimalists like Carl Andre and Robert Morris, we should not interpret this as a formal decision, or at least as a formal decision separate from its political and allegorical significance. The Minimalists – notably Dan Flavin – took over aspects of Constructivism, which they knew largely from Camilla Gray's book *The Russian Experiment in Art 1863–1922*, published in 1962, to use as formal structuring devices to phenomenological ends. Araeen moves in the opposite direction, taking a form and, while it is detached from function (therefore distinct from the Constructivist trajectory), releasing its social and allegorical implications. Caro drew on pre-existing steel units from engineering, like beams and plates – like his forerunner David Smith – and organized them in an open and transparent way. Yet his approach is fundamentally compositional, based on intuitive judgements concerning balance and tension, and therefore implicitly hierarchical in its implications. By contrast, Araeen's approach is egalitarian, in that it does not posit any special compositional judgement – genius – at work in the creation of the object, and the elements don't assert themselves in different ways in relation to the whole. Araeen preferred to call these objects 'Structures' rather than sculptures. On the one hand this alludes to their origin in engineering and architecture, and on the other suggests a parallel with the theory of structuralism, which was then being developed in linguistics, anthropology, and social science. It sought to uncover the basic structures that governed language, society, and subjectivity. One might also include here the Frankfurt School philosopher Theodor Adorno's idea that the form of the work of art and the relation of its parts to the whole reflected both the totalization imposed by the subject and the resistance to that form on the part of what he called the 'non-identical'.[8] Closer to home was the interest in the combination of sociology, information theory, and diagramming in the work of Stephen Willats from the mid-1970s, with the implication that art could chart social life and organization, and record the views and aspirations of the participants who are effectively collaborators in its making. Indeed, there are parallels with Araeen, in that Willats' approach to work with specific social content grew out of drawings based on cybernetics and ideas of self-organizing systems.[9] Altogether these phenomena contribute to the idea that a work of art, through the way its elements are related to each other, could model social relations.

The question for an artist undertaking social critique is on what basis, from what position, can the critique be made and by what value or ethical claim is it supported? For many making work in the 1980s, the answer was from the standpoint of a distinctive identity based on difference. This was considered to be a critical alternative to a critical approach based on equality, which was taken to neglect the specific claims of difference and identity. But why should identity as such make a political claim? What would enable a judgement to be made concerning the claim of an identity – for example, one that might be considered racist, exclusionary, or repressive? Or, are all identity claims equally valid? Araeen moved towards the engagement with questions of identity in the 1970s, concurrent with his turn to intervention in discourse with the four-panel collage work *For Oluwale* (1971–1973 / 1975), documenting the victimization of black people in Britain, his engagement in civil rights by joining the Black Panther movement in 1972, up to his co-founding of the journal *Black Phoenix* in 1978. But the basis for critique in Araeen's approach to identity was precisely not to assert the intrinsic claim of his 'ethnicity' or hybrid identity, but rather to consider, more in the manner of the theorist of colonialism Frantz Fanon, the way that he is positioned and his desires expropriated by the dominant white power in order to be excluded.[10] To assert ethnic identity as such would be to perpetuate this structure of oppression rather than defeat it.

Consequently, we can see the relevance and importance of the early abstract Structures – that continue to feature throughout the work – to Araeen's approach to critique: the value of identity is grounded in universality, which implies equality, which in turn is not to be understood as sameness, but is rather related to the singular irreplaceability of every person. The strategy, therefore, is to take both approaches – the claim of identity, and of universality and equality – simultaneously, in order to provide a basis from which representation might be decoded and critiqued. If equality is to be an ethical-political value, rather than simply one form of distribution among others, it needs to be grounded in universality.[11] But how are we to take into account that universality has been subject to critique as partial and contextual – white, male, Western, colonialist, et cetera? The doxa is that Araeen's work, insofar as it stands for the black, marginalized artist, must also involve a critique of universality. I think this claim is based on a misunderstanding of the role of universality in Araeen's work and discourse. What it fails to recognize is the distinction between a historically contextualized 'universality' – that may function ideologically to support racism and colonialism – and the universality, which, while it has historical beginnings, marks a break with the phenomenal and historical world, that is to say, the universality that comes into being with geometry. In my view, it is this 'geometric' universality that is referred to by Araeen's lattice Structures, and that it emerges from his experience as an engineer. It is partly through this universality that Araeen avoids the pitfalls of identity politics without falling back onto ideological claims to hegemonic universality.

This alternative approach to universality, with its necessary corollary of equality, is provided by Michel Serres in his book *Geometry: The Third Book of Foundations* (in French in 1995 and English in 2017). According to Serres, as a just reaction to a 'universal' reducible to an imperialist and invading phenomenon, difference has become a dogma. If the problem that called for the assertion of difference was totalization, now it is 'splitting up'. We need to think of a new universal outside those dominances. The language of mathematics shows the universal without dominance, and we are compelled to obey something other than ourselves, a new universe, according to Serres, different from our differences. The invention of axiomatic geometry involved a shift from the field of the measurers to the world through the traces of the shadow made by the sun when Thales compared the shadow cast by a measuring stick, the *gnomon*, to the shadow cast by the Great Pyramid in order to calculate the height of the latter: 'geometry writes a universal language that neither engraves nor traces any mark on any medium.'[12] The break is between an instrument that measures, and an axiomatic proof. It specifically arises around the diagonal as an irrational number. This opens up a third sphere that is neither that of the human nor of the measuring instrument. The area of the square of the diagonal of a right triangle cannot be stated as an integer or a rational number since it is the square root of the product of the squares of the two right sides. That the issue is the diagonal, which is also so central to what Araeen learned from engineering about the resolution of structural tension, is intriguing. Geometry passes from small plot of ground to world: first, by using the relation of the sun to the gnomon it established a point of view above the world; and in a second move, through the use of an irrational number that can't be derived from measuring but requires a theorem or proof in Pythagoras' theorem (that states that the square of the hypotenuse is equal to the sum of the squares of the other two sides), it creates a space that is outside the social space of measuring fields and pyramids, that moves beyond the Babylonian-Egyptian algorithmic operation. As Serres writes: 'The existence of knowledge outside the *gnomon* authorises that we seek what we do not know – what knowledge itself does not know, what memory has not recorded.'[13] This opens up a new, universal, atopic world: 'The world that's as measurable as you please, by algorithm, approximation, even exactness, borders immediately on another world that's infinitely distant, that's without dimension since the metric exhausts itself reaching it: an absent hole in the drawing.'[14] This is a world of abstraction that is categorically different to that of abstract art, which is still measurable and traced. 'The abstract line without any dimension other than its own is extracted from the wooden or marble ruler, is drawn from it in every sense.... Why does the theory of abstraction unfold its splendours in an imaginary space separating the true senses from the pure understanding?'[15] This is theoretical space that is not a representation of real space, but a jump to another order. Interesting that Serres writes of it as an operation of the imagination given the importance of imagination to Araeen.

Serres also writes of the 'surprising equivalence between geometry and equality'.[16] Socrates says 'you forget that geometrical equality rules, all-powerful, among the gods as among men. You think that we must strive to get the better of all the others: because you forget geometry' (Plato, Gorgias 507e–508a). This new space of universality supposes a collectivity of equal subjects, which will become the community of science. 'There is no science without constancy, without the equals sign. There is no knowledge without an invariance. This notion and this operation are also and again equivalent to order, justice, harmony, the social bond. Equality conditions community.'[17] What does it mean for community to be conditioned by the science that arises from axiomatic geometry? '...[T]here exists an object or objects for us, for the collective, for this society whose iron law usually consists in acting as though they didn't exist. Science forms a paradoxical realist group in the ordinarily idealist collective. In it we, together, relate to a thing whose laws don't in any way relate to our relations.'[18] That is to say, equality cannot be based on a measurement or distribution within society, an immanent comparison of its members or groups, which would always result in a relative equality dependent on inequality, but in relation to a domain that is indifferent to us, a relation to that which doesn't relate to our relations. The basis of equality is not comparison but the non-relation to the axiomatic world discovered by an imaginative leap prompted by the diagonal.

This doesn't mean that the axiomatic world does not have a social dimension. Rather than measuring land (in Ancient Egypt by the *harpedonaptai* who measured the fields after the flooding of the Nile, establishing the tax proportional to their areas that may have changed due to the washing away of the banks), or being dependent on speech and memory, it involves a structure of proportion or balance: 'Proportion-logos chases out discourse-logos; a law or an order exists that doesn't know or isn't known by social order or law, and the pharaoh does anew. What remains is an empty polyhedron, a luminous and transparent box',[19] which replaces the opaque pyramid holding the mummified corpse of the pharaoh. This is not a 'distribution of the sensible' in Jacques Rancière's sense, which would be relevant to the geometric stage of the flooding of the Nile and the harpadenoptai's distribution of land.[20] The point of Rancière's argument is that there would be different and also historically changing distributions of the sensible, which might be judged – measured – as equitable or not. The axiometric geometry of proofs would have rather to do with the non-relation of different distributions of the sensible to a non-sensible, the difference between the ideal or abstract line and point, and the inscribed. This difference derives from an operation of purification or subtraction,[21] an extirpation of the sensible to create a space of intelligibility. The surpassing of hierarchy has political implications, but not simply in the direction of universal equality, since exclusion is involved in its very operation. Using a diagram,[22] Serres shows that the egalitarian space of the democratic circle with a speaker at the centre and equal listeners who may in turn become speakers in a circle around him, is produced by a quarter turn on a future that elevates the king above the privileged class above the people. A hierarchical structure is turned into an exclusionary structure where the circumference centralizes in order to exclude.[23] What is resisted by this is that on an even more fundamental level 'in truth the universe anarchically scatters'.[24] Geometric abstraction is a second-order operation on the indefinite infinite that the Greeks called *apeiron*. The first geometric operation would be measurement, associated with hierarchy (measuring out the formlessly silted fields for the purposes of taxation). The next would be subtraction/exclusion, the emptying of the field, rendering it transparent and without qualities. Seeing things in relation to an indefinite (called to attention in the fragment of the Greek philosopher Anaximander) means seeing them from outside the world, above the king.[25] The world, then, is between the apeiron, the indefinite infinite, and the transcendental abstraction. The geometric operation creating an above or outside the world renders the world a projection, a theatre. There is thus an intrinsic relation between geometry and tragedy.

An installation Araeen made in 1994 is titled *Aflatoon (So You Think You Are Plato)* where the title refers to the Arabic, Persian, and Urdu name for the philosopher. Paul Overy reports that 'Araeen originally thought of including a bust of Plato in the work but he could not find one in Britain.'[26] A single white Sol LeWitt-like cube sits on top of a black pyramid of diagonal-lattice cubes – the white supported by and dominating the black. We could take this as a critique of universality, but does it not rather establish the difference between egalitarian, critical universality and a hierarchical idealism? The latter would be based on ideas of ascent towards a combination of complete intelligibility and maximal being,[27] very different from the immanent egalitarianism of the lattice that is also present in its very formation and reception, and not postponed to the future as a teleological ideal. The distinction is not only between black and white, in an allegory of colonialism and racist exploitation, but also between the representation of universality as idealization, the elevation of a god or ideal, and structural or, better, infrastructural equality.

We can see here how Araeen's representational work – dealing precisely with the point of view in terms of position and power from which subjects, particularly black, colonialized, and immigrant subjects, are represented – was not a break from his Structures. This is a point strengthened by the inclusion of Structures in the photographic and other works, and the use of abstract yet symbolic formations like the cross. The space of abstraction, understood as axiomatic and based in equality, facilitates the critique of the entwinement of power and representation, and the relation of representation to exclusion. Identity, to be recognized in its difference, is not taken as a value in itself or a basis for political action, but articulated in its (non)relation to equality, which is indifferent and without qualities. The direction of Araeen's work is not so much that of abstracting from everyday practices such as building and measurement, but rather to draw the abstract axiomatic geometry into the everyday. This is after all precisely the function of the engineer, and we might see Araeen's large-scale scaffolding structures, such as *To Whom It May Concern* installed outside the Serpentine Gallery in London in 1996, at approximately fifty square feet, built of used scaffolding metal tubes, as in the tradition of the artist-engineer or artist-architect, like Tatlin. The difference with the Constructivist lies in the egalitarianism inherent to the structure, and its relation to everyday social life: after three months returning to the work normally done by those who had installed it. This is not only a work of directed construction, it also draws attention to the anonymous labour that made it possible for it to be built.

As Serres realizes, we may be at the end of the 'geometric' epoch situated between apeiron and axiomatic subtraction and at the emergence of a new formation: 'Now bodies, messages, information, knowledge, light in its speed more than its brightness circulate in mass: a new space of new transports is installed on a global Earth, a space more mixed than pure, more blended, variegated, tiger-striped, zebra-striped, in multiple and connected networks, than smooth or homogenous.'[28] There is a question of what equality and universality might mean in such a world. Would it still devolve from a relation without relation to an axiomatic space? Serres' account is predicated on a distinction – a leap – from the algorithmic geometry of the gnomon to the axiomatic realm of proof. The subsequent space that he hints at coincides with a resurgence of the algorithm in relation to big data and artificial intelligence (which maybe means we are Babylonian rather than Greek[29] – that not only algorithms but Pythagoras' theorem was discovered much earlier – but this only strengthens the non-contextual argument). The history is not that of a progressive paradigm shift in any simple sense: the algorithmic predates the axiomatic, as it seems the axiomatic predates itself. The Euclidean geometric realm discovered supposedly by the Greeks (it could have been earlier) was also the discovery of the transcendental. The return to the algorithm as a set of operations of measurement implies an ontological 'flattening'. This would mean the loss of the transcendental-axiomatic sphere as a basis for community; that is, the loss of the relation to non-relation. In the networked world, there are only relations: non-relations count for nothing. This means that there cannot be any basis for equality other than immanent relations. Equality in the previous sense – established first of all through a non-relation rather than distribution, which comes afterwards – becomes unthinkable: where there are only comparisons and targeted individualization based on surveillance and big data, there can be no true equality.

Universality also shifts. It is no longer non-differential: a sphere other than the sphere of differences and identities. Universality becomes flattened into access to relations as global networks. In this context, the link between equality and universality, which had been subject to criticism on the basis of difference, itself becomes critical in a new way. On the basis of this, we can see that Araeen's work reaches a new stage of critique, involving a return to the lattice and to abstraction. The first stage was the criticism through the insistence on 'equal access' to modernist universality (as if it were of the same nature as the universality of geometry) of subaltern neo-colonialism and the 'ethnicization' of non-white artists. The second stage is the critique of the colonization of desire (Fanon), the conceptual and performative work on being subject to projections of what dominant white society thinks that a black artist should be (even in this Araeen rejects the solutions of identifying with an identity, or hybridity). The third stage would be the return to the lattice and the diagonal in a context where the flattening of ontology and politics (society governed by algorithmic metrics) poses algorithmic individualization as a threat to the very possibility and even thinkability of social equality. Far from being a conservative return to abstraction, Araeen's recent work should rather be seen as the beginning of a new critical project.

This third aspect involves participation as a localized realization of the universal and critical ideals of the Structures and conceptual works. American Minimalism involves a phenomenological integration of the viewer. Contrast this with the active involvement of the viewer in reorganizing Araeen's work, so that it is continually changing according to the participation of multiple viewers. This integrates the activism of Constructivism, but with a different conception of the participant. If the initial configuration of cube forms with diagonal cross-bracing of *Zero to* 305
Infinity (1968–2004) is symmetrical, the participation of the audience in moving the shapes produces an asymmetry that is also unpredictable, but within a situation of equality among the members of the participating public.[30] It marks a break with the authoritative remoteness of a work that cannot be touched or altered, even if, as with Minimalism, the phenomenological experience of visitors is engaged. The participation of the public in transforming the work parallels works by the Brazilian artists Lygia Clark, Hélio Oiticica, and Filipino artist David Medalla.[31]

In 2017 Araeen presented two works for documenta 14, both of them involving participation by the public, and both of them incorporating paintings and Structures with abstract designs. In both cases, the effect was celebratory and welcoming. In Kassel's Neue Neue Galerie he installed a reading room with the 356
complete edition of *Third Text* under his editorship. Inside, the tables and chairs were made using his module cubes with diagonal braces, thus bringing together his Structures with his path-making intervention into the critical discourse of postcolonialism and globalization though writing and editing. Different versions of *The Reading Room* were installed at ZKM Centre for Art and Media, Karlsruhe, 287
2011–2012 and the Gwangju Biennale, 2012.[32] His contribution to the section of documenta in Athens was *Shamiyaana–Food for Thought: Thought for Change*, a 358
functioning restaurant where a free, simple meal could be shared at tables seating eight by anyone who queued for a ticket.[33] By situating the restaurant outside in Kotsia Square, Araeen made it accessible to those who could not afford to enter the official venues. The shared meal creates an equality and fellowship between the participants, realizing in social terms, at least for the duration of the meal, the equality implied by the Structures referred to in the temporary building that Araeen had designed, fulfilling his early interest in architecture, particularly that of Frank Lloyd Wright, who also used structures to generate potential relationships between users (Araeen's earliest work of this kind combining function with abstract form was perhaps the lattice-structured window grills he designed for 27
his parents' house in Karachi).[34] The brightly coloured cubic tent structures, and the panels of abstract patterns forming the walls, allude to the equalizing serial shapes of the early Structures: the equality inherent in the world of geometry is related to the equality achieved among the fellowship of diners. Furthermore, Araeen's *Shamiyaana* restaurant was situated between the municipal Town Hall of Athens on one side of the square, and the Greek National Bank on the other, thus drawing attention to its situation in the aftermath of the Greek financial crisis and subjection to EU neoliberal economics, and its relation to the community's self-organization and obligation of care. Finally, the provision of this food and the occasion for sociality is a gift, which may be understood in all its complexity as both something given gratuitously and potentially a 'poison',[35] providing a critical reflection on documenta's presence in Athens, as well as being an act of hospitality.[36] Both installations provide occasions for conversation between strangers. This gesture reflects Araeen's art more generally, which is at once critical, even stern, while being unfailingly generous.

Such generosity raises the question of the relation of equality, which we have discussed in terms of universality, to the gift. To reciprocate a gift is to 'economize' it, to turn it into an exchange. Would the basis of equality, then, be equal reciprocal exchange? As a form of balancing, as in a weighing scale, this would be the economic form of the equation, which is the basis of mathematical universality. Strictly speaking a gift does not remain a gift if it is returned, even if not literally but in terms of an equivalent.[37] Thus, in a way, the gift needs always to be unbalanced, and hence, as Araeen himself argues, the necessity for asymmetry. It is through asymmetry that the equality of universality gives into singularity, which is gratuitous. Rather than through the top-down formative genius of the artist, this happens through participation by others. The symmetric, grid-based Structures become rearranged into a unique and unpredictable pattern of relationships. Identities and forms of collectivity are negotiated in the space – perhaps topological rather than Euclidean, and even chaotic – of the 'impossible relation' between critical universality and ethical singularity.

1 Rasheed Araeen, *Art Beyond Art, Ecoaesthetics: A Manifesto for the 21st Century* (London: Third Text Publications, 2010), 8–12.
2 For the artist's own construction of his development, see ibid.; and for other views the excellent essays in Jean Fisher, ed., *The Triumph of Icarus: Life and Art of Rasheed Araeen* (Karachi: Millennium Media, 2014) and David Elliott, 'The Danger and the Flame', in *Rasheed Araeen: Going East* (Hong Kong: Rossi and Rossi, 2016), 3–27.
3 Araeen won a John Moore's 7 prize at the Liverpool Biennale, 1969, for *BoO*, which comprises four thin, vertical lattice Structures attached to painted board, qualifying as a relief for the painting prize.
4 See Paul Warmington, *Black British Intellectuals and Education: Multiculturalism's Hidden History* (London: Routledge, 2014), 39; also the path-breaking study by Paul Gilroy, *There Ain't No Black in the Union Jack: The Cultural Politics of Race and Nation* (London: Hutchinson, 1987), 43–71.
5 Araeen describes this in Araeen, *Art Beyond Art*, 12–14.
6 For an argument concerning Minimalism's evacuation of interiority, see Rosalind Krauss, *The Originality of the Avant-Garde and Other Modernist Myths* (Cambridge, MA: MIT Press, 1985). It seems to me that Araeen's rejection of the interior has more to do with a combination of Caro's open construction combined with the principle of intelligibility Constructivism.
7 PCL also housed an important photography department where Victor Burgin taught, and which was consequently a nexus for Conceptual art at the time.
8 See Theodor Adorno, *Minima Moralia: Reflections on a Damaged Life*, trans. Edmund Jephcott (London: Verso, 1974), 152; *Philosophy of New Music*, trans. Robert Hullot-Kentor (Minneapolis: University of Minnesota Press, 2006); and *Aesthetic Theory* (Minneapolis: University of Minnesota Press, 1997), 22–23.
9 See www.stephenwillats.com/work/homeostat-drawing and Andrew Wilson, 'Stephen Willats. Work 1962-69', Raven Row, gallery website, www.ravenrow.org/texts/54.
10 Frantz Fanon, *Black Skin, White Masks* (New York: Grove Press, 1967) was an important book for Araeen.
11 For the philosopher Immanuel Kant in his *Grounding for the Metaphysics of Morals* (1785), what makes a maxim moral is its universalizability.
12 Michel Serres, *Geometry: The Third Book of Foundations*, trans. Randolph Burks (London: Bloomsbury Academic, 2017), xiv.
13 Ibid., 171.
14 Ibid., 174.
15 Ibid., 180.
16 Ibid., 181.
17 Ibid.
18 Ibid., 185.
19 Ibid., 189.
20 See Jacques Rancière, *The Politics of Aesthetics: The Distribution of the Sensible* (London: Continuum, 2006), 12–19.
21 Serres, *Geometry*, xiv.
22 Ibid., 44.
23 Ibid., 45.
24 Ibid.
25 Ibid., 47.
26 Fisher, *The Triumph of Icarus*, 126.
27 See Gregory Vlastos, 'Degrees of Reality in Plato', in *New Essays on Plato and Aristotle*, ed. Renford Brambough (New York: Humanities Press, 1965).
28 Serres, *Geometry*, 211.
29 See Maev Kennedy, 'Mathematical Secrets of Ancient Tablet Unlocked After Nearly a Century of Study', *The Guardian*, 24 August 2017, www.theguardian.com/science/2017/aug/24/mathematical-secrets-of-ancient-tablet-unlocked-after-nearly-a-century-of-study.
30 Araeen points out this generation of asymmetry in a statement of 2012 reproduced in Fisher, *The Triumph of Icarus*, 176. The work was conceived in 1968, and realized in 2004 with audience participation at 198 Gallery in London.
31 For Araeen's own account of his 'Minimalist' work, see 'A Chronology of what led to my Minimalist Work in 1965', and the notes by Tate curator Andreas Leventis, in *Minimalism and Beyond: Rasheed Araeen at Tate Britain, April – August 2007* (London: Third Text Publications with Tate Britain, 2007).
32 See Fisher, *The Triumph of Icarus*, 172–175.
33 The artist restaurant or restaurant as social artwork goes at least as far back as FOOD, the artist-run restaurant in SoHo, New York City, run by Carol Gooden, Tina Girouard, and Gordon Matta-Clark from 1971–1974. For hospitality and the sharing of food as art, see Stephanie Smith, *Feast: Radical Hospitality in Contemporary Art* (Chicago: Smart Museum of Art, University of Chicago, 2013), the publication of the exhibition *Feast: Radical Hospitality in Contemporary Art*, Smart Museum of Art, Chicago, 2012. For further information and talks, see http://smartmuseum.uchicago.edu/exhibitions/feast.
34 Functional window lattices he designed from 1957 and 1961 are illustrated in *Minimalism and Beyond*, 1. See *Rasheed Araeen: Going East*, 5 and note 9; and Jon Wood, 'Caro/Araeen: A Conversation', Grosvenor Gallery, overview on gallery website, July 2017, http://grosvenorgallery.com/exhibitions/41/overview.
35 Playing on the German term for poison, *das Gift*. See Jacques Derrida, *The Gift of Death* (Chicago: University of Chicago Press, 1995) and *Given Time* (Chicago: University of Chicago Press, 1992).
36 On hospitality, see Jacques Derrida 'Hostipitality' (*sic*) in *Angelaki: Journal of the Theoretical Humanities* 5, no. 3 (December 2000).
37 Derrida discusses the non-reciprocity of the gift in *Given Time I: Counterfeit Money* (Chicago: University of Chicago Press, 2007), 13–15.

The Politics of Symmetry Marcus du Sautoy

Artists have always had an ambiguous relationship to the concept of symmetry. Many sympathize with Thomas Mann, when his central character in *The Magic Mountain* reacts to a snowflake that lands on this arm: 'he shuddered at its perfect precision, found it deathly, the very marrow of death.'[1] For some artists the rigidity of perfect symmetry boxes one in, forces things to be too predictable.

Symmetry is a central theme in much of Rasheed Araeen's work. Rather than cramping his imagination, it is a constraint that leads to new creative territory. Igor Stravinsky wrote about the importance of such constraints to creativity: 'My freedom consists in my moving about within the narrow frame that I have assigned myself for each one of my undertakings. I shall go even further: my freedom will be so much the greater and more meaningful the more narrowly I limit my field of action and the more I surround myself with obstacles.'[2]

It would be easy to tie Araeen's obsession with symmetry to the importance of symmetry in the Islamic world. One thinks of the wonderful tiles that adorn the palace in the Alhambra in Granada or the mosques of Pakistan, Araeen's country of birth. Araeen is quick to dismiss this easy connection. In fact he admits that he only became aware of the importance of symmetry in Islamic art when he attended an exhibition in 1972 in the UK.[3] It was that same year that he visited the Alhambra for the first time, a place to which he would love to return, but due to the pressure of work keeps postponing. His new work, combining colour and symmetry, might be that return, if only mentally.

Although Araeen initially reacted against critics' attempts to categorize his art as Islamic, he has more recently softened his resistant stance. 'I have changed my mind in the last ten years. If they want me to be Islamic, why not be Islamic!' This turn has inspired his recent exploration of Islamic calligraphy through the perspective of symmetry, a body of work he calls 'Homecoming' (2010–2014).

The desire to lazily bundle Islamic art with symmetry probably reflects a Western colonial attitude. After all, symmetry has a deep universal appeal that transcends any cultural or geographical borders. In the natural world, symmetry is usually a signal. It denotes something that should be noticed. In the chaos of the jungle if you suddenly spot something with symmetry it is likely to be an animal that you could eat or could eat you. Those who can spot symmetry survive.

Symmetry is used by nature as a language to communicate information. For example, a bee's eyesight is extremely limited. As it flies through the air in search of food, it has to find some way to make sense of the onslaught of images that bombard it. Evolution has tuned the bee in such a way that it is able to recognize shapes full of symmetry: this is where it will find the sustenance to keep it alive. The flower is equally dependent on the bee for its survival, its symmetrical shape an evolutionary step towards attracting the bee.

For humans, too, symmetry is fundamental to the way we converse with the universe. The poet Alexander Pushkin wrote in a letter to Prince Vyazemsky: 'Symmetry is a characteristic of the human mind.' Poet Paul Valéry also recognized symmetry's place at the heart of how we perceive our surroundings: 'The universe is built on a plan, the profound symmetry of which is somehow present in the inner structure of our intellect.'[4]

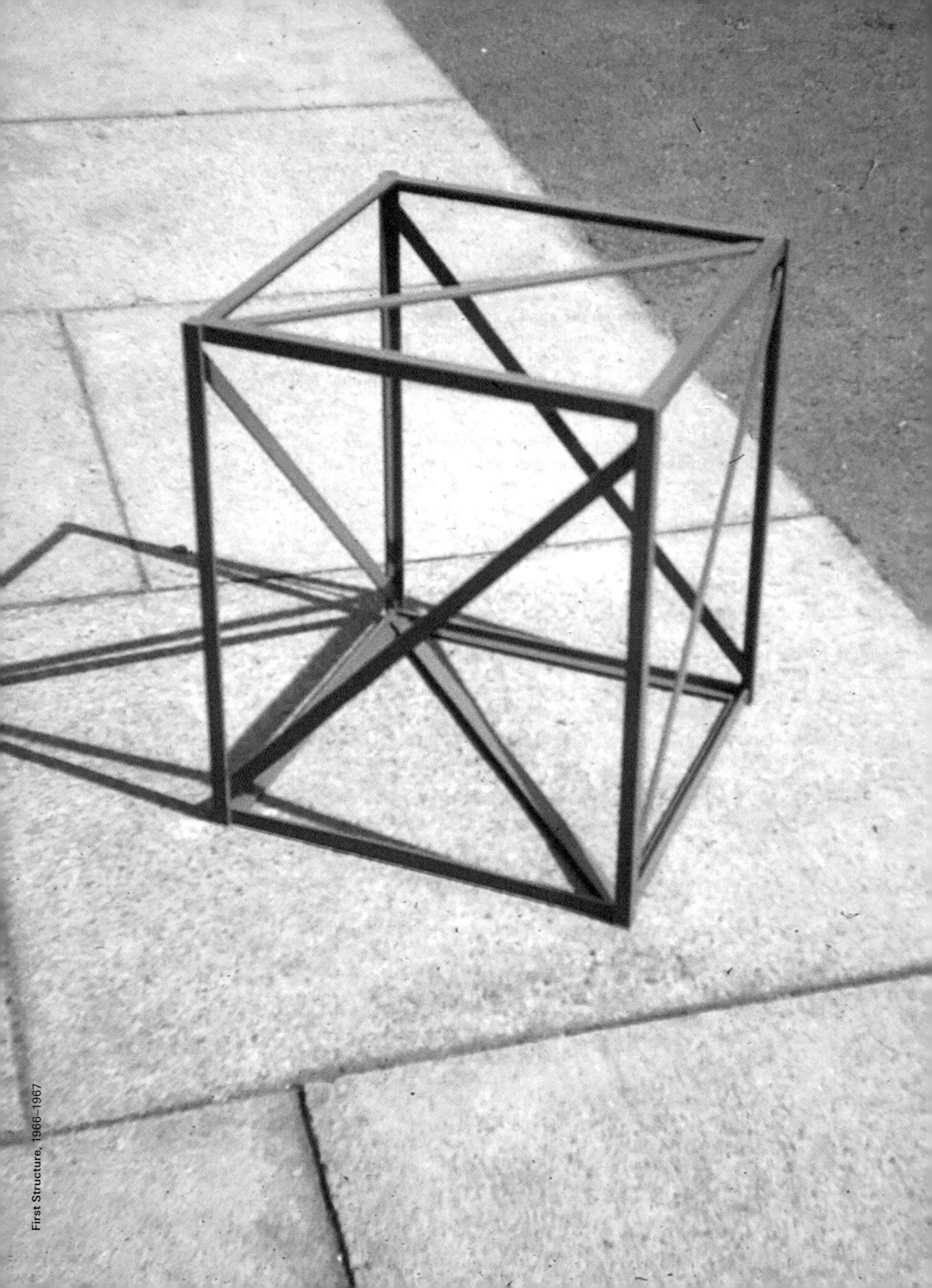

First Structure, 1966–1967

So I was interested in what message hid in Araeen's use of symmetry. 'It's political. Asymmetry is a symbol of capitalism. The big versus the small. Symmetry tries to react against these inequalities inherent in capitalism.' It was a striking and surprising response but one that had some resonance for my own journey through the world of symmetry. While researching *Finding Moonshine*, my book about symmetry, I discovered that at the beginning of the nineteenth century French revolutionaries had dreamt of creating a perfect spherical building in the heart of Paris. It would be a symbol of égalité – no direction favoured over any other. Their dream was eventually realized in the twentieth century with the construction of La Géode in Parc de la Villette – they might be disappointed to discover that the sphere has become home to an Omnimax theatre, not a terribly revolutionary venture.

> My ultimate aim is to create symmetry within human relationships. Not just between humans but humans and other forms of life. That is the political aspect of my work. You can use geometry and symmetry in art to realize equality in the world.[5]

At first sight it might seem strange to effect transformation through symmetry, something that appears so static – but that would be a misreading of what symmetry entails. For a mathematician, symmetry is all about movement and transformation. A cube sitting on a floor can be rotated, and can then return to its original form but realized in a new arrangement. The various symmetries of the cube for a mathematician are all these movements one can make. For example, I can rotate it by 90 degrees around an axis running through the centre of opposite faces or by 120 degrees through an axis passing through opposite corners. There are twenty-four different moves I can make which constitute the different symmetries of the cube. Symmetry is something active. We even call these transformations. It is this idea of the active nature of symmetry that I believe Araeen taps into when he uses the concept as a political act in his work.

Araeen also talks about the way symmetry appeals to the non-verbal side of communication allowing one to access forms that are pre-aesthetics, pre-thought, pre-conditioning, pre-language. Given that mathematics seeks to extract the patterns and universal structures underlying the particularities of the physical world, perhaps this would inevitably lead Araeen to forms that are at the heart of the mathematician's world, shapes that are universal and not bound by cultural reference.

The symmetrical shape that dominates Araeen's work is the cube. It is an obsession that started when he built his first cubes in the 1960s and that appear throughout his work to this day. At first sight one might question how much personal expression there is in something as simple as a cube. And yet as one starts to explore its geometry it has some startling surprises hidden inside it. One of my favourite questions to ask students, in order to judge their geometric intuition, involves the cube.

Imagining Shapes

Imagine hanging a cube-shaped decoration on a tree with the string attached to one of the corners or vertices. If you cut the cube horizontally between the point at the top and point at the bottom you have two pieces, each with a new face. What is the shape of that new face?

Araeen is interested not just in creating but also disrupting symmetry. This is a classic move by artists working with symmetry: use it to set up expectations that are then disrupted. The Islamic carpet weavers would deliberately sew imperfections into their designs because they did not wish to aspire to the perfection that only God can achieve. The Kaaba (which means cube) in Mecca, the most sacred site in Islam, is not in fact a perfect cube. Not only are its dimensions not perfectly cubic, but also further disrupting its symmetry is the Black Stone in its eastern corner. Even Bach in the *Goldberg Variations*, a veritable song for symmetry, disrupts one's expectations by making the final variation a musical joke. It has nothing to do with previous variations intricately interwoven with ideas of symmetry. But this disruption only highlights the symmetry one has experienced up to that point.

Araeen too has been fascinated by the disruption that diagonal struts introduce into his cubic structures. These struts often help to reveal further unexpected hidden symmetries inside the cube. For example, as Araeen discovered in his piece *Structure Blue* (1967), if you arrange the struts in a particular way a tetrahedron 102 appears inside the cube. His favourite configuration, used, for example, in the cubes featured in *Zero to Infinity* (1968–2004), has an arrangement of struts that 305 destroys reflectional symmetry but retains an element of rotational symmetry. Before the struts are introduced, the cube has twenty-four rotations that preserve the cube's structure. These twenty-four rotations include one that might seem rather strange: just leaving the cube where it is without moving it. This is rather like the number zero. After introducing the struts in the cubes of *Zero to Infinity*, there are only four rotations that preserve the structural arrangement. Three rotations of 180 degrees around the three axes run through opposite faces together with the zero symmetry. These four rotations permute the struts but leave the cube looking as you did before you rotated it. The other twenty rotations will move the struts into new positions.

Looking through Araeen's sketches for his cubes another dominant quality of the mathematical mind at work comes to the fore: classification and exploration of all that is possible. How many different strut arrangements are there? We see this desire for classification early on in the history of mathematics. Euclid's *Elements* ends with a proof that the five Platonic solids are all the symmetrical dice you can make in three dimensions. At the end of the nineteenth century mathematicians used the work of the French revolutionary Évariste Galois to prove that there are only seventeen symmetrical games you can play on the walls of the Alhambra. When M. C. Escher visited the Alhambra in 1922, he started creating variations on these walls. Instead of the triangles, hexagons, and squares that the Moorish artists had used, Escher tessellated the page with angels, devils, birds, and fish. It was already known that the images could vary infinitely. Yet as hard as Escher tried he could not produce an eighteenth-century symmetrical design that hadn't already been found by the Moorish artists.

Andrea Palladio's sketchbooks are full of possibilities for piecing together rooms with whole number proportions to make his symmetrical villas. He believed that rooms that had proportions of 2 to 1 or 3 to 2 had a frozen harmony encoded in them and his sketchbooks show how he tried in the fashion of a jigsaw puzzle to build up designs for villas with rooms having these harmonic proportions. Le Corbusier's notebooks are likewise full of asymmetrical designs made from his favourite Fibonacci-like numbers. The Fibonacci numbers 1,1,2,3,5,8,13... have the property that the next number is the sum of the two previous numbers and can be found all over the natural world. Le Corbusier was drawn to the organic sense of growth these numbers have and how they can instil a building with a connection to the natural world. Like Palladio his notebooks investigate all the ways you might build structures using these Fibonacci proportions. In the case of Araeen you can see him exploring different ways to place the struts in his symmetrical cubes. Each arrangement creates a different character in the respective cube. Often the struts destroy reflectional symmetry. They instead allow for a twisting rotational

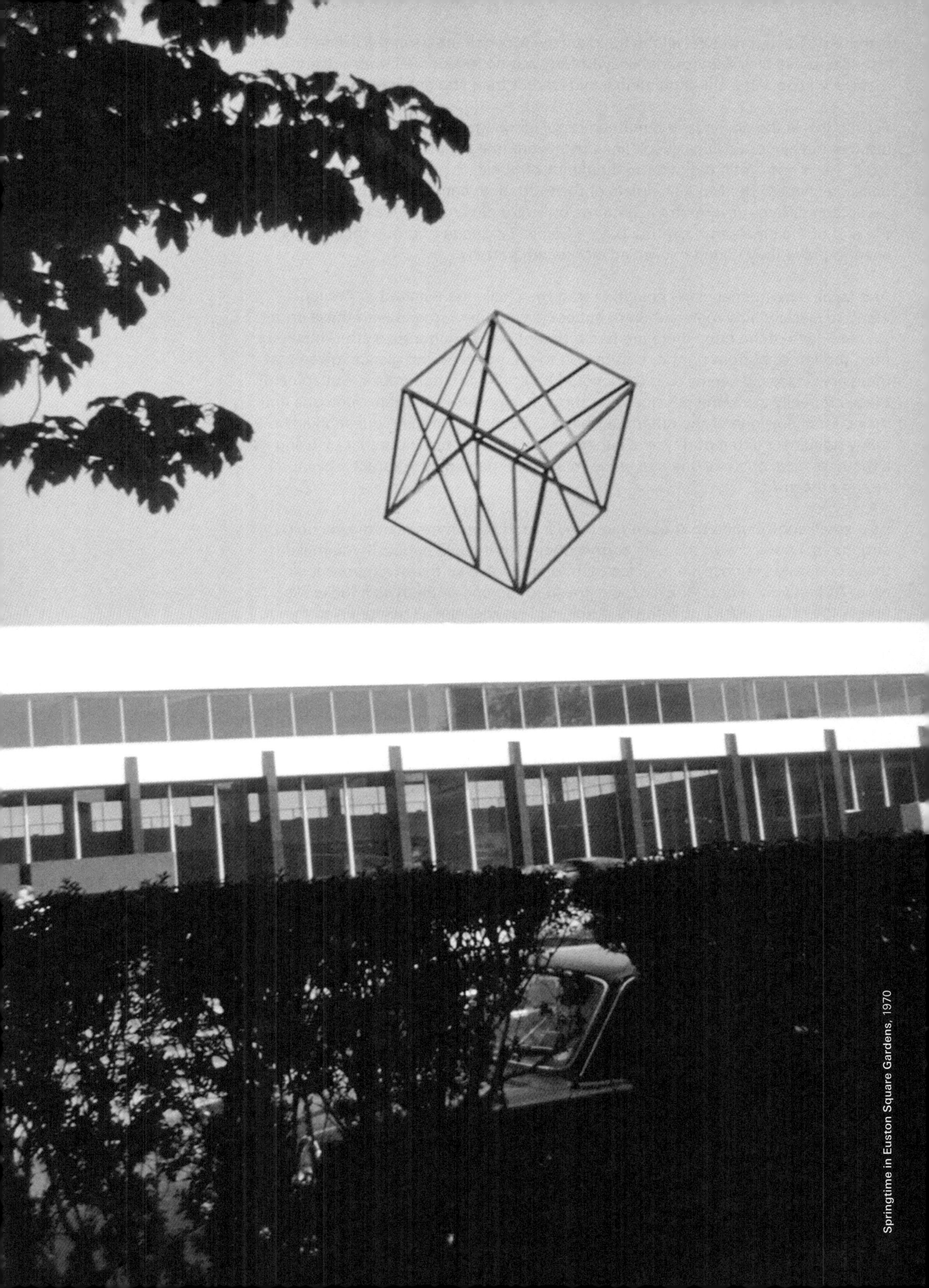

Springtime in Euston Square Gardens, 1970

symmetry. Such moves recall the tricks by the Moorish artists in the Alhambra who also like to use tiles with rotational symmetry but no reflectional symmetry, like the triangle whose sides are undulating waves rather than straight lines.

For me this is the power of the mathematical language: it allows one to articulate discovering all possibilities. Neolithic artists were making platonic solids as early as 5,000 years ago. Yet it took the mathematics of Euclid to prove there are only five possible shapes. The Moorish artists of the fourteenth century painted all possible seventeen different symmetrical patterns on a two dimensional wall. It took until the end of the nineteenth century before Galois' language of group theory was used to prove they hadn't missed an eighteenth pattern.

And so as a mathematician I couldn't resist the challenge inherent in Araeen's work: to classify how many different cubes he could have made with these struts. On each face of the cube there are two different ways to arrange a strut. It can run from top left to bottom right or bottom left to top right. At first glance, given that there are 6 faces, it seems as if there could be $2^6=64$ different cubes. But some of these are really the same physical structures. It is possible to rotate one cube and make it look like one of the other possibilities. So the challenging question is: how many genuinely different physical cubes do you have? It turns out that by using a mathematical analysis one can prove there are 8 genuinely different ways to arrange the struts.

As a small contribution to Araeen's journey into the symmetries of these cubic structures, I have drawn the nets corresponding to these 8 cubes. If you make these cubes it is impossible to place them on the table so that two cubes look alike. At first you might think it is possible to rotate one of them so it looks like one of the other cubes but with the struts in place they are all genuinely different. Similarly you won't find a ninth cube with struts different from these. Any cube you try to make can be placed on the table in such a way that it is identical to one of these 8 cubes.

Symmetry is generally associated with some sort of perfection so I was quite struck by Araeen's statement: 'Perfection is to be avoided as it is the symbol of absolute power.' *Zero to Infinity* starts with 100 cubes laid out in a perfect 10 x 10 grid. It is the audience's interaction with Araeen's cubes that breaks the perfection, symmetry, and absolute power that these ordered cubes seem to assert. They are encouraged to disrupt the order laid out in the gallery. This movement from order to chaos resonates with many ideas of symmetry in science. The universe went from a highly ordered state in the moment of the Big Bang to one in which this symmetry broke, creating the distinct fundamental forces that control the universe. The discovery by Yoichiro Nambu, Makoto Kobayashi, and Toshihide Maskawa that the breaking of symmetry is responsible for the fundamental forces we see today was rewarded a Nobel Prize in 2008. The news of the award was particularly exciting for Araeen as he felt that his body of work perfectly captured the scientific story they were telling. The second law of thermodynamics, states that the universe's trajectory from a state of order to one with many different possible arrangements is a fundamental law of nature. The different possible arrangements of any physical system are measured by something called entropy. An unbroken egg has low entropy because the atoms in the shell are bound together in the shape of the egg. But once it smashes to the floor, the entropy of the egg increases because there are many more ways that the bits of broken eggshell can be arranged. We can see this idea of increasing in play in Araeen's work, especially in the interactive piece *Zero to Infinity*.

The 10 x 10 grid of cubes with which the piece begins is a low entropy state. There is one arrangement of the cubes prescribed by the artist. But then the audience is allowed to interact and move the cubes. Even if you keep these cubes in the 10 x 10 grid and just rotate individual cubes it is striking how many different arrangements are possible. Each single cube (with the struts chosen by Araeen) can be arranged in 6 genuinely distinct orientations. There are 100 cubes. So that makes 6^{100} possible arrangements before you even disrupt the grid. That is a number with 78 digits, more than the number of atoms in our Milky Way galaxy, a number that requires only 69 digits to count them. Once you break the 10 x 10 grid the possibilities are endless. As the visitors interact more and more, you see more disorderly arrangements emerging: cubes on their sides, cubes balancing between other cubes. Araeen's title *Zero to Infinity* is an expression of the change in entropy that the piece experiences over time.

His most recent paintings return again to the theme of symmetry. As he said to me: 'Symmetry is an enigma.' It is a sentiment I agree with given that my own research life is still faced with the challenge of unwrapping this thorny subject. In these paintings we see a 3 x 3 grid standing on one of its corners with each square cell divided into two triangles. Surrounding the central 3 x 3 grid is a lattice of black and white squares giving the impression that the 3 x 3 grid is sitting on a checkerboard. In contrast to the black and white checkerboard, the 18 triangles that make up the 3 x 3 grid are painted with different colours. I wondered if there was any logic to the colours used. It turns out that there is a certain degree of randomness that Araeen applies to the choice of colours. But unlike Gerhard Richter's use of total randomness to choose the colours in his piece *4900 Farben* (2007), at some point the randomness stops and pattern takes over to fill the remaining cells. We then see Araeen's symmetry emerging.

The pieces represent an important tension between chaos and order, something that we enjoy in music, in art, even in the mathematics we create. As John Cawelti wrote in his book *Adventure, Mystery, and Romance*: 'If we seek order and security the result is likely to be boredom and sameness. But rejecting order for the sake of change and novelty brings danger and uncertainty... the history of culture can be interpreted as a dynamic tension between the quest for order and the flight from ennui.' These new images that Araeen produces strike a perfect balance between the two.

The images also have a distinctly Buddhist feel to them. Specifically, the symbol of the mandala is central to Buddhist practice and again fragility is inherent to its symmetry. The mandala is always destroyed as soon as it is finished to avoid us becoming attached to it. The mandala and symmetry has often been viewed as a window into the mind. Carl Jung used them in his psychological practice, getting his patients to draw mandalas during sessions under the belief that 'a mandala is the psychological expression of the totality of the self'.[6] Perhaps these new pieces are giving us a view into Araeen's current internal world. But as Araeen once scribbled in his notebook: 'At this stage I must keep silent because I might be doing more than I know.'

Rather, let the symmetry do the talking.

Answer to my challenge to cut the cube: a hexagon. The slice cuts all six faces. Each face contributes an edge to the new face. The shape should be symmetrical. Hence you get a hexagon.

Notes on the 8 strutted cubes. There are 24 rotations of a cube. With struts only a subset of these will be symmetries of the broken symmetrical structure. The number of different arrangements of each strutted cube will therefore be 24 divided by the number of symmetries of the strutted cube. Cube 1 is the cube used in *Zero to Infinity*. Cube 2 sees the struts mark out a tetrahedron, which is why we

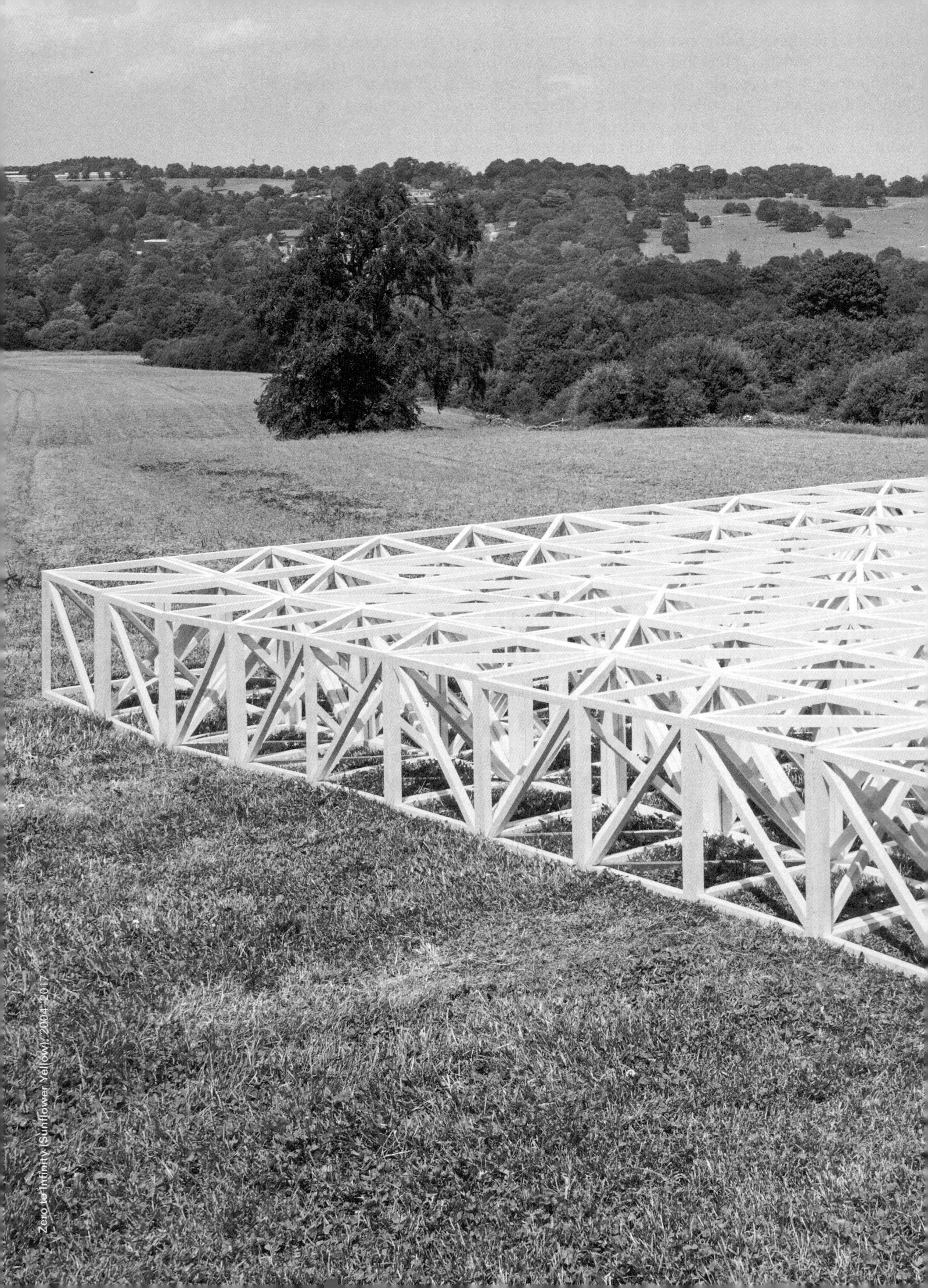

Zero to Infinity (Sunflower Yellow), 2004–2017

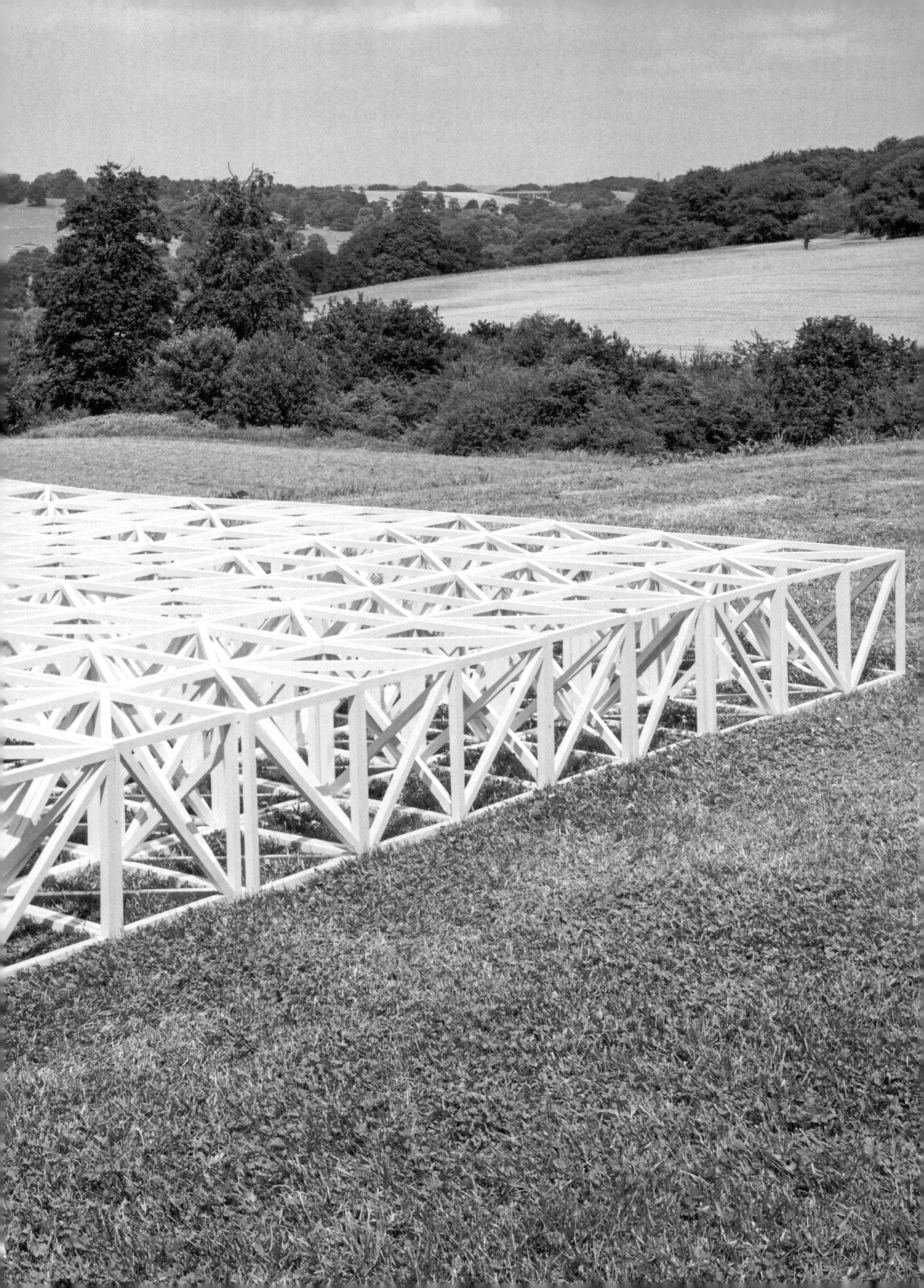

see the biggest symmetry group. Araeen's *First Structure*, (1966–1967) is on the way to realizing this form, which appears in *First Structure (Blue)*, (1966–1967 / 2013). Cube 5 is the most asymmetrical. Cube 4 is arrived at by rotating all lines in Cube 3 by 90 degrees. Cube 8 is arrived at by rotating all the lines in Cube 7 by 90 degrees. These are dual shapes with the same symmetry groups.

Cube Number	Symmetry Group	Size of Symmetry Group	Number of Distinct Arrangements
1	V_4	4	6
2	A_4	12	2
3	S_3	6	4
4	S_3	6	4
5	1	1	24
6	C_2	2	12
7	V_4	4	6
8	V_4	4	6

1 See Thomas Mann, *The Magic Mountain* (New York: Knopf, 1927).
2 Igor Stravinsky, *Poetics of Music in the Form of Six Lessons* (Cambridge, MA: Harvard University Press, 1970), 65.
3 Conversation between myself and Rasheed Araeen, 17 January 2017.
4 See Paul Valéry, *Sea Shells* (Boston: Beacon Press, 1998).
5 Conversation between myself and Rasheed Araeen, Ibid.
6 Carl Jung, *Mandala Symbolism* (Princeton: Princeton University Press, 1973), 20.

The Play of Structure: Rasheed Araeen's Chakras and Related Works

Dominic Rahtz

In February 1970 Rasheed Araeen released sixteen plywood discs coated in red fluorescent paint into the water off St. Katharine Docks in London. *Chakras* 136
(1969–1970) would be the first work in a series to continue throughout 1970 involving discs launched into water: *White Discs* and *Canalevent* both in London, 137, 138
and *Discs in River Seine* in Paris.[1] A photograph from December 1969 shows 139
Araeen in his studio, one of the original artist-run S.P.A.C.E. studios that occupied a disused warehouse at the Docks; the discs lean against the wall alongside other structural works from the same period, an idiom in which Araeen had been working since the mid-1960s.[2] The circular forms of *Chakras*, as single flat elements, do not have the same complexity of interior relations as the structural works, and, formally, seem to represent a change of direction. A series of photographs show Araeen, with participants from the other studios observing the discs from the edge of the dock as the discs float east, eventually becoming mixed in with various drift material in the corner of the eastern dock.

The play of the work is not confined to a predetermined structure: it is open to the contingent determinations of its environment – the movement of water and wind. The lack of interior formal relations diverts attention outwards to relations between the work and what is around it. The way in which its form produces its relationship to its environment finds similarity with Daniel Buren's *Affichages sauvages* from the same period, where Buren pasted up coloured striped paper of varying dimensions on advertisement hoardings or walls in Paris and other cities. Each circular element of *Chakras* has the same absence of interior composition as the repetition of stripes, producing a kind of 'zero degree' of form that acted as the condition for the work's capacity to establish relations with its exterior environment. In connection with a later realization of the work in 1974, Araeen writes: 'It is essential that the same size and colour is used to eliminate the RELATIONS which exist between the elements or objects owing to their difference in size and colour.' This elimination of interior formal relations allows for an awareness of the 'RELATIONS which exist between equal elements/objects in time and space and their relationship with environment'.[3] His statement can be compared to Buren's analysis of his own work in his 1969 text 'Beware', where he claims the 'formal neutrality' of the work's interiority gives it an '*indicative*' or '*critical*' character with respect to its exteriority.[4] And, like Buren's work, *Chakras* is photogenic. The sense of its visual separateness from its environment – while being immersed in it – is necessary for its identity as art. The red colour is picked up so strongly by the emulsion of the slide film used to document the event that, against the greyness of the surrounding docks and buildings, the discs look as if they are painted onto the film itself. The painterly effect may be supplementary to the event, as it is an attribute of its medium of documentation. Nonetheless, since the original work, like Buren's *Affichages sauvages*, and indeed many process works of the late 1960s and early 1970s, is no longer extant, the photographs inevitably stand in for and mediate its continuing existence.

The absence of interior relations or composition within each element mean that *Chakras* establishes its identity and formal unity through the dispersing and gathering relations between its circular elements, determined by natural forces.

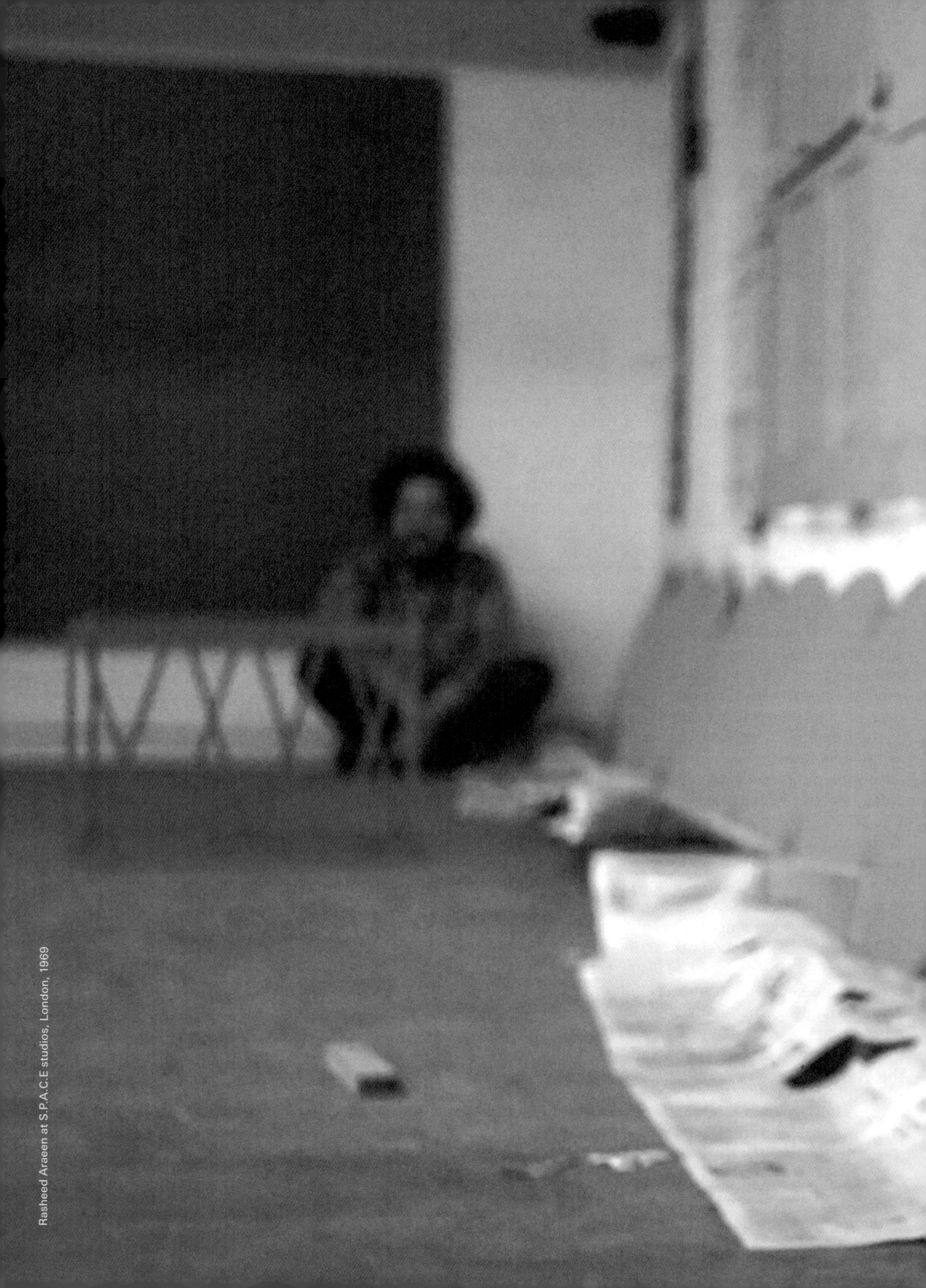

Rasheed Araeen at S.P.A.C.E studios, London, 1969

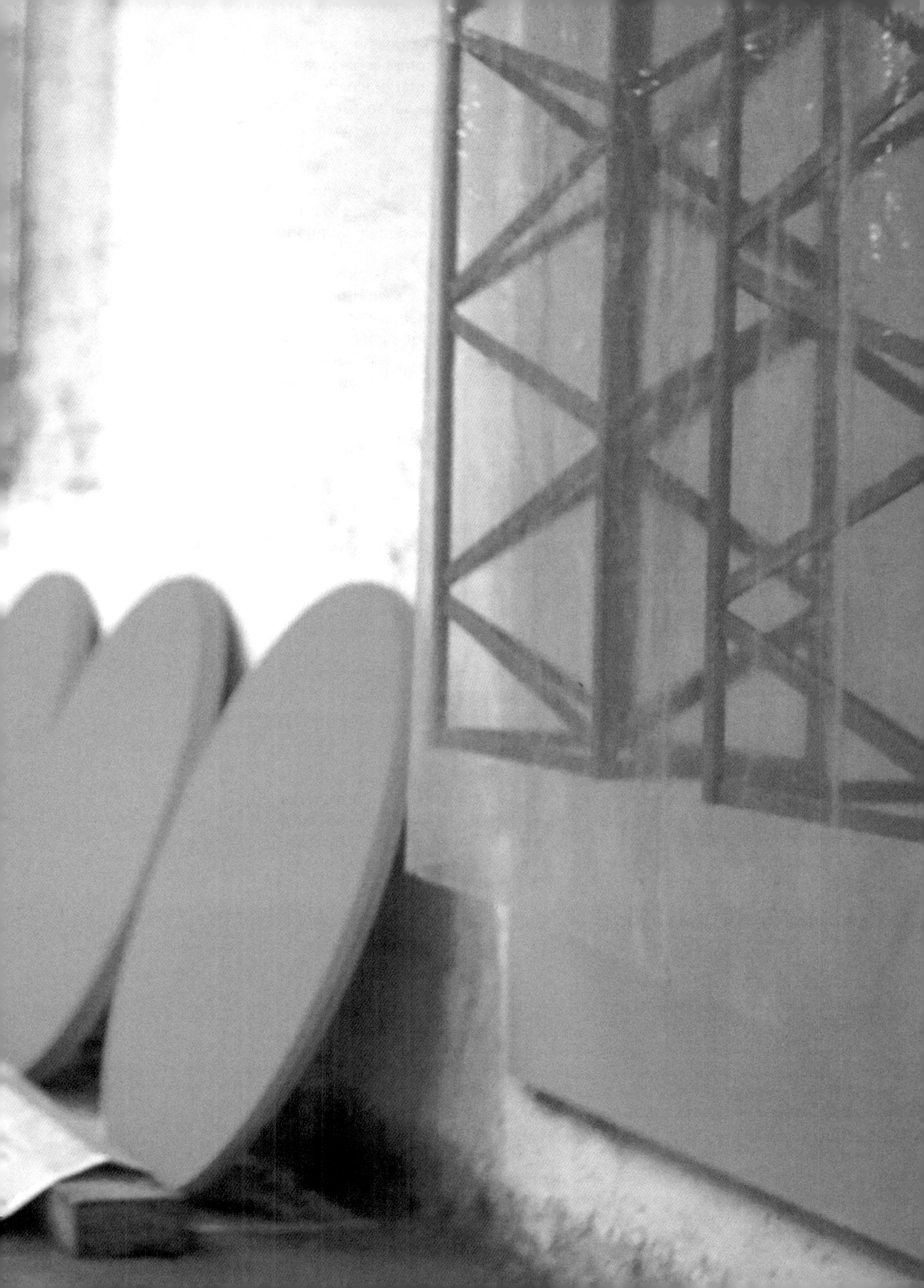

Unlike Araeen's earlier structural works, the play of the work does not depend on the viewer. The incorporation of diagonals, in the more complex pieces such as *BoO* (1969), introduce a sense of movement through an interior illusion of 133 spiralling activated by the movement of the beholder.[5] In this sense, *Chakras* is indifferent to its viewer. Although Araeen invites participation in the making of the work, the work is not dependent on the participants for its continuing mode of existence. Once in play, launched into the water, the work has its own life and suffers its own fate. Its form constitutes the precondition for the open-ended play of identity and difference that defines this life, a play that extends to its subsequent variations and the relationships between these and their situations.

In this respect, a helpful distinction might be drawn between *Chakras* and a work that explicitly depends on action and participation. In 1968, Araeen proposed a work to the Institute of Contemporary Arts (ICA) in London with the title *Bio-structural Play*.[6] The work was only realized much later, with the changed title *Zero to Infinity* (1968–2004). It consisted of 100 open cube structures arranged in 305 a 10 x 10 square pattern on the ground intended to be freely reordered into any kind of structure by its audience who, through their physical involvement, became participants. The wooden cubes incorporate diagonal struts, and are painted (blue in a later realization of the work now owned by the Tate). The diagonals are slightly displaced since the cut end is joined, for strength, to a vertical or horizontal strut, producing a slight change in angle. Within the structure there is thus an initial play between a geometrical order of linearity and points and an order that resulted from the width of the actual material used to make it, which must have been a matter of practical knowledge for Araeen, who was a trained engineer. The basic structure of the cubes follows that of earlier works, including a precursor for *Bio-structural Play*, titled *Chaar Yaar* (1968 / 2014), 122 which comprises four cubes painted red, blue, orange, and yellow that could be composed in different ways (square, line, or vertical stack). In one sense, *Bio-structural Play*, and its later realized version, *Zero to Infinity*, take the interior illusion of play within the earlier structural works and exteriorize it through a physical engagement with participants, actualizing a potentiality already contained in the work. Like *Chakras*, it depends on the action of play, but this agency resides in persons rather than environment.

The original title, *Bio-structural Play*, suggests theoretical parameters to interpret the development in Araeen's work from the earlier Minimalist structural works to the post-Minimalist work from the late 1960s and early 1970s. The word 'play' contains a polysemy, which is brought out by its relationship to the other two terms. Play can pertain to a movement within an already existing structure, as in, for example, the play in a mechanism, or in a game with rules. Play, however, can also infer an absence or excess of structure, consisting in free action; here it is closer to life, in which new forms and relations are continually emerging. *Bio-structural Play* invokes this continuum of meanings, and the terms suggest some affinities with the contemporary philosophical thinking concerned with the structurality of structure. Both Jacques Derrida's 'Structure, Sign and Play in the Discourse of the Human Sciences' first published in 1967, and Gilles Deleuze's text, also from 1967, 'How Do We Recognize Structuralism?' draw attention to the necessity of the indeterminacy of play in defining structure, from Derrida's concept of play as 'a field of infinite substitutions' within a finite structure to Deleuze's metaphor of the 'empty square' in a game to refer to the serial organization of structure as the actualization of its properly virtual existence.[7] Structure and play are inseparable, and each conditions the other.

It is impossible to dissociate Araeen's work of the late 1960s and early 1970s from a general tendency in art to explore the social and political potential of participation and play (and its complex interactions with other currents, including the kinetic and cybernetic). Probably the first overview of these trends is Frank Popper's 1975 book, *Art – Action and Participation*, which includes a discussion of Araeen's *Canalevent*. In Britain, Popper identified such exhibitions as *Play Orbit*, shown at the ICA in late 1969, and *Popa at Moma: Pioneers of Part-Art* ('Part-Art' short for 'Participation Art'), at the Museum of Modern Art, Oxford in early 1971, as representative of this tendency.[8] The first identified art with play through toys and games, while the second included works that were intended for participation (although in practice this proved too chaotic).[9] Several of the artists involved in the latter had been associated with the avant-garde gallery Signals, London during the mid-1960s, including David Medalla, Lygia Clark, and Hélio Oiticica, of which Araeen would have been aware. Medalla's early 'biokinetic' works, and others by Clark including her rearrangeable *Bichos* (shown at Signals in 1965) and *Monument in All Situations* (1964) give some sense of the artistic milieu in which *Bio-structural Play* might be positioned. Much of the work addressed in *Art – Action and Participation* was processual and participatory. It was often intended to produce a sensory awareness of the environment, but also in its combination of technical innovation and play typified a kind of technological optimism absent in *Chakras*.

Popper discussed some of the theoretical resources for this tendency, ranging from Johan Huizinga to Herbert Marcuse, but the social and political meaning of art as a form of play may be traced back to Friedrich Schiller, and to the promise of reconciling art and life through the free play of the aesthetic.[10] One could argue that play and participation in art in the 1960s took on its political meaning as an expression of this promise. The institutional art world was often identified with the repressive structures of work and state, and so artists often attempted to address a wider community. Araeen certainly saw the participatory aspect of works such as *Chakras* as in opposition to a separation between the artist and public. In a statement from 1970 published in Popper's book, Araeen comments on this as being a consequence of the artist's relationship to the 'elitist-cultural tradition of the past'.[11] Photographs of *Canalevent*, part of a community arts festival in 1970, show participants, including children, throwing discs – this time made of polystyrene – into the Grand Union Canal in West London. This event also gave Araeen the idea for another form of art as participatory play, *Waterplay* (1971) (later given the title *Disco Sailing*), after seeing two people floating on the canal on a large piece of polystyrene. This work was not realized then, but it involved participants directly by having them float, and sail, on the discs.[12] Although Araeen's work from this time could take up some of the democratic and utopian meanings associated with the artistic explorations of play and participation surveyed by Popper, this reading is complicated by the proviso that the universalized participatory subject might be seen as an ideological illusion given certain subsequent variations of *Chakras* and Araeen's later trajectory.[13]

While *Chakras* begins with actions of participants, the patterns it produces in the water are determined by natural or material agency. Whereas the earlier work, *Bio-structural Play*, could be related to the idea of play thematized in an exhibition such as *Play Orbit*, the material determination of *Chakras* brings it closer to the concerns of another exhibition staged at the ICA: the London showing in September 1969 of *When Attitudes Become Form* following its appearances at Bern Kunsthalle and Museum Haus Lange in Krefeld. This exhibition brought together a diverse range of recent work concerned with material process, site, and information – from American 'anti-form' to Italian Arte Povera. The patterning of the elements in *Chakras* identify it as a process piece, since its forming is, like the other materials floating in the docks, in a state of continual gathering and dispersal caused by the material actions of water and wind. *Chakras* is not, however, concerned with a materiality per se in the same way as the work in *When Attitudes Become Form*. The immediate materials of *Chakras*, plywood and paint, were shaped according

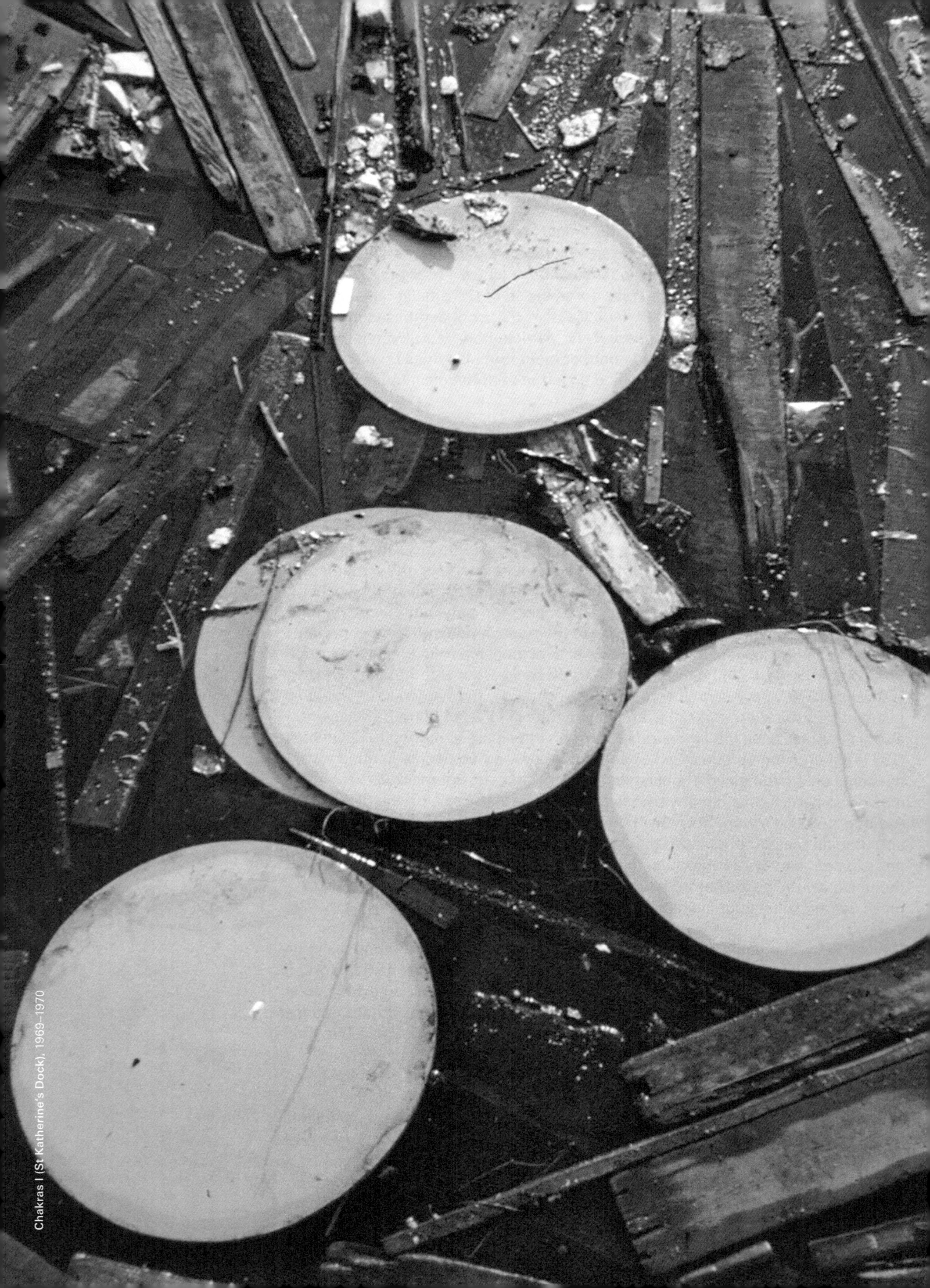

Chakras I (St Katherine's Dock), 1969–1970

to a particular form, a circle, and the identical shape and number of these circles constitutes a more general form. These circular elements retain an intentionality orientated to form and meaning – that is, a figural dimension. (The title of the work, which employs an esoteric term found in Indian religions, also contributes to this dimension.) At the same time that *Chakras* is shaped by its environment, it also shapes this environment by referring to it. The work thus intends relationships to its environment, St. Katharine Docks that as part of London's industrial infrastructure is itself subject to processes of history.[14]

When seen according to the registers of material determination and reference, *Chakras* appears less concerned with the utopian promise of play and participation than with the actual locations in which its versions are enacted – the relations produced between the work and the social and political realities in which it is immersed. For instance, later in 1970 with *Discs in River Seine* in Paris, white polystyrene discs are released at the foot of some steps next to the Petit Pont by the Notre-Dame Cathedral. In a photograph that documents the event, taken from the other side of the Seine, the figures involved in the action are completely dominated by the size of the cathedral, but more significantly by the Préfecture de Police located immediately next to the bridge where they stand. This location must have been meaningful, given Araeen's statement from 1970 relating to this work:

> [I]n the circumstances of not being able to organize the event in such a way when I could have given the information to the public beforehand about my intentions (although it is not always necessary to do so), I should not have expected much more spontaneous response. As a matter of fact, to some extent, it was my own apprehension of the police which prevented me from involving the public directly. ... Therefore instead of throwing the discs from the bridge with the participation of the public, I myself alone went down to the river bank and started throwing/releasing the discs into the river. I must say when I was doing so, some young men came down from the bridge and to my surprise asked me for the discs, which I gave them. Then we threw the discs together. You can imagine how happy I was to receive this unexpected response from the public.[15]

This work was enacted in the wider context of the 'return to order' following the mass action of workers and students in May and June 1968 in Paris, characterized by increased police presence, surveillance, and state repression.[16] The unauthorized nature of Araeen's event necessitated the spontaneity of the participation he described, and thus registers the real limits placed on it.

In 1974, writing in relation to *Chakras* – albeit a later version, *Discs in Jheel* 218
Park, Karachi – Araeen is much more trenchant in its distinctions between the 'dominating class' and people who are 'exploit[ed]' and 'depriv[ed]' of culture.[17] This statement reflects the shift in Araeen's work towards a more politicized mode of address that begins in the 1970s with *For Oluwale* (1971–1973 / 1975). Although 210
community-orientated participation can be seen as political and oppositional, particularly in the early 1970s when the British institutional art world was firmly bourgeois in its class composition, it did not explicitly provoke an awareness of social distinctions in its public to the extent that Araeen's later work would. These two statements by Araeen from 1970 and 1974 amount to a critical attitude towards the tendency in which his work from the late 1960s and early 1970s was historically immersed, since the utopian promise of art as participatory play tended to ignore actual material conditions. Araeen's work from the late 1960s and early 1970s, although abstract in form, contains within it the possibility of both readings. The poetic character of *Chakras*, and its historical meaning as art, lies in its state of being suspended between the incompatible positions that characterized its moment, without resolution.

1 Related works such as *Touch* and *Triangles*, which were made of the material that remained after the circles were cut, also took place that year. All of these works are reproduced in Rasheed Araeen, *Making Myself Visible* (London: Kala Press, 1984), 43–47, 49, and 51–54. In general, I have followed *Making Myself Visible* for titles of works.

2 Rasheed Araeen archive, Grosvenor Gallery, London. I would like to thank Conor Macklin from the gallery for facilitating access to these slides.

3 Statement made by Rasheed Araeen in Karachi, 11 April 1974. Araeen, *Making Myself Visible*, 64–65.

4 Daniel Buren, 'Beware', in Buren, *Five Texts* (London and New York: Jack Wendler Gallery and John Weber Gallery, 1973), 14; the phrase 'zero degree' was one that Buren appropriated from Roland Barthes.

5 See Patricia Bickers, 'From Object to Subject' (1987) and Jean Fisher, 'An Art of Transformation' (1993), in ed. Jean Fisher, *The Triumph of Icarus: Life and Art of Rasheed Araeen* (Karachi: Millennium Media, 2014), 20 and 107.

6 See Rasheed Araeen, *Art Beyond Art: Ecoaeshetics: A Manifesto for the 21st Century* (London: Third Text Publications, 2010), 45. In Araeen, *Making Myself Visible*, 175 the title is given as *Spatiostructural Play*, but Araeen has confirmed that it was originally *Bio-structural Play*.

7 Jacques Derrida, 'Structure, Sign and Play in the Discourse of the Human Sciences', *Writing and Difference* (London: Routledge, 2001), 365; Gilles Deleuze, 'How Do We Recognize Structuralism?', *Desert Islands and Other Texts*, 1953–1974 (Los Angeles and New York: Semiotext(e), 2004), 184.

8 Frank Popper, *Art – Action and Participation* (London: Studio Vista, 1975), 180 and 189.

9 See Hilary Floe, '"Everything Was Getting Smashed": Three Case Studies of Play and Participation, 1965–71', *Tate Papers*, no. 22 (fall 2014), www.tate.org.uk/research/publications/tate-papers/22/everything-was-getting-smashed-three-case-studies-of-play-and-participation-1965-71.

10 On Schiller and the '"original scene" of aesthetics', see Jacques Rancière, 'The Aesthetic Revolution and its Outcomes: Emplotments of Autonomy and Heteronomy', *New Left Review* 14 (March – April 2002):133–151.

11 Popper, *Art – Action and Participation*, 192.

12 See the description of this project in Araeen, *Making Myself Visible*, 175 and the account in Araeen, *Art Beyond Art*, 51–54.

13 This distinction concerning the participating subject may also be read in Claire Bishop's more recent critique of Nicholas Bourriaud's *Relational Aesthetics*, 'Antagonism and Relational Aesthetics', *October*, no. 110 (fall 2004):51–79.

14 See Courtney J. Martin's interpretation of *Chakras* for which Araeen's radicalized work of the mid-1970s and 1980s provides the allegorical pretext: 'Araeen's later social justice and political art actions position *Chakras* as a comment on the ways in which difference (be it class, race, ethnicity, or gender) was an uneasy fit in Britain in the late 1960s. … Floating a symbolic object with bodily connotations drawn from Eastern spiritual traditions (chakras occur in both Hinduism and Buddhism) in water that leads to the open sea is a performance of reclaiming, of liberation from imperialism, and with it, slavery, colonialism, and all it implies.' Courtney J. Martin, 'The Studio and the City: S.P.A.C.E. Ltd. and Rasheed Araeen's *Chakras*', in *The Studio Reader: On the Space of Artists*, ed. Mary Jane Jacob and Michelle Grabner (Chicago and London: University of Chicago Press, 2010), 306–307.

15 Popper, *Art – Action and Participation*, 192.

16 See Kristin Ross, *May '68 and Its Afterlives* (Chicago and London: University of Chicago Press, 2002), 60–64.

17 Araeen, *Making Myself Visible*, 65.

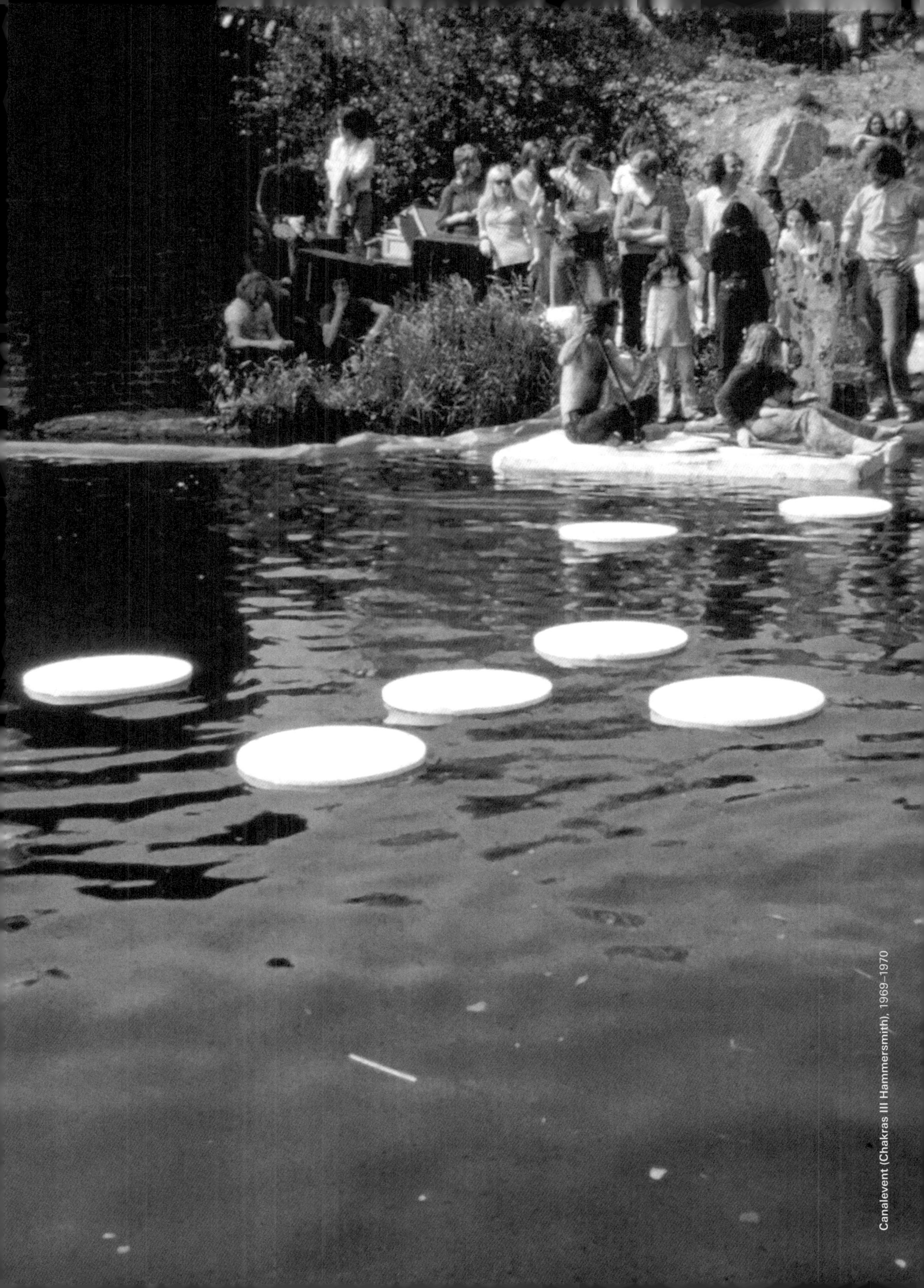

Canalevent (Chakras III Hammersmith), 1969–1970

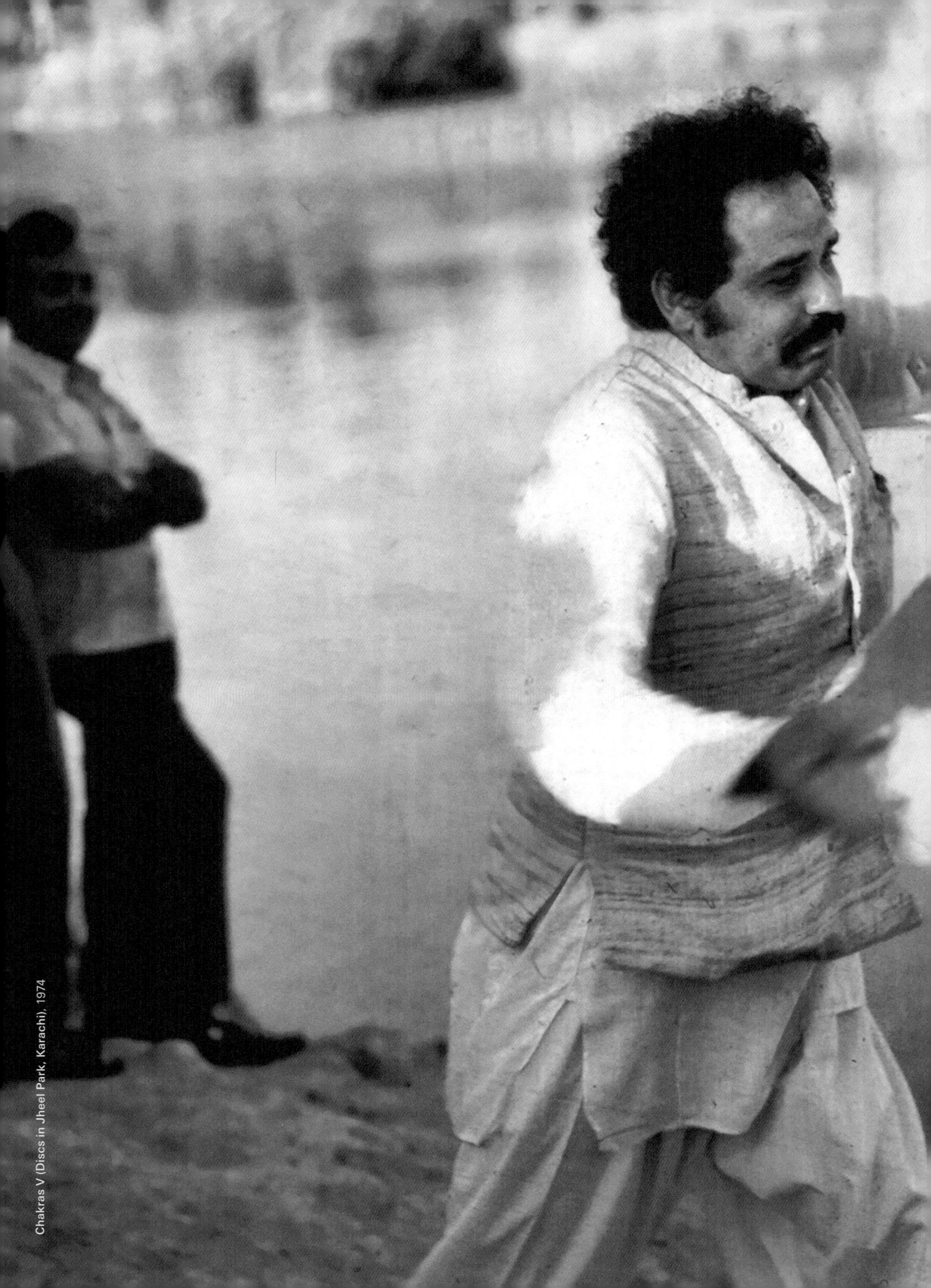

Chakras V (Discs in Jheel Park, Karachi), 1974

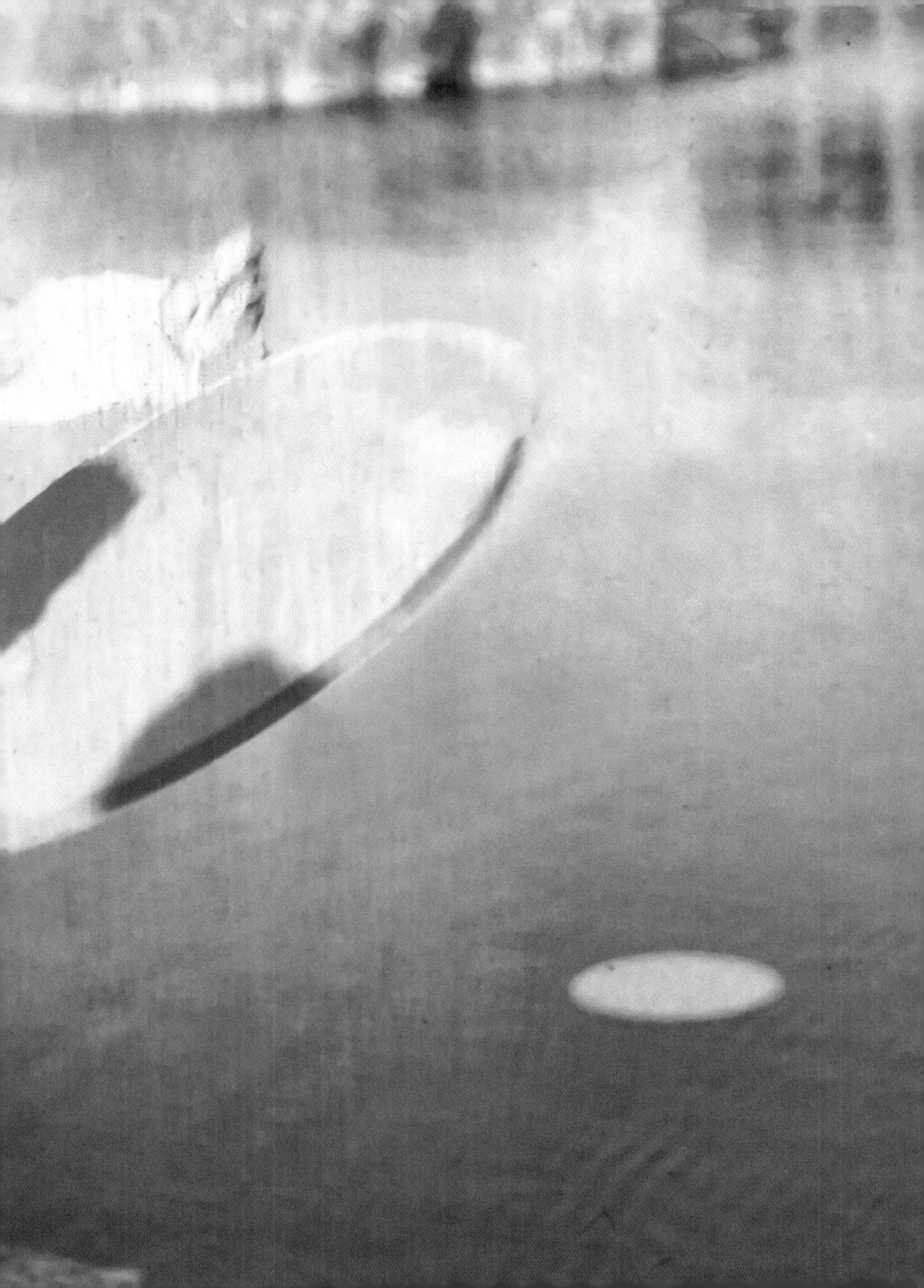

Untitled (Painting No. 1), 1965
pencil on graph paper, 25 x 20 cm
Drawing for Sculpture, 1965
graphite on paper, 25 x 20 cm
Tate: Presented by Tate Members 2011

Drawing for Sculpture, 1965
graphite on paper, 25 x 20 cm
Tate: Presented by Tate Members 2011
Drawing for Sculpture No. 3, 1965
graphite on paper, 25 x 20 cm
Private collection, London

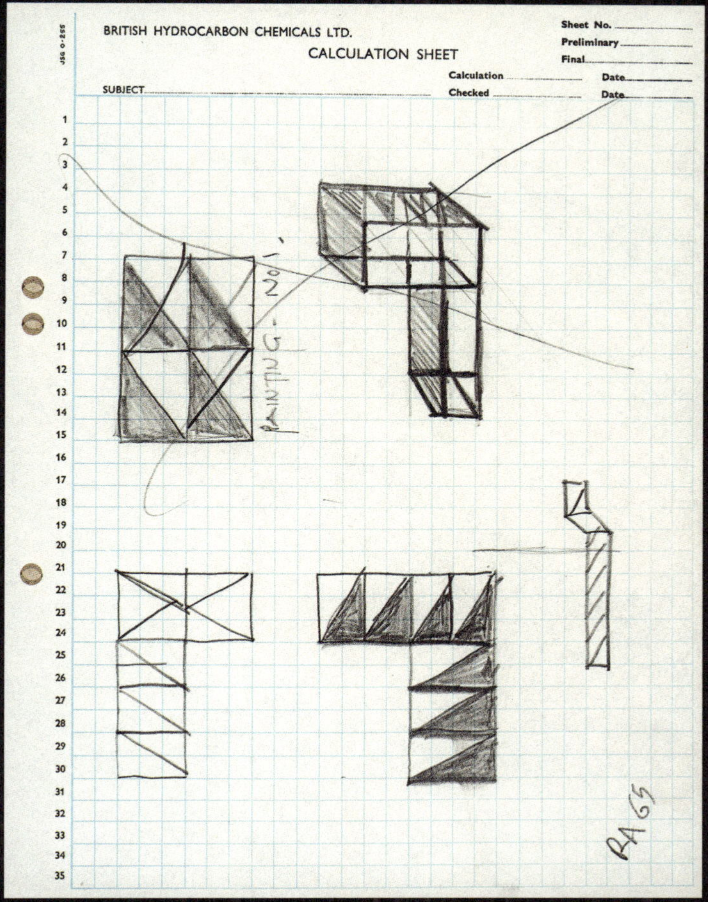

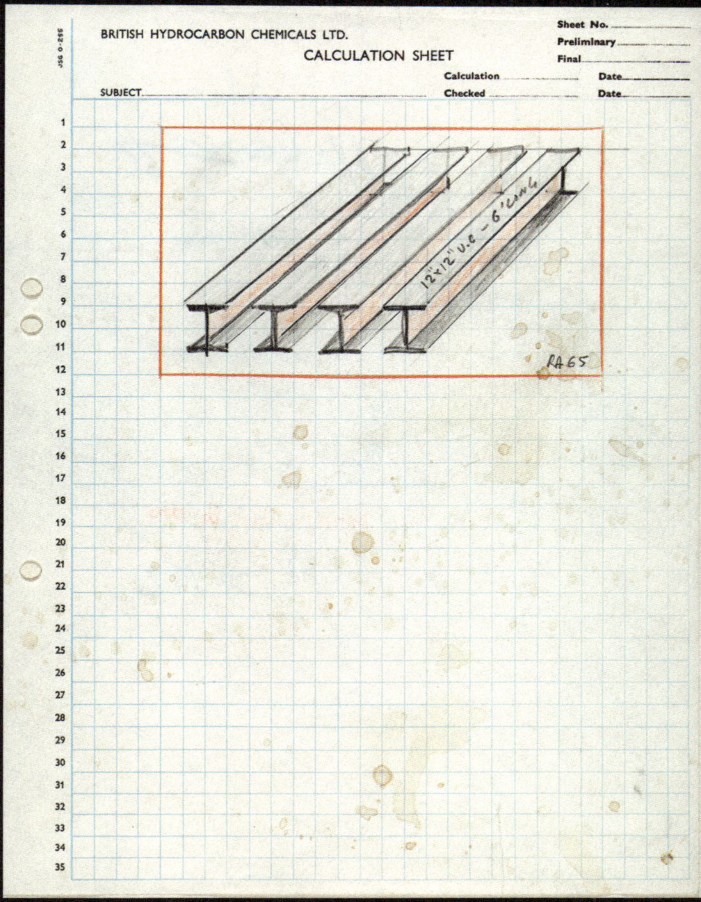

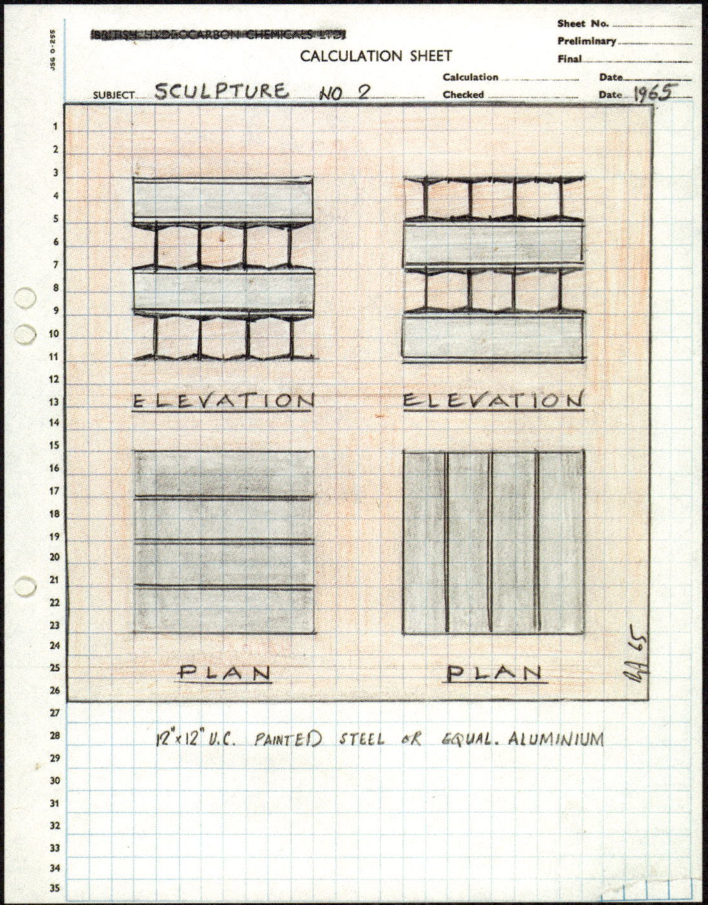

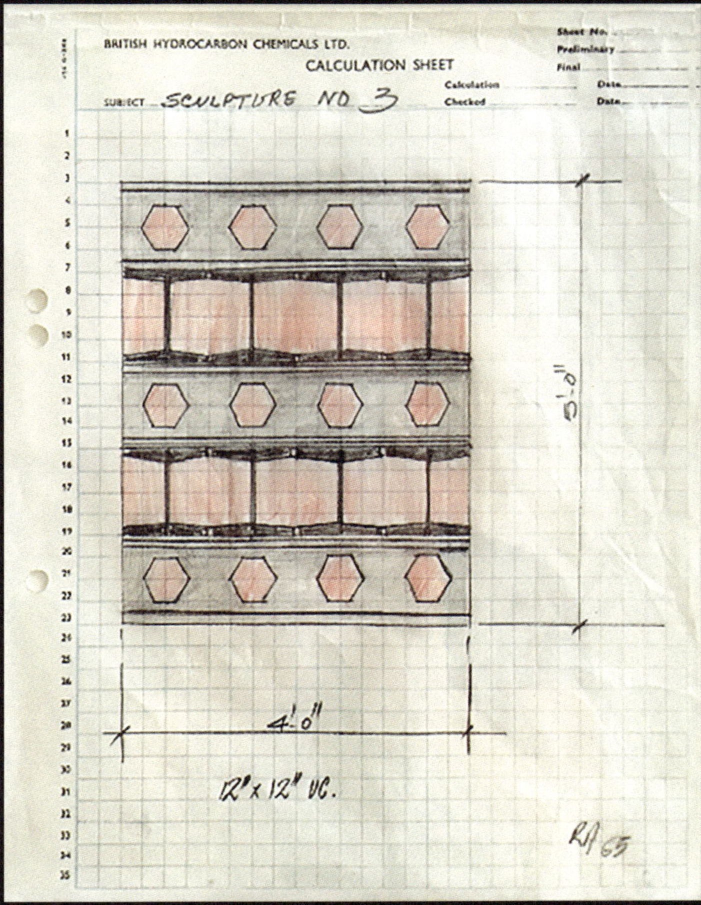

Sculpture No. 1 (Red), 1965 / 2010
painted steel, 31 x 183 x 183 cm

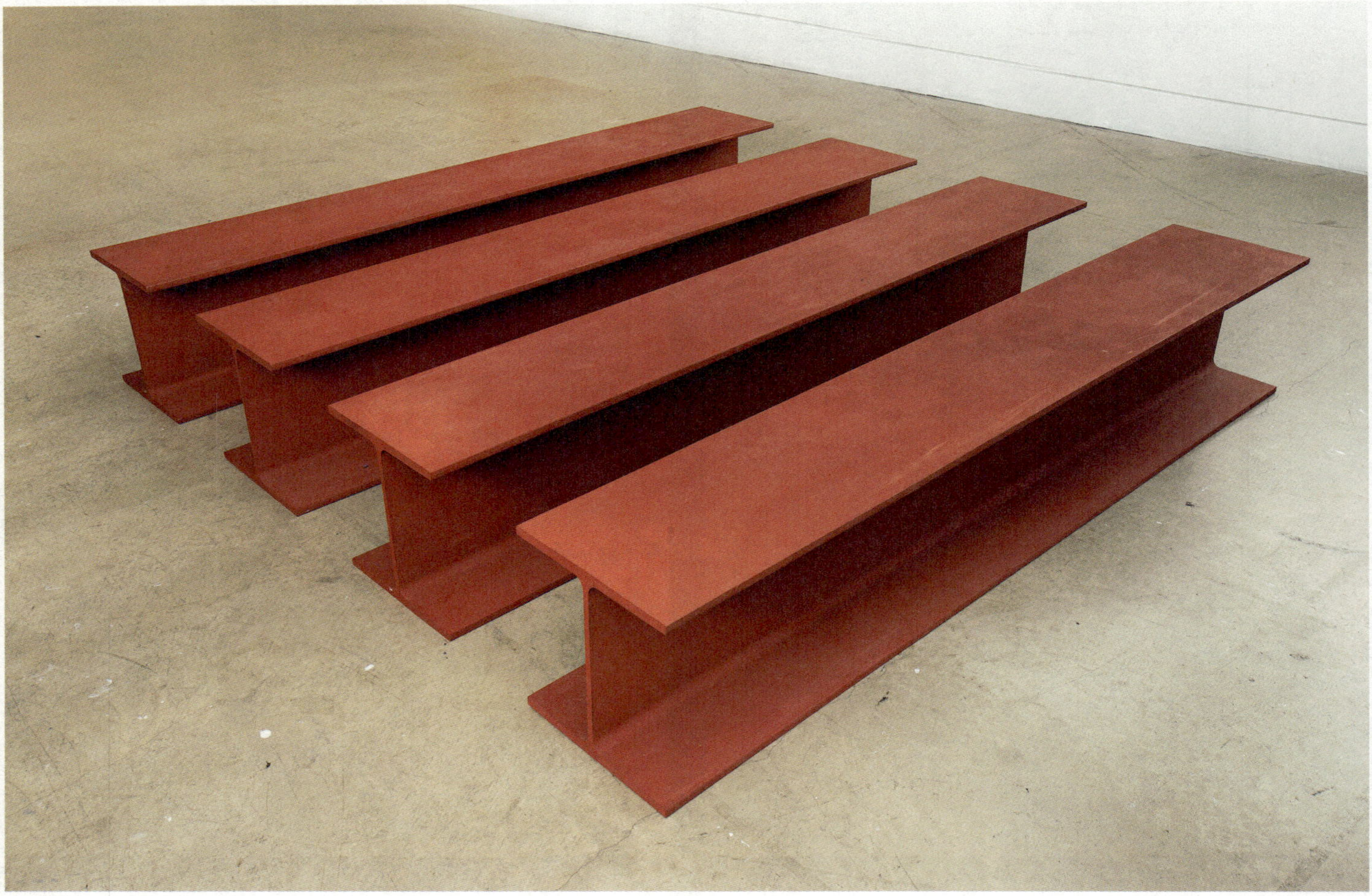

Sculpture No. 1 (Blue), 1965 / 2010
painted steel, 31 x 183 x 183 cm
Sharjah Art Foundation Collection

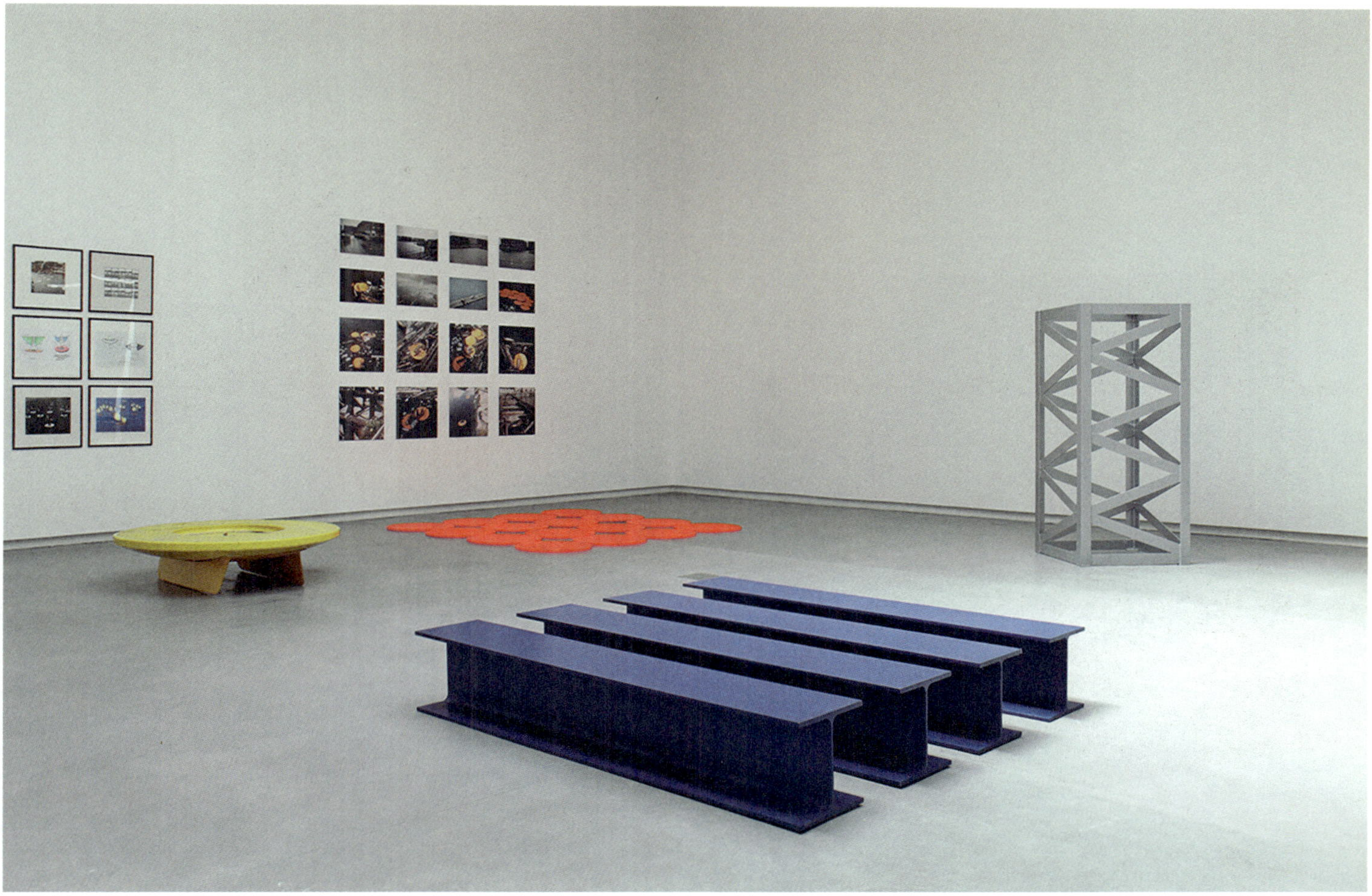

Sculpture No. 2 (Red), 1965 / 2015
painted steel, 120 x 120 x 120 cm
Sharjah Art Foundation Collection
Sculpture No. 2 (Blue), 1965 / 2015
painted steel, 120 x 120 x 120 cm

Sculpture No. 2 (Silver), 1965 / 2015
painted steel, 120 x 120 x 120 cm
M+ Collection, Hong Kong

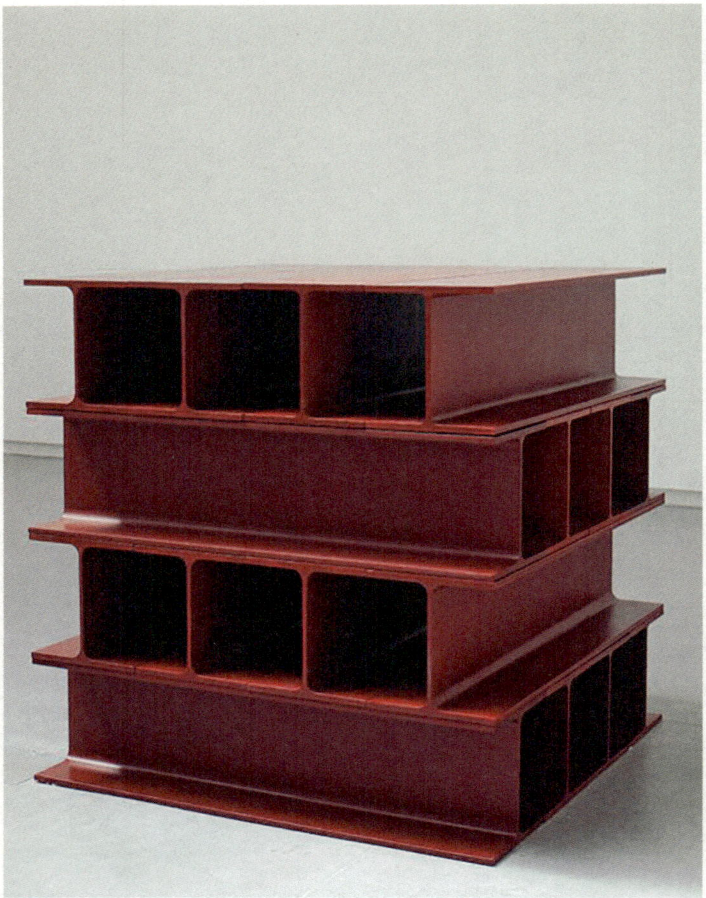

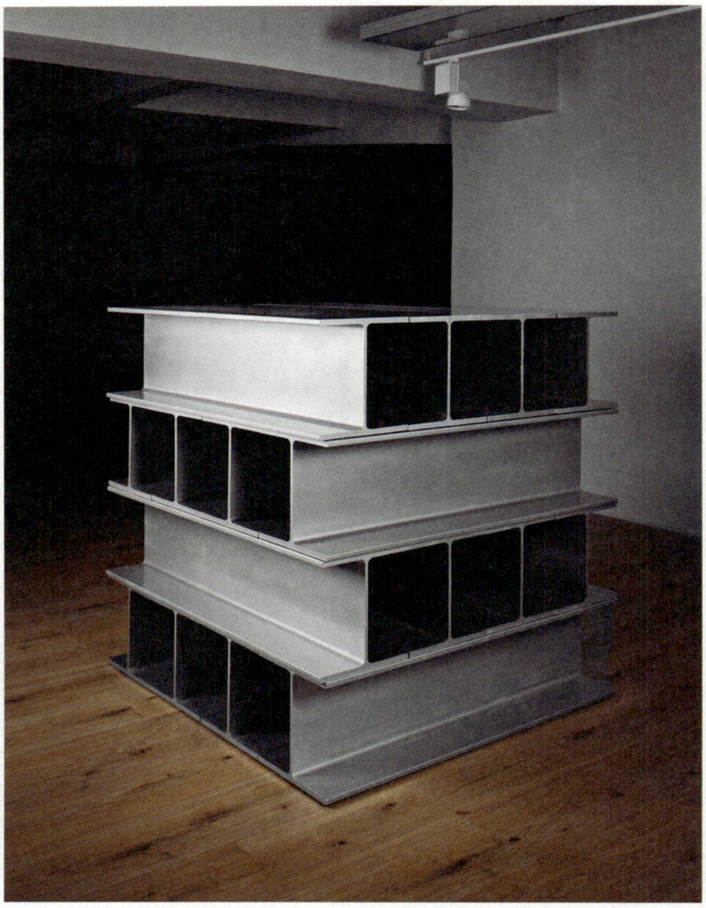

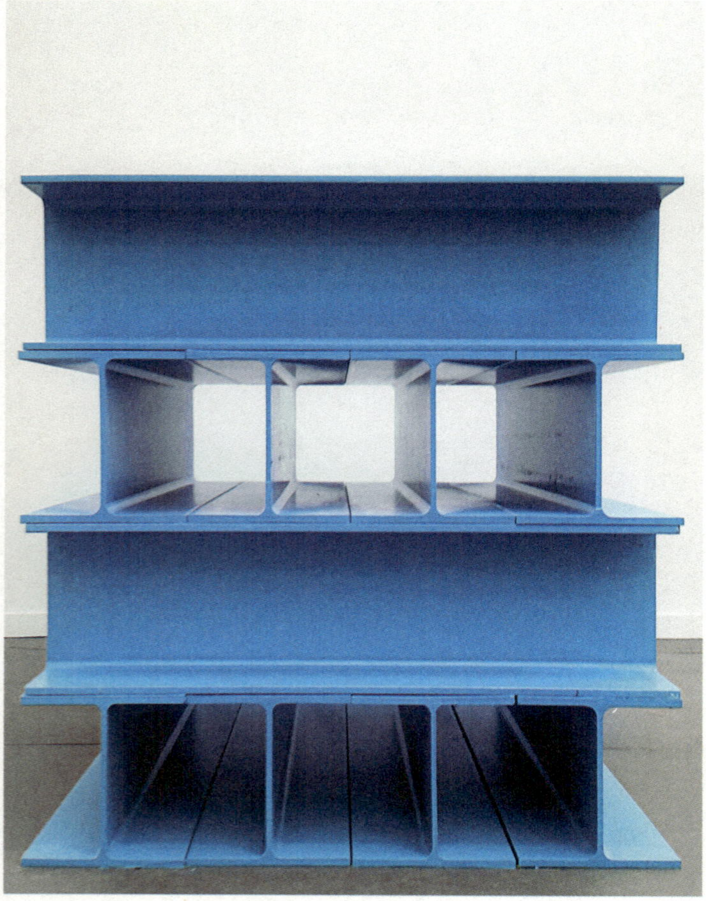

First Structure, 1966–1967
emulsion on wood, 25 x 25 x 25 cm
Red Structure, 1967–1968
emulsion on wood, 33 x 25 x 25 cm
Blue Cube, 1968
acrylic on wood, 92 x 92 x 92 cm

Brown Structure, 1967
emulsion on wood, 33 x 25 x 25 cm
Yellow Structure, 1968
emulsion on wood, 33 x 25 x 25 cm
Red and Yellow Structure, 1968
emulsion on wood, 33 x 50 x 25 cm, destroyed

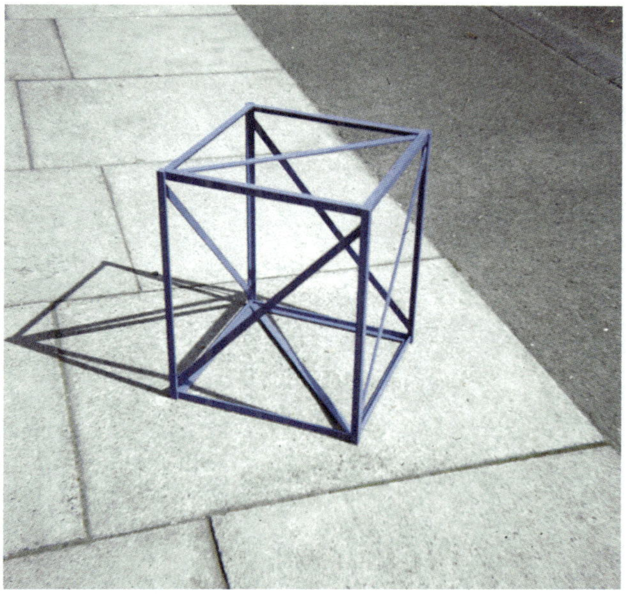
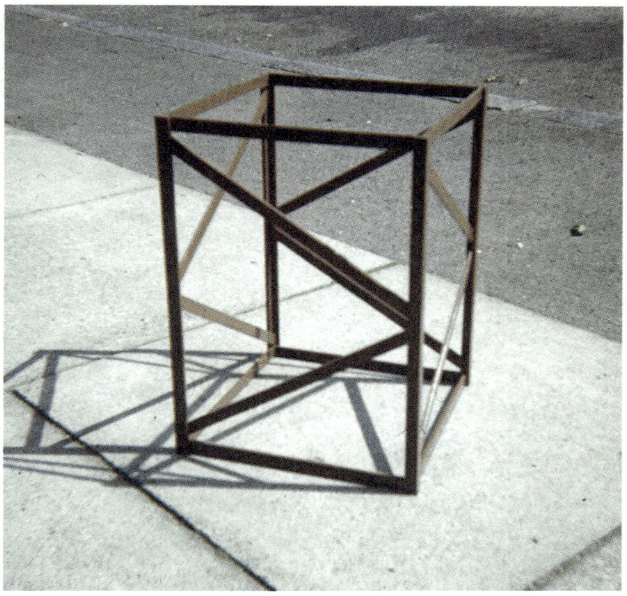
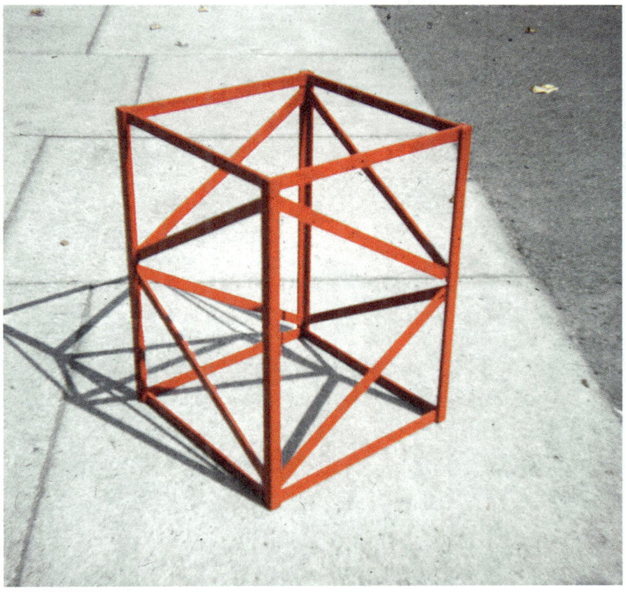
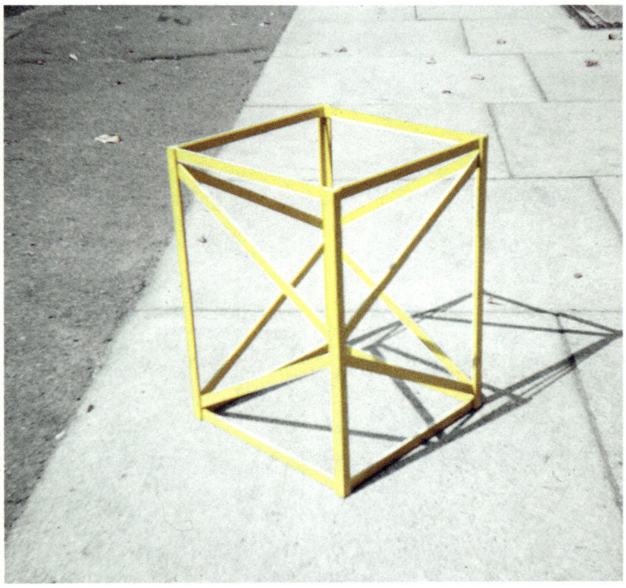
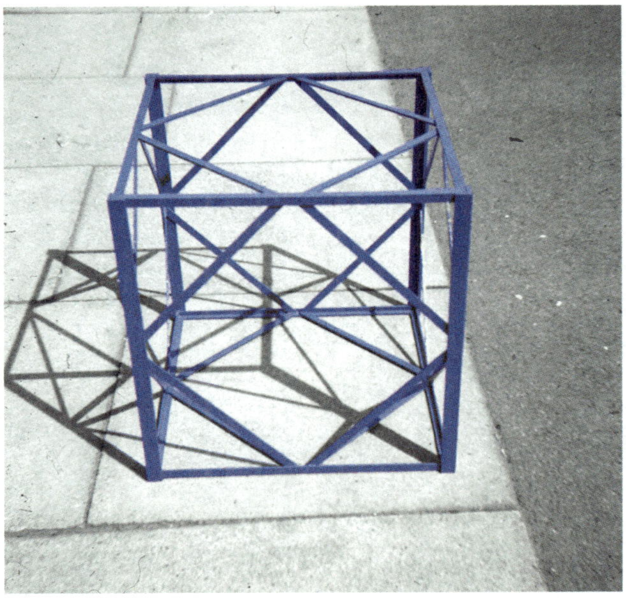
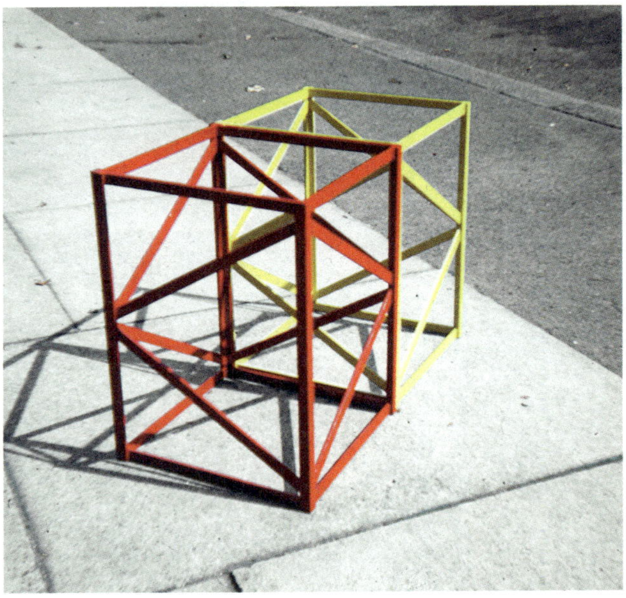

First Structure (Blue), 1966–1967 / 2013
painted steel, 140 x 140 x 140 cm

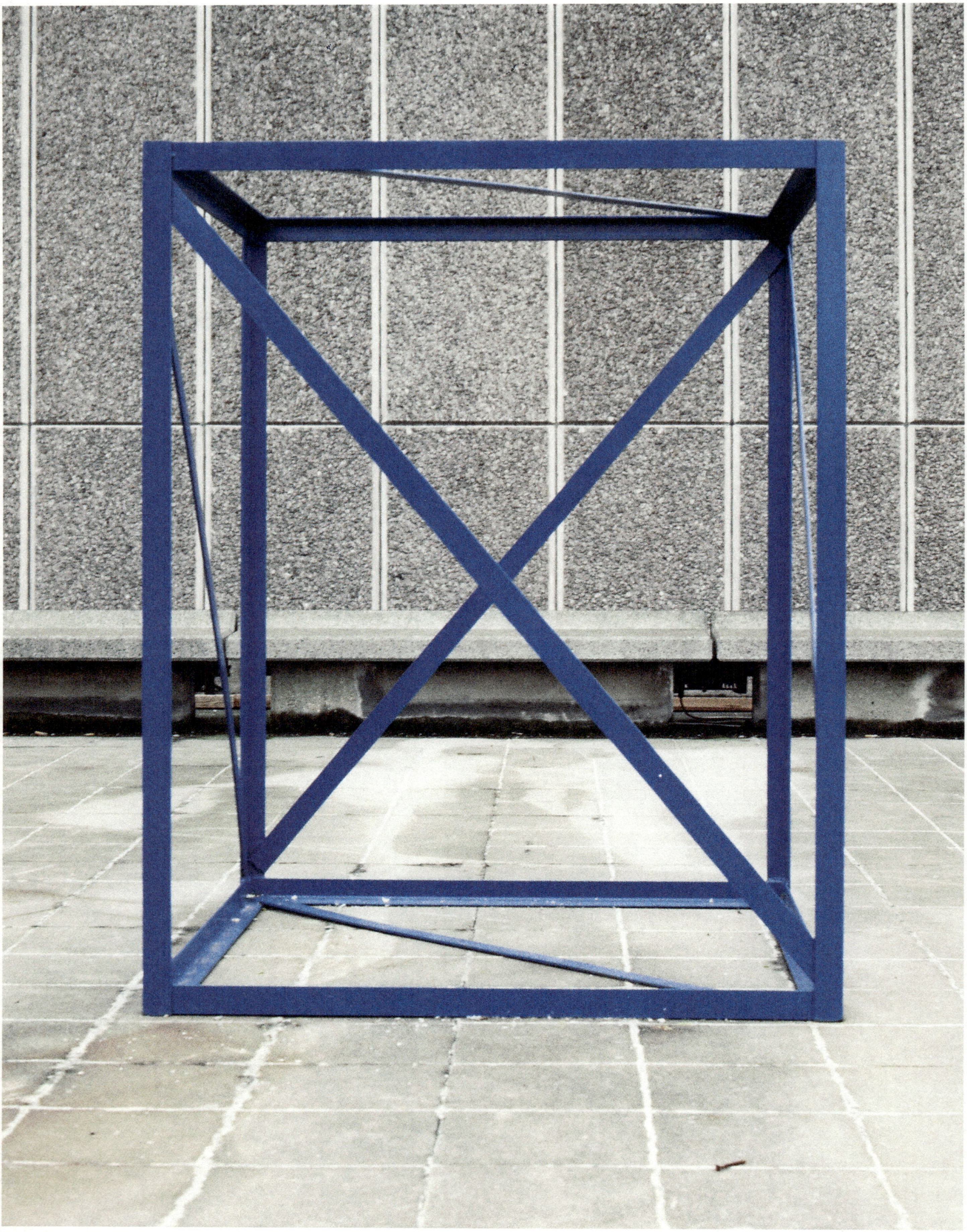

Second Structure, 1966–1967 / 2010
painted steel, 183 x 81 x 81 cm

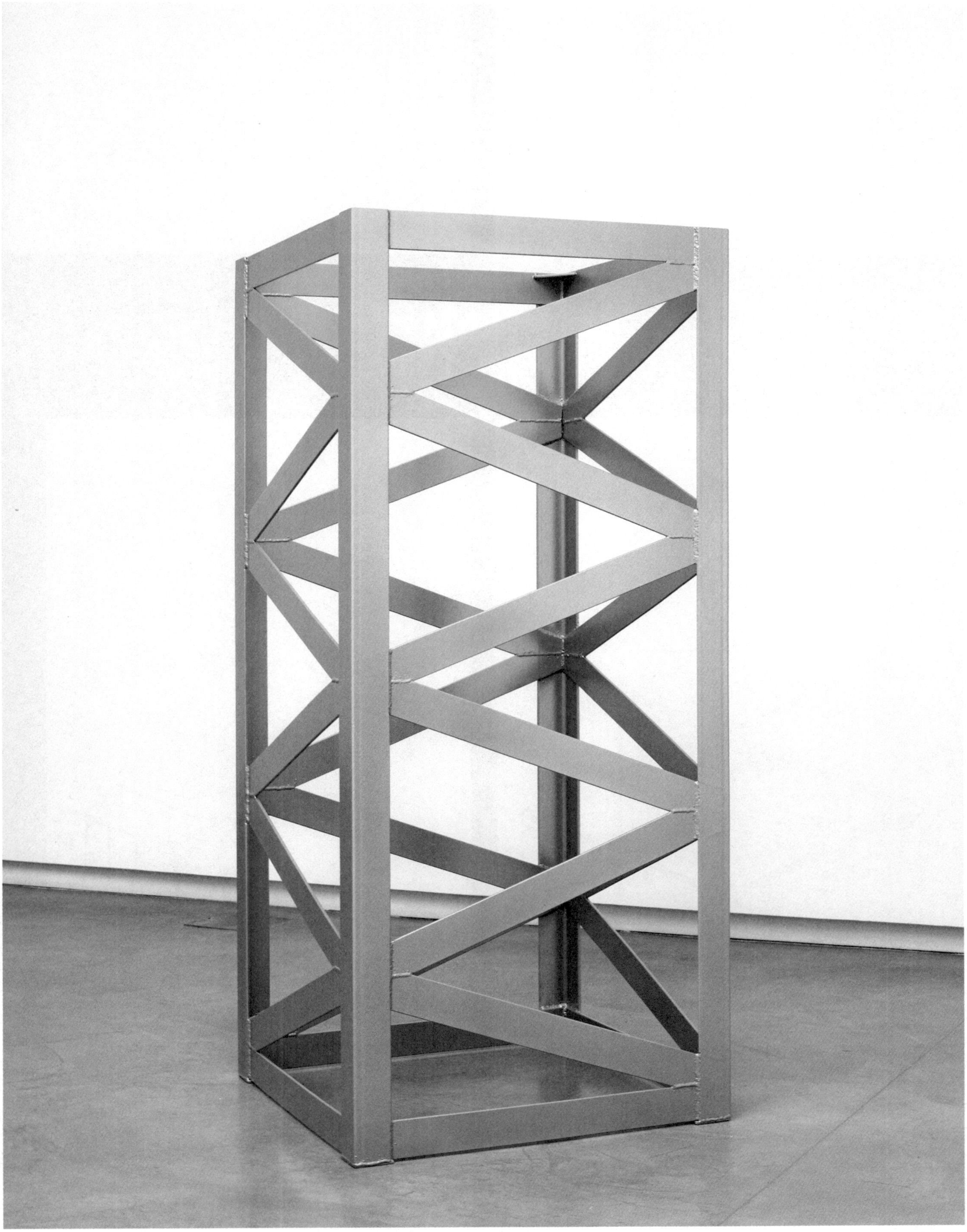

Untitled, 1966
pencil and crayon on paper, 10 x 19 cm
Untitled, 1966
pencil and crayon on paper, 27 x 20 cm

Untitled, 1966
pencil on paper, 10 x 16 cm
Untitled (St MK2), 1966
pencil on paper, 19 x 10 cm

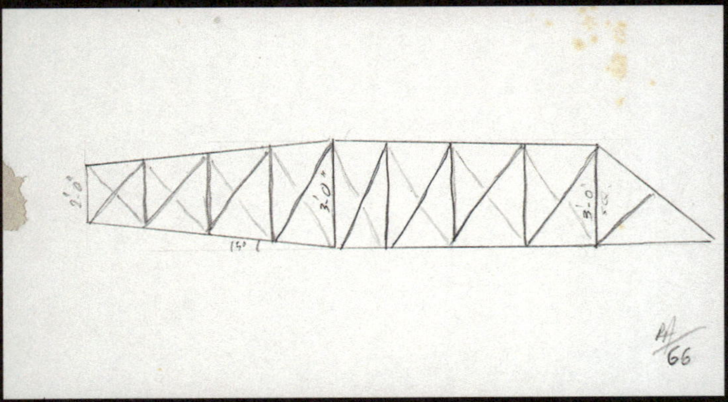

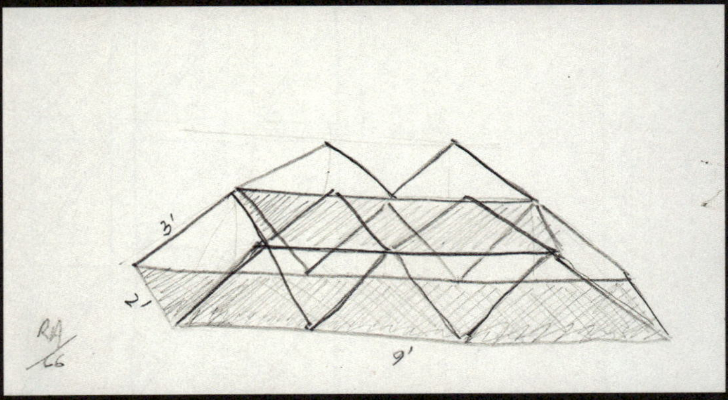

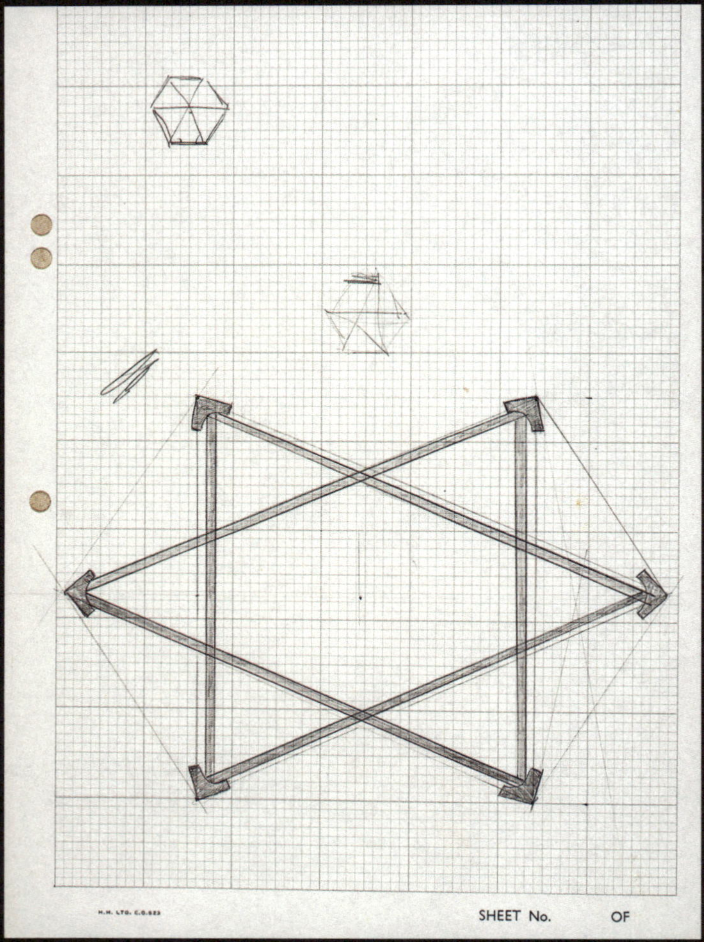

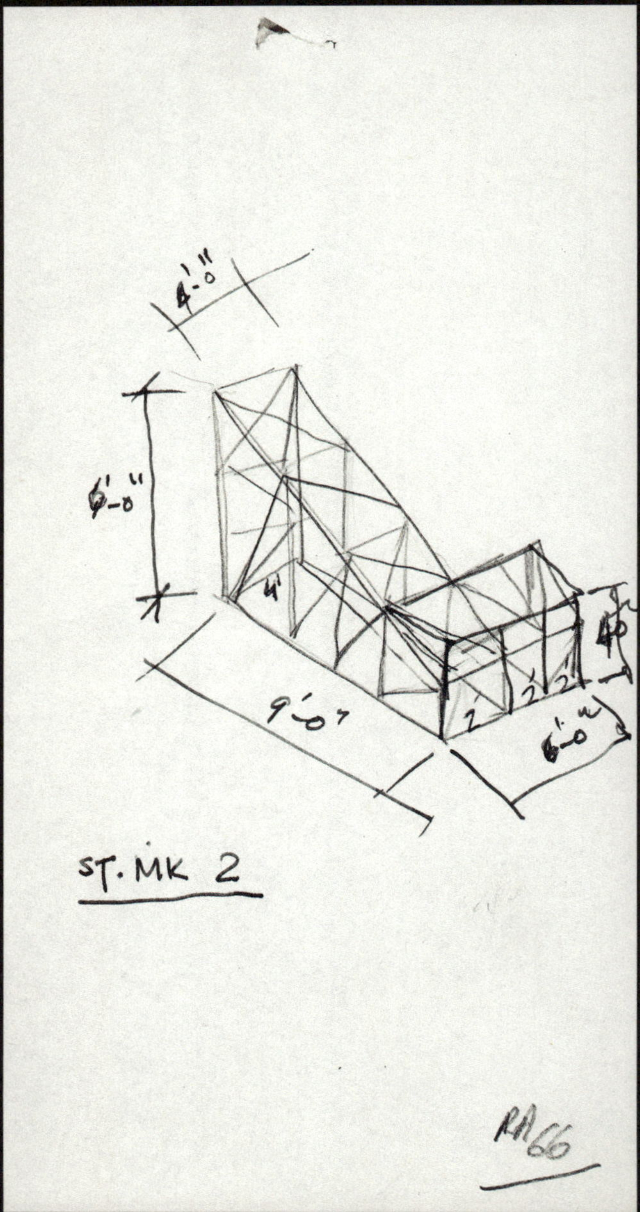

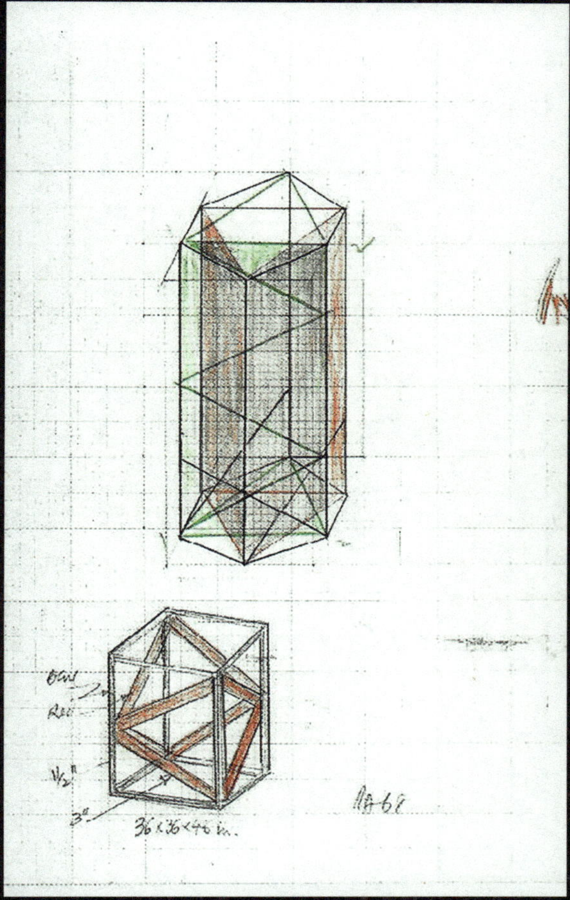
36 x 36 x 46 in.
RA 68

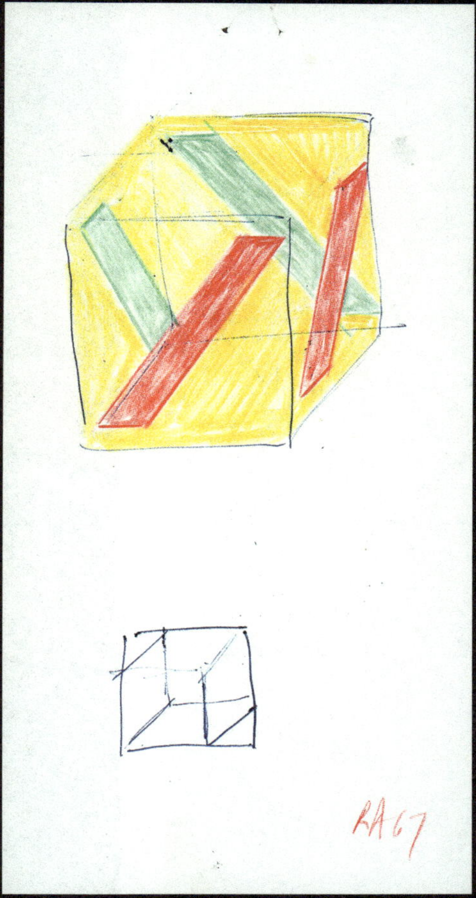
RA 67

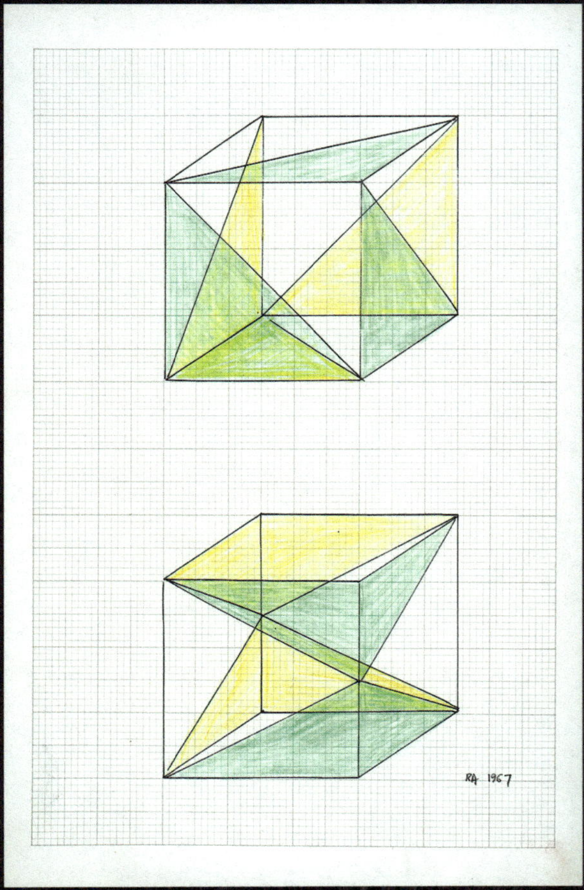
RA 1967

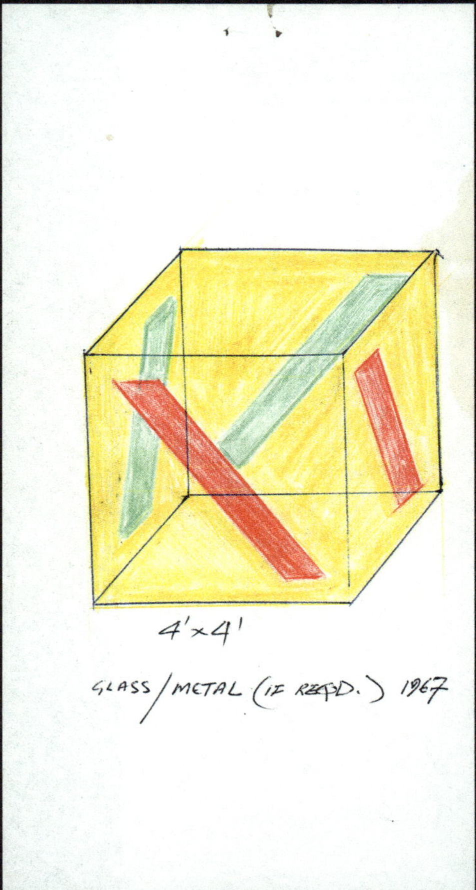
4'x4'
GLASS / METAL (IF REQ'D.) 1967

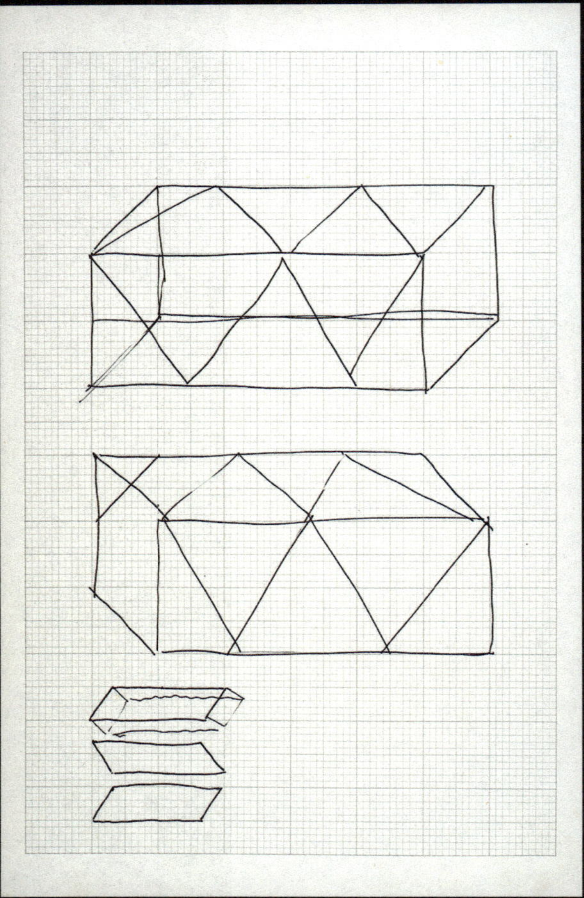

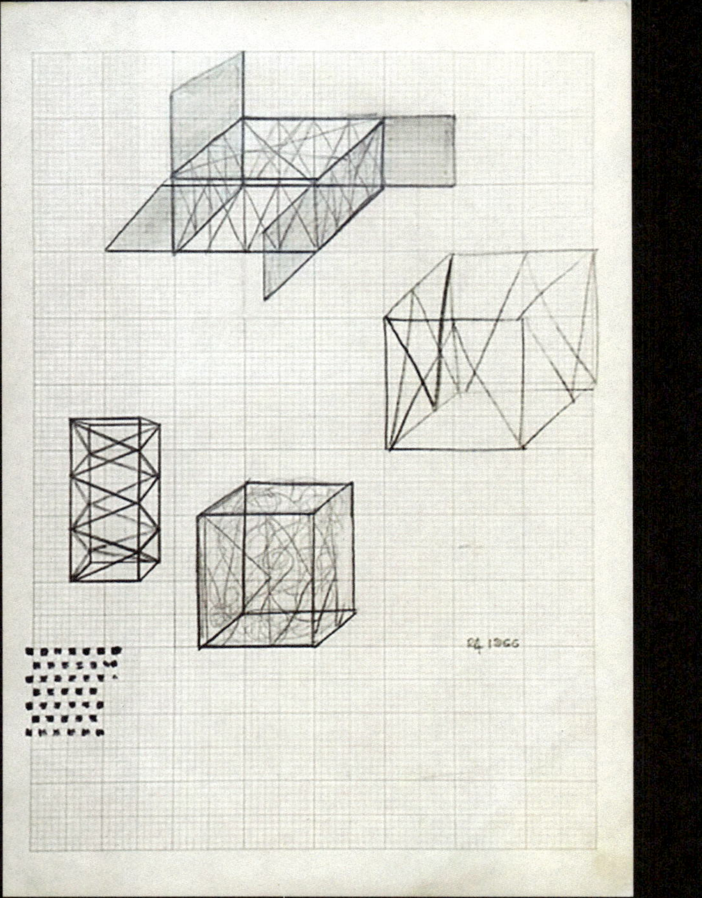
1966

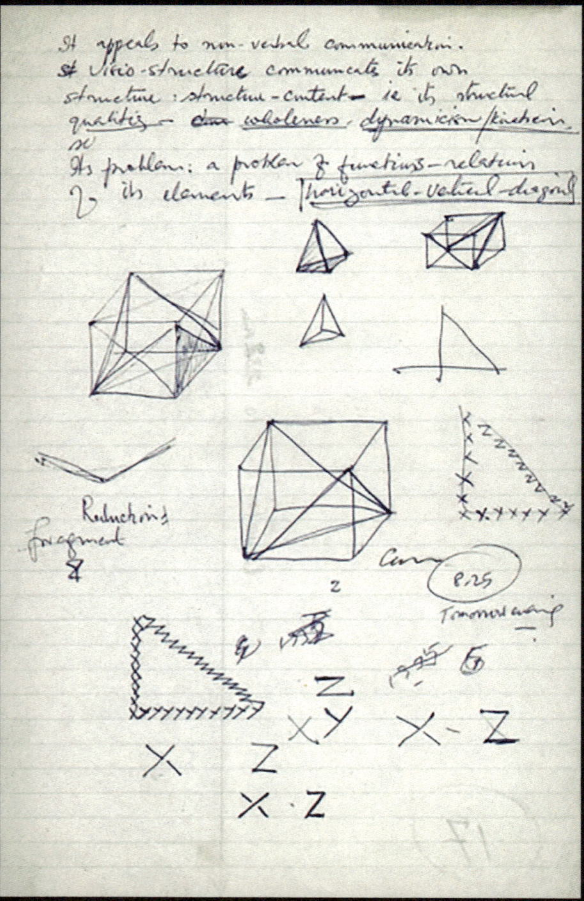
It appeals to non-verbal communication.
It Visio-structure communicates its own
structure: structure-content - ie its structural
qualities - wholeness, dynamicism/kinetic
Its problem: a problem of functions-relations
of its elements - horizontal-vertical-diagonal
Reductions
fragment
X - Z
X
Z
X - Z

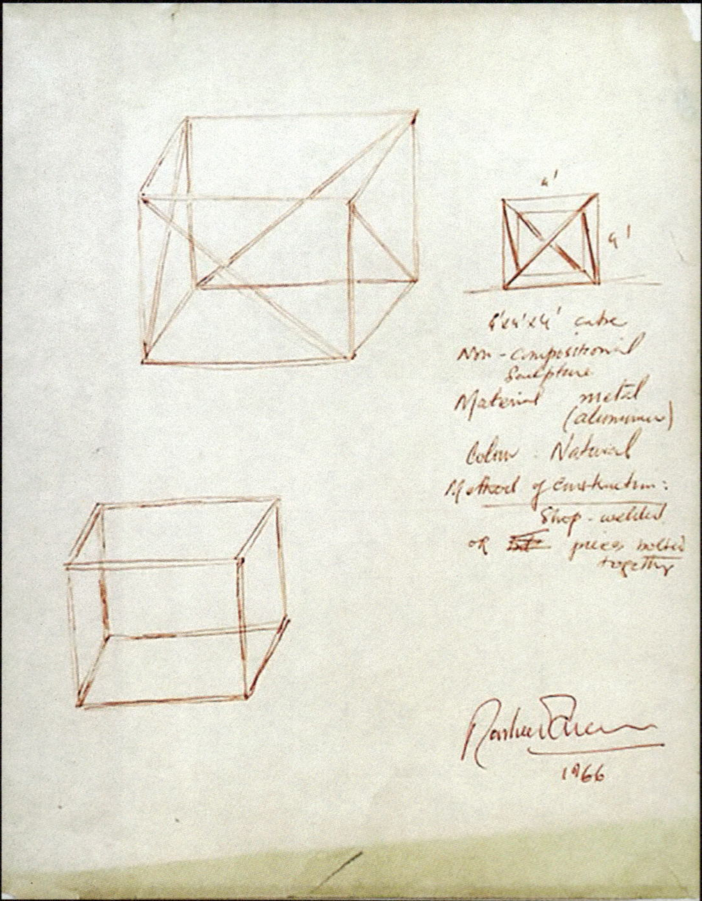
4'
4'
Non-compositional
Sculpture
Material metal
(aluminum)
Color Natural
Method of construction:
Shop-welded
or pieces bolted
together
1966

graphite on paper, 32 x 22 cm
Tate: Presented by Tate Members 2011

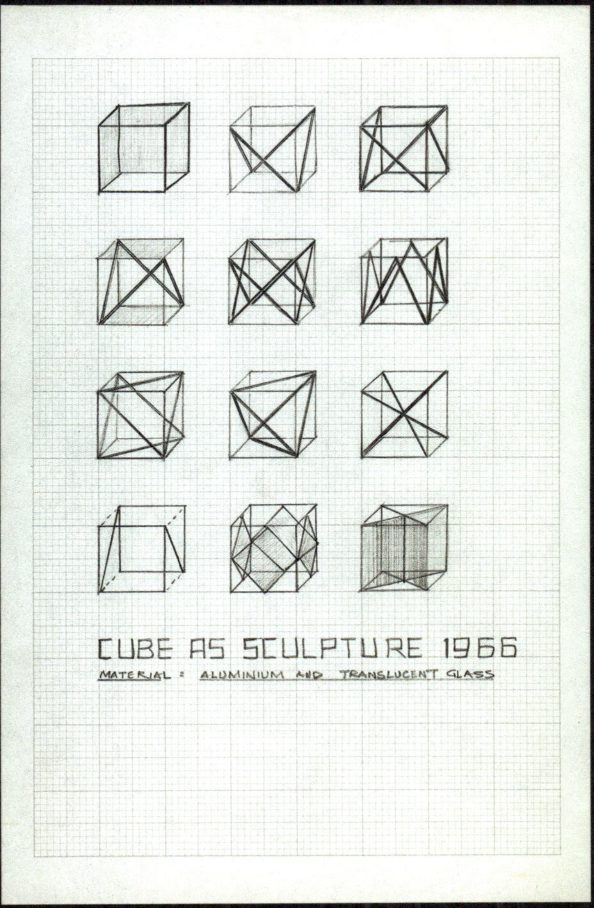

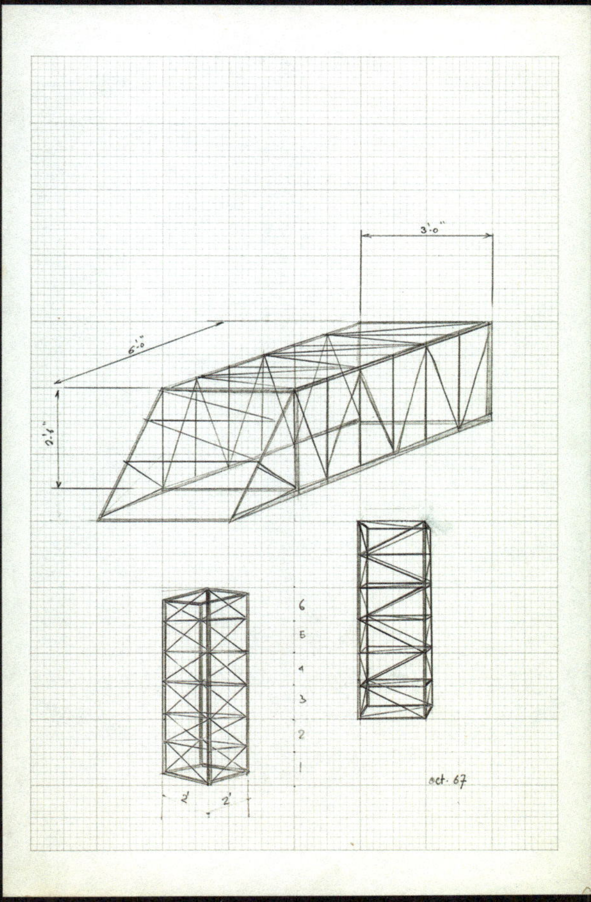

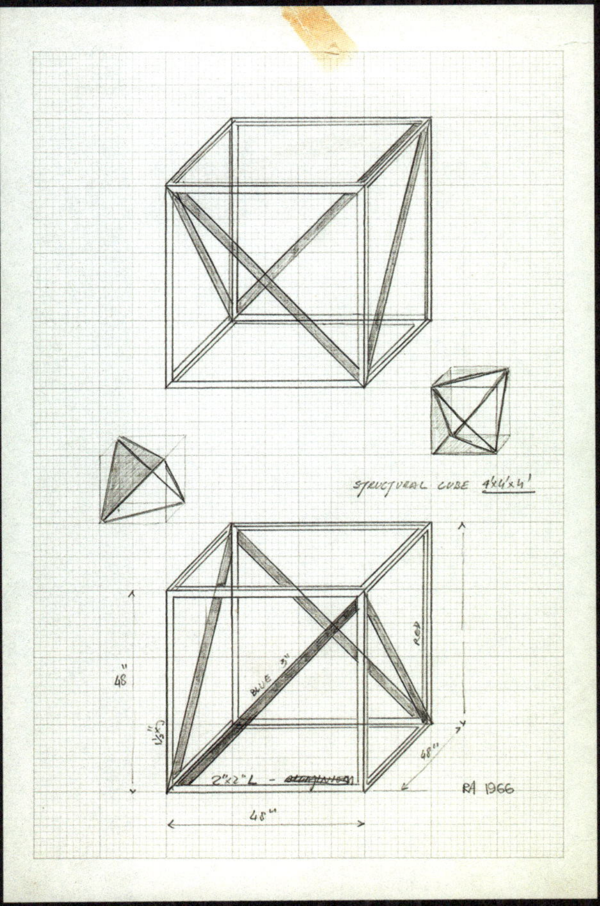

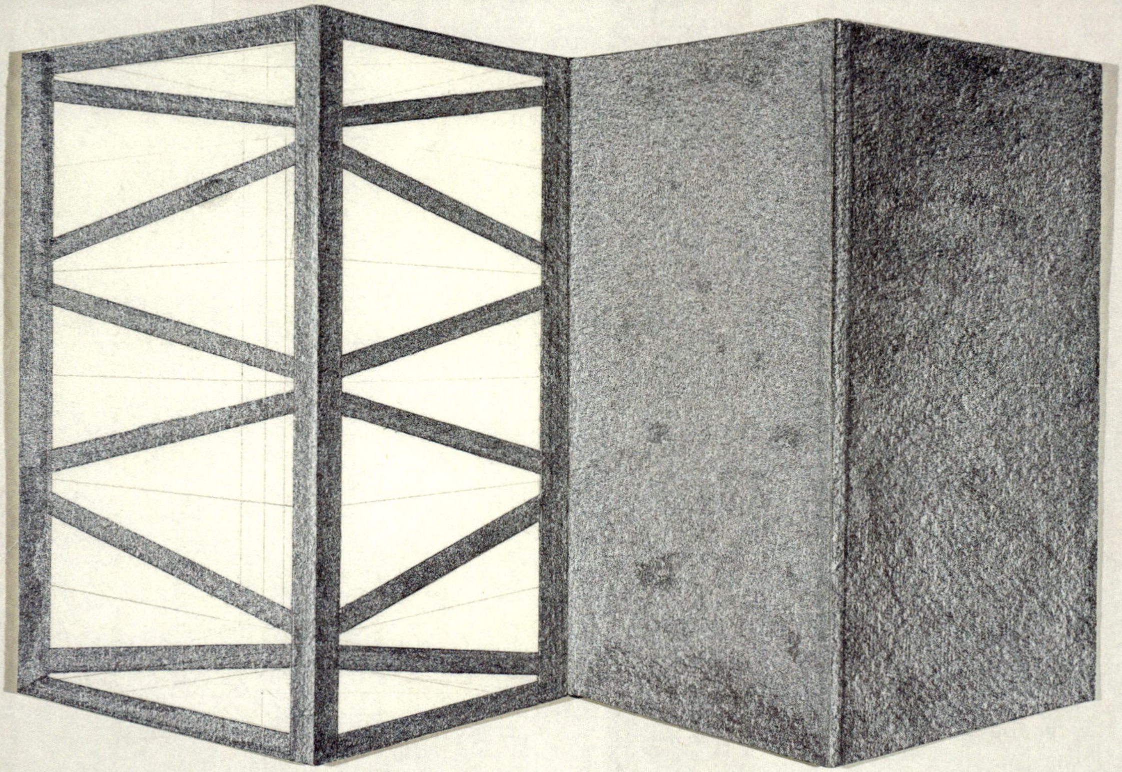

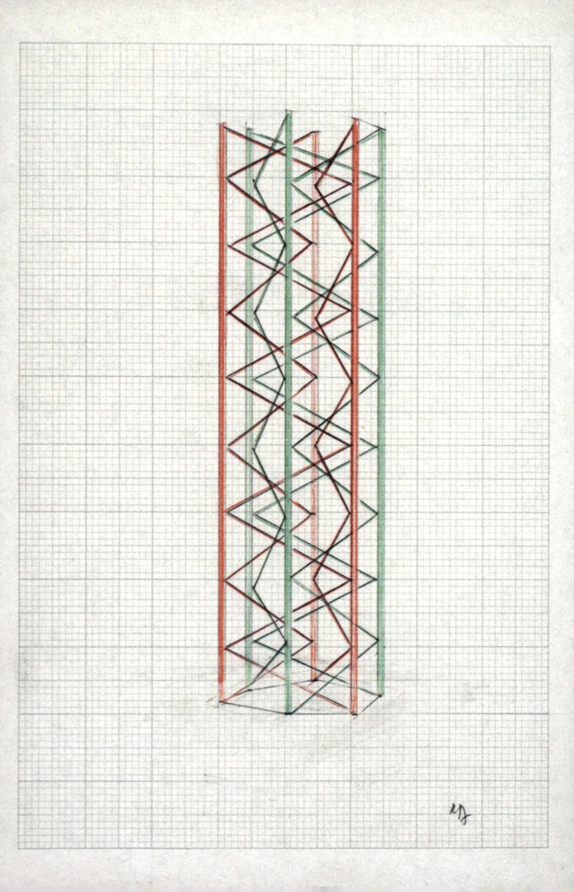

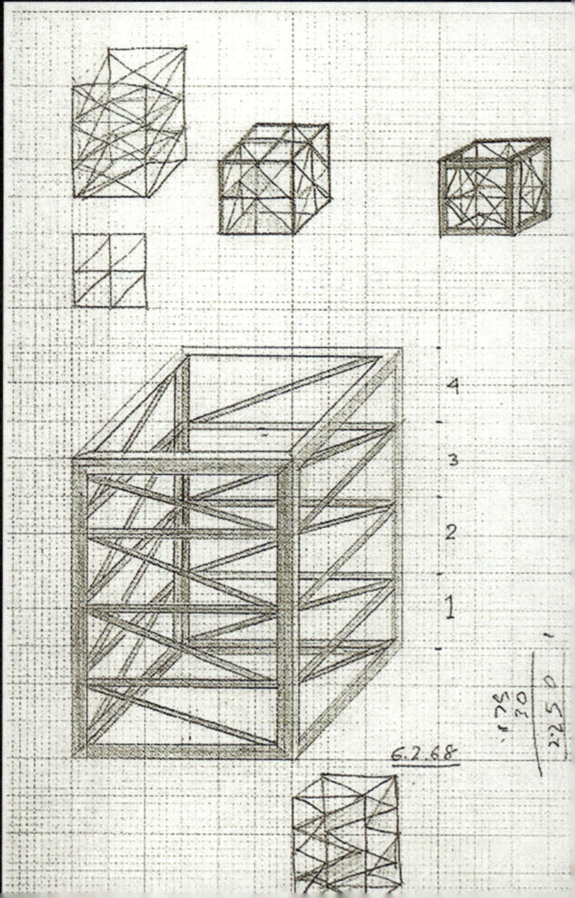
4
3
2
1
6.2.68

CALCULATION SHEET

BP CHEMICALS (U.K.) LIMITED, ENGINEERING DIVISION
ENFORD HOUSE, 139-151 MARYLEBONE ROAD, LONDON N.W.1

FACTORY JOB No. DATE
SECTION & SECTION No. CALCULATION BY
CALCULATION FOR CHECK BY

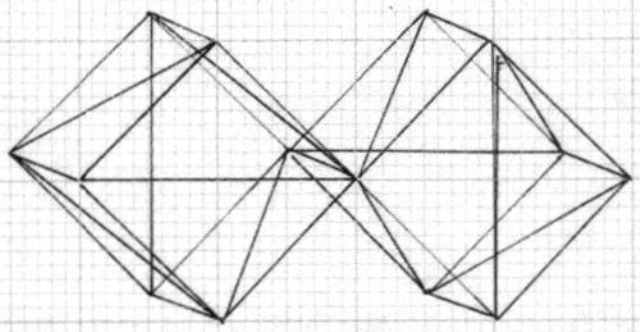

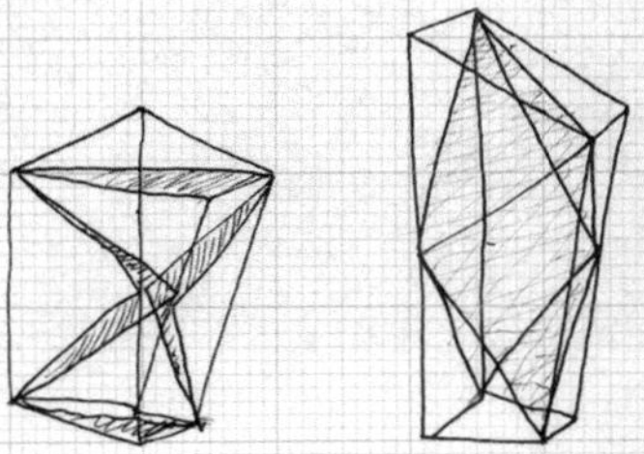

It derives its energy, its irrationality and its mysterious power from the id, which is to be regarded as the source of what we usually call inspiration. It is given formal synthesis and unity by the ego; and finally it may be assimilated to those ideologies or spiritual aspirations which are the peculiar creations of the super-ego:

SHEET No. OF

CALCULATION SHEET

BP CHEMICALS (U.K.) LIMITED, ENGINEERING DIVISION
ENFORD HOUSE, 139-151 MARYLEBONE ROAD, LONDON N.W.1

FACTORY JOB No. DATE
SECTION & SECTION No. CALCULATION BY
CALCULATION FOR CHECK BY

Art cannot survive indifference. But to flourish it needs the involvement of the audience. The galleries generally do not accept this phenomenon* with the result their interest only lies in the artists who would create (or make) "art object to art" for their limited customers.

* or responsibility:

making Art subordinate to philosophical point of view:

The design is a design — art for art's sake — and only acquires its extra-aesthetic or ideological significance from its environment — its position in time and place:

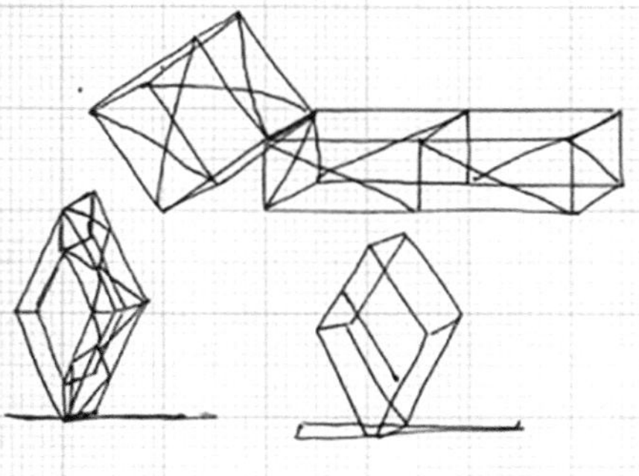

SHEET No. OF

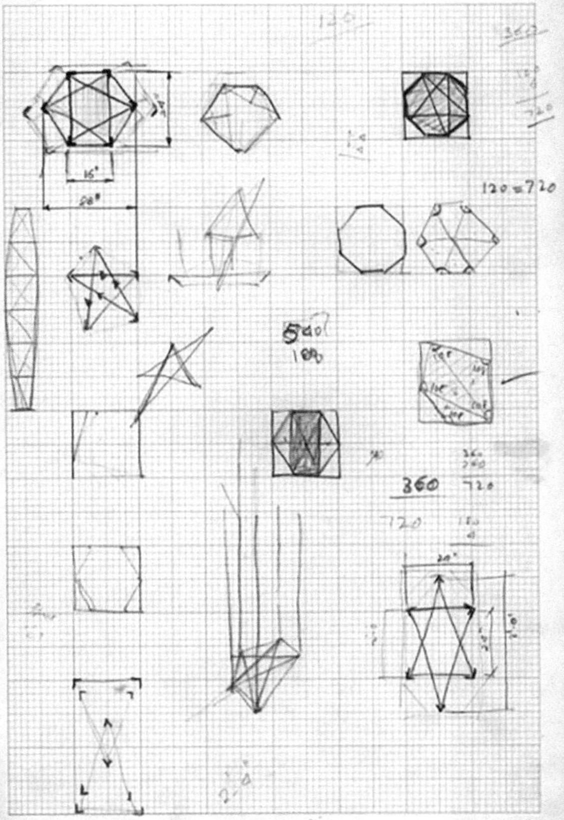

Untitled, 1966
pencil on paper, 34 x 23 cm
Untitled, 1967
pencil and pen on paper, 23 x 34 cm

Untitled, 1967
pencil on paper, 9 x 21 cm
Untitled, 1966
pencil and crayon on paper, 10 x 19 cm
Untitled (3H SQ), 1966
pencil on paper, 19 x 10 cm

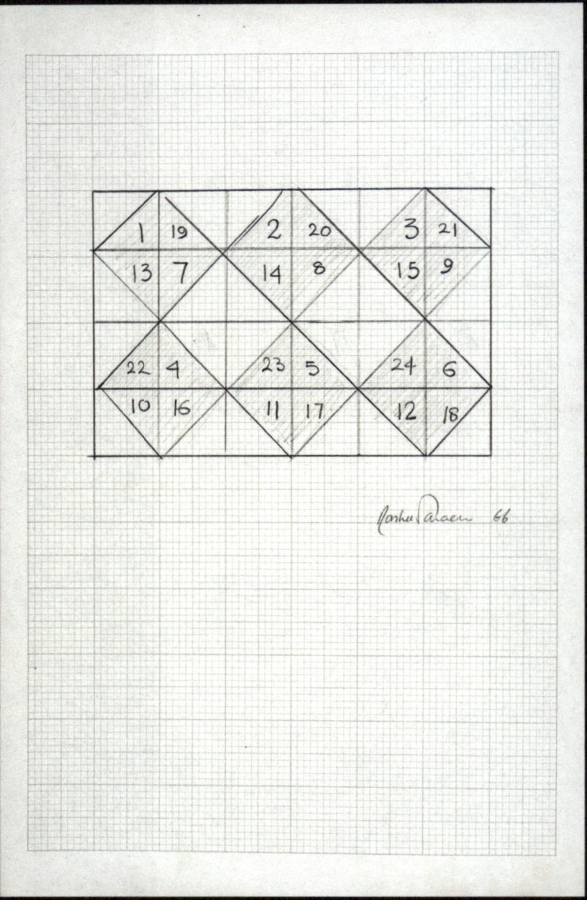

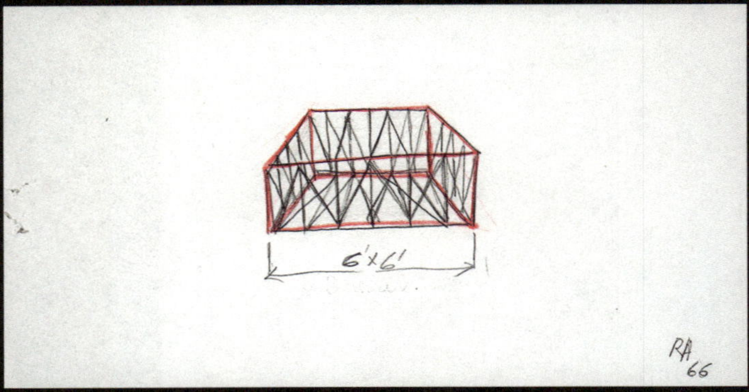

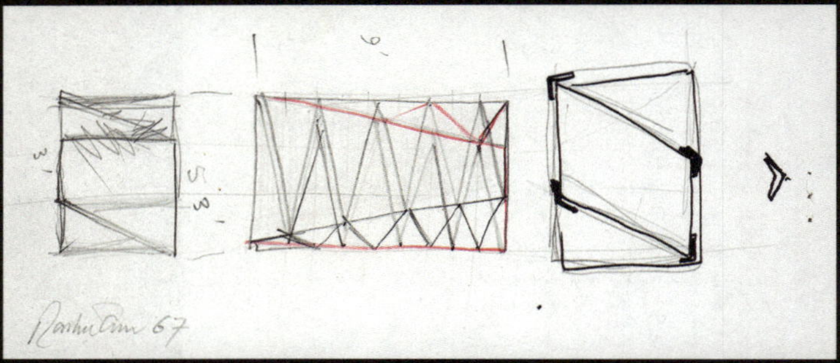

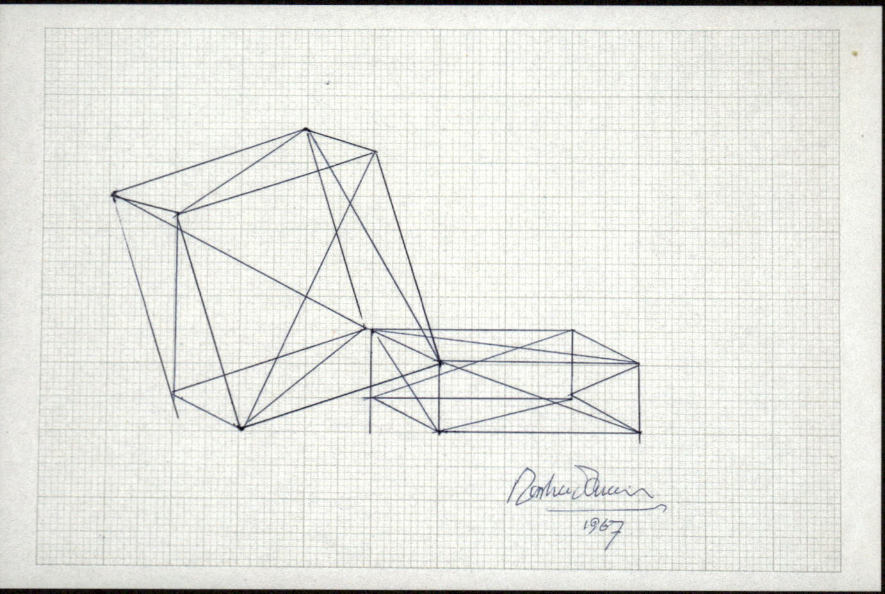

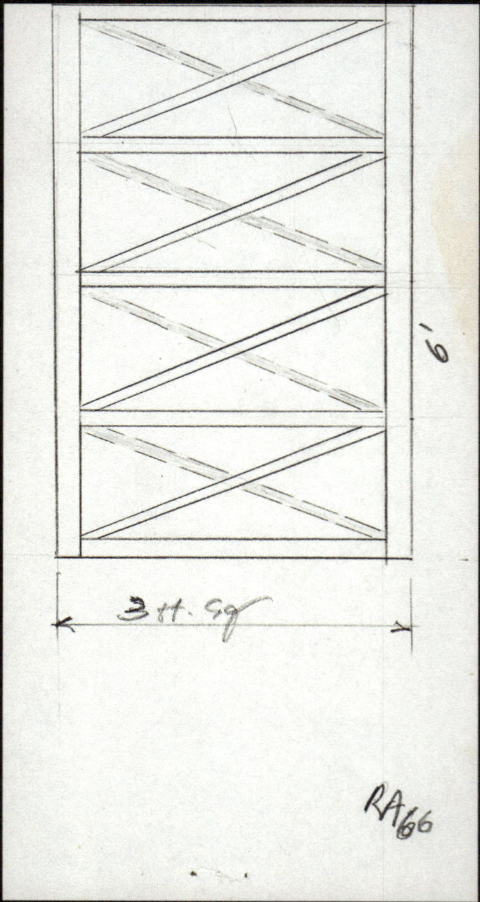

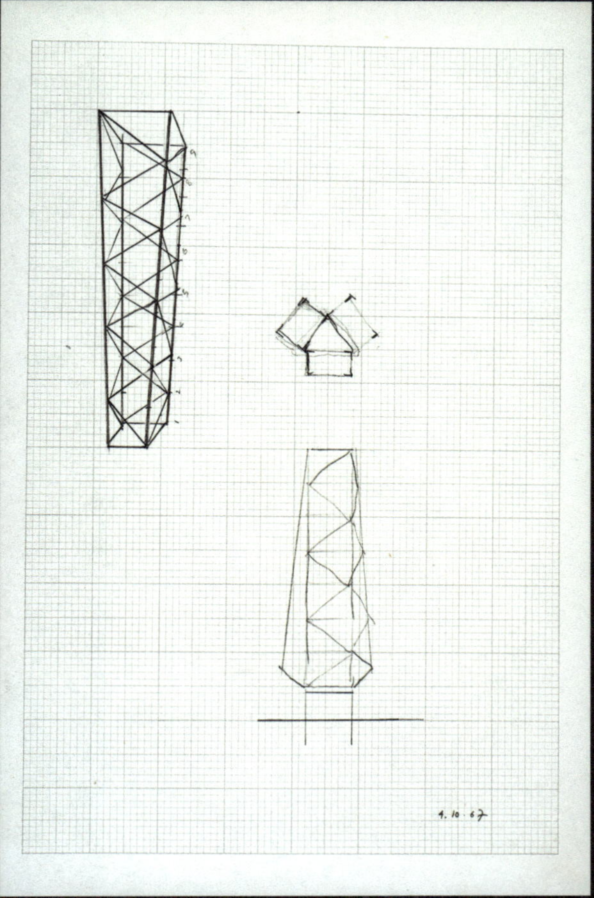
4.10.67

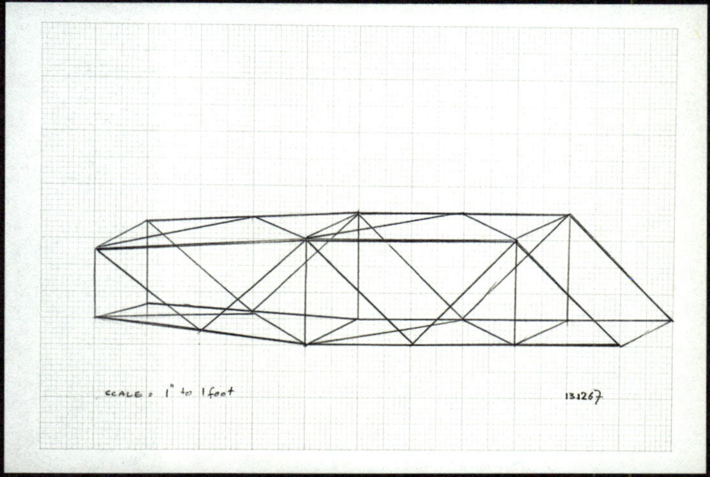
SCALE: 1" to 1 foot
13.12.67

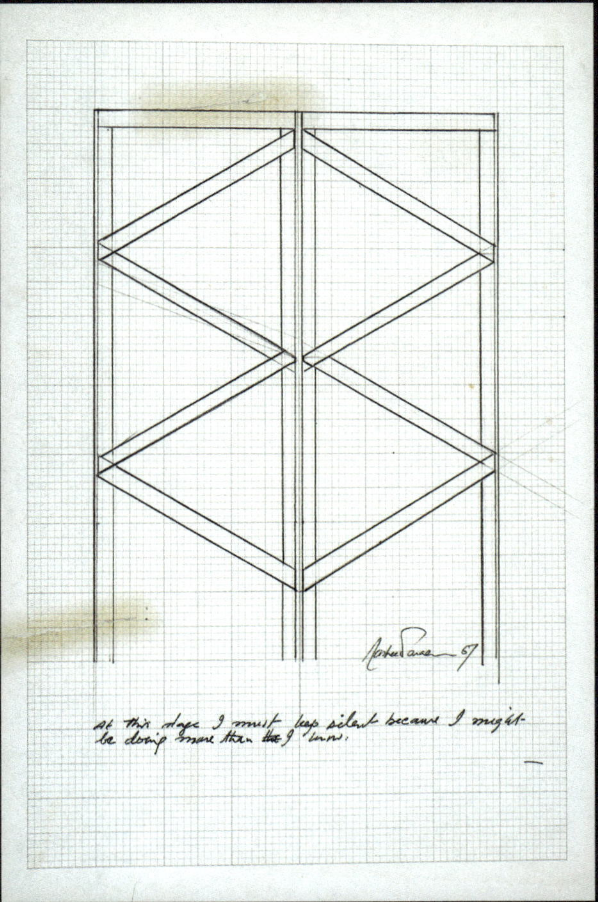
67
At this stage I must keep silent because I might be doing more than I know.

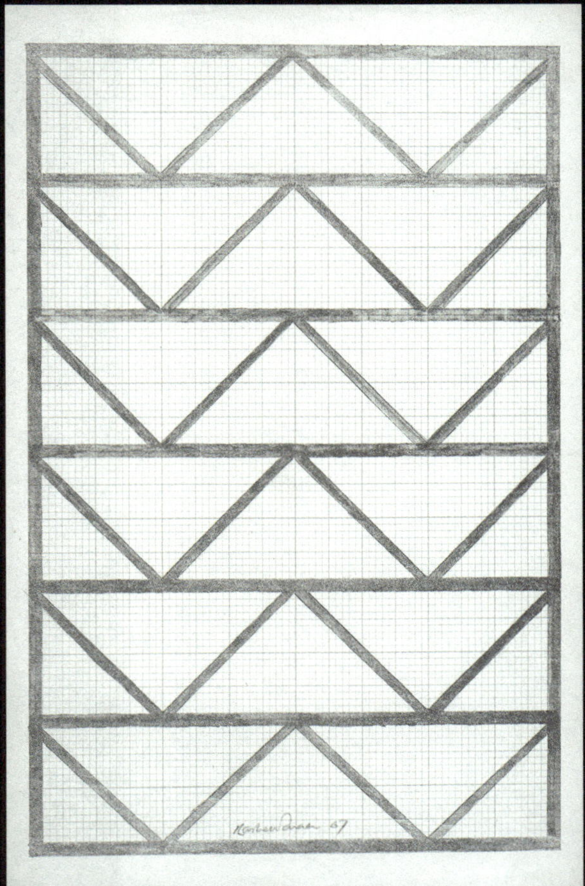
67

Untitled, 1968
ink on paper, 29 x 20 cm
Untitled, 1968,
pencil and crayon on paper, 34 x 23 cm

Untitled (Red), 1968
crayon on paper, 34 x 23 cm
Untitled (Jan 68), 1968
pencil on paper, 34 x 23 cm

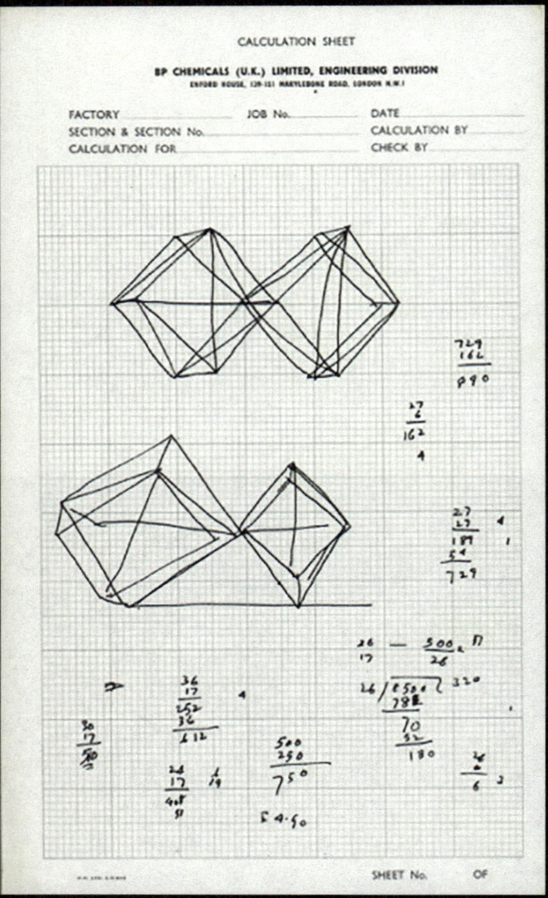

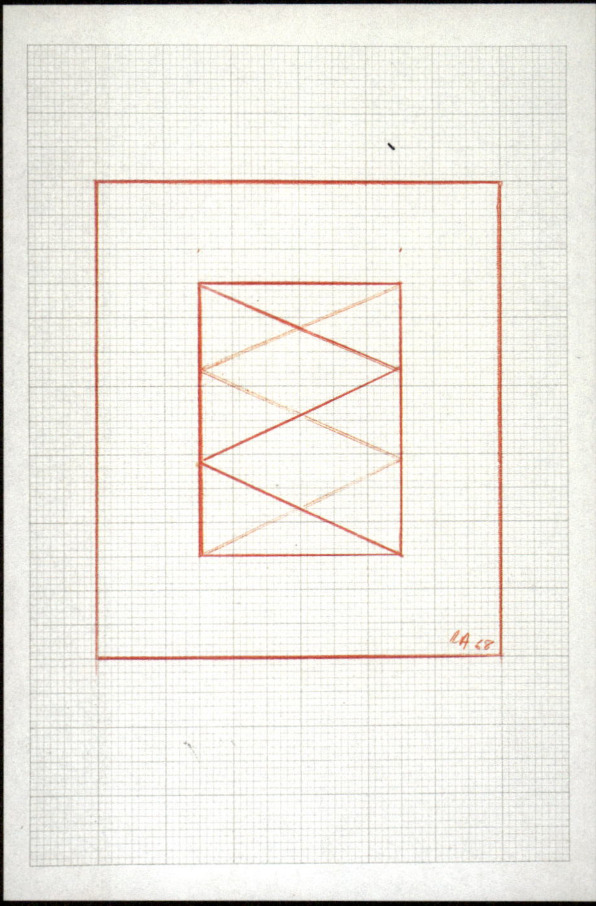

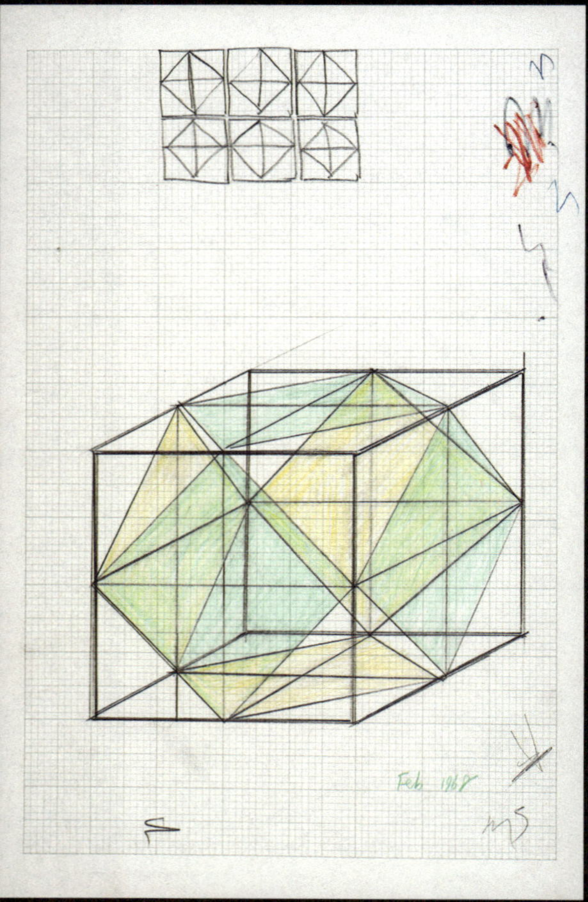

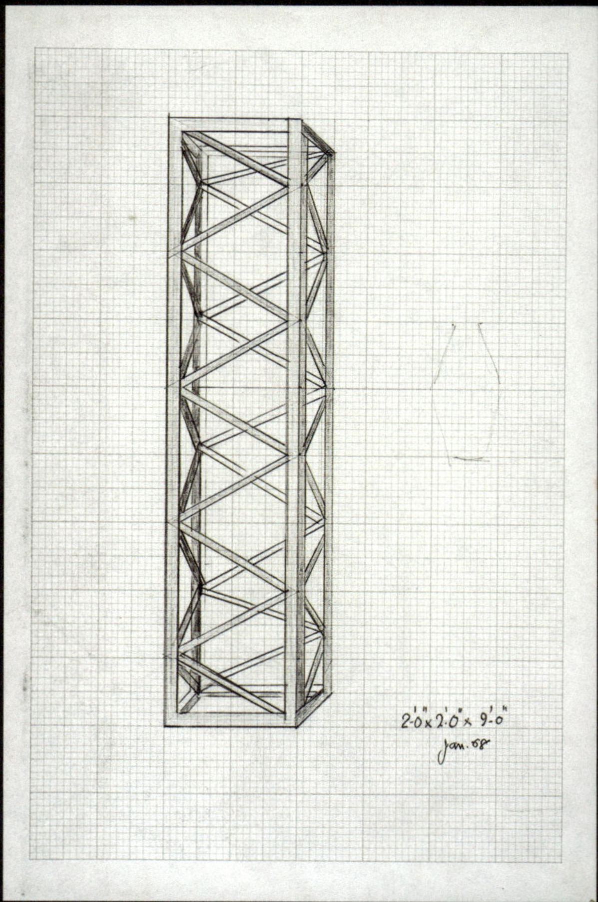

Untitled, 1968
pencil and crayon on paper, 34 x 23 cm
Untitled, 1968
crayon on paper, 29 x 20 cm

Untitled, 1968
pencil and crayon on paper, 34 x 23 cm
Untitled, 1968
ink on paper, 29 x 20 cm

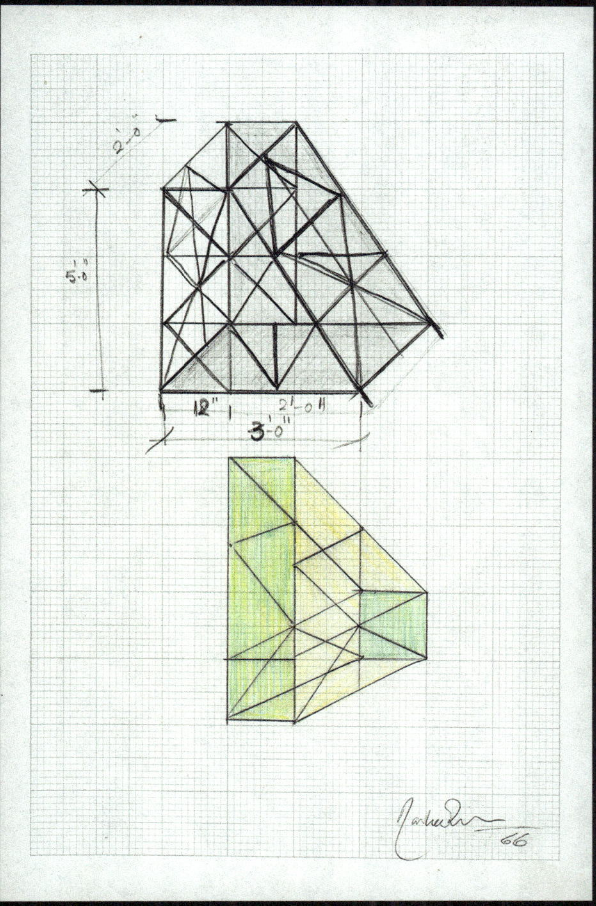

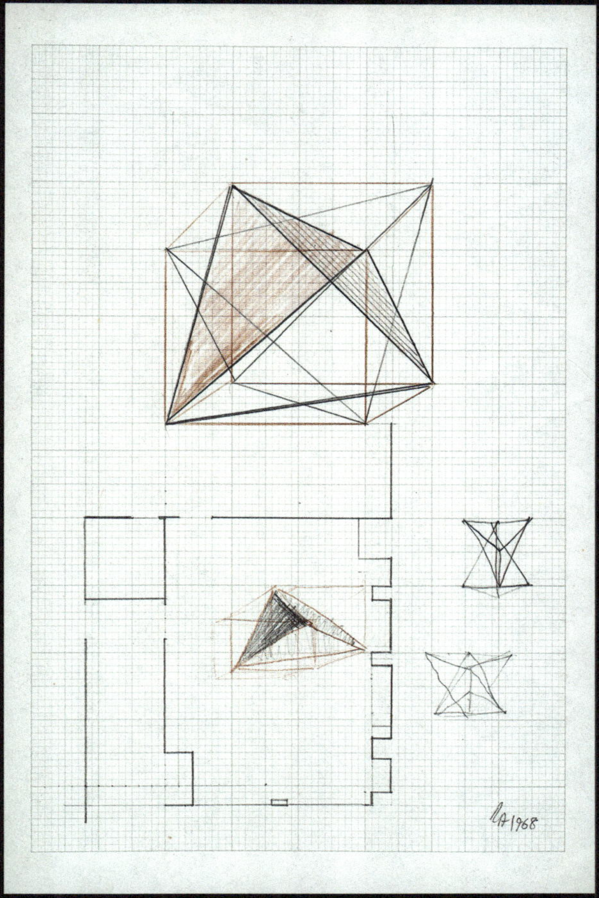

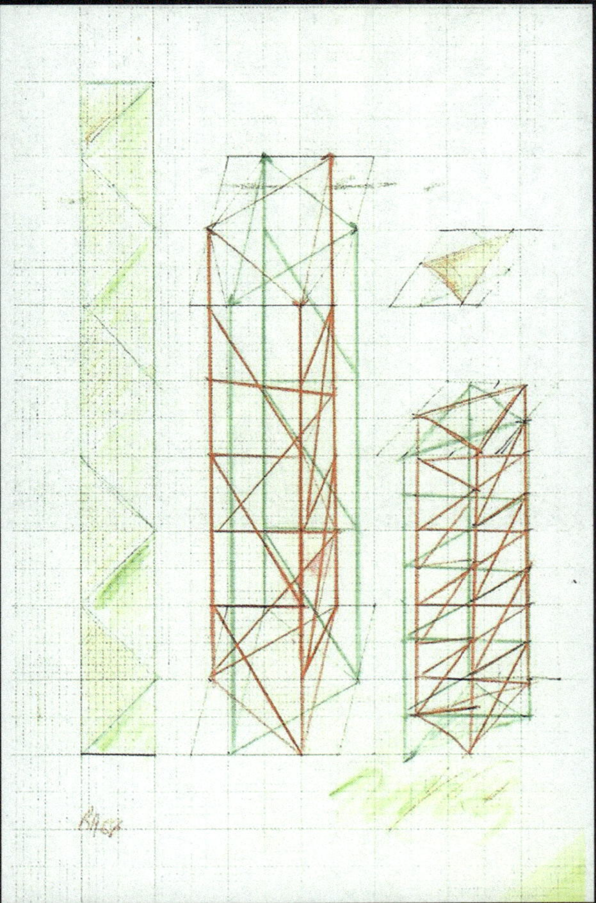

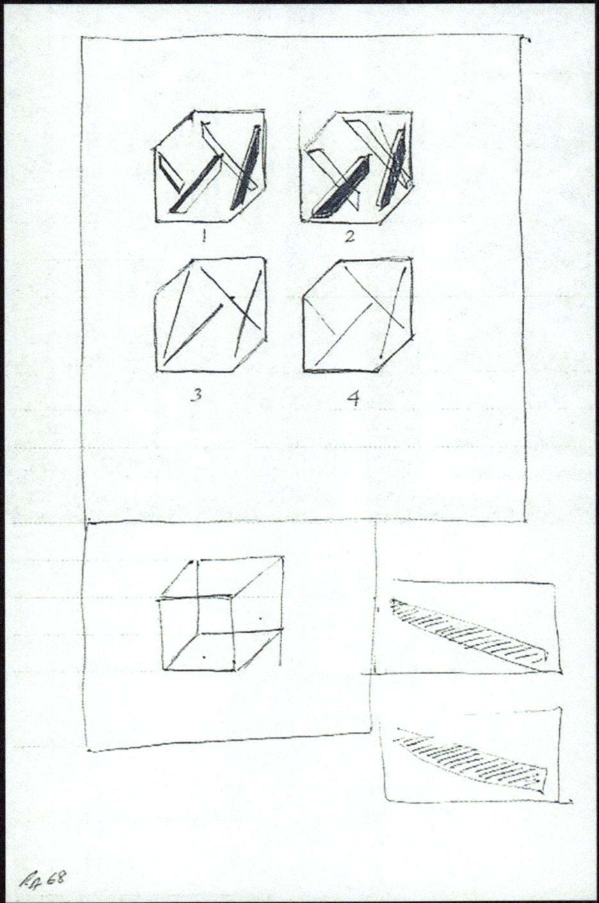

Untitled (A), 1967
emulsion on wood, 69 x 10 x 10 cm

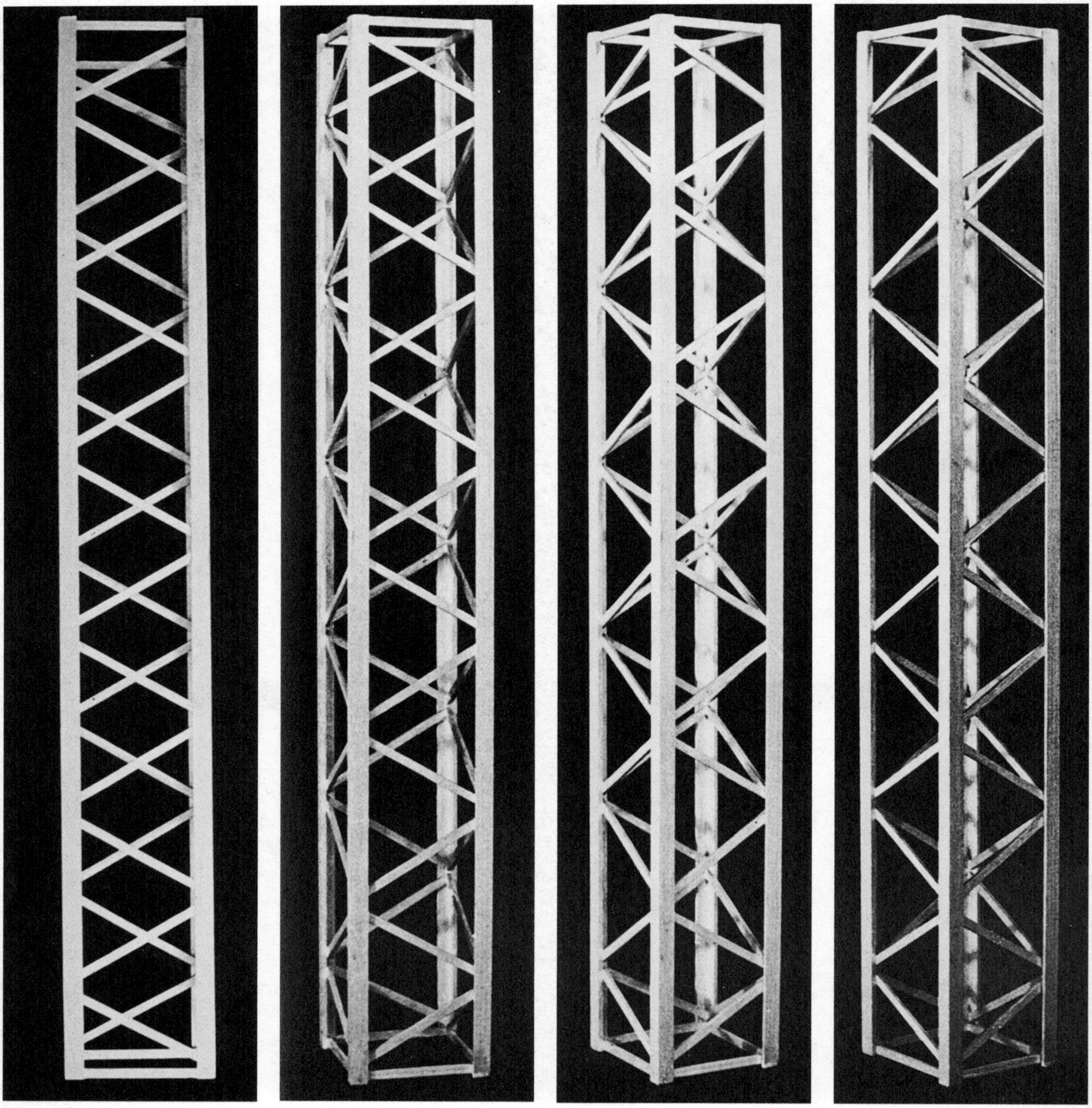

Winter Blue, 1968
acrylic on wood, 38 x 46 x 12 cm
Collection Anne and Conor Macklin

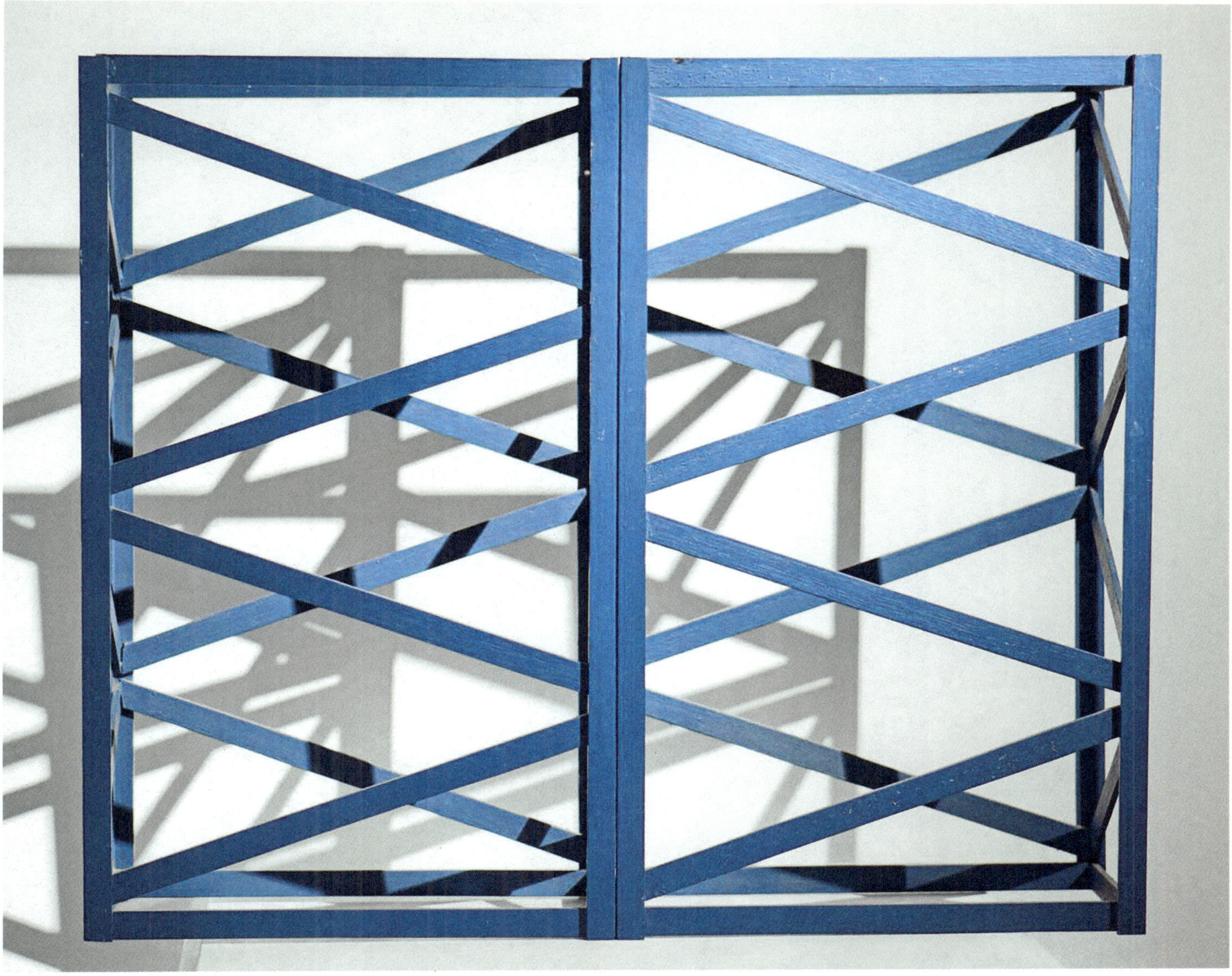

Homage to Tatlin, 1968
emulsion on wood, 69 x 24 x 24 cm

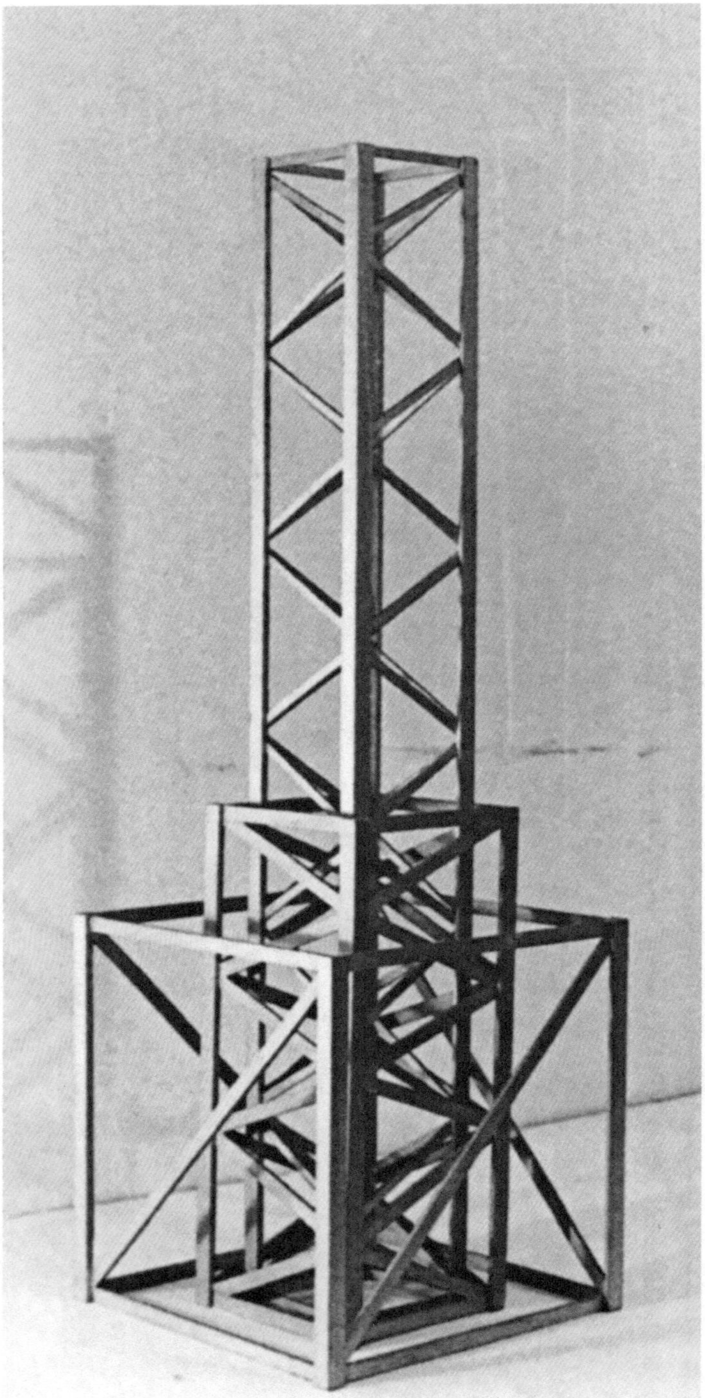

Untitled (B), 1968
emulsion on wood, 51 x 76 x 274 cm, destroyed

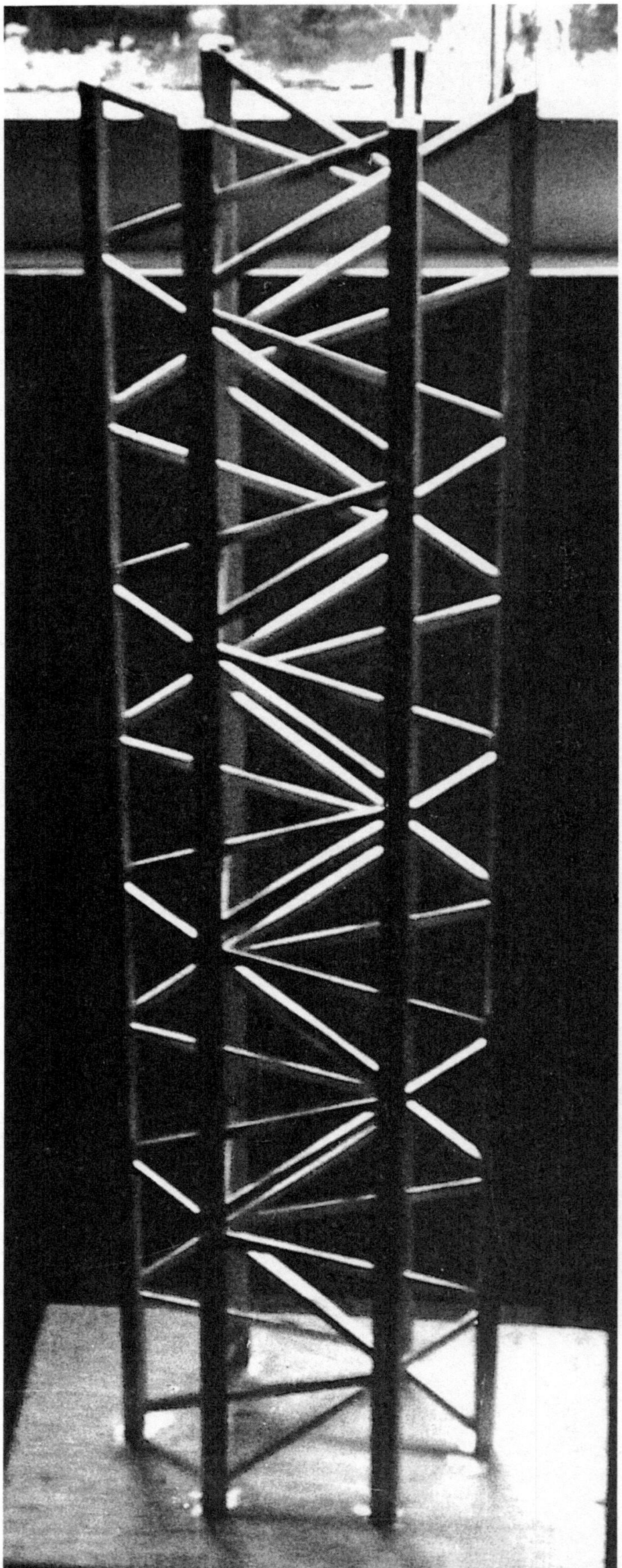

SR One, 1968
acrylic on wood, 122 x 64 x 13 cm, destroyed
Untitled, 1968
emulsion on wood, dimensions unknown, destroyed

SR Two, 1968
acrylic on wood, 122 x 76 x 13 cm, destroyed

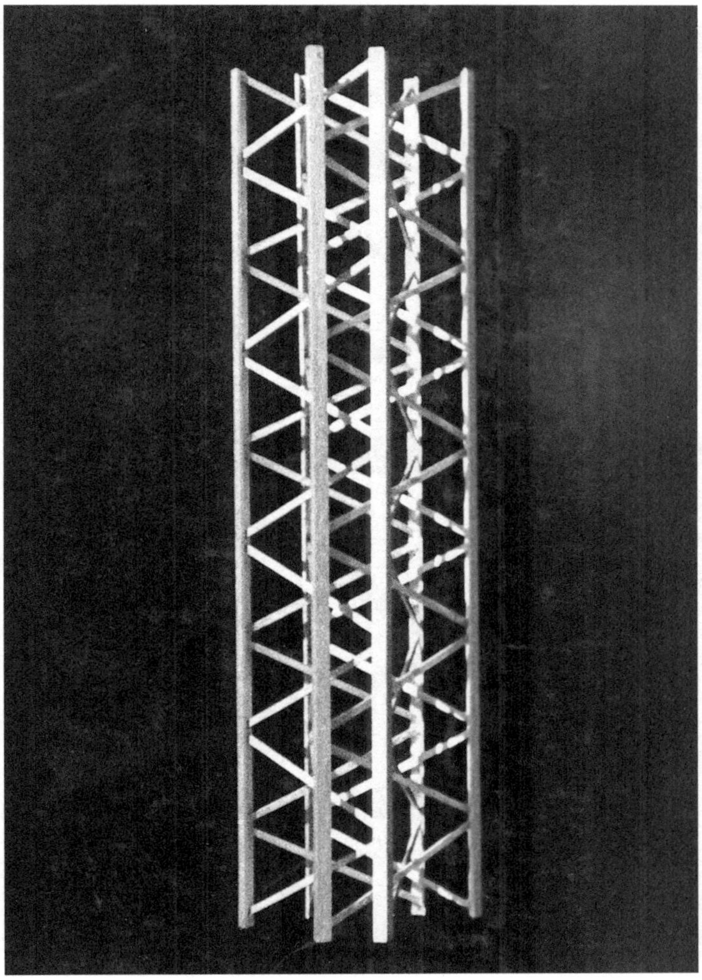

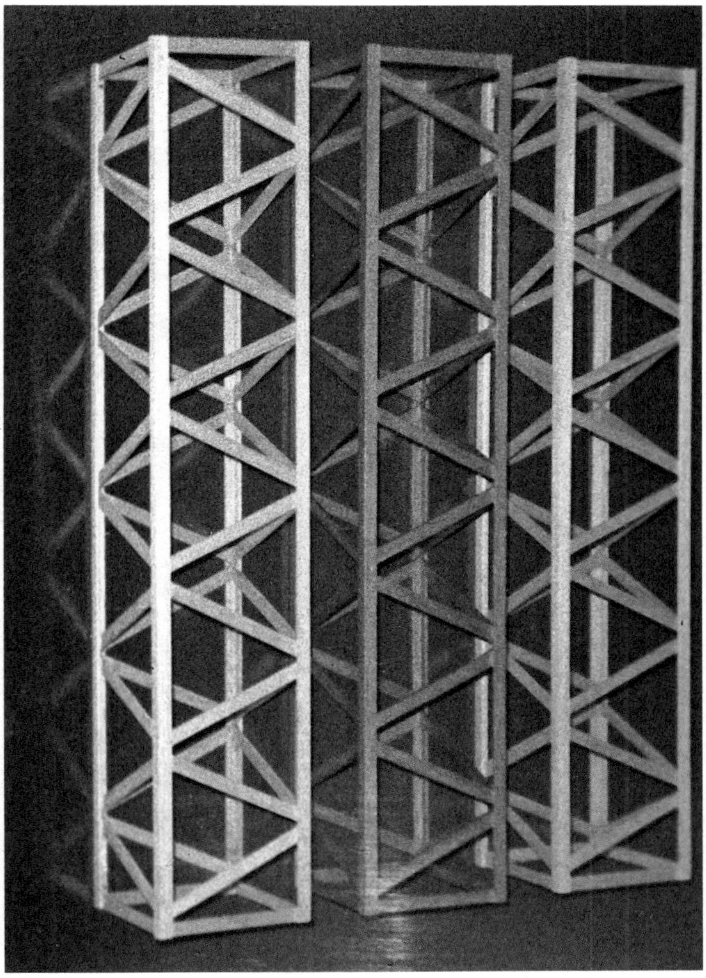

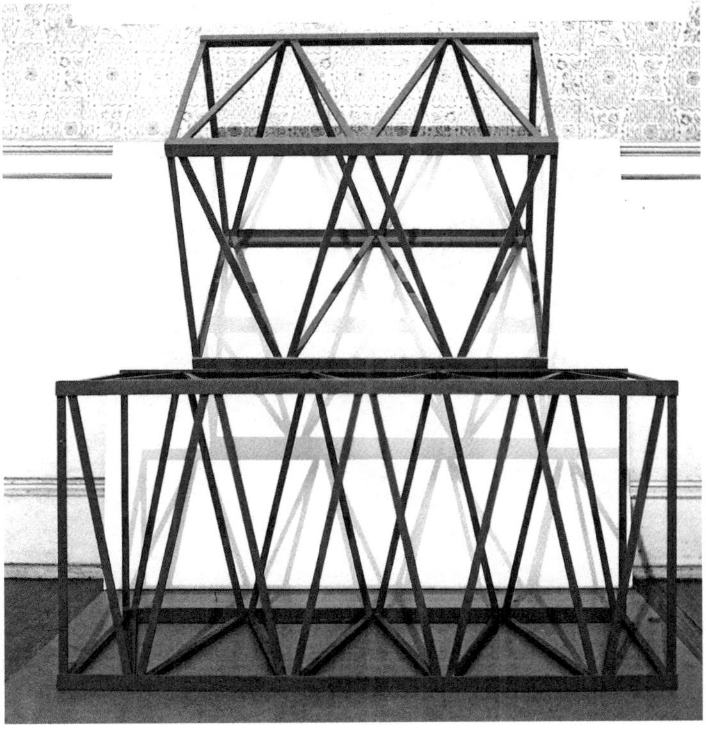

Blue Structure, 1968
emulsion on wood, 89 x 89 x 183 cm, destroyed

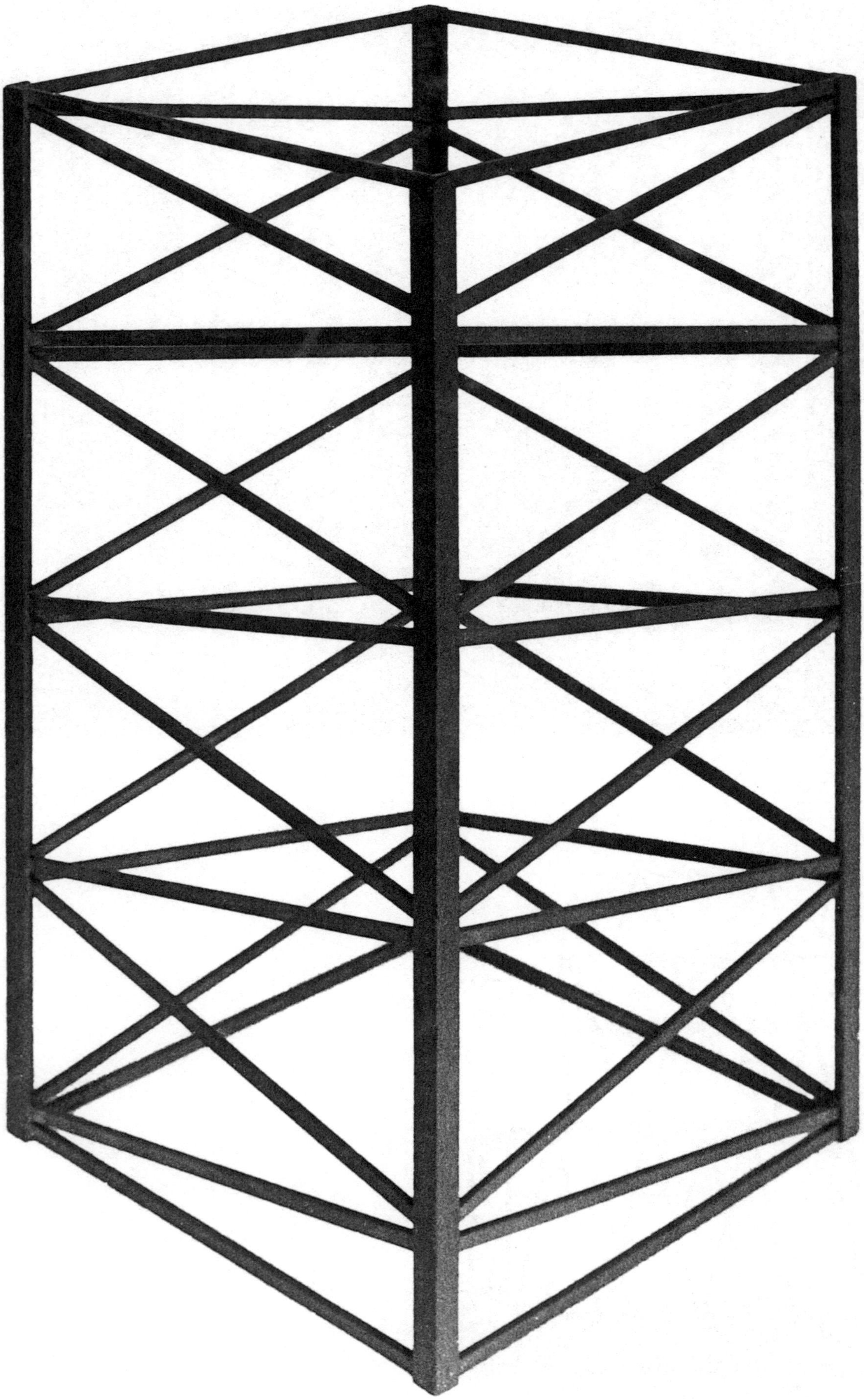

Red Structure B, 1968
emulsion on wood, 89 x 89 x 132 cm, destroyed

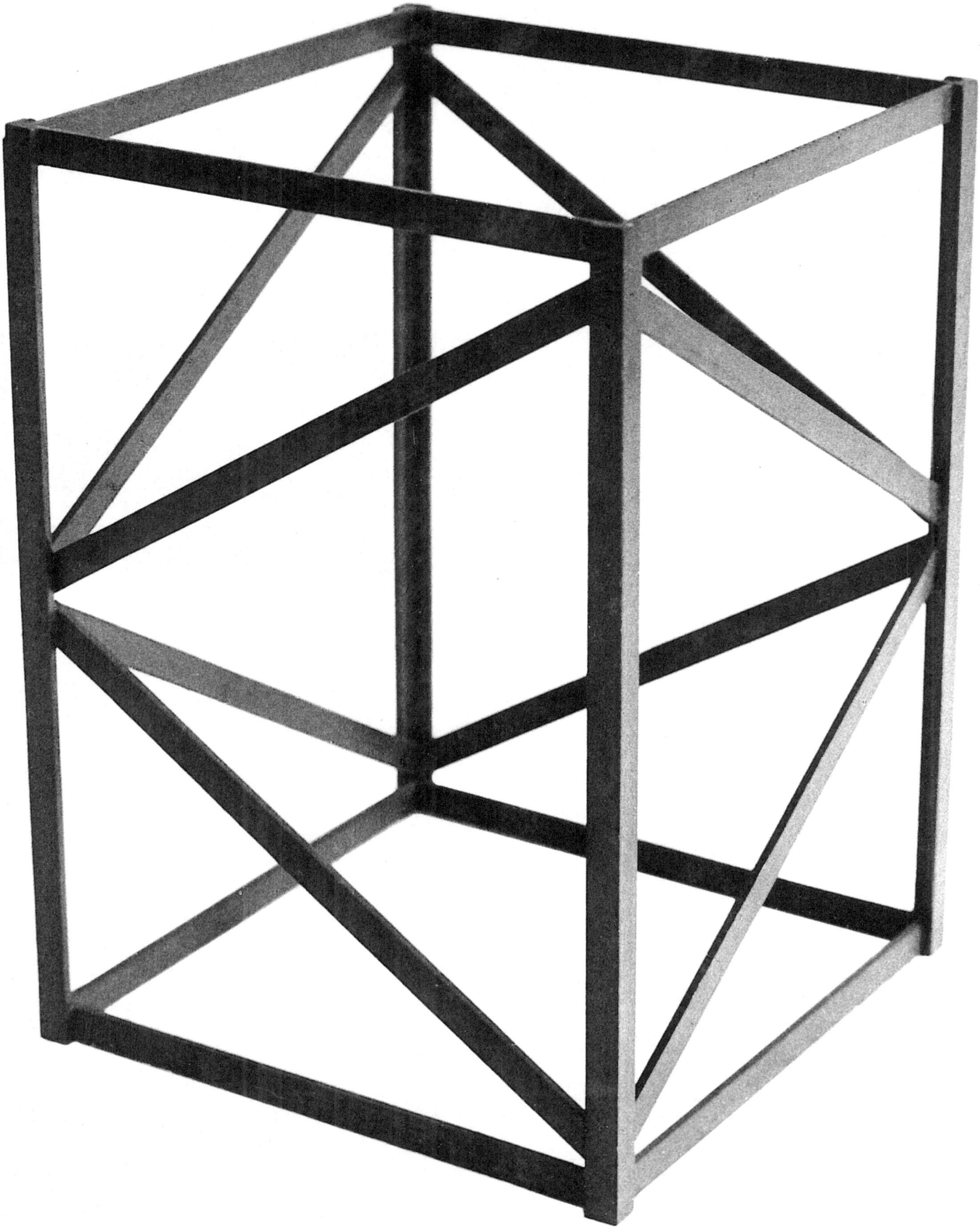

One Summer Afternoon, 1968
6 acrylic on wood Structures, various dimensions
Centre Pompidou Collection
Blues Four, 1968 / 2004,
4 acrylic on wood Structures, 50 x 50 x 50 cm each

Yellow Structure, 1968
emulsion on wood, 142 x 142 x 152 cm, destroyed
Chaar Pellay, 1968 / 2017
4 acrylic on wood Structures, 61 x 61 x 61 cm each

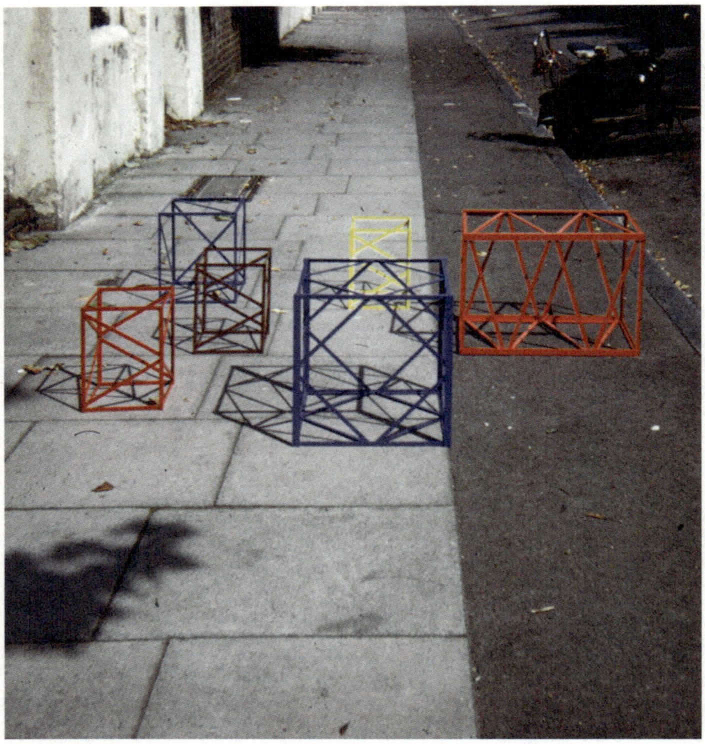

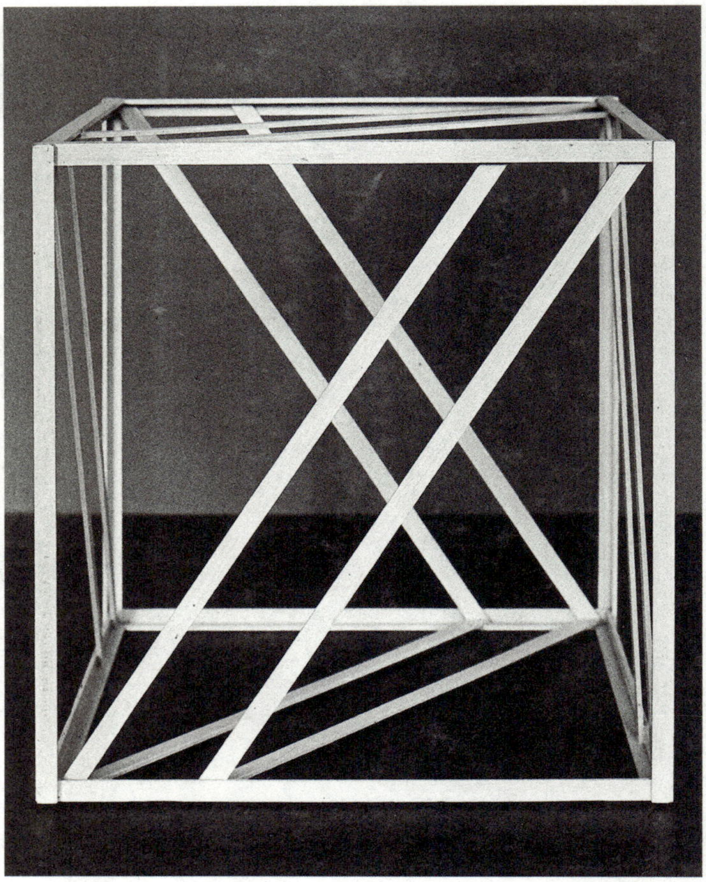

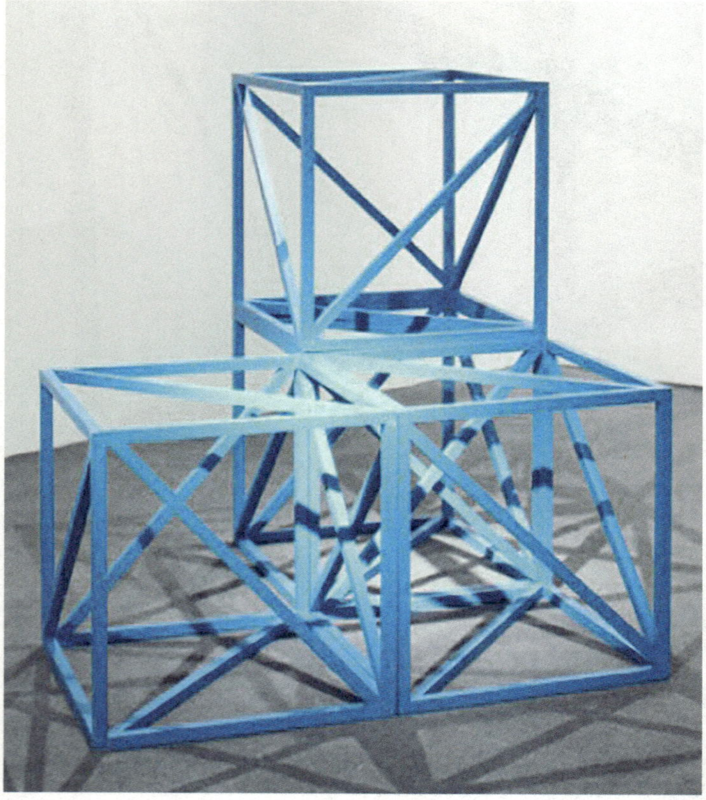

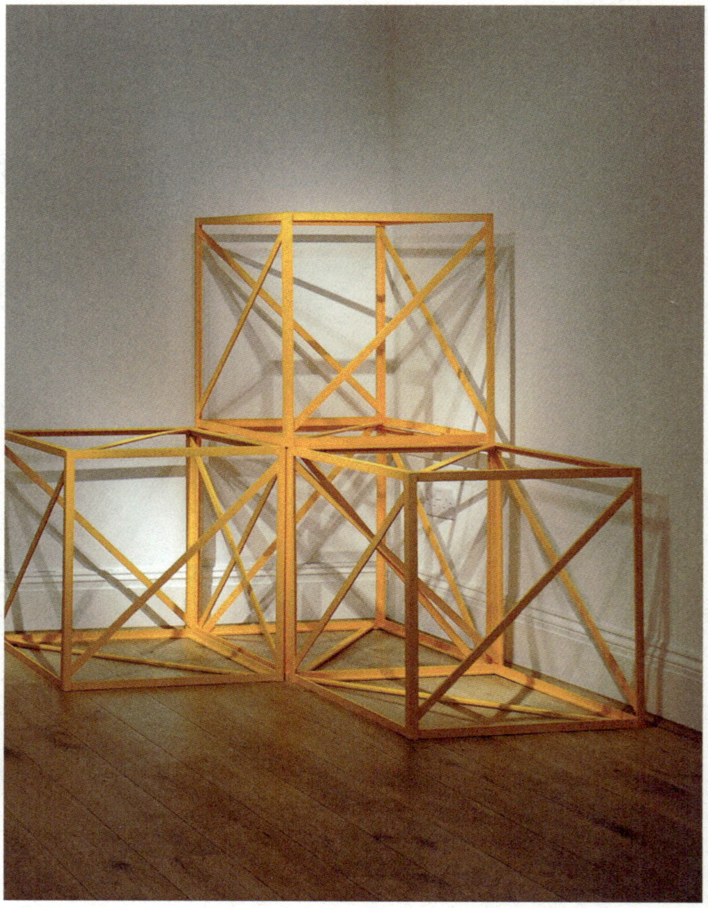

Chaar Yaar, 1968
4 emulsion on wood Structures, 23 x 23 x 23 cm each

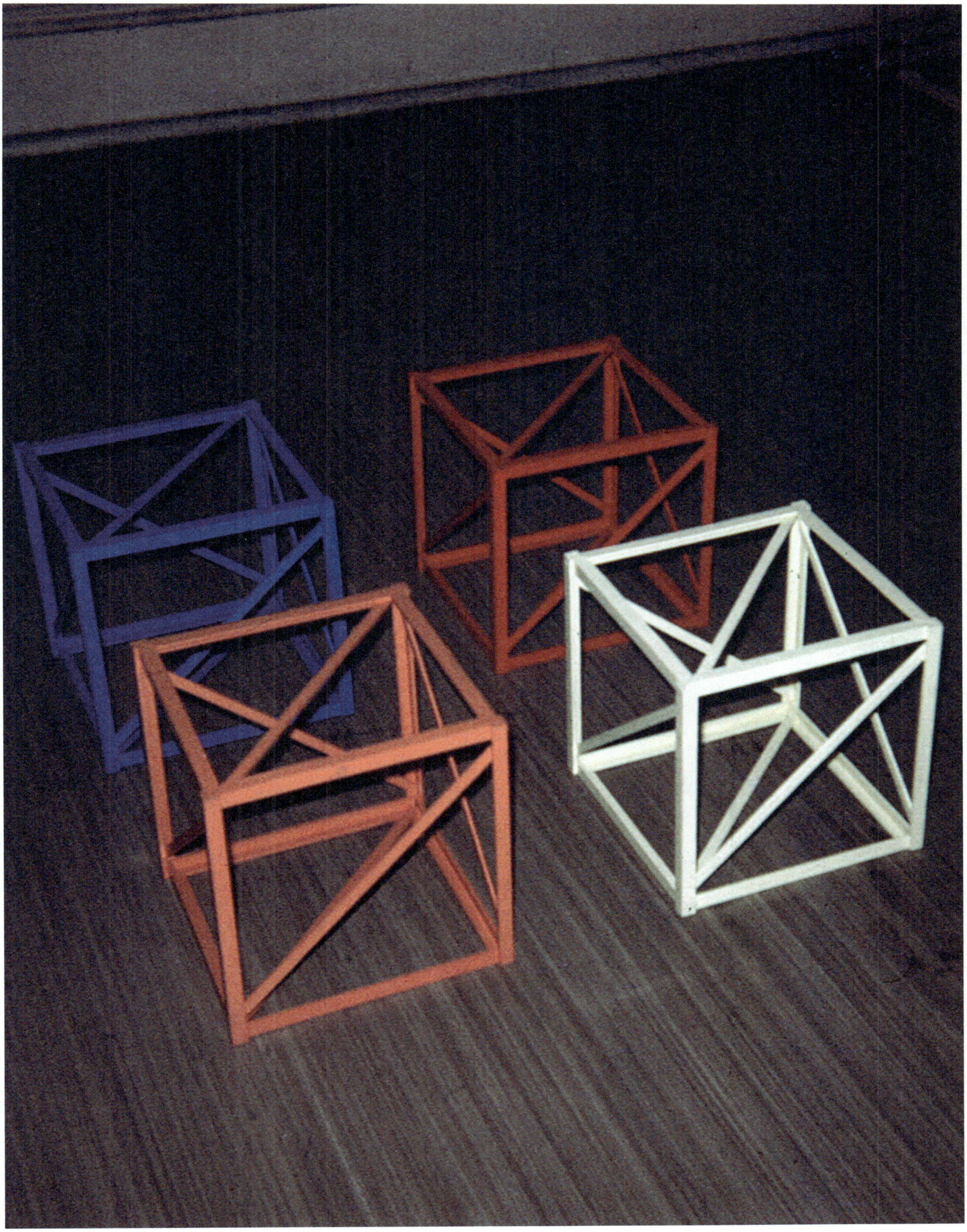

Chaar Yaar I (Four Friends), 1968 / 2014
4 acrylic on wood Structures, 61 x 61 x 61 cm each
The Art Gallery of New South Wales

Chaar Yaar II (Four Friends), 1968 / 2014
4 acrylic on wood Structures, 61 x 61 x 61 cm each
Metropolitan Museum, New York

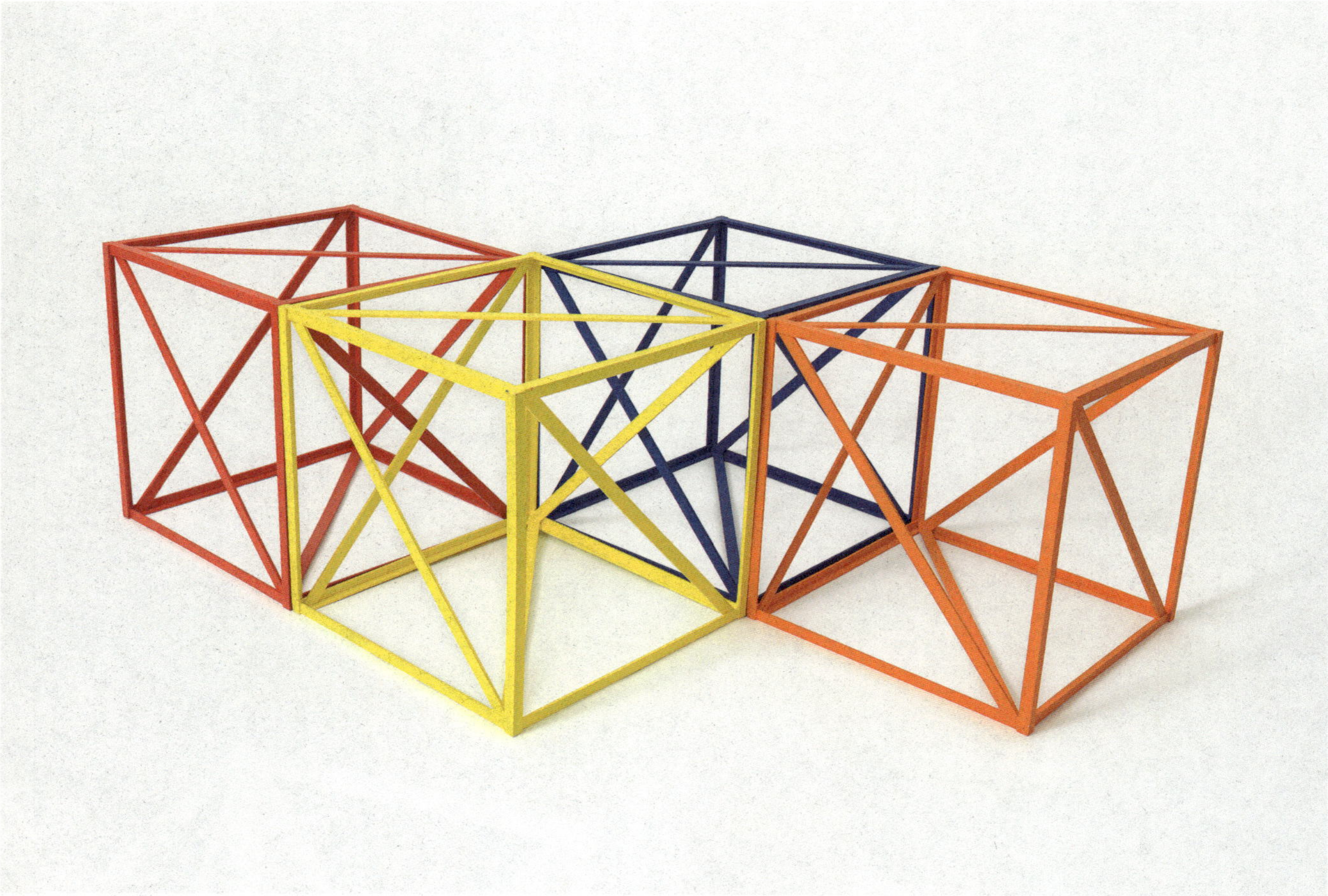

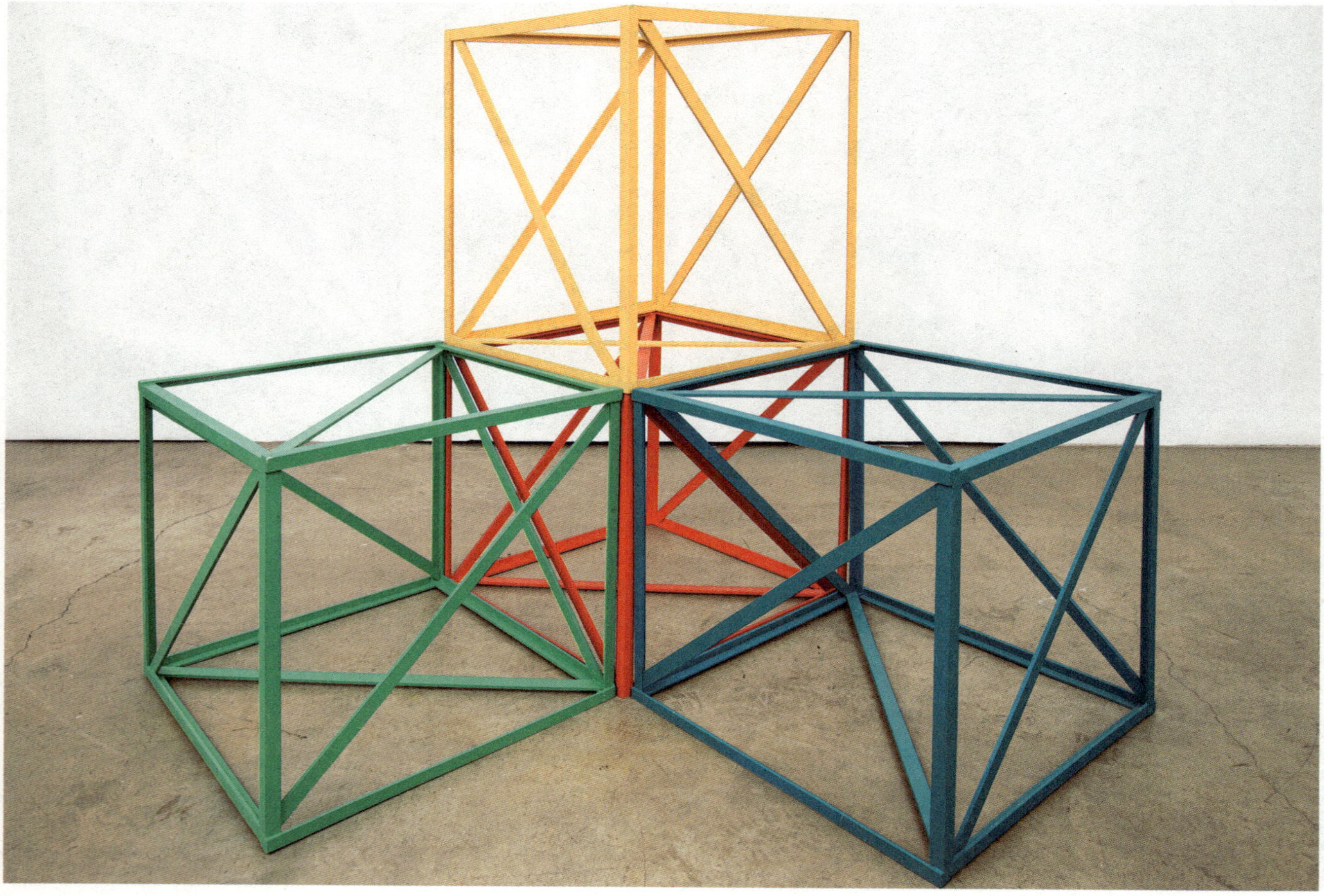

Mill Gaye Phir Chaaron Yaar (Have Met Again, Four Friends), 1968 / 2015
acrylic on wood, 88 x 256 x 183 cm
Burger Collection, Hong Kong

Milaap, 1968 / 2016
acrylic on wood, 81 x 173 x 81 cm

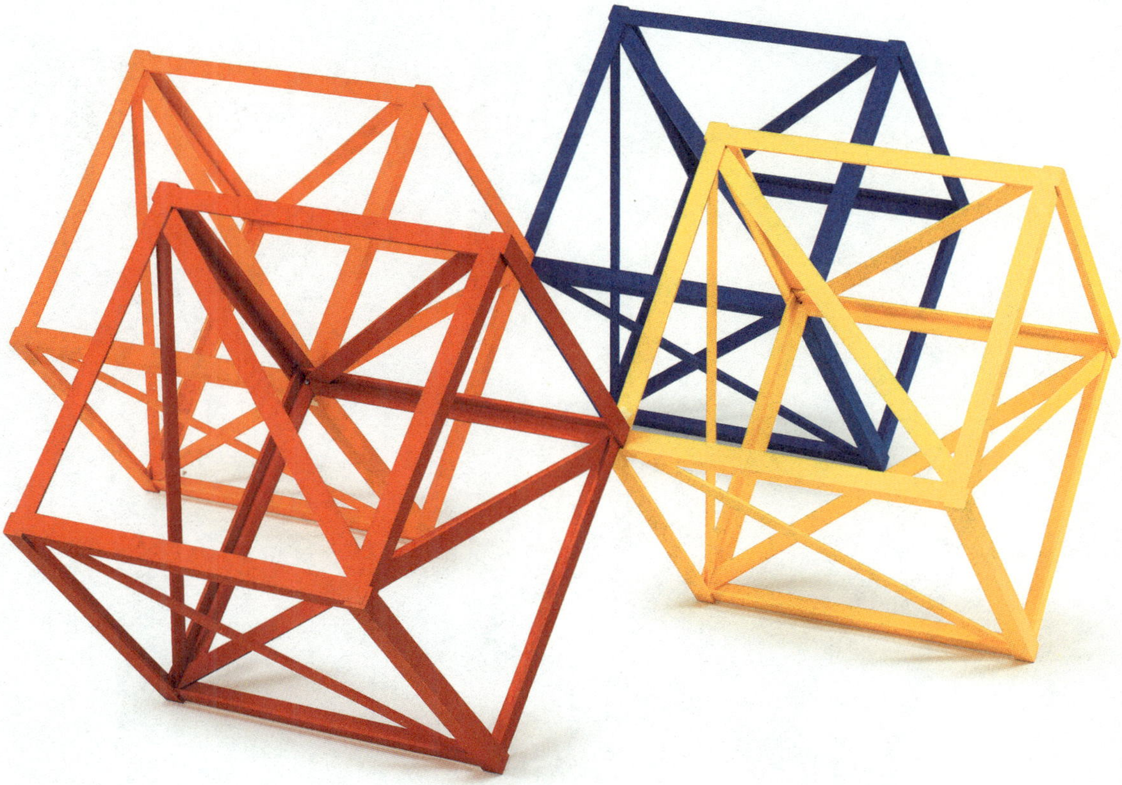

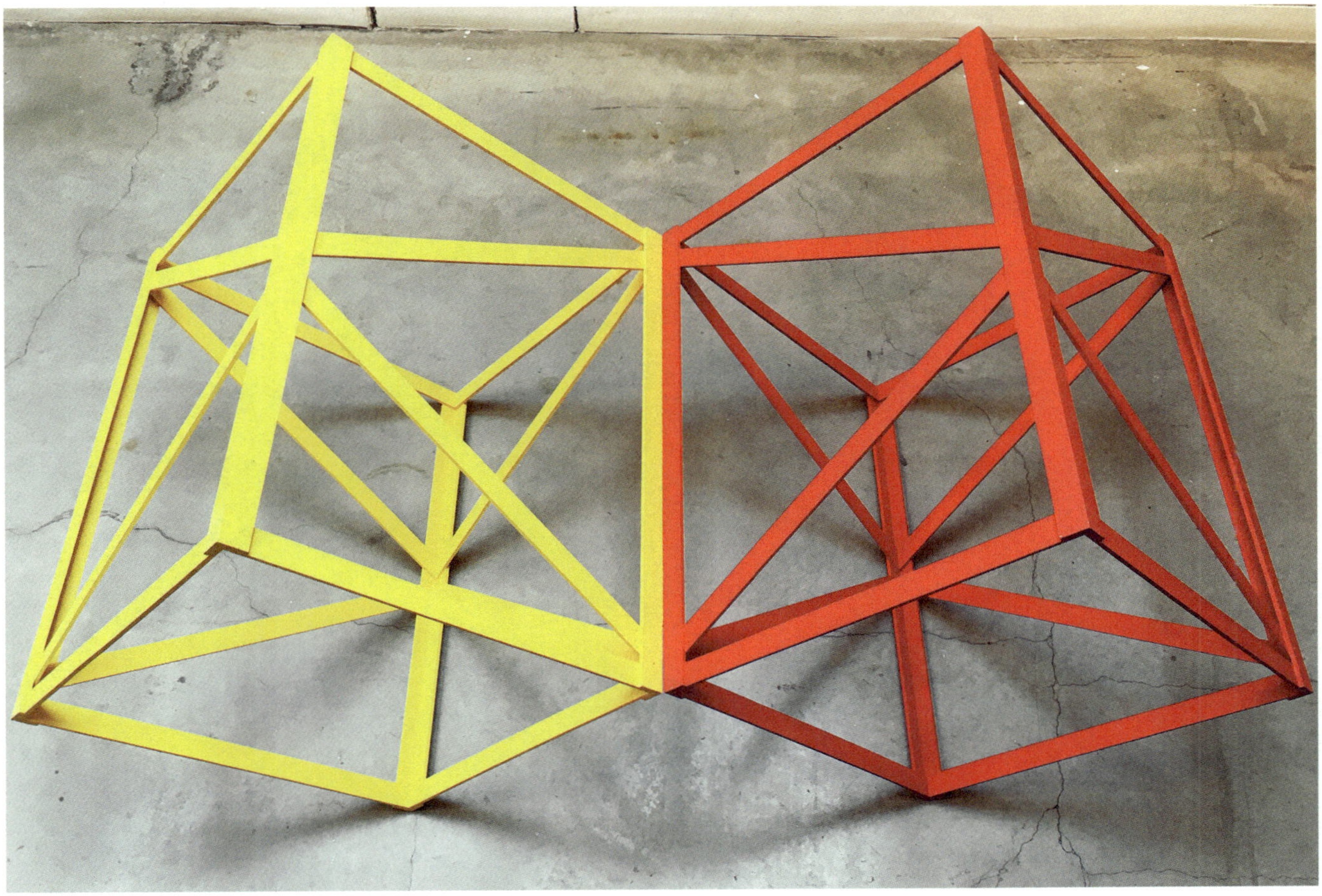

Nine, 1968–1975 / 1987 / 2016
9 acrylic on wood Structures, 61 x 61 x 61 cm each

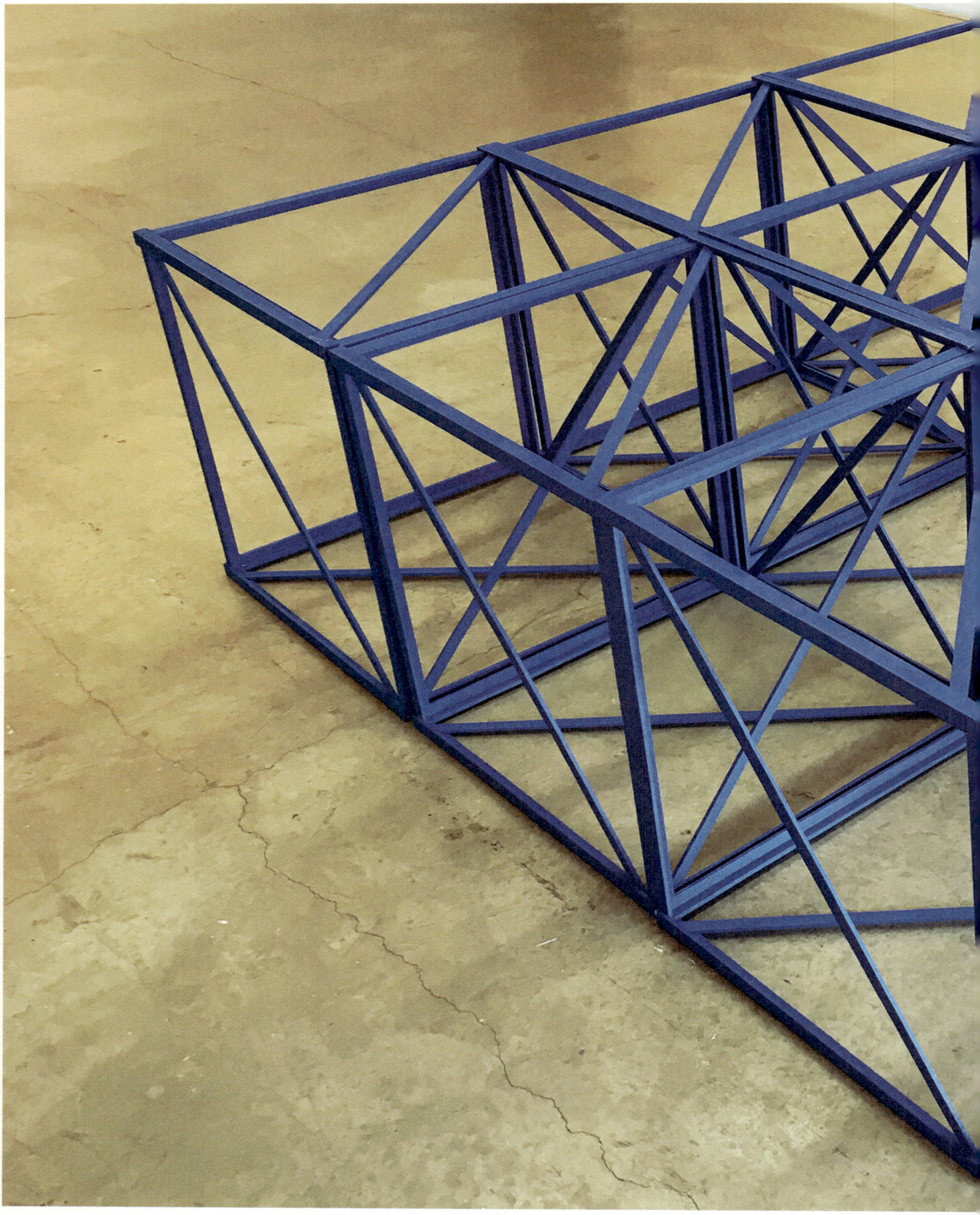

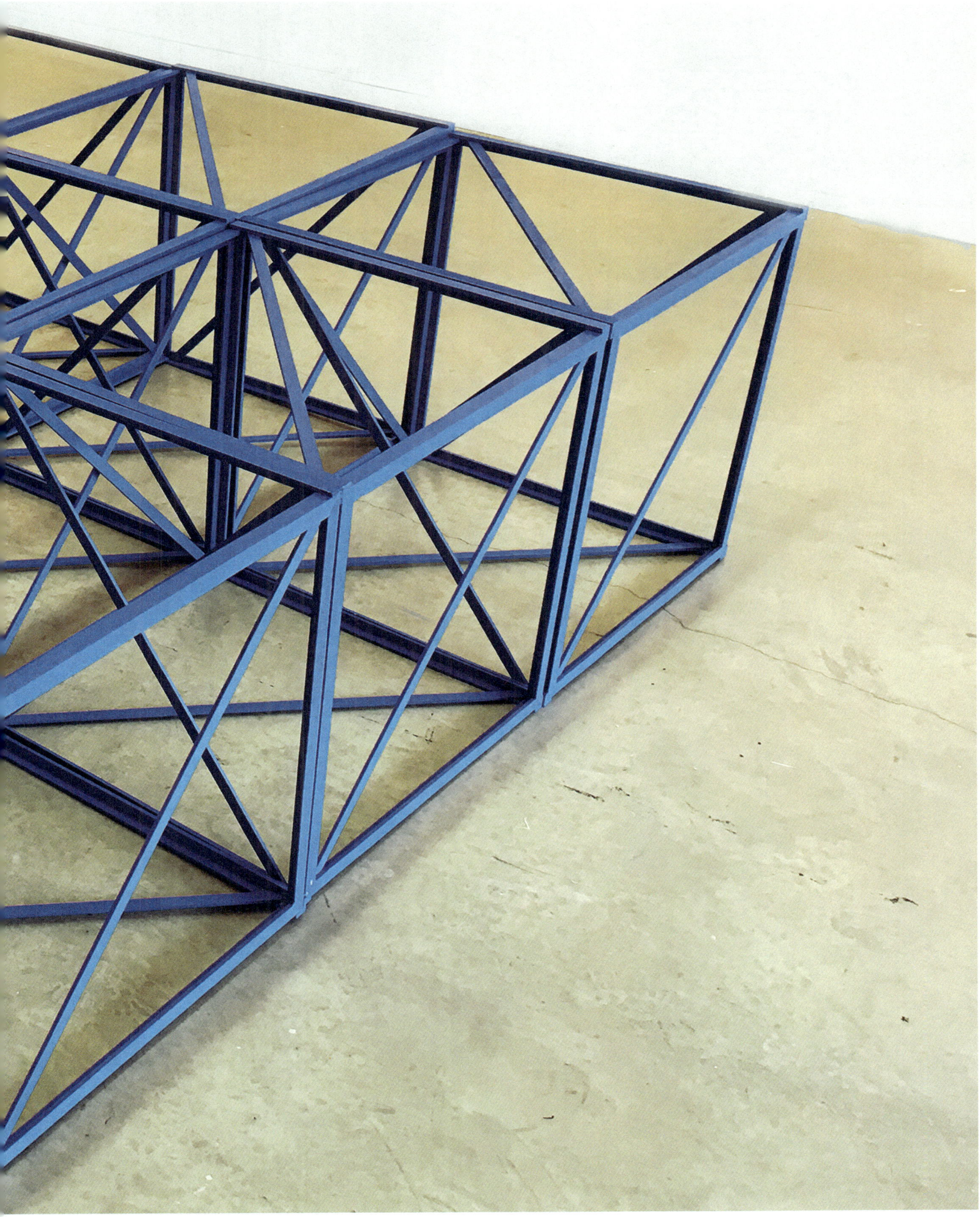

Nine Minus One, 1968–1975
8 acrylic on wood Structures, 61 x 61 x 61 cm each

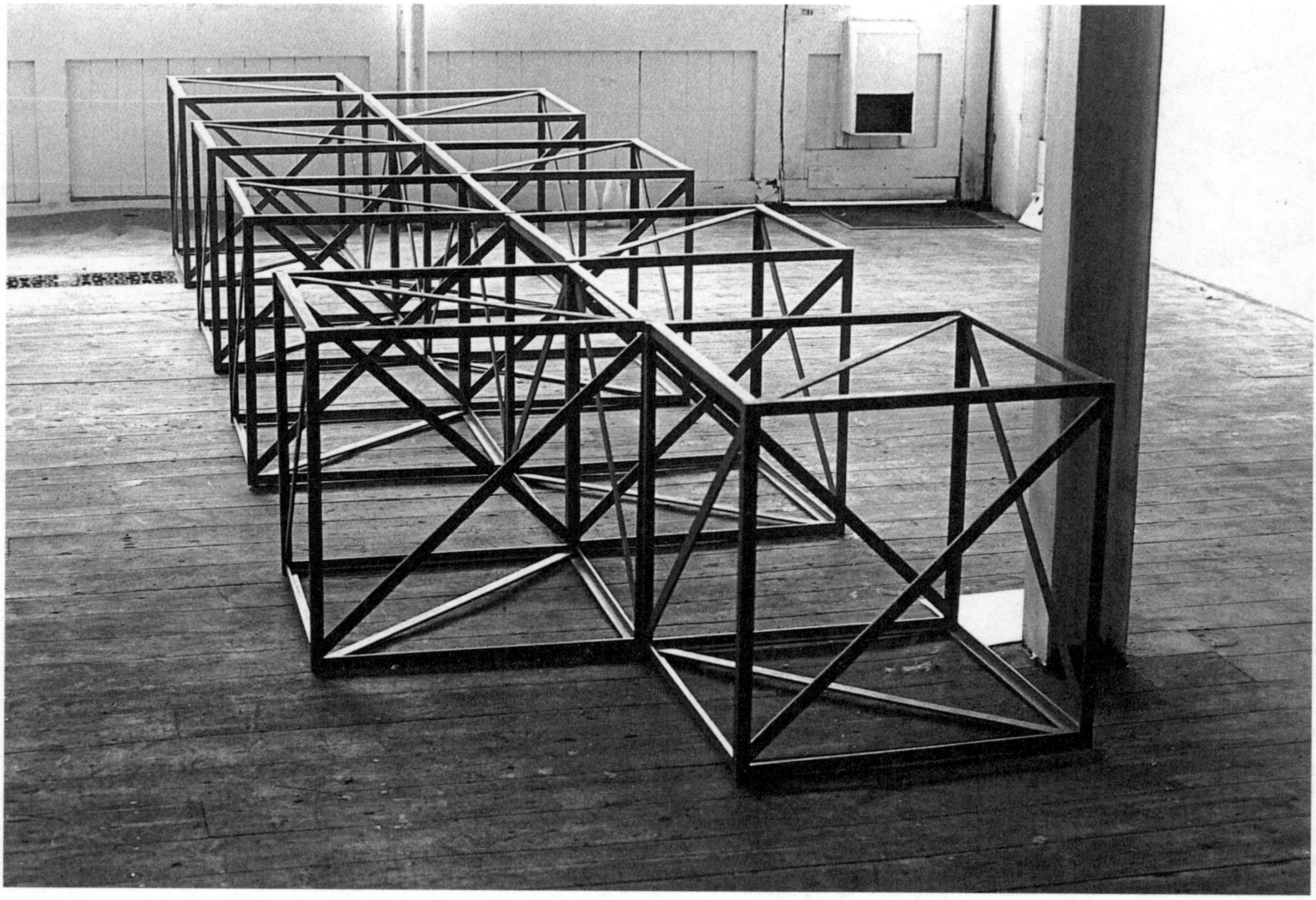

Lovers, 1968
acrylic on wood, 92 x 92 x 92 cm
Tate: Presented by Tate Members 2011

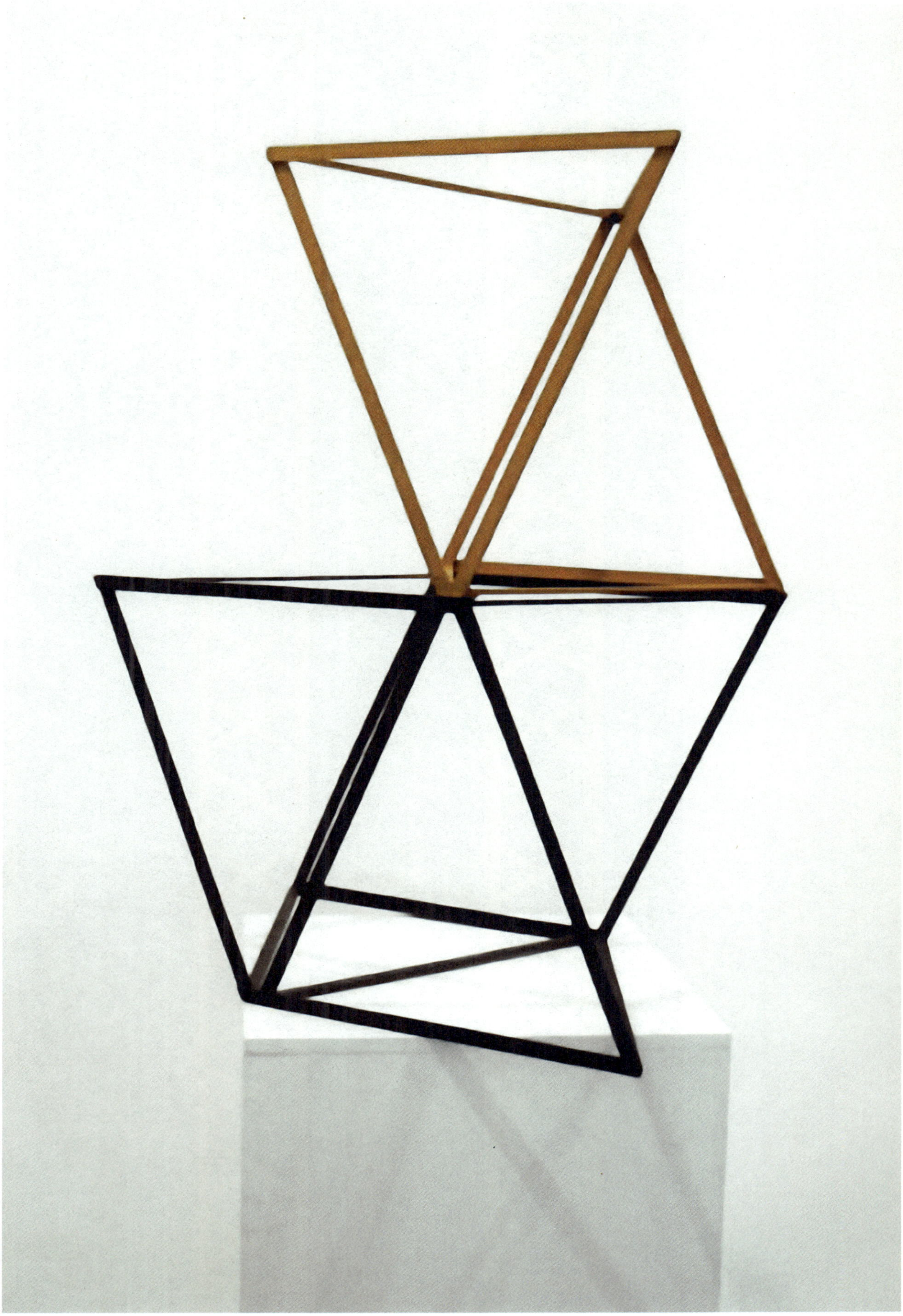

3Y + 3B, 1968–1969
acrylic on metal and wood, 183 x 244 x 14 cm
Tate: Purchased 2007

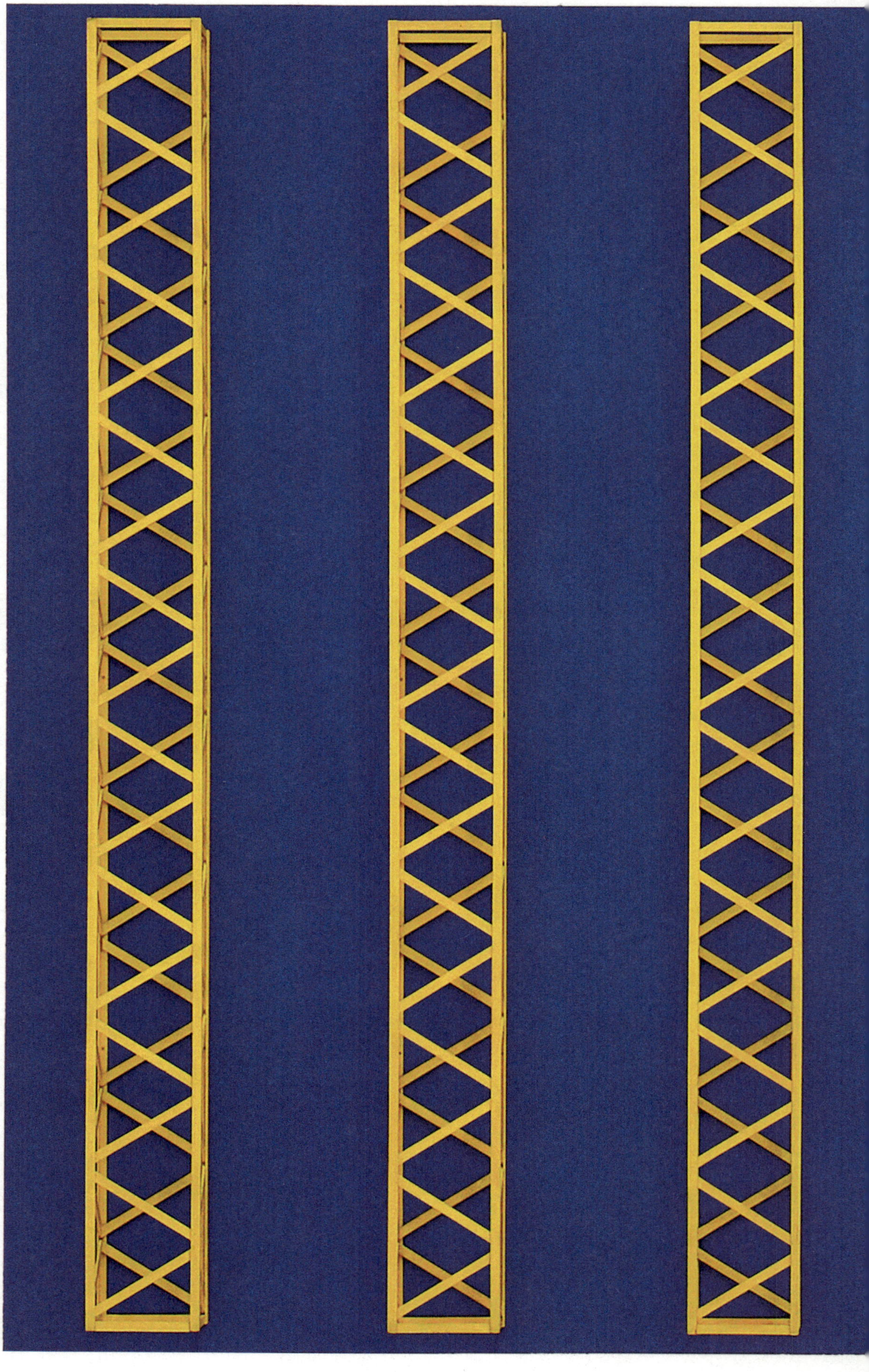

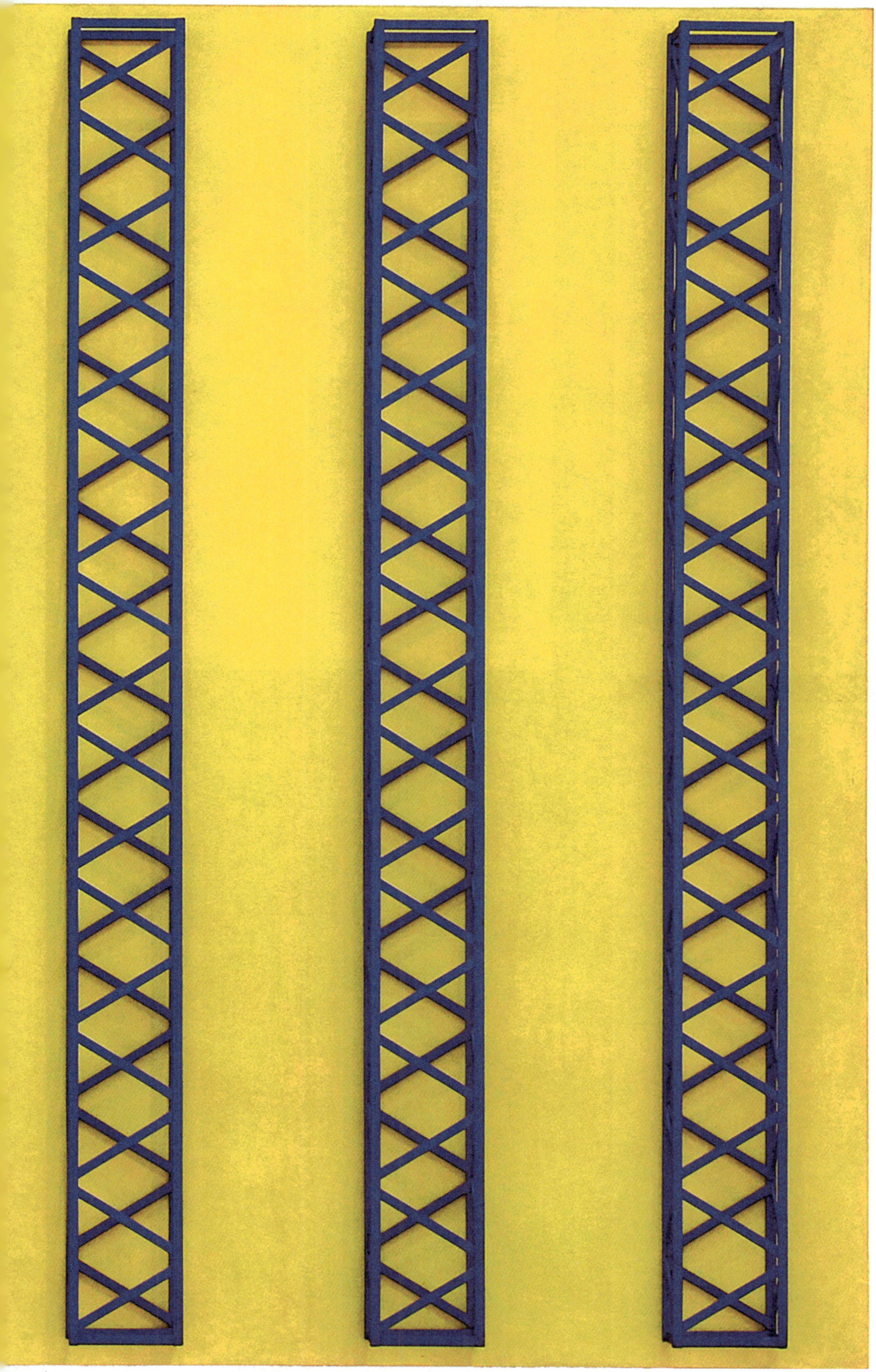

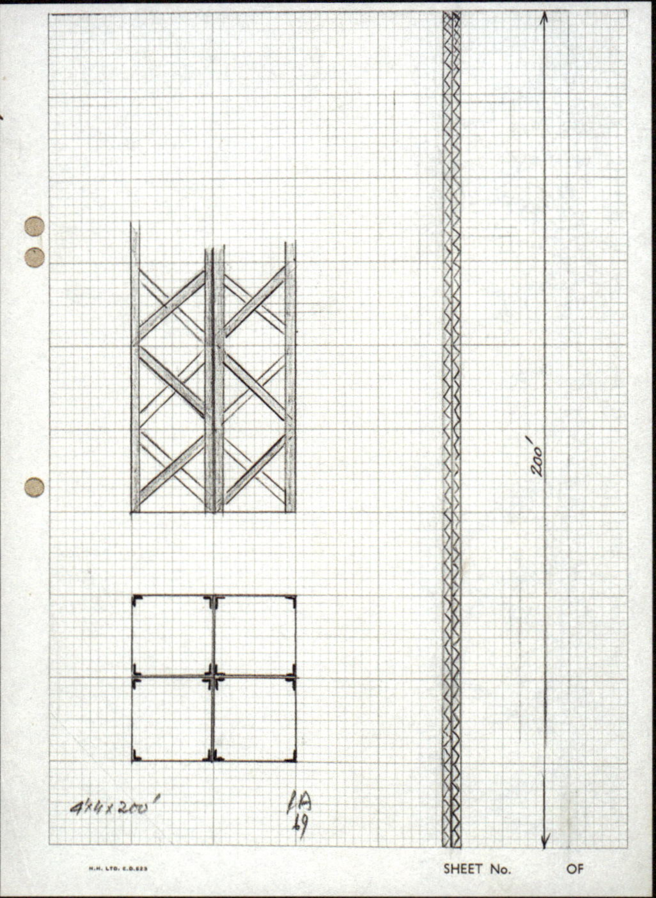
200'
4x4x200'
AA
69
SHEET No.
OF

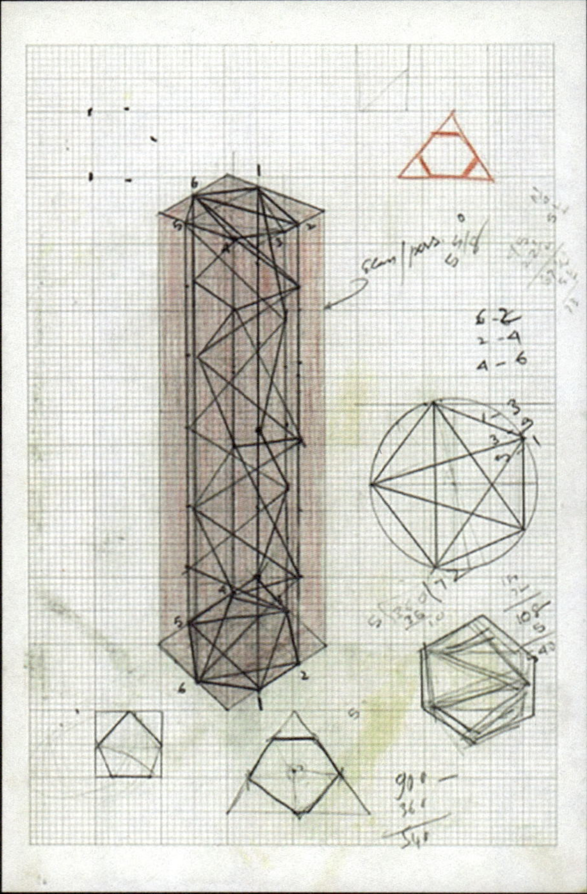
6-2
2-4
4-6

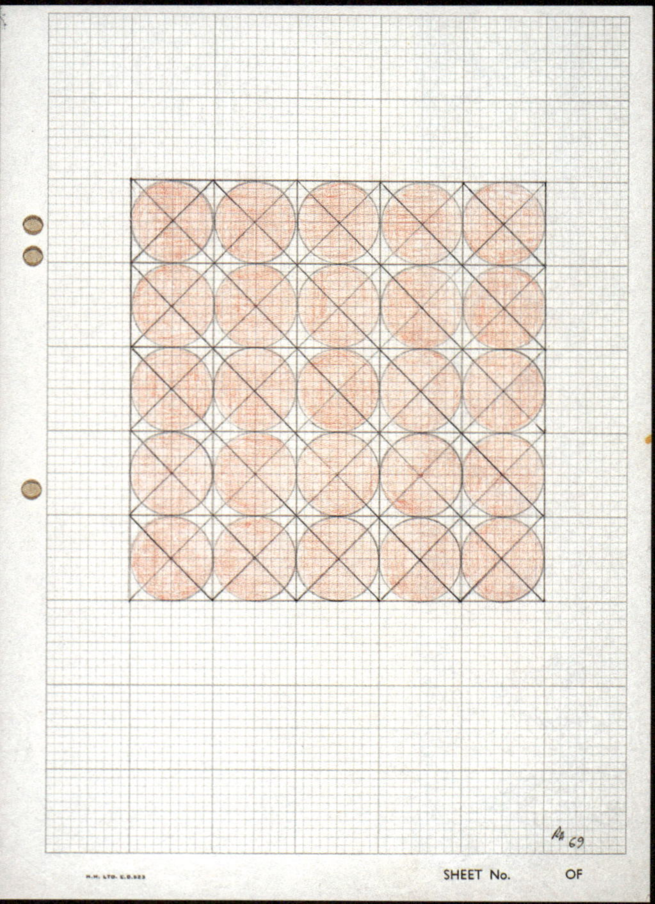
AA 69
SHEET No.
OF

Lal Kona, 1969
acrylic on wood, 145 x 31 x 31 cm
Collection Amrita Jhavery

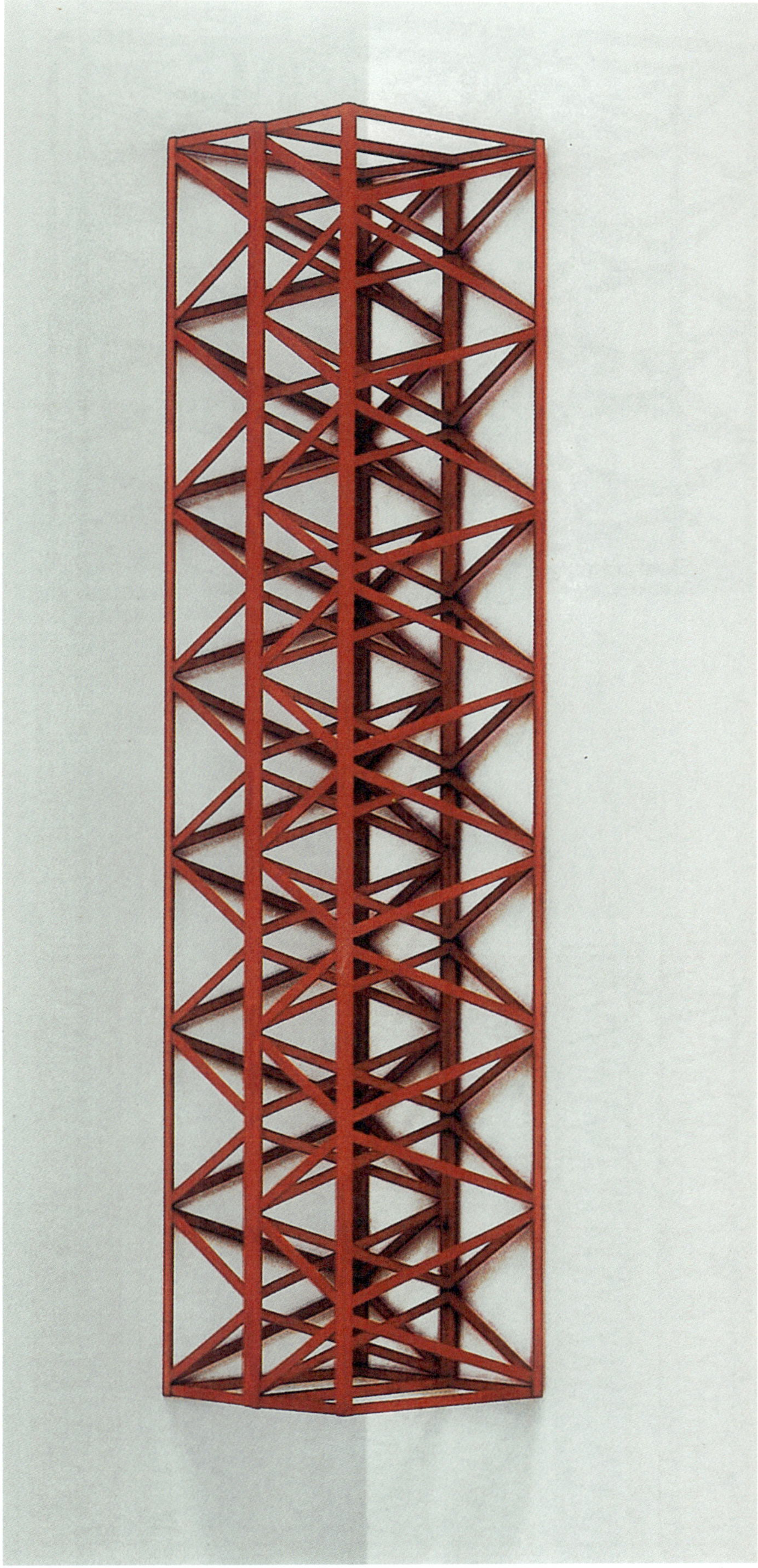

3PS, 1969
acrylic on wood, 140 x 107 x 31 cm
(3 + 4) SR, 1969
acrylic on wood, 170 x 221 x 10 cm

Twins, 1969
acrylic on wood, 61 x 145 x 15 cm

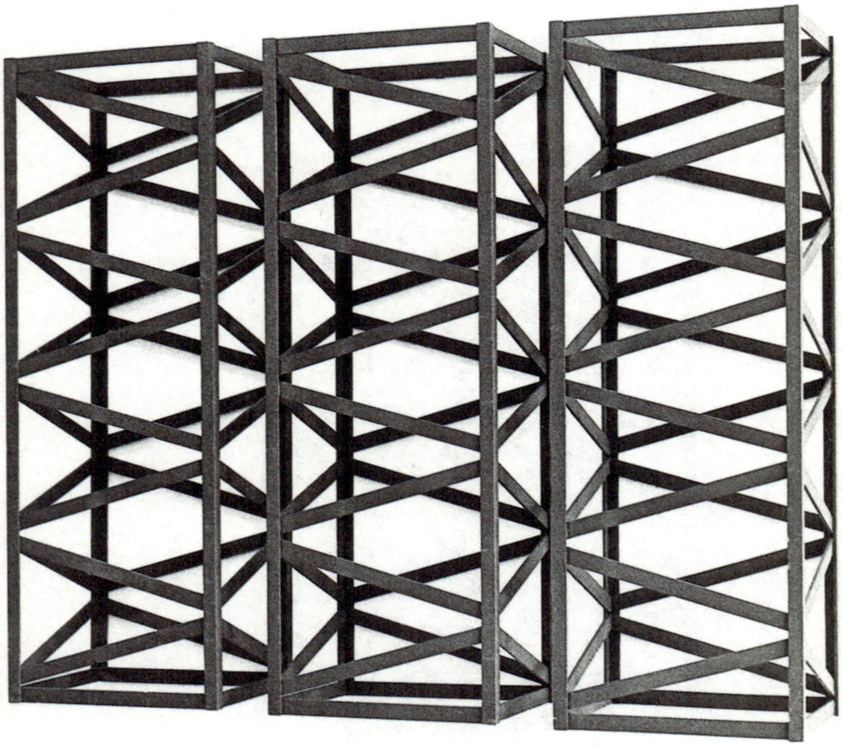

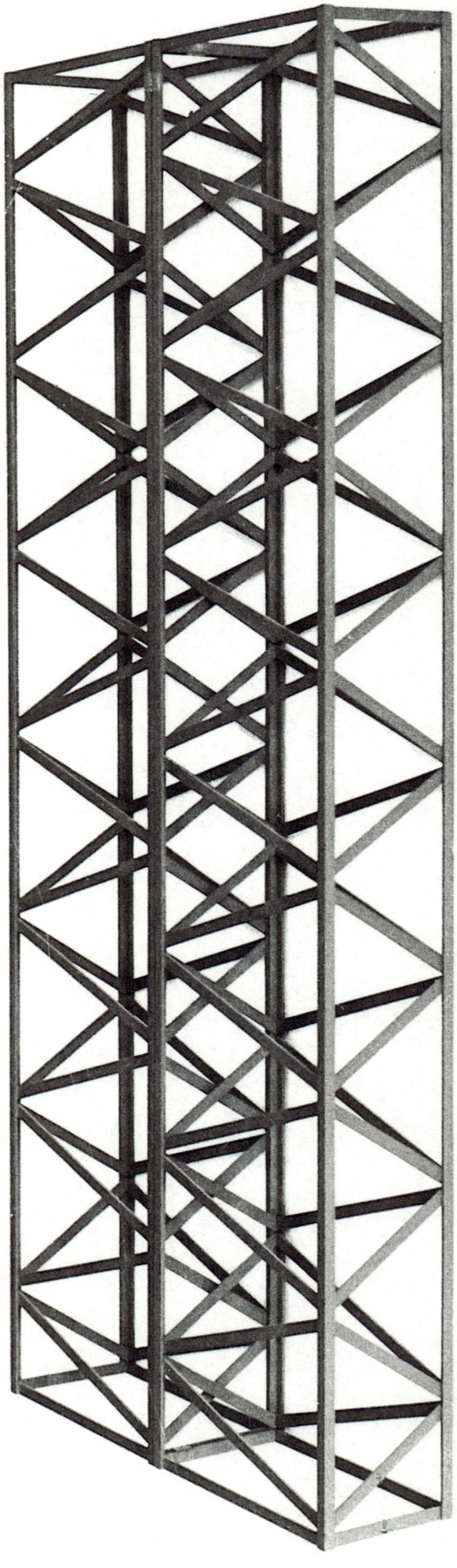

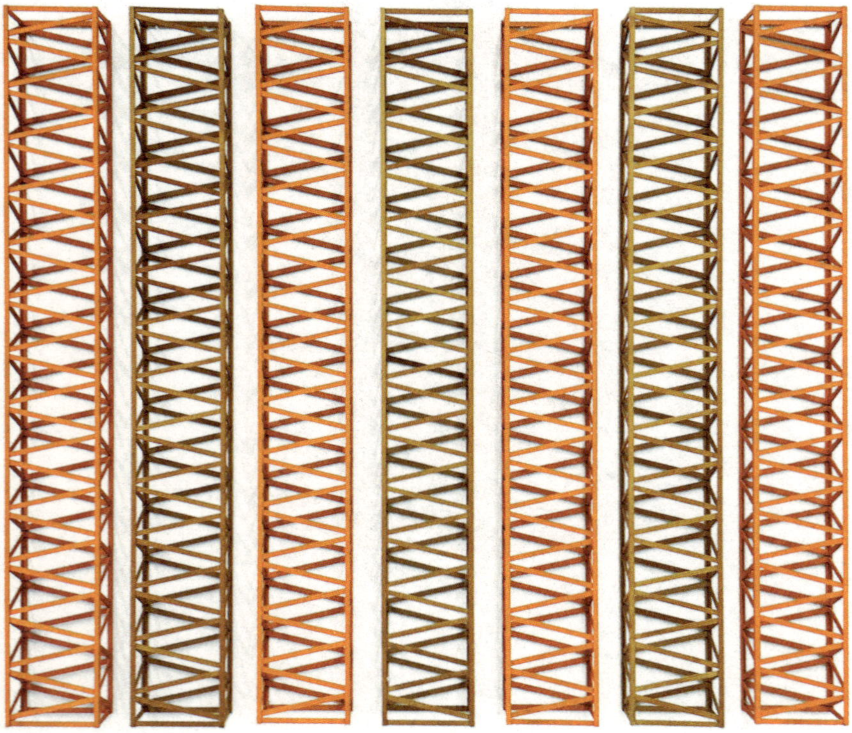

BoO, 1969
acrylic on wood, 122 x 183 x 13 cm
National Museums Liverpool, Walker Art Gallery

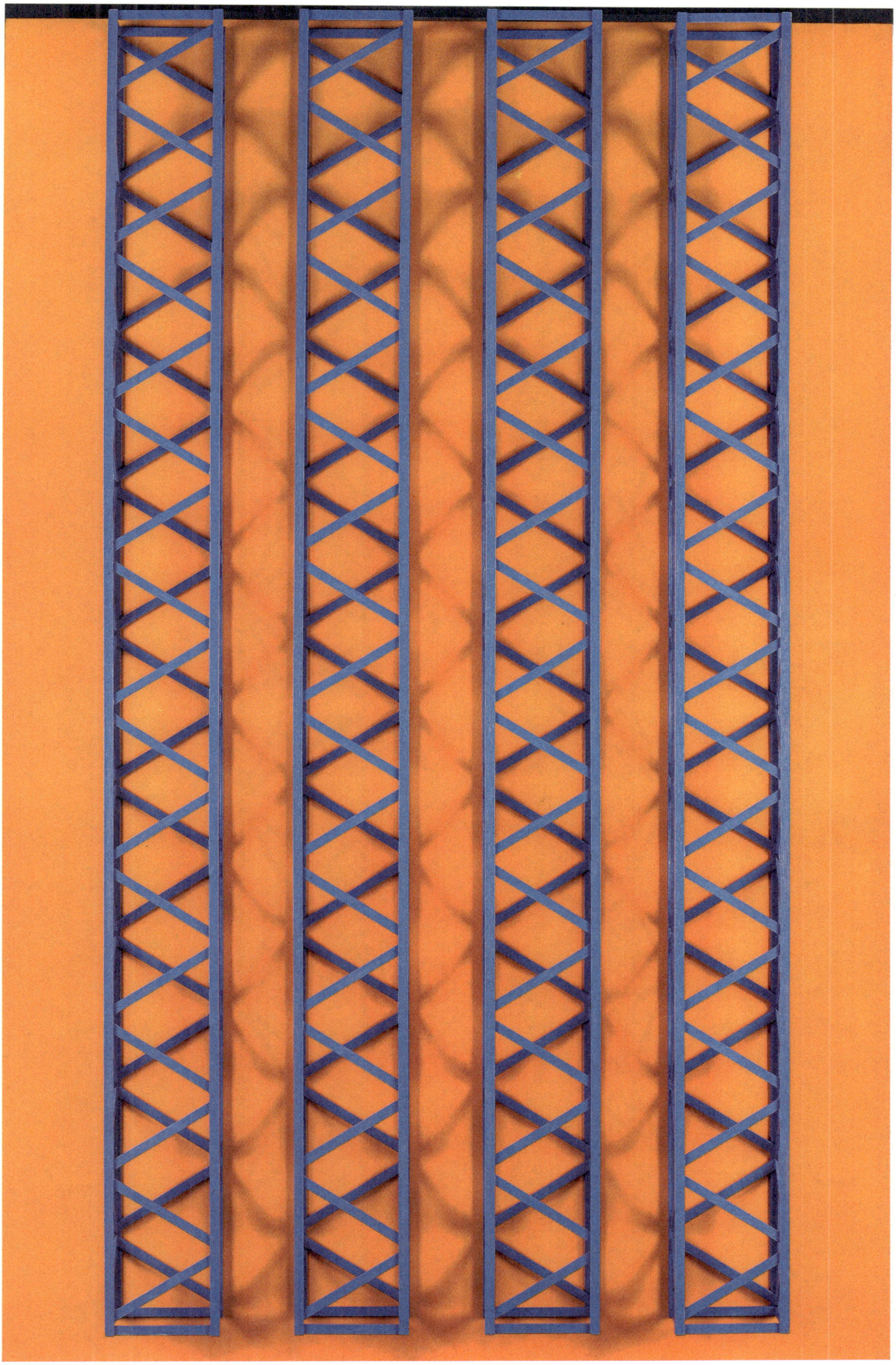

Rang Baranga I, 1969
acrylic on wood, 182 x 61 x 46 cm
Tate: Presented by Tate Members 2007

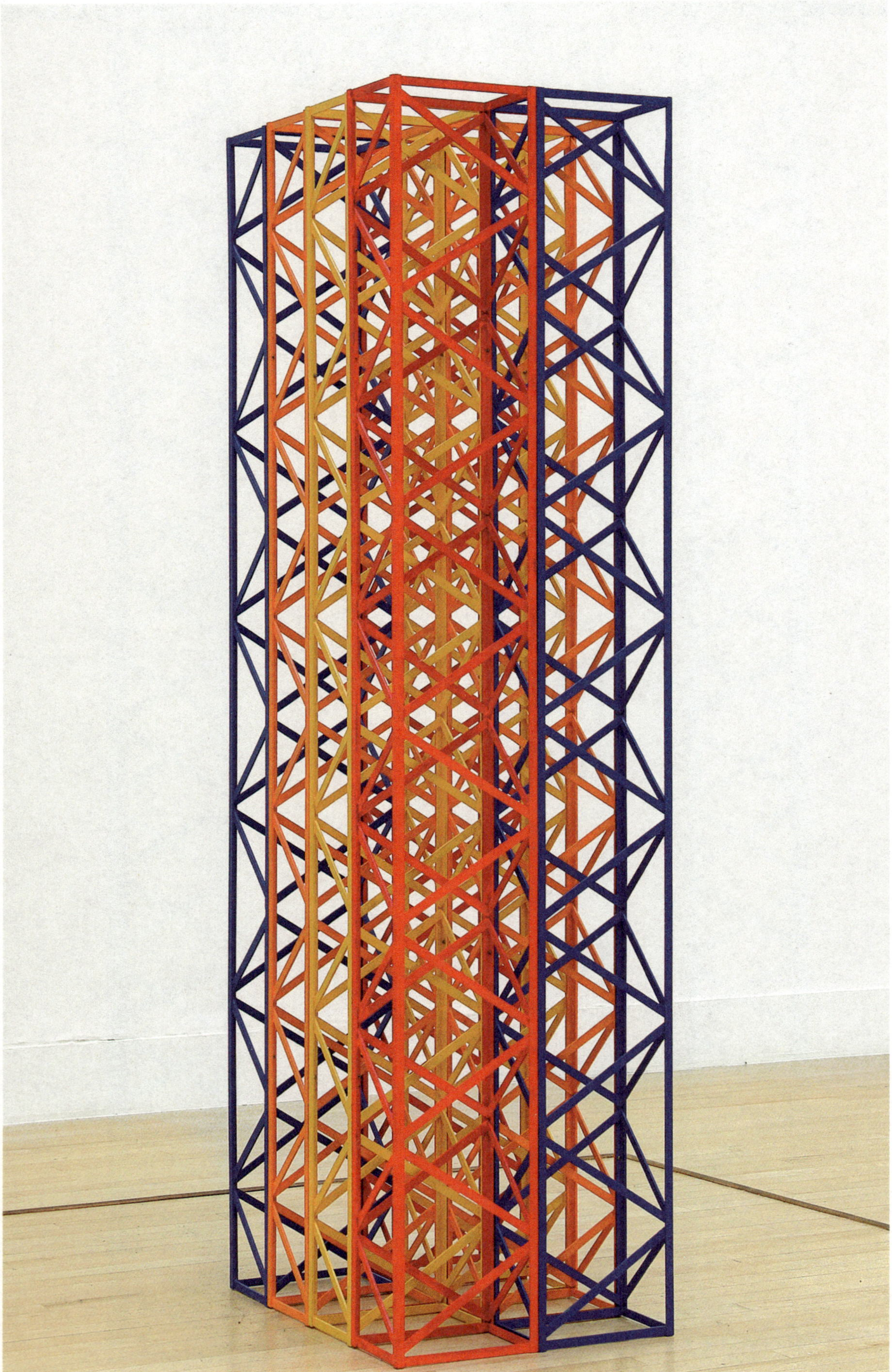

Rang Baranga II, 1969 / 2014
acrylic on wood, 182 x 61 x 46 cm
Kiran Nadar Museum of Art Collection

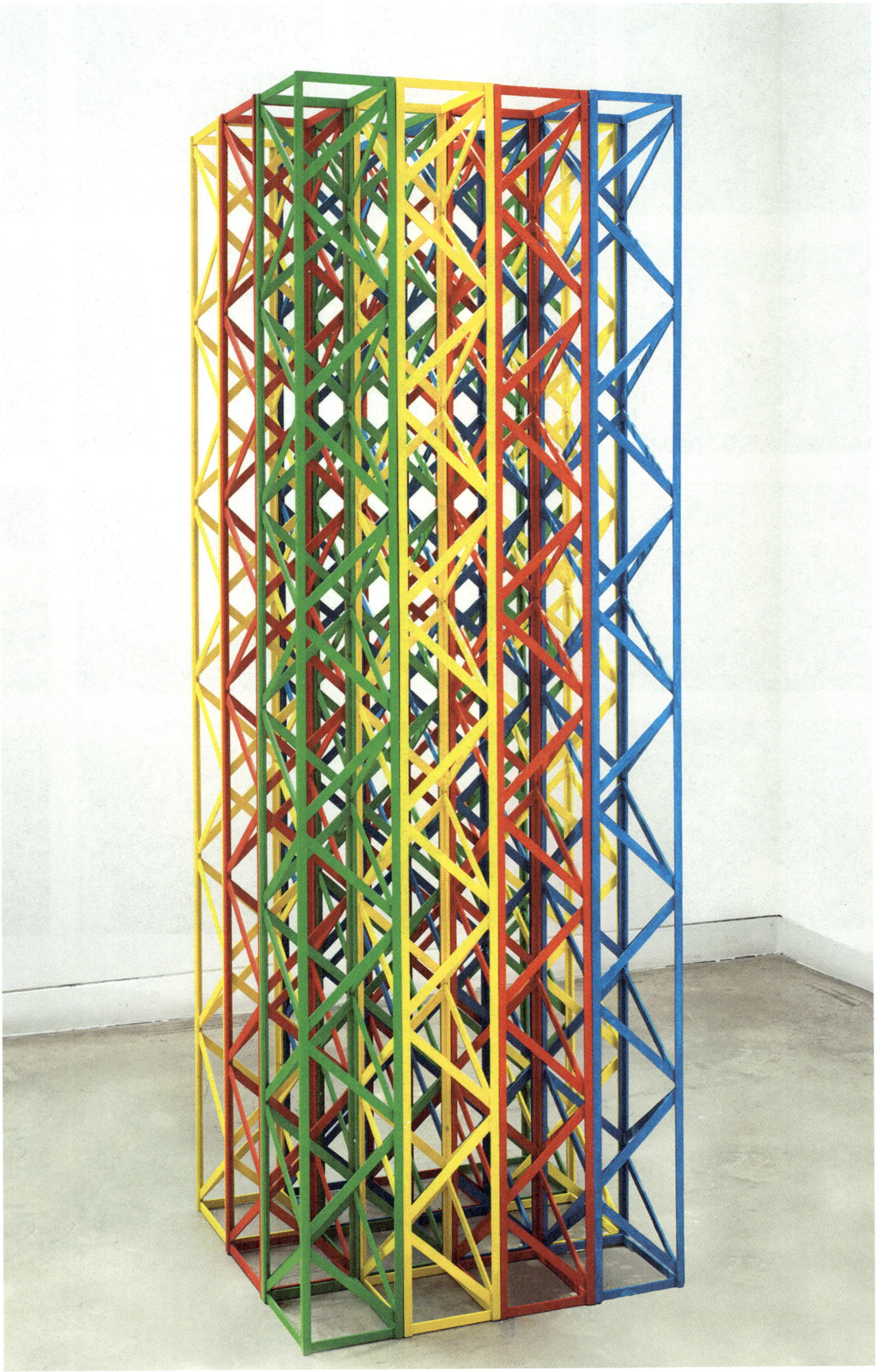

Chakras I (St. Katherine Docks), 1969–1970 / 1987
16 wood discs and 16 photographs, dimensions variable
Guggenheim Abu Dhabi

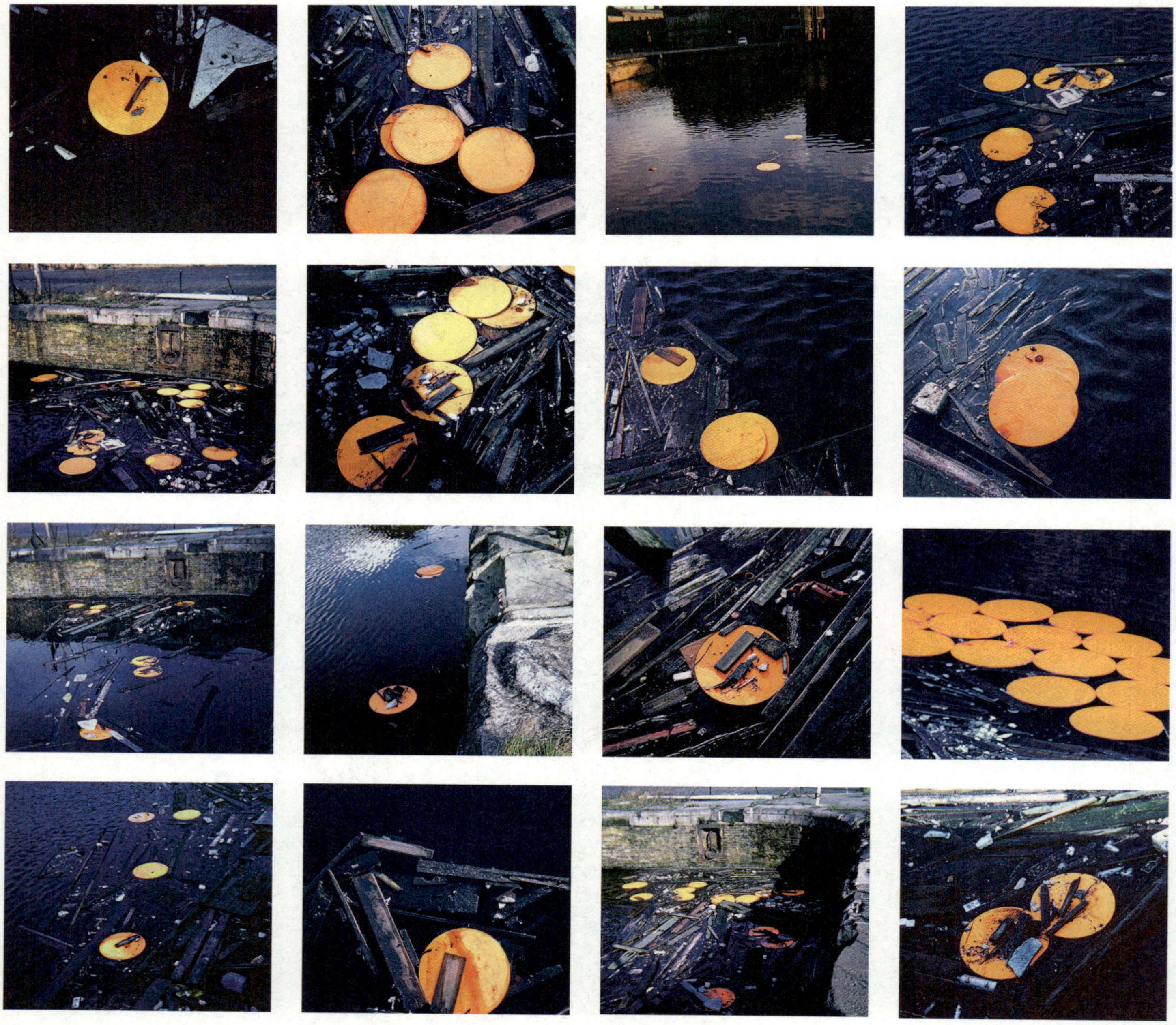

White Discs (Chakras II, Black Heath), 1969–1970
16 polystyrene discs and 16 photographs
dimensions variable

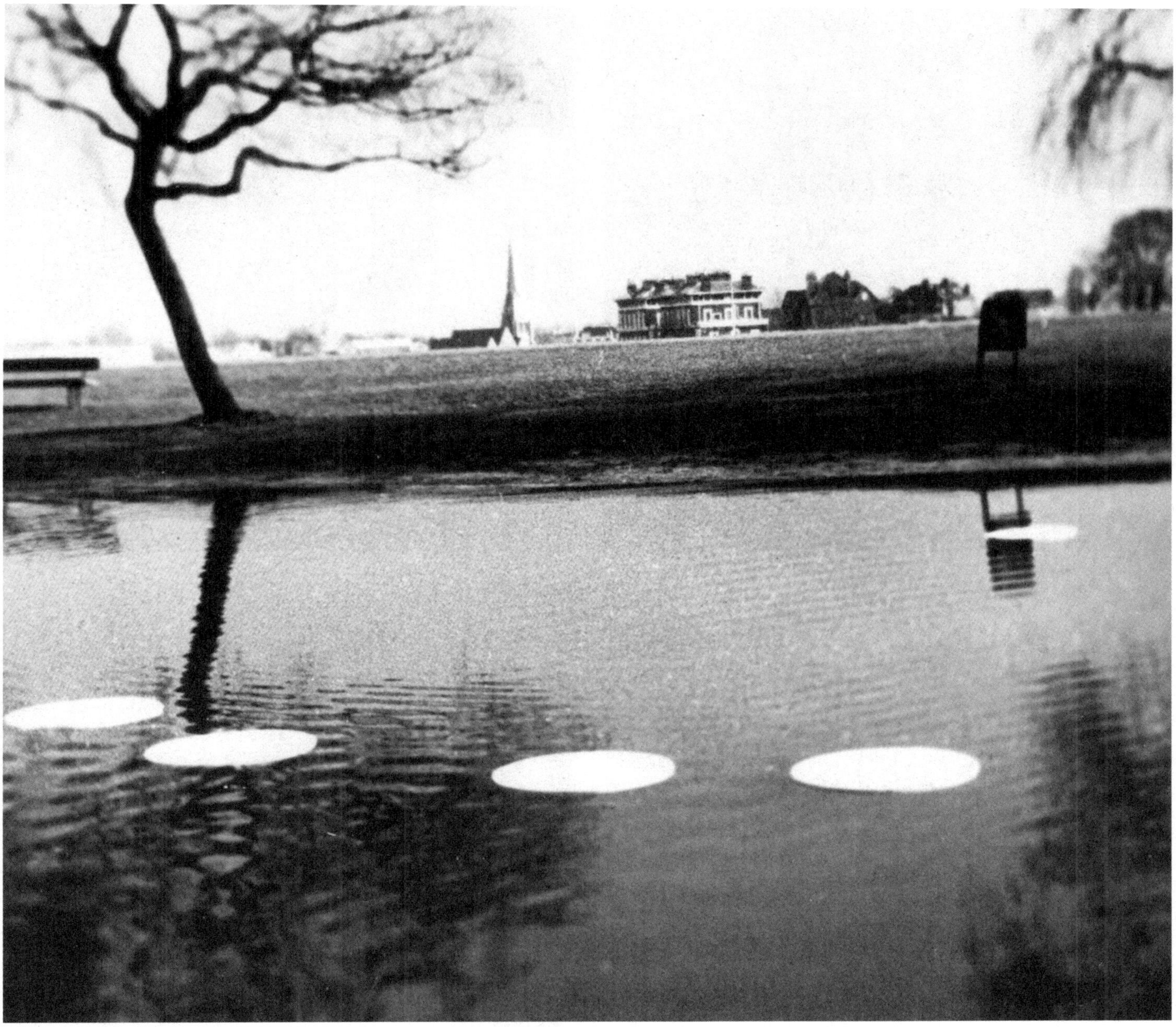

Canalevent (Chakras III, Hammersmith), 1969–1970
16 polystyrene discs and 16 photographs
dimensions variable

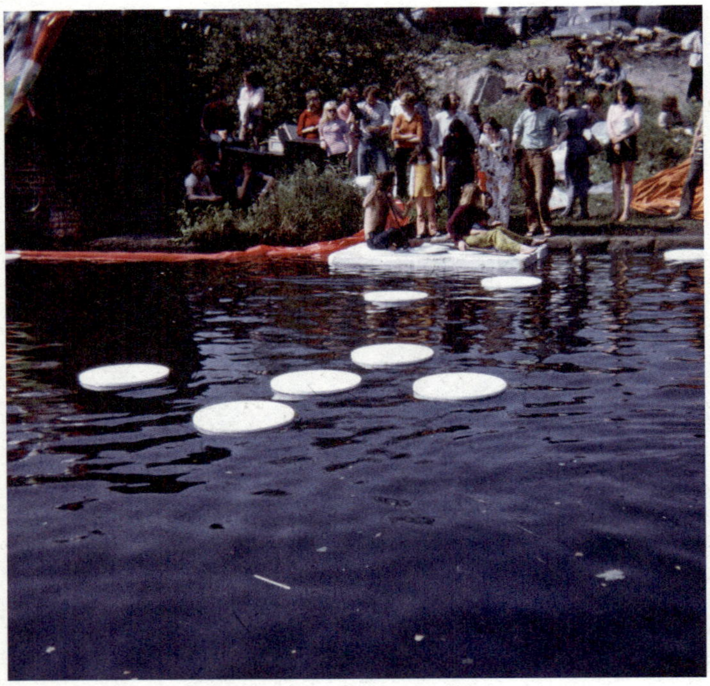

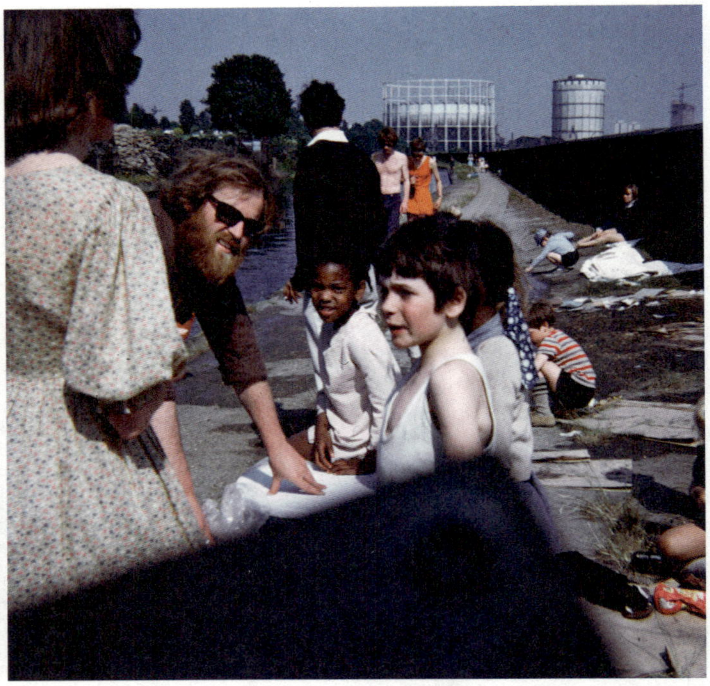

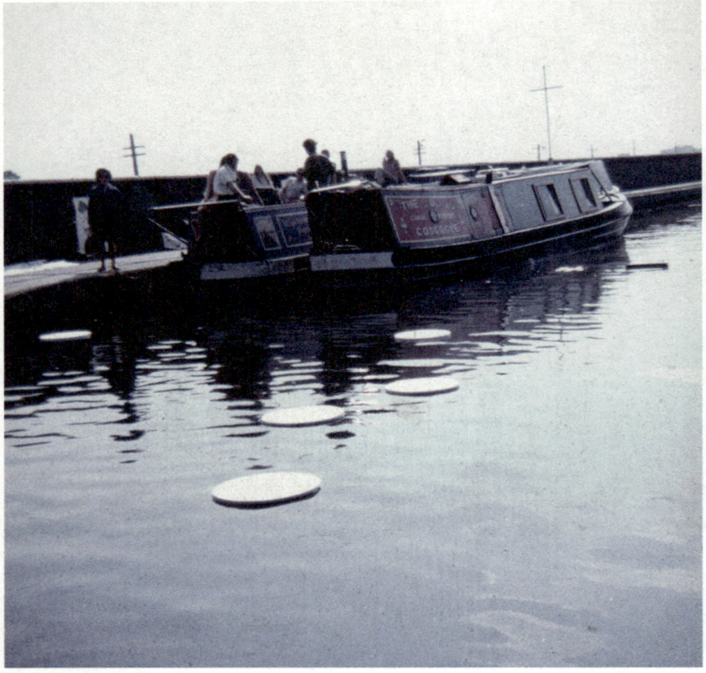

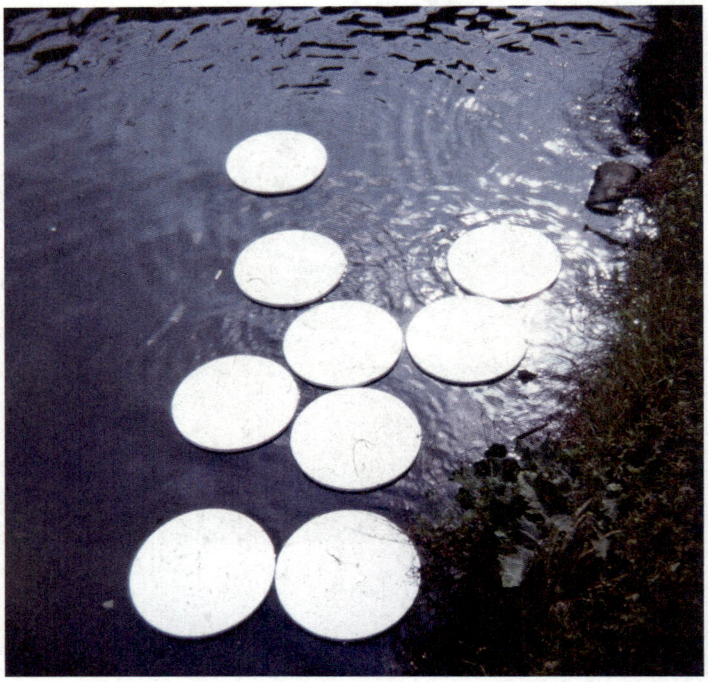

Discs in the River (Chakras IV, La Seine, Paris), 1970
16 polystyrene discs and 16 photographs
dimensions variable

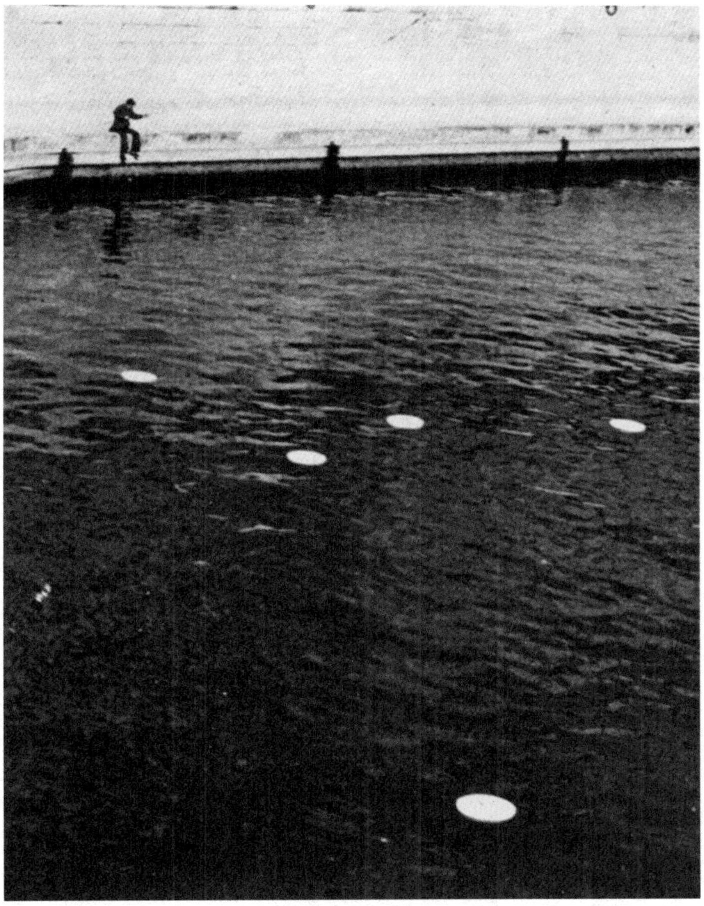

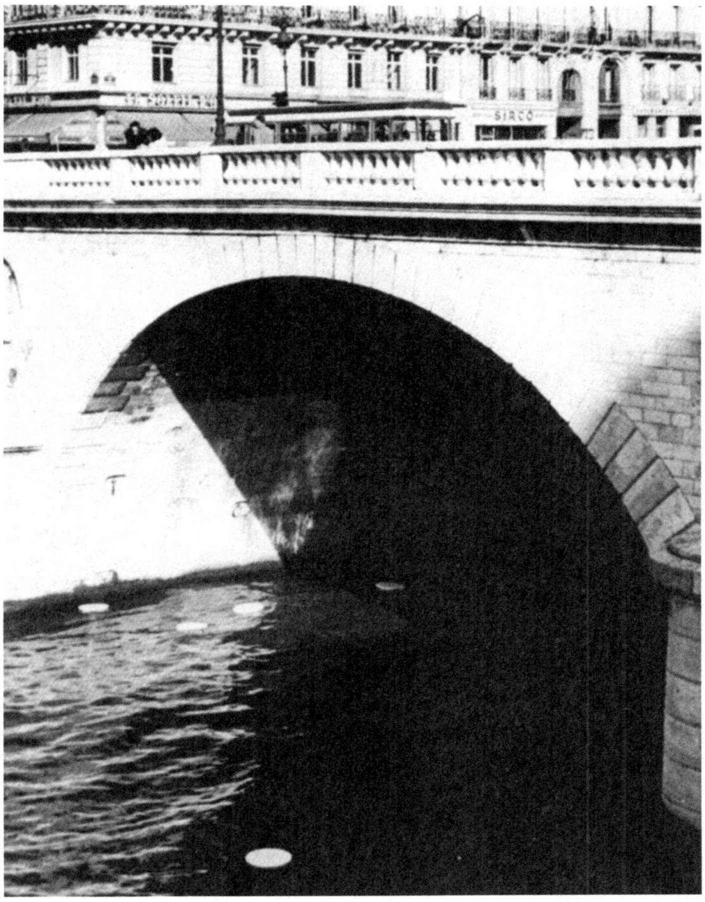

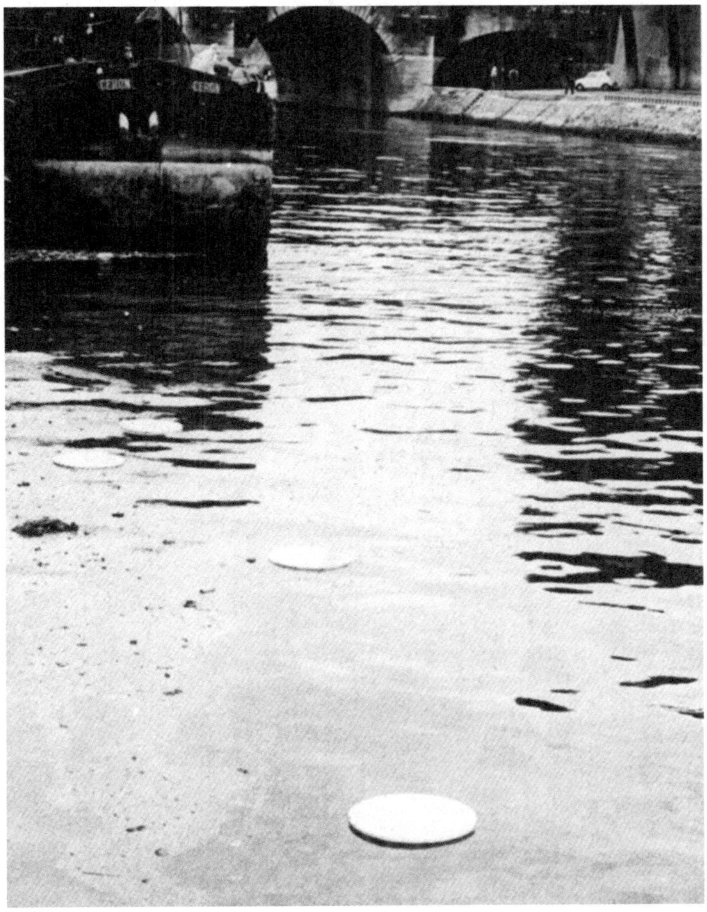

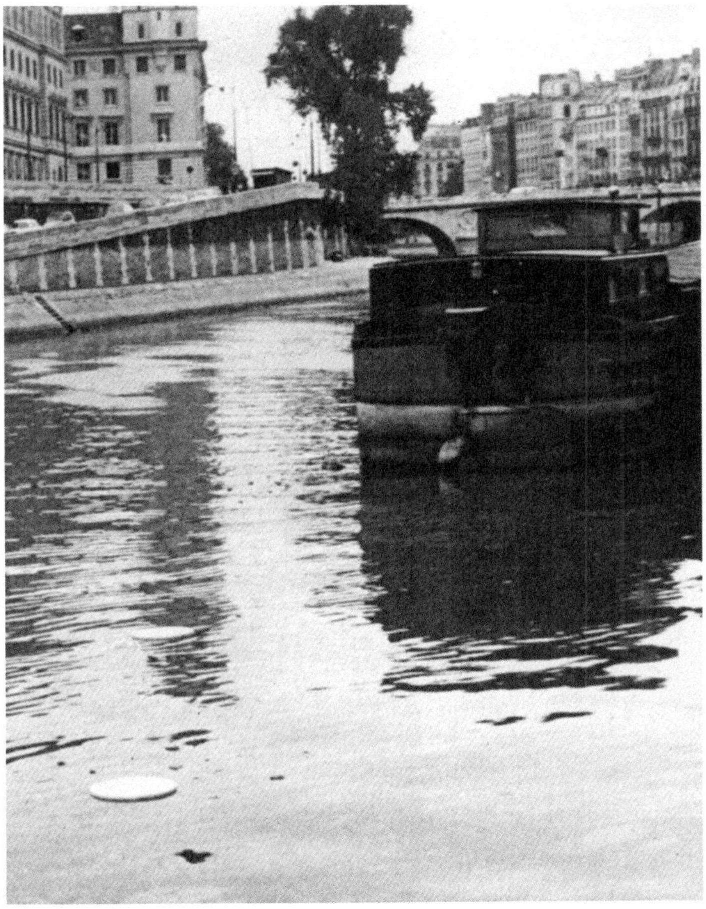

The One That Could Not Float Away, 1970
4 photographs, 64 x 64 cm each

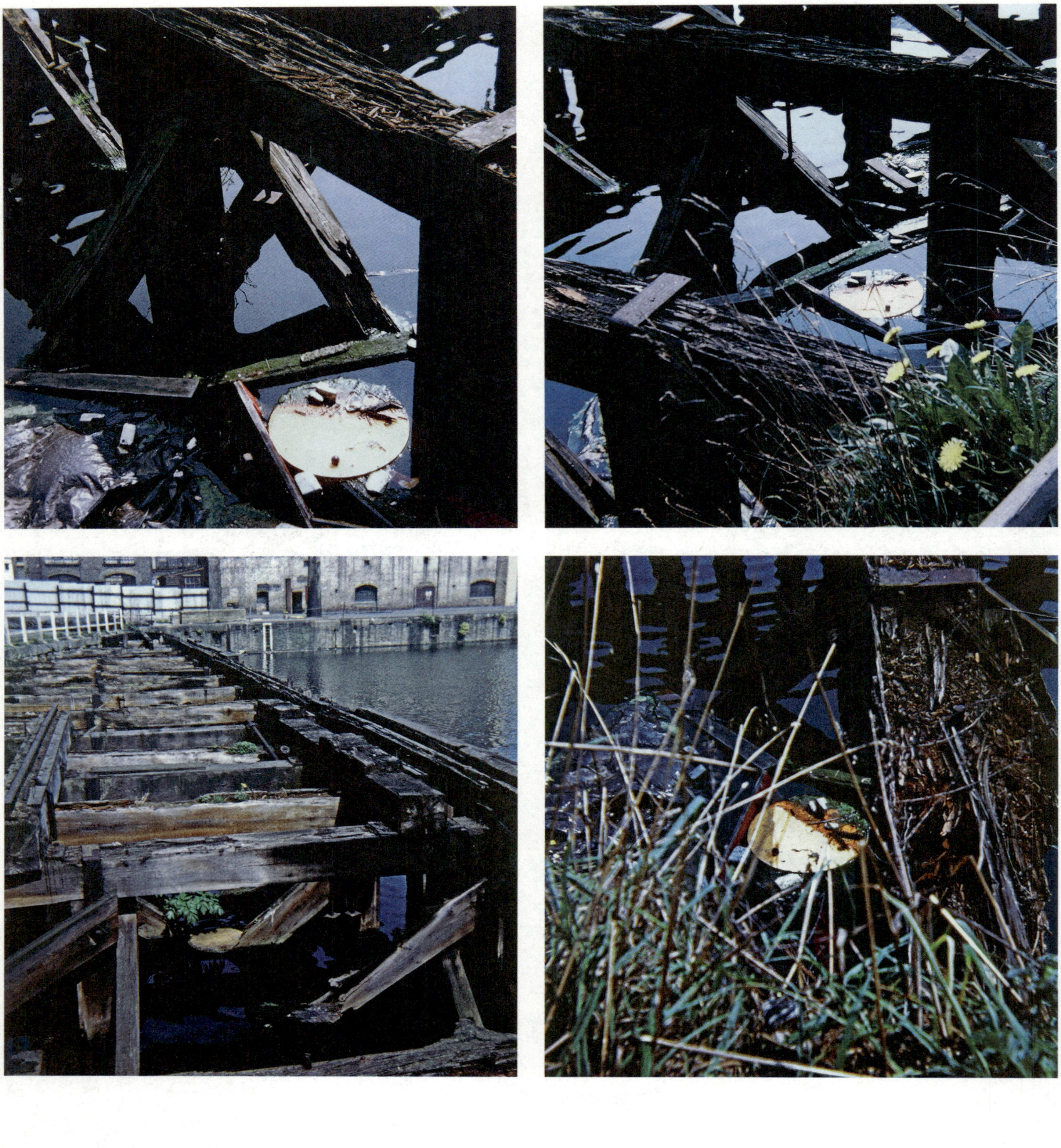

Triangles, 1970
wood triangles and 12 photographs
dimensions variable

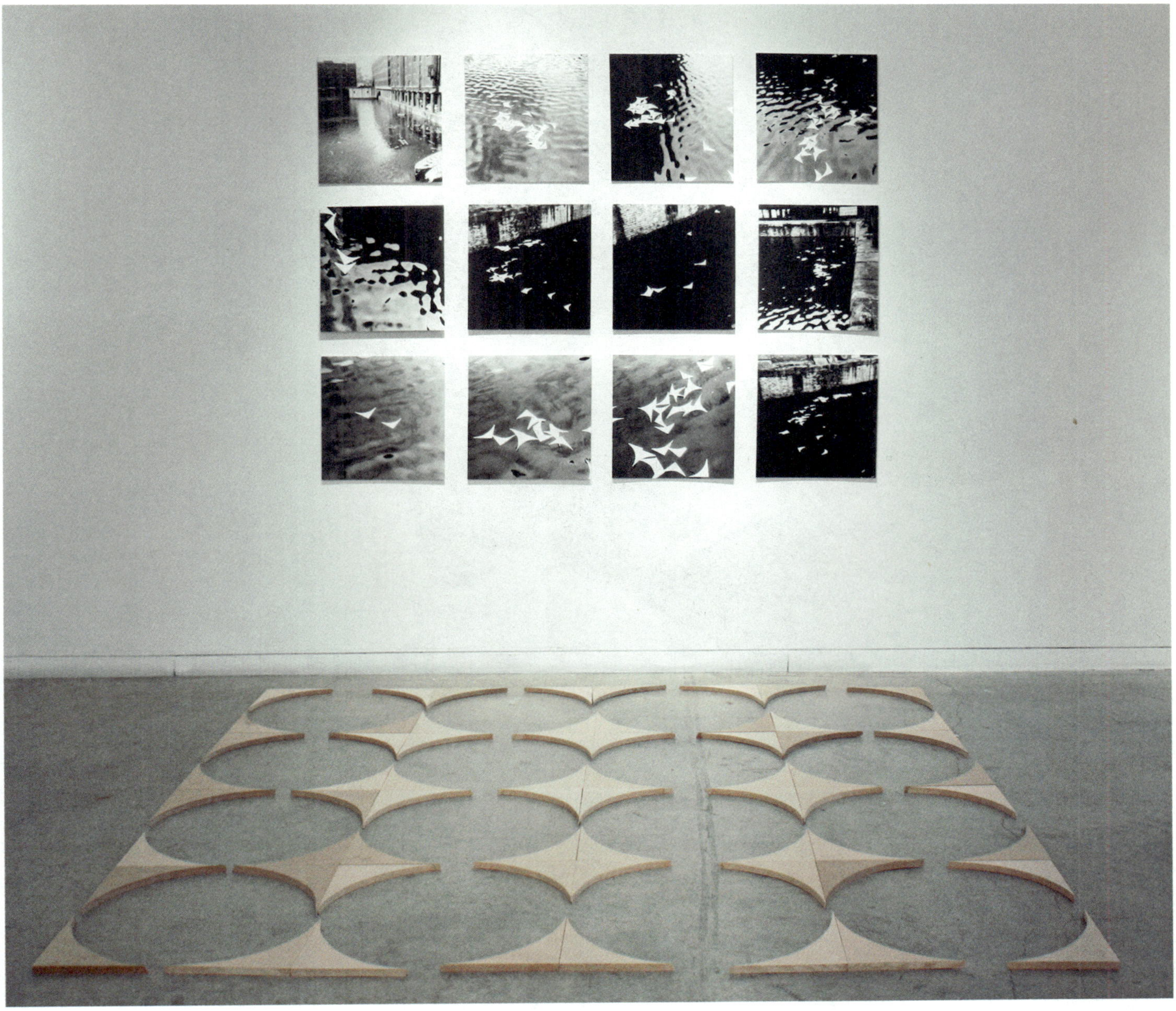

Touch, 1970
5 photographs, 142 x 112 cm

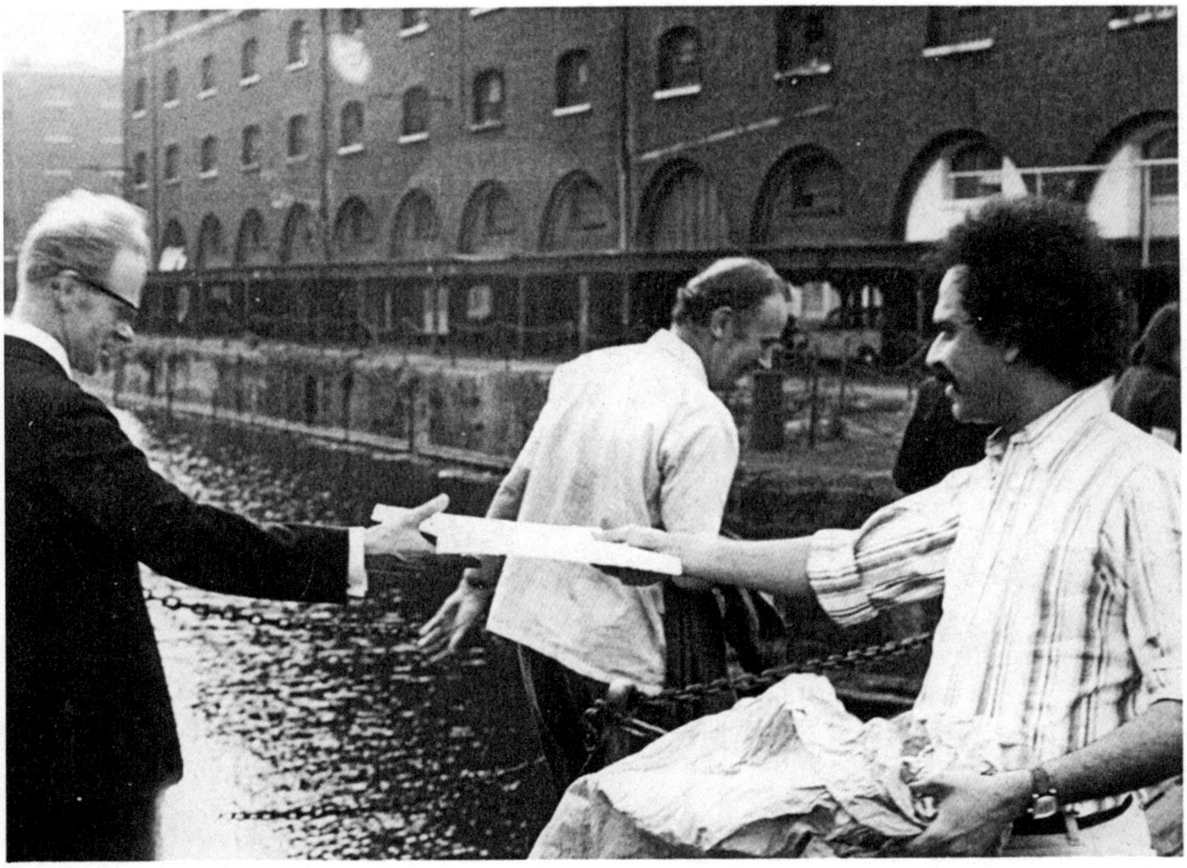

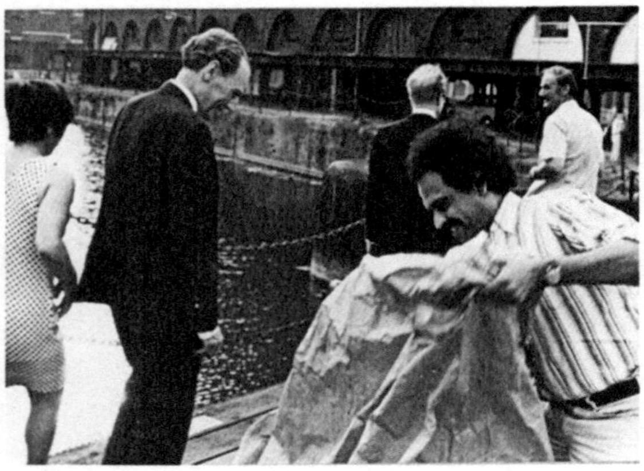

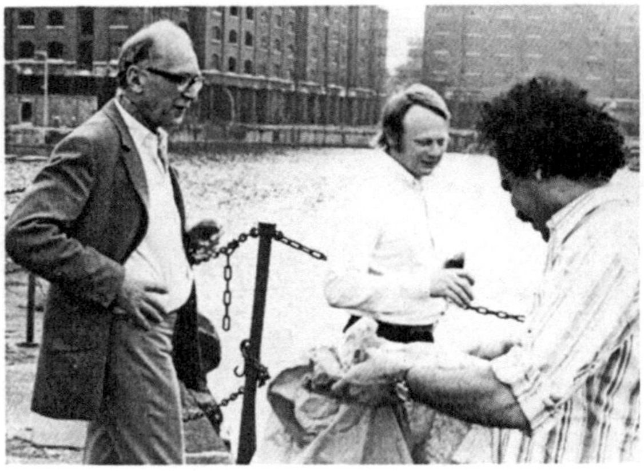

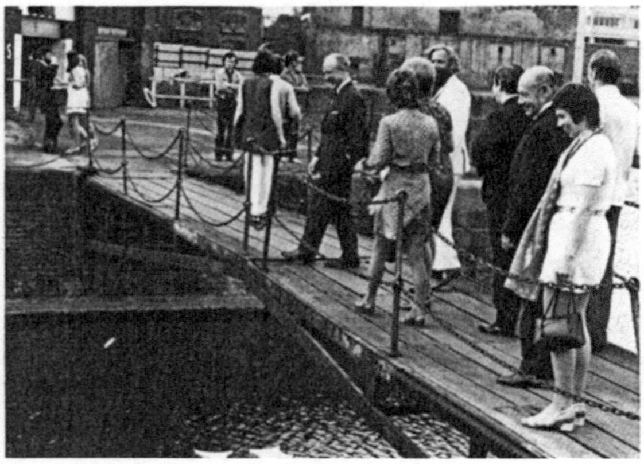

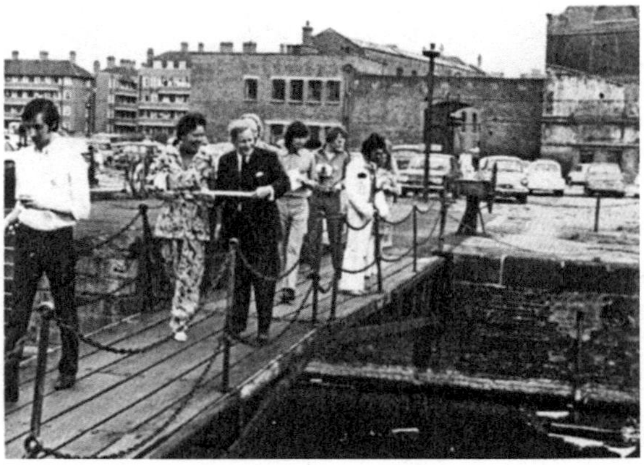

Disco Sailing, 1970–1973 / 2001
6 photographs and drawings, and fibreglass disc
dimensions variable
Sharjah Art Foundation Collection

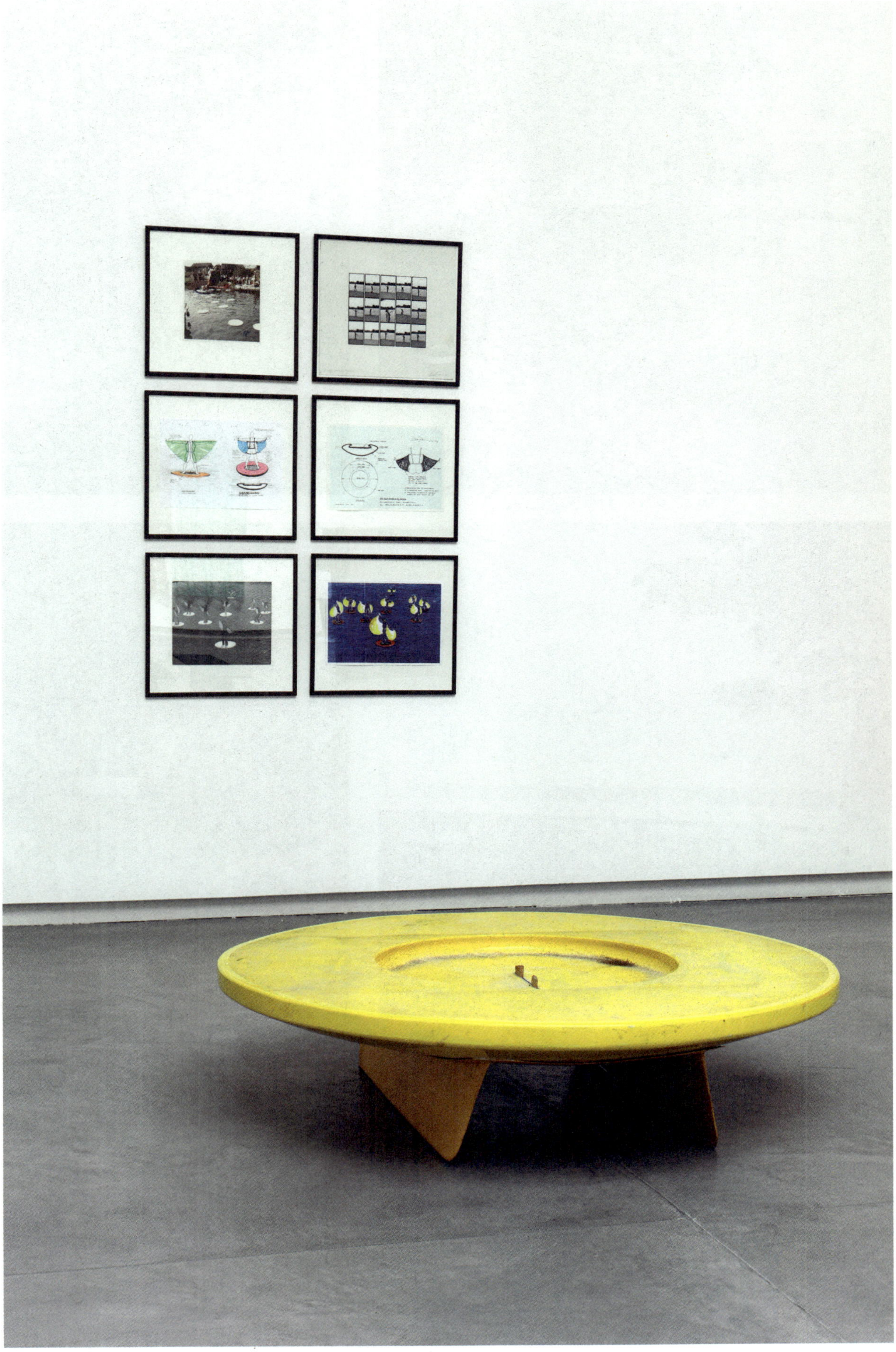

Springtime in Euston Square Gardens, 1970 / 2015
8 photographs, and 4 acrylic on wood Structures
dimensions variable

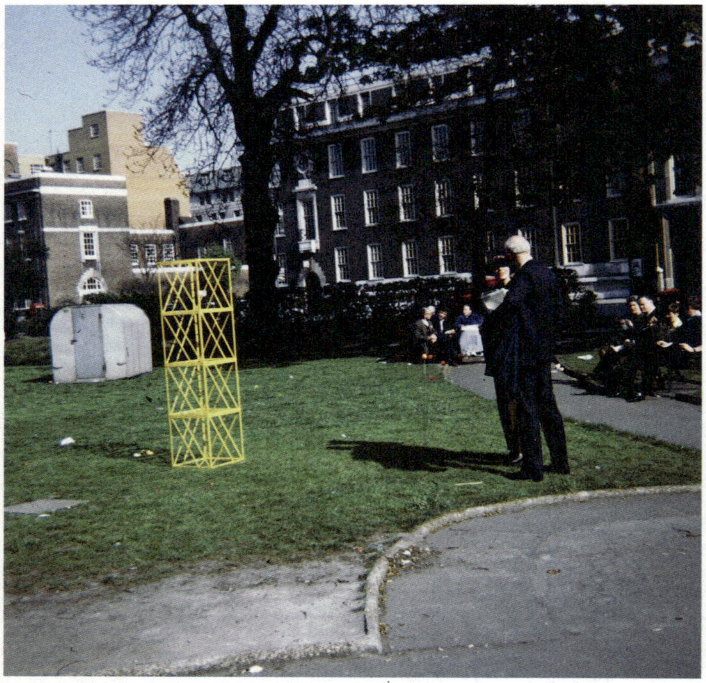

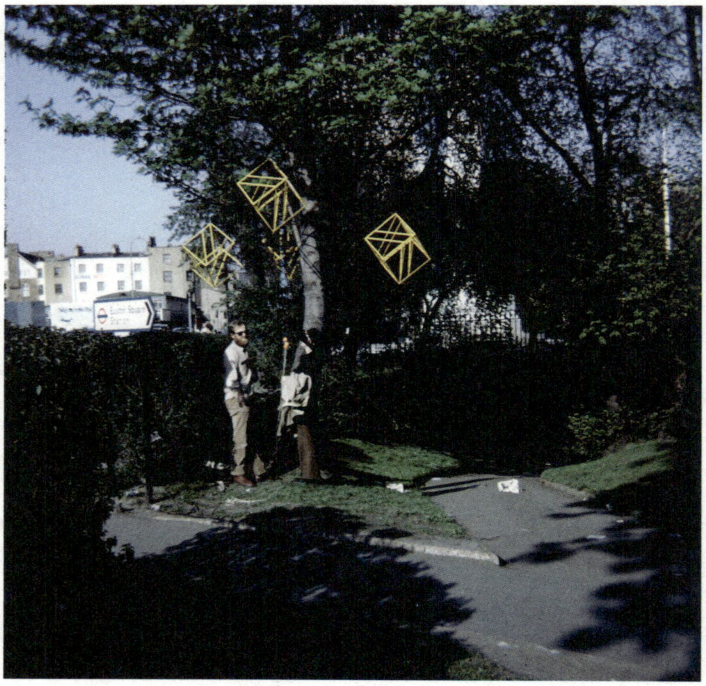

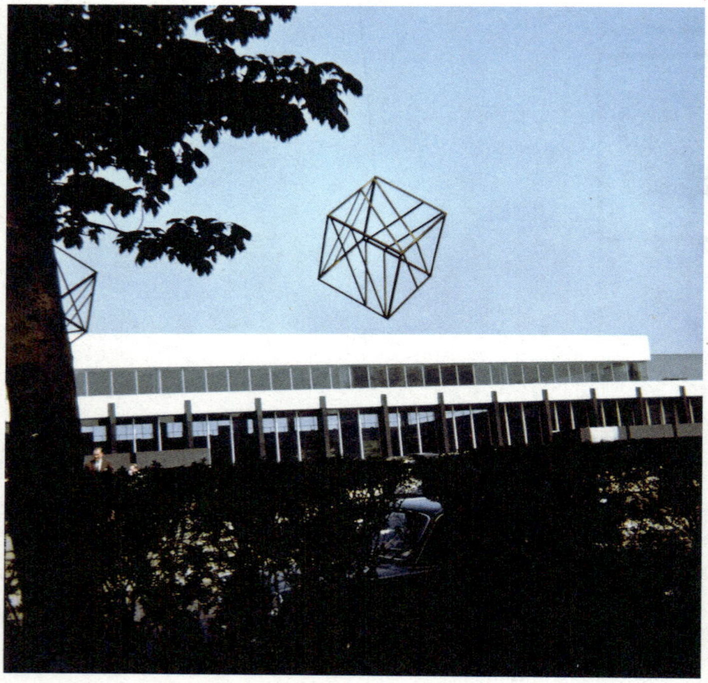

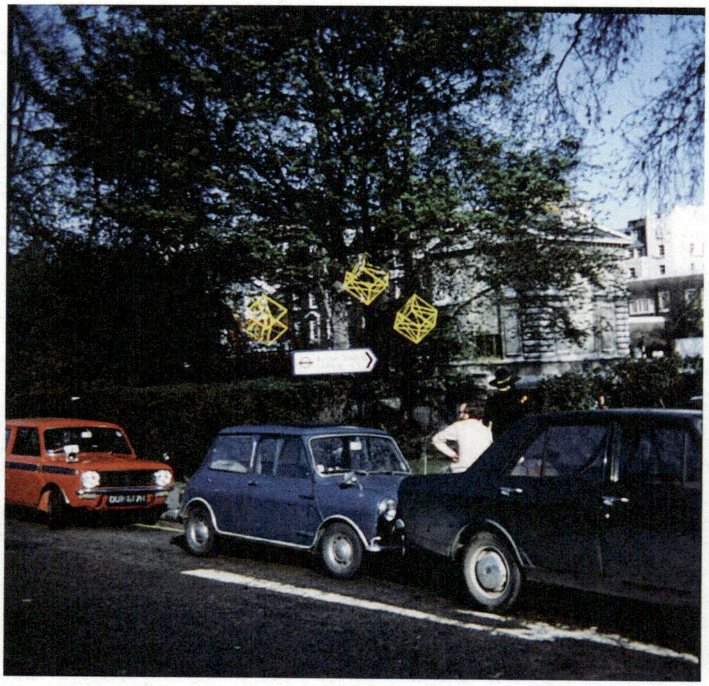

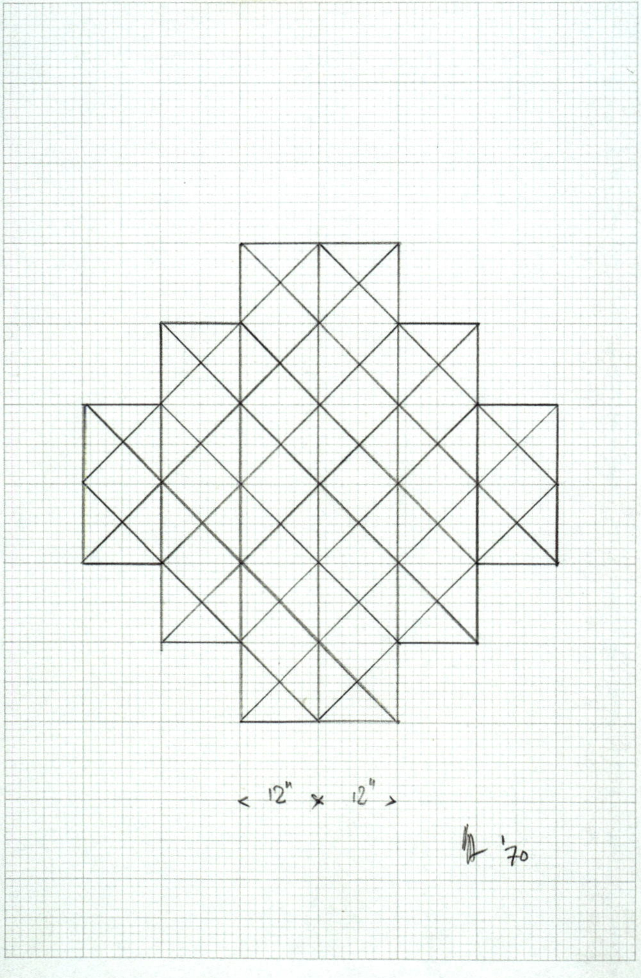
< 12" × 12" >
'70

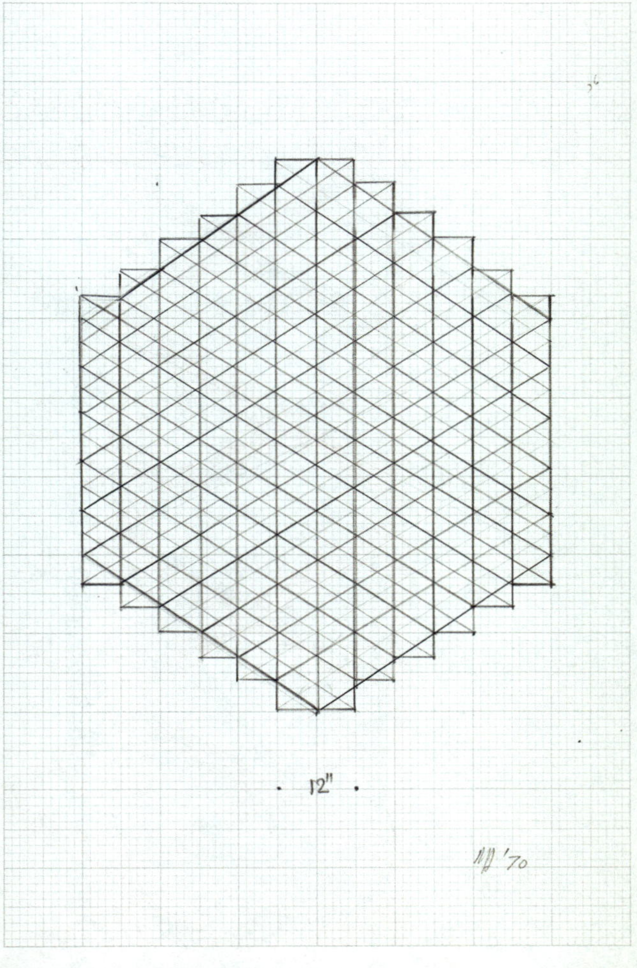
12"
'70

Piaray Lal, 1970
acrylic on wood, 84 x 31 x 15 cm

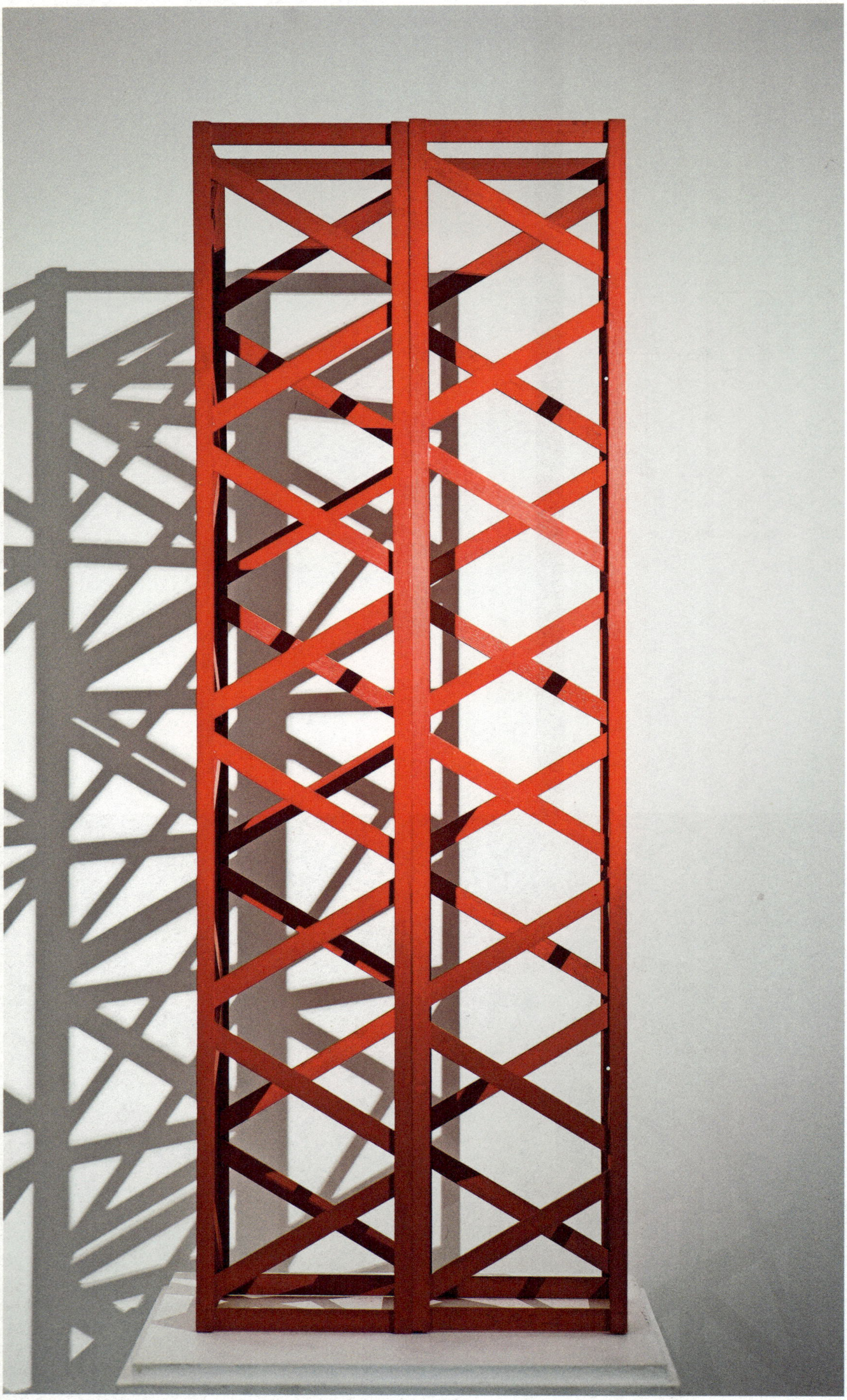

Basant, 1970
acrylic on wood, 104 x 46 x 10 cm
Collection Elaine W. Ng and Fabio Rossi

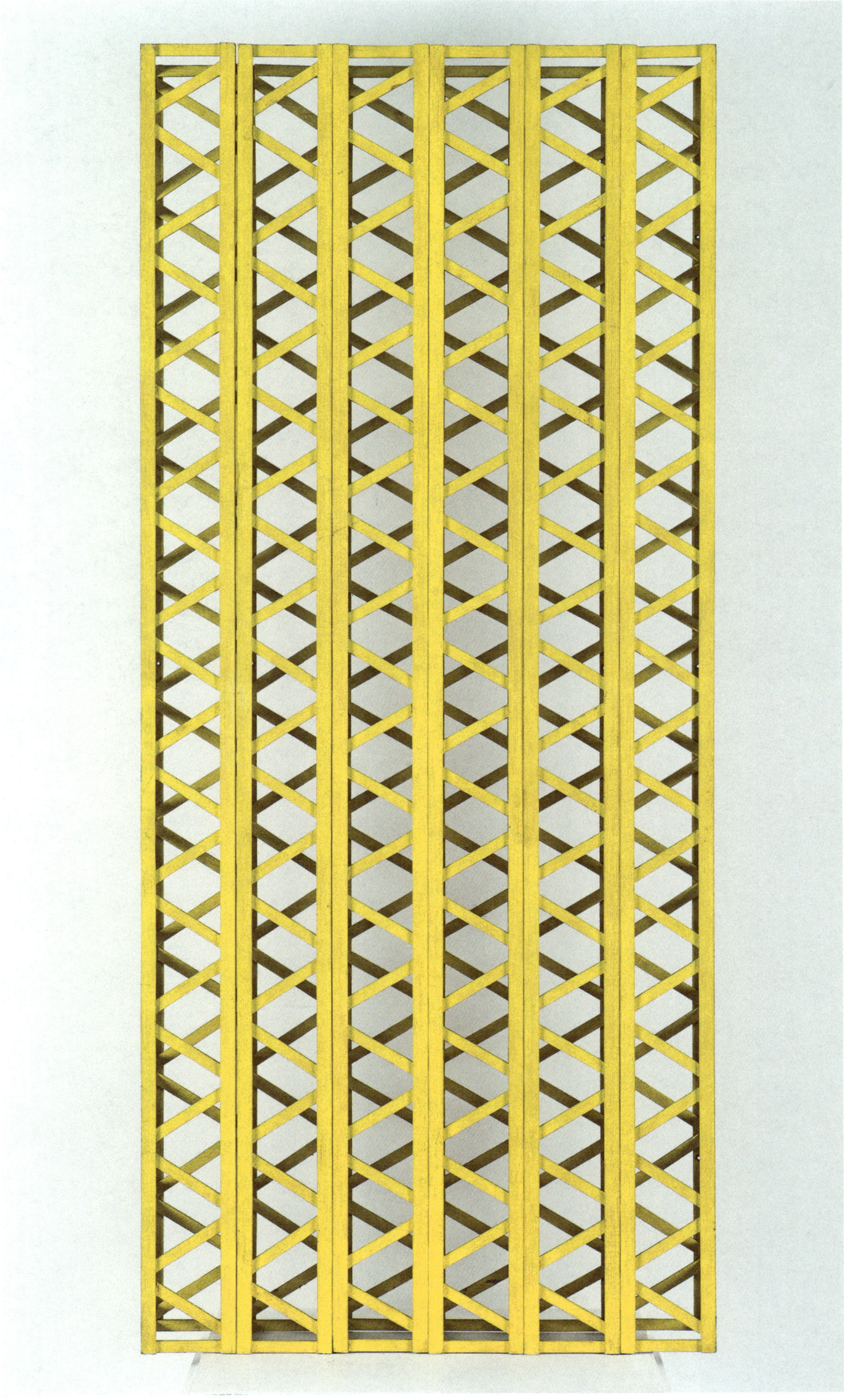

Untitled (Blue), 1970
acrylic on wood, 122 x 61 x 61 cm

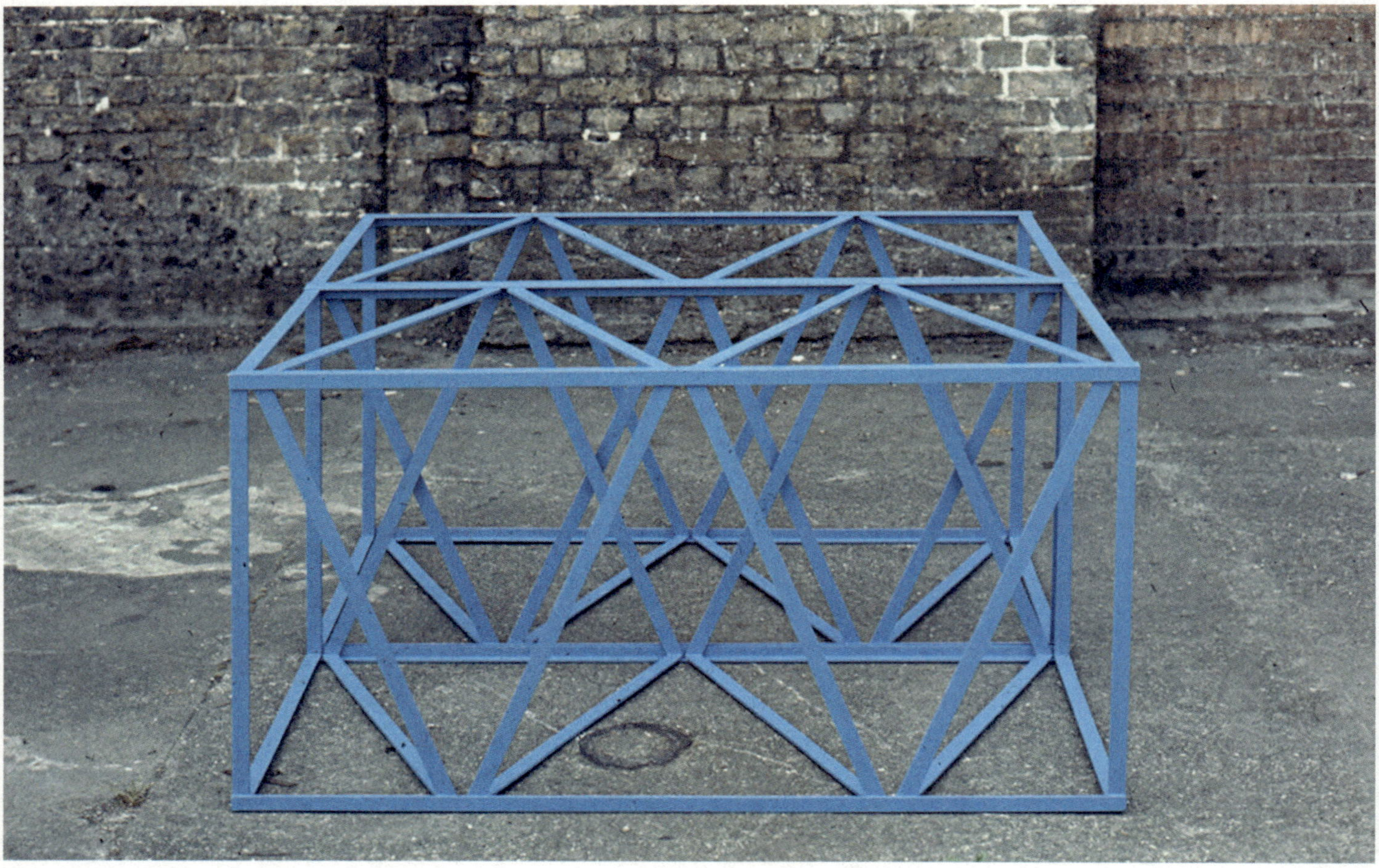

4bS, 1970
acrylic on wood, 183 x 152 x 38 cm

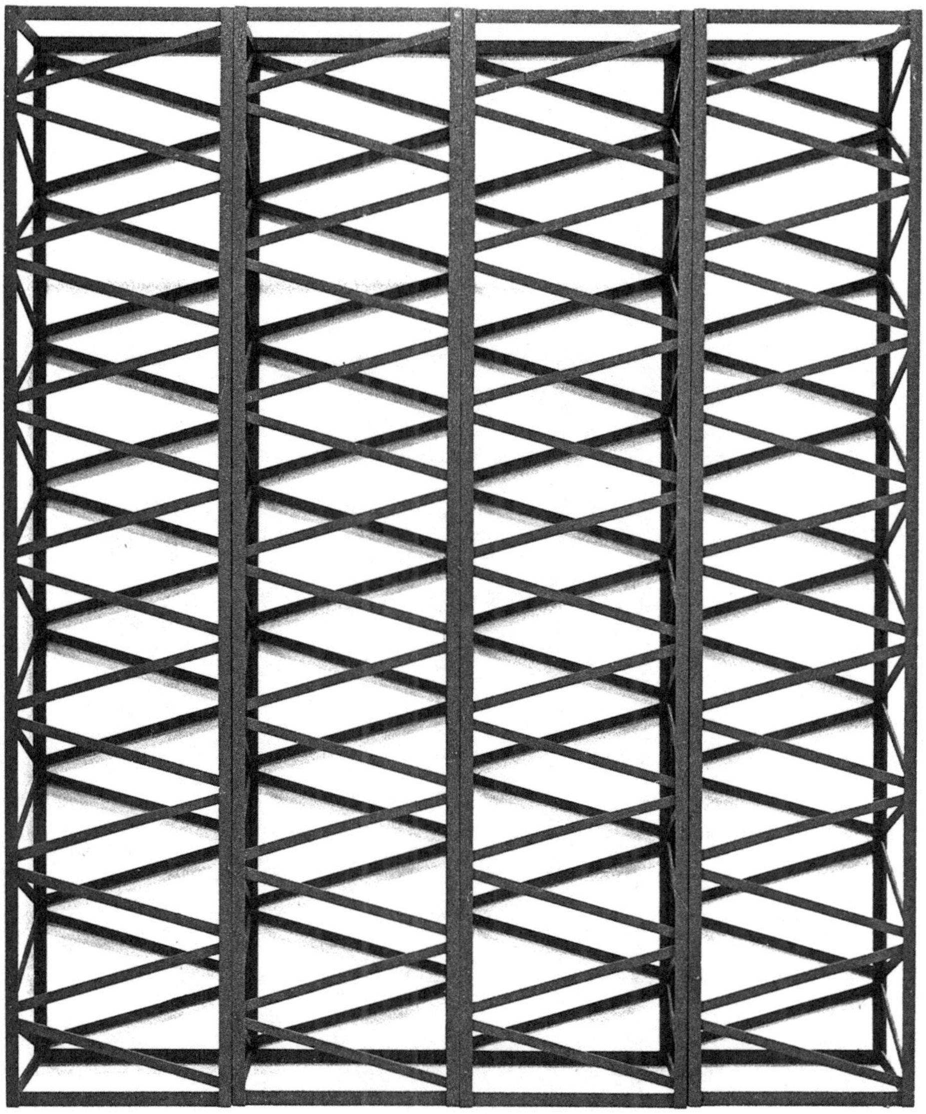

Unit Structure, 1970
acrylic on wood, 183 x 152 x 38 cm

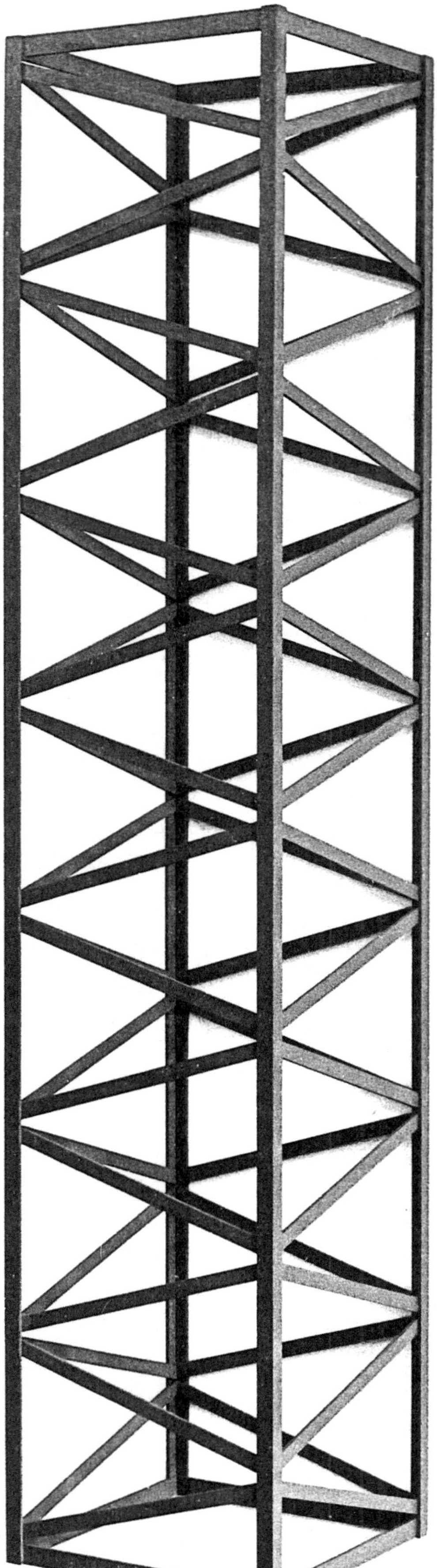

8bS, 1970
acrylic on wood, 183 x 394 x 28 cm

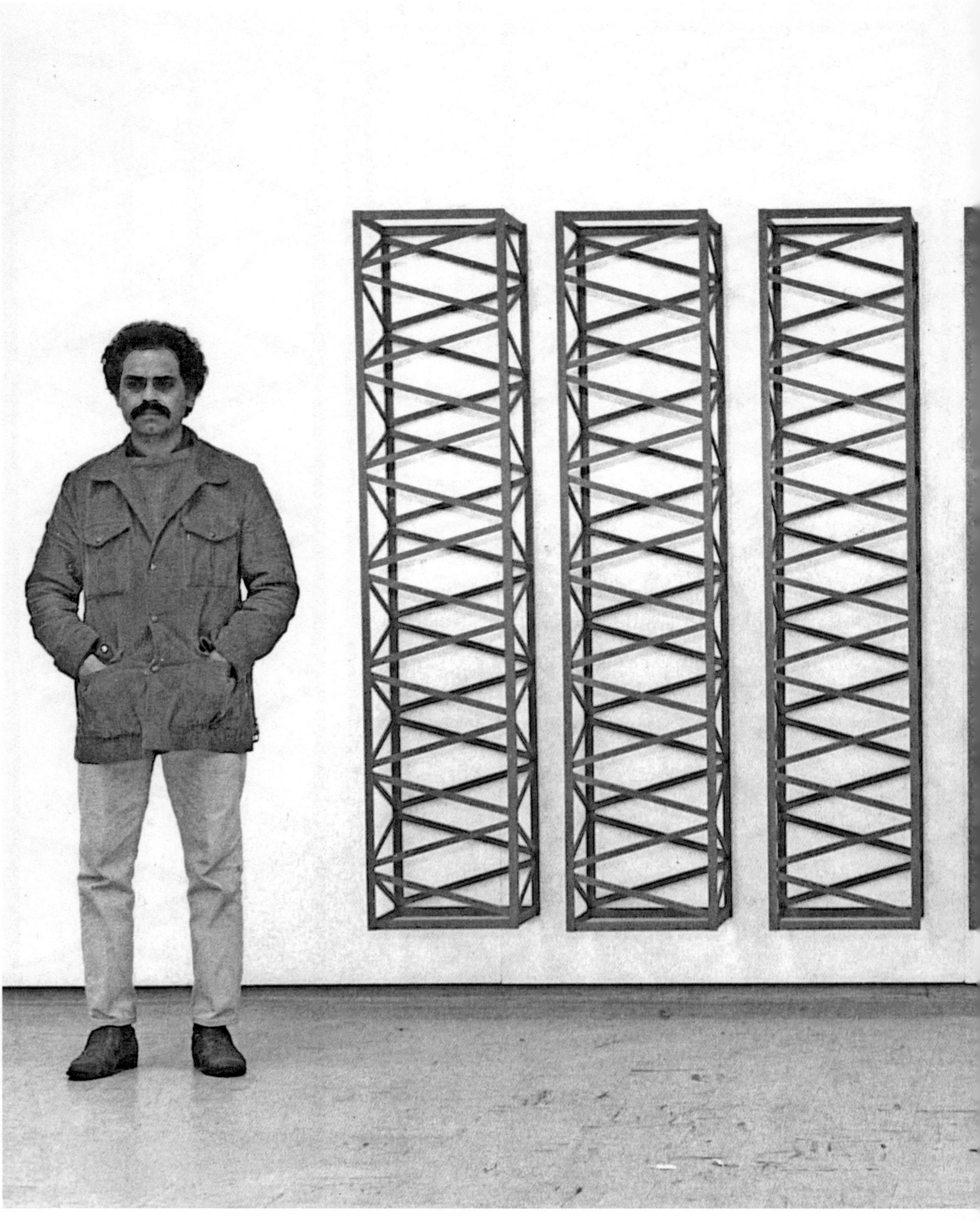

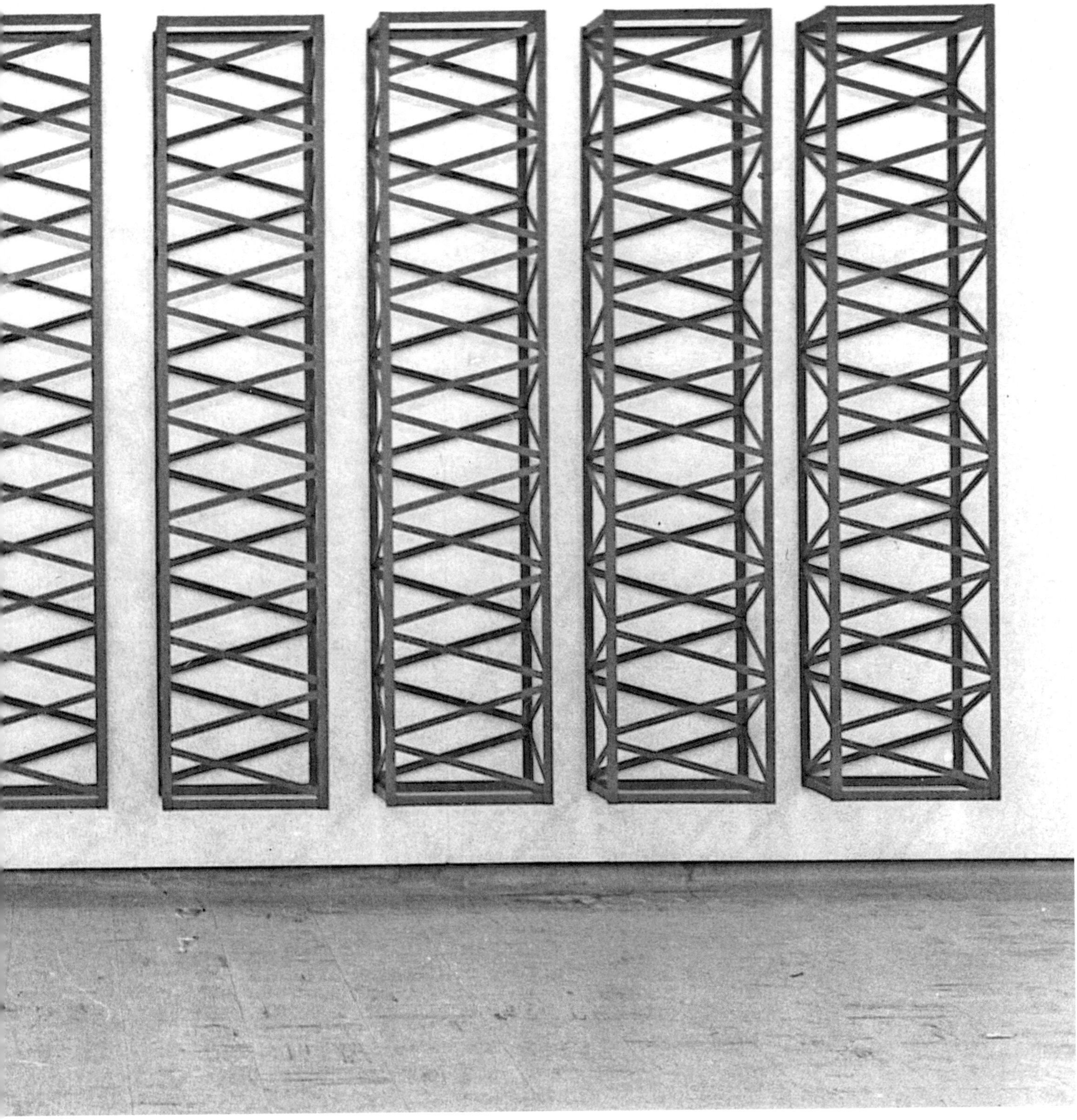

8BS II, 1970
acrylic on wood, 183 x 152 x 76 cm
Uno, 1970
acrylic on wood, 183 x 183 x 15 cm

Punj Neelay (Five Blues), 1970
acrylic on wood, 170 x 156 x 13 cm
Collection Art Institute of Chicago
4rS, 1970
acrylic on wood, 178 x 76 x 76 cm

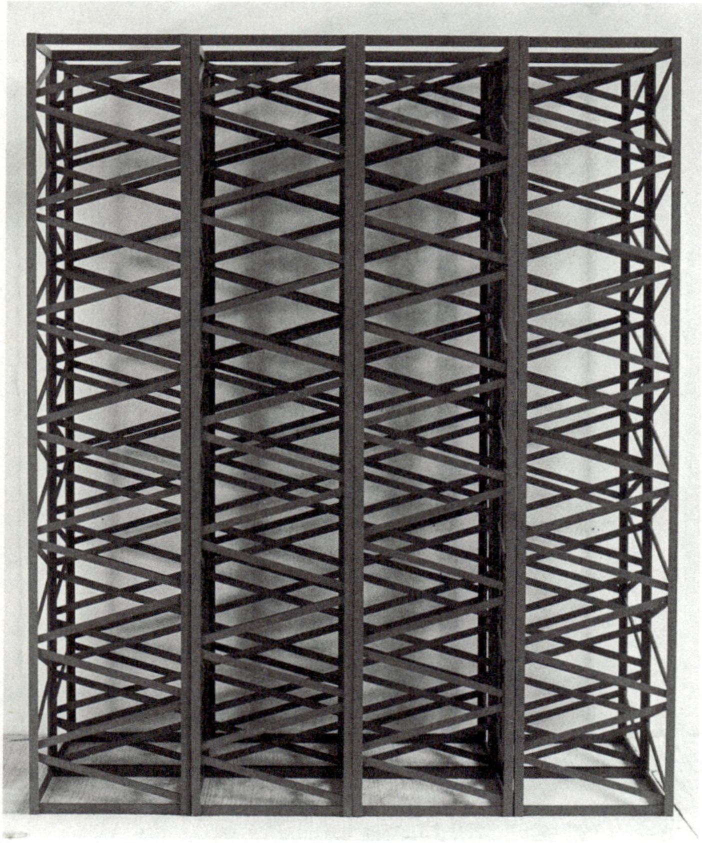

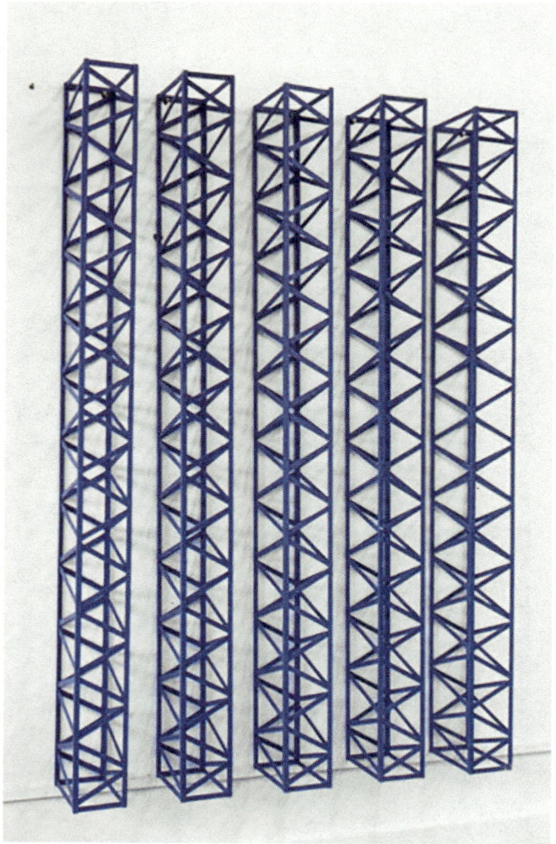

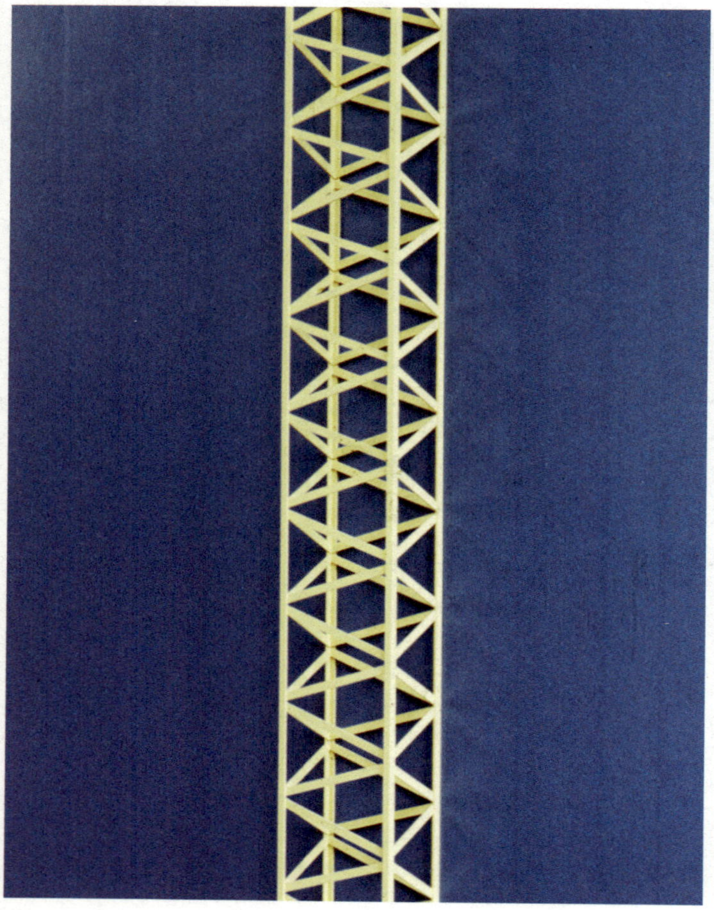

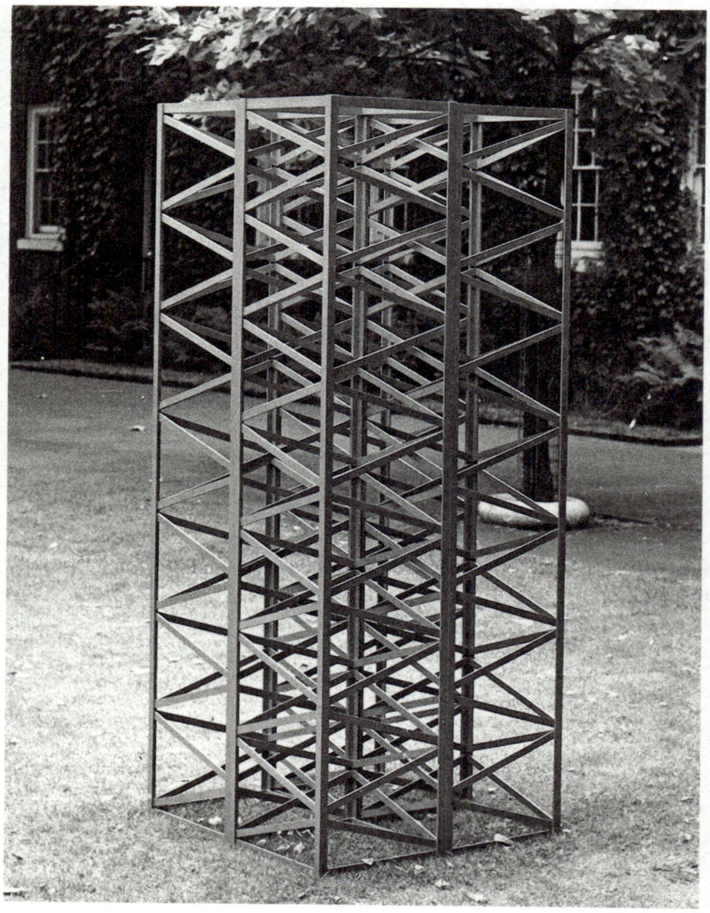

Red Orange on Blue, 1970
acrylic on wood, 183 x 122 x 15 cm

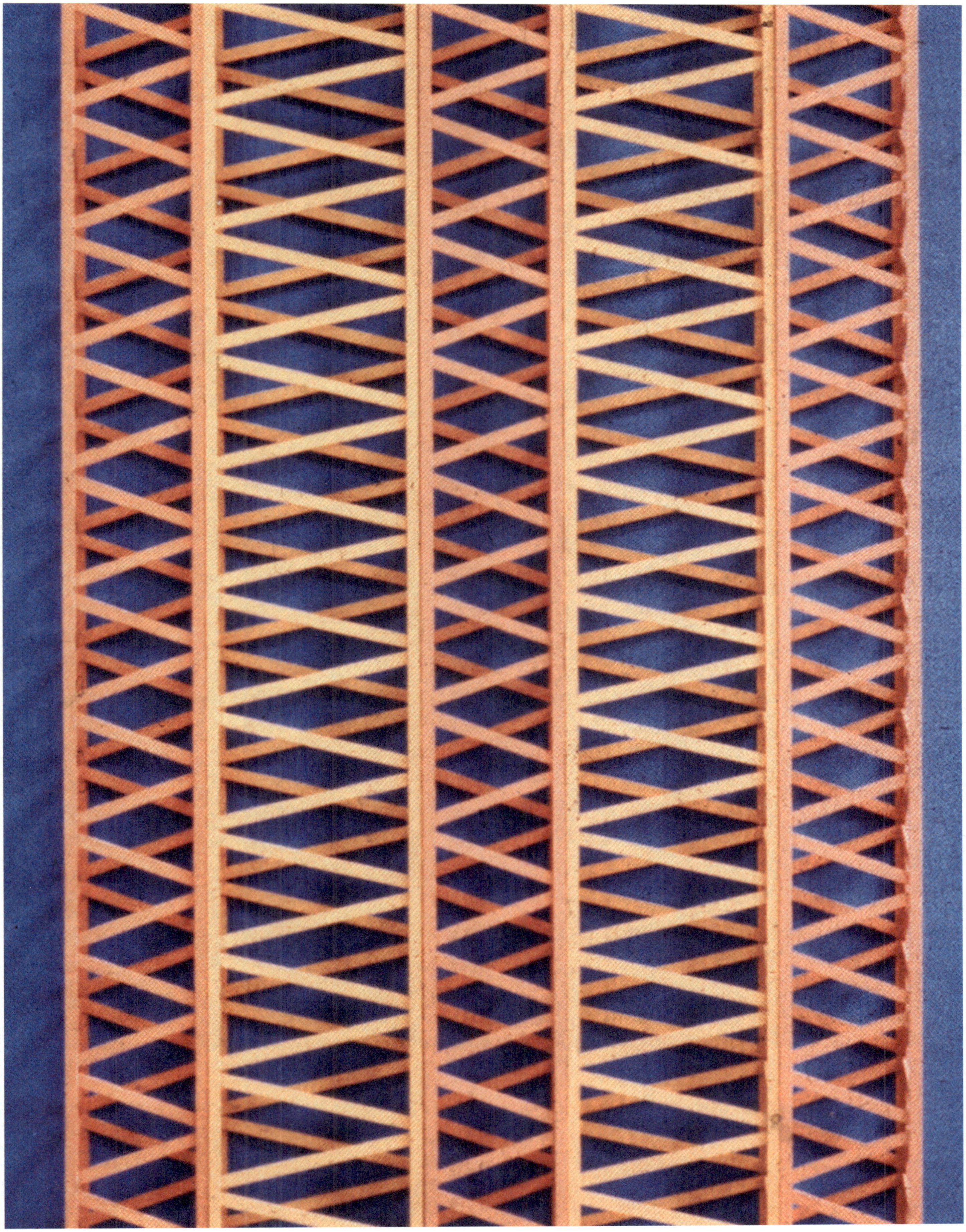

Neela Peela, 1970 / 2016
acrylic on wood, 183 x 183 x 15 cm

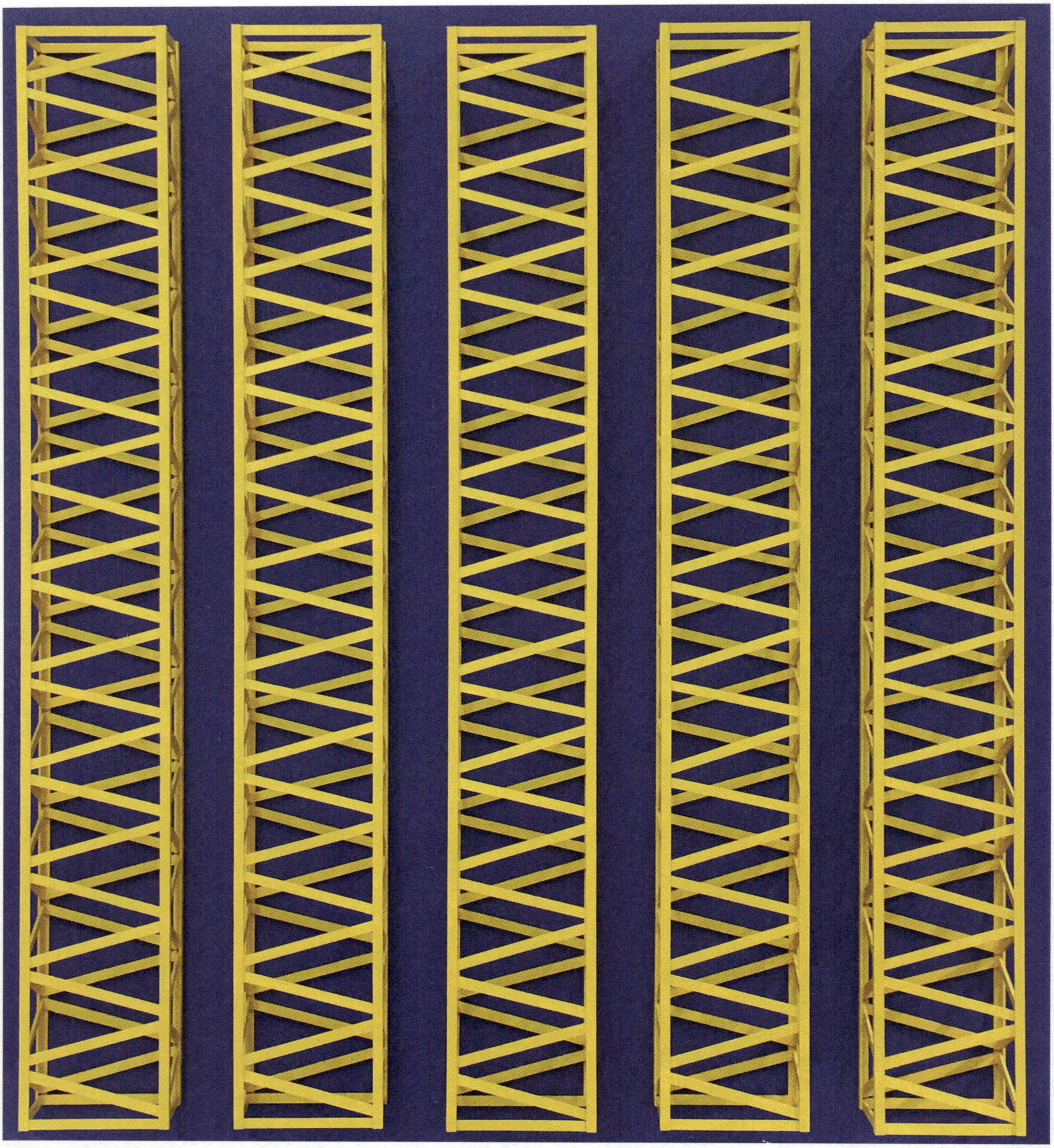

(3R+2B) SW, 1971
acrylic on wood, 76 x 74 x 15 cm
Private collection

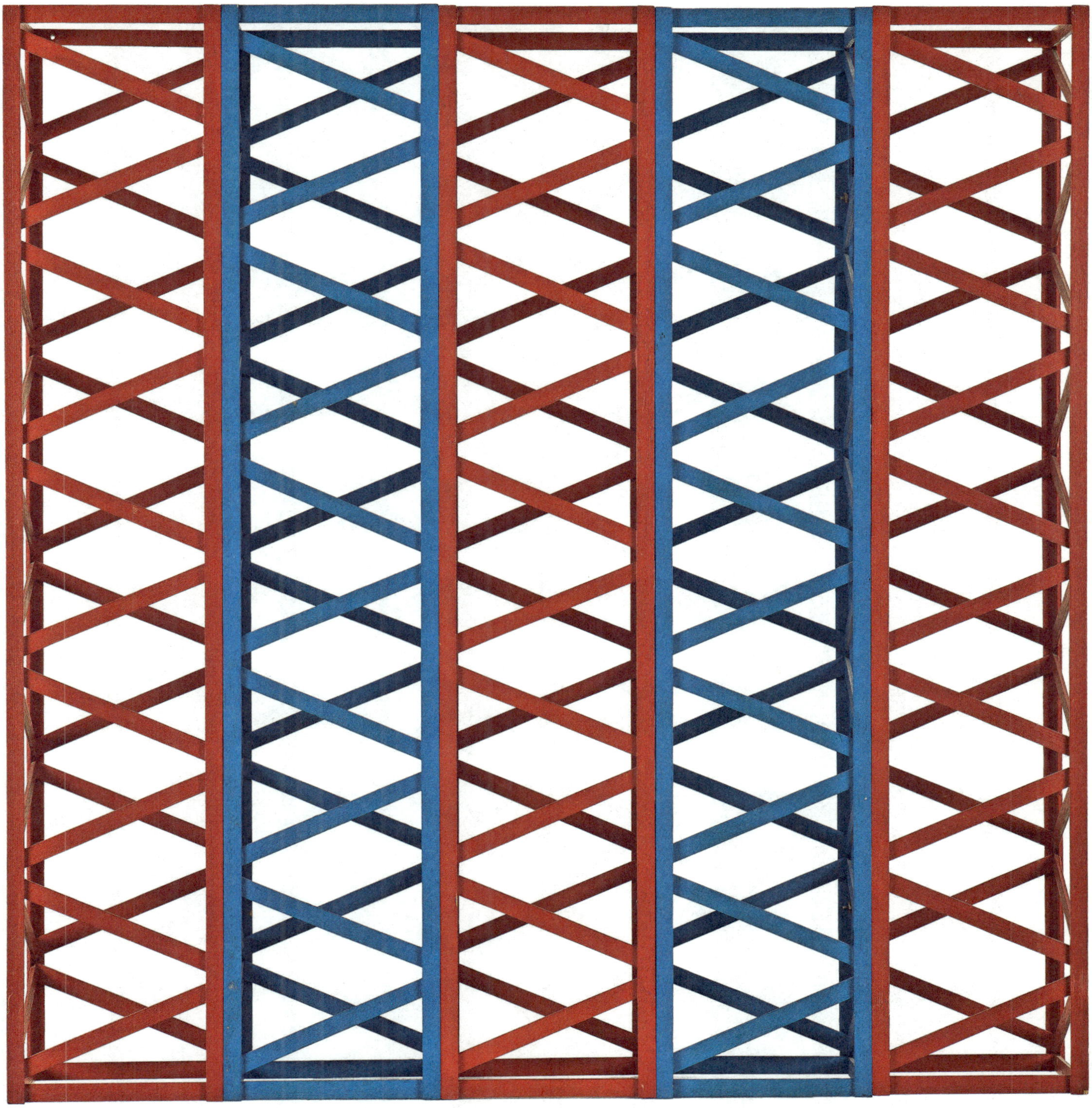

Burgundy Dark, 1971
acrylic on wood, 104 x 69 x 13 cm
Collection Gayathri and Priyam Jhaveri

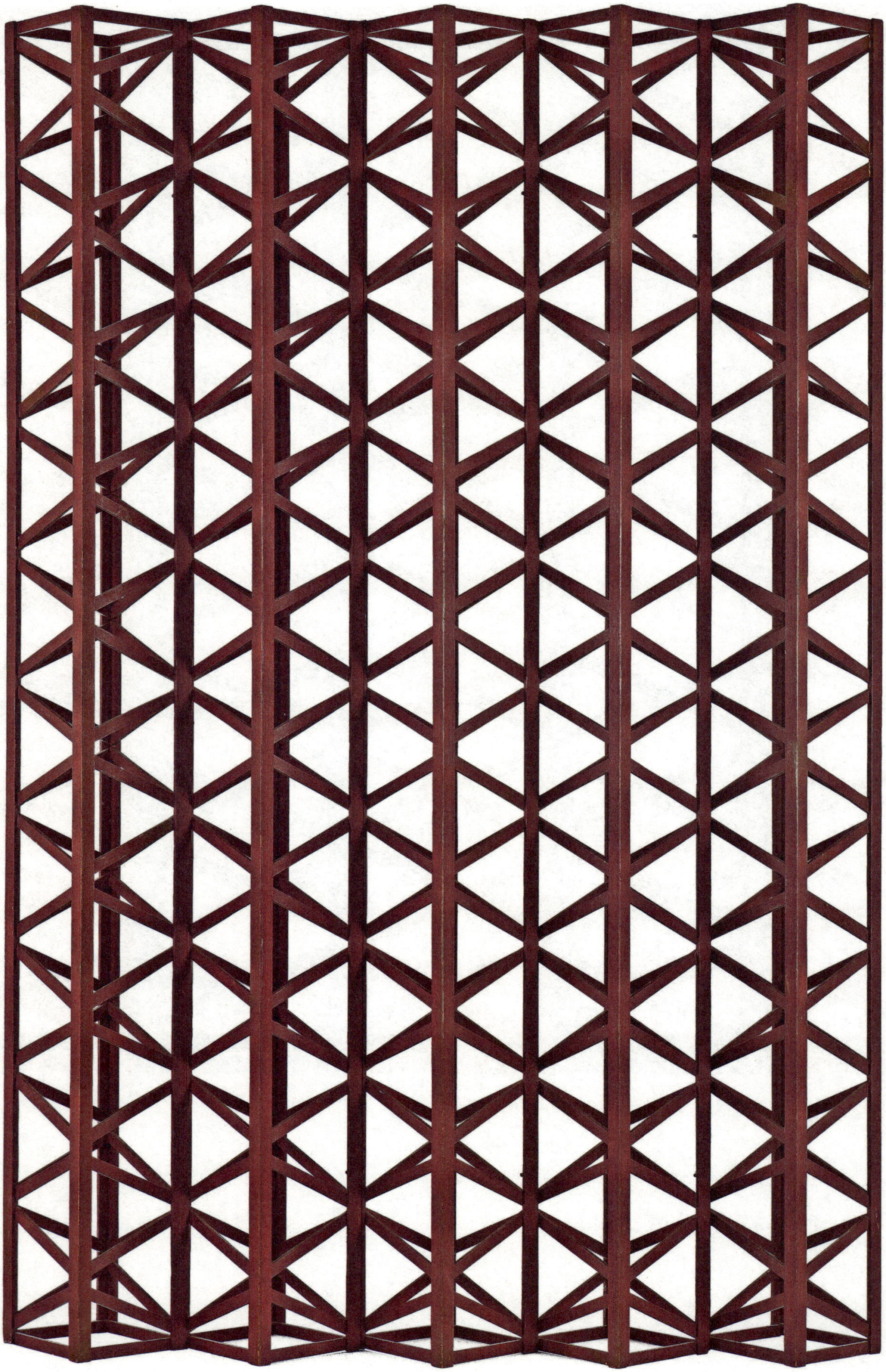

Burgundy Light, 1971
acrylic on wood, 104 x 69 x 13 cm
Samdani Art Foundation Collection

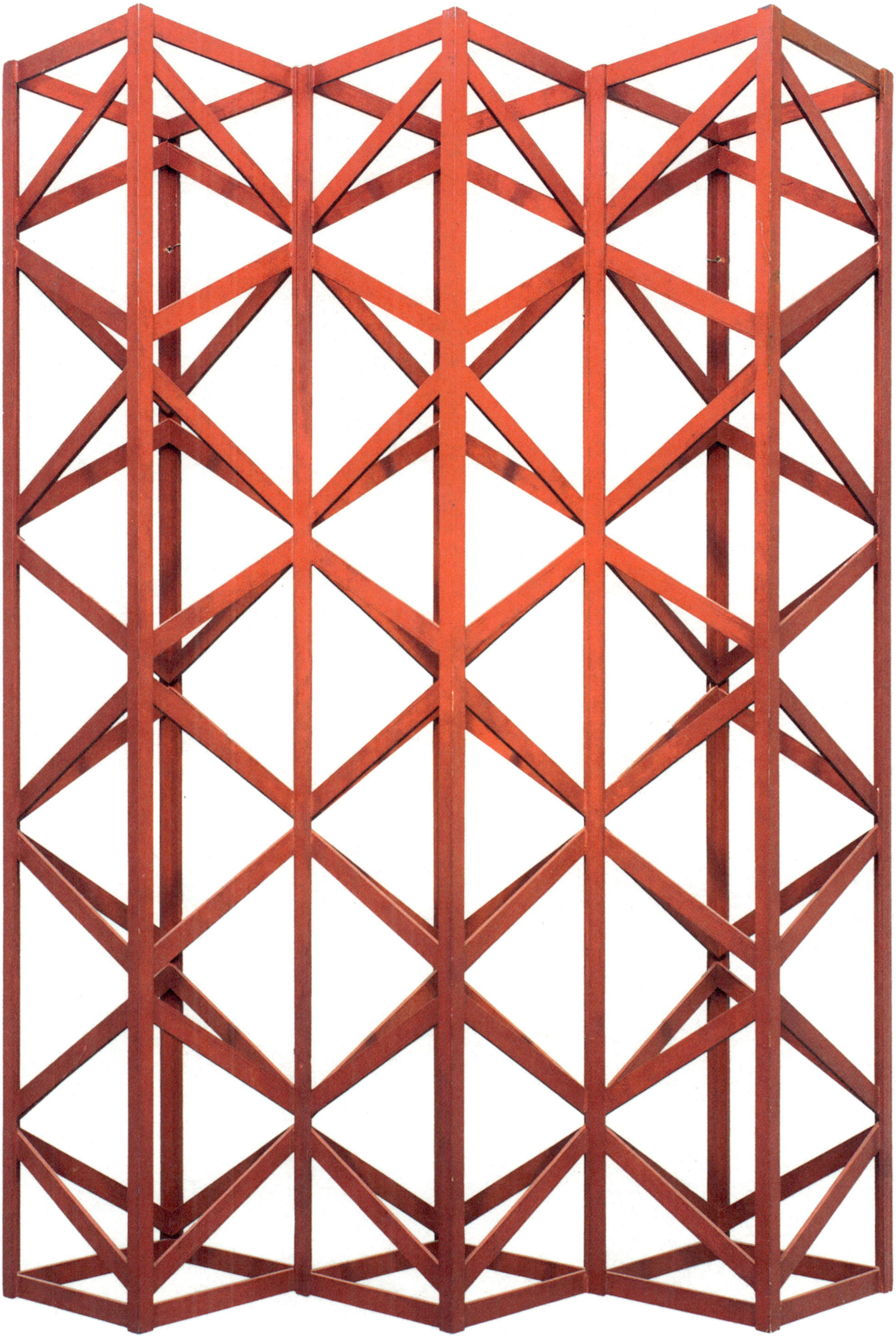

Fall, 1971
acrylic on wood, 216 x 183 x 53 cm

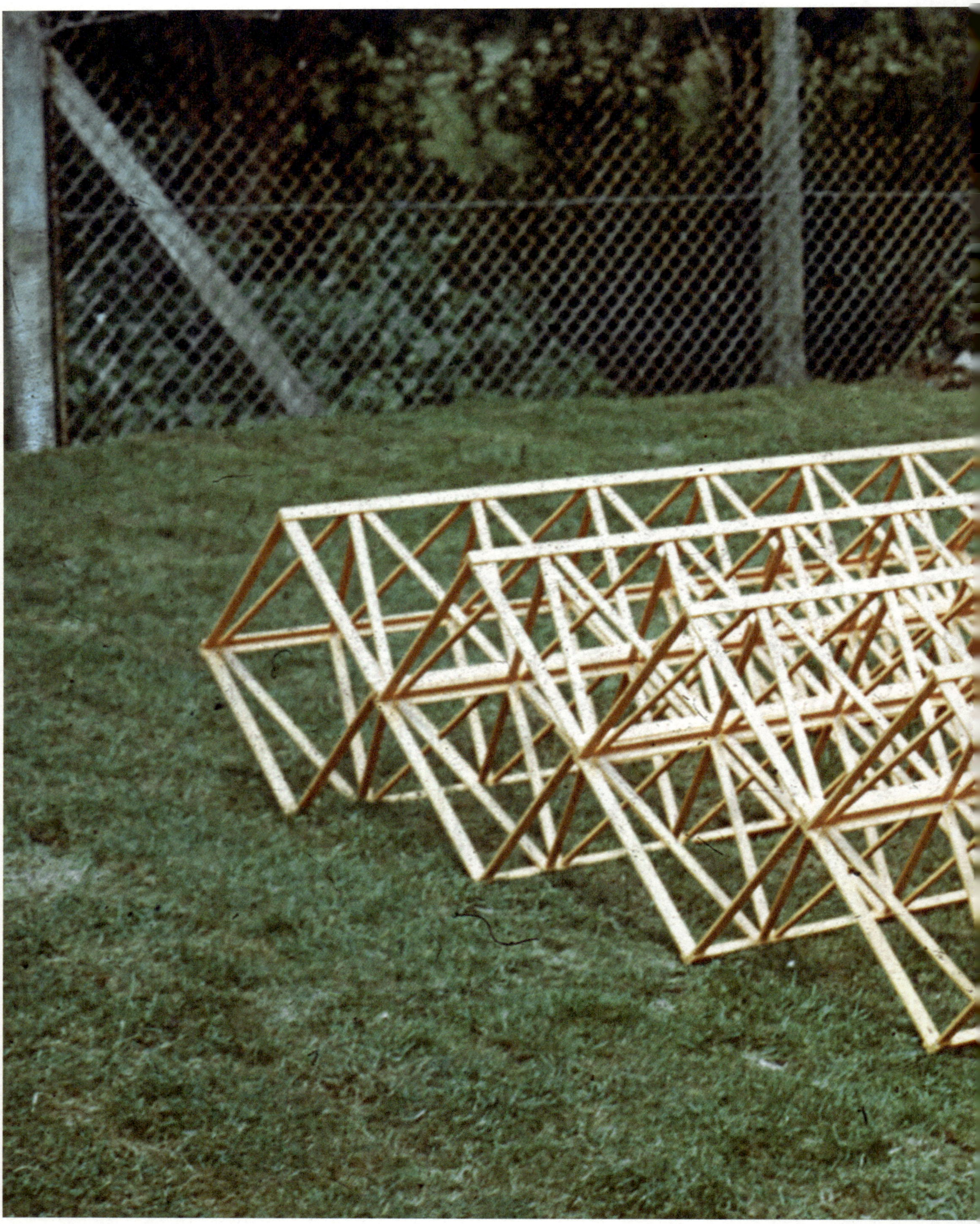

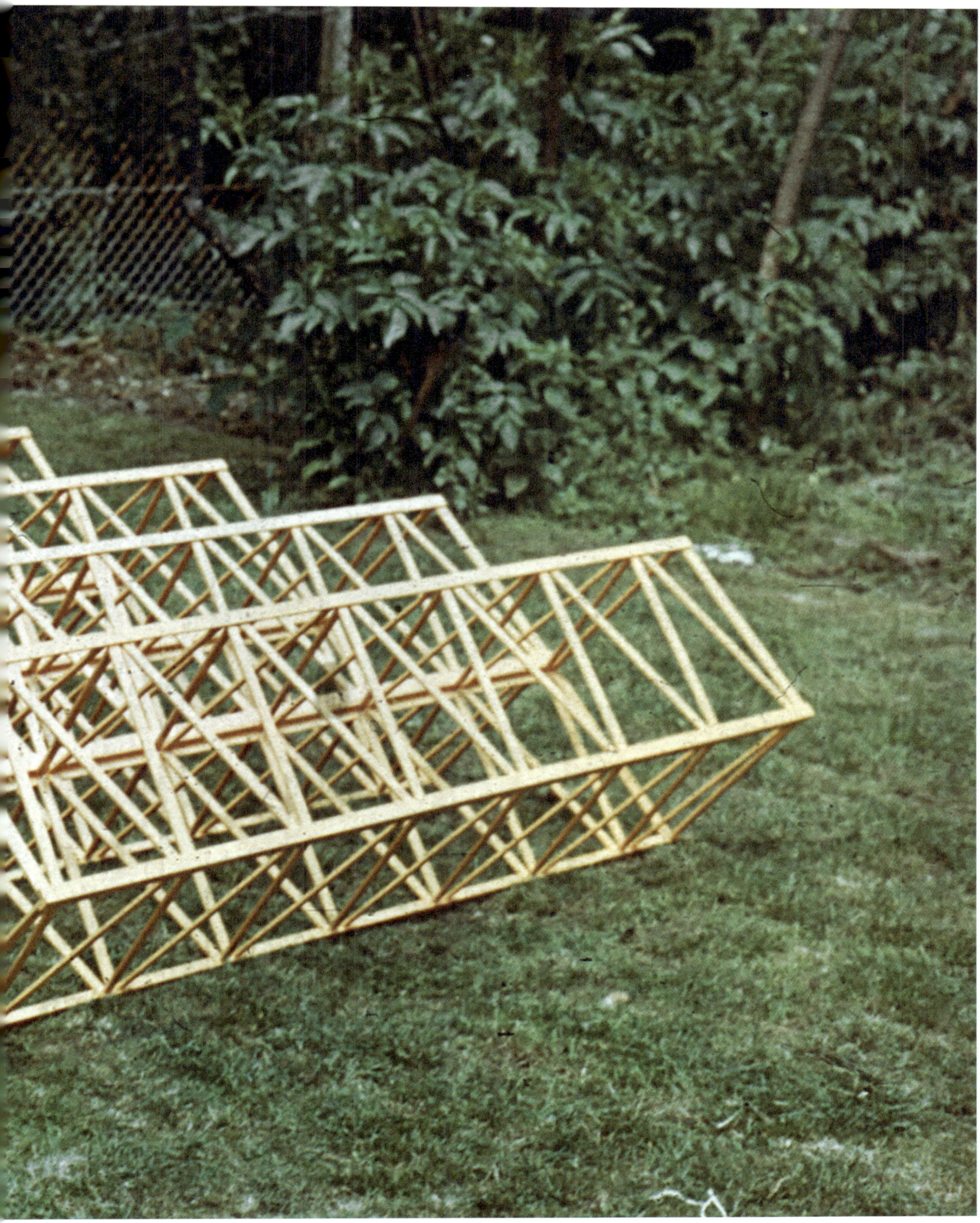

Pehli Si Muhabut, 1971 / 2014
acrylic on wood, 185 x 211 x 25 cm
Collection Albright-Knox Art Gallery

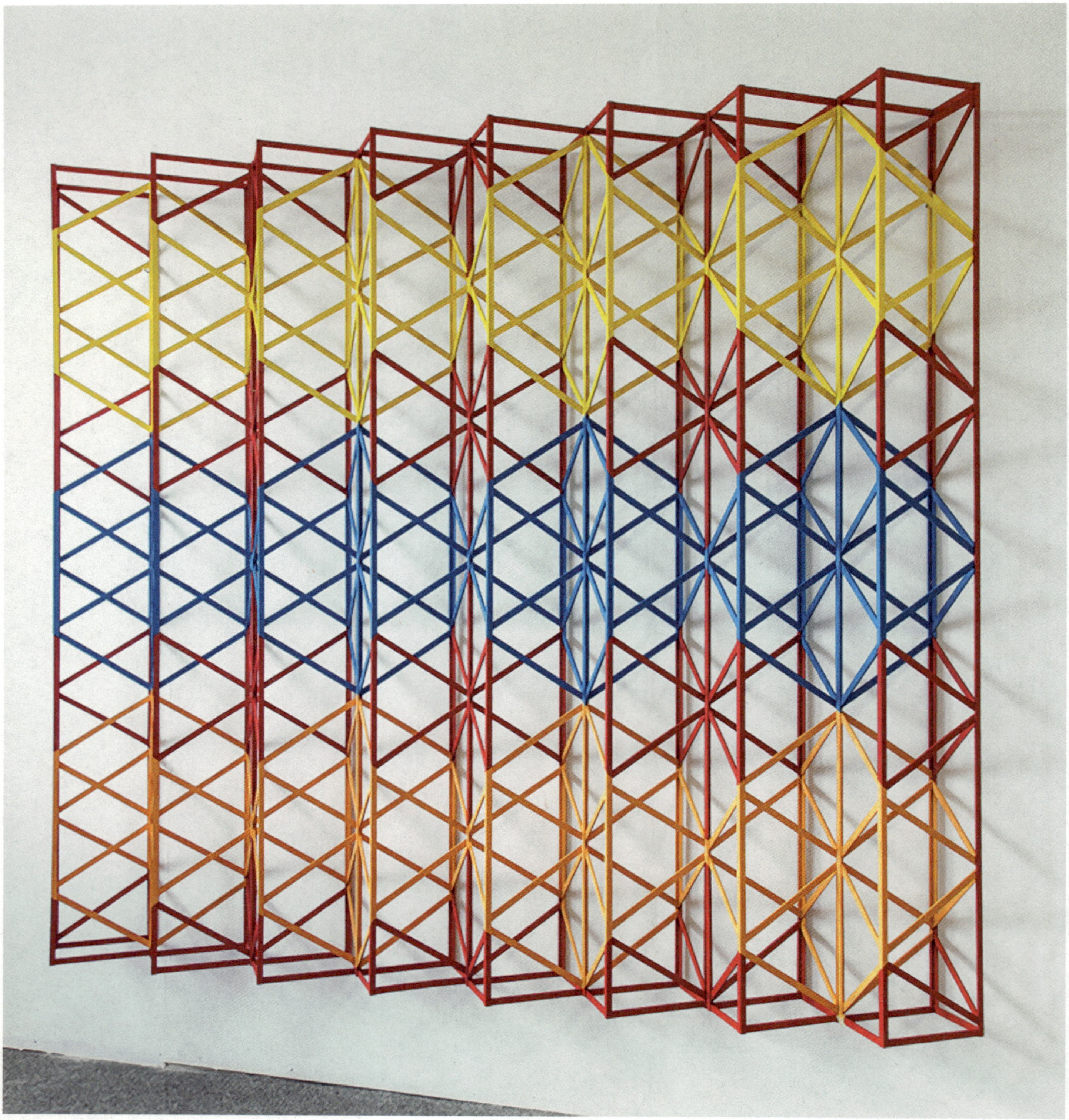

5SR, 1971
acrylic on wood, 114 x 91 x 10 cm, destroyed

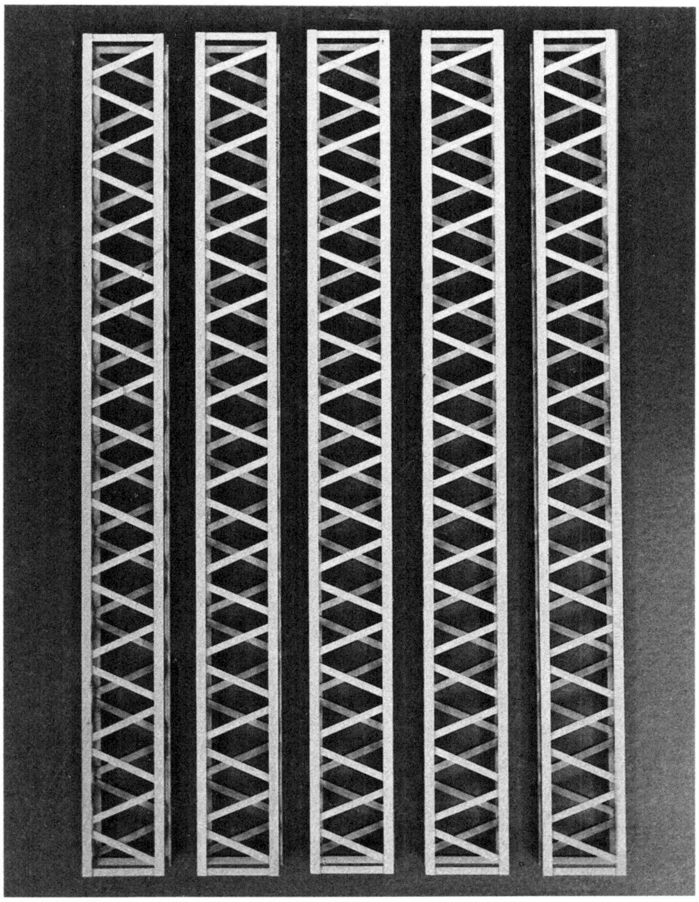

TRE, 1971
acrylic on wood, 183 x 183 x 15 cm

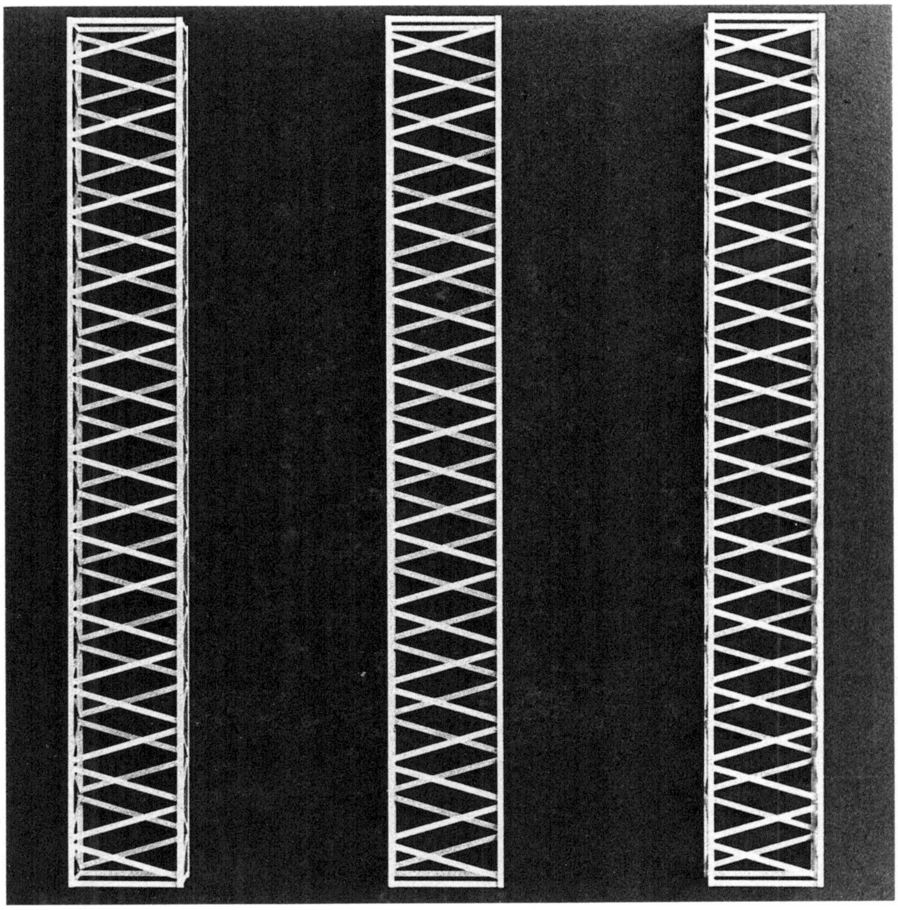

Untitled 4R, 1971
acrylic on wood, 178 x 89 x 10 cm
Untitled 4R+3W, 1971
acrylic on wood, 178 x 160 x 10 cm

Untitled 4R II, 1971
acrylic on wood, 178 x 89 x 10 cm

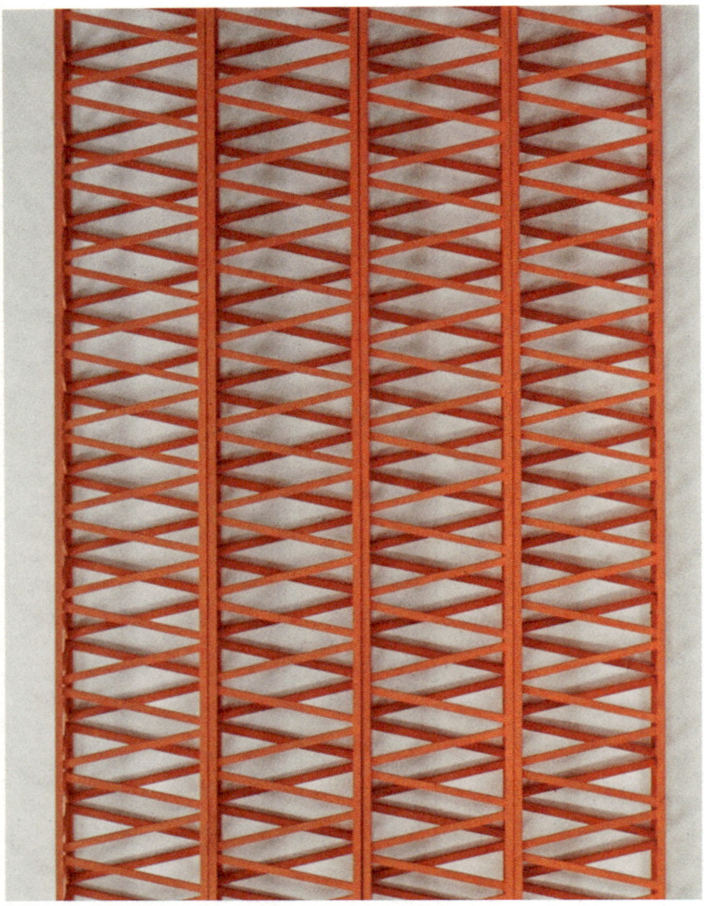

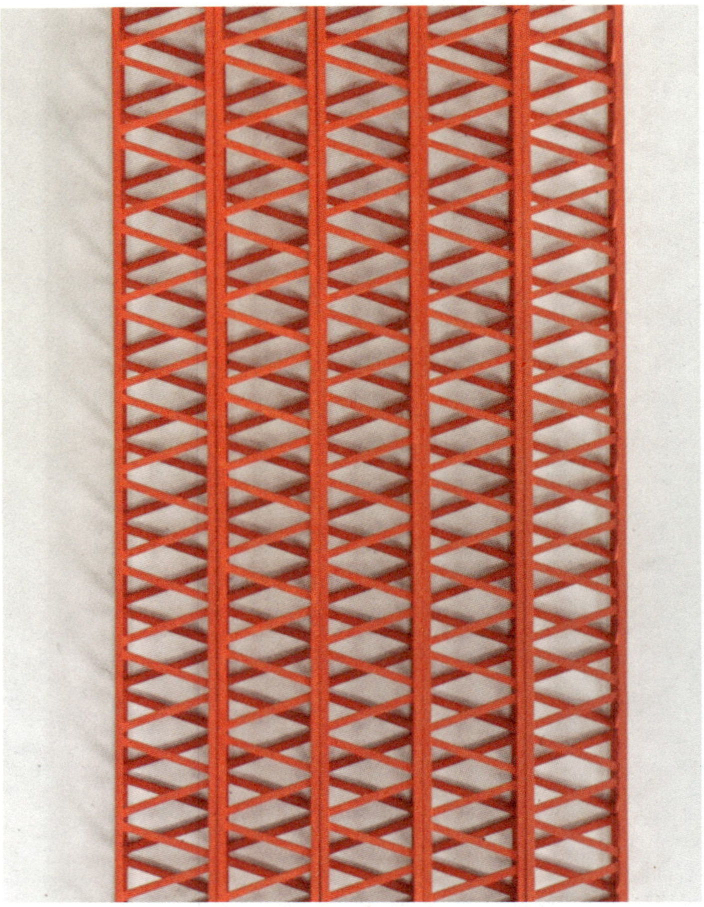

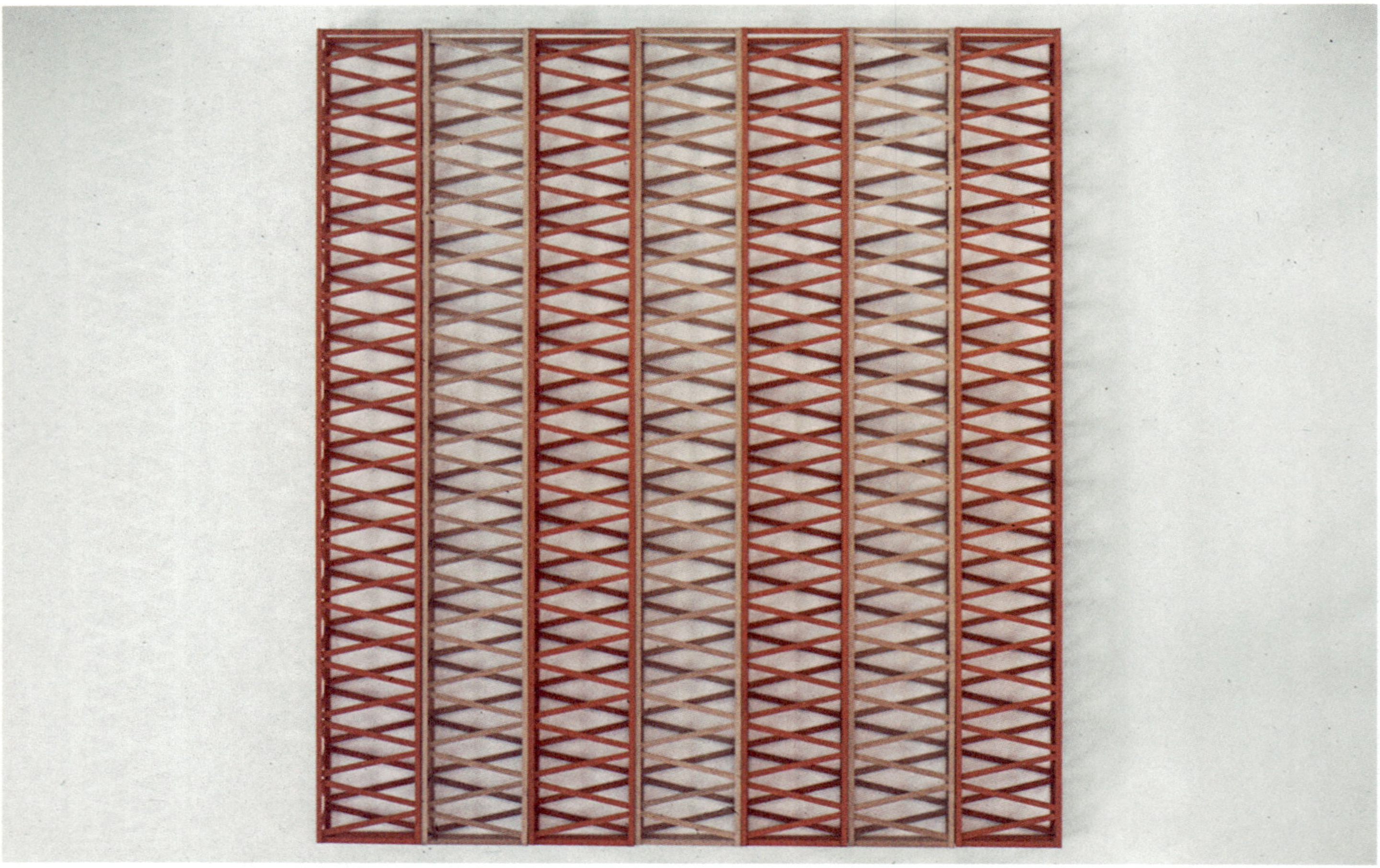

Dewar Per Neela (Blue Wall Piece), 1971
acrylic on wood, 114 x 152 x 31 cm

Burgundy and Red, 1971
acrylic on wood, 91 x 122 x 10 cm

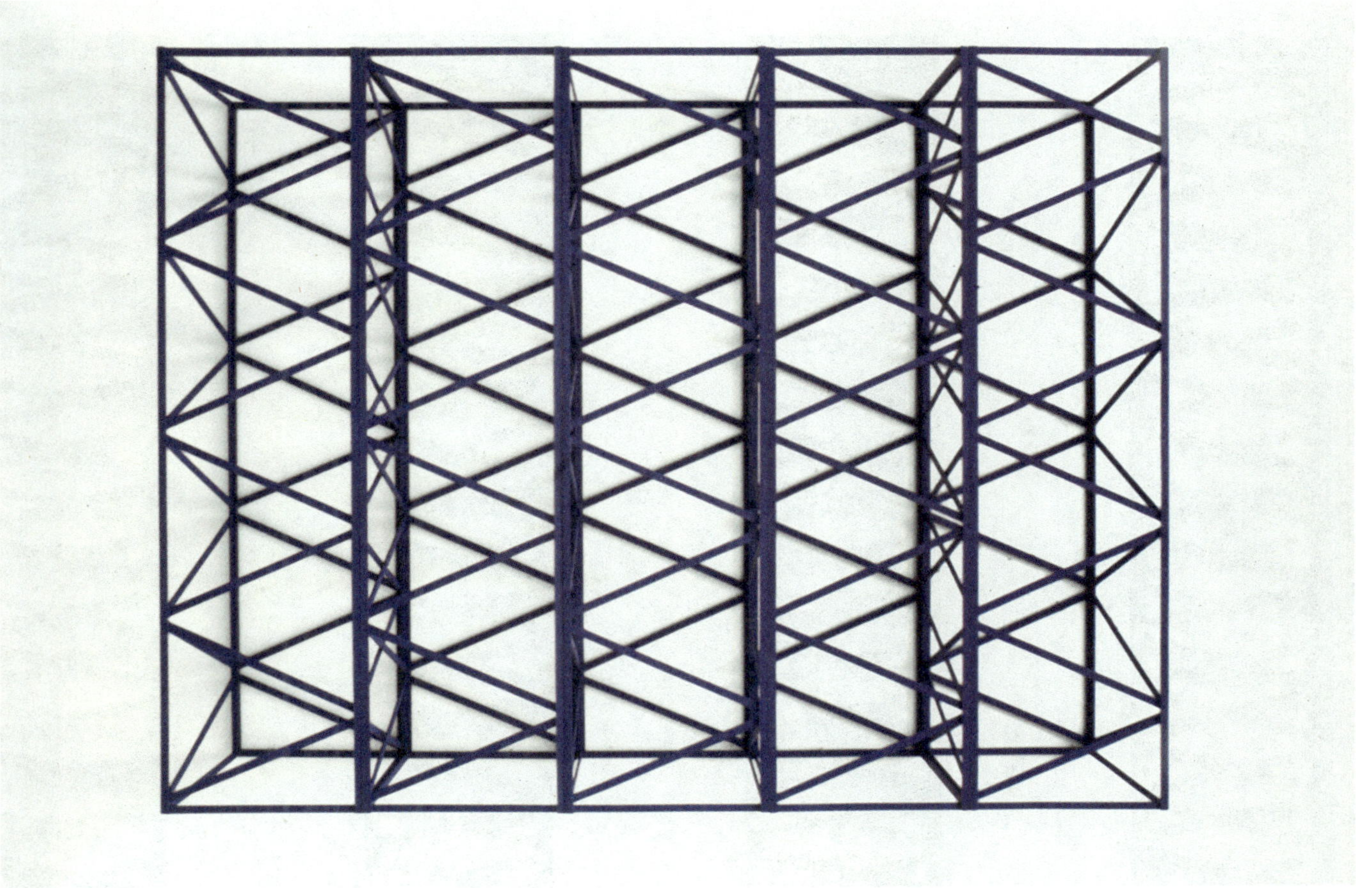

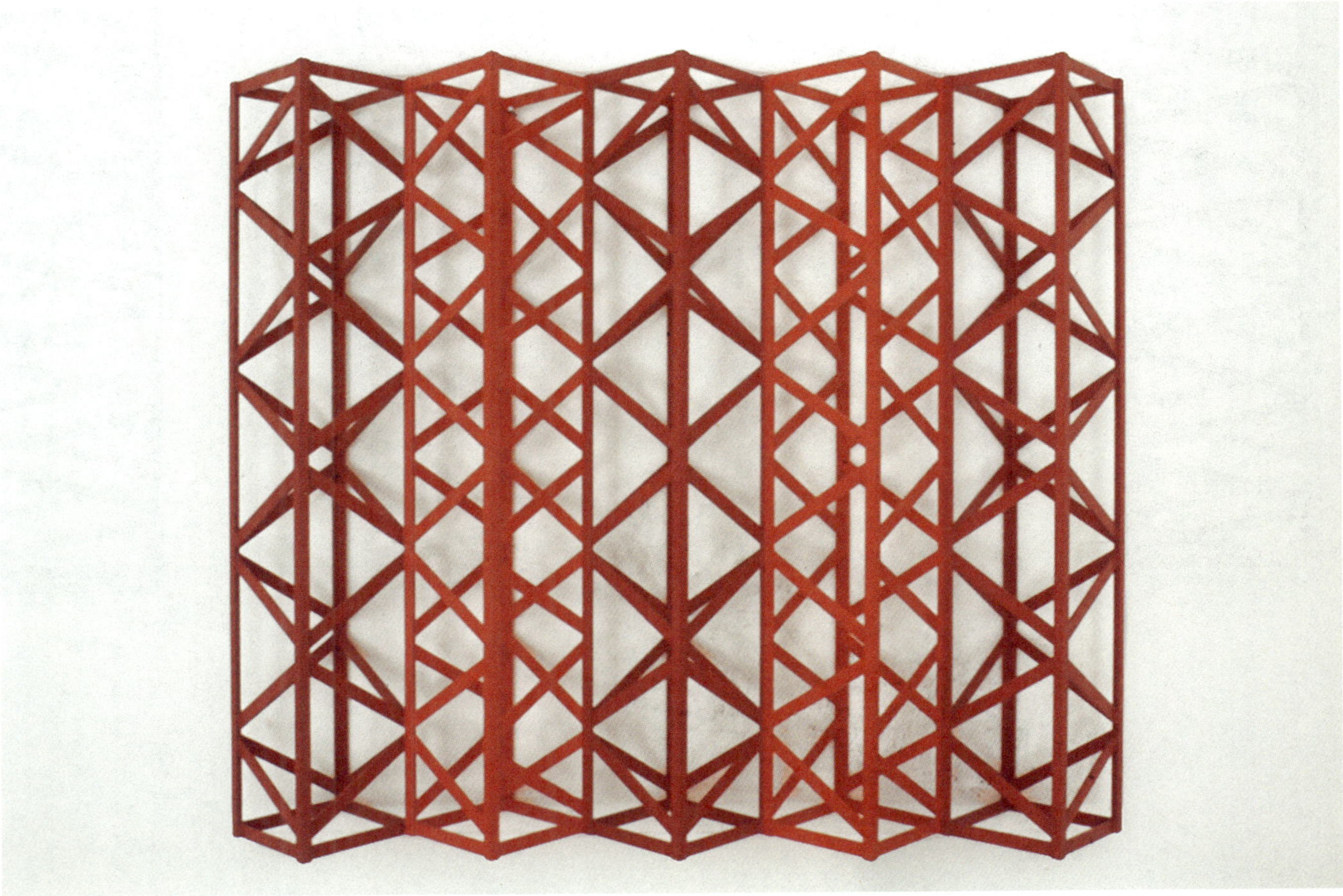

Four Blue Apart, 1971–1972
4 acrylic on wood Structures, 23 x 173 x 10 cm each

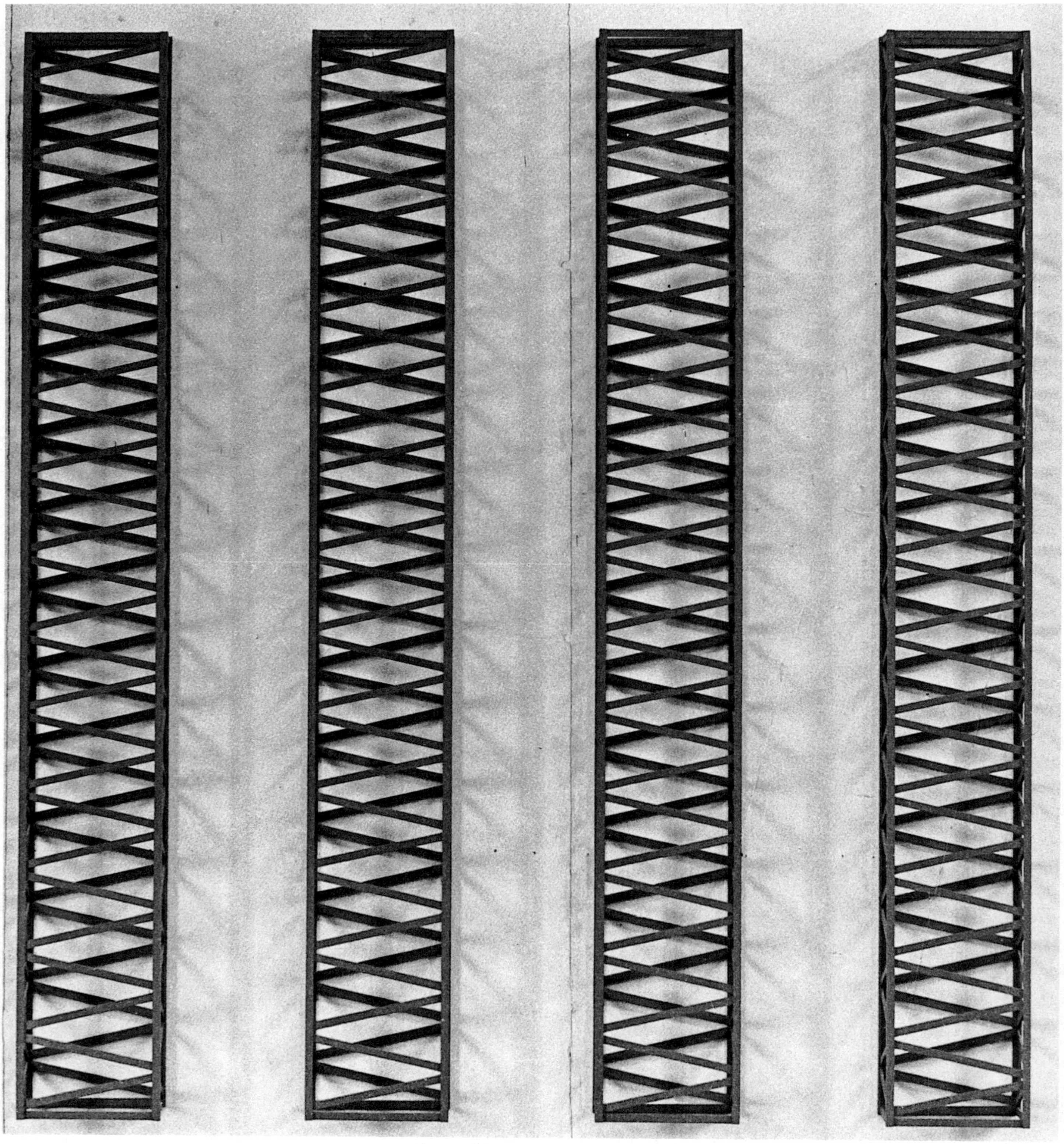

Zig-Zag, 1972
acrylic on wood, 183 x 183 x 13 cm
YOOB, 1972
acrylic on wood, 152 x 152 x 13 cm

4YSR, 1972
acrylic on wood, 122 x 183 x 15 cm
Five Together, 1972
acrylic on wood, 91 x 162 x 10 cm

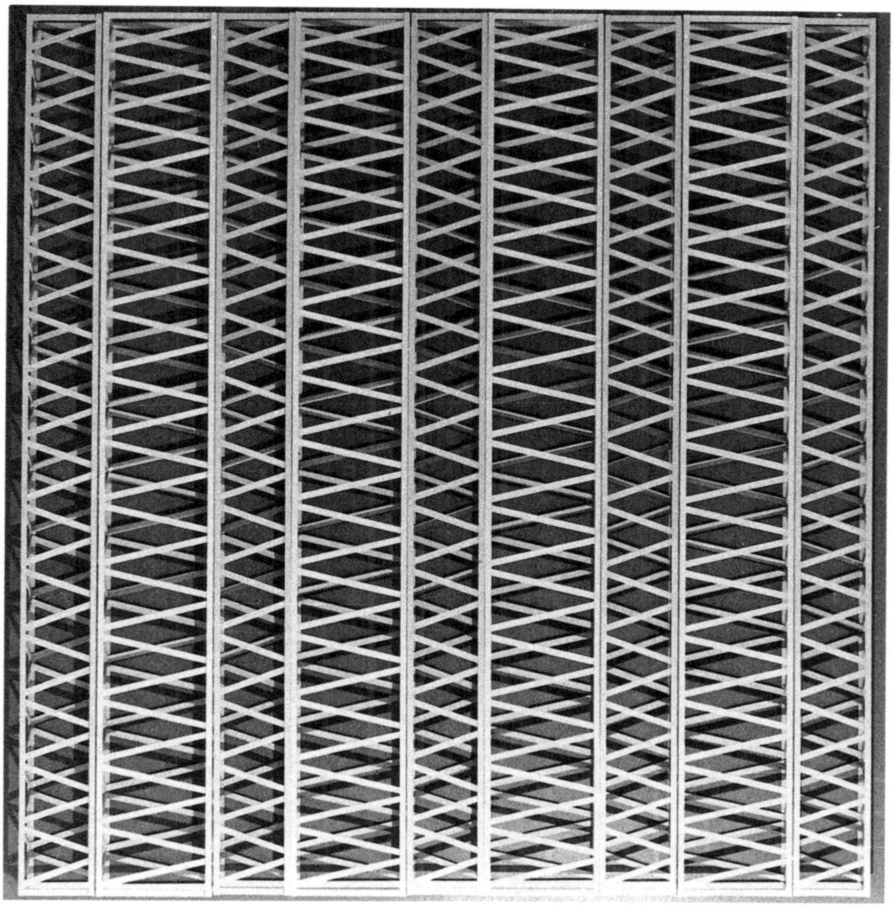

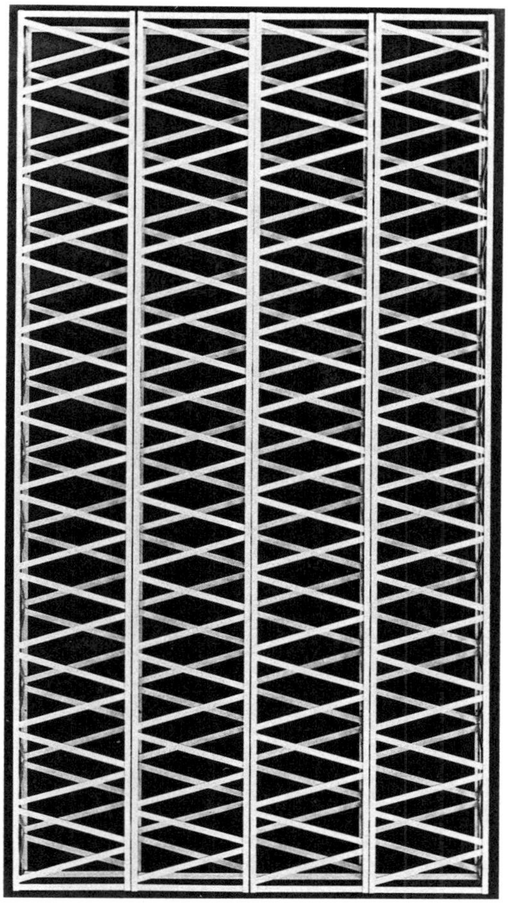

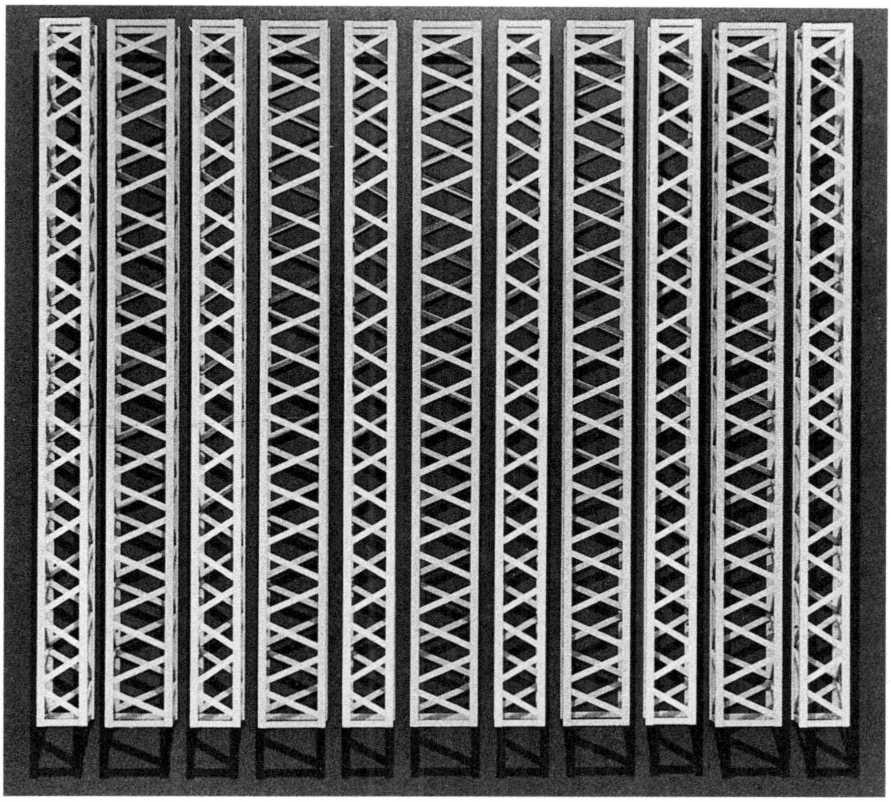

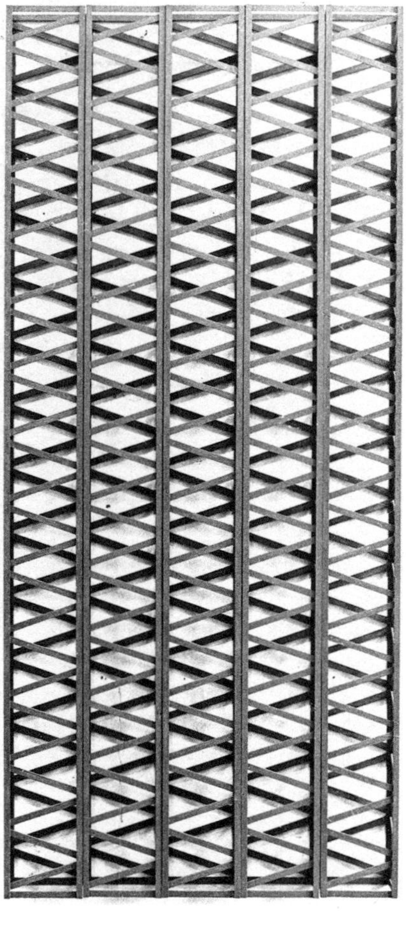

Neela, 1971 / 2017
acrylic on wood, 114 x 91 x 91 cm

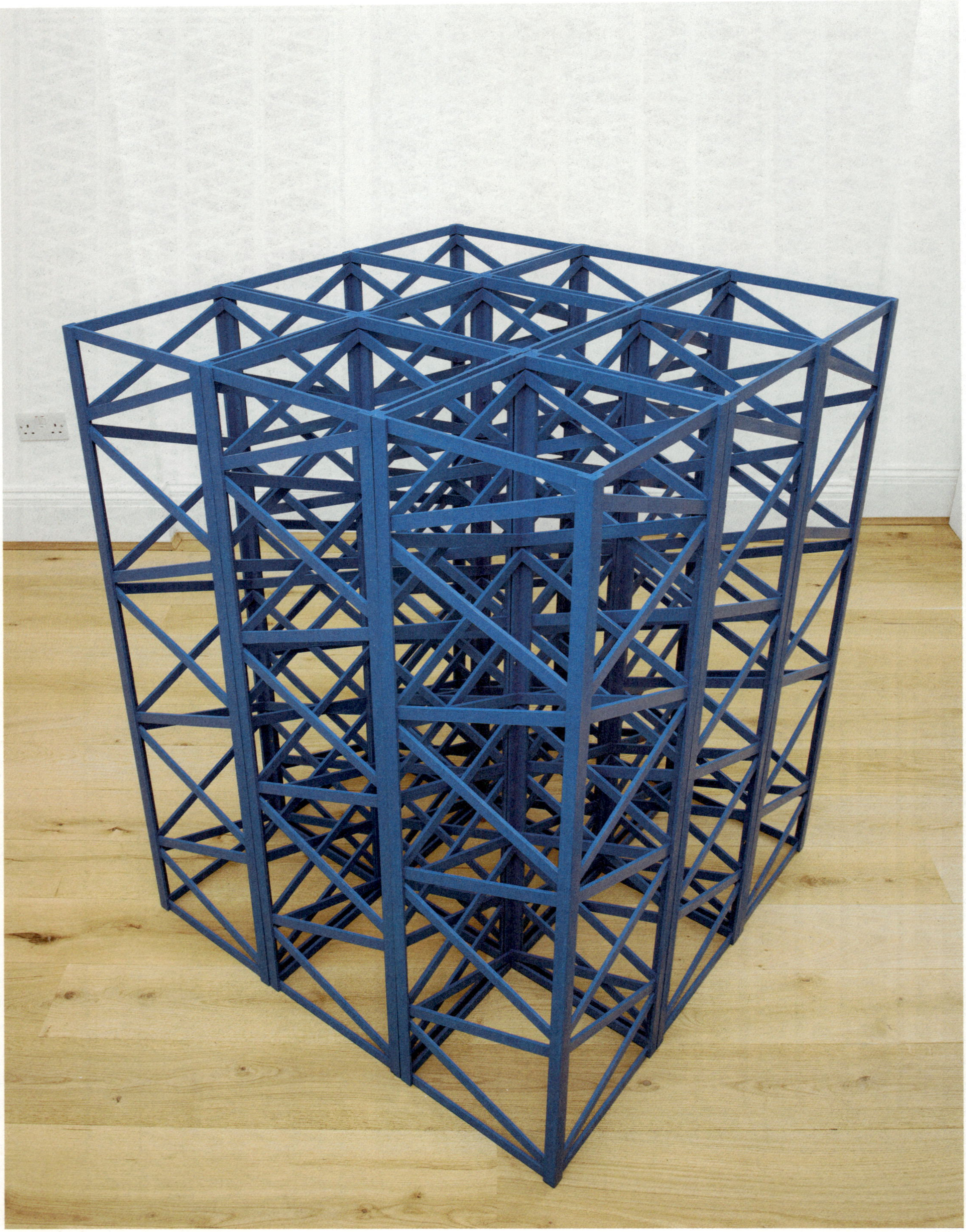

Untitled (Yellow on Red), 1971 / 2016
acrylic on wood, 183 x 122 x 15 cm

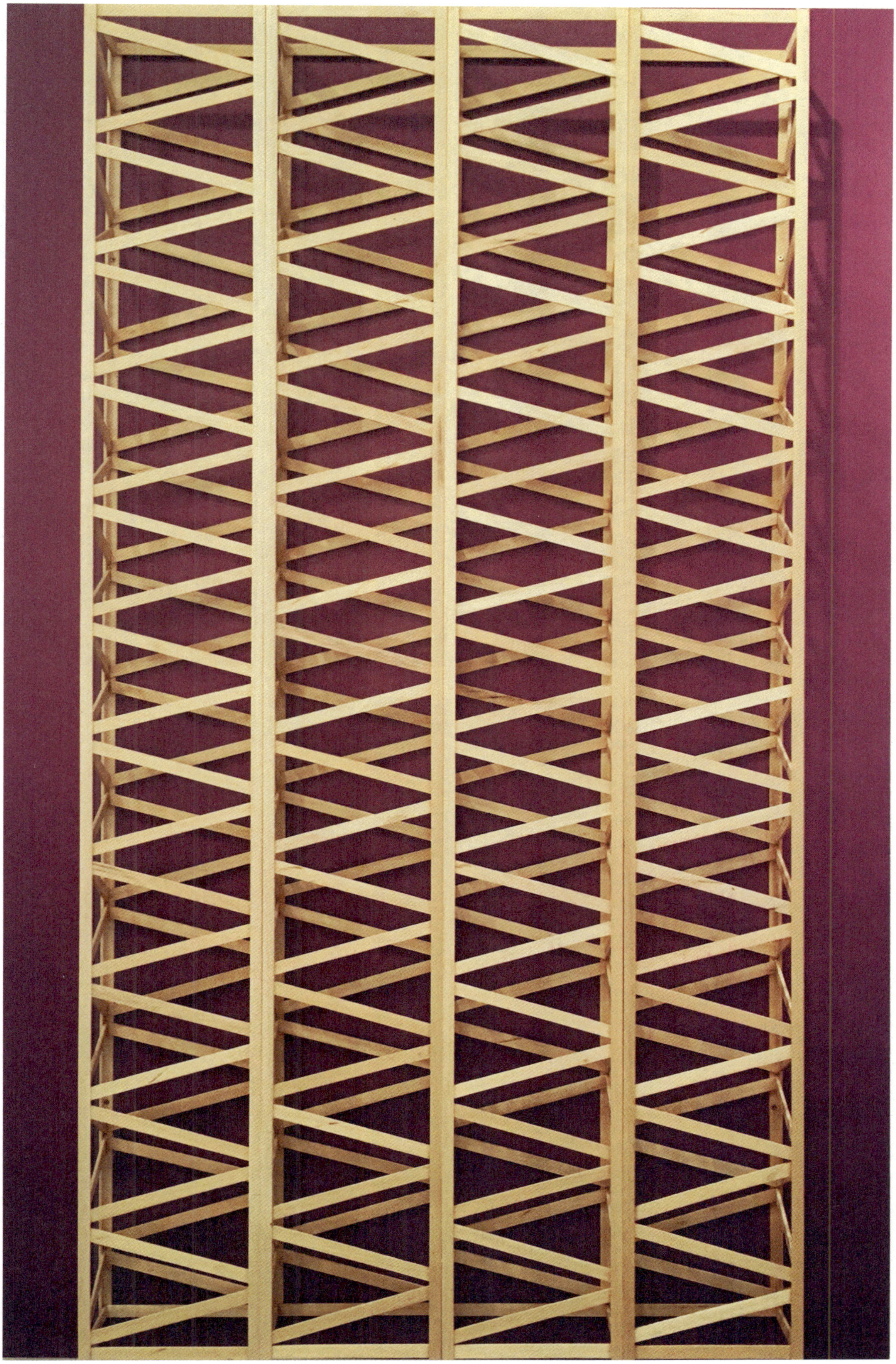

Yellow On Blue, 1972
acrylic on wood, 183 x 183 x 15 cm
Red On Blue (Five together), 1972
acrylic on wood, 183 x 122 x 15 cm

Red On Blue (Five apart), 1972
acrylic on wood, 183 x 183 x 15 cm

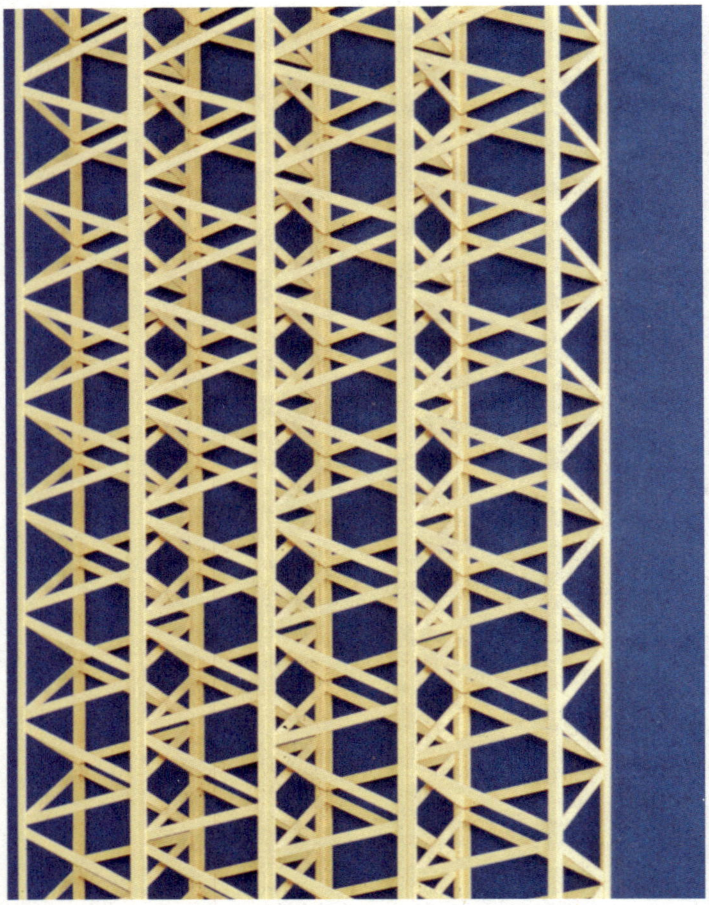

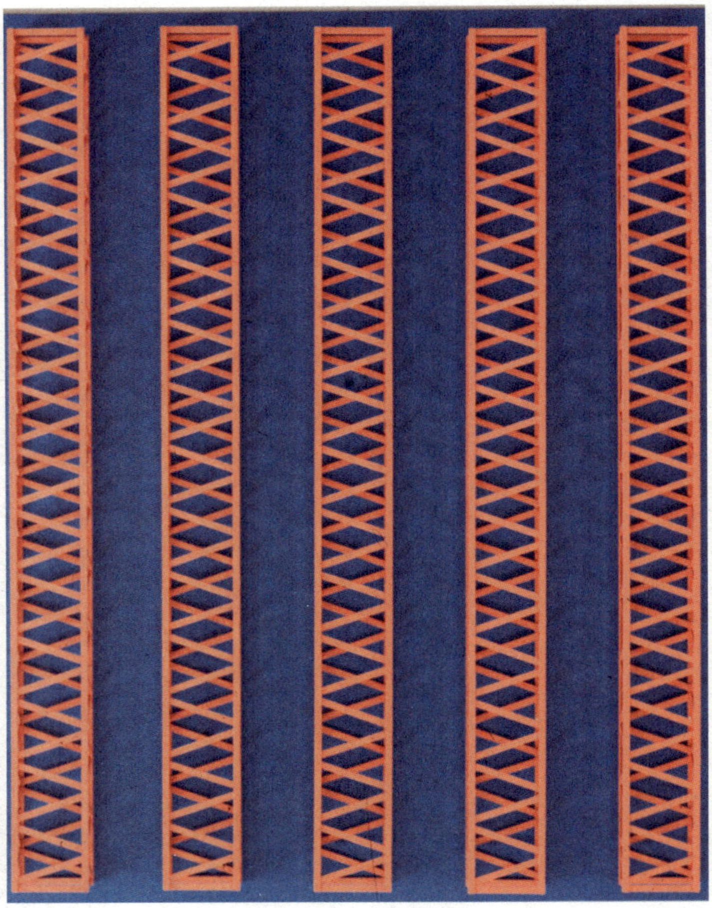

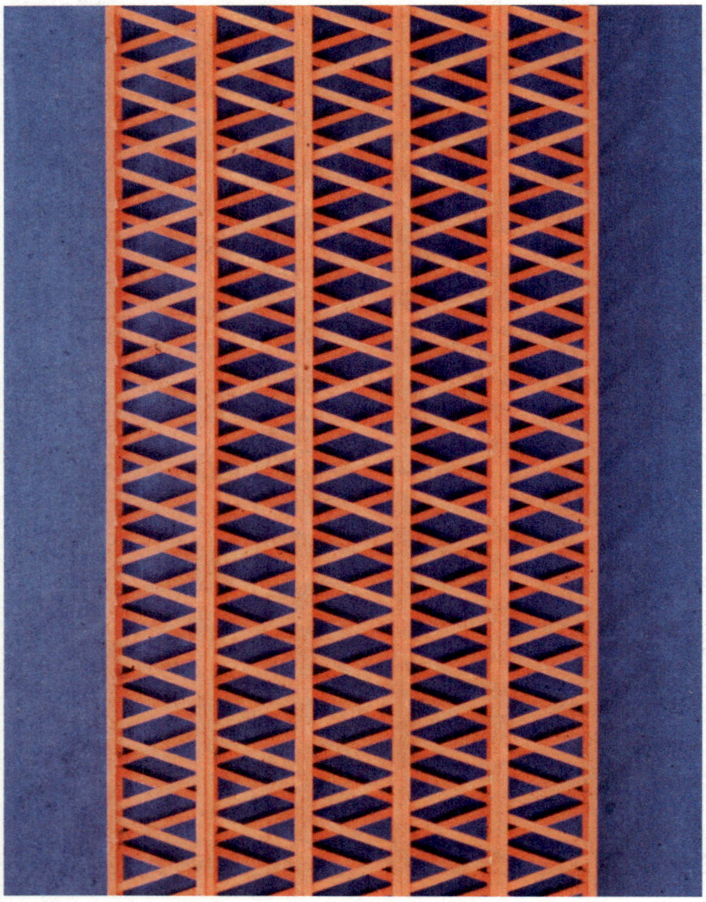

Orange On Blue (Four apart), 1972
acrylic on wood, 183 x 122 x 15 cm
5W On Red, 1972
acrylic on wood, 183 x 122 x 15 cm

Orange On Blue (Four Together), 1972
acrylic on wood, 183 x 122 x 15 cm
3Ws On Blue, 1972
acrylic on wood, 183 x 122 x 15 cm

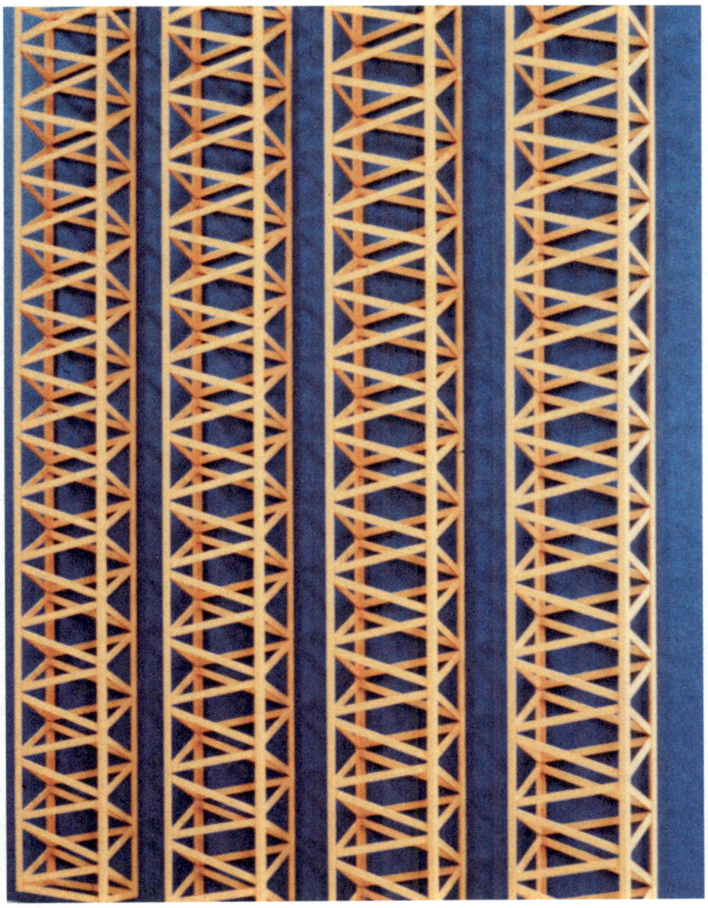

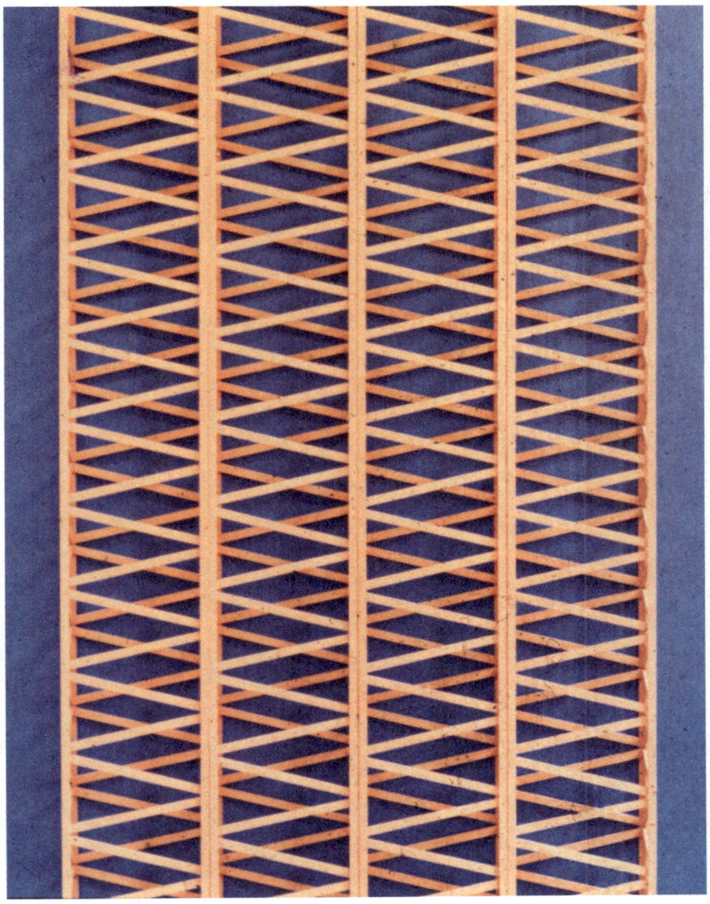

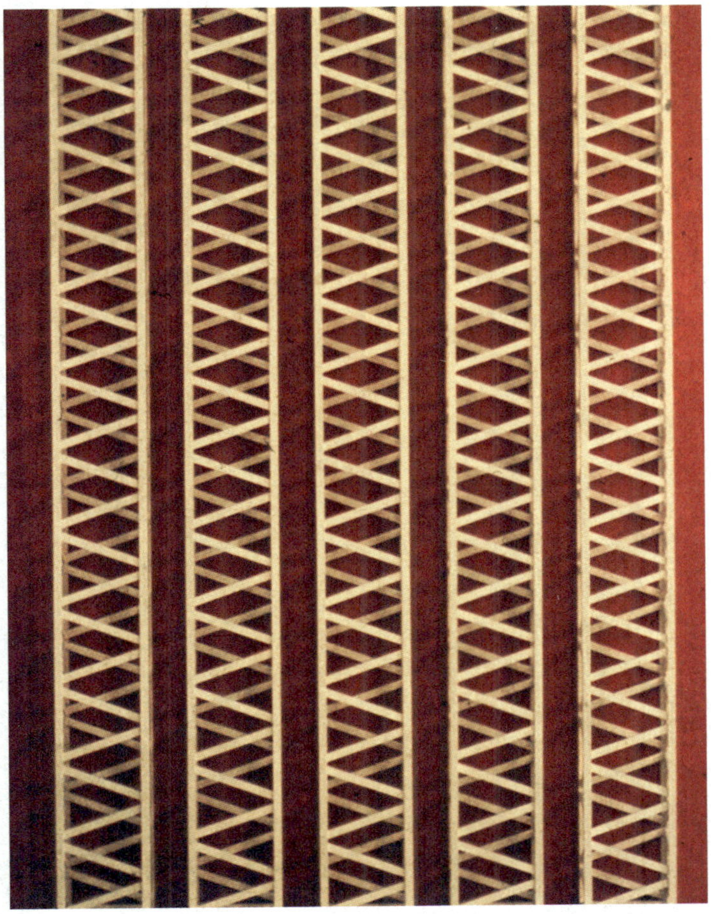

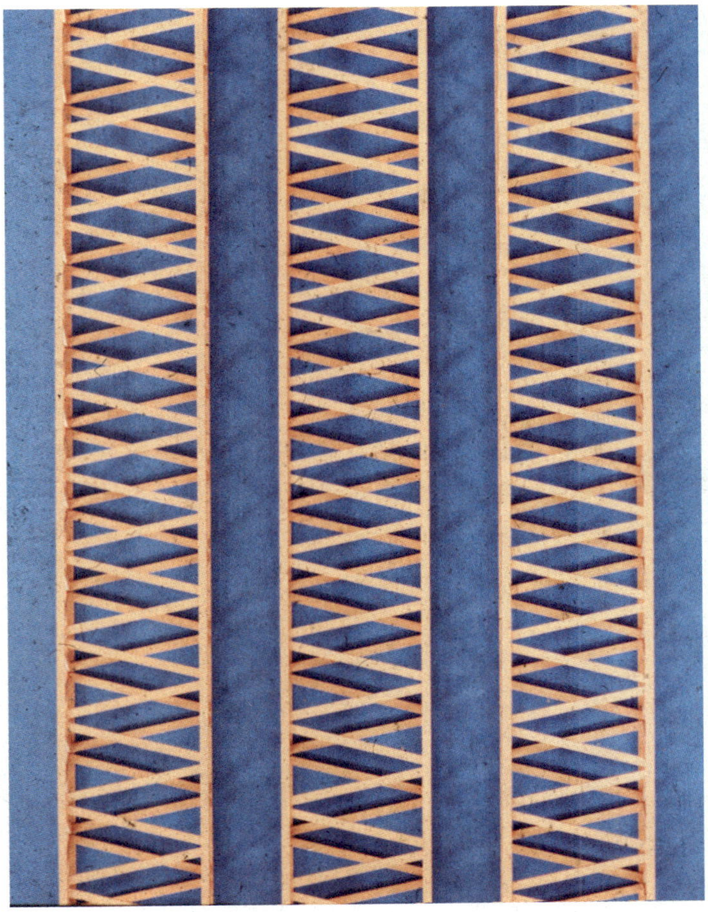

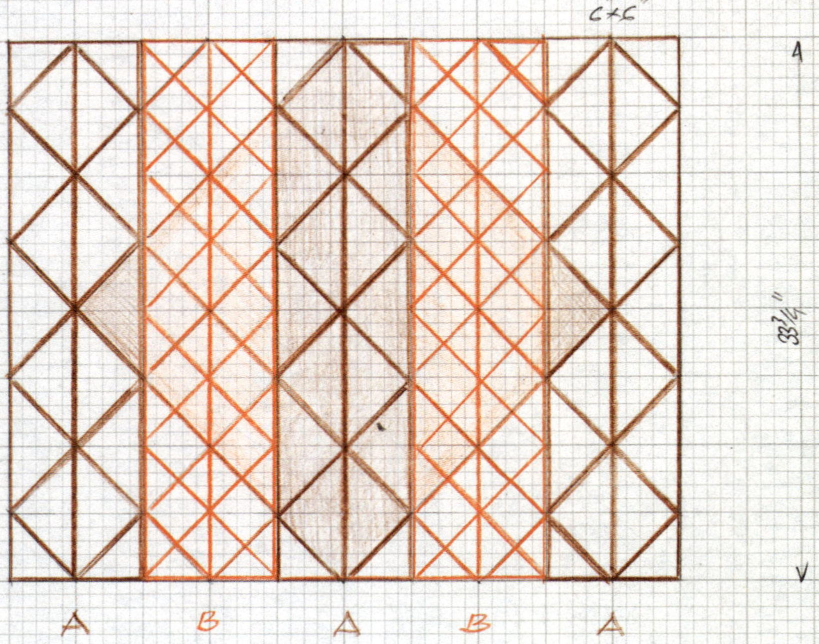

1) A A A A A
2) B B B B B
3) A B A B A —— 1972
4) B A B A B

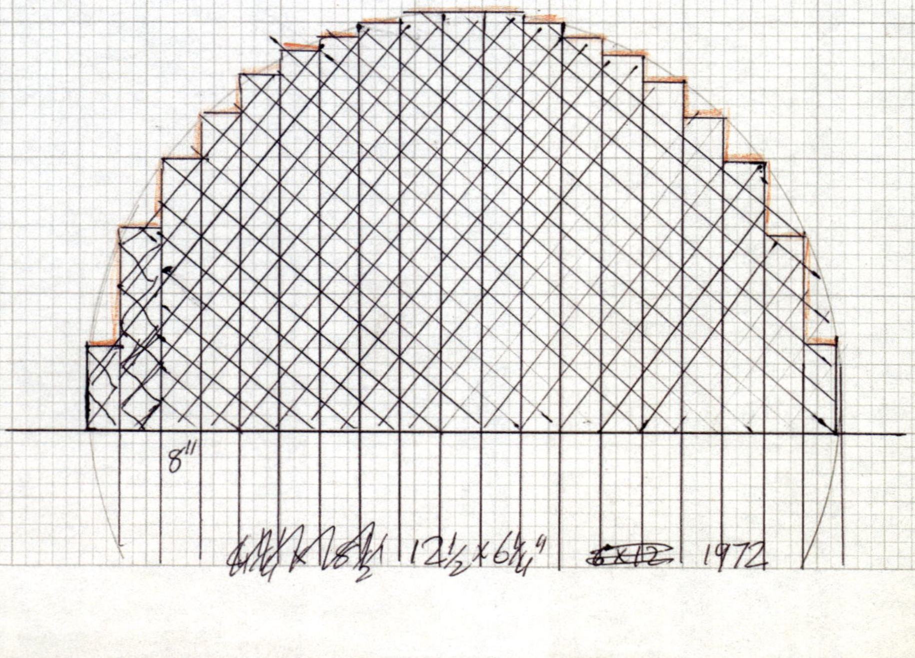

Untitled (6H54), 1972
pencil on paper, 34 x 23 cm
Untitled, 1972
pencil on paper, 23 x 20 cm

Untitled, 1972
pencil on paper, 34 x 23 cm

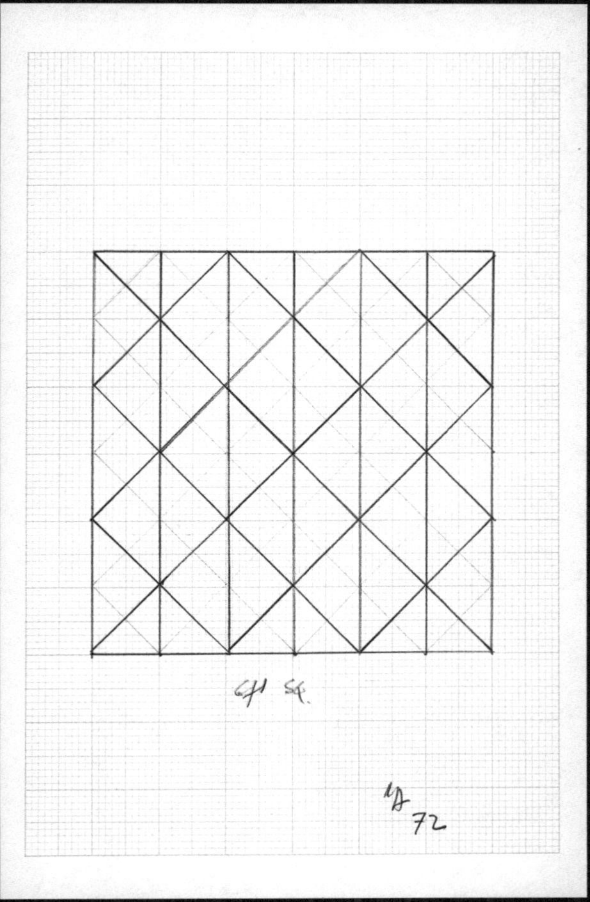

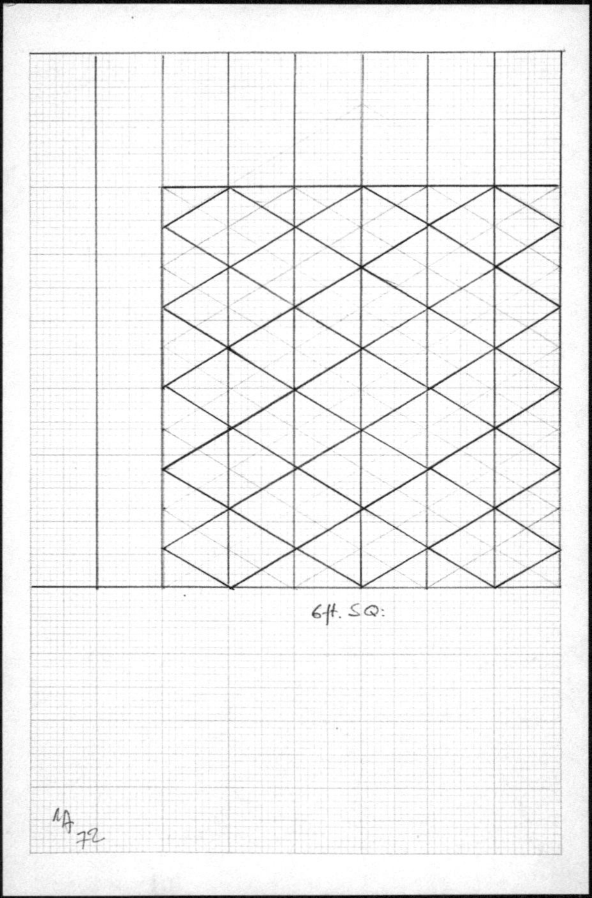

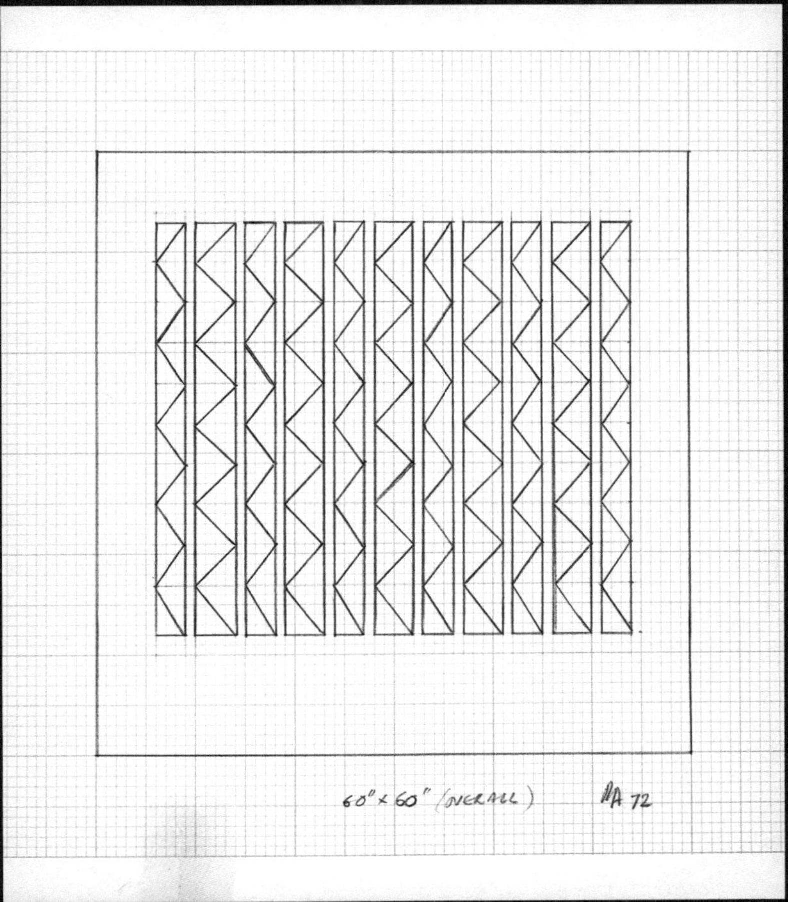

RYRY, 1972
acrylic on wood, 183 x 91 x 15 cm
RRYOOYBB, 1972 / 2014
acrylic on wood, 185 x 290 x 10 cm

RYOOYR, 1972
acrylic on wood, 183 x 137 x 15 cm
YOBR, 1972
acrylic on wood, 183 x 91 x 15 cm

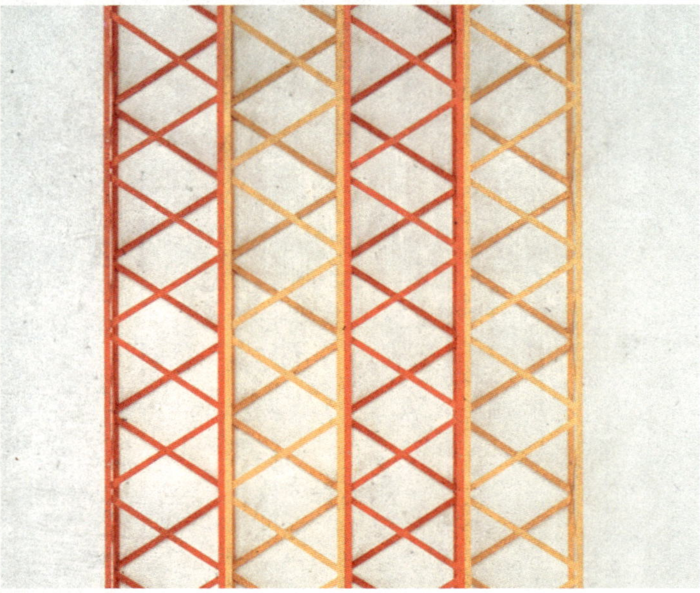

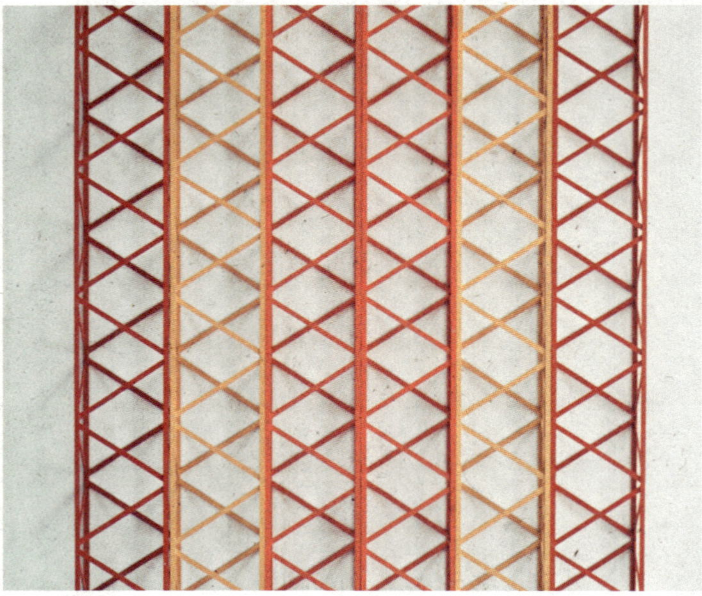

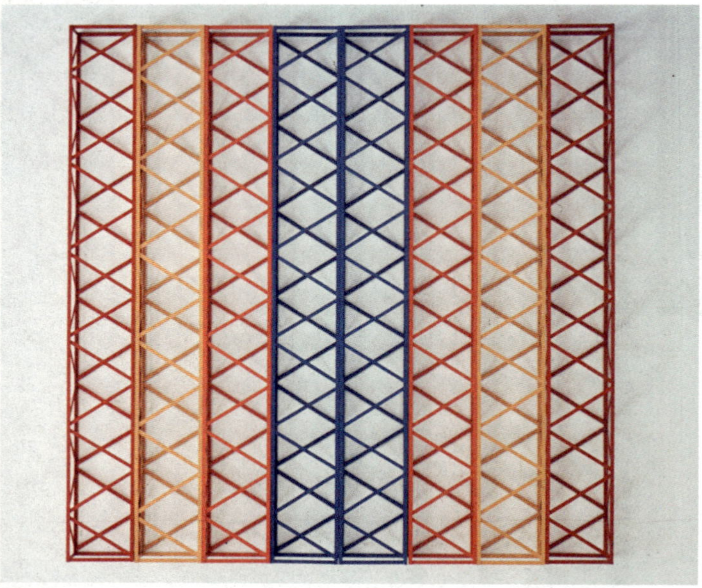

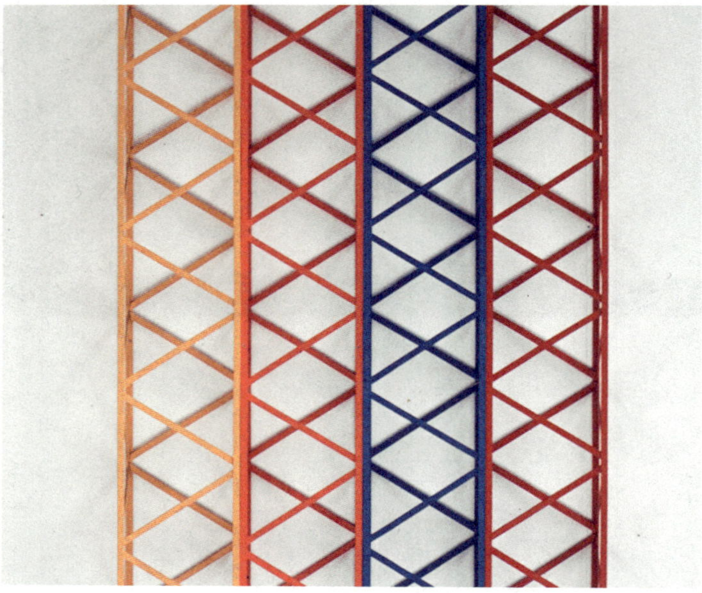

Untitled 2W+2R, 1972
acrylic on wood, 178 x 81 x 15 cm
BROYYORB, 1972
acrylic on wood, 183 x 183 x 15 cm

BRBR, 1972
acrylic on wood, 183 x 91 x 15 cm
BRYOOYRB, 1972
acrylic on wood, 183 x 183 x 15 cm

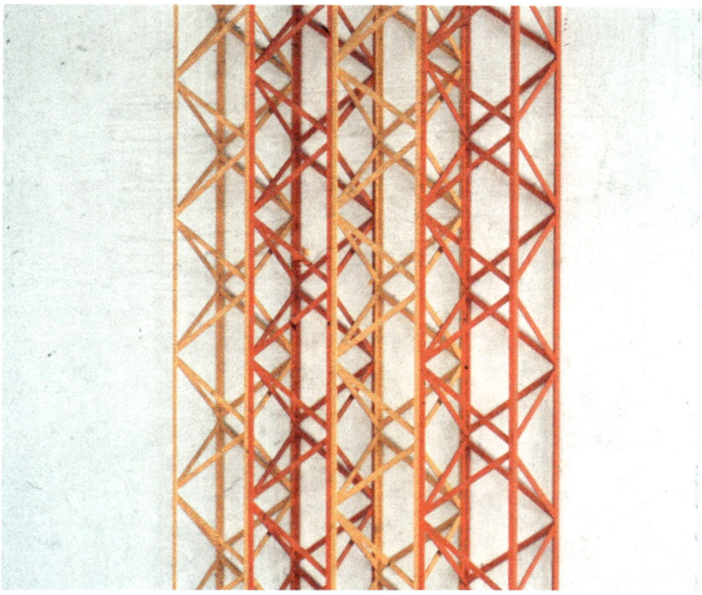

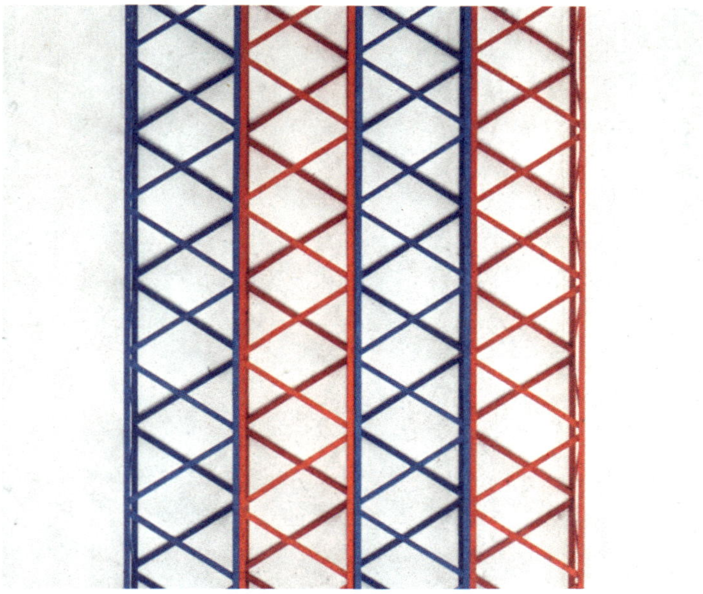

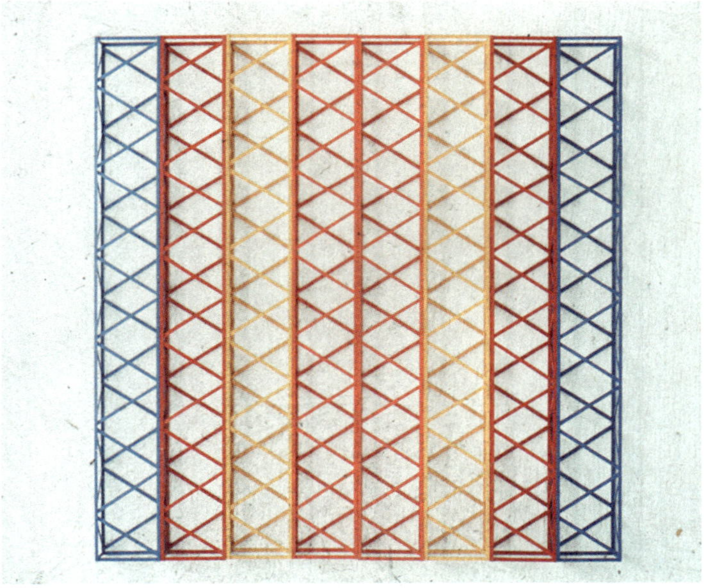

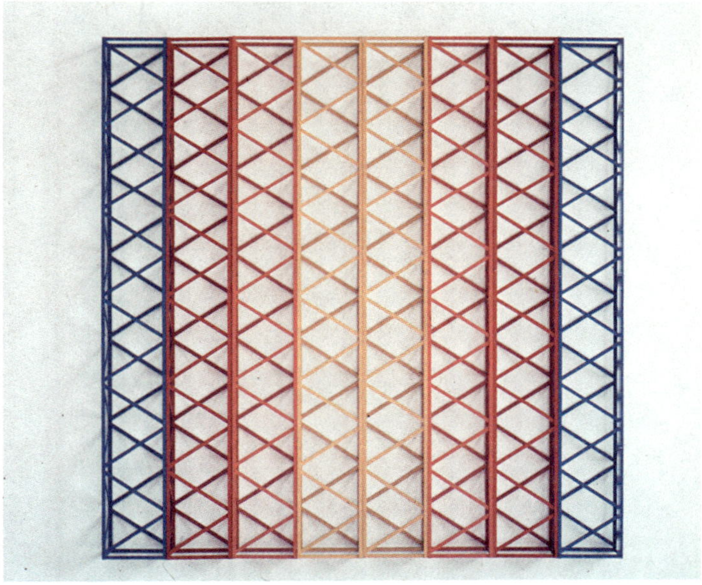

Burgundy II, 1972
acrylic on wood, 178 x 64 x 13 cm

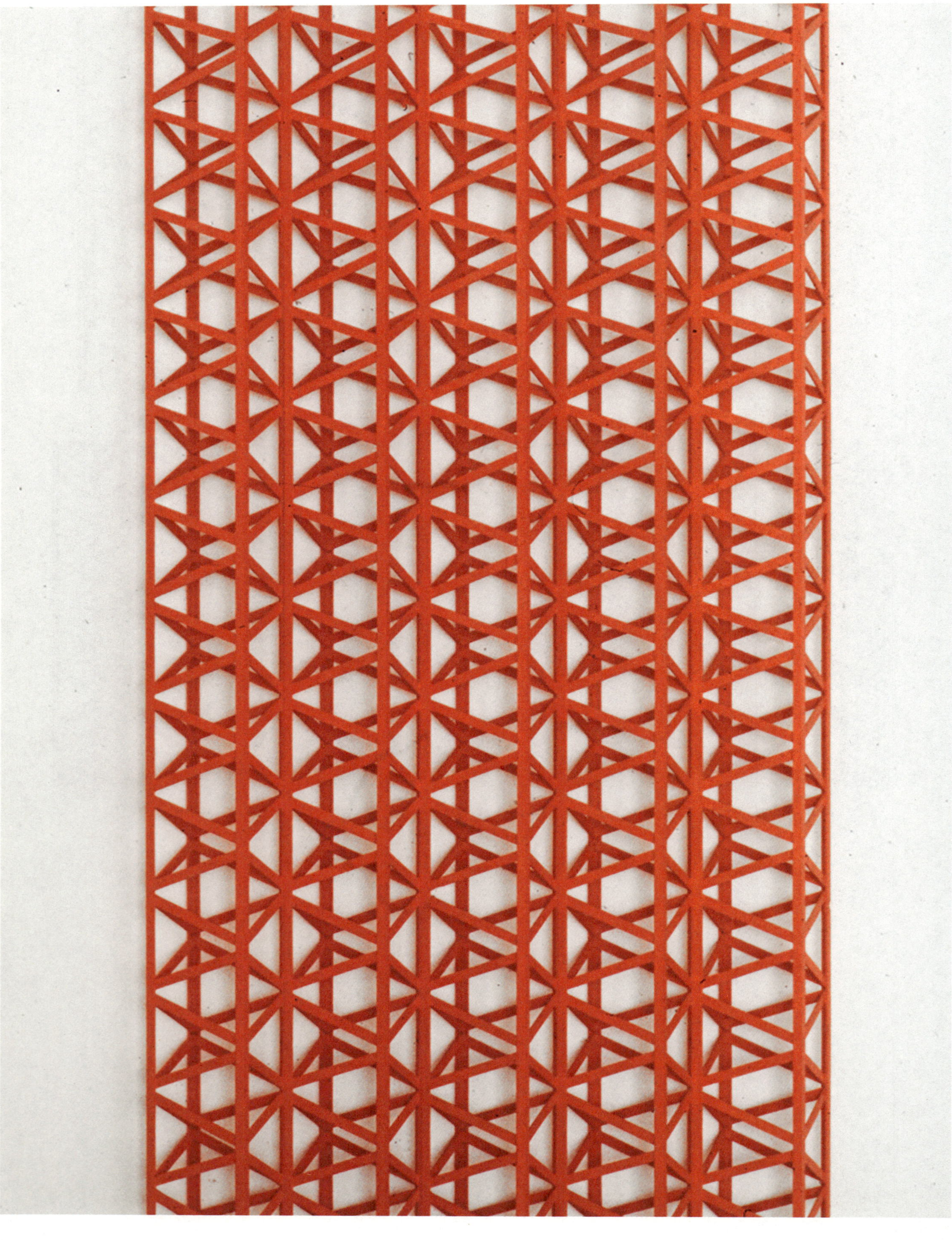

OYBRRBYO, 1972
acrylic on wood, 183 x 183 x 15 cm
RBYORBYO, 1972
acrylic on wood, 183 x 183 x 15 cm
OYBRRBYO, 1972
acrylic on wood, 183 x 183 x 15 cm

OYRBBRYO, 1972
acrylic on wood, 183 x 183 x 15 cm
RY+RB+OY+RB, 1972
acrylic on wood, 183 x 229 x 15 cm
RYBYR, 1972
acrylic on wood, 71 x 43 x 15 cm

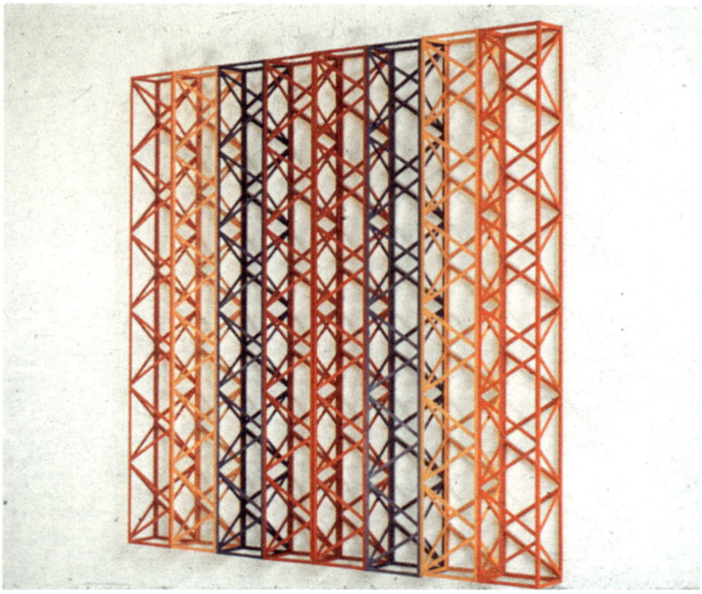

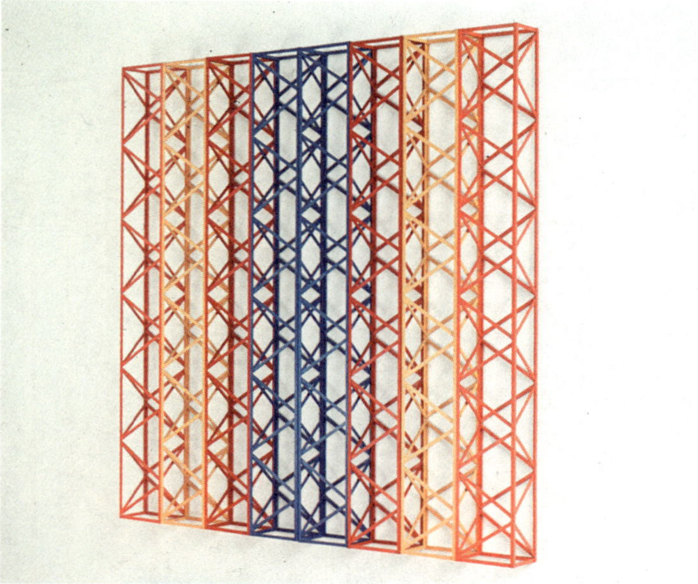

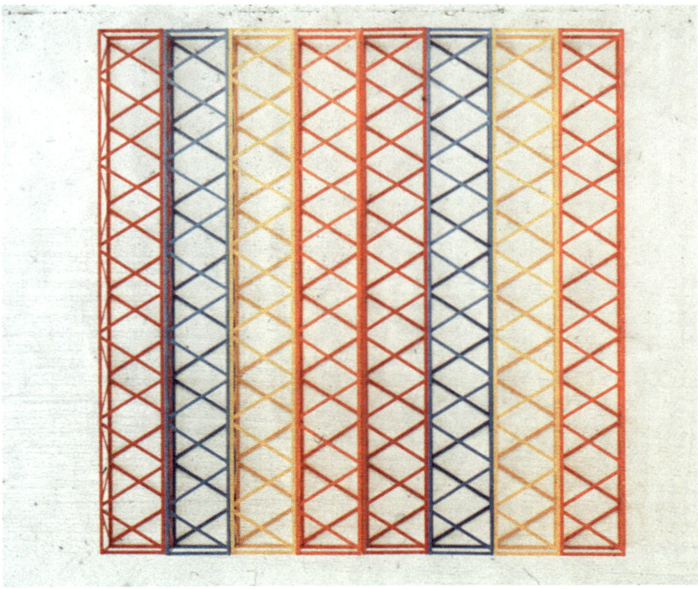

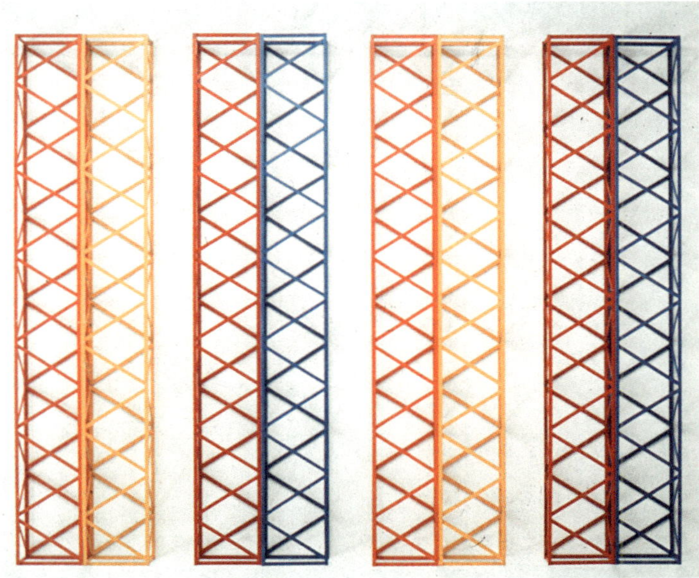

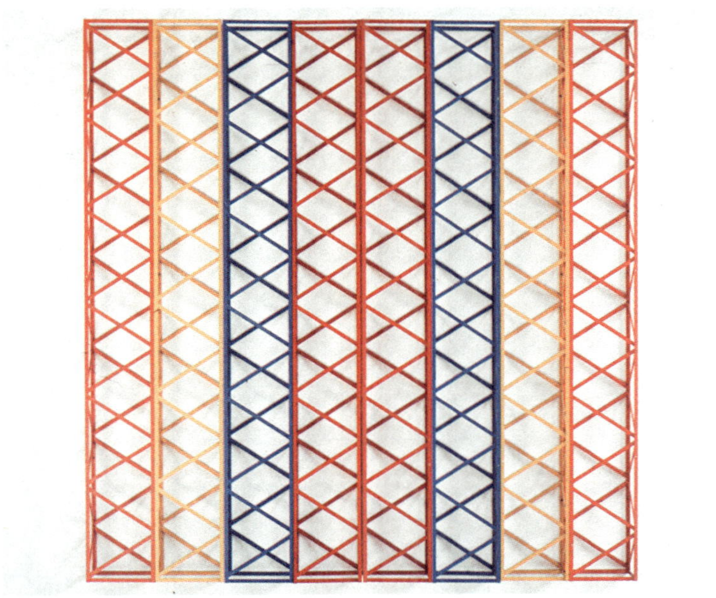

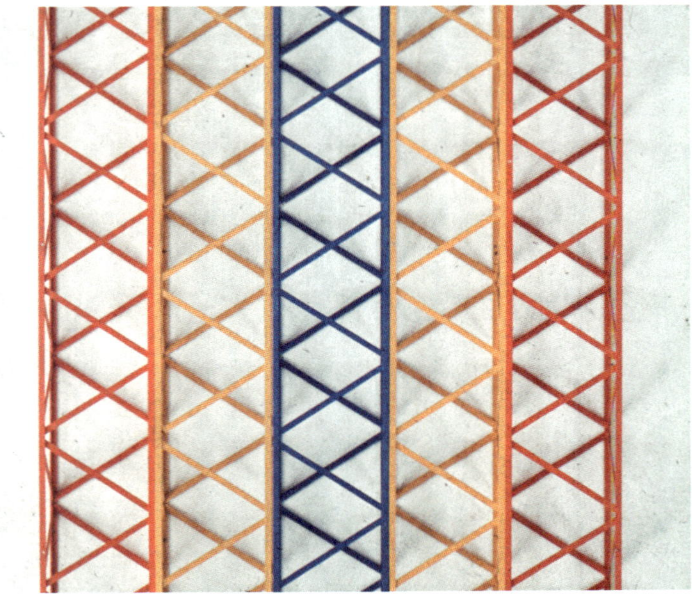

RRYOOYBB, 1972 / 2014
acrylic on wood, 185 x 290 x 10 cm
Private collection

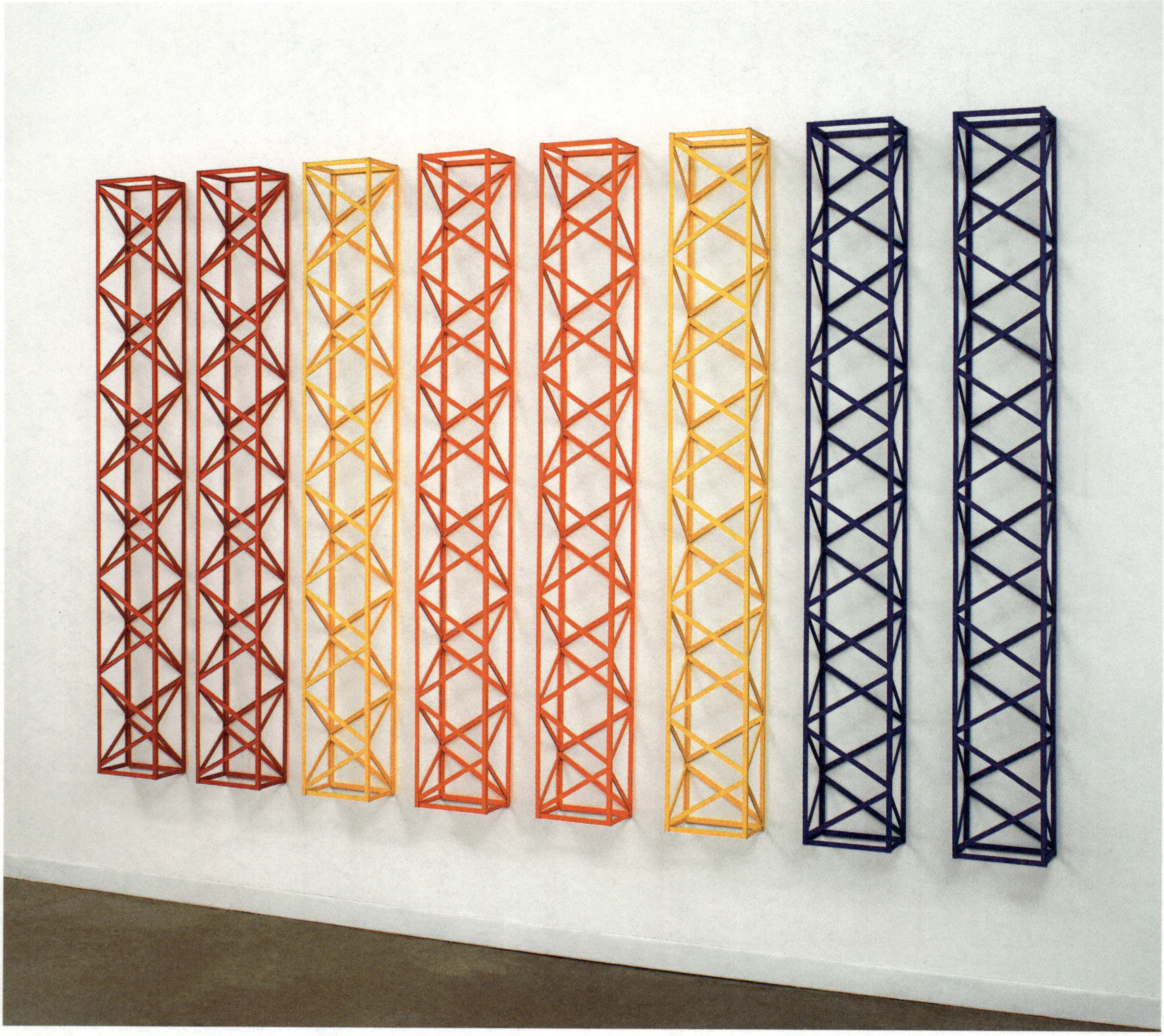

Sculptor, Performer, Critic: Rasheed Araeen, Circa 1970

Courtney J. Martin

At the outset of the 1970s Rasheed Araeen's life and career hinged between two seemingly opposite poles. He continued to make and show the spare, formalist handmade objects that he called Structures begun in the previous decade. Related but distinct from these Structures was his interest in politics. The latter positioned him as both an arbiter of social injustice in his London surroundings as well as a target and sometimes victim. What could have led to a complete bifurcation (work and life) for another artist, led Araeen to an incorporation of object making and activism. Ten years on he embarked on a new studio practice, shifting him from sculptor to performer, editor, writer, and theorist. Since each role saw him explore a new medium or practice, materiality and method would always be at stake.

From the very beginning of his work as an artist in 1965, Araeen was unquestionably situated within a sculptural practice that was formally and critically inside a Minimalist vernacular. But, by the mid-1970s, his subjectivity began to emerge: first in a conceptual installation that mapped the plight of another immigrant from Britain's former colonies, not dissimilar to him in age or public perception. In concert with this overtly textual work, he began to perform live in front of audiences. His foray into body art allowed him to disassemble his sculpture publicly. By the close of the decade, sculpture was firmly in the background for Araeen, foregrounded by his refashioned role as editor and critic. The anonymity of his earlier studio practice had given way to a public personification of the politics of personhood, specifically his own. In this essay, I plot the points of each of these iterations on the path to his decade-long aesthetic transformation.

Artists for Democracy

Though he had been a painter in Karachi, when Araeen arrived in London in the mid-1960s, he began making geometric, industrially derived sculpture. Soon, he encountered Signals, London, a locus for showing experimental art and international artists in the city. Begun in 1964 as the Centre for Advanced Creative Study, Signals was an avant-garde space where artists, musicians, and counter-cultural types met. Collectively founded and run by writer Guy Brett, artists David Medalla and Gustav Metzger, along with Marcello Salvadori and Paul Keeler, the gallery also incubated a bulletin that expanded their international scope.[1] By 1964, the gallery settled into a space on Wigmore Street. In the following year, Araeen saw the Jesus Rafael Soto show there. By 1968, he had met Medalla, an artist well known for his street performances, organization of public happenings, and other forms of participatory art practices that dealt with social injustice.

In 1971 Araeen was one in the group that assembled for Medalla's participatory-artwork, *Down with the Slave Trade* (1968–1971), which attempted to publicize then contemporary forms of international slavery (and its historical antecedents) by literalizing human bondage, with willing participants physically tethered to one another. Following Augusto Pinochet's coup against Chilean President Salvador Allende on 11 September 1973, Brett, American artist John Dugger, and Medalla joined with Chilean artist Cecilia Vicuña to form Artists for Democracy (AFD). As a group, they sought to offer artistic responses to the coup and publicize its atrocities to Britons.

In October of 1974, the group, with the participation and support of several other artists, launched the Arts Festival for Democracy in Chile at the Royal College of Art (RCA) in London.[2] Araeen was one of the artists asked to support the multi-day rota of performances, lectures, and an auction to raise money for and awareness of Chilean resistance.[3] According to the exhibition checklist, Araeen was one among an international roster that included Su Braden, Christo, Jon Hendricks, David Hockney, Jorg Immendorf, Tina Keane, R. B. Kitaj, Sol LeWitt, Roberto Matta, Claes Oldenburg, and Meret Oppenheim.

Works (1965–75)

Though AFD as a group dissolved shortly after the RCA festival ended, the name, and the idealism that it purported, morphed into another entity: an exhibition and performance space run by a collective that included Medalla. As an outgrowth of his relationship to both the previous group and its new incarnation as a tangible organization, Araeen was invited to hold a solo exhibition in 1975. AFD's Whitfield Street location was a conventional storefront interrupting a block of terraced houses, located near University College London. Installed on the ground floor, Araeen's show featured a group of modular, geometric, freestanding and wall-mounted structures: a series of process photographs mounted to the wall; a slide projector from which images were projected onto the wall; and a five-panel, text-based wall installation located in the rear of the room. As Araeen's first one-person exhibition, it showed the range of his output up to that point and signalled the directions that his studio practice might take in the coming years.

The selection of objects was neither happenstance nor a display of all objects in his studio. Rather, the show was carefully planned and executed in a manner that displayed Araeen's eye for detail and his attentiveness to viewer experience. As such, I count *Works (1965–75)*, as one of his first curatorial outings. The functional 226
and numerical title of the show was the number of years that he had lived in London, following his arrival in 1964. The subtle nod towards his time in the city made the seemingly clinical title a personal disclosure.[4] Though many emerging artists working in alternative spaces in the seventies were chiefly charged with selecting, planning, and installing their own work, Araeen seems to have played a larger, curatorial role in this exhibition, one that suggested he wanted more participation and less passive viewership from visitors. The exhibition had a determined path through which viewers/participants were to follow. This path, starting from either the front door or from the rear of the gallery space, guided the viewer/participant to move between and around the objects (photographs, reliefs, works on paper and board) on the wall and the larger (in height and expanse) freestanding sculpture in the middle of the room. His curatorial outline placed the three-dimensional objects firmly in Robert Morris' sculptural dictum of 'space, light and materials'.[5] Where the gallery conditions allowed, Araeen organized the objects to maximize the viewer's experience of all three and to extend the amount of time that viewers/participants spent with each work and among groups of works. One needed to endure the confines of the small space (and its attendant grittiness), pace his/her gait through the winding path of objects and stay long enough to notice the nuanced inter-relation of freestanding and wall-mounted pieces. Duration was the performative connection between this show and his later performance practice.

Take, for example, the sculptural remnants of *Burning Bicycle Tyres* (1959, 38
reconstructed in 1975). Placed on the floor and against the wall underneath the photo documentation of this performance, the sculpture was the only three-dimensional object in the show not given space around it for interaction. Instead, it was placed on a square, white surface flush with the floor. While not a pedestal, the white square isolated the small object. If viewers might have walked by it or

overlooked it due to its insubstantial manufacture, they were alerted to its presence by way of the white support.

Where the other floor-based Structures were cubic, the object was a single piece of continuous wire, a circle twisted into a shape of two circular forms. It appeared to be moveable and different in character – as well as size, scale, and composition – from the other freestanding sculpture directly across from it. Rather than being shown, the work was proficiently *staged*, in a manner that both alluded to (by being placed on the floor) and rejected (through the interjection of the white surface between the object and the floor) the presentation style of 'New Generation' sculpture to which many of his contemporaries adhered.[6]

This arrangement of objects was wholly different from Araeen's later, more well-known curatorial efforts, such as *Essential Black Art* (1988) and *The Other Story: Afro-Asian Artists in Post-War Britain* (1989). Araeen's later style made use of all of the space available, characterized by densely over-hung objects on the wall and freestanding work crammed close together on the floor. Those shows were often essayistic, meaning that Araeen led with a thesis, such as the absence of black (here meant to denote African, Asian, and Caribbean) artists in British art history or the political nature or certain types of art making, that was then developed into an exhibition of objects. Quite often the thesis was pursued (in the exhibition ephemera, the catalogue, or in his writing about the shows) in the installation to a greater degree than the organization of the objects. Unlike those exhibitions, the AFD show was edited – a clear presentation of some, but not all, of the items in his studio. And the sculptural objects on view were, within the confines of the small gallery, given what Morris called 'literal space', the physical space accorded to the object that recognized its physical autonomy.[7] The AFD show suggested that the display was an immersive environment in which the objects and the viewers/participants were in communication. Moreover, Araeen placed less emphasis on thematic or topical aspects of his work and more on their formal and participatory possibilities.

For Oluwale

Araeen installed a text-based wall construction in the rear of the AFD gallery. Titled, *For Oluwale* (1971–1973 / 1975) (reconstructed for the AFD show in 1975), the four-panel installation consisted of newspaper clippings and paper photocopies pasted onto a board. Drawn mainly from alternate news sources like *Black People's News Service*, the weekly newsletter of the Black Panthers in London, some of the black and white text concerned the death of Nigerian immigrant, David Oluwale in Leeds in 1969, while other text referenced the national investigation of the Leeds police force following Oluwale's death.[8] *For Oluwale* shared little surface quality or materials with the sculptural work that comprised the rest of the exhibition. Araeen had long worked in space, meaning that some of his sculptural works had always been freestanding and changeable in orientation, or in positions relative to each other. To step back from the three-dimensional into the almost-flat against the wall, without colour and with little assembly suggested a shift in his sensibility, utilized perhaps, to properly explore a different set of aesthetic goals. 210

Similarities between the two bodies of work existed elsewhere. Each paper sheet is placed on the board in a gridded pattern and those grids are similar to the geometric organization of the Structures. On one board, for example, photocopies of newspaper articles appear in a grid of four columns and three rows. The top two rows are identical, each with a squared photograph of the slain man in the same position. The bottom row contains four slightly longer pages of text, without the picture. In the three other boards, the reproduced news article with Oluwale's face appears in the bottom row of a two-row set.

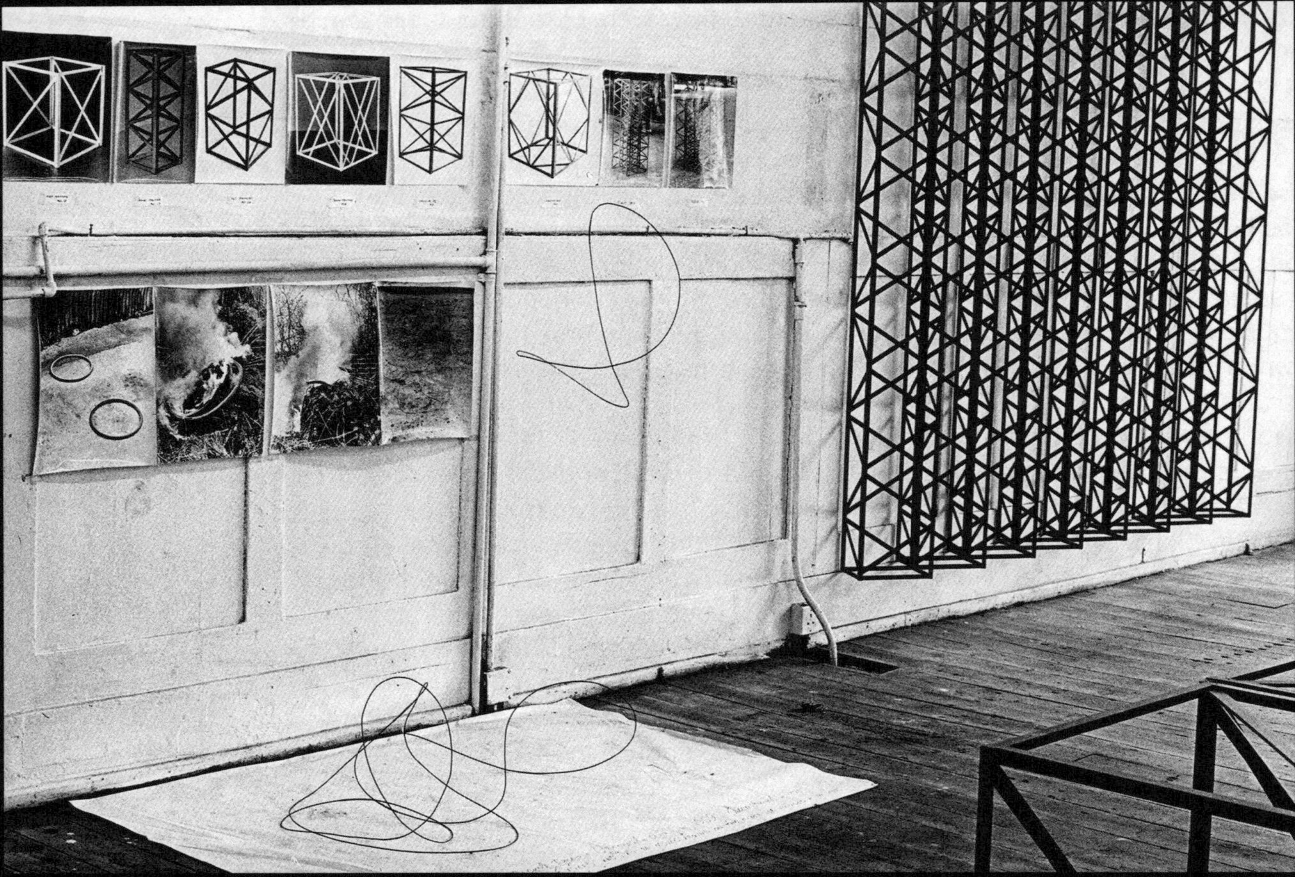

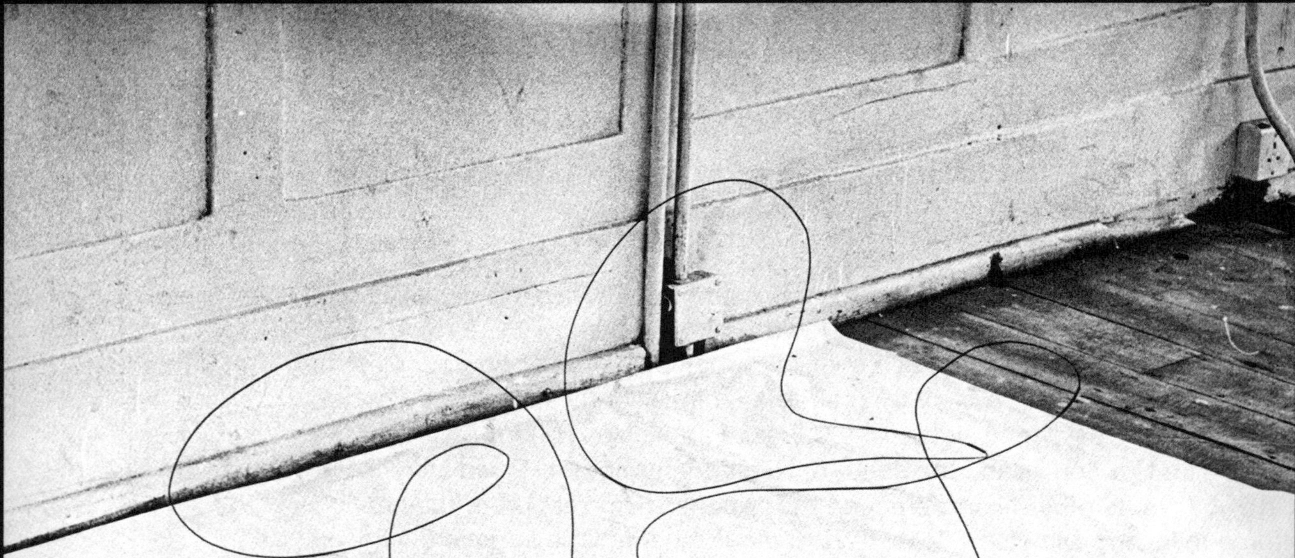

Installation views of **Works (1965-75)**, 1975
Artists for Democracy, London

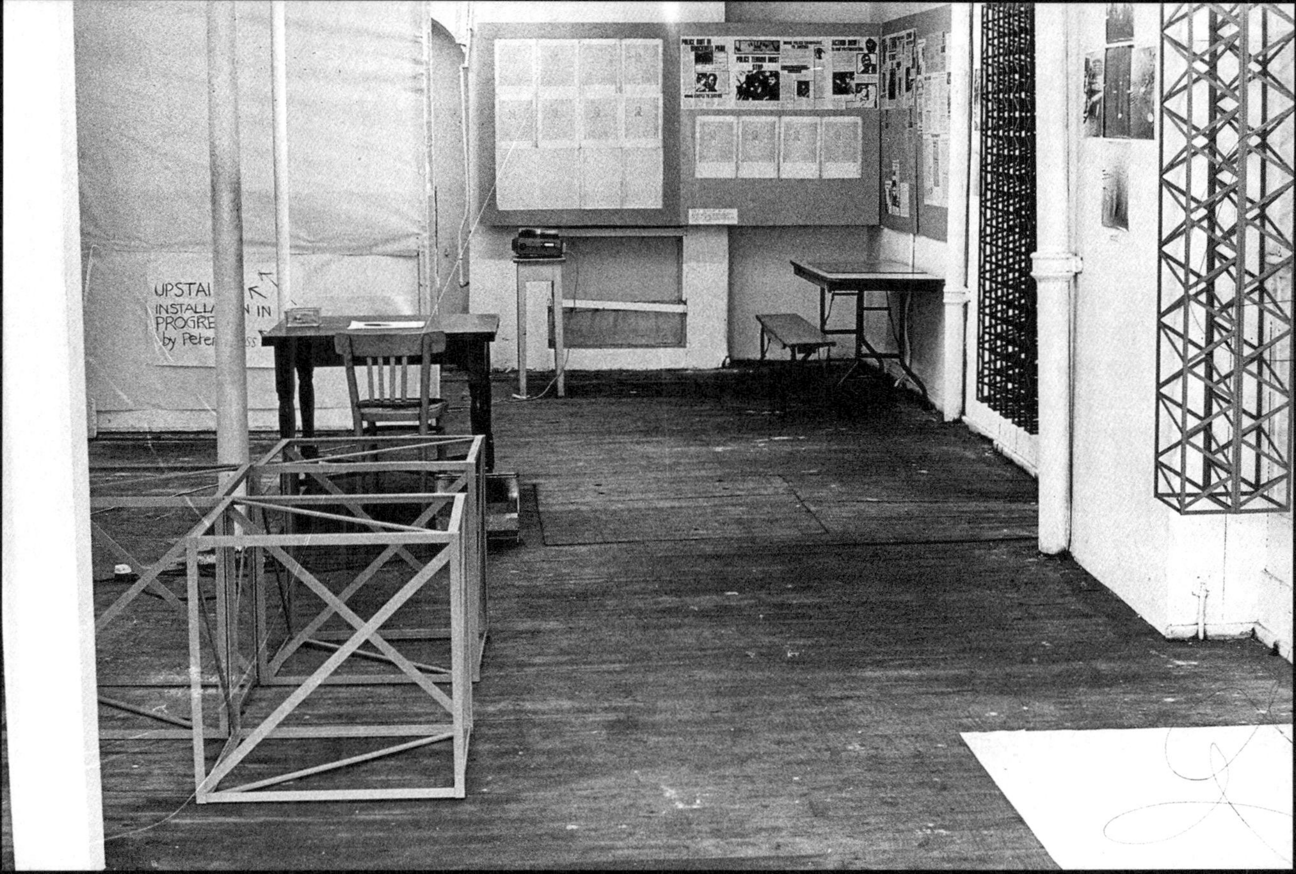

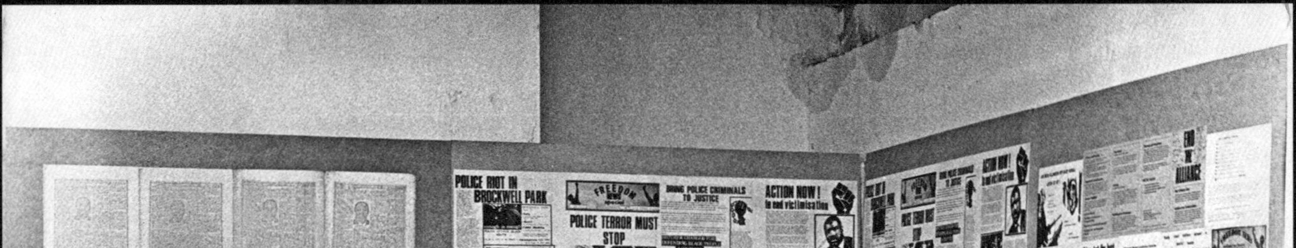
POLICE RIOT IN BROCKWELL PARK
BRING CASTLE TO JUSTICE
POLICE TERROR MUST STOP
BRING POLICE CRIMINALS TO JUSTICE
ACTION NOW!
to end victimisation

The rows are distinct and do not line up vertically as continuous columns. The top row is wider on the board, meeting it side to side. The pages in that row bear headlines such as 'Police Terror Must Stop' and 'Bring Police Criminals to Justice' and graphic designs of a raised clenched fist and a fist grabbing a loose chain. These visual and textual devices move the commemorative aspect of the installation towards one of active engagement with the audience.

Though Araeen described *For Oluwale* as the 'first work in Britain which raised the issue of racism', it was, largely, a conceptual text-based object with little impact as an activist intervention. Its construction – paper on board – however unselfconsciously, asserts its claim to space for low media within high art. This is true of the object's distinction, as well as its relationship to the other Structures in the AFD exhibition. If *For Oluwale* was not radical enough to express Araeen's outrage at Oluwale's death or his full potential for a political artwork or too clinical and, largely circumspect, as a memorial to death or specific call for action, it is of a piece with other British Conceptual undertakings, like those by the Art & Language collective, John Hilliard, Michael Craig-Martin, Stephen Willats, and others. All, including Araeen, pointed to a specifically national tendency that saw *concept* as an idealistic undertaking rooted in both word and deed. The repeated exclusion of Araeen from this (art) history, and its subsequent exhibitions, is noteworthy given both the subject of his work and its method of delivery. It is only the former that seems out of line with the expectations of what British Conceptual art should and would be.[9]

For Oluwale was one of Araeen's earliest transitions into the roughly made and legibly provocative political art through which he would explore various forms of media. In the 1970s after *For Oluwale*, this aesthetic (materially and compositionally rough) would come to define his art and help to shape his role as a political artist, first seen widely in 1977, in his performance, *'Paki Bastard' (Portrait of the Artist as a Black Person)*. 234
Following the show at AFD, Araeen was invited to debut his new performance in the space that had two years before hosted his first solo exhibition. *'Paki Bastard'* was first performed at AFD on 31 July 1977.[10] As live art, it was rough in its allusion to the lived experiences of non-white people in Britain. Unlike *For Oluwale*, where the body, name, and circumstances of an actual person formed the context and content of the work, here Araeen stood in for the bodies politic that were threatened: people finding themselves the objects of scorn who sought retribution, if often futilely, in Britain. The performance was physically demanding, and also emotionally draining for Araeen. Yet, AFD was the ideal location for such an overt shift in media from sculpture and installation to body art. It was a space that he knew well: one that he had already blocked, in a theatrical sense, for his earlier exhibition. There was an easy connection between the display of objects in which he sought viewer engagement, and the performance that relied heavily on the viewers' ability and willingness to follow him visually and emotively; he moved about in front of them breaking up and sitting on objects, while the changing slides and music altered their sensory experience.

Black Phoenix

During the winter after the first performance of *'Paki Bastard'* in 1977, Araeen started a publication with writer Mahmood Jamal, *Black Phoenix*.[11] Subtitled *Journal of Contemporary Art & Culture in the Third World*, *Black Phoenix* was a hybrid periodical that foreshadowed the high-concept ideas of postcolonial and postmodernist theory that were later bought together in *Third Text*, and the specificity of Araeen's political awakening in London. Though Araeen founded the magazine with Jamal, he was the driving force behind its editorial decisions, financial management, distribution, and overall spirit. Despite *Black Phoenix*'s public function, it came directly from the persona and aesthetic sensibilities of Araeen as an artist.

To call forth the publication's autobiographical elements does not in any way diminish its import. After all, Araeen the artist and Araeen the Pakistani person were often conflated by the audiences who wanted to project an unnuanced diaristic reading of Araeen onto *'Paki Bastard'*. His personal narrative as an artist and as an immigrant in London typified a generation of British cultural workers invested equally in aesthetics and the politics of British imperialism and class dynamics. Like the artwork that preceded it and the studio practice that he maintained concurrently, *Black Phoenix* examined art through a range of theoretical and methodological means, such as criticism (art and literature), poetry, and opinion pieces. The other writers and artists that contributed to the three issues of *Black Phoenix* were just that – contributors to Araeen's project, rather than equal collaborators in a group enterprise, as he had been in the various iterations of Artists for Democracy. Years later, when Araeen launched *Third Text*, the journal and role for which he is most well-known internationally, he called it a continuation of *Black Phoenix*, though the two are radically different in content, scope, and size. Their similarity – the continuation as it were – is the presence of Araeen and his conceptualization of both *Black Phoenix* and *Third Text.*

Both publications are no different from any of the other works that emerged from his studio, including *For Oluwale* and *'Paki Bastard'*. We might think of the publications in the same vein as other post-studio Conceptual practices favoured by his contemporaries from the period. Robert Morris' exploration of dance, Donald Judd's architecture, or Carl Andre's poems are other examples of the ways in which these artists expanded their object-based art making in ways that both complemented and complicated both outputs.

Preliminary Notes for a BLACK MANIFESTO

Araeen's foray into writing and editing also mirrored the Conceptual and Minimalist tendencies towards criticism and art writing that self-diagnosed their approach to art. Andre, Judd, and Morris, along with LeWitt and Mel Bochner, wrote some of the key texts of this period to publicly refine their own artistic practices and define them in relationship to or against those of their peers. But the maker-writer (or artist-critic) is not the sole product of the mid-century and certainly not of America. *Black Phoenix*, the magazine-cum-art project, was a modernist strategy in line with the history of 'little magazines', and artists' periodicals from the early part of the twentieth century, like British painter Wyndham Lewis' *Blast*. And, like Lewis' first issue of *Blast*, which debuted the polemical Vorticist manifesto, the first issue of *Black Phoenix* contained Araeen's manifesto as an editorial, 'Preliminary Notes for a BLACK MANIFESTO'. The manifesto was Araeen's first exploration of the relationship between the Third World and the West. Drawing on the spirit of the *Communist Manifesto* (1848) in suggestive terms and didactic prose, Araeen followed the incendiary rhetoric set forth in the art historical models of the Futurist (1909), Vorticist (1914), Dada (1918), and other manifestos that formed around an aesthetic concept. If the whole of *Black Phoenix* was a new medium (print) in which to work, 'BLACK MANIFESTO' was Araeen's central object, just as performance had been to *'Paki Bastard'* and installation to *For Oluwale*. 230

'BLACK MANIFESTO' also mirrored another form with which Araeen was familiar: *Black People's News Service* later called *Freedom News*. Throughout, the Marxist-fuelled language in the manifesto positions art as the pawn of Western imperialism, but art is also the avenue for society's redemption. It is the tool for artists to reclaim and repair all that capitalism has broken.

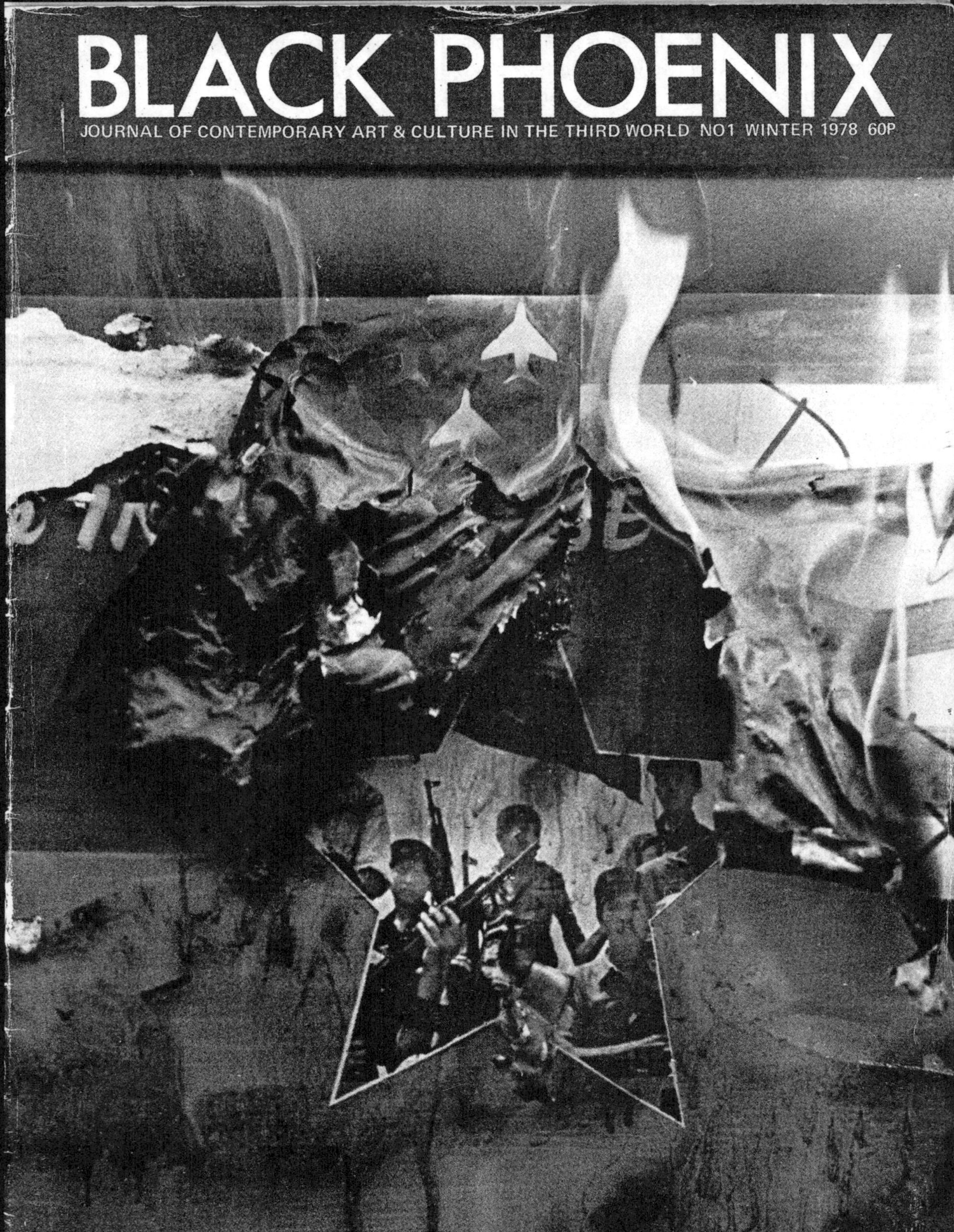

Front covers of **Black Phoenix** (1978–1979)

BLACK PHOENIX

THIRD WORLD PERSPECTIVE ON CONTEMPORARY ART AND CULTURE No 2 SUMMER 1978 60p

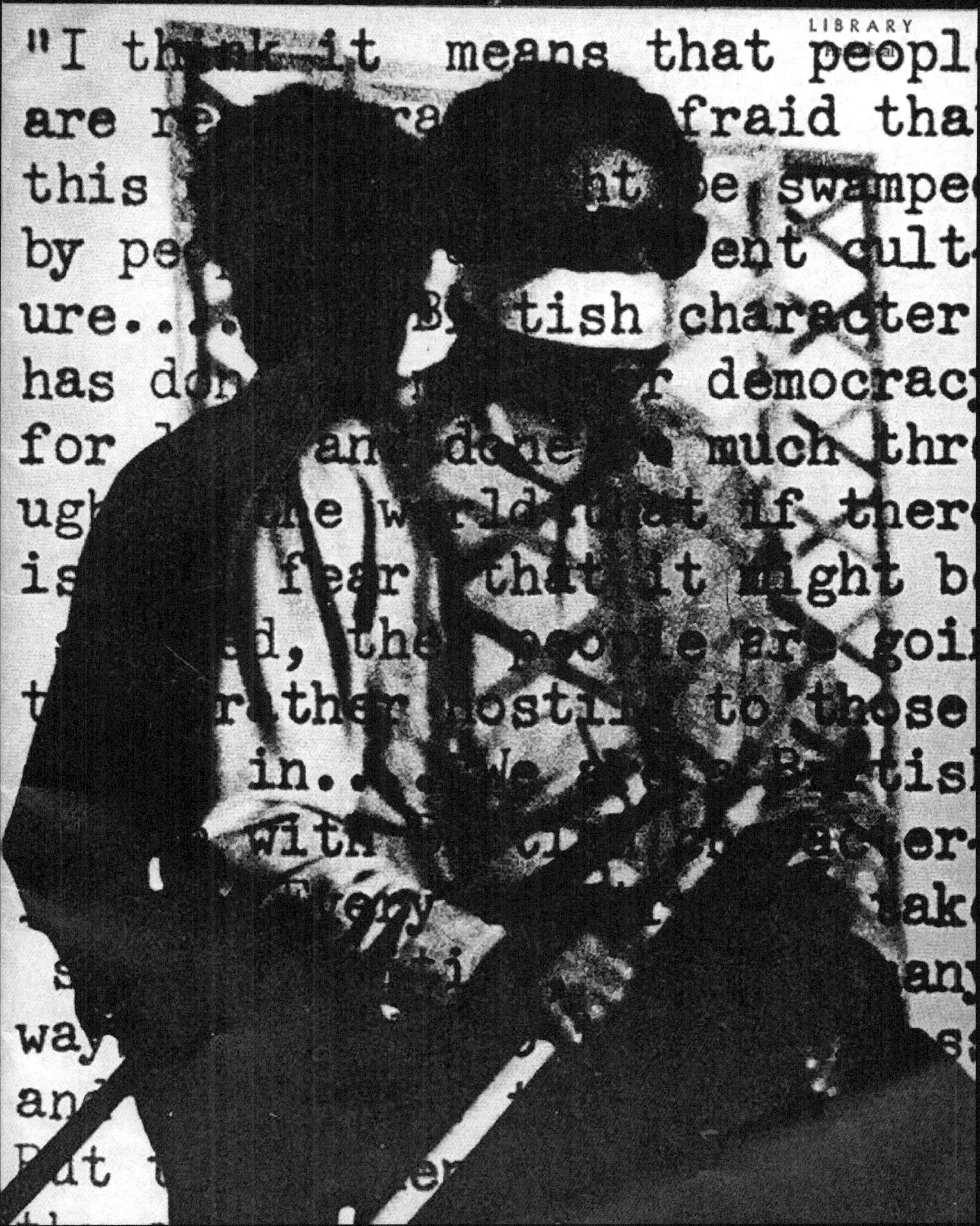

BLACK PHOENIX

THIRD WORLD PERSPECTIVE ON CONTEMPORARY ART AND CULTURE No 3 SPRING 1978 60p

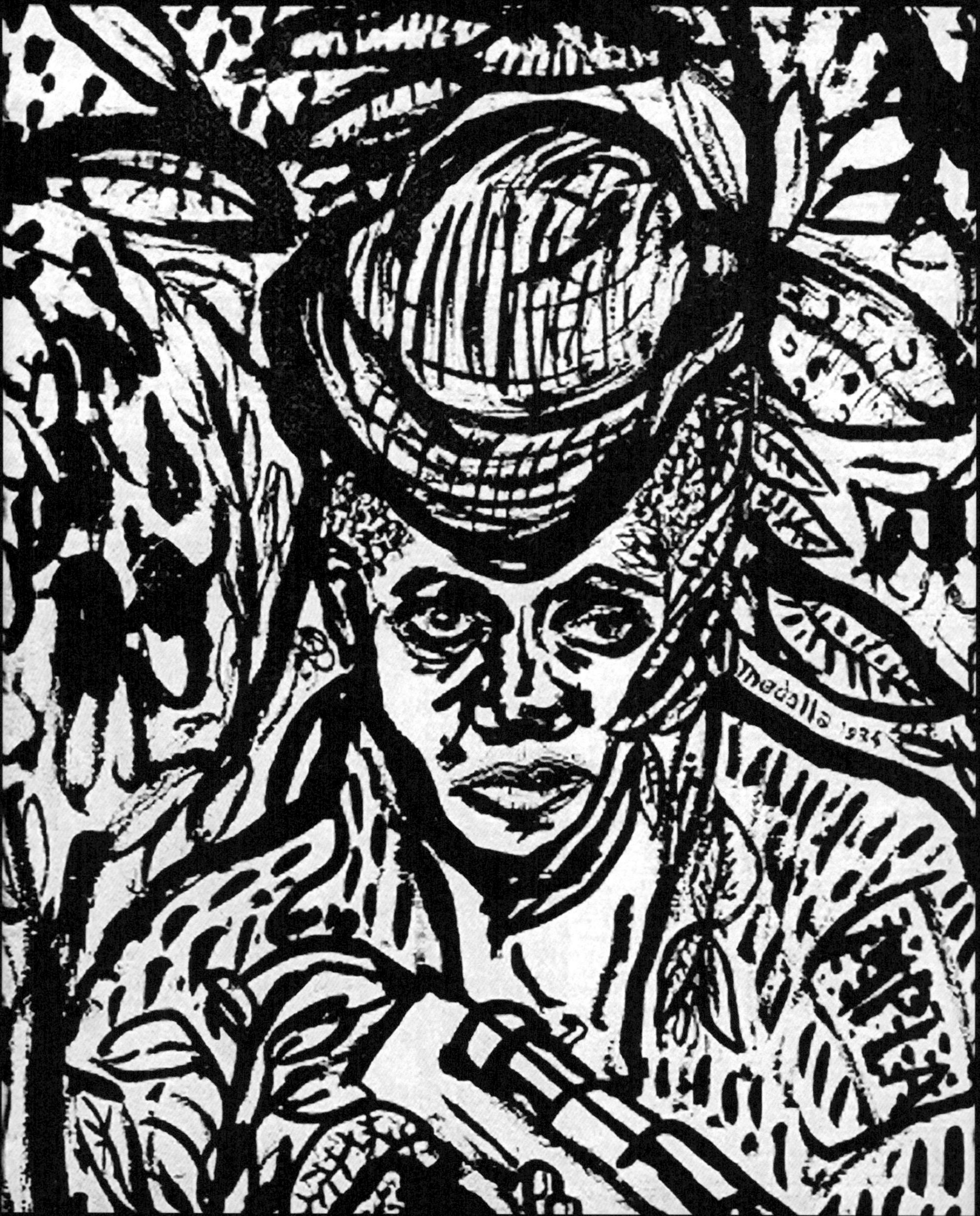

For example, Araeen used Jasper Johns' *Flag* (1954) to illustrate how American art through Pop art and consumer culture work in tandem to 'undermine the indigenous values and their contemporary developments in the third world'.[12] Completed in the mid-1950s, before events in 1968 or the Vietnam War, *Flag* feels as if it is, as Araeen suggests, 'imperialist art', his phrase for straightforward propaganda.[13] In a chapter on *Flag*, Anne Wagner also contests its assumed neutrality by tying it into a complex argument about nationalism and art, specifically painting.[14] Araeen's assessment of *Flag* as a totem for nationality purporting to be painting/assemblage spoke to how he understood the function of art. Yet he recognized the flag's (any flag's) subversive potential because he too had employed a flag – Britain's Union Jack – in collages (1974–1976) that were 220 critical of colonialism.

In his analysis of *Flag*, Araeen makes use of recent developments in art history without naming his efforts as such. Throughout the manifesto, and in subsequent writing, he employs the so-called 'new art history', a form of social art history that attempts to place objects within the discursive frame of Marxism, semiotics, and other theoretical modernist modes. The new art history was opposed to the tradition of art history as a compilation of connoisseurship, iconography, literature, and patronage. Seen in this way, Araeen's advance onto Johns' *Flag* is less about the painting of the flag as an object of imperialism and more connected to an art history that had not accounted for imperialism within a discussion of the painting of a flag. That Araeen never explicitly stated his art historical undertaking is curious, but not unexpected. None of his artist-critic contemporaries (Judd, Morris, et cetera) ever specifically state their art historical methodologies, yet their writings are frequently read within the field as both primary sources for their work and the period and secondary sources for other artists of the period.

But Araeen's criticism of the Johns painting as imperialist had precedence in British art discourse. The British painter Patrick Heron railed against the 'intense artistic chauvinism' of American art in *Studio International* in 1966.[15] Later, Heron would define the presence of American art in Britain as 'cultural imperialism'.[16] In both essays he adopted the language used to describe America's relationship to the 'third world', specifically Vietnam, to define American art's hegemonic relationship to British art and artists. In 1978, Heron returned to this argument, calling it 'a political stance' during 'The State of British Art' conference in which he shared a panel with Araeen who performed a condensed spoken-word version of 'BLACK MANIFESTO'.[17] In instances such as these, Araeen was keenly focused on concerns shared by many in Britain's art world, yet he argued them from a transnational perspective, rarely making the claim that his location in Britain affected his perspective on the ambiguous geography of the art world or the binary construction of Western art.

In addition to its attentiveness to the polemics of art and imperialism, Araeen configured the manifesto around his interest in and attention to a set of similar documents that gathered artists around a single idea towards the creation of a movement. Pierre Restany's 'Constitutive Declaration of New Realism', which inaugurated a group of artists into Nouveau Réalisme in 1960 and Victor Vasarely's 'Manifeste jaune' (1955) that lent the theoretical dimension to the kinetic artists, are predecessors to what he hoped to achieve.[18] A closer model existed in Gustav Metzger, an artist Araeen knew. His first manifesto on destruction appeared as Auto Destructive Art on 4 November 1959 in London. In this first (there were several) iteration, Metzger identified a self-guided (defined by the titular auto), auteurist practice that would produce 'a total unity of idea, site, form, colour, method, and timing of the disintegrative process'. Throughout the 1960s and 1970s, Metzger made (and destroyed) art in disruptive public exhibitions and participated in direct action campaigns. Art and activism were, according to the manifesto, activities of his practice. Similarly, Araeen's manifesto was a call for interaction, an acknowledgement of his ongoing plan of building a community among artists and increasing engagement between himself and a larger public by way of his art practice.

'BLACK MANIFESTO' ends with Araeen's invitation to others to join him in the 'conceptual structure of THE PROPOSED WORK...' outlining a plan for a participatory project that would be fulfilled by contributing to *Black Phoenix*.[19] The invitation also explains why the manifesto was a preliminary enterprise, one that would be completed by the audience's engagement in the process and the production of a collaborative work.

Co-published in *Studio International* (SI) in the same month, 'BLACK MANIFESTO' revealed itself as a textual performance, like those of Art & Language that had graced the pages of their eponymous publication. The manifesto's appearance in SI made sense for the art world of which Araeen was part. In SI, the manifesto was a feature, rather than an editorial. It included the same illustrations that accompanied its first printing, like a single panel of *For Oluwale*, which then publicized the ongoing investigation into the murder of David Oluwale. Because it was the most widely circulated art magazine in Britain, it called out to a wider audience, educating them about imperialism, attempting to gather converts against American art, and hoping for allies in the fight for equality within British art. Co-publishing the manifesto was a strategic manoeuvre that gave Araeen credibility as a writer and theorist, just as it helped him to wrest control of his shifting public persona from an object maker to performer and writer.

In June of 1979, Lucy Lippard curated an exhibition at Artists Space in New York, *Art from the British Left* that showed 'socially concerned art intended to expand international communication and to form an archive of political art'.[20] Araeen was selected to show work alongside Conrad Atkinson, Margaret Harrison, Alexis Hunter, Mary Kelly, Tony Rickaby, and Marie Yates, all of whom fell on the more crude (in terms of the visual display of their technical skills as artists) side of the political art aesthetic. This was also one of few times in his career that Araeen was given the opportunity to show with other Conceptual artists. In a letter to Lippard in preparation for the installation, Araeen advised her that either 'blown-up copies of the pages of BLACK MANIFESTO could be put on the wall' or 'six pages of my piece, *Paki Bastard*, could be taken out from the magazine and displayed on the wall'.[21] Araeen's options indicate that the magazine served as an extension of his studio practice, one in which their previous mediums (in this case writing and performance) were collapsed by the magazine as an exhibition space. This was a full revolution away from the way that he thought about exhibiting art in the previous decade.

Looking back from the vantage of the end of the decade, Araeen's AFD show in 1975 looks like a coda to one part of his career as well as the announcement of the next part. The Structures in the front of the gallery showed viewers what he had made and how he understood the physical and technical processes of making art. In the back of the gallery, *For Oluwale* asked viewers to understand the new directions that his art might be taking and why he and his art had to do so.

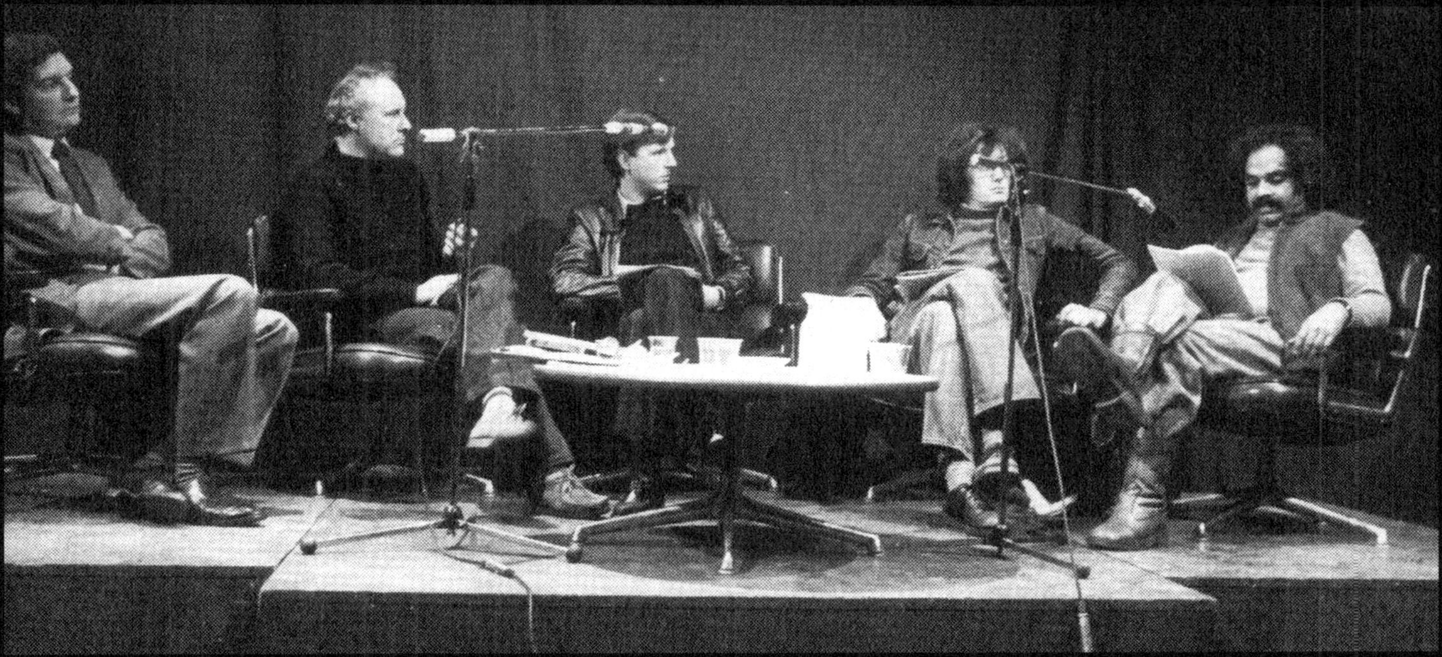

'The State of British Art' conference, ICA, London, 10–12 February 1978.
From left: Alan Bowness (Director, Tate Gallery), Patrick Heron (artist),
John Tagg (critic and historian), Richard Cork (art critic) and Rasheed Araeen
(reading **BLACK MANIFESTO**)

1 I have written elsewhere about Araeen's interaction with Signals gallery, see 'Exiles, Emigrés, and Cosmopolitans: London's Postwar Art World', in *Postwar – Art Between the Pacific and the Atlantic, 1945-1965*, ed. Okwui Enwezor (Munich: Prestel, 2017), 572.

2 I offer a longer discussion of the festival in 'Collectivity, Temporality and Festival Culture in John Dugger's Quasi-Architecture, 1970-1974', *London Art Worlds*, ed. Jo Applin, Catherine Spencer, and Amy Tobin (University Park, PA: Penn State University Press, 2018).

3 A decade after the event, Araeen reflected on his involvement with the group, see Rasheed Araeen, 'Black Umbrella', organization proposal (January 1984), Panchayat Archive, University of Westminster, Harrow.

4 Rasheed Araeen, *Making Myself Visible* (London: Kala Press, 1984), 174.

5 Robert Morris, 'Notes on Sculpture, Part II', *Artforum* 5, no. 2 (October 1966):43.

6 Araeen's reflections on Anthony Caro and 'New Generation' sculpture began to appear in the 1990s, see Araeen, 'How I Discovered My Oriental Soul in the Wilderness of the West', *Third Text* 6, no. 19 (summer 1992):94–95. His more recent musings on Caro can be found here: Rasheed Araeen, 'Rasheed Araeen on Anthony Caro', *ArtAsiaPacific* (July/August 2017). See also my examination of Araeen's relationship to the New Generation in '"Non-compositional and Non-hierarchical": Rasheed Araeen's Search for the Conceptual and the Political in British Sculpture', in *Anglo-American Exchange in Post-War Sculpture, 1945-1975*, ed. Rebecca Peabody (Los Angeles: J. Paul Getty Museum and Getty Research Institute, 2011), 122–132.

7 Morris, 'Notes on Sculpture', 43.

8 For a longer discussion of David Oluwale's death in 1969 and the Leeds police investigation in 1971, see Kester Aspden, *Nationality: Wog – The Hounding of David Oluwale* (London: Jonathan Cape, 2007).

9 The most recent and glaring omission is *Conceptual Art in Britain 1964–1979*, which was on view at Tate Britain from 12 April to 29 August 2016. Though the show aligned itself with a chronology and thematic premise of national politics inherent in Conceptual art in which Araeen could have been included, he was not, thereby furthering his outsider status with respect to a period and movement in which he was firmly present.

10 *'Paki Bastard' (Portrait of the Artist as a Black Person)* is the subject of my essay 'Rasheed Araeen, Live Art and Radical Politics in Britain', *Getty Research Journal*, no. 2 (2010):107–124. It is also one of the primary topics under review in my forthcoming book, *Rasheed Araeen: What is Black Art?*

11 The launch of *Black Phoenix* receives more attention in my essay 'Rasheed Araeen, Live Art and Radical Politics in Britain', 116–119.

12 Rasheed Araeen, 'Preliminary Notes for a BLACK MANIFESTO', *Black Phoenix*, no. 1 (winter 1978):7.

13 Ibid.

14 Anne Wagner, *A House Divided: American Art Since 1955* (Berkeley: University of California Press, 2012), 24.

15 'The Ascendancy of London in the Sixties', *Studio International* 172, no. 884 (December 1966):280–281.

16 'A Kind of Cultural Imperialism?', *Studio International* 175, no. 897 (February 1968):62–64.

17 For the conference transcript, see 'The State of British Art: A Debate', *Studio International* 193, no. 987 (February 1978):76–140.

18 Restany's short tract was signed by Yves Klein, Arman, Martial Raysse, Francois Dufrêne, Raymond Hains, Jacques de la Villeglé, Daniel Spoerri, and Jean Tinguely on 27 October 1960 at Klein's apartment. Vasarely's text entered into the discourse of *Le Mouvement* (6–30 April 1955) when it appeared in the material that accompanied the exhibition at Galerie Denise René in Paris. The other artists in the show – Yaacov Agam, Pol Bury, Alexander Calder, Marcel Duchamp, Robert Jacobsen, Jesús Rafael Soto, and Jean Tinguely – saw it after publication. They were not necessarily in agreement with Vasarely's approach to colour, light, motion, and time – the major themes in the text.

19 Araeen, 'BLACK MANIFESTO', 10.

20 Lucy Lippard, exhibition notes (1979), PAD/D Pamphlet File, Museum of Modern Art, New York.

21 Letter from Rasheed Araeen to Lucy Lippard, 24 March 1979, PAD/D Pamphlet File, Museum of Modern Art, New York.

Dialectics of Modernity and Counter-Modernity: Rasheed Araeen's Cruciform Works

Zöe Sutherland

In 1974, in an open letter to *The Guardian* and the Institute of Contemporary Arts, London, Rasheed Araeen challenged the radical posturing of what he pointedly called 'the Western international art world', emphasizing its historical dependency on the economic legacies of colonialism.[1] He later developed this critique in his 1978 text 'Preliminary Notes for A BLACK MANIFESTO', calling the pretensions to 'internationalism' little more than 'a function of Western politico-economic power and the imposition of its values on other people'.[2] The 'international' networks that gave the art world its shape remained, in reality, predominantly transatlantic – an imprint, for Araeen, of monopoly capital and its imperialist ethos.[3] And the generalization and development of the modernist techniques of abstraction and dematerialization characterizing that art world – the flight from material specificities towards an abstract universal, epitomized by some works of Conceptual art – obscured and distracted even further from real material forms of domination. Thus, as the West's art institutions and neo-avant-garde artists, were proclaiming a new universalism, Araeen embarked upon a radical critique of their Eurocentricity.

While the ideology of post-war cultural internationalism increasingly proclaimed art's radical democratization and potential for inclusion, and purported to offer unlimited artistic freedom, for Araeen, 'Third World' artists were struggling to play a significant role as avant-gardists in the development of modernist art's trajectory. Participation for non-Western artists was largely conditional on their occupation of an impossible space: they could either tolerate a weak form of inclusion, in which their work was rendered derivative of, and inferior to, Western modernist forms, or else give up all association with modernism and instead embrace a fetishized identity as an "ethnic" artist. Either way, their position within the system appeared predetermined. Although in the 1970s, Araeen still hoped for the realization of a true international spirit of men and women through Third World struggle – a true universal – within which radical artistic practice might play a role, this hope later dissipated. With the consolidation of what Araeen called the 'Race Relations Industry', which essentialized non-Western artists for the sake of 'phoney racial harmony', he saw the submergence and containment of radical consciousness under the single universal of an increasingly global capitalist market. A central question of Araeen's career thus became how to make art that is politically radical and conscious,[4] *within and against* the institutionalized spaces of the art world, such that those spaces might be transformed.

From the mid-1980s to the early 1990s – in the context of the ebbing of Third World struggle, the end of the Cold War, the consolidation of a restructured capitalism, and a new round of imperialist wars – Araeen made a series of artworks that have since been dubbed his 'cruciform' works.[5] In the construction of these works, Araeen gathered and placed together disparate and fragmented images from the world around him, often iconic art-historical, religious, or else political. In addition to using such 'readymade' images, these collage-type compositions rework or recycle key themes and forms from Araeen's previous work, creating a dynamic snapshot of the development of the artist's own identity over time. Each work thus becomes readable as a window through which to view

Araeen's interrogations of a central artistic and political problematic, situated in relation to a range of global economic and geopolitical shifts. However, their often quite jarring fragments find particular resonance when the works are taken together as a series.

The 'cruciform' works share the basic form of a nine-panel grid system, which creates the shape of a cross at its centre, a form developed through Araeen's earlier investigation of industrial 'Structures' in the 1960s. In *First Structure* (1966–1967) 101 Araeen made a single, open-faced cube, each face bisected by a diagonal, which acts to highlight, but also hold or contain tension between its parts. In *Nine* (1968–1975) Araeen made a 3 x 3 grid system of such cubes, whose static 124 symmetrical – and Minimalist – form appeared potentially disrupted through the movement suggested by such tension. The dialectical logic of these works was carried over into Araeen's cruciform.

Araeen first recycled this cruciform structure when making *Fair and Lovely* (1985), 255 named after a whitening cream he saw advertised in a newspaper in Pakistan. This and other creams, such as EMEX, used photographs of white, Western women, and Pakistani women who resembled them, to sell their products. Struck by the disparate realities expressed by these images, Araeen arranged them into a nine-panel grid system, with the white women in the centre making the figure of the cross. While his aim was to illustrate the effect of Western culture on the rest of the world, Araeen also discovered a new, critical aesthetic language through which to transcend the formal limits of Minimalism in order to express the contradictions of the Western modernity it represented. Transposed into pictorial form, the cruciform could allude to the symmetrical structures of Minimalism, while presenting more concrete tensions between two seemingly disparate realities.[6]

Araeen has emphasized procedure in the making of his subsequent 'cruciform' works, which he describes as a process of 'cutting' and 'rupturing' a green-coloured monochrome.[7] Making a horizontal and vertical cut through the middle of the monochrome in the shape of a cross, Araeen would then separate out the four sections and 'fill' the cross-shaped cavity with a range of material he considered 'incongruent to the purity of Minimalism'.[8] If Lucio Fontana signals the limits of Western modernist painting, rendering material the historical and ideological nature of the medium – albeit negatively, through slashes and perforations – in his 'cruciform' works, Araeen uses the same destructive procedure to indicate the limits of Western modernity itself, pointing at the global structures on which it was founded: colonialism, imperialism, and their attendant mechanisms of abjection. While Fontana's act belongs to the era of high modernism, before the crumbling of Western colonialism had really begun, Araeen's embodies disillusionment with both Western modernism and with the outcomes of Third Worldist struggle.

Green Painting I (1985)

In *Green Painting I*, four dark green painted plywood panels have been separated 262 out and their cross-shaped interiors filled with five distinct photographs, each showing the bloodstained ground, following the ritualistic killing of animals during the *Eid-ul-Azha* festival. Running underneath each of these images is a green strip of calligraphic Urdu script. The simple coloured panels carry a complex set of significations. While the use of monochrome clearly invokes Western modernism, Araeen's choice of this green avowedly as 'an allusion to nature/raw/young/immature/underdeveloped etc.,[9] surely also refers to its constructed 'Other' – green (and particularly this tone) having a multilayered significance within Islam: associated with paradise in the Quran; the dynastic colour of the Fatimids; the colour of the dome over the tomb of Muhammad in Medina; and so on.

Due to such connotations it is also, of course, the core colour of Arab and Islamic universalisms – religious and secular – and nationalisms, appearing in flags from Bangladesh to Western Sahara; in those of the Arab League, the Ba'ath Party, Palestine, the Arab Revolt against Ottoman rule in World War I; in the monochrome flag of Muammar Gaddafi's Libya and on the cover of the book in which he laid out his political philosophy *The Green Book* (1975)... One might draw a parallel between these connotations of a universalism rooted in a world religion and those of the colour white in Western tradition, conjuring up the lamb of Christ, the Virgin Mary, Dante's 'snow-white rose, consecrated to Christ' and so on – but also the exemplary colour of high modernity: of the white cube space; Robert Rauschenberg's *White Paintings* (1951); Fontana's canvases; the typical field on which Conceptualist text was laid out, et cetera. This is the green of another attempted universalism, grounded in a particular religious history and mediated in the modern epoch through many ill-fated nation-building projects, and it seems plausible that it is deployed here in part with a view to particularizing that of the West.

In many of the photographs – except, perhaps, the middle one – the blood has mixed quite heavily with other substances on the ground, producing a dirty greenish colour, akin to the water that results from cleaning a paintbrush. The distinct images show varying proportions of dominance between the red and green. In the far left image, the green stain seems to encircle a puddle of blood, while in the right image it appears to have flooded or washed over the bloodstain. In the top image, only the edges of a very striking and dominant red bloodstain are tinged with dirty green patches, as well as little fragments of the Pakistani flag, while in the bottom image the two sit together, fragmented, as though of an Abstract Expressionist drip painting.

The grid system allows for the images to be clearly and sharply demarcated from each other. Yet Araeen's specific compositions are designed to complicate these demarcations, prompting us to look more closely at the continuities, overlaps, and erasures at work. While the visceral images of blood evoke ritual sacrifice in contrast to the Minimalism signalled by the green panels, in blending the two colours together within the interior space of the panels, Araeen points to their co-dependence as two poles within the same structure. Moreover, laid out in cruciform shape, the blood shed in *Eid* can of course take on Christian connotations, pointing transculturally to a "primitive" moment at the heart of Western tradition.

By blending together, and presenting as reversible, multiple aesthetic references – ritualistic performance, Abstract Expressionist painting, and Minimalism – Araeen captures the entanglement of these concepts as they developed within the art making of post-war neo-avant-gardism. Not only was the idea of ritualistic performance popularized, and presented as a supposed counter-tendency to the abstractions of high modernism, but also an element of the fetishization of ritual is present in the painting techniques of Abstract Expressionism. This is reinforced by the way in which the real bloodstains can be read as compositions when placed beside the monochromes, suggesting an ambivalence between visceral violence and modernist abstraction.

While potentially appearing to a Western audience as merely decorative, or as fragments of some sacred text – and thereby instantiating the audience's ignorance – the rows of Urdu script are in fact composed of current newspaper headlines: Richard Nixon's visit to Pakistan, or Benazir Bhutto placed under house arrest. As the centralization of text within the ontology of the contemporary artwork has acted to challenge ideas of the universality of the image, it has also produced the dependence upon the text as offering the final authority in its interpretation – particularly with abstract or Conceptual works. In contrast, here the non-Urdu reader is confronted by their own ignorance of the full meaning of the work.

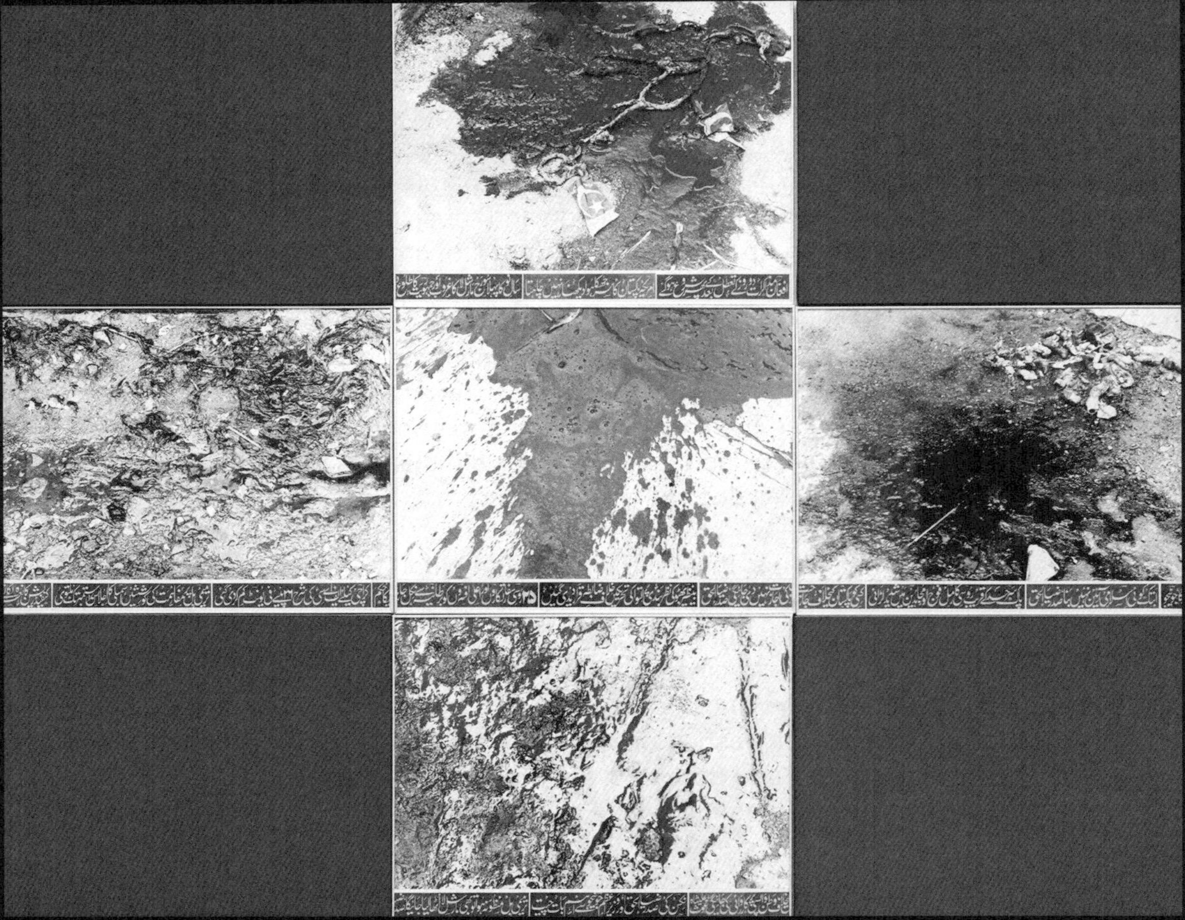

Green Painting I, 1985–1986

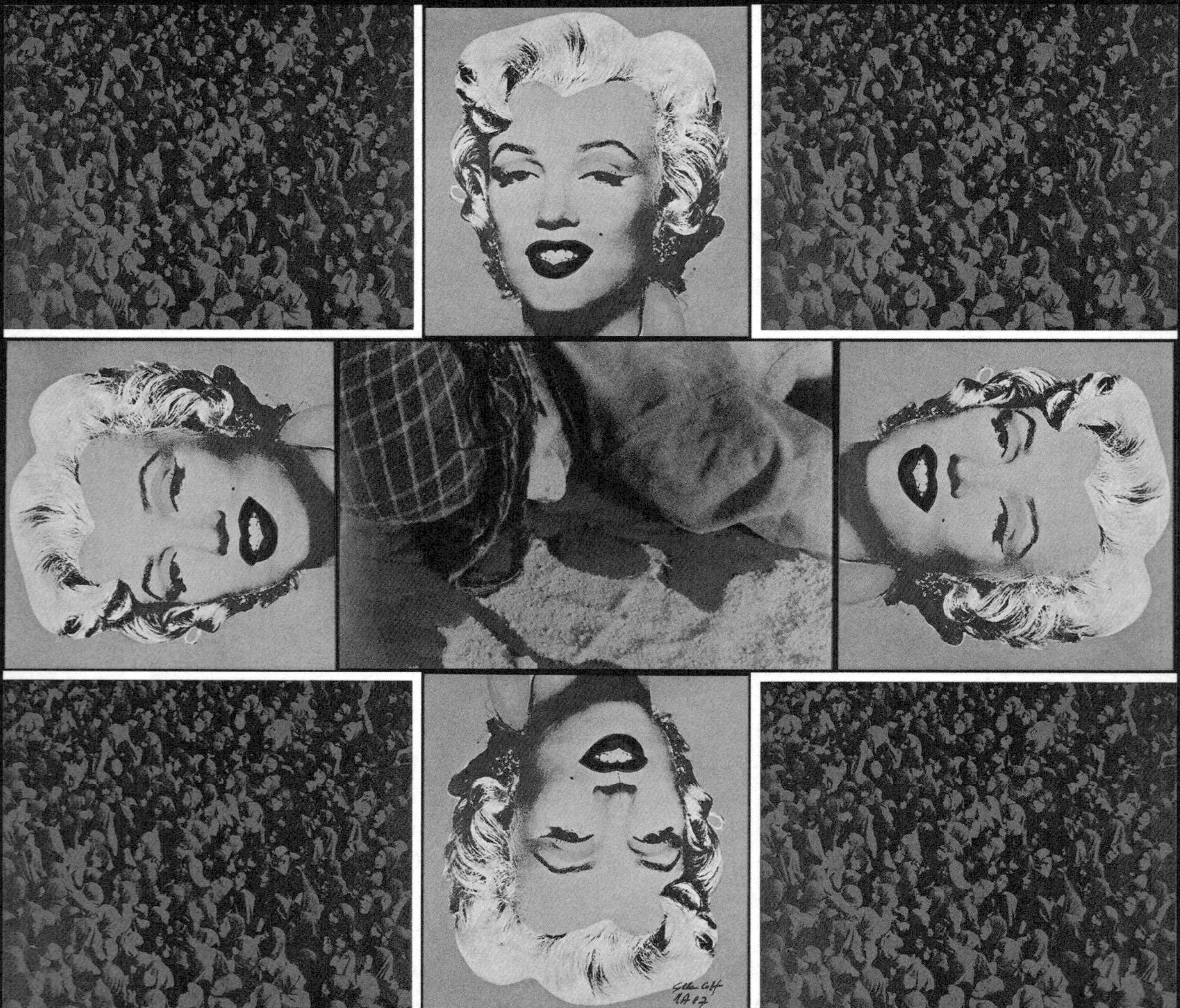

Golden Calf, 1987

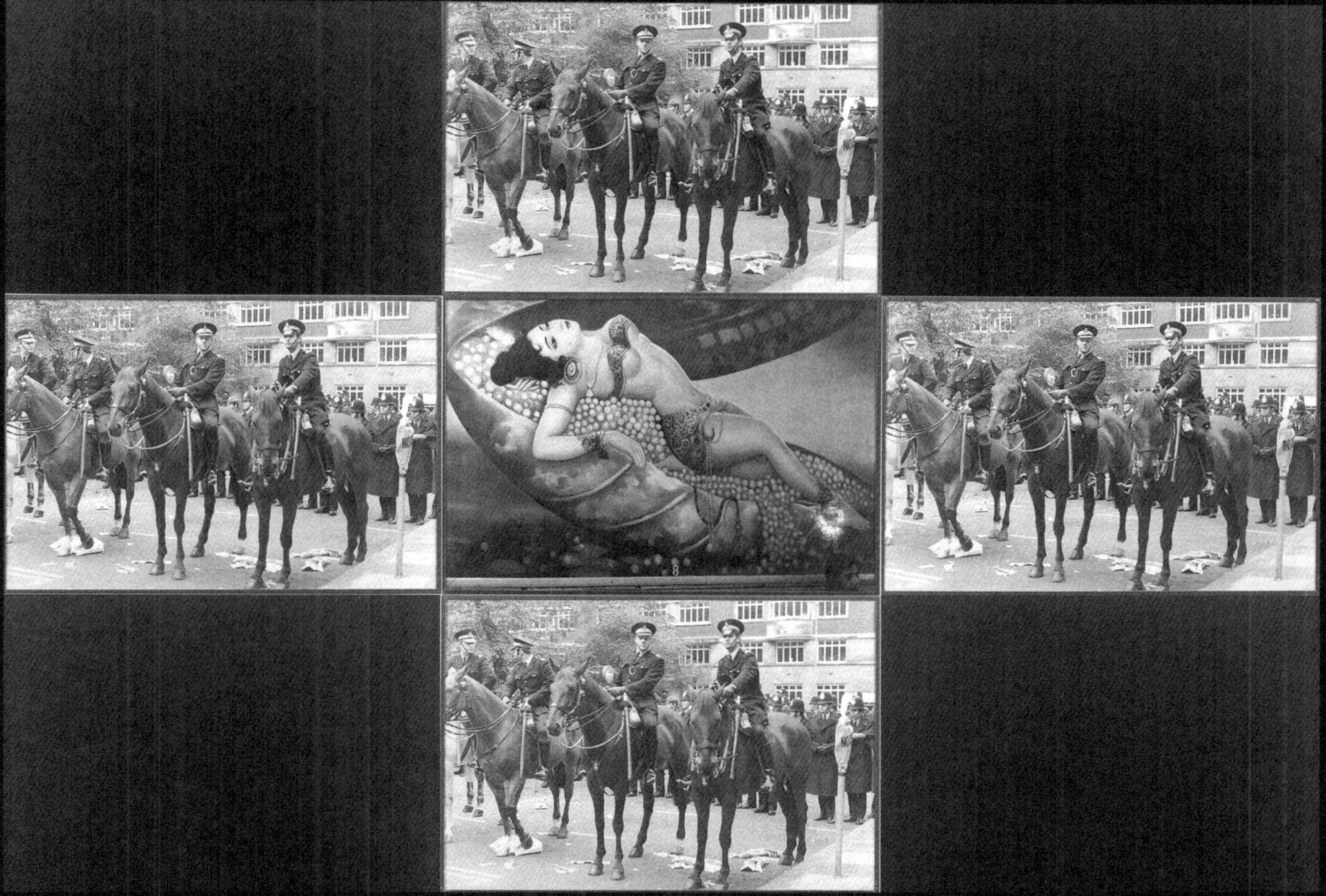

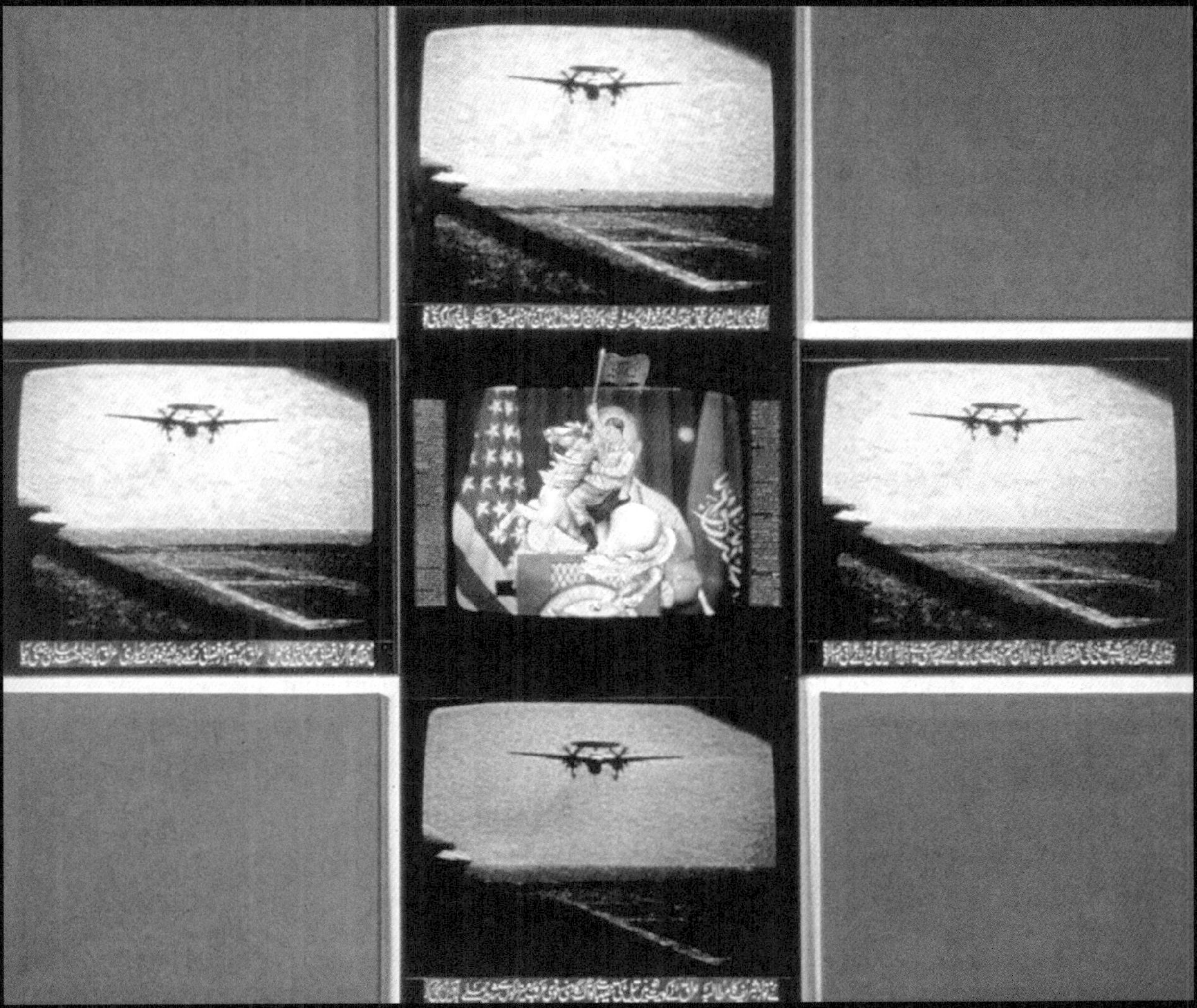

Golden Calf (1987)

269

In *Golden Calf*, violence is more forcefully foregrounded as the abstracted bloodstain in the central panel of *Green Painting I* has been replaced with an image of a dead Iranian man lying face down in the sand in a pool of blood. Despite this rupturing of what could appear in *Green Painting I* as mere formal abstraction, through the introduction of a human figure, the fact that the soldier's identity is hidden, highlights the abstract nature of the man's death, especially for those in the West. On the surrounding four panels of the cross-shape are Andy Warhol's screen prints of Marilyn Monroe, whose fully visible, smiling face – in stark contrast to the Iranian man's – is instantly recognizable, albeit for its abstract iconography. As an archetypal work of 1960s Pop art, a cultural form, which, for Araeen, is expressive of the fully fledged consolidation of US economic and cultural imperialism,[10] the work's recycling within *Golden Calf* points to the continuation of this imperialism through the US backing of Iraq in the Iraq-Iran war. The 'golden calf' of the work's title, which could be seen to refer interchangeably to either the dead Iranian man, or Warhol's constructed image of Marilyn, alludes to a history of real human sacrifice in the name of false idolatry. However, both are rendered abstract within the totality of the composition.

The violence of masculinity also reappears powerfully in *Golden Calf*. While Warhol's Marilyn pouts and smiles sinisterly over and around the Iranian man, she appears herself as what Jean Fisher has termed, 'the commodified icon of Euroamerican masculine desire',[11] an aggressively hyper-sexualized and Westernized concept of beauty. The Iranian man in turn appears emasculated, the sacrificial signification reducing him to the status of a slaughtered animal. In the four corner panels, the green monochromes have now been filled with what appears at first glance as a pattern, as though a small sponge has been used to make black dabs across the panel's surface. On closer inspection, the black dabs are imprints of the image of a crowd of mourning Iranian women. Thus Pop art is used to represent the sacrifice and loss resulting from aggressive masculinity and imperialism, just as the historical emergence and 'universalization' of Pop art coincides with the ascendency and consolidation of US economic and cultural power.

Tableau Noir (1987)

256

In *Tableau Noir*, these themes are re-examined from a British context, where the question of class is brought into dialogue with that of race and gender. In the central panel is a painted image of a reclining Asian woman, which Araeen reports to have taken from the wall of a Bangladeshi restaurant in Brick Lane.[12] In the context of the other panels, and also the other 'cruciform' works, the image seems to point to a sexualized and fetishized notion of the Asian female, but could also resemble the figure of a female deity. Surrounding this, in the shape of the cross, are four black and white photographs, taken by Araeen himself, of rows of mounted riot police, and behind them a row of policemen on foot, protecting a meeting of the National Front at Conway Hall in London in 1973. That the police gave little protection in the 1970s to South Asian people – including many Bangladeshis who were brutally, and sometimes fatally, attacked by the National Front – makes this configuration particularly pointed.

Here, in place of the Urdu of *Green Painting 1*, chalked on the 'blackboard' (*tableau noir*) is text from a newspaper report describing how the majority of injuries inflicted by police on the predominantly South Asian women of the famous Grunwick strike in the late 1970s were to the genitals and the breasts. Araeen thus alludes to the deeply psychosexual nature of state violence and oppression towards racialized groups. The figure of the striker is – like the face of the Iranian man in *Golden Calf* – absent, yet she is evoked negatively, through the image of her aggressors, and mythicized in the central figure of the Asian woman. As Simone de Beauvoir argued, the mythical elevation of the concept of 'woman' by men, typically through the worshipping of her sexual power and beauty, constitutes the flipside of a lack of real socio-economic power. While the ascription of such mythical status is often presented as though it brings with it a form of social and cultural power, it is both limited and limiting: it assists in keeping the female entrapped within her inferior socio-economic position.

White Stallion (1991)

In *White Stallion*, the central panel shows Saddam Hussein on a white horse, waving a green flag that reads 'Allah is Great' in Arabic. This figure is superimposed onto a photo of US General Schwarzkopf, a field commander in the Gulf War, as he appears on TV giving a press conference, on a podium draped with the flags of the US and Saudi Arabia, while columns of Arabic text on either side discuss various racehorses. Surrounding this are four photographs, again of a TV screen, with identical images of a US AWACS reconnaissance plane landing on an aircraft carrier, underneath which are strips of Urdu text. The four corner panels are a bright green monochrome, which contrasts the grainy images from the TV. In this work, Araeen uses the ambiguous figure of Saddam to draw out the complicated historical and political character of the entanglement between the West and the Middle East, within Western hegemony. 268

The image of Saddam is derived from Jacques-Louis David's painting *Napoleon at St. Bernard* (1800). As Paul Overy explains, the characterization of Saddam on the horse not only aligns him with Bonaparte, but also has mythical status for Muslims, as Muhammad's grandson Hussein – Saddam's seventh-century namesake – rode on a white horse to fight against the tyrant Yazid in the 680 AD Battle of Karbala, in what is now Iraq.[13] Yet, while this image evokes a culturally specific historical and mythological imaginary, the figure of Saddam carries contradictory significations, acting to illustrate the entanglement of Western and non-Western power. While Saddam presented himself as leader and representative of the identity and interests of the Middle East, he was backed economically and militarily by the West against a revolutionary Iran. Superimposed on General Schwarzkopf and enclosed by descending US planes, this mythological status is reduced to ineffectuality; Saddam appears small and puppet-like against the economic and military power of the US. Araeen is also, of course, commenting upon the notorious role of media in this war – most famously analysed by Jean Baudrillard in *The Gulf War Did Not Take Place* (1991) – but also in the construction of a personality cult around Saddam Hussein: the image of Saddam on horseback, as the reincarnation of a legendary representative of Islam, apparently sold two million copies in Pakistan alone.[14]

—

Araeen's 'cruciform' works interrogate the economic, military, and cultural hegemony of the West and its universalist pretensions. By setting up a dynamic interaction between symbols of modernism on the one hand and images of war, masculinity, racism, sexism, violence, sacrifice, and commercialism on the other, they highlight that culture's dependence on legacies of colonialism, imperialism, and the related mechanisms of abjection and control that safeguard white male power. At the same time, the subtle tensions within these works, which operate across and between the more obvious demarcations of the Minimalist grid system, effect a critical deconstruction that suggests a more dialectical relationship between the two poles. By rupturing and filling an archetypal aesthetic symbol of modernity with what it would hide, Araeen disrupts its purity and presents 'centre' and 'periphery' as co-constituting. As he explains:

> For me this system represents our divided world, the centre – white, male, Christian and globally dominant – and the periphery which aspires to the centre but cannot get there due to this division. Yet both are tied together in a violent nexus. Both are dependent on each other. The centre defines the periphery and in turn is defined by it.[15]

Araeen's revisiting, in the 1980s through 1990s, of this problematic that he had articulated in the 1970s, could be read as anticipating his later scepticism about the limitations of postcolonialism and multiculturalism, and his belief that the emergent global unification typically described as "globalization" – which would be celebrated as levelling the playing field, both in the abstract space of art and in the world beyond – was still essentially an imperialist one, under the unity of a single world market. Within these new conditions, the cruciform provided an aesthetic structure through which Araeen could – while recycling and combining the themes, techniques, and media that had accumulated through his artistic career – transcend the formal constraints of Minimalism and develop his own critical language.

1. Rasheed Araeen, 'Conspiracy of Silence' (1974), in Rasheed Araeen, *Making Myself Visible* (London: Kala Press, 1984), 67.
2. Araeen, 'Preliminary Notes for a BLACK MANIFESTO', in ibid., 83. First published in *Black Phoenix* (winter 1978):3–12.
3. Araeen, 'Epilogue', in *Making Myself Visible*, 5.
4. For an account of Araeen's position on the question of political art see Araeen and Eddie Chambers, 'Black Art: A Discussion', *Third Text* 2, no.5 (winter, 1988):51–77.
5. These works were first shown together in Britain in 1994 at the exhibition *Rasheed Araeen* at South London Gallery.
6. A selection of works from this period by Araeen were on view as part of the *Back to the Future* section at Artissima, Turin, 3–5 November 2017.
7. Ibid.
8. Ibid.
9. Rasheed Araeen, 'I Had No Choice but to Deal with This Gaze Which Was Making Me Invisible', interview with Helena Pivec, *M'Ars: Casopis Moderne Galerije Ljubljana* 6, no. 1–4 (1994). Quoted in Paul Overy, 'The New Works of Rasheed Araeen' (exhibition catalogue) (London: South London 1994), 17.
10. Araeen, 'BLACK MANIFESTO', 83.
11. Jean Fisher, 'An Art of Transformation', in *Rasheed Araeen: STRIFE and/or STRUCTURE* (exhibition catalogue) (Fukuoka: Fukuoka Asian Art Museum, 1993). Reprinted in *The Triumph of Icarus: Life and Art of Rasheed Araeen*, ed. Jean Fisher (Karachi: Millennium Media, 2014), 113.
12. See note 6.
13. Overy, 'The New Works', 129.
14. Ibid.
15. See Rasheed Araeen, 'From Innovation to Deconstruction: My Own Story', *Undo.net*, http://1995-2015.undo.net/cgi-bin/openframe.pl?x=/Pinto/Eng/earaeen.htm.

In Conversation: Nick Aikens and Rasheed Araeen

Nick Aikens (NA) In Professor Majnoon Gorakhpuri's article 'Why Art?' published in *Dawn*, a Karachi newspaper, in February 1976, he opens with the statement: 'Art is the expression of beauty.' You wrote a response, taking him to task over this definition of art, saying that the meaning of art must be finely attuned to the realities of the present. I wonder, now in 2017, forty years after that text was written, how would you describe the meaning of art?

Rasheed Araeen (RA) I would still define the meaning of art in terms of the production of beauty. I know this does not answer your question, because we will have to first ask ourselves what we mean by 'beauty'. Who defines it? My response to Majnoon Gorakhpuri (who was a highly respected, eminent literary critic of Urdu literature) was to question and challenge his notion of beauty,[1] which was taken from the West, and which is still prevalent and dominant not only in Pakistan but the whole world. Art today suffers from this globally dominant notion of beauty.

NA In that text you talk about artists having to be attuned to the realities of the world around them. The realities you have experienced as an artist in Karachi, and then in England, have changed quite dramatically in that time.

RA In England, things happened differently. I got trapped between my artistic sensibility and political consciousness. I tried to negotiate the relationship: sometimes I became very political, but without losing my artistic sensibility; at other times my artistic sensibility suffered from my politics. My art became confrontational – explicitly confrontational towards the system that then became an obstacle in my pursuit of beauty in art.

NA I want to focus in this conversation on your relationship to modernism. When I look at the different moments in your trajectory as an artist, your relationship to modernism – or modernisms we could say – undergoes many different turns. It is a relationship that has formal, cultural, and political implications within your practice. When you began painting portraits of people in the streets of Karachi in your early twenties, what was your awareness, or understanding, of modernism – in either artistic or more broadly cultural terms?

RA Well, we had a big idea of modernism in Pakistan: modernism as a progressive thing, or a progressive view of the world. It was visible in many aspects of the city, as Karachi was not an old city but developed under the British Raj. Once it was considered one of the most beautiful modern cities of Asia, with all the modern amenities, such as the availability of electricity and running water even in the poor areas of the city, and its tram network, which connected all its different parts. However, things began to change when Karachi became the capital of the newly emergent country of Pakistan, as with it also emerged the post-independence bourgeois class that began to see everything imported from the West as embodying modernism. This also influenced the modernism of art in Pakistan.

When I began to do art I was only interested in doing drawings and paintings of what I saw around me – particularly the portraits of ordinary people you have mentioned. Although artists in Karachi began to get involved in the debate and discussion about modernism, which interested me a great deal, I kept my interest in doing things in my own way. The thing that did interest me, however, was that I didn't have to reproduce in my work realistically what I experienced visually. I could instead engage myself freely in the medium I was using to make art. My first interest in modernism was in what I found in architecture, not only in Karachi but also in the work of Frank Lloyd Wright whose work I discovered in the United States Information Service (USIS) library in Karachi in 1955; and I expressed this in the house I myself designed for my parents in 1957 (when I was still a civil engineering student). My interest in the modernism of art was aroused when I came across some books on art in 1958, particularly of Herbert Read and Roger Fry, which it seemed I then studied thoroughly, as I marked up many sentences and passages when I read them. In the same year, I began to play with the various mediums of art and produced some works that were the results of thinking about modernism rather than what I had produced until then by looking at things. What was most important in this respect was the somewhat abstract form of boats, which emerged from a play of horizontal, 28 vertical, and diagonal lines drawn on a piece of paper and the in-between spaces filled with water colour. What actually emerged from this was geometry: the formation of triangles by the intersection of horizontal, vertical, and diagonal lines, which in fact has persisted in my work until today.

A year later, in 1959, another important thing happened to me. I picked up a piece of metal, a twisted circular wire, from the street, took it home, and turned it into *My First Sculpture*. Its circular form was twisted in such way 32 that it formed two circles; when I looked at it recently I realized it represents infinity. It is now lying in my studio.

When I picked up this piece from the street I didn't know what I was doing, because I did it innocently and instinctively, without realizing what it meant. Only when I took it home, put it on the table, and looked at it, did I think of it as a modern sculpture. Some months later, I burned two bicycle tyres, from which emerged four similar metal pieces. I did both of these works without knowing what the avant-garde was, when in fact similar things were happening in the avant-garde in the West. We never heard the name Duchamp in Karachi. And, now, when art historians look at these works they contextualize them within the avant-garde while these works had nothing to do with what was a movement of the West that emerged from its own socio-historical conditions. One critic actually called these works Fluxus-like, while Fluxus did not then exist – not even in the West.

Also, at that time, I had no idea that art was meant to confront. I was doing things innocently; perhaps there was some invisible force behind it. I don't know how to describe it otherwise; maybe we can describe it as a manifestation of free imagination – an imagination that is not burdened with already determined ideas. That's why many critics have problems dealing with my work.

NA In this regard the fact that you had no formal training as an artist is significant. You were not positioning yourself in relation to a history or discourse as that knowledge wasn't there.

RA When you want to be an artist, you go to art school where you are taught not only how to make art but also what is contained in the whole history of art. You become aware of the existing knowledge, and then you respond to that knowledge to become an artist. I didn't have that. I didn't have anything in front of me to respond to. I did have some idea of modernism, but not its full history, let alone that of the avant-garde.

NA And was that idea of modernism, as understood through Wright, Read, and Fry, what made you get on a boat and leave Pakistan? And how did that idea change when you arrived in Britain in 1964?

RA Yes, they did influence my decision to leave. In Britain things were different. I became aware of what was already there as historical knowledge. When I saw and became fascinated by the work of Anthony Caro, I knew that his work was already part of the mainstream history of modernism. So what I faced then was a historical discourse, and I had to respond to it historically. But I couldn't, with the kind of resources it required. I had no training as a sculptor, and no means to join an art school and learn the skill of making, or experimenting with what is involved in the making of sculpture. But, since my fascination for the modernity of Caro's work became obsessive, it created in me a state of mind in which I constantly thought about what could be the new form of sculpture.

NA It's interesting that you say your relationship with the modernity of Caro's work was obsessive. But your approach in the Structures and specifically lattice works of the 1960s is very different from Caro's compositions. Your wish to think, rather than compose new forms of sculpture, through geometry and symmetry, is also the difference between a conceptual and gestural approach to making art.

RA In the beginning my fascination for Caro's work was obsessive, as I kept on thinking about how to make sculpture like him. But this desire didn't last very long, and my thinking began to change. I began to contemplate sculpture rather than what Caro was doing. At the end of 1965, while making some drawings of I-beam girders in different arrangements, during the lunchtime in the drawing office of BHC Ltd (a subsidiary of BP), I noticed their symmetry; I then realized that I had found something new and different from Caro.

NA And what drew you to symmetry?

RA Perhaps my education in engineering.

NA By the late 1960s you were starting to experiment with the relationship between your geometric forms, the audience, and public space – most famously in works such as *Chakras* (1969–1970) or *Triangles* (1970). This was 136, 141
a further development in how you *thought*, rather than composed sculpture. In that sense it's a deeply conceptual piece. But at that time in London were you not aware of conceptual practices elsewhere?

RA Then, I didn't yet know much about what Conceptual art was, although I did come to know the work of Gustav Metzger. But I wasn't yet aware that it should be called 'conceptual'. Only in the late 1960s, when people began to talk about art as conceptual, did I begin to know that there was something called 'conceptual'. It was then that I began to read about art. It was also then that by chance in 1967 I stumbled upon the special issue of *Art and Artists* about Duchamp and first came to know about him and his work. I became somewhat fascinated by his work, which might have influenced what I did subsequently.

NA And thinking, Rasheed, again about this evolving relationship to and understanding of modernism, how did it change in the late 1960s, and

1970s, in terms of your understanding of modernism as a European or Western project?

RA Well I didn't see art in those terms when I arrived in London. The idea that art might represent society wasn't on my mind at that time. I was only interested in the so-called art. I didn't think along the lines of the relationship between art and society explicitly until the early 1970s, when I became more acutely aware of the nature of British society.

NA Could you talk about the awareness of the society in which you found yourself in the early 1970s and how that affected your art?

RA When I arrived in London in 1964, racism was everywhere. It was spirited, overt, and it was legal. There was no law against overt racism. However, in the beginning it didn't bother me much. But when I moved out of the friend's house where I was living since I arrived, and had to find myself a place to live, everywhere I went, I was received with the constant signs of 'No Blacks, No Coloureds'. And when I eventually found a small room it was in a house owned by an Indian woman. Again, when I had to look for a larger place to live, I faced the same situation. Once, ultimately, I did find a large bedsitter it was in the household of a Polish family. But I didn't see all this in terms of its relationship with art. I thought art was free from it. Why confuse it with that? So I carried on with my work.

I am not saying that everything was racist, or everyone I met was a racist. I spent three years working with the petro-chemical subsidiary of BP, and on no occasion did I face racism there. On the contrary, when I left BP the head of its engineering section, Mr. Ritchie, was extremely upset. Anyway, racism didn't affect my practice as an artist until 1971, when I went around looking for a gallery to show my work. And everywhere I went, they said, 'No'. It was the same experience that I had when I went around looking for a place to live. There was a gallery who explicitly said: 'We love your work, but sorry we only show American and English artists.' It was a shattering experience, and I got disorientated, and I didn't know what to do with myself. I couldn't carry on with my work.

NA And then you made a decision that you had to confront racism?

RA Yes. Then I also met people who were one kind of artist or another, like poets and writers, who were already involved in politics. We would usually meet in the pubs, and talk about the relationship of art to politics. During this time, I also met David Medalla, who was then highly political, and I often heard him saying that art should reflect society, and that art should be involved in the struggle against oppressive forces. He would frequently talk about the writing of Marx and Mao. So, I got my training from these people, particularly from David. I can now say that he actually played a major role in my politicization in relation to art.

NA Were you then beginning to think about modernism's relationship to imperialism? Was there a consciousness that these two things were interlinked?

RA Not in the beginning, except for racism, which I realized was enshrined in the legacy of colonial imperialism. This awareness came to me from reading Frantz Fanon. Also, I read other anti-colonial writers, such as Amilcar Cabral and Paulo Freire; and I then got involved with the work of the Black Panthers in London. Only when I began to write 'Preliminary Notes for a BLACK

MANIFESTO' in 1975, did I become aware of the relationship between modernism and imperialism.

230

NA In this regard, the work *For Oluwale*, conceived in 1971 was a turning point. 210

RA Yes, it was a turning point. I was shocked when I read how David Oluwale was treated by the police and how it lead to his death in Leeds. So, on that day, when I read about his death, I decided I would make a work dedicated to him.

NA Not only did *For Oluwale* mark a turning point in the direct politicization of your practice, it also marked a new approach to working with materials.

RA In the 1970s I started experimenting a lot with the language or the medium of art. I would use whatever material I would find or that was suitable for the work, often newspaper and magazine clippings, with which I would make collages. In *For Oluwale* I used the most unusual method of making a collage. It comprised four panels, yet they were not done together at the same time, but as a movement from one panel to another inside an art exhibition space. Although the work was conceived in 1971 it was realized in 1973. In the beginning I wasn't aware of its form. It came to me in 1973 when the director of the Camden Arts Centre called me, and asked me to participate in a show he was organizing at the Swiss Cottage Library.

I put a 4 x 4 foot panel there on the first day of opening, and then put the information about Oluwale on it, how he died in Leeds. In the second week, I changed the material of the panel, by including in it two pages from the newspaper of the Black Panthers, which showed the violence of racism against black people. For the third week, the panel included the information about Fascist Portugese dictator Salazar's state visit to London, and so on, until the fourth week panel appeared and included what was going on around outside the art exhibition. In fact, in the week Salazar came to London, there was a public demonstration against his visit. So, the work was connected to what was happening outside an art exhibition space. *For Oluwale* was not just about the death of Oluwale, but also about what was there in the public domain in the summer of 1973 – the struggle of all people against oppressive forces.

Following that, I went to Karachi where I did a version of *Chakras*. Back in London, I wrote an open letter to the art critic of *The Guardian*, in which I tried to suggest the relationship between modernism and imperialism. This was the beginning of my writing discourse, which then led me to the writing of 'BLACK MANIFESTO' (1975–1976). 218

NA And what about *Fire*, the work you did in 1975. This seems one of your most overt confrontations with imperialism. 228

RA This was about the relationship between two flags: American and Vietnamese flags, the former representing the American aggression against Vietnam, and the latter the victorious struggle of Vietnam against America. I placed the American flag on top of the Vietnamese flag, making the Vietnamese flag invisible. But when I burned the American flag, the Vietnamese flag emerged and became visible. The use of fire in the making of this work was a sort of recurrence of what I did in 1959 when I burned bicycle tyres. In fact, the phenomenon of recurrence has been common throughout my work.

NA Yes – it reappears in the highly evocative *Burning Ties* (1976–1979), also in the '70s. Fire here – as elsewhere in your work is both destructive and generative. Were you aware at the time of your recurring use of fire? 232

RA I was aware of the use of fire in the making of art when I did it in 1975, as part of the exhibition at Artists for Democracy to celebrate the victory of Indo-Chinese people against American imperialism.

NA In the first half the 1970s you made a series of works that directly confronted different aspects of imperial Britain. But at a certain moment you start appearing in the work. As Courtney J. Martin points out in her essay in this book, it was a dramatic shift considering how absent you – or the artists' hands we could say – had been form the work. Why was that?

RA After *For Oluwale* (1971–1973 / 1975), I did a series of collages, referring 220 to British imperialism; and then I also photographed the police protecting the National Front meeting at the Conway Hall, London. All this was about the struggle of people against oppressive forces, but it excluded my own struggle. So, I began to ask myself, why do I not put myself into what I do as an artist? It was this question that led me into: first, doing the performance 234 of *'Paki Bastard' (Portrait of the Artist as a Black Person)* in 1977; and then a series of what appear to be 'self-portraits'. But they are not self-portraits as such. I used my own face in these works to question and critique the idea of self-portraiture representing the self. The idea of representing oneself in the form of self-portraiture comes from the iconographic tradition of Western art, representing the power of the narcissistic self, which was denied the colonized self; it is this colonized self you see in these so-called 'self-portraits'.

If you look at the whole body of work of the 1970s, you would see collages, photo works, performances, and, finally, a series of the so-called 'self-portraits'. Most of them have to do with the problems of identity in a racist/ imperialist society. There is no particular medium or style that I pursued. I would do whatever was suitable – I even started doing painting, which I had not done for fifteen years.

NA You not only addressed questions of representation towards you as a black artist at this time – you also addressed the representation of women, for which you have been criticized.

RA Yes – I have been criticized for using images of naked white women, taken 223 from soft-porn magazines, in one of the collages. Underlying this criticism is an assumption that women are the victims of male power, which is true. Yet, this work tries to address the fact that white women are also participants in the West's domination of the world, from which they derive their privileges within world culture. All these glossy magazines published in the West containing images of white women are not only for people in the West, but they are circulated worldwide, as a result of which women in the rest of the world see these images as examples of superior beauty. And they often try to look like white women, particularly by using whitening cream, which is produced and marketed by the multinationals.

255

NA This was the subject of *Fair and Lovely* in 1985, which was the first of the nine-panel works later to become the 'cruciform' series. Here, your engagement with modernism evolves into an engagement with postmodernism to some extent, a bringing together or clash of different references, cultures, and ideologies. It is also a return to a much more formal approach with the use of green monochrome panels that form the four corners of the works.

Do you see the 'cruciform' works as bringing together some of the concerns of the 1960s with those of the '70s? Going back to what you said at the beginning, was there a certain synthesis that was happening at that moment between your formal concerns and political concerns?

RA I had already used the number nine in some works in 1960s, first with the work *Nine* (1968–1975), in order to give them a symmetrical structure. 124 The nine-panel works of the eighties also have this symmetry, but their symmetrical order is broken and has become divided by two conflicting realities. Let me go back to what I said earlier, that I was caught between aesthetic sensibility and political awareness. In the 1970s, my tendency began to turn more towards the political, rather than ideological. One can deal with conflicting realities, ideologically, without developing an artistic style, which represents the artist's identity. But in the seventies I realized that I needed an identity, even when it might be a problematic one. I don't know if it was a good or bad thing that I did develop a work with a style that could be attributed to me. What is interesting here is the fact that I developed this nine-panel work without thinking about my identity. However, in this work, I managed to bring together both of my concerns: aesthetics and the political. These works look beautiful. But within their beauty are disturbing realities.

NA What fascinates me about the 'cruciform' works is they seem to be the place where many of the conflicts and concerns within your practice are laid bare. I read the monochrome greens as both the abstraction of high modernism and, as you have described, referencing the Pakistani flag, the embodiment of nature, youth. How we read those monochromes speaks to our political and cultural formation. And these oscillating monochromes are intersected with images that reference contemporaneous imperial forays (the Gulf War, the Falklands War) and their embodiment in the history of art (Pollock, Warhol). The relationship between cultures, between modernism as understood through art and imperialism is centrifugal, by which I mean different elements and references are not simply presented as different but understood through the force of the dominant, central culture – that of the West.

RA It is not just the breaking and splitting of the monochrome (the ultimate manifestation of modernism, particularly the *Black Square* (1915) by Malevich), but my own identity as a modern artist. In 1979 and 1980, I did a series of works by cutting up my own image on paper (a photograph that I used for the poster for the performance *'Paki Bastard'* in 1977), and then rearranging the cut parts in different ways. In one work, I cut the image into four parts and arranged them to form an empty cross between them, and titled it *Crossed*. When I began to do the 'cruciform' works in 1985, it 246 seemed I filled this empty cross with images while I had forgotten this work. Only recently, while looking at *Crossed*, which now hangs in my studio, did I realize that the 'cruciform' works are also to do with my identity. In other words, the green monochromes represent my identity, which has been pushed out into the periphery of the corners by the images you see inside the cross.

NA It is of course in 1987, while making the 'cruciform' works that you launched *Third Text*, whose first issue was green, I should say. In this issue you outline how the journal should be understood as an effort to confront and move away from the centre. Two years later at the Hayward Gallery *The Other Story:*

Afro-Asian Artists in Post-War Britain opened, with the aim of redressing the history of modernism so it might include the contribution of black artists – a project you have been invested in throughout your career. At the time, how did you understand the project of *Third Text* and *The Other Story* in relation to or as a part of your art practice?

RA *Third Text* was the resurrection of the magazine *Black Phoenix: Journal of Contemporary Art & Culture in the Third World* (1978–1979), which included my 'BLACK MANIFESTO' and thus provided the framework for my subsequent work, with a shift from 'black' to 'green'. As I have pointed out before, 'green' had become the periphery of the centre (the cross), but this move to the periphery provided a necessary critical distance from the centre to look at the centre. When I began to do my first modernist works (1958–1959), I wasn't at the centre. And yet I was able to produce something that in some way was innovatively ahead of the mainstream of the centre. So, moving to the periphery could be extremely productive.

However, my understanding of both came from my own practice as an artist and what it faced in relation to Eurocentric modernism and its history. At the same time, I realized that it was not what I faced alone but also the whole body of modernist works produced by artists from all over the world. Why was it that then the prevailing history of modernism was – and still is – the history of only white artists? It was this question that lead me to the projects of *Third Text* and then *The Other Story*, as a conceptual extension of what I was producing as art objects.

NA After you were removed from *Third Text* in 2011 you returned to painting. Within the 'Opus' and 'Homecoming' series' there seems to be a further shift in your relationship with modernism, or a reappraisal of it. These new paintings comprising geometry and symmetry, abstraction, one could read as references to twentieth-century European modernism: De Stijl, and Constructivism, which are important reference points for you. But you could also look to the history of geometry and symmetry within Islam, as well, which I know is an equally important reference point. I was wondering if you could talk about what is happening with these new paintings, in terms of a repositioning of modernism, both historically and geographically?

RA I don't know if what was produced by Islamic civilization in art was called 'modern', or it was conceived as 'modern', but the use of geometry and symmetry in Islamic art was a progressive thing, ideologically as well as historically. Ideologically, it defied and confronted the iconography of art based on the images of living being, particularly of humans, and particularly originating from the Greeks and Romans and then becoming fundamental to Christian art. The geometry of Islamic art thus created a shift, historically, from what the eye could see and is represented in art to what could be conceived imaginatively beyond the experience of the eye. In other words, it was a move towards an abstraction – an abstraction not only of art but intellectual thinking, which has been fundamental to the progress of ideas in human history. This achievement by Islamic civilization took place eleven centuries before the modern artists of the twentieth century in Europe understood the importance of abstraction. But this cannot be and is not recognized by the Eurocentrism of modern art history; it does, however, recognize the connection between the Renaissance and Greek art, despite the gap of 1,500 years between them. In fact, this is the problem I constantly face when I want to connect, historically, my work, especially the work I'm doing now that you see here in the studio, with not only the modernism you have mentioned but also the achievement of Islamic civilization.

NA I know that artisanal craft was also an inspiration in making these recent works.

RA When the potter makes a piece of pottery, he or she doesn't think about ideology or politics. I wish I could be like a potter. In my present work I am trying to be like a potter, although I cannot remove from what I produce its ideological level, which is implicit rather than explicit. Also, I'm now trying to bring together, in some other works, the creativity of everyday life and what we do as artists.

NA And without formal training as an artist.

RA Although I didn't go to an art school, I did train myself to be an artist. So, as an artist I know I cannot be innocent. I wish I were innocent.

NA But it's interesting that you've never had training as an artist, or in English, in writing, in theory. So, the sense of perpetual amateurism, or not being professionalized to a certain extent, has consistently run through your practice and is something that you now want to hold on to. In the introduction to *Making Myself Visible*, Guy Brett quotes Antonio Gramsci and references the Gramscian notion of the organic intellectual. Thinking of your relationship to amateurism, and your crossing of many different fields as part of your practice, how do you relate to the idea of the 'organic intellectual'?

RA Under capitalism, you cannot be an organic intellectual.

NA Why not?

RA Well, you can be, in terms of relating to the struggle, to a political struggle, particularly in the context of class struggle. I think that's what Gramsci had in mind. But there is a problem. The common perception of the relationship of artists to class struggle tends to be simplistic, promoted particularly by those who believe in the primacy of political struggle and expect the artist to be subservient to this, which, as a result becomes an obstacle to free imagination, fundamental to creativity.

NA And you would say that creativity, or that function of the imagination is in fact a more powerful political force, than being subservient to – or representing – a specific struggle.

RA Yes. I'm not denying the importance of the political struggle. But the artist should be free to relate to this in his or her own way, rather than taking instruction from politically engaged people.

NA How do you see that in relation to some of the ideas that you've put forward in *Art Beyond Art, Ecoaesthetics: A Manifesto for the 21st Century* (2010)? It constitutes another fascinating move in terms of your relationship to modernism and the ongoing negotiation we have talked about between political awareness and aesthetic sensibility. The centrality of the art object and the artist as author, both fundamental to the modernist paradigm, are made to give way to a practice conceived with and for a public.

RA There's a gap, a hierarchical gap, between what artists do and what ordinary people do in terms of expressing their own creativity. Artistic expression is seen as something higher, something precious. I want to demolish that gap. I don't know if I will be successful or not, but in my future projects I want to bring these things together, so that people can express their own creativity

366, 356
358

through what I can initiate. And then I will leave people to carry on what I have initiated. This year I have initiated three such projects: *Zero to Infinity* for the Venice Biennale, and *The Reading Room Kassel* and *Shamiyaana–Food for Thought: Thought for Change* in Athens for documenta 14. These projects would have not been possible without public 'participation'.

NA Returning to where we started, the 'production of beauty' in works such as *Shamiyaana* and *Zero to Infinity* takes place with and through the public, the users of the project. And, as you pointed out at the beginning of our conversation beauty can mean different things to different people at different times. Such understandings – from the craftsman or the people running *Shamiyaana* in Athens to New Generation sculptors in Britain in the '60s – do not have to be contradictory. Rather, they open up infinite ways of conceiving and relating to beauty, the project of modernism and our understanding of art.

RA Although these projects are generally understood in terms of public participation, 'participation' is not the right word here, because it means you are allowing people to enter your work, which has already been completed, and they thus then become participants in it. In the case of the projects I have mentioned, they don't just involve the participation of the public but also their creativity. For *Shamiyaana*, I only did the initial work such as the drawings of the pavilion. Then I went to Athens, and discussed the project with the people who would be involved in making *Shamiyaana*. I returned to London and left them to do everything. They, in fact, did the whole thing themselves. They were not only participants, but the makers of the work, and they themselves ran the project for two months – without my involvement, without my supervision, or anything else.

1 Rasheed Araeen, *Morning News*, 22 February 1976.

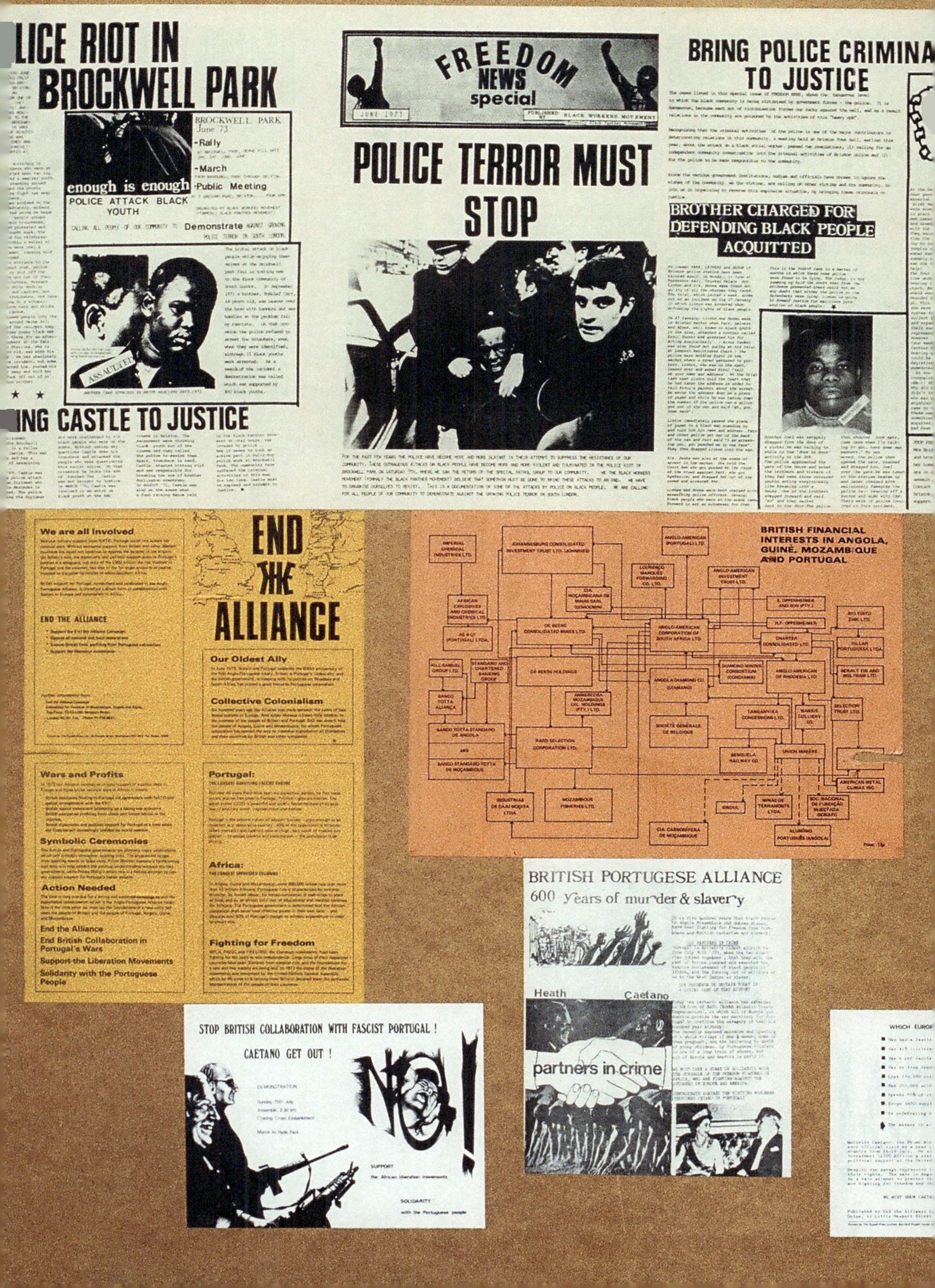
LICE RIOT IN BROCKWELL PARK
BROCKWELL PARK June 73
-Rally
-March
-Public Meeting
enough is enough
POLICE ATTACK BLACK YOUTH
Demonstrate
ASSAULTED
ING CASTLE TO JUSTICE
FREEDOM NEWS special
JUNE 1973
PUBLISHED BY BLACK WORKERS MOVEMENT
POLICE TERROR MUST STOP
BRING POLICE CRIMINA
TO JUSTICE
BROTHER CHARGED FOR DEFENDING BLACK PEOPLE ACQUITTED
We are all Involved
END THE ALLIANCE
END THE ALLIANCE
Our Oldest Ally
Collective Colonialism
Wars and Profits
Symbolic Ceremonies
Action Needed
End the Alliance
End British Collaboration in Portugal's Wars
Support the Liberation Movements
Solidarity with the Portuguese People
Portugal:
Africa:
Fighting for Freedom
BRITISH FINANCIAL INTERESTS IN ANGOLA, GUINE, MOZAMBIQUE AND PORTUGAL
BRITISH PORTUGESE ALLIANCE
600 years of murder & slavery
Heath
Caetano
partners in crime
STOP BRITISH COLLABORATION WITH FASCIST PORTUGAL !
CAETANO GET OUT !
NO!
SUPPORT
the African liberation movements
SOLIDARITY
with the Portuguese people

For Oluwale, 1971–1973 / 1975
4 mixed-media collages on board

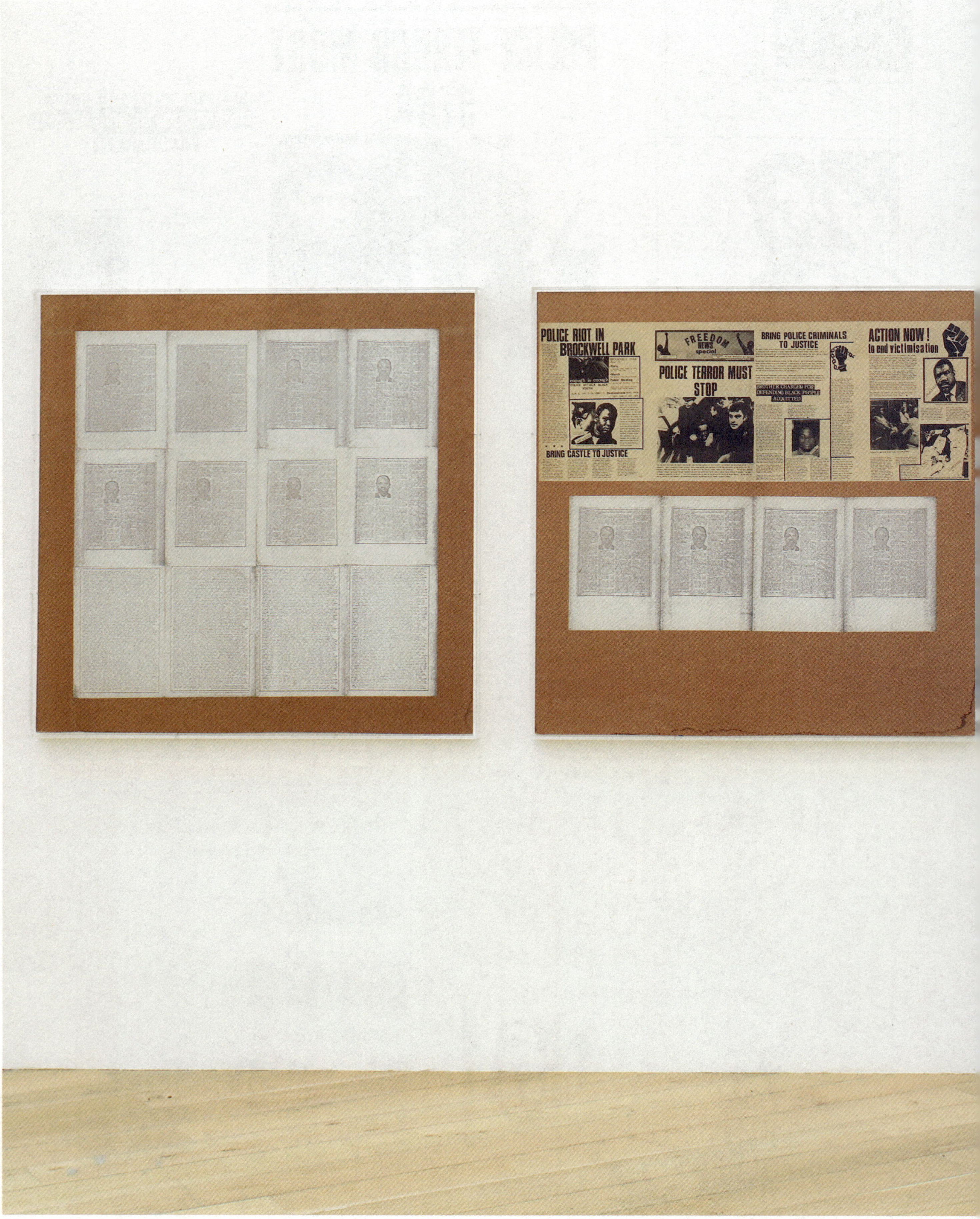

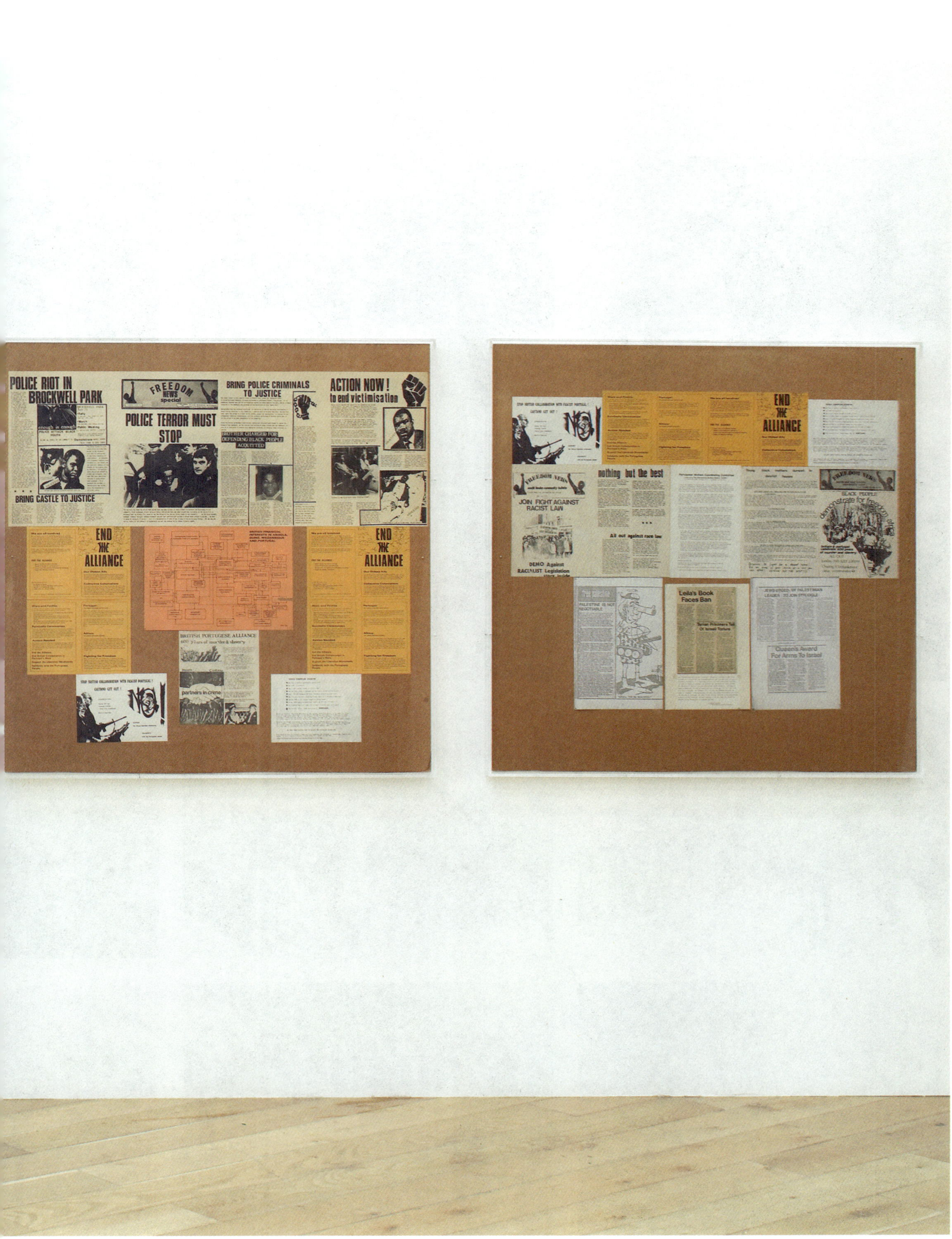
POLICE RIOT IN BROCKWELL PARK
BRING CASTLE TO JUSTICE
FREEDOM NEWS special
POLICE TERROR MUST STOP
BRING POLICE CRIMINALS TO JUSTICE
BROTHER CHARGED FOR DEFENDING BLACK PEOPLE ACQUITTED
ACTION NOW! to end victimisation
END THE ALLIANCE
END THE ALLIANCE
BRITISH PORTUGESE ALLIANCE
partners in crime
STOP BRITISH COLLABORATION WITH FASCIST PORTUGAL!
NO!
END THE ALLIANCE
FREEDOM NEWS
JOIN FIGHT AGAINST RACIST LAW
DEMO Against RACIALIST Legislation
nothing but the best
All out against race law
FREEDOM NEWS
BLACK PEOPLE
demonstrate for freedom
PALESTINE IS NOT NEGOTIABLE
Leila's Book Faces Ban
Queen's Award For Arms To Israel

When They Meet, 1973
photographic series, dimensions variable

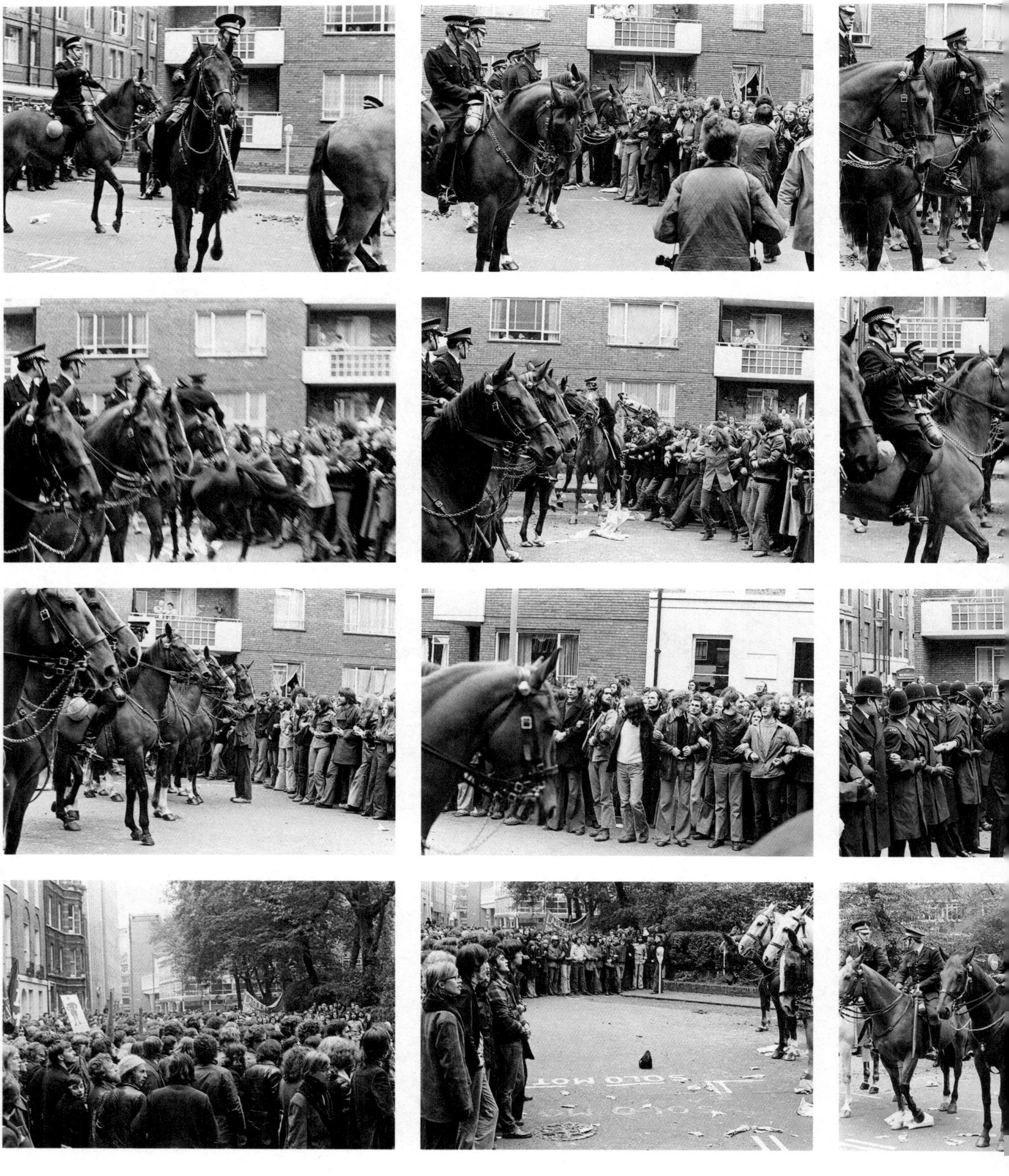

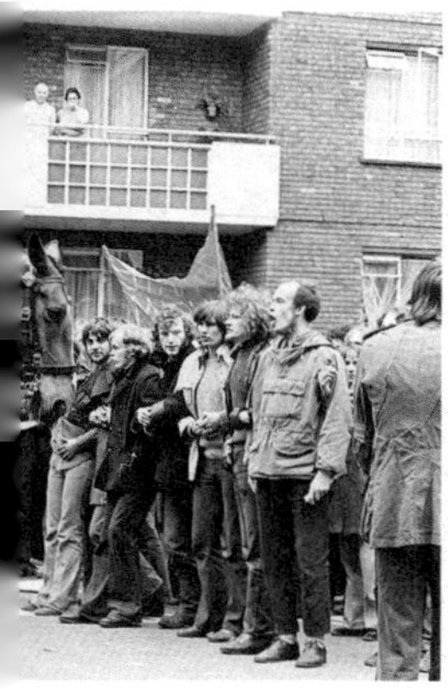
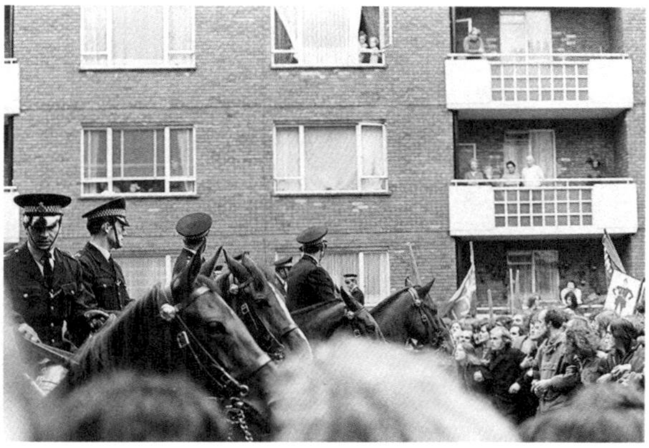
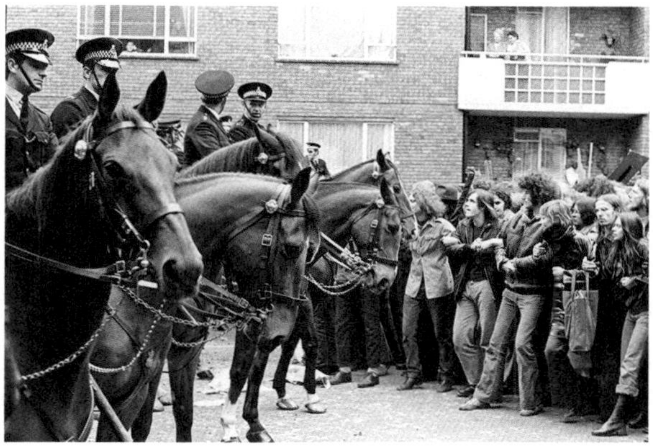
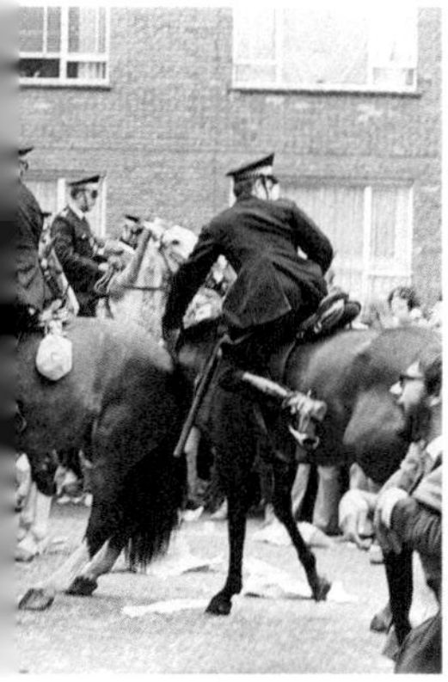
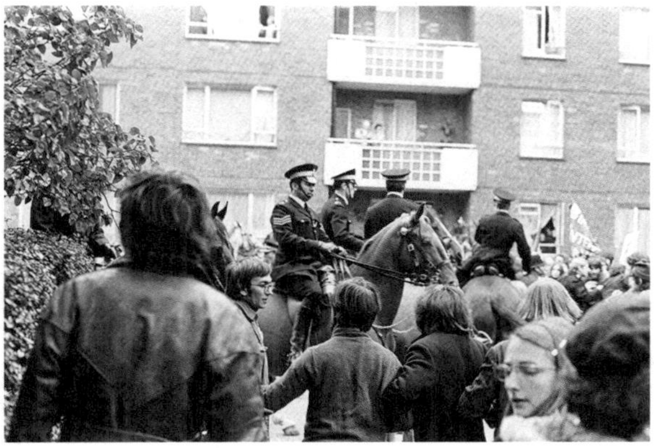
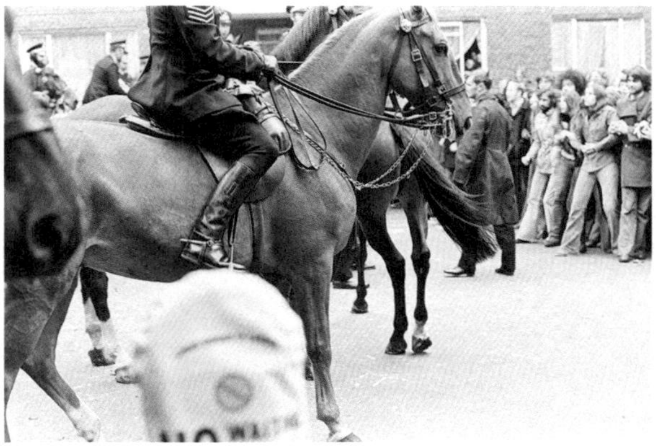
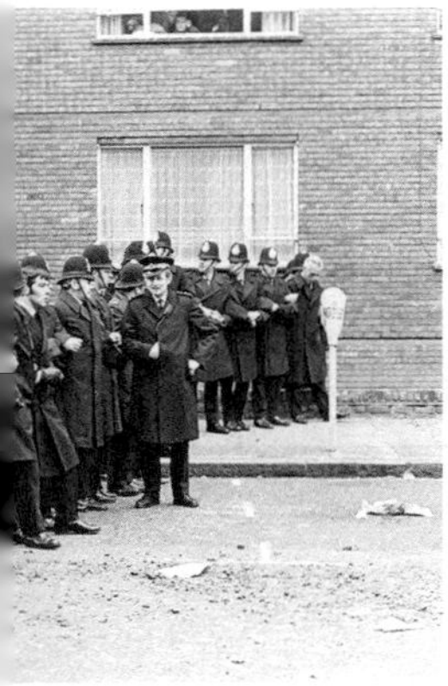
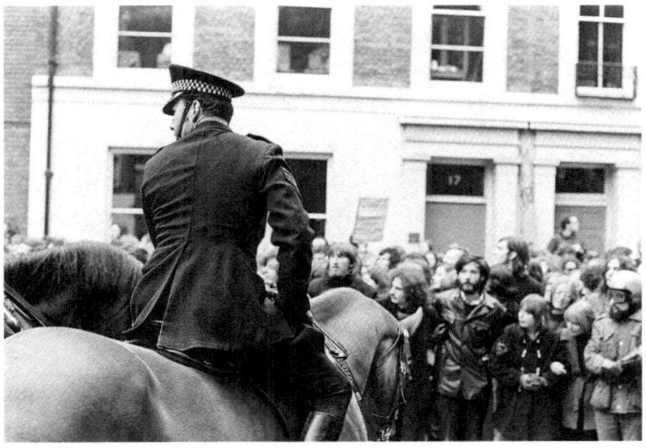
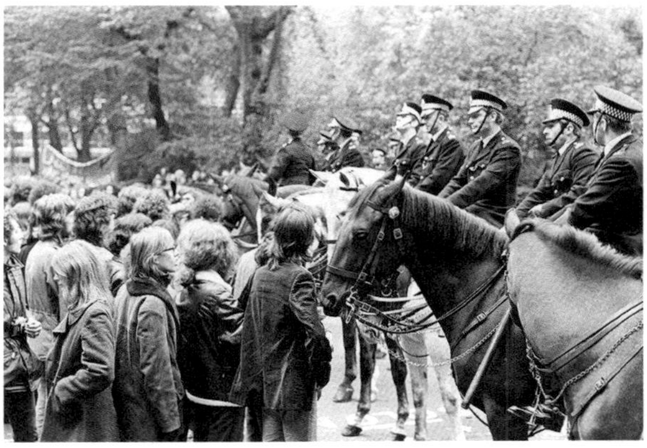
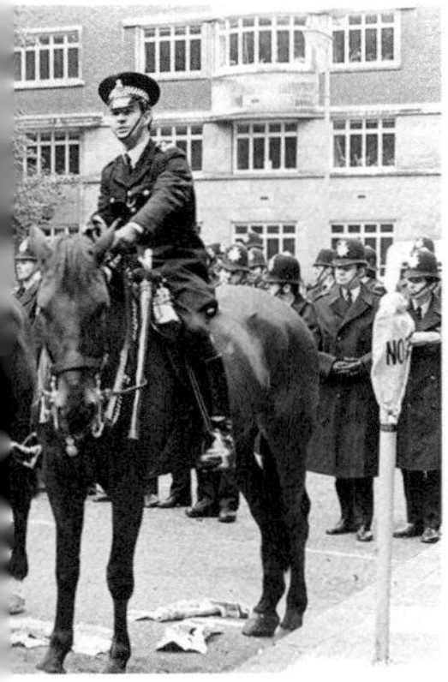
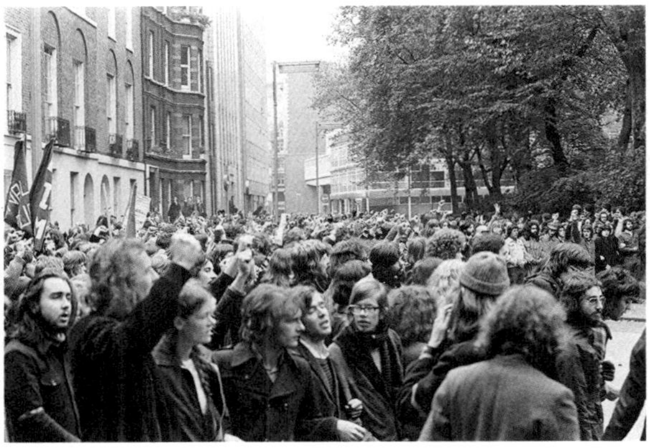
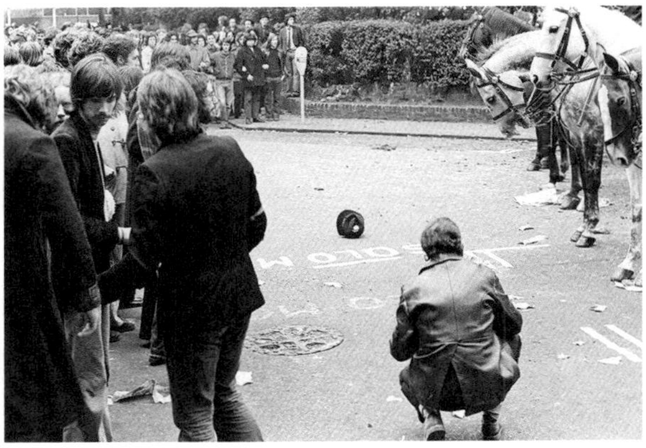

Sharbati: Forty Years On, 1973 / 2013
3 acrylic on wood Structures, 173 x 69 x 15 cm each

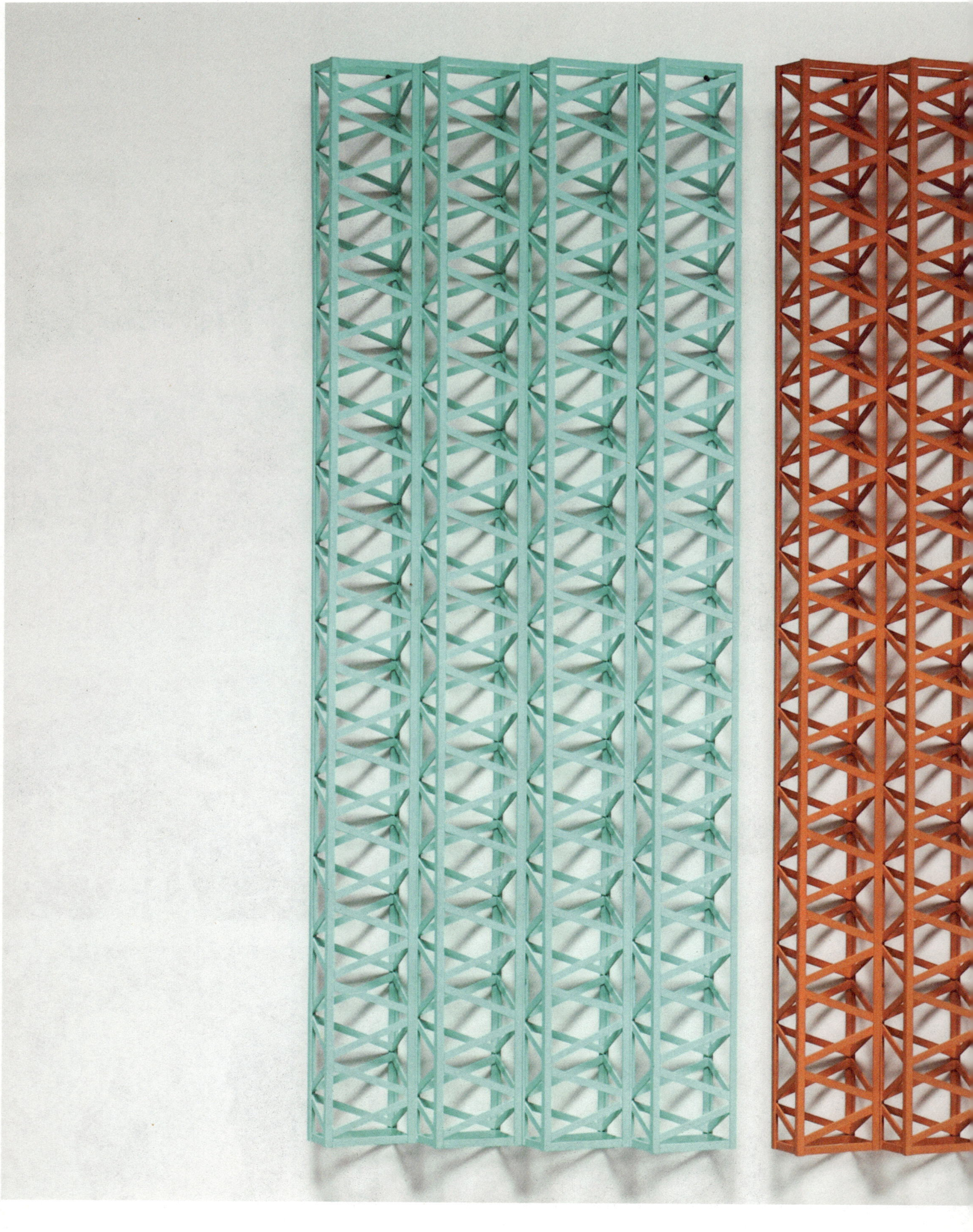

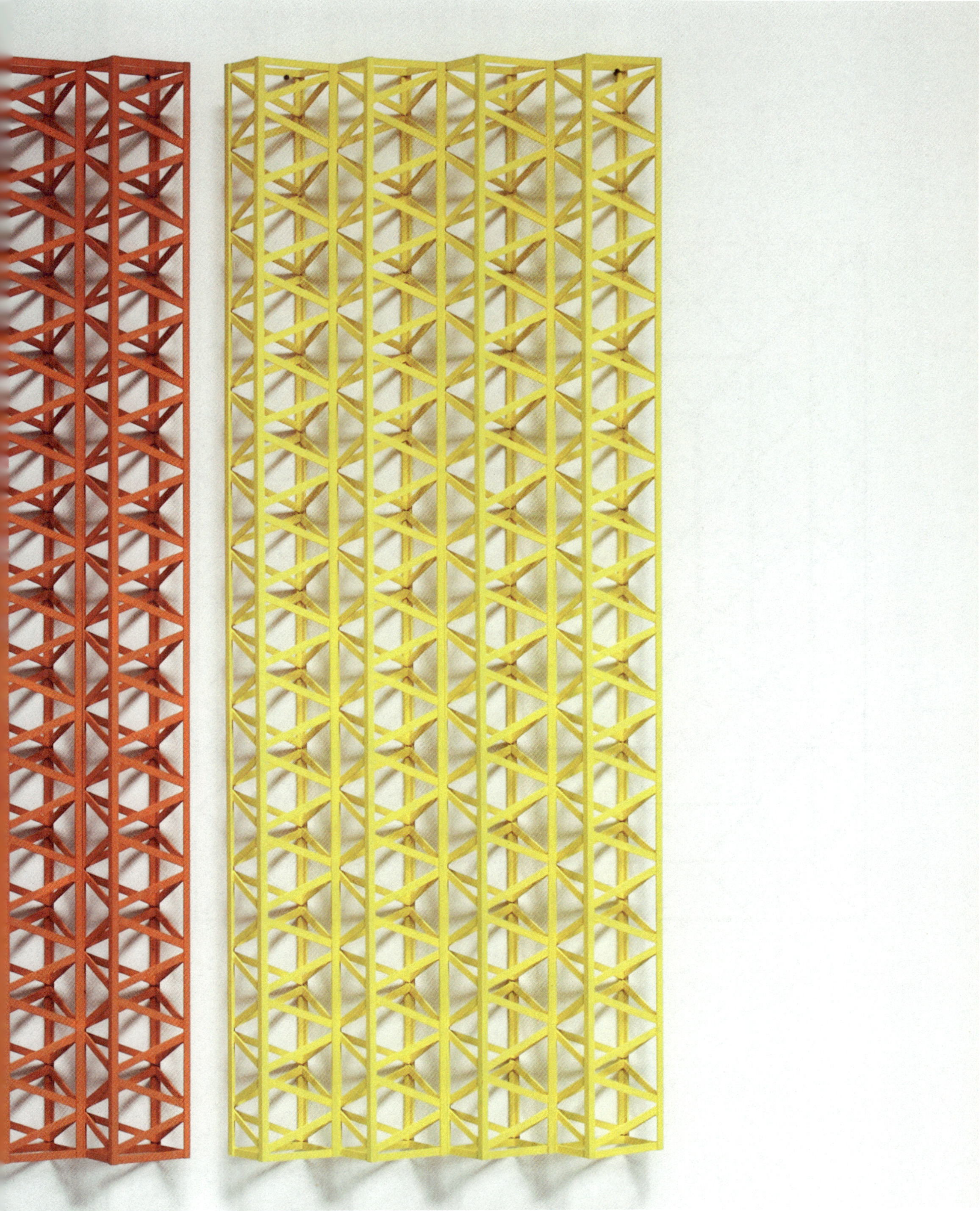

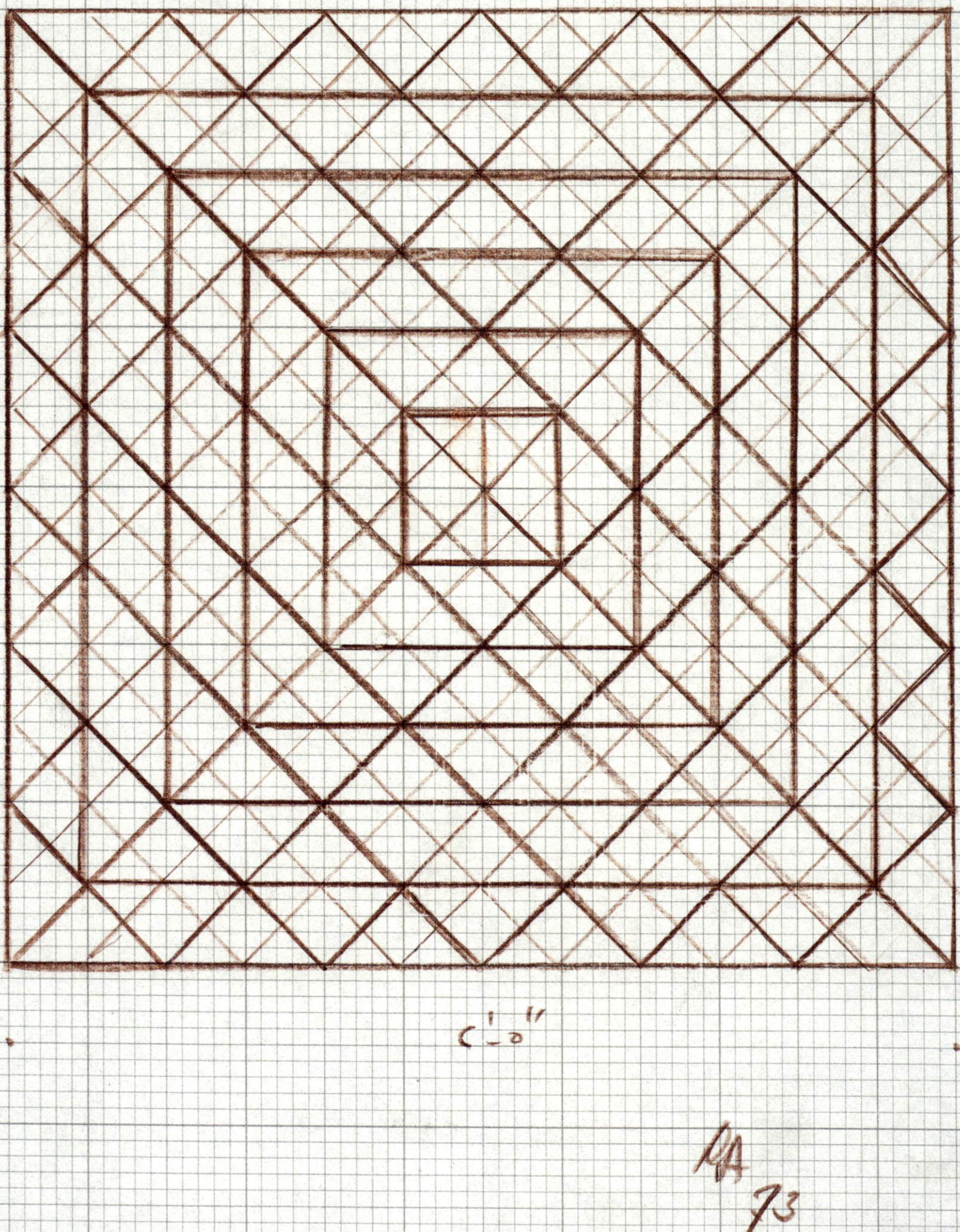

H.H. LTD. E.D.523

SHEET No. OF

Kagzi, 1974
mixed-media, dimensions unknown

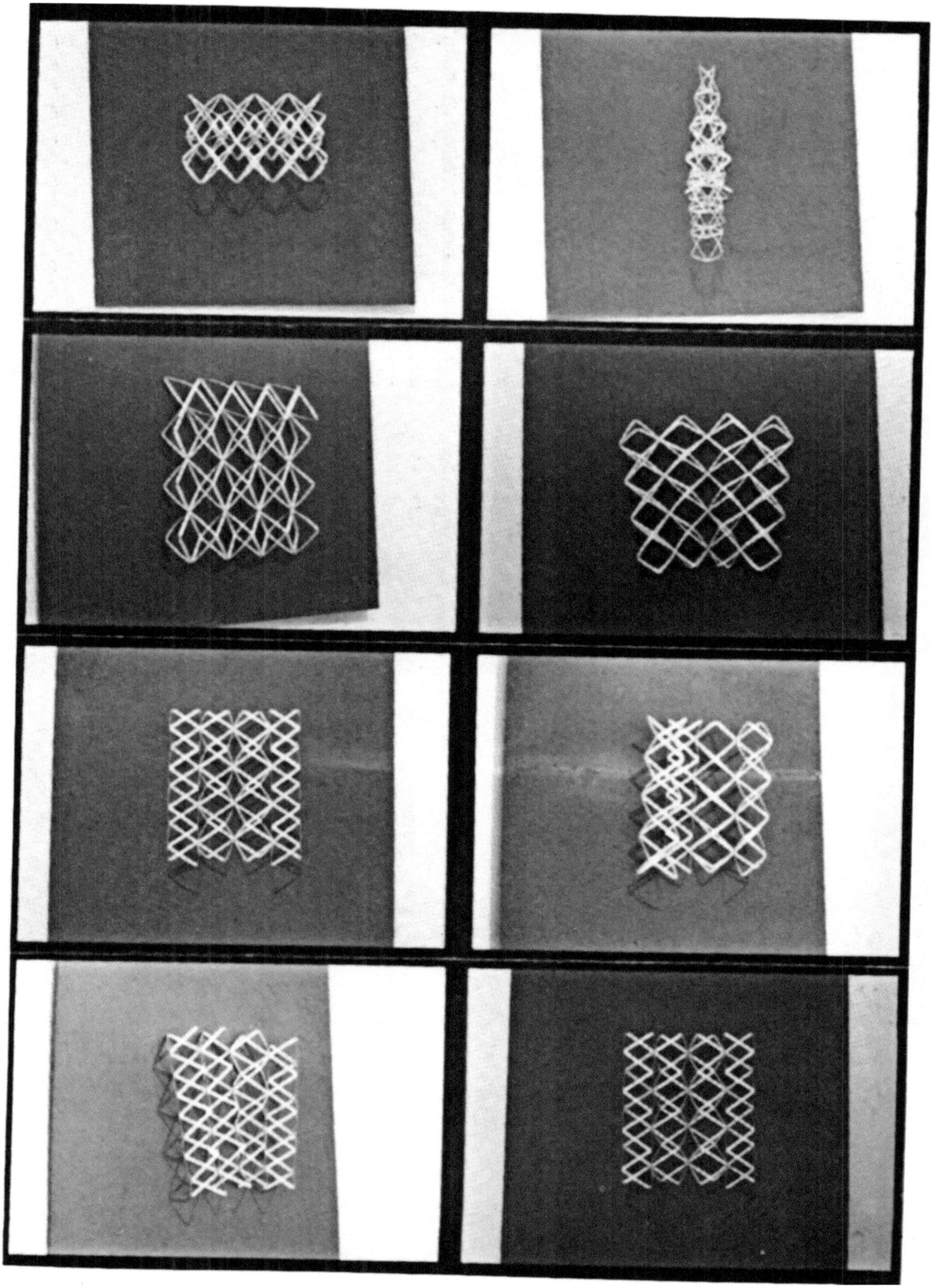

Chakras V (Discs in Jheel Park, Karachi), 1974
16 wood discs and 9 photographs, dimensions variable

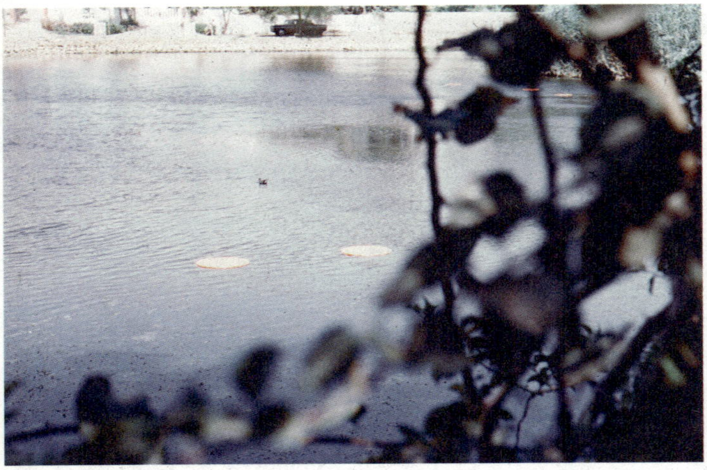

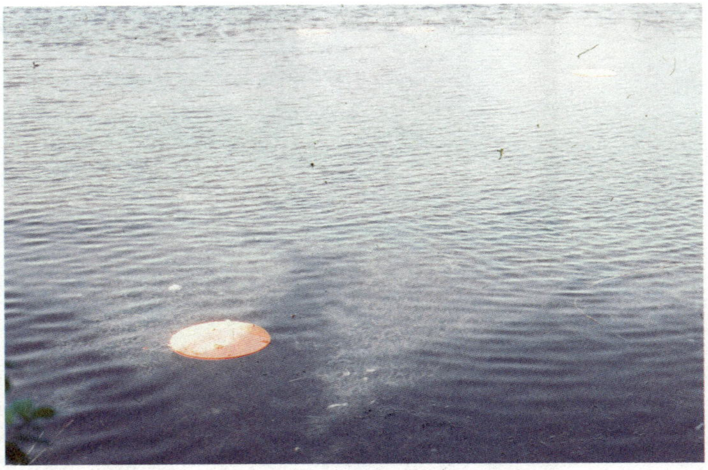

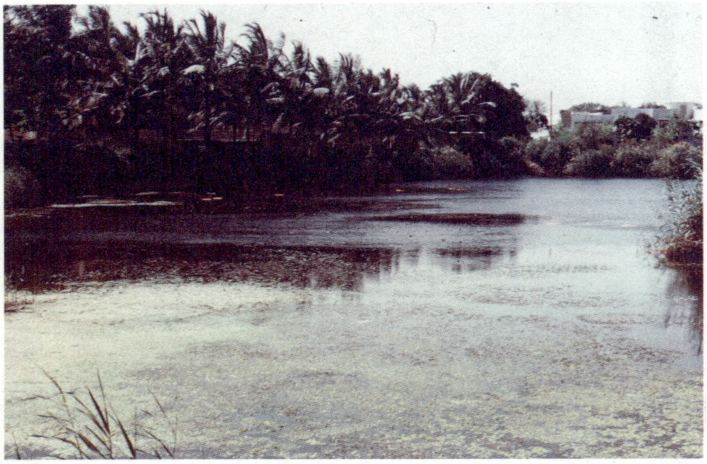

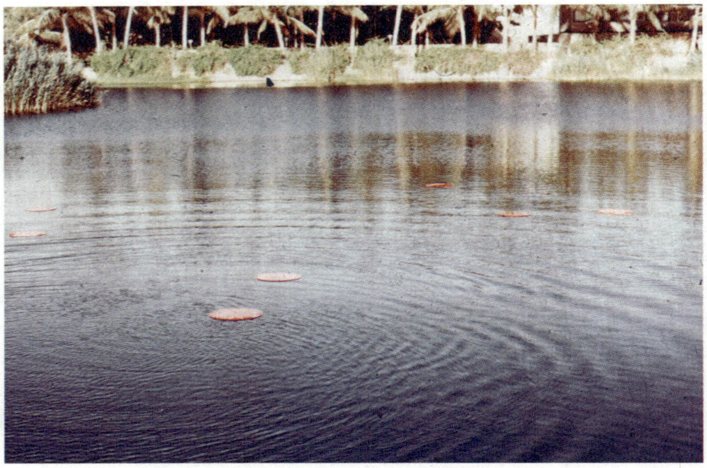

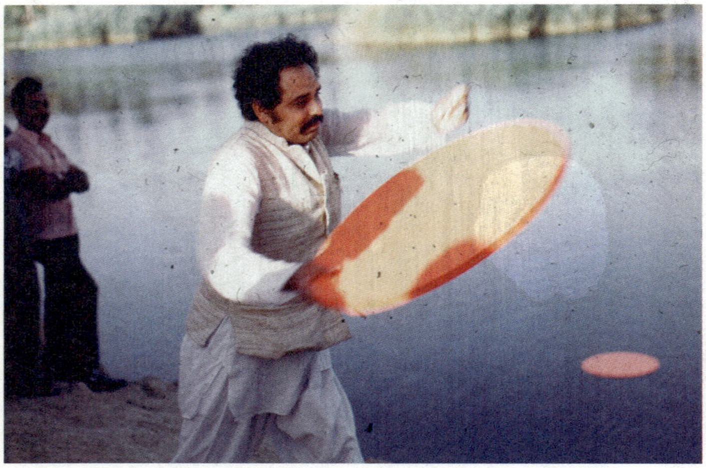

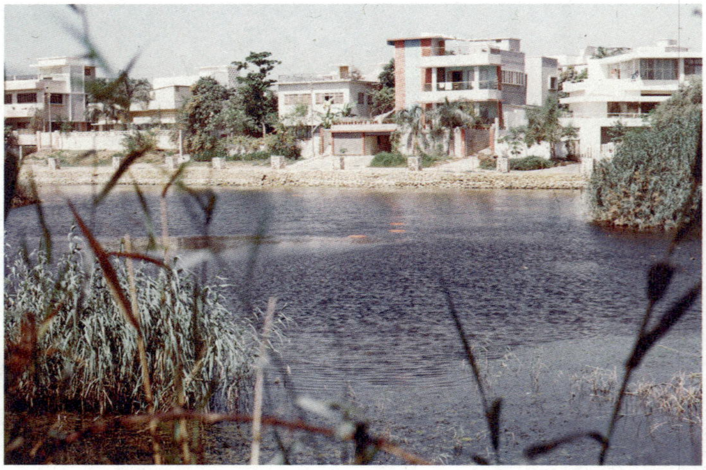

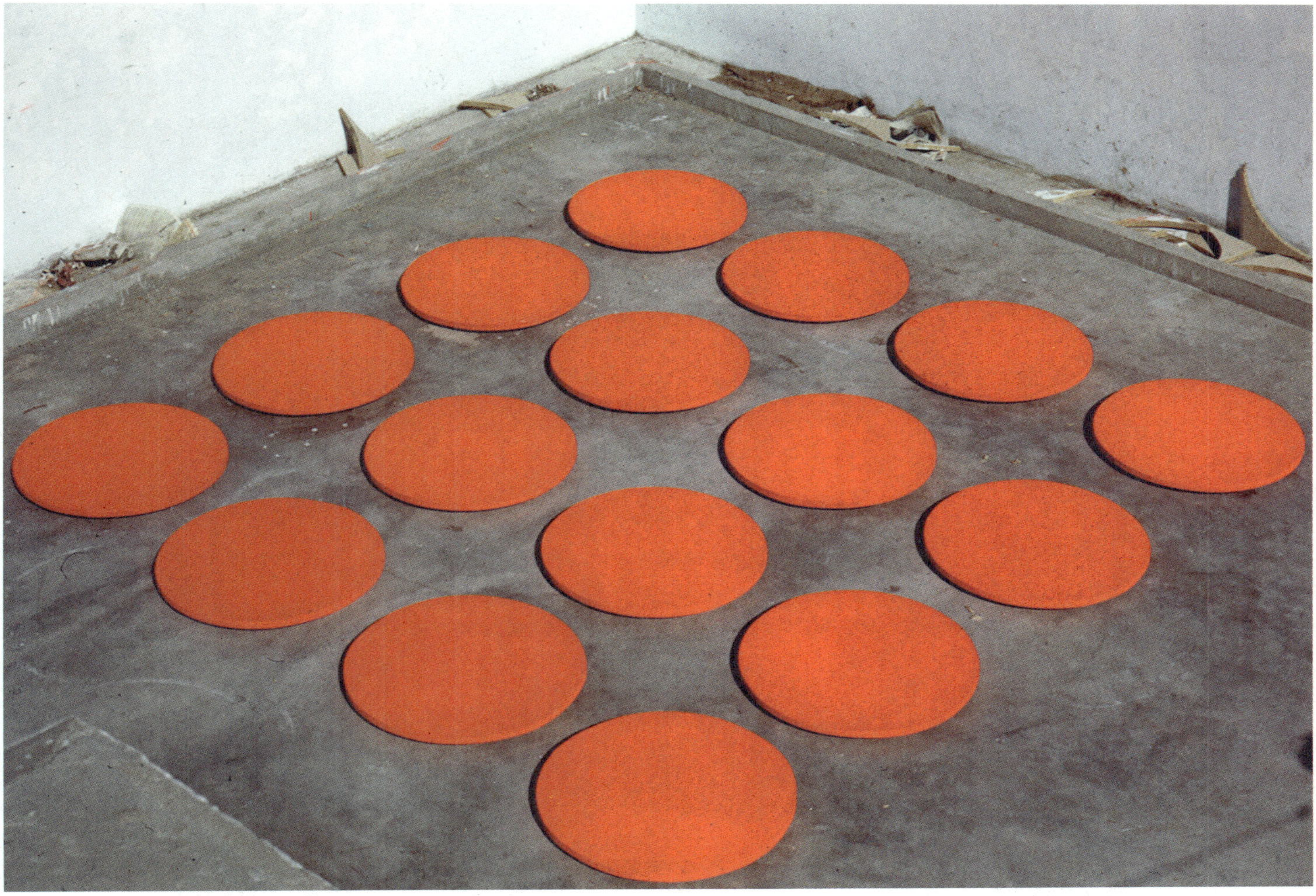

Civilisation, 1974
mixed-media on board, 122 x 102 cm

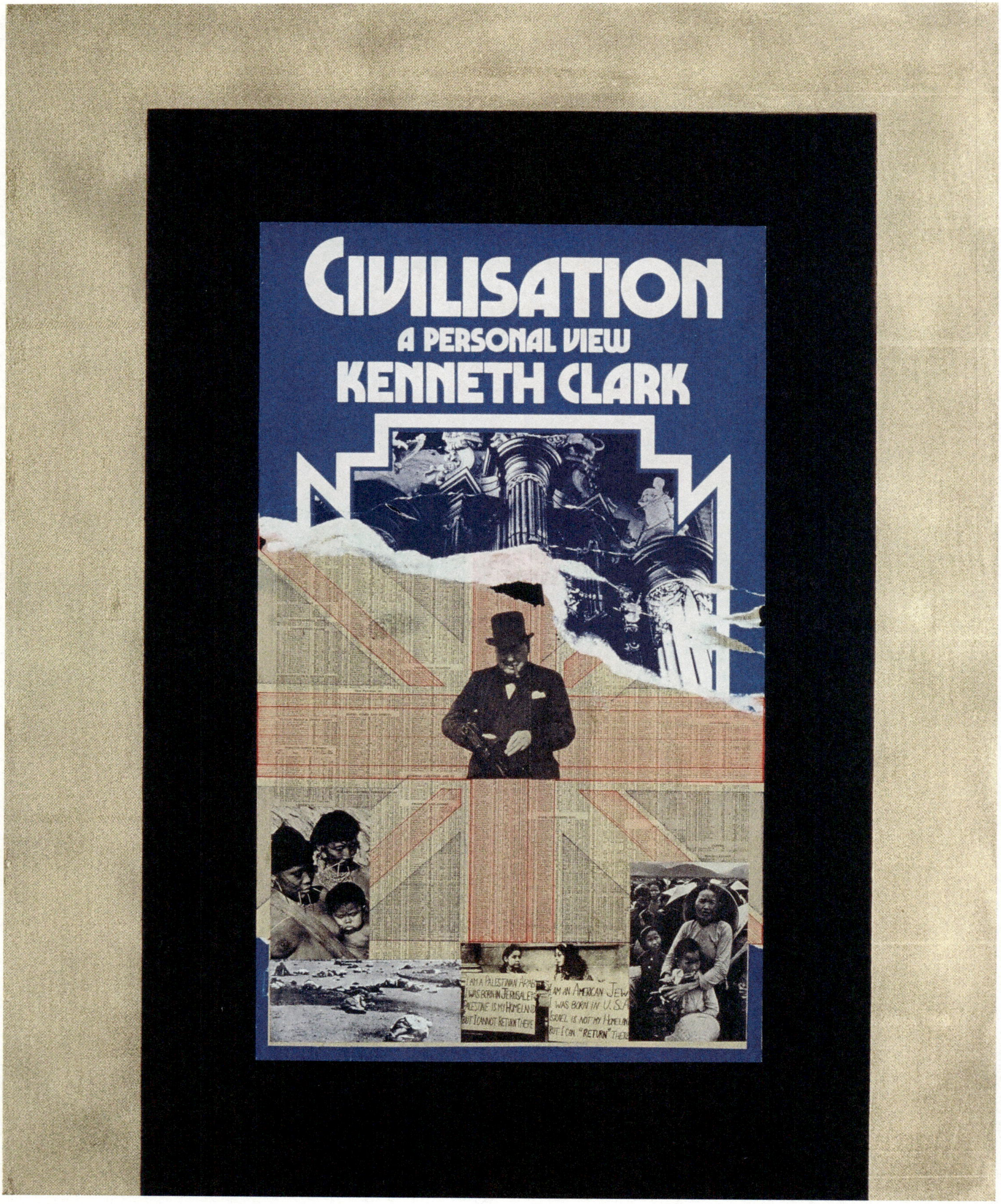

Disaster, 1974–1975
mixed-media on board, 122 x 102 cm

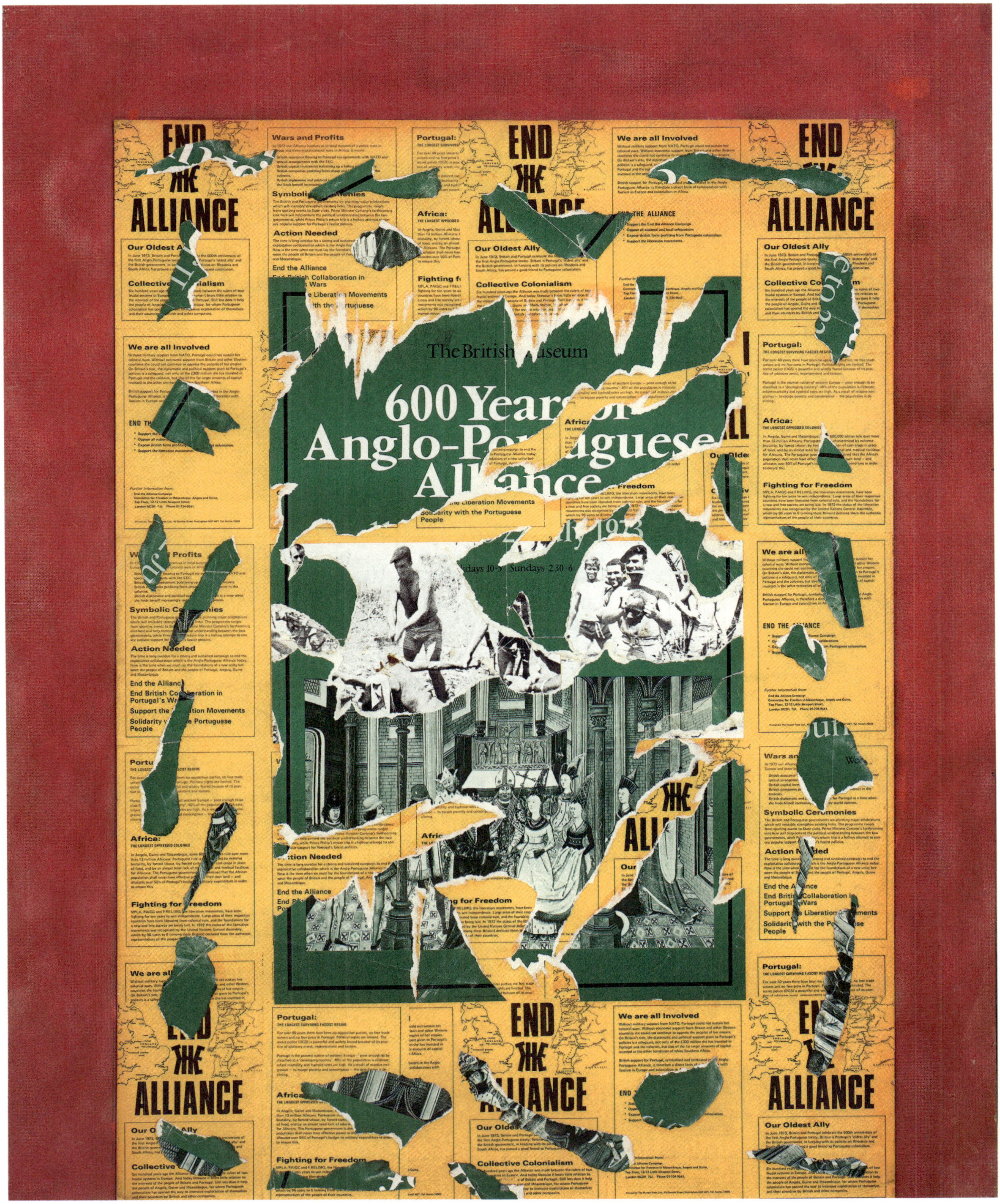

Playing Anguish, 1974–1979
36-slide projection with sound, 18 minutes

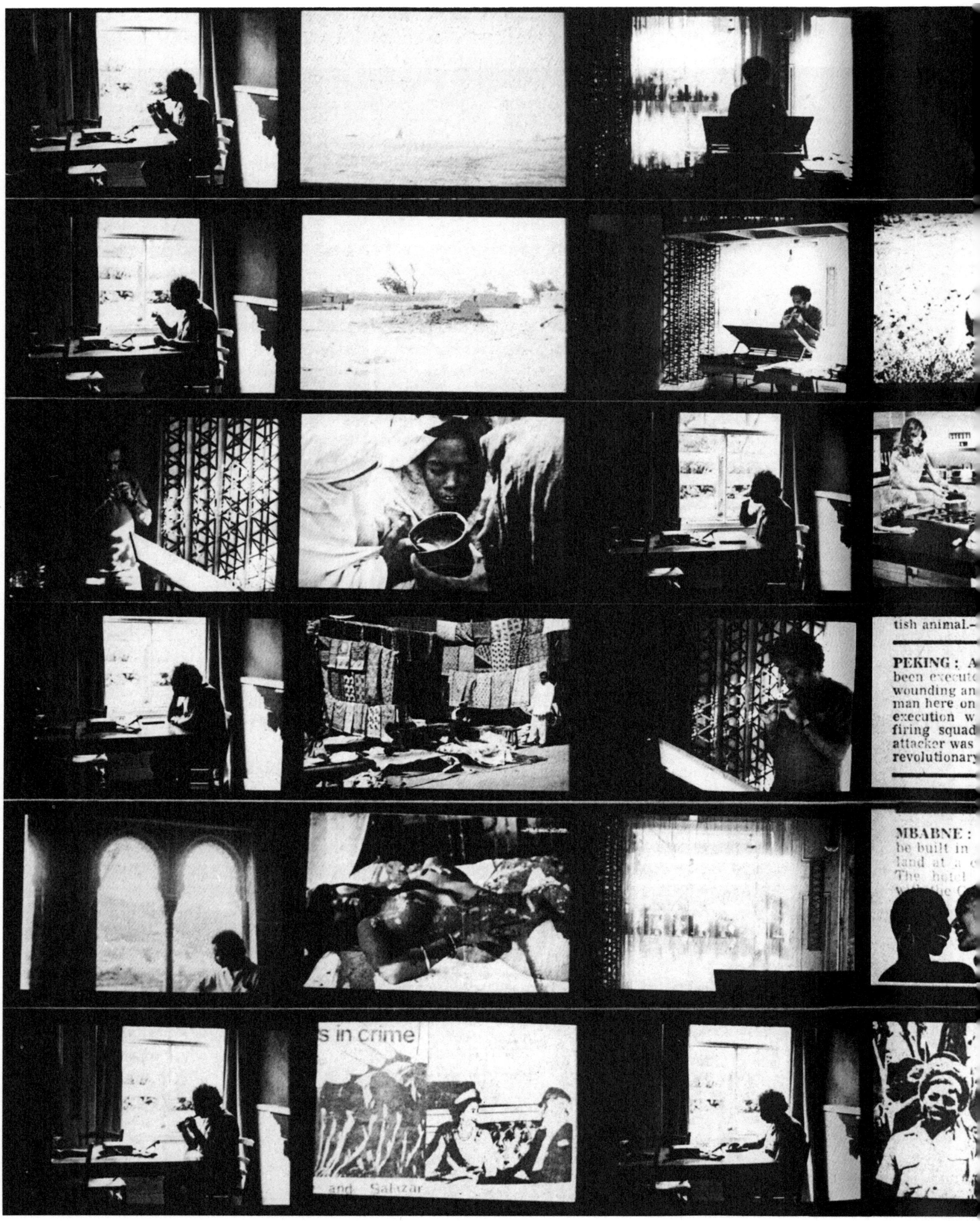

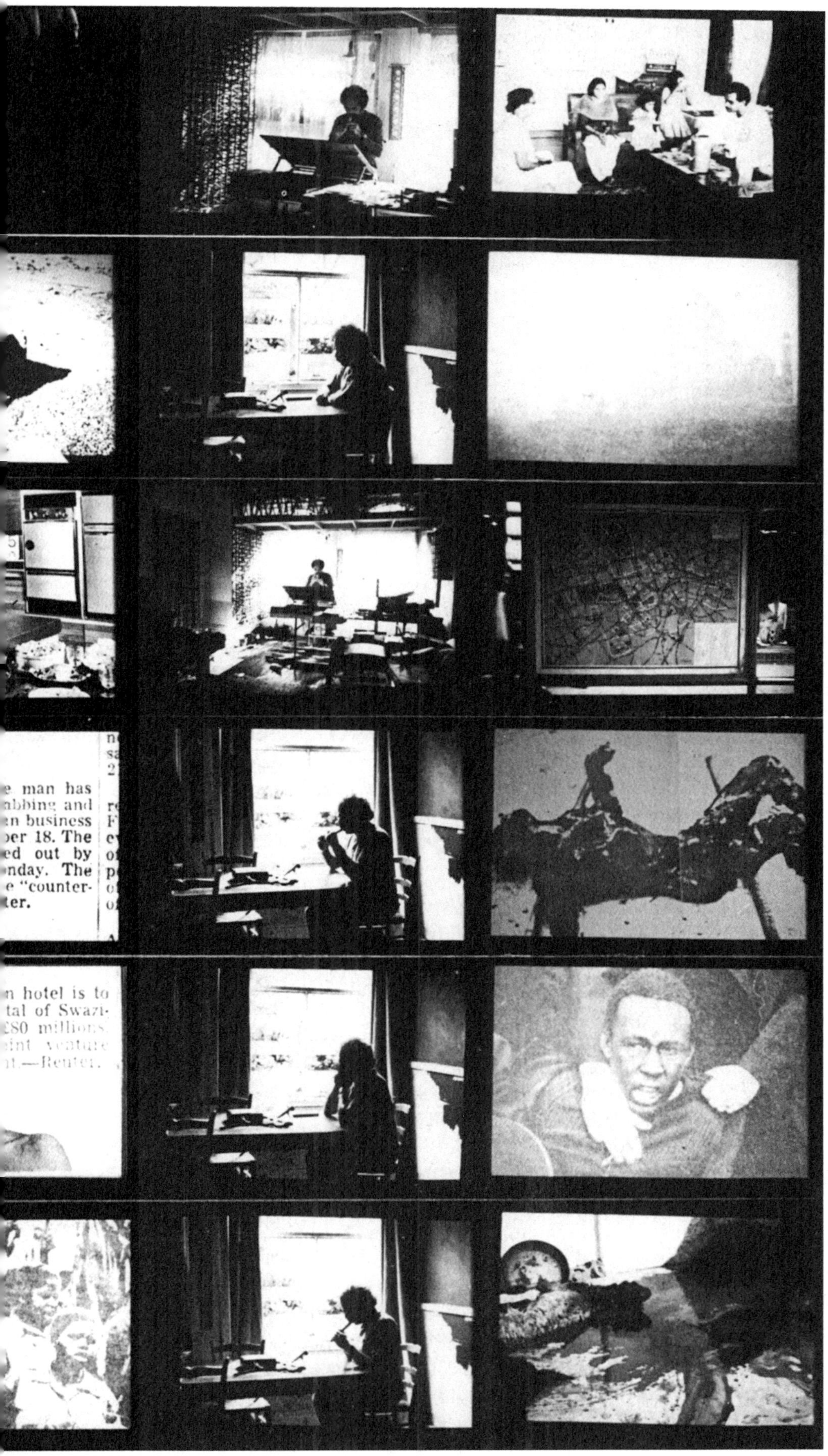

Works 1965–1975, 1975
installation at Artists for Democracy, London
dimensions variable

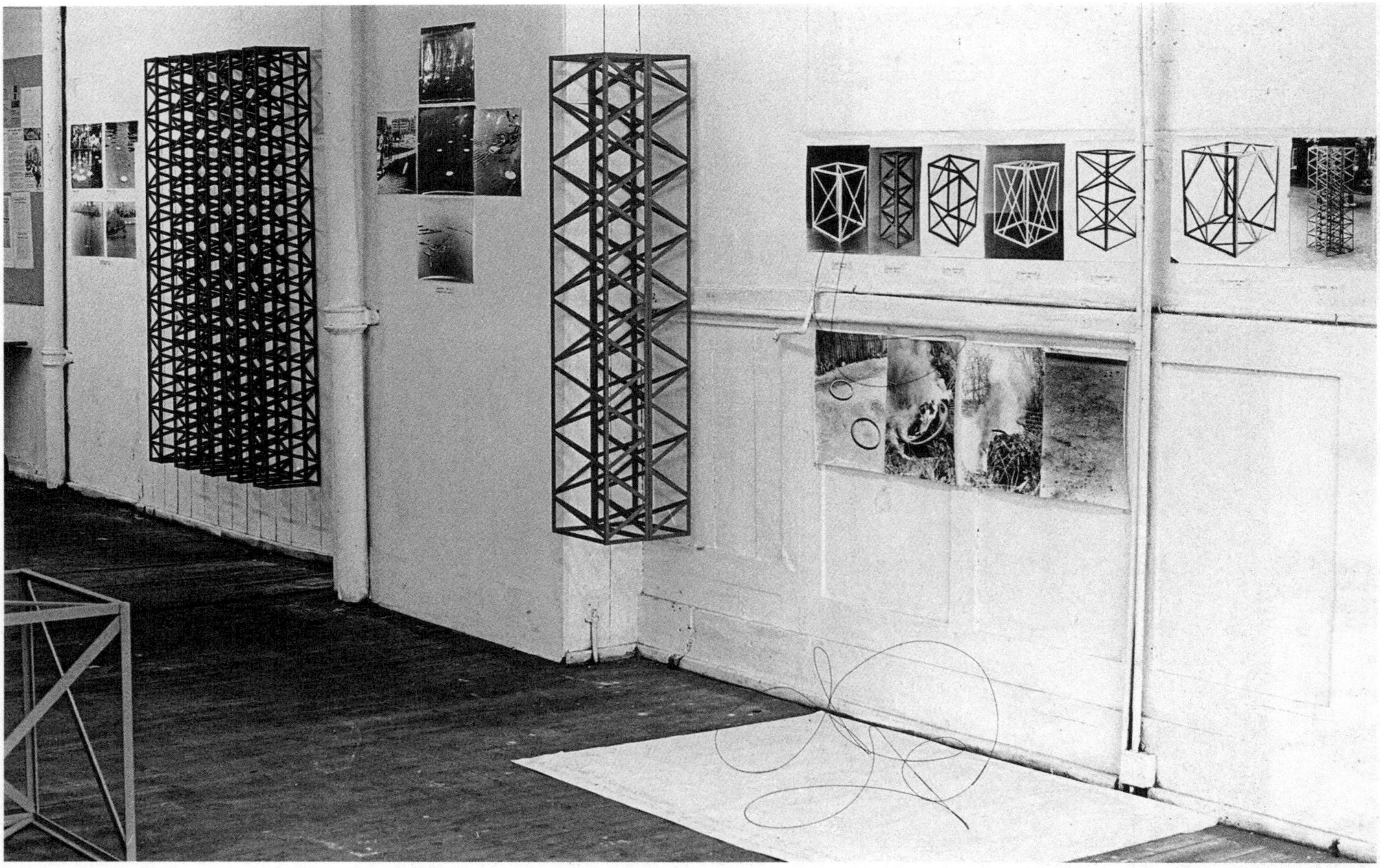

Holes on Earth, 1975
mixed-media installation, dimensions variable

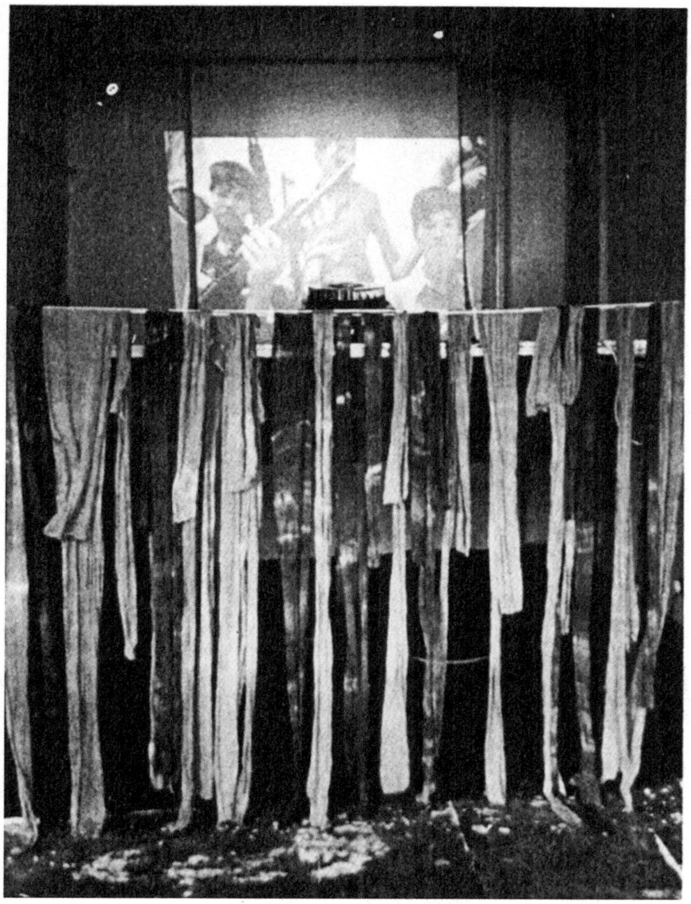

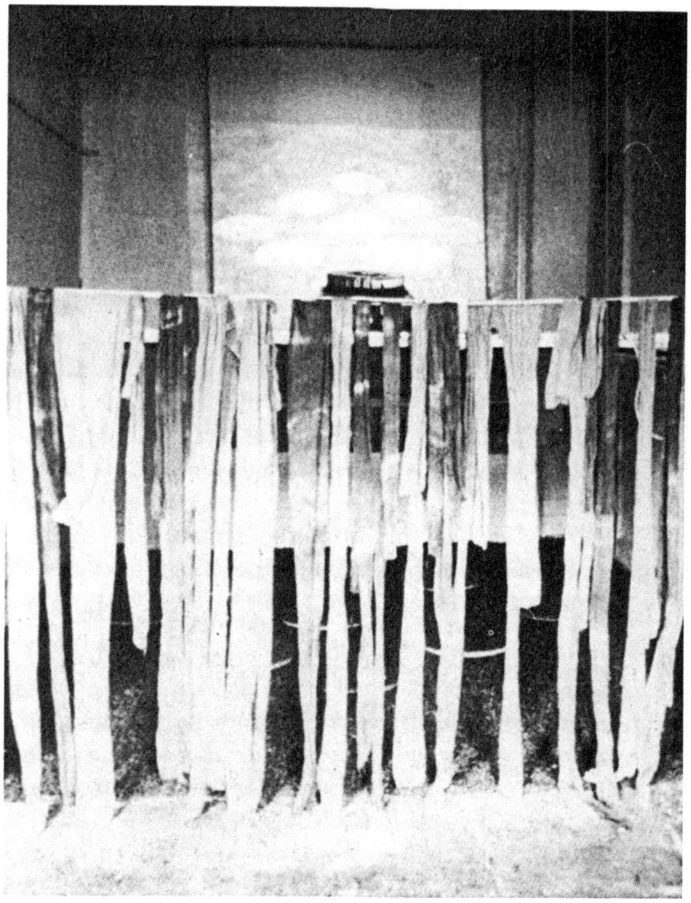

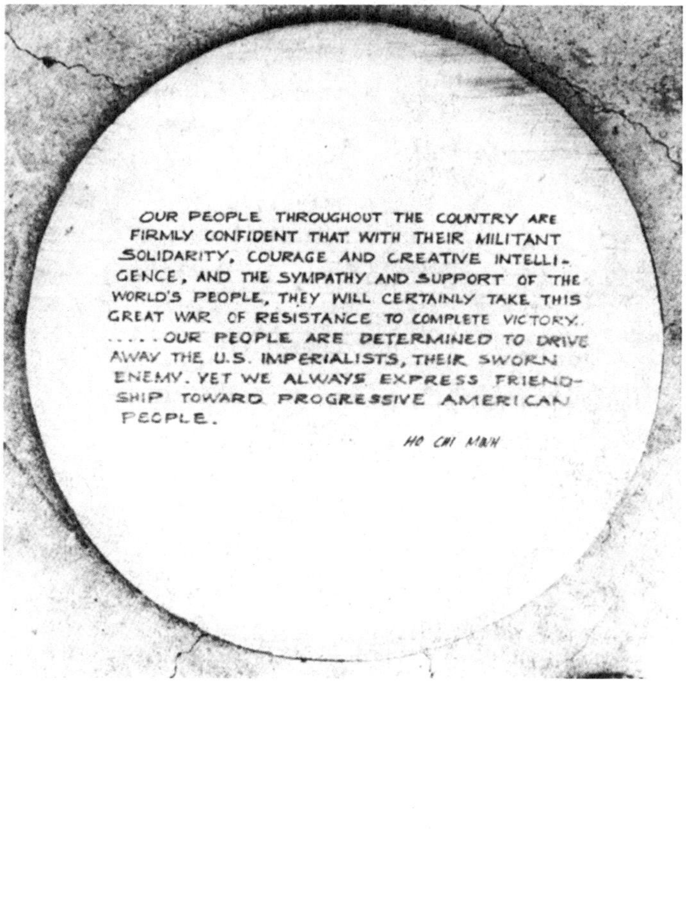

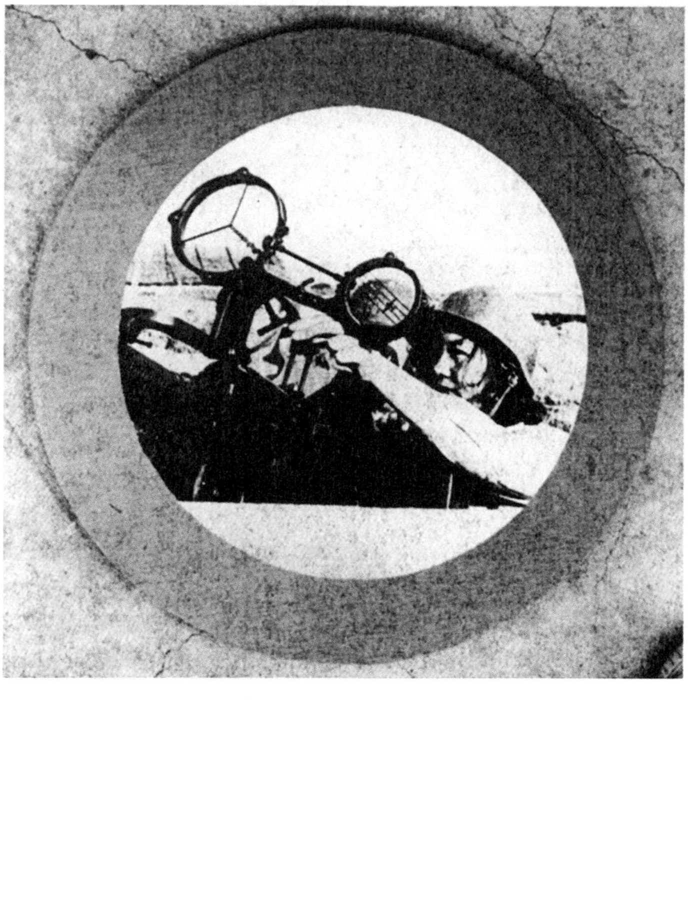

Fire!, 1975
24 photographs, dimensions variable

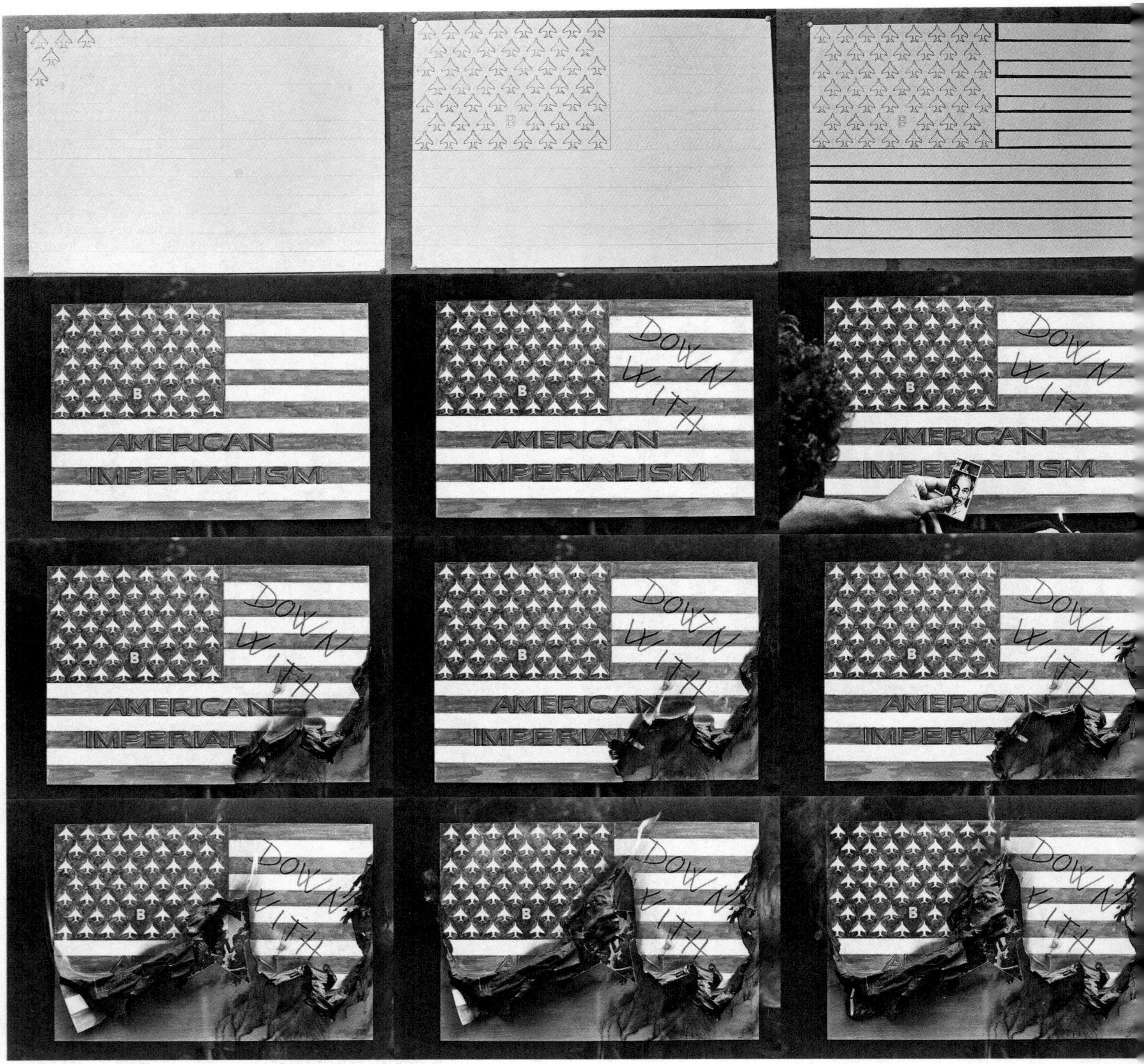

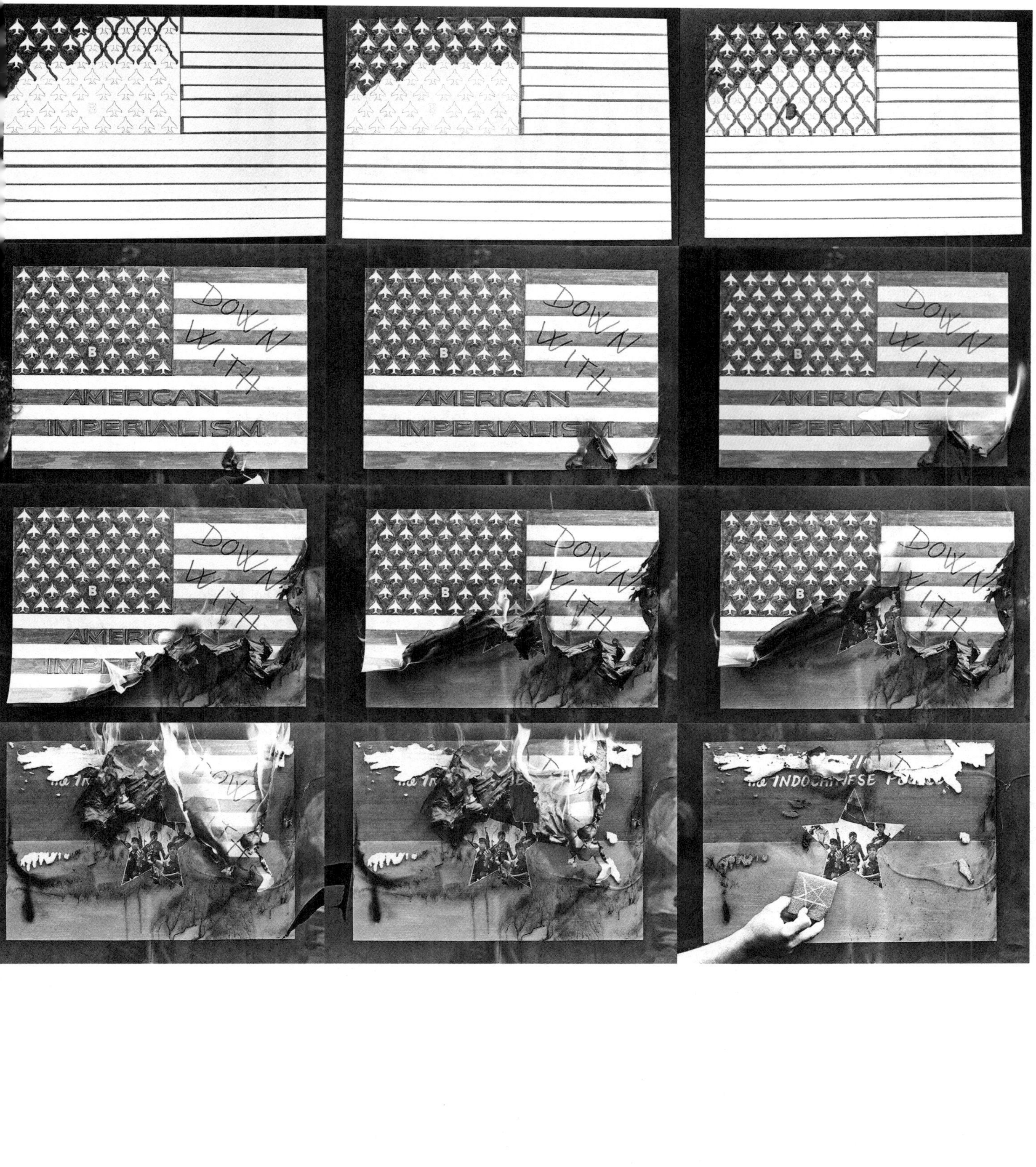
DOWN WITH
AMERICAN
IMPERIALISM
the INDOCHINESE

Preliminary Notes for a
BLACK MANIFESTO

Rasheed Araeen

Introduction

The problems of contemporary art in the Third World today are part of its socio-economic and political predicaments, resulting from colonialism and its present relationship with the West. We must therefore go beyond formal and aesthetic considerations and look into the historical factors which influenced or suppressed artistic developments in the last few centuries, as well as those forces which are today predominant, in the Third World.

By Third World we mean Asia, Africa, Latin America, and the Caribbean. But we *must* also include in it all those non-European peoples (whom we shall collectively call 'blacks' or 'black people') who now live in various Western countries and find themselves in a similar predicament to that of the actual Third World.

What concerns us here specifically is the situation of contemporary visual art in the Third World. But we cannot meaningfully deal with the problems of visual art alone isolated from the cultural context. What affects culture as a whole is also reflected in art activity.

A cursory glance at the Third World today shows that, even after years of 'independence', its contemporary cultures in general and the visual arts in particular remain what could be described as the stagnant *backwaters* of Western developments or what Paulo Freire[1] calls the 'culture of silence' of the masses.

There does exist, however, an increasing awareness of the situation and efforts are being made to confront the problems. We must therefore look into how this problematic situation is actually being dealt with. **How are Third World people trying to enter the modern era or/and create their own contemporary history? If their voice is muted or not heard at all, what are the underlying causes? And what are the actual alternatives open to them?**

The awareness that the Third World must now find a direction which is different from that imposed on it by the West has been growing; and, in fact, organised attempts pointing towards this goal have recently been made. But these efforts[2] have either remained confined within different regions or lacked a clear (ideological) perspective. They have not therefore made any unifying impact on the overall situation or offered a real challenge to those forces which have been responsible for the present predicament of its art and culture. This is partly due to the lack of *direct* communication of ideas between the Third World countries; and the problem has been further compounded by the extremely oppressive political situation in many Third World countries today—and which is, in most cases, the legacy of colonialism or/and the result of Western imperialist domination.

Although there does exist an opposition to imperialism and questions are being asked about the growing domination of Western culture, the general situation *in practice* remains West-oriented. That is, even when there is a strong tendency among many Afro-Asian countries to maintain the continuity of their own traditions, resulting in the preservation and revival of old forms—particularly their reintroduction in contemporary works, the actual result or its underlying criterion often tends to conform to the standards created in the West. This could be explained by the fact that it is not unusual today for many Afro-Asian countries to seek advice from the so-called Western experts of Oriental/African Art in understanding their own traditional past and to depend on the guidance from the West for contemporary developments.

And therefore Third World artists today are *in general* accepting the 'supremacy' of Western developments in the contemporary field by following whatever styles are developed or produced in the major art centres of the West. This not only uproots them from the reality of their own culture and history, but leads them into an alienated situation which cannot question the domination of foreign values, thereby also denying them any opportunity to develop their art indigenously.

This is not, of course, due to what many Western critics would have us believe. As Edward Lucie-Smith has put it: "In places such as India and Japan, traditional culture between the wars was already in a state of decay; it was natural therefore that artists in those countries should try and rebuild upon the European and American model."[3]

It is typical of many (if not most) Western critics not to see things in the correct historical perspective. Mr Lucie-Smith has very cleverly tried to conceal the actual truth. He might have impressed his own lot, but he cannot fool us. Who does not know that Western colonialism in India—and for that matter in the whole Third World—was directly responsible for what he himself calls 'a state of decay' of traditional culture? And then he has the arrogance to suggest that it should be *natural* for the people, who have been subjected to the traumatic experience of colonialism, to rebuild their future on the model created by those who once were, and still are, their oppressors. This is no more than an attempt to keep the Third World people perpetually under Western domination so that apologists like Lucie-Smith may continue enjoying their international privileges granted by the system they unashamedly serve.

It is essential not to fall into the pitfalls of the Western attitude that tends to disguise the truth. On the one hand, Western interpretation of human history is often extremely biased against non-European peoples and their achievements; and on the other, while ignoring the real dynamics of historical developments, it lays a great emphasis on the *individual* achievements of Western men supposedly struggling against all odds. The fact is that socio-economic and political forces play a fundamental role in moulding, nourishing, supporting, and sustaining all human productive and creative activities, both physically and psychologically.

This brings us face to face with the question of the developments of our own socio-economic and political institutions. The question here really is: what actually happened to these institutions, and why did they fail to play an historical role in providing support to the indigenous developments of arts in the Third World in the colonial period of the last few centuries? The answer to this is, of course, well-known but not widely and fully acknowledged, particularly in the West, for reasons which we hope would become more clear by the end of this manifesto.

Contrary to what we are often told by the West, the colonial era was one of the most exploitative and oppressive periods in human history; and its legacies are still with us today as part of neo-colonialism. This was the period when the West preached **human liberty, equality,** and **fraternity.** But at the same time, it was the very same West which, in brutal and blatant violation of basic human dignity and in contradiction to its own presumed human values, actually enslaved and subjugated the majority of the world's population and plundered its resources for the West's interest alone. The wealth it thus acquired helped the West develop its various institutions. This development was in fact achieved at the expense of ignoring, if not actually suppressing, the historical developments of indigenous institutions. And on top of this, it had the audacity to perpetrate lies about the 'primitiveness' of indigenous Third World peoples whom, as most Western people still believe, the West *only* wanted to 'civilize'.

The truth of the matter is, whether one likes it or not, that the actual aim of colonialism was to merely appropriate other peoples' wealth and resources, by hook or by crook, as a result of which the West was able to become what it is today. As Frantz Fanon has rightly said: **"This European opulence is literally scandalous, for it has been founded on slavery, it has been nourished with the blood of slaves and it comes directly from the soil and from the subsoil of that under-developed world. The well-being and the progress of Europe have been built up with the sweat and the dead bodies of Negroes, Arabs, Indians, and the yellow races.** *We have decided not to overlook this any longer.*"[4] (italics added).

While the West flourished during colonialism, Western art also flourished along with the emergence of its various institutions. The historical developments of Western art of the modern era took place not because of the mental 'superiority' of Western artists (as is commonly believed in the West), but due to the advantage they had by being placed within the complex totality of developing forces of an historical process. And this was made possible to a large extent with the material resources from the Third World. While the historical process in the West provided Western artists with necessary incentives or driving force for their creativity, colonialism suppressed the developments of indigenous art and culture in the Third World by preventing the historical development of the productive forces of its peoples.

For this reason the history of Western art over the last few centuries also becomes an issue here; not only for the fact that its developments took place at the cost of Third World people, but more essentially because of the West's assertion today that its history must be accepted as the mainstream of human development and that in the light of this all human achievements must be seen. THE ESTABLISHMENT OF EUROPEAN CIVILIZATION AS THE MAINSTREAM IS ONE OF THE MOST CATASTROPHIC DEVELOPMENTS THAT HAVE TAKEN PLACE IN HUMAN HISTORY, DESTROYING OR SUPPRESSING OTHER CULTURES AND CIVILIZATIONS. And today this European/MAINSTREAM is used to measure the achievements of the peoples whose very historical developments were suppressed by it. It is therefore not a surprise that the West either ignores other peoples' contributions to human knowledge or history, or it allocates them an inferior status determined by an attitude that sees all non-European phenomena as ahistorical.

This is, of course, a fundamental feature of the dominant ideology that perceives the world in terms of its different parts arranged in a hierarchical order, so that this system serves the interests of those who control it from the top. As such, the West sees the rest of the world as its own appendage and expects all the world resources, natural as well as human, to serve the interests of Western civilization alone. THIS WESTERN PERCEPTION OF THE WORLD HAS REDUCED TODAY THE WHOLE WORLD INTO A 'GLOBAL VILLAGE' WITH A VULGARLY AFFLUENT WEST AT ITS CENTRE SURROUNDED BY STARVING PEOPLE WITH BEGGING BOWLS IN THEIR HANDS.

Moral double standards, arrogance, hypocrisy, and racism are some of the manifestations of the ideology which maintains that Western people alone have a civilized existence and that they should constantly maintain and protect this even at the expense of denying other peoples their humanity. WHILE EUROPEANS ARE HAILED AS PATRIOTS, FREEDOM FIGHTERS AND HEROES, OTHERS ARE DENOUNCED AS BLOODTHIRSTY TERRORISTS. The various attempts of some pseudo-scientists to prove the 'superiority' of the white race, is also part of the same apparatus which deliberately perpetuates lies about non-European peoples. And these attempts to give scientific respectability to racism only reveals the hideous designs of those who are an integral part of the Western imperialist domination of the world today.

The present state of affairs in the Third World is not the result of the 'natural laziness' or 'a lack of imagination' of its peoples, as we are often told by the West, neither is it the legacy of the devastation of some oriental 'barbarian'. It is in fact the direct consequence of the colonial pillage by the 'civilized' West whose pretentious claims to all humanity have now turned out to be no more than a mask to hide its pathologically excessive greed and which has today reached dangerous proportions. The Western obsession for more and more material wealth (mostly in the form of consumer goods), which in the West is euphemistically called 'a higher standard of living', cannot be perpetually fulfilled without further exploitation and appropriation by the West of *resources which are not its own resources*. These resources actually belong to Third World peoples who themselves should now utilize them to fulfil their own needs, by developing their own productive forces and rebuilding their own socio-economic, political, educational, cultural, and artistic institutions *which must be free from foreign domination*.

Against this historical background, therefore, we must place the present predicaments of our art and culture. We must recognise that as long as we allow the West (and for that matter anybody else), willingly or unwillingly, to dominate our lives, we will only be exploited. As long as our physical and mental resources are under its direct or indirect control, our development will either be suppressed or used for the benefit of the West alone, its art and culture, and its civilization. In other words, **we must free ourselves from foreign domination before we can create our own contemporary art and culture.**

But this does not mean that we have no option open to us at present or that we cannot carry on an art activity. Of course, if we continue accepting the general situation today which demands our subservience to the West we are doomed as a people. On the other hand, we can and must stand on our feet and oppose those alien values, as well as our own, which obstruct radical change by preventing the development of internal dynamism of our people; and in the process of confronting these values we can and shall discover new art forms that will authentically reflect our own reality today. However, before we proceed further to look into possible alternatives, we must examine here the various aspects of those forces which are holding us back.

The Third World Today

One of the important features of colonialism was and is to violently suppress the indigenous culture of the colonized country and then impose its own cultural values on the colonial people. In many instances, colonialism imposed an actual ban on native cultural practices, taking away by force from the people their cultural artifacts. The loot was then transferred to the West. As a result, most of the Third World heritage is today either hidden away stored in the basement lockers of Western museums[5] or insolently displayed in their glass cases as part of the evidence of the West's pride and precious possessions. AFTER EXTERMINATING MILLIONS OF PEOPLE AND THEN LOOTING THEIR BELONGINGS, THE WEST TODAY HAS THE AUDACITY

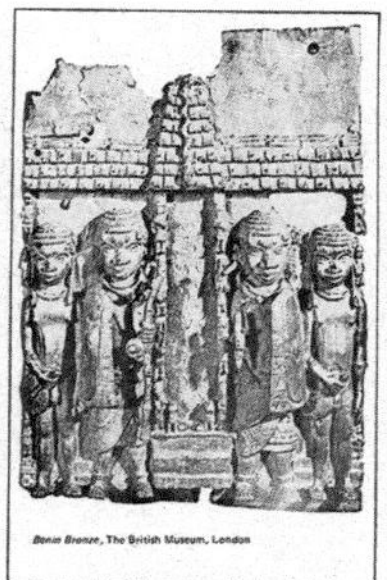

Benin Bronze, The British Museum, London

"The deplorable state of most Benin work is due to the fact that it was eventually plundered by the British when, in 1897, they sacked and burnt the city. In some of the pieces part of the bronze has melted; in others there are gashes caused by their being torn roughly from their places. These, and the burnt ivories, are the mute record of the city's rape."

Boris de Rachewitz, *Introduction to* ***AFRICAN ART***

TO CALL ITSELF THE PROTECTOR OF THE ARTISTIC AND CULTURAL HERITAGE OF THE WORLD.

At the same time, colonialism created and creates a native bourgeoisie by giving some of the native population Western colonial education, and by awarding them some socio-economic privileges and a share in political power. In turn, this native class, to quote Amilcar Cabral, "assimilates the colonizer's mentality, considers itself culturally superior to its own people and ignores or looks down upon their cultural values."[6]

With the coming to power of *this* native bourgeoisie, after 'independence', colonialism is only replaced by neo-colonialism; which in fact is a general phenomenon in the Third World today. One of the most important characteristics of neo-colonialism is the perpetuation of Western imperialist domination in the 'decolonized' countries through Western cultural penetration, against which the native bourgeoisie cannot and does not act as a shield. On the contrary, its own lifestyle facilitates further propagation of Western values, which openly relegate the indigenous cultural life. In effect, it virtually becomes an instrument through which Western culture is projected as civilized and progressive vis-à-vis the 'primitive' and 'backward' native culture.

It is therefore no surprise that, immediately, after the Second World War, Western imperialism under the leadership of its most powerful country, the US, unleashed an unprecedented cultural propaganda in the major cities of the Third World, particularly in Asia and Africa, through its control of mass media (films, TV, glossy publications, etc.). The whole purpose of this propaganda, which constantly assaulted people's senses with alien images of the values of Western life, was to inflict their minds with the illusions of a better life (in the West) and to lure them into believing that they could also possess this life, if only they would

'Sadat, oh Sadat, you dress in the latest fashion while we sleep 12 to a room'

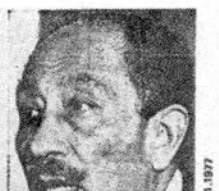

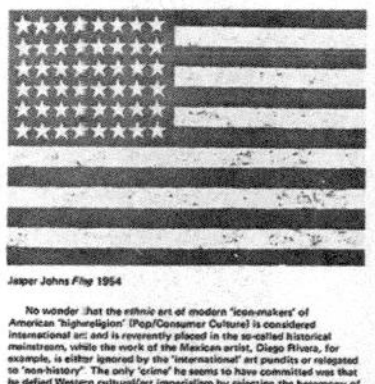

Jasper Johns Flag 1954

... international art and is reverently placed in the so-called historical mainstream, while the work of the Mexican artist, Diego Rivera, for example, is either ignored by the 'international' art pundits or relegated to 'non-history'. The only 'crime' he seems to have committed was that he defied Western cultural/art imperialism by rejecting the hegemony of art styles created in the art centres of Europe alone. Instead of merely serving the interests of Western civilization and history, he returned to his own people and committed himself to their reality. His work is a reflection of the socio-cultural, economic, and political environment in which he lived. Instead of understanding him in the context of his own socio-historical forces, his work has been dismissed by the Western art pundits as mere propaganda.[8] We do not necessarily agree *fully* with the populist and propagandist philosophy in art, but **is Pop Art not propaganda?** If the West is only concerned with narrow boundaries of stylistic evolution within its own history and considers only the developments taking place in its metropolises, at the expense of other contemporary developments, **what right has it to champion the cause of internationalism in art and culture?**

The myth of the internationalism of Western art must be now exploded. The fact is that there does not yet exist an art which truly reflects international spirit of Man and Woman today. Western art only reflects the particularity of the West and has little to do with the actual reality of the world. It can therefore be said that WESTERN ART IS NOT INTERNATIONAL; IT IS MERELY TRANSATLANTIC ART. IT ONLY REFLECTS TRANSATLANTIC CULTURE OF EUROPE AND NORTH AMERICA. The present 'internationalism' of Western art is no more than a function of Western politico-economic power and its imposition of its values on other people. Therefore, in an international context, it would be more appropriate to call it IMPERIALIST ART.

We are not playing here with semantics. If by internationalism is *only* meant an expression of a phenomenon taking place in more than one country, an art movement emerging simultaneously at more than one place across national boundaries as a reflection of their cultural interrelationship, we would have no hesitation at all in accepting the 'internationalism' of Western art. A style of wood carving is still being ...

Ceremonial Ground Painting/Sculpture by Australian Aborigines

Photograph: The Museum of Mankind, London

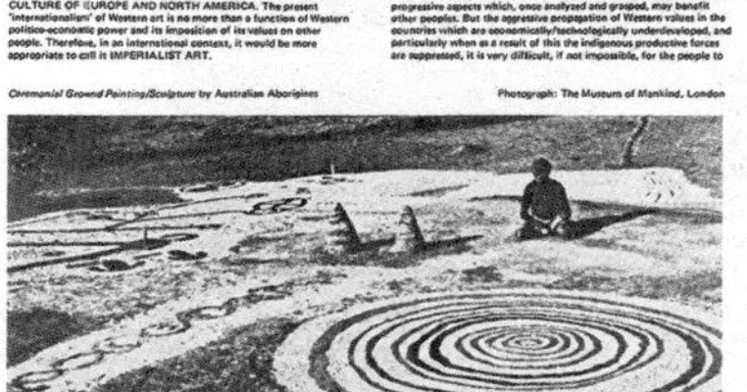

... ourselves here to our own predicament in Britain, but we do recognise that a similar pattern of racism and exploitation exists in other Western countries employing foreign labour,[9] not forgetting, of course, the US and those Afro-Asian peoples who are still living under the yoke of racist colonial/imperialist rule.

Black people in Britain today cannot be treated in the same way as 25 years ago when we, after being uprooted from our native soils, were railroaded into menial jobs. The aspirations of the younger generation of blacks, particularly those born in Britain, are very different. We cannot, and will not, accept only shitwork. If society cannot fulfil our expectations just because it does not wish to see us rising above our present existence at the bottom of the heap, we shall continue fighting ourselves for our rights. If some black kids are in the street, and a few have become what the establishment calls 'muggers', the fault does not *totally* lie with them but with this society.

HOWEVER, TWO MILLION BLACKS AREN'T GOING BACK

RASHEED ARAEEN *Ghulab* (3rd of 4 collage-panels) 1971-73

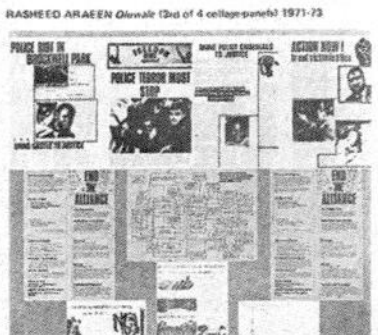

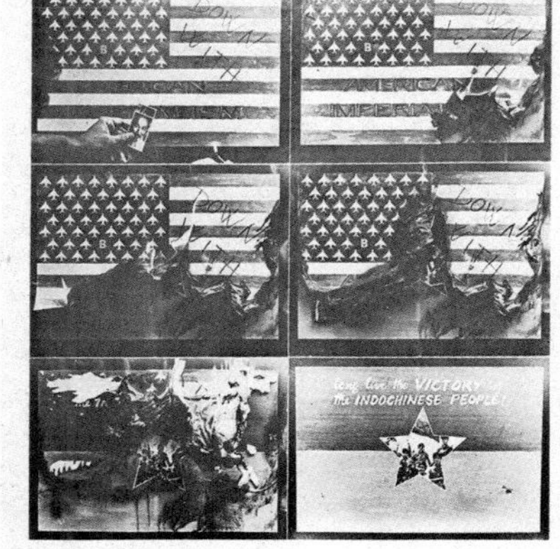

RASHEED ARAEEN *Fire* (6 of 30 or so photo-anal'aagsi) 1975

What is important now is not WHAT WE WERE IN THE PAST, but WHAT WE ARE TODAY. Whether we live in our own countries of origin or in the West, neither a mechanistic revival of our traditional forms nor a trailing behind on the paths formed by the so-called historical styles of Western art can offer us a positive direction. While rejecting both these options, but still finding ourselves surrounded and dominated by the forces which either demand our return to ethnic traditions or make us accept the hegemony of Western developments, WE HAVE NO CHOICE BUT TO OPPOSE THEM BOTH; AND OUT OF THIS CONFRONTATION WILL EMERGE NEW FORMS THAT TRULY REFLECT OUR PARTICULARITY IN THE WORLD TODAY.

We are no longer *national* entities, in the literal sense of the word. The problems facing us today are not necessarily of national dimensions or characteristics. They are in fact the consequences of the dominating forces *internationally* unleashed by the West. Our efforts, ...

... predicament of dominated people, etc., manipulating them only to perpetrate a new formalism. The radical polemics/rhetoric of most Western artists, however, is not applicable to Third World conditions.

We ourselves do not need to look for any material outside our own existential reality, which is in fact part of our peoples' predicaments. We do not have any art-historical axe to grind. We have no art-historical pedestal to stand on and defend bourgeois values or preach sermons about beauty and aesthetics, nor shall we indulge in the futile activity of *art for art's sake*. Our history is in fact the history of the pillage and plundering by colonialism. We must grasp *this* truth and turn it into a weapon of our cultural struggle. FROM CENTURIES OF OPPRESSED EXISTENCE, FROM THE WILDERNESS OF COLONIALISM, THE THIRD WORLD MUST NOW EMERGE, LIKE A BLACK PHOENIX RISING FROM WHITE ASHES.

"... it is necessary to totally destroy, to break, to reduce to ash all aspects of colonial state in our country in order to make everything possible for our people."
- AMILCAR CABRAL

It does not follow from this that we must cut off ourselves from the activities of our Western contemporaries, particularly those who are also aware of their role in society and are aiming at the radical change. Since many of us live in the West, we must avoid isolation and separatism which is no recipe for the positive development of a society in which all people, irrespective of race and colour, must interrelate. But in the present situation it is very difficult. *So long* as Western people speak from their privileged positions and with their usual paternalistic attitude and arrogance, there is no possibility whatsoever for the development of a real dialogue between THEM and US.

The development of a true international platform/movement, from/to which all cultures could make their unique contributions, is not only possible but desirable in the long run. But if this is to serve the true interests of all peoples rather than become another instrument of selfish Western interests, it must be based on the clear rejection of ...

Burning Ties, 1976–1979
8 photographs, 75 x 50 cm each
Burger Collection, Hong Kong

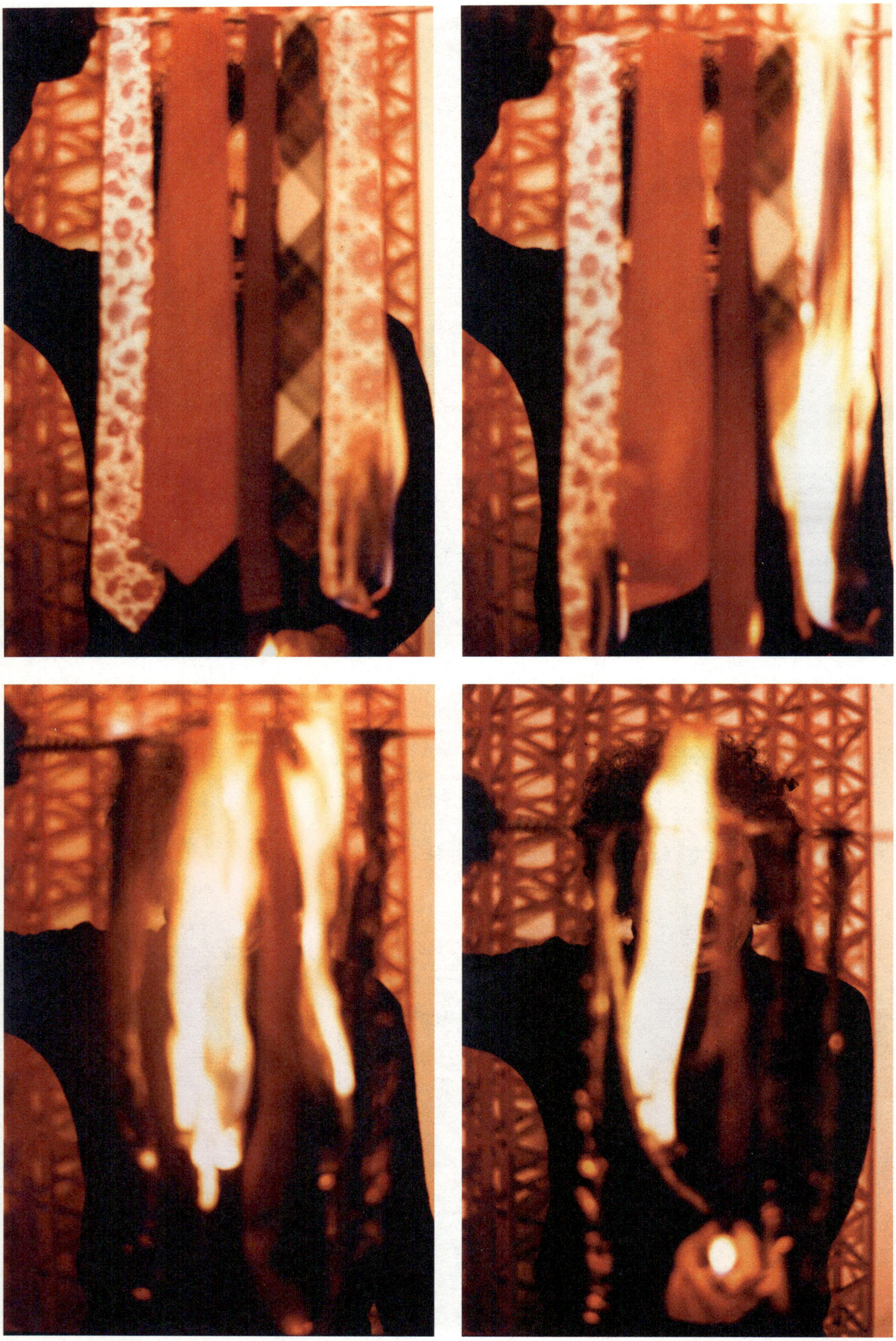

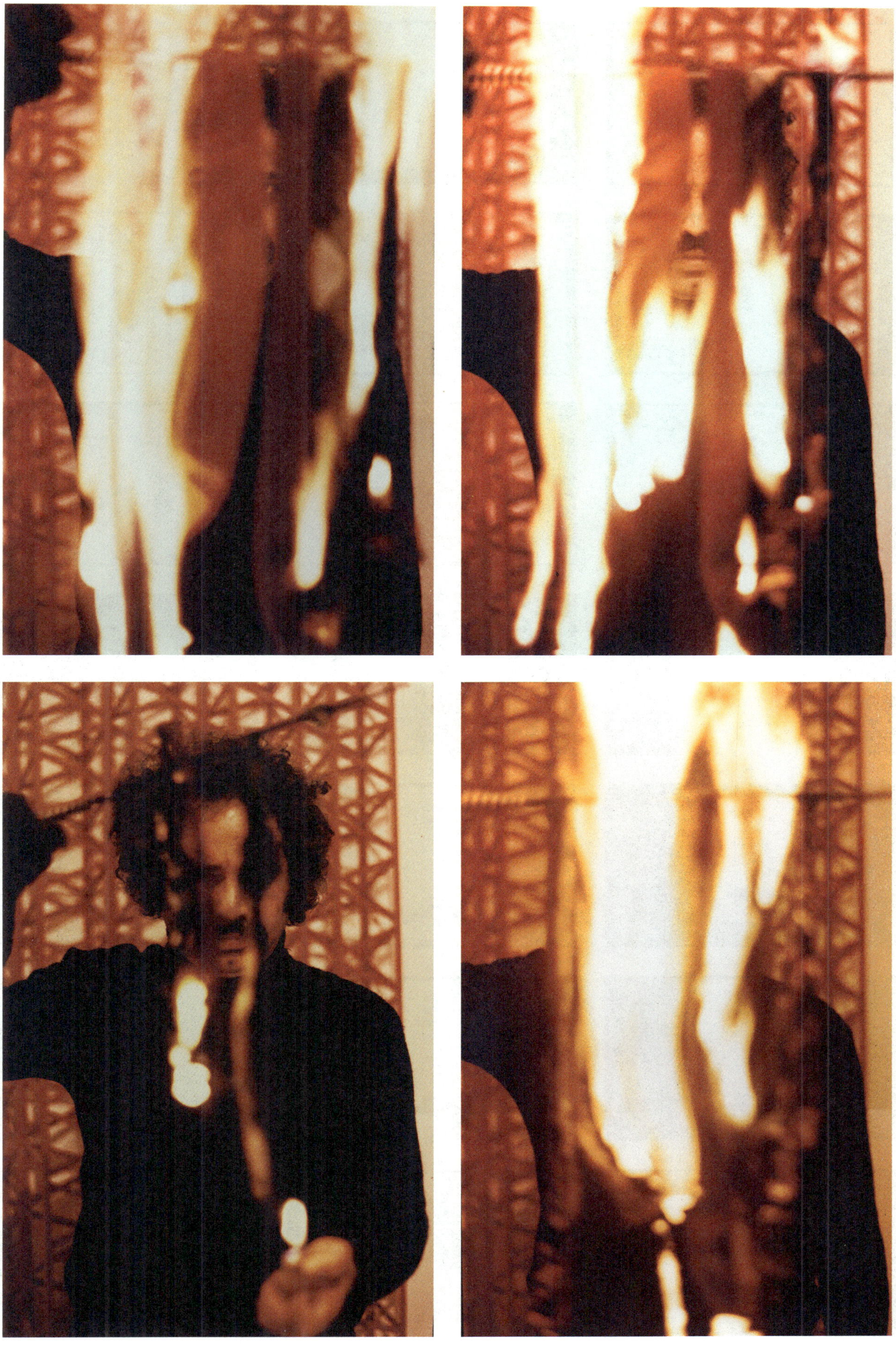

Paki Bastard, 1977
slide projection with sound and performance

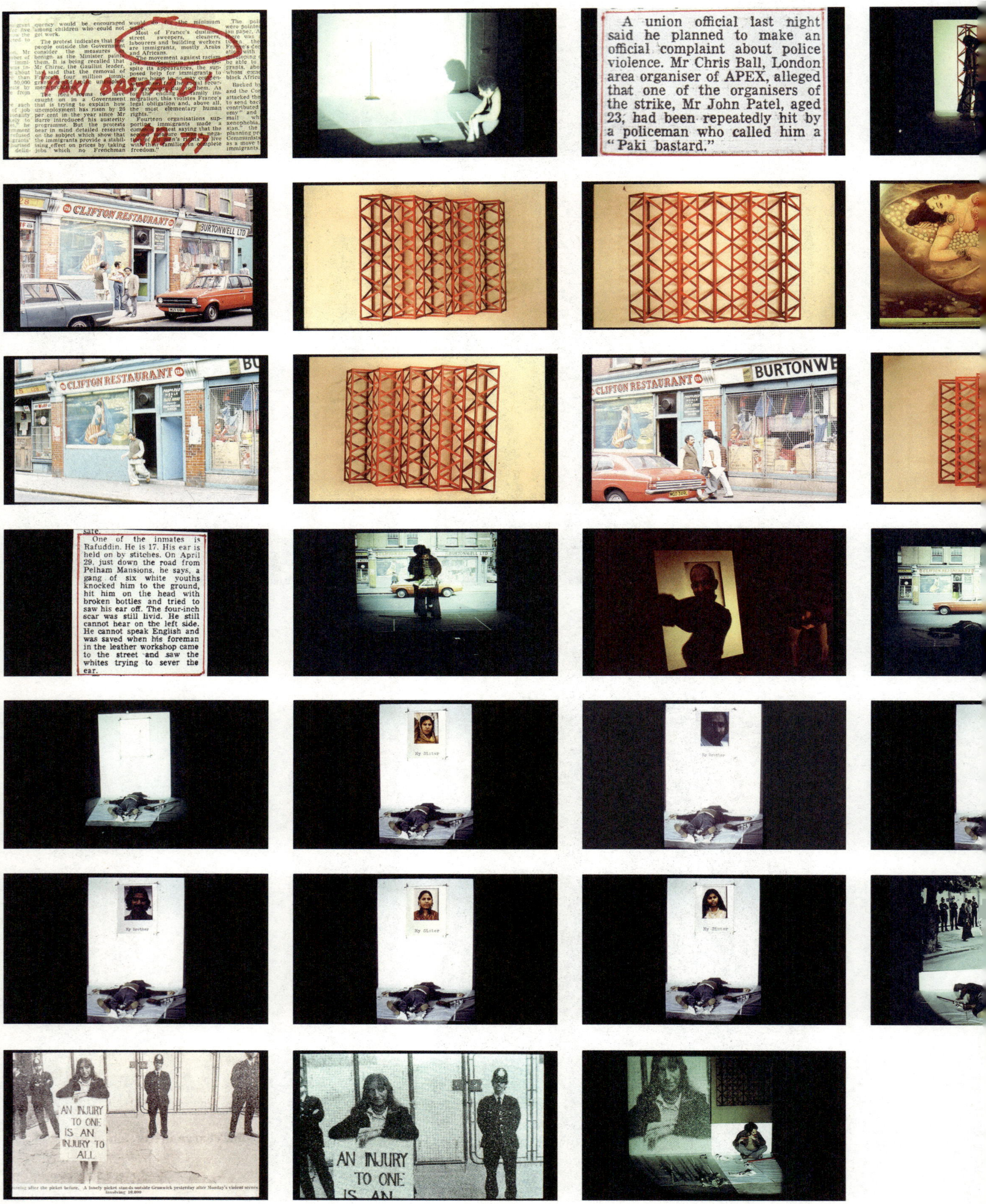

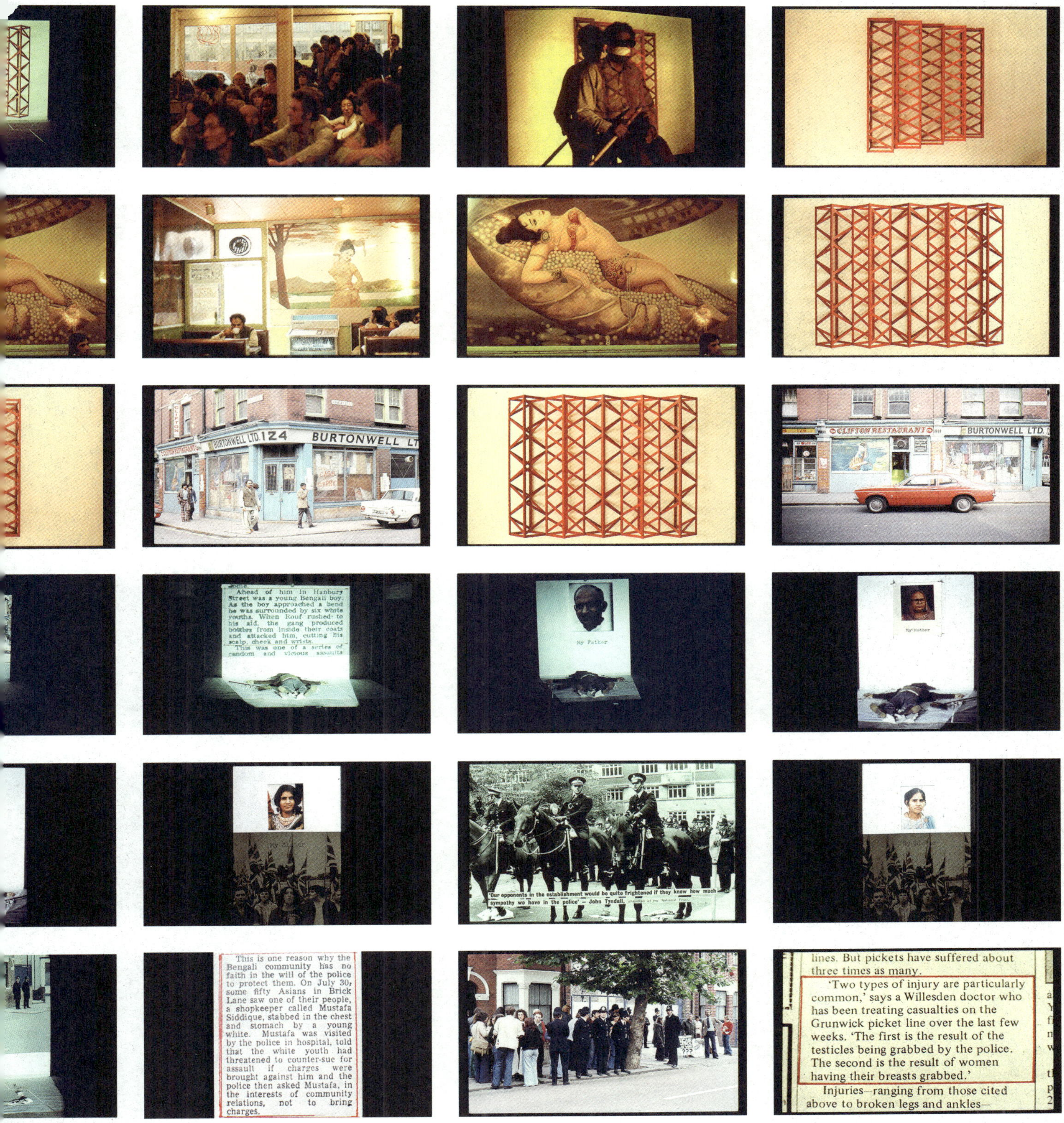
BURTONWELL LTD. 124
BURTONWELL LT
CLIFTON RESTAURANT
BURTONWELL LTD.
Ahead of him in Hanbury Street was a young Bengali boy. As the boy approached a bend he was surrounded by six white youths. When Rouf rushed to his aid, the gang produced bottles from inside their coats and attacked him, cutting his scalp, cheek and wrists.
This was one of a series of random and vicious assaults
My Father
'Our opponents in the establishment would be quite frightened if they knew how much sympathy we have in the police' – John Tyndall,
This is one reason why the Bengali community has no faith in the will of the police to protect them. On July 30, some fifty Asians in Brick Lane saw one of their people, a shopkeeper called Mustafa Siddique, stabbed in the chest and stomach by a young white. Mustafa was visited by the police in hospital, told that the white youth had threatened to counter-sue for assault if charges were brought against him and the police then asked Mustafa, in the interests of community relations, not to bring charges.
lines. But pickets have suffered about three times as many.
'Two types of injury are particularly common,' says a Willesden doctor who has been treating casualties on the Grunwick picket line over the last few weeks. 'The first is the result of the testicles being grabbed by the police. The second is the result of women having their breasts grabbed.'
Injuries—ranging from those cited above to broken legs and ankles—

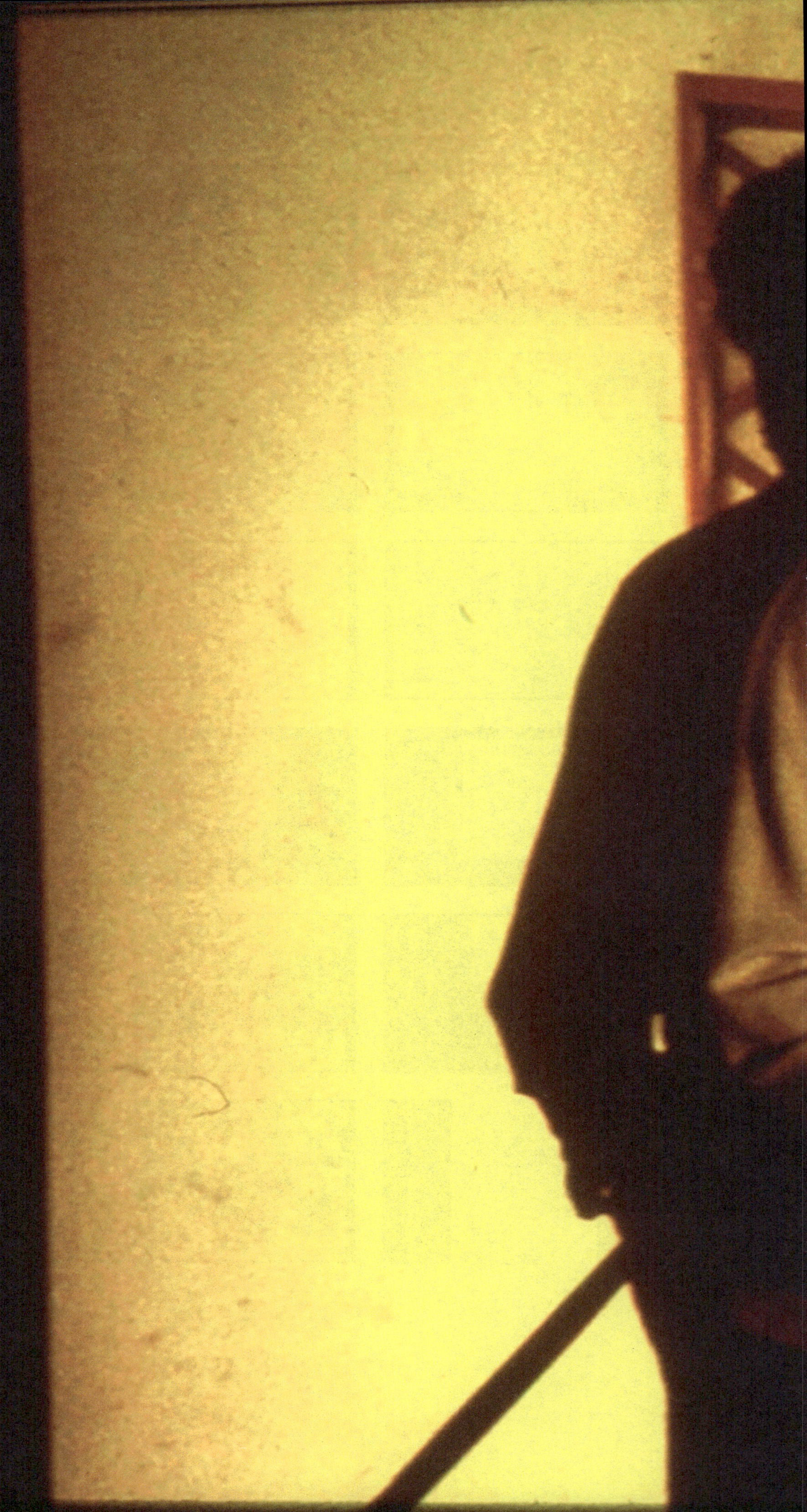

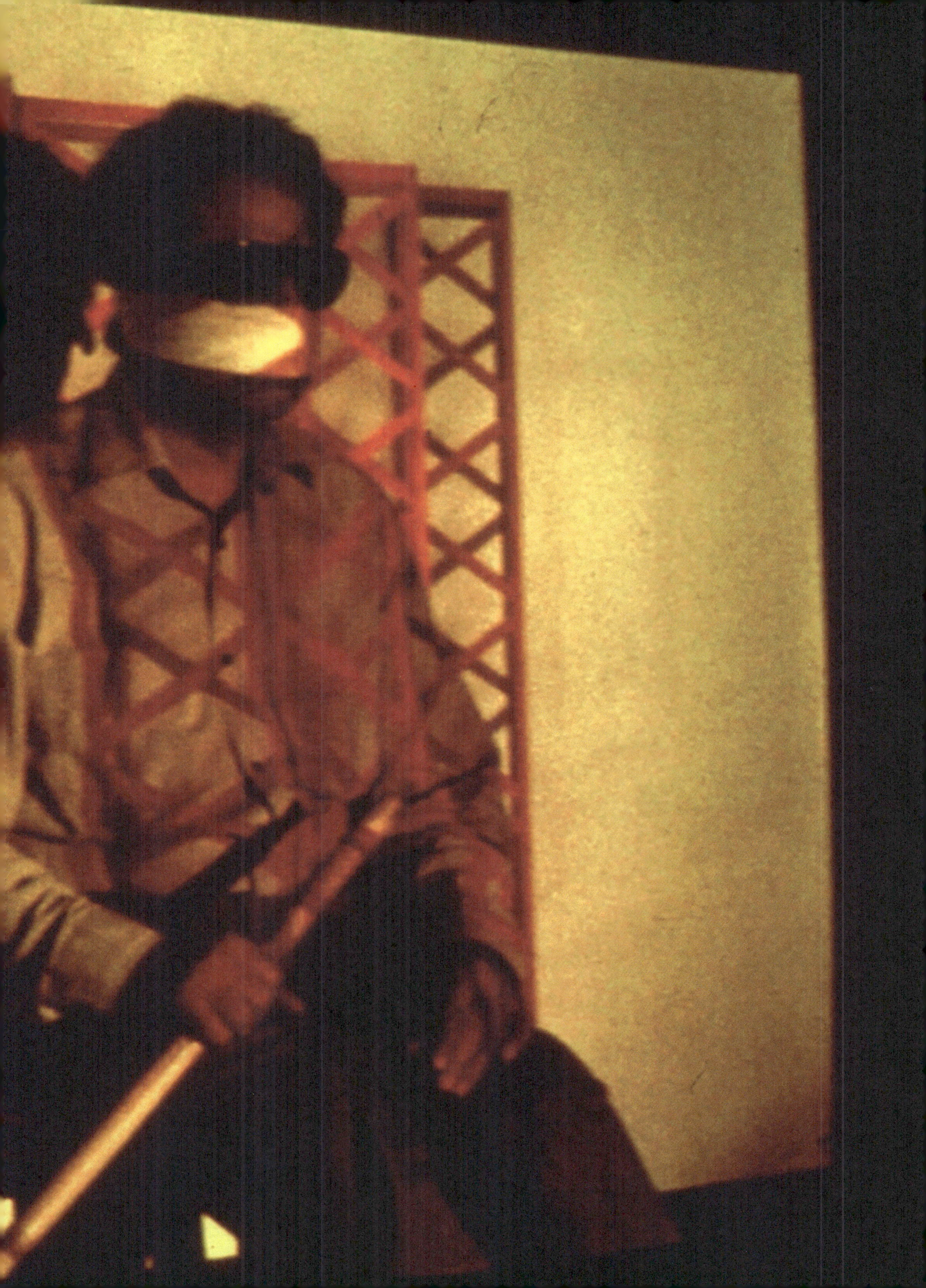

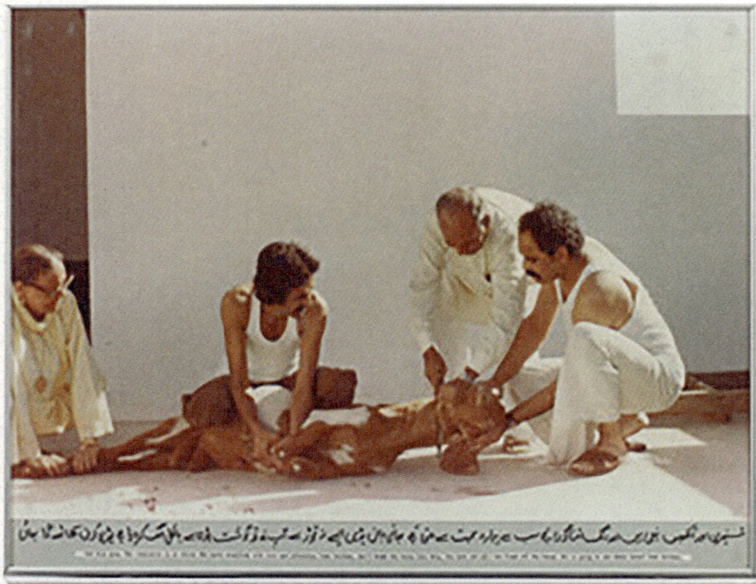

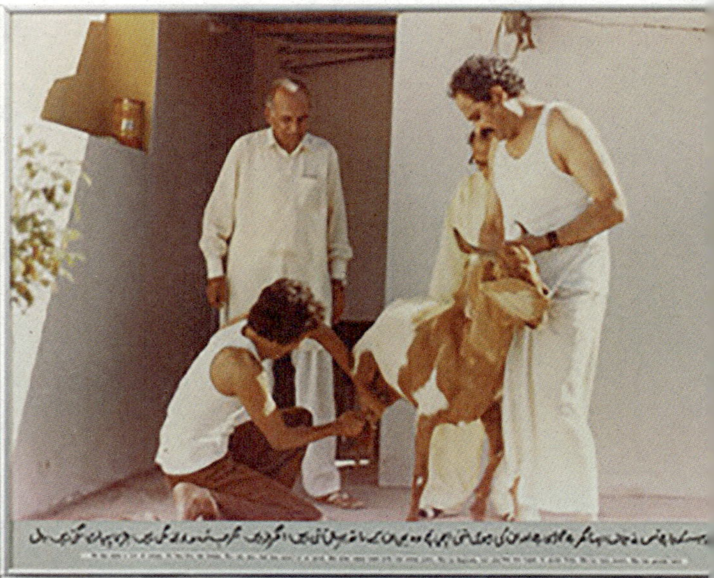

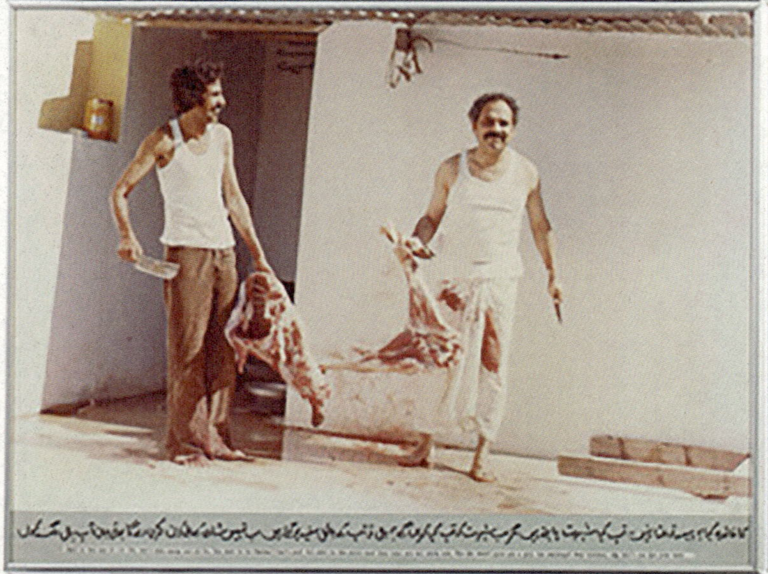

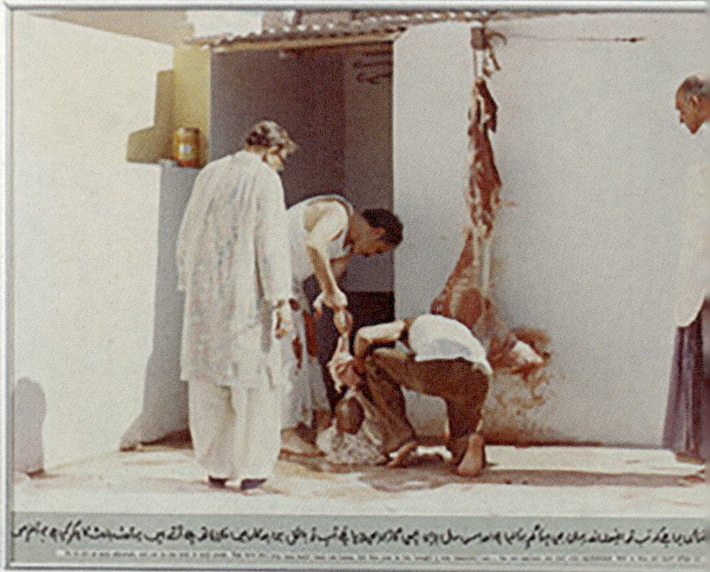

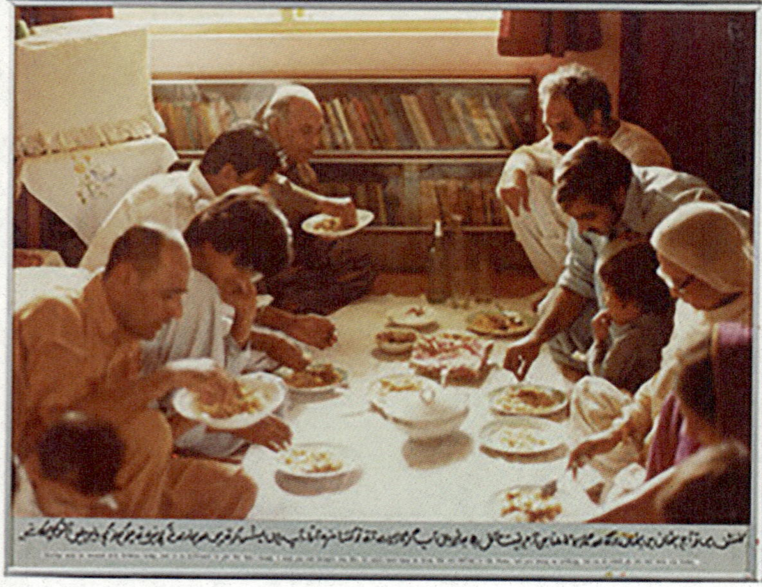

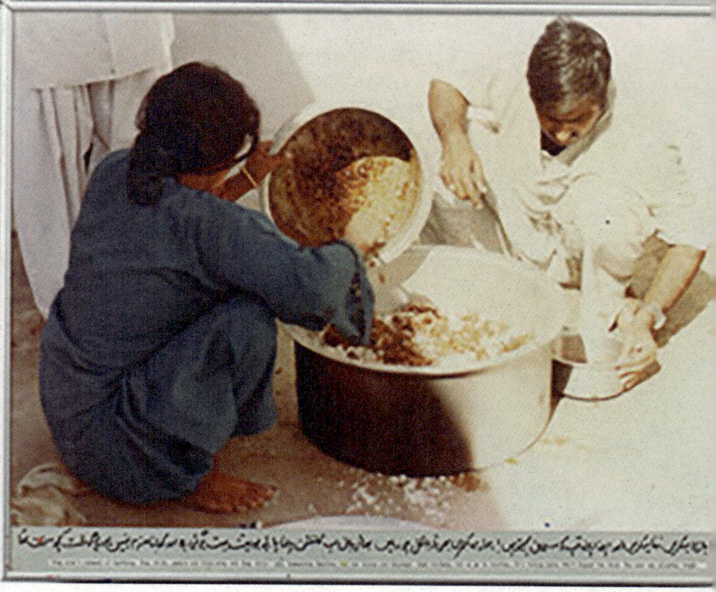

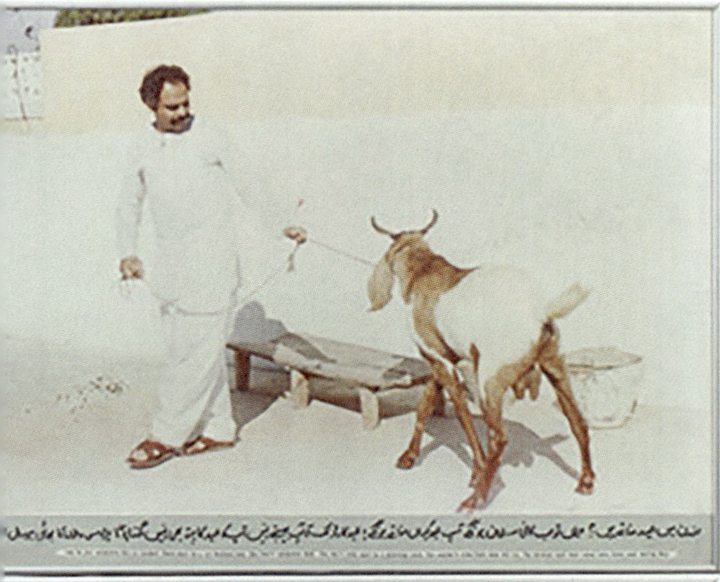

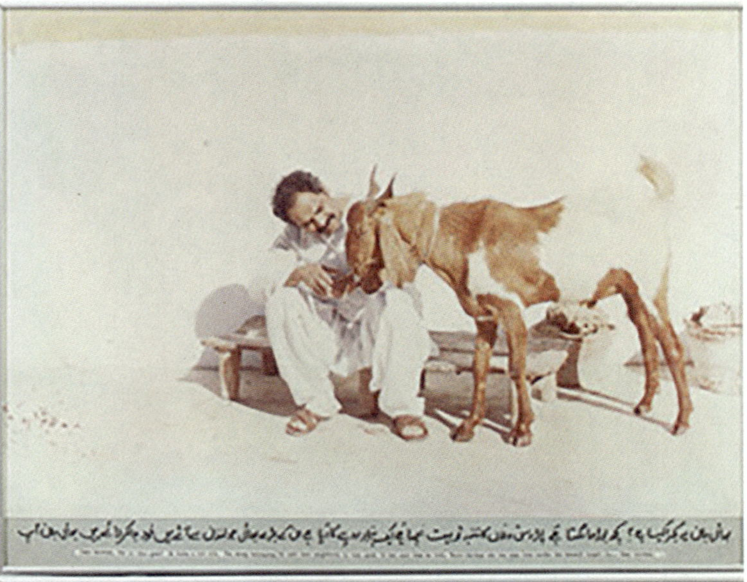

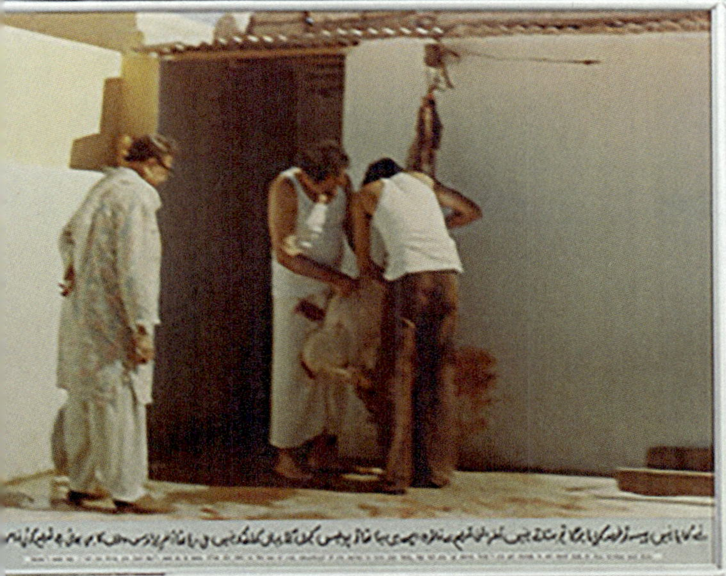

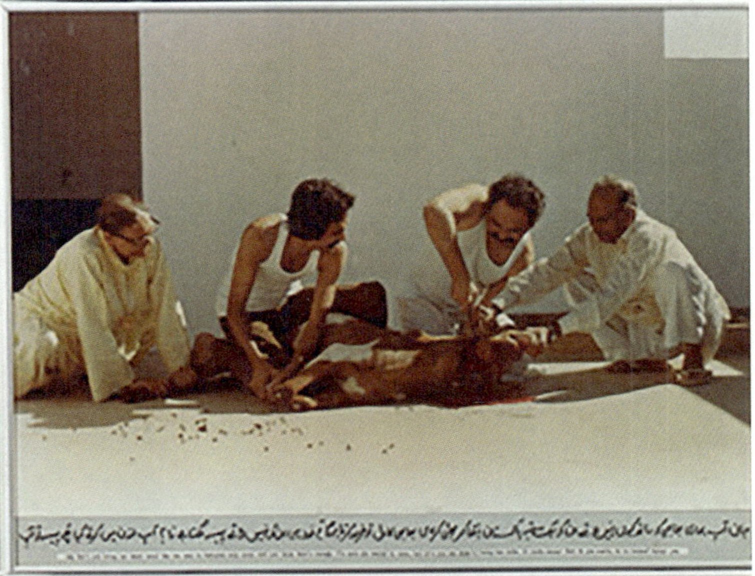

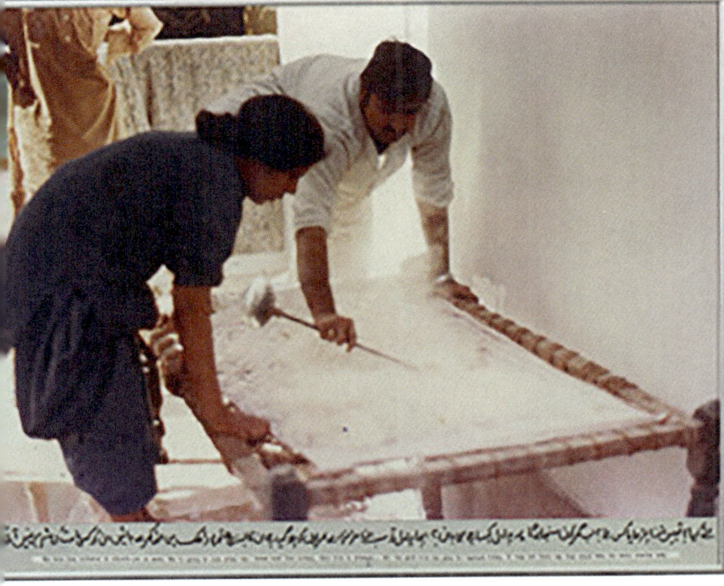

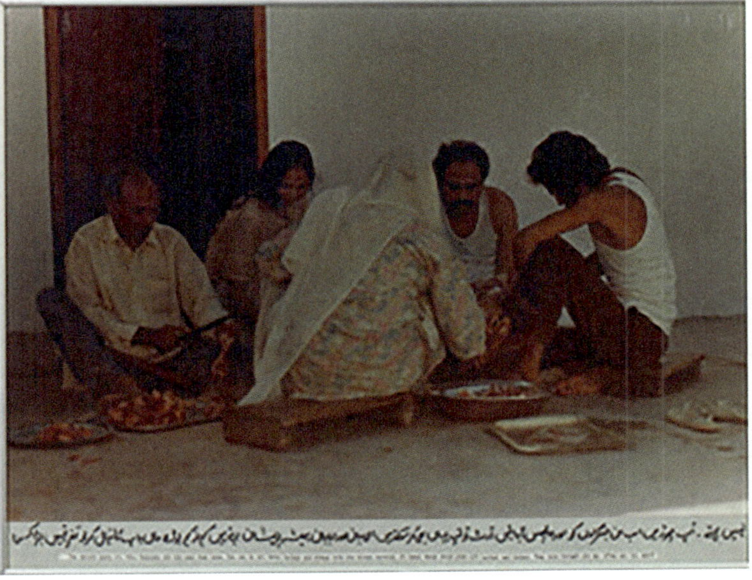

How Could One Paint a Self-Portrait, 1978
mixed-media on paper, 122 x 102 cm
Sharjah Art Foundation Collection

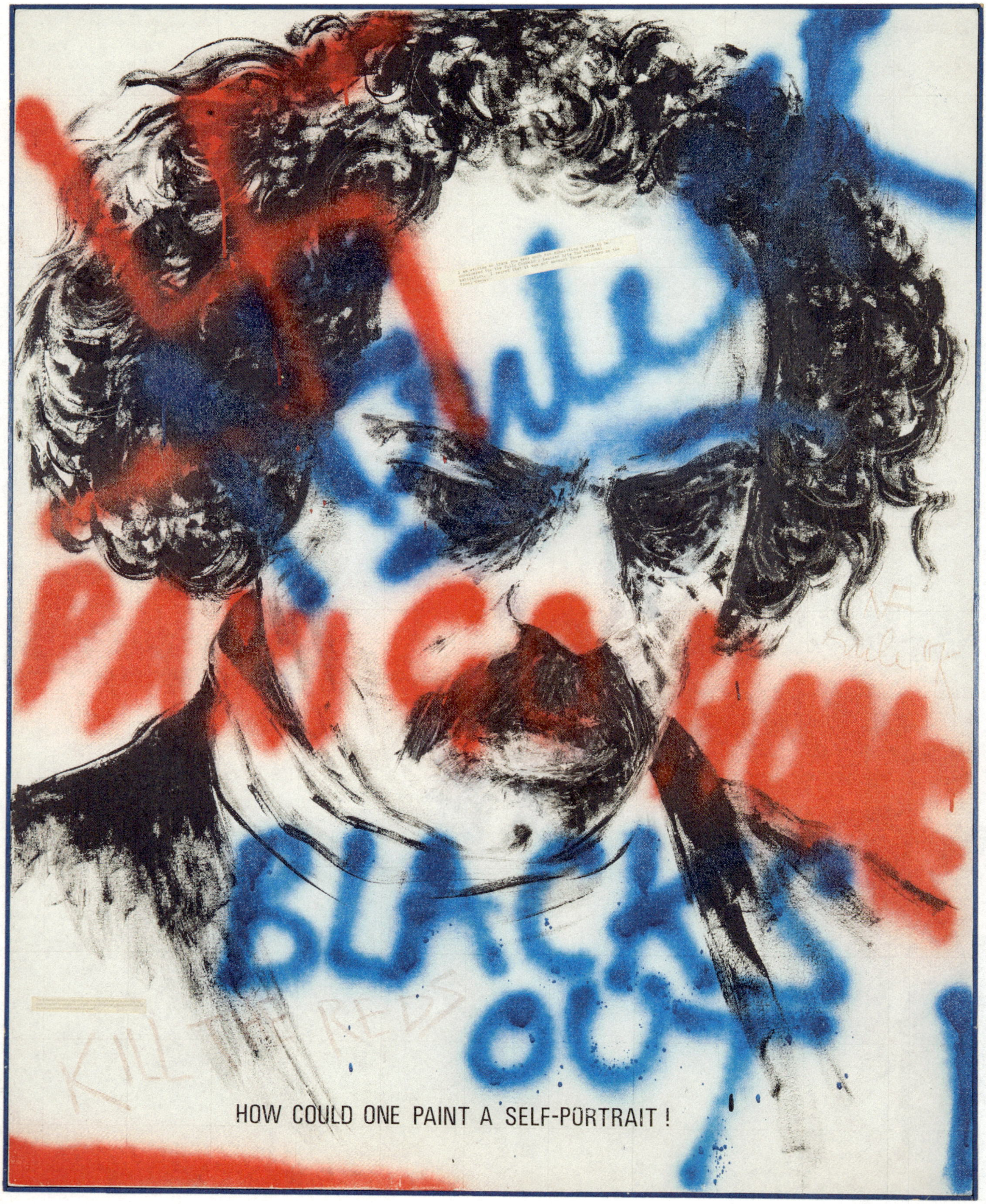

Homecoming, 1982
mixed-media on board, 122 x 102 cm
Sharjah Art Foundation Collection

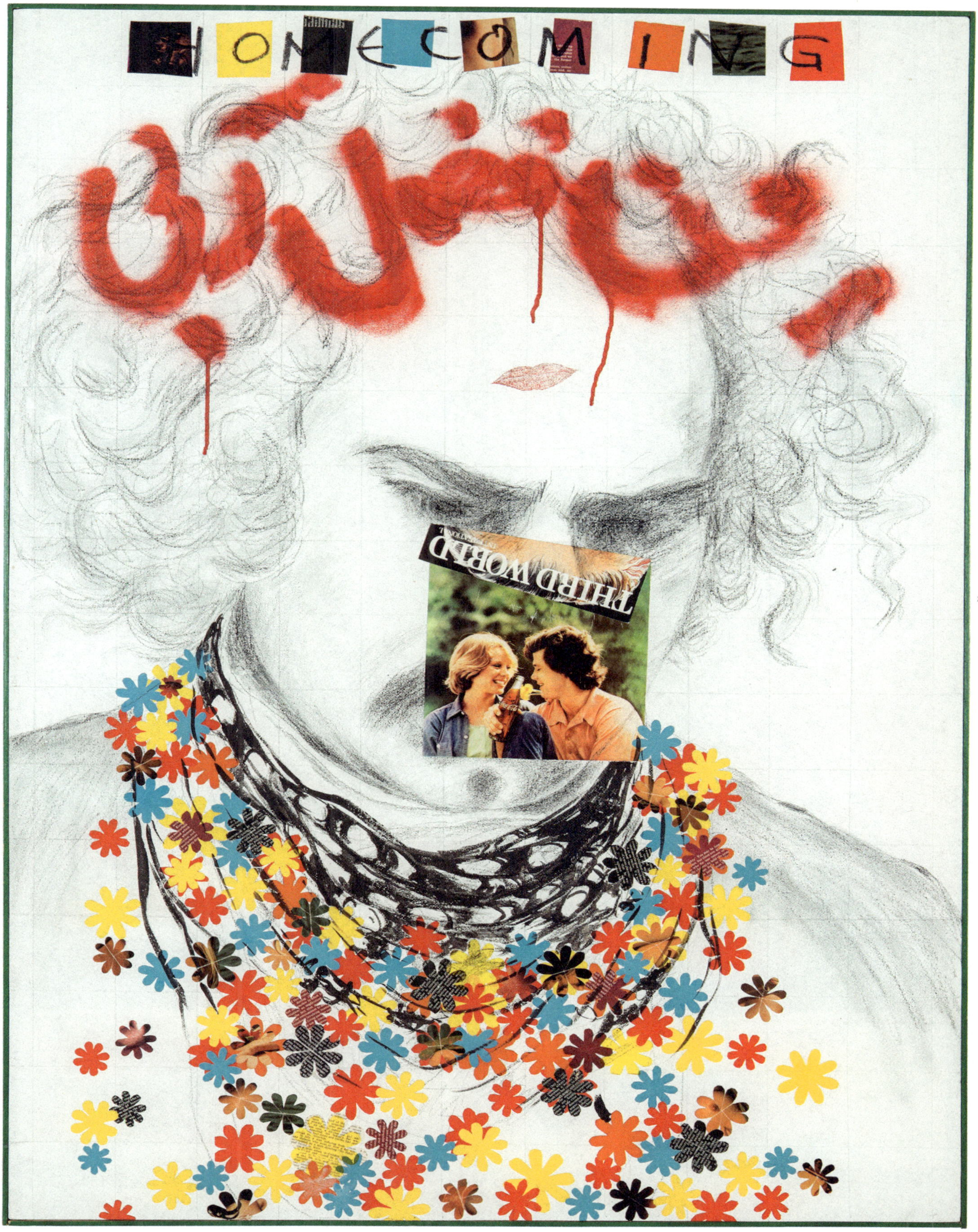

Happy Christmas, 1979–1983
mixed-media on board, 122 x 102 cm
Sharjah Art Foundation Collection

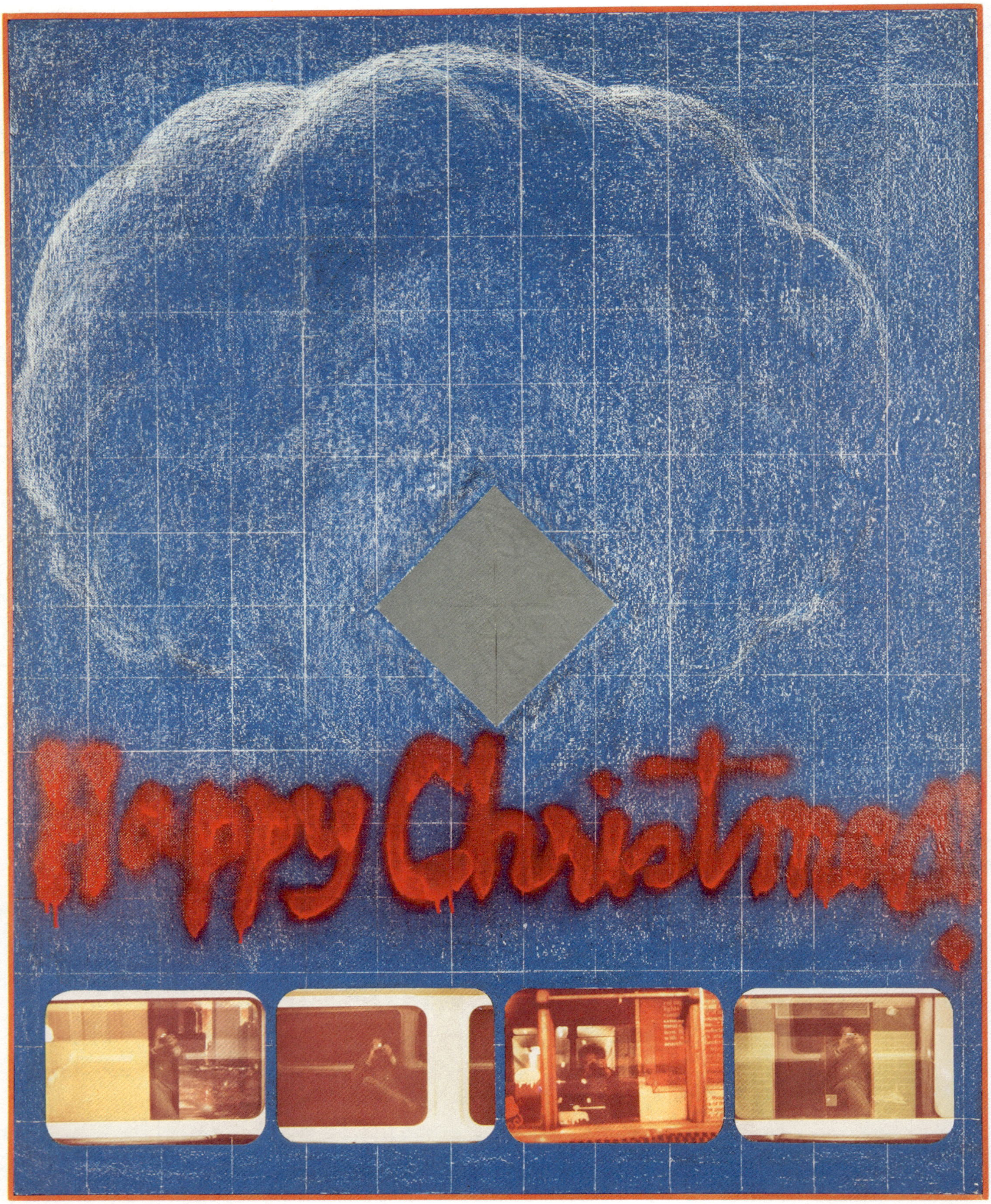

Narcissus, 1979–1983
mixed-media on on board, 122 x 102 cm
Sharjah Art Foundation Collection

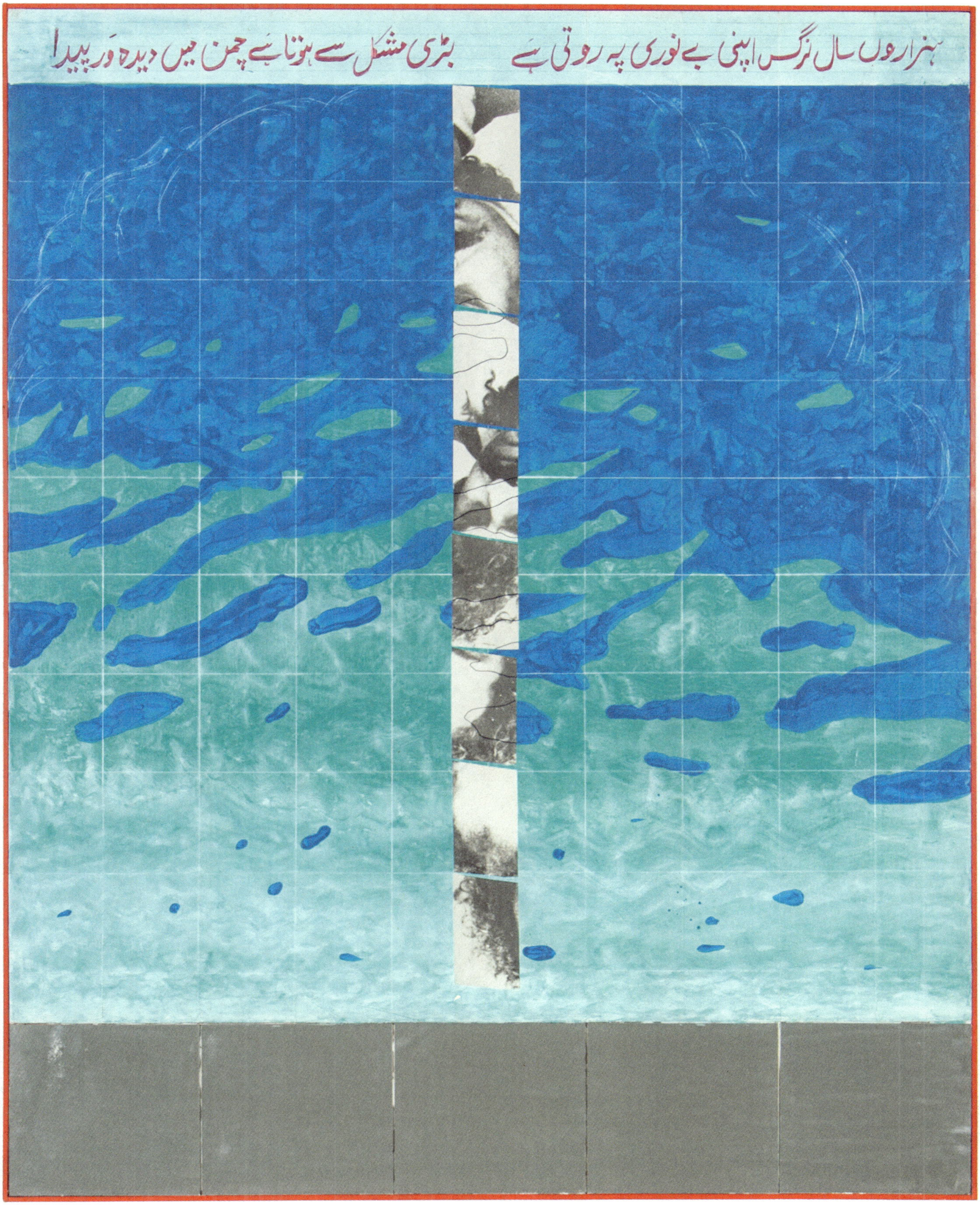

Black Sheep, 1983–1984
mixed-media on board, 122 x 102 cm
Sharjah Art Foundation Collection

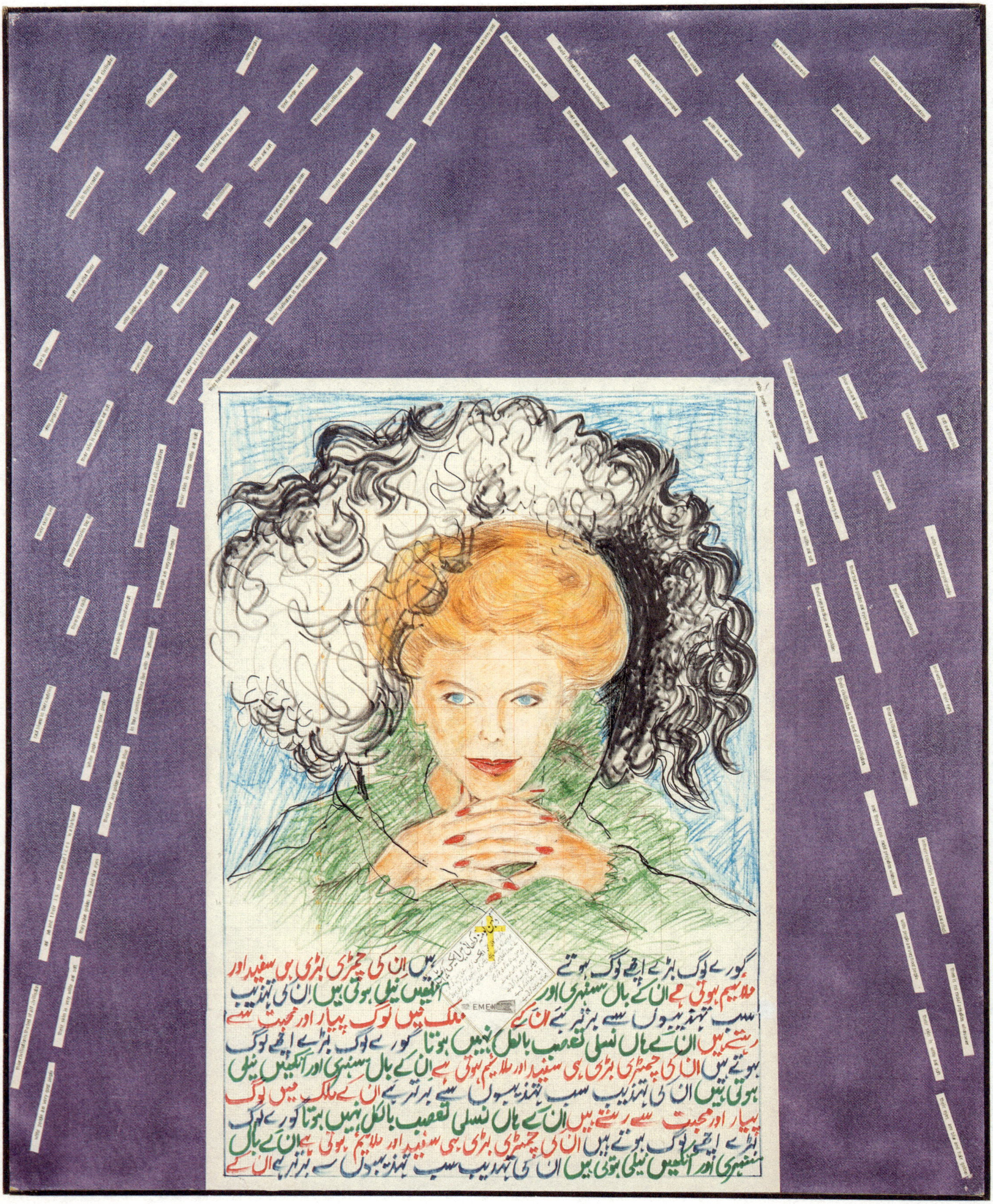

White Wash, Coloured and a Long Afternoon, 1979–1980
mixed-media on paper, 91 x 91 cm each

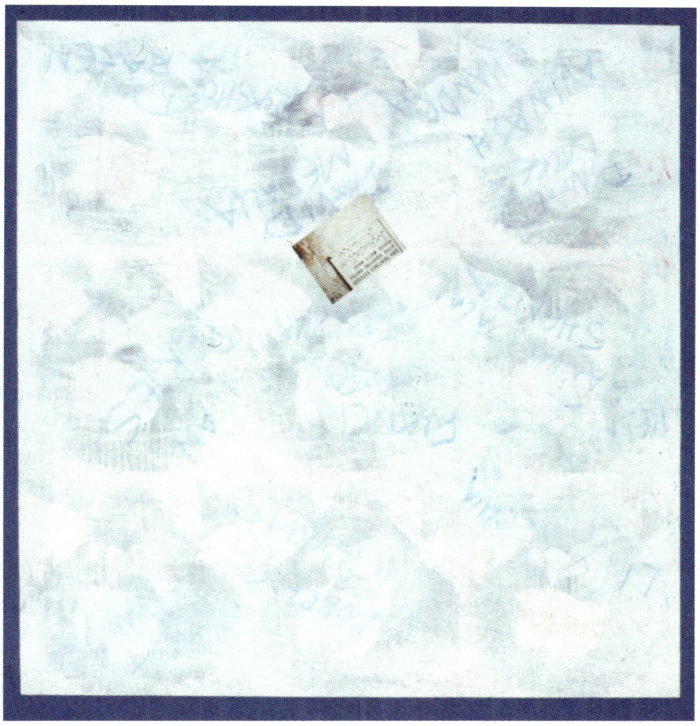

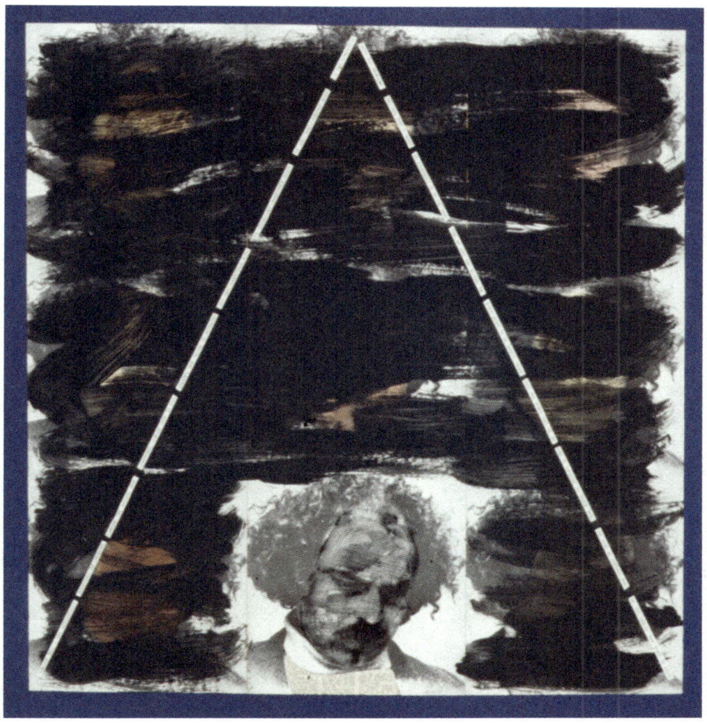

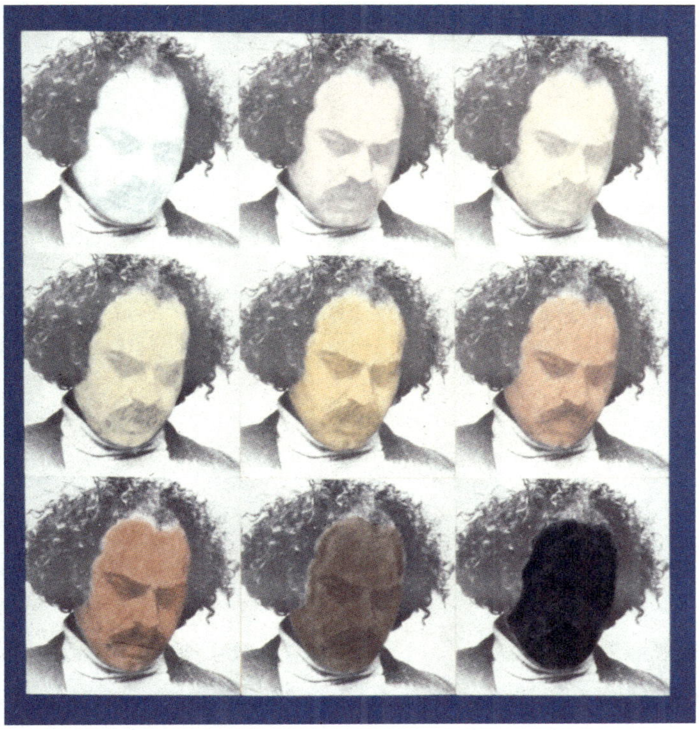

Art History, Brilliant White and Crossed, 1979
mixed-media on paper, 91 x 91 cm each

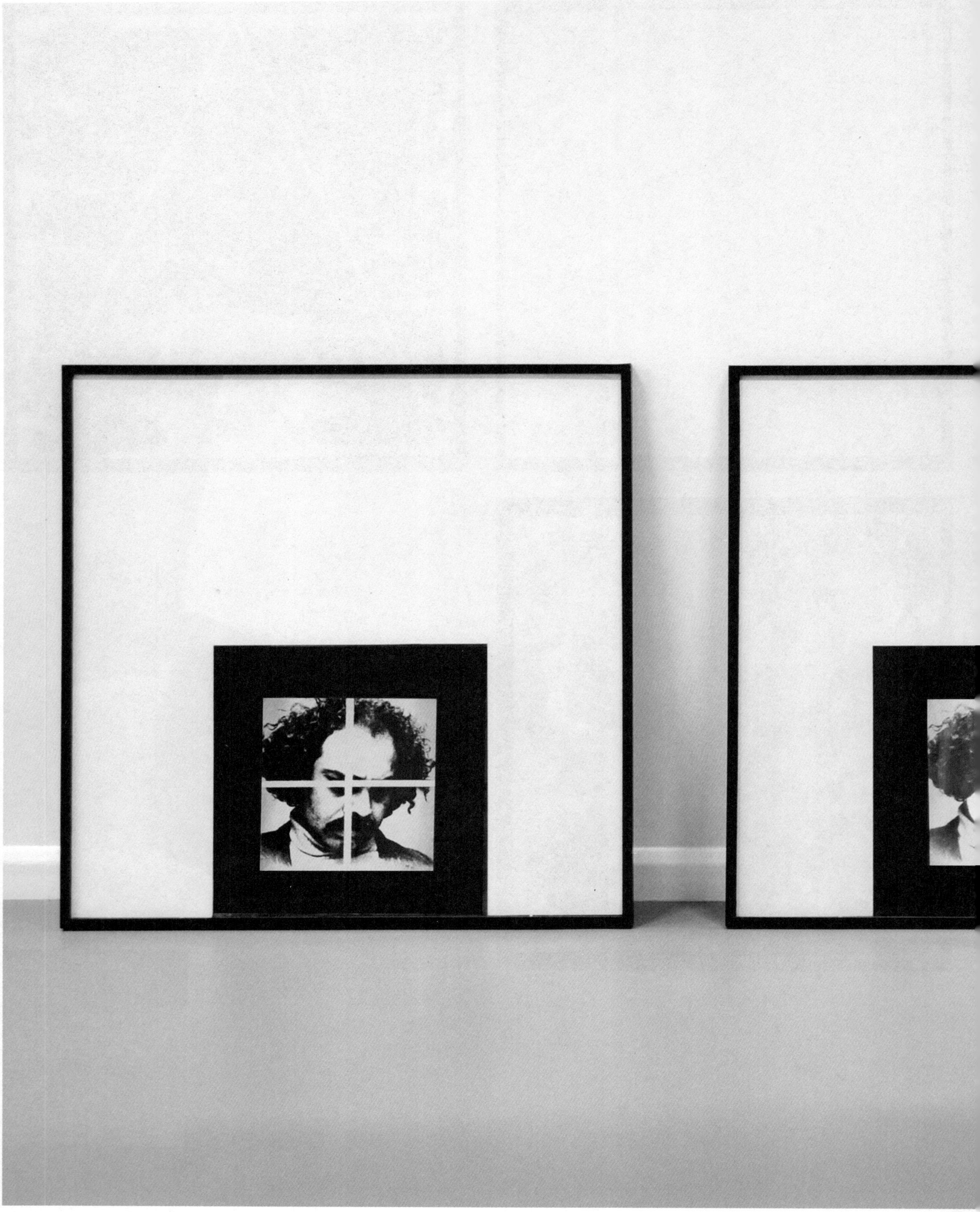

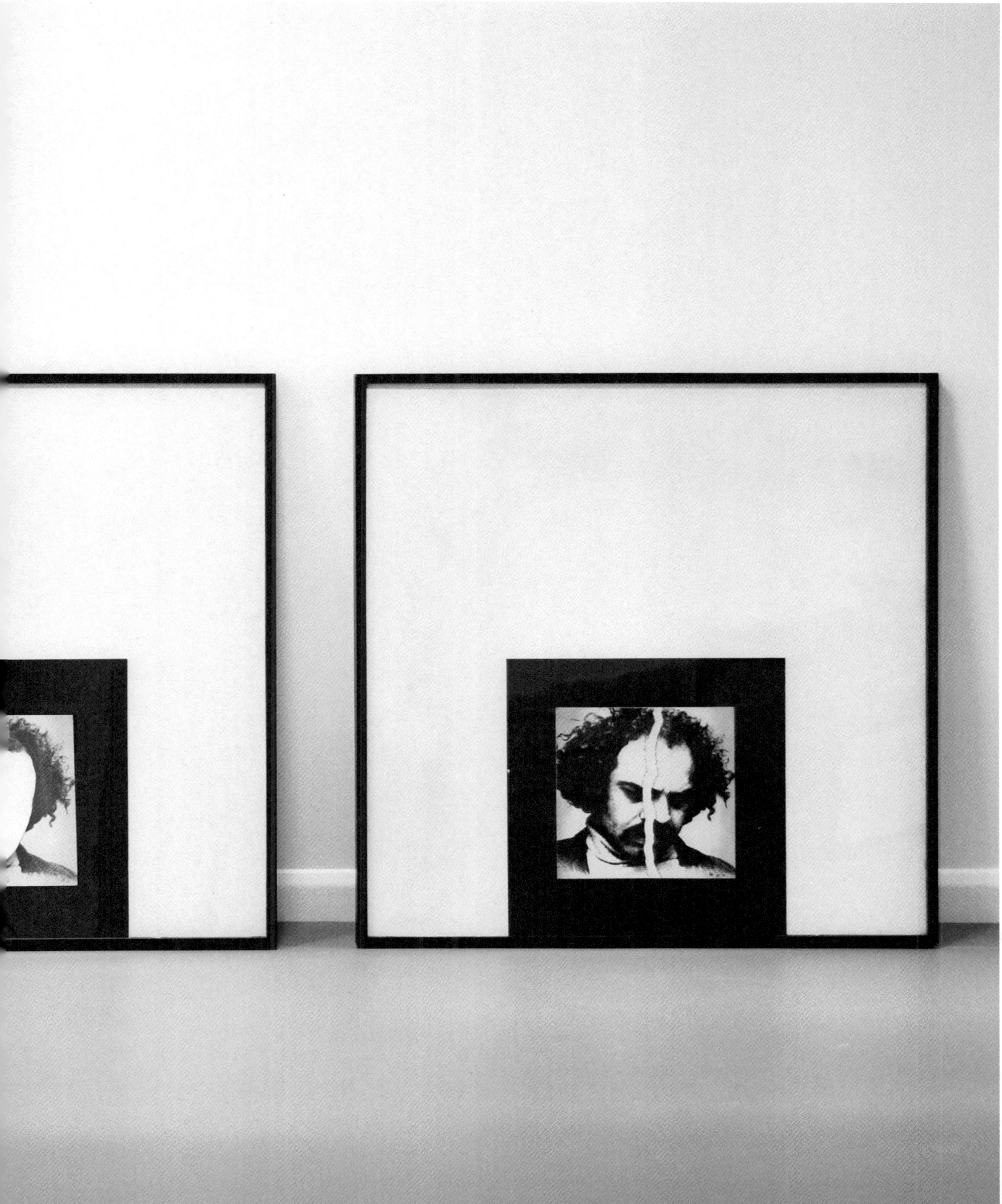

EXISTE-T'IL UN ART ANGLAIS ?

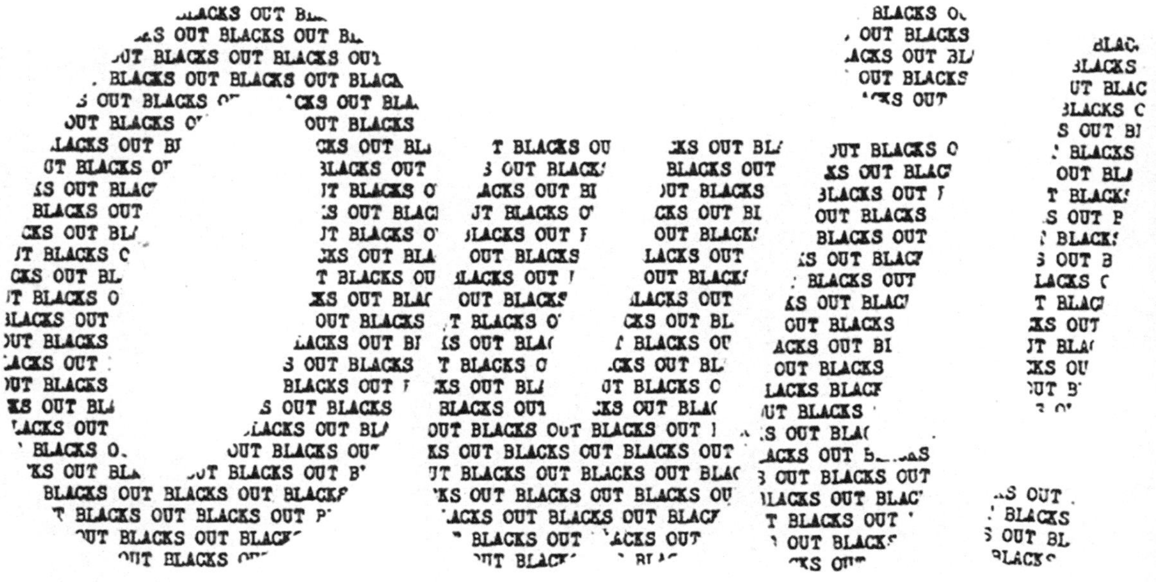

Christmas Day, 1979
4 photographs, 51 x 76 cm each

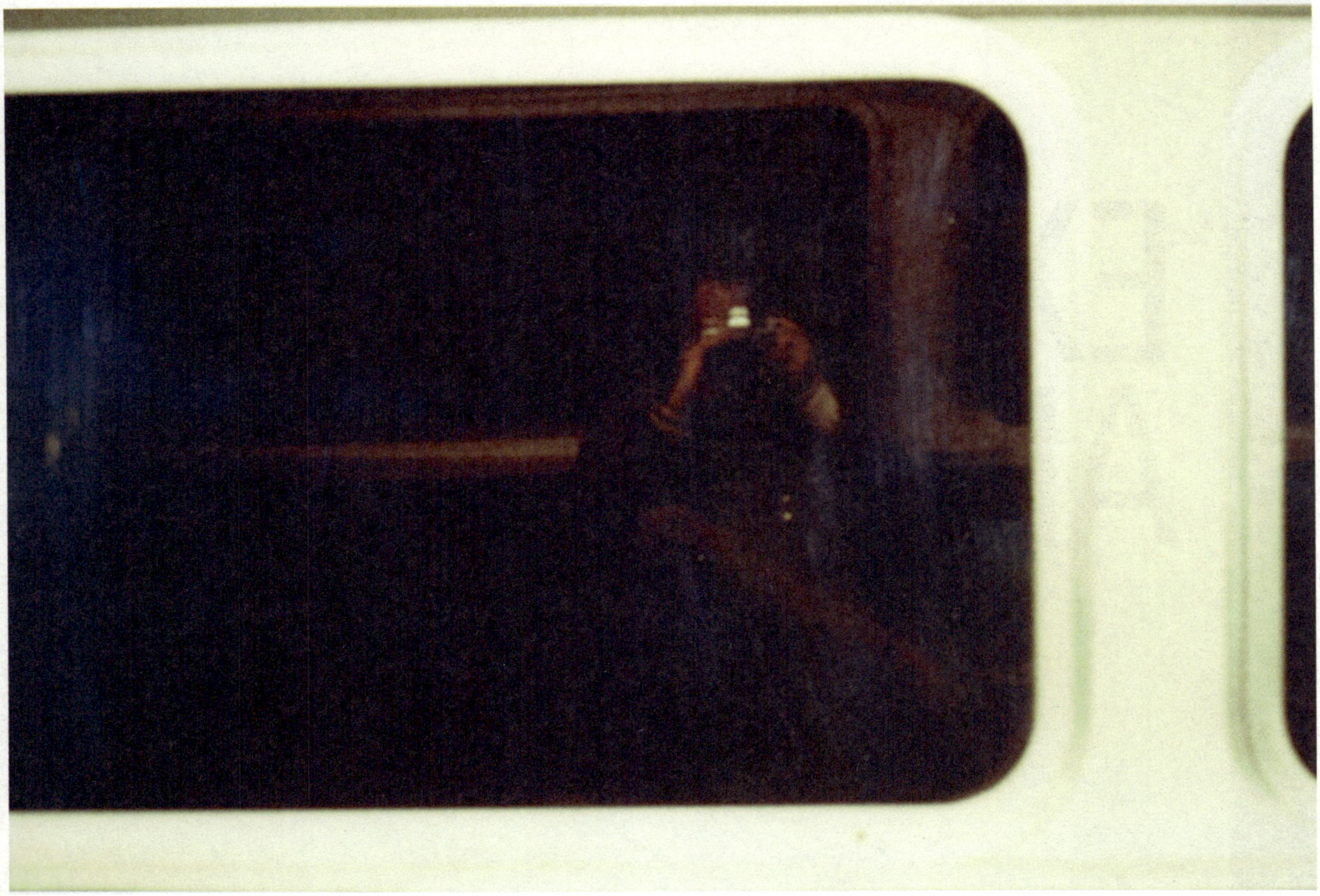

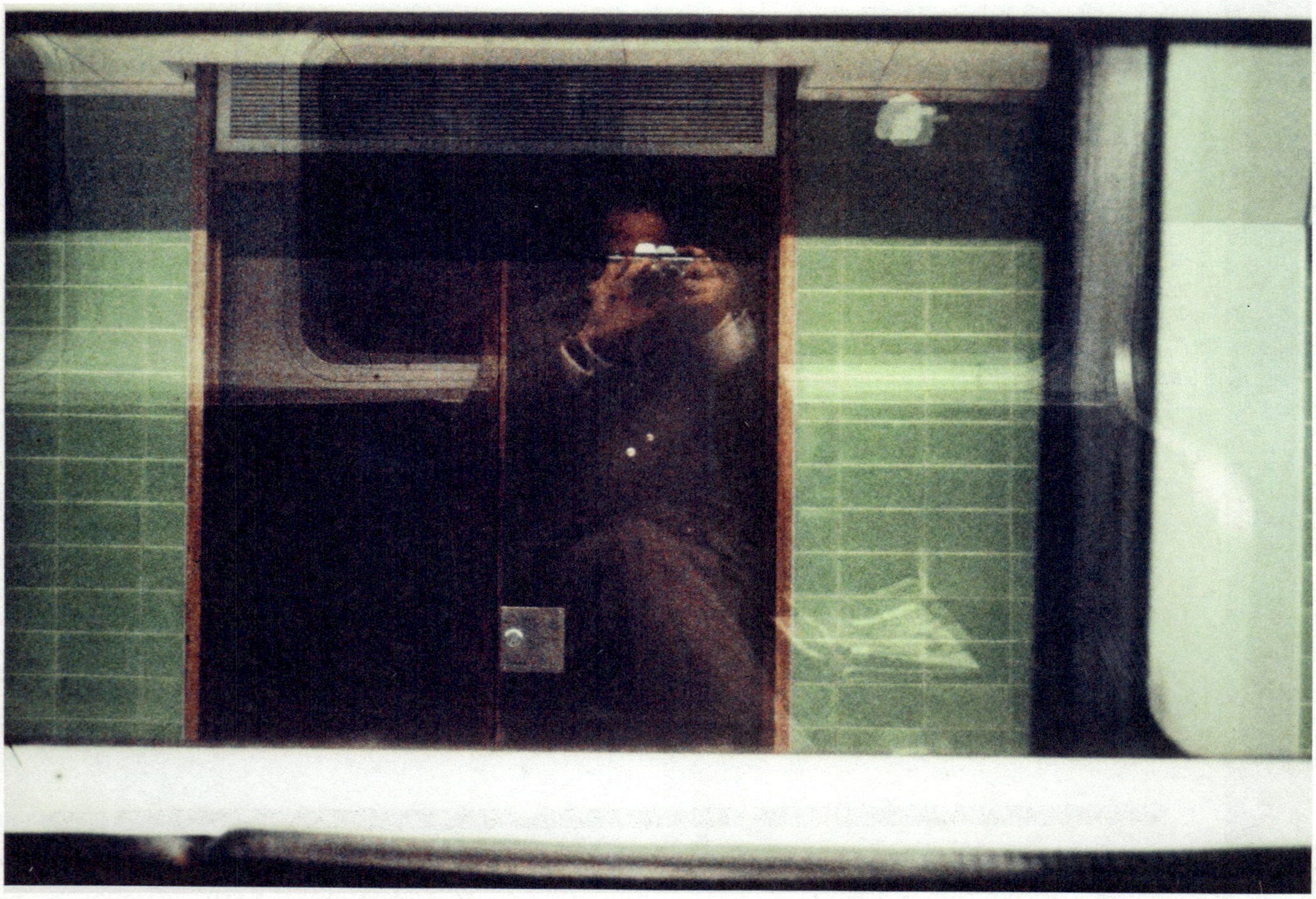

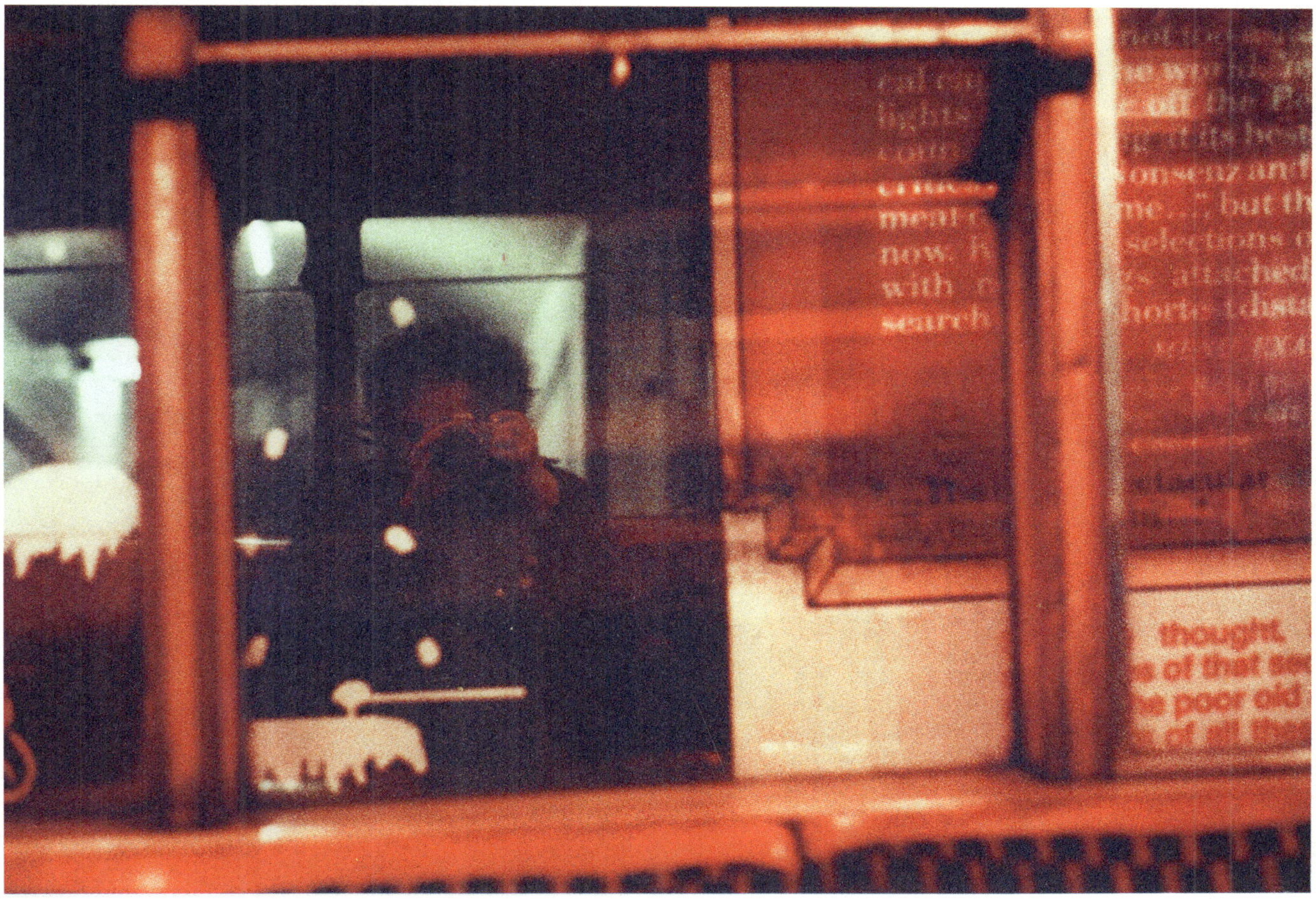
thought,

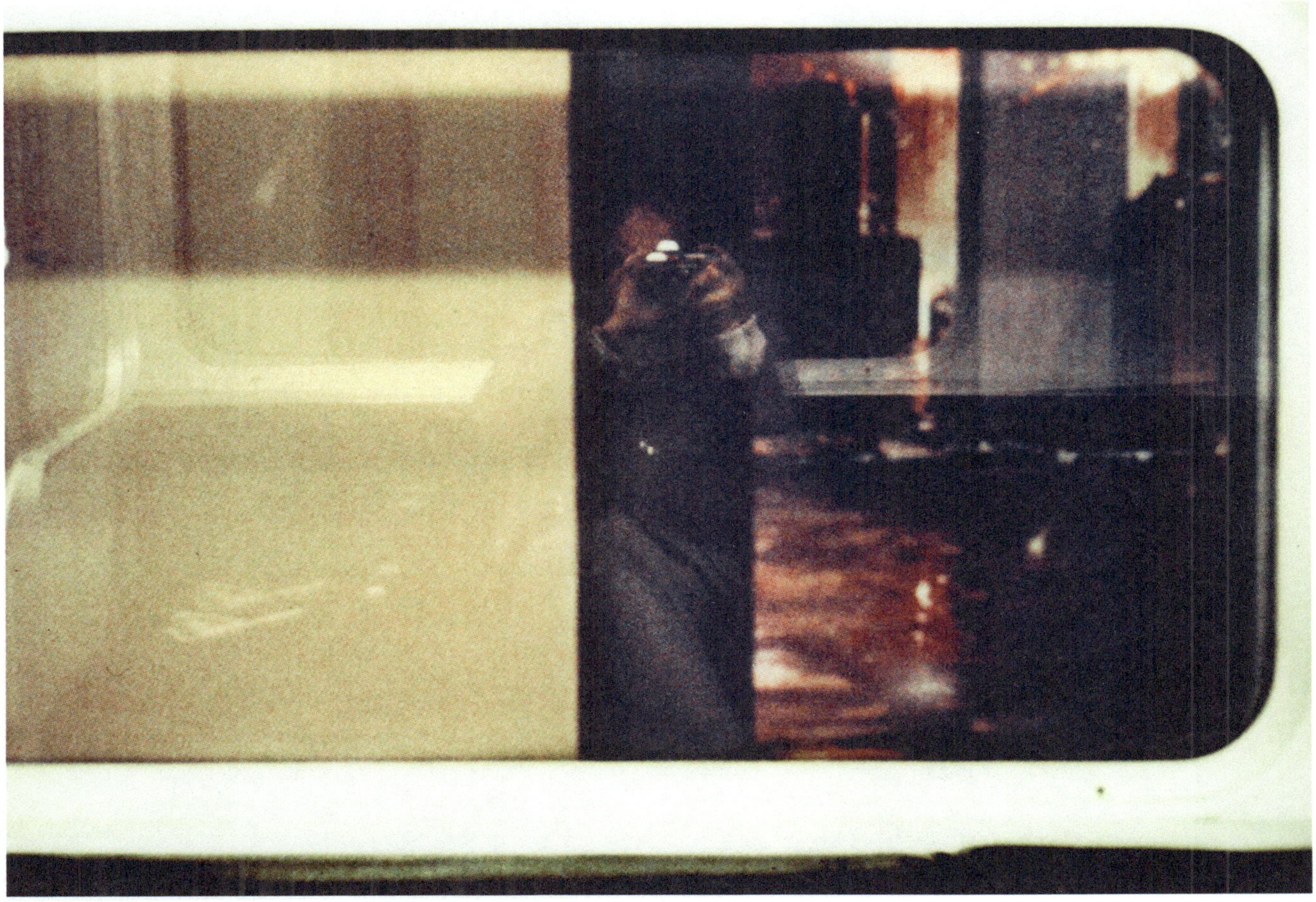

Gastkünstler, 1980
collage in wooden suitcase, 110 x 140 cm

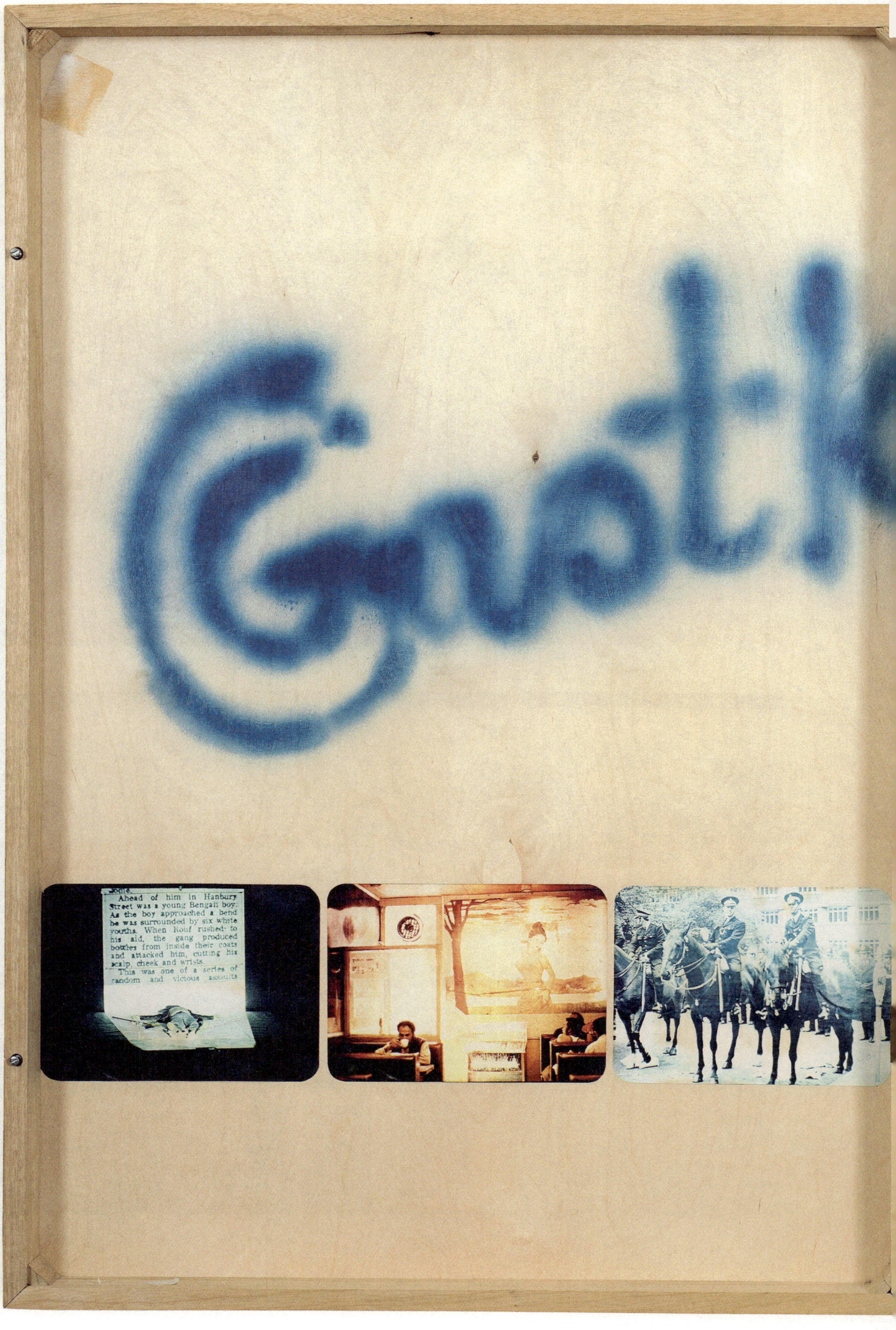

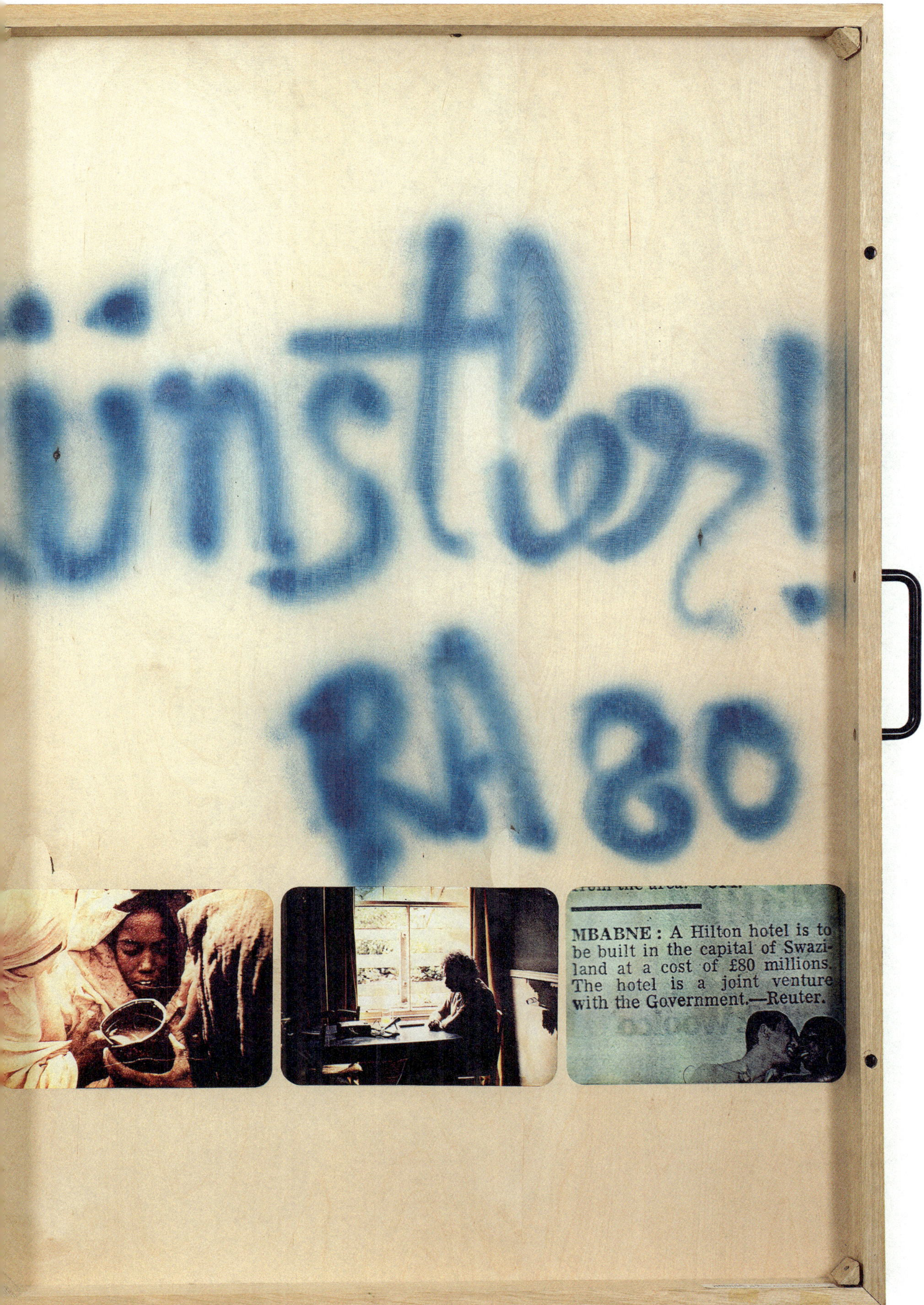
ünstler!
RA 80
MBABNE : A Hilton hotel is to be built in the capital of Swaziland at a cost of £80 millions. The hotel is a joint venture with the Government.—Reuter.

Ethnic Drawings, 1982
4 drawings, pencil and pen on paper, 79 x 53 cm each
Arts Council Collection, Southbank Centre, London

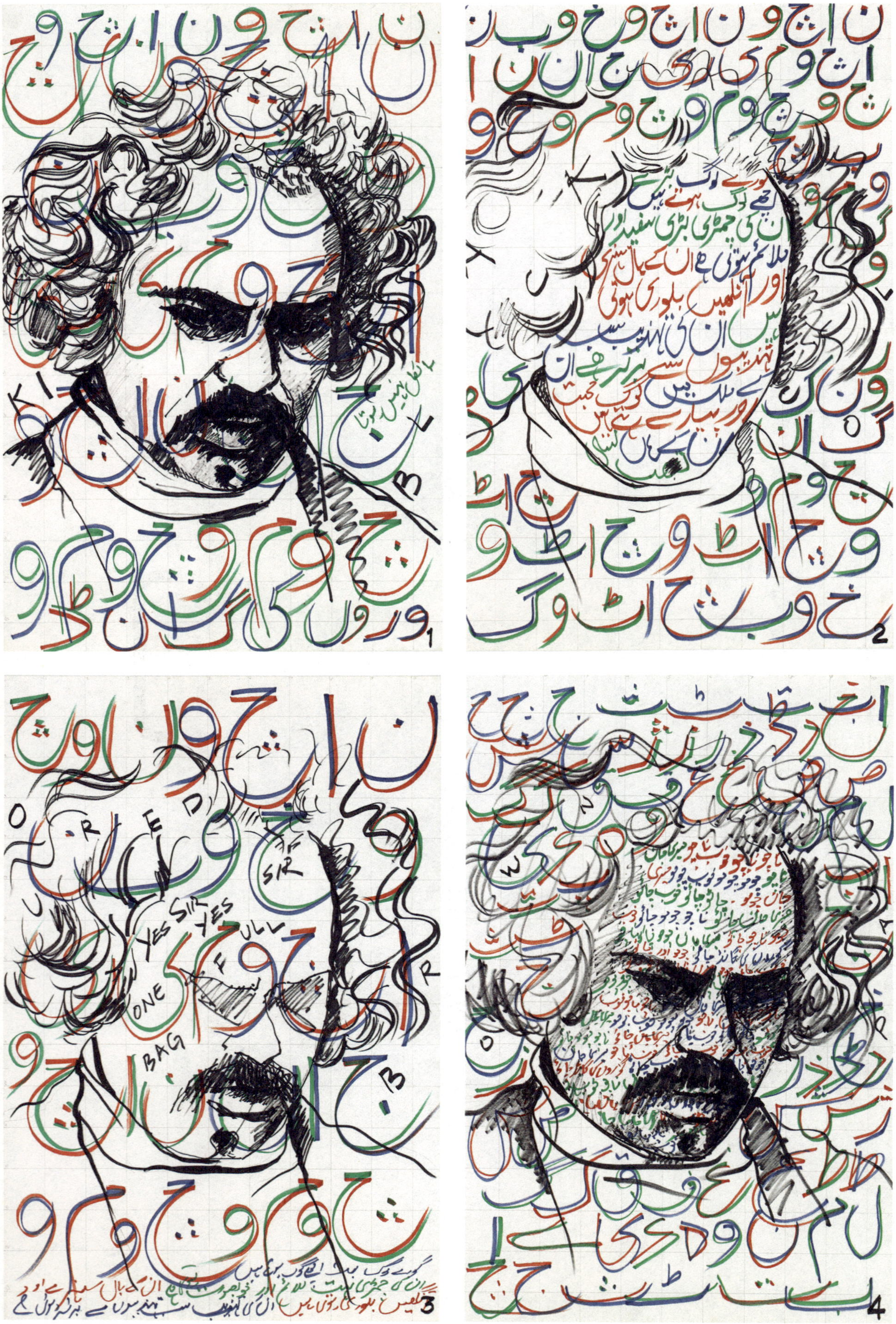

Fair and Lovely, 1985
mixed-media collage, 183 x 218 cm

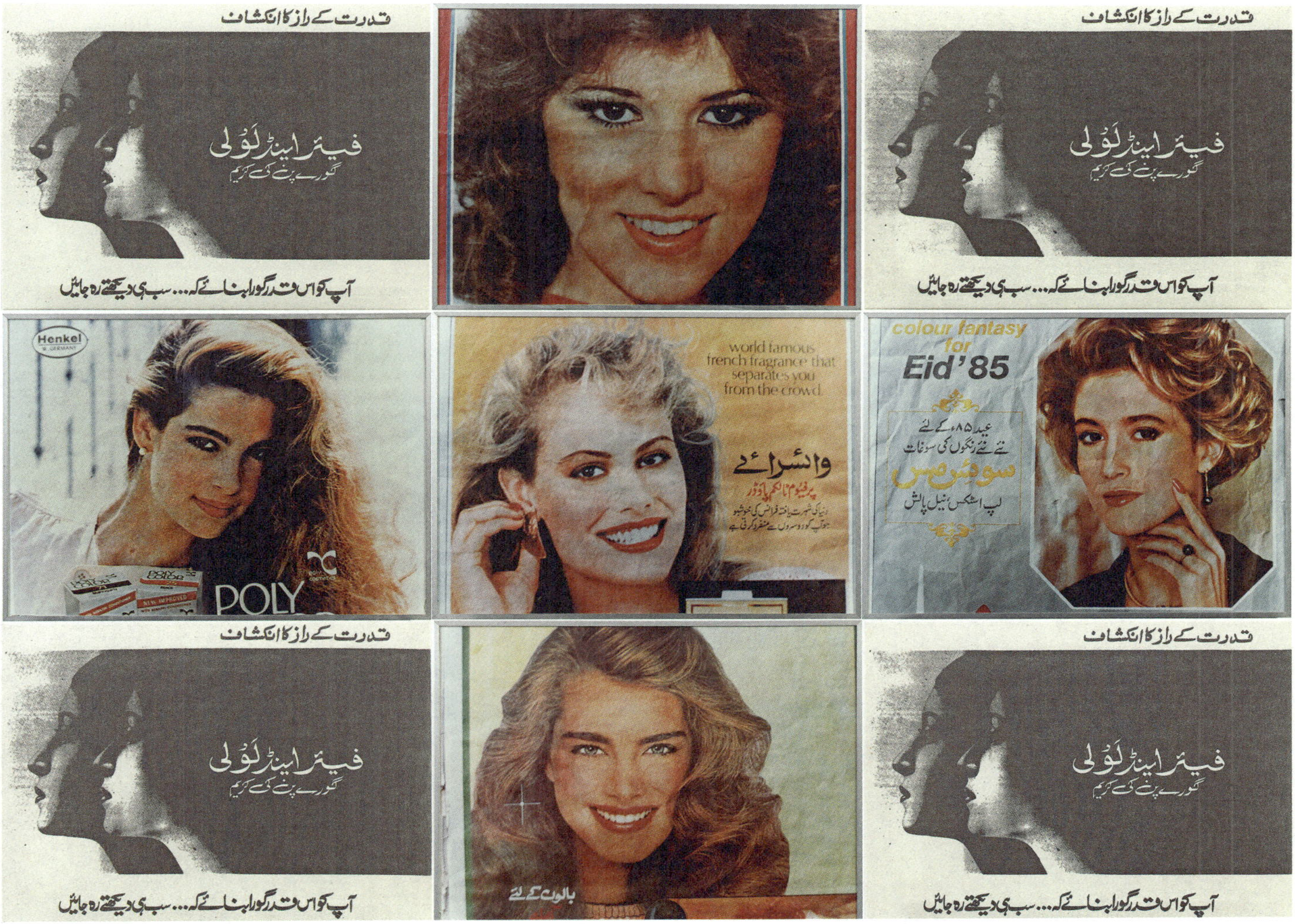

Look Mamma...Macho!, 1983–1986
mixed-media, 153 x 457 x 8 cm
Collection JM Patras / Paris

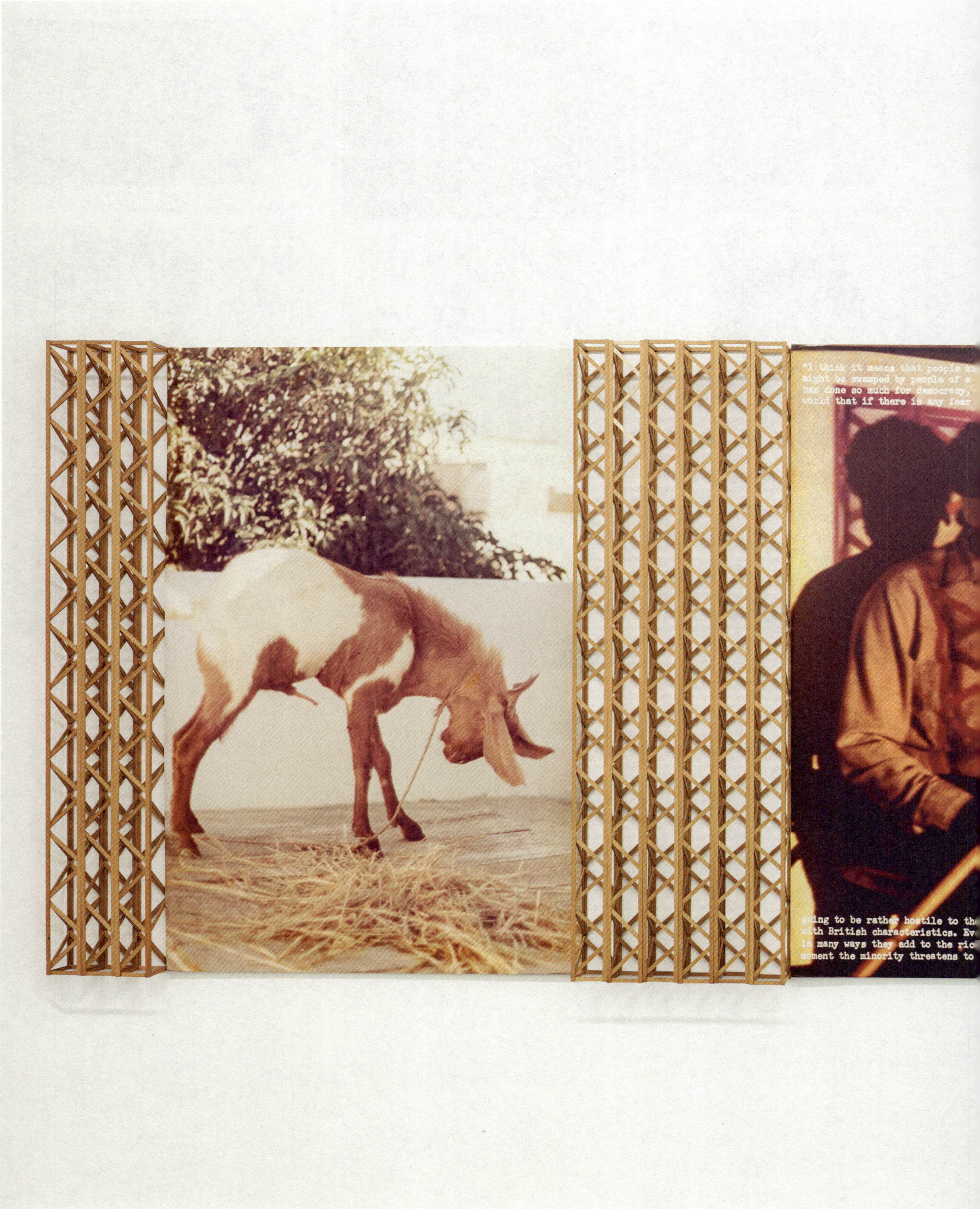

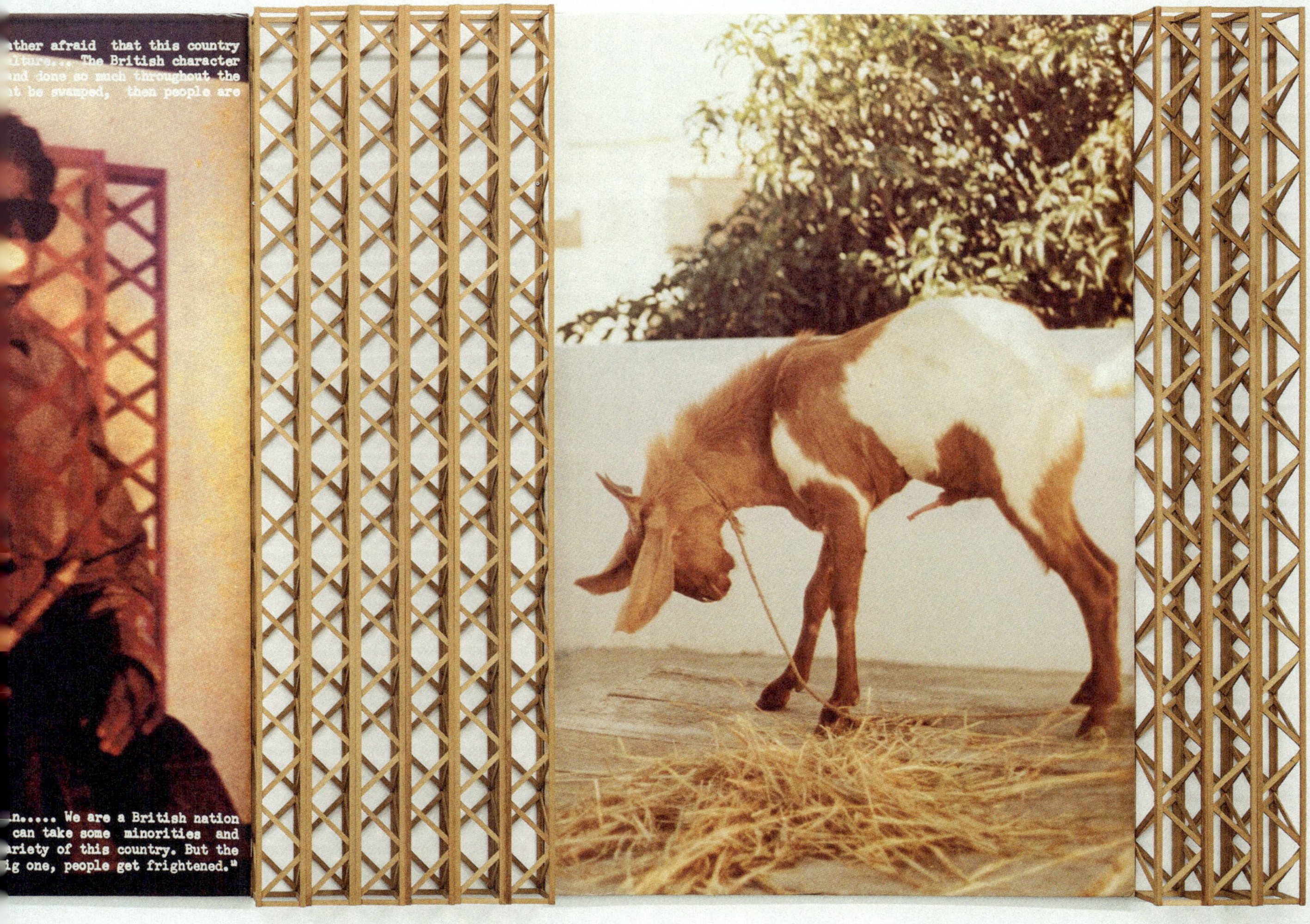
ather afraid that this country
ulture... The British character
and done so much throughout the
t be swamped, then people are
n..... We are a British nation
can take some minorities and
ariety of this country. But the
ig one, people get frightened."

Arctic Circle, 1983–1987 / 2017
wine and beer bottle, dimensions variable

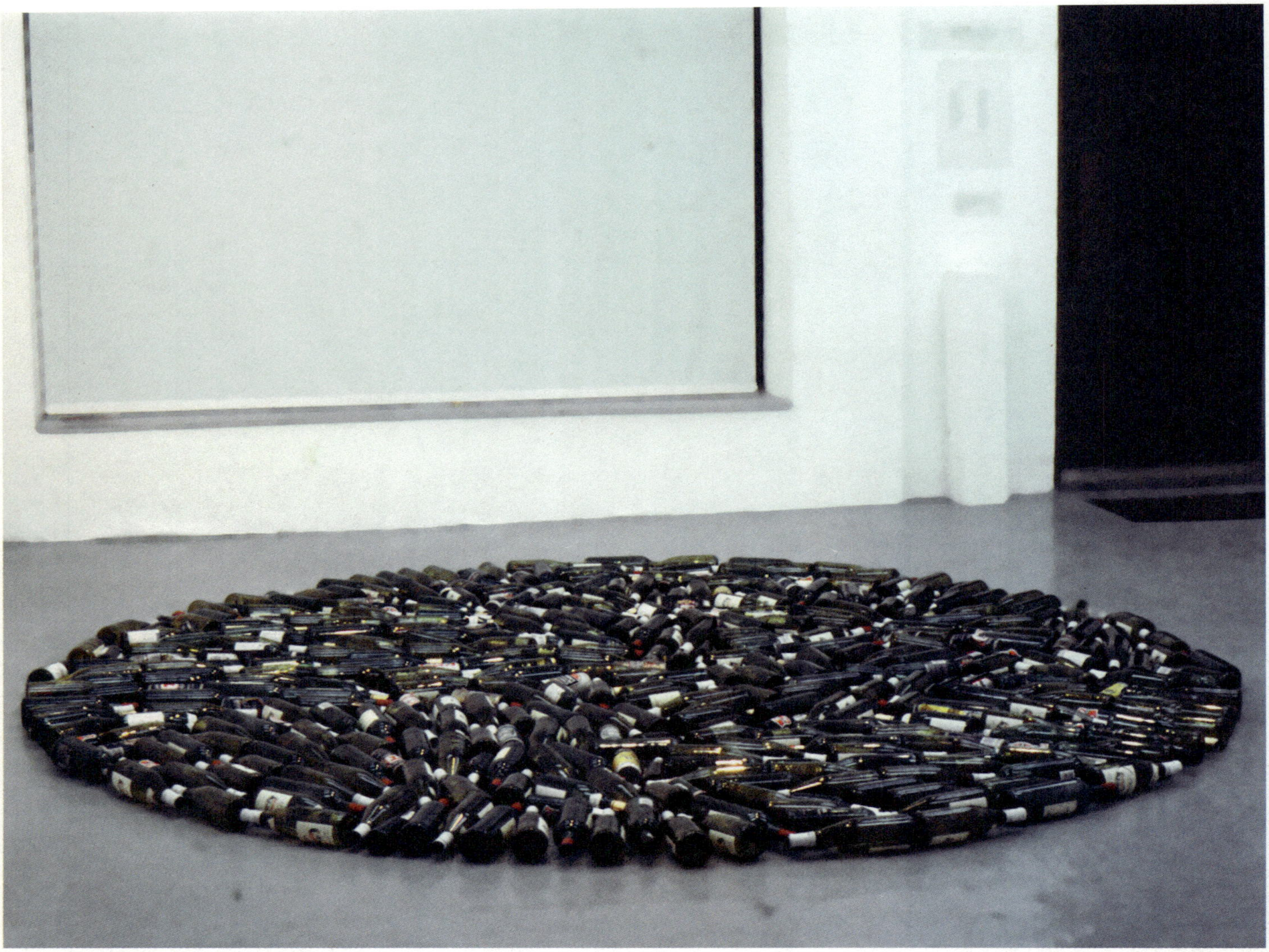

Mon St V, 1985
acrylic on wood, 183 x 224 x 13 cm

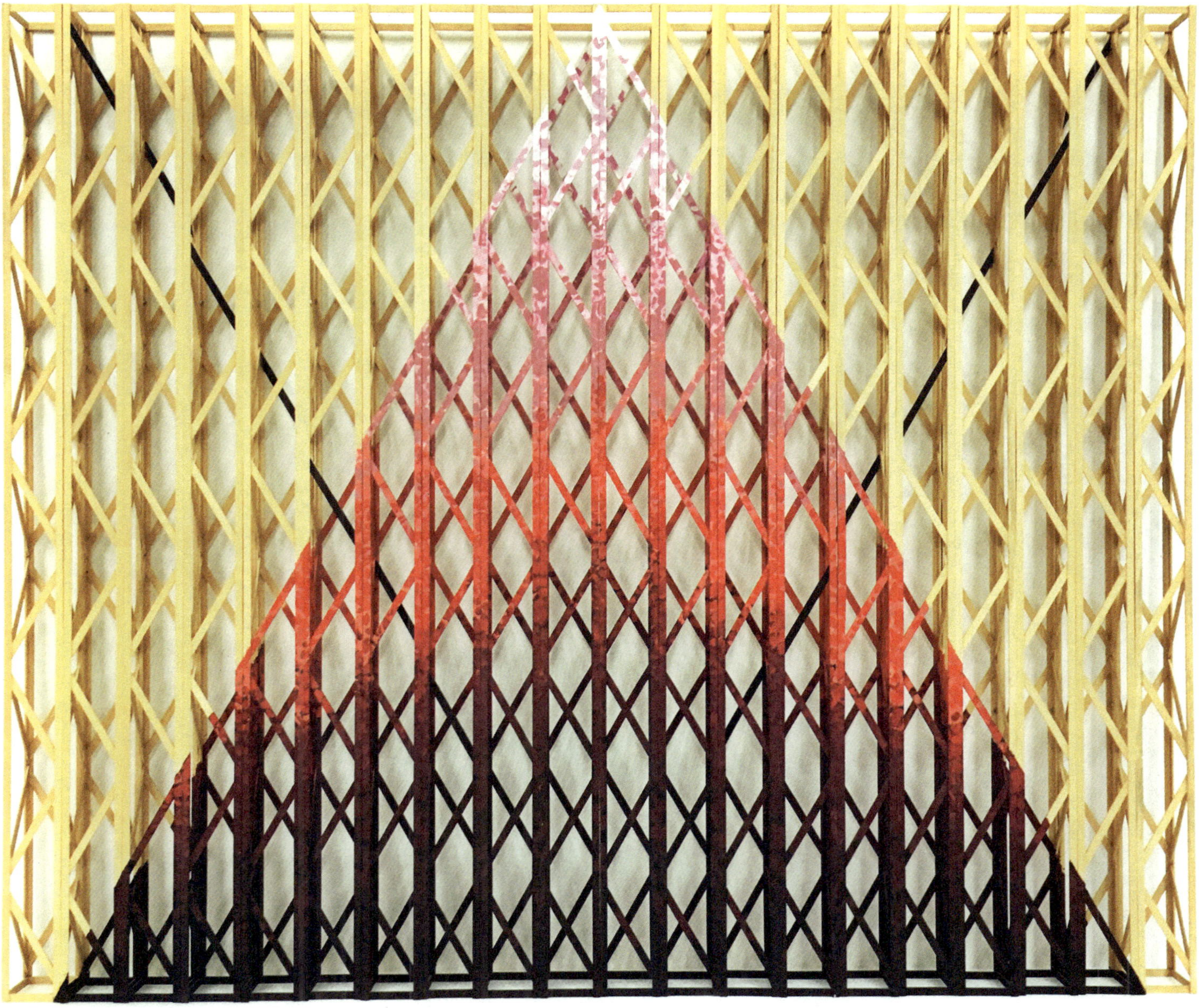

We Always Loved You Darling!, 1986
collage, dimensions unknown

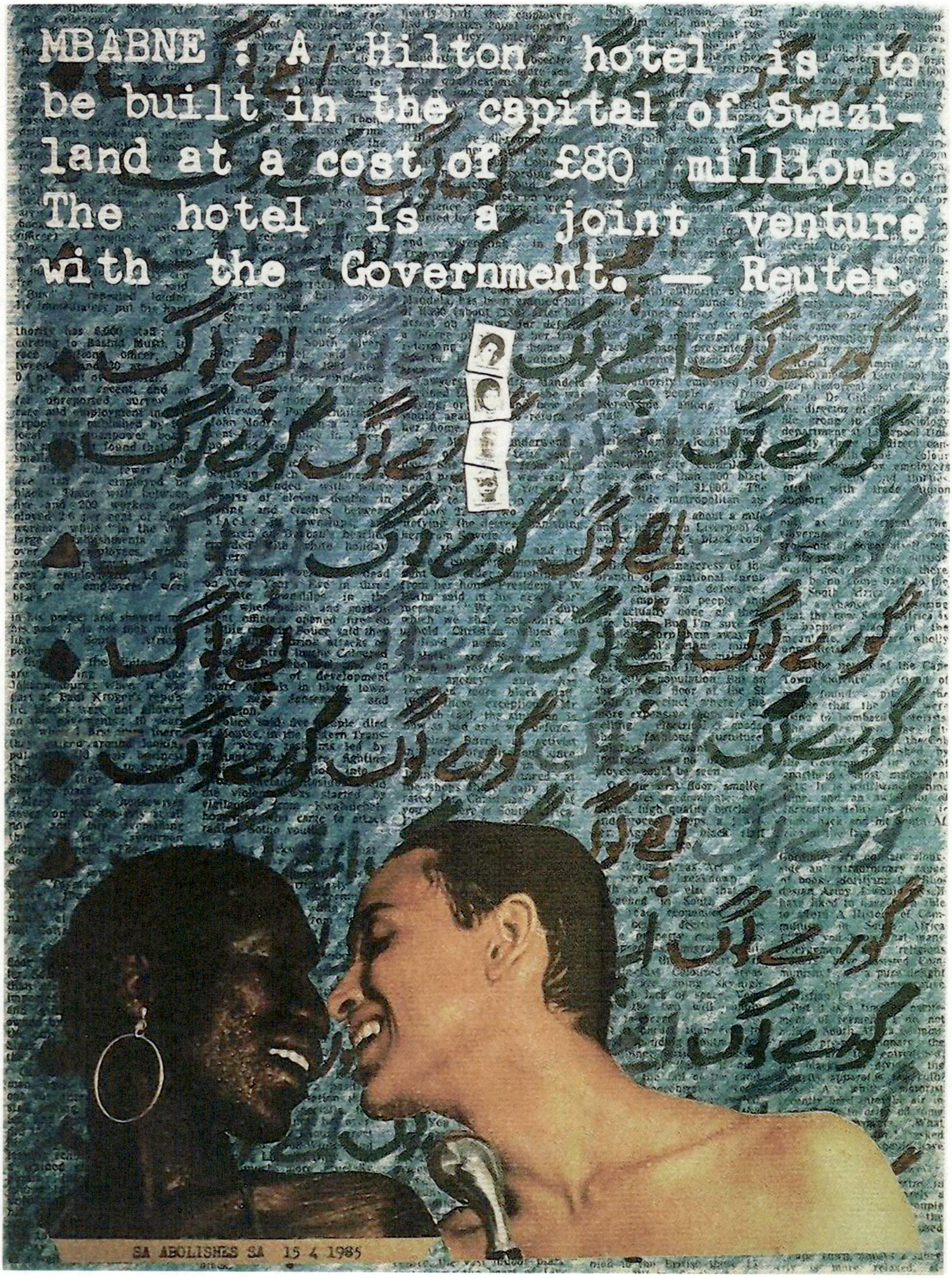

Sonay Ke Chirya (Golden Bird), 1986
mixed-media on wood, 238 x 270 x 14 cm
Fukuoka Asian Art Museum Collection

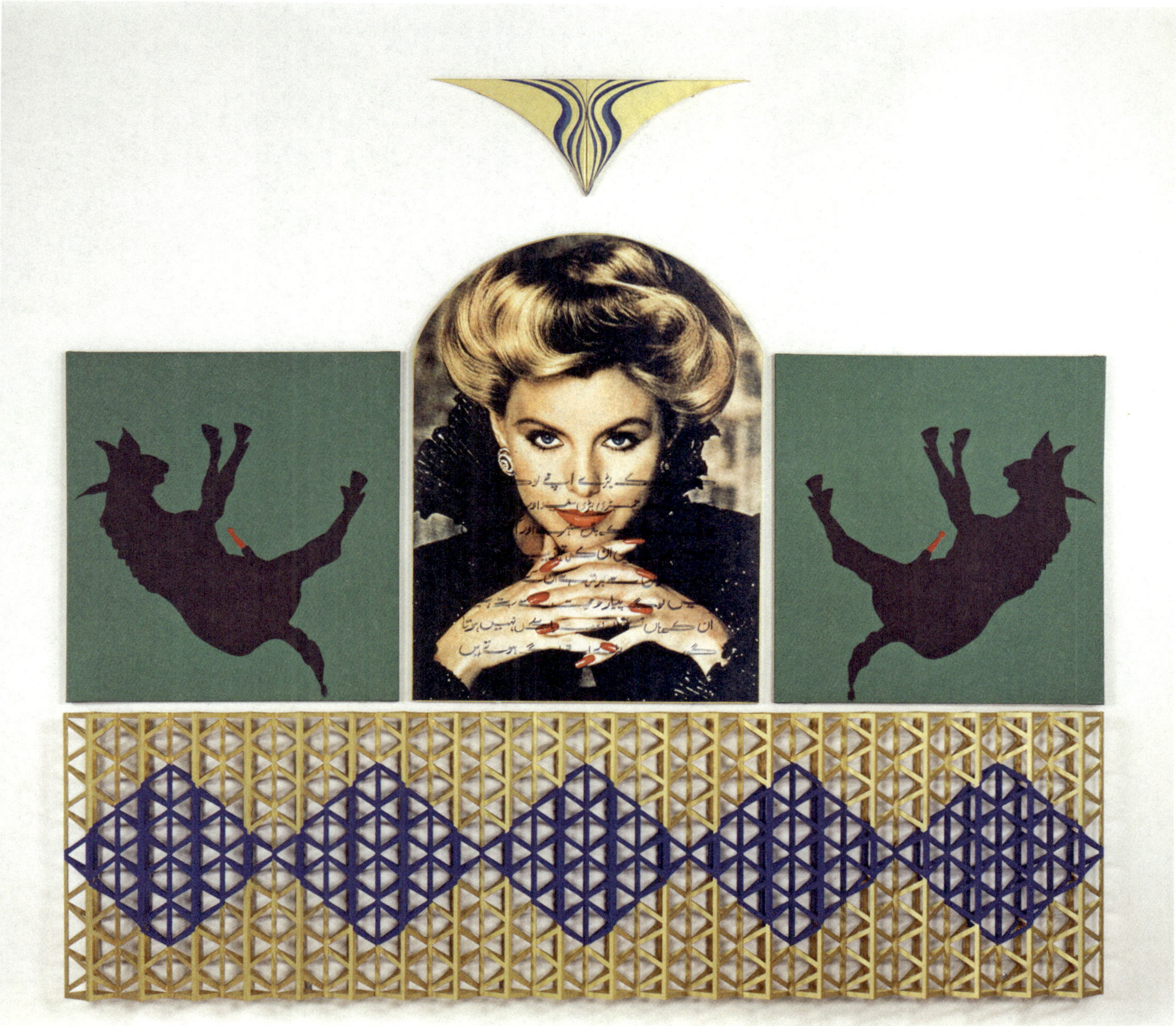

Green Painting I, 1985–1986
photographs, acrylic on plywood, 173 x 226 cm
Arts Council Collection, Southbank Centre, London

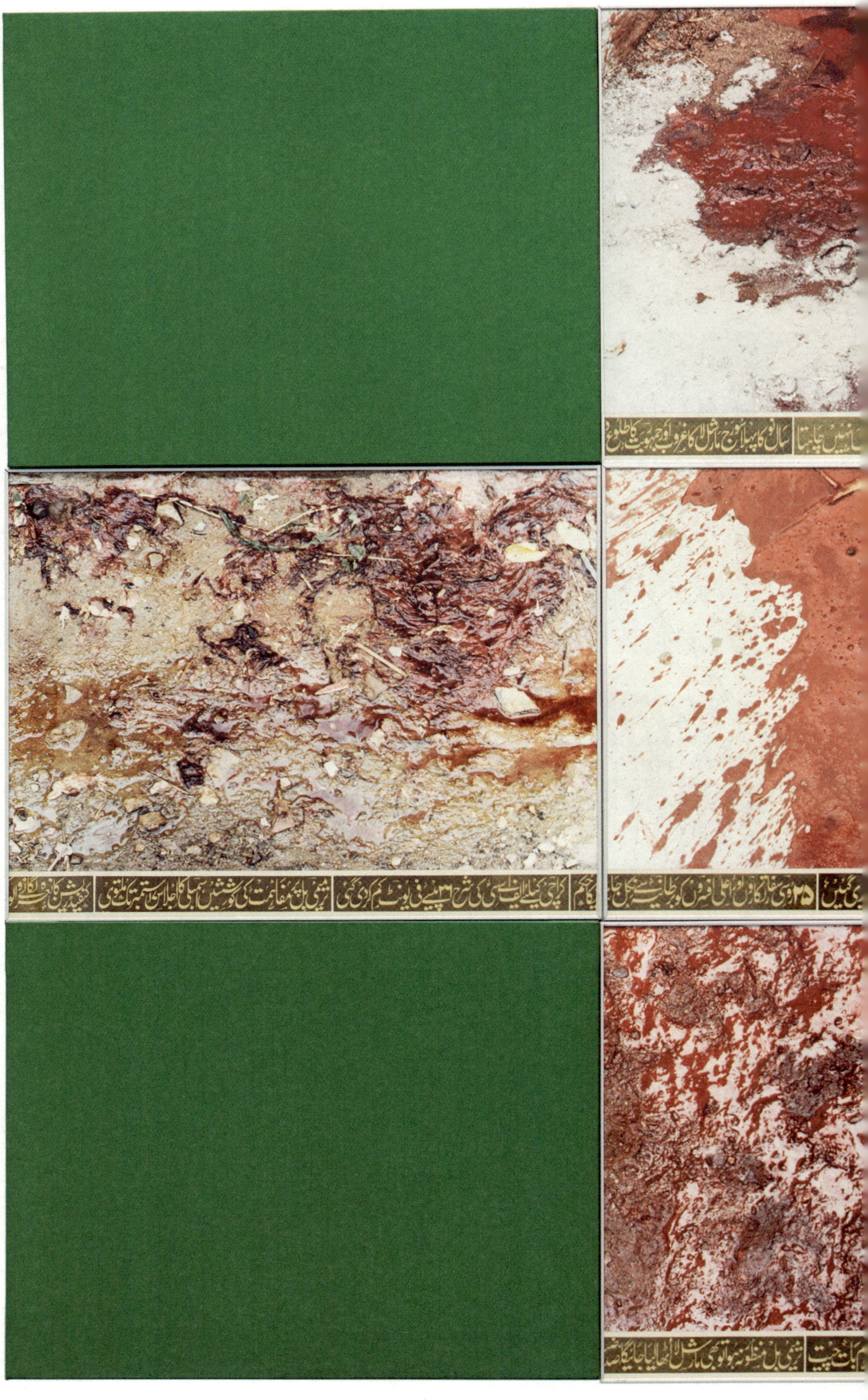

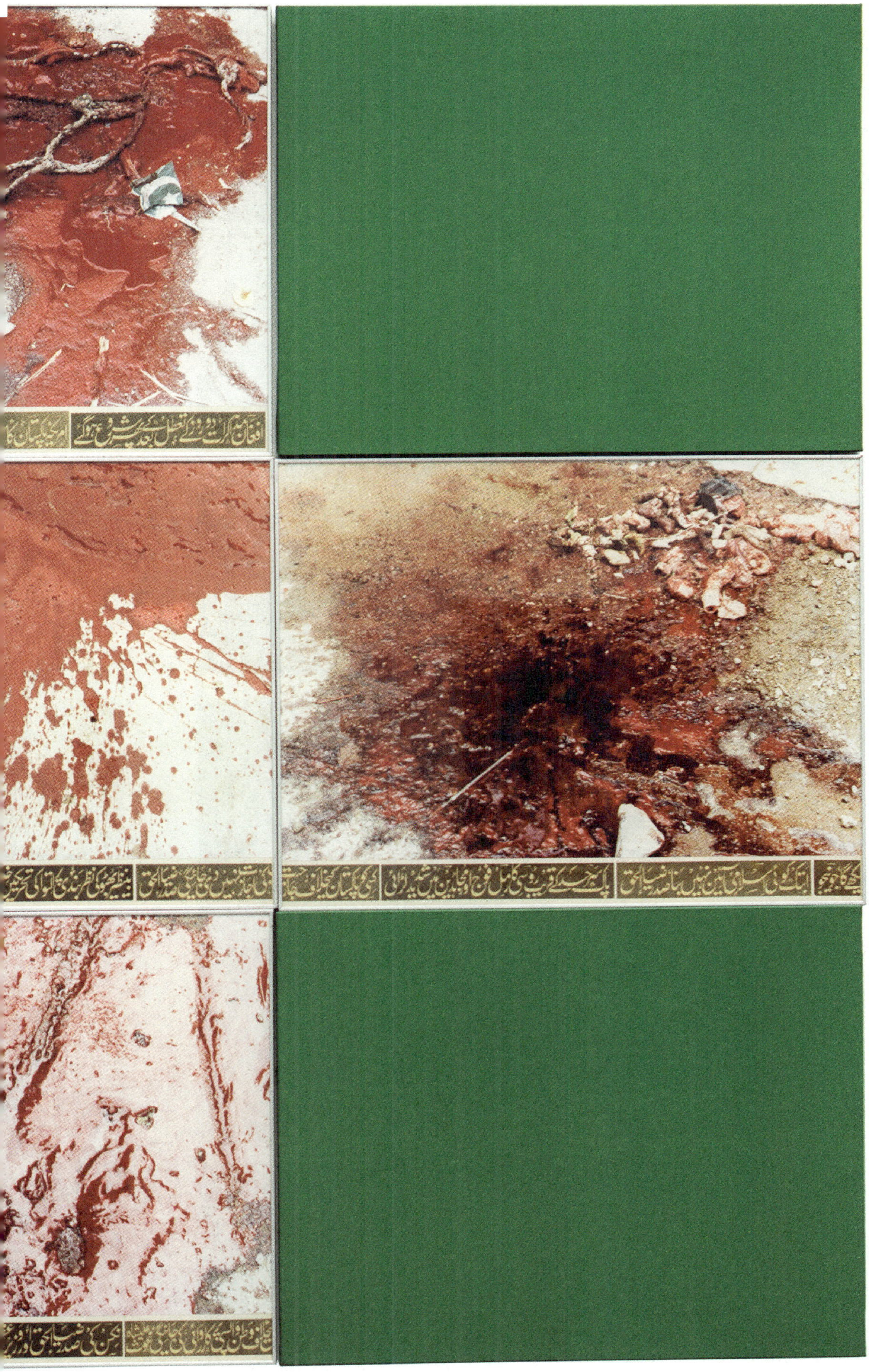

Green Painting II, 1987–1992
photographs, acrylic on plywood, 170 x 226 cm
Fukuoka Asian Art Museum Collection

Green Painting III, 1987–1994
photographs, acrylic on plywood, 168 x 208 cm

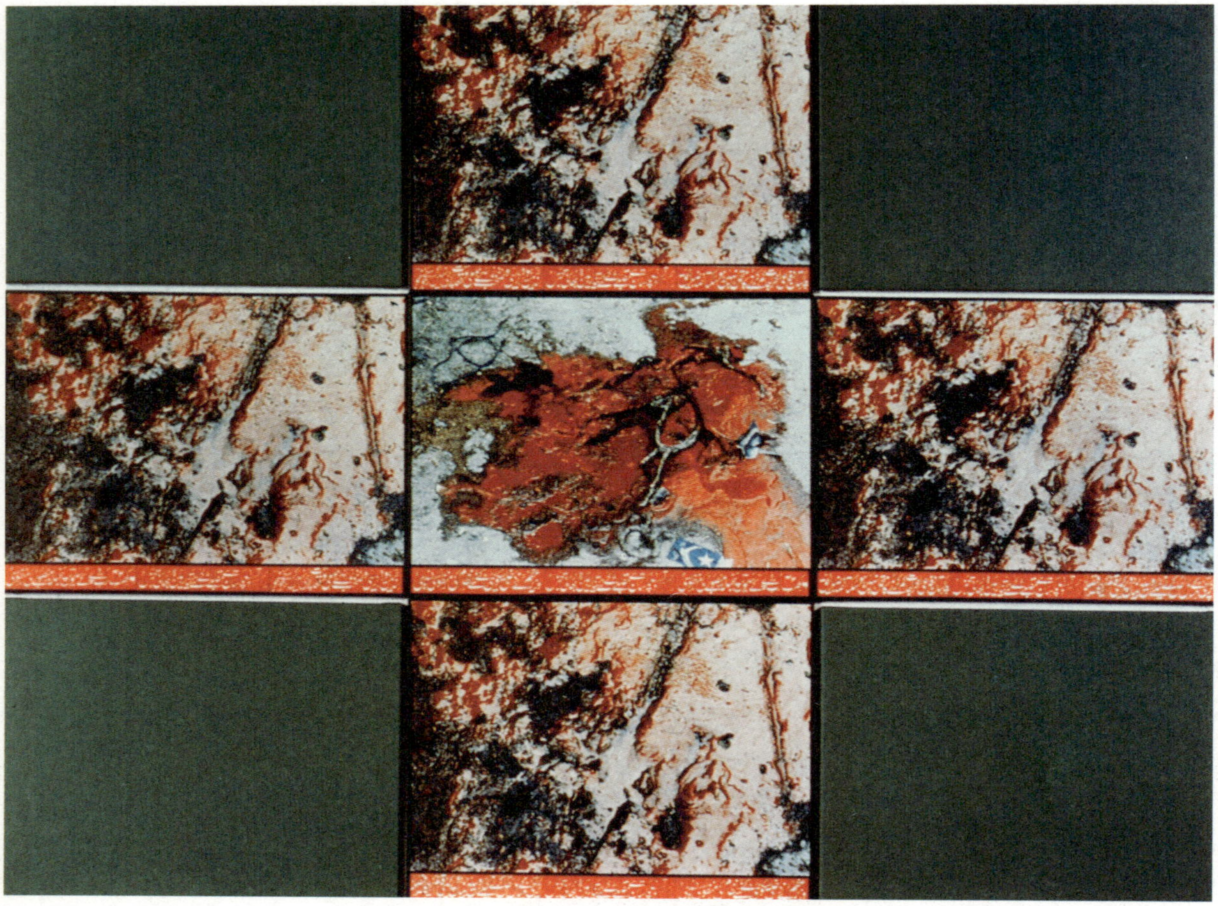

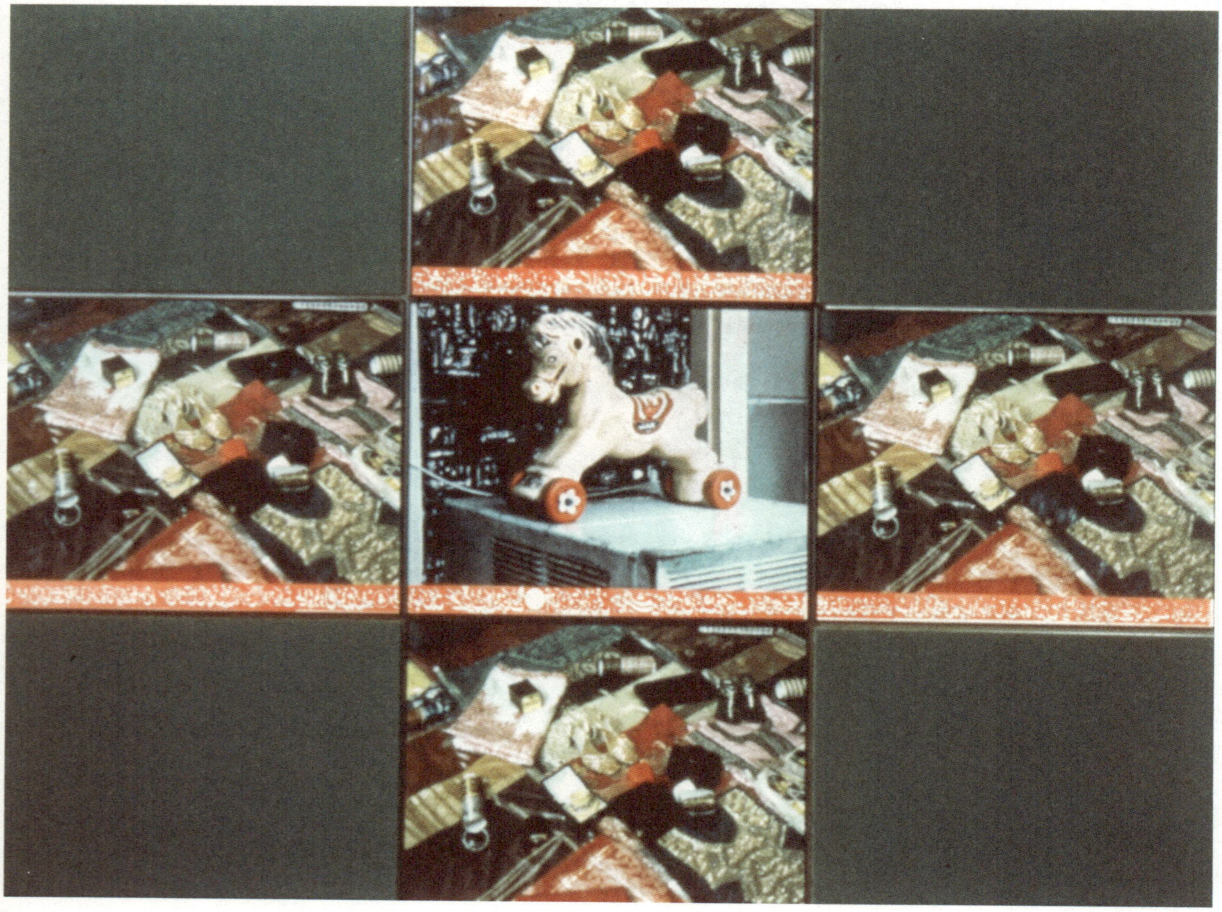

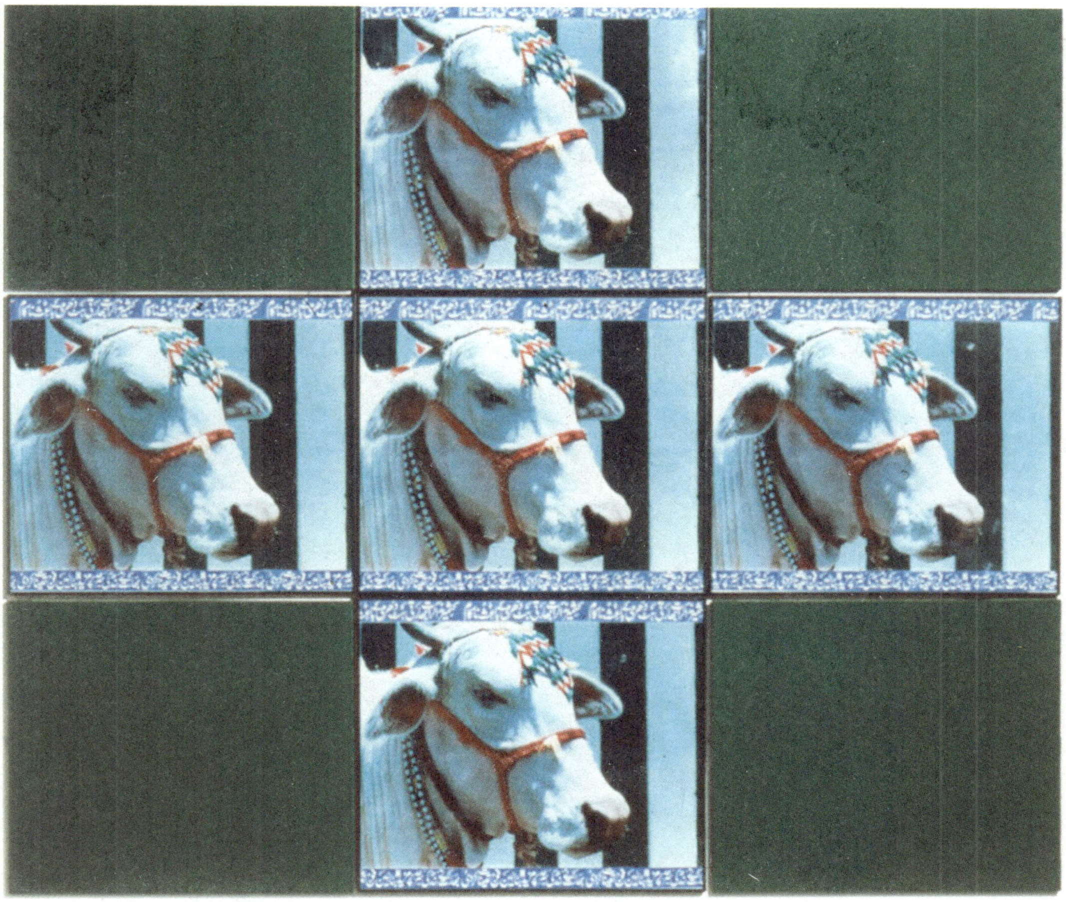

Green Painting IV, 1987–1994
photographs, acrylic on plywood, 175 x 208 cm

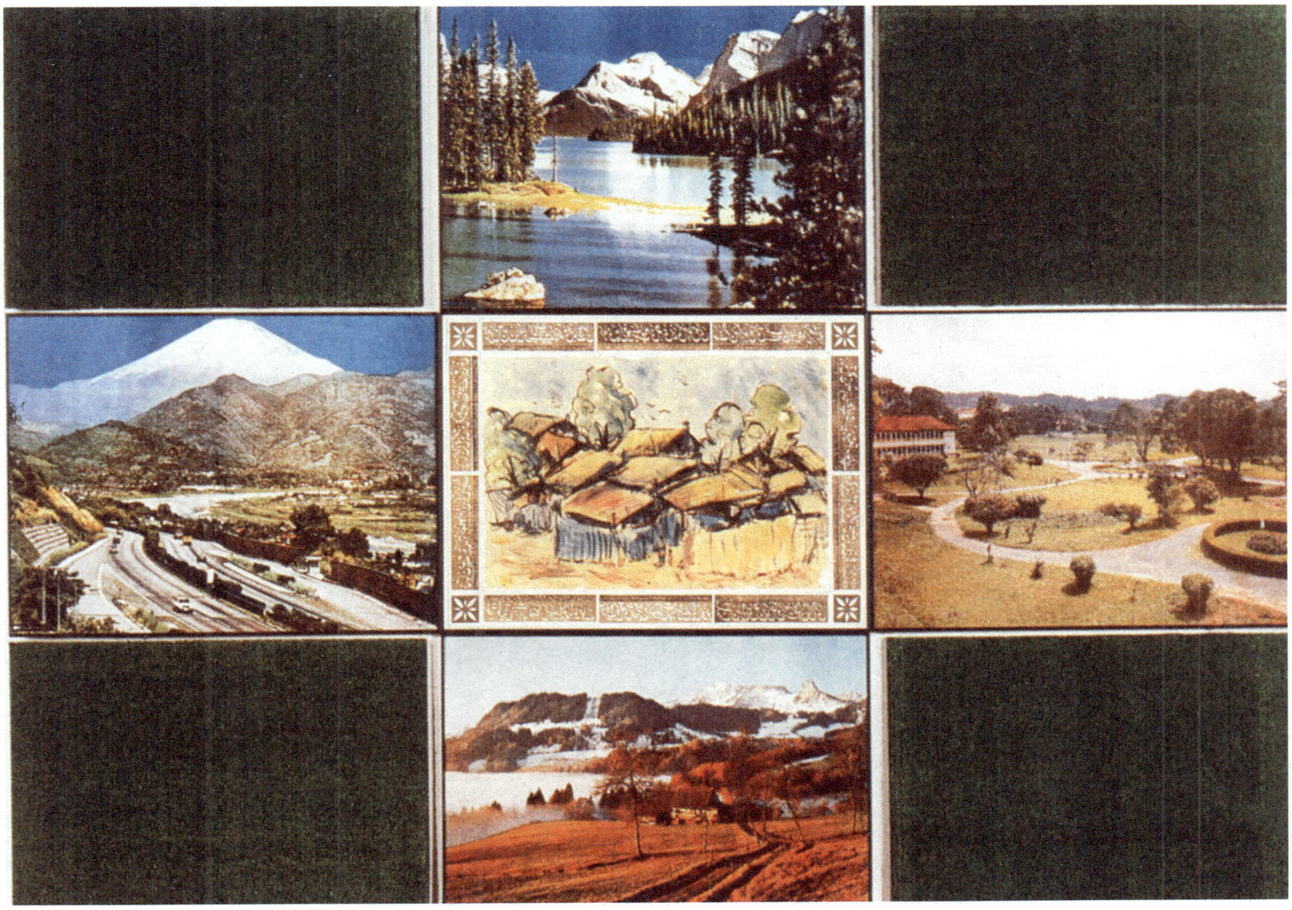

Forever Green, 1987–1994
photographs, watercolour, artificial grass, 206 x 282 cm

Tableau Noir, 1987
photographs, acrylic on plywood, 152 x 229 cm

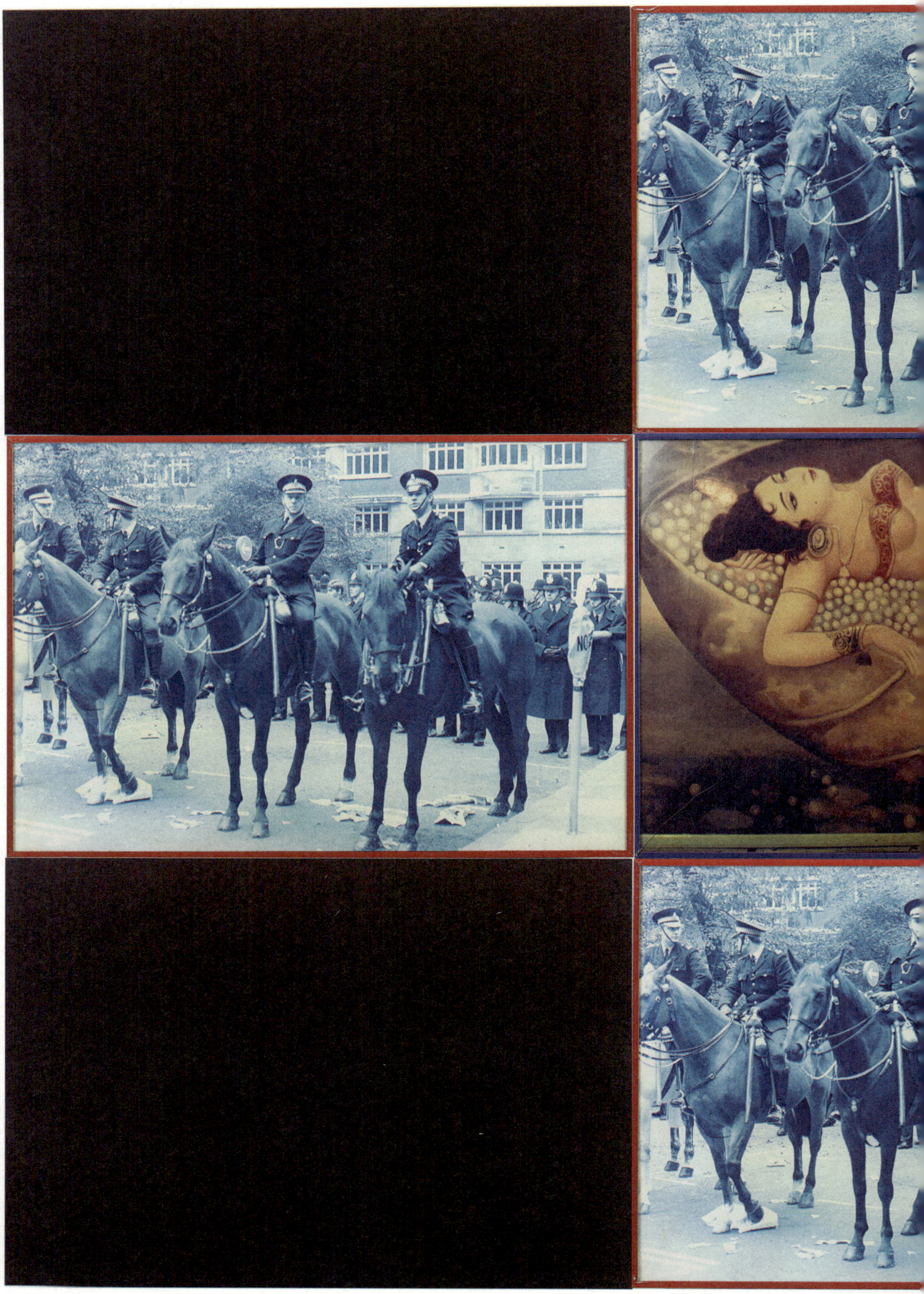

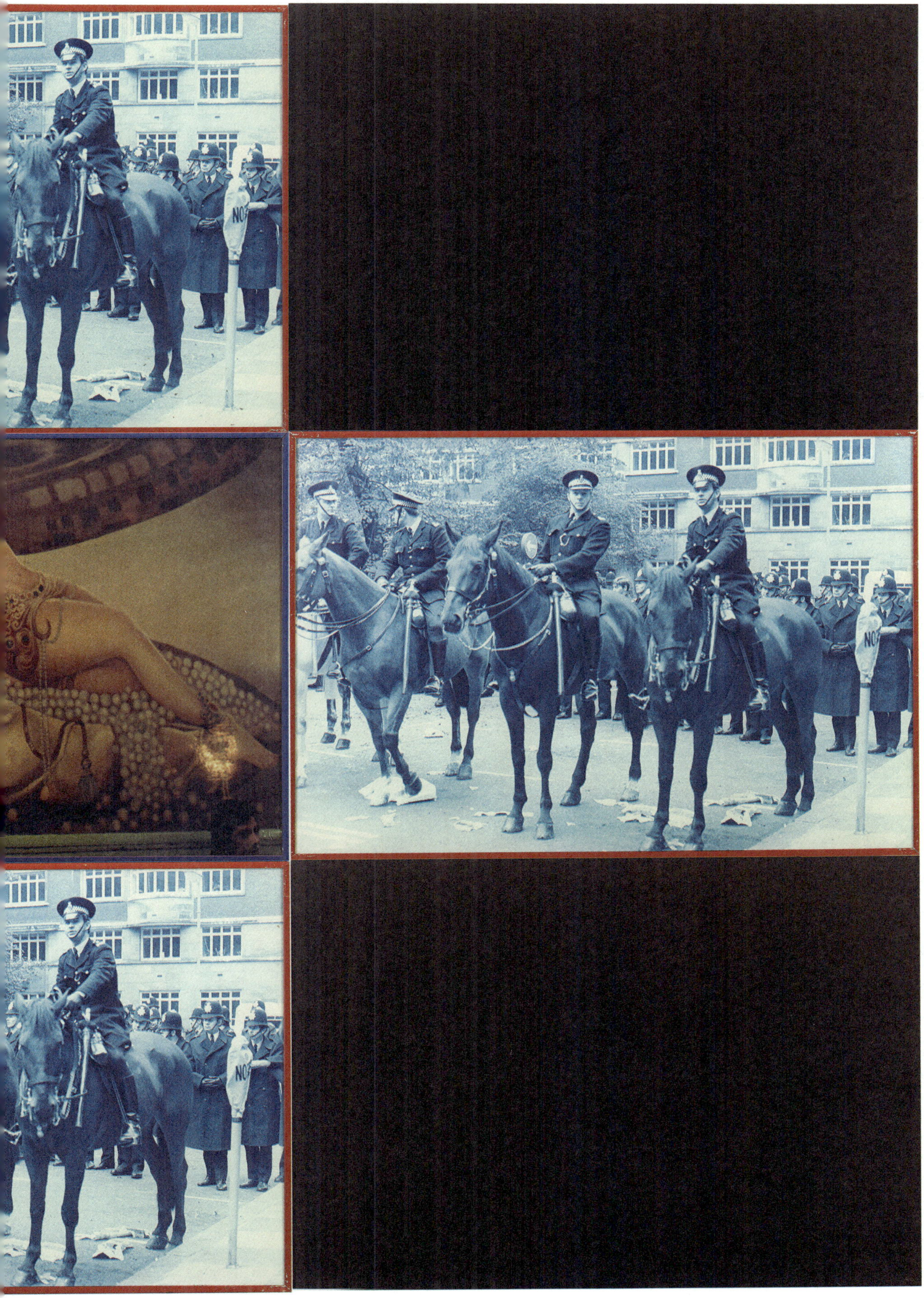

White Stallion, 1987–1991
photographs, acrylic on plywood, 163 x 199 cm
Imperial War Museum

Flowers, 1987–1994
photographs, acrylic on plywood, 152 x 229 cm

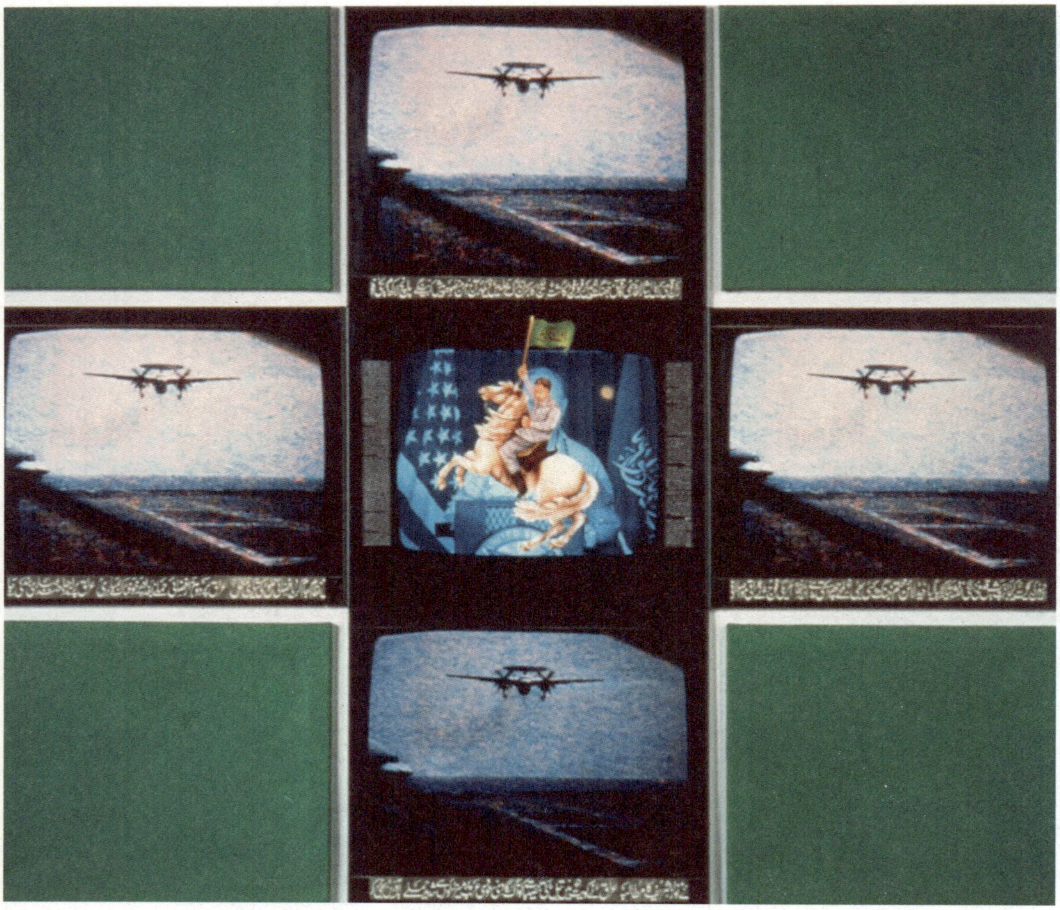

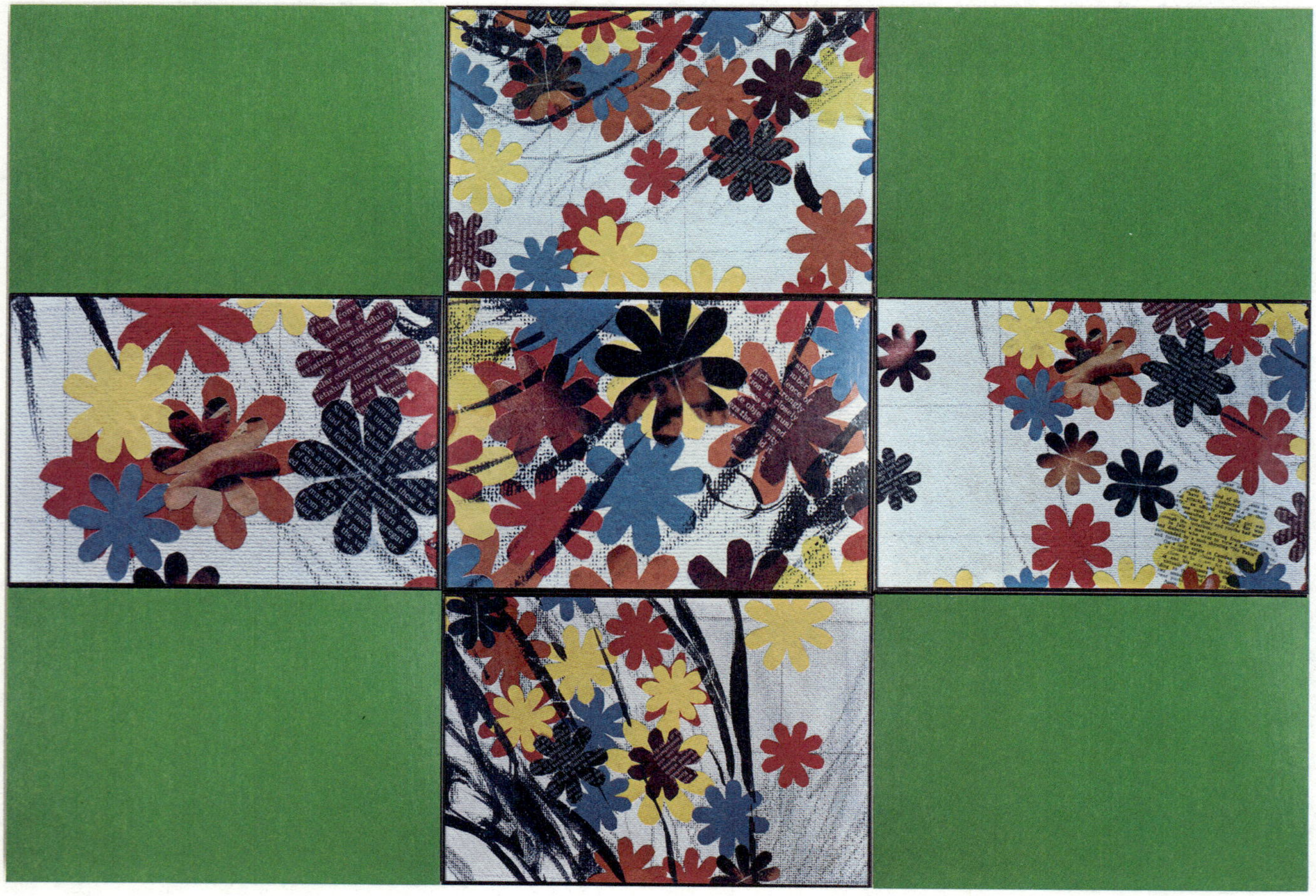

Golden Calf, 1987
photographs, silkscreen on canvas, 152 x 178 cm

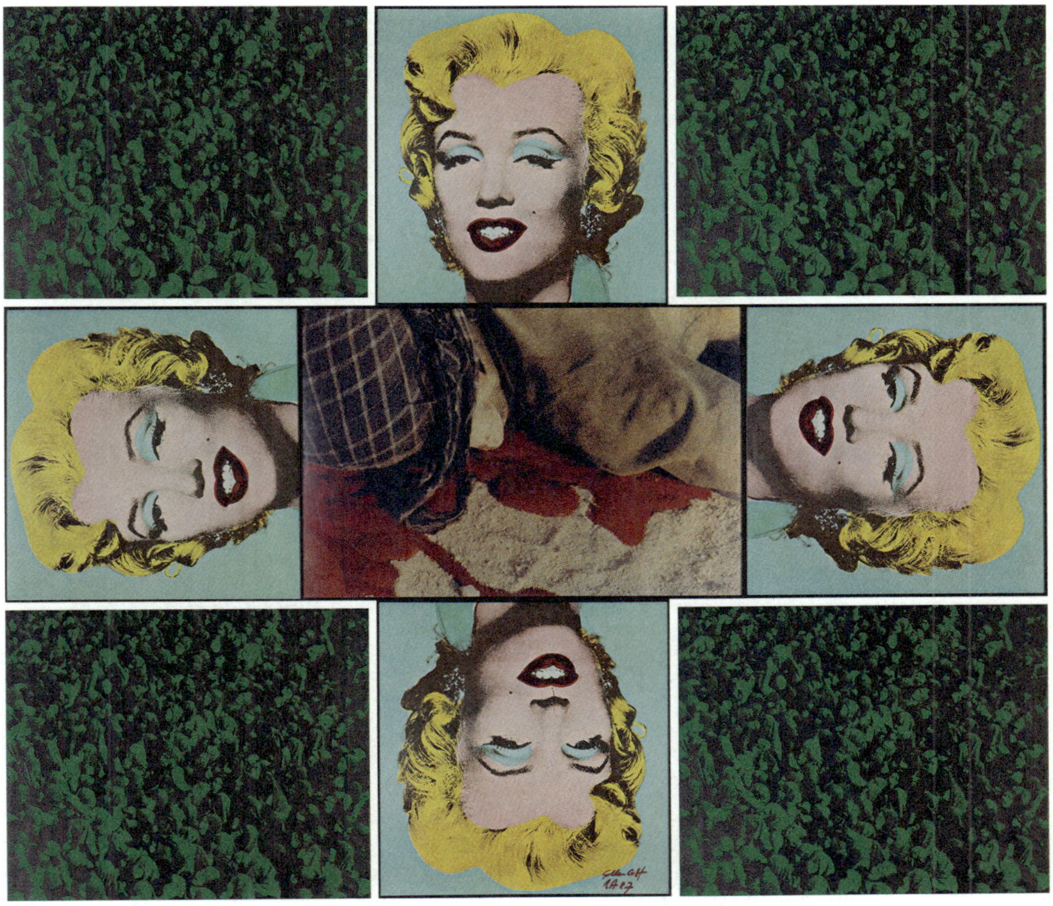

La Grande Jatte, 1987–1994
photographs, acrylic on plywood, 175 x 218 cm

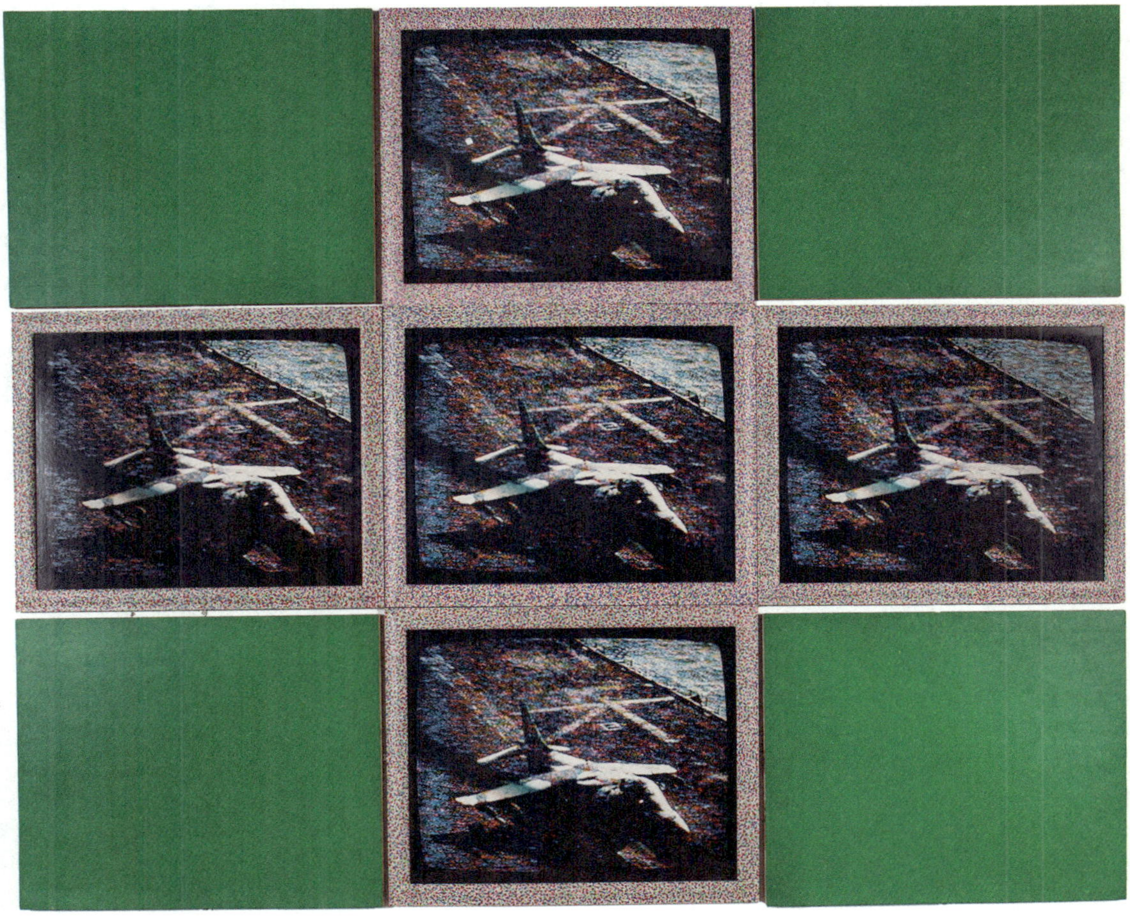

History Painting, 1987–1994
photographs, acrylic on plywood, 185 x 274 cm

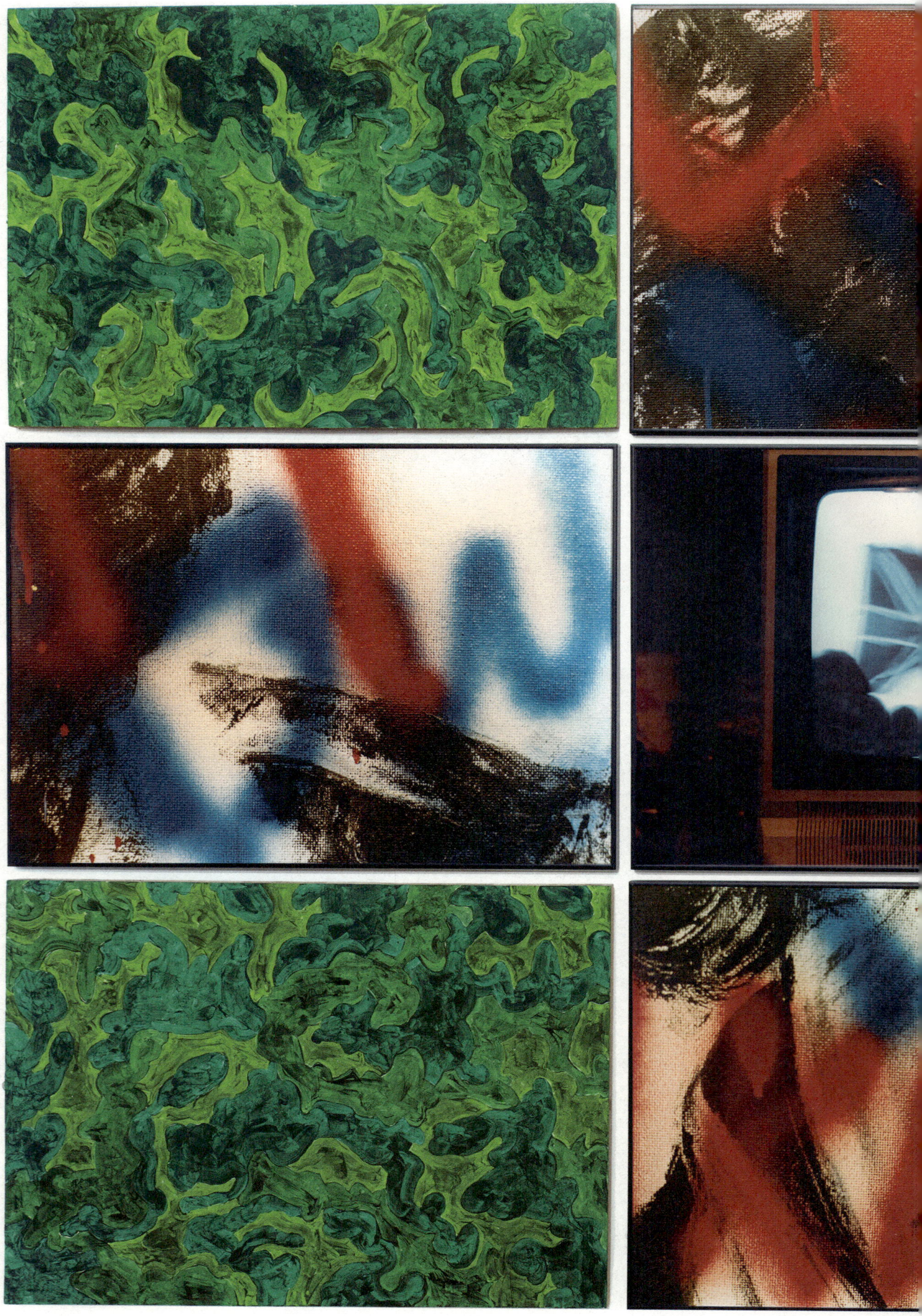

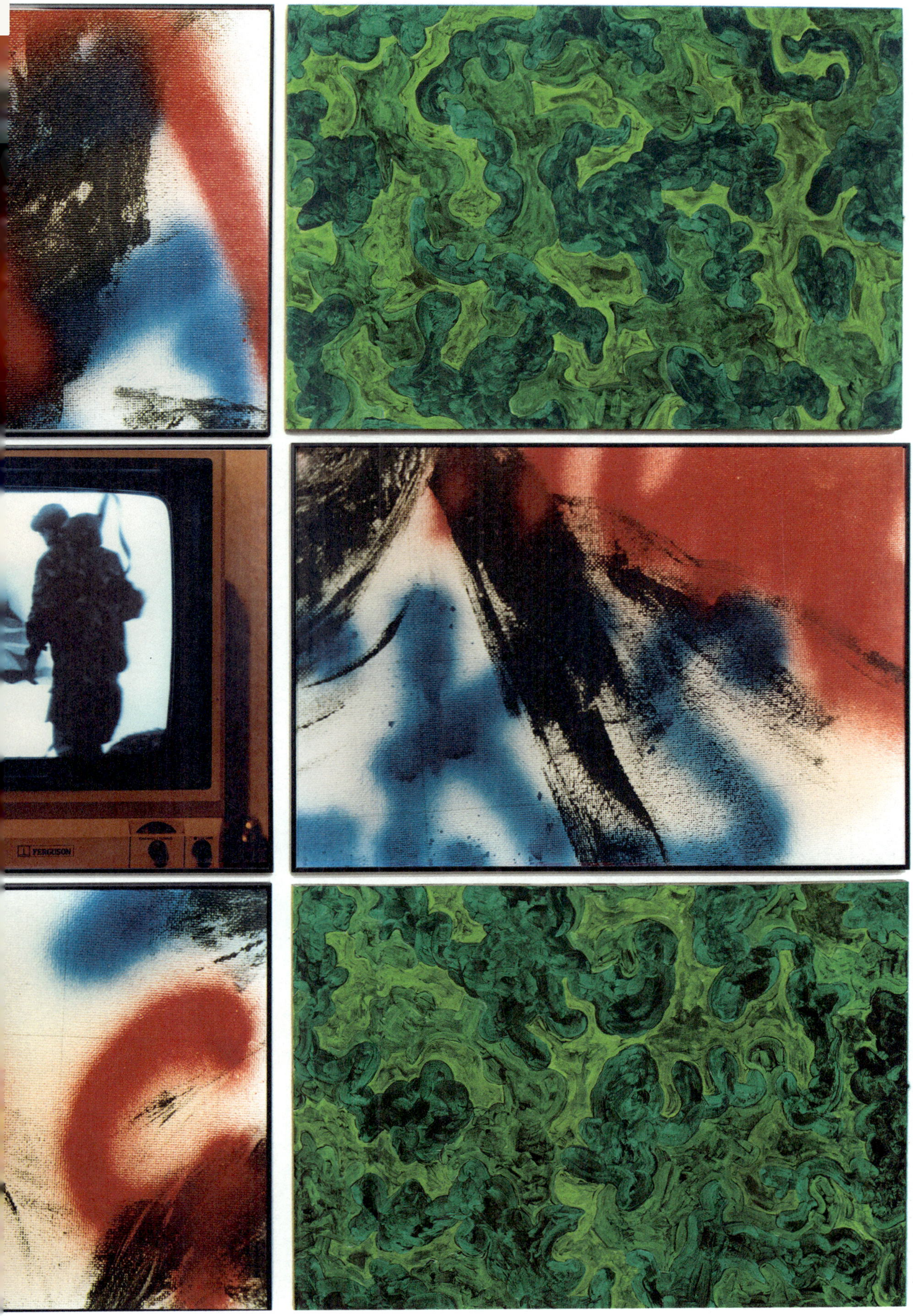
FERGUSON

Jouissance, 1987–1994
photographs, acrylic on plywood, 185 x 277 cm

The End of His Days, 1987–1994
cotton bedspreads, acrylic on plywood, TV set,
130 x 155 cm

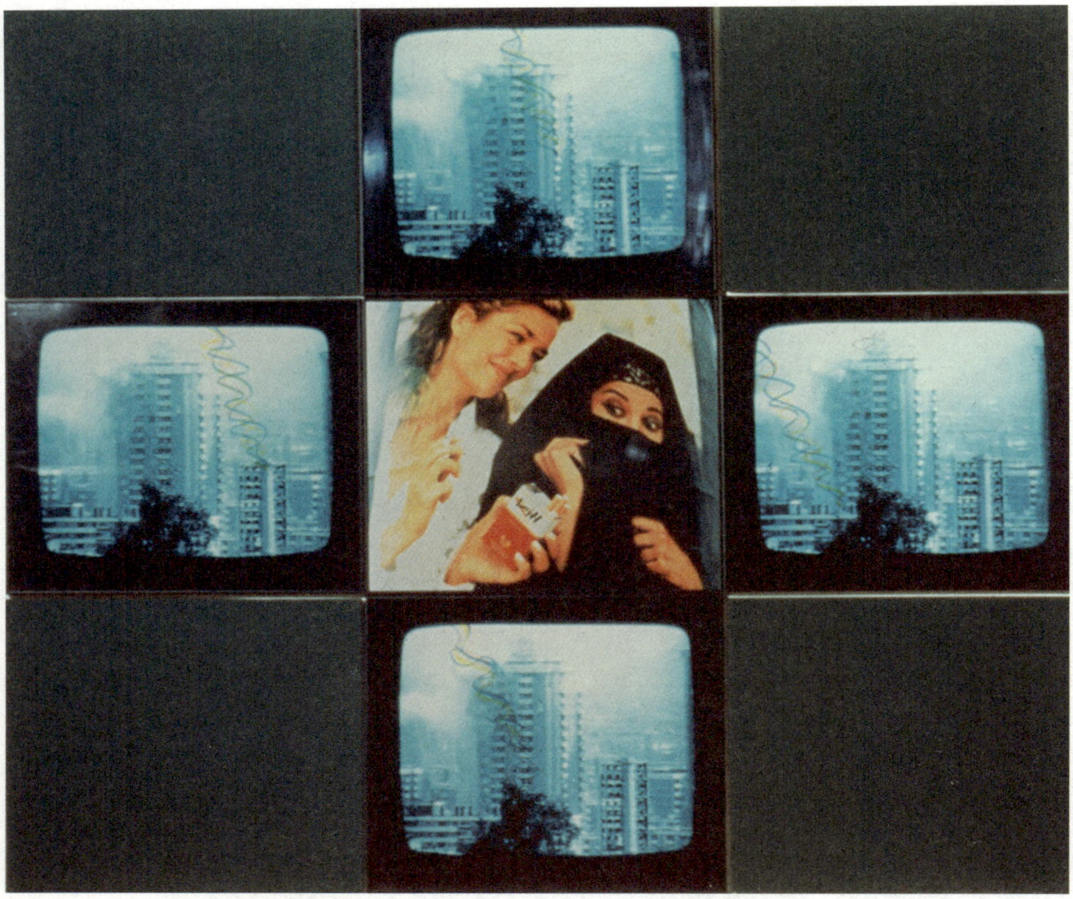

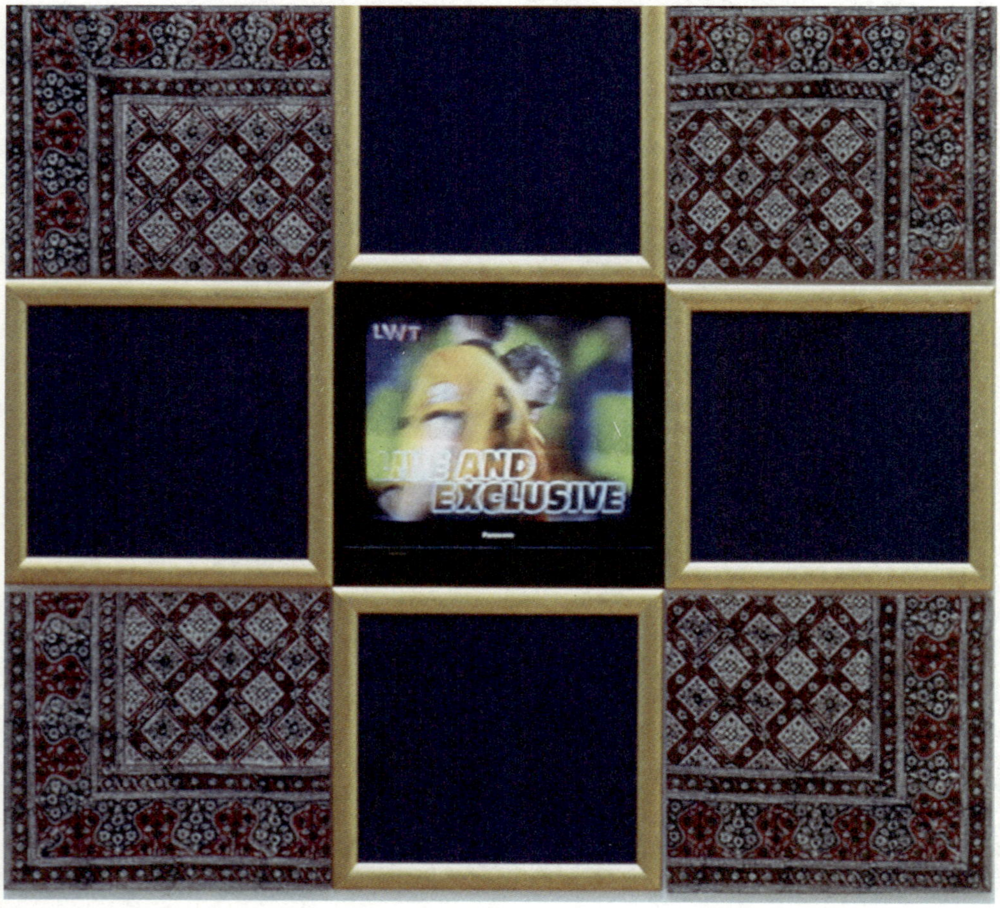

Oh Dear, Oh Dear What A Mess You Have Made!, 1987–1994
emulsion and acrylic on plywood and cardboard
185 x 277 cm

Hallelujah, 1987–1994
photographs, acrylic on plywood, 193 x 226 cm

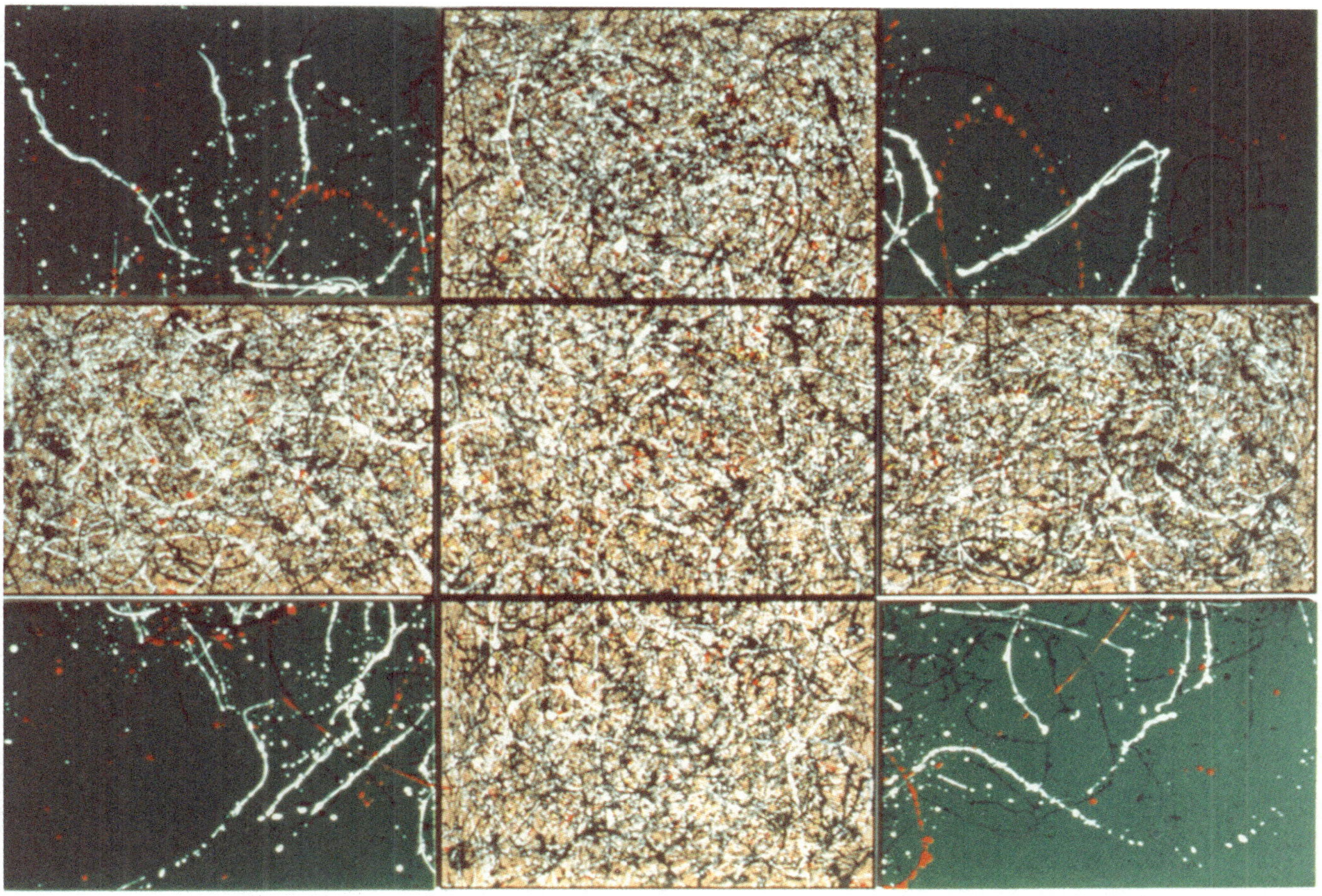

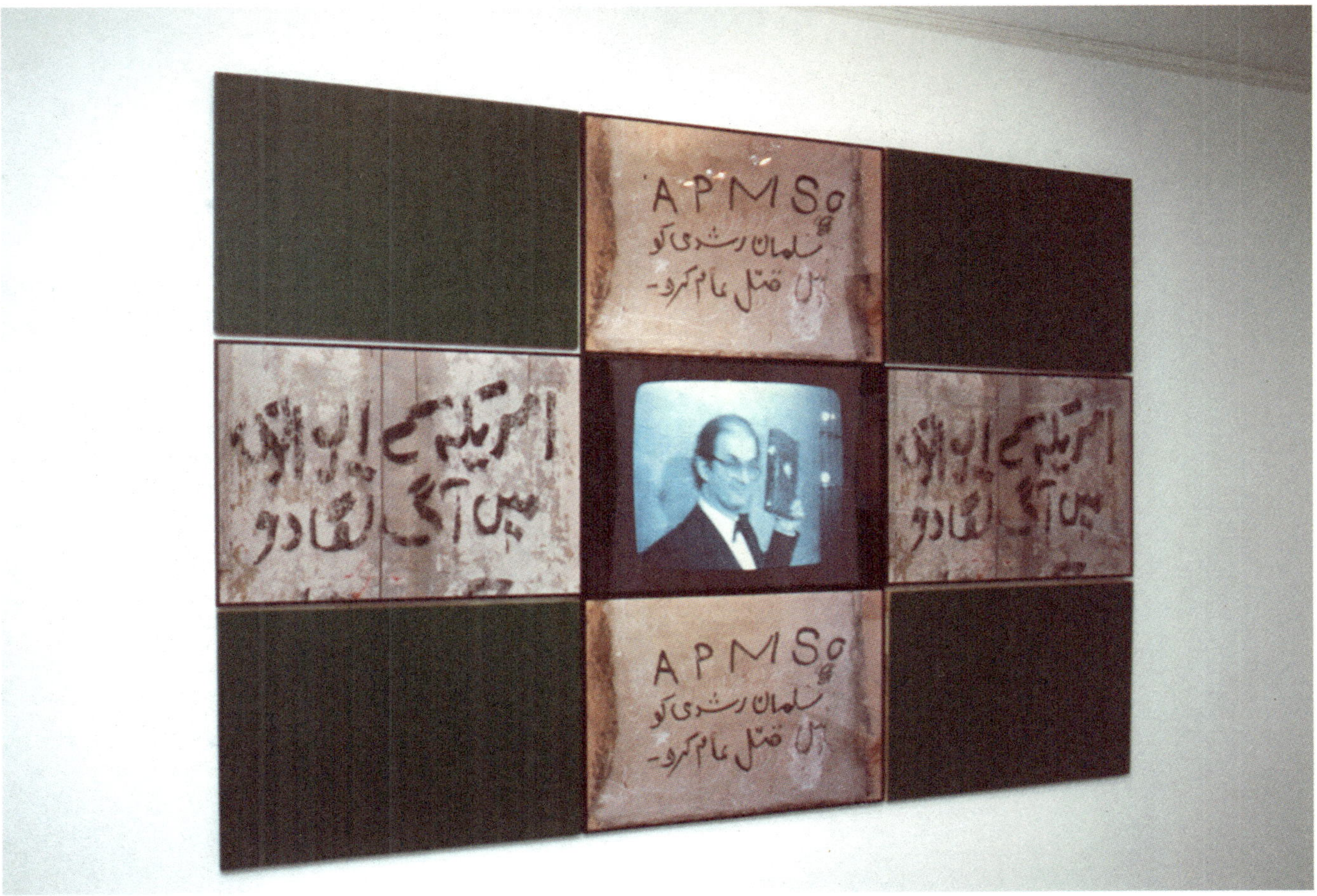

Bismullah, 1988
photographs, acrylic on canvas, 155 x 230 cm
Tate: Purchased 1995

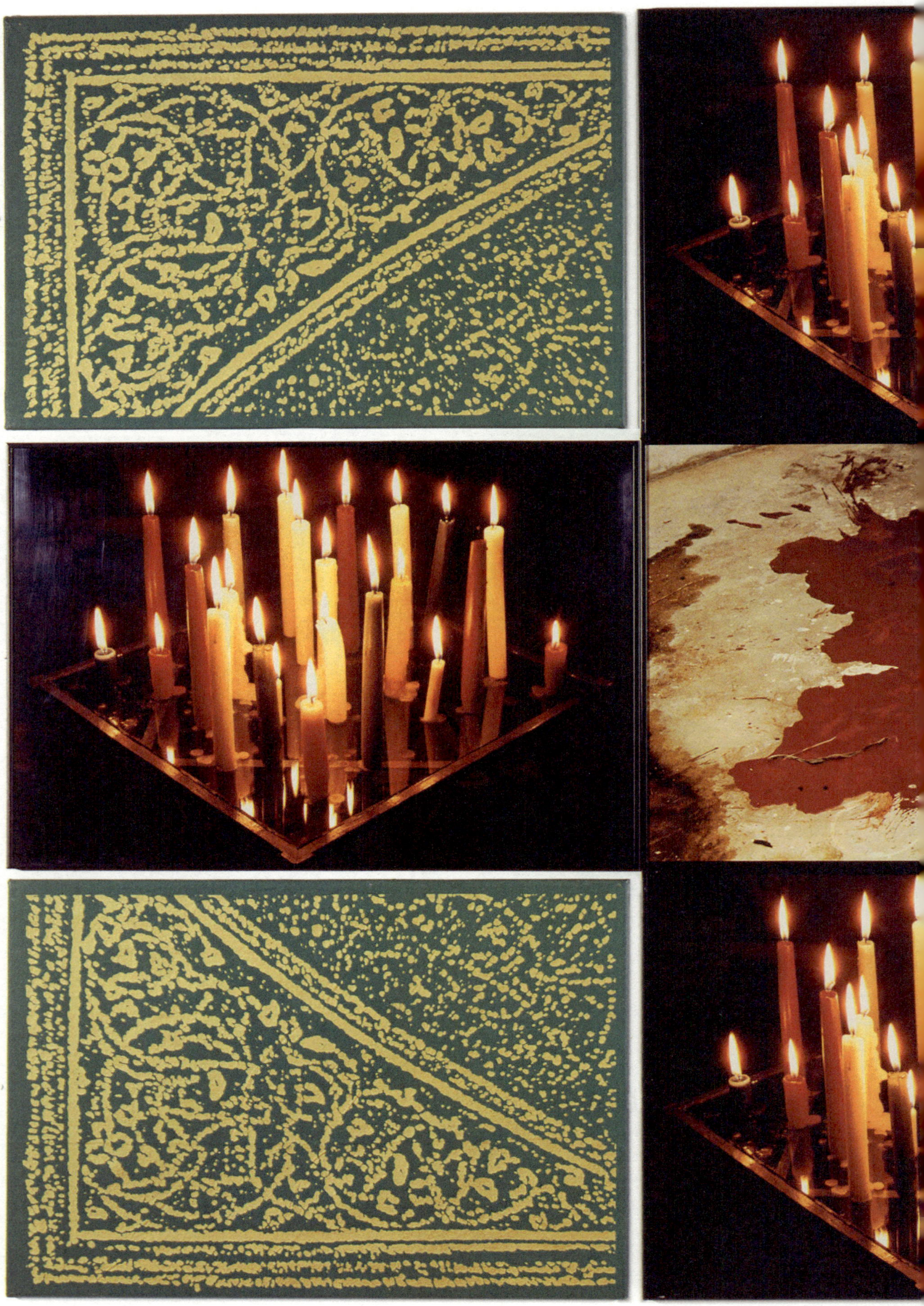

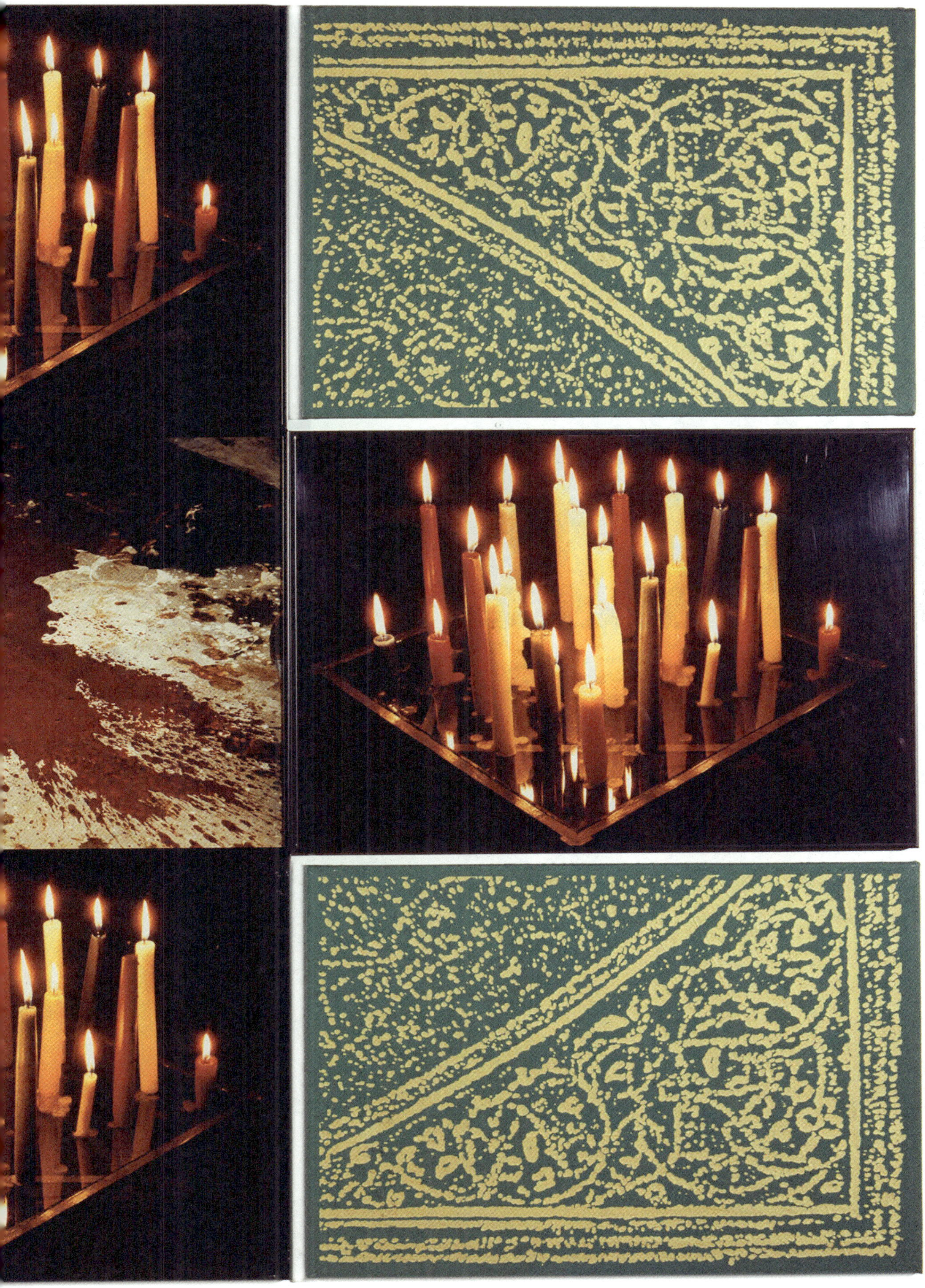

Sheesh Mahal (Place of Glass), 1989
installation at Centre Pompidou, Paris
dimensions unknown

Garden of Love, 1990
scaffolding installation at Gateshead, UK
dimensions unknown

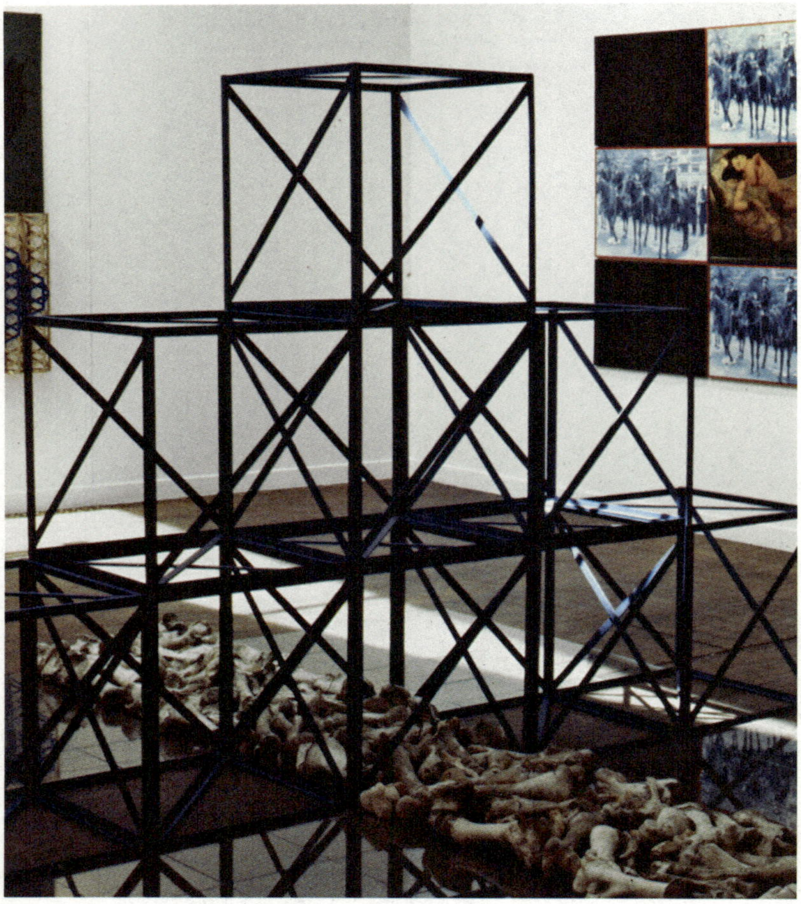

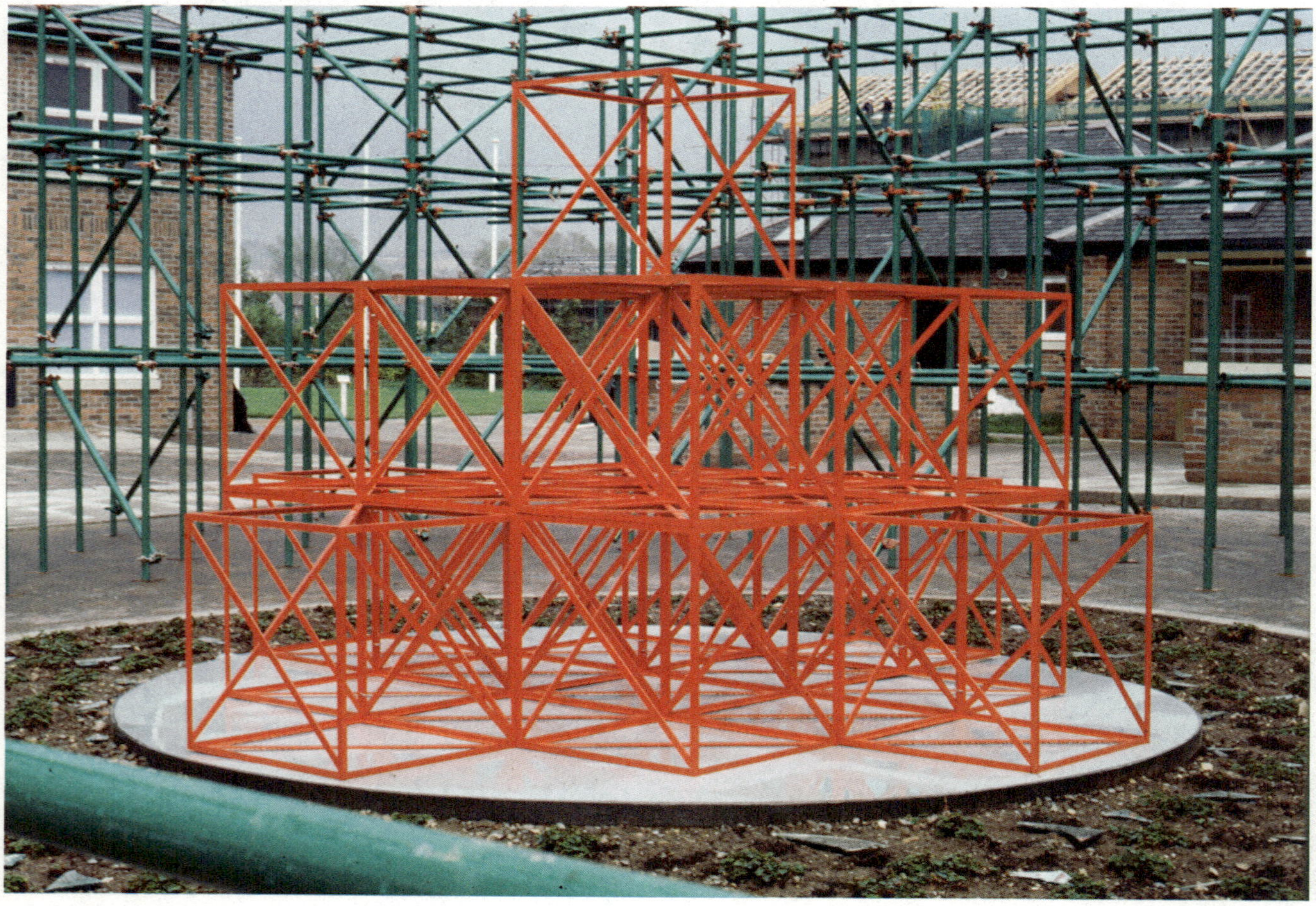

The Golden Verses, 1990
a series of billboards
in association with Artangel Trust, London
305 x 633 cm each

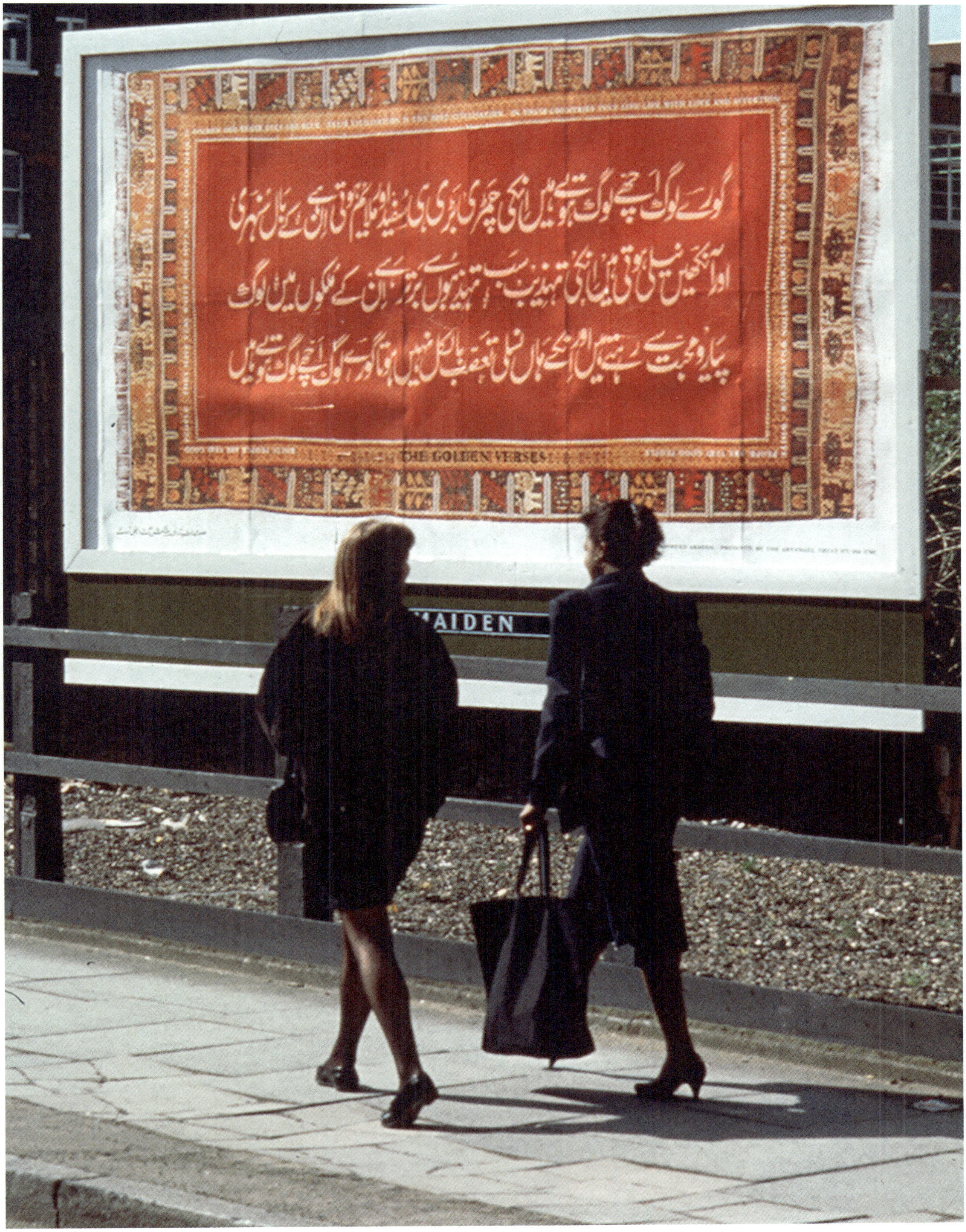

What's It All About, Bongo?, 1991
installation at Central Space, London
dimensions unknown

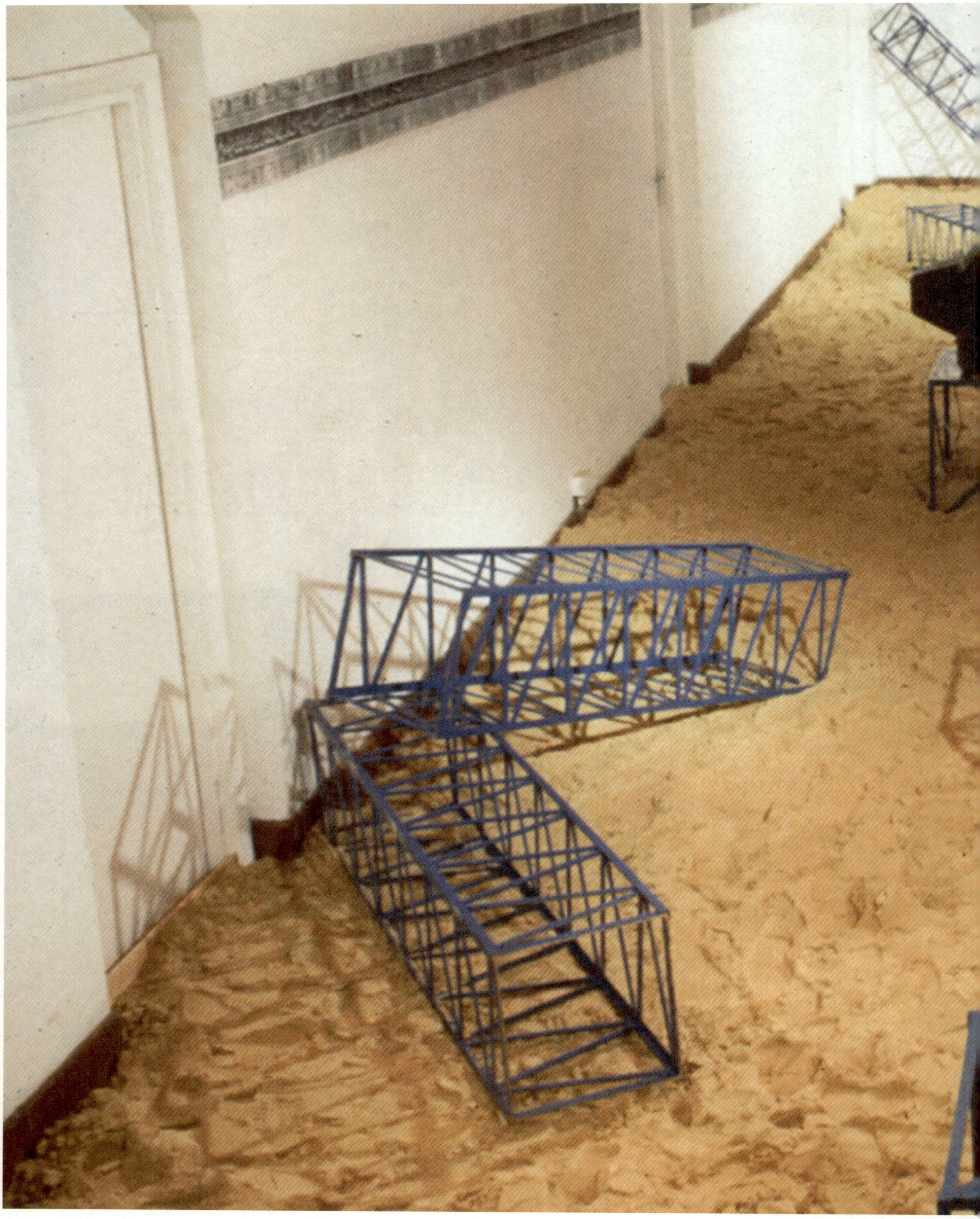

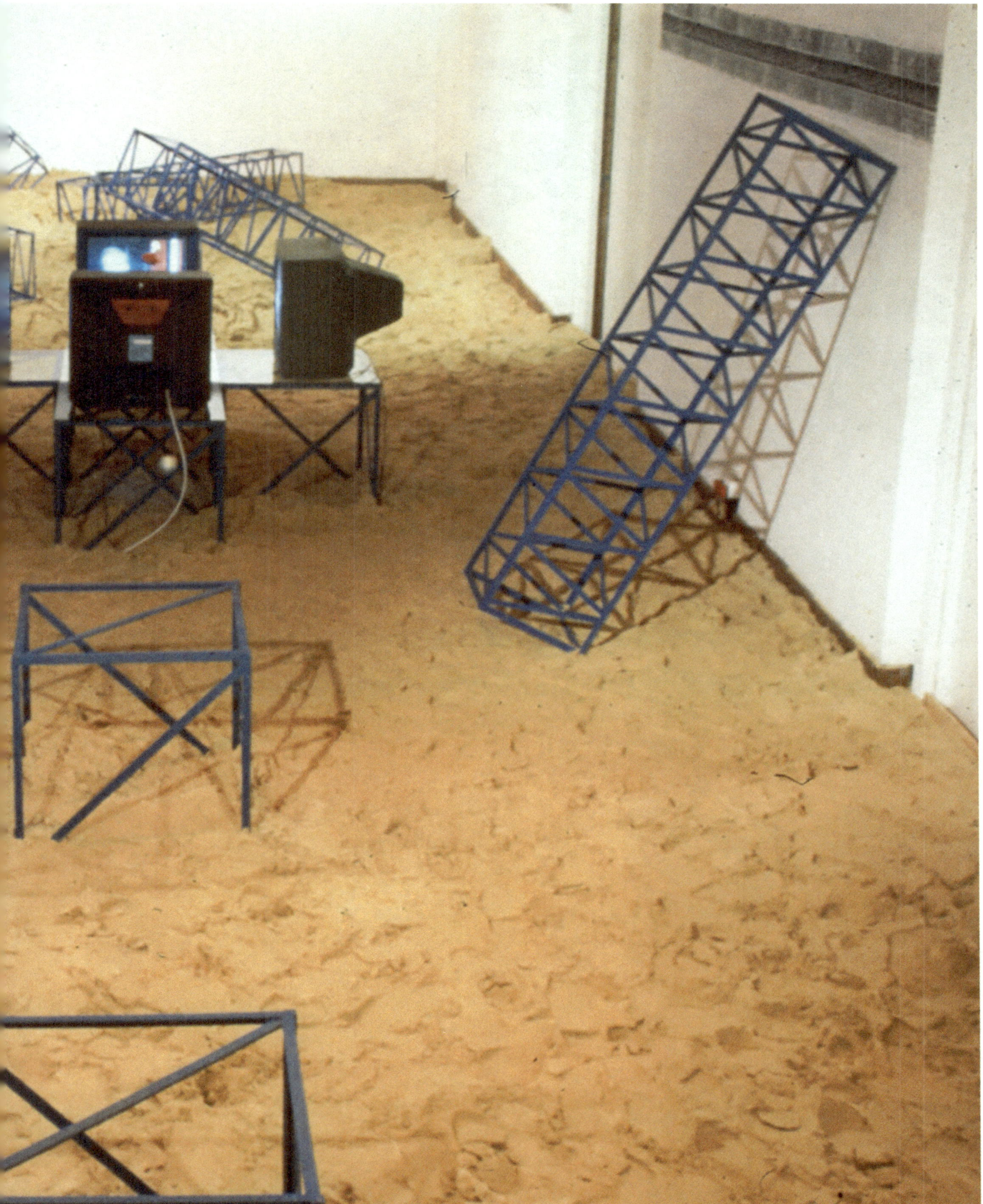

A Long Walk In The Wilderness, 1991
shoe installation at Vancouver Art Gallery
dimensions unknown

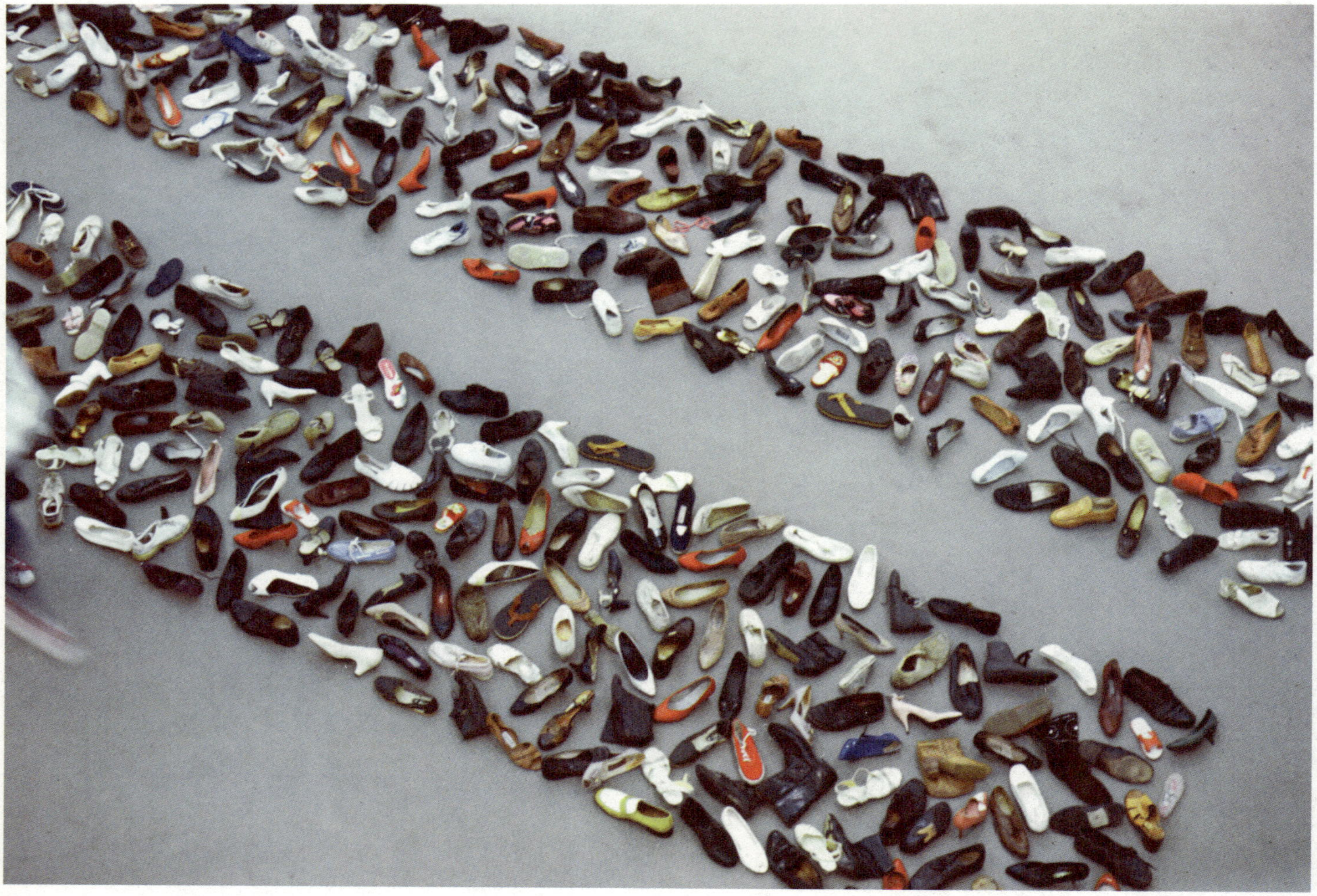

Heroes, 1991–1992
photographs, newspaper, acrylic on plywood
185 x 276 cm

No Big Tragedy, 1991–1992
installation Fukuoka Asian Art Museum
dimensions unknown
Fukuoka Asian Art Museum Collection

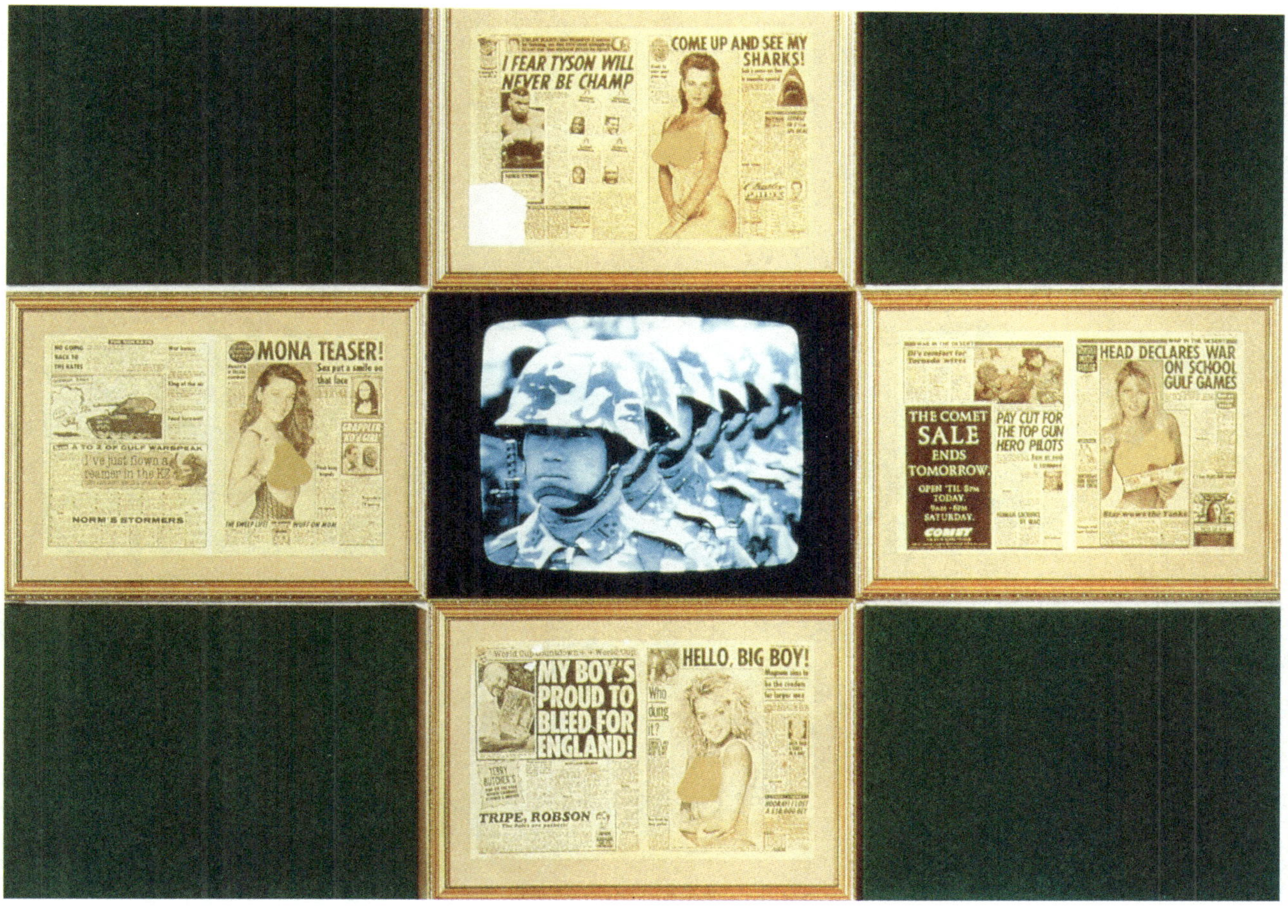

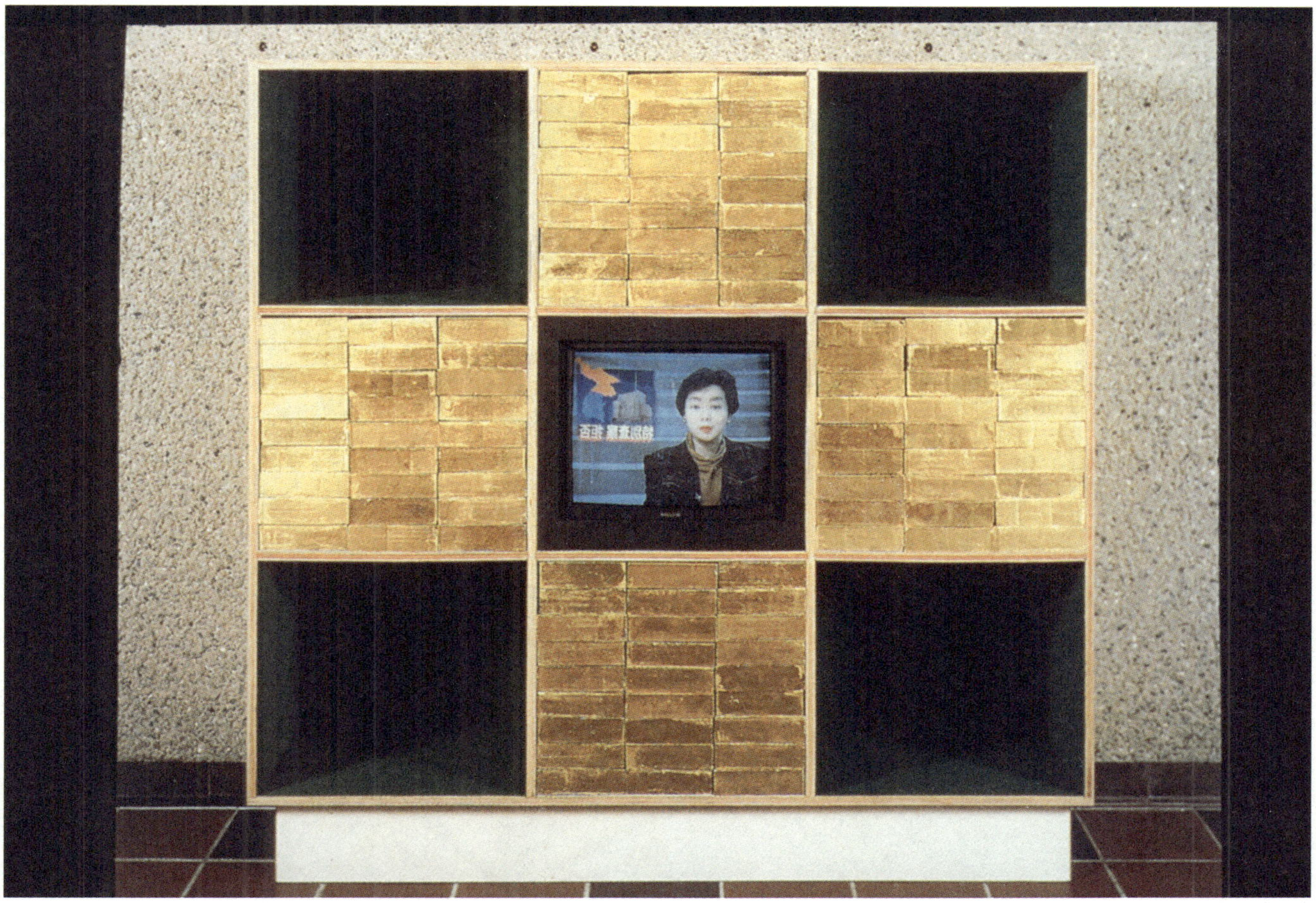

Tigris, 1992
mixed-media installation, 91 x 183 x 183 cm
Fukuoka Asian Art Museum Collection

Tigerjee, 1992–1997
mixed-media installation, 100 x 150 x 150 cm
Installation Middlesbrough Art Gallery

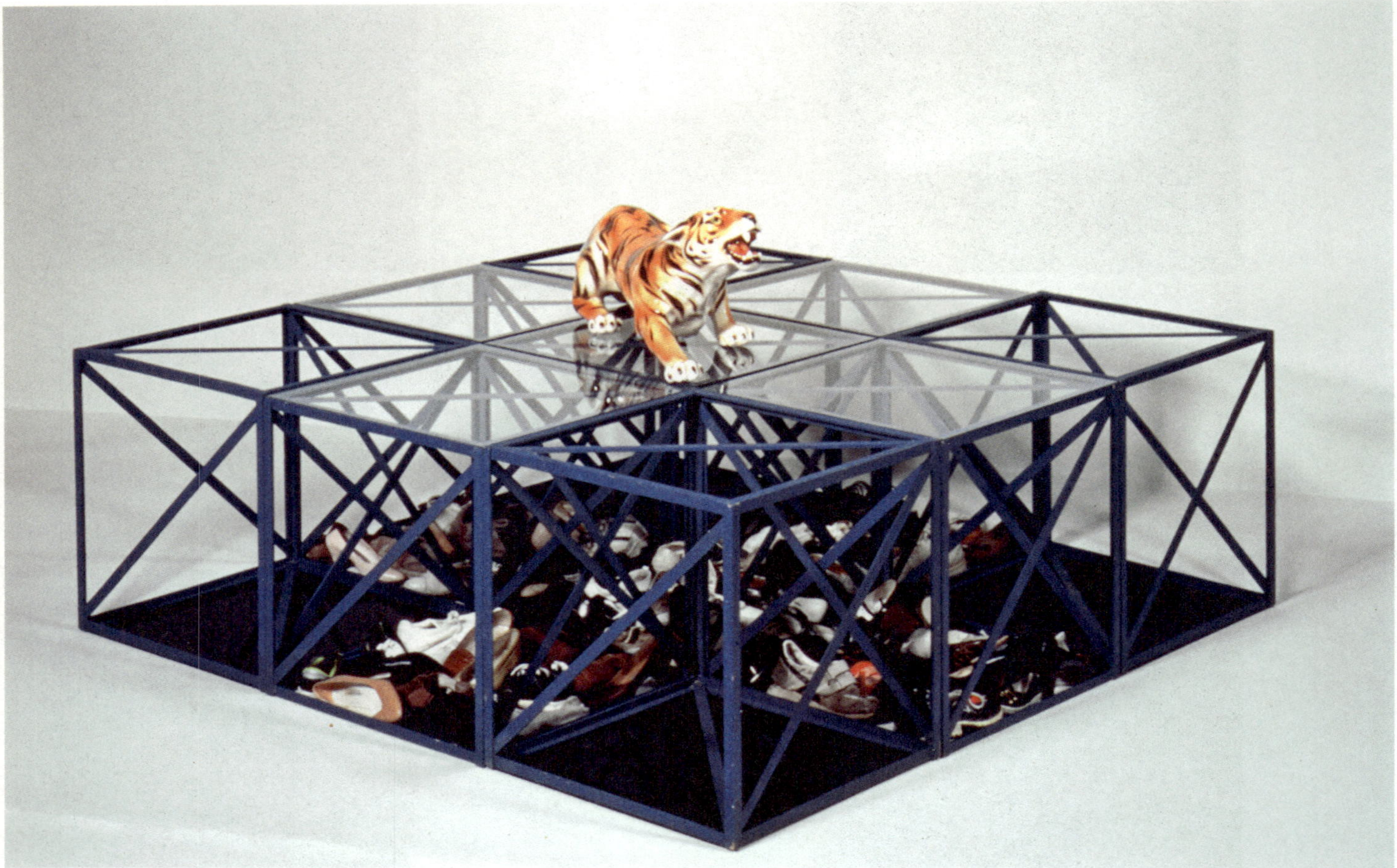

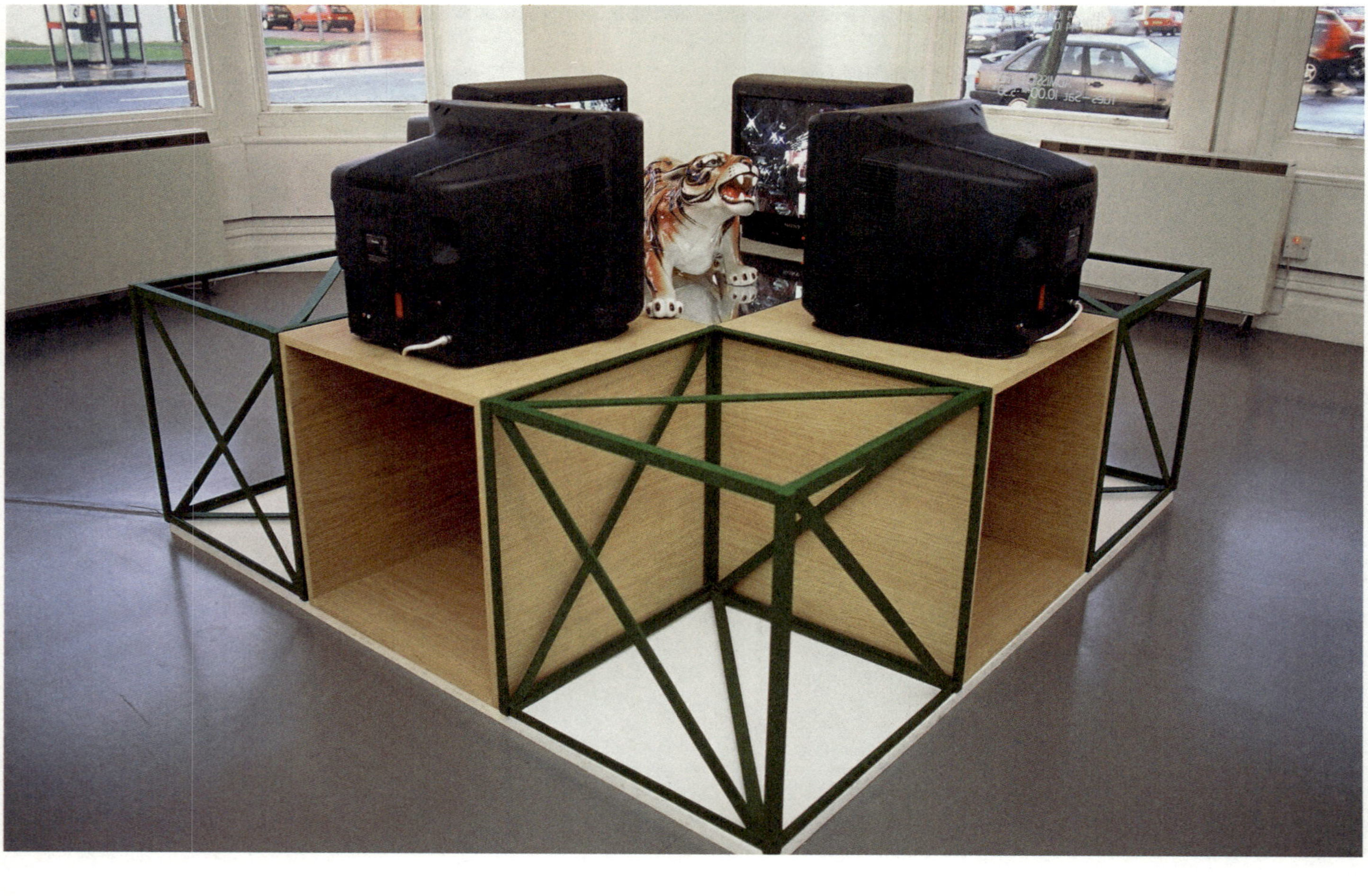

Once Upon A Time, 1994
mixed-media installation, 160 x 185 x 185 cm
installation South London Gallery

Aflatoon (So You Think You Are Plato), 1994
acrylic on wood, 183 x 185 x 185 cm
installation South London Gallery

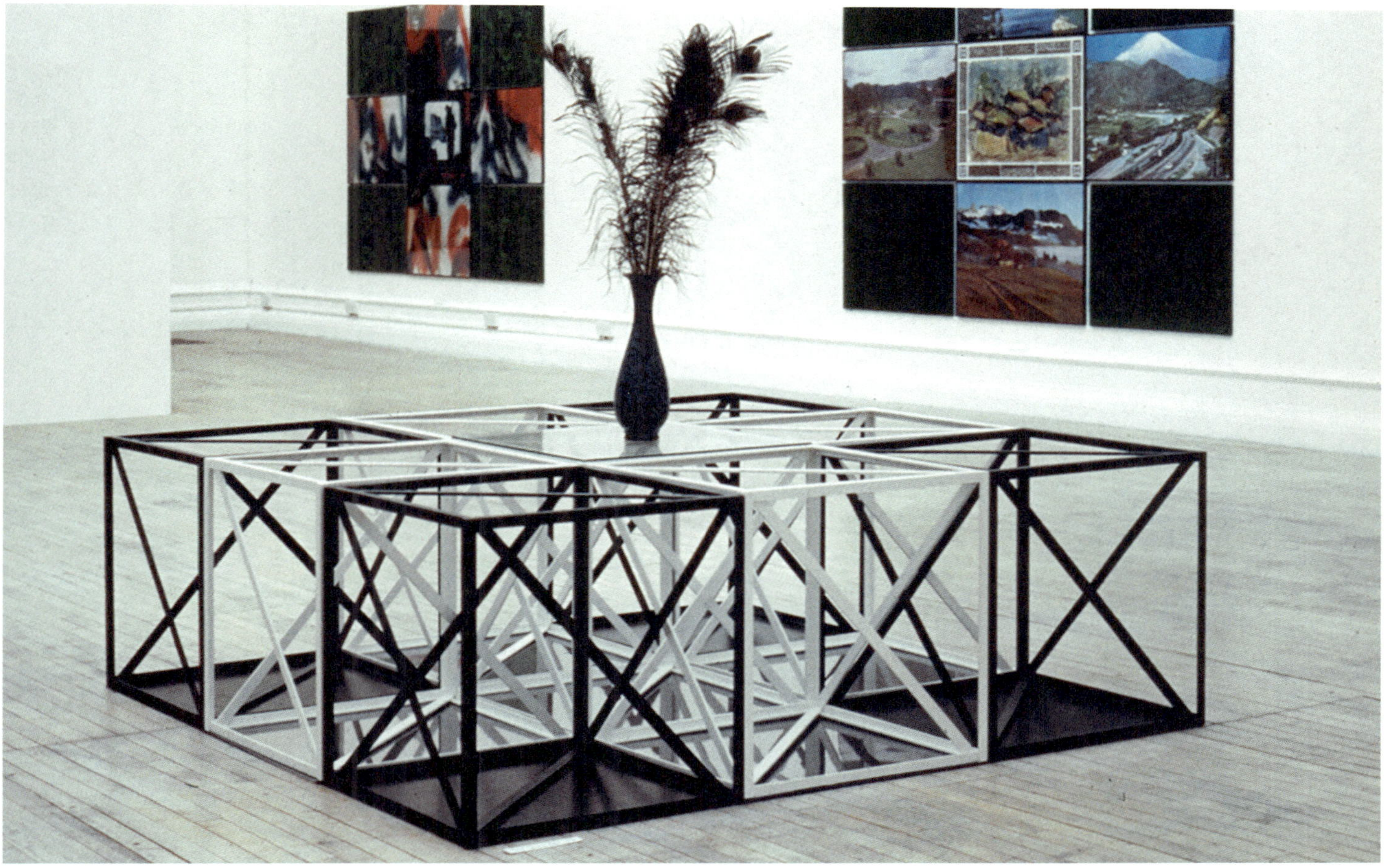

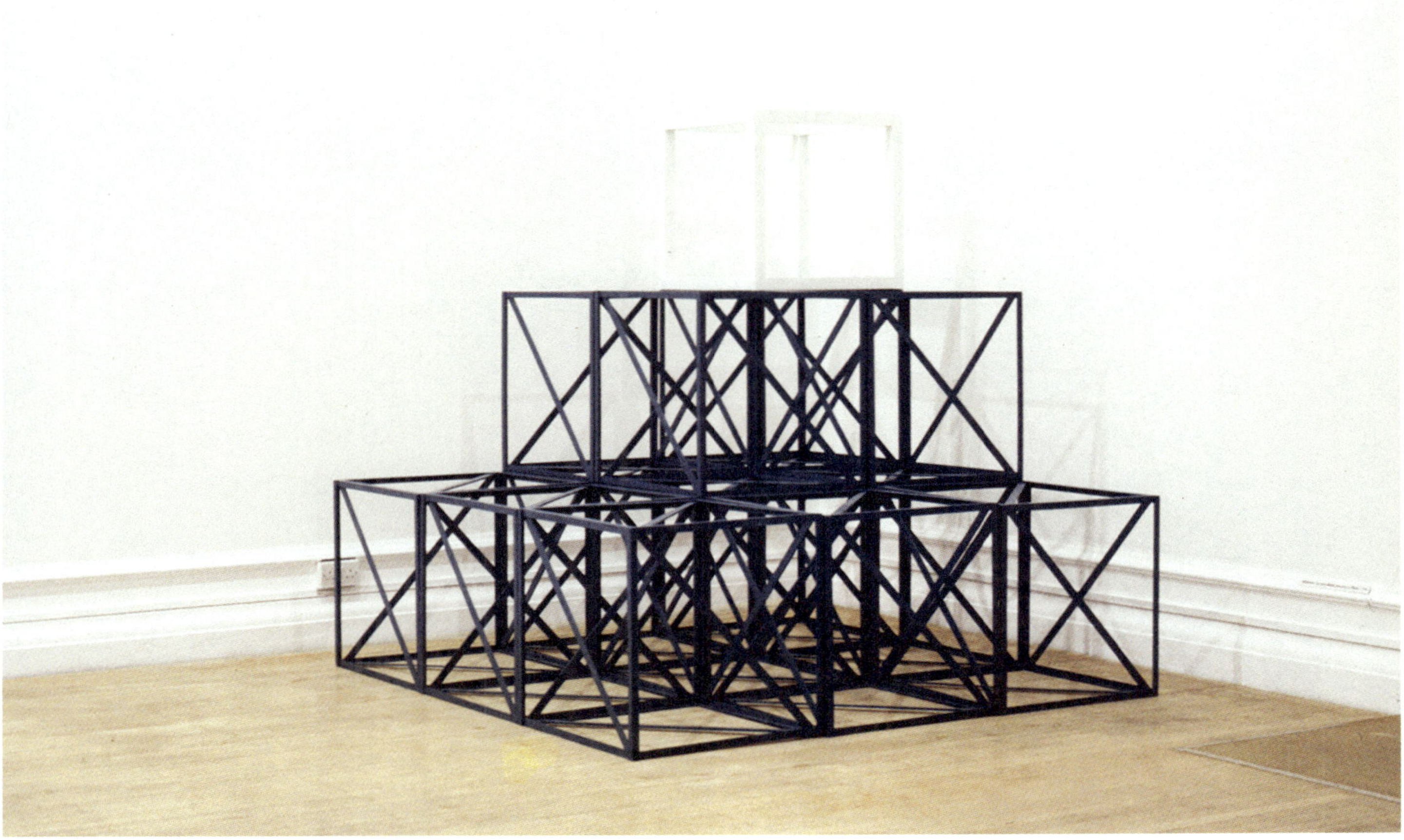

Untitled, 1995
painted steel installation
United Nations Building, Geneva
dimensions unknown

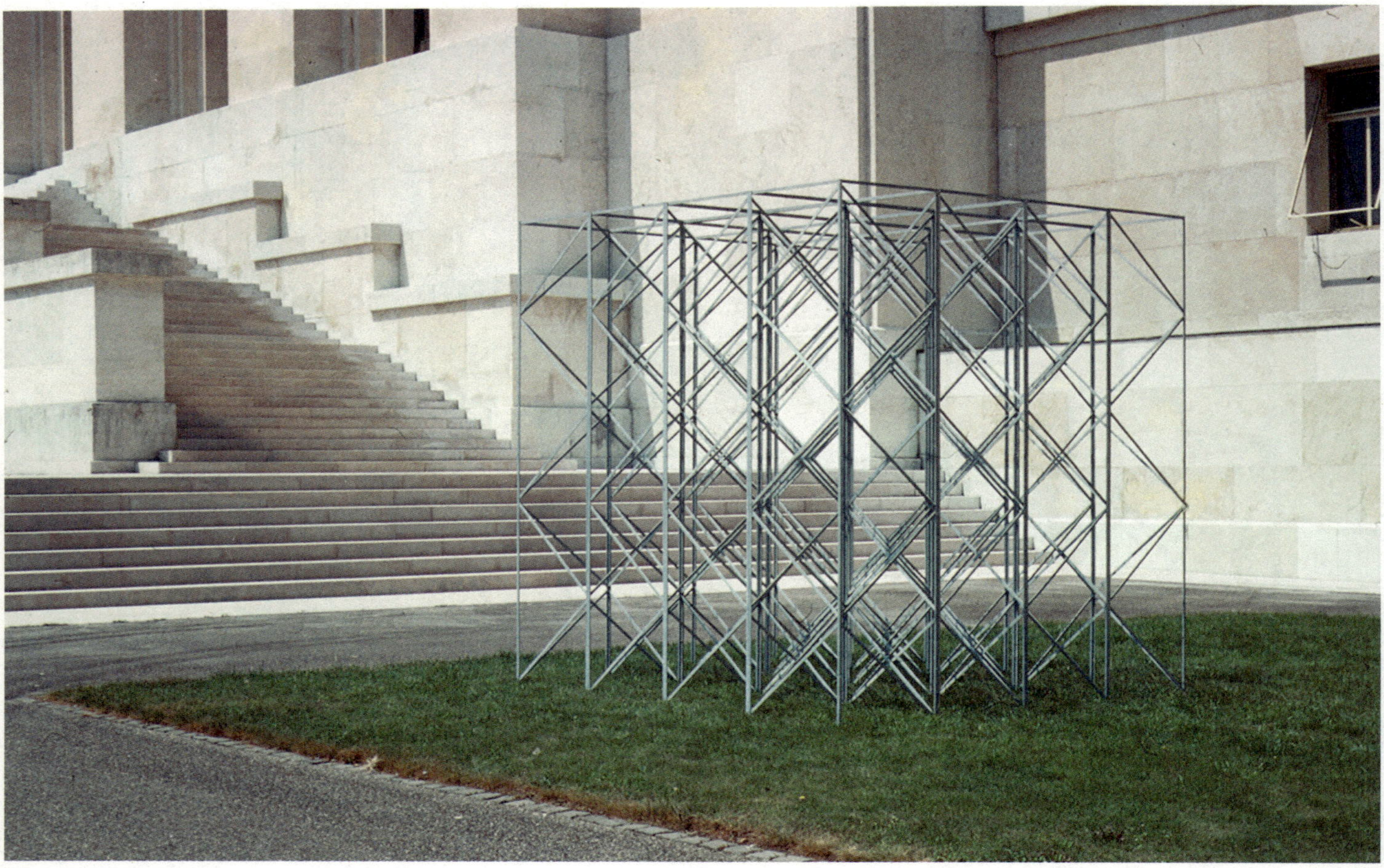

To Whom It May Concern, 1996
scaffolding installation at Serpentine Gallery, London
1219 x 1219 x 1219 cm

When There's A Will There's A Way, 1998
scaffolding installation at Sydney Biennale, Australia
1199 x 1199 x 1199 cm

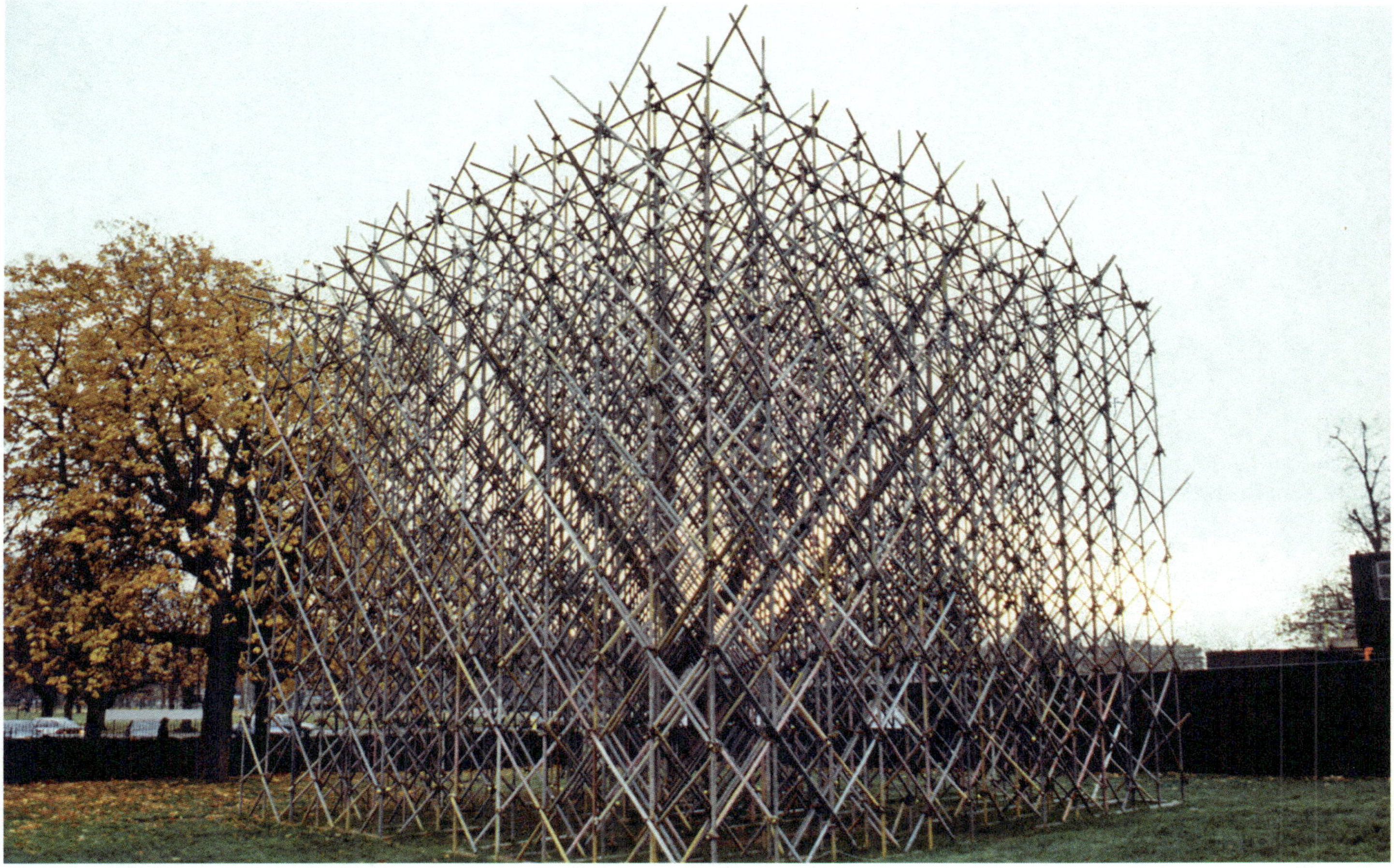

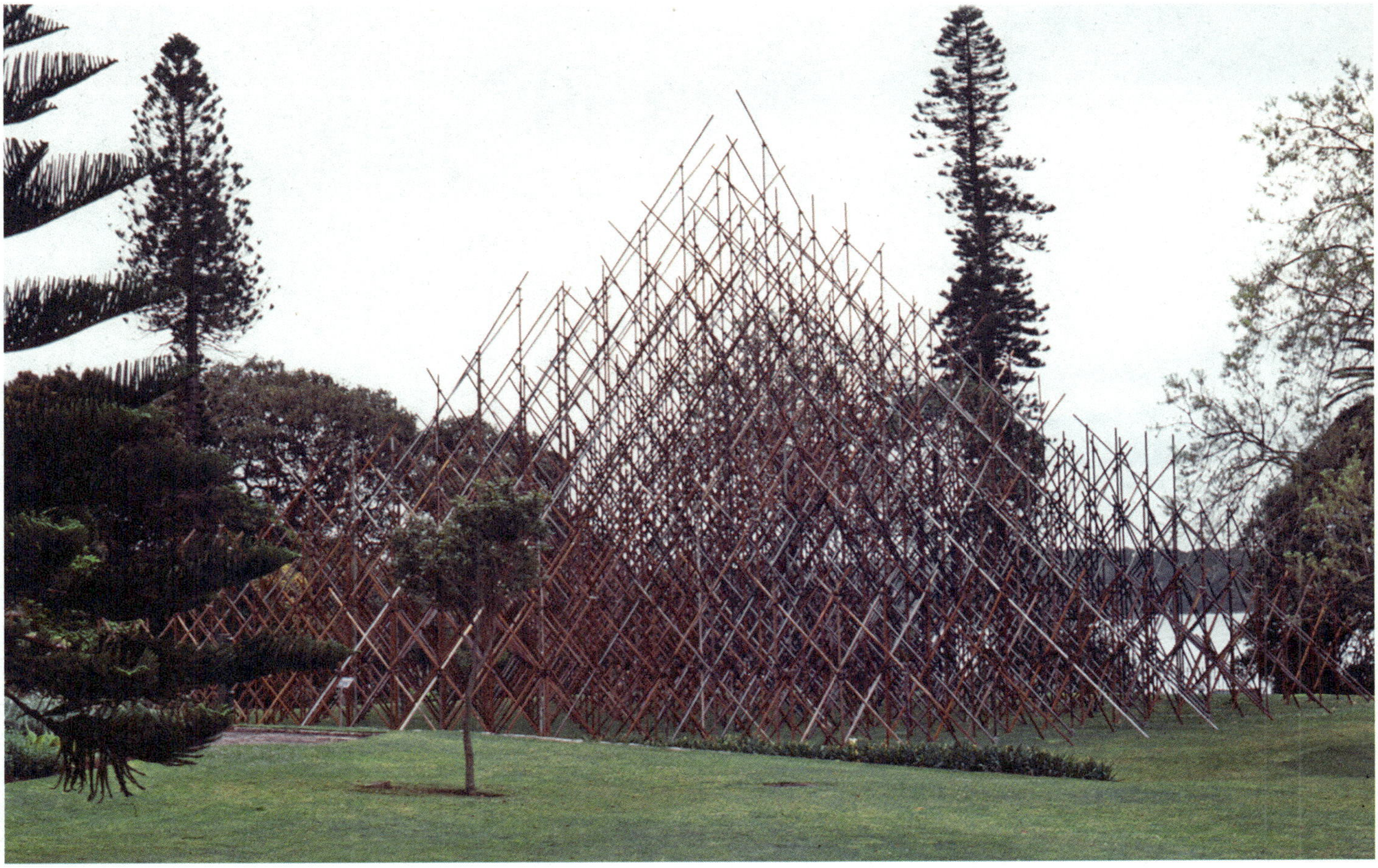

Anything Goes in Post Modernity, 1996
collage on paper, 41 x 38 cm

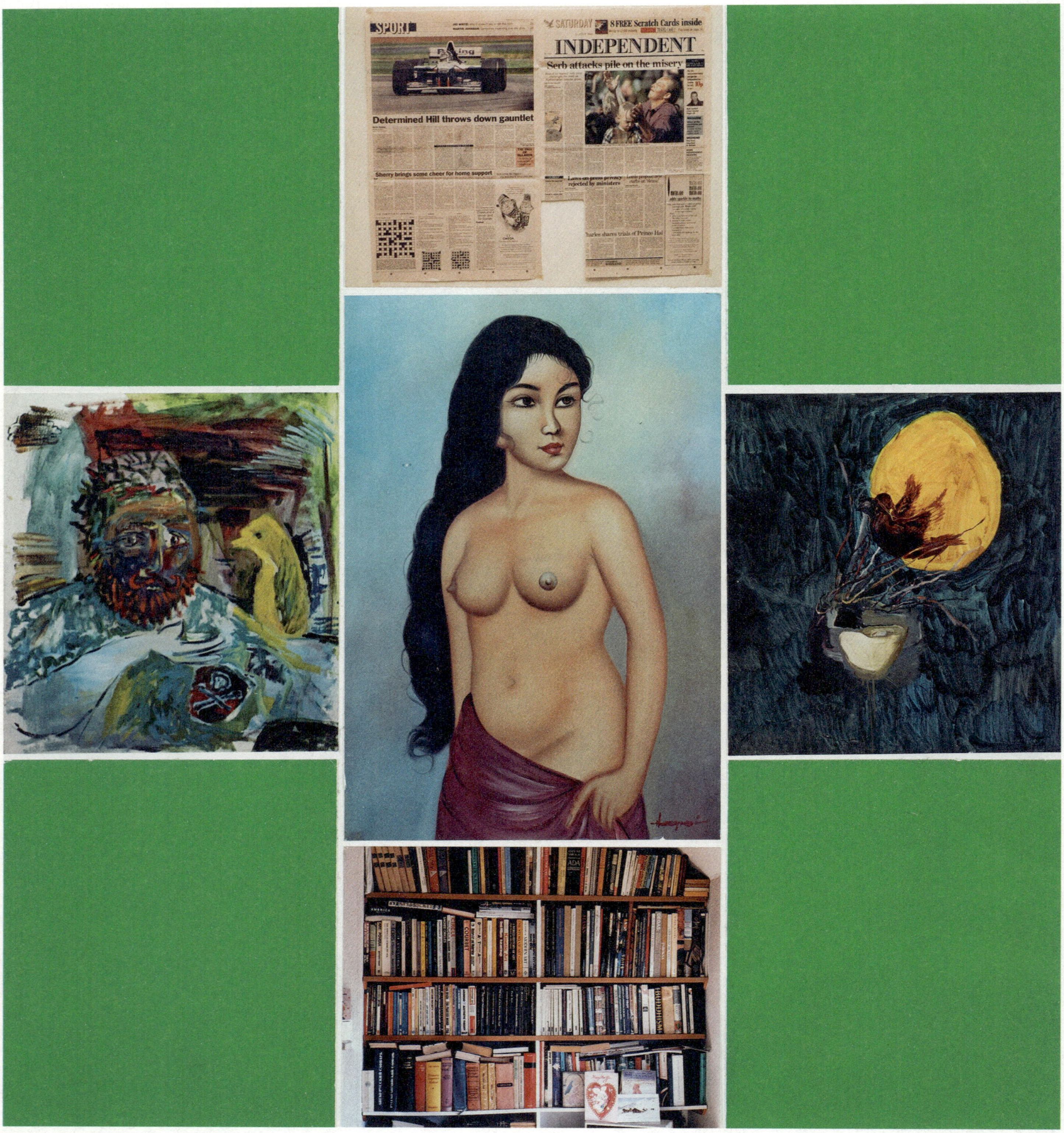

The ZKM Reading Room, 1997–2011
interactive mixed-media installation, Karlsruhe
dimensions unknown
ZKM Centre for Art and Media Collection

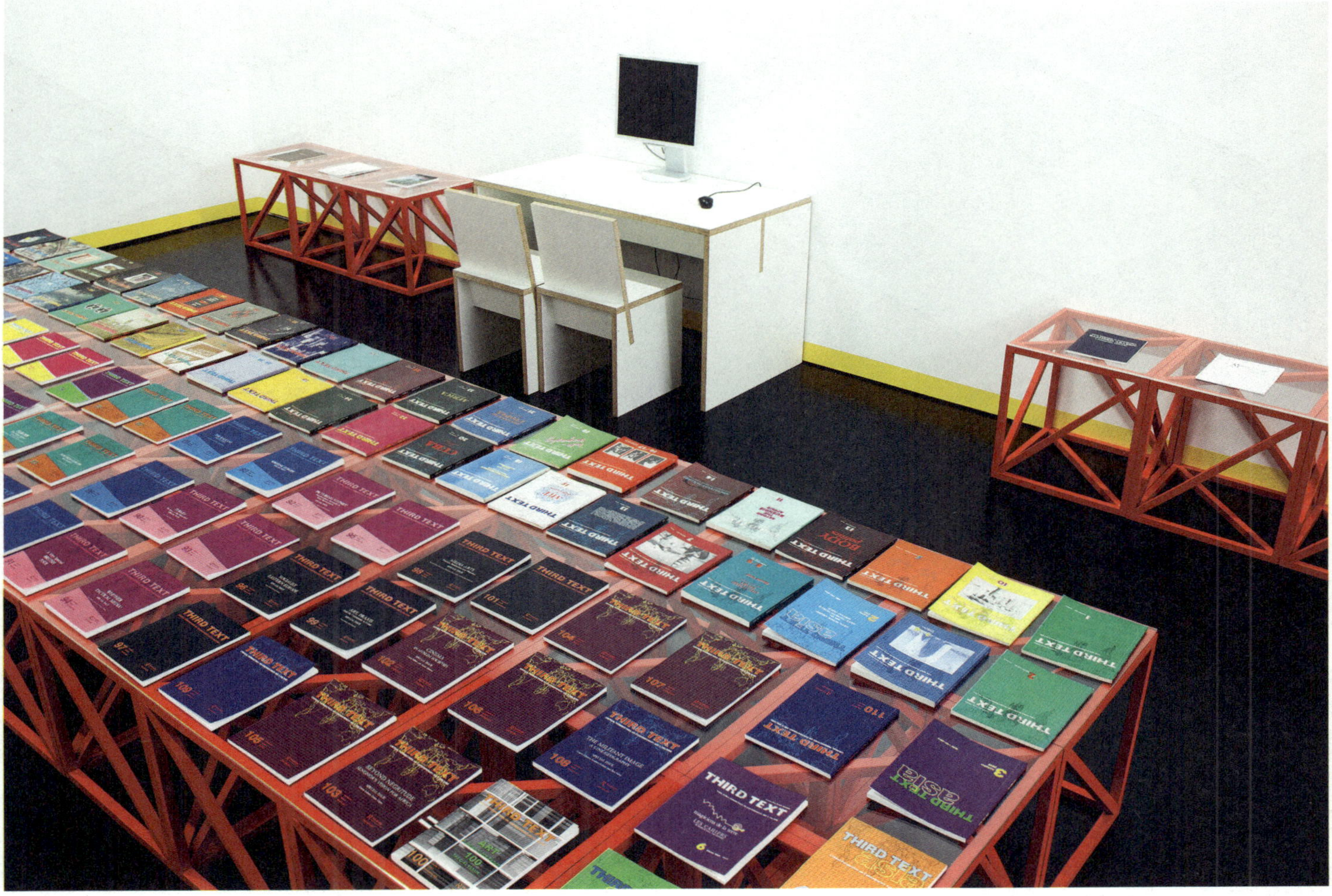

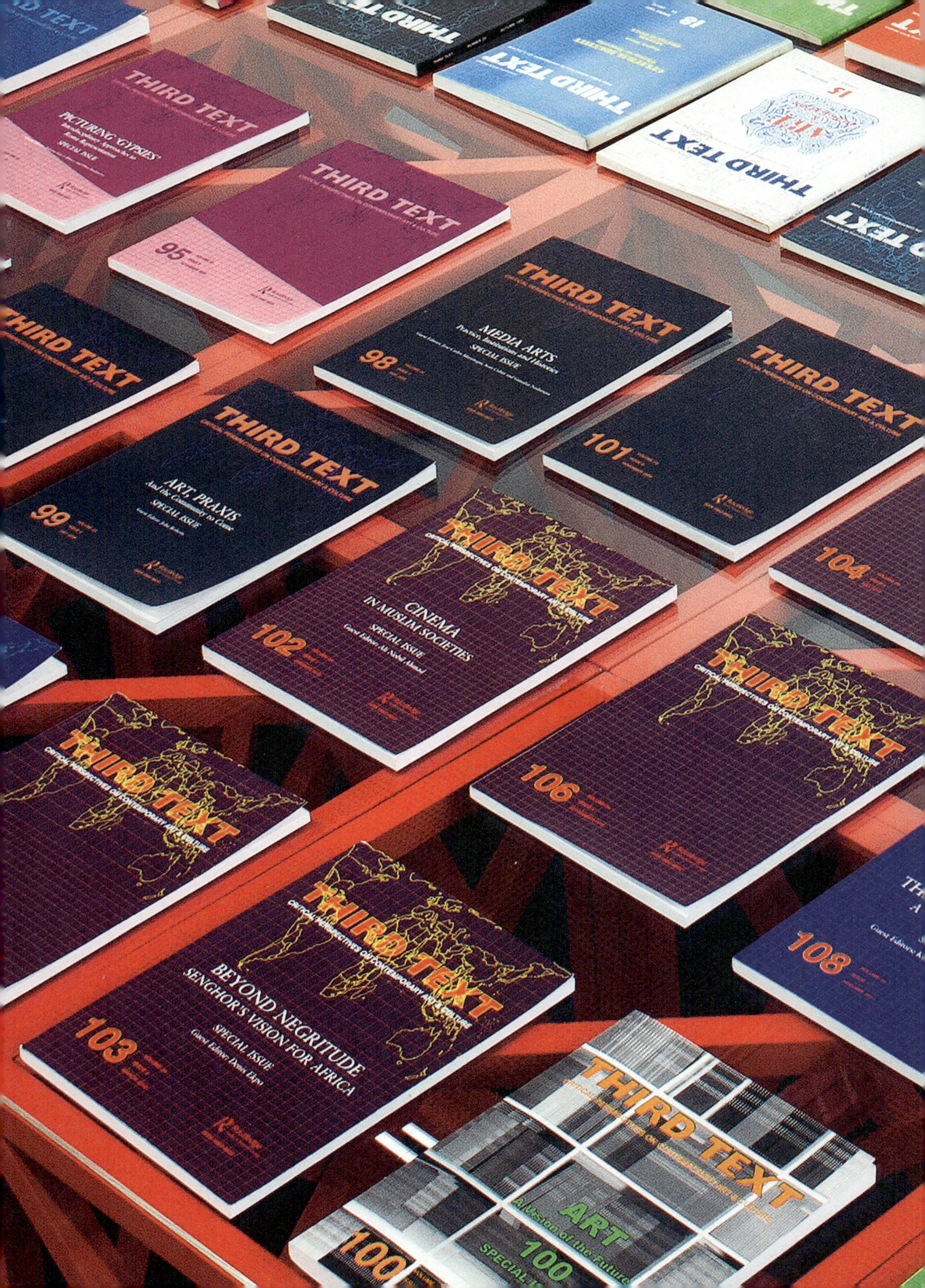
THIRD TEXT
PICTURING 'GYPSIES'
SPECIAL ISSUE
95
MEDIA ARTS
SPECIAL ISSUE
98
101
ART, PRAXIS
SPECIAL ISSUE
99
CINEMA
IN MUSLIM SOCIETIES
SPECIAL ISSUE
102
104
106
108
BEYOND NEGRITUDE
SENGHOR'S VISION FOR AFRICA
SPECIAL ISSUE
103
ART
A Vision of the Future
100

Third Text: Modernism, Negritude, and the Critique of Ethnicity[1]

John Roberts

The origins of the journal *Third Text* founded by Rasheed Araeen in 1987 (editor in chief through 2011) lie in the rich and explosive resistance to racism, colonialism, and imperialism between the early 1970s and mid-1980s in Britain. This is a period in which the struggles of Afro-Caribbean, African, and Asian (hereafter 'black') workers who having arrived as immigrants in the 1950s and 1960s, began to reshape the British state's national and domestic response to decolonization and the legacy of colonialism and imperialism. Their struggles against racism at work, and for equal pay and union recognition [as in the extraordinary strike for union recognition led by Indian women workers at the photo-processing plant Grunwick in London, (1976–1977)], shifted the political self-perception of the British state and the politicians that had brought these workers to Britain: namely, the fact, that black immigrants were here to stay. More pointedly though, they were here to stay and contribute far more than their poorly paid labour-power, for the immigrants not only brought with them their own native cultures, allegiances, and histories, but also their own cultural ambitions. However much the British state may have welcomed and tolerated the marginal and largely private manifestations of these immigrant cultures when they had the air of exotic imports, it didn't know how to deal with manifestations of public assertiveness once black workers began to realize their collective independence. Indeed, it was in the early 1970s, the highpoint of a racist backlash against black immigrants' resistance to their silent integration, when a seismic shift in post-war British culture gained definition that British culture – the host culture, so to speak – could no longer disguise the fact that it was *itself* a part of the process of decolonization. The multi-glottal had invaded the mono-cultural citadel.

Consequently it was at this point that the various cultural organs of the British state, in order to defuse the worst effects of a chronic institutional racism and race-blindness, began to promulgate the notions of 'multiculturalism' and 'ethnic' arts. Multiculturalism and ethnic arts, in their original forms, at least, were seen as a way to integrate native immigrant cultures into public life along pathways of separate development. That is, they were formulated primarily to protect immigrant cultures from their newly imposed alien host culture by giving assent to their traditional and pre-modern aspects, encouraging artists, as a result, to identify with their ethnicity above all else. As such what was seen as an act of benign and progressive grace, was actually a continuation of racial difference by other means: immigrant cultures were held to be at their most authentic when they were attached to their traditional forms and patterns of allegiance.

It was at this point that Rasheed Araeen entered the debate. Having just arrived in Britain from Karachi in 1964 to continue to make a career for himself as an artist, he soon came up against the overt racism of the host culture, the beginnings of multiculturalism and the fetishization of ethnicity. This situation sought either to push him into the category of ethnic arts, or subtly or blatantly denigrate him as a failed modernist. In the mid-1970s, then, there was a clear ideological struggle facing newly arrived and long-standing immigrant artists of ambition: a head-on confrontation with the categories and working practices of "ethnic" arts. Through this black artists hoped to define their ambitions within the extra-artistic struggle for equality and internationalism. In 1978, Araeen set up the forerunner of *Third Text*, *Black Phoenix: Journal of Contemporary Art & Culture in the Third World*, to do precisely this. The inaugural issue included what was to be the first radical manifesto of black liberation and art practice since the beginnings of the black liberation movement in the United States in the mid-1960s and the debates on modernism and negritude in the 1930s. The new black artist, and black artist of the recent past contributes to contemporary development in their own right, by their own original ideas, concepts and synthesis/antithesis; and more importantly, they offer a challenge to Western domination by defying the hegemony of art styles perpetuated and promoted internationally by the *transatlantic* gallery circuit of the Western world.[2] It was soon republished in *Studio International*.[3]

In this respect Araeen's writing during that period acts as focus for the struggles of two earlier generations: the postcolonial intellectuals and artists from Africa, the Caribbean, and Asia, newly arrived in the 1950s and 1960s, who go on to shape the intellectual framework of cultural resistance for the first generation immigrants (such as Ambalavaner Sivanandan and his journal, *Race & Class*, the British Black Workers Movement, Artists for Democracy, and Stuart Hall, editor, from 1959–1961, of the *New Left Review*) and – behind these British pioneers – the great modernist legacy of black liberation and resistance (James Baldwin, W. E. B. Du Bois, Angela Davis, Frantz Fanon, Paulo Freire, Langston Hughes, C. L. R. James, Huey P. Newton, and Malcolm X). There was already some residual knowledge in the early 1980s of this modernist legacy, derived from its impact on elements of 1960s British counter-culture and the revolutionary left, just as in the early 1970s the formative attempts, derived from the Black Panthers and other movements in the US, to reconfigure the place of anti-racism within the Western Marxist tradition, had left their traces.[4] But the theoretical implications of this modernist legacy had yet to be employed systematically in addressing the cultural impact of new forms of racism in Britain in the wake of the delayed impact of Caribbean immigration and the postcolonial diaspora.

Third Text arrives, therefore, at the point where Araeen and others' mediation of these legacies are finding a tentative hold in the emergence of a new generation of black British writers and artists in the British art school system, such as Sonia Boyce, Zarina Bhimji, Eddie Chambers, Lubaina Himid, and Keith Piper. In the spirit of Araeen, this generation demanded the recognition of their autonomy as artists, and their collective contribution to definitions of the modern, without any kind of fealty to ethnicity. Yet, initially there was residual tension between this emergent bloc and Araeen's project, around the status of black nationalism in art in Britain, particularly given the fact that outside of the academy black nationalism in Britain was one of the few popular sources of radicalization for young Afro-Caribbean Britons, with its overlaps with Rastafarianism and the Nation of Islam. Chambers and Piper, as children of first generation Caribbean immigrants, were, as such, closer to the American writer Frank Kofsky's black nationalist reading of black modernism, in his writings on American jazz[5]: it was the job of the black artist to forge a singular 'black language', a negritude *écriture* from the bounds of racism. Despite Araeen's sympathy for a defence of immigrant and indigenous practices as a way to define a space free from overt racism and the colonial legacy – this smacked too much of race essentialism – in its first issues *Third Text* began to address the questions surrounding this space in depth. As such, by the late 1980s *Third Text*, became the primary site of debate on race, representation, and British and global culture, in an extraordinary outpouring of critical and theoretical creativity within this emergent second-generation modernist – and then latterly postmodernist – formation. Questions of black identity were systematically taken apart, as much as the exclusions and occlusions of Western art history. Thus, in these formative years, one of the critical jobs Araeen also undertook was to produce a new postcolonial canon of art in Britain. In the introduction to his curated Hayward Gallery exhibition *The Other Story: Afro-Asian Artists in Post-War Britain* (1989) a survey of post-1950s first- and second-generation immigrant

Afro-Asian artists (Frank Bowling, Boyce, Chambers, Mona Hatoum, Piper, and Aubrey Williams) he attacks the Western 'master narrative' in which its self-proclaimed civilizational values speak for historical objectivity. In this he emphasizes, less individual racism, and more so the institutional conditions under which postcolonial artists were received.

But it must be remembered that the objective of post-war American cultural imperialism was not just anti-communism but also its assertion of its own cultural hegemony over the world. Freedom of expression in newly independent countries was inevitably affected. It seems that the eventual disappearance of Afro-Asian art from the British art scene was not fortuitous, nor can it be explained simply as a result of the emergence of a new racism, epitomized by the famous speech of Enoch Powell in 1968 in which he demanded the return of the new Commonwealth peoples to the countries of their origin. It is no coincidence that the British art world became completely white by the end of the 1960s – so much so that no major gallery showed work other than English, American, and, to a lesser extent, European. Subsequently no national or international survey of post-war art in Britain has mentioned or included any non-European artist.[6]

Hence, as the product of postcolonial and post-Empire Britain, *Third Text* is in an important sense a forerunner and critical under-labourer for the massive global transformation in art production and art theory in the 1980s and 1990s. This was just as the flourishing of postcolonial modes of thinking became identified with the crisis of Western modernism itself – or a particular post-war US-centric reading of modernism. The immanent race-blindness and gender-blindness of post-war US modernism – a radical culture indifferent to its own black modernist legacy – acts as the fulcrum for the development of a wide range of theoretical deconstructions and historical reconstructions. These, of course, eventually lead to the formation of critical postmodernism, which in its earlier version was driven by the critique of white, male Western presumptions.

But if US postmodernism in the late 1980s is quick to develop a critique of Eurocentrism, and then in turn, a theory of the postcolonial subject and the black and immigrant modernist subject as a hybrid construction – a subject lying between 'blackness' and white European culture, nativism, and modernism – the condition of the new culture and its theoretical problems are rarely addressed with such consistency and from within a genuinely global framework as in *Third Text*. Indeed, as postmodernism declines as a postcolonial formation within the American and British academy in the 1990s, the discussion of Eurocentrism, race, and imperialism drops out of the picture, falling back into 'race studies' or moving into a postcolonial adaptation of cultural theory. Thus, in the face of these retreats and omissions, *Third Text* continues to be one of the few cultural journals that continues to operate consistently within a global, anti-imperialist framework, drawing on new theoretical thinking in response to the changing demands of a postcolonial world, and mainstream modernist cultural practices from around the globe in a period of mass immigrations (and racist immigration policy).

In this respect, by the early 1990s the journal had become preoccupied – in addition to its foundational work on ethnicity, identity, and multiculturalism – with two new major issues: firstly, the limits of postcolonial critique in a world of expanded migrations and rebarbative nationalisms; and secondly, the hyper-globalization of art and growth of advanced practice globally – the latter partly being the result of internationalization of artistic production, but also a consequence of the expansion of the biennale circuit under the rise of neoliberalism. Hence, from a position concerned with British native introversion in the late 1980s – dominated by the editors' complaints about British provincialism and cultural essentialism – by the late 1990s the journal had become a significant international forum for the analysis and critique of the new circuits of advanced postcolonial and non-Western practice. This is reflected in a widening cohort of contributors from around the globe and an expanded readership. A few titles of *Third Text* special issues in the new millennium, give a sense of these changes: 'Post-Soviet Russia', edited by Victor Tupitsyn (no. 65, 2003), 'Palestine & Israel', edited by Haim Bresheeth and Haifa Hammami (no. 80–81, 2006), 'Fortress Europe', edited by Yosefa Loshitzky (no. 83, 2006), 'Turkey: The Space of the Min(d) Field', edited by Gülsen Bal (no. 90, 2008), 'Picturing "Gypsies": Interdisciplinary Approaches to Roma Representation', edited by Paloma Gay y Blasco and Dina Iordanova (no. 92, 2008), 'Socialist Eastern Europe', edited by Reuben Fowkes (no. 96, 2009), 'Cinema in Muslim Countries', edited by Ali Nobil Ahmad (no. 102, 2010), 'Beyond Negritude: Senghor's Vision for Africa', edited by Denis Ekpo (no. 103, 2010), and 'The Militant Image: A Ciné-Geography', edited by Kodwo Eshun and Ros Gray (no. 108, 2011).

The richness of these subjects is self-evident, and shows the intellectual resources *Third Text* was able to call on to orchestrate its analyses and critique of 'business as usual'. But what is of particular significance in this period of the journal's 'post-postcolonial' expansion is the issue on negritude.

The failure of negritude as a cultural policy in various post-independence states in Africa is well documented; its metaphysics of the 'black soul' and 'black identity' are part of an egregious essentialism, which had derailed the ambitions of black artists and black struggle in both Africa and Europe; and indeed, a critique of one of its leading ideologues Léopold Sédar Senghor [(1906–2001), the president of Senegal from 1960–1980] forms part of the special issue (although Senghor was in no sense a black nationalist; the post-independent states, he argued, should not turn their back on Europe). So, clearly in lieu of *Third Text*'s foundational work on 'ethnicity' and racial essentialism, the legacy of negritude is something of which the journal should be especially critical. But negritude as the name – or strategy – for that which refuses to be assimilated by a newly hegemonic postcolonial modernity, is another matter. In this sense 'negritude' is not necessarily coeval with 'black nationalism'. As Araeen argues in his introduction to the special issue, negritude is also, prior to its conservative and defensive racialist appropriation, 'the historical necessity to recognize the specificity of a culture's own ground from which to speak'.[7] In other words: geography and native culture are places in which to *begin* the process of signification, not its home or destiny. Accordingly, once negritude is separated from cultural or racial essentialism, it becomes another name for cultural autonomy, and as such marshals another possible dynamic within the multicultural zones and strictures of postcolonialism: the *mutual liberation* of the colonizer and colonized, periphery and centre, through the shared participation of Western and non-Western cultures in an expanded and emancipatory universality. And part of this mutual liberation is that 'negritude' or its cognates determine the content of this universality, as opposed simply to giving itself up to its pregiven parameters. Hence the wider postcolonial, anti-imperialist, and anti-racist struggle is not for multicultural parity and participation but for *global cultural interdependence without preconceptions*. This I believe, is fundamental to *Third Text*'s theoretical project under Araeen and as such returns the debate on culture and racism to the very core of the colonial experience and imperialism: the *making* of blackness.

Under colonialism and imperialism native peoples *became* black, insofar as skin colour became the mark of a defining and visible inferiority and otherness, expressed in its most direct and violent form, of course, through the slave economy as a racialized category of 'just privation'; blackness and the absolute privations of colonialism and slavery becoming synonymous. This produces what Domenico Losurdo and Louis Sala-Molins in their respective ways have called the racial delimitation of democracy, liberty, and social identity during the Enlightenment and after. The exclusion of the colonial subject and black slave from humanity and reason produces, in the period of slave emancipation and decolonization, a call for the reparation of blackness separate from racist discourse. Yet, if blackness is separated from racism it is not separated from race. After colonialism, after slavery, blackness remains fixed in its racialized place as that which has to be given a new racial dignity.[8] And, indeed, in spite of anti-racist struggle and postcolonial liberation, the peoples of Africa, Asia, and the Caribbean and the peoples in other areas of the Americas, as well as in Australia and the Pacific, today *remain* black – that is subject to a blackness defined as a racial category.

One of the struggles then for first-generation immigrant and second-generation artists, activists, and intellectuals in Britain in the 1980s and 1990s, was to define and defend blackness, while resisting a given or received black identity, insofar as if blackness was a fiction, it was a necessary fiction, given the realities of racism.[9] This bifurcation, however, is a troubled and exhausting one: on either side of this divide – race-as-blackness, race as the pre-determinate of anti-racist struggle – is constituted as a 'problem'. 'Everyone has skin color, but not everyone's skin color counts as race',[10] as Karen E. Fields and Barbara J. Fields put it succinctly. Indeed, the problem is not race – which has no biological reality – but *racism*, as a *practice*, inscribed and re-inscribed in the belief in the actuality of race as identity. This was very much part of what Sivanandan described in the 1970s as the cultural schizophrenia of the postcolonial immigrant worker and artist, the 'creature of two worlds', as he called it, confronted with the construction 'race' in these terms and as such struggling to find a place and voice – certainly for the sons and daughters of first-generation immigrants – in a culture both alien and homely.

Today, though, the necessary fiction of blackness faces another struggle: the disappearance of the black or Afro-Asian artist into the exoticized global and multicultural artistic diaspora, that inflates 'race' as identity at the expense of racism as practice. Hence Araeen and *Third Text*'s interest in a modernized and retooled negritude: negritude is that politicized space, where the necessary fiction of blackness contributes to the possibility of a post-Western universality in the name of a globalizing and post-capitalist modernity (and not the globalization of multiculturalisms in the name of an enlightened Western capitalist modernization – the old liberal story). This is a powerful utopian vision, and as such, it draws on Sivanandan's fundamental critique of the parochial descent of post-1980s multiculturalism into an unfortunate 'enclave' mentality. But perhaps more pointedly, it reveals the historical stakes of *Third Text*. The journal seems increasingly less attached to anything resembling a First World art journal monitoring what appears to be a bewildering global scene, but is rather, an unfolding place of attachment to a new world of values, a place for old new worlds and new old worlds; in this, *Third Text*'s persistence, vision, and creativity under Araeen was quite remarkable.

1 A version of this text was presented at 'Publicaciones (no solo) de arte: usos culturales, sociales y políticos', Universidad Internacional de Andalucía, Seville, 15–18 June 2011. Held in collaboration with Centro experimental y tecnológico para la cultura y las artes de Sevilla and Librería La Fuga and organized by Pablo Lafuente, Pauline van Mourik Broekman, and Joaquín Vázquez.

2 Rasheed Araeen, 'Preliminary Notes for a BLACK MANIFESTO', *Black Phoenix,* no. 1 (winter 1978) republished in *Making Myself Visible* (London: Kala Press, 1984), 82.

3 Rasheed Araeen, 'Preliminary Notes for a BLACK MANIFESTO', *Studio International*, no. 194 (1978).

4 See, for example, A. X. Cambridge's journal *The Black Liberator* from the early 1970s.

5 See Frank Kofsky, *Black Nationalism and the Revolution in Music* (New York: Pathfinder Press, 1970).

6 Rasheed Araeen, 'When Chickens Come Home to Roost', in *The Other Story: Afro-Asian Artists in Post-War Britain* (exhibition catalogue) (London: Southbank Centre, 1989), 14–15.

7 Rasheed Araeen, 'Why "Beyond" Negritude?', special issue, *Beyond Negritude: Senghor's Vision for Africa*, ed. Denis Ekpo, *Third Text* 24, no. 103, issue 2 (March 2010):172.

8 See Domenico Losurdo, *Liberalism: A Counter-History* (London: Verso, 2011) and Louis Sala-Molins, *Dark Side of the Light: Slavery and the French Enlightenment*, trans. John Conteh-Morgan (Minneapolis: University of Minnesota Press, 2006).

9 For an extension of this position, see Karen E. Fields and Barbara J. Fields, *Racecraft: The Soul of Inequality in American Life* (London: Verso, 2012).

10 Ibid., 27.

THE OTHER STORY

History of Afro/Asian Artists in Britain

A Historical Survey Exhibition

Proposed and Selected by

Rasheed Araeen

Preliminary Research work
Submitted to the Arts Council
in 1987

Missing History

Kate Fowle

> In fact the history of mainstream art of the last fifty or so years in Britain is a story of a great achievement of a modern, postcolonial, and multiracial society, an achievement realised by the freedom of imagination and human interactions, exchange of ideas and influences. [...]
>
> If we seriously look at the work of African/Asian artists, in the same way we look at the work of artists of European origins, using a common criteria – both aesthetic and historical – what we would encounter is not an exotic addition to the postwar British art scene, as has been seen by many, but that which occupies a central position within historical developments of modernism.[1]

The statement above is part of a project proposal written by Rasheed Araeen to the Arts Council of England in 2000 and updated in 2003. It reiterates a sentiment that the artist has been championing his entire career: until black artists are written into the canon of art history on the basis of their contribution to modernism, there is no common ground from which to tell – or analyse – the story of post-war art.[2]

Titled *The Whole Story: Art in Postwar Britain*, the document is one of many the artist has written on the subject since the 1970s.[3] Each has sought to outline the discrimination towards the standing of black artists in the development of modern art, shifting focus to the work that they make, rather than the politics or discourses they represent. Buried within the paragraphs are fault lines that have created the rifts and allegiances between artists, curators, academics, and institutions, preventing this endeavour from being realized. Among them – and of repeated significance to Araeen – are the legacies of colonial imperialism, institutional benevolence, multiculturalism, and the divides within the Black Arts Movement. This essay charts some of those fault lines, looking at Araeen's efforts to redress the exclusions within the accepted canon of modernism and the struggle this has entailed with the British art establishment.

Araeen's call for critical equality in his proposal for *The Whole Story* was timely, reflecting a sentiment that was beginning to gain political resonance. For example, in a national conference held in November 1999 in Manchester – *Whose Heritage: The Impact of Cultural Diversity on Britain's Cultural Heritage* – Chris Smith, then Secretary of State for Culture, made a speech, which Araeen quoted from in his proposal:

> If we have a national identity, as I'm sure we do, then that pre-supposes we have developed a common cultural heritage and history, and we are aware that we have developed it. ... Cultural professionals should be aware of how narrowly based their own interpreters of history can be. ... They need both to employ people with a wider vision and undertake projects that focus on missing history. As Secretary of State for Culture, I want to see organisations working in this field and – I would put this very strongly – providing a more complete version of the truth.[4]

In Araeen's bid to provide 'the truth' he began by describing common non-Western influences that both Henry Moore and Ronald Moody sought out at the British Museum in the late 1920s; the inspiration found by both Patrick Heron and Aubrey Williams on visiting the *Modern Art in the United States* show at the Tate Gallery in 1957; and the innovations developed by Anthony Caro and David Medalla, which motivated younger generations in the late 1960s. With each example – in spite of shared impetus – Araeen pointed out that there was no art history that recognized the artists as contemporaries, 'let alone their relative merits'. Moody, Williams, and Medalla are barely in the footnotes of mainstream art historical discourse.

Araeen went on to outline his own entry into the British art scene from Pakistan in 1964 as one driven by wanting to be 'at the forefront of avant-garde developments'. As such, he explained that when he was pioneering new structural forms in sculpture in the 1960s, by some 'sad paradox' they were not recognized as unique contributions to Minimalism. If they had, it could have been seen as an important development in British art that ran in parallel with the American movement. Generally, just as Britain's demographic changed through the advent of decolonization and the creation of the Commonwealth of Nations in 1949, 'the history of British art should be a reflection of Britain, not as a pre-war white/colonial society, but a post-war postcolonial multiracial society'.[5] To move forward with equality, and without the cultural constraints of the past, it was time to reassess who and what constituted art history.

To create *The Whole Story*, Araeen proposed to 'undertake research into what has been produced as art by all artists, irrespective of their cultural or racial origins and ignoring all those presumptions and preconceptions which are associated with particular races or cultures'.[6] A team of art historians would create an archive with materials charting both the Eurocentric imperialist art history *and* the more dispersed, postcolonial discourses of African/Asian artists in Britain. Practitioners would be grouped according to the historical periods and movements in which they worked so that publications, exhibitions, films, and programmes of workshops, seminars, and conferences could be produced in light of the newfound correlations. Together, it was proposed, these platforms would help revise national legacies, and in turn the modernist European/North American bias in twentieth-century art history.

Seventeen years have passed since this proposal was written and the project remains nascent, yet no less important to Araeen.[7] That such a protracted time-lag could happen would seem inconceivable, if it wasn't for the fact that the artist had experienced it in the development of a proposal before.

The Other Story

The first lag was eleven years. It began on 28 October 1978, when Araeen wrote a letter to Andrew Dempsey, then assistant director of London exhibitions at the Arts Council, suggesting that the institution should organize a survey show of black artists in Britain. The exhibition would be titled *The Other Story: Afro/Asian Artists in Post-War Britain*. While Araeen acknowledged that such a distinction could be problematic, possibly even exacerbating racial separatism, he saw few alternatives: 'there doesn't seem to be any choice for us except in asserting now our historical presence here separately, 'til the cultural institutions of the country come to terms with the multiracial aspects of this society by fully recognizing the equal abilities of all peoples irrespective of colour and race.'

According to the artist, what prompted this letter was the second *Hayward Annual* in August 1978, which was the first Arts Council-funded exhibition to be curated by women, presenting twenty-three artists, of whom sixteen were women.[8]
In a published statement, Araeen championed it as 'an important event against the forces of discrimination in Britain', before pointing out that 'if women artists are "2nd class citizens" … black artists have no position whatsoever in the British art world'.[9] This conviction against discrimination was already manifest in his art practice and involvement in political activism from the early '70s. It was also a driver behind his co-founding of the journal *Black Phoenix* in 1978, which is

BLACK PHOENIX

Third World Perspective on Contemporary Art & Culture

[redacted],
London NW6 3PJ

28 October 1978

Andrew Dempsey,
The Arts Council of Great Britain,
105 Piccadilly,
London W1V OAU

Dear Andrew Dempsey,

Just to suggest that the Arts Council of Great Britain should now look into the possibility of organising a survey exhibition of the works of black artists in Britain. Although I'm aware of the pitfalls in approaching art from a point of view that may lead to separate groups based on sex, race, etc., the separateness already exists and it is not of our own making but a result of the attitude of the society. Moreover there doesn't seem to be any choice for us except in asserting now our historical presence here separately, till the cultural institutions of the country come to terms with the multi-racial aspect of this society by fully recognising the equal abilities of all peoples irrespective of colour and race.

I would therefore like to propose a study project which should look into what has actually been produced by black artists in Britain for the last thirty or so years, by placing them in their socio-historical context, and then making this information available to public. This could take the form of a book as well as become a basis for a comprehensive exhibition.

This information is crucial at this particular time when the progressive forces of the country are moving towards recognising the fact that black people are here to stay and they shall, and will, become permanent part of British society. It is important therefore for the people to know that black people constitute not only those who by their hard work have been contributing to the material prosperity of the country but also those who have been engaged in artistic and cultural activities.

The ignorance of the work of professional black artists in this country is in fact responsible for the lack of incentive among the younger generation of blacks (40% of them are born here) to enter the field of visual arts. The situation now requires an urgent redress and this cannot be achieved by merely providing new opportunities, nor by pigeonholing black people into various ethnic categories and then placing them in the context of the countries of their origin, but by fully recognising their past achievements in this country. The presence of black artists in Britain is part of recent British history, as well as the world at large, and this aspect of the history must be brought to surface if we as black people are expected to contribute positively towards the development of this society into a truly multi-racial society.

I would therefore like to know if the Arts Council is prepared to consider this proposal. However I shall be away in Pakistan for the next six weeks and this will give you enough time to think and discuss the matter with your collegues. I shall be back in London sometime in the middle of December and then, if you wish, we can discuss the matter further and, if possible, give the proposal a concrete framework.

With regards,

Rasheed Araeen

the first of a number of autonomous platforms he would initiate to encourage independent thinking against cultural imperialism. But, until the letter to Dempsey, Araeen had not directly approached the seat of power, nor had he been engaged in exhibition making. *The Other Story*, was his first curatorial proposal, signalling a shift in his modus operandi: whereas initiating alternative discourses, publishing, and activism challenged dominant social and political constructs, ultimately he needed to turn attention to the art object, not the artist or the politics of race. To produce exhibitions for mainstream art institutions so that artworks can be experienced, understood, and historicized, he believed, was a way to do this.

Almost a year after receiving the letter, Dempsey, on behalf of the Arts Council exhibition committee, finally responded to Araeen, only to reject the proposal because it was felt that the suggested artists already had exposure. He did add, however, it was a 'subject' that should be revisited 'to remind the committee of an area of work which has not been considered in the past as seriously as it should have been'.[10] In his reply, Araeen noted the committee's double standards with respect to artistic 'exposure'; their lack of foresight in not initiating a 'preliminary investigation' before rejecting the proposal; and their 'extraordinary' neglect to take responsibility for the position of black artists in Britain. Araeen then ended the letter on a positive note, stating that he looked forward to hearing from the Arts Council again, should their attitude change.

That change came in March 1986 following his second approach to Dempsey, which resulted in *The Other Story* proposal being accepted. With hindsight it's possible to see this was not an epiphany by the committee, but the likely consequence of the 'Ethnic Minority Arts Action Plan' that had just been initiated by the Arts Council.[11] This had spawned a number of exhibitions and initiatives that were to represent the mandate for a more inclusive agenda in museums and non-profits. Araeen made reference to the 'Action Plan' in his acceptance of Dempsey's invitation, indicating he was aware of the strategic reasons for the change of heart, but wrote that he was glad the Arts Council was now recognizing what he had been saying for the last decade.[12]

In the meantime, the artist had established *Project MRB* in 1982, receiving seed funding from the Greater London Art Association (GLAA) and the Greater London Council (GLC) to research the history of black artists in Britain, with the intention of setting up an archive and research centre. An offshoot of this initiative was the launch of Kala Press, instituted to publish reports, newsletters, and books from the findings, incorporating *Black Phoenix* into its back catalogue. In 1984, the two entities were merged under a new name, *Black Umbrella*, which defined itself as the 'AfroAsian People's Visual Arts Resource & Information Centre'. Primarily self-funded, this is a quasi-institutional structure through which Araeen has since developed his expanded practice.[13]

When the acceptance letter from Dempsey arrived, Araeen was in the process of mounting *THIRD WORLD WITHIN: a cross section of work by AfroAsian artists in Britain* at the Brixton Art Gallery in London under the auspices of *Black Umbrella*. This was, according to the press release, a 'hurriedly put together' alternative to the exhibition, *Essential Black Art*, that had not received GLC funding in time. The latter would eventually be presented at Chisenhale Gallery and then tour from early 1988.

With both shows, emphasis was placed on contemporary politics, young artists, and the fundamental misuses of the term Black Art, in that 'whatever is produced by black artists is seen as Black Art', rather than it being a specific socio-historical term.[14] In effect, both shows were prequels to Araeen's quest for AfroAsian art-historical inclusivity, which was the intention of *The Other Story*.

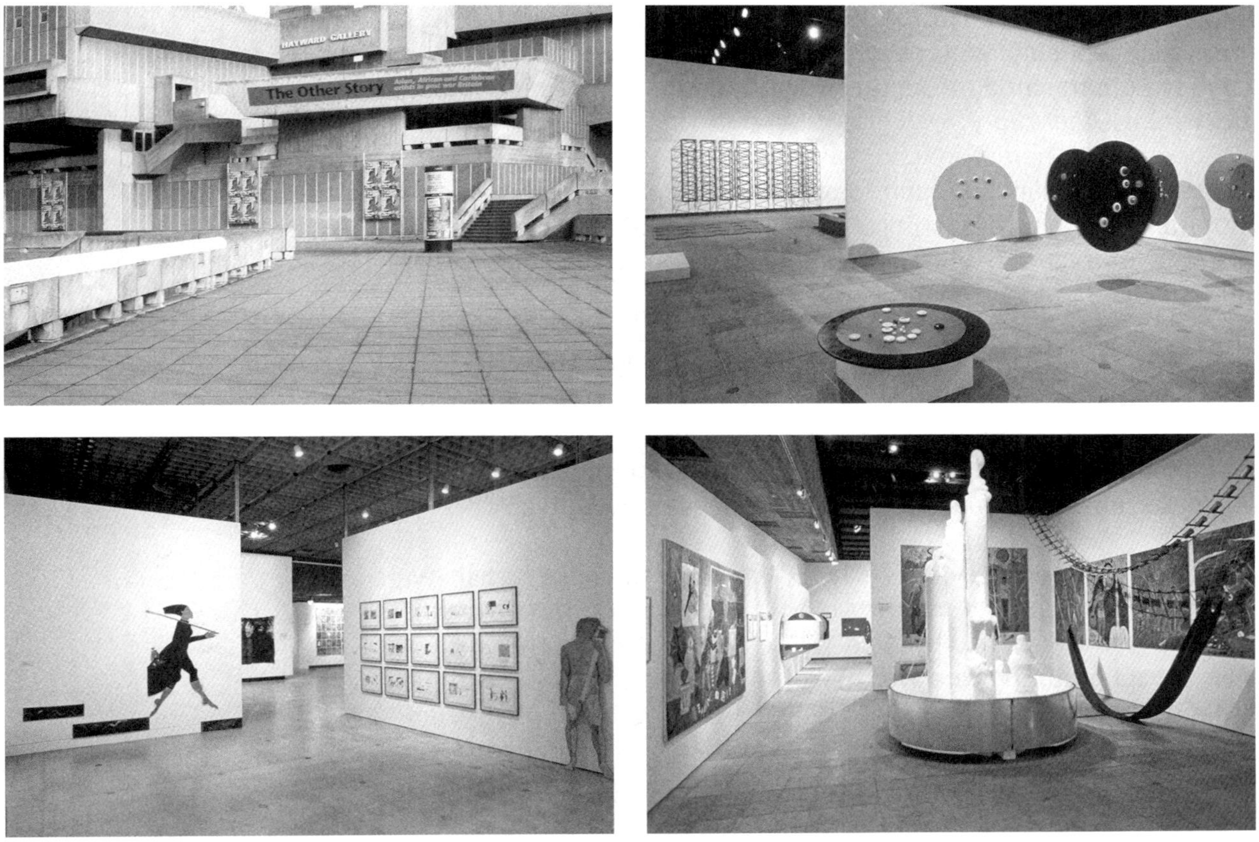

Installation views of **The Other Story**
Hayward Gallery, London, 1989

During the development of *The Other Story* a series of meetings took place with Dempsey and an advisory group (Richard Cork, Balraj Khanna, David Thompson, Aubrey Williams). During the discussions, as the archives of the Southbank Centre record, discrepancies between the advisor's political mandate – motivated by the inclusive tendencies of the 'Ethnic Arts' imperative – and Araeen's corrective mission met head on. The main difference in perspective was the remit of the show. The advisors were advocating for the inclusion of all types of AfroAsian practices, including artists who worked with traditional materials and forms. For Araeen the only criterion should be 'historical and critical considerations'.

Eventually the show opened at Hayward Gallery on 29 November 1989 before travelling to Wolverhampton Art Gallery, Manchester City Art Gallery, and Cornerhouse, also in Manchester, closing in June 1990. It included twenty-four artists, divided into four chronological sections – In the Citadel of Modernism; Taking the Bull by the Horns; Confronting the System; and Recovering Cultural Metaphors – with works ranging from the late 1930s by artists who had immigrated to the UK from British colonies, through to the 1980s with first-generation black British artists.[15] In the press release *The Other Story* was described as 'an exhibition which celebrates the contribution of artists from the countries of Africa, Asia, and the Caribbean to art in Britain in the post-war period'. The press, however, did not pick up on the cause for celebration.

Media reaction to the exhibition instead generally reflected the prejudice and pompous attitudes that were rife within the art establishment at the time. Journalists took a defensive stance in reviews, as in Marina Vaizey's piece for *The Sunday Times*: '…but racism is endemic, to our shame, in most societies that have more than one race…'; or William Packer for the *Financial Times*: 'The charge inferred by the "Other" of the title is that so substantial a body of work can only have been neglected by virtue of a critico-cultural conspiracy on our, the host society's part'. If the question of art historical inclusion was raised, many suggested that it was the lack of talent, or a focus on politics, that was the root cause of the artist's so-called non-acceptance into the mainstream. To cite one review, Andrew Graham Dixon wrote in *The Independent*: '...you are just left with the impression that their work is uninteresting, and that race has nothing to do with it', suggesting later in the article, 'but art history demands innovation rather than political effectiveness'.

Column inches were dedicated in large part to artists' biographies, giving readers potted histories of trajectories and accomplishments rather than descriptions of their work. After citing some of the older generation artists' academic credentials, Brian Sewell of the *Evening Standard* wrote:

> All this they adduce for their argument that they are despised, rejected, ignored and invisible, when they are nothing of the kind. Let me now suggest that perhaps they should be. ... Talent in the white West is an extremely rare phenomenon and most Western art is indifferent at best. I see no reason to distort the judgement that damns it so as to praise the work of artists just as bad, or worse, because they make the noisy business of being black.

It was frequently stated – as Dempsey had in 1978 – that the exhibiting artists were actually *not* overlooked, particularly during the glory days of the Commonwealth Institute exhibition programme, and in the late 1980s when, some journalists claimed, artists of all backgrounds were well represented in commercial galleries and museums. Many reasons were given as to why the show excused AfroAsian mediocrity: Vaizey, Graham Dixon, and Sewell among others all mentioned Anish Kapoor was representing Britain at Venice that year and the many 'successful' artists – Kapoor, Shirazeh Houshiary, and Dhruva Mistry, to name a few – who had refused to be in the show as they were not into 'special pleading' (Vaizey).[16] In short, the hypothesis and ambitions of *The Other Story* were eclipsed by the public anxieties of multiculturalism and at times blatant racism.

Araeen's long-time friend and collaborator, Jean Fisher, pre-empted this kind of response in her editorial for the special issue of *Third Text*, intended as a supplement to *The Other Story*, released at the time of the show. In this, she posits that it is 'history itself' at stake. As a Western form of narrative used to prop up national identity, Fisher writes, it cannot be viewed as some kind of universal truth, but 'an interpretation of a set of events conditioned by the ideological demands of a dominant or hegemonic group'. It follows, therefore, that so-called history is ultimately just a series of myths that must be protected: 'For the Modernist art critic avant-gardism is as much an "essentialist" European art movement as stasis is the culture of others.'[17]

Smokescreens and Roadblocks

In spite of debates ignited by *The Other Story*, it has taken years for the exhibition to be re-evaluated, in large part due to the increased attention paid to identity politics and postcolonial discourse – as opposed to historiography – in exhibitions, conferences, and writing during the ensuing decade. In the 1990s, Araeen turned his activism back towards publishing, developing *Third Text*, while the Arts Council focused on infrastructures that would champion their diversity mandate. A prime example is the Institute for International Visual Arts (Iniva), which was inaugurated in 1994 with the conference *Global Visions: Towards a New Internationalism*. Under the premise 'Postmodernity demands a different concept of internationalism', esteemed professionals were asked to outline what their questions were with respect to 'curatorial work, collecting and the construction of postmodern art history' in a new, expanded art world.[18]

Araeen was an outspoken participant, probing the motivations for founding Iniva, describing the personal experiences on which his apprehensions were based: 'Having lived and struggled as an artist in Britain for the last thirty years, and often finding myself at loggerheads with the art establishment, I'm too well aware of the difficulties one faces when trying to change the system.' His argument was: how did such establishments – the forces that he saw as undermining the struggle – become leaders of the debate? 'Does this represent a genuine change on the part of our art institutions or a smokescreen?' he asked.

What Araeen didn't reveal in his presentation were his own efforts at institutional formation: a year before Iniva was inaugurated, his outline for the further development of *Black Umbrella* proposed creating archives, discursive platforms, and exhibitions. This proposal was rejected by the Arts Council, who then established Iniva with that very premise.[19] Instead, during the conference he took another tack, probing whether Iniva was established to eliminate, instead of reflect difference: 'If "new internationalism" means a global projection of the idea of cultural pluralism, or multiculturalism, as it has been formed in the West, then I am afraid we are on shaky ground.'

To this point, he cited the exhibition *Magiciens de la terre* (curated by Jean-Hubert Martin at the Centre George Pompidou and Grande Halle at Parc de la Villette in Paris in 1989, the same year as *The Other Story*), which had gathered artworks from all over the world 'without any regard for a common artistic criterion or framework', but that were also 'legitimized differently as art in terms of preconceived distinctions between the West and non-West'. He then went on to talk about *The Other Story* in contrast to the trend of multicultural expressions of identity: 'The obsession with cultural difference is now being institutionally legitimized through the construction of the "postcolonial other", who is allowed to express itself only as long as it speaks of its own otherness', suggesting that this was a fundamental roadblock to the critical assessment of artworks.[20]

In relation to this distorted criterion for evaluation, Araeen brought up the (then) recent article in *October*, the journal's first published roundtable discussion. Focusing on the 1993 Biennial Exhibition at the Whitney Museum of American Art in New York, the roundtable explored how the show tackled issues of multiculturalism and the Culture Wars by presenting artists whose practices engaged with migration, diaspora, gender, and race in the US.[21] In the article, Benjamin Buchloh, Hal Foster, Silvia Kolbowski, Rosalind Krauss, and Miwon Kwon deliberated how political, socio-economic, and institutional change was affecting the frames through which art was being produced and understood. This, it was determined, had transformed how meaning in art was conveyed.[22] Drawing a parallel to what was happening in Britain, Araeen surmised that it was actually the Western notion of multiculturalism that prevented the development of an international standard, 'in terms of aesthetics, historical formation, location and significance, rules not necessarily derived from any one or originary culture'.[23]

Expanding this transatlantic debate, in 2001 Duke University presented the conference, *Shades of Black*, on the 1980s Black Arts Movement in Britain. Here, the arguments that emerged in the 1990s were incorporated to assess the changing relationship between art, politics, and culture both in Britain and the US. In his paper, 'Iconography After Identity', art historian Kobena Mercer addressed many issues that Araeen had been speaking out against over the preceding two decades. Mercer's perspective was that, in part, the problem was institutional 'shallow memory', wherein the drive to seize 'the contemporary moment' led to a policy of exhibition making that created historical oversight: 'In my view there is a strong tendency in much of this discourse to shuttle between two extremes, between a sort of low grade celebrationism of multicultural murmuring and a highly charged, explosive and divisive controversy, both of which deflect attention from the work of art itself'. He put this down to the basic fact that there is 'conceptual chaos and confusion' both in writing and curating about where to focus, between the biography of an artist – their cultural identity – or the work of art. This results in what he describes as the 'optical wobble' between background and foreground, so that 'the dignity of objecthood is very rarely bestowed on the diaspora's works of art'. [24]

Mercer's observations have since been credited with inspiring the first comprehensive research initiative – Black Artists and Modernism (BAM) – to focus on how artists of African and Asian descent feature in the story of twentieth century art. Sonia Boyce – an artist who was included in *The Other Story* and principal investigator of BAM – says it was Mercer's paper at the *Shades of Black* conference that triggered the leading research question, which she paraphrased as: 'How have we missed talking about the work and contextualizing it in its historical moment?'[25] It's impossible Boyce would have 'missed' the fact that *The Other Story* was premised on this intention long before Mercer's text was written – indeed the exhibition was the subject of a BAM conference – but the fact of Araeen's sustained insistence on redressing the modernist canon and his long time proposition to create *The Whole Story*, is largely missing from the history currently being created.[26]

Ultimately, Fisher's proposition from 1989 – that history is an interpretation of events, not a "universal truth" – remains perhaps the only universal truth. *The Other Story* is now recognized as an important event in history, but its underlying premise is still unanswered. Chris Smith's call for 'a more complete version of the truth', is perhaps put in motion through the building of initiatives such as BAM, but for Araeen, it could be said, history is simply repeating itself:

> Nothing has changed. The art history of modernism continues to be exclusively the history of white artists, behind which still lurks the ideas of white supremacy, which rules the world. ... The problem to my mind is that the real agenda of the art establishment has always been to create a black functionary class which would pretend do something to bring about a radical change in the system, but who would, in fact, serve the imperial interests in art of the British state.[27]

In Pursuit of Truth

Following Araeen's statement, and by way of an (incomplete) conclusion, it is important to consider whether the turn to addressing exhibition histories could be seen as yet another act of institutional deflection. Increasingly deployed by museums and academia, this form of analysis has enabled exhibitions such as *The Other Story* to be revisited and their impact reconsidered, yet it remains to be seen if this changes the presented works' standing in art history. In this new form of historicization lies a danger of forgetting that curatorial intervention is only a temporary corrective to the problematics of discourse at any given time. An exhibition, in other words, cannot be the institutional answer to abiding responsibility towards building the art historical canon.

Fisher further expands on these problematics in her coherent critique of *The Other Story* presented at the conference *Exhibitions and the World at Large* in 2009. She explained that Araeen, as with a number of his colleagues in the 1980s, turned to curating and writing because of the absence of institutionally driven initiatives 'to construct a cultural and archival counter memory'. This, however, created a paradox insofar as the exhibition 'implied a desire for inclusion in and approbation from a system regarded at the outset as unjust and corrupt'.[28] What she calls the 'oppositional politics' of this double bind caused an endgame played out both by critics then and posthumously. While *The Other Story* was important in its anti-colonial critique, it produced and fetishized difference by its very existence, rather than pointing to the commonalities of the selected artists' works to the modernist tradition as Araeen intended. But, to focus on this, Fisher states, misses the main point: Araeen, as part of the Commonwealth generation and one of the founders of the Black Arts Movement, is a bridge. As such, his curatorial pursuit is important because the selected work connects the two generations art historically. Until the show existed this had not occurred in either writing or exhibitions. It was the first initiative to give the younger generation an awareness of an otherwise obscured context.

While sitting with Araeen in his south London studio, I asked him numerous questions about his curatorial work and track record of establishing institutional structures as platforms for debate, from Kala Press to *Third Text* to *Black Umbrella*. But, despite my enthusiasm, he was wearied in his responses, asserting that he was not a curator, a professor, a historian, nor a critic, and had never pursued these professions as a career. Instead he saw exhibitions as Conceptual art projects, and the institutional structures he builds as a form of social practice: one he was happy to give up once European institutions were no longer the legacy of empires.

For him making art has never ceased to be his raison d'être, but this doesn't happen in a vacuum. His concern is also with the knowledge of ideas and the fact that there are gaps in what we recognize as knowledge. The information is there, he says, but it's not institutionally embedded. This is why he continues to push the development of *The Whole Story* – particularly in published form – and with it an inclusive, revised British art history. But, this has met with resistance from the Tate and the Arts Council among other institutions.[29] In the end, the problem is perhaps with misconstrued intentions, which remains the case today as it was in 1978 when *The Other Story* was first proposed, which Fisher has subsequently brought to the fore, and why Araeen will seemingly have to repeat himself as he did, probably for the umpteenth time that February afternoon: 'I'm not doing it for myself, for black artists, or for the Third World. My main focus is modernism, but institutions don't understand that. They think I want something from them.'[30]

1 Rasheed Araeen, unpublished project proposal e-mailed to the author, 'The Whole Story: Art in Postwar Britain', August 2000/October 2003.

2 For one recent summary of Araeen's use of the term 'black' and 'Afro-Asian' see Jens Hoffman, 'Countless (Untold) Stories. Rasheed Araeen in Conversation with Jens Hoffman', *Mousse Magazine* 58 (April – May 2017):139: 'The difference lay in the nature of racism in Britain, as you suggested, which was the legacy of colonialism: whoever was colonized was "black" (in the 1960s, racism was also directed against Irish people). It was this colonial "blackness" that united Asian, African, and Caribbean people in Britain, resulting in a common identity. Historically and politically, this unity of African and Asian people was also formed and asserted by the Bandung Conference in 1955.' For an understanding of Araeen's use of the term 'modernism' see Rasheed Araeen, 'In The Citadel of Modernism', in *The Other Story: Afro-Asian Artists in Post-War Britain*, ed. Rasheed Araeen (London: Southbank Centre, 1989), 16: '"Modernism" here signifies that broad philosophical framework within which the modern art movement has taken place in the twentieth century, with all its diversity and disunity of forms and styles, and which also provides theoretical discourse for the evaluation and legitimization of modern works of art. ... To simplify the matter, we can say that what is under consideration is the art of an epoch dominated by the bourgeois society of late capitalism, not only in its metropolis but also in the colonial and postcolonial outposts. ... so that the citadel of its modernism is protected from any possible intrusion from the outside ... the very fear of the Other being within has produced a whole philosophical discourse that is unable to resolve this contradiction.'

3 Key texts by Araeen include: 'Preliminary Notes for a BLACK MANIFESTO', *Black Phoenix* 1 (winter 1978):3–12, reprinted in *Making Myself Visible,* ed. Rasheed Araeen (London: Kala Press, 1984), 73–97; 'From Primitivism to Ethnic Arts', *Third Text* 1, no. 1 (fall 1987):6–25; 'The Emergence of Black Consciousness in Contemporary Art in Britain: Seventeen Years of Neglected History', in *The Essential Black Art* (London: Chisenhale Gallery, 1988), 5–11; 'Our Bauhaus, Others' Mudhouse', *Third Text* 3, no. 6 (spring 1989):3–14; 'A New Beginning: Beyond Postcolonial Cultural Theory and Identity Politics', *Third Text* 14, no. 50 (spring 2000):3–21; 'The Art of Benevolent Racism', *Third Text* 14, no. 51 (summer 2000):57–64; 'Return to the Source', in *Art Beyond Art, Ecoaesthetics: A Manifesto for the 21st Century* (London: Third Text Publications, 2010), 111–128.

4 Quotes taken from the unpublished project proposal 'The Whole Story'.

5 Ibid.

6 Ibid.

7 The Arts Council of England rejected the proposal twice, then gave it seed funding, and now maintains it's interested in the project. As told to the author in an interview at the artist's studio, London, 8 February 2017.

8 Hoffman, 'Countless (Untold) Stories', 140. For a detailed account of the second *Hayward Annual*, critical responses, and the rise of feminist discourse around contemporary art in Britain see Griselda Pollock, 'Feminism, Femininity and the Hayward Annual Exhibition 1978', *Feminist Review* 2, no. 1 (July 1979):33–35. The curators were Liliane Lijn, Rita Donagh, Kim Lim, Tess Jaray, and Gillian Wise Ciobaratu.

9 Statement written by *Black Phoenix*, 2 August 1978, quoted in Araeen, *Making Myself Visible*, 162.

10 All quotations taken from correspondence of *The Other Story: Afro-Asian Artists in Post-War Britain*, Hayward Gallery Art Library, Southbank Centre archive, London.

11 The 'Action Plan' was part of a wider shift in the UK throughout the decade, as institutions were forced to reassess their policies in light of the racial division and exclusion endemic in the cultural sector and Thatcherite Britain. See *Arts Council of Great Britain: records, 1928–1997: Ethnic Minority Arts Unit Papers, 1976–1989* (ref: ACGB/79), http://media.vam.ac.uk/media/website/acgb/acgb-79.html.

12 Araeen's first responses were triggered by a published report, Naseem Kahn, 'The Art that Britain Ignores' (London: Commission for Racial Equality, 1976) based on commissioned research. This led to the establishment of Minorities Arts Advisory Service and an advisory group to the arts in the Commission for Racial Equality. It also established the term 'Ethnic Arts', which was replaced by 'Diversity Arts' in 1988–1989. For Araeen's response read 'The Art That Britain *Really* Ignores', in *Making Myself Visible*, 100–105. For a description of the outcome of Ethnic Arts initiatives see Naseem Khan, 'The Arts Of Ethnic Minorities In Britain', *Journal of the Royal Society Of Arts* 128, no. 5290 (September 1980):676–688. Apart from Araeen's curatorial initiatives during the time of the 'Action Plan', other exhibitions include *From Two Worlds*, Whitechapel Gallery, London, 30 July – 7 September 1986, curated by Nicholas Serota and Gavin Jantjes; *The Image Employed: the use of narrative in Black art,* Cornerhouse, Manchester, 13 June – 19 July 1987, curated by Keith Piper and Marlene Smith; *Rasheed Araeen*, Ikon Gallery, Birmingham, 21 November 1987 – 9 January 1988; *Black Art: Plotting the Course*, Oldham Art Gallery, 22 October – 3 December 1988, curated by Eddie Chambers at: Wolverhampton Art Gallery; Bluecoat Gallery, Liverpool; and Camden Arts Center, London.

13 Documents describing the history of *Project MRB* and *Black Umbrella* are now part of the artist's archive at Asia Art Archive, Hong Kong.

14 Araeen, *Essential Black Art*, press release, 1988, http://chisenhale.org.uk/archive/exhibitions/index.php?id=142. *Third World Within* included Araeen, Saleem Arif, David Bailey, Sutapa Biswas, Avtarjeet Dhanjal, Uzo Egonu, Mona Hatoum, Gavin Jantjes, Merdelle J-Irving, Houria Niati, Keith Piper, and Kumiko Shimuzu, Brixton Art Gallery, London, 31 March – 22 April 1986; *Essential Black Art* included Araeen, Zarina Bhimji, Biswas, Sonia Boyce, Eddie Chambers, Hatoum, Lubaina Himid, Gavin Jantjes, Piper, and Alan de Souza, Chisenhale Gallery, London, 5 February – 5 March 1988; it travelled to: Laing Art Gallery, Newcastle-upon-Tyne; Huddersfield Art Gallery; Herbert Art Gallery, Coventry; Gardner Arts Centre, Sussex University, Brighton; and Cooper Gallery, Barnsley.

15 Artists involved: Araeen, Arif, Frank Bowling, Boyce, Chambers, Avinash Chandra, Dhanjal, Egonu, Iqbal Geoffrey, Hatoum, Himid, Jantjes, Balraj Khanna, Donald Locke, David Medalla, Ronald Moody, Ahmed Parvez, Ivan Peries, Piper, Anwar Jalal Shemza, Kumiko Shimizu, Francis Newton Souza, Aubrey Williams, and Li Yuan Chia. From the Southbank Centre press release, Hayward Gallery archive.

16 Press coverage of *The Other Story*, Southbank Centre archive includes: Dalya Alberge, 'When White Is The Acceptable Colour Of Art', *The Independent*, 27 November 1989; John Cunningham, 'Scaling The Walls', *The Guardian*, 28 November 1989; Amanda Sebestyen, 'The Other Story', *City Limits*, November 30 – 7 December 1989; William Feaver, 'The Empire Strikes Back', *The Observer*, 3 December 1989; James Hall, 'Black, British And Coming Into View', *Correspondent*, 3 December 1989; Andrew Graham-Dixon, 'Pride And Prejudice', *The Independent*, 5 December 1989; William Packer, 'Immigrant Issues', *Financial Times*, 5 December 1989; Richard Cork, 'Buried Treasures', *The Listener*, 7 December 1989; Richard Dorment, 'Vexed Questions Of Colour', *The Telegraph*, 9 December 1989; Marina Vaizey, 'Why Partiality Doesn't Tell The Whole Story', *The Sunday Times*, 10 December 1989; Jeff Sawtell, 'Pictures of The Resistance', *Morning Star*, 13 December 1989; Sutapa Biswas, 'The Wrong Story', *The New Statesman*, 15 December 1989; Tim Hilton, 'Collision Culture', *The Guardian*, 20 December 1989; Gregory Jensen, 'Art's "Other Story" Stirs Up a Buzz', *Compass Arts*, 22 December 1989; Quentin Williams, 'The Centrality Crippling The Arts in Britain', *The Guardian*, 30 December 1989; Brian Sewell, 'Black Pride And Prejudice', *Evening Standard*, 4 January 1990; Petrine Archer-Straw, 'The Other Story', *Art Monthly* 2 (1990):14–16; Jo-Anne Birnie Danzker, 'Cultural Apartheid', *Muse*, (fall 1990):20–26; and Corinna Lotz, 'The Other Story: Afro-Asian Artists in Post-War Britain', *The Marxist Monthly* 1 (1990):480–486.

17 Jean Fisher, 'editorial', *Third Text* 3, no. 8–9 (fall/winter 1989):3–4.

18 Gavin Jantjes, preface to *Global Visions: Towards a New Internationalism in the Visual Arts*, ed. Jean Fisher (London: Kala Press with Institute of International Visual Arts, 1994), 2. The conference was held at the Tate Gallery.

19 As discussed at length with the author during the interview in Araeen's studio on 8 February 2017 and expanded upon in an e-mail from Araeen on 15 August 2017, *The Whole Story* was initiated in 2000 due to the failure of Iniva to follow-up with the arguments outlined in *The Other Story*, which aimed to integrate AfroAsian art into mainstream British Art History.

20 All quotes from Araeen, 'New Internationalism, or, The Multiculturalism of Global Bantustans', in *Global Visions*, 3–11.

21 Curated by Elisabeth Sussman with co-curators Thelma Golden, John G. Hanhardt, and Lisa Phillips. The subject of multiculturalism was widespread in exhibitions at the time, such as: *Aperto*, Venice, 1993; *Poliphonies*, Budapest, 1993; and *Culture in Action*, Chicago, 1993 as just a few examples outside Britain.

22 Hal Foster, Rosalind Krauss, Silvia Kolbowski, Miwon Kwon, and Benjamin Buchloh, 'The Politics of the Signifier: A Conversation on the Whitney Biennial', *October* 66 (1993):3–27. For further details on Araeen's perspective on *Magiciens de la terre* see his 'Our Bauhaus, Others' Mudhouse', *Third Text* 3, no. 6 (spring 1989): 3–14. For a more in-depth analysis of *Magiciens de la terre*, the 1993 Whitney Biennial, and the subsequent *October* roundtable discussion see Kate Fowle, 'Action Research: Generative Curatorial Practices', in *Curating Research*, ed. Paul O'Neill and Mick Wilson (London: Open Editions, 2015), 153–172.

23 Araeen, 'New Internationalism', 10.

24 Mercer, 'Iconography after Identity', in *Shades of Black: Assembling Black Arts in 1980s Britain*, ed. David A. Bailey, Sonia Boyce, and Ian Baucom (Durham: Duke University Press, 2005), 49–58.

25 Black Artists and Modernism (BAM) is a research project established in 2013 funded by the Arts and Humanities Research Council (AHRC) as a collaboration between University of the Arts London and Middlesex University. The conference *Now & Then... Here & There: Black Artists & Modernism*, where Boyce makes the statement on the influences for BAM, took place at Chelsea College of Art and Clore Auditorium, Tate Britain, 6–8 October 2016. For Boyce's introduction see video documenation on the BAM website, www.blackartistsmodernism.co.uk/2016/12/12/nowthenherethere-keynote-kobenamercer.

26 The one-day symposium *'The Work Between Us': Black British Artists and Exhibition Histories* took place at Bluecoat Gallery, Liverpool, 20 January 2016. For Lucy Steeds' keynote speech on *The Other Story* see www.blackartistsmodernism.co.uk/2016/07/29/the-work-between-us-keynote-lucy-steeds.

27 As written in an e-mail to the author, 15 August 2017.

28 Jean Fisher, 'The Other Story and the Past Imperfect', *Tate Papers* 12 (2009) was based on a talk given at the symposium *Exhibitions and the World at Large*, Tate Britain, 3 April 2009, commissioned by *Afterall* and TrAIN, www.tate.org.uk/download/file/fid/7273.

29 As of August 2017 Araeen has commissioned eighteen art historians to revise the various movements through which post-war British art history is currently told and has received ten texts, with the rest of the writers agreeing to complete essays once the artist has found a publisher. Araeen has pursued Tate Publishing, via Sir Nicholas Serota, from 2002 through May 2017, with no success. As written in an e-mail to the author, 15 August 2017. See notes 7 and 19 for details of the Arts Council dealings.

30 As told to the author in an interview at the artist's studio in south London, 8 February 2017.

Zero to Infinity, 1968–2004
installation at 198 Gallery, Spitalfields, 100 acrylic on wood Structures, 50 x 50 x 50 cm each

Zero to Infinity, 1968–2004 / 2007
installation at Tate, London, 100 acrylic on wood Structures, 50 x 50 x 50 cm each
Tate: Purchased 2009

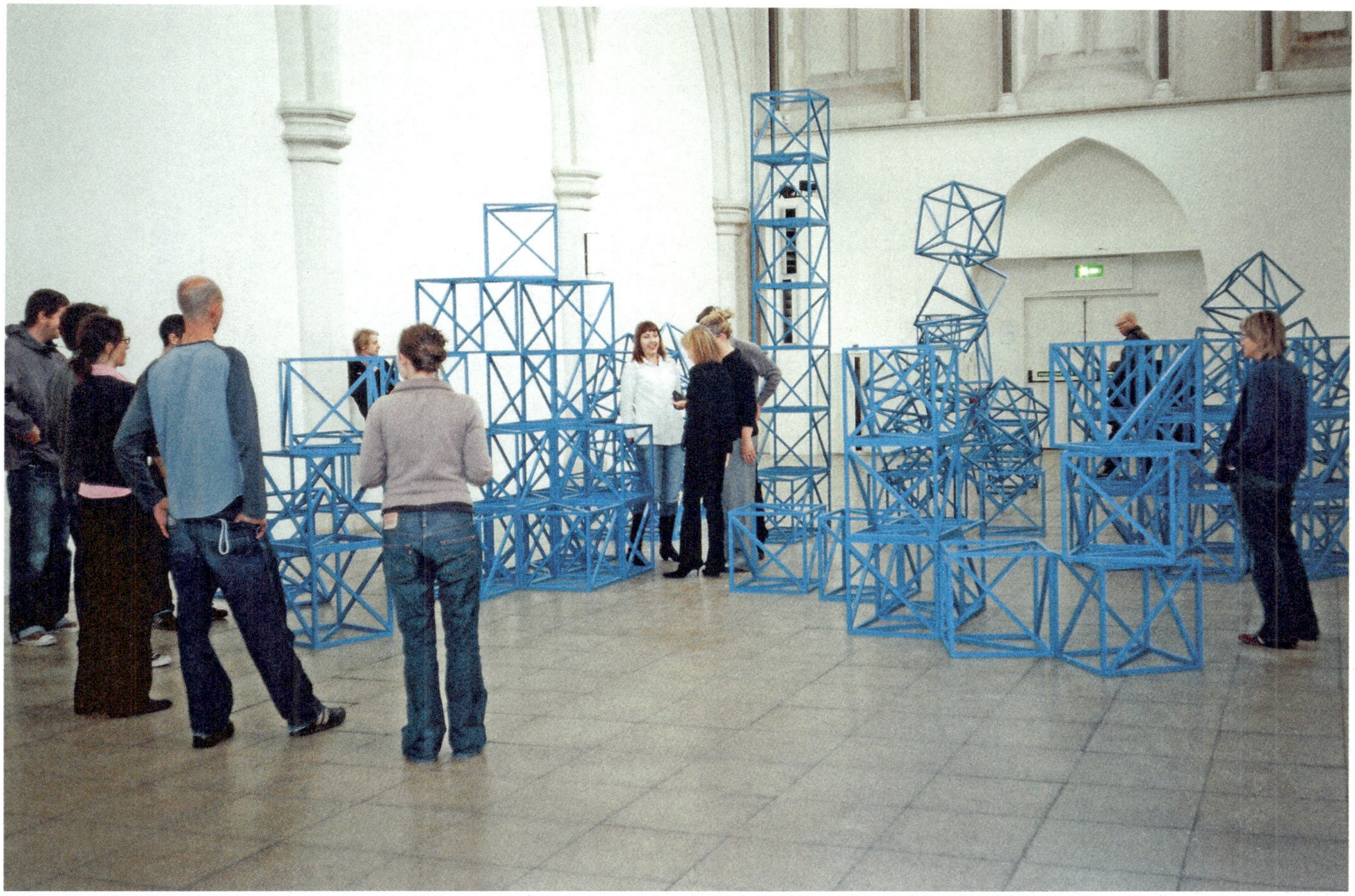

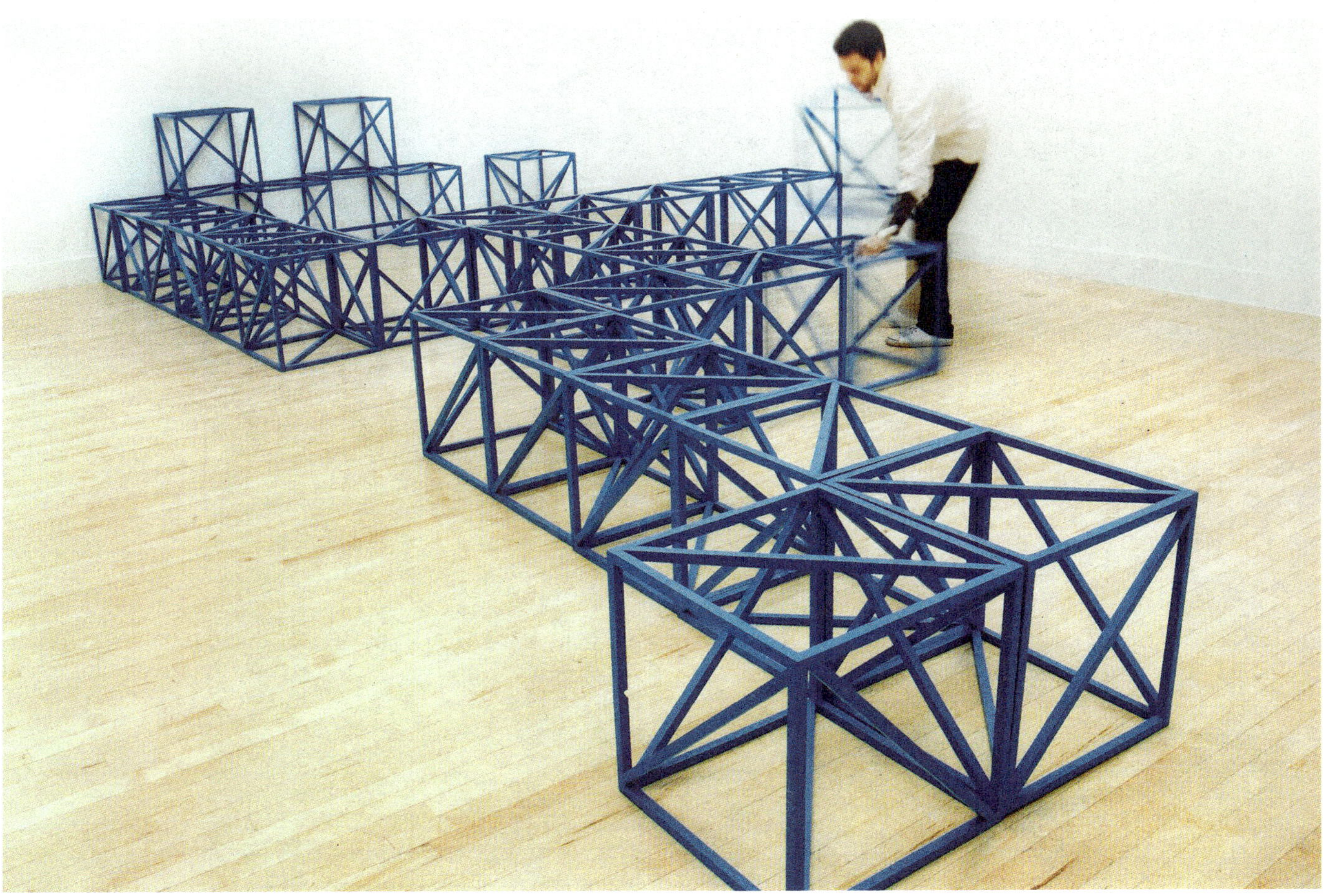

A Proposal for a Collective Farm in Balochistan, 1998
pen on paper, 60 x 42 cm

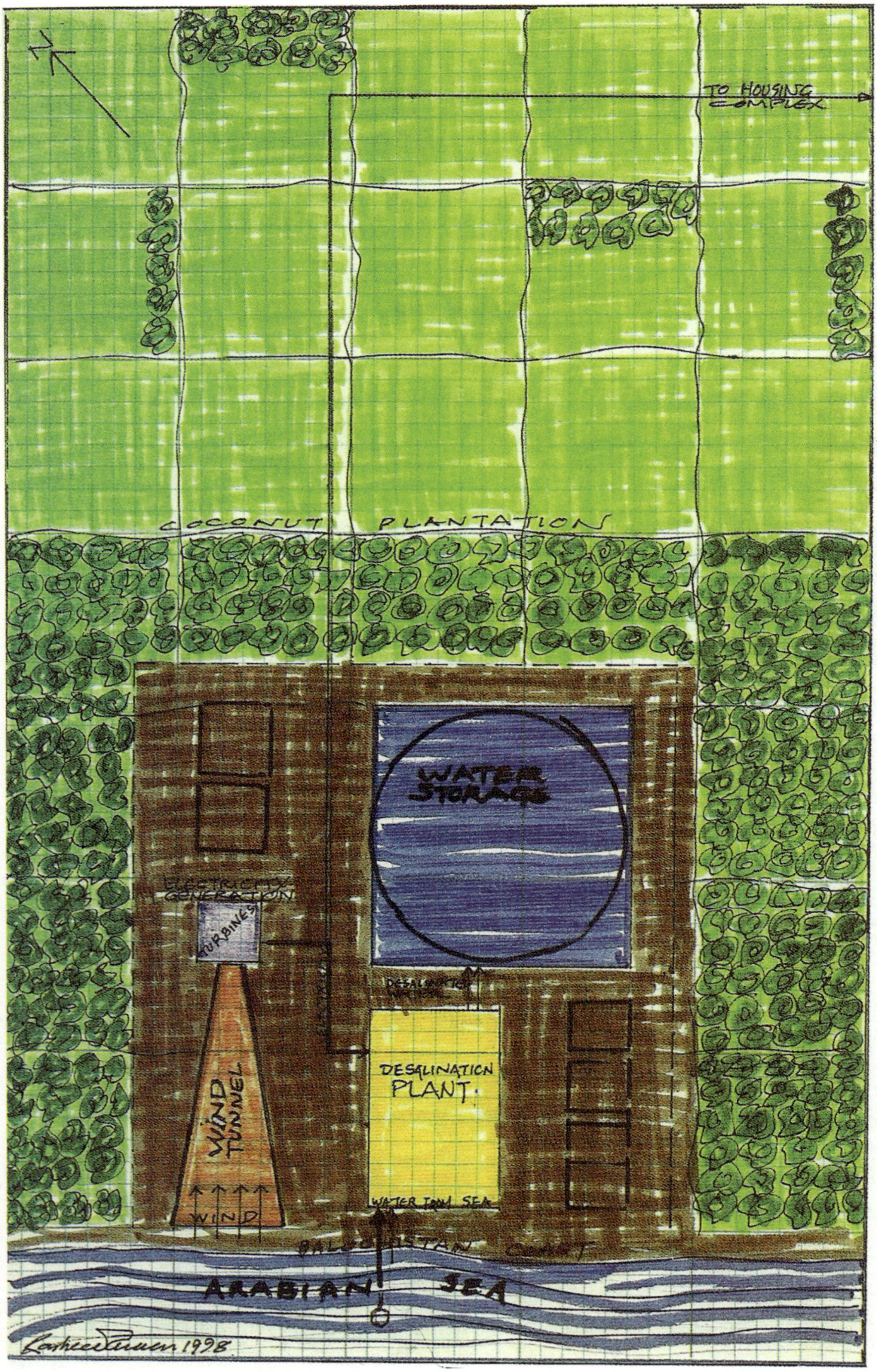

Asthesis, 2005
4 drawings, marker and pen on paper, 30 x 21 cm each

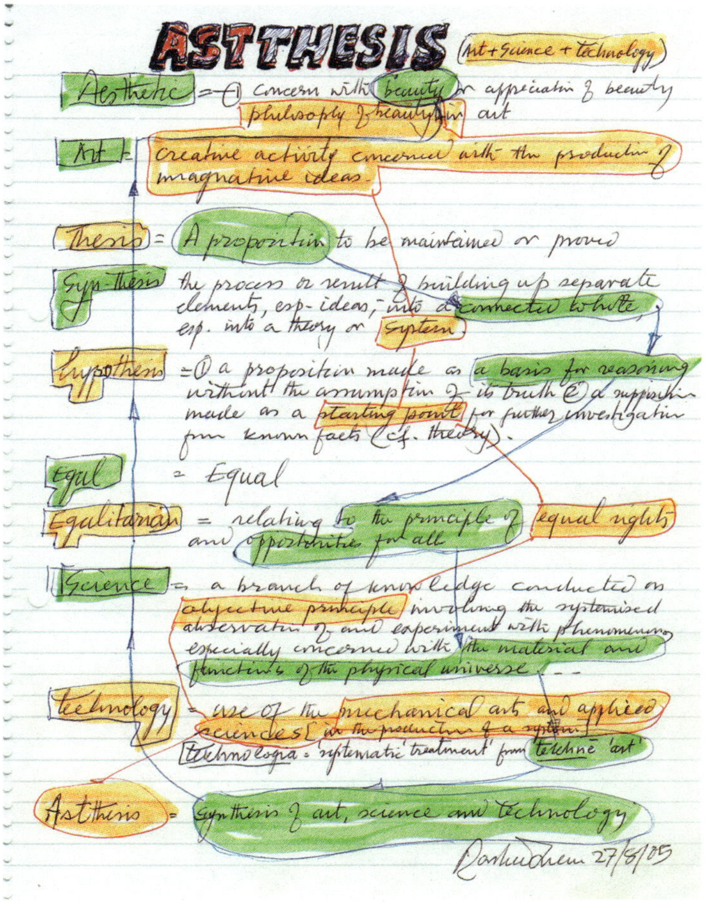

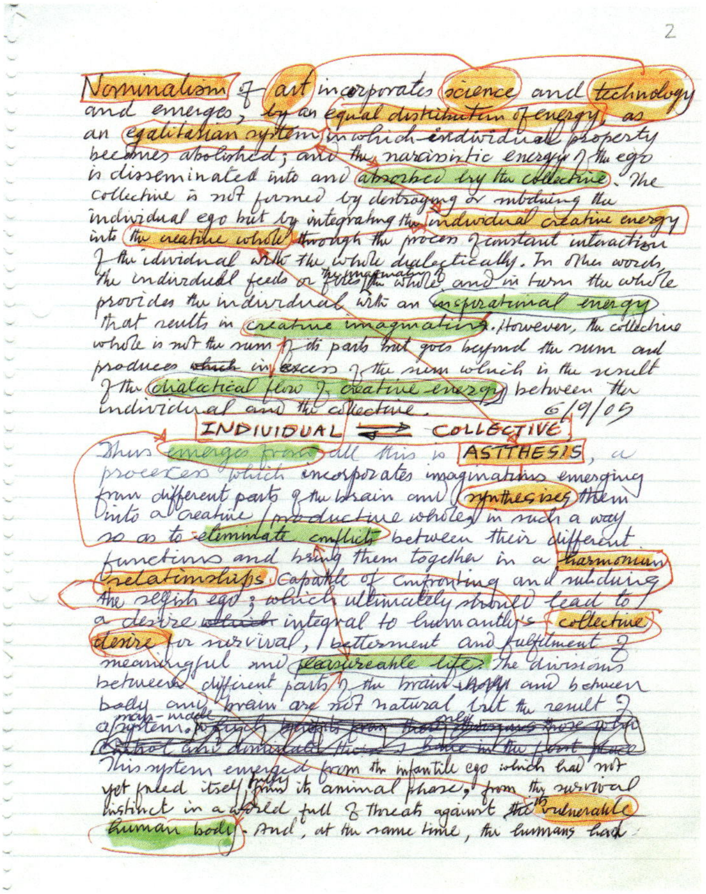

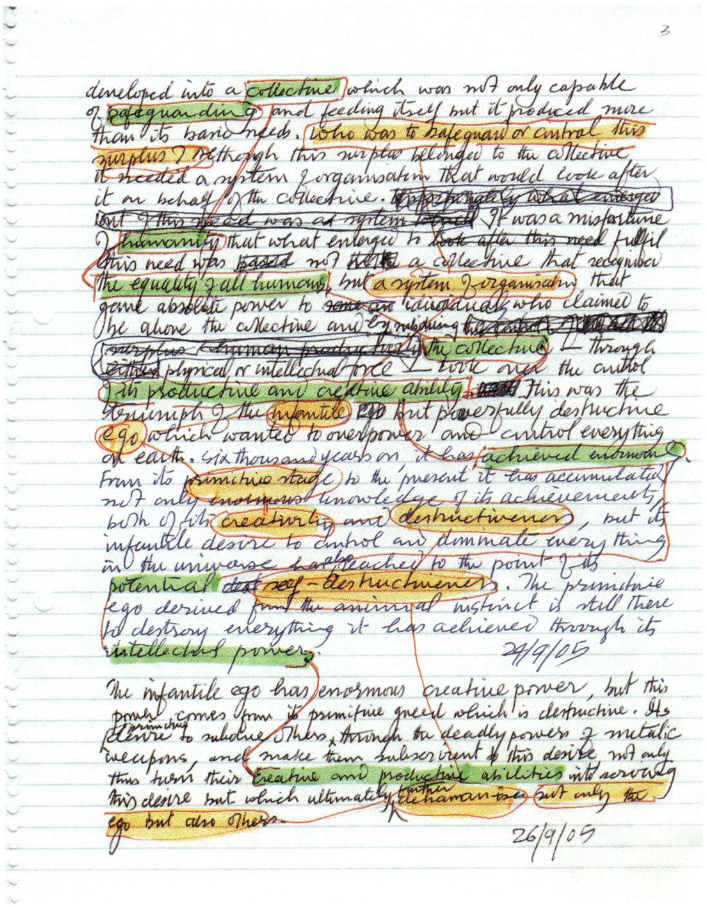

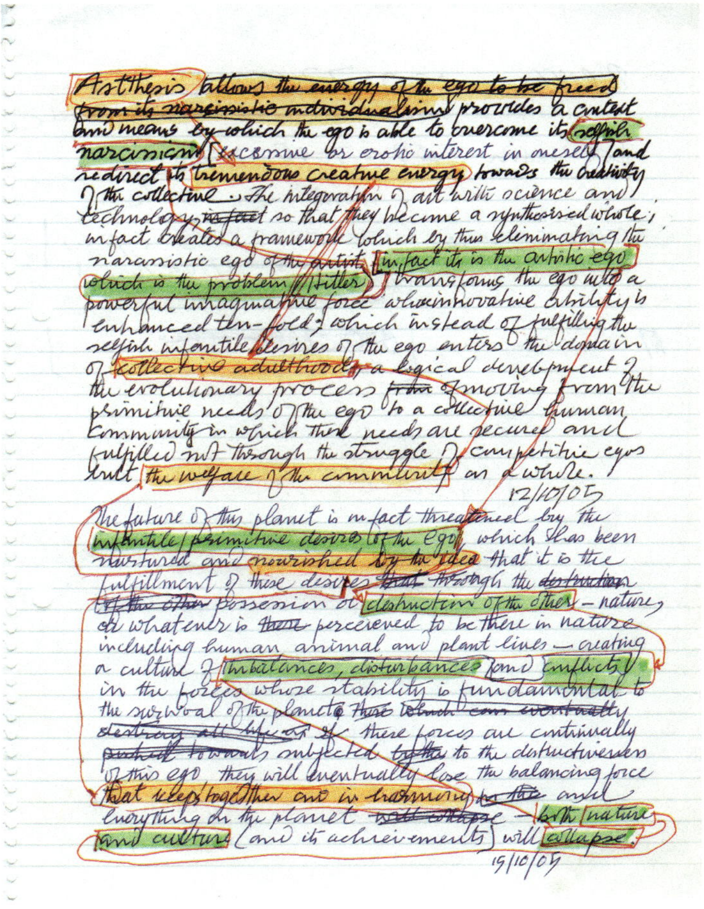

Between The Black Lines, 2002
pen on printed map, 21 x 30 cm
Mediterranean Union, 2002
felt-tip marker and pen on printed map, 21 x 30 cm
Union of Mediterranean Countries, 2009
felt-tip marker on printed map, 21 x 30 cm

Mediterranea, 2001–2002
series of 3 drawings, felt-tip marker and pen on printed map, 21 x 30 cm each (selection)
Mediterranismo, 2002
pen on printed map, 21 x 30 cm
Preliminary Drawing for Mediterranea 1, 2009
felt-tip marker on printed map, 21 x 30 cm

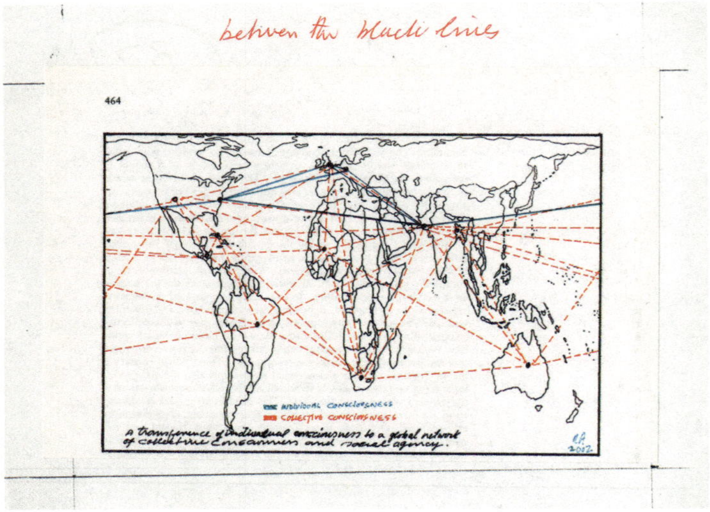

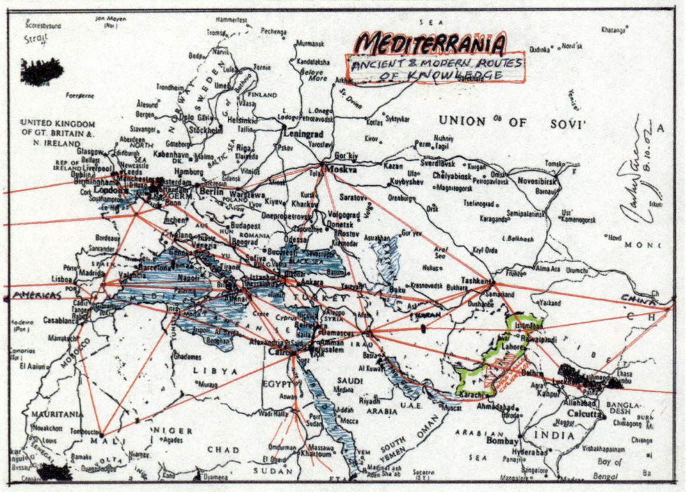

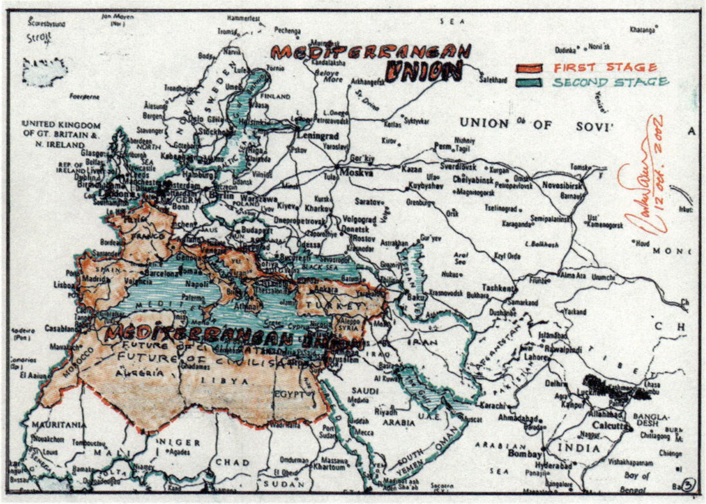

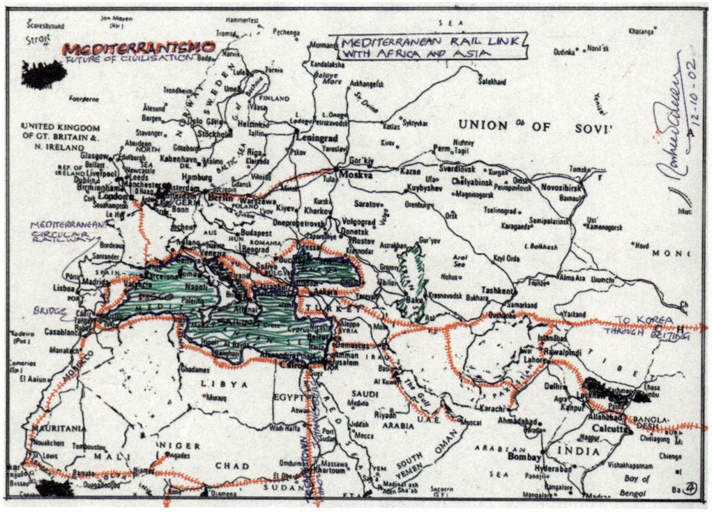

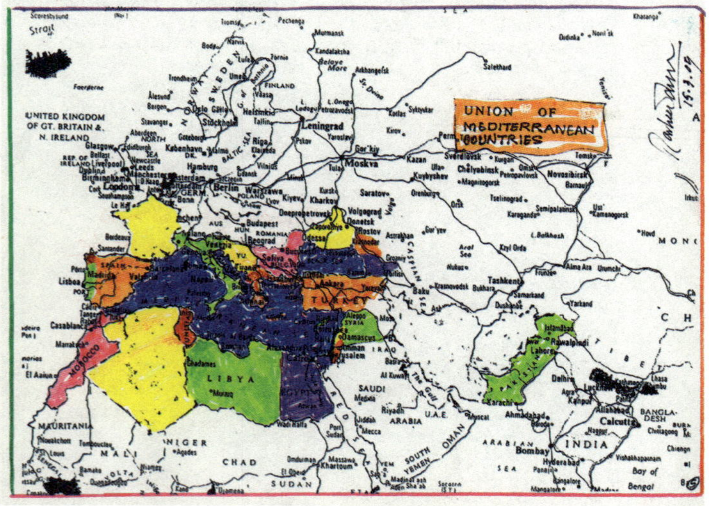

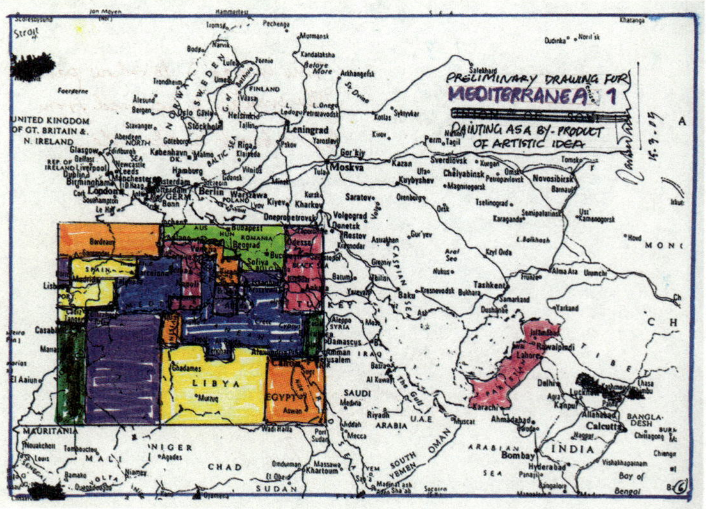

Preliminary Drawing for Mediterranea 2, 2009
felt-tip marker on printed map, 21 x 30 cm

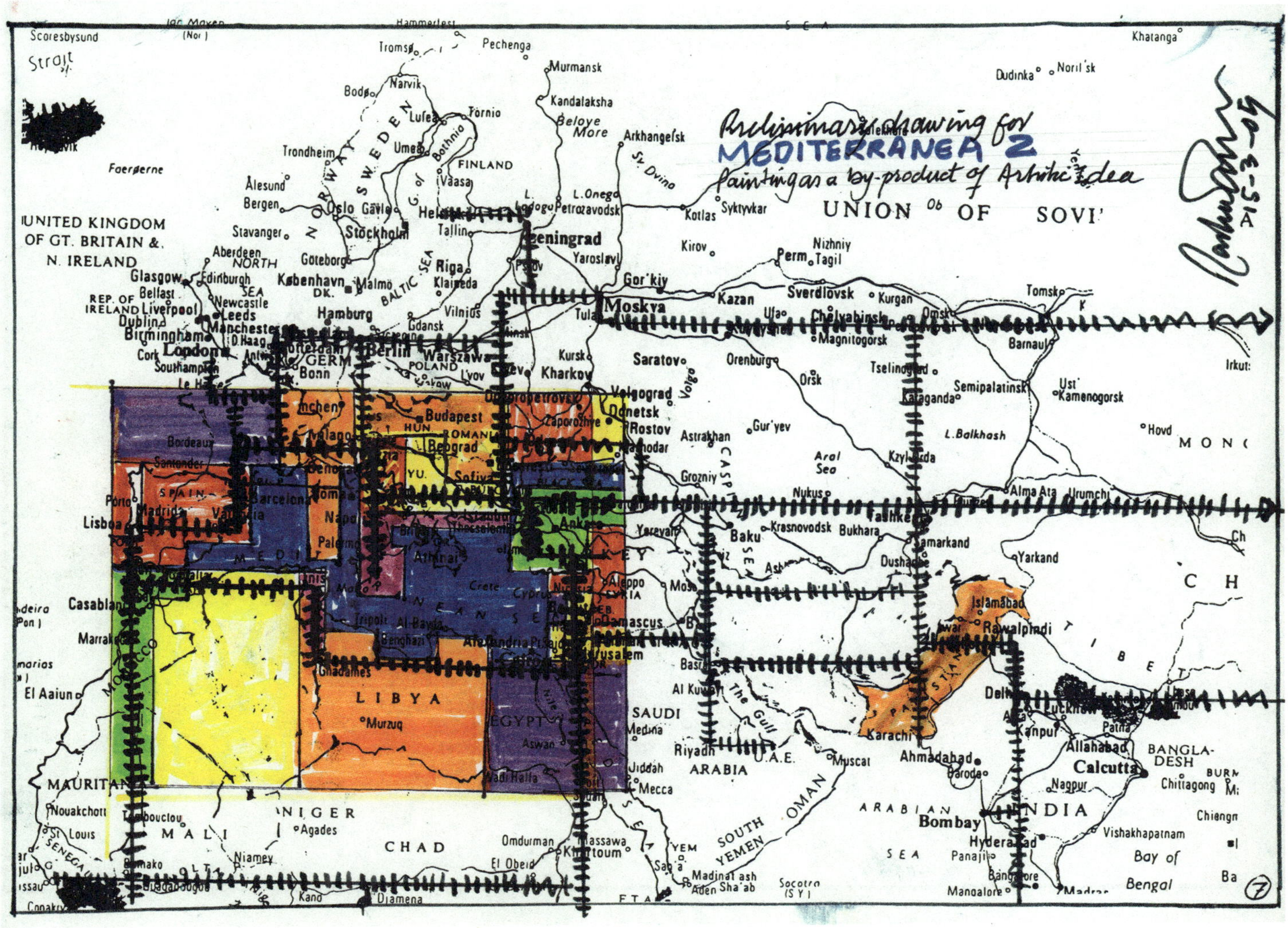

A Chronology of Events That Led to the Mediterranean Project and its Subsequent Ideas and Propositions, 2007
pen on printed map, 21 x 30 cm

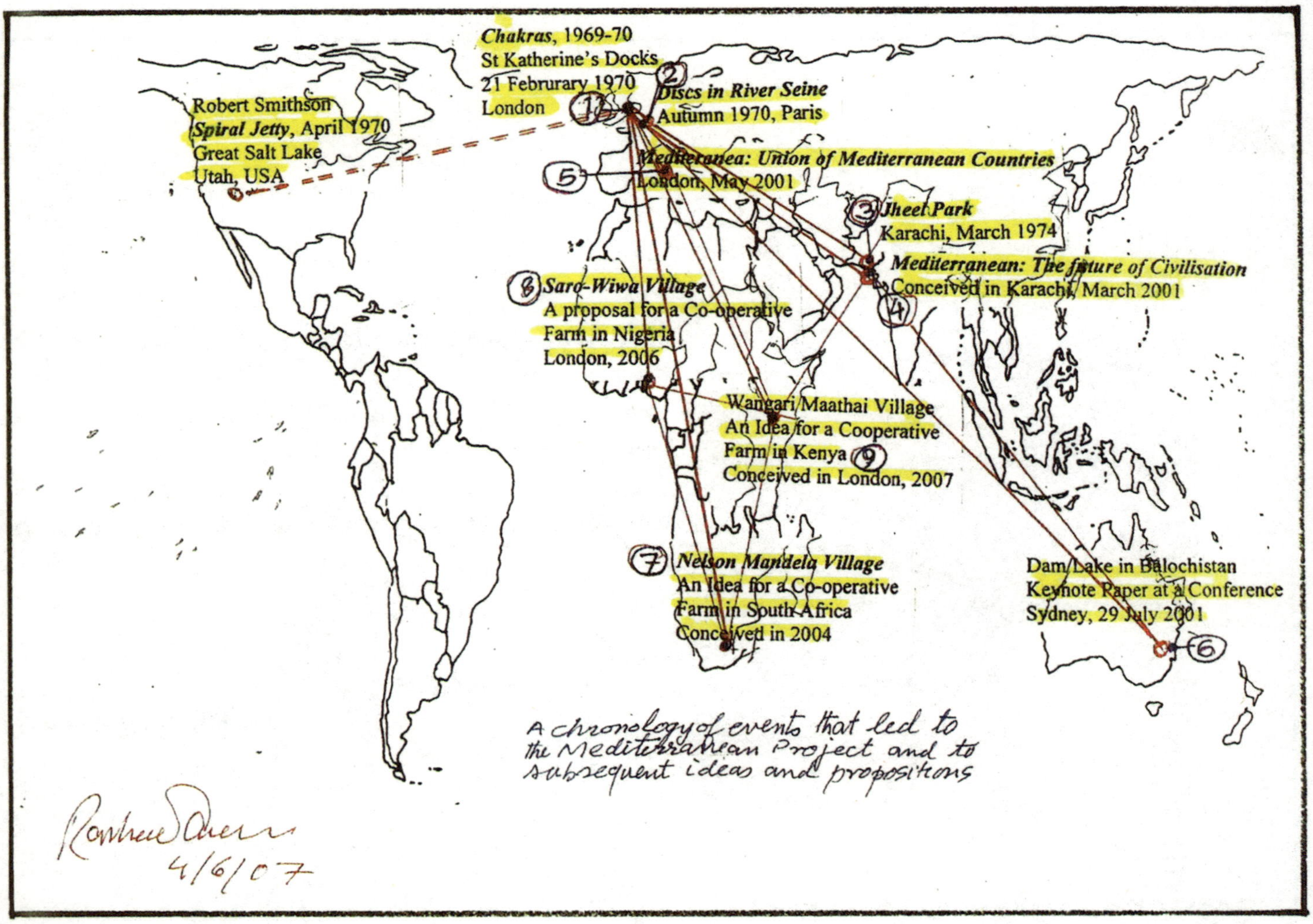

The Caribbean, 2008
2 drawings, felt-tip marker and pen on printed map 104 x 69 cm

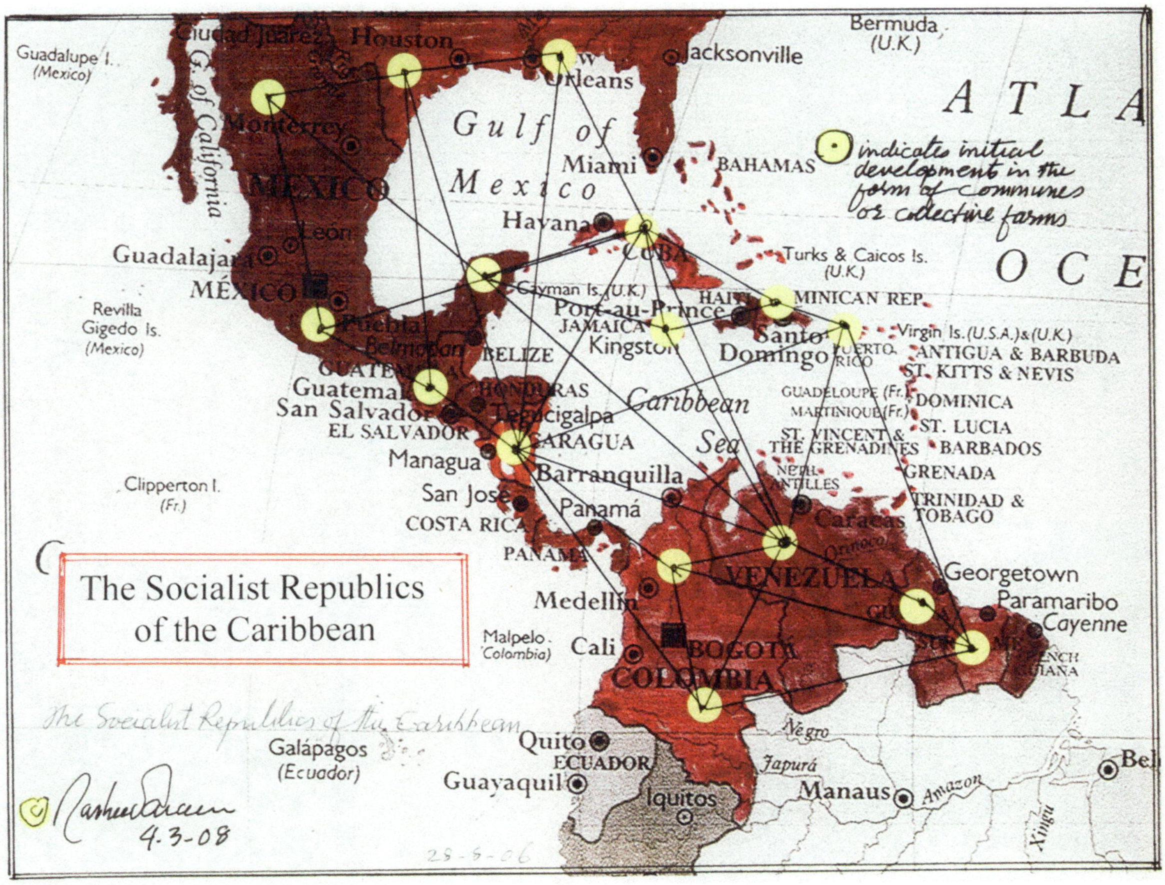

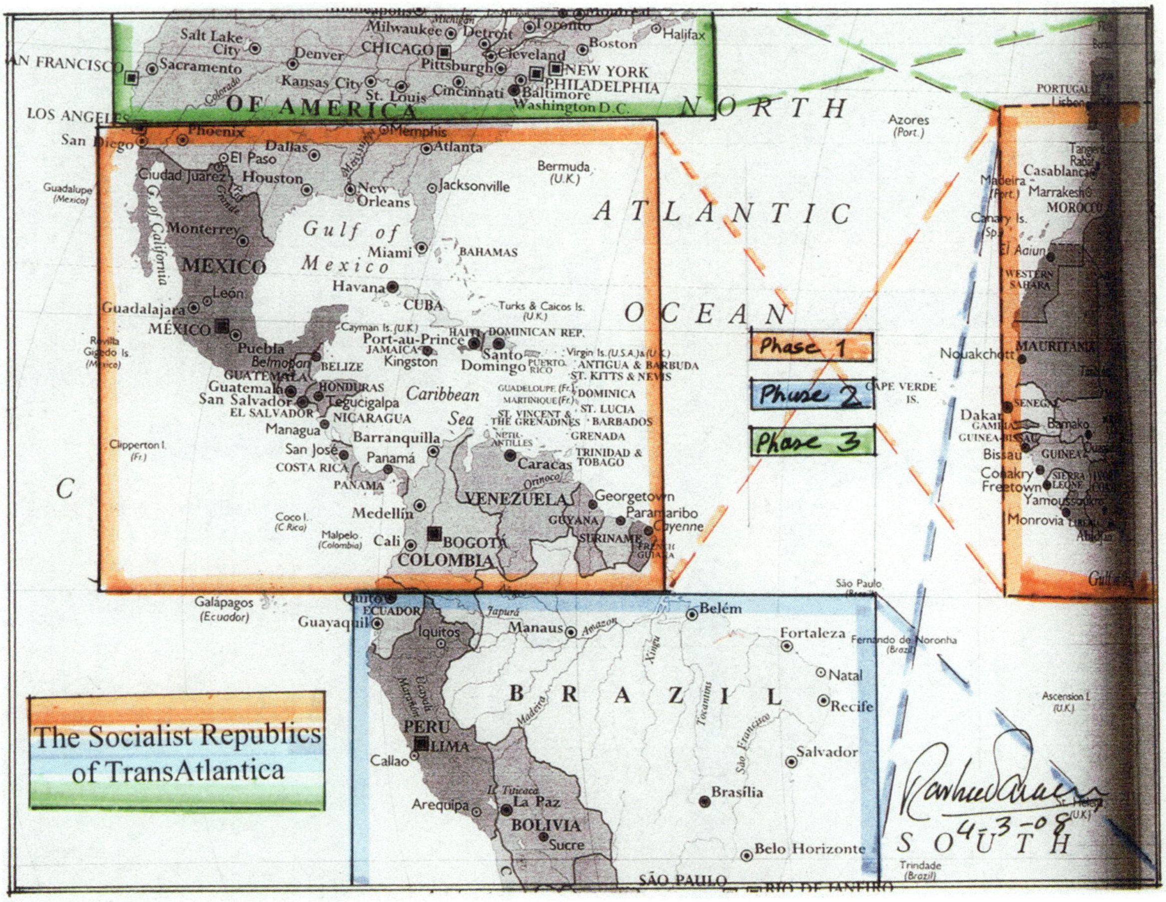

AlkindiAlKindiAlKindiAlkindi, 2010–2013
emulsion on canvas, 152 x 203 cm

AlFarabiAlFarabiAlFarabi, 2010–2013
emulsion on canvas, 152 x 203 cm

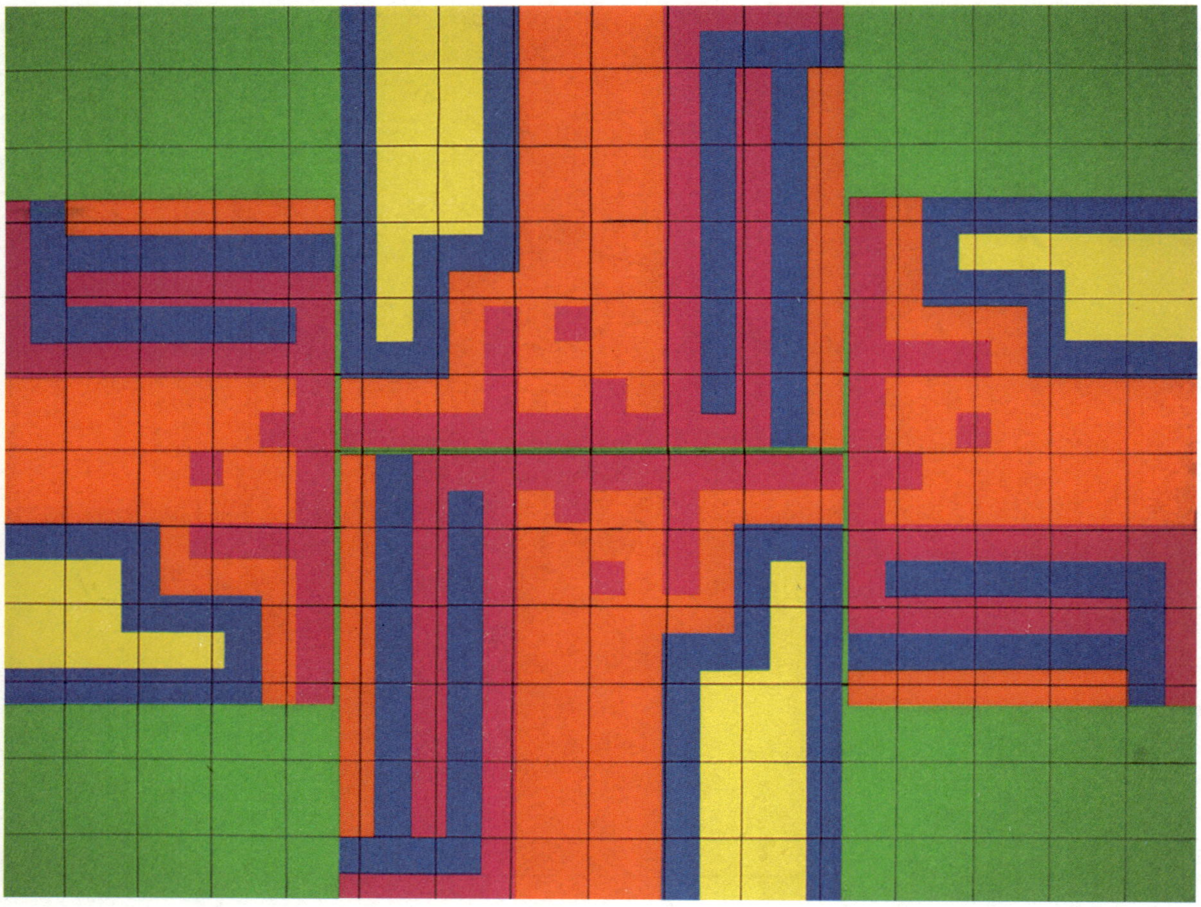

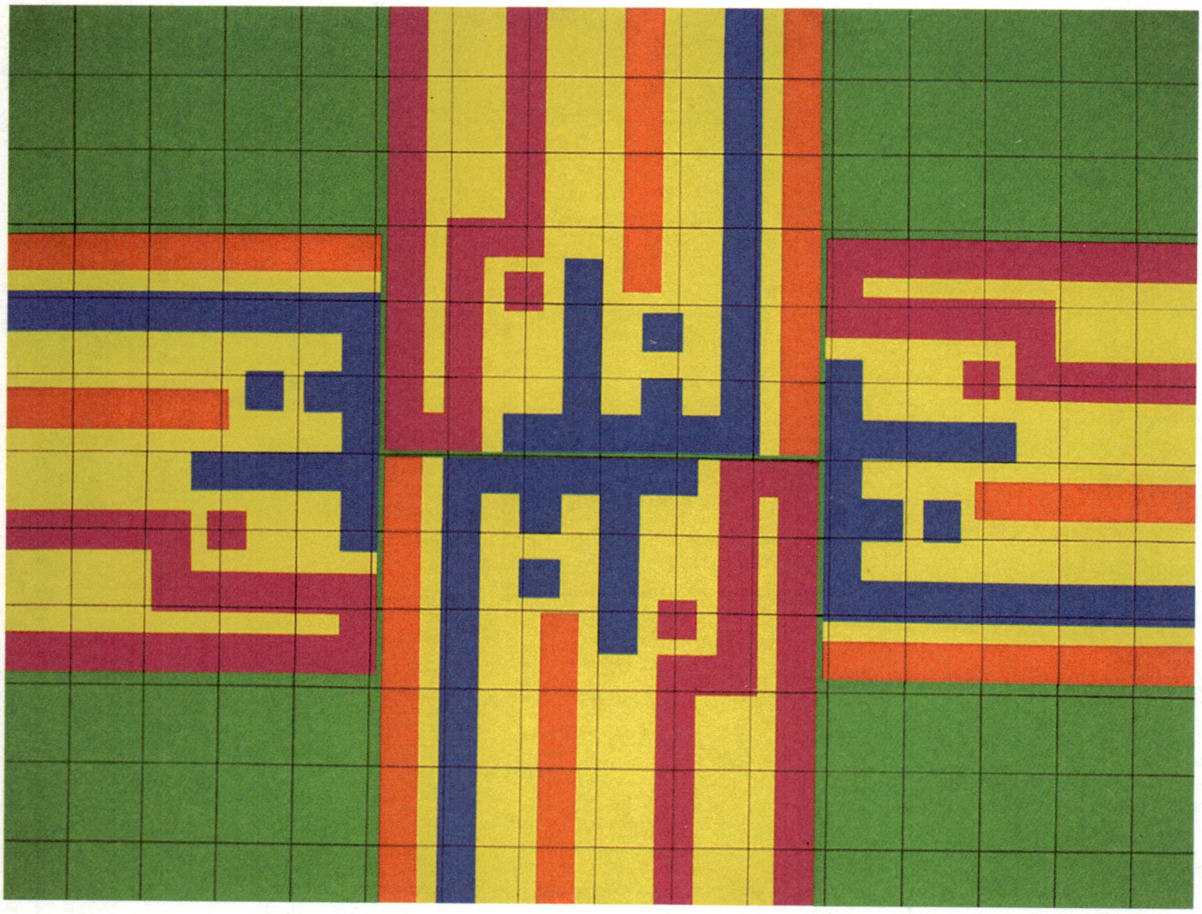

IbnRushdibnRushibnRushibnRushd, 2010–2013
emulsion on canvas, 152 x 203 cm

IbnSinalibnSinalibnSinalibnSina, 2010–2013
emulsion on canvas, 152 x 203 cm

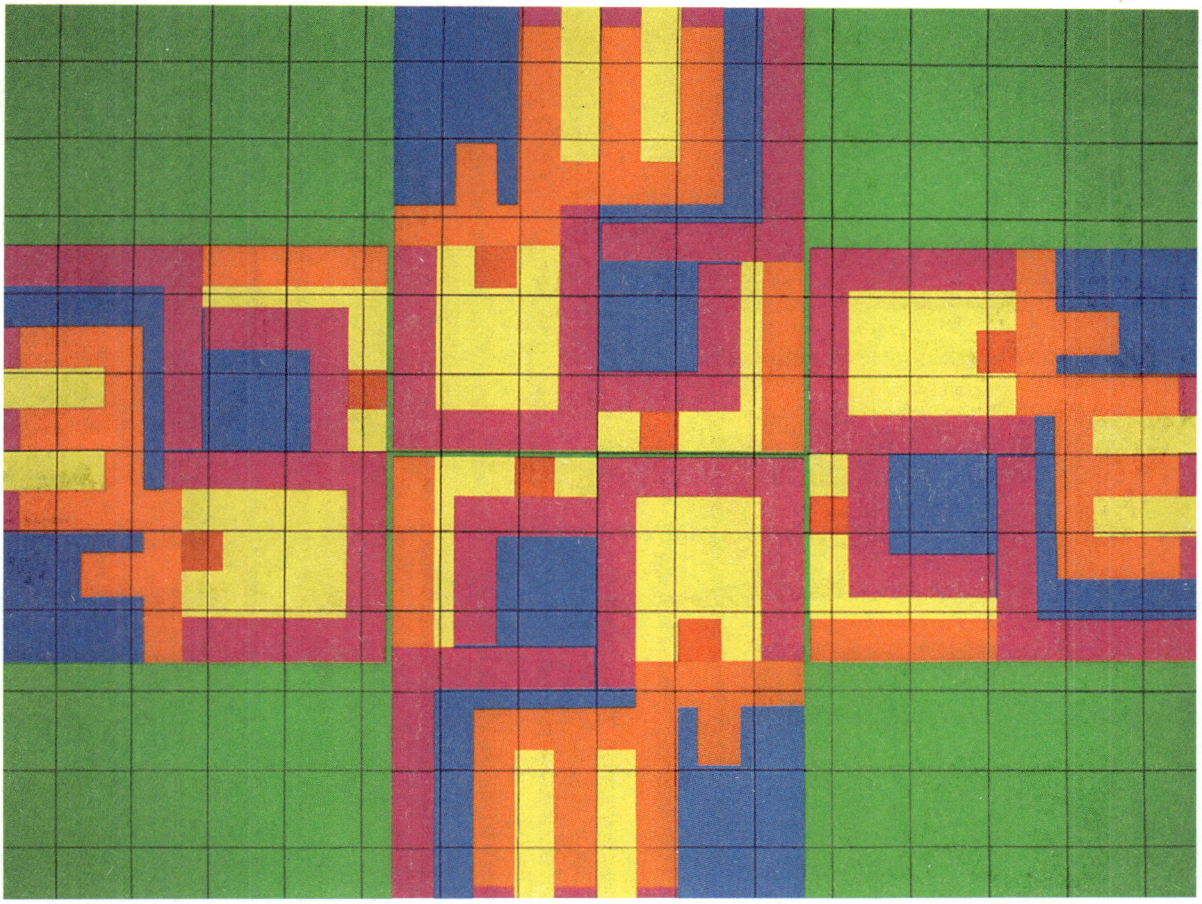

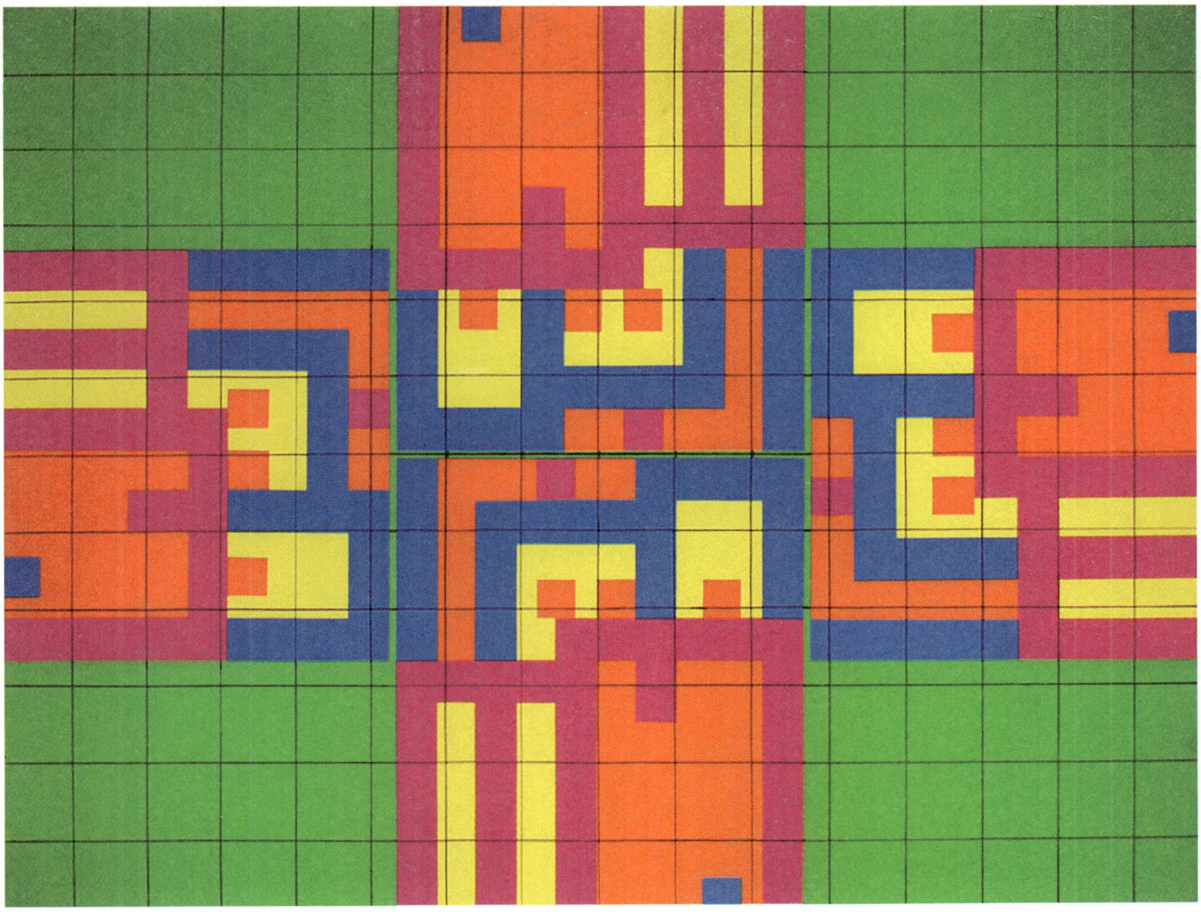

Al-Gazali, 2010–2011
emulsion on canvas, 152 x 203 cm

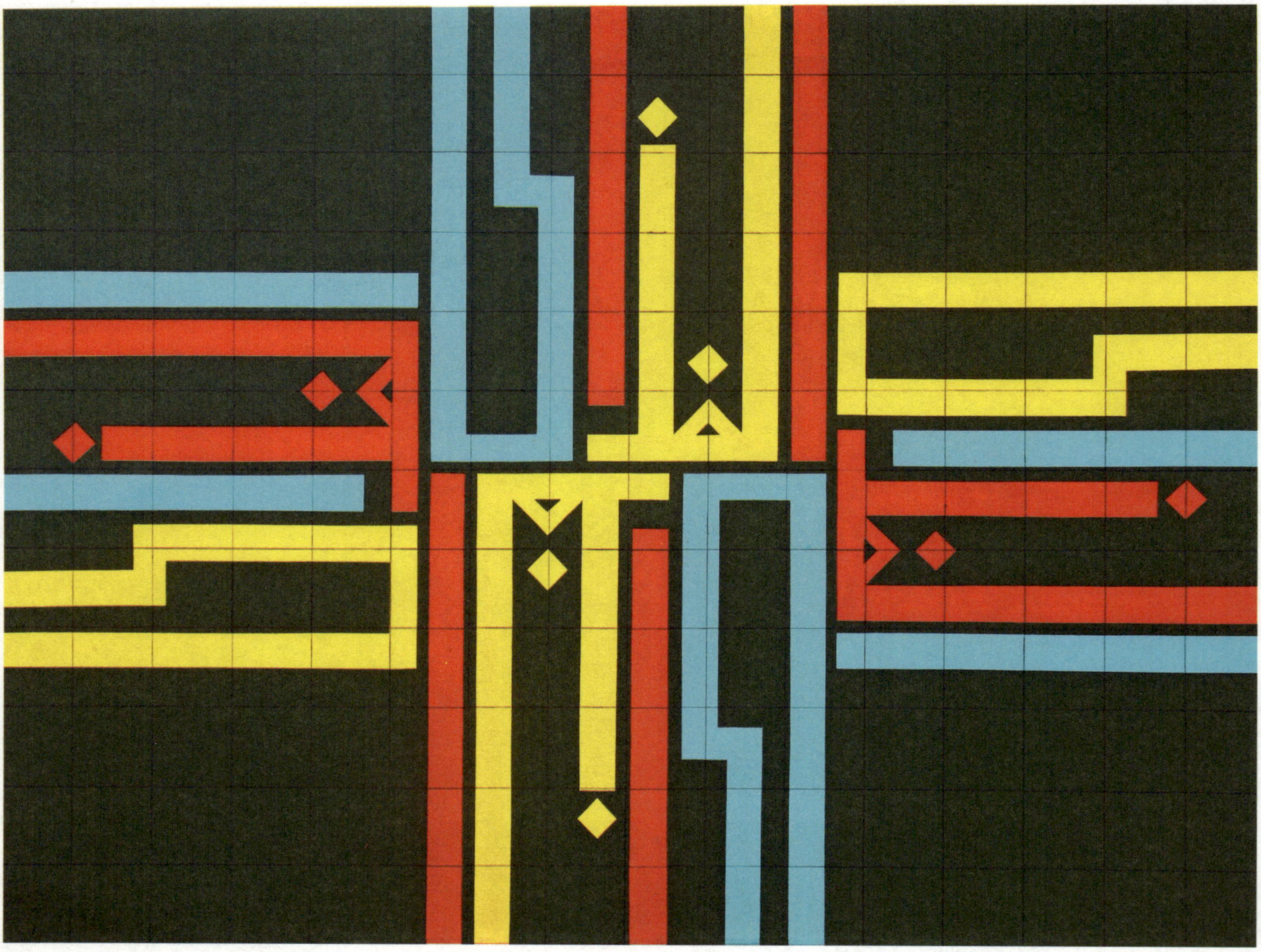

The Greatness of Islamic Civilisation (Ibn Rushd, Umer-Khayyam, Al-Ghazali, Ibn Sina, Al-Farabi and A-Kindi), 2011–2012
6 paintings, acrylic on canvas, 152 x 122 cm each

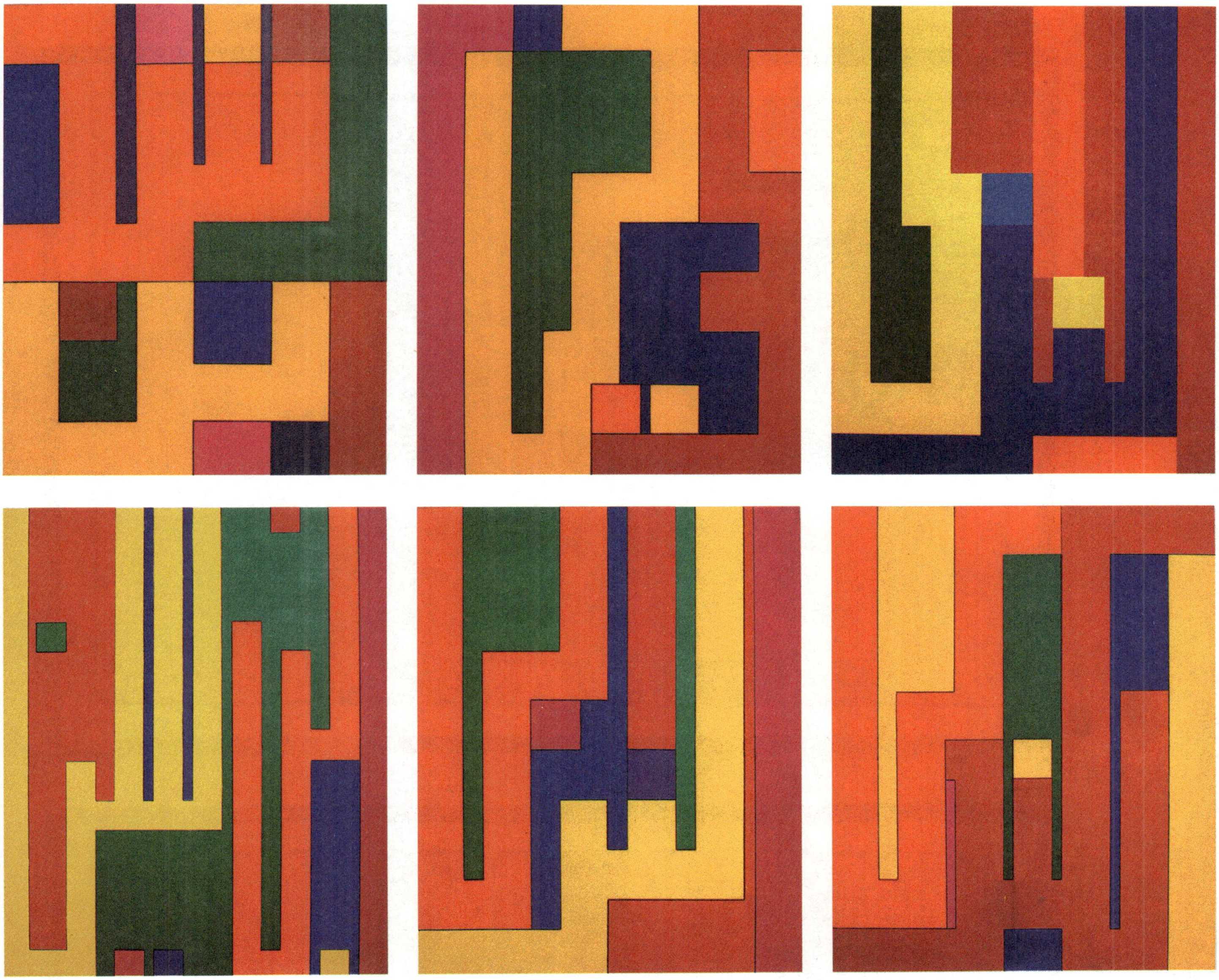

Studies for In the Midst of Darkness, 2012–2013
series of 4 drawings, pencil on paper, 60 x 90 cm

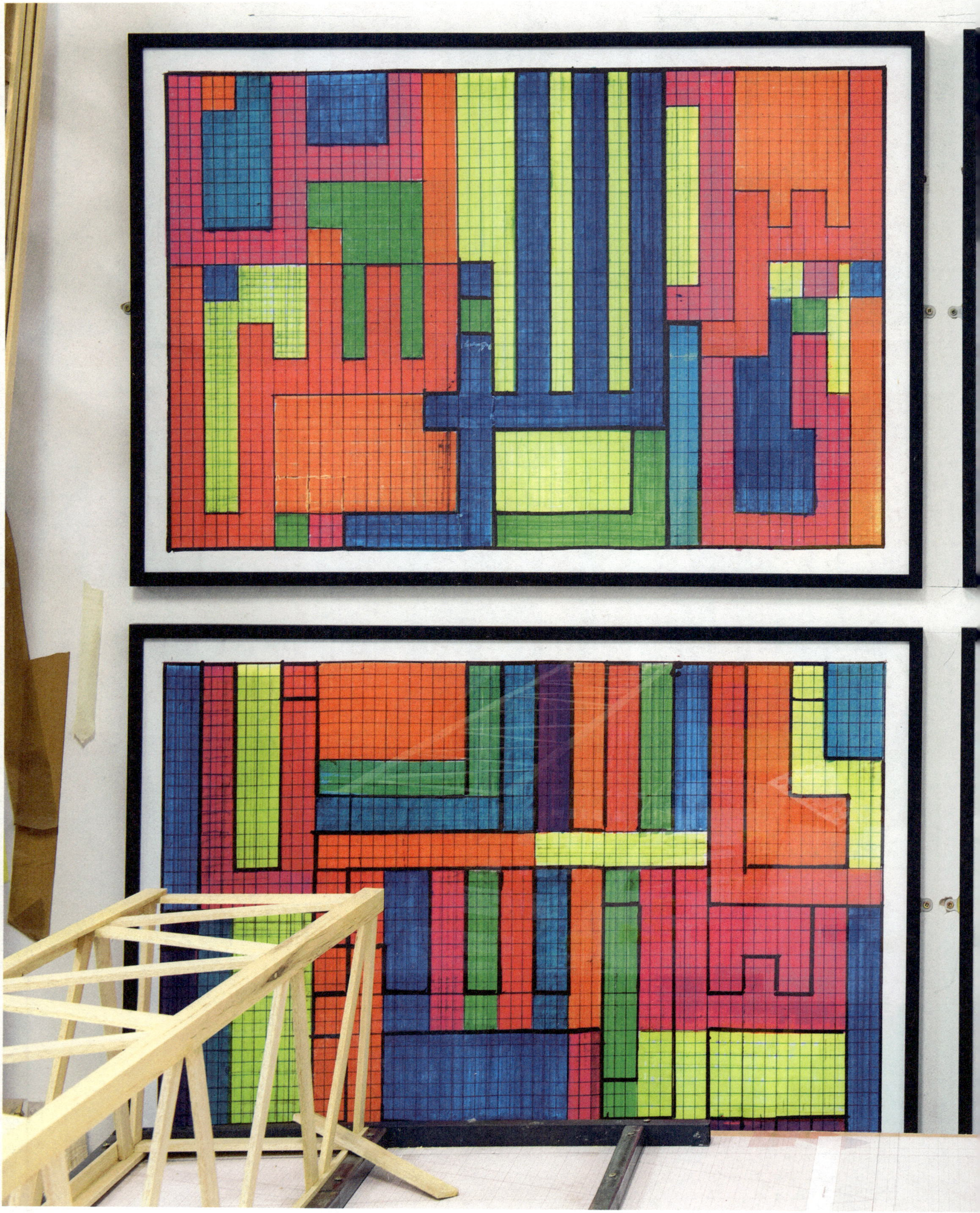

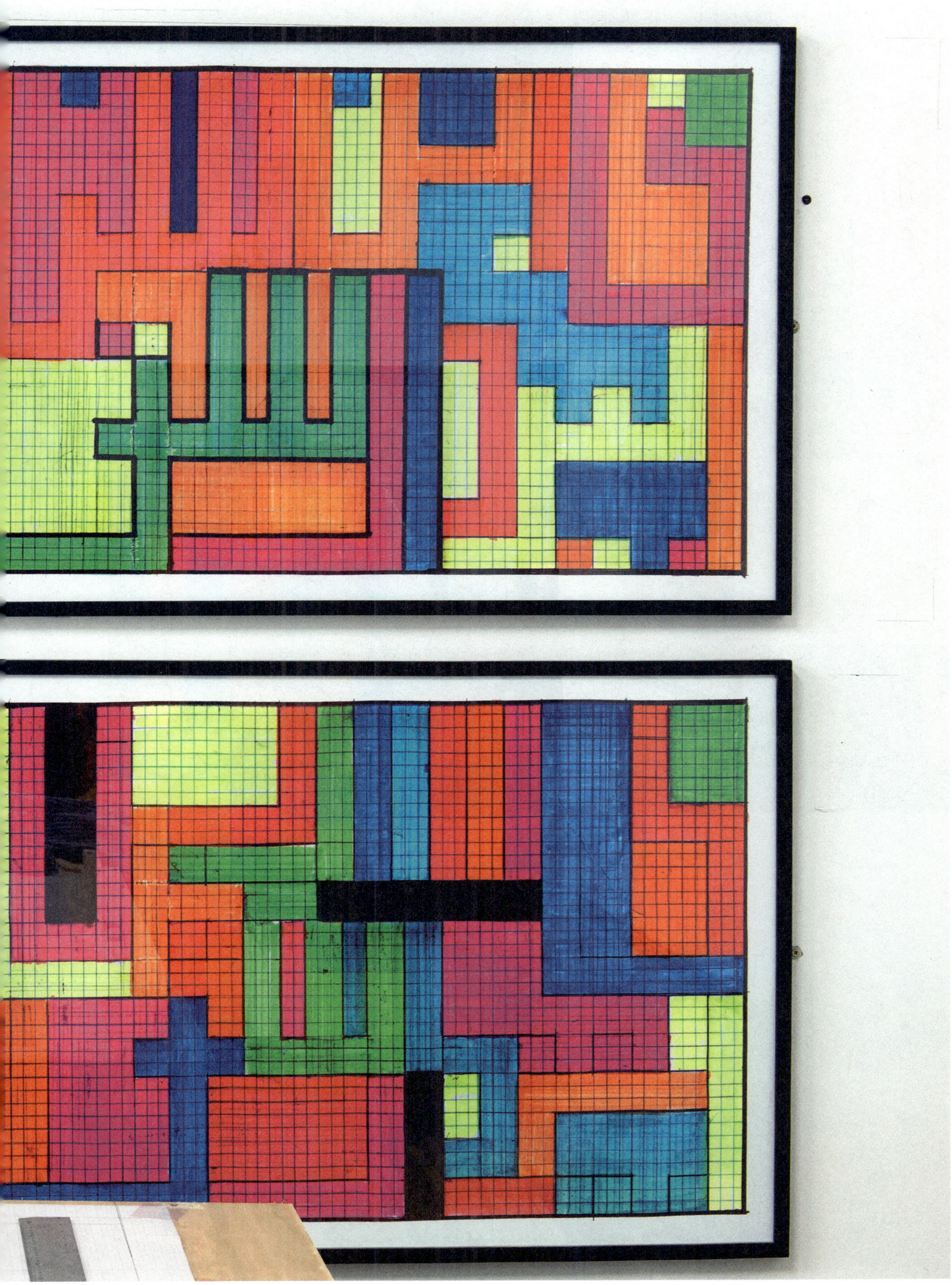

In The Midst Of Darkness I, 2012–2013
acrylic on canvas, 114 x 140 cm

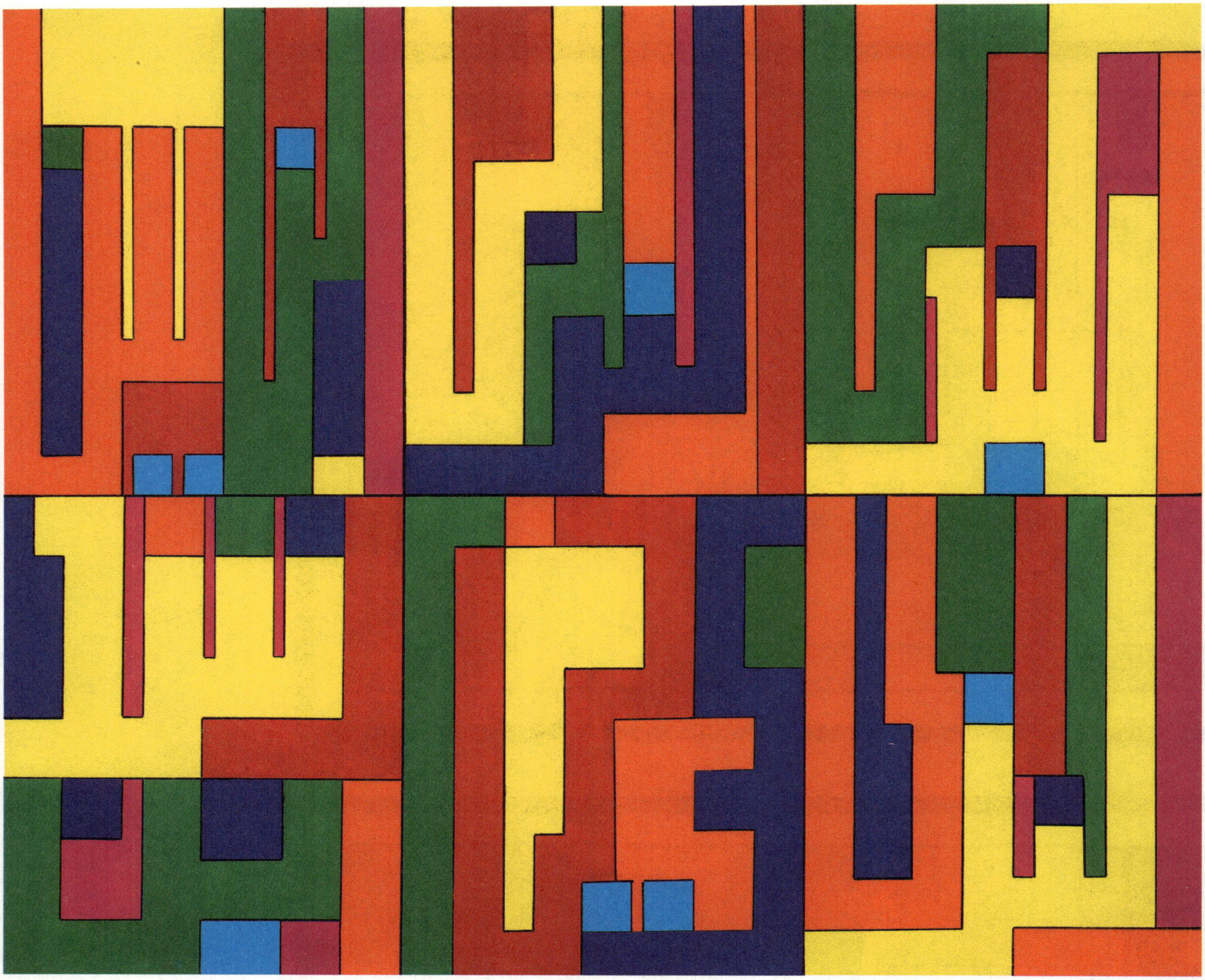

In The Midst Of Darkness 1A, 2012–2013
painting, acrylic on canvas, 152 x 203 cm

In The Midst Of Darkness 2A, 2012–2013
painting, acrylic on canvas, 152 x 203 cm

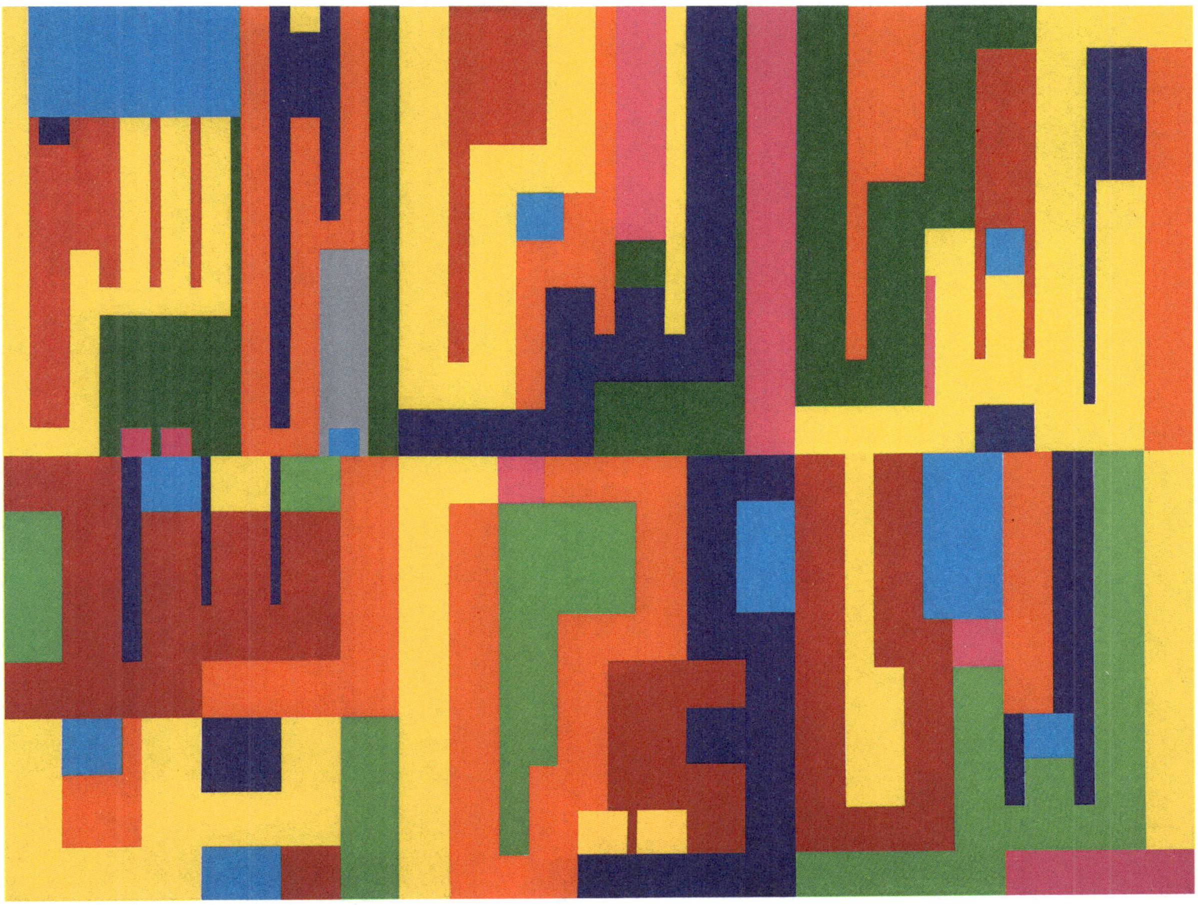

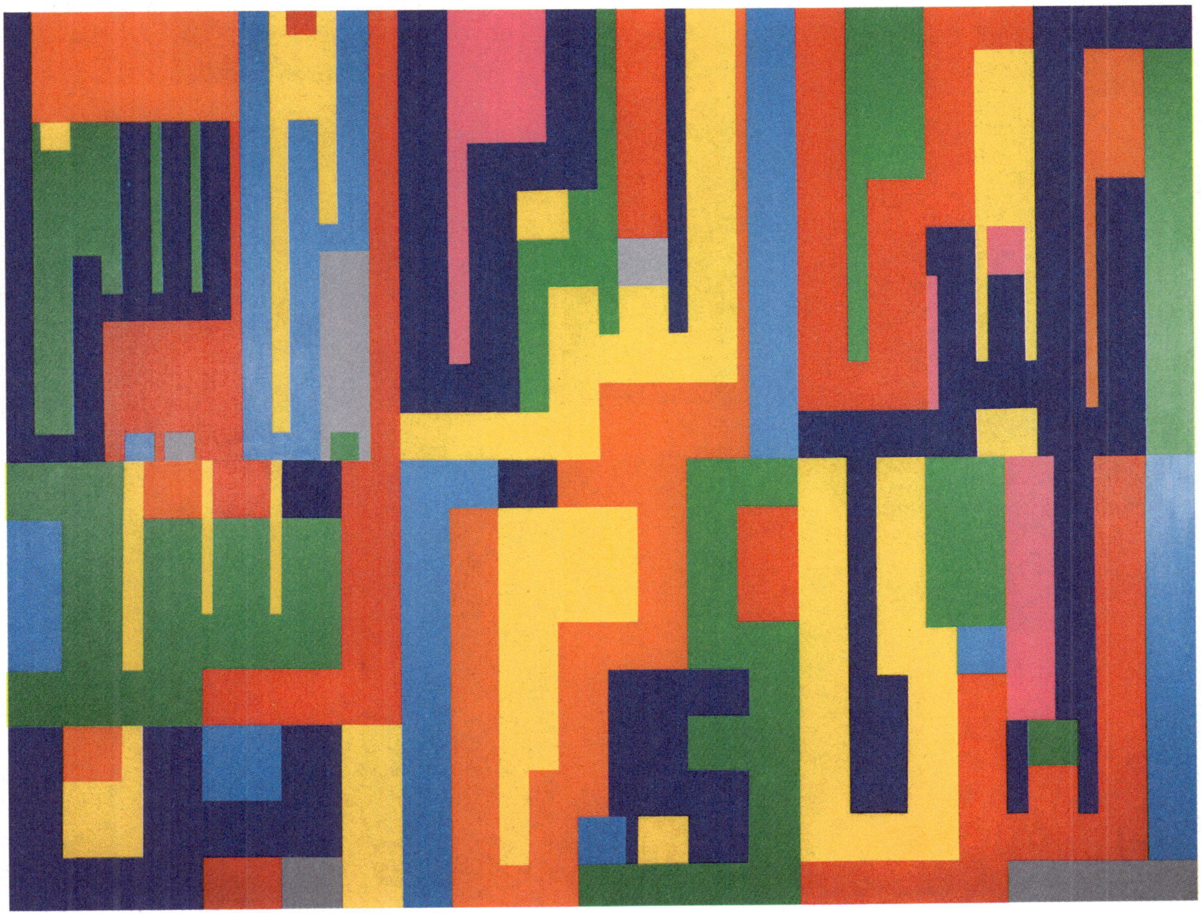

In The Midst Of Darkness 3A, 2012–2013
acrylic on canvas, 114 x 140 cm

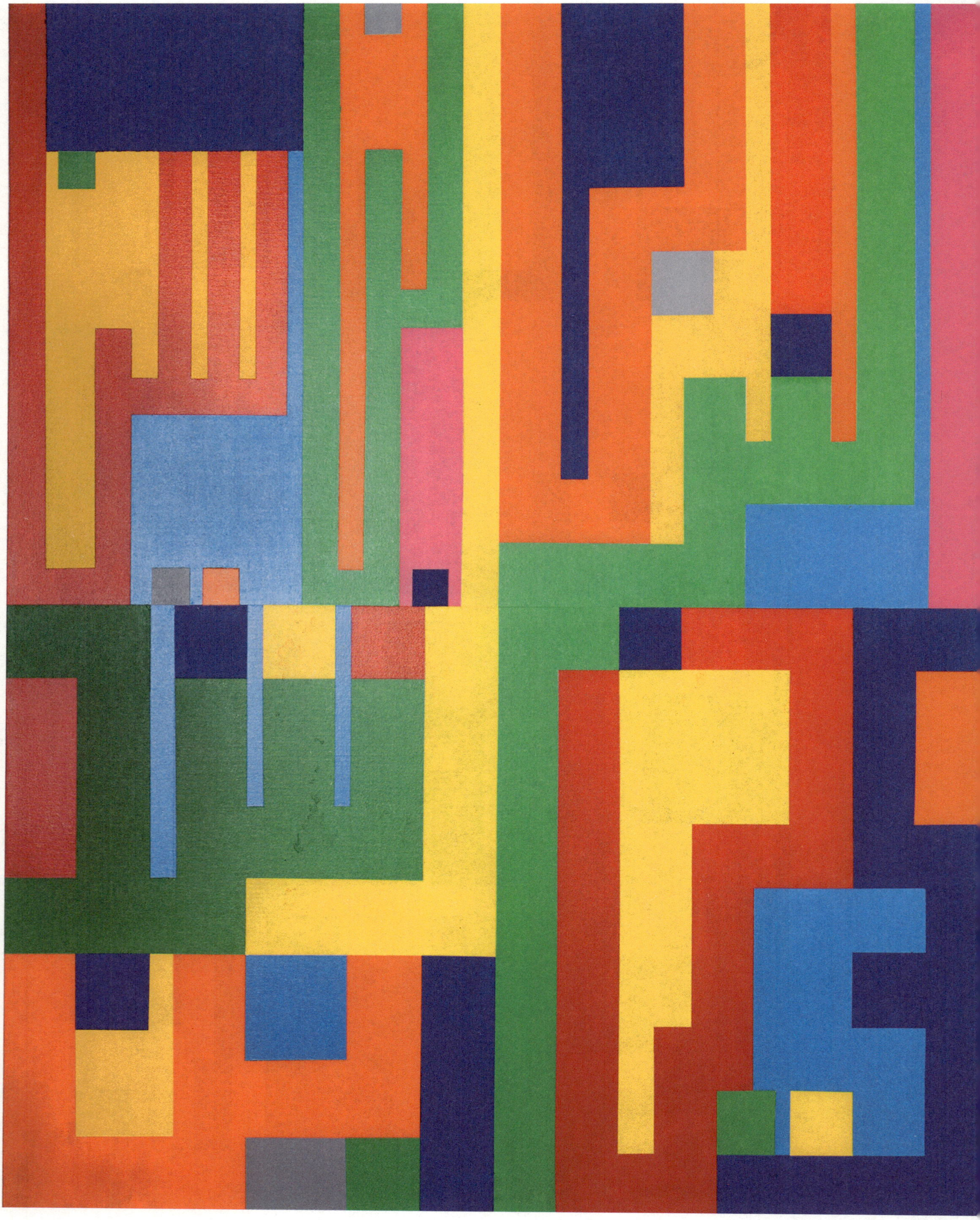

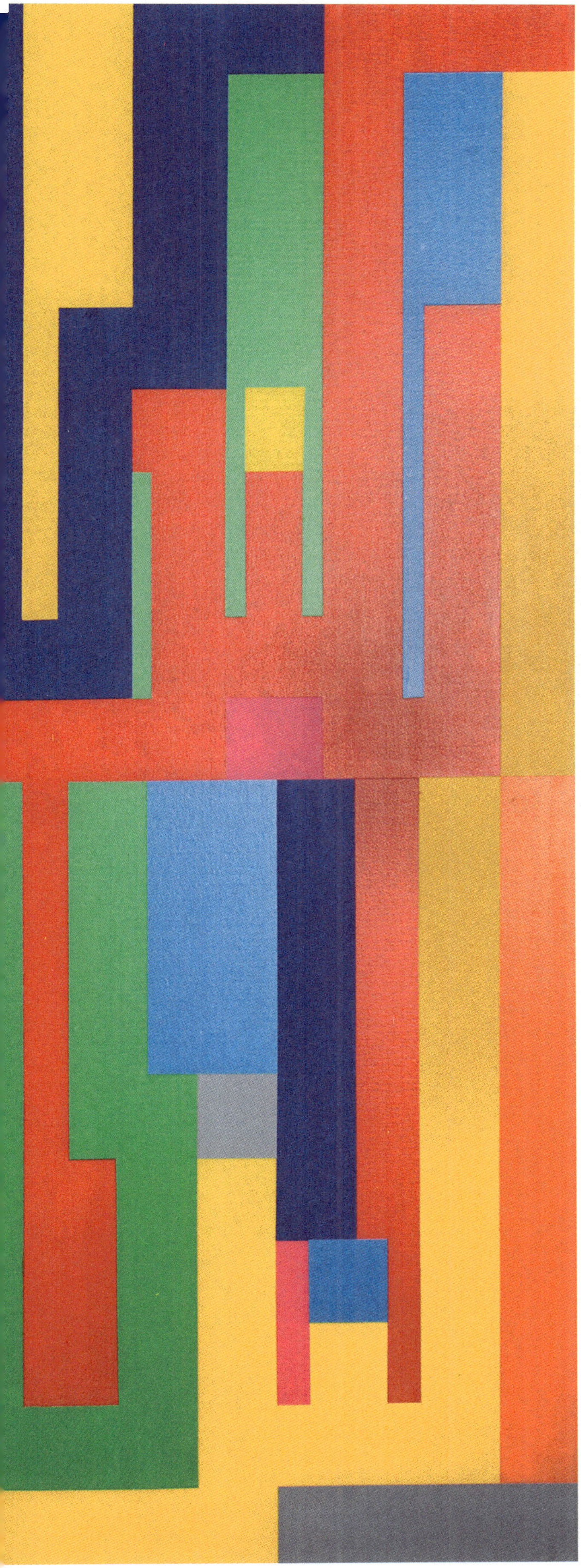

Sharjah Blues, 2013
metallic paint on steel, 312 x 43 x 43 cm
Sharjah Art Foundation Collection

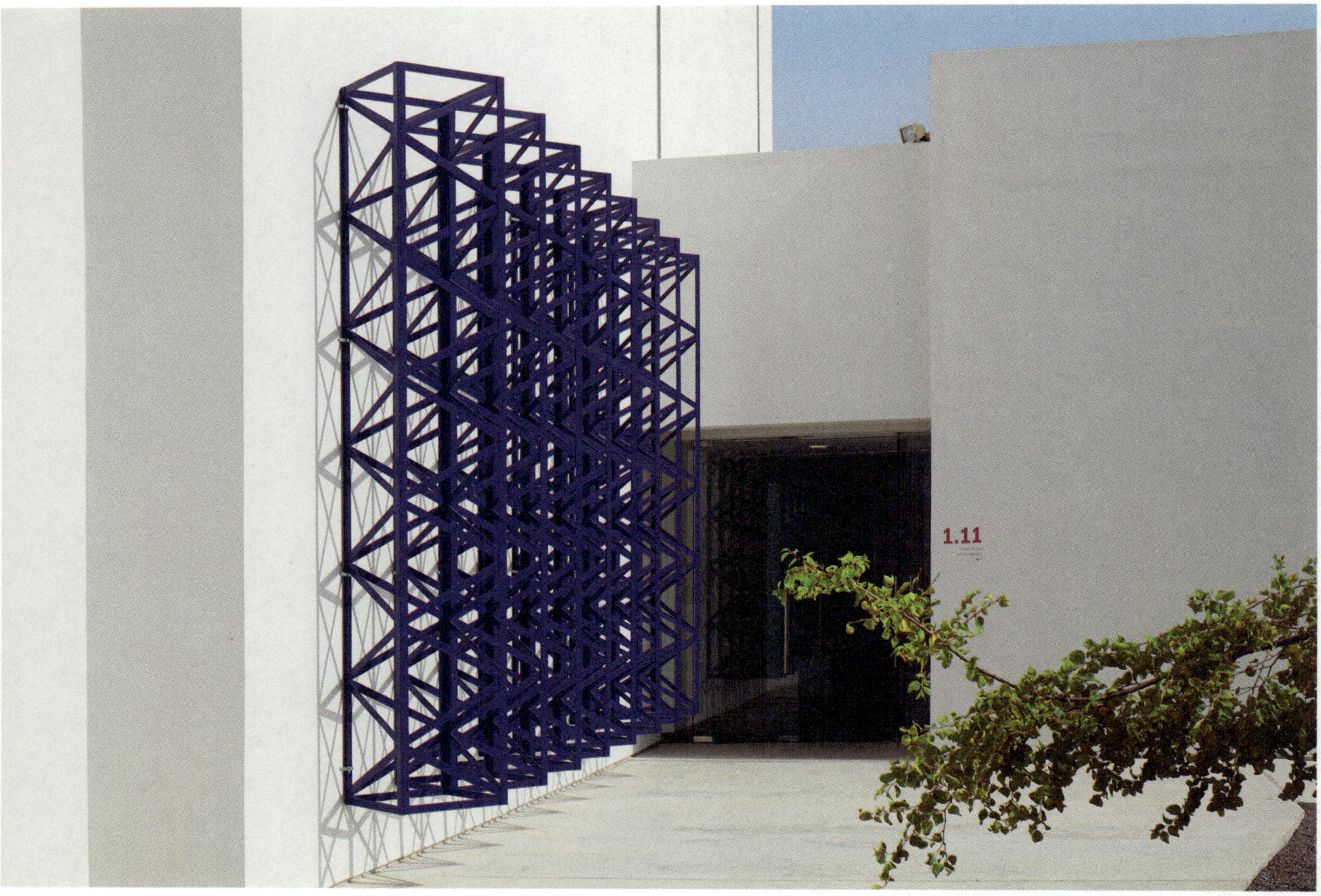

Zero to Infinity, 1968–2004 / 2013
installation at Museo de Arte de Lima, Peru
100 acrylic on wood Structures, 50 x 50 x 50 cm each

Zero to Infinity, 1968–2004 / 2014
installation at Athr Gallery, Jeddah
26 acrylic on wood Structures, 50 x 50 x 50 cm each

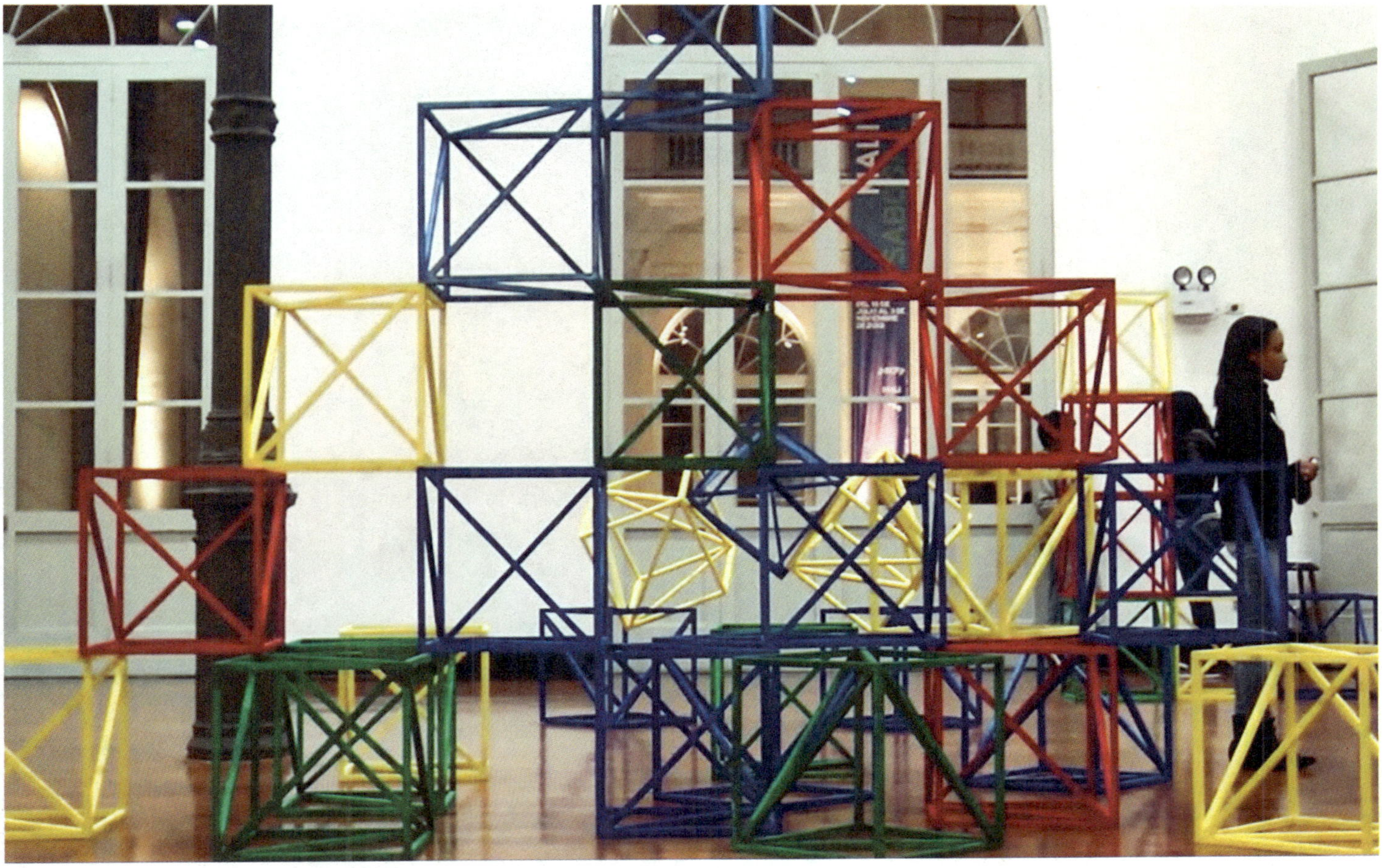

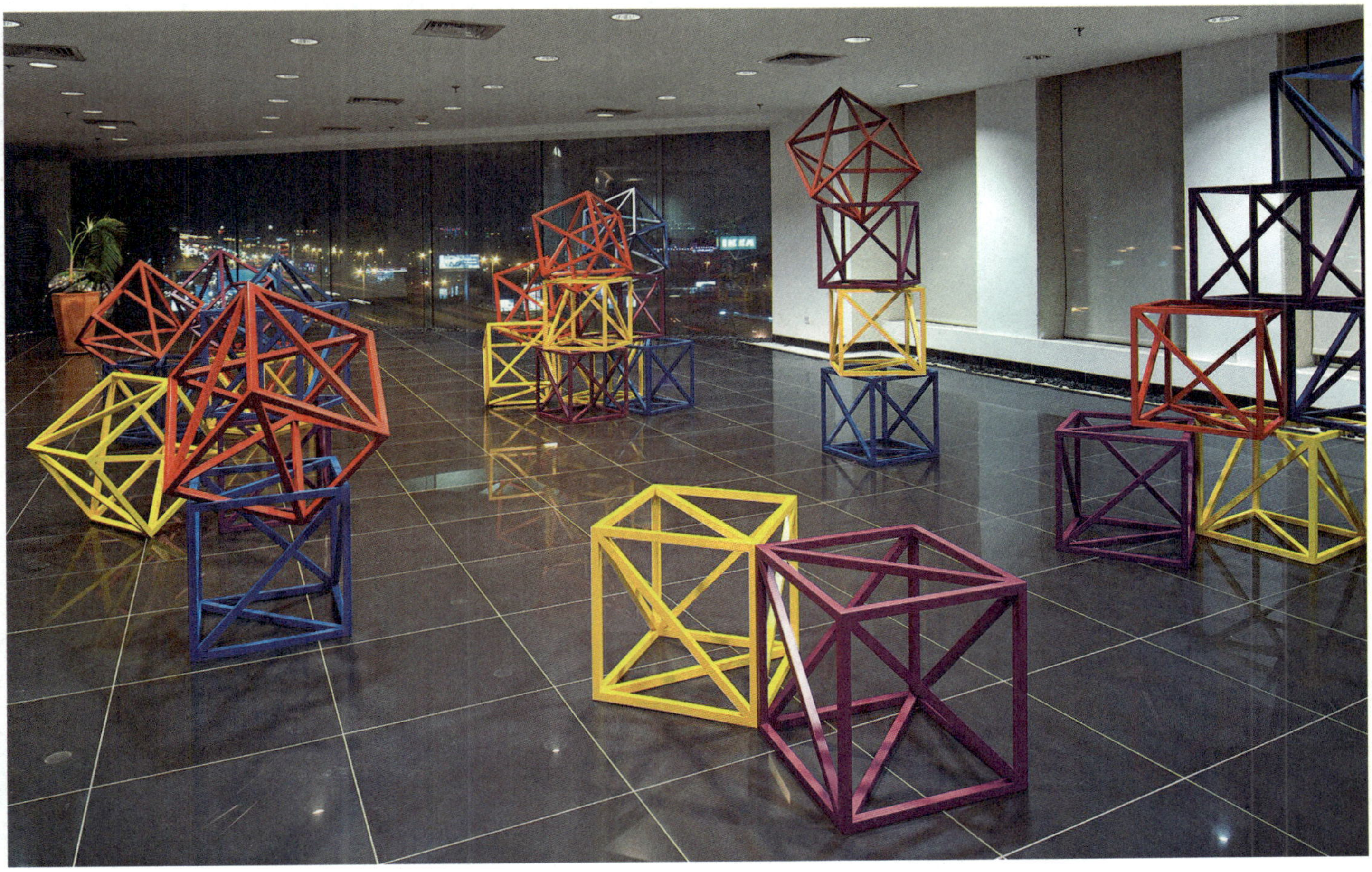

Guftugu I (A Conversation Between Al Baruni and Ibn Sina), 2014
acrylic on canvas, 160 x 239 cm

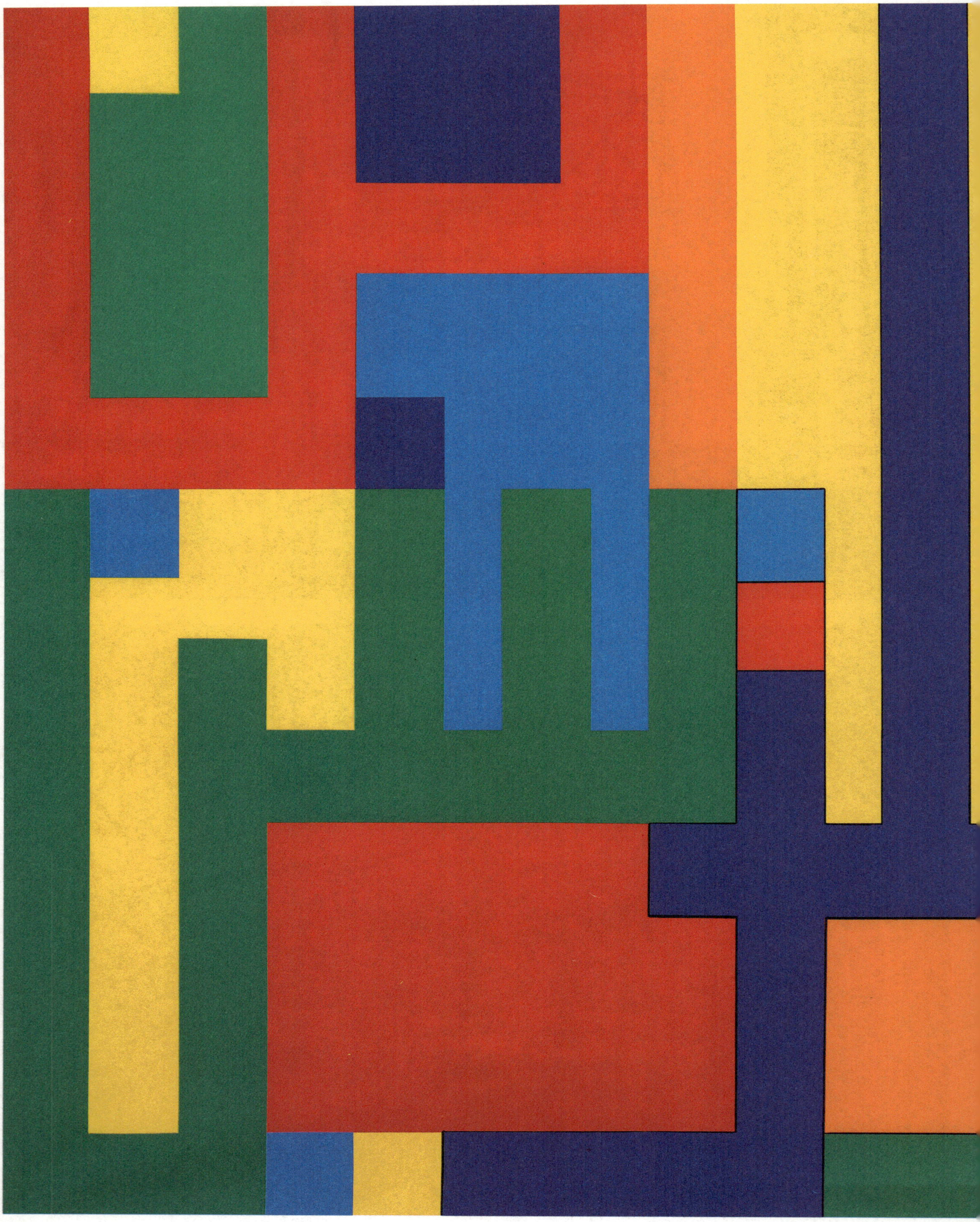

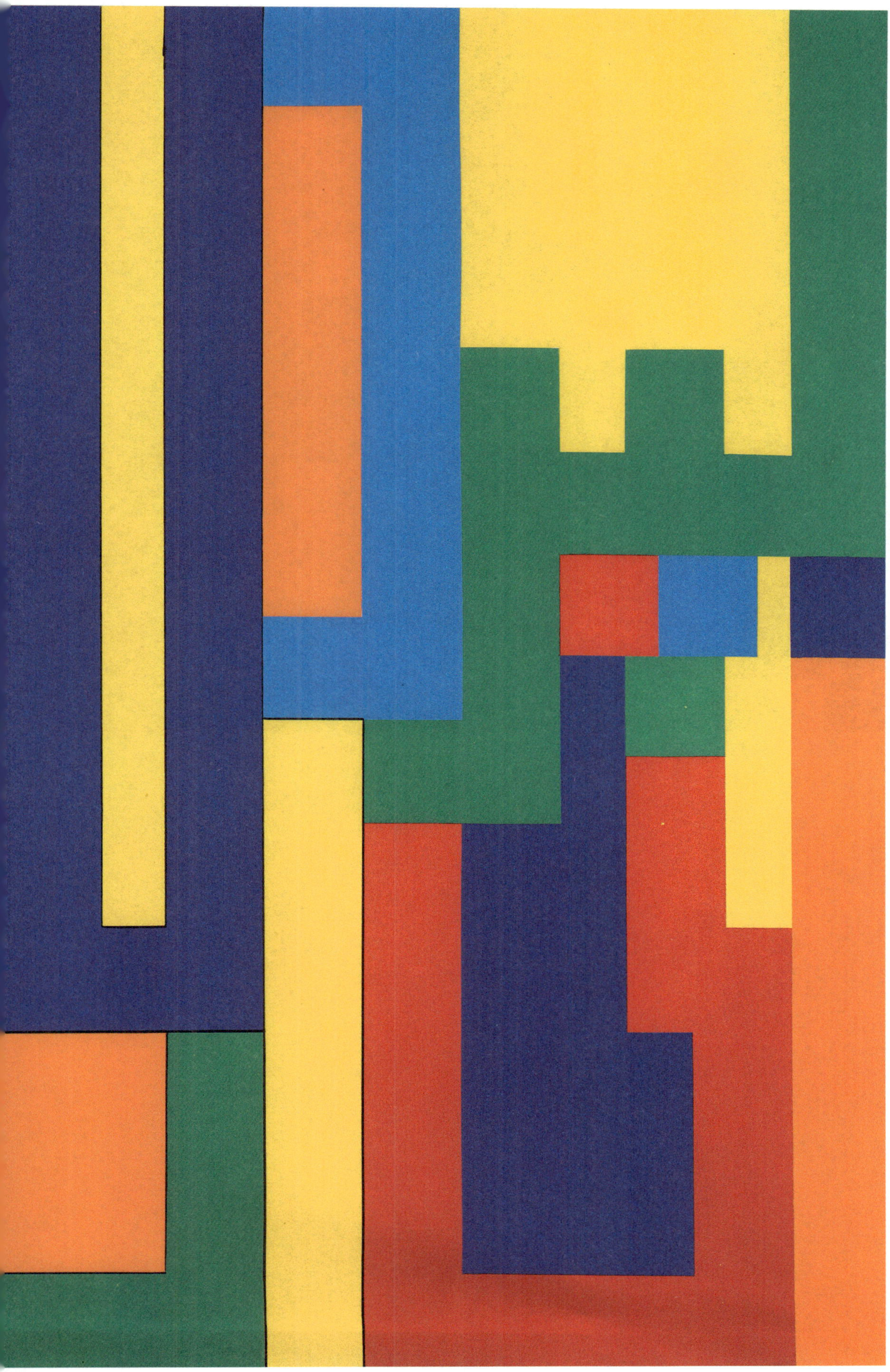

Guftugu II (A Conversation Between Al Baruni and Ibn Sina), 2014
acrylic on canvas, 160 x 239 cm

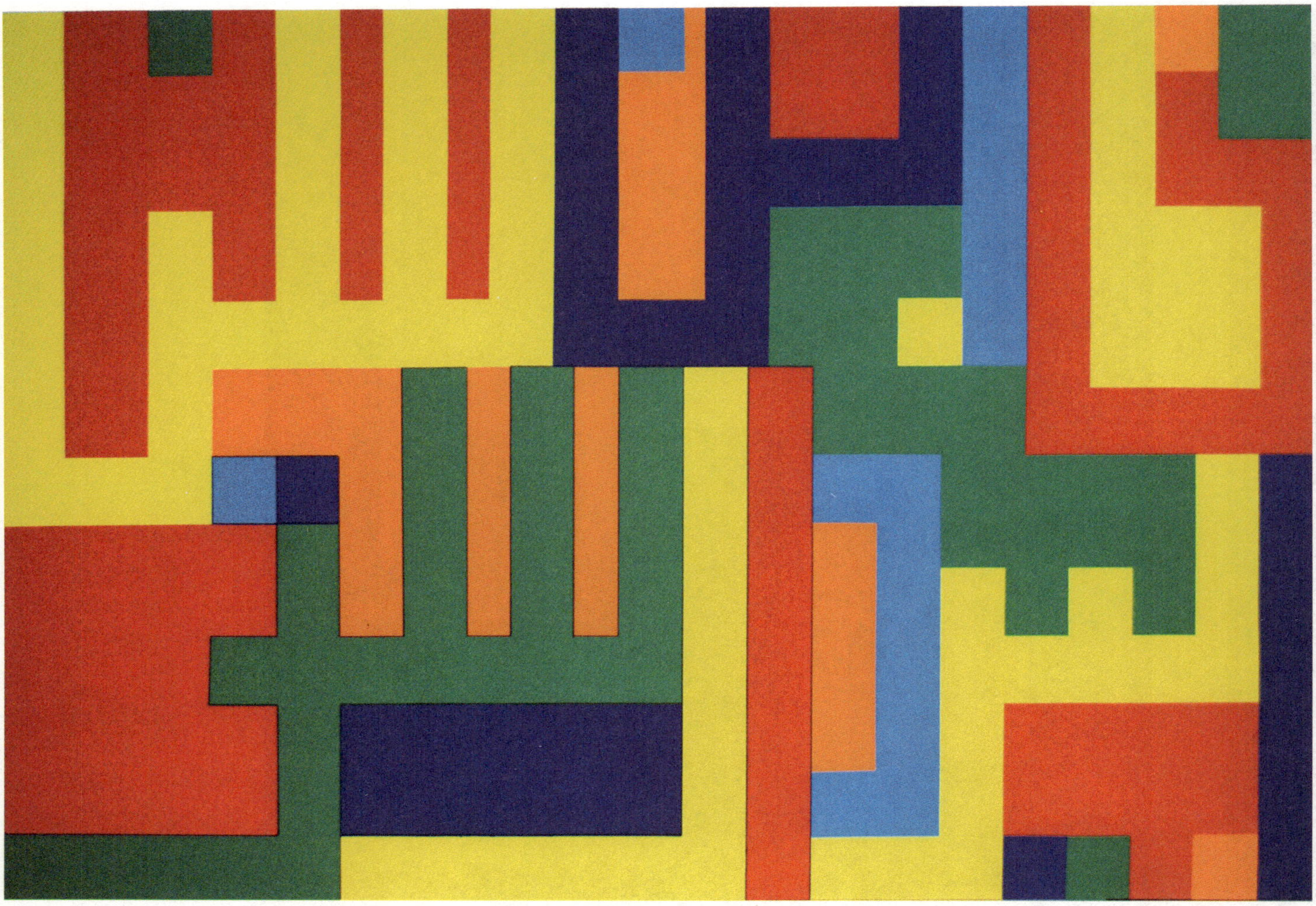

Guftugu III (A Conversation Between Al Baruni and Ibn Sina), 2014
acrylic on canvas, 160 x 239 cm

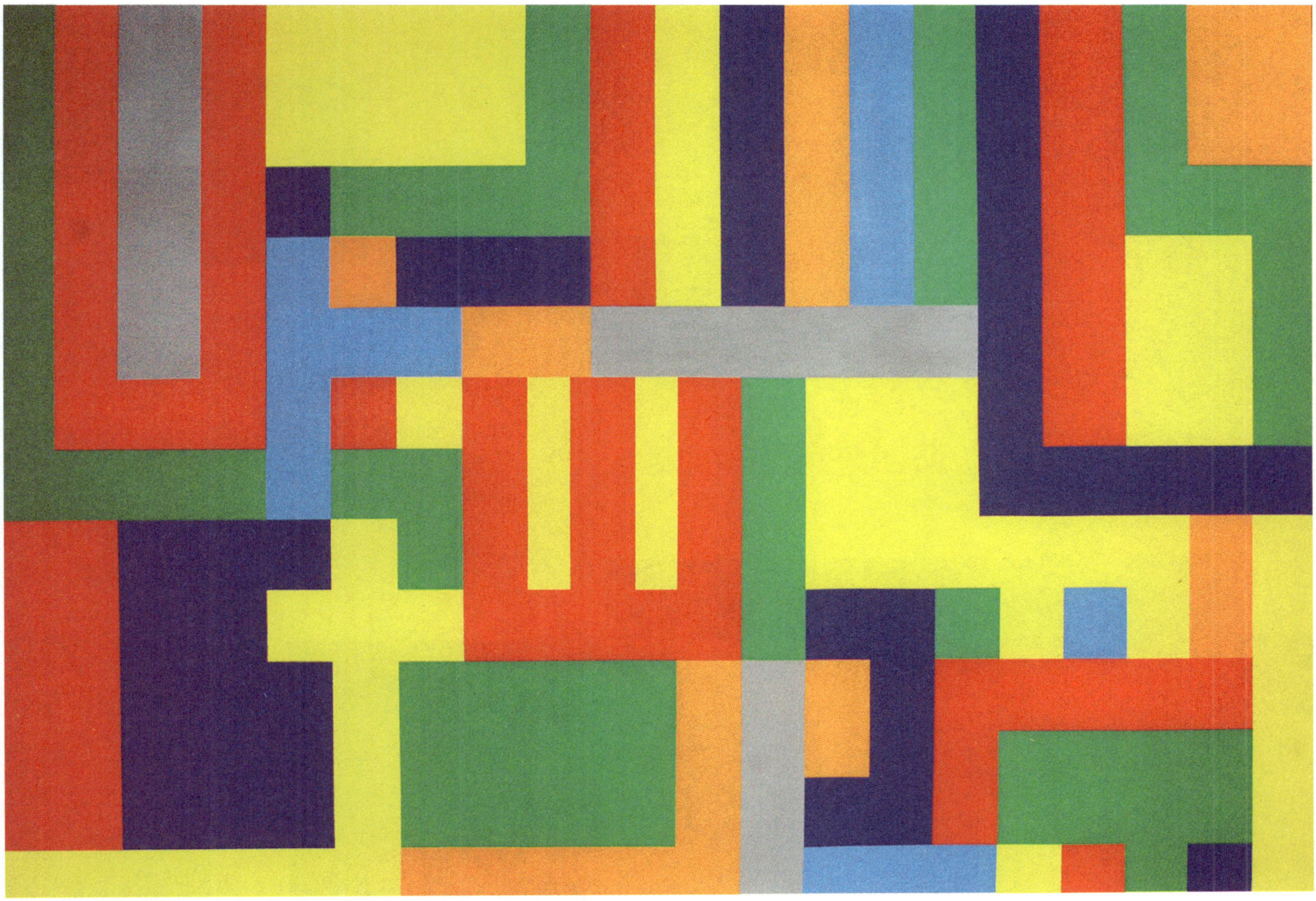

Ishq Haqiqi, Ishq Majazi, 2013
emulsion on canvas, 160 x 198 cm

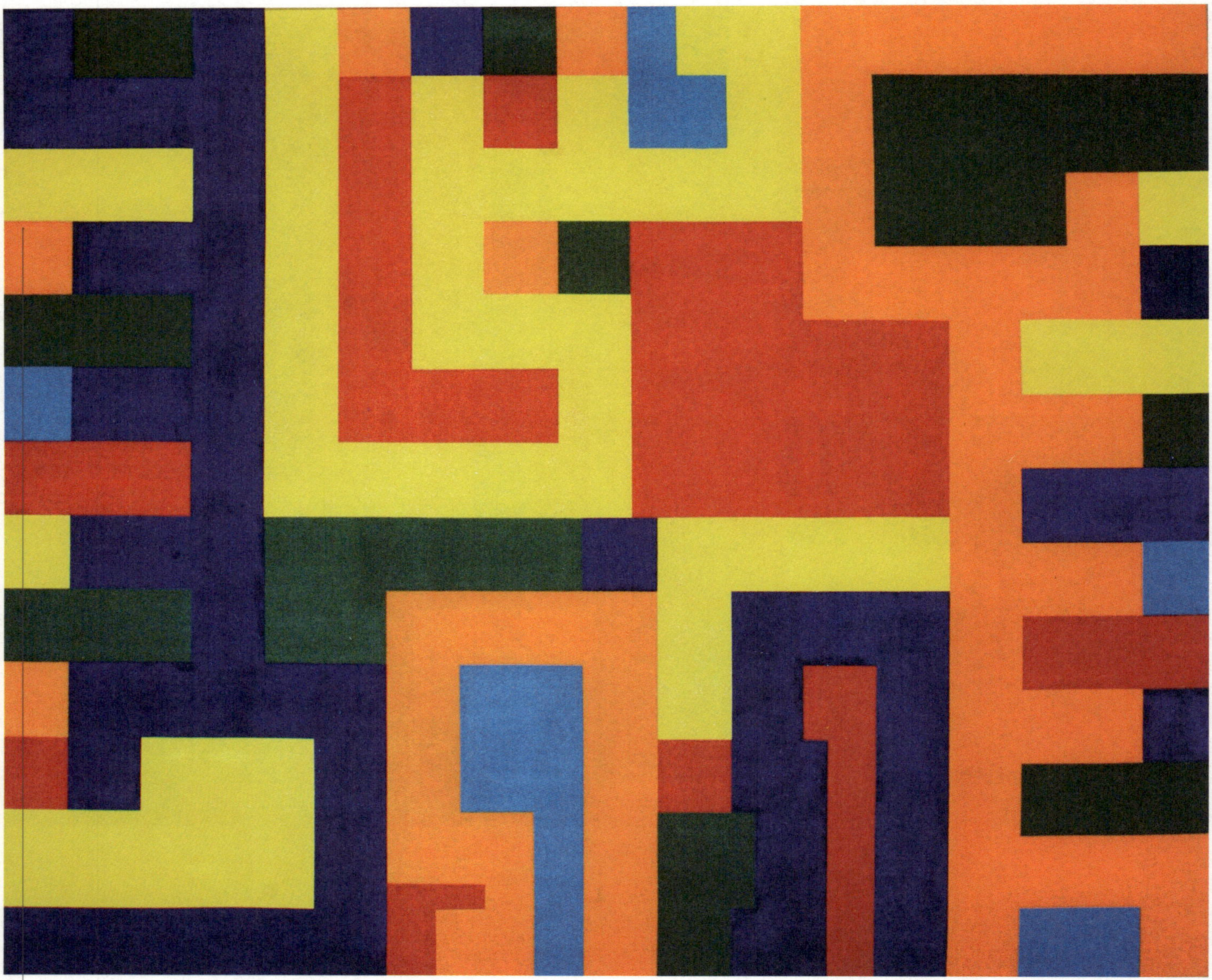

Ishq Haqiqi, Ishq Majazi 1A, 2014
emulsion on canvas, 198 x 160 cm

Ishq Haqiqi, Ishq Majazi 2A, 2014
emulsion on canvas, 160 x 198 cm
Ishq Haqiqi, Ishq Majazi 2B, 2014
emulsion on canvas, 160 x 198 cm

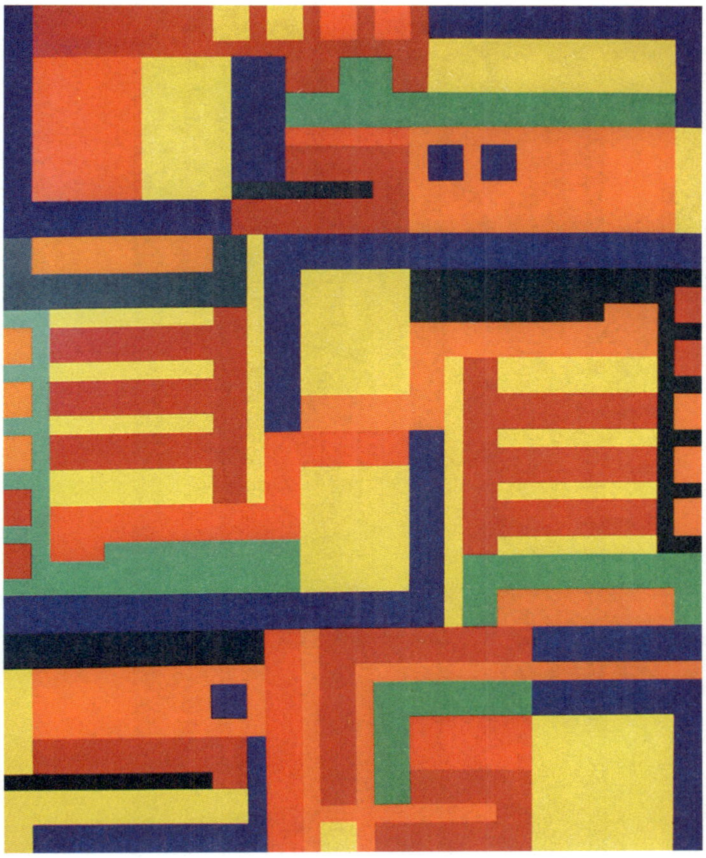

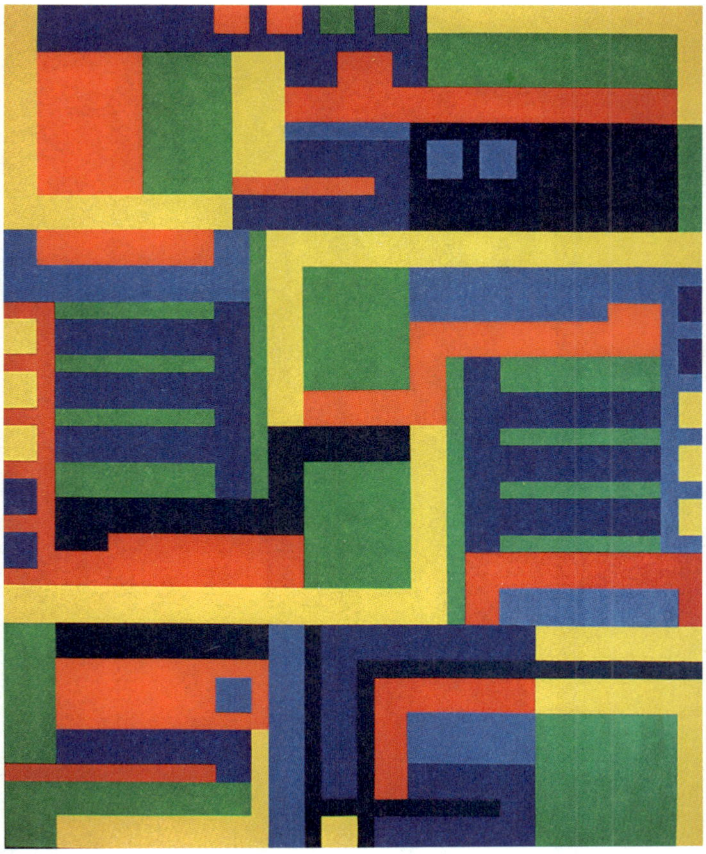

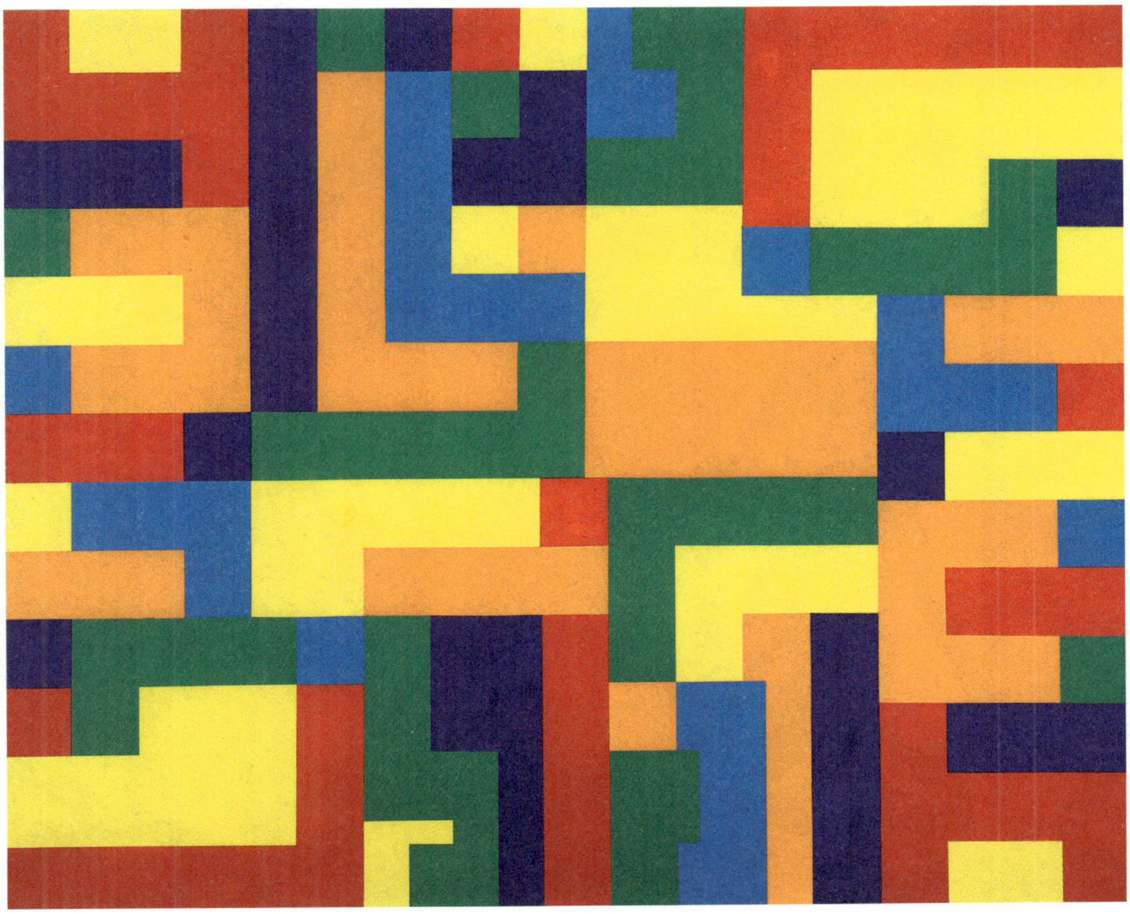

Summer Blue, 2014
acrylic on wood, 76 x 56 x 13 cm

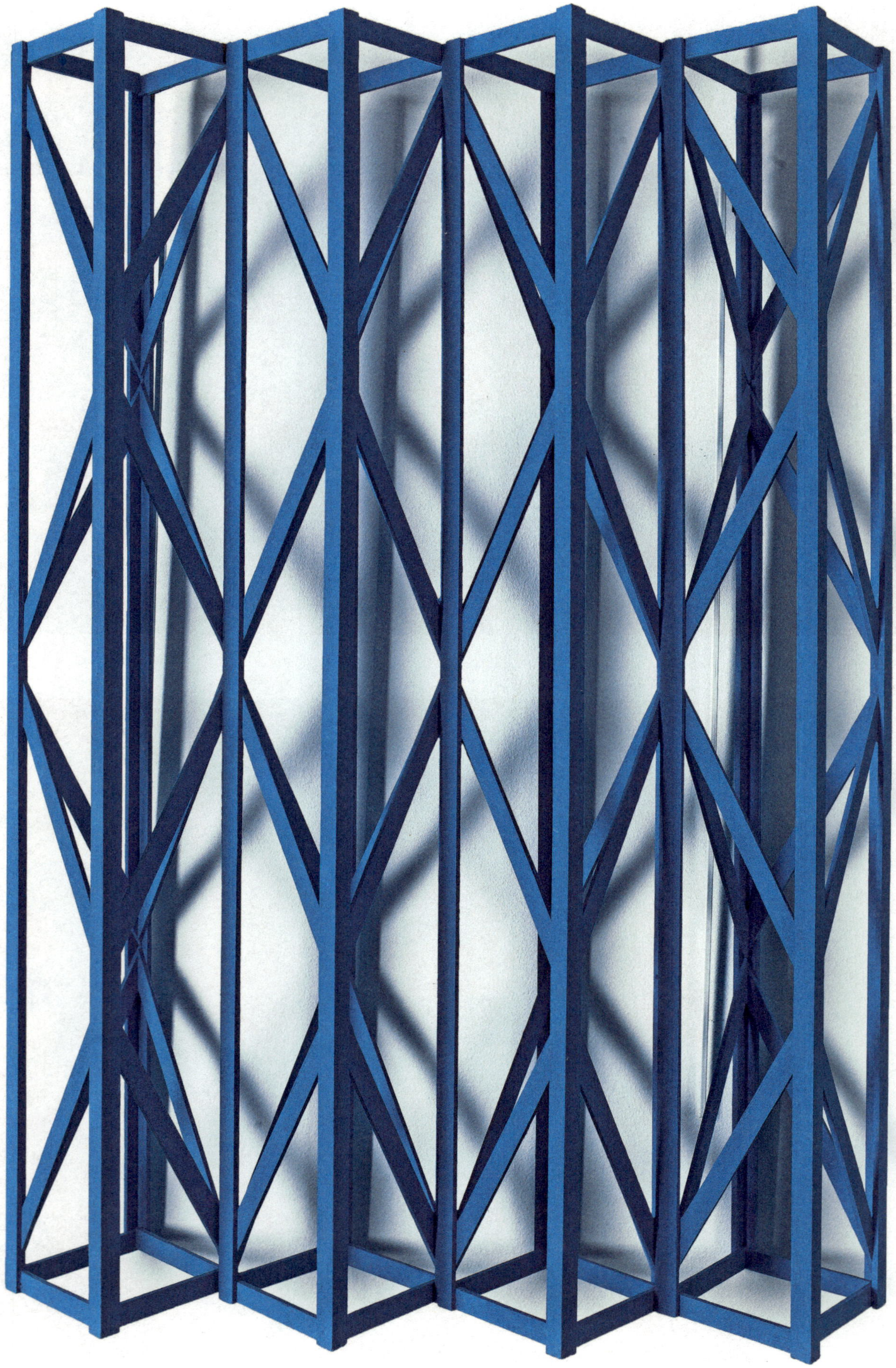

Cricklewood Broadway, 2014
acrylic on wood, 53 x 58 x 10 cm

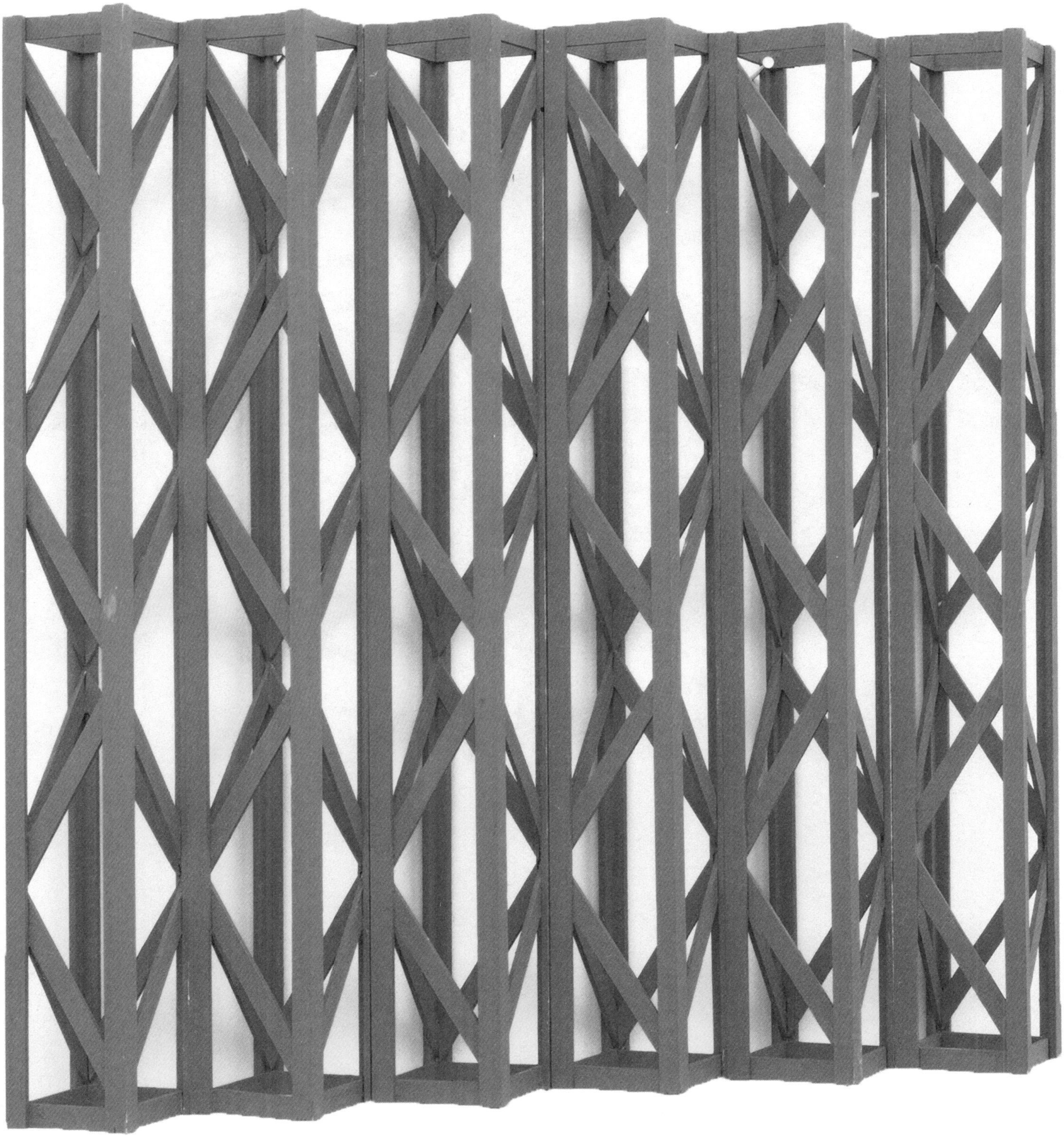

Jaamni (Purple Diamond), 2014
acrylic on wood, 79 x 119 x 18 cm

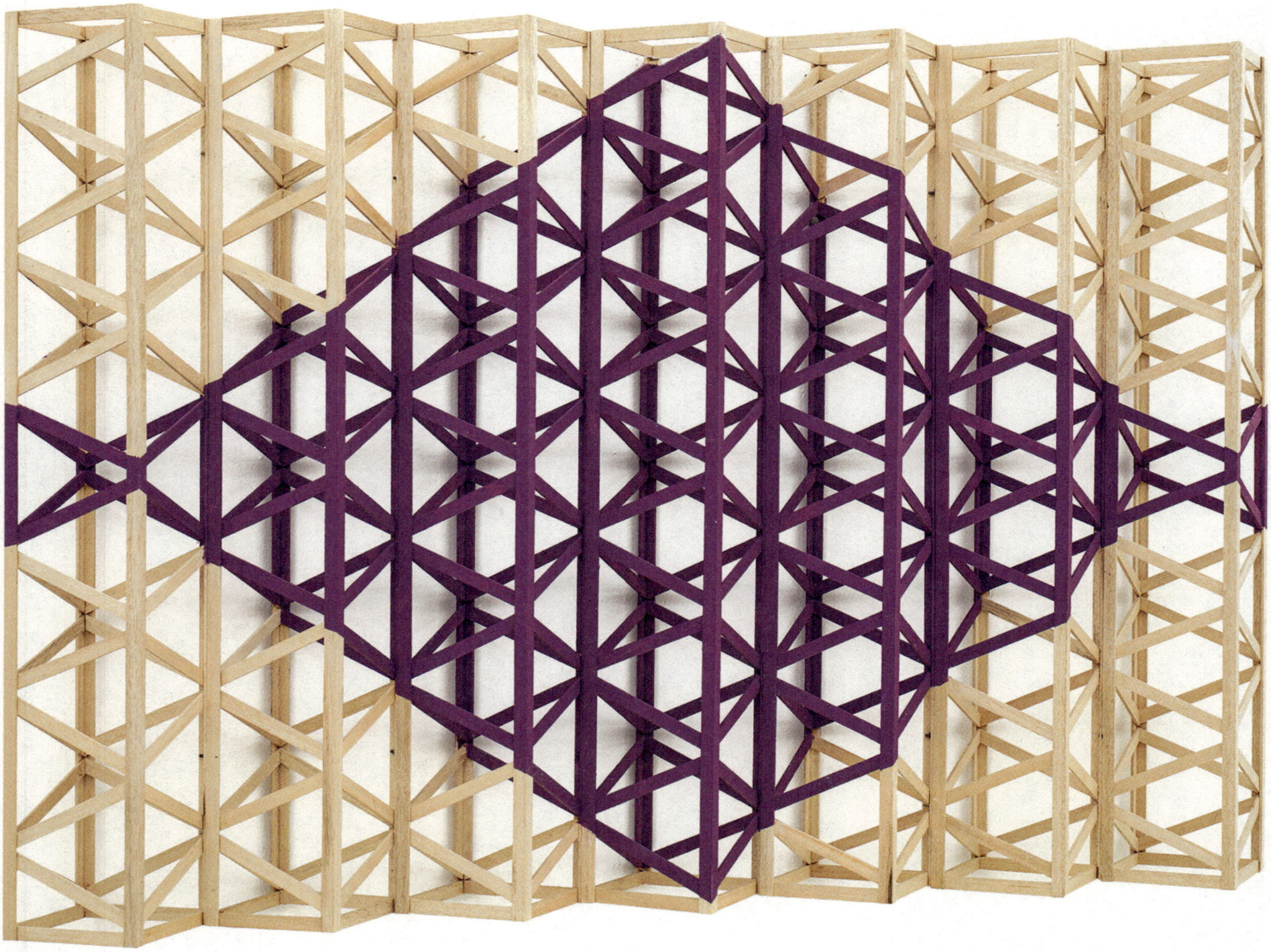

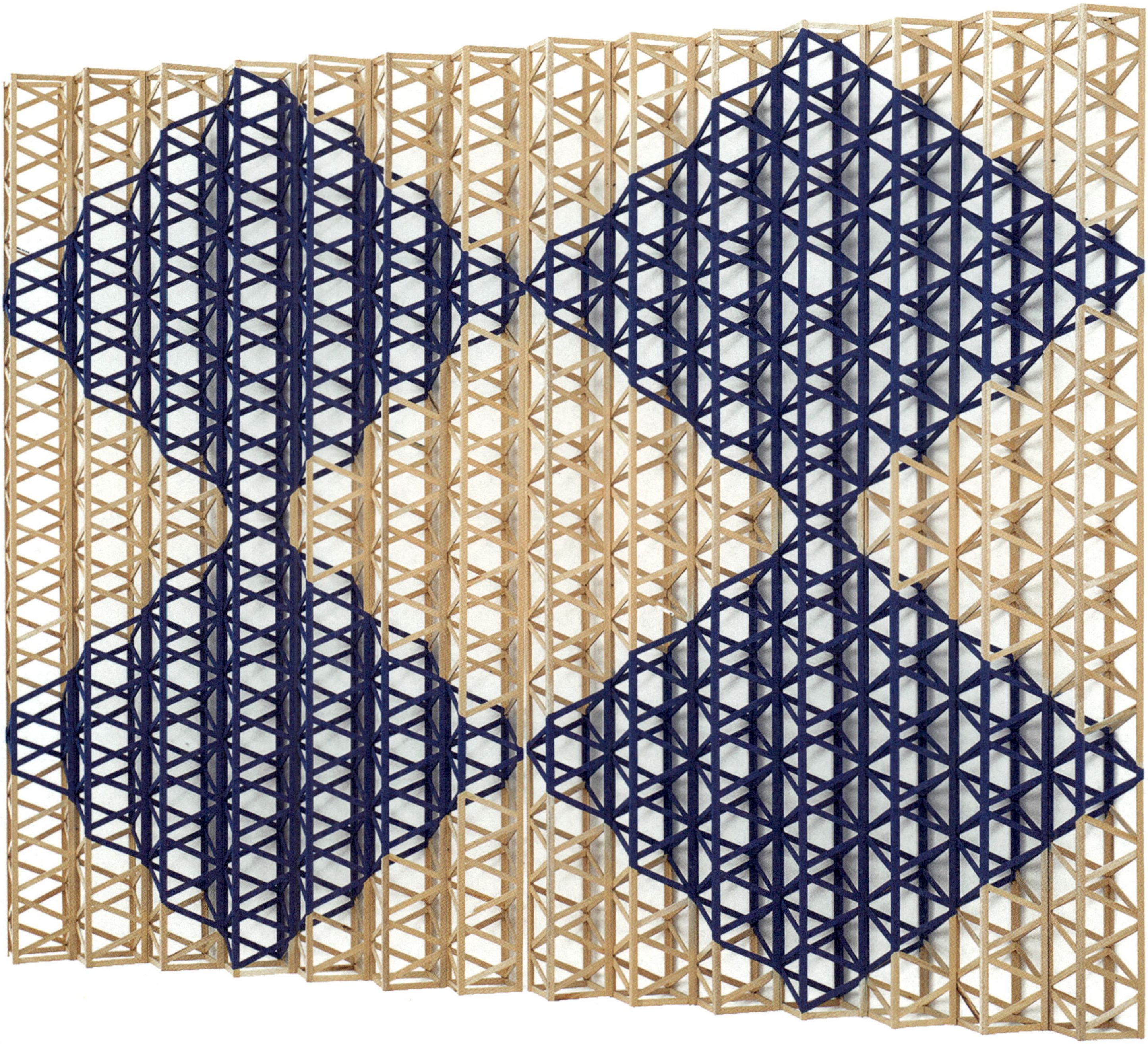

Chaar Neelay Heeray (Four Blue Diamonds), 2014
acrylic on wood, 180 x 239 x 18 cm
Kiran Nadar Museum of Art Collection

Three Cheers For Rodchenko, 2015
acrylic on wood, 155 x 340 x 18 cm

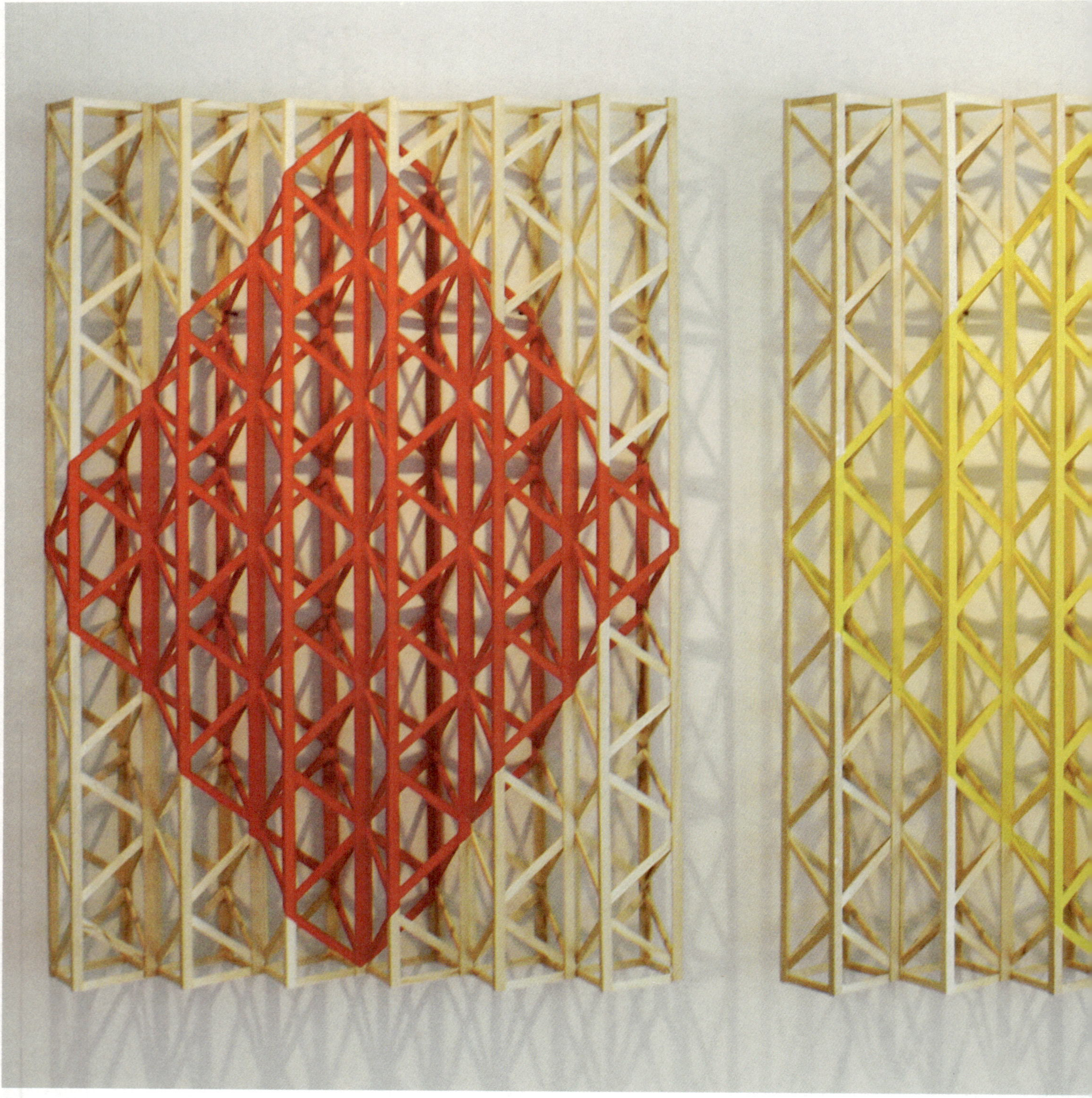

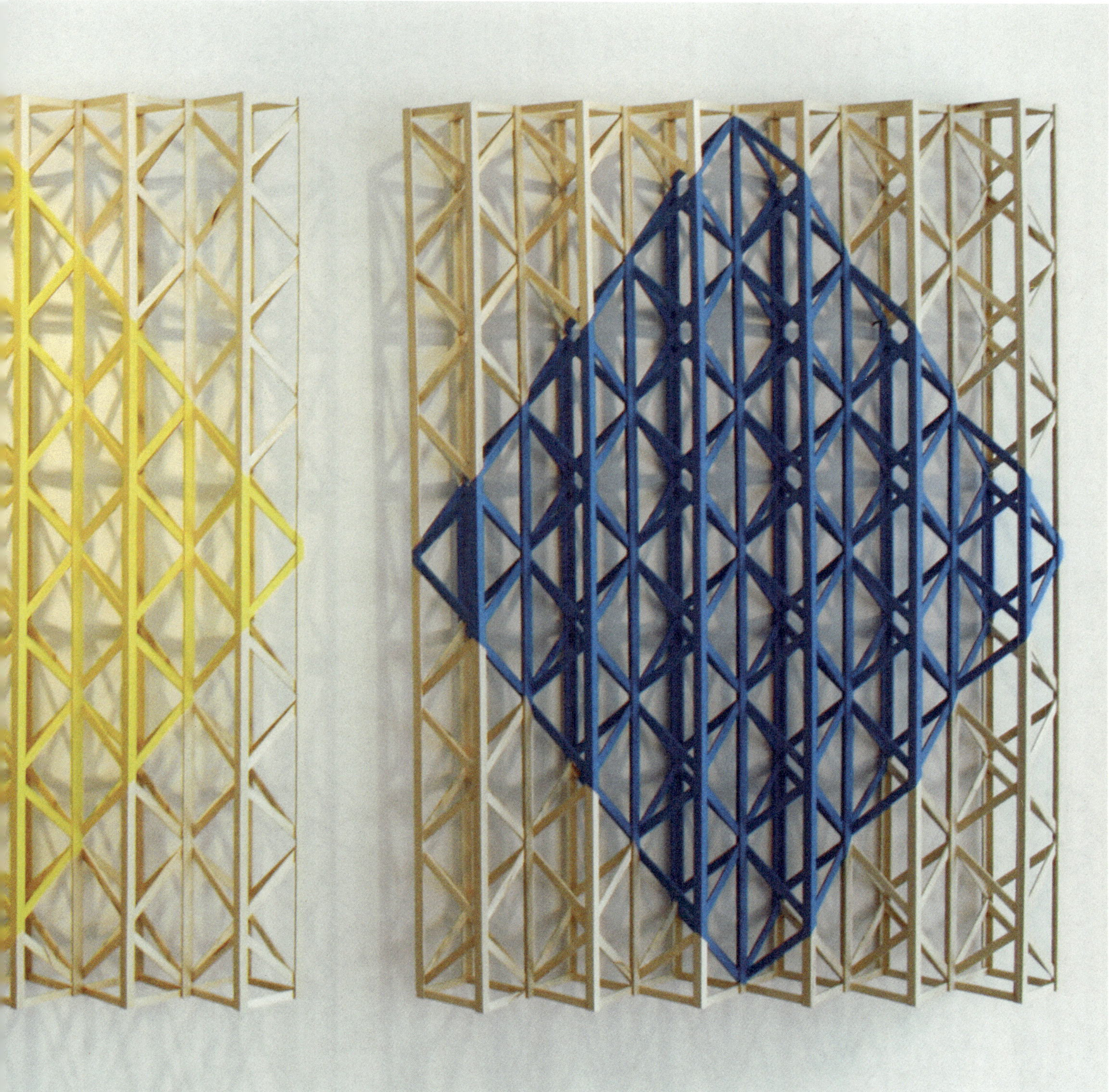

Red Square (After Malevich), 2015
acrylic on wood, 160 x 160 x 18 cm
Red Square Surrounded by Blue and Pink, 2015
acrylic on wood, 160 x 160 x 18 cm

Indigo Square, 2015
acrylic on wood, 160 x 160 x 18 cm
Black Square Breaking Into Rainbow Colours, 2015
acrylic on wood, 160 x 160 x 18 cm

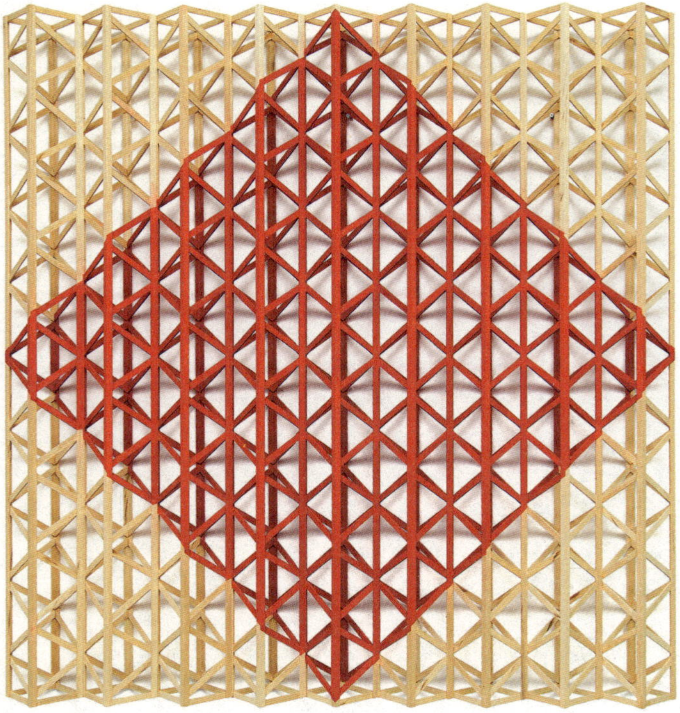

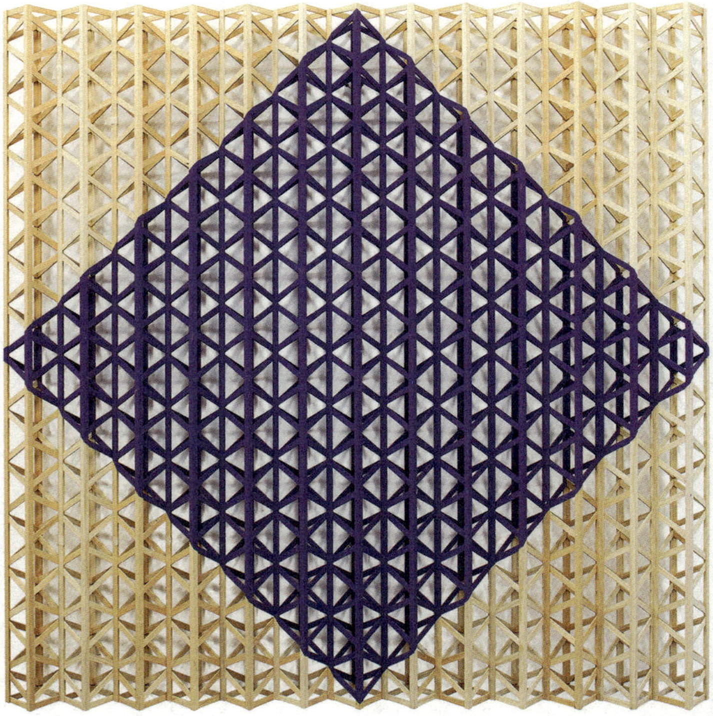

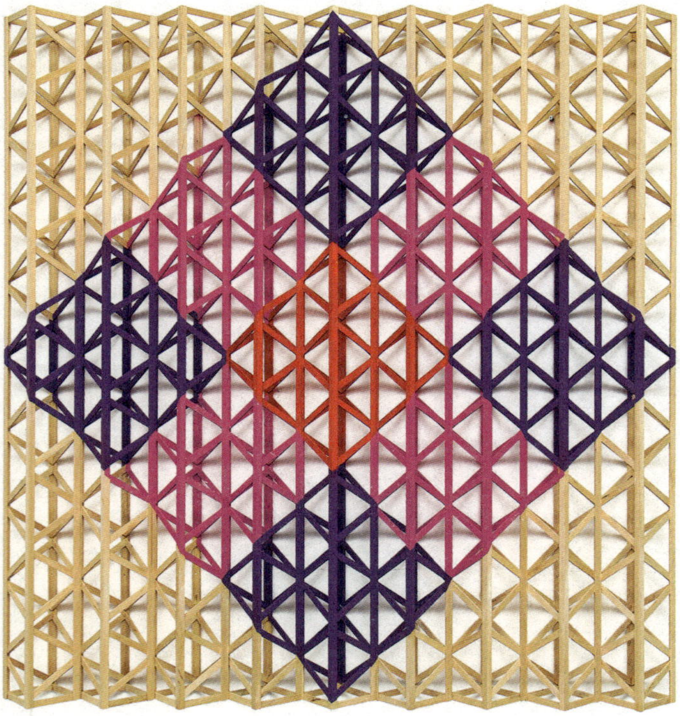

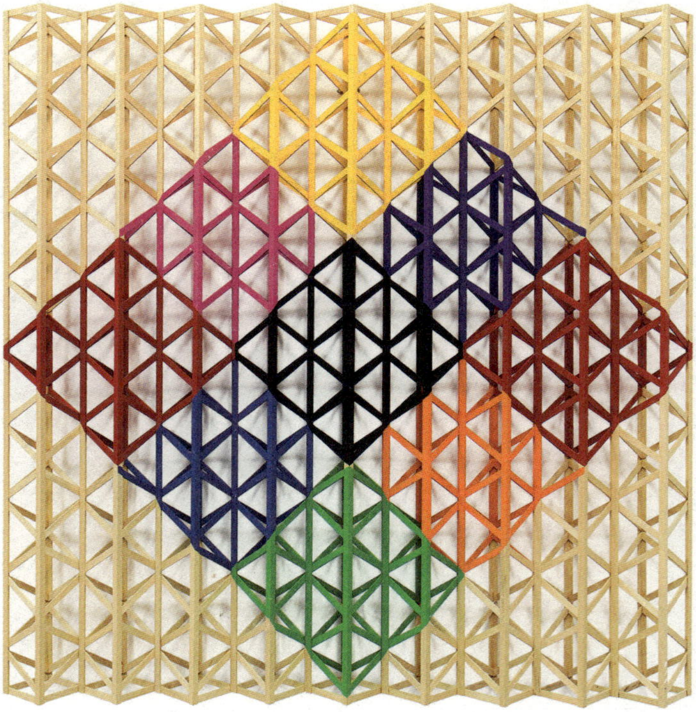

Red Square Breaking Into Primary Colours, 2015
acrylic on wood, 160 x 160 x 18 cm

Bahar Ayie, Khushyaan Lyie, 2015
acrylic on wood, 160 x 213 x 18 cm

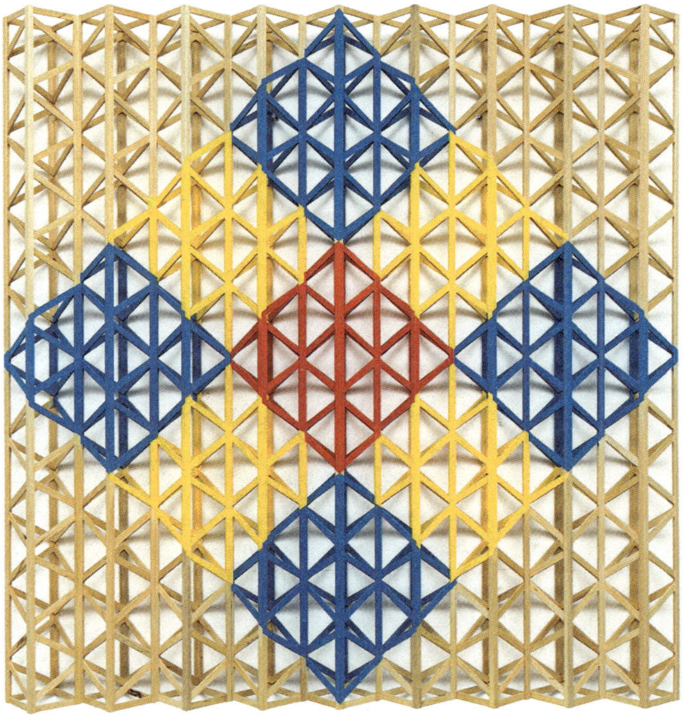

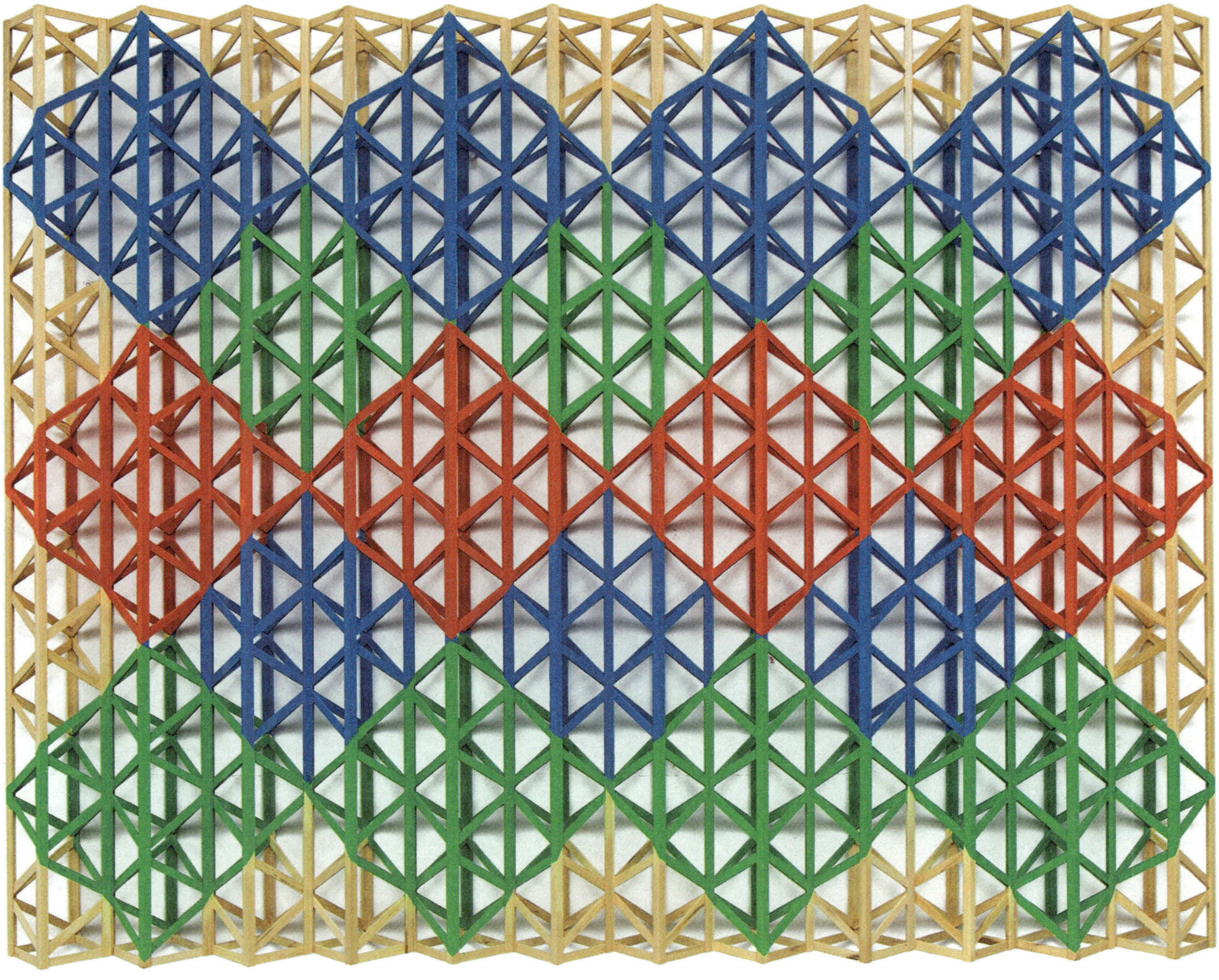

Black Square Breaking into Primary Colours, 2016
acrylic on wood, 162 x 487 x 20 cm

Black Square Breaking into Rainbow Colours, 2016
acrylic on wood, 162 x 20 x 487 cm

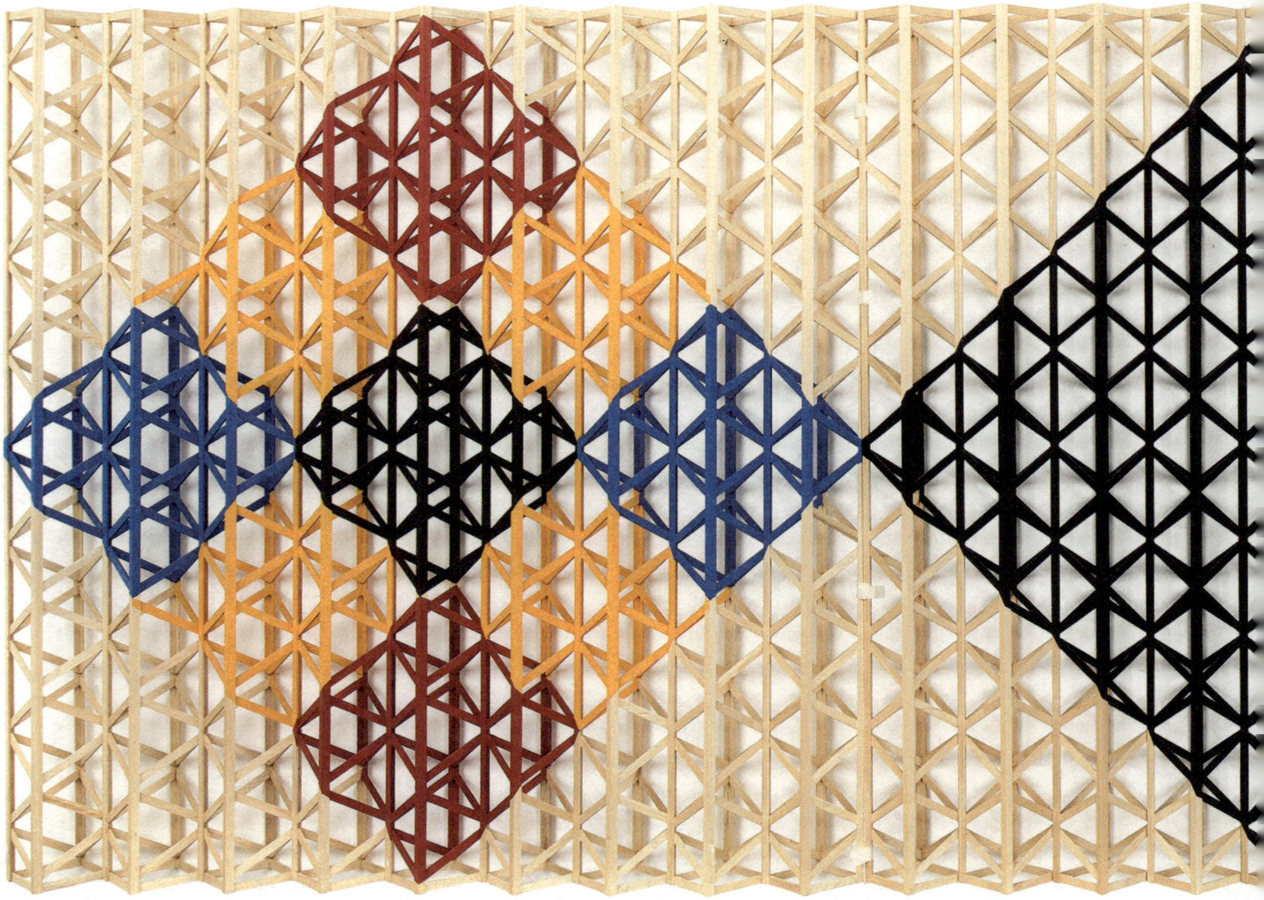

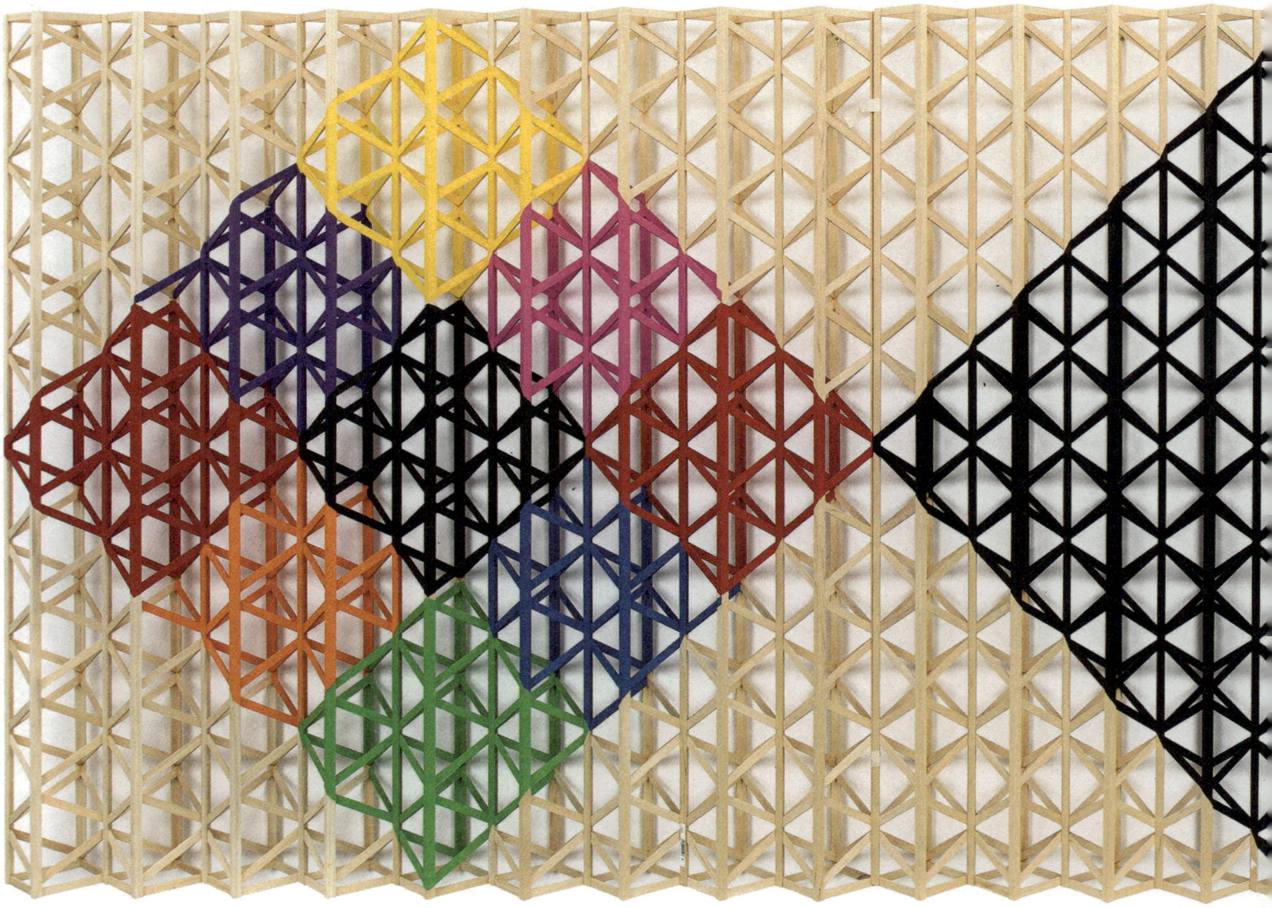

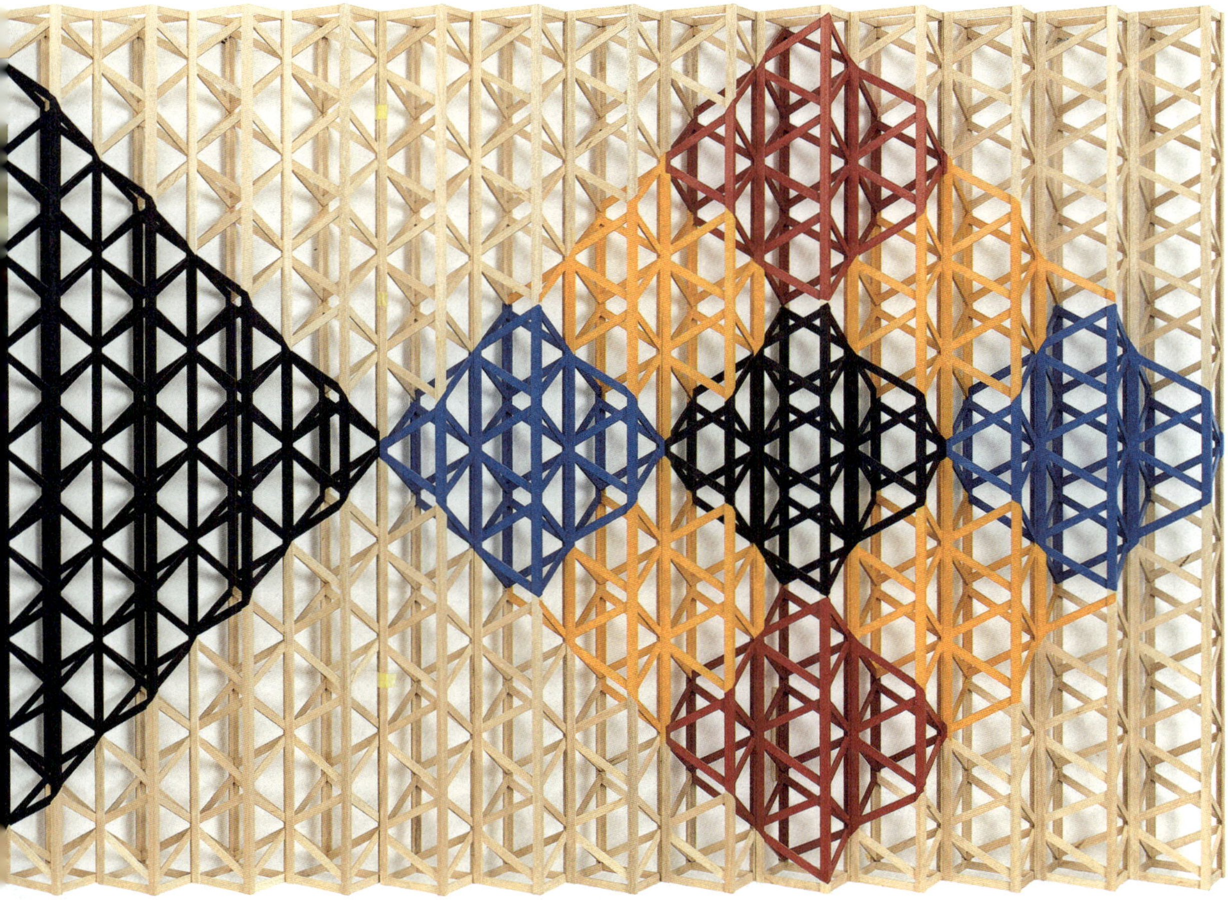

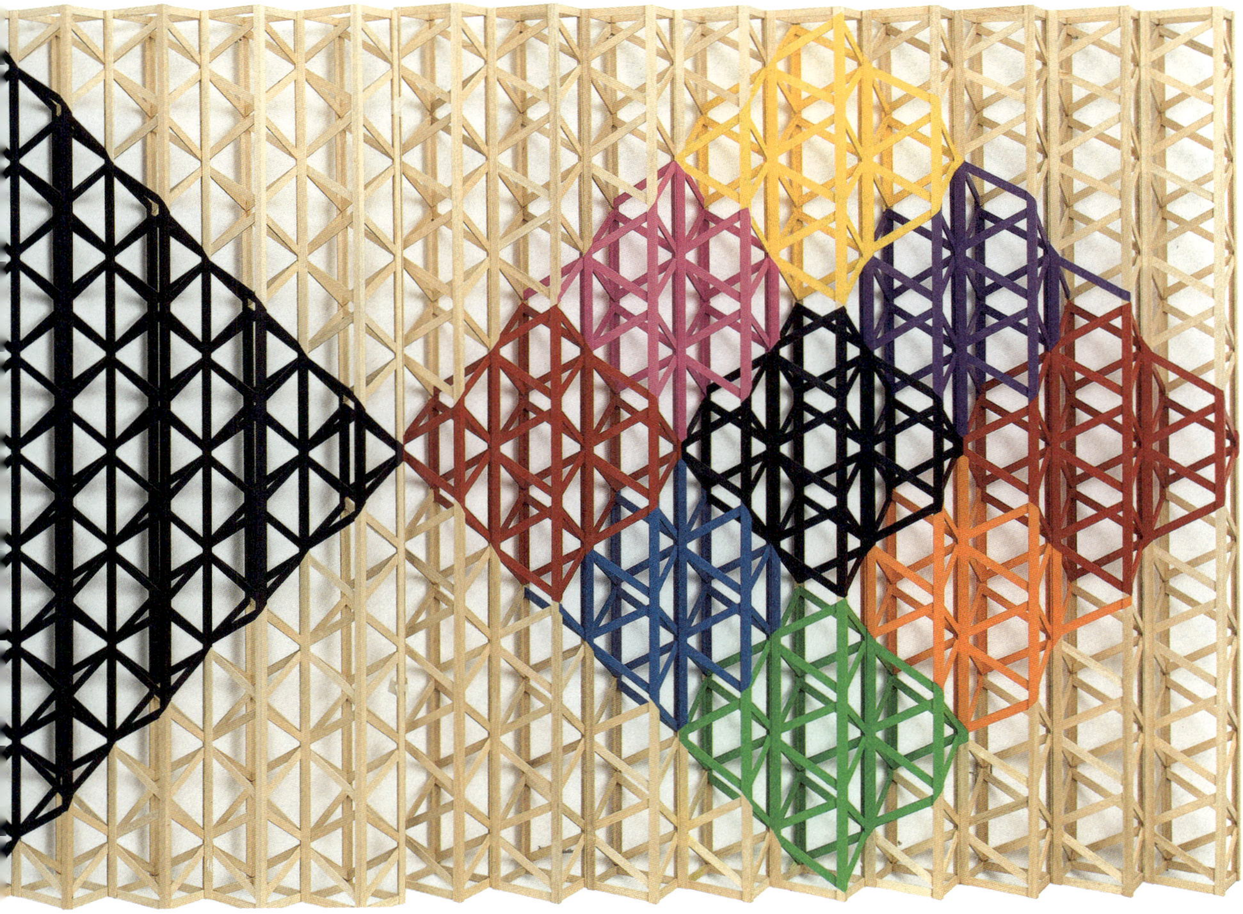

Two Rainbows, 2017
acrylic on wood, 160 x 269 x 17 cm
Hutchison Family Collection

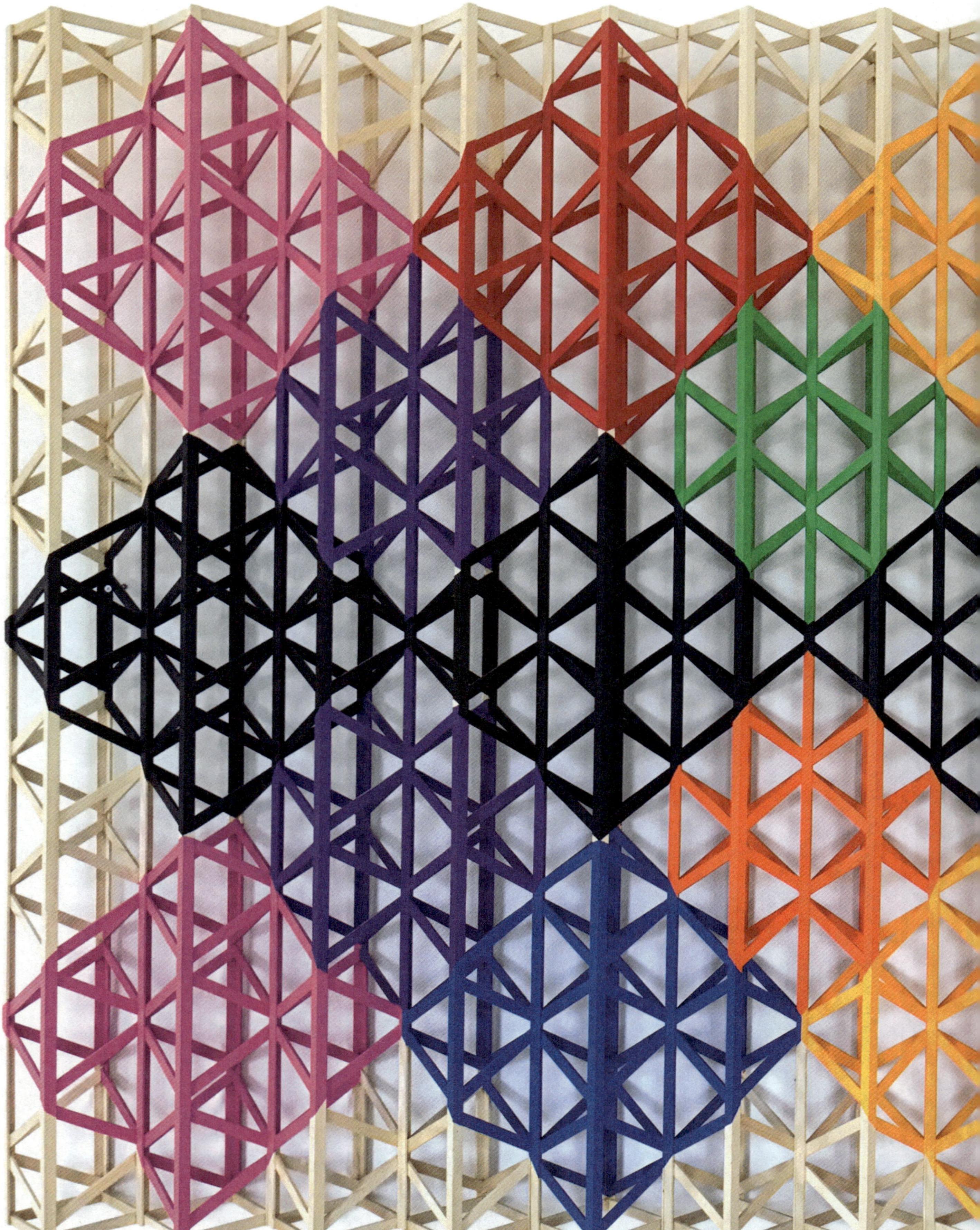

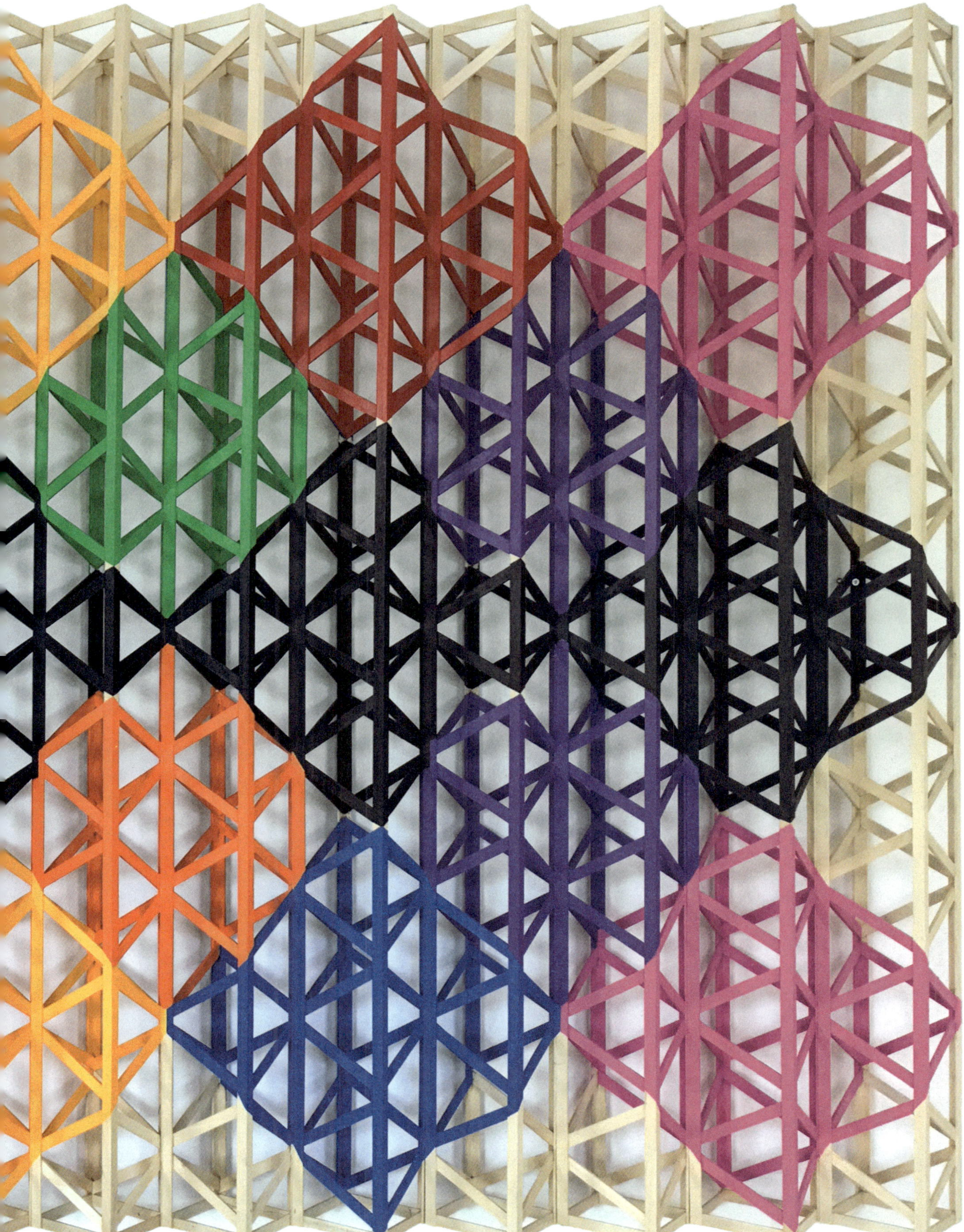

Rainbow, 2015
7 acrylic on wood Structures, 31 x 31 x 31 cm each
British Council Collection

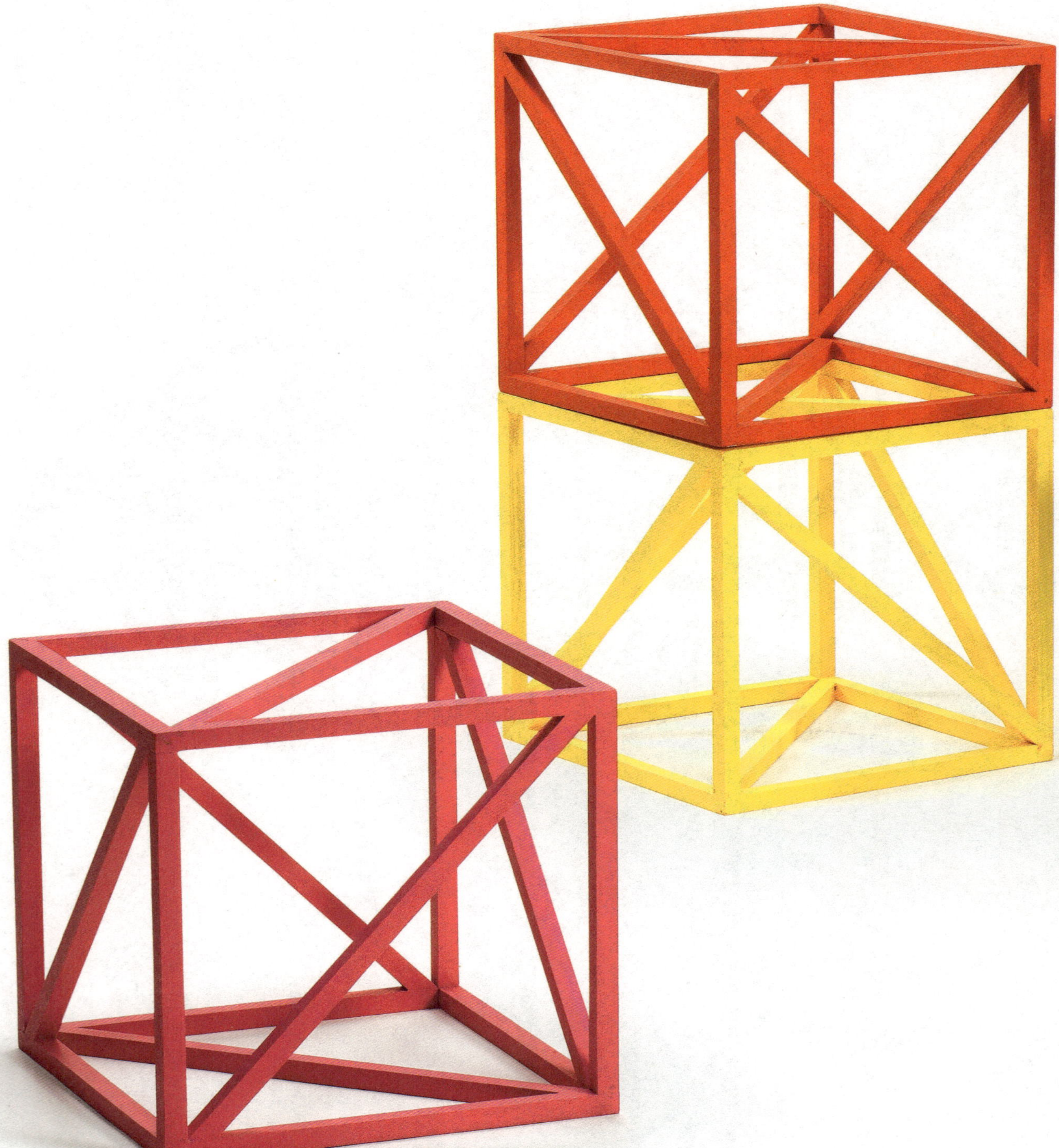

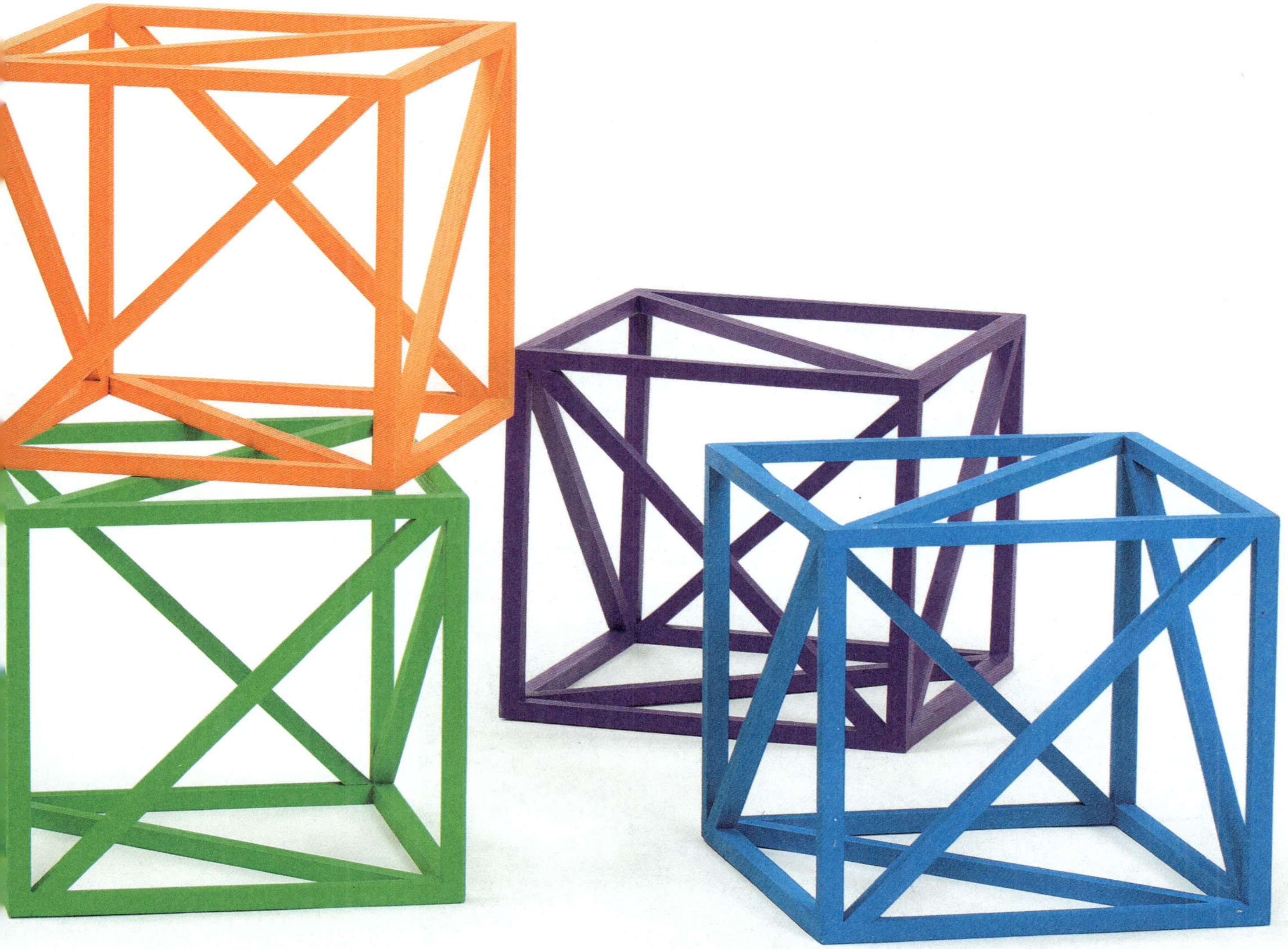

Go On, Sing The Blues, Again, 2015
acrylic on wood, 91 x 91 x 91 cm
Private collection

Quoon Iyes Yaad Phir Uskey, 2015
acrylic on wood, 91 x 91 x 91 cm

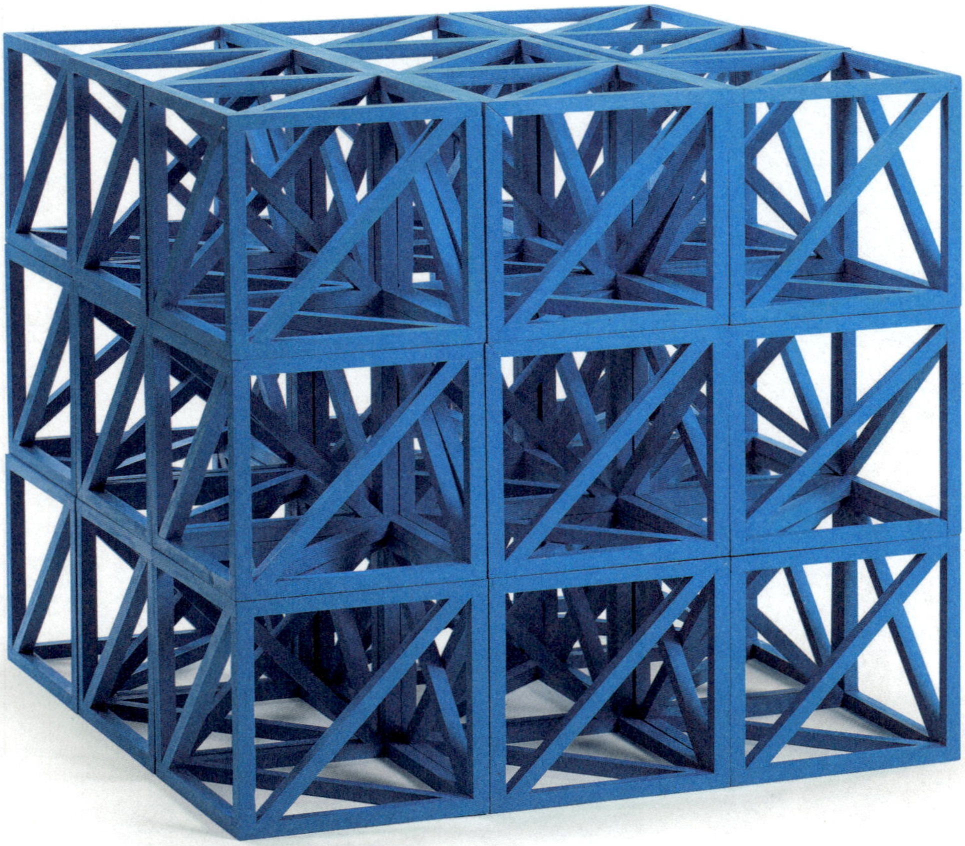

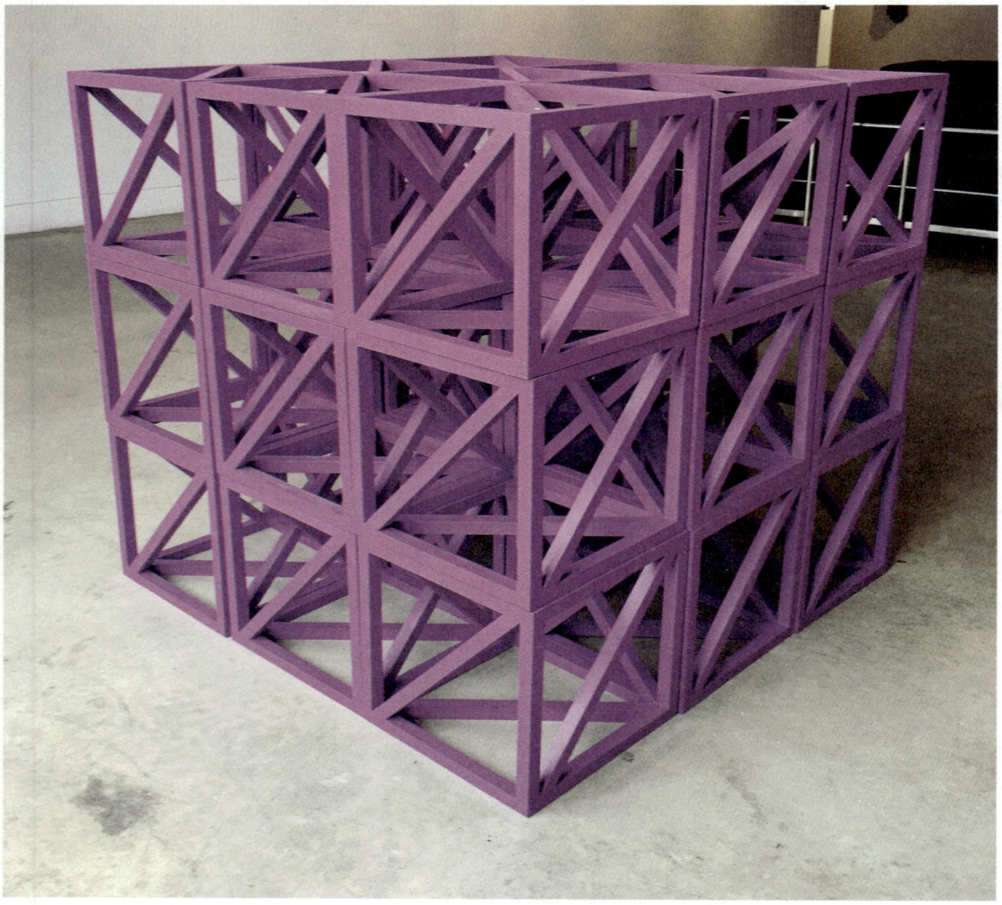

Rainbow Colours Surrounding Black, 2015
acrylic on wood, 152 x 152 x 31 cm

Zero to Infinity, 1968–2004 / 2015
installation at Aicon Gallery, New York
24 acrylic on wood structures, 48 x 48 x 48 cm each

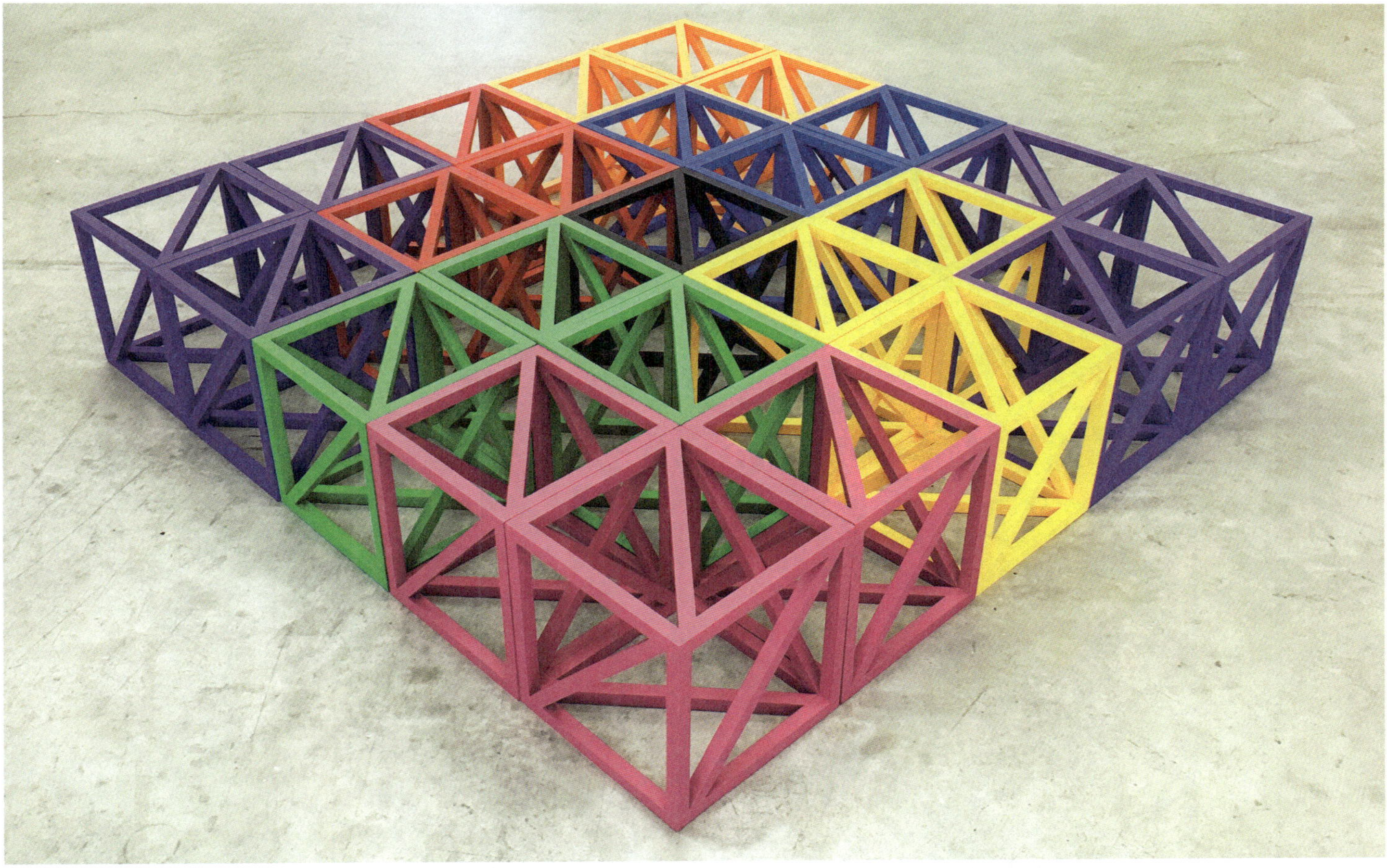

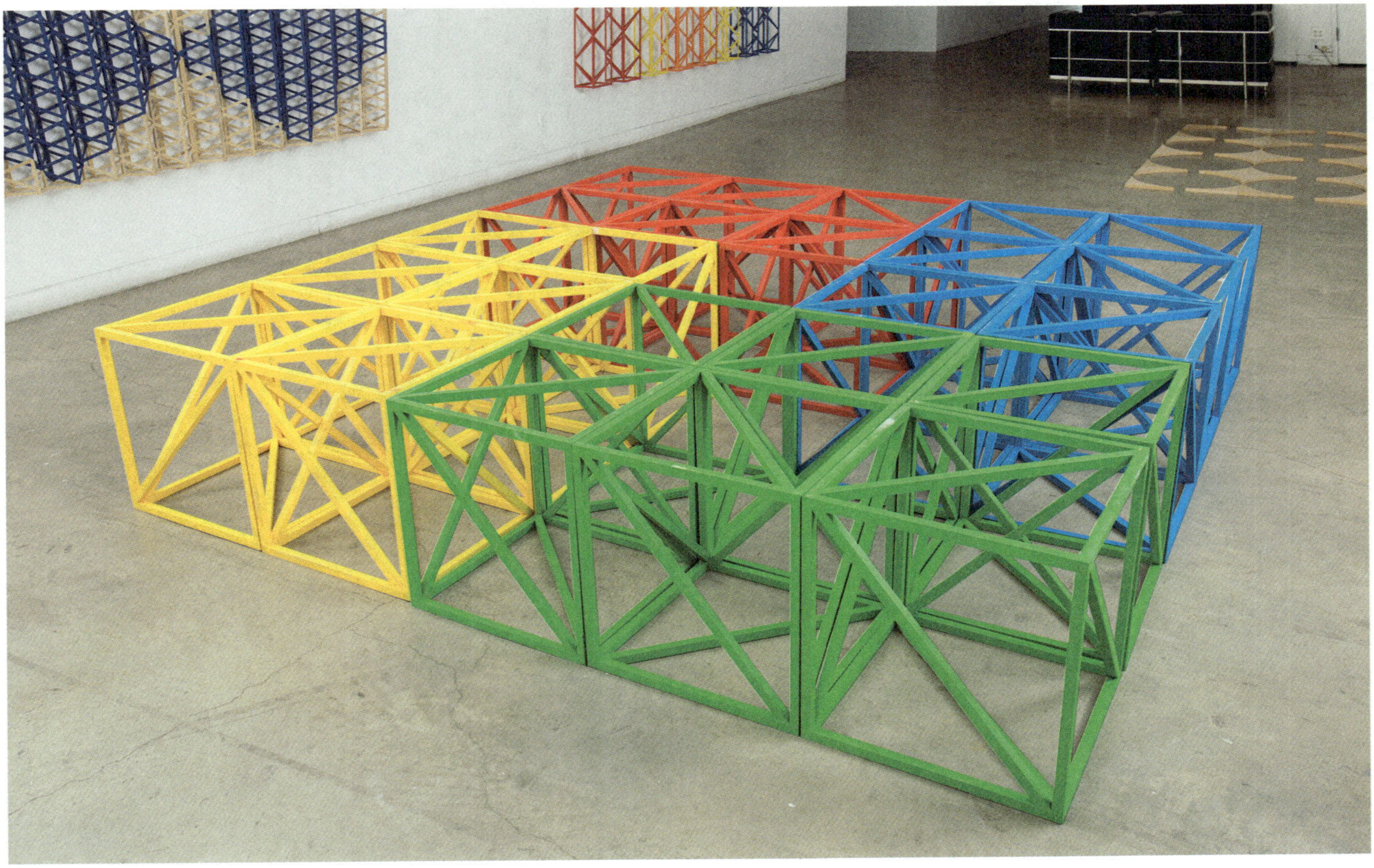

Farunghi Mahal (Palace of the Foreigners), 2016
acrylic on wood, 170 x 153 x 153 cm

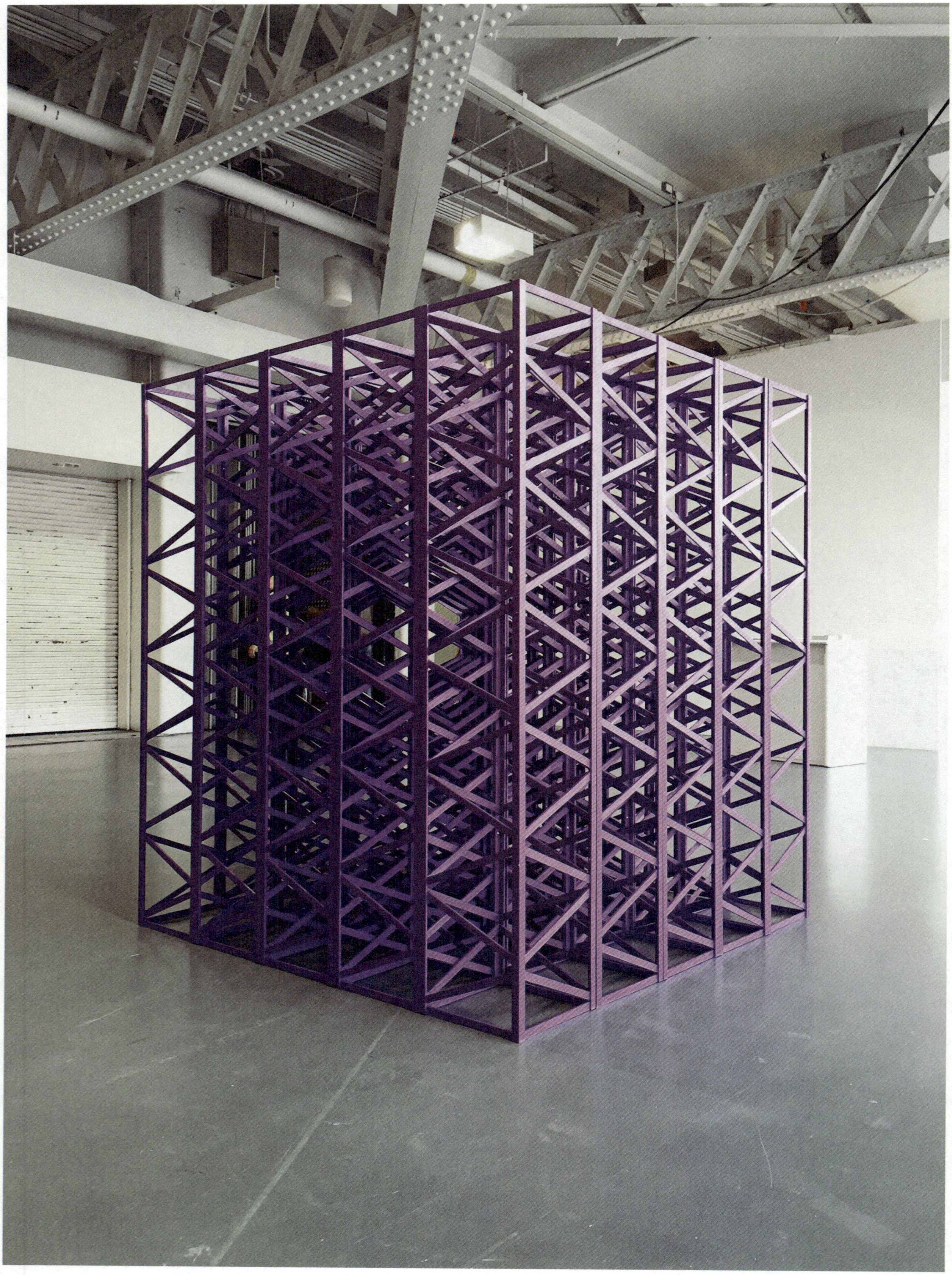

Teen Rungh Upper Nechay, 2016
acrylic on wood, 183 x 274 x 15 cm

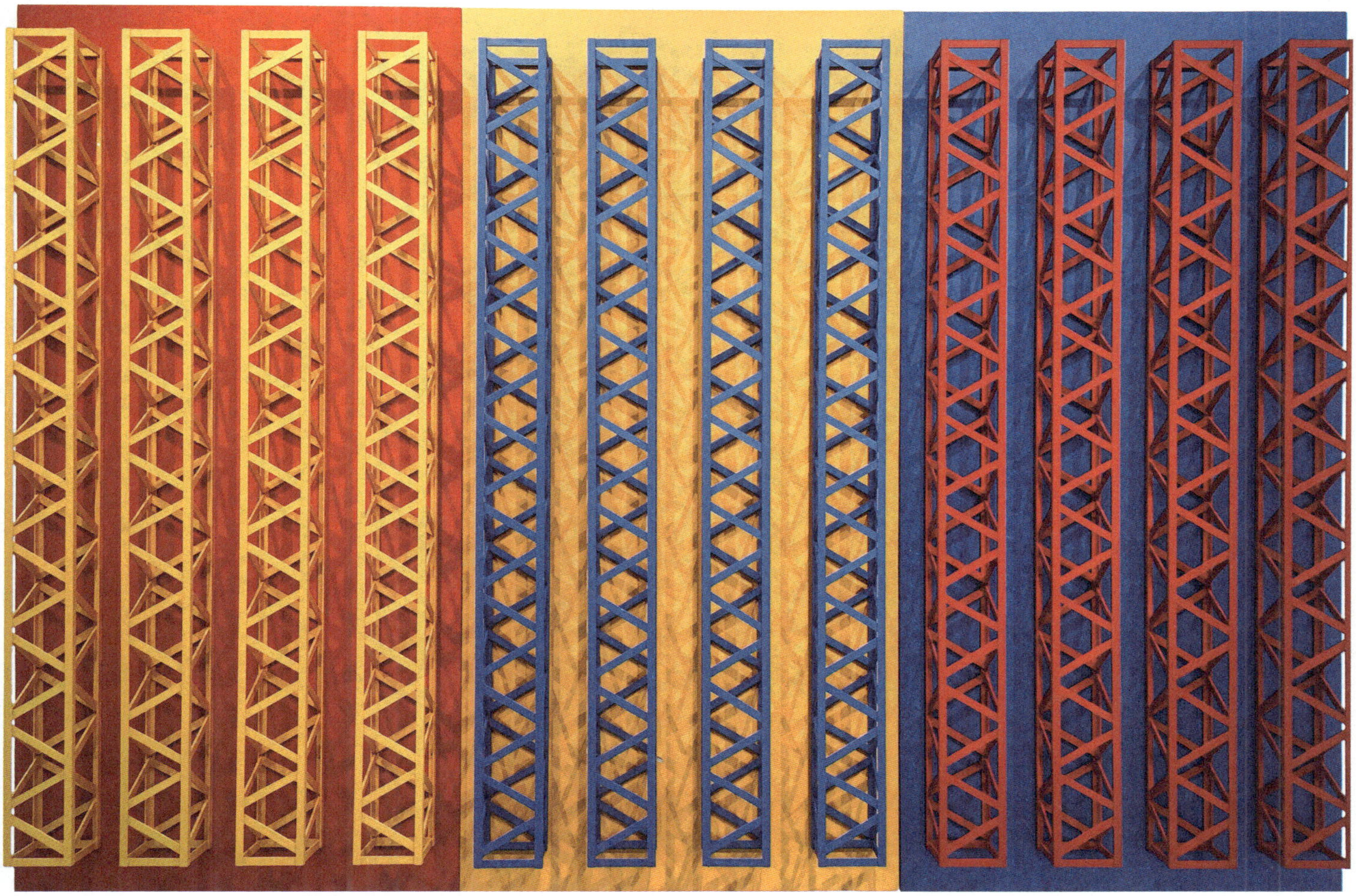

Neelay Hey Neelay (Blues and Blues), 2016
acrylic on wood, 168 x 366 cm

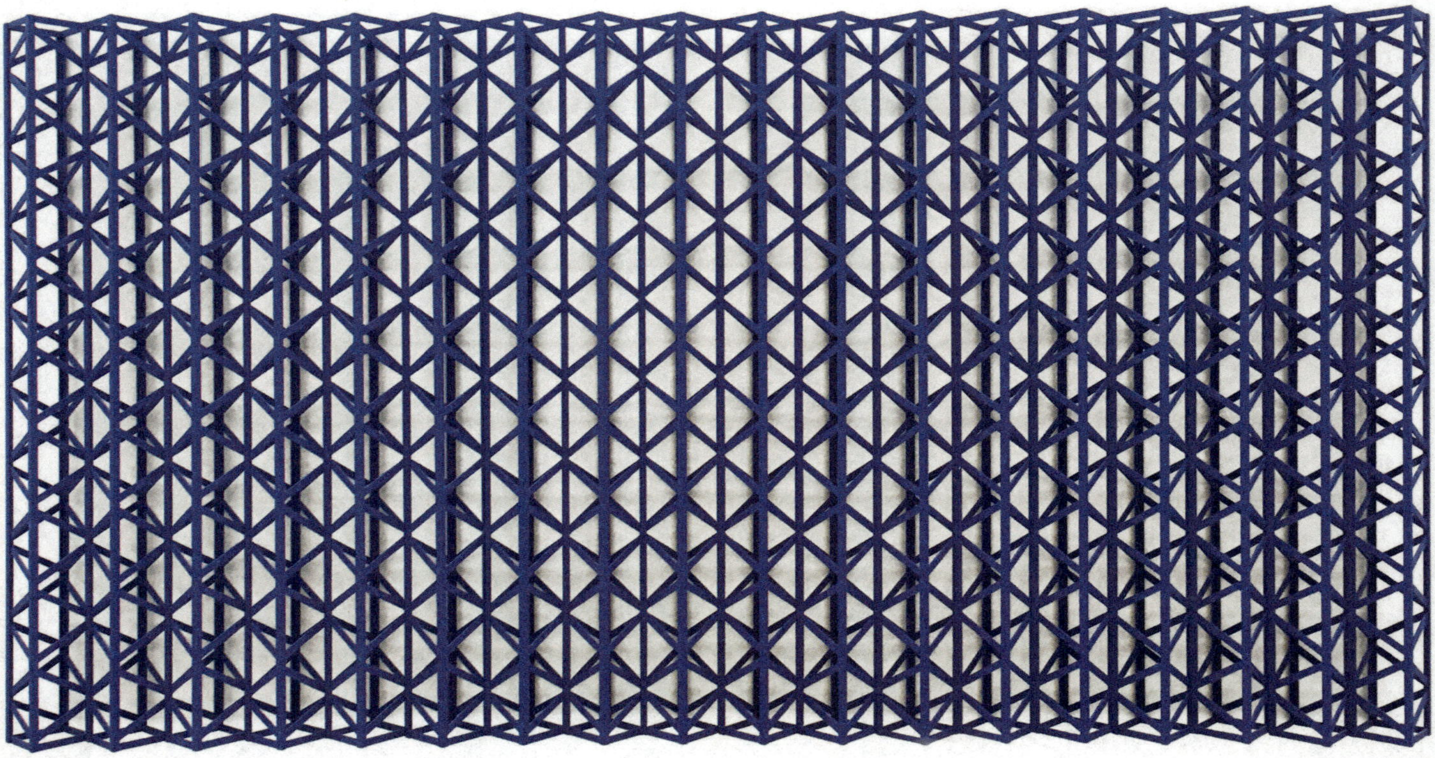

Zero to Infinity, 1968–2004 / 2016
installation at Museu de Arte de São Paulo
400 acrylic on wood Structures, 50 x 50 x 50 cm each
São Paulo Museum of Art Collection

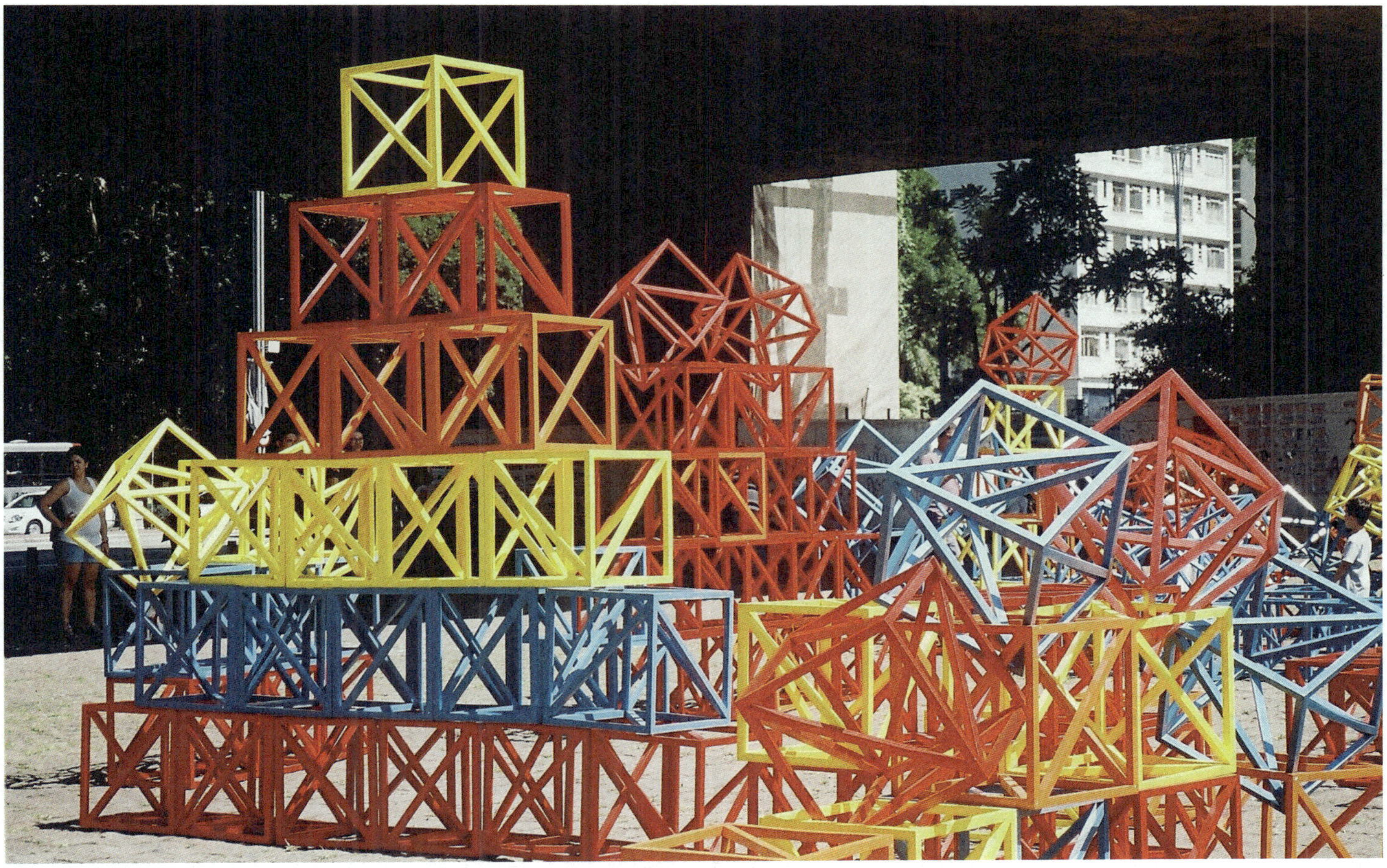

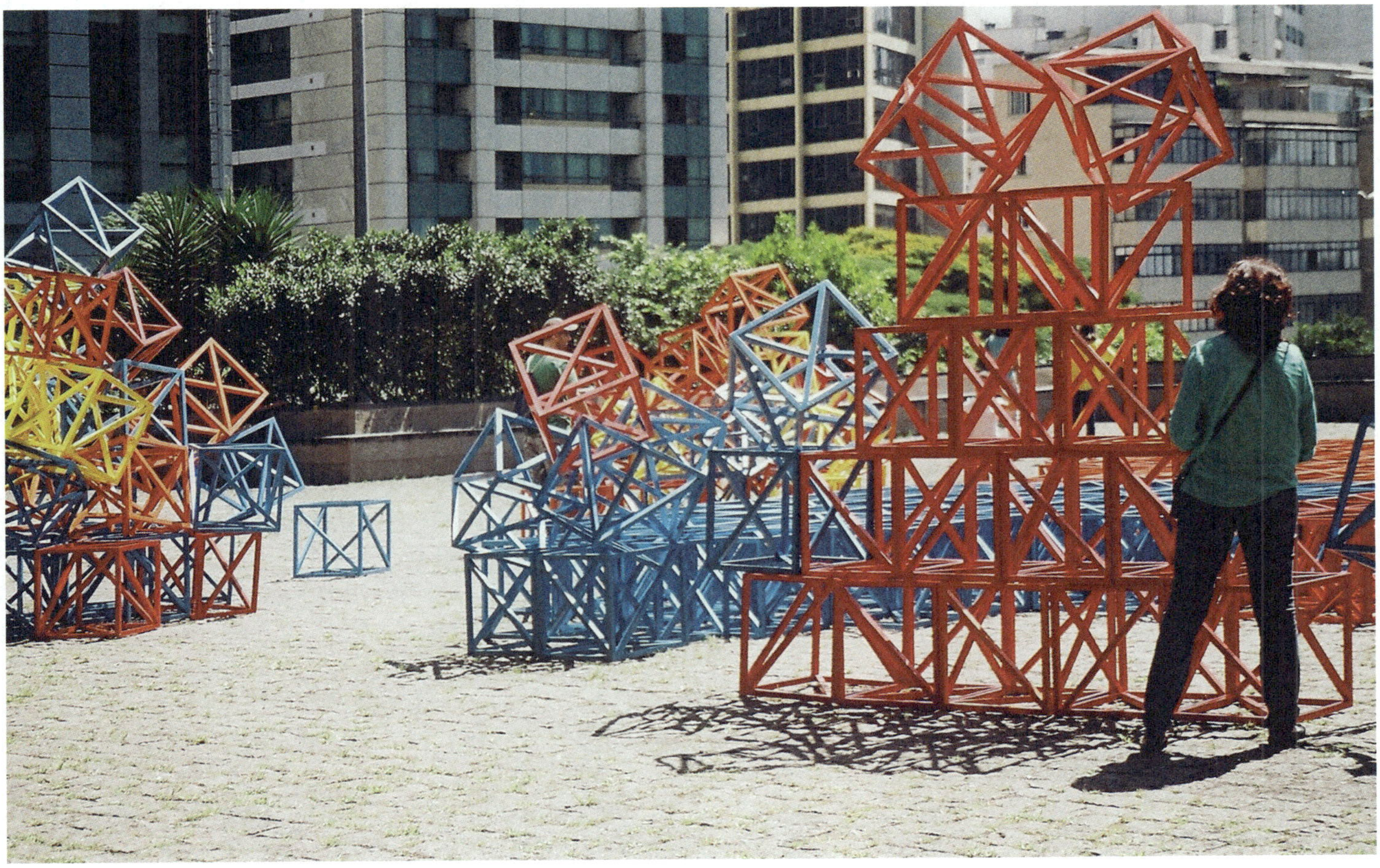

Opus B1, 2016
acrylic on canvas, 160 x 160 cm
Opus B3, 2016
acrylic on canvas, 160 x 160 cm

Opus B2, 2016
acrylic on canvas, 160 x 160 cm
Opus B4, 2016
acrylic on canvas, 160 x 160 cm

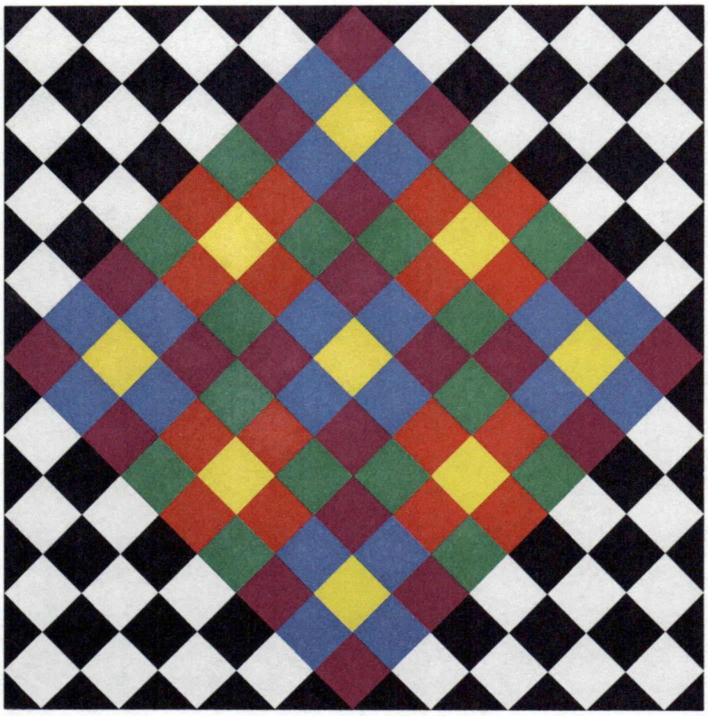

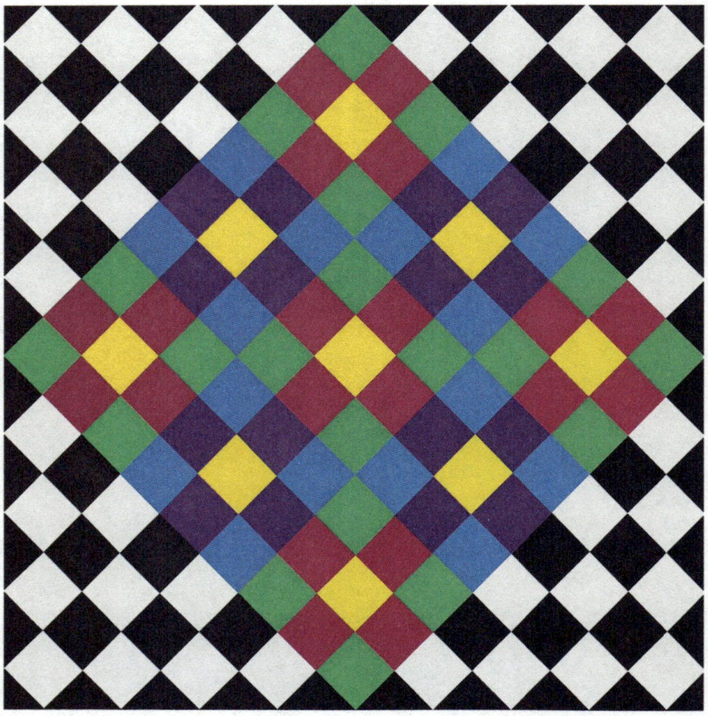

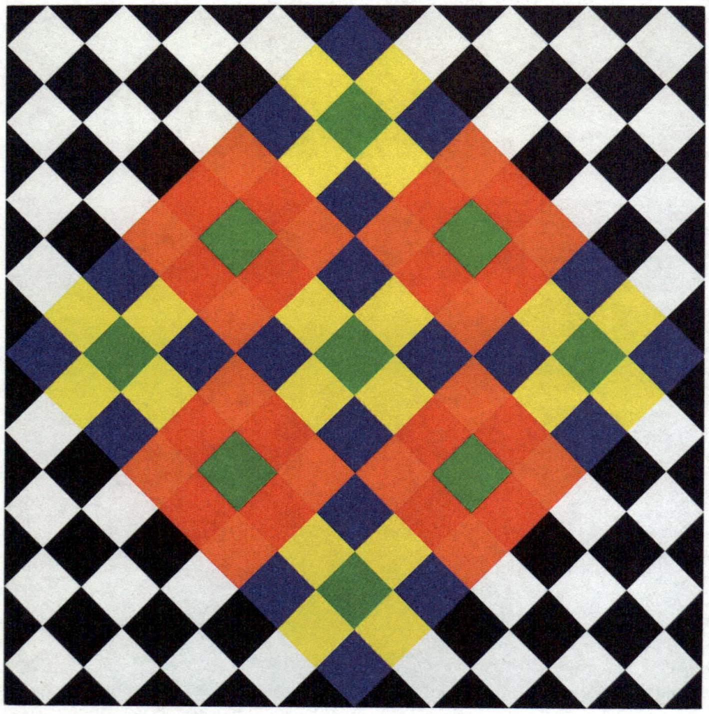

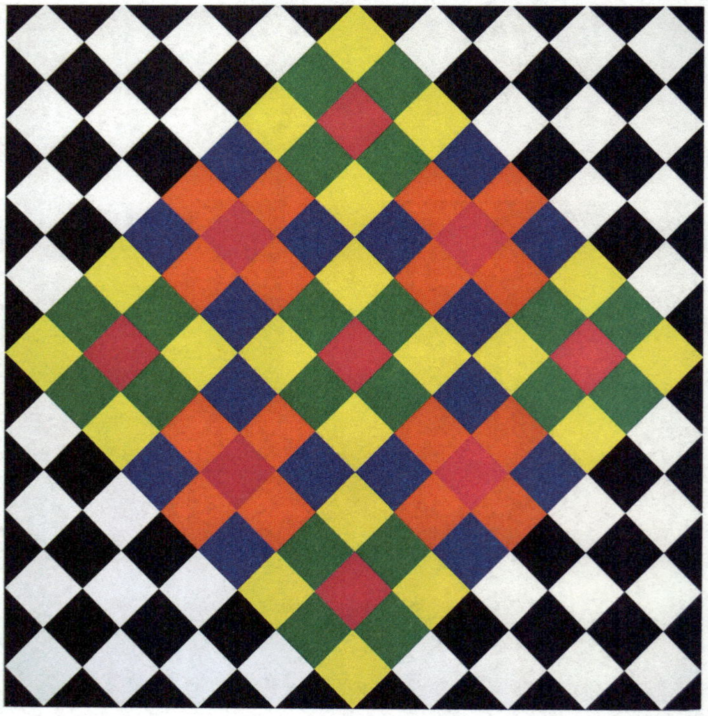

Opus D1, 2016
acrylic on canvas, 160 x 160 cm
Opus D3, 2016
acrylic on canvas, 160 x 160 cm

Opus D2, 2016
acrylic on canvas, 160 x 160 cm
Opus D4, 2016
acrylic on canvas, 160 x 160 cm

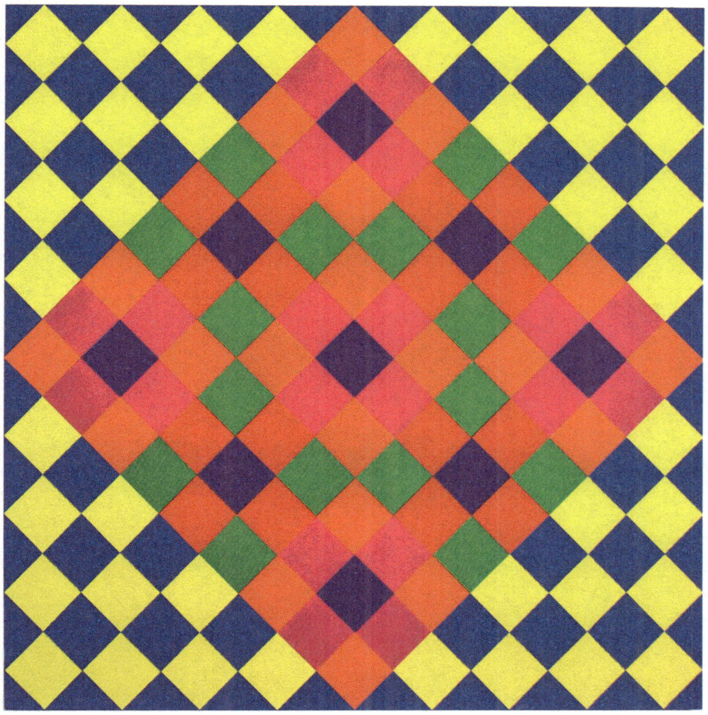

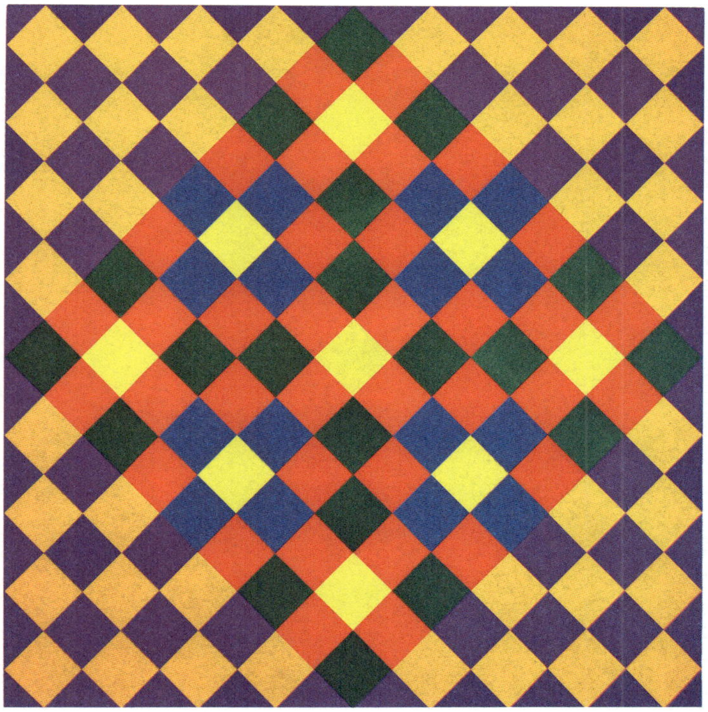

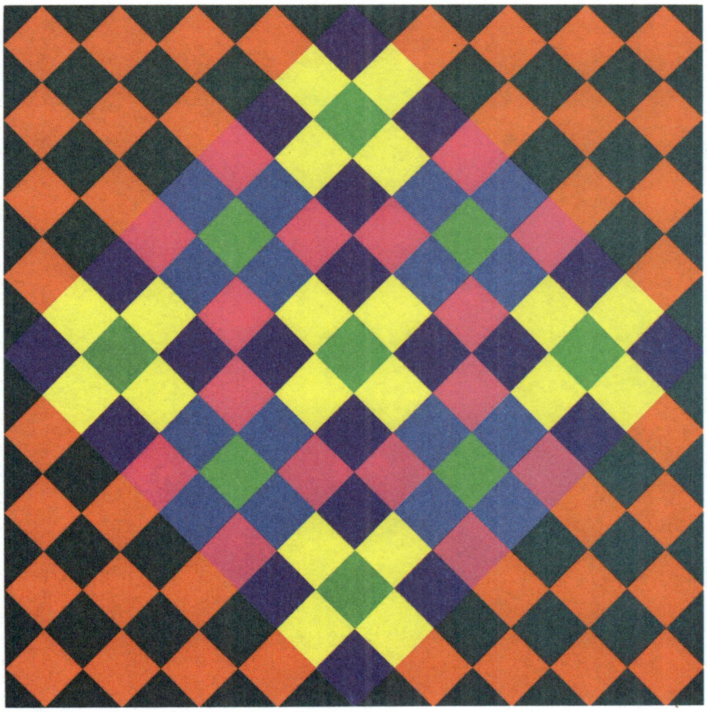

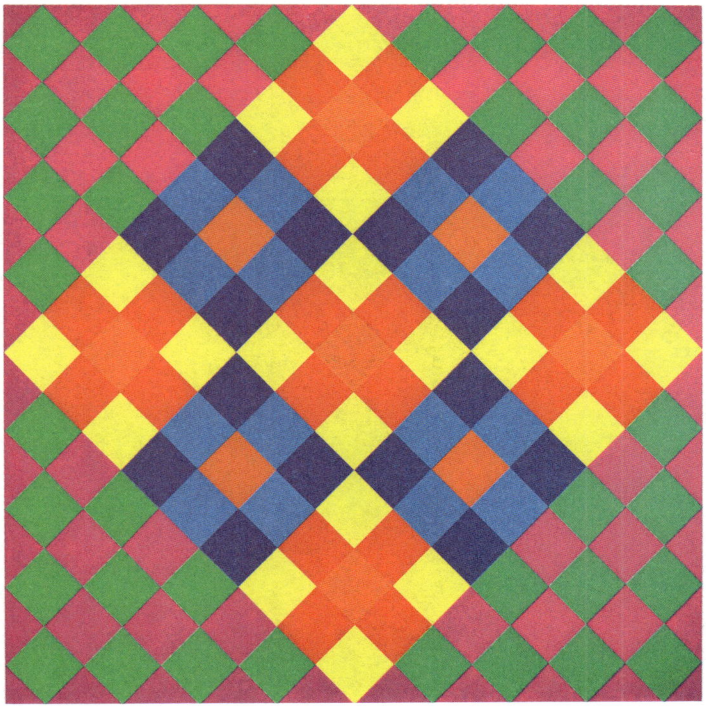

Opus F1, 2016
acrylic on canvas, 160 x 160 cm
Opus F3, 2016
acrylic on canvas, 160 x 160 cm

Opus F2, 2016
acrylic on canvas, 160 x 160 cm
Opus F4, 2016
acrylic on canvas, 160 x 160 cm

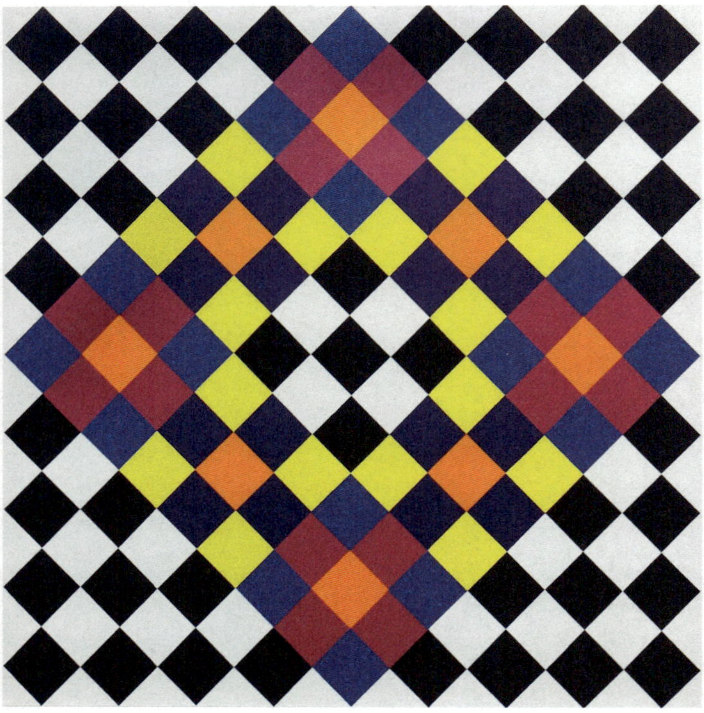

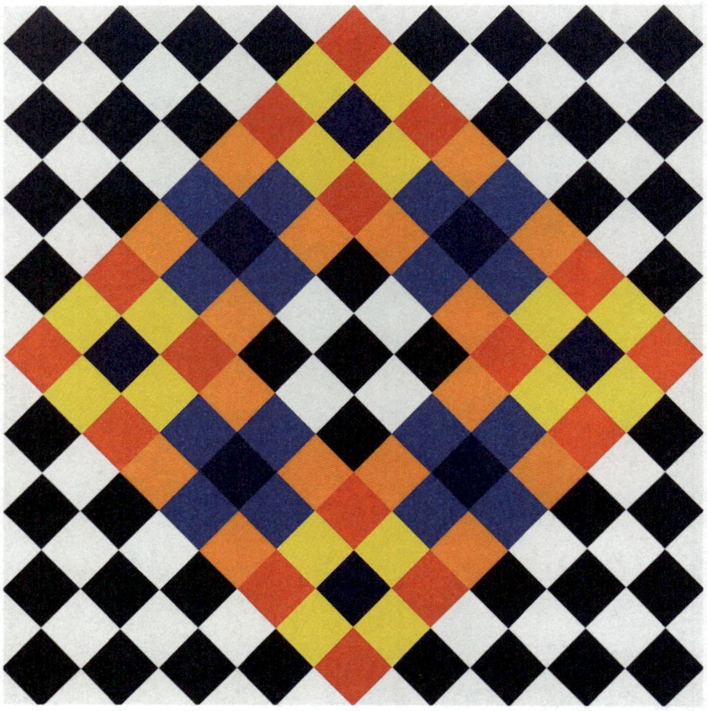

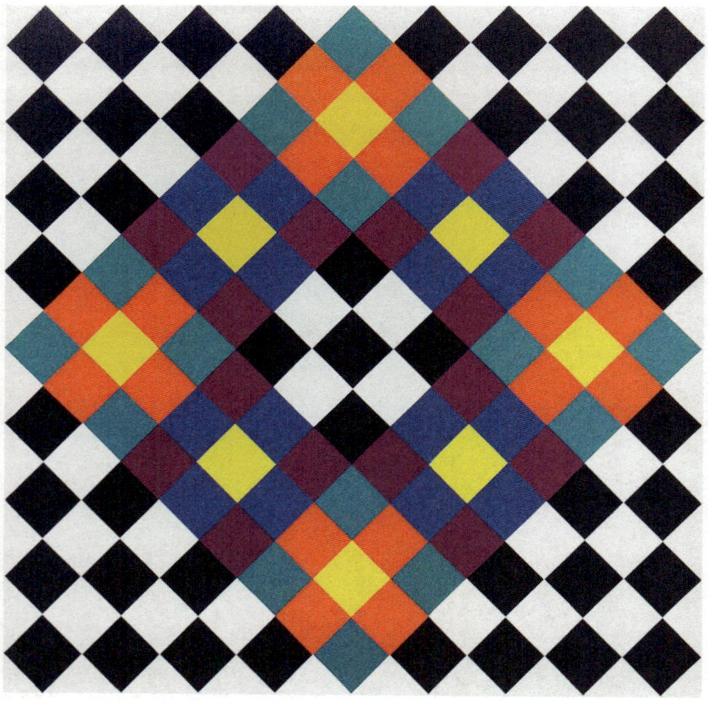

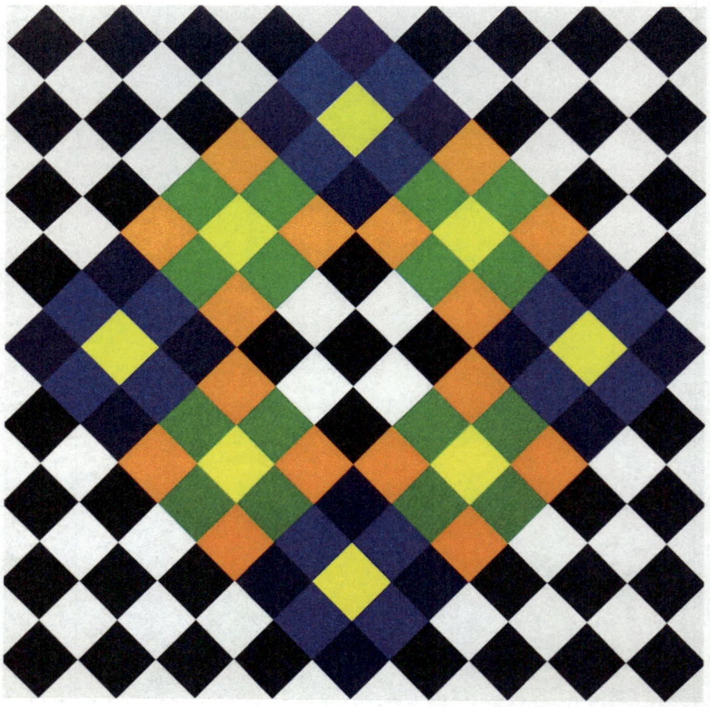

Opus AA1, 2016
acrylic on canvas, 160 x 160 cm
Opus AA3, 2016
acrylic on canvas, 160 x 160 cm

Opus AA2, 2016
acrylic on canvas, 160 x 160 cm
Opus AA4, 2016
acrylic on canvas, 160 x 160 cm

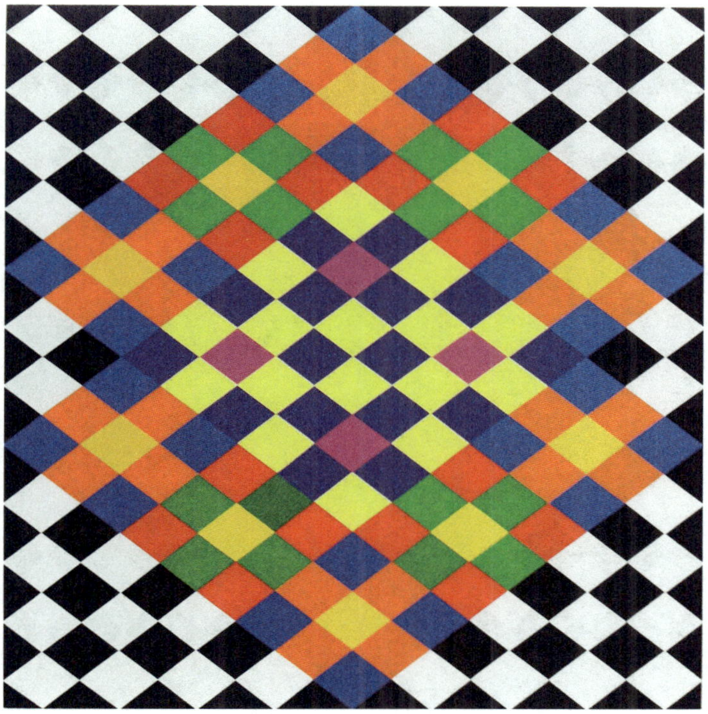

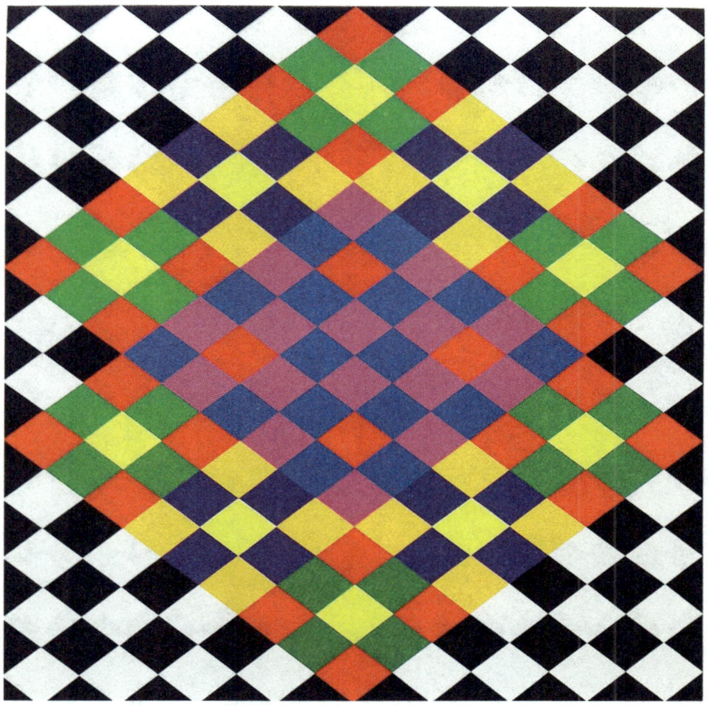

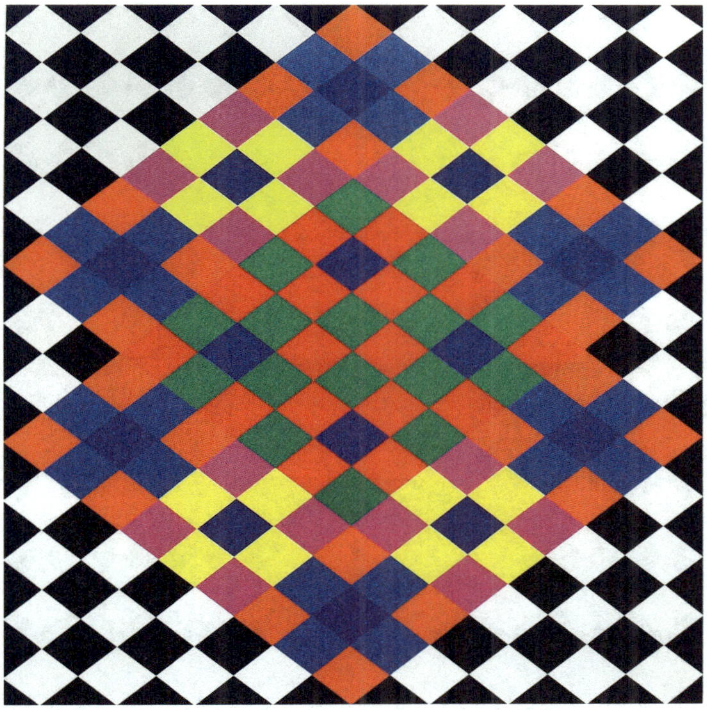

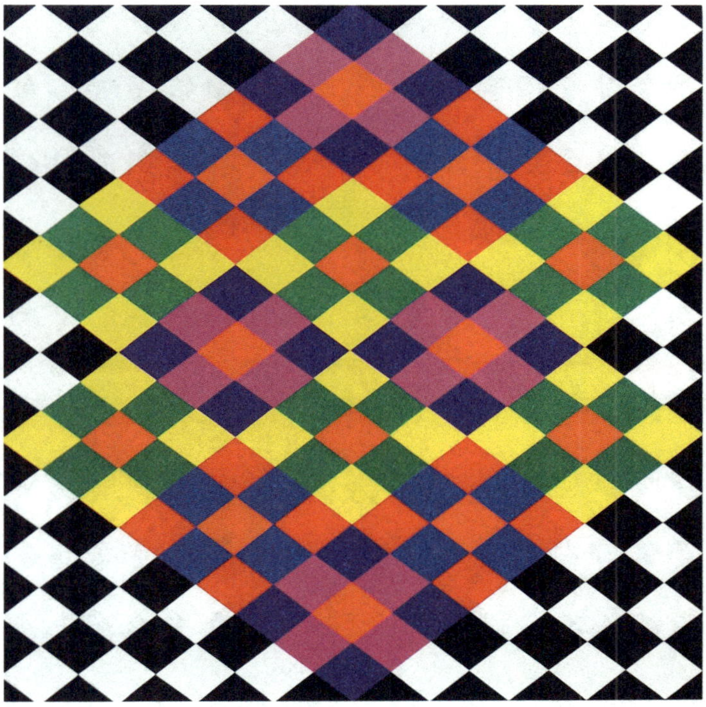

Opus TA1, 2016
acrylic on canvas, 160 x 160 cm
Opus TA2, 2016
acrylic on canvas, 160 x 160 cm
Opus TA3, 2016
acrylic on canvas, 160 x 160 cm
Opus TA4, 2016
acrylic on canvas, 160 x 160 cm

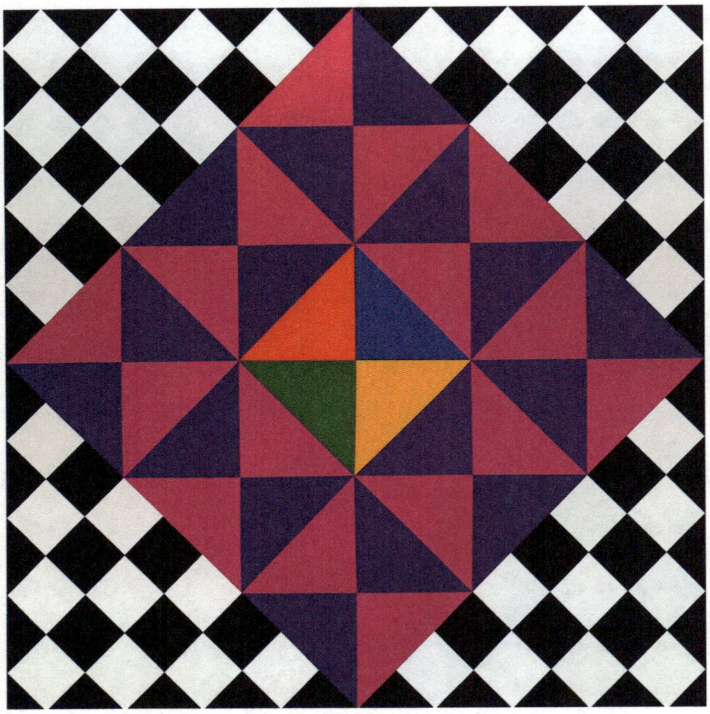

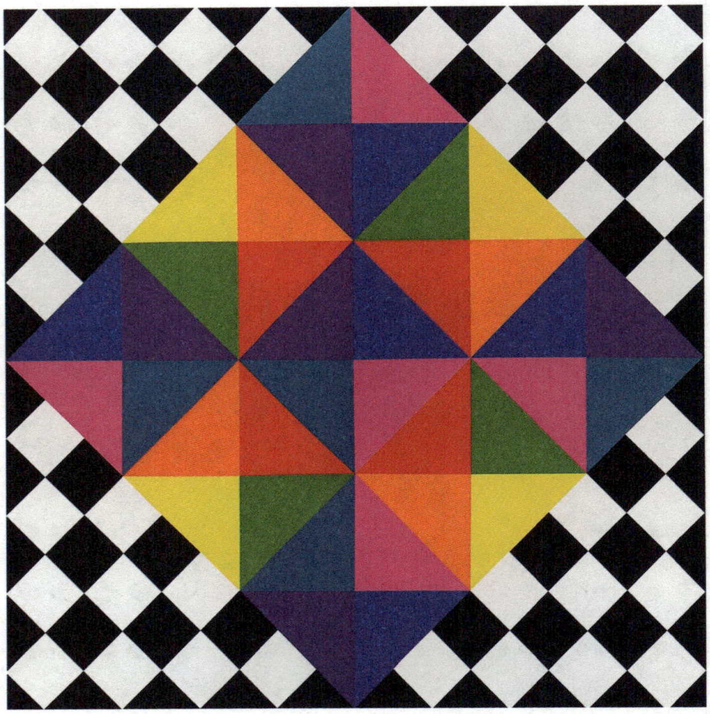

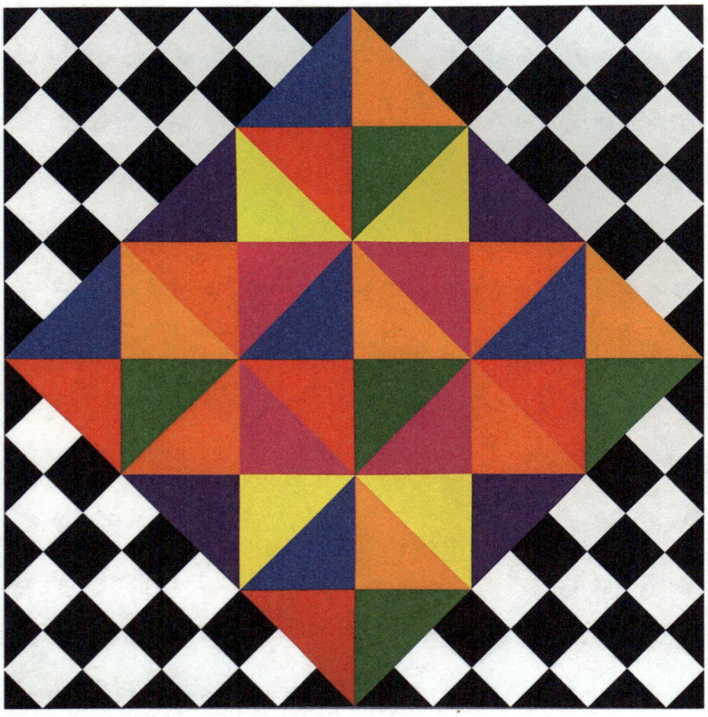

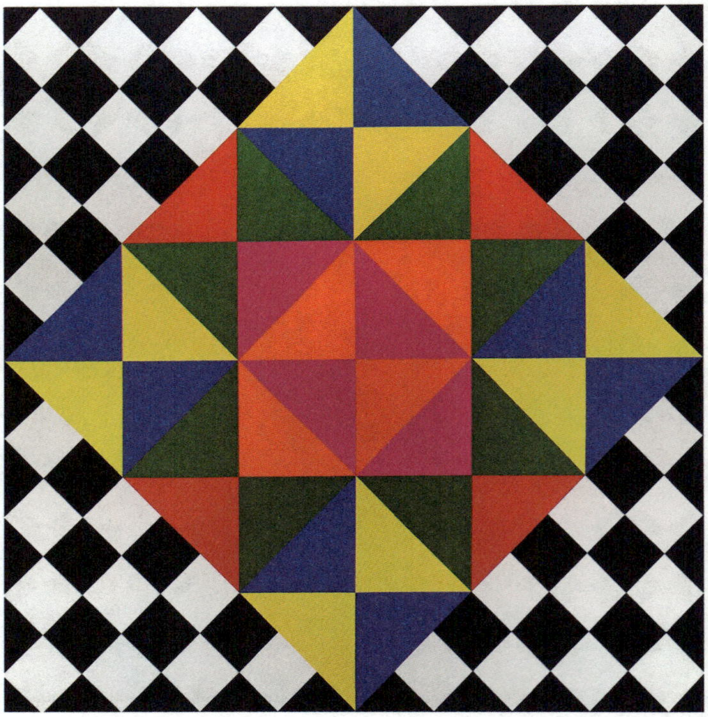

Opus TC1, 2016
acrylic on canvas, 160 x 160 cm
Opus TC3, 2016
acrylic on canvas, 160 x 160 cm

Opus TC2, 2016
acrylic on canvas, 160 x 160 cm
Opus TC4, 2016
acrylic on canvas, 160 x 160 cm

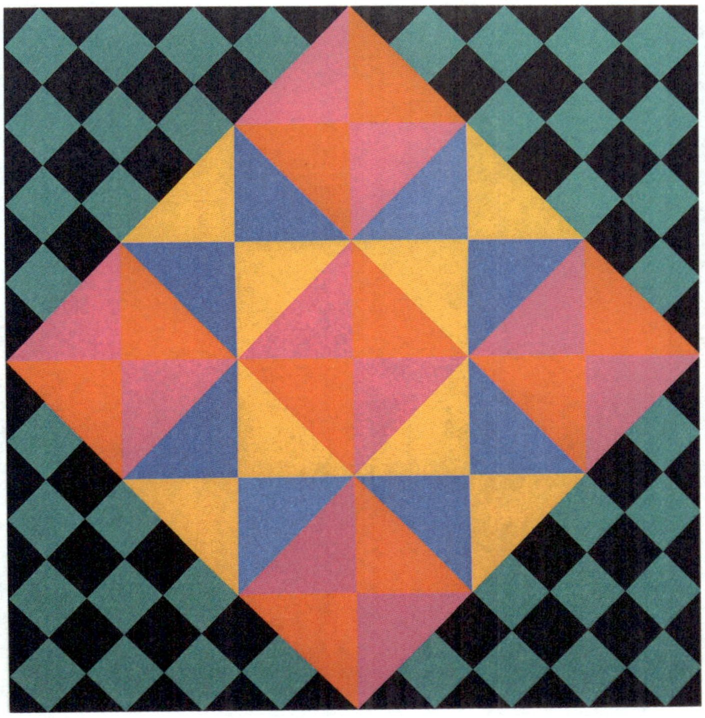

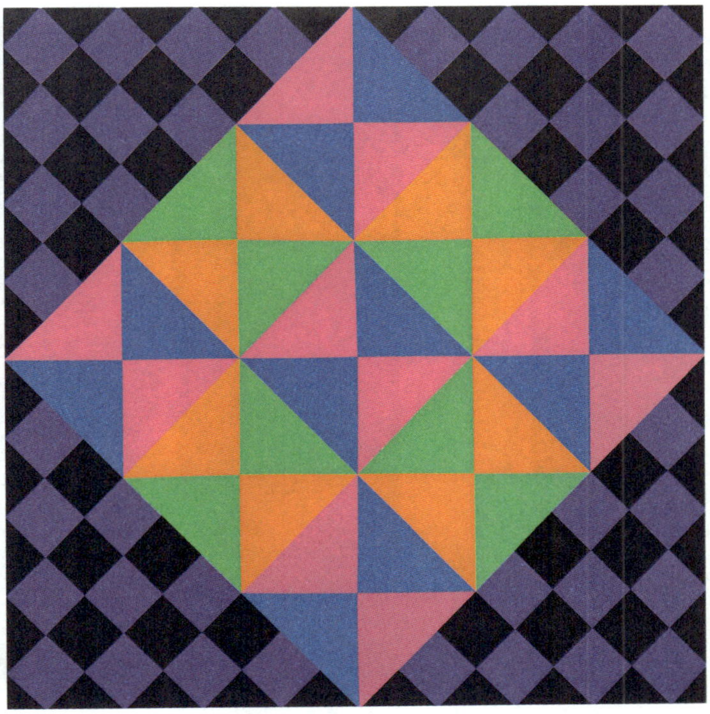

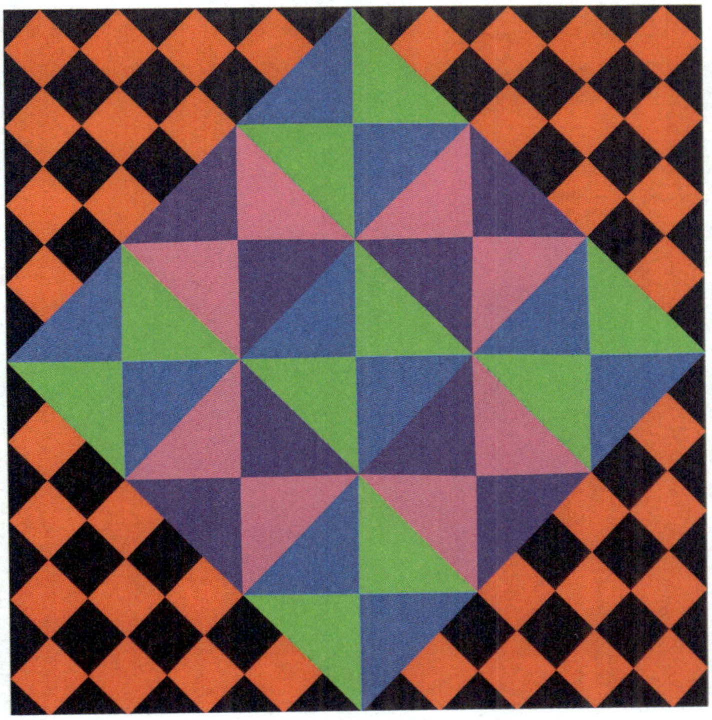

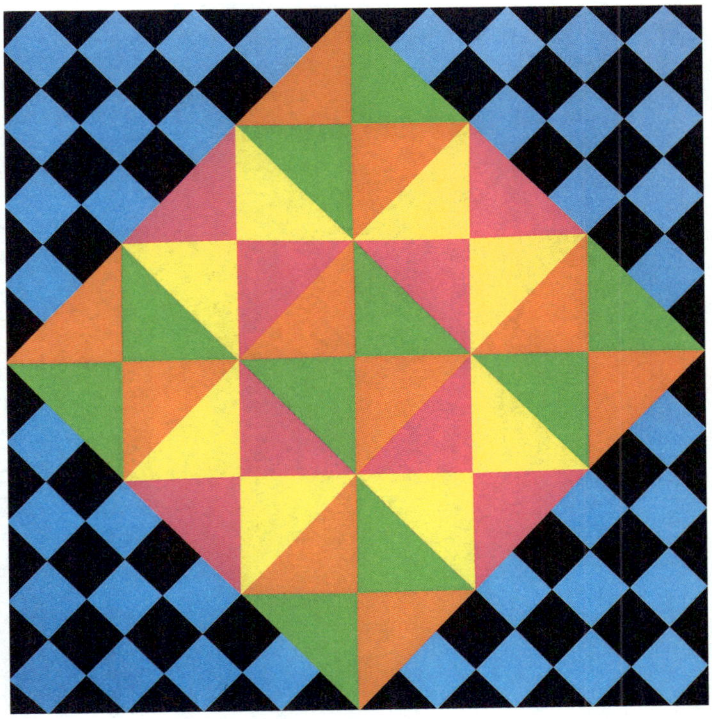

The Reading Room Kassel, 1997–2011 / 2016–2017
interactive mixed-media installation at documenta 14
160 x 1280 cm overall

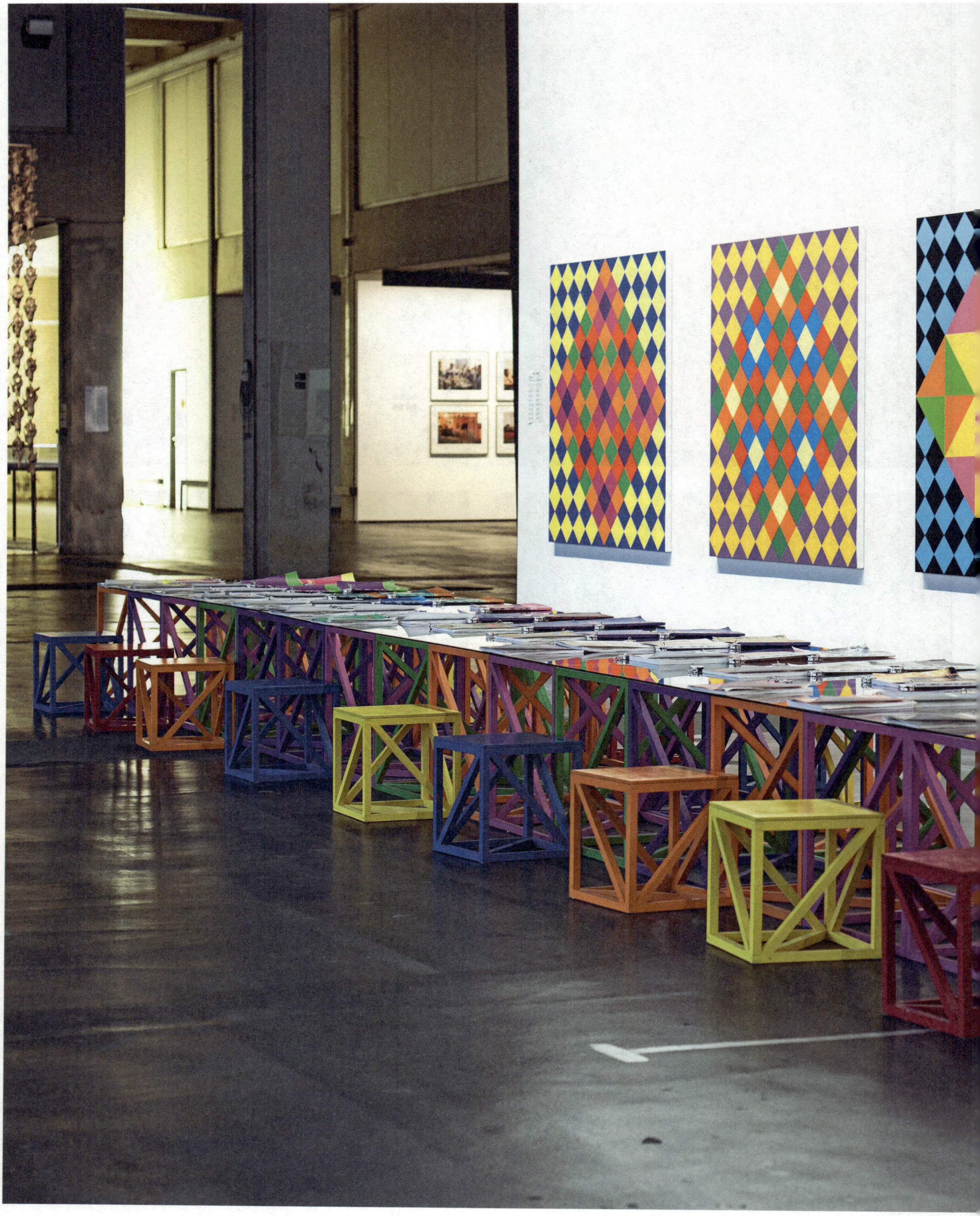

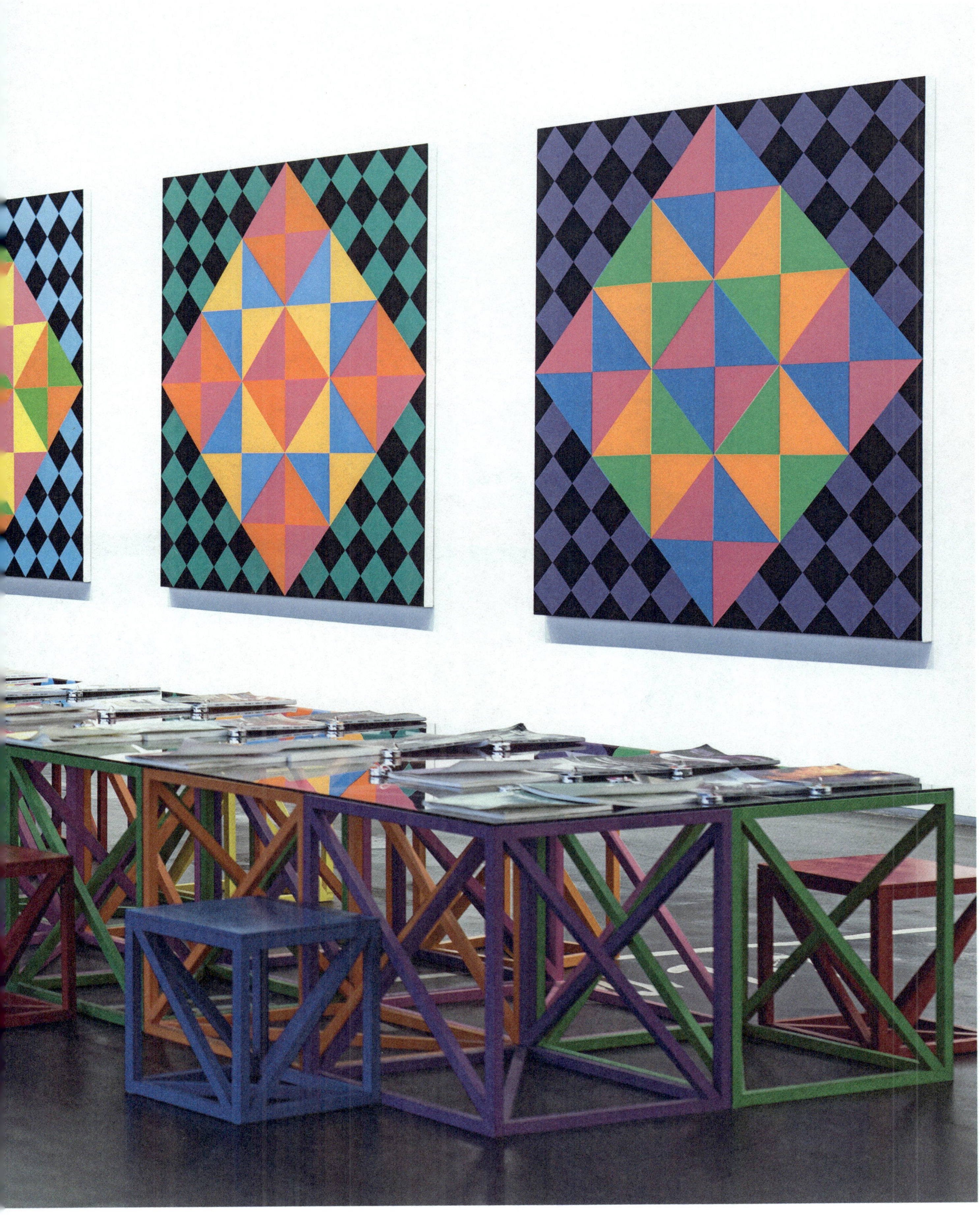

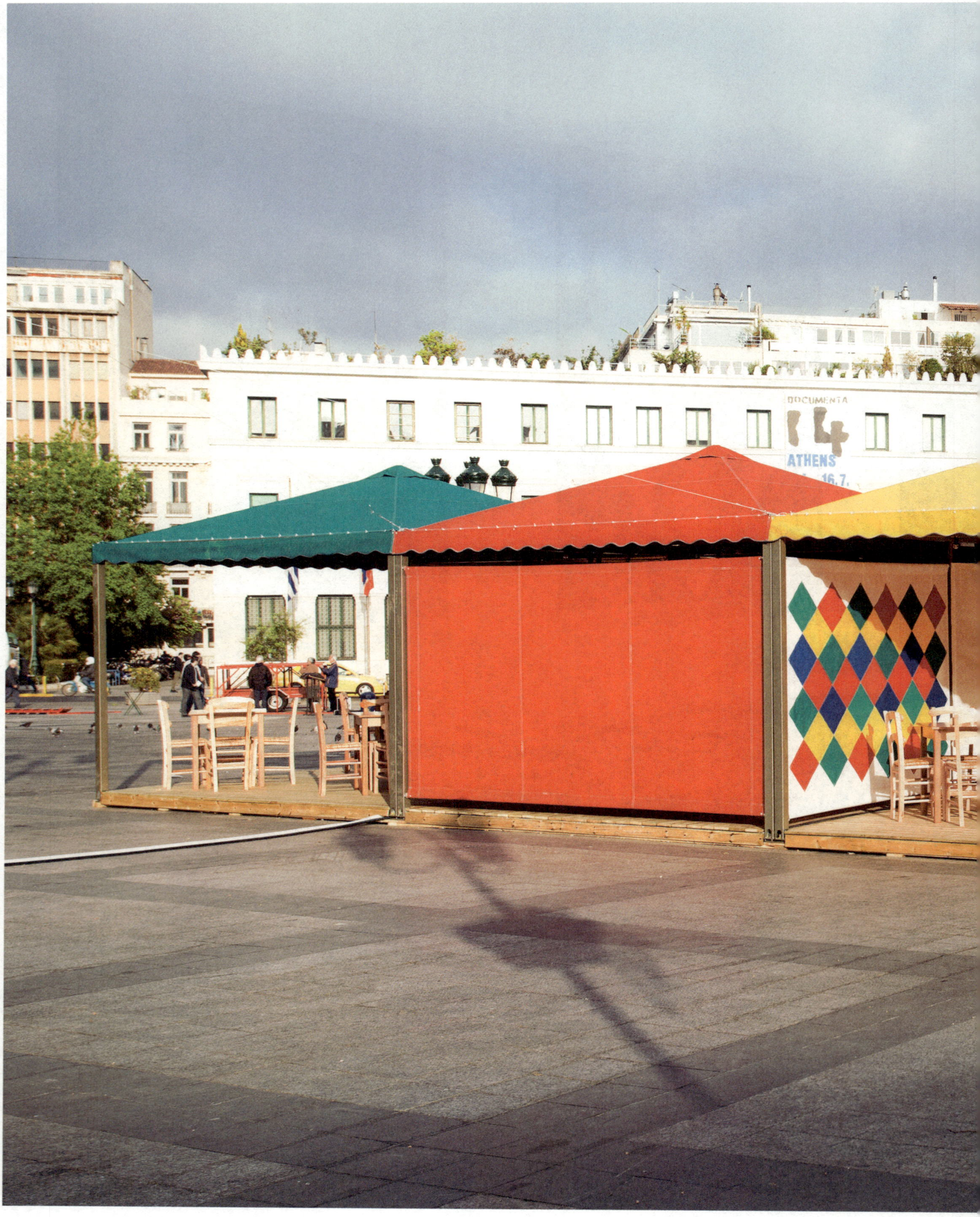
DOCUMENTA
14
ATHENS

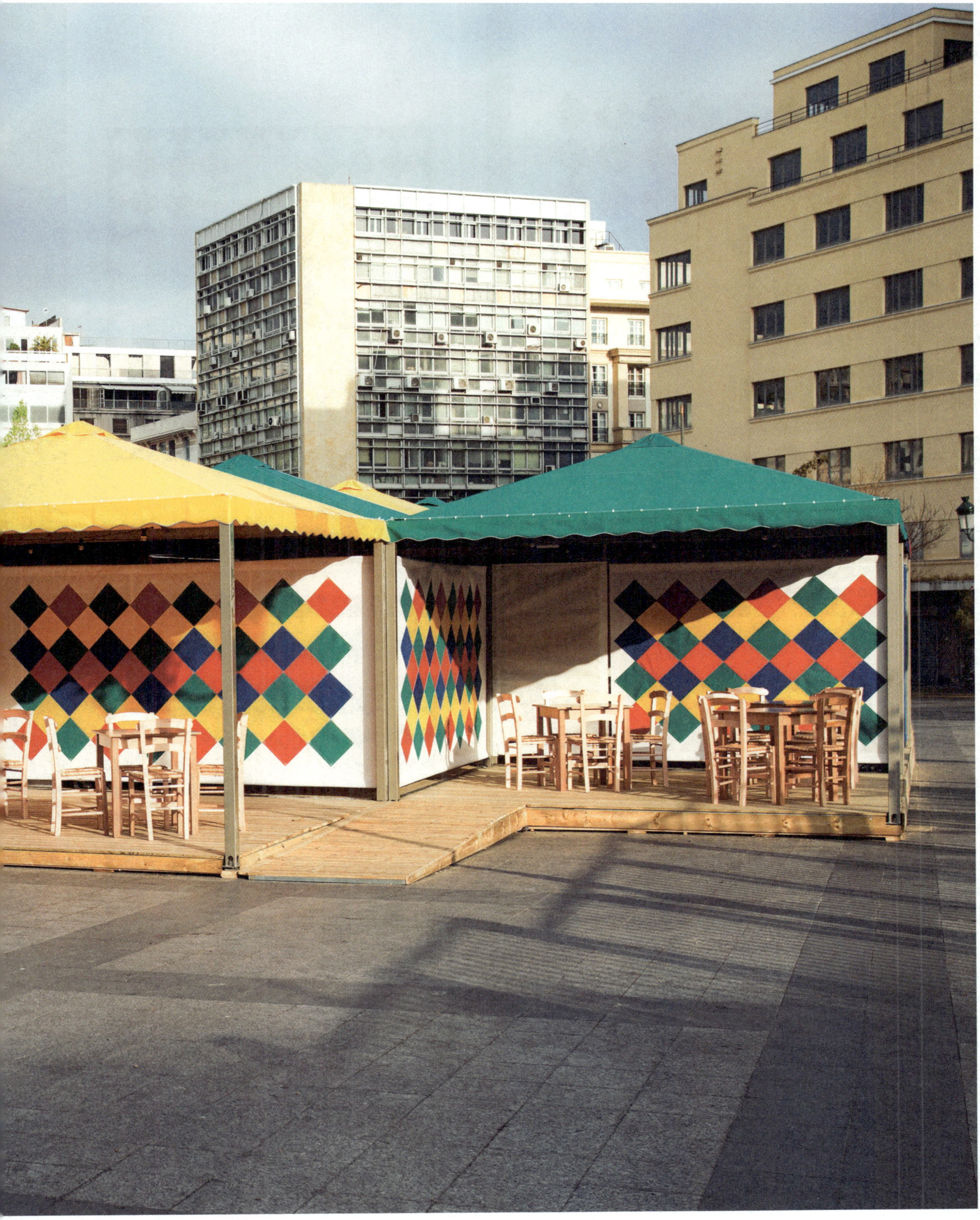

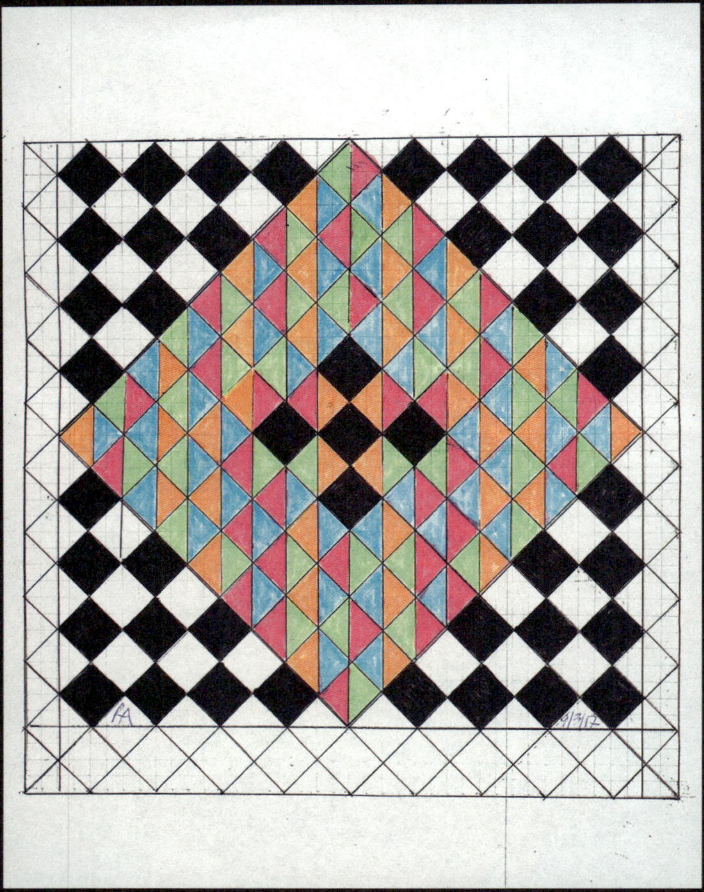
PA
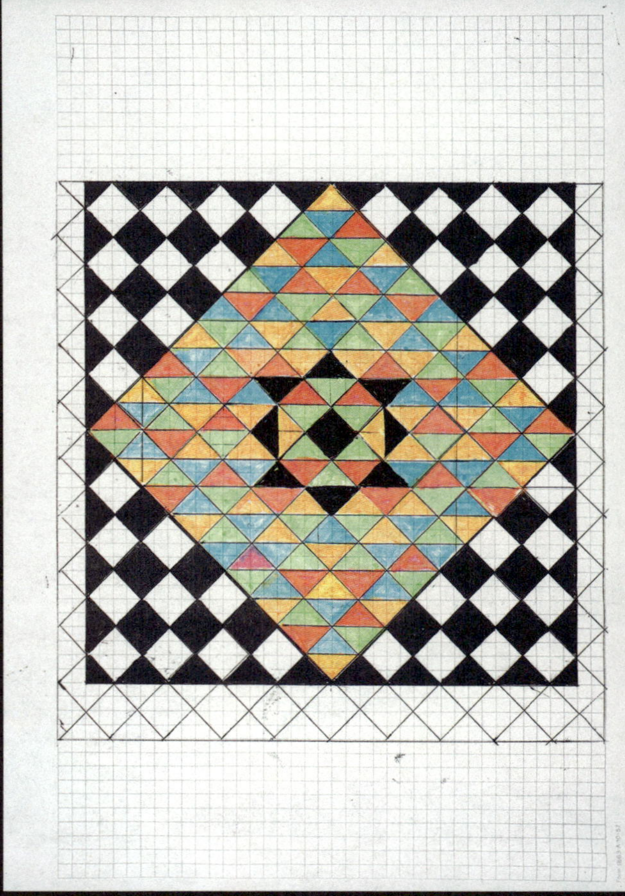
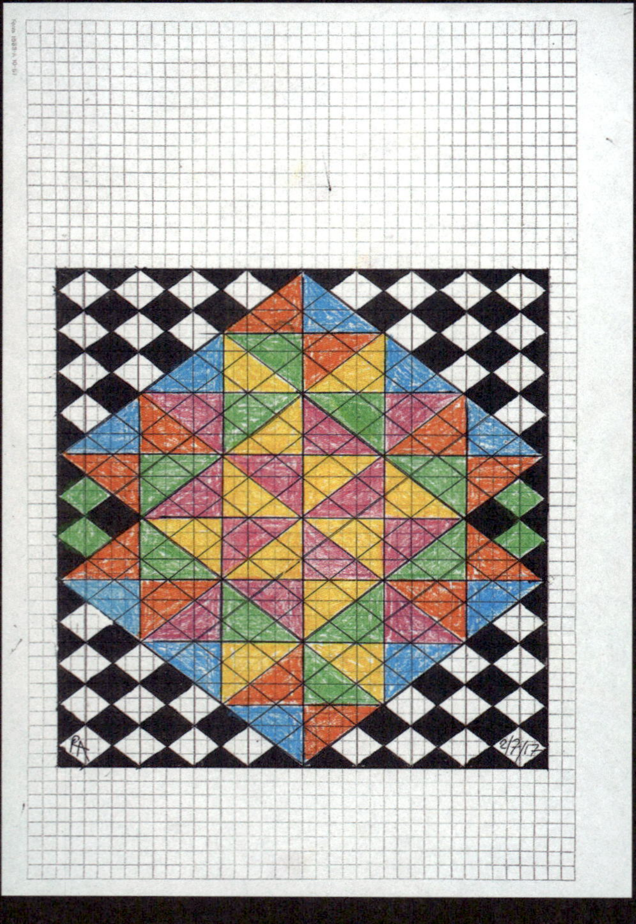
PA
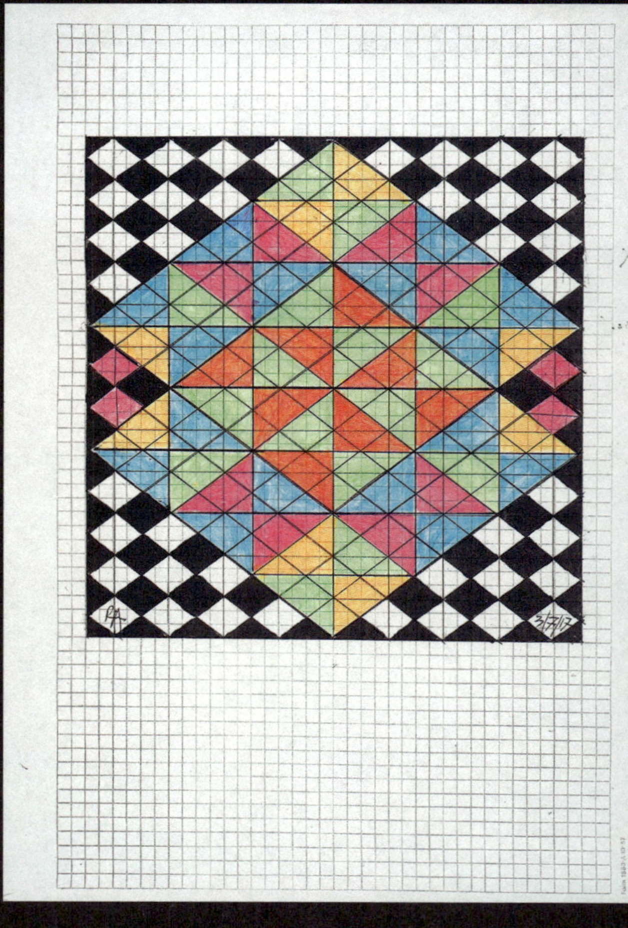
PA

Untitled (Study for Opus), 2017
crayon on paper, 40 x 30 cm

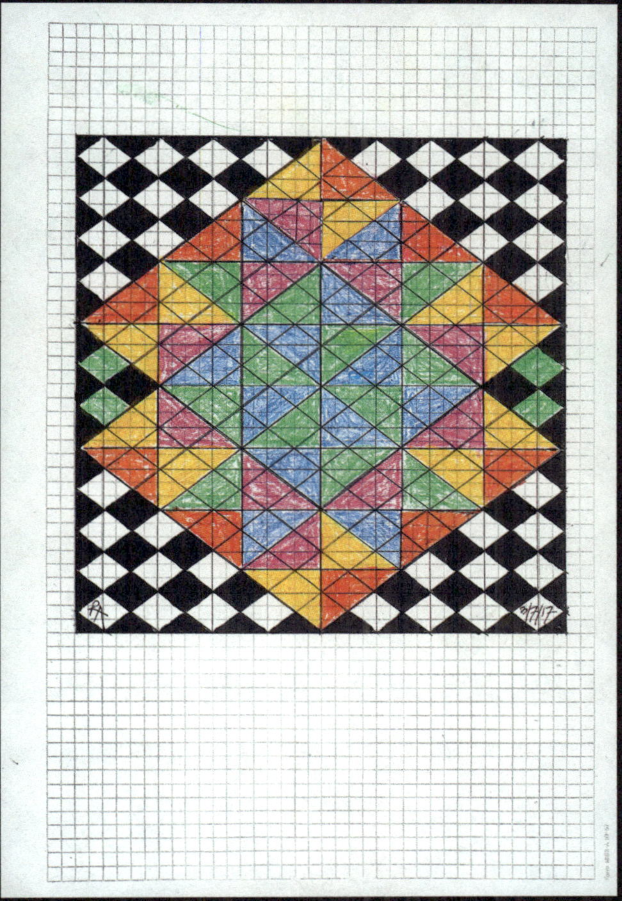

Untitled (Study for Opus), 2017
crayon on paper, 40 x 30 cm

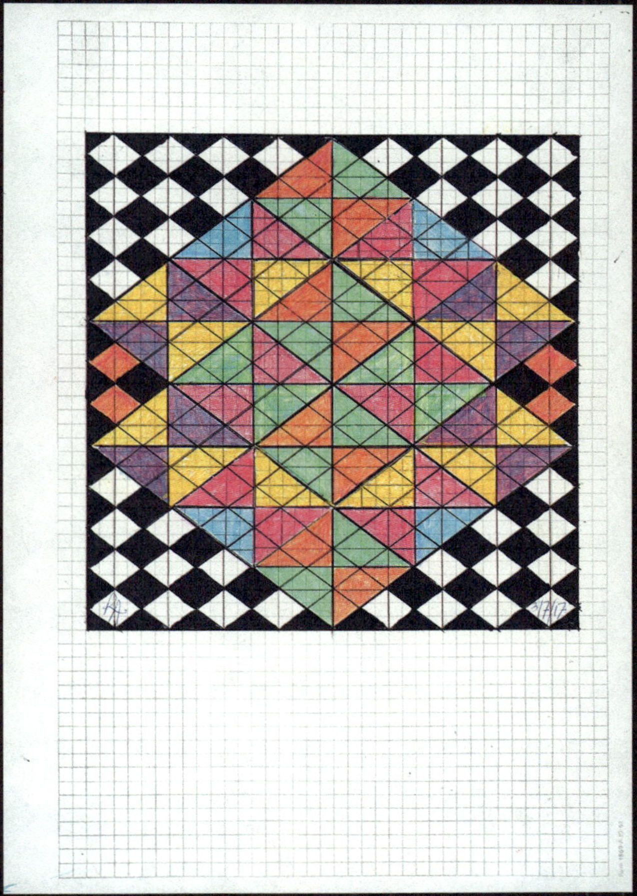

Opus TA1, 2017
acrylic on canvas, 160 x 160 cm
Opus TA3, 2017
acrylic on canvas, 160 x 160 cm

Opus TA2, 2017
acrylic on canvas, 160 x 160 cm
Opus TA4, 2017
acrylic on canvas, 160 x 160 cm

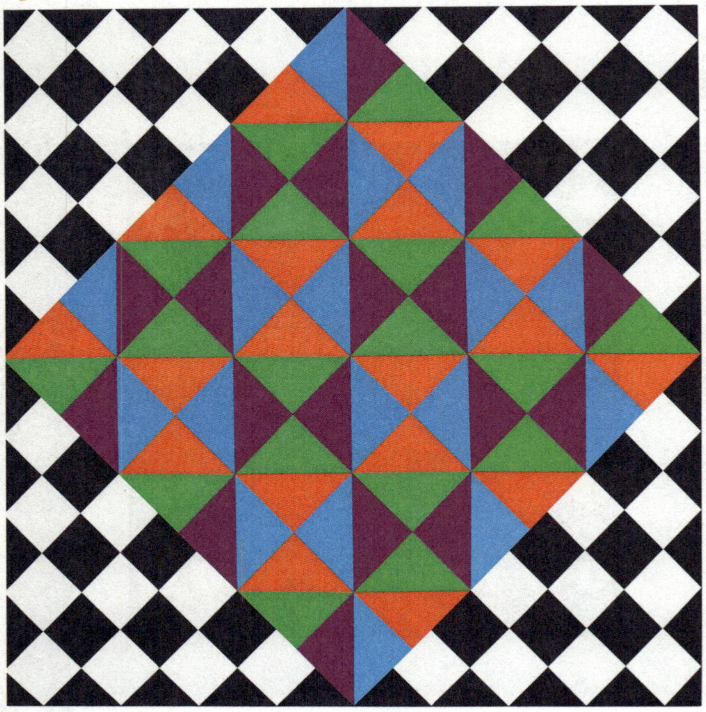

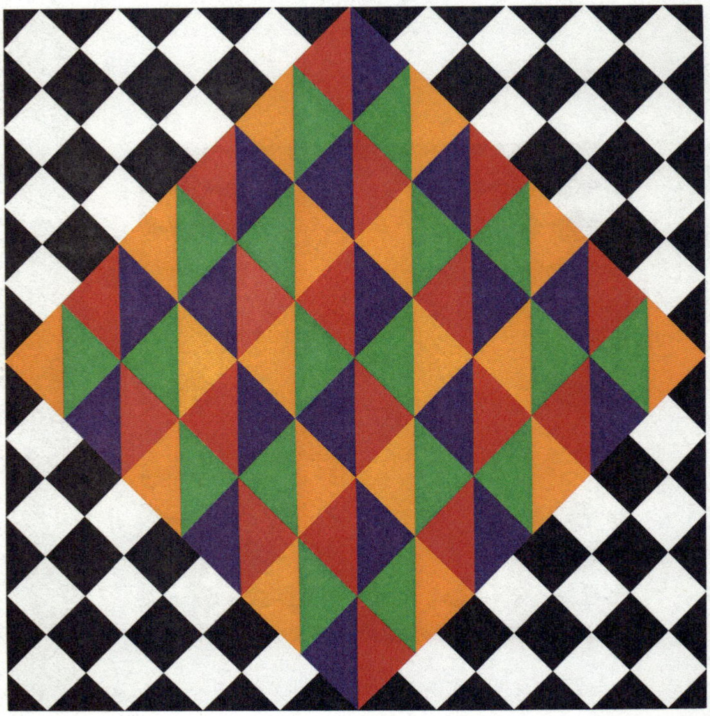

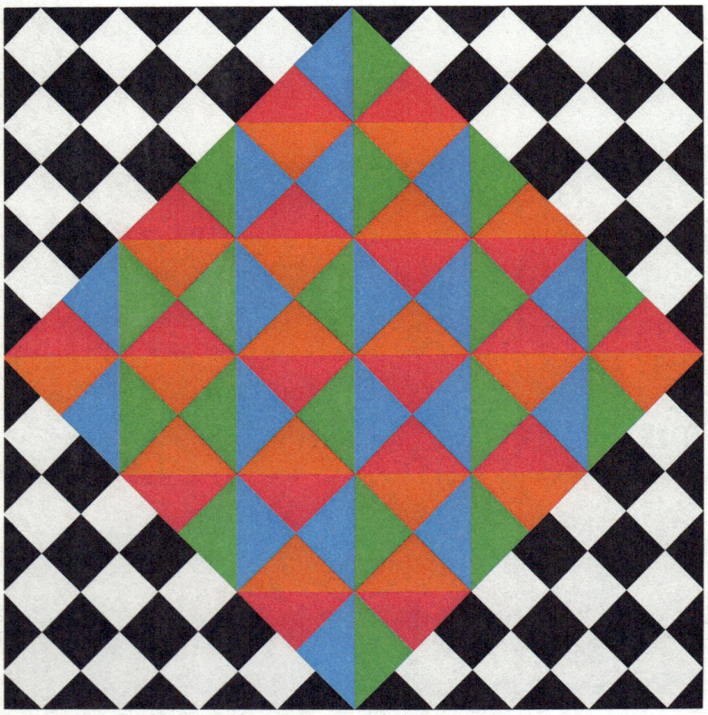

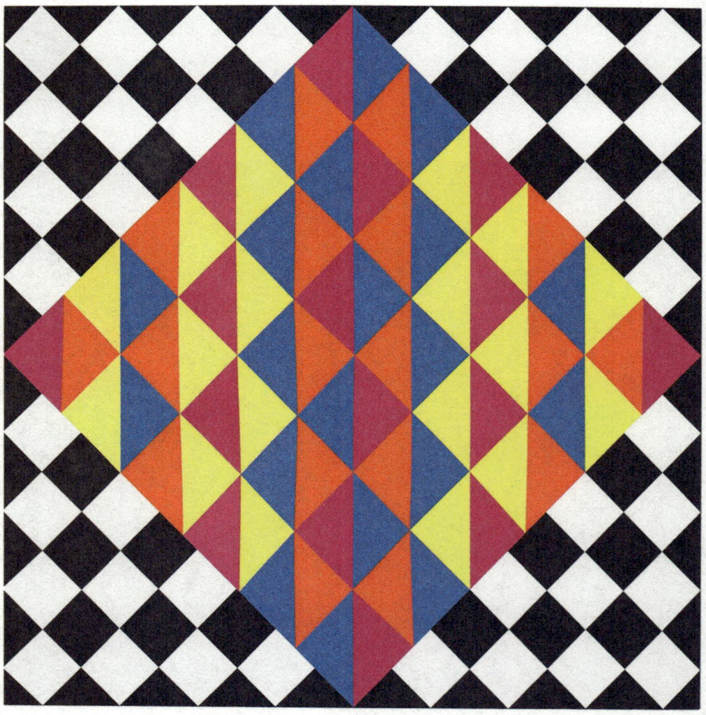

Opus TAA1, 2017
acrylic on canvas, 160 x 160 cm
Opus TAA3, 2017
acrylic on canvas, 160 x 160 cm

Opus TAA2, 2017
acrylic on canvas, 160 x 160 cm
Opus TAA4, 2017
acrylic on canvas, 160 x 160 cm

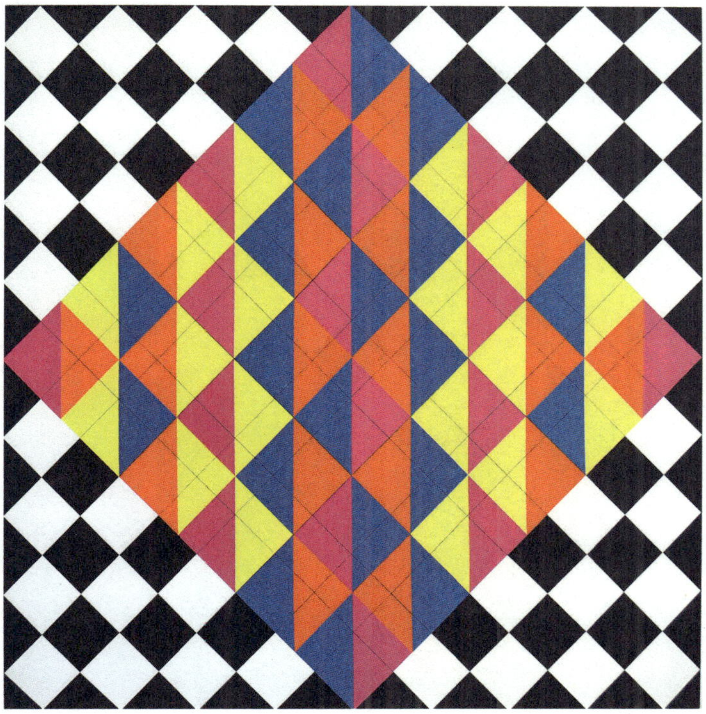

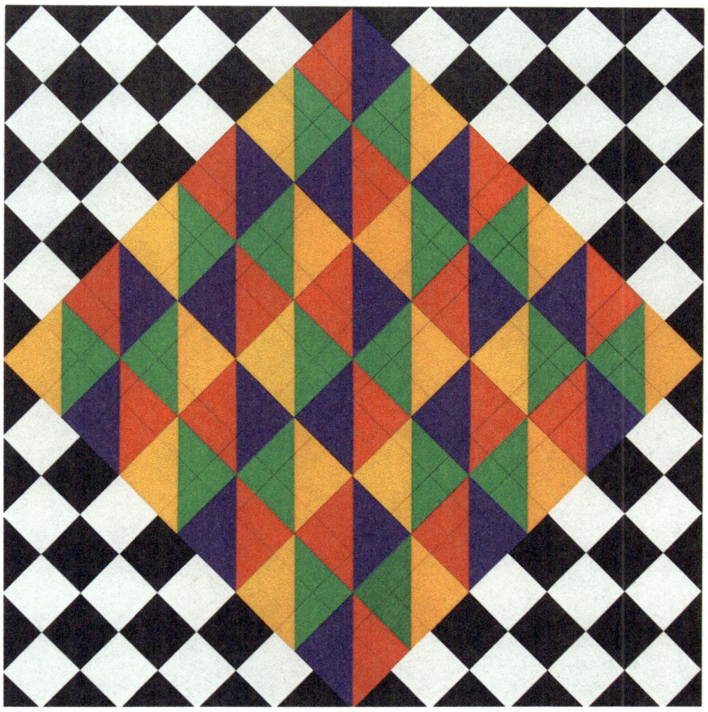

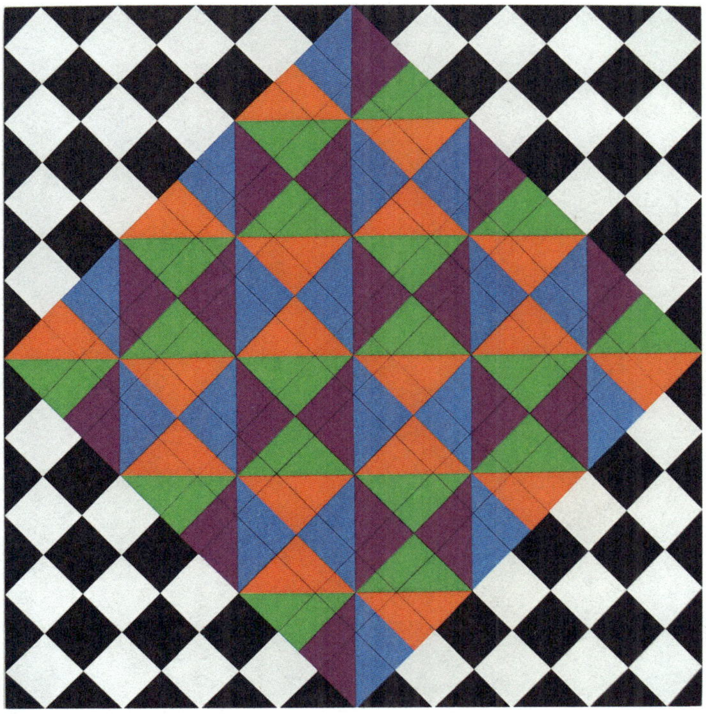

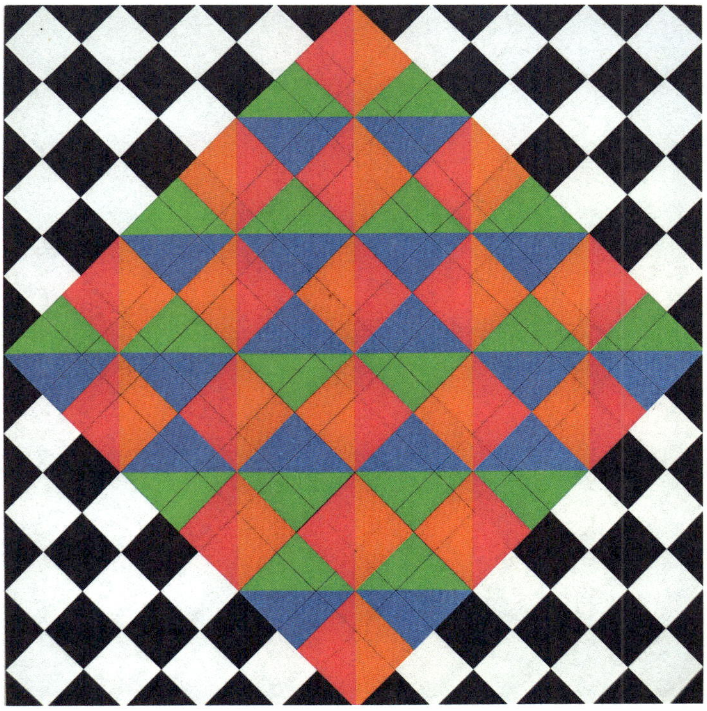

Opus TD1, 2017
acrylic on canvas, 160 x 160 cm

Opus TD2, 2017
acrylic on canvas, 160 x 160 cm

Opus TD3, 2017
acrylic on canvas, 160 x 160 cm

Opus TD4, 2017
acrylic on canvas, 160 x 160 cm

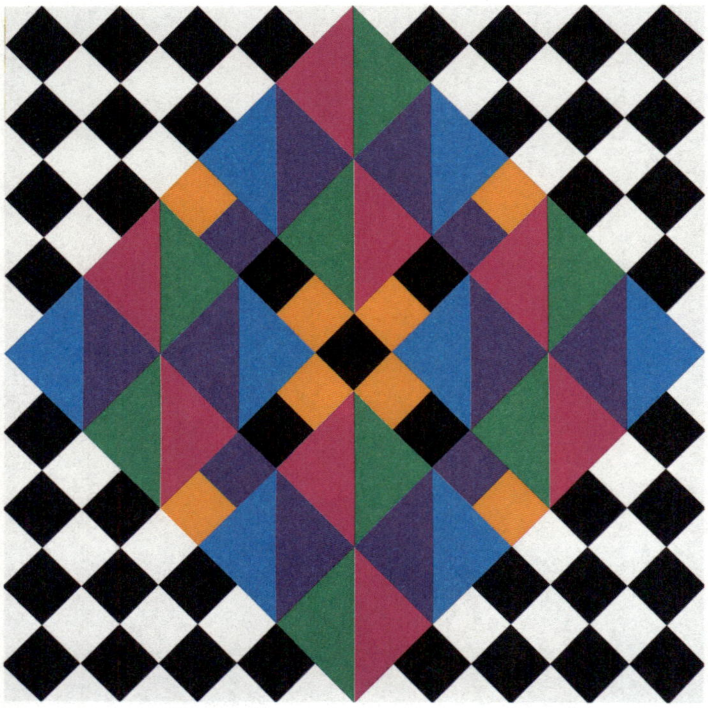

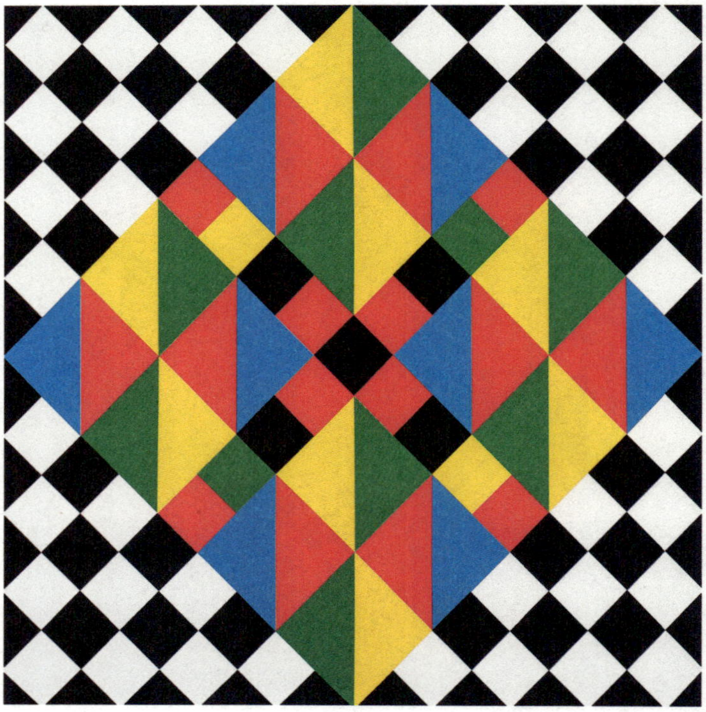

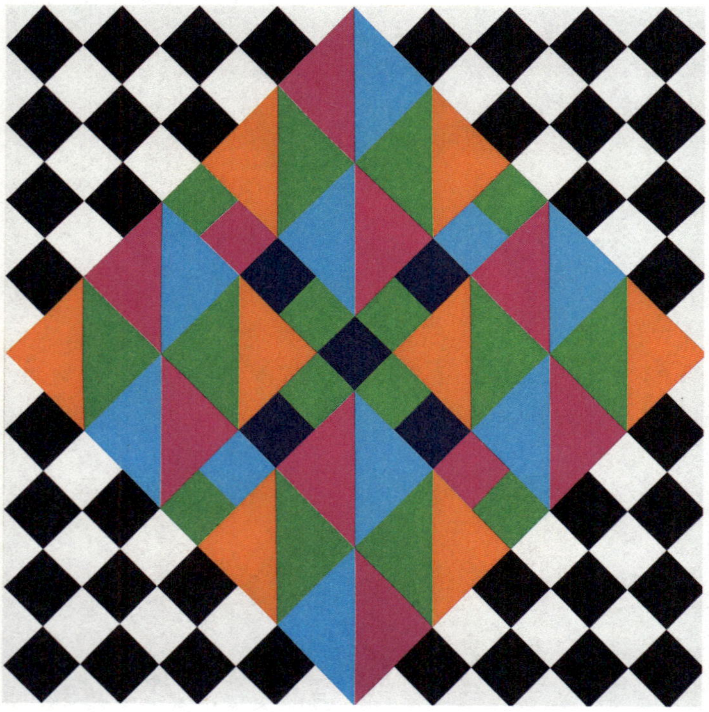

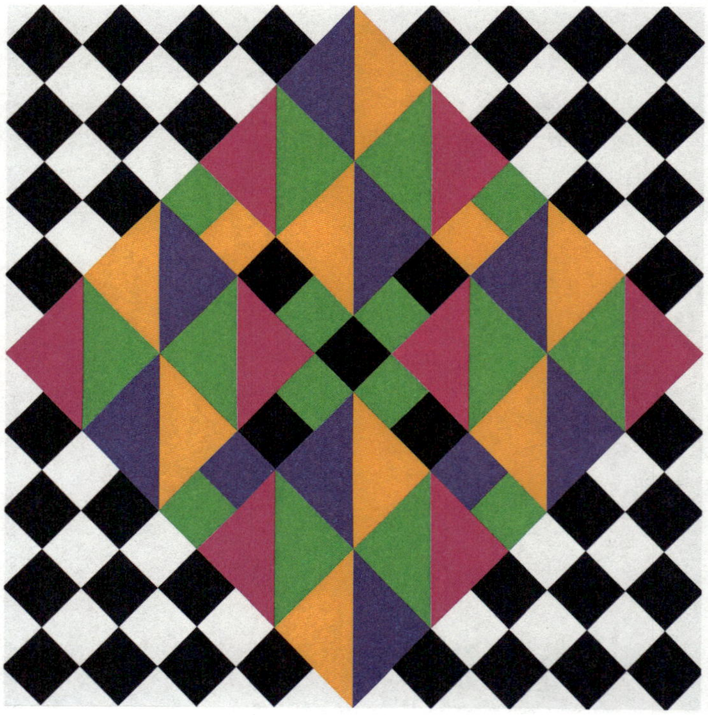

Opus TEE1, 2017
acrylic on canvas, 160 x 160 cm
Opus TEE3, 2017
acrylic on canvas, 160 x 160 cm

Opus TEE2, 2017
acrylic on canvas, 160 x 160 cm
Opus TEE4, 2017
acrylic on canvas, 160 x 160 cm

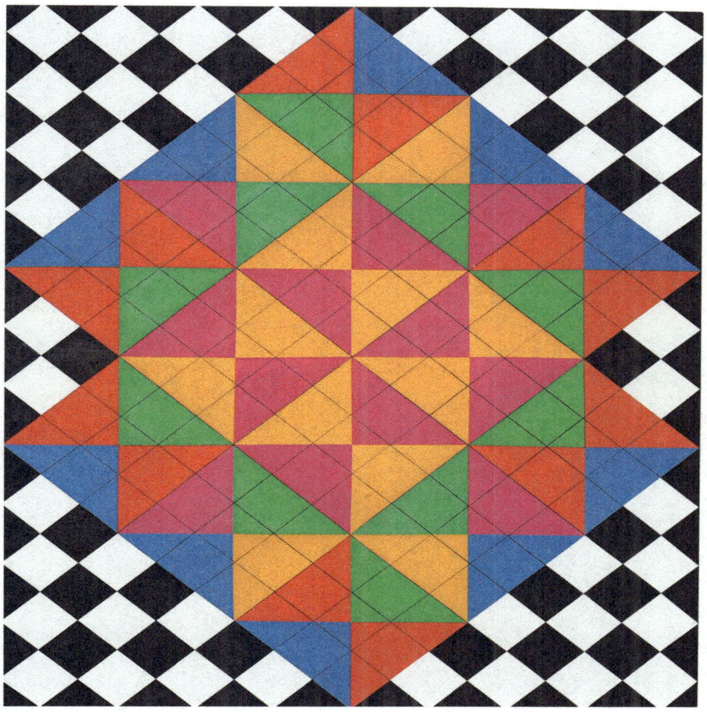

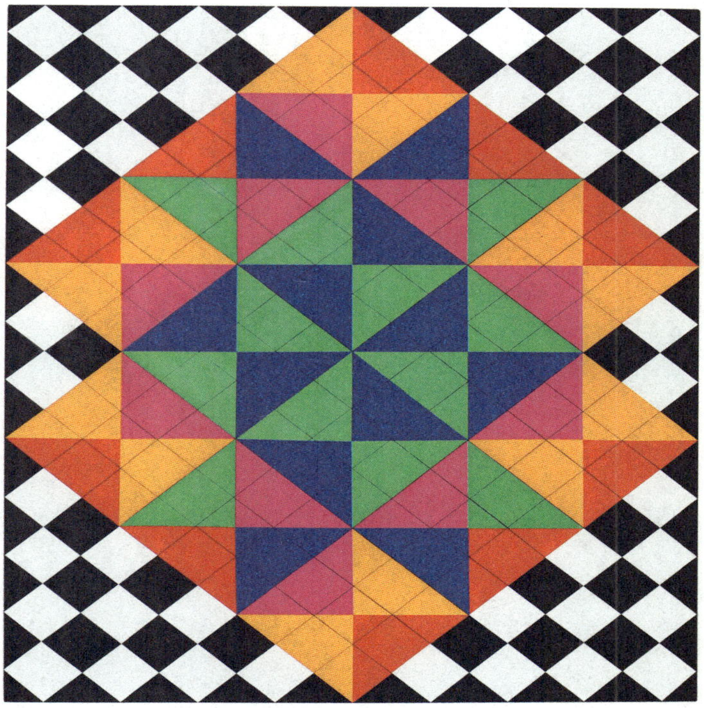

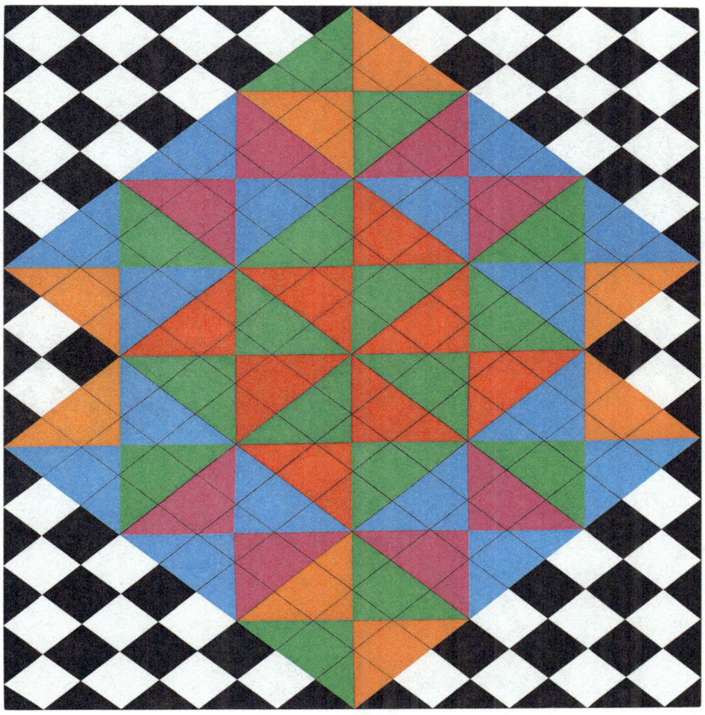

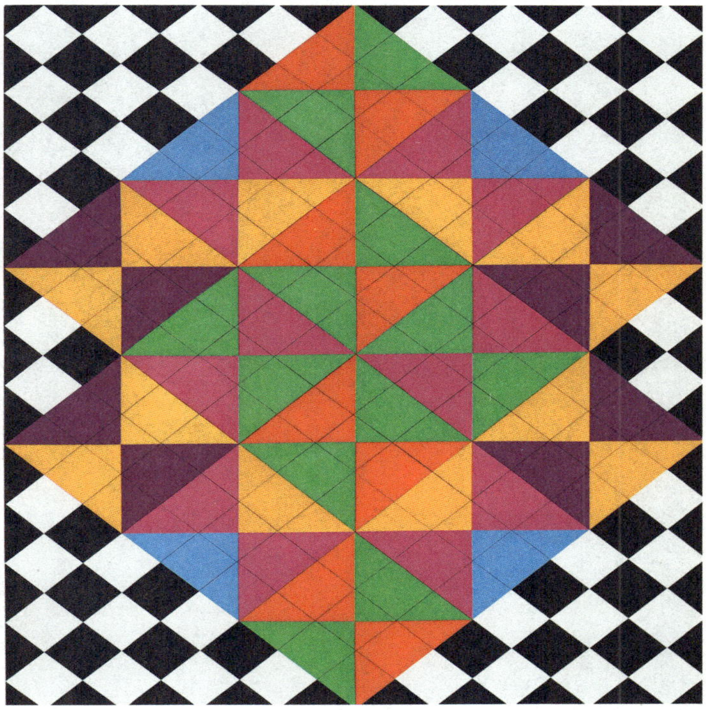

Zero to Infinity, 1968–2004 / 2017
installation at Venice Art Biennale
100 acrylic on wood Structures, 50 x 50 x 50 cm each

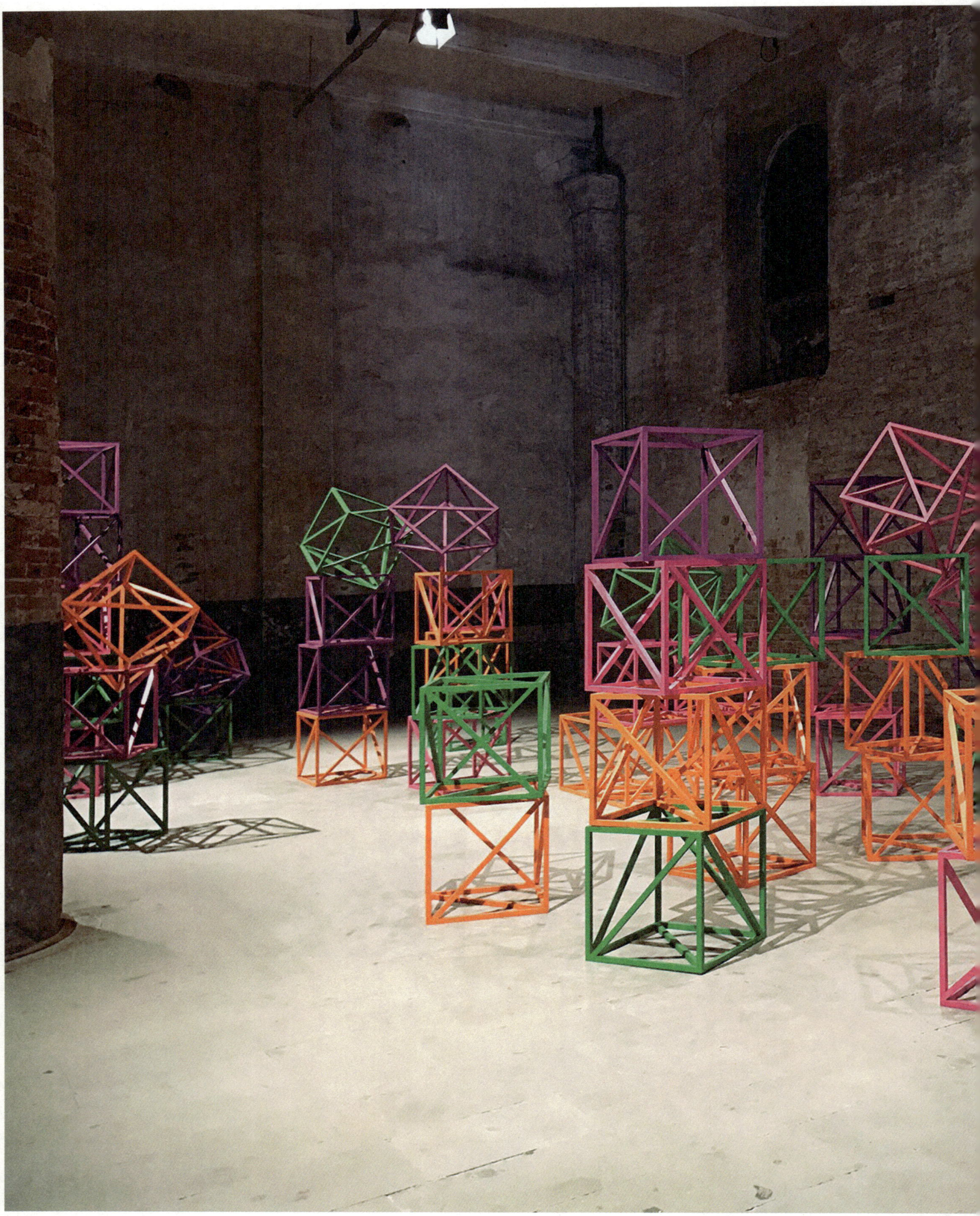

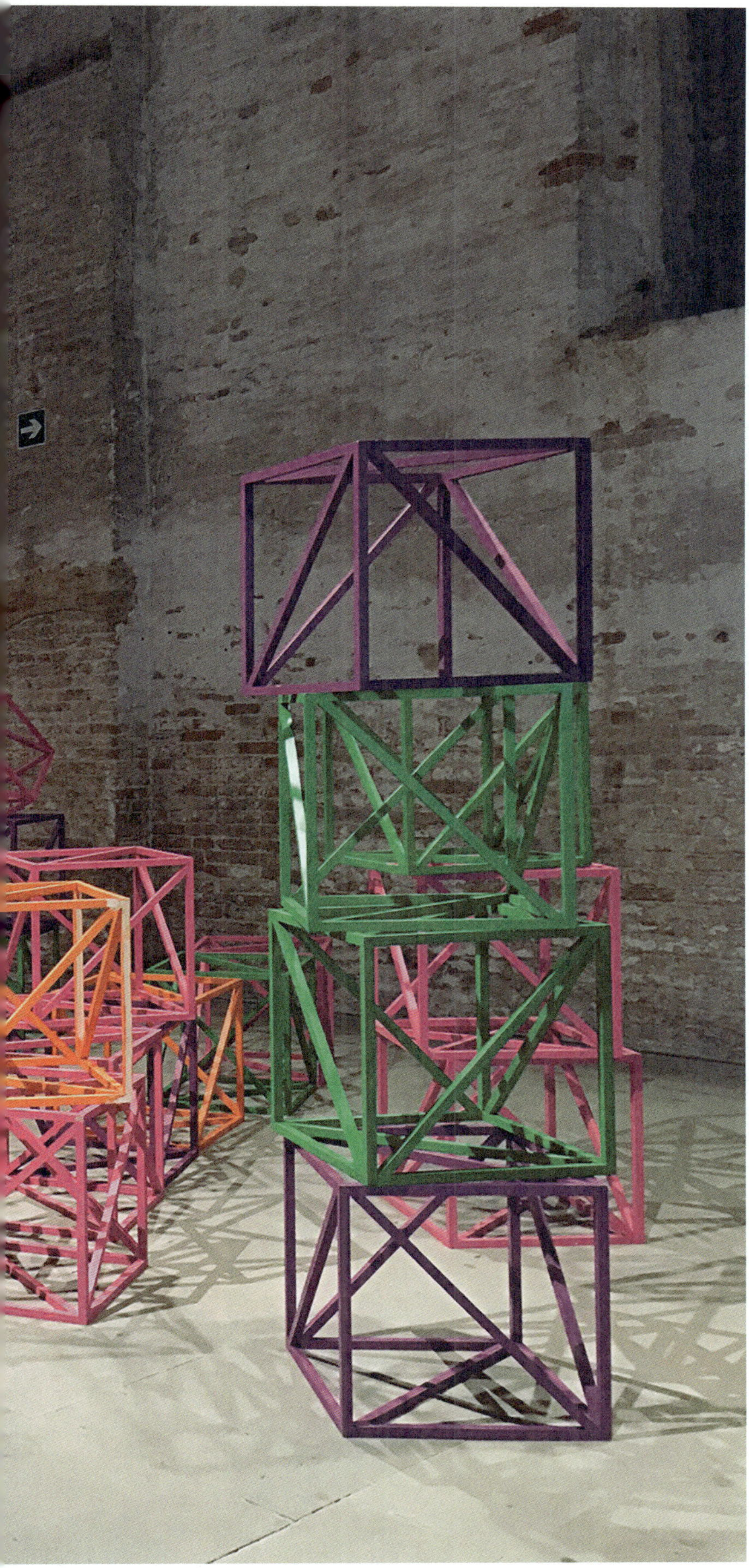

Zero to Infinity, 1968–2004 / 2017
installation at Yorkshire Sculpture Park
100 acrylic on wood Structures, 40 x 40 x 40 cm each

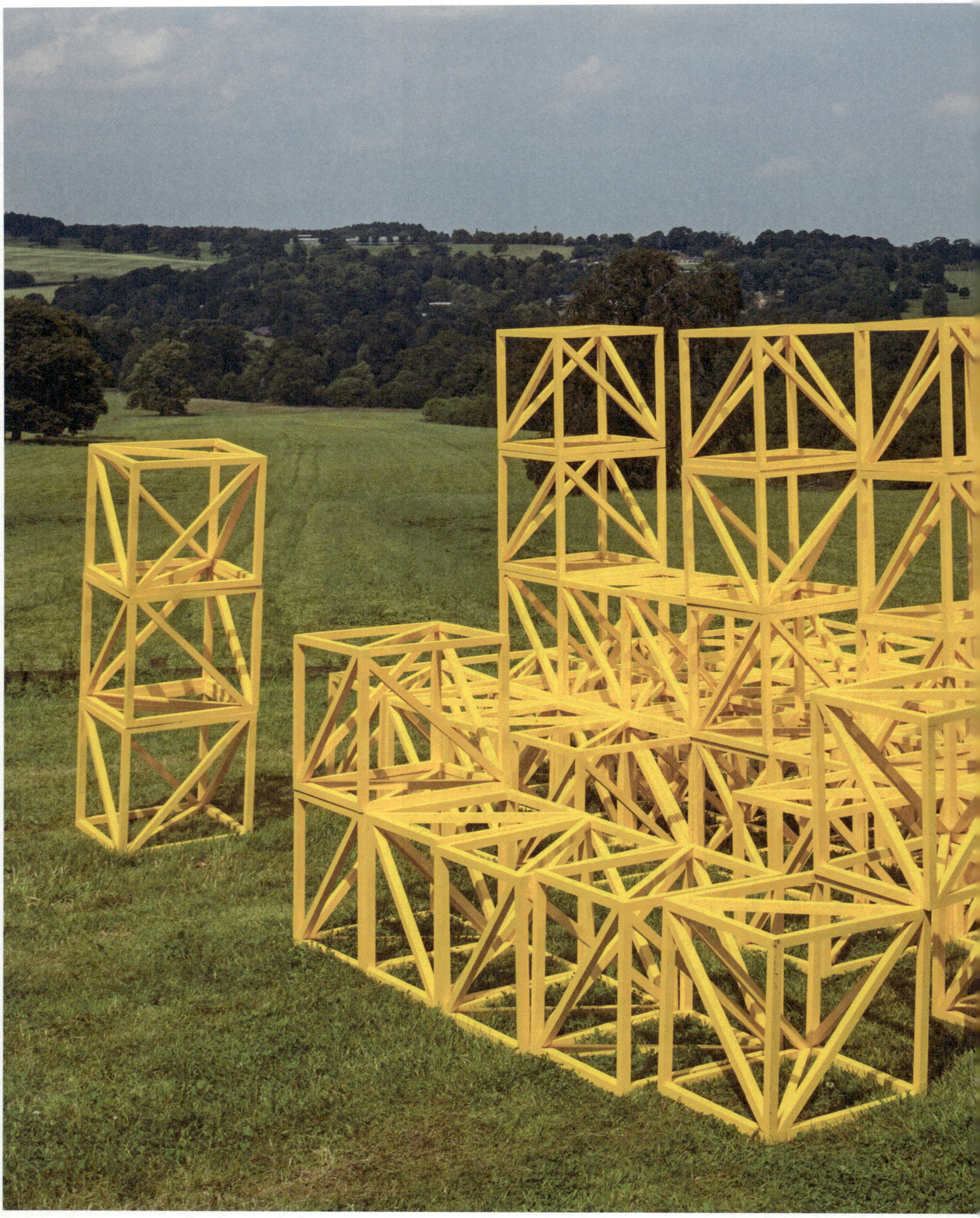

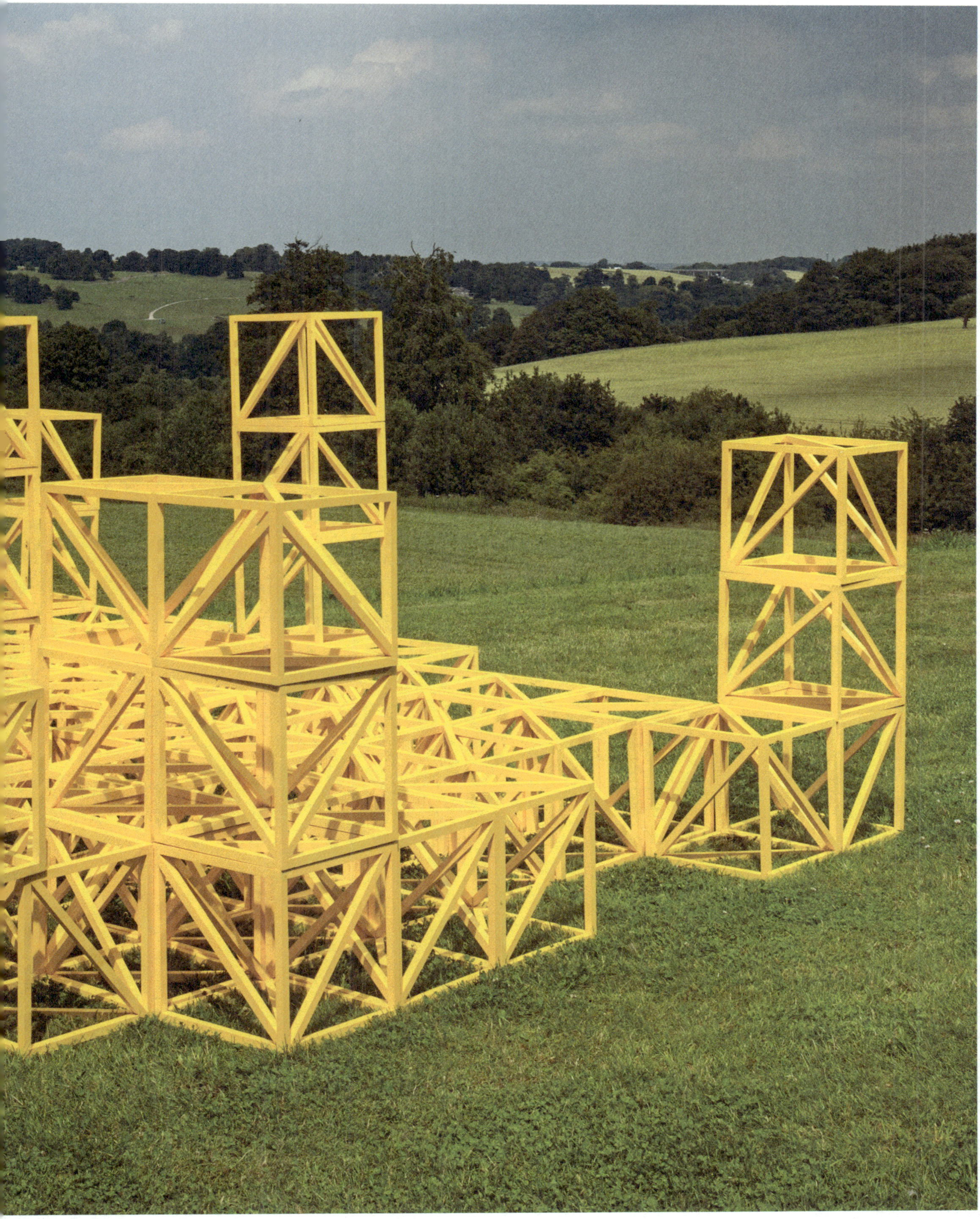

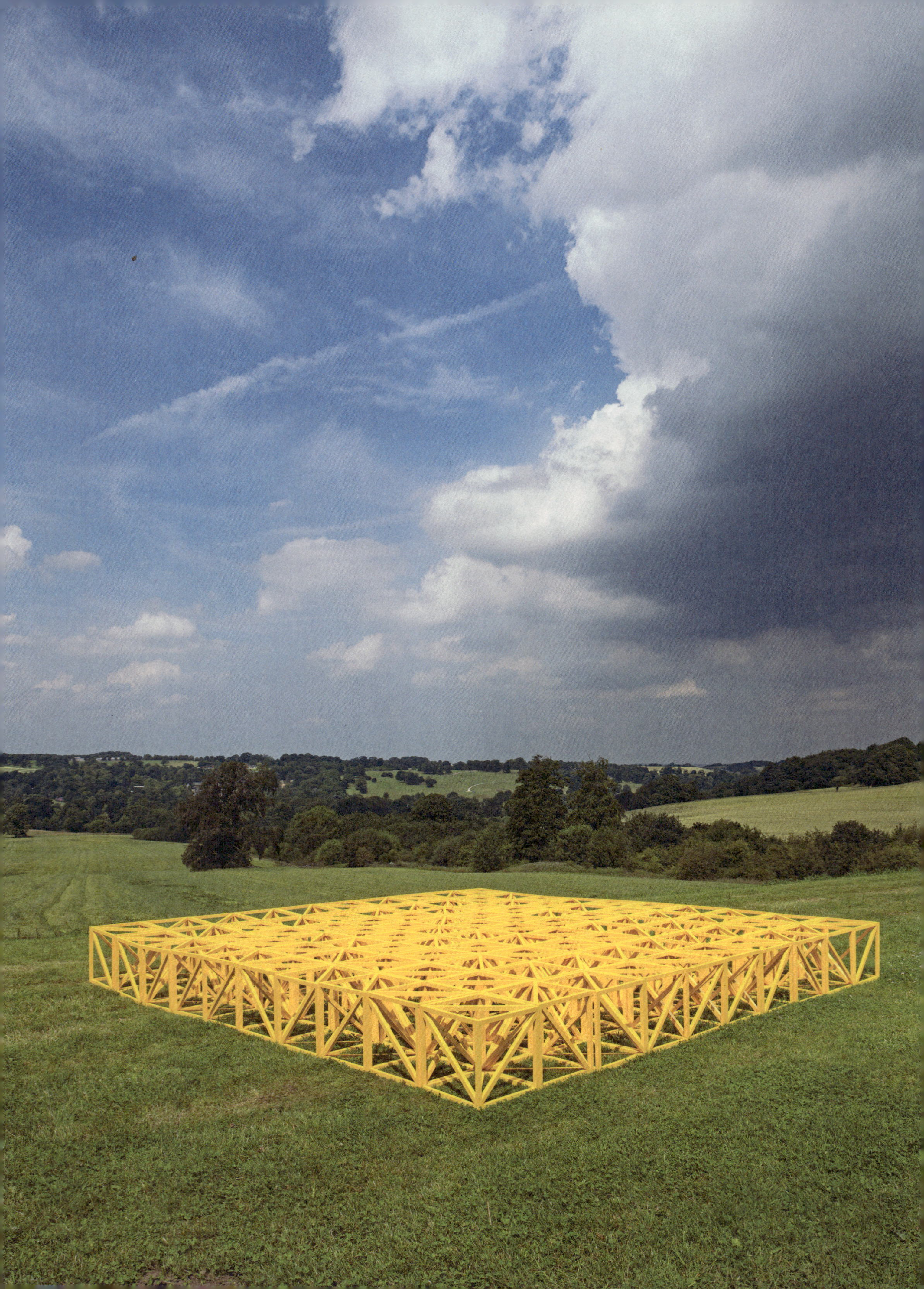

Chakras VI (Phir Agaye Sub Chakar), 2017
16 wood discs, 16 photographs, dimensions variable
Yorkshire Sculpture Park Collection

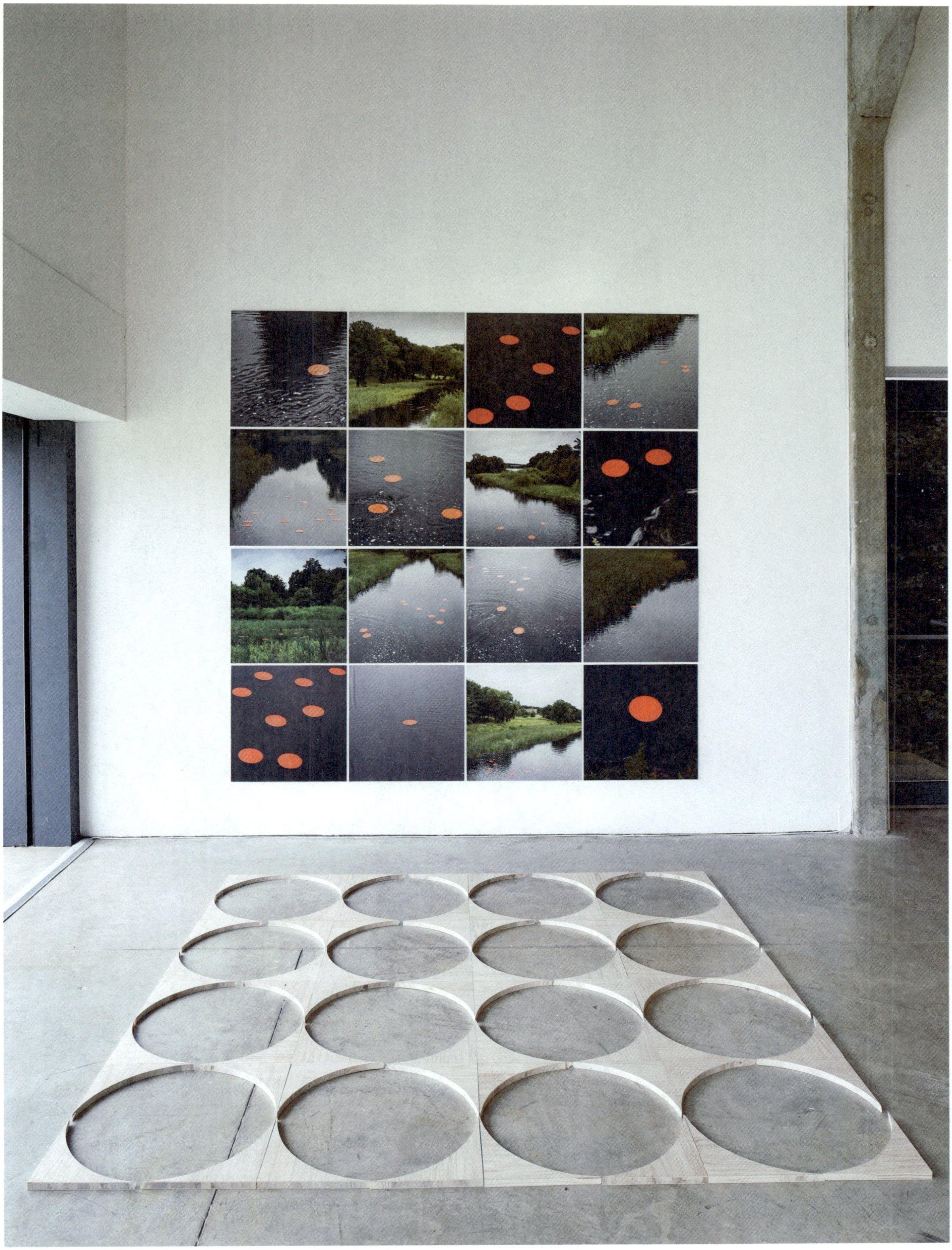

House of Red Bamboo, 2017
installation at Art Basel Hong Kong
acrylic on bamboo, 450 x 450 x 450 cm

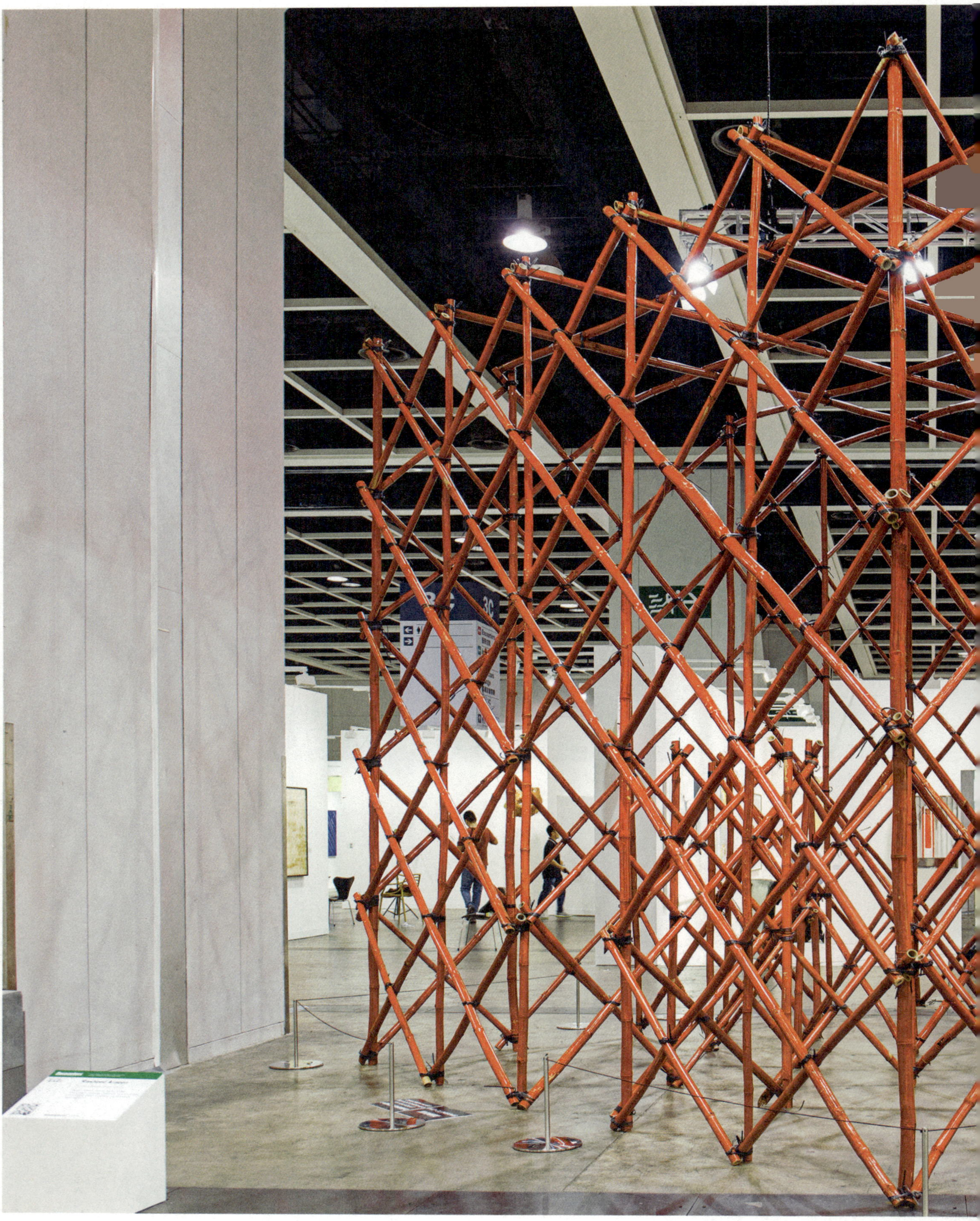

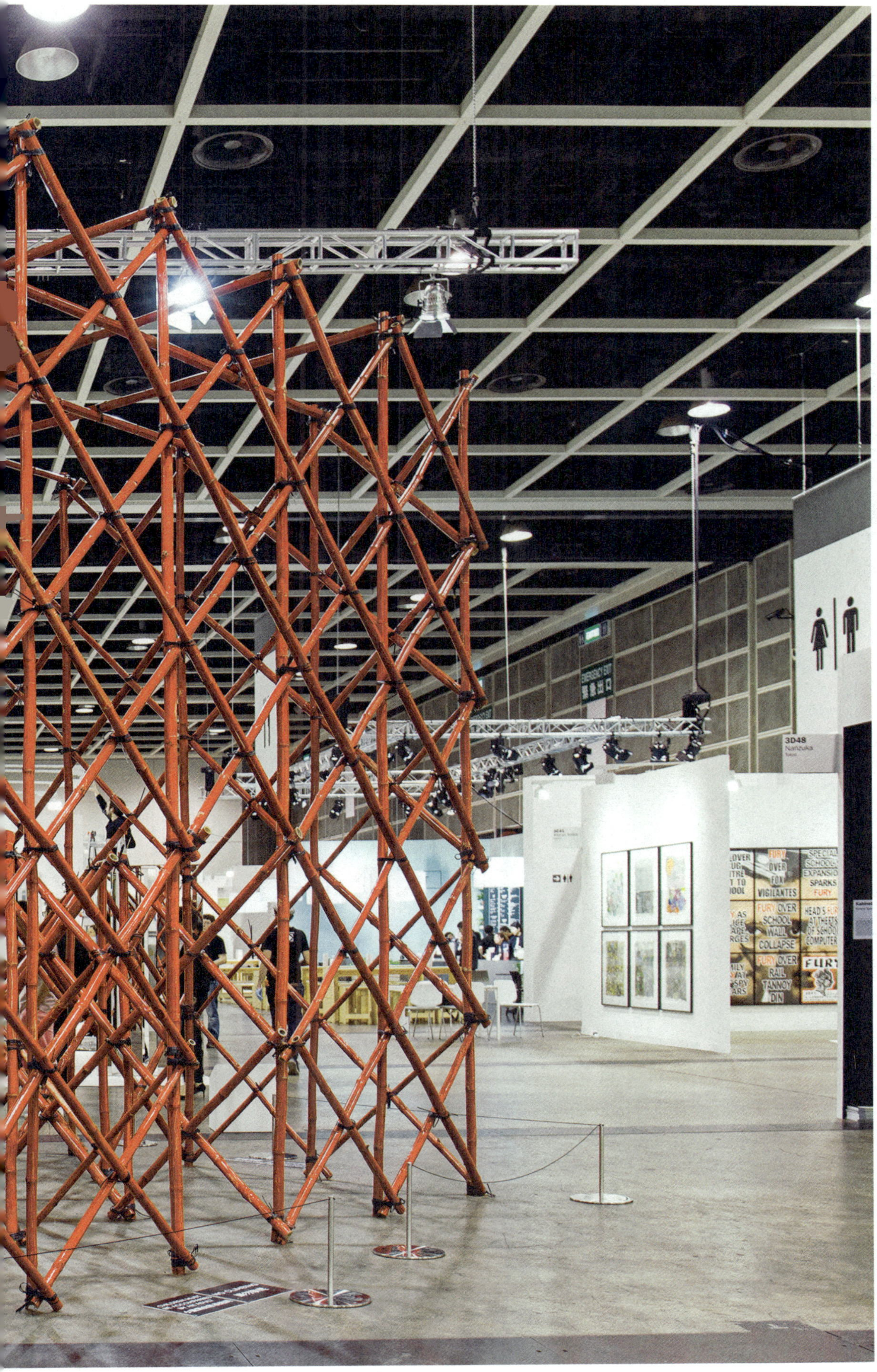
EMERGENCY EXIT
緊急出口
3D48
Nanzuka
FURY OVER FOX VIGILANTES
FURY OVER SCHOOL WALL COLLAPSE
FURY OVER RAIL TANNOY DIN

Summertime, 2017
powder-coated steel, edition of 5
193 x 183 x 183 cm

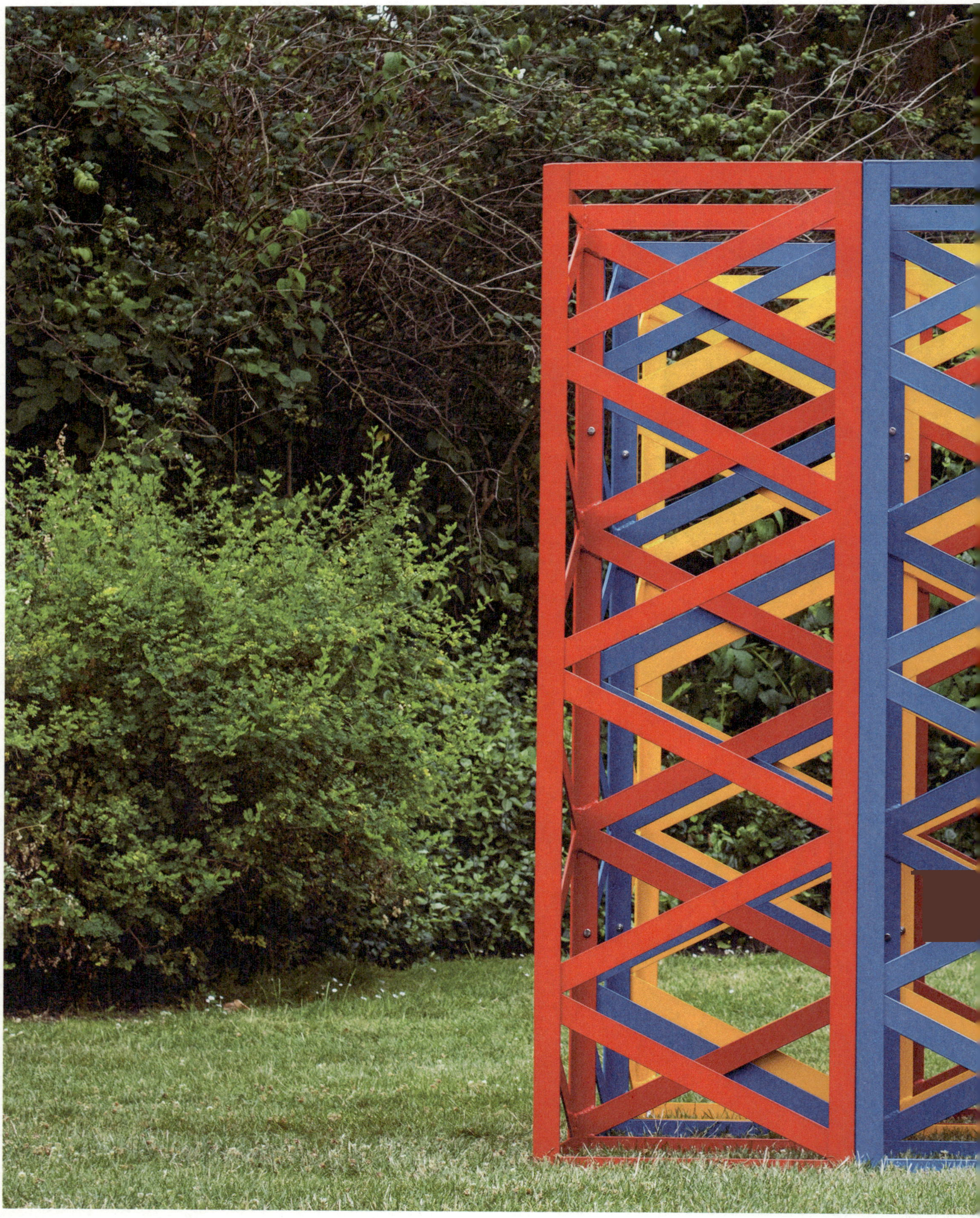

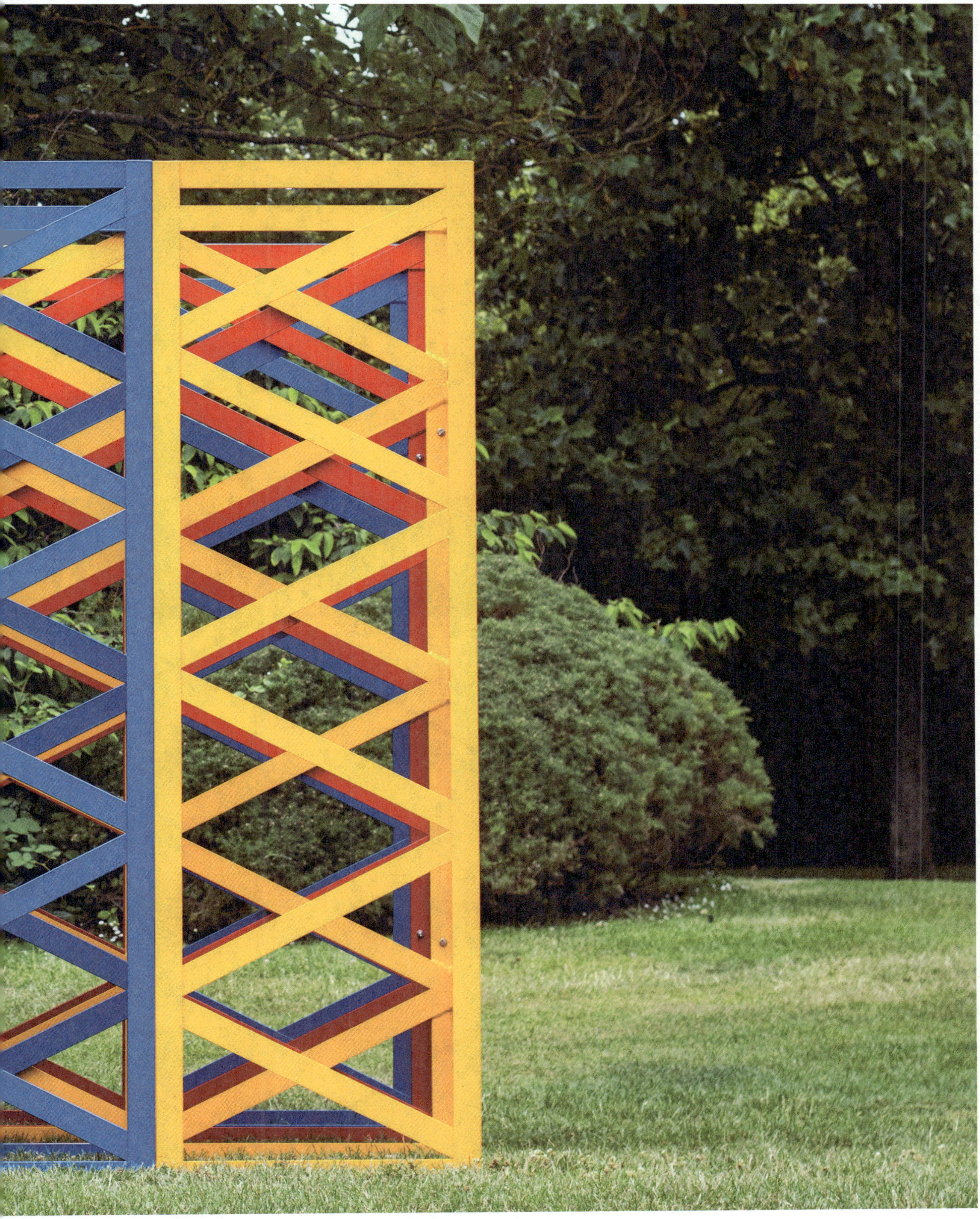

Untitled (Study for Opus), 2017
crayon on paper, 40 x 30 cm
Untitled (Study for Opus), 2017
crayon on paper, 40 x 30 cm

Untitled (Study for Opus), 2017
crayon on paper, 40 x 30 cm
Untitled (Study for Opus), 2017
crayon on paper, 40 x 30 cm

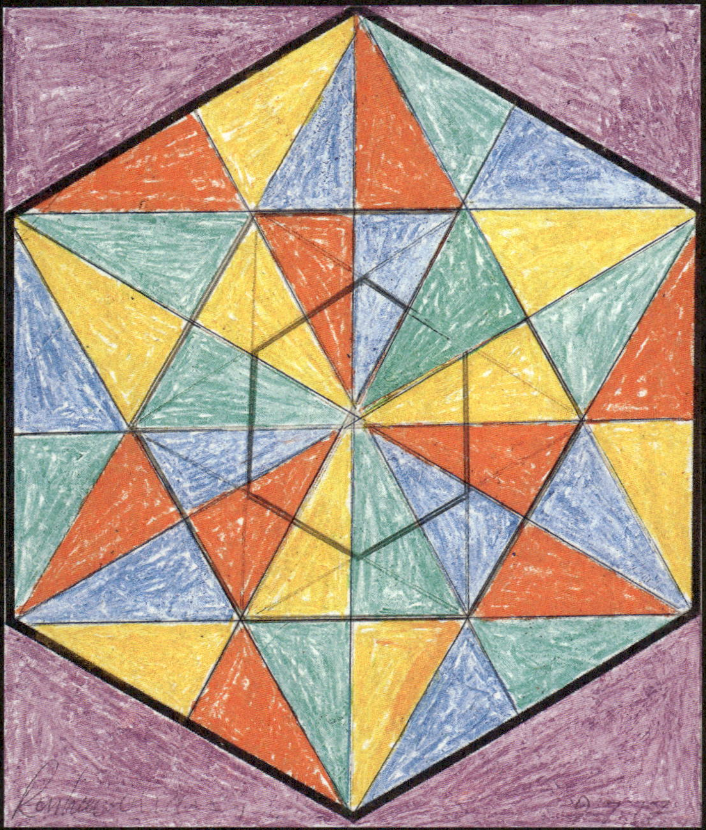

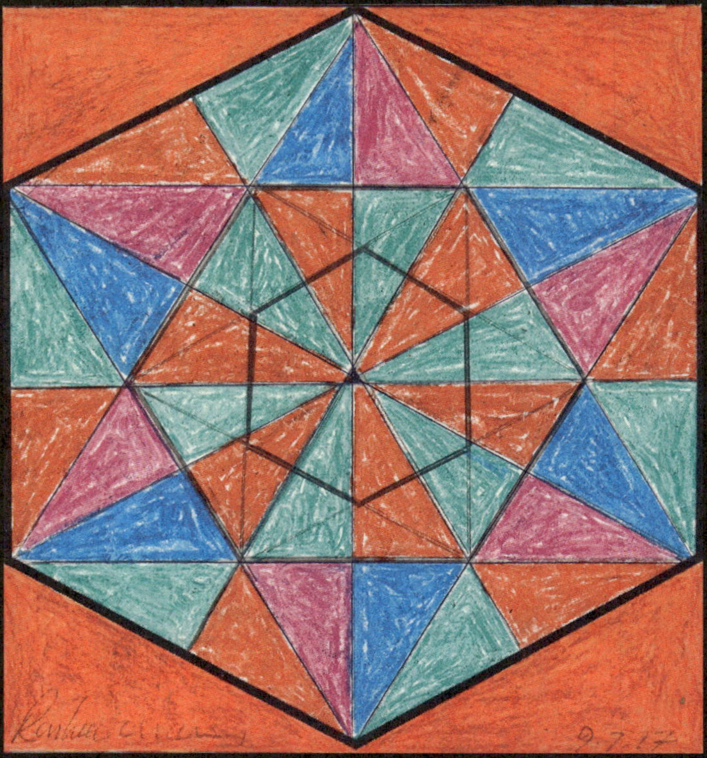

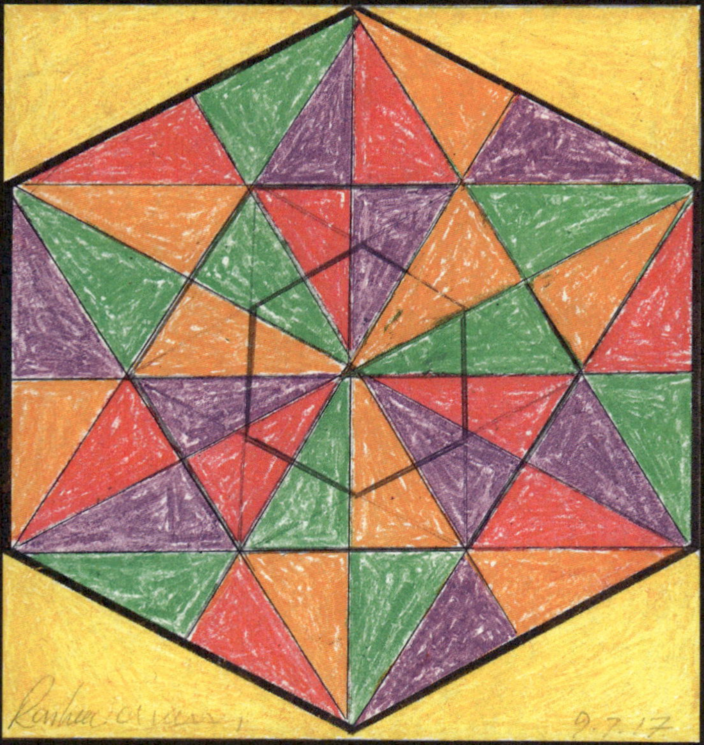

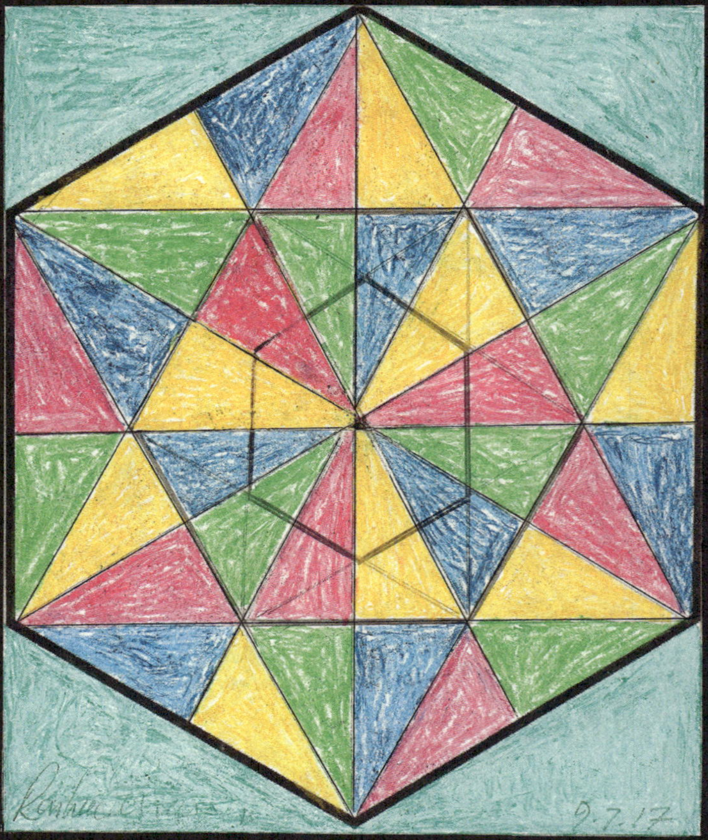

Opus HA1, 2017
acrylic on canvas, 160 x 140 cm

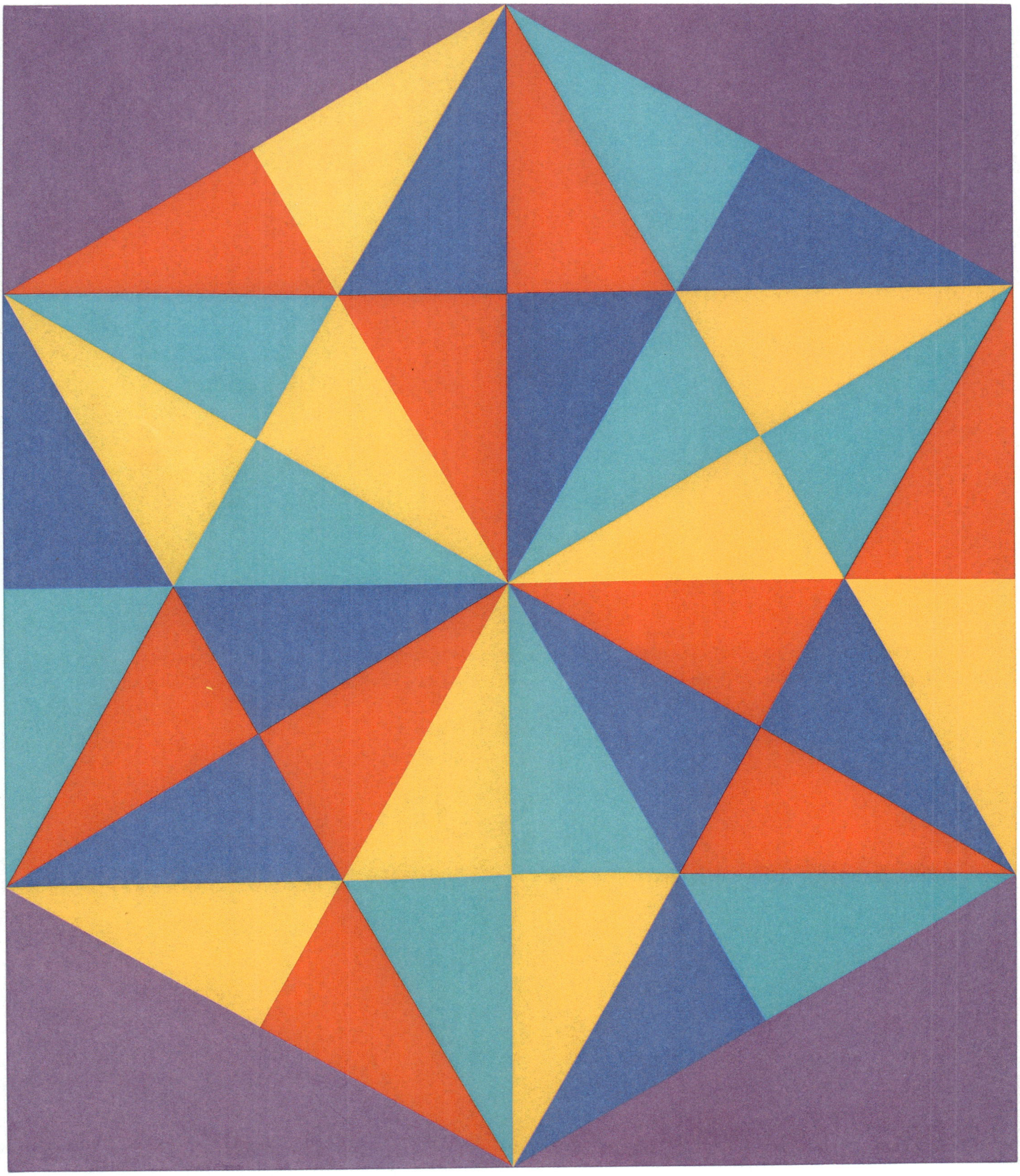

Opus HB2, 2017
acrylic on canvas, 160 x 140 cm

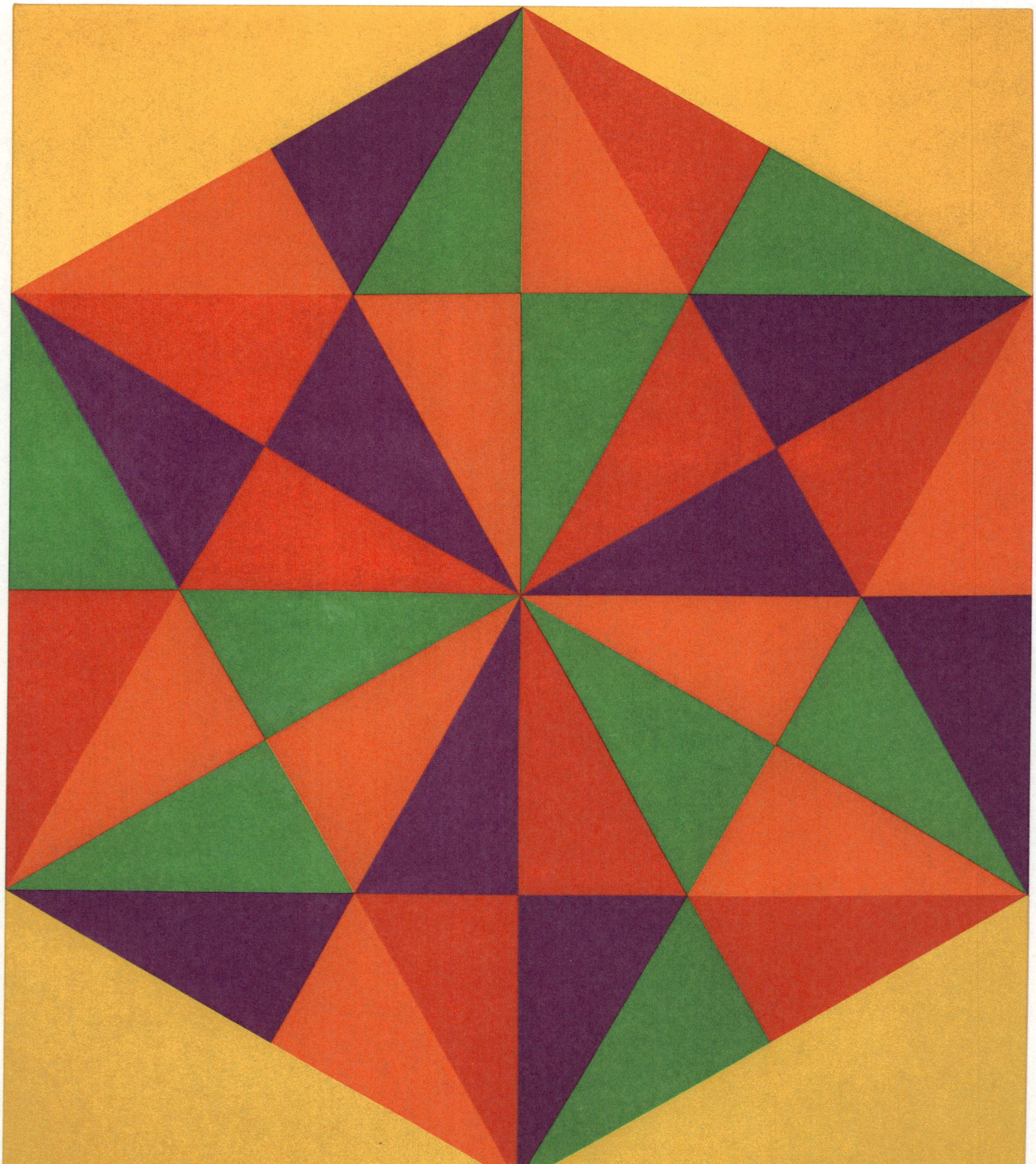

Opus HA3, 2017
acrylic on canvas, 160 x 140 cm

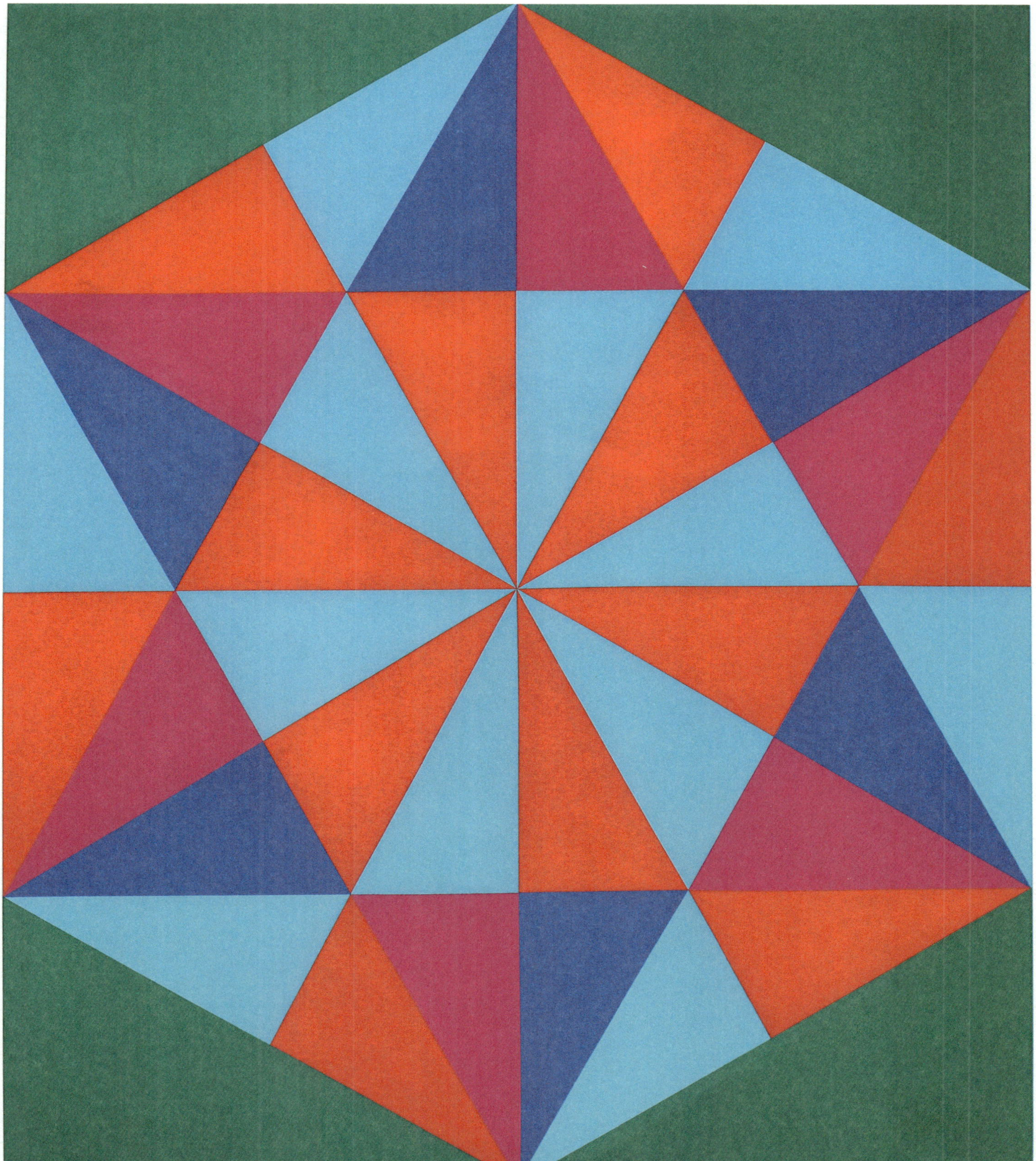

Opus HA4, 2017
acrylic on canvas, 160 x 140 cm

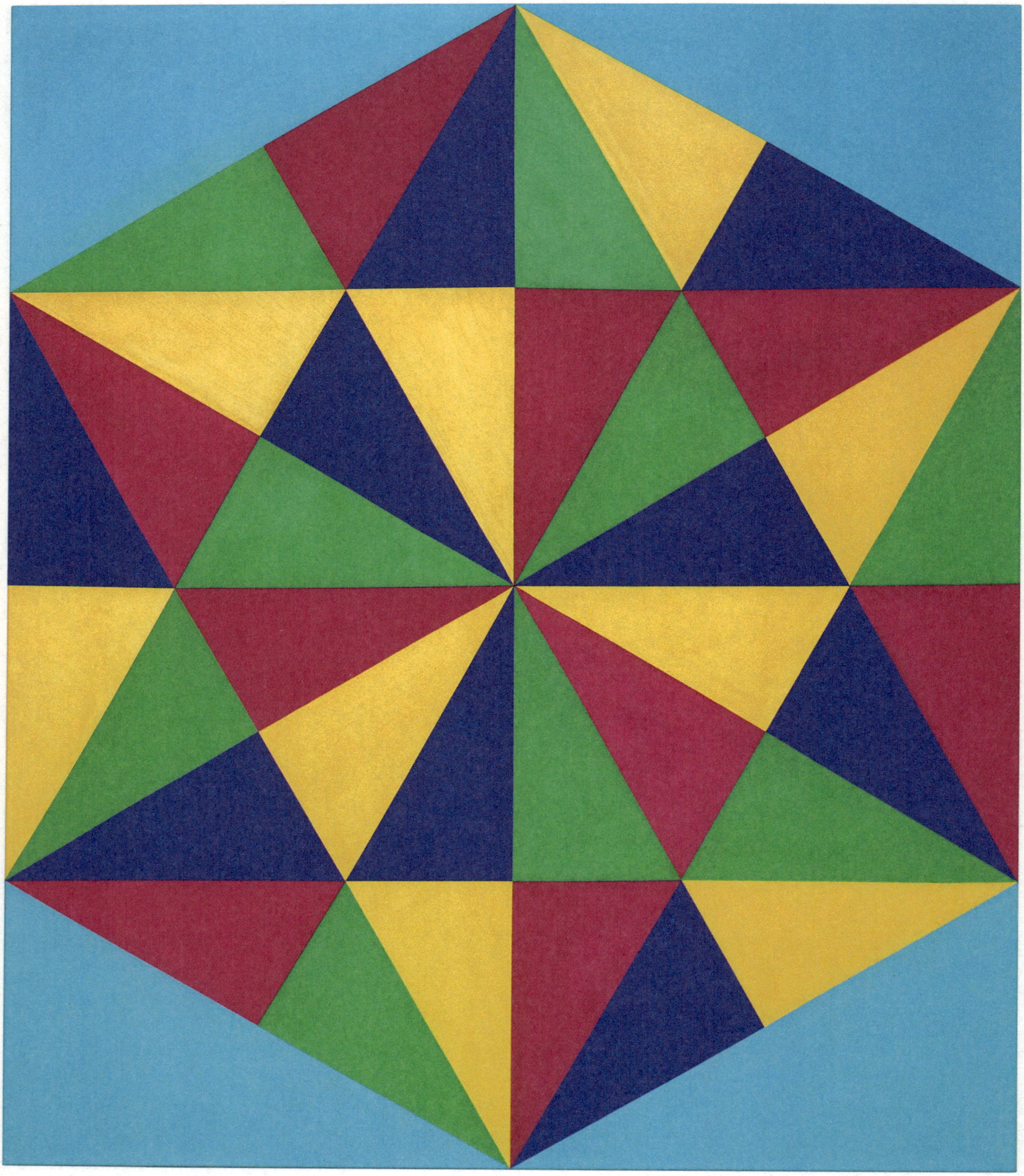

Opus HB1, 2017
acrylic on canvas, 160 x 140 cm

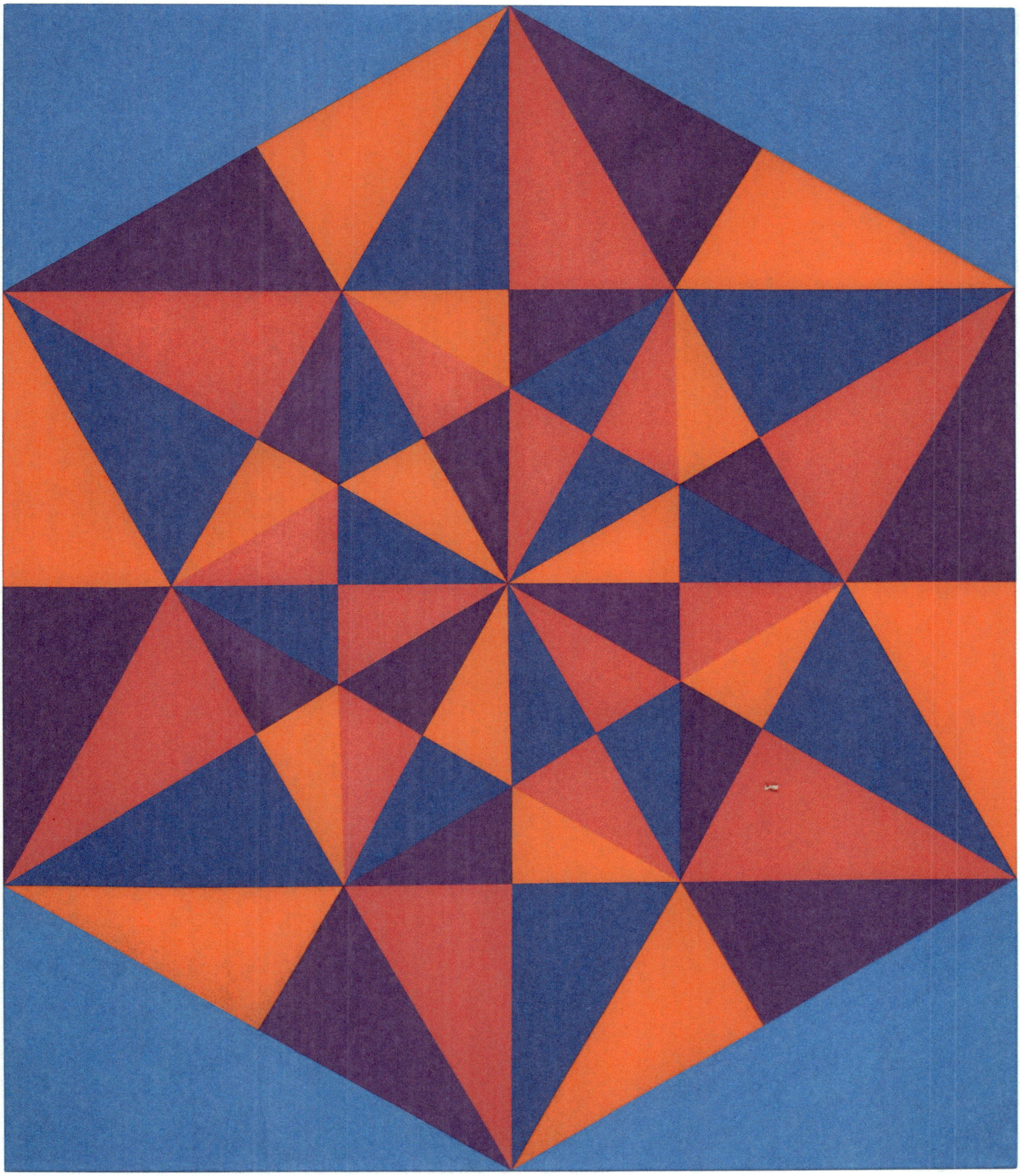

Opus HB2, 2017
acrylic on canvas, 1160 x 140 cm

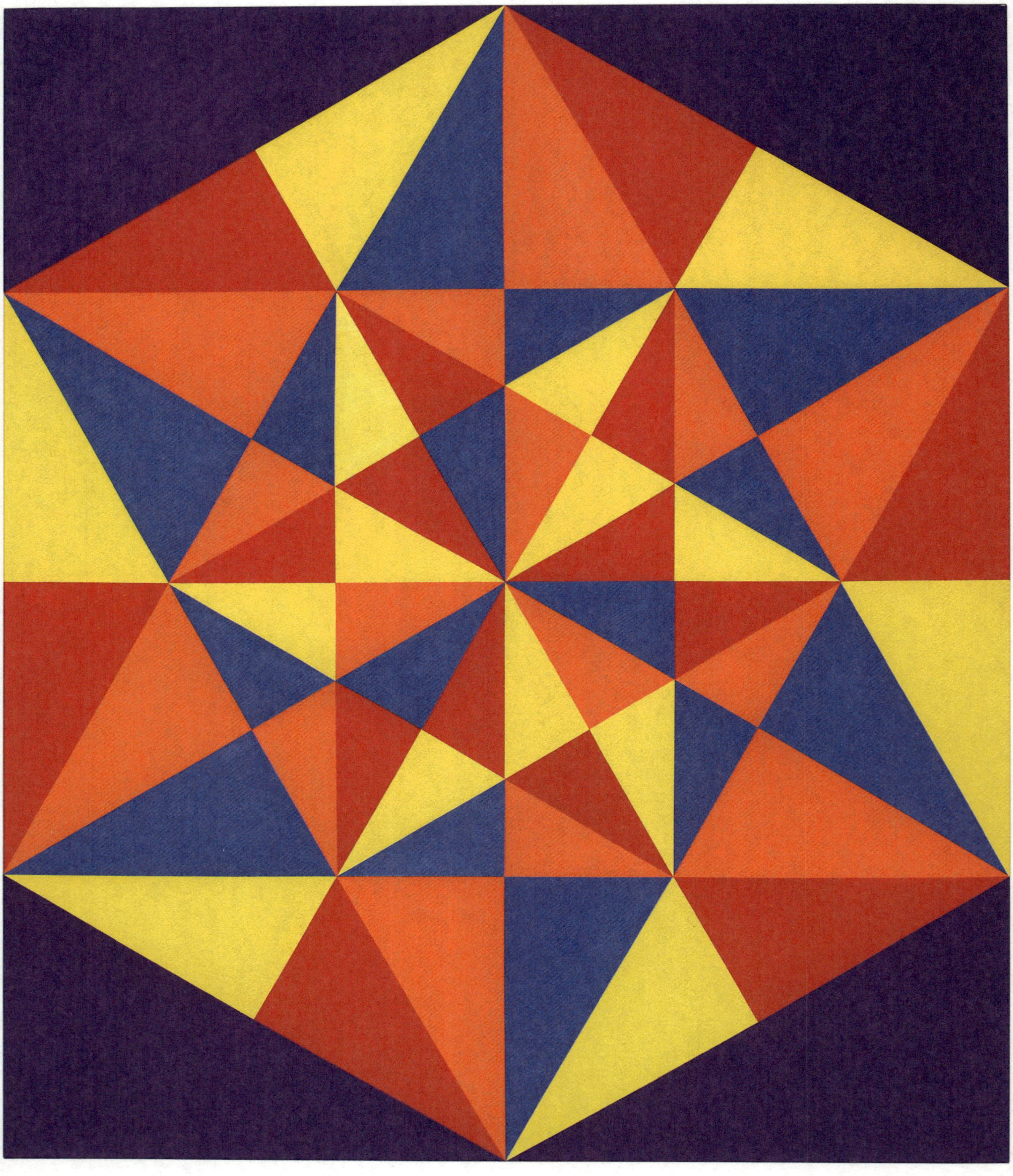

Opus HB3, 2017
acrylic on canvas, 160 x 140 cm

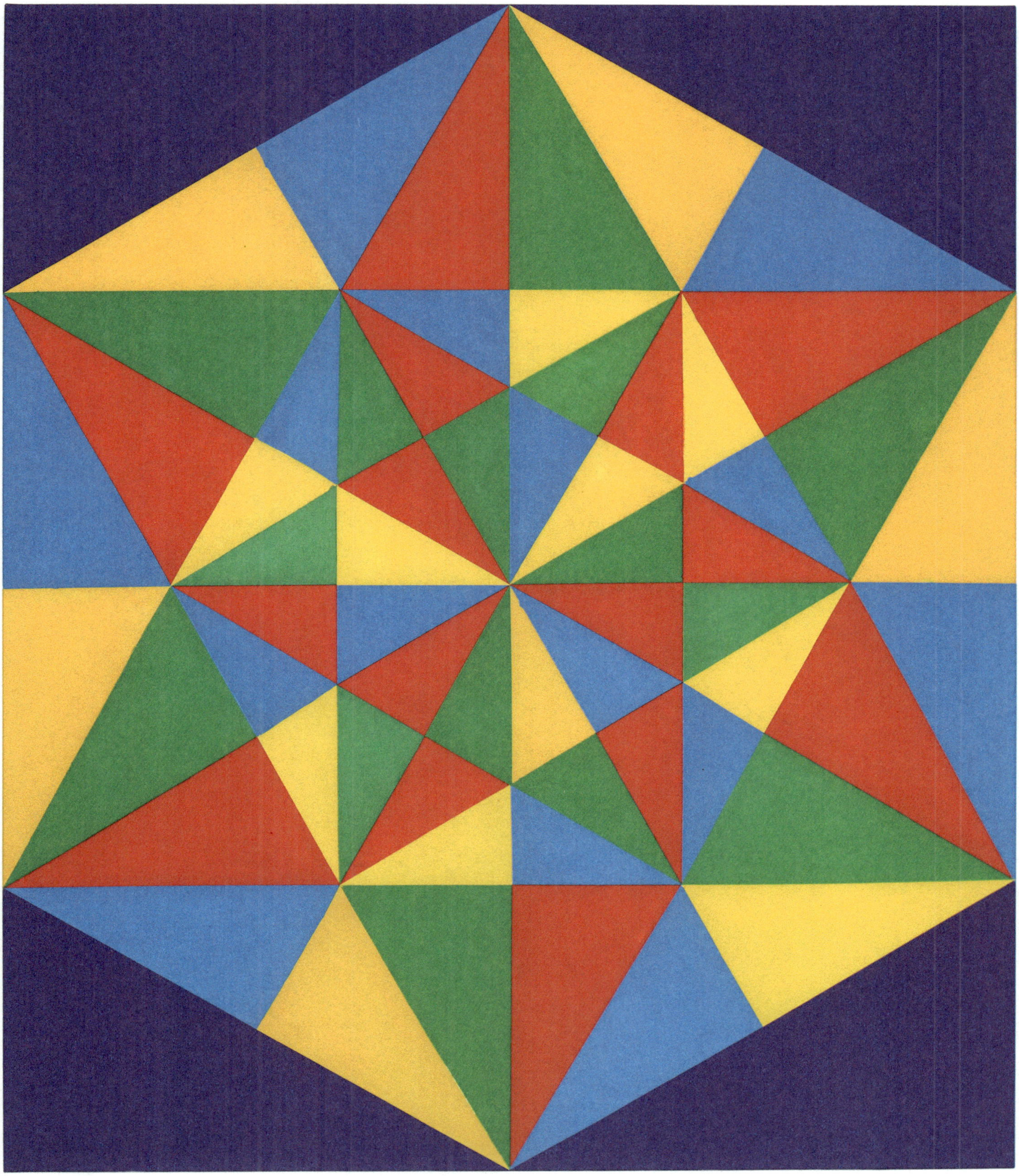

Opus HB4, 2017
acrylic on canvas, 160 x 140 cm

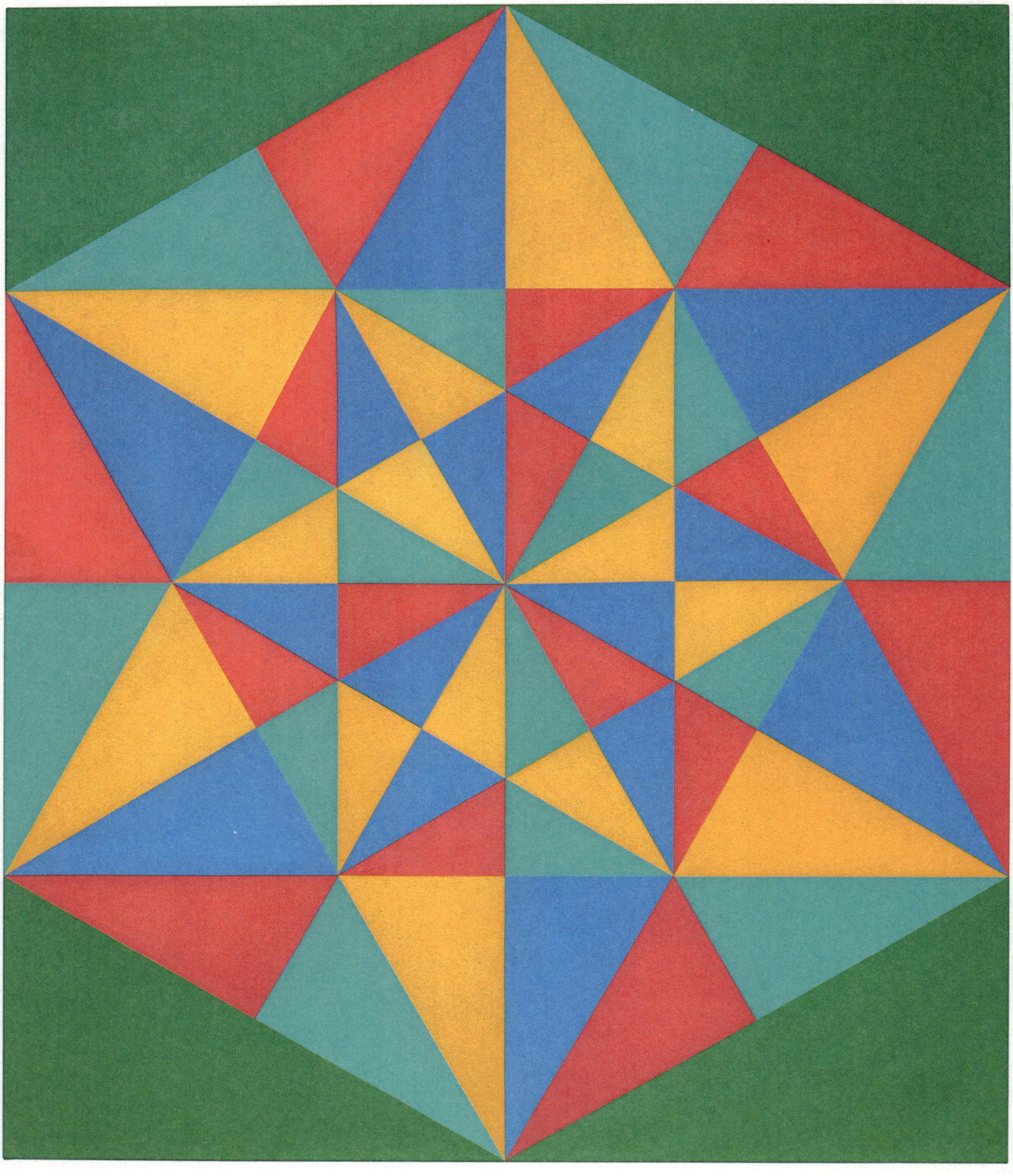

The Revolution Will Be Beautiful

Kaelen Wilson-Goldie

In 2014, Rasheed Araeen began a series of paintings titled 'Opus', which he continued adding to for another three years. Made of acrylic on canvas, the paintings are large, square, and colourful. They are also extremely smooth, without so much as a brushstroke in evidence on their surfaces. Individually named with short sequences of letters and numbers – such as *Opus F1*, *Opus AA4*, and 352, 353
Opus TC1, all 2016 – each painting consists of a grid tipped on the diagonal. 355
Eye-popping patterns of either diamonds alone or diamonds and triangles are set against orderly backgrounds in black and white or other such two-colour combinations (blue and yellow, for example, or purple and black). The backgrounds look like checkerboard tiles. The colours of the central patterns vary considerably while the compositional rules (so to speak) remain fixed. To walk through a room filled with the 'Opus' paintings is to run playfully through many of the permutations available in a geometric sequence. There is something vaguely childlike about the changing roster of pinks, blues, yellows, oranges, purples, teals, greens, and indigos. The paintings seem like exercises done with a child's mosaics kit in mind. They appear – at least they did so to me the first time I saw them – purely joyful, drily mathematical, archly conceptual, and decidedly mischievous all at once.

Five of the 'Opus' paintings were on view throughout the summer of 2017. They lined the prominent, outward-facing front wall of the ground floor exhibition space in the Neue Neue Galerie, the name given to a Brutalist former post 356
office in the central German city of Kassel by the curatorial team, led by Adam Szymczyk, of documenta 14. The paintings were hung before a long, open space, which featured a tidy arrangement of one of Araeen's 'reading rooms'. Steel and wooden cubes resembling the Minimalist sculptures he had started making in London in the 1960s had been placed there as tables and chairs for the presumed study of *Third Text*, the influential journal that Araeen established in 1987 and edited until 2011. An orderly grid of back issues covered a sea of glass tabletops. It was a kind of social space awaiting readers, who might sit and read and then turn towards the paintings to look and think. The combination of library furniture, reading material, and wall décor seemed like a deliberate attempt to use geometric abstraction as a prompt for the imagination, the paintings as brain teasers to further one's thinking about streamlined spatial forms and/or dense theoretical texts.

Like the reading rooms themselves, the 'Opus' paintings exemplify a number of works that might be grouped together and described as Araeen's late style. This holds true in the simple chronological sense that the artist, who was born in Karachi in 1935, had essentially stopped making art by the end of the 1990s, only to return to it with a flurry of new projects starting around 2010. 'Opus' and the other paintings, sculptures, and installations that Araeen has been working on in the past seven years also constitute late style in the more pointed, precise sense of the phrase as it was defined by Edward Said, who, in the essay collection *On Late Style: Music and Literature Against the Grain*, published posthumously in 2006, writes about how the mature works of Beethoven among others are characterized not by the reflection and melancholy of elderly figures looking back on their lives but rather by a stubborn and seemingly youthful intransigence and unresolved contradiction. Late style in this vein is daring, difficult, eccentric, and above all out of time. It is produced in a spirit of productive discontinuity and going against – against the grain, against the artist's previous work, against the social order or general flow of culture and learning in his or her time.[1]

Consider another late collection of paintings, known as the 'Homecoming' series, which Araeen initiated in 2010. The 'Homecoming' paintings employ a colour palette as vibrant as the 'Opus' series, but instead of pure geometric patterning, they take the names of prominent Muslim thinkers from the Abbasid era – Arab and Persian polymaths including Ibn Sina, Ibn Rushd, Al-Ghazali, and Al-Farabi 312
– and fan them out in four directions from the centre of each canvas. The names are rendered in a highly stylized Arabic script, where the lines of the letters and diacritical marks have been fattened into thick, interlocking geometric forms. The 'Opus' and 'Homecoming' paintings repeat certain visual motifs in Araeen's oeuvre – the square, the diamond, the diagonal – but at the same time they seem to radically reposition some of the artist's long-standing ideas about modernism and the meaning (or purpose) of geometric abstraction.

The works of Araeen's late style belong to the same formal universe as his earlier
works – including the Structures he made in 1965, using industrial I-beams placed 98
or stacked on the floor; the lattice-like structures produced throughout the 1960s and 1970s, which were often mounted on walls or, in at least one instance, in
London's Euston Square Gardens in 1970, hung like ornaments from trees; and the 144
'cruciform' collages, each arranged on a grid of nine squares, four monochromatic and green, five figurative consisting of found photographs or prints – but they shuffle the sources of his visual language. The late works mark a provocative change in Araeen's conception of modernism in relation to time (when it appeared most meaningfully, not necessarily in the twentieth century but rather in the seventh, eleventh, or twelfth) and place (where it made the greatest contribution to the advancement of human achievement, less in Western Europe or the United States than in Umayyad Damascus or Abbasid Baghdad). If Araeen has developed a new idiom in the work he has been doing in the elder stages of his life, to borrow the terms of Edward Said's argument on late style, then it is one unexpectedly, even counter-intuitively engaged with the history and philosophy of Islam. On first impression, this would seem unusual for an artist who has spent virtually all of his life professing total indifference to religion; who has for decades dismissed the idea of rooting one's artwork in ethnic, religious, or even cultural identities; and who insists to this day that even as he pays homage to the ideas and achievements of medieval Muslim scholars, he is still completely uninterested in Islam as a religious or spiritual practice. What, then, do the late works signify in the context of Araeen's art from the 1950s until today? Are they a break or a dramatic departure from his own past, or do they simply come at some of the same questions that have long occupied Araeen – about modernism, history, equality, and justice – from a very different place, a new set of tools, an additional constellation of ideas?

I was surprised by the 'Opus' paintings in documenta 14. I had expected 356
sculptures. I might have imagined something like *Red Square*, from 2015, his nod 336
to Malevich, which sits like a sculpture stuck on the wall and echoes Araeen's
Mon St V, from 1985, a clever reference to Cézanne. I had assumed the artist 259
would convey a hypercritical and possibly humorous incision into the art history and political inheritance (via colonialism and a domineering modernism) of the West. But I hadn't imagined paintings so smooth or pleasing to the eye, or seemingly so invested in the discourse of Islamic art. Also, in person, I was expecting to meet the most cantankerous man in Europe, or at the very least, the grumpiest traveller coming a long way from North London. And to a certain extent, though disarmingly gentle and jovial, Araeen did occasionally play the part, complaining bitterly that his 'reading room' had been reduced to a corridor,

slamming in blunt language some of the more arrogant and spectacle-driven works on view. But when I asked Araeen what had motivated him to make the 'Opus' paintings, he told me, somewhat improbably, that he had wanted to make something beautiful.[2]

'Going around contemporary art and the so-called avant-garde', he said, 'I realized there's nothing beautiful. I had to go back to geometric patterning. I was thinking about how to celebrate people who make beautiful things who are not artists', he explained, citing not only medieval artisans but also people working with household crafts in present-day Pakistan. 'I'm fed up with artists. I'm fed up with the so-called avant-garde and I want to get out of it. The notion of abstraction is seen to be a twentieth-century phenomenon. Historically it happened 1,200 years ago in Damascus. Europeans don't want to hear about it.' Here he paused and smiled like Yoda. 'I'm trying to connect to this forgotten history, which is not the history of Islam alone but the history of humanity, how geometric thinking allows us to perceive the world in terms of equality for all.'[3]

The emergence of Araeen's late style dates to 2010, the year that began the process of his unceremonious removal from *Third Text*. 'I didn't know what to do', he said. 'I had no job, no money. I borrowed money from the bank and set up a studio in Karachi. I had gone a long time without making work.' Araeen began working on the 'Homecoming' series around that time. He also started playing with the notion of the grid, looking at how to make different arrangements of colour within a fixed pattern. At first he worked with highlighter pens, which were easy for him to use – now in his eighties, Araeen is less dexterous than he once was – and these exercises or sketches eventually segued into the 'Opus' works. 'I build them like children do', he said. Araeen had studied civil engineering in Pakistan and had worked in the field in London. Some of the drawings where he planned out his early sculptures were drafted under BP Chemicals (UK) Ltd, Engineering Division letterhead. He had also secured an international patent for a prototype he made for one of his wilder performance works from the 1970s, *Disco Sailing*, involving a floating fibreglass disc with two rudders. I wondered if he had developed a system for assigning the colours to the 'Opus' paintings. I wondered if he had written some piece of computer code to generate their patterns and permutations. 'The selection of colours in the new works is totally arbitrary', Araeen told me. 'There's no assigned meaning, no symbolism. It's like childhood', he insisted.[4]

And yet, the 'Opus' and 'Homecoming' paintings are also complex intellectual statements about the history of modernism, abstraction, and Islam, as a body of knowledge if not, for Araeen, a religion per se. He described the new works as an 'enunciation and celebration' of the achievements of medieval Islamic thinkers, who devised geometric abstraction as a means of representing, or making visible in two-dimensional form, that which was otherwise invisible in the world, including the divine.[5] It is that capacity for giving shape to abstract thought that interests Araeen, the process of developing the new and necessary philosophical concepts to perceive the world more clearly, down to the essence of everything in it. Those were among the achievements behind what is now called Islamic art. Araeen had been more or less aware of the history of Islamic art since the 1970s, but it wasn't until eight years ago, when he was invited in 2009 to give a talk for a conference on Arab identity in Damascus, that he figured out for himself how to position the geometric abstraction of medieval Islam in relation to the discourse and history of modernism in the twentieth century. For Araeen, the kind of thinking that led to the achievements of the Abbasid era, widely considered the golden age of Islamic thought in art as well as science, is the essential historical glue that binds Ancient Greece to the Renaissance and the Enlightenment in Europe.[6] It is also a possible key for restoring the emancipatory promises of modernism, which was not, in itself, conceived as a method of domination and exploitation but as a rational means of making rational progress towards equality.[7] Araeen told me he wanted his next 'reading room' to be filled not with old issues of *Third Text* but rather with books on Islamic history.[8]

I should confess that up until 2014, I knew nothing of Araeen's work as an artist. I had never lived in the United Kingdom or Europe and had spent virtually all of my life in the Unites States and the Middle East. I knew nothing of Araeen's relationship to the work of Anthony Caro or his shifting positions with respect to the discourse of British modernism. I knew nothing of his blistering one-man
performance *'Paki-Bastard' (Portrait of the artist as a Black Person)*, staged in 234
London in 1977, with Araeen appearing at times bound and gagged, with slide projections and Bollywood songs and his Minimalist sculptures used as props. I had never seen his graffiti-esque paintings, his scribbled self-portraits series, and his explicitly anti-war collages. And scan through the artist's exhibition history and you'll see that I wasn't wholly oblivious or out of touch – Araeen has shown only spottily in New York, never in the Arab world until three years ago, and even then, only in the Gulf and not, as yet, anywhere in the Levant or North Africa. (Aside from some very notable exceptions, such as the Havana and Johannesburg biennials, Araeen's CV remains curiously, almost stubbornly Eurocentric.)

Prior to the opening, in 2014, of Araeen's fairly mind-blowing retrospective at the Sharjah Art Foundation – a show that, as several critics later noted, carefully elided much of the artist's most politically explosive art from the middle period of his life – I knew Araeen only, and exclusively, as a writer, as the critic who panned the blockbuster exhibition *Magiciens de la terre* in Paris, as the founder of *Third Text*. As a forum on the colonial, imperial condition, on power politics in relation to the mechanisms of global contemporary art, the journal was and for many still is a landmark. It is especially popular among American university students of certain disciplinary dispositions (comparative literature, postcolonial theory, women's studies), and it has been crucial reading among left-leaning artists and intellectuals in cities ranging from Algiers to Cairo to Beirut. It was therefore a moment of considerable revelation to walk through a relentlessly chronological show featuring fifty years of Araeen's drawings, paintings, sculptures, and performance documentation. (The curator Hammad Nasar promptly chided me in person and in print for deigning to discover Araeen's artwork so late.) Most striking to me at the time were not the muscular or industrial or precise geometric sculptures but the more delicately abstract works on paper, especially the watercolours with wiggly
lines and sensuous swirls titled *'Dancing Bodies (Hula-Hoop Series)'* (1959–1961). 35
These works on paper seemed to mark a tremendous pivot in Araeen's work, between the fey, figurative landscapes and portraits he was making as a young man taking art classes in Karachi, and everything that followed. Now, how do those early, tentative abstractions relate to Araeen's most recent paintings? How does the movement between them highlight his changing ideas about modernism, history, and Islam? Can the early and late works be reconciled? Beyond the common visual language of lines, shapes, and colours, is there any real sense of continuity to be found between them or do the late works represent a necessary disjuncture? And how do they each in their own way fulfill Araeen's promise that modernism, at its best, will create the conditions for greater equality, and that the core force of Islam, as knowledge and philosophy, can be revived to spark a revolution in intellectual thought as consequential as the Renaissance?

In the lore of Araeen's life, his origins as an artist were the work of his mother. Growing up between Karachi and a small coastal village in Balochistan, Araeen didn't go to school or begin his formal education until he was eleven years old. Before that time, he was at home with his mother, whom he credits, somewhat jokingly, for initiating him into art by asking him to help her trace out flower patterns to incorporate into her embroidery. He took to drawing and continued on his own. One day, when he was older, he stumbled upon a library in Karachi that was run by the United States Information Service (USIS), a public diplomacy arm of the US government that was later renamed the US Information Agency (USIA), eventually folded into the State Department, and dissolved in the late 1990s (the broadcast service Voice of America, whose heyday was at the height of the Cold War, also emerged from these agencies). Among its educational programmes, the USIS library in Karachi offered weekly drawing sessions under the auspices of its Sketch Club, which Araeen promptly joined. He soon discovered another artists' club in the city offering more classes that helped him to develop his skills as a draughtsman. The club also allowed him a sense of camaraderie with other artists, an ongoing conversation about what art was, what it could do, and what could be pursued in its name.

By this time Araeen was in his early twenties and studying civil engineering. If his mother sparked in him a love of drawing, then it was engineering – as well as his intense observations of the fishing boats in Karachi harbour and the wind towers characterizing the architecture in the southeastern Pakistani city of Hyderabad – that instilled a love of geometry. Araeen was, in these days, essentially a hobbyist as far as art was concerned, a young Sunday painter. 'Until 1958', he says, 'I did drawings and watercolours by looking at things'.[9] He made portraits of ordinary people, where he concentrated all of his detail in the face and then trailed off at the shoulders. He made perspectival landscapes of waterways and trees. He faithfully captured the tumble of urban housing as it was above the coastline of Karachi and reflected in the Arabian Sea.

In the late 1950s, abstraction was a topic of conversation among artists in Karachi – Araeen said that among the practitioners he knew there was some knowledge of abstraction as a school or a style – but as a methodology of subtraction and elimination, it wasn't something that he was particularly interested in doing himself. Then, on a day in 1958, while he was sitting at his study table at home, he took out a piece of paper from a drawer, placed it in front of him, and began to draw without looking at or thinking about anything. 'What I drew were just vertical, horizontal, and diagonal lines', Araeen recalled. 'I then filled the spaces between them with watercolours. The result was a sort of abstraction, resembling boats', he explained, 'which I used to paint from life; which in fact surprised me because I did something unique now without knowing what I was doing – it was unique because I had not seen this kind of work among my fellow artists in Karachi; and which subsequently led me into pursuing, consciously, this kind of abstraction'.[10]

The series 'Boats: Toward Abstraction' (1958–1962), composed of watercolour, 30
pastel, and black ink on paper, represents one of several essential turning points in Araeen's oeuvre, many of them clustered together in the years before and after his departure from Pakistan. In one of the paintings, a collection of jagged triangles appear like sails that have been sewn from fabric scraps and frozen in stained glass, all set against a dark stormy sky, with the slightest evocation of a sun or moon (or an eye to ward off spirits) echoes the more clearly drawn shape of a fish at the hull. Whispers of light seem to be sneaking up from beneath a gloomy horizon line. Squint at the painting and one might find a dramatic X stretching in two lines diagonally from all four corners of the composition. Another picture in the series replaces sea with fire, and stitched together sails with a fleet of small boats that might have been thrown to the flames of hell. Or perhaps it is a more joyous, or at least more ambiguous, painting than that. Whatever the case these are some of the most intriguing and equivocal works of Araeen's career.

'The geometry of this work in 1958', he says of his first stab at drawing from nothing, 'produced by the interaction of vertical, horizontal, and diagonal lines, is still fundamental to my work today'. It is present in the sculptural works he calls 'Structures', starting in 1965. It finds full-blooded expression in the 'Opus' series, starting in 2014. And for Araeen it is important to say that this process was always purely intuitive, never spiritual or supernatural or conditioned by the wider culture or guided by faith. He admits to having an interest in Sufism, the mystical arm of Islam, from which much of the religious life of Pakistan originally stems, but only in the sense that Sufism confronts and questions the orthodoxies of organized religion.

The Syrian poet Adonis, in his book *An Introduction to Arab Poetics*, from 1985, and later, in *Sufism and Surrealism*, from 1995, places the advent of modernity in the Arab world precisely with the Sufi mystics in eighth-century Baghdad. Like Araeen, he argues in deliberate, contentious contrast to the West's twentieth-century modernism:

> We must place some of the mystics... firmly at the heart of [the] modernist movement, and help rescue them from neglect and oblivion and restore them the consideration they deserve... Modernity... had its origins in a climate which brought together two independent elements: awareness of new urban culture which developed in Baghdad in the eighth century, and a new use of the language to embrace this awareness and express it in poetry.[11]

And indeed, although Adonis was a believer in the past and converted from one religion to another, there is considerable common ground between him and Araeen, not least in their respective involvements in small but intellectually consequential magazines (Adonis was one of the key figures behind the revolutionary modernist literary journals *Shi'r* and *Muwaqif* in Beirut in the 1960s), and their shared conviction that the contemporary Arab and Muslim worlds are in states of total disarray (younger artists and intellectuals in the region tend to regard this view, either gently or dismissively, as a generational affliction on the part of their elders).

But unlike Adonis, Araeen insists that he is in no way remotely even stirred by an interest in Islam as an organized religion or spiritual pursuit. It interests him solely as philosophy, as history, as a body of knowledge that was produced by some force of imagination or mechanism of thought, which could in turn be revived to produce a new set of concepts, capable of bringing the Arab and Muslim worlds out of their generalized dysfunction through rational and abstract thought.[12] Writes Araeen in 'Preliminary Notes for the Understanding of the Historical Significance of Geometry in Arab/Islamic Through, and its Suppressed Role in the Genealogy of World History' published in *Third Text* in the summer of 2010:

> The whole process of contemplation and articulation of geometry, from its basic forms of square, circle and triangle to its complex multilayered configurations based on symmetry and seriality, produced not only a unique art form of its own making unprecedented in history; but more significantly, it enshrined and revealed a rationality that produced Islamic civilization with all its achievements in art, science and philosophy. The artistic form of geometry not only represents the ability of the mind to deal with complex problems of an abstract nature but it demands that we look at things and understand them through the rationality of science. The symmetry of geometry in Islamic art offers, in my understanding, an allegory for human equality (*Musawaat*), something that humanity now desperately needs.[13]

Araeen arrived in London in 1964. He took an interest in the sculptures of Anthony Caro and the modernist discourse as it was evolving in Britain at the time. He also developed a deep and inherent distrust in hierarchy, exclusivity, and elitism. This added to his abiding affection for geometry, which in his practice proposed symmetry as an antidote to compositional hierarchy, combined in such a way as to produce the Structures he made in 1965, which he placed directly on the floor, never on plinths, equal to man and things and as subject to gravity as anything else.

When critics and viewers first saw his Structures and interpreted them through references to Islamic art, Araeen was baffled – first because he had never heard the term and had no idea what Islamic art was; second because he wasn't interested in religion at all, not personally, politically, or artistically. This was in 1970, and soon after a man named Paul Keeler, who had been running an experimental art collective known as the Exploding Galaxy with the artist David Medalla, began organizing festivals, assembling exhibitions, and publishing books about Islamic art in London. As an academic category in the discipline of art history, Islamic art is, like many such designations, a little forced, inaccurate, serviceable, and artificial. Keeler, who converted to Islam in 1975 and adopted the name Ahmed, took an exuberant, maximalist approach to the field. Araeen saw those shows and paged through those books and sensed a gap, a missing link, not only in his own intellectual development but in how the history of the world had been written to account for the movement of ideas from Mesopotamia through Ancient Greece into the Renaissance and on until today. This didn't exactly compel Araeen to pursue Islamic art per se, but it did make him read, and it did make him rethink his intellectual position vis-à-vis Islam.

However, it wasn't until 2010 that Araaen turned his attention to Islam as a subject of sustained intellectual and artistic inquiry. 'Preliminary Notes for the Understanding of the Historical Significance of Geometry in Arab/Islamic Thought, and its Suppressed Role in the Genealogy of Ideas' quoted earlier, pulls together a number of different ideas that Araeen had pursued elsewhere into a cogent narrative, framed within a set of tough questions and brutal critiques concerning the sad, dysfunctional state of what constitutes the Muslim world today. His argument, in effect, is that the general understanding of the ban on image making in Islam is misconstrued. When the inhabitants of Mesopotamia and Ancient Egypt figured out how to farm and stockpile food, they were able to turn their attention to how the world was made. In thinking about that, they began to make art in their own image. For Araeen, the natural progression moves on to Ancient Greece where men have begun to portray gods in their own image. This is wonderful, Araeen argues, but also narcissistic and ultimately limiting.

'A system would emerge to receive the divine message and also follow its multilayered complexity in encouraging the human mind to independence and creation', Araeen writes, explaining:

> What was most extraordinary about this message was a repudiation of any physical relationship of the Divine with humanity, creating both an infinity of distance and a nearness between the Divine and humans, which could only be penetrated and grasped through the contemplative power of imagination. Imagination could now wander freely in the universe and explore its vastness.... It was this relationship of a revelatory knowledge that engendered a "secular" rational discourse that underlies the spirit of Islam.[14]

While Europe plunged itself into the darkness of the Middle Ages, the golden age of Islam took hold. Instead of picturing god as a man, artisans of the Abbasid era in Baghdad, in particular (when the ideas of the Greeks were translated into Arabic and used to give science a boost), pushed it further. If god was invisible, how could an invisible thing be pictured? If god was an abstract concept, perhaps geometry could be applied to express it and give it form. Perhaps geometry could be used to see that which was otherwise unseen. And in that sense, the inherently rational, science-minded spirit of medieval Islamic culture, its ethos of critical reception transformed into creative imagination, led to freedom, and in freedom, to equality. Writes Araeen:

> The art that emerged in the Muslim world could not therefore be based on the human body or on images of living beings, but had to go beyond, whence the spirit was free from the sensuous physicality of the body and could reveal itself as the abstract ability of the mind,…Geometry in Islamic art thus represents a paradigm shift in the evolution of human thought from the observation of things and their representation as they appear to the eye to the creation of an art form whose sensuousness is the product of pure abstract thinking, thus giving the imagination enhanced power to think but also unprecedented power to create.[15]

This is of course an over-simplification of Araeen's ideas but he does accept the notion that in a sense, his late paintings try to realize in artworks the arguments he makes in 'Preliminary Notes'. Those paintings themselves won't bring about the revolution needed to restore Islamic philosophy to its place in the world of ideas between the Greeks and the Renaissance (Araeen effectively blames Hegel for taking it out and making Europe feel smug, dominant, superior, and intellectual sufficient unto itself). They won't pull the Muslim world of today out of its own dark ages and malaise. They might not even convince subsequent generations of writers and thinkers in the region that Araeen is actually on their side, and still fighting their fight. But the very act of painting, and of letting those paintings work their way into the imagination of viewers, might start to give the status quo a little shake, and that, in turn, might be quite an accomplishment for a set of pretty pictures.

1 Edward Said, 'Timeliness and Lateness', in *On Late Style: Music and Literature Against the Grain* (New York, Pantheon, 2006), 3–24.
2 Conversation with the author, Kassel, 9 June 2017.
3 Ibid.
4 Ibid.
5 Correspondence with the author, 26 August 2017.
6 Ibid.
7 'Art is also about thinking, about perception and about an ability to innovate and create. It requires a free imagination to express its vision through a product that is original and has a profound social meaning, not only for the individual but also for the community or society of which the artist is a member.... Modernity began its journey in Europe, and on its way to conquer the world it turned itself into a tool of barbarity. But there was another side to the coin, which articulated and promised a modern world in which all human beings would be equal, and this equality would be achieved with the rational ideas of progress.... But has modernity fulfilled its promises? If the answer is no, then we must examine its failure.... If these ideas of modernity are trapped in a system of domination and exploitation, then the need is not to condemn it as Eurocentric but to liberate its ideas from their Western grip.... What we need... is a body of new philosophical ideas capable of not only exposing and confronting the inhumanity of the Eurocentric vision, but which can also present a new interpretation of modernity so that it becomes a tool for the liberation of humanity, not only in Africa but universally.' Rasheed Araeen, 'Modernity, Modernism and Africa's Place in the History of Art of Our Age. Postcolonialism and the Dependency Syndrome', *Dakar—Art, Minorities, Majorities*, AICA, Africa, July 2003.
8 Conversation with the author, Kassel, 9 June 2017.
9 Correspondence with the author, 26 August 2017.
10 Ibid.
11 Adonis, *An Introduction to Arab Poetics*, trans. Catherine Cobham (London: Saqi Books, 1990), 88–89.
12 'There is a gap of more than 1500 years between the end of the Greek period and the Renaissance, but this gap was filled by what emerged as knowledge during the Renaissance, and what continued to happen subsequently. The Renaissance was a Revolution, which opened the way for the West to achieve what it has achieved, and created a sense of continuity between them and the Greeks. There is of course a missing factor in this equation, Islamic achievement, whose continuity can be restored only if there is a Revolution in the Arab/Muslim world similar to the Renaissance.' Art, among other things, 'can lead this revolution', says Araeen. Correspondence with the author, 26 August 2017.
13 Rasheed Araeen, 'Preliminary Notes for the Understanding of the Historical Significance of Geometry in Arab/Islamic Thought, and its Suppressed Role in the Genealogy of World History', *Third Text* 24, no. 5 (summer 2010):518.
14 Ibid., 511.
15 Ibid., 513.

Imagining Mutuality: A Reading of Rasheed Araeen's Art Beyond Art

Gene Ray

Rasheed Araeen's *Art Beyond Art* (2010) testifies to one artist's ceaseless questioning of art's powers and places in the world. Araeen is not concerned with art's capacities to represent and symbolize the world, nor even to respond to the world expressively or affectively. He is searching rather for visions and bases of decolonized mutuality; these would be nothing less than kinds of elusive inspirations, which, sometimes in history, move and encourage people to alter the restricting patterns of everyday life. This searching, this aim, is lived as a passion. In *Art Beyond Art*, Araeen's passion becomes legible through various metaphors, stories, project proposals, and a running dialogue with art history. The transformative mutuality sought here is driven by what he calls 'the creative energy of the free collective imagination'.[1] Araeen's quest repeatedly brings him up against the limits of modern art's fixation on the conventions and signatures of individualized artistic production. The aim of this passionate searching, therefore, can only be collective; it desires an art of shared process rather than objects, an art vitally linked to a collective empowerment that moves beyond the vicious circles of the 'narcissistic ego' and the unbounded social and ecological violence of globalized accumulation.

Collecting fourteen essays, *Art Beyond Art* was published in 2010 in the context of *Third Text*, the journal and collective publishing adventure that Araeen founded in 1987 and continued to catalyse until 2012. The texts of this book, their author insists, do not constitute an academic work; they should be read as the evolving retrospections and propositions of an artist who began as an engineer, who moved from Karachi to metropolitan London in 1964, and who was initially inspired by the possibilities opened up by modernist sculpture. But while Araeen's searching was stimulated by modernism, it could not be contained by it. His questions, always opening new questions, were too insistent – his aims, his passion, too expansive, generous, and fertile.

In the pages of *Art Beyond Art*, a qualified utopian impulse is undoubtedly at work. The passion just described, which actively seeks as well as merely endures, is strongly critical – anti-colonial, anti-imperialist, anti-racist, as well as, in certain moments, openly anti-capitalist. But Araeen remains suspicious of facile political postures. He comments caustically on the failures of confrontational vanguardism. And he rejects as naïve the suggestion that there are any simple or easy escapes from modernity and its logics. He acknowledges the unsolved practical and theoretical dilemmas of radical history and does not pretend to solve them himself. And yet, these pages evince an abiding commitment to what he calls 'the journey of the idea' ('idea' in Araeen's sense is hereafter italicized).

This *idea*, the first formulations of which open *Art Beyond Art*, denotes the generative migration of art into life. Ultimately, by the last pages of this book, the *idea* comes to stand for a dynamic articulation of energies, generosities, and capacities for cooperation and mutuality. This shifting and renewable constellation of human powers and desires is, for Araeen, an abiding source of artistic creation and performance. Or, at least, it is the source of practices that reach both before and beyond all modernisms. This constellation of energies, generosities, and capacities is also, if my reading is correct, something like a subtle motor of history: always novel in its responses to urgencies, always unpredictable in its transversal effects, always a call that may be answered at any time and without warning from the heart of the collective. This, in any case, may be the gift that an artist can give – the artistic and intellectual restlessness out of which Araeen shapes a practice that also aims to be ethical and political.

The subtitle of *Art Beyond Art* is *Ecoaesthetics: A Manifesto for the 21st Century*. In the seven years since this book appeared, public knowledge about ecocide has made denial untenable. Most of the world is now well aware of climate chaos, planetary toxification, and the mass extinction of species and cultures – the socially driven processes of the so-called Anthropocene. Every day now, local experience confirms the consensus of networked science. And yet, our mainstream political cultures and agencies of governance continue to defer the moment of full avowal and mobilized action. Entrenched dogmas of growth and accumulation continue to dominate the metabolic interactions between globalized society and the planet. Faced with technocratic inaction, grassroots movements for food, water, and energy sovereignty seek to reshape this metabolic interaction from below. Biophilic cultures and movements (such as permaculture, the Transition movement, eco-villages, even Slow Food) are emerging, sometimes in alliance with resurgent Indigenous struggles, such as that at Standing Rock, North Dakota, in 2016. While these diverse cultures cannot be reduced to univocal aims and motivations, they seem to share a call for respect, cooperation, and mutuality. Some of the impulses that animate this spreading intervention into everyday life are registered and anticipated in *Art Beyond Art*. Araeen's growing concerns about the social threats to the life of the planet are legible across these pages. The critique of urban-industrial society that grounds his notion of 'cosmoruralism' is reflected in his visions and proposals for establishing networks of peoples' collectives and cooperative farms. These project proposals share with the grassroots movements for food, water, and energy sovereignty a desire to rethink, reinvent, and locally reinvigorate co-opted concepts such as sustainability and resilience. At several moments, Araeen also makes a striking move beyond anthropocentrism, or what I call 'human species supremacism'.[2] The attempt to refuse human supremacism, and to rethink ethics and politics on the basis of multispecies care and mutual flourishing, is, I suggest, a crucial intellectual and cultural shift underway today. If it takes hold, a major headlock of modernity would be transformed, opening pathways for re-patterning the metabolic interaction with the planet's everyday life. The projects Araeen proposes in the second half of *Art Beyond Art*, such as *Food for Thought: Thought for Change* (2008), reach in this direction.

The Journey of the Idea

There is no journey without difficulties or an obstacle.[3]

Araeen opens *Art Beyond Art* by retelling the story of his own artistic formation and early engagement with modernist sculpture. What he calls the *idea* in the first two chapters, or rather texts, of this book gradually becomes clear. In both art and everyday life, the creative and inventive energies liberated by the free play of imagination are empowering, transforming, and contagious. But in the system of modernist art, the energies gathered and released in artistic production are traditionally cordoned off from the energies of free intellectual speculation, scientific research, and emancipatory critique. Confined to institutional circuits and commodified relays, these energies are not allowed to flow freely into and enliven the collective existence of the majority of people. One main means by which this boundary between art and life energies is enforced is the fostering of an individualized artistic identity anchored in the narcissistic ego, or 'narego' as Araeen will call it, and focused on the rewarded production of precious cultural assets. The *idea* appears in moments of insight, as Araeen reflects on the stimulations and challenges of his evolving artistic practice. Above all, the *idea* must move; in its forms and details, it cannot be fixed or arrested. The tendential content of the movement, however, can be described: the energies of art and life can be joined, if the artist lets go of the narego that supports art world career imperatives, coming to view art as a free process to be joined generously to the collective dimensions of everyday life. In those collective dimensions, where ordinary people seek to satisfy needs and cope with the stresses of contemporary existence, the free play of imagination can respond to issues of urgency with surprising and inspiring results. The *idea*, itself a movement of thinking, evokes a potential movement from individualist narego to collective membership, from object production to open process, and from the pursuit of self-advantage to generous mutuality. Art itself becomes 'a process of transformation within the everyday'.

The metaphor Araeen chooses to describe this movement by which the *idea* is discovered, clarified, and continuously expressed in new forms, is the 'constantly interrupted journey that has continually struggled against all attempts to stop or end it'. A journey, in Araeen's sense, is no mere tracing of a pre-given route, or unbroken line in space. Instead, a journey takes shape through encounters with blockage and resistance. Thus, his journey of the *idea* 'has taken all sorts of routes, sometimes going forward but other times, when it faces an unexpected obstacle, adopting a position that might appear to be a regression'. For Araeen, the resistance of obstacles becomes productive when it stimulates more movement, when the questions thrown up on the way bring into view another aspect of the *idea*. Stimulated by his encounters with the work of Anthony Caro in the mid-1960s, for example, Araeen developed a form of modernist sculpture based on symmetries of geometric structures, but that was non-compositional and non-hierarchical. Eventually experiencing the results as too static and limiting, Araeen opened a new space for movement. From fixed symmetrical Structures signed by an individualist ego, he develops a process to actively involve the audience in the continuous reorganization of sculptural fragments. Thus,

> in 1968, the idea becomes a concept postulating a constant transformation within and through the public domain. It is no longer the individualism of the artist but the collective energy of the public, which produces the dynamism of the journey and sustains its movement. By dismantling the artist's initial fixed symmetrical configuration and the producing of its own variations, it is the collective that turns the whole thing into an unending continuous process.

This invited participation that transforms the structured artwork becomes a metaphor for the popular transformation of social structures.

Zero to Infinity, the project opening the symmetrical monument to continuous reorganization by the public, was proposed to the Institute of Contemporary Arts (ICA) in London in 1968. While the project was finally realized in 2004, the ICA at the time never bothered to respond to Araeen's proposal. This disrespect, among others, exposed the biases and institutional power of modernist art, causing Araeen to ask: who writes art history, the history of Minimalism, for example, and for whose benefit? Who decides which artists are exhibited and which are excluded? The museum and gallery system, he comes to see, fuels the competitive narego and channels its activities into the reproduction of hierarchical power relations: 'Separated and disconnected from collective life, the narcissistic ego makes the idea whirl around its own axis, emitting an enormous centrifugal force that not only destroys the creative energy of the free collective imagination but subjects whatever is there in its way to bloody violence.' 305

For the next thirty years, he will try 'through a self-consciously critical process to confront and remove [the] obstacle [of institutional power]'. White supremacism is an unacknowledged aspect of that power and the ways in which it is exercised and performed. The journey does not, as Araeen puts it, 'carry with it the ID card

230
234

of its ethnicity.' The demand for and control of such IDs come, as it were, from the institutions. The confrontation with the racism of the art institutions of London opens another passage of the journey: the text 'Preliminary Notes for a BLACK MANIFESTO' (1975–1976), the performance *'Paki Bastard' (Portrait of the Artist as a Black Person)* (1977), and the anti-imperialist, anti-racist collaborative publication *Black Phoenix: Journal of Contemporary Art & Culture in the Third World* (1978–1979) were some of the productive results that Araeen marks in passing.[3] An 'extremely difficult dilemma' then emerges: 'Should [the idea] try to bypass the obstacle or come to terms with this institutional power?' Eventually, Araeen would reject the strategies of confrontation that he associates with some of the historical avant-gardes and which perhaps were enacted in some of his own texts and performances during the mid-to-late 1970s. 'There can be no absolute escape from the bourgeois socioeconomic and political system and its art institution, and that leaves us no choice but to negotiate our position – even when it is becoming extremely frustrating to maintain one's critical position within it.'

The attempt to move beyond direct confrontation and to negotiate a critical position within the institutions of art resulted in Araeen's founding of the journal and cooperative project *Third Text* in 1987. But the continuing reflection on institutional power and violence leads to a swerve in the journey that over time joins the search for collectivity to ecological concerns. As awareness of planetary ecocide grows, this energy becomes an urgent agency of survival. 'Only then, by thus freeing itself from the destructive narcissism of the bourgeois ego, art can and must now indicate a new way of constructing and organizing the life, a life which protects, nourishes and enriches *everything and everyone on this planet*.'[4] In that 'everything and everyone', human exceptionalism is refused. Survival will be a multi-species collaboration. In the project proposals and discussions of 'nominalism' and *cosmoruralism* that follow, Araeen elaborates this aspect of the *idea* and offers some practical visions.

From Land Art to Cosmoruralism

In the twenty-first century, Araeen has returned to the ideas of collective values and open public participation that inspired him in the 1960s. Under the pressure of planetary ecocide, it seems to me, these ideas evolved into the visionary projects of more-than-human mutuality, which take up the second half of *Art Beyond Art.* The journey or process by which these projects emerged are described by Araeen as new aspects and moments of the *idea*. Revisiting the landscapes of his native Pakistan, he began to reconsider Land Art. While exciting to Araeen, the large-scale projects of Robert Smithson and others were mostly, he now concludes, the self-indulgent interventions of artist-naregos, sometimes inflicted violently on landscapes and the living beings inhabiting them. Arguably, Land Art remained within the frameworks of modernist violence and human species supremacism. William Morris and the Arts and Crafts Movement seemed to offer Araeen a more promising and generous model for joining the creative energies of the free imagination to collective needs. Another key stimulus was *7000 Oaks*, Joseph Beuys' tree-planting project initiated in 1982 at documenta 7. Beuys' project activated possibilities for public participation and the deliberation of ecological concerns, but the German artist's shamanic persona was a form of *narego* still too distorted by the rivalries of the art system. Araeen was now searching for a form that would give scope to the free play of the imagination in addressing contemporary social and ecological urgencies, but which would at the same time inspire and invite collaboration and mutuality.

He explores the possibilities of what he first calls 'nominalism', or, as I read it, a reorganizing artistic attention directed to the material processes and systems of everyday life. Araeen's project proposals enact an intentional shift from artistic individualism to an aspiration for collective empowerment. 'If this shift could produce a collective agency capable of resisting individualism by its *self-sustaining creative and productive labour, it would produce its own legitimation*.' But if this agency would be a mobilization, as it were, of other people and their labour, which inspires them actively to transform their everyday situations into more mutually beneficial and sustainable patterns, then how will these people be engaged or enlisted? Araeen sees the formal dilemma here: his project proposals can only be invitations extended in openness; consent and collaboration can never be coerced.

Araeen's proposals are often addressed to people in the global South; they would be realized there, in collaboration with local communities. Indeed, these communities would be transformed by Araeen's projects. The 'artist' here is proposing visions that would re-pattern the local metabolic interaction with nature according to the values of mutuality, sustainability, and resilience. They are utopian prospective models, although Araeen insists that they are practical and realizable, rather than 'romantic'.

But how would such a collective agency and aim be organized or self-organized? The process begins with deliberation: 'Only when all the ideas are acceptable to the people and they are prepared to carry them forward, with their full understanding of its ideology and active material collaboration, [will] the project be pursued.' His 'artistic' projects constitute 'a body of propositions whose realization depends on the collective consciousness, vision and struggle of people themselves.' Even when the projects are grounded in the repurposing of existing and readily available technologies, realization is contingent on the vicissitudes of human desire and commitment. Certain theoretical, but also practical, tensions remain, then, but these would be common to most of the admired proposals of utopian literature and the history of communes.

For his efforts to defend the Niger Delta from the ecocidal violence of Royal Dutch Shell and other multinational energy corporations, the Ogoni writer and environmental justice activist Ken Saro-Wiwa was executed, along with eight comrades, by the Nigerian military regime in 1995. A coalition led by the London-based art group PLATFORM organized an open call for artistic proposals for a 'Living Memorial' to Saro-Wiwa on the tenth anniversary of his murder. In this context, Araeen developed his 'Saro-Wiwa Village' project proposal, which he shared with PLATFORM and others, but did not formally submit to the selection process. *Art Beyond Art* includes the proposal, which begins to constellate the concerns and approaches impressively at work in Araeen's other visions and projects. He is seeking here to re-establish the sustainable and regenerative circles of mutuality that have been pulled apart by colonialism, enclosure, profit, and extraction. In this aim, he comes close to the design methods of permaculture, a biophilic and mutualistic approach to growing food that draws on traditional and Indigenous practices – except that Araeen lets his artistic imagination and experience, in this case informed by his early engineering training, take the lead. As a 'living memorial' to Saro-Wiwa, he imagines a new village of about 100 families in Nigeria.

> While the basic economy of the village will be dependent on farming, using indigenous knowledge about agriculture combined with the scientific work done in organic farming, it should be supplemented by reviving African traditional arts and crafts, such as wood carving, pottery making, handmade textiles, rug making, etc.... [E]lectricity will be generated by solar power, an alternative to the oil which is the basis of the exploitation and oppression of the people in the Delta region of Nigeria.

The proposed village could 'also develop as a Pan-African centre for research in the field[s] of agriculture, water and energy resources specifically needed for developments in Africa.' Araeen attempts to support traditional and vernacular knowledges and skills, and to link them with some of the metabolic infrastructures of modernity; the village 'must have all the basic modern facilities such as electricity, clean water supply and sewerage system'.

The ethico-political impulse legible in this proposal is widely shared today, as many communities strive to work out their own local forms of sustainable and just inhabitation and their own hybrid assemblages of the modern and traditional. In the global North, networked grassroots movements are again experimenting with eco-villages and Transition Towns, based on the mutualities of shared commons, and DIY cultures of resilience are focused on re-skilling and skill sharing beyond the competitive economies of capital. In the global South, many Indigenous peoples, increasingly organized into alliances and networks such as La Via Campesina, are defending the life and water of local places from the disasters of imposed "development", are refusing the chemical-genetic monocultures of industrial agriculture, and are supporting sustainable alternative visions of *buen vivir* or 'good living'.[5] These movements and struggles for food, water, and energy sovereignty are undoubtedly enervated by the growing general awareness of planetary emergency and the systemic threats to life in what I call the 'endgame of modernity'.[6] In this sense, Araeen's *Art Beyond Art* is a pertinent document of awakening.

Food for Thought: Thought for Change

Araeen has continued to reflect on the workings of Eurocentrism and the still
unrealized promises of decolonization. *Mediterranea* (2007) one of the projects 309
elaborated in *Art Beyond Art*, reclaims the Mediterranean as the mutually enriching cultural crossroads of Europe, Asia, and Africa that it was before the force fields of modernity imposed relations of colonial domination. Instead of the European Union, Araeen proposes the imaginary multicultural community of a Mediterranean Union, connected by coastal railways (rather than airports) and sea lanes for wind- and sun-ships (not the giant container ships of capitalist economies). The Mediterranean, re-envisioned as an alternative to the exercise of European power through debt regimes and deadly border controls, seems indeed to be, for Araeen, a passionate enthusiasm of the imagination. In his essay 'Return to the Source: Art History as an Indicator of the Future', Araeen contributes an incisive reading of modernism and Africa that restores to visibility the erased figure of South African sculptor and painter Ernest Mancoba. For Araeen, Mancoba is 'Africa's most original modern artist', one who 'enters the space of modernism formed and perpetuated by the colonial myth of white racial supremacy and superiority – the very same myth on which apartheid was based and its violence justified – and demolishes it from within. He thus rejects the view that the colonized had no choice but to resort to mimicry.' In the same essay, Araeen pays tribute to Wangari Maathai, the Kenyan activist who was awarded the Nobel Peace Prize in 2004. 'Should one now be surprised that [the ecological vision of Beuys' *7000 Oaks*] had in fact already emerged in Africa, six or seven years before Beuys' work, and led to a systematic programme of tree planting?' In Maathai's Green Belt Movement, which has succeeded in planting millions of trees, Araeen finds a more generous enactment of the *idea*.

Araeen goes on, in the next text of *Art Beyond Art*, to regather these threads of thought, elaborating further his notion of cosmoruralism. Noting the obscene daily wastage of food in the global North (£12 billion's worth every year in Great Britain alone), he reviews the destructive insanities of modernity's industrial food system. The chemical and toxic inputs of industrial agriculture kill the life of the soil and establish vicious circles of depletion and desertification: as forests are replaced by fields and monocultural plantations, the rain and snow decreases, and the fossil aquifers are sucked down to make up the difference. Tree planting – reforestation – is thus central to Araeen's cosmorural vision: '[Wangari] Maathai knew, right from the start, that the destruction of trees was part of the destruction of traditional methods of farming in Africa, and both the poverty of people and environmental degradation were the results of this destruction.' An alliance between science and tradition, for the sustainable production of safe food and restored landscapes, is now possible, Araeen argues. Indeed, permaculture and what La Via Campesina calls 'agroecology' are dedicated to developing and sharing proven alternatives to the chemical-genetic industrial methods still pushed today by multinationals and the agencies of global governance.[7]

Araeen begins to imagine a network of collective farms organized on principals of sustainability and mutuality, which goes beyond the faltering altruism of the global North and aims at restoring the local forms of self-reliance that modernity has deliberately undermined and destroyed. 'The idea of collective farms or cooperatives in Africa may appear an unrealizable utopian dream, but it is not.' Araeen now seeks a practical project that would model a new mutuality between global North and South. He proposes 'a chain of restaurants throughout Britain, run largely on the rescued surplus food from the supermarkets before it is destined to dustbins'. Running the numbers, he finds that each restaurant could 'be started with an initial modest capital of £250,000, repaid within a year'. The money that the restaurants thereafter earn could, he proposes, be used to establish a sustainable village in Africa, working with and through local organizations such as the one already run by Wangari Maathai. 'This idea of such [an] African village is primarily to recover a tradition of agriculture that was organic and holistically productive, which not only provided sustenance but had a creative culture.' If the project is embraced by its intended collaborators, the model village might in time be extended to networks of villages on the same principals of mutuality, sustainability, and restored self-reliance.

Cosmoruralism, as Araeen elaborates it, thus entails a critique of modernity and its urban-industrial values and logics. The promise of these values and logics – cosmopolitanism – entered history as a transformative and emancipatory energy. But that promise and energy are now, Araeen asserts, exhausted. For documenta 14 in 2017, Araeen created a variation on *Food for Thought: Thought for Change*, called *Shamiyaana*, after the word for the colourful traditional Pakistani wedding tent. In Kotzia Square in central Athens, *Shamiyaana* served smeals to the public twice a day, at small tables conducive to discussion. The food was sourced and prepared by Organization Earth, a local NGO committed to preserving methods of sustainable traditional agriculture and to teaching 'environmental and social intelligence' to young people. 358

Precaution and Mutuality

> Only when all that constitutes the earth – its biosphere, its rivers, seas and oceans (and the life they contain), its forests, the icecaps of its northern and southern spheres, its animal and insect lives, its flora and fauna – is left alone, freed from the insatiable greed of the urbanized human desire, [will] humanity recover from its present state of violence and brutality not only against itself but what is in nature necessary for the life's survival and its betterment in the future.[8]

Critics of the term 'Anthropocene' have noted that the social processes and logics actually driving climate chaos and ecocide are obscured under an abstracted 'human species'. Critical counter-terms – such as 'Capitalocene' (Jason Moore, Andreas Malm, and Donna Haraway), 'Necrocene' (Justin McBrien), and 'Chthulucene' (Haraway) – have enabled a fuller political discussion of the causes and stakes of the planetary emergency.[9] The global oligarchs and the governments of dominant nation-states continue to defend the competitive economics of accumulation, as if this core logic of modernity was not the major driver of ecocide. The refusal to subordinate economic growth to ecological realities supports a number of political tendencies. National energy security, so-called, will be pursued to the detriment of all initiatives from below for local and sustainable energy sovereignty. Extreme energy extraction, such as hydraulic fracturing, mountaintop removal, and tar sands extraction, will continue so long as it is profitable, and every government effort will be made to ensure that it remains profitable. Greenhouse gas emissions will in practice, therefore, not be contained or reduced, and climate chaos, global warming, and species extinction will continue to accelerate. States, corporations, and financial institutions will continue to support the spread of profitable chemical-genetic-industrial monoculture, regardless of their ecocidal effects. New enclosures and land-grabs will continue to drive communities of traditional small farmers and peasants off their land bases, and the shift to agroecology and permaculture will continue to be blocked from above. Given these tendencies, so-called adaptation to global warming becomes the obvious national security imperative, which will generate unending new conflicts among rival nation-states. What states, which citizens, will be able or willing to shore up inundated cities or extend refuge to climate refugees fleeing drought, famine, or super storms? As the result of all the foregoing tendencies, the pathways of political least resistance lead to geo-engineering experiments on a planetary scale, for these appear to address the "problem" without disturbing established economies and power relations.

There are alternatives to these tendencies, and these alternatives begin with cultural shifts in values and localized efforts to change the energetics and metabolics of everyday life. These shifts and efforts are underway, and in *Art Beyond Art*, Araeen brings the artistic imagination to bear in supporting them. This support is a timely and helpful contribution, full of generosity and an admirable reach for a more-than-human mutuality. The one worry I would have about this work is that the commitment to the journey of the *idea*, understood as the free play of the creative imagination, is not enough qualified, and the enthusiasm for engineering solutions not enough moderated; while Araeen's projects are very different from the dangerous geo-engineering schemes now steadily being normalized and prepared, they do seem to share a certain enthusiasm for designed solutions. The risk is that the ecological effects of such interventions cannot be known and anticipated, and that, as has happened so often before, the unintended consequences may cause new or greater harm. This risk would be one of the theoretical implications that Araeen acknowledged in passing. More differentiation between his cosmoruralist projects and the schemes of the new geo-engineers, as well as discussion in this context of the precautionary principle, would be welcome. The truly radical move of *Art Beyond Art*, and the necessary one in my view, is the refusal of human species supremacism. Araeen's call for a culture of more-than-human mutuality is clear. However, we don't know enough about the processes by which such a culture could spread, gain practical traction, and gradually change the patterns of everyday life. Neither the social scientists, nor the critical theorists, nor the activists can, I believe, justly claim to understand these processes of change. But I would wager, with Araeen, that social change always needs the energies and inspirations of the creative imagination and the generosities of the opened heart.[10]

1 Rasheed Araeen, *Art Beyond Art, Ecoaesthetics: A Manifesto for the 21st Century* (London: Third Text Publications, 2010), 39.
2 Gene Ray, 'Resisting Extinction: Standing Rock, Eco-Genocide, and Survival', *South as a State of Mind*, no. 9, documenta 14 special guest issue, no. 4 (2017).
3 See Araeen, *Art Beyond Art*.
4 Araeen, *Art Beyond Art*, 40, my emphasis.
5 On La Via Campesina and *buen vivir*, see https://viacampesina.org/fr/index.php.
6 See Gene Ray, 'Writing the Ecocide-Genocide Knot: Indigenous Knowledge and Critical Theory in the Endgame', *South as a State of Mind*, no. 8, documenta 14 special guest issue, no. 3 (2016).
7 On La Via Campesina and agroecology, see website cited previously.
8 See Araeen, *Art Beyond Art*.
9 See Jason W. Moore, ed., *Anthropocene or Capitalocene?: Nature, History, and the Crisis of Capitalism* (Oakland: PM Press, 2016).
10 Warm thanks to Gabriella Calchi Novati for her careful critical reading of this text, and to Rasheed Araeen for many years of generous discussion and friendly support.

Nick Aikens is a curator at the Van Abbemuseum, Eindhoven since 2012. He is a Research Affiliate of the CCC Research Master Program, HEAD – Geneva School of Art and Design and a member of the editorial board for L'Internationale Online. He is a course leader at the Dutch Art Institute and was recently a tutor at the Design Academy Eindhoven.

Kate Fowle is chief curator at Garage Museum of Contemporary Art, Moscow and director-at-large at Independent Curators International (ICI) in New York. From 2009 to 2013 she was executive director of ICI. Previously she was the inaugural international curator at the Ullens Center for Contemporary Art in Beijing and chair of the Master's Program in Curatorial Practice, which she co-founded in 2002 for California College of the Arts in San Francisco. Before moving to the United States Fowle was co-director of Smith + Fowle in London. From 1994 to 1996 she was curator at Towner Art Gallery and Museum in Eastbourne, East Sussex.

Courtney J. Martin is deputy director and chief curator at Dia Art Foundation. Her previous positions include: Assistant Professor in the History of Art and Architecture Department, Brown University; Assistant Professor in the History of Art Department, Vanderbilt University; Chancellor's Postdoctoral Fellow in the History of Art, University of California, Berkeley; Fellow at Getty Research Institute; and a Henry Moore Institute Research Fellow. In 2015 she received an Andy Warhol Foundation Arts Writers Grant. She has also worked in the media, arts, and culture unit of the Ford Foundation in New York. In 2012, she curated a focus display at Tate Britain, *Drop, Roll, Slide, Drip... Frank Bowling's Poured Paintings 1973–8*. In 2014, she co-curated the group show, *Minimal Baroque: Post-Minimalism and Contemporary Art*, at Rønnebæksholm, Næstved, Denmark. From 2008 to 2015 she co-led a research project on the Anglo-American art critic Lawrence Alloway at Getty Research Institute and is co-editor of *Lawrence Alloway: Critic and Curator* (Getty Publications, 2015, winner of the 2016 Historians of British Art Book Award). In 2015 she curated an exhibition of the American painter, Robert Ryman at Dia Art Foundation. She is the editor of *Four Generations: The Joyner Giuffrida Collection of Abstract Art* (2016).

Michael Newman is Professor of Art Writing at Goldsmiths, University of London. He has published numerous essays on modern and contemporary artists, as well as thematic essays on the wound, the horizon, contingency, memory, drawing, and nonsense. He is the author of 'Stuart Brisley: Performing the Political Body and Eating Shit' in *Stuart Brisley* (2015), *Price, Seth* (2010), *Jeff Wall: Works and Writings* (2007), and *Richard Prince Untitled (couple)* (2006). He is co-editor of *The State of Art Criticism* (2007) and *Rewriting Conceptual Art* (1999). He has curated exhibitions including: *Drawing after Bellmer in Europe, North America and Japan*, The Drawing Room, London, upcoming; *Revolver II* (co-curated with Robin Klassnik), Matt's Gallery, London, 2014; and *Tacita Dean*, Art Gallery of York University, Toronto, 2000. The first volume of his selected writings, *'I know very well...but all the same': Essays on Artists of the Still and Moving Image* is forthcoming with Ridinghouse.

Dominic Rahtz is Reader in History and Theory of Contemporary Art at University for the Creative Arts in Canterbury. His research lies principally in the area of 1960s and 1970s American and European art. Recent publications include 'Dematerialization and /Cloud/' in *In Terms of Painting* (2016), 'Indifference of Material in the Work of Carl Andre and Robert Smithson' in *Oxford Art Journal* (2012), and 'Daniel Buren's Theoretical Practice' in *Spatialities: The Geographies of Art and Architecture* (2012).

Gene Ray is Associate Professor of Critical Studies in the CCC Research Master Program, HEAD – Geneva School of Art and Design. He is author of *Terror and the Sublime in Art and Critical Theory* (2005) and his essays have appeared in *Third Text*, *Brumaria*, *Historical Materialism*, *Yale Journal of Criticism*, and *South as a State of Mind*.

John Roberts is Professor of Art & Aesthetics at the University of Wolverhampton, and the author of a number of books including, *Thoughts on an Index Not Freely Given* (2016), *Revolutionary Time and the Avant-Garde* (2015), *The Necessity of Errors* (2011), *and The Intangibilities of Form: Skill and Deskilling in Art After the Readymade* (2007). His *The Reasoning of Unreason* is forthcoming from Bloomsbury.

Marcus du Sautoy is Simonyi Professor for the Public Understanding of Science and Professor of Mathematics at University of Oxford and a Fellow of New College. In 2016 he was made a Fellow of the Royal Society. He is the author of four popular science books including his most recent book *What We Cannot Know* (2016). He has presented numerous radio and TV series' including the four-part landmark for the BBC called *The Story of Maths* (2008). He works extensively with a range of arts organizations, from The Royal Opera House to the Glastonbury Festival, to bring science to life for the public. In 2009 he was awarded the Royal Society's Faraday Prize, the UK's premiere award for excellence in communicating science. He received an OBE for services to science in the 2010 New Year's Honours List.

Zöe Sutherland is Senior Lecturer at University of Brighton, where she teaches philosophy, critical theory, radical politics, and aesthetics. Her current research is on twentieth- and twenty-first-century art practices, with a focus on the so-called "global" character of the contemporary art world. Her recent article 'The World as Gallery: Conceptualism and Global Neo-Avant-Garde' published in *New Left Review*, critically analyses the claim that Conceptual art of the 1960s through 1970s was the first truly global movement. In addition to contemporary art theory and practice, she also writes in the area of materialist and Marxist feminisms, focusing on debates around social reproduction.

Kaelen Wilson-Goldie is a contributing editor for *Bidoun* who writes regularly for *Artforum*, *Bookforum*, and *Frieze*. She has travelled extensively in the Middle East and North Africa to report on the relationship between contemporary art and political upheaval, writing for newspapers, magazines, and journals including *Afterall*, *Aperture*, *Parkett*, and *New York Times* among others. In 2007 she was a fellow in the USC Annenberg Getty Arts Journalism Program. She won a grant from the Creative Capital Andy Warhol Foundation Arts Writers Program in 2014. She is working on a book about contemporary art in post-war reconstruction-era Beirut, to be published by Kaph Books in 2019.

Rasheed Araeen

1935 born in Karachi, Pakistan
1962 receives Bachelor of Engineering in Civil Engineering, NED Engineering College, University of Karachi
1964 arrives in London
1964–1965 architectural draughtsman with Wimpey Construction Co, London
1965–1969 assistant architect/civil engineer, BHC/BP, London
1972 joins the Black Panther movement
1978 co-founds *Black Phoenix: Journal of Contemporary Art & Culture in the Third World* (three issues until 1979)
1982 founds *Project MRB*, to conduct research into the history of black artists
1984 publishes *Making Myself Visible* (Kala Press)
1987 founds *Third Text* (editor until 2011)
1988 initiates and curates *Essential Black Art*, Chisenhale Gallery, London
1989 initiates and curates *The Other Story: Afro-Asian Artists in Post-War Britain*, Hayward Gallery, London
2008 founds *Third Text Asia*
2010 publishes *Art Beyond Art, Ecoaesthetics: A Manifesto for the 21st Century* (Third Text Publications)

Select Solo Exhibitions

2017–2019 *Rasheed Araeen: A Retrospective*, Van Abbemuseum, Eindhoven; MAMCO, Musée d'art moderne et contemporain, Geneva; BALTIC Centre for Contemporary Art, Gateshead; Garage Museum of Contemporary Art, Moscow
2016 *Geometry and Symmetry, New Works by Rasheed Araeen*, Aicon Gallery, New York
2015 *Rasheed Araeen–Minimalism Then and Now*, 1960 – present, Aicon Gallery, New York
Going East, Rossi & Rossi, Hong Kong
2014 *Rasheed Araeen: Before and After Minimalism*, Sharjah Art Foundation
Rasheed Araeen: Homecoming, VM Art Gallery, Karachi
2013 *Zero to Infinity*, Museo de Arte de Lima – MALI
2012 *Zero to Infinity*, Tate Modern, London
2010 *Before and After Minimalism, 1959–1974*, Aicon Gallery, London
2004 *Zero to Infinity*, 198 Gallery, London
1997 The Art Gallery of New South Wales, Sydney
Middlesbrough Art Gallery, Middlesbrough, UK
1996 The Contemporary Art Centre, Vilnius
To Whom It May Concern, Serpentine Gallery (external project), London
1995 John Hansard Gallery, Southampton
1994 South London Gallery
Škuc Gallery, Ljubljana
5th Havana Biennial
1993 *Rasheed Araeen: Strife and/or Structure*, Fukuoka Asian Art Museum, Fukuoka, Japan
1991 *What's it All Bongo*, Central Space, London
The Golden Verses, in collaboration with the Artangel Trust, London
1988 *Rasheed Araeen: When the Innocent Begins to Walk the Earth*, The Showroom, London
1987 *From Modernism to Postmodernism: Rasheed Araeen, A Retrospective*, Ikon Gallery, Birmingham; Cornerhouse, Manchester; John Hansard Gallery, Southampton; and Chapter, Cardiff
1986 *White Power, Black Sexuality*, Pentonville Gallery, London
1984 *Rasheed Araeen: Recent Work*, Pentonville Gallery, London
1977 *'Paki Bastard' (Portrait of the Artist as a Black Person)*, Artists for Democracy, London
1975 *Works 1965–75*, Artists for Democracy, London
1974 Indus Gallery, Karachi
1963 Arts Council of Pakistan Gallery, Karachi

Select Group Exhibitions

2017 *Learning from Athens*, documenta 14, Athens and Kassel
Viva Arte Viva, 57th International Art Exhibition, Venice Biennale
Occasional Geometries, Yorkshire Sculpture Park, Wakefield, UK
Caro/Araeen: A Conversation, Grosvenor Gallery, London
The Creative Act: Performance, Process, Presence, Guggenheim Abu Dhabi
The Place Is Here, Nottingham Contemporary; Middlesbrough Institute of Modern Art; and South London Gallery
2016 *Playgrounds 2016*, Museu de Arte de São Paulo
The 1980s: Today's Beginnings?, Van Abbemuseum, Eindhoven
Postwar: Art Between the Pacific and the Atlantic, 1945–1965, Haus der Kunst, Munich

Picking up the Pieces: Collage in Post-War Britain, Grosvenor Gallery, London
Jameel Prize 4, Pera Museum, Istanbul
BMW Tate Live, Tate Modern, London
Between Structure and Matter: Other Minimal Futures, Aicon Gallery, New York

2015 *Adventures of the Black Square: Abstract Art and Society 1915–2015*, Whitechapel Gallery, London

2014 *Dark Waters*, Galerie Chantal Crousel, Paris
Other Primary Structures, The Jewish Museum, New York
As Exciting as We Can Make It: Ikon in the 1980s, Ikon Gallery, Birmingham
The Language of Human Consciousness, Athr Gallery, Jeddah, Saudi Arabia

2012 ROUNDTABLE, 9th Gwangju Biennale
Migrations: Journeys into British Art, Tate Britain, London
Reactivation, 9th Shanghai Biennale

2011 *Old Intersections – Make It New*, 3rd Thessaloniki Biennial of Contemporary Art, Greek State Museum of Contemporary Art, Thessaloniki
Situation Z, Art-cade, Galerie des grands bains douches de la plaine, Marseille
The Global Contemporary: Art Worlds After 1989, ZKM Centre for Art and Media, Karlsruhe
Super Farmers' Market, Handel Street Projects, London
Modern British Sculpture, Royal Academy, London

2010 *Raising Dust*, Calvert 22 Foundation, London
A Missing History: 'The Other Story' Re-visited, Aicon Gallery, London

2009 *The Death of the Audience*, Vienna Secession

2007 BP Annual Display, Tate Britain, London

2001 *Live in Your Head: Concept and Experiment in Great Britain 1965–75*, National Museum of Contemporary Art – Museu do Chiado Lisbon

2000 *Live in Your Head: Concept and Experiment in Great Britain 1965–75*, Whitechapel Gallery, London

1999 *Art-Worlds in Dialogue: From Gauguin to the Global Present*, Museum Ludwig, Cologne

1998 *Every Day*, 11th Biennale of Sydney

1997 *Trade Routes: History and Geography*, 2nd Johannesburg Biennale, South Africa

1996 *Inklusion: Exklusion*, Steirischer Herbst, Graz, Austria

1995 *Dialogue for PEACE*, Palais de Nations, Geneva
Art/Politics, Kean College of New Jersey

1991 *Lost Illusions: Recent Landscape Art*, Vancouver Art Gallery, Canada
The Challenge of Colonisation, 4th Havana Biennial
Interrogating Identity, Grey Art Gallery and Study Center, New York University; Museum of Fine Arts, Boston; Walker Art Center, Minneapolis; Madison Art Center, Wisconsin; Center for the Fine Arts, Miami; Oberlin College Gallery, Ohio; and Duke University Museum of Art, Durham

1990 *A New Necessity*, First Tyne International of Contemporary Art, Gateshead, UK

1989 *The Other Story: Afro-Asian Artists in Post-War Britain*, Hayward Gallery, London; Wolverhampton Art Gallery; Manchester City Art Gallery; and Cornerhouse, Manchester
Magiciens de la terre, Centre George Pompidou and Grande Halle de la Villette, Paris

1988 *Essential Black Art*, Chisenhale Gallery, London; Laing Art Gallery, Newcastle-upon-Tyne; Huddersfield Art Gallery; Herbert Art Gallery and Museum, Coventry; Gardner Art Centre, Sussex University; and Cooper Gallery, Barnsley

1987 *Heroes*, A.I.R. Gallery, London
State of the Nation, Herbert Art Gallery and Museum, Coventry
Conceptual Clothing, Ikon Gallery, Birmingham
From Two Worlds, Whitechapel Gallery, London

1986 *THIRD WORLD WITHIN: a cross section of work by AfroAsian artists in Britain*, Brixton Art Gallery, London

1985 *Roadworks*, Brixton Art Gallery, London

1984 *Creation for Liberation Open Exhibition*, Brixton Art Gallery, London

1983 *New Beginning*, Pentonville Gallery, London

1982 *New Art Platform*, Midland Group Gallery, Nottingham

1980 *Accrochage*, Gimpel Fils, London
Koffer fur Rottweil, Forum Kunst, Rottweil and Kunstverein, Freiburg, Germany
Kontact: From Contemplation to Agitation, Galleria MDM, Warsaw

1979 *Art from the British Left*, Artists Space, New York
Tape/Slide Show, Audio Arts, Riverside Studios, London
Art/Politics, Kean College of New Jersey

1978 *Art for Society*, Whitechapel Gallery, London

1975 *Vietnam Festival*, Artists for Democracy, London

1973 *Artists from Five Continents*, Swiss Cottage Library, London

1971 *SPACE*, Midland Group Gallery, Nottingham
SPACE, Geffrye Museum, London

1970 *Manufactured Art*, Camden Arts Centre, London

1969 John Moore's Liverpool Biennial

Public Collections

Albright-Knox Art Gallery, Buffalo
Art Institute of Chicago, Chicago
Arts Council England
Athr Gallery, Jeddah, Saudi Arabia
Burger Collection, Hong Kong
Centre Georges Pompidou, Paris
Contemporary Art Centre, Vilnius
Fukuoka Asian Art Museum, Fukuoka, Japan
Guggenheim Abu Dhabi
Gwangju Biennale Foundation
Imperial War Museum, London
Kiran Nadar Museum of Art, New Delhi
M+, Hong Kong
Metropolitan Museum of Art, New York
Museum of Modern Art, Rio de Janeiro
Queensland Art Gallery and Gallery of Modern Art
Samdani Foundation, Bangladesh
Sharjah Art Foundation
Tate, London
National Museums Liverpool, Walker Art Gallery, Liverpool
Wifredo Lam Centre, Havana
ZKM Centre for Art and Media, Karlsruhe

Prizes and Awards

2014 ArtNow Lifetime Achievement Award, Karachi Dubai

2003 Honorary Doctor of Arts (PhD), University of Wolverhampton

1997 Honorary Doctor of Arts (PhD), University of East London

1995 Honorary Doctor of Letters (PhD), University of Southampton

1984 GLC's Antiracist Painting Prize, London

1978 Award, Arts Council of Great Britain

1969 John Moore's 7, Walker Art Gallery, Liverpool

1955 Burmah-Shell Greeting Cards Competition prize, Karachi

Select Bibliography and Catalogues

2016 Araeen, Rasheed. *Going East*. Hong Kong: Rossi Rossi. (exh. cat.)
Orlando, Sophie. *British Black Art: Debates on Western Art History*. Paris: Dis Voir.

2014 Ali, Amra (ed.). *Rasheed Araeen: Homecoming*. Karachi: VM Art Gallery.
Araeen, Rasheed et al. *The Triumph of Icarus: Life and Art of Rasheed Araeen*. Ed. Jean Fisher. Karachi: Millennium Media.
Chambers, Eddie. *Black Artists in British Art: A History since the 1950s*. London: I. B. Tauris.

2013 Araeen, Rasheed, McEvilley, Thomas, Buchloh, Benjamin, and Lucy Steeds. *Making Art Global (Part 2): 'Magiciens de la Terre' 1989* (Exhibition Histories). London: Afterall Books.
Rasheed Araeen: Before and After Minimalism. Sharjah: Sharjah Art Foundation.
Bäckström, Per and Benedikt Hjartarson (ed.). *Decentring the Avant-Garde (Avant-Garde Critical Studies)*. Amsterdam: Rodopi.
Belting, Hans, Buddensieg, Andrea, and Peter Weibel (ed.). *The Global Contemporary and the Rise of New Art Worlds*. Cambridge, MA: MIT Press.
Moxey, Keith. *Visual Time: The Image in History*. Durham: Duke University Press.

2012 Chambers, Eddie. *Things Done Change: The Cultural Politics of Recent Black Artists in Britain* (Cross Cultures 144). Amsterdam: Rodopi.
Dewdney, Andrew, Dibosa, David, and Victoria Walsh. *Post-Critical Museology: Theory and Practice in the Art Museum*. London: Routledge.
Manz, Stefan and Panikos Panayi (ed.). 'Refugees and Cultural Transfer to Britain.' In *Immigrants & Minorities* 30, no. 2–3.
Newall, Diana and Grant Pooke (ed.). *Fifty Key Texts in Art History*. New York: Routledge.
Papastergiadis, Nikos. *Cosmopolitanism and Culture*. Cambridge: Polity Press.

2011 Allen, Gwen. *Artists' Magazines: An Alternative Space for Art*. Cambridge, MA: MIT Press.
Harris, Jonathan (ed.). *Globalization and Contemporary Art*. Hoboken, NJ: Wiley-Blackwell.
Mirza, Munira. *The Politics of Culture: The Case for Universalism*. London: Palgrave Macmillan.
Pooke, Grant. *Contemporary British Art: An Introduction*. London: Routledge.

2010 Appignanesi, Richard (ed.). *Beyond Cultural Diversity: The Case for Creativity*. London: Third Text Publications.
Araeen, Rasheed, Gooding, Mel, and Leon Wainwright. *Aubrey Williams*. London: October Gallery. (exh. cat.)
Araeen, Rasheed. *Art Beyond Art, Ecoaesthetics: A Manifesto for the 21st Century*. London: Third Text Publications.
Dadi, Iftikhar. *Modernism and the Art of Muslim South Asia*. Chapel Hill: University of North Carolina Press.
Elkins, James, Valiavicharska, Zhivka, and Alice Kim (ed.). *Art and Globalization*. University Park, PA: Pennsylvania State University Press.
Jacob, Mary Jane and Michelle Grabner (ed.). *The Studio Reader: On the Space of Artists*. Chicago: University of Chicago Press.
Philipsen, Lotte. *Globalizing Contemporary Art*. Aarhus: Aarhus University Press.
Malik, Amna. *Rasheed Araeen: Before and After Minimalism 1959–1974*. London: Aicon Gallery. (exh. cat.)

2009 Alberro, Alexander and Blake Stimson (ed.). *Institutional Critique: An Anthology of Artists' Writings*. Cambridge, MA: MIT Press.
Mersmann, Birgit and Alexandra Schneider (ed.). *Transmission Image: Visual Translation and Cultural Agency*. Newcastle: Cambridge Scholars Publishing.

2008 Araeen, Rasheed (ed.). *Third Text* 21, no. 5–6
González, Jennifer A. *Subject to Display: Reframing Race in Contemporary Installation Art*. Cambridge, MA: MIT Press.
Mercer, Kobena (ed.). *Exiles, Diasporas & Strangers*. Cambridge, MA: MIT Press.

2007 Araeen, Rasheed (ed.). *Third Text* 21, no. 1–4.
Brandon, Laura. *Art and War*. London: I. B. Tauris.
Buddensieg, Andrea and Peter Weibel (ed.). *Contemporary Art and the Museum: A Global Perspective*. Ostfildern: Hatje Cantz.
Jeffery, Celina and Gregory Minissale (ed.). *Global and Local Art Histories*. Newcastle: Cambridge Scholars Publishing.
Ramadan, Khaled D. (ed.). *Peripheral Insider: Perspectives on Contemporary Internationalism in Visual Culture*. Copenhagen: Museum Tusculanum.

2006 Jones, Amelia (ed.). *A Companion to Contemporary Art since 1945*. Malden, MA: Blackwell Publishing.
Stallabrass, Julian. *Contemporary Art: A Very Short Introduction*. Oxford: Oxford University Press.

2005 Bailey, David A., Baucom, Ian, and Sonia Boyce. *Shades of Black: Assembling Black Arts in 1980s Britain*. Durham: Duke University Press.
Mercer, Kobena (ed.). *Cosmopolitan Modernisms*. Cambridge, MA and London: MIT Press and Institute of International Visual Arts.
Taylor, Brandon. *Contemporary Art: Art Since 1970*. Upper Saddle River, NJ: Pearson Prentice Hall.

2004 Arana, R. Victoria and Lauri Ramey (ed.). *Black British Writing*. New York: Palgrave Macmillan.
Stallabrass, Julian. *Art Incorporated: The Story of Contemporary Art*. Oxford: Oxford University Press.

2003 Addison, Nicholas and Lesley Burgess (ed.). *Issues in Art and Design Teaching*. London: RoutledgeFalmer.

2002 Araeen, Rasheed (ed.). *The Third Text Reader: On Art, Culture, and Theory*. London: Continuum.
Donnell, Alison (ed.). *Companion to Contemporary Black British Culture*. London: Routledge.
Pinder, Kymberly N. *Race-ing Art History: Critical Readings in Race and Art History*. New York: Routledge.
Walker, John Albert. *Left Shift: Radical Art in 1970s Britain*. London: I. B. Tauris.

2001 Araeen, Rasheed et al. *Das Museum als Arena Institutionskritische Texte von Künstlerinnen* (The Museum as Arena: Artists on Institutional Critique). Cologne: König.
Araeen, Rasheed et al. *Remarks on Interventive Tendencies: Meetings between Different Economies in Contemporary Art*. Copenhagen: Borgens.
Carson, Fiona and Claire Pajaczkowska. *Feminist Visual Culture*. New York: Routledge.
Davies, Alistair, and Alan Sinfield (ed.). *British Culture of the Postwar: An Introduction to Literature and Society 1945–1995*. London: Routledge.
Welchman, John C. *Art after Appropriation: Essays on Art in the 1990s*. London: Routledge.

2000 Doy, Gen. *Black Visual Culture: Modernity and Postmodernity*. London: I. B. Tauris.
Owusu, Kwesi (ed.). *Black British Culture & Society: A Text Reader*. London: Routledge.

1999 Giles, Judy and Tim Middleton. *Studying Culture: A Practical Introduction*. Oxford: Blackwell.
King, Catherine (ed.). *Views of Difference: Different Views of Art (Art and Its Histories Series)*. New Haven: Yale University Press.

1996 Baker, Houston A., Diawara, Manthia, and Ruth

Lindeborg (ed.). *Black British Cultural Studies: A Reader*. Chicago: University of Chicago Press.

1994 Araeen, Rasheed and Jean Fisher. *Global Visions: Towards a New Internationalism in the Visual Arts*. London: Kala Press with the Institute of International Visual Arts.

Mercer, Kobena. *Welcome to the Jungle: New Positions in Black Cultural Studies*. New York: Routledge.

Overy, Paul. *Rasheed Araeen*. London: South London Gallery. (exh. cat.)

Weedon, Chris and Glenn Jordan. *Cultural Politics: Class, Gender, Race and the Postmodern World*. London: Blackwell.

1993 Araeen, Rasheed (et al.). *Disparities and Connection: The Excluded on Postmodernism*. Chicago: Axe St. Arena, (exh. cat.)

Gilroy, Paul. *Small Acts: Thoughts on the Politics of Black Cultures*. London: Serpent's Tail.

Kuroda, Raiji (ed.). *Rasheed Araeen: Strife and/or Structure*. Fukuoka: Fukuoka Asian Art Museum.

1991 Araeen, Rasheed (ed.). 'Spectacular Failures'. Special Issue. *Third Text* 5, no. 14 (spring).

Hiller, Susan (ed.). *The Myth of Primitivism: Perspectives on Art*. London: Routledge.

Disparities and Connection: The Excluded on Postmodernism (introduction by Elizam Escobar). Chicago: Axe St. Arena.

Jones, Kellie, Phillips, Meredith L., and Sokolowski, Thomas W. *Interrogating Identity*. New York: Grey Art Gallery and Study Center.

1990 *Third Text* 4, no. 10–12 (spring/summer/fall).

Roberts, John. *Approaches to Realism*. Liverpool: Bluecoat Gallery.

The Golden Verses: A Billboard Artwork by Rasheed Araeen. London: Artangel Trust.

1989 Araeen, Rasheed (ed.). *Third Text* 3, no. 7–9 (summer/autumn/winter). London: Kala Press.

-----*The Other Story: Afro-Asian Artists in Post-War Britain*. London: Southbank Centre.

1988 Araeen, Rasheed. *The Essential Black Art*. London: Chisenhale Gallery.

Thorp, David. *Rasheed Araeen: When the Innocent Begins to Walk the Earth*. London: The Showroom.

1987 Araeen, Rasheed, Kingston, Angela, and Antonia Payne (ed.). *From Modernism to Postmodernism: Rasheed Araeen: A Retrospective: 1959–1987*. Birmingham: Ikon Gallery.

1986 Araeen, Rasheed, Serota, Nicholas, Kirby, Rachel, and Whitechapel Gallery. *From Two Worlds*. London: Whitechapel Gallery.

Newman, Michael. *Rasheed Araeen: White Power, Black Sexuality*. London: Pentonville Gallery.

1984 Araeen, Rasheed. *Making Myself Visible*. London: Kala Press.

Rasheed Araeen: Recent Work. London: Pentonville Gallery.

Rasheed Araeen: A Retrospective

Exhibition List

All works courtesy the artist and Araeen Family Collection, unless otherwise stated

In the Beginning: 1953–

Views of Karachi, 1953–1956
series of 11 watercolours on paper
various dimensions

People of Karachi I, 1955–1959
series of 24 works on paper, 56 x 41 cm each

Boats: Towards Abstraction, 1958–1962
series of 9 works on paper, various dimensions
M+ Museum Collection, Hong Kong

My First Sculpture, 1959
steel wire, dimensions variable

Ham Raqs, 1959
painting, oil on canvas, 64 x 41 cm

Dancing Bodies (Hula-Hoop Series), 1959–1962
series of 10 works on paper, various dimensions
Sharjah Art Foundation Collection

Burning Bicycle Tyres, 1959 (1975 reconstruction)
series of 9 photographs, twisted metal
dimensions variable

Red and Yellow, 1961
oil on board, 91 x 61 cm

Aag ka Naach, 1961
oil on board, 91 x 61 cm

Aag, 1961
oil on board, 91 x 61cm

Untitled (B Series), 1962
series of 6 works on paper, 28 x 41 cm

Hyderabad Series, 1962–1963
six works on paper, various dimensions

Before Departure (Black Painting No. IV), 1963
oil on canvas, 91 x 99 cm
Sharjah Art Foundation Collection

Before Departure (Black Painting No. V), 1963
oil on canvas, 91 x 122 cm
Sharjah Art Foundation Collection

Before Departure (Black Painting No. VI), 1963
oil on canvas, 91 x 73 cm
Sharjah Art Foundation Collection

Before Departure (Painting 71), 1964
oil on canvas, 91 x 91 cm
Sharjah Art Foundation Collection

Before Departure (Black Painting No. VIII), 1964
oil on canvas, 91 x 139 cm
Sharjah Art Foundation Collection

Geometry and Symmetry: 1964–

Sculpture No. 1 (Purple), 1965 / 2017
powder coated steel, 31 x 183 x 183 cm

Sculpture No. 3 (Silver Grey), 1965 / 2017
powder coated steel, 150 x 120 x 120 cm

Drawing for Sculpture No. 3, 1965
graphite on paper, 25 x 20 cm
Private collection, London

Drawing for Sculpture, 1965
graphite on paper, 25 x 20 cm
Tate: Presented by Tate Members 2011

Drawing for Sculpture, 1965
graphite on paper, 25 x 20 cm
Tate: Presented by Tate Members 2011

Drawing for Sculpture, 1966
graphite on paper, 32 x 20 cm
Tate: Presented by Tate Members 2011

Drawing for Sculpture, 1966
graphite on paper, 32 x 22 cm
Tate: Presented by Tate Members 2011

Drawing for Sculpture, 1968
graphite on paper, 50 x 20 cm

First Structure, 1966 / 2013
painted steel, 140 x 140 x 140 cm

Second Structure, 1966–1967 / 2010
painted steel, 183 x 81 x 81 cm

Drawing for Sculpture, 1968
ink on paper, 29 x 20 cm
Tate: Presented by Tate Members 2011

Chaar Yaar, 1968
4 emulsion on wood Structures
23 x 23 x 23 cm each

Untitled Maquettes, 1968
emulsion on wood,
various dimensions

Chaar Pellay, 1968 / 2017
4 acrylic on wood Structures
61 x 61 x 61 cm each

3Y + 3B, 1968–1969
acrylic on metal and wood
183 x 244 x 14 cm
Tate: Purchased: 2007

Nine, 1968–1975 / 1987 / 2016
9 acrylic on wood Structures
61 x 61 x 61 cm each

Lal Kona, 1969
acrylic on wood, 145 x 31 x 31 cm
Collection Amrita Jhavery

Rang Baranga I, 1969
acrylic on wood, 182 x 61 x 46 cm
Tate: Presented by Tate Members 2007

Touch, 1970
5 photographs, 142 x 112 cm

Drawing for Sculpture, 1970
graphite on paper, 32 x 22 cm
Tate: Presented by Tate Members 2011

The One That Could Not Float Away, 1970
4 photographs, 64 x 64 cm each

Disco Sailing, 1970–1973 / 2001
6 photographs and drawings, and fibreglass disc
dimensions variable
Sharjah Art Foundation Collection

Chakar Chakeroon May
(Circles Inside Circles), 1970 / 2017
16 discs, acrylic on wood, photographs
dimensions variable

Drawing for Sculpture, 1972
graphite on paper, 32 x 22 cm
Tate: Presented by Tate Members 2011

8bS, 1970
acrylic on wood, 183 x 394 x 28 cm

Springtime in Euston Square Gardens, 1970 /2015
9 photographs and 4 acrylic on wood Structures
dimensions variable

Triangles, 1970
6 photographs, 61 x 61 cm each

YYOBOBRR, 1972 / 2017
acrylic on wood, 183 x 183 x 15 cm

Sharbati: Forty Years On, 1973 / 2013
three structures, acrylic on wood,
173 x 67 x 15 cm each

Return of the Chakras, 2017
wood, 16 photographs, 60 x 60 cm each

Becoming Political: 1971–

BoO, 1969
acrylic on wood, 122 x 183 x 13 cm
National Museums Liverpool, Walker Art Gallery

For Oluwale, 1971–1973 / 1975
4 mixed-media collages on board, 122 x 122 cm each

When They Meet, 1973
20 photographs, dimensions variable

Civilisation, 1974
mixed-media on board, 122 x 102 cm

No Politics Please!, 1974–1975
mixed-media on board, 122 x 102 cm

Disaster, 1974–1975
mixed-media on board, 122 x 102 cm

Must We Always Wait For Pictures Like This, 1974–1976
mixed-media on board, 122 x 102 cm

Holes in the Earth, 1975 / 2017
mixed-media installation, dimensions variable

Preliminary Notes for a BLACK MANIFESTO
1975–1976 / 2017
vinyl on forex, 10 panels, 60 x 42 cm each

Fire!, 1975–1987
24 photographs, dimensions variable

Burning Ties, 1976–1979
8 photographs, 75 x 50 cm each
Burger Collection, Hong Kong

'Paki Bastard'
(Portrait of the Artist as a Black Person), 1977 / 2016
video with sound

I Love It, It Loves I, 1978–1983
12 photographs, 43 x 58 cm each

How Could One Paint a Self-Portrait, 1978
mixed-media on paper, 122 x 102 cm
Sharjah Art Foundation Collection

Christmas Day, 1979
four photographs, 51 x 76 cm each

Happy Christmas, 1979–1983
mixed-media on board, 122 x 102 cm
Sharjah Art Foundation Collection

Narcissus, 1979–1983
mixed-media on on board, 122 x 102 cm
Sharjah Art Foundation Collection

Gastkünstler, 1980
collage in wooden suitcase, 110 x 140 cm

Homecoming, 1982
mixed-media on board, 122 x 102 cm
Sharjah Art Foundation Collection

Ethnic Drawings, 1982
4 drawings, pencil and pen on paper
79 x 53 cm each
Arts Council Collection, Southbank Centre, London

Black Sheep, 1983–1984
mixed-media on board, 122 x 102 cm
Sharjah Art Foundation Collection

Arctic Circle, 1983–87 / 2017
installation, wine and beer bottles,
dimensions variable

In Pursuit of Significant Language: 1983–

Look Mamma... Macho!, 1983–1986
mixed-media, 153 x 457 x 8 cm
Collection JM Patras / Paris

Mon St V, 1985
acrylic on wood, 183 x 224 x 13 cm

Fair and Lovely, 1985
mixed-media collage, 183 x 218 cm

Green Painting I, 1985–1986
photographs, acrylic on plywood, 173 x 226 cm
Arts Council Collection, Southbank Centre, London

Sonay Ke Chirya (Golden Bird), 1986
mixed-media on wood, 238 x 270 x 14 cm
Fukuoka Asian Art Museum Collection

Tableau Noir, 1987
photographs, acrylic on plywood, 152 x 229 cm

Golden Calf, 1987
photographs, silkscreen on canvas, 152 x 178 cm

White Stallion, 1987–1991
photographs, acrylic on plywood, 163 x 199 cm
Imperial War Museum

Archival material relating Third World Within, 1986
and **Essential Black Art**, 1987
Andrew Hurman / Brixton Gallery Archive

History Painting, 1987–1994
photographs, acrylic on plywood, 185 x 274 cm

Jouissance, 1987–1994
photographs, acrylic on plywood, 185 x 277 cm

Bismullah, 1988
photographs, acrylic on canvas, 155 x 230 cm
Tate: Purchased 1995

Archival material relating to **The Other Story: Afro-Asian artists in Post-War Britain**, 1989
Asia Art Archive

Tigerjee, 1992–1997
mixed-media installation, 100 x 150 x 150 cm

Aflatoon (So You Think You Are Plato), 1994
acrylic on wood, 183 x 185 x 185 cm

Once Upon A Time, 1994
mixed-media installation, 160 x 185 x 185 cm

Homecoming: 2012–

In The Midst Of Darkness 2A, 2012–2013
acrylic on canvas, 152 x 203 cm

In The Midst Of Darkness 1A, 2012–2013
acrylic on canvas, 152 x 203 cm

Guftugu (A Conversation Between Al Baruni and Ibn Sina), 2014, acrylic on canvas, 160 x 238 cm

Opus B1, 2016
oil on canvas, 160 x 160 cm

Opus B2, 2016
oil on canvas, 160 x 160 cm

Opus TA2, 2017
oil on canvas, 160 x 160 cm

Opus TAA2, 2017
oil on canvas, 160 x 160 cm

Opus HB3, 2017
oil on canvas, 160 x 140 cm

Black Square Breaking into Primary Colours, 2016
acrylic on wood, 162 x 487 x 20 cm

Black Square Breaking into Rainbow Colours, 2016
acrylic on wood, 162 x 20 x 487 cm

Zero to Infinity, 2017
64 painted wood Structures, 40 x 40 x 40 cm each

Reading Room

A Proposal for a Collective Farm in Balochistan, 1998
print, 60 x 42 cm

Mediterranea, 2001–2002
three drawings, felt-tipped marker and ink pen on printed map, 21 x 30 cm each

Between the Black Lines, 2002
pen on printed map, 21 x 30 cm

Mediterranean Union, 2002
felt-tipped marker and ink pen on printed map, 21 x 30 cm

Mediterranismo, 2002
drawing, pen and ink on printed map, 21 x 30 cm

Asthesis, 2005
four drawings, marker and ink on paper
30 x 21 cm each

Preparatory map for Mediterranean, 2007
pen on printed map, 20 x 3 0cm

The Caribbean, 2008
vinyl reproduction, 104 x 70 cm

Union of Mediterranean Countries, 2009
felt-tipped marker on printed map, 21 x 30 cm

Preliminary Drawing for Mediterranea 1, 2009
felt-tipped marker on printed map, 21 x 30 cm

Preliminary Drawing for Mediterranea 2, 2009
felt-tipped marker on printed map, 21 x 30 cm each

Union of Mediterranean Countries, 2010
felt-tipped marker and ink on printed map, 20 x 30 cm

Reading Room, 2017
installation of issues of **Third Text** (1987–2011) on 36 painted wood Structures, 50 x 50 x 50 cm each

Image Credits

All images courtesy Rasheed Araeen, Aicon Gallery, and Grosvenor Gallery, and Rossi Rossi, unless otherwise stated. Every effort has been made to identify and trace image rights holders. The publishers apologize for any omissions that may have been inadvertently made.

1–3 Rasheed Araeen's studio; 97 Untitled (Painting No. 1), 1965; 104 Untitled, 1966; 104 Untitled, 1966; 104 Untitled, 1966; 104 Untitled (St MK2), 1966; 105 Untitled, 1967; 105 Untitled, 1967; 105 Untitled (4x4), 1967; 105 Untitled, 1967; 106 Untitled, 1966; 106 A Scribble, 1966; 106 Untitled, 1966; 106 Untitled, 1966; 108 Cut Out Collage, 1967; 108 Untitled, 1968; 108 Untitled, 1968; 109 Untitled, 1968; 109 Untitled, 1968; 109 Untitled, 1968; 109 Untitled, 1968; 110 Untitled, 1966; 110 Untitled, 1967; 110 Untitled, 1967; 110 Untitled, 1966; 110 Untitled (3H SQ), 1966; 111 Untitled (4.10.67), 1967; 111 Untitled (At This Stage), 1967; 111 Untitled (scale 1 x 1 foot), 1967; 111 Untitled (Silver), 1967; 112 Untitled, 1968; 112 Untitled, 1968; 112 Untitled (Red), 1968; 112 Untitled (Jan 68), 1968; 113 Untitled, 1968; 113 Untitled, 1968; 113 Untitled, 1968; 113 Untitled, 1968; 130 Untitled, 1969; 130 Untitled (red), 1969; 130 Untitled, 1969; 145 Untitled (12 x 12), 1970; 171 Untitled (6H54), 1972; 171 Untitled, 1972; 171 Untitled, 1972; p216 Untitled (Brown), 1973; 286 Anything Goes in Post Modernity, 1996; 314 Al-Gazali, 2010–2011; 326 Guftugu II (A Conversation Between Al Baruni and Ibn Sina), 2014; 329 Ishq Haqiqi, Ishq Majazi 2B, 2014; 338–339 Black Square Breaking into Primary Colours, 2016; 338–339 Black Square Breaking into Rainbow Colours, 2016; 360 Untitled (Study for Opus), 2017; 360 Untitled (Study for Opus), 2017; 360 Untitled (Study for Opus), 2017; 360 Untitled (Study for Opus), 2017; p361 Untitled (Study for Opus), 2017; 361 Untitled (Study for Opus), 2017; 362 Opus TA1, 2017; 362 Opus TA2, 2017; 362 Opus TA3, 2017; 362 Opus TA4, 2017; 363 Opus TAA1, 2017; 363 Opus TAA2, 2017; 363 Opus TAA3, 2017; 363 Opus TAA4, 2017; 364 Opus TD1, 2017; 364 Opus TD2, 2017; 364 Opus TD3, 2017; 364 Opus TD4, 2017; 365 Opus TEE1, 2017; 365 Opus TEE2, 2017; 365 Opus TEE3, 2017; 365 Opus TEE4, 2017; 376 Untitled (Study for Opus), 2017; 376 Untitled (Study for Opus), 2017; 376 Untitled (Study for Opus), 2017; 376 Untitled (Study for Opus), 2017; 377 Opus HA1, 2017; 378 Opus HB2, 2017; 379 Opus HA3, 2017; 380 Opus HA4, 2017; 381 Opus HB1, 2017; 382 Opus HB2, 2017; 383 Opus HB3, 2017; 384 Opus HB4, 2017
Photos Justin Piperger

8, 232–233 Burning Ties, 1976–1979; 228–230 Fire!, 1975–1987
Photos Elena Bonzanigo

19 A Memory of My Childhood in Punjab, 1953; 26 Waves at Sandspit, 1956; 28 Untitled Green I, 1958; 28 Untitled Green II, 1958; 28 Nightmare, 1958; 37 Untitled, 1961; 45 Demand of Life (A Scribble), 1961; 52 Windcatchers in Pink, 1963; 55 Hyderabad, 1963; 55 Houses, 1963; 156 Burgundy Dark, 1971; 312 AlFarabiAlFarabiAlFarabi, 2010–2013; 312 AlkindiAlKindiAlKindiAlkindi, 2010–2013; 313 IbnRushdibnRushibnRushibnRushd, 2010–2013; 313 IbnSinaIbnSinaIbnSinaIbnSina; 315 The Greatness of Islamic Civilisation (Ibn Rushd, Umer-Khayyam, Al-Ghazali, Ibn Sina, Al-Farabi and A-Kindi), 2011–2012; 318 In The Midst of Darkness 1, 2012–2013; 319 In The Midst Of Darkness 1A, 2012–2013, 324 Guftugu I (A Conversation Between Al Baruni and Ibn Sina), 2014; 327 Guftugu III (A Conversation Between Al Baruni and Ibn Sina), 2014; 328 Ishq Haqiqi, Ishq Majazi, 2013; 329 Ishq Haqiqi, Ishq Majazi 1A, 2014; 329 Ishq Haqiqi, Ishq Majazi 2A, 2014
Courtesy V.M. Gallery
Photos Wahid Khairi

20 Views of Karachi, 1953–1956; 21–22 People of Karachi I, 1955–1959; 23–24 People of Karachi II, 1957–1959; 25 People of Karachi III, 1957–1959; 29 Boats at Keamari, 1958; 30–31 Boats: Towards Abstraction, 1958–1962
Courtesy V.M. Gallery
Photos Akram Spaul

30–31 Boats: Towards Abstraction, 1958–1962
Courtesy M+ Museum; 35–36 Dancing Bodies (Hula-Hoop Series), 1959–1962; 60 Before Departure (Black Painting No. IV), 1963; 60 Before Departure (Black Painting No. V), 1963; 61 Before Departure (Black Painting No. VI), 1963; 61 Before Departure (Painting 71), 1964; 62 Before Departure (Black Painting No. VIII), 1964; 99 Sculpture No. 1 (Blue), 1965 / 2010; 100 Sculpture No. 2 (Red), 1965 / 2015; 103 Second Structure, 1966–1967 / 2010; 143 Disco Sailing, 1970–1973 / 2001; 214 Sharbati: Forty Years On, 1973 / 2013; 240 How Could One Paint a Self-Portrait, 1978; 241 Homecoming, 1982; 242 Happy Christmas, 1979–1983; 243 Narcissus, 1979–1983; 244 Black Sheep, 1983–1984; 322 Sharjah Blues, 2013
Courtesy Sharjah Art Foundation Collection
Photos Sharjah Art Foundation

43 Aag, 1961, 256 Look Mamma...Macho!, 1983–1986
Photos Perry van Duijnhoven

49 Untitled B10, 1962; 49 Untitled B9, 1962; 49 Untitled B7, 1962; 49 Untitled B8, 1962; 50 Cats and Lips, 1962
Photos Matt Pia

97 Drawing for Sculpture No. 3, 1965
Courtesy Private collection, London

101 Blue Cube, 1968; 123 Mill Gaye Phir Chaaron Yaar (Have Met Again, Four Friends), 1968; 342 Rainbow, 2015; 344 Go On, Sing The Blues, Again, 2015
Photos Mark French

97 Drawing for Sculpture No. 2, 1965; 97 Untitled (Original Drawing for Sculpture No. 2), 1965; 107 Drawing for Sculpture, 1966; 107 Drawing for Sculpture, 1966; 107 Drawing for Sculpture, 1966; 109 Drawing for Sculpture, 1968; 127 Lovers, 1968; 128 3Y + 3B, 1968–1969; 134 Rang Baranga I, 1969; 145 Drawing for Sculpture, 1970; 170 Drawing for Sculpture, 1970; 274 Bismullah, 1988; 305 Zero to Infinity, 1968–2004 / 2007
Courtesy Tate, London 2017
Photos Tate, London 2017

115 Winter Blue, 1968; 146 Piaray Lal, 1970; 147 Basant, 1970; 155 (3R+2B) SW, 1971; 156 Burgundy Dark, 1971; 330 Summer Blue, 2014
Photos Andrew Barklem

122 Chaar Yaar I (Four Friends), 1968 / 2014
Photo Todd White

122 Chaar Yaar II (Four Friends), 1968 / 2014; 135 Rang Baranga II, 1969 / 2014; 144 Springtime in Euston Square Gardens, 1970 / 2015; 331 Cricklewood Broadway, 2014; 332 Jaamni (Purple Diamond), 2014; 333 Chaar Neelay Heeray (Four Blue Diamonds), 2014
Photos Bill Orcutt

131 Lal Kona, 1969
Photo Socrates Mitsos

133 BoO, 1969
Courtesy National Museums Liverpool, Walker Art Gallery

157 Burgundy Light, 1971
Courtesy Samdani Art Foundation Collection
Photo Sarker Protick

210–211 For Oluwale, 1971–73 / 1975
Courtesy Nottingham Contemporary
Photo Andy Keate

254 Ethnic Drawings, 1982
Courtesy Arts Council Collection, Southbank Centre, London

262 Green Painting I, 1985–86
Courtesy Van Abbemuseum
Photo Peter Cox

299 The Other Story, 1989
Courtesy Rasheed Araeen and Asia Art Archive

354 Opus TA1, 2016; 354 Opus TA2, 2016; 354 Opus TA3, 2016; 354 Opus TA4, 2016
Courtesy Baro Gallery
Photo Martin Bernard

368–370 Zero to Infinity, 1968–2004 / 2017; 371 Chakras VI (Phir Agaye Sub Chakar), 2017
Courtesy Yorkshire Sculpture Park
Photo Jonty Wilde

350 Opus B1, 2016; Opus B3, 2016; Opus B2, 2016; Opus B4, 2016; Opus D1, 2016; Opus D3, 2016; Opus D2, 2016; Opus D4, 2016; 355 Opus TC1, 2016; Opus TC3, 2016; Opus TC2, 2016; Opus TC4, 2016; 363 Opus TAA1, 2017; Opus TAA3, 2017; Opus TAA2, 2017; 377 Opus HA1, 2017; 378 HA2, 2017; 379 HA3, 2017; 380 HA4, 2017; 381 HB1, 2017; 382 HB2, 2017; 383 HB3, 2017, 384 HB4, 2017
Photos Majella Dowdican

358 Shamiyaana–Food for Thought: Thought for Change, 2016–2017
Courtesy documenta 14
Photo Yiannis Hadjiaslanis

356 The Reading Room in Kassel, 2016–2017
Courtesy documenta 14
Photo Milan Soremski

366 Zero to Infinity, 1968–2004 / 2017
Courtesy La Biennale di Venezia
Photo Italo Rondinella

374 Summertime, 2017
Photo Simon Booth

This book is published to accompany the exhibition *Rasheed Araeen: A Retrospective*

2 December 2017 – 25 March 2018
Van Abbemuseum, Eindhoven
curated by Nick Aikens

30 May – 9 September 2018
MAMCO, Musée d'art moderne et contemporain, Geneva
curated by Nick Aikens with Paul Bernard

19 October 2018 – 27 January 2019
BALTIC Centre for Contemporary Art, Gateshead
curated by Nick Aikens with Katharine Welsh

27 February to 12 May 2019
Garage Museum of Contemporary Art, Moscow
curated by Nick Aikens with Kate Fowle

Editor: Nick Aikens
Texts: Nick Aikens, Rasheed Araeen, Charles Esche, Kate Fowle, Courtney J. Martin, Michael Newman, Dominic Rahtz, Gene Ray, John Roberts, Marcus du Sautoy, Zöe Sutherland, Kaelen Wilson-Goldie

Copy and line editor: Janine Armin
Editorial assistant: Nadine Botha
Design: Bardhi Haliti
Inventory: Compiled by Conor Macklin and Grosvenor Gallery, London in collaboration with Rasheed Araeen. Additional support by Nadine Botha, Gaia Giammusso, Kajoli Khanna, Toby Kid, Charles Moore, Ananya Mukhophadyay, Laura Peh
Lithography: Marc Gijzen
Printing: UNICUM | Gianotten Printed Media

Publishers:
BALTIC Centre for Contemporary Art
baltic.art
Garage Museum of Contemporary Art
garagemca.org
MAMCO, Musée d'art moderne et contemporain
mamco.ch
Van Abbemuseum
vanabbemuseum.nl

The book is generously supported by
Aicon Gallery, New York
Grosvenor Gallery, London
Rossi Rossi, Hong Kong

Printed in Europe

Distributor:
JRP|Ringier
Limmatstrasse 270
CH–8005 Zurich
jrp-ringier.com

ISBN 978-3-03764-515-4

JRP|Ringier publications are available internationally at selected bookstores and from the following distribution partners:

Switzerland
AVA Verlagsauslieferung AG
Centralweg 16
CH–8910 Affoltern
avainfo@ava.ch
ava.ch

Germany and Austria
Vice Versa Distribution GmbH
Potsdamer Str. 93
D-10785 Berlin
info@viceversaartbooks.com
viceversaartbooks.com

France
Les presses du réel
35 rue Colson
F–21000 Dijon
info@lespressesdureel.com
lespressesdureel.com

UK and other European countries
Cornerhouse Publications, HOME
2 Tony Wilson Place
UK–Manchester M15 4FN
publications@cornerhouse.org
cornerhousepublications.org

USA, Canada, Asia, and Australia
ARTBOOK | D.A.P.
75 Broad Street, Suite 630
US-New York, NY 10004
orders@dapinc.com
artbook.com

For a list of our partner bookshops or for any general questions, please contact JRP|Ringier directly at info@jrp-ringier.com, or visit our homepage www.jrp-ringier.com for further information about our programme.

BALTIC GARAGE MAMCO GENEVE VAN ABBE MUSEUM

Acknowledgements

Nick Aikens and Rasheed Araeen would like to give a warm thank you to Amra Ali, Janine Armin, Paul Bernard, Nadine Botha, Elena Bonzanigo, Lionel Bovier, Burger Collection Hong Kong, Majella Dowdican, Prajit Dutta, Charles Esche, Peter Fillingham, Kate Fowle, Marc Gijzen, Bardhi Haliti, Taimur Hassan, Andrew Hurman, Harry Hutchinson, Amrita Jhaveri, Kajoly Khanna, Conor Macklin, Courtney J. Martin, Charles Moore, Tauqeer Muhajir, Sarah Munro, Mohammed Mushtaq, Michael Newman, Jean-Marc Patras, Laure Prouvost, Hoor Al Qasimi, Will de Quetteville, Dominic Rahtz, Gene Ray, Mauro Ribero, John Roberts, Fabio Rossi, Marcus du Sautoy, Lucy Steeds, Zoë Sutherland, Katharine Welsh, and Kaelen Wilson-Goldie. We would also like to extend sincere thanks to the teams at Van Abbemuseum Eindhoven; MAMCO, Musée d'art moderne et contemporain, Geneva; BALTIC Centre for Contemporary Art, Gateshead; Garage Museum of Contemporary Art, Moscow; and the institutions who have loaned works for the exhibition.

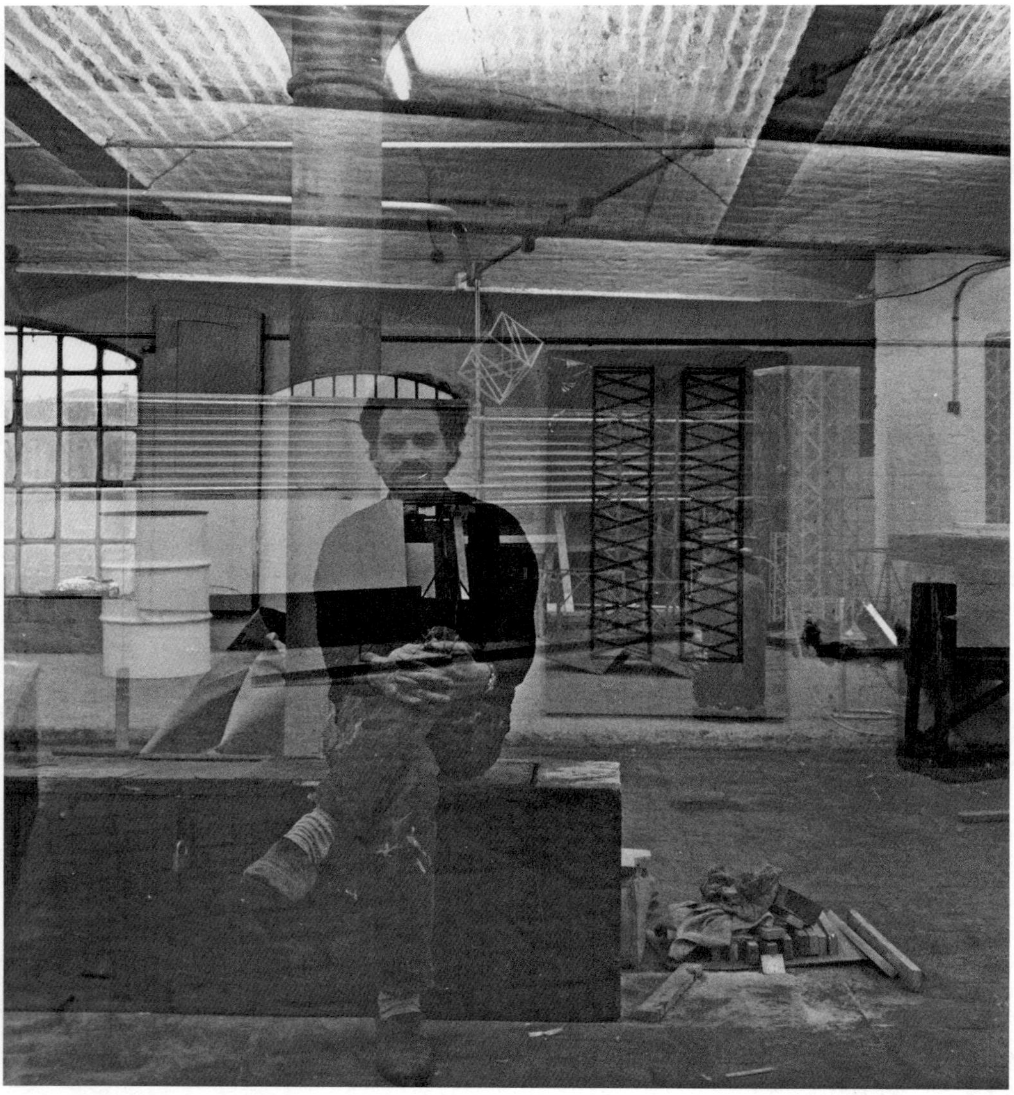

MORNING NEWS

June 12, 1955.

A BUDDING ARTIST

TWENTY - year - old Abdur Rashid Araeen, a student of Inter Science of D. J. Sind Government Science College, Karachi, has won the 2nd Prize (Rs. 300|-) in the Pakistan Day Greeting Cards Competition held by the Burmah Shell last week.

This budding student-artist, who had also won the 2nd Prize in Landscape in the 3rd Inter-Collegiate Fine Arts and Crafts Exhibition held last year at the Sind Muslim College, Karachi. had depicted a merry crowd at a carnival around merry-go-rounds.

The vivid and harmonious colours used by him received applause of almost all the visitors to the exhibition held on Saturday last.

A member of the Artists' Club (Turab Studio) and also the USIS Sketch Club, Mr. Araeen, has, by winning the 2nd Prize, amazed the innumerable experienced and qualified artists of Pakistan, who had participated in this All-Pakistan Competition.

ENGINEER-TURNED ARTIST DISPLAYS HIS WARES

BY M. T. BOKHARI

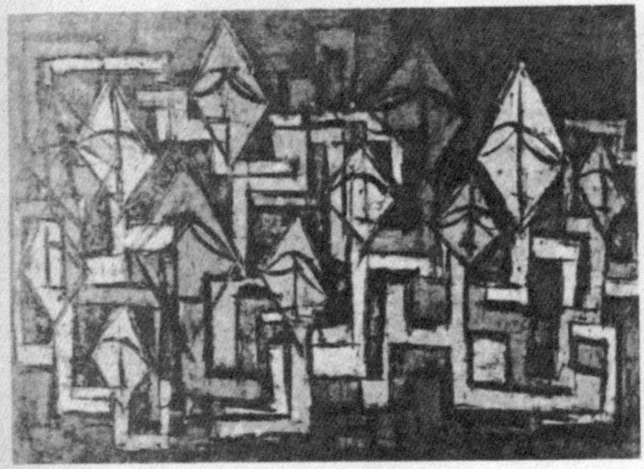

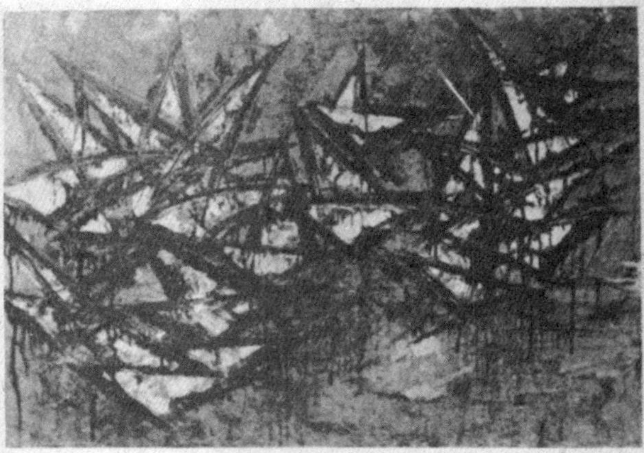

The artist & his compositions

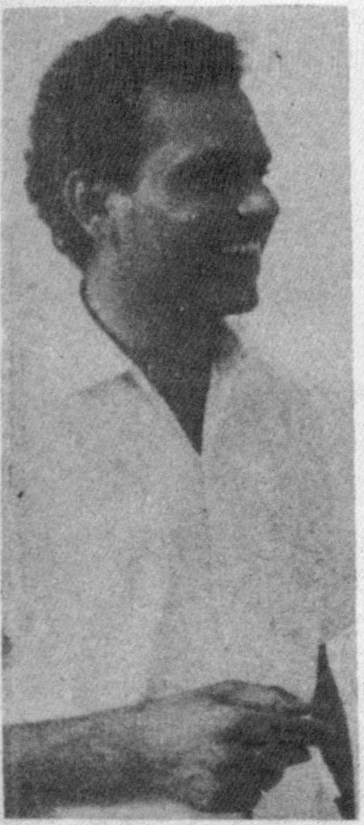

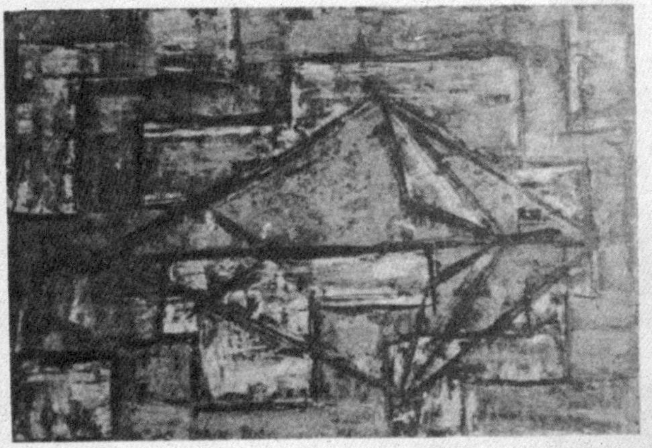

The exhibition of paintings of Rashid Araeen, one of our promising young abstractioinists, opened here at the Art Council on July 9 with twitching of noses by the 'old world' and thunderous clappings by the 'new'.

Karachi-born Rashid Araeen, began as a qualified engineer, jaywalked into painting a few years ago and decided to stay permamently in the artisitic world. Ever since then abstract painting has been his staple diet.

He came as an artist before the public for the first tidme in 1961 at the Pakistan American Cultural Centre in a group exhibition with works that showed nothing but curves.

The presnt hangings are a far cry from his older prefrences and are noticeably devoid of all traces of curves. There place has been taken instead by straight lines. Here bright colours also have given way to drab ones. Black predominates.

According to the Sudanese Ambassador Mr. Fakhr-ed-din Mohommad, who inaugurated his exhibition Rashid's paintings "conjure up numerous reminisceneces through the selection of colours, shapes and forms and are complete in themselves as pieces of good balancing and harmonious composition."

In all Rashid has put on view 35 of his works which include paintings, drawing and woodcuts.

رشید آرائیں —— ایک فنکار

—— جنھوں نے ایک خوبصورت فن سے پاکستان کو متعارف کرایا! -

لندن میں رہنے والے پاکستانی فنکار رشید آرائیں پچھلے دنوں مختصر قیام کے لئے پاکستان آئے تو انہوں نے کراچی کی ایک مقامی جھیل میں اپنے فن "KINETIC ART" کا مظاہرہ کر کے تماشائیوں کو حیرت میں ڈال دیا۔ رشید آرائیں عرصہ دراز سے لندن میں مقیم ہیں اور یورپ کے بیشتر ممالک میں اپنے فن کا مظاہرہ کر چکے ہیں۔

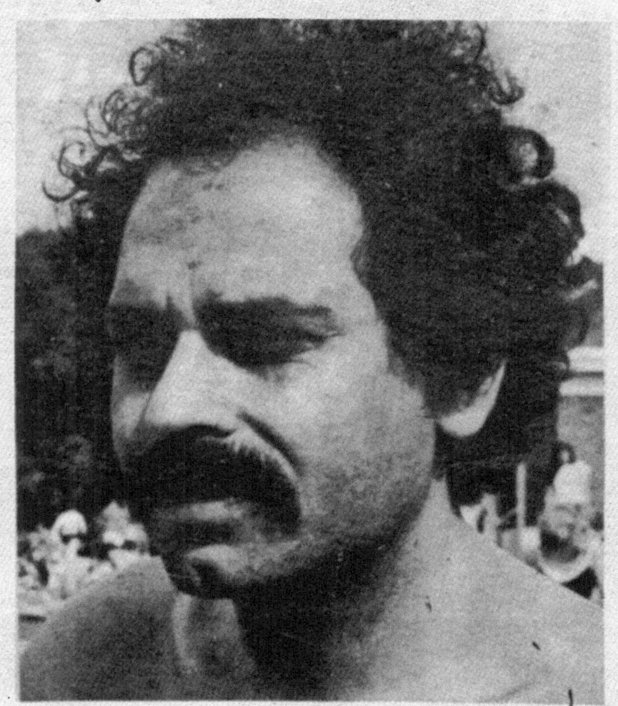

رشید آرائیں پلاسٹک یا ہلکی لکڑی سے بنی ہوئی پلیٹیں کچھ اس انداز سے پانی کی ہموار سطح پر پھینکتے ہیں کہ پلیٹ سطح آب پر مختلف قسم کی رنگین لہریں اور ڈیزائن بناتی ہوئی یوں پھسلتی چلی جاتی ہیں جیسے وہ برقی طاقت سے چل رہی ہوں بقول رشید صاحب رکابیاں پھینک کر سطح آب پر دلکش مناظر پیدا کرنے کا فن پاکستان میں تو پہلی مرتبہ پیش کیا ہے لیکن یورپین باشندوں کے لئے یہ فن نیا نہیں اور وہ اسے بڑی دلچسپی سے دیکھتے ہیں۔

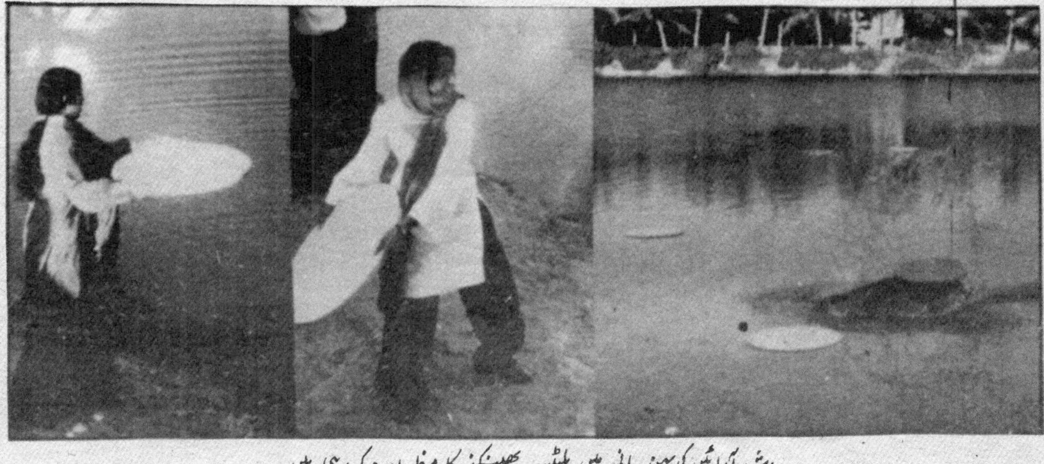

رشید آرائیں کی بہن پانی میں پلیٹیں پھینکنے کا مظاہرہ کر رہی ہیں

THE GUARDIAN
Wednesday March 26 1975

WHITFIELD STREET

Caroline Tisdall

Democratic art

ARTISTS FOR DEMOCRACY is the name of the latest platform for London's radical artists. It's a gallery-cum-meeting place run in a cooperative way and on a tight budget, and looks as if it could last until the demolisher's ball hits the rest of the Tandoori belt of Whitfield Street. The emphasis of the gallery is emphatically third world, and the aim is to try to combine that kind of interest with progressive art forms, discussions, and poetry readings. Exhibitions to date have included participational e n v i r o n m e n t s, an investigation into the relationship between social organisation and forms of agriculture, and a photo-documentation display by Guy Brett tracing the theme of the fruits of the earth running through the decorative art of all parts of the world.

The current exhibition presents the work of a Pakistani artist, Rasheed Araeen, who has in the past been justifiably vociferous in his condemnation of the lack of thought given to the position of the third world artist in western discussions of art. His own work started with paintings that depicted the movement of fire, and shifted to movement itself, the use of fire and water, in environmental works with which he hoped to involve people more directly. Another side of his art has to do with structures in which each part relates to the whole, providing the spectator with a familiar social parallel.

More recently he has been working with collage: the juxtaposition of pieces of information to give a message or provide a new context. Here the problem is that the ground is almost too well-trodden to be effective: the placing together of Kenneth Clark's Civilisation with Churchill and his tommy gun over a background of world violence and hunger is the kind of callous coexistence often criticised in the colour supplements. The hope is always that an artist can go a bit further than formulating questions that have already been asked, and maybe indicate the next step.

Artists for Democracy, 143 Whitfield Street W 1 until April 9.